Short Story Criticism

Guide to Gale Literary Criticism Series

When you need to review criticism of literary works, these are the Gale series to use:

If the author's death date is:

You should turn to:

After Dec. 31, 1959
(or author is still living)

CONTEMPORARY LITERARY CRITICISM

for example: Jorge Luis Borges, Anthony Burgess,
William Faulkner, Mary Gordon,
Ernest Hemingway, Iris Murdoch

1900 through 1959

TWENTIETH-CENTURY LITERARY CRITICISM

for example: Willa Cather, F. Scott Fitzgerald,
Henry James, Mark Twain, Virginia Woolf

1800 through 1899

NINETEENTH-CENTURY LITERATURE CRITICISM

for example: Fyodor Dostoevski, Nathaniel Hawthorne,
George Sand, William Wordsworth

1400 through 1799

LITERATURE CRITICISM FROM 1400 TO 1800
(excluding Shakespeare)

for example: Anne Bradstreet, Daniel Defoe,
Alexander Pope, François Rabelais,
Jonathan Swift, Phillis Wheatley

SHAKESPEAREAN CRITICISM

Shakespeare's plays and poetry

Antiquity through 1399

CLASSICAL AND MEDIEVAL LITERATURE CRITICISM

for example: Dante, Homer, Plato, Sophocles, Vergil,
the Beowulf Poet

Gale also publishes related criticism series:

CHILDREN'S LITERATURE REVIEW

This series covers authors of all eras who have written for the preschool through high school audience.

SHORT STORY CRITICISM

This series covers the major short fiction writers of all nationalities and periods of literary history.

POETRY CRITICISM

This series covers poets of all nationalities and periods of literary history.

DRAMA CRITICISM

This series covers playwrights of all nationalities and periods of literary history.

ISSN 0895-9439

Volume 10

Short Story Criticism

Excerpts from Criticism of the Works of Short Fiction Writers

8792

David Segal
Editor

Laurie DiMauro
Marie Lazzari
Thomas Ligotti
Sean R. Pollock
Bridget Travers
Robyn Young
Associate Editors

Gale Research Inc. • *DETROIT* • *LONDON*

STAFF

David Segal, *Editor*

Laurie DiMauro, Marie Lazzari, Thomas Ligotti, Sean R. Pollock,
Bridget Travers, Robyn Young, *Associate Editors*

Jennifer Brostrom, Cristina Cramer, Rogene M. Fisher, Christopher
Giroux, Ian A. Goodhall, Elizabeth P. Henry, Kyung-Sun Lim, Dale R.
Miller, Kristin Palm, Alexander C. Sweda, Debra A. Wells, Janet M.
Witalec, Allyson J. Wylie, *Assistant Editors*

Jeanne A. Gough, *Permissions & Production Manager*

Linda M. Pugliese, *Production Supervisor*

Paul Lewon, Maureen Puhl, Camille Robinson, Jennifer VanSickle,
Editorial Associates

Donna Craft, Rosita D'Souza, Brandy C. Johnson, Sheila Walencewicz,
Editorial Assistants

Sandra C. Davis, *Permissions Supervisor (Text)*

Maria L. Franklin, Josephine M. Keene, Michele M. Lonoconus, Denise
M. Singleton, Kimberly F. Smilay, *Permissions Associates*

Brandy Johnson, Shelly Rakoczy, Shalice Shah, *Permissions Assistants*

Margaret A. Chamberlain, *Permissions Supervisor (Pictures)*

Pamela A. Hayes, *Permissions Associate*

Amy Lynn Emrich, Karla Kulkis, Nancy Rattenbury, Keith Reed,
Permissions Assistants

Victoria B. Cariappa, *Research Manager*

Maureen Richards, *Research Supervisor*

Mary Beth McElmeel, Tamara C. Nott, *Editorial Associates*

Andrea Ghorai, Daniel J. Jankowski, Julie K. Karmazin, Robert S.
Lazich, Julie A. Synkonis, *Editorial Assistants*

Mary Beth Trimper, *Production Director*

Mary Winterhalter, *Production Assistant*

Cynthia Baldwin, *Art Director*

Nicholas Jakubiak, C. J. Jonik, Yolanda Y. Latham, *Keyliner*

Since this page cannot legibly accommodate all the copyright notices, the Acknowledgments constitute an extension of the copyright page.

The paper used in this publication meets the minimum requirements of American National Standard for Information Sciences—Permanence Paper for Printed Library Materials, ANSI Z39.48-1984 ∞

Library of Congress Catalog Card Number 88-641014
ISBN 0-8103-2559-4
ISSN 0895-9439
Printed in the United States of America
Published simultaneously in the United Kingdom
by Gale Research International Limited
(An affiliated company of Gale Research Inc.)

Contents

Preface   vii

Acknowledgments   ix

Preface

Short Story Criticism (SSC) presents significant passages from criticism of the world's greatest short story writers and provides supplementary biographical and bibliographical materials to guide the interested reader to a greater understanding of the authors of short fiction. This series was developed in response to suggestions from librarians serving high school, college, and public library patrons, who had noted a considerable number of requests for critical material on short story writers. Although major short story writers are covered in such Gale series as *Contemporary Literary Criticism (CLC), Twentieth-Century Literary Criticism (TCLC), Nineteenth-Century Literature Criticism (NCLC),* and *Literature Criticism from 1400 to 1800 (LC),* librarians perceived the need for a series devoted solely to writers of the short story genre.

Scope of the Work

SSC is designed to serve as an introduction to major short story writers of all eras and nationalities. Since these authors have inspired a great deal of relevant critical material, *SSC* is necessarily selective, and the editors have chosen the most important published criticism to aid readers and students in their research.

Approximately ten to fifteen authors are included in each volume, and each entry presents a historical survey of the critical response to that author's work. The length of an entry is intended to reflect the amount of critical attention the author has received from critics writing in English and from foreign critics in translation. Every attempt has been made to identify and include excerpts from the most significant essays on each author's work. In order to provide these important critical pieces, the editors will sometimes reprint essays that have appeared in previous volumes of Gale's Literary Criticism Series. Such duplication, however, never exceeds twenty percent of an *SSC* volume.

Organization of the Book

An *SSC* author entry consists of the following elements:

- The **author heading** cites the name under which the author most commonly wrote, followed by birth and death dates. If the author wrote consistently under a pseudonym, the pseudonym will be listed in the author heading and the author's actual name given in parentheses on the first line of the biographical and critical introduction.

- The **biographical and critical introduction** contains background information designed to introduce a reader to the author and the critical debates surrounding his or her work. Parenthetical material following the introduction provides references to other biographical and critical series published by Gale, including *CLC, TCLC, NCLC, Contemporary Authors,* and *Dictionary of Literary Biography.*

- A **portrait of the author** is included when available. Many entries also contain illustrations of materials pertinent to an author's career, including holographs of manuscript pages, title pages, dust jackets, letters, or representations of important people, places, and events in the author's life.

- The list of **principal works** is chronological by date of first publication and lists the most important works by the author. The first section comprises short story collections, novellas, and novella collections. The second section gives information on other major works by the author. For foreign authors, the editors have provided original foreign-language publication information and have selected what are considered the best and most complete English-language editions of their works.

- **Criticism** is arranged chronologically in each author entry to provide a useful perspective on changes in critical evaluation over the years. All short story, novella, and collection titles by the author featured in the entry are printed in boldface type to enable a reader to ascertain without difficulty the works discussed. Also for purposes of easier identification, the critic's name and the publication date of the essay are given at the beginning of each piece of criticism. Unsigned criticism is preceded by the title of the journal in which it appeared.

- Critical essays are prefaced with **explanatory notes** as an additional aid to students and readers using *SSC*. The explanatory notes provide several types of useful information, including: the reputation of a critic, the importance of a work of criticism, and the specific type of criticism (biographical, psychoanalytic, structuralist, etc.).

- A complete **bibliographical citation,** designed to help the interested reader locate the original essay or book, follows each piece of criticism.

- The **further reading list** appearing at the end of each author entry suggests additional materials on the author. In some cases it includes essays for which the editors could not obtain reprint rights.

Beginning with volume six, *SSC* contains two additional features designed to enhance the reader's understanding of short fiction writers and their works:

- Each *SSC* entry now includes, when available, **comments by the author** that illuminate his or her own works or the short story genre in general. These statements are set within boxes or bold rules to distinguish them from the criticism.

- A **select bibliography of general sources on short fiction** is included as an appendix. Updated and amended with each new *SSC* volume, this listing of materials for further research provides readers with a selection of the best available general studies of the short story genre.

Other Features

A **cumulative author index** lists all the authors who have appeared in *SSC, CLC, TCLC, NCLC, LC,* and *Classical and Medieval Literature Criticism (CMLC),* as well as cross-references to other Gale series. Users will welcome this cumulated index as a useful tool for locating an author within the Literary Criticism Series.

A **cumulative nationality index** lists all authors featured in *SSC* by nationality, followed by the number of the *SSC* volume in which their entry appears.

A **cumulative title index** lists in alphabetical order all short story, novella, and collection titles contained in the *SSC* series. Titles of short story collections, separately published novellas, and novella collections are printed in italics, while titles of individual short stories are printed in roman type with quotation marks. Each title is followed by the author's name and the corresponding volume and page numbers where commentary on the work may be located. English-language translations of original foreign-language titles are cross-referenced to the foreign titles so that all references to discussion of a work are combined in one listing.

A Note to the Reader

When writing papers, students who quote directly from any volume in the Literary Criticism Series may use the following general forms to footnote reprinted criticism. The first example pertains to material drawn from periodicals, the second to material reprinted from books:

[1] Henry James, Jr., "Honoré de Balzac," *The Galaxy* 20 (December 1875), 814-36; excerpted and reprinted in *Short Story Criticism,* Vol. 5, ed. Thomas Votteler (Detroit: Gale Research, 1990), pp. 8-11.

[2] F. R. Leavis, *D. H. Lawrence: Novelist* (Alfred A. Knopf, 1956); excerpted and reprinted in *Short Story Criticism,* Vol. 4, ed. Thomas Votteler (Detroit: Gale Research, 1990), pp. 202-06.

Suggestions Are Welcome

Readers who wish to suggest authors to appear in future volumes, or who have other suggestions, are invited to contact the editors by writing to Gale Research, Inc., Literary Criticism Division, 835 Penobscot Building, Detroit, MI., 48226-4094.

ACKNOWLEDGMENTS

The editors wish to thank the copyright holders of the excerpted criticism included in this volume, the permissions managers of many book and magazine publishing companies for assisting us in securing reprint rights, and Anthony Bogucki for assistance with copyright research. We are also grateful to the staffs of the Detroit Public Library, the Library of Congress, the University of Detroit Library, Wayne State University Purdy/Kresge Library Complex, and the University of Michigan Libraries for making their resources available to us. Following is a list of the copyright holders who have granted us permission to reprint material in this volume of *SSC*. Every effort has been made to trace copyright, but if omissions have been made, please let us know.

COPYRIGHT EXCERPTS IN *SSC*, VOLUME 10, WERE REPRINTED FROM THE FOLLOWING PERIODICALS:

The American Scholar, v. 53, Autumn, 1984 for "Herself" by Donna Rifkind. © 1984 Donna Rifkind. Reprinted by permission of the publishers.—*The Atlantic Monthly,* v. 220, August, 1967 for "The Literature of Exhaustion" by John Barth. Copyright 1967 by The Atlantic Monthly Company, Boston, MA Reprinted by permission of Wylie, Aitken & Stone, Inc.—*Book Week—New York Herald Tribune,* September 29, 1963. © 1963, *The Washington Post.* Reprinted by permission of the publisher.—*The Centennial Review,* v. XXIV, Spring, 1980. © 1980 by *The Centennial Review.* Reprinted by permission of the publisher.—*Chicago Tribune—Books,* May 27, 1990. © copyrighted 1990, Chicago Tribune Company. All rights reserved. Used with permission.—*CLA Journal,* v. XXIX, December, 1985. Copyright, 1985 by The College Language Association. Used by permission of The College Lanuage Association.—*The Commonweal,* v. LXVII, January 3, 1958; v. LXXVI, June 8, 1962. Copyright © 1958, renewed 1986; copyright © 1962, renewed 1990 Commonweal Publishing Co., Inc. Both reprinted by permission of Commonweal Foundation.—*Contemporary Literature,* v. 26, Winter, 1985; v. 29, Winter, 1988. © 1985, 1988 by the Board of Regents of the University of Wisconsin System. Both reprinted by permission of The University of Wisconsin Press.—*The Critic,* Chicago, v. 33, January-February, 1975. © *The Critic* 1975. Reprinted with the permission of the Thomas More Association, Chicago, IL.—*Critique: Studies in Modern Fiction,* v. XVIII, 1976. Copyright © 1976 Helen Dwight Reid Educational Foundation. Reprinted with permission of the Helen Dwight Reid Educational Foundation, published by Heldref Publications, 1319 18th Street, N.W., Washington, DC 20036-1802.—*The Georgia Review,* v. XXIV, Winter, 1970 for "The Non-Regionalism of Peter Taylor" by Jan Pinkerton. Copyright, 1970, by the University of Georgia. Reprinted by permission of the publisher and the author.—*The Hollins Critic,* v. II, December, 1965. Copyright 1965 by Hollins College. Reprinted by permission of the publisher.—*The Hudson Review,* v. XXXVIII, Summer, 1985. Copyright © 1985 by The Hudson Review, Inc. Reprinted by permission of the publisher./ v. I, Autumn, 1948. Copyright 1948, renewed 1976 by The Hudson Review, Inc. Reprinted by permission of the publisher.—*The International Fiction Review,* v. 6, Summer, 1979 for "James Baldwin's Blues and the Function of Art" by Edward Lobb; v. 11, Summer, 1984 for "Literature, Self-Consciousness, and Writing: The Example of Barth's 'Lost in the Funhouse' " by Steven M. Bell. © copyright 1979, 1984 International Fiction Association. Both reprinted by permission of the publisher and the respective authors.—*Journal of the Short Story in English,* n. 9, Autumn, 1987. © Universite d'Angers, 1987. Reprinted by permission of the publisher./ *The Listener,* v. 117, April 30, 1987 for "Spark on the Horizon" by Valerie Shaw. © British Broadcasting Corp. 1987. Reprinted by permission of the author.—*The Massachusetts Review,* v. XXVIII, Autumn, 1987. © 1987. Reprinted from *The Massachusetts Review,* The Massachusetts Review, Inc. by permission.—*Modern Fiction Studies,* v. XIV, Winter, 1968-69. Copyright © 1969 by Purdue Research Foundation, West Lafayette, IN 47907. All rights reserved. Reprinted with permission.—*The Nation,* New York, v. 201, December 13, 1965. Copyright 1965 *The Nation* magazine/ The Nation Company, Inc. Reprinted by permission of the publisher.—*Negro American Literature Forum,* v. 4, July, 1970 for " 'Sonny's Blues': James Baldwin's Image of Black Community" by John M. Reilly. Copyright © Indiana State University 1970. Reprinted with the permission of *African American Review* and the author./ v. 3, Spring, 1969. Copyright © Indiana State University 1969. Reprinted with the permission of *African American Review.*—*The New Criterion,* v. 6, March, 1988 for "H. E. Bates, Storyteller" by Brock Baker. Copyright © 1988 by The Foundation for Cultural Review. Reprinted by permission of the author.—*The New Republic,* v. 153, November 27, 1965. © 1965 The New Republic, Inc. Reprinted by permission of *The New Republic.*—*New York Herald Tribune Books,* November 6, 1932. Copyright 1932, *The Washington Post.* Reprinted with permission of the publisher./ August 25, 1929. Copyright 1929, renewed 1957, *The Washington Post.* Reprinted with permission of the publisher.—*The New York Review of Books,* v. V, December 9, 1965. Copyright © 1965 Nyrev, Inc. Reprinted with permission from *The New York Review of Books.*—*The New York Times,* September 18, 1985. Copyright © 1985 by The New York Times Company. Reprinted by permission of the publisher./ November 28, 1943. Copyright 1943, renewed 1971 by The New York Times Company. Reprinted by permission of the publisher.—*The New*

permission of the publisher.—Westcott, Glenway. From an introduction to *Short Novels of Colette.* Dial Press, 1951. Copyright, 1951, The Dial Press, Inc. Renewed 1979 by Glenway Westcott. Used by permission of Doubleday, a division of Bantam, Doubleday, Dell Publishing Group, Inc.—Ziegler, Heide. From *John Barth.* Methuen, 1987. © 1987 Heide Ziegler. All rights reserved. Reprinted by permission of the publisher.

PHOTOGRAPHS AND ILLUSTRATIONS APPEARING IN *SSC,* VOLUME 10 WERE RECEIVED FROM THE FOLLOWING SOURCES:

AP/Wide World Photos: **p. 1;** © Jerry Bauer: **pp. 29, 329;** © William Denison: **p. 57;** Photograph by Mark Gerson: **pp. 109, 349;** Herbert Gehr, *LIFE* Magazine © Time Warner Inc.: **p. 141;** Photograph by Margo Moore: **p. 298;** Photograph by Jill Krementz: **p. 308;** Photograph by Mark Morrow: **p. 373;** Dust jacket of *In the Miro District and Other Stories,* by Peter Taylor. Alfred A. Knopf, 1977. Reprinted by permission of Alfred A. Knopf Inc.: **p. 395.**

James Baldwin

1924-1987

(Full name James Arthur Baldwin) American novelist, essayist, dramatist, nonfiction and short story writer, poet, scriptwriter, and author of children's books.

INTRODUCTION

One of the most eminent writers in post–World War II American literature, Baldwin garnered acclaim for such works as the essay collection *Notes of a Native Son* and the novel *Go Tell It on the Mountain,* in which he called attention to the racial and sexual polarization of American society. In *Going to Meet the Man,* his only volume of short fiction, Baldwin drew on many of his own experiences to explore the issues of racial conflict, individual identity, and the complexity of human motivations. Several of his short stories, including "Sonny's Blues" and "Going to Meet the Man," are regarded as important to a full understanding of his oeuvre. According to Harry L. Jones: "An examination of Baldwin's short fiction should provide a basis for some studies on his development as a writer, for the short works seem to contain in microcosm the universe that later manifests itself in Baldwin's major works."

Many of the stories collected in *Going to Meet the Man* were written between 1948 and 1960 and focus on such themes as racial integration and the destruction of childhood innocence by adult experience. While some initial reviewers faulted the stories as self-indulgent, trite, or unconvincing, others praised the authenticity and sincerity of Baldwin's writing. The most highly regarded and frequently discussed of the stories include "Previous Condition," "Sonny's Blues," and the title story of the collection. In "Previous Condition," Baldwin examined the limitations and contradictions of white liberalism and addressed racial alienation through his portrayal of Peter, an unemployed African-American actor who attempts to overcome his racial insecurities through relationships with liberal white friends. These include his Jewish friend Jules, who, as a member of an ethnic minority, purports to understand Peter's ambivalence toward white society, and Ida, Peter's white Protestant girlfriend who chastises him for his feelings of racial inferiority. At the story's climax, Peter is evicted from his apartment building—where most of the residents are white—by a bigoted landlady who tells him "All my tenants are complainin'. Women afraid to come home nights." Never certain of the boundaries between sympathy and hatred, Peter finds that the bigotry evident in some white people ultimately subverts his relationships with others.

Critics generally appraise "Sonny's Blues" as a succinct and moving treatment of the themes of suffering and redemption expressed in his longer works. In this story a conservative black teacher narrates his attempts to com-

prehend the alienated perspective of his brother Sonny, an unemployed jazz pianist and occasional heroin user. Upon hearing that Sonny has been arrested for possession of narcotics, the unnamed teacher refuses to become involved. As the story proceeds he is led to a personal awareness of human frailty through the death of his young daughter. Recalling how his mother sympathetically comforted his father when his father's brother was intentionally hit and killed by a car driven by a drunken white man, the narrator acts on his mother's request that he offer the same sympathy to Sonny in times of duress. Listening to Sonny's jazz solo at a bar in Greenwich Village, the narrator is finally led to an understanding of universal suffering and of his brother's attitudes. John M. Reilly commented: "An outstanding quality of the Black literary tradition in America is its attention to the interdependence of personal and social experience. . . . James Baldwin significantly adds to this aspect of the tradition in 'Sonny's Blues' by showing that artful expression of personal yet typical experience is one way to freedom."

One of Baldwin's most provocative stories, "Going to Meet the Man," alludes to events that transpired in the American South in the early 1960s, and, as in "Sonny's

1

Blues," uses the past as a means of understanding the present. In 1963 Baldwin traveled to Selma, Alabama, to help launch a black voter registration drive. There he encountered James Clark, a Dallas County sheriff who has been suggested as Baldwin's model for the protagonist of "Going to Meet the Man." The story begins the morning after a white deputy sheriff has beaten a young black man for refusing to order his fellow civil rights demonstrators to disperse. In bed with his wife, the sheriff experiences sexual impotence and recalls a childhood episode during which he witnessed the lynching of a black man during a picnic with his parents. Remembering in vivid detail how the man was castrated, dismembered, and burned in front of the crowd, he recalls the mixture of fear, repugnance, and sexual fascination the experience aroused. As this flashback sequence concludes, the sheriff's sexual potency is restored, suggesting a psychological link between his aggressively racist actions and his ability to perform sexually. Although some commentators have considered this treatment of the psychology of racism stereotyped and unconvincing, others have agreed with Peter Freese that "Going to Meet the Man" "probes deeply into the hidden connexions between distorted sexuality, mindless bigotry, and violent racism; and the very fact that Baldwin, through the choice of his narrative perspective, remains sufficiently detached to stand back completely and to let his protagonist reveal himself as both victimizer and victim makes it a compelling and deeply moving story about the havoc worked by racial prejudice among the oppressed and oppressors alike."

PRINCIPAL WORKS

SHORT FICTION

"The Death of the Prophet"   1950; published in journal
    Commentary
Going to Meet the Man   1965

OTHER MAJOR WORKS

Autobiographical Notes (autobiography) 1953
Go Tell It on the Mountain (novel) 1953
The Amen Corner (drama) 1955
Notes of a Native Son (essays) 1955
Giovanni's Room (novel) 1956
*Giovanni's Room (drama) 1957
Nobody Knows My Name: More Notes of a Native Son
    (essays) 1961
Another Country (novel) 1962
The Fire Next Time (essays) 1963
Blues for Mister Charlie (drama) 1964
This Morning, This Evening, So Soon (novel) 1967
Tell Me How Long the Train's Been Gone (novel) 1968
Black Anti-Semitism and Jewish Racism [with others]
    (essays) 1969
A Rap on Race [with Margaret Mead] (dialogue)
    1971
No Name in the Street (essays) 1972
One Day, When I Was Lost: A Scenario Based on 'The Autobiography of Malcolm X' [adaptor; from the novel of the same title by Alex Haley] (screenplay) 1972
A Dialogue [with Nikki Giovanni] (dialogue) 1973

If Beale Street Could Talk (novel) 1974
The Devil Finds Work (essays) 1976
Little Man, Little Man: A Story of Childhood (novel)
    1976
Just above My Head (novel) 1979
The Evidence of Things Not Seen (nonfiction) 1985
Jimmy's Blues: Selected Poems (poetry) 1985
The Price of the Ticket: Collected Nonfiction, 1948-1985
    (nonfiction) 1985
Harlem Quartet (novel) 1987

*This drama is an adaptation of the novel *Giovanni's Room.*

Joseph Featherstone   (essay date 1965)

[*Featherstone is an American educator and critic. In the following review of* Going to Meet the Man, *he faults Baldwin's tendency to treat secular ideas as a means of salvation but praises self-revelatory aspects of his fiction.*]

The blues are an attempt to retain the memory of pain, to transcend catastrophe, not by taking thought—for that often only adds to the pain—but by an attitude, a nearly comic, nearly tragic lyricism. The best stories in James Baldwin's new collection [*Going to Meet the Man*] are blues, fragments of his vast and cureless sorrow. One, **"The Outing,"** is a beautifully disciplined piece of writing. It is hard to know which to admire more, the ironic precision of the characters or the despairing eloquence with which Baldwin spells out a vision of their fate. In subject and time, **"The Outing"** is an early effort. The Hudson River excursion of a Harlem church evokes the world of Baldwin's first and best novel, *Go Tell It On The Mountain* (1953). Here again he describes the tension in the Negro community between the saved and the wavering young, whose burning time is upon them. The hearts of the saints are easy; they know, in their cosmic smugness, the peace that passes understanding. But for the unsaved, growing into consciousness of evil on the Harlem streets and within themselves, there is no peace. The prose is bleak; there is an ugly spareness to the church life. There is none of the rhetorical grandeur that lifted up the experience of the store front churches in *Go Tell It On the Mountain,* none of the Pentecostal ecstasies of God's hand striking the redeemed down onto the dust of the floor, the world rocking on its foundations. Here the lives of the saints are empty too, and the poetry is mostly pathos: the iron of the trap, the defenselessness of the young flesh caught in it.

"Come Out the Wilderness" and **"Sonny's Blues"** were both written in the late fifties. The first again renders Baldwin's ghastly vision of the moral chaos of New York, this time through the eyes of a Negro girl who has escaped North into the dreary landscape of fulfillment. She is sharply seen, a study in pity and rage. She loves a white artist who is sure to leave her; and in one scene, where she lunches with a young Negro executive, Baldwin marvelously creates her scorn and self-hatred, her brave, hopeless love for the white artist, her panic as she realizes the un-likelihood of love flowering in this wilderness. **"Sonny's Blues"** is poised on the edge of certain of the unsolved problems of Baldwin's grand failure, *Another Country* (1962). In its own right, though, **"Sonny's Blues"** is close to a success, the most completely imagined story of the collection, next to **"The Outing."** It is written with detach-ment; sweet objectivity rare for Baldwin who in much of his recent writing has been unable to distinguish between himself and his characters. The story relates the attempt of a Negro schoolteacher, very square, to understand his brother Sonny, a jazz musician and on-and-off dope ad-dict. Variations on its theme have filled all of Baldwin's works: it concerns what Robert Bone has described as the priestly function of the sufferer in Baldwin's fiction. He who manages to endure suffering is set free; more impor-tant, he can set others free through his sacramental minis-trations. Sonny's jazz solo flows from his cracked heart and his sickness. As he plays, the broken pieces of his life fuse for once into a whole which his brother hears and comprehends. It is an extraordinary story, but its testimo-ny is not, in the end, altogether persuasive. There is, first of all, the problem of language, which constantly dogs Bal-dwin: for all his eloquence, he has a hard time sticking to any one tone. Here the brother's sober, square speech is set against Sonny's hip idioms, which in their inarticulate way are meant to point to deeper levels of experience. Yet at the final, the deepest level of experience, the transform-ing power of the jazz solo is described in unexpectedly reli-gious terms: "And he was giving it back, as everything must be given back, so that, passing through death, it can live forever." The terms seem wrong; clearly this is not the voice of Sonny or his brother, it is the intrusive voice of Baldwin the boy preacher who has turned his back on the store front tabernacles but cannot forget the sound of angel's wings beating around his head.

Despite Baldwin's scornful rejection of the "God-shops," life is constantly weighed in the balance against an un-earthly time when he rode the whirlwind of absolute love. The lives of the characters in these stories seem to possess an extra dimension of emptiness, because he sees them against the possibility of a very different kind of life: a life of ceremonies and mysteries touching the absolute. He is searching for another city and another country. Like the great moralizing novelists, he is a preacher; he writes to bear witness. It would be ridiculous, as well as rude, to tell him he should take another tack.

My complaint is simply that the total hunger aching inside him has driven him on to invest certain aspects of secular life—notably sex—with a blasphemous grace, and, alas, the grace is artistically unconvincing. The beauty of the language in *Go Tell It On the Mountain* brought the hero's experience of salvation to life; and, faithful to the spirit of the blues, Baldwin left much of the book's anguish unre-solved. But in recent works he has made larger and larger claims for his various instruments of salvation, while the instruments themselves have become less and less con-vincing. When, in *Another Country,* Baldwin gives us the word about the redeeming majesty of the orgasm—multiracial, heterosexual, or homosexual—you sense a

> **James Baldwin is at his best as himself. His finest work is self-revelatory. . . . This is a source of both weakness and strength. The weakness centers around his difficulty seeing his characters plainly through the distorted lenses of his self-pity and self-love. The strength lies in his ability to endow his experience, his feelings, with universal significance.**
>
> **—*Joseph Featherstone***

lack of artistic control, to say nothing of a loss of common sense.

The stories in this collection thus leave us with the prob-lematic Baldwin of *Another Country,* with his rich prom-ise, his prophet's ambition, his magnificent sense of urban desolation, his lapses of tone, and the spurious religiosity of his sex. There are no resolutions here, no new depar-tures. The four first-rate stories—**"The Outing," "Sonny's Blues," "Come Out the Wilderness,"** and **"Previous Con-dition,"**—were all written before 1958. The title story seems to be a recent effort; it is reminiscent of, though not quite as terrible as, Baldwin's misguided play, *Blues for Mister Charlie* (1964). Here again, he attempts the com-passionate feat of entering into the mind of a Southern rac-ist, in this case a deputy sheriff dealing with civil rights demonstrations. Despite its gruesome stylized lynching scene, **"Going to Meet the Man"** has the same trivial ef-fect as *Blues for Mister Charlie*: it appears that what all this racial fuss stems from is the white man's inability to get it up. After so much suffering and anguish, so many thousands gone, the indictment of the South that emerges is that it's square.

In *Notes of a Native Son* (1955) and *Nobody Knows My Name* (1961) Baldwin argued that part of the race prob-lem was white America's refusal to confront reality, espe-cially the reality of pain, tragedy, violence, sex, and death. This inability to understand forbidden impulses and secret terrors made it hard for the American to know himself; and from a crazy structure of inhibitions and lies followed the fantasies and projections which were the white picture of the Negro. It was a complex and profound argument, full of anger and understanding. Reading **"Going to Meet the Man,"** you dimly recognize the outlines of the argu-ment, reduced to inanely simple terms. It is almost like reading the Book of Job in the form of a comic.

James Baldwin is at his best as himself. His finest work is self-revelatory: the fictional selves who walk the troubled regions of his mind, or the dramatic self created in essays like *The Fire Next Time* (1963). This is a source of both weakness and strength. The weakness centers around his difficulty seeing his characters plainly through the distort-ed lenses of his self-pity and self-love. The strength lies in his ability to endow his experience, his feelings, with uni-versal significance. This one figure, surrounded by darkness, is lit with light of unbelievable intensity. Thus when Baldwin speaks of beauty, a particular undertone of yearning reminds you of the ugly child who put pennies over his eyes to make them go back. Nor are his encounters with the Negro churches or the Black Muslims simply reported; they are aspects of his lost self, the child who wondered in Harlem whose little boy he was. And the race troubles of America are the intersection of James Baldwin and history. Look what you have done to me, says the prophet whose country has endangered his salvation; look at my wounds. What is heard is something more, and something less, than the voice of the Negro. It is the voice of James Baldwin, crying to you from his private wilderness. (pp. 34-6)

Joseph Featherstone, "Blues for Mister Baldwin," in The New Republic, *Vol. 153, No. 22, November 27, 1965, pp. 34-6.*

John Rees Moore (essay date 1965)

[*Moore is an American educator and critic. In the following excerpt, he unfavorably compares Baldwin's* Going to Meet the Man *with his previous works.*]

James Baldwin's most valuable quality as a writer is authenticity. In his new collection of stories, **Going to Meet the Man,** we can trace in little the testing out of experience that is writ large in the novels. The first two stories, **"The Rockpile"** and **"The Outing,"** take us back to Baldwin's memorable first novel, *Go Tell It On the Mountain,* dealing as they do with young John (the hero of the novel) and his attempt to discover in what ways he belongs and doesn't belong to his family. The scene in which Roy, John's younger brother and the father's favorite, is the center of family tensions as he lies savagely wounded in the forehead as the result of a gang fight is brought to life in the novel with all the painful freshness of a physical blow. In **"The Rockpile"** both the racial implications and the violent family antagonisms are much less fully developed, and the story is far less powerful than the corresponding episode in the novel.

A trip up the Hudson to Bear Mountain is the setting for the annual outing of "the saints" in the second story reminiscent of *Go Tell,* though it has no real analogue in the novel. John and Roy, on the brink of adolescence, and their hatred and feared father are all in this story, too; in it John makes the unnerving discovery that David, the slightly older friend to whom he has entrusted the love nobody else wants from him, is growing away from him as he develops an interest in girls. John is left with a feeling of panicky loneliness. The story has a richer potential than Baldwin is able to realize fully within the limits he has imposed upon himself, but the characters and situations are sharply evoked. These stories, like the novel, are close to the marrow of personal experience.

By contrast **"The Man Child"** is a *made up* horror story. Two men have gone through the war together; one has land and wife and son—the other, at thirty-four, has nothing but his dog. His love-hate for his relatively successful and only friend leads the failure to kill his friend's little boy. It cannot be denied that this chilling story is unforget-

table, and the flow of feeling among the four characters is projected with subtlety and skill. Nevertheless, it is *too* well made to carry conviction. One is left with an unpleasant sensation of the author's self-indulgence, not with a sense of tragic inevitability.

Baldwin is a very conscious artist in all his fiction. Represented experience must have a meaning. And he applies all his skill and intelligence to making sure that the shock and pain of this meaning will not be lost on the reader. His people are lonely, frustrated, fearful, often angry, and above all lovelorn. They reach out for the security of love like a drowning swimmer trying to grab a spar from the wreckage to keep himself afloat in the wide, wide ocean. Most of them have a vision of a better land, a better life, but their moments of happiness are always precarious and the surrender to love costs not less than catastrophe. As soon as they are old enough to have a sense of themselves becoming adults (if they live that long), his children, at least the gifted ones, must construct a strategy for finding and then trying to maintain their identities. In expressing the strain and suffering of a person trying to be true to himself and to others Baldwin almost always gives us, often powerfully, a sense of authenticity. But when his imagination is overwhelmed by fantasies of sadism or masochism, the objective reality of his art blurs and the result is bizarre, repellent, and unconvincing. The difficulty is that the territory Baldwin is exploring *does* lie between blatant social fact and nightmare. Besides, he writes on controversial subjects about which "everybody" has strong opinions and, even more to the point, deep-rooted feelings. To Baldwin the distinction between bad dreams and waking horror, or the attempt to make the distinction (even though some of his characters worry about this very thing), may well seem academic. Nevertheless, he knows that for the artist the truth that is stranger than fiction has no place there. At least not in his kind of fiction.

Childhood is frequently important in the five later stories of **Going to Meet the Man,** but the focus is on adult problems, and we don't see these problems from a child's standpoint as we do in the first three. "You are full of nightmares," says Harriet to her worried young husband, who has become a famous musician during his twelve-year stay in Europe. He has just made a film in Paris and is on the point of leaving for America with his wife and sister and seven-year-old son. He is a Negro from Alabama; his wife is Swedish. By leaving America he was able to establish a life of his own; otherwise he could not have entered his own life.

> For everyone's life begins on a level where races, armies, and churches stop. And yet everyone's life is always shaped by races, churches, and armies; races, churches, armies menace, and have taken, many lives. If Harriet had been born in America, it would have taken her a long time, perhaps forever, to look on me as a man like other men; if I had met her in America, I would never have been able to look on her as a woman like all other women. The habits of public rage and power would have blinded our eyes. We would never have been able to love each other. And Paul would never have been born.

And because it saved his life, he loves Paris. He remembers his three-month trip to America when his mother died eight years ago. And how glad he was to get back to Paris. In the film he has just made he played the part of Chico, a half-breed troubadour who, hating his father and mother, flees from Martinique to descend "into the underworld of Paris, where he dies." At first he tried to base his characterization on the Algerians he had known in the city, but the famous director, Vidal, shows him that his performance is not truthful; it becomes truthful when he keeps in the bottom of his mind all the possible fates in store for his son Paul. Nightmares in art ring true when they are based on nightmares in life. **"This Morning, This Evening, So Soon"** exhibits one of Baldwin's recurring themes: the dread of the exile *returning* home. And yet, ironically, a bad thing happens the last night in Paris, of a kind that would be unlikely in New York. The narrator and Vidal have met some young American Negro college students and gone to a Spanish night spot where Boona, an Arab from Tunis who once befriended the narrator, joins them. He apparently steals ten dollars from one of the girls. Amid protestations of trust on both sides, the mistrust is a glaring fact. The Arab is in a worse position than they are (in Paris)—lonelier, poorer, more *unknown*.

In contrast to the "blessed" life possible in Paris for a Negro, **"Previous Condition"** assures us of the purgatorial necessities of the poor but emancipated Negro in New York who has white friends and a white girl, but is never sure that he may not return home at night to find himself forced out of his lodgings. The hatred of the young unemployed actor for *some* whites poisons the liking he wants to have for others. Nor is Baldwin unaware of the difficulties this situation creates for the whites. But a still harder and more poignant problem confronts the hero of **"Sonny's Blues"** when he discovers his younger brother has been arrested as a heroin addict. His first reaction is not to get involved: let Sonny sink or swim, even if he is a kid brother. As usual in a Baldwin story, we are brought to an understanding of a present crisis by an exploration of the past. Just before he was married, the older brother learned from his mother how his father, who had always seemed such a tough and independent man, would have collapsed after an accident in which *his* brother had been killed by some drunken white boys who ran over him, if the mother hadn't supported him by being there—"to see his tears." His mother had only smiled when her eldest son had said he wouldn't let anything happen to Sonny. "You may not be able to stop nothing from happening. But you got to let him know you's *there.*" After his release, Sonny comes to live with his brother and sister-in-law. And one day Sonny talks about what taking the drug, what music, what life, has meant to him, even while he is telling his brother that there is no way he can tell him these things. It is beautifully done. But the climax of the story comes when Sonny takes his brother to his "kingdom" in Greenwich Village and succeeds in saying through the music he creates what he could never say in words. This, I should say, is the most unequivocally successful story in the book.

Love, the poets tell us, is what makes the world go round. Modern novelists show us varieties of sexual experience,

often with the suggestion that "love" is a neurotic disorder that can only interfere with our pleasure and ruin our mental health. In Baldwin's work lovers carry the additional burden of racial consciousness, of revolt against social convention, of a guilt that self-righteousness cannot absolve them from. Yet the very obstacles that make love all but impossible for them give it a peculiar preciousness. Most of them *do* believe in love with a primitive intensity that civilization cannot destroy, though it often destroys *them* for so believing. Ruth in **"Come Out the Wilderness"** is a country girl who has come to the big city to find love and fortune. She is living in Greenwich Village with a young artist, Paul. She is black and he is white. And she knows that the end of their affair is approaching, that Paul will soon leave her. The insurance company she works for in midtown Manhattan has recently hired Negroes; she finds herself "in an atmosphere so positively electric with interracial good will that no one ever dreamed of telling the truth about anything." Ruth thinks of her parents who, though they have labored all their lives in the South, would not have a penny for burial clothes if they should drop dead tomorrow, and of her older brother, almost thirty, still unmarried, "drinking and living off the woman he murdered with his love-making." She wishes she had never left home and never met Paul. She is called into the inner office of Mr. Davis, the only other Negro employee, who tells her she is to be his secretary if she will take the job; he is choosing her not for any racial reason but because she seems the most sensible girl available. She does not really find him attractive but is touched by his humanity. Her love for Paul is "like a toothache," but love ought to be something else, "a means of being released from guilt and terror." Paul would never be able to give her this release. And yet because of Paul she is ashamed and unable to give herself to Mr. Davis. After work, as she sits by herself in a bar, unable to reach Paul by phone and finding the thought of going home to wait for him intolerable, she catches sight of a young fellow whom she finally recognizes as a rising actor. He is pale and fair and boyish and he reminds her of other men she has known—in spite of his coming fame she sees in his face and head that he is "lost." She has seen that look on many, including Paul. And she thinks, "The sons of the masters were roaming the world, looking for arms to hold them. And the arms that might have held them—could not forgive." She stumbles out into the rain, not knowing where to go or where she is going. Her capacity for love combined with her need to use it is her undoing. But here we do feel a potentially "happy" ending withheld. Mr. Davis is an undeniable comfort to have in the background.

In **"Going To Meet the Man,"** the last story in the collection, no such comfort is in sight. Sex, violence, history, the Negro and the South are brought together in a shocker as up to date as tomorrow's newspaper. A deputy sheriff, in bed with his wife, is dismayed to find himself impotent. He tells how he has beaten up a young Negro leader who refused to order his followers to disperse and stop their singing. He remembers a night long ago, riding in a car, sleepy, between his father and his mother. They were one of a long caravan of cars coming back from a lynching. Like a Fourth of July picnic, white men, women, and children had gathered to witness the last rites of a Negro who had, apparently, knocked down a white woman. The boy Jesse was terrified by what he saw—and the burning, castrating, and dismemberment are described in meticulous detail. The boy notices the faces of the watchers as he is perched on his father's shoulders. His mother's "eyes were very bright, her mouth was open: she was more beautiful than he had ever seen her, and more strange. He began to feel a joy he had never felt before." He wishes he were the man with the knife approaching the hanging, naked black body. And when it is over, Jesse feels a great love for his father. "He felt that his father had carried him through a mighty test, had revealed to him a great secret which would be the key to his life forever." Reliving it all, the deputy feels his manhood return to him, and he takes his wife with triumphant violence. With sardonic irony, Baldwin leaves his little fable to speak for itself. It is a tale of outrage and grief and yet of the greatest possible ambivalence, like a ritual at once sacred and obscene. (pp. 1-6)

At this stage in his career it is evident Baldwin is out for the championship. If his novels give the impression that life is over at thirty-five, this will no doubt change with time. He has brains, talent, and a conviction of what art should do: make us change our lives. The unwary reader might get the impression from *Another Country* that sex is the only alternative to a solution of the world's problems. Or perhaps the only solution there is. But Baldwin does not make this mistake. His endeavor is to show us—even to the point of hallucination—that the public life and the private life are an indivisible whole, that sanity cannot exist half slave and half free. (p. 12)

> *John Rees Moore, "An Embarrassment of Riches: Baldwin's 'Going to Meet the Man',"* in The Hollins Critic, *Vol. II, No. 5, December, 1965, pp. 1-12.*

Denis Donoghue   (essay date 1965)

[*Donoghue is an Irish educator, essayist, and critic. In the following review of* Going to Meet the Man, *he identifies the merits and weaknesses of Baldwin's writing style and praises the stories "Sonny's Blues" and "This Morning, This Evening, So Soon."*]

One of the short stories in James Baldwin's new collection [***Going to Meet the Man***] tells of a well-adjusted Negro schoolteacher and his young brother Sonny, a jazz pianist, drug-addict, drop-out. The relationship is heavy with care, constricted with fear, until one night Sonny brings his brother to a place in the Village. The music starts, a man named Creole leads off (bass fiddle), Sonny moves in on the piano, the burdens are suddenly lifted, and in the intensity of the playing (as Keats said of *King Lear*) all disagreeables evaporate. In another story a responsive Frenchman visiting the Negro hero puts on a record: Mahalia Jackson singing "I'm Going to Live the Life I Sing About in My Song." Mr. Baldwin seems to think of his art in similar terms; as a great release, redemption, a long blast on the horn, a flare; afterwards, rest. "Then it was over. Creole and Sonny let out their breath, both soaking wet, and grinning." Hence, in Mr. Baldwin's fiction, sex is the jazz of life; preferably homosexual. Dreams of fair

women are fine for men who like that sort of thing, but the real jazz is a homosexual relation between Black and White. Mr. Baldwin introduced this nuptial image for the first time, as far as my researches go, in his famous lecture at Kalamazoo College. It is featured again in *Another Country,* when Vivaldo meditates on the death of Rufus Scott and thinks of a redemptive opportunity lost. In *Nobody Knows My Name* it is implicated in the notion of "accepting our humanity." By now, it has become enormously extended: everything now depends upon a Negro of homosexual and heterosexual capacities who marries the whole white world. That way, we get Love.

I do not offer this image as an example of Mr. Baldwin's straight thinking, but to suggest that his celebrated eloquence is partly the pressure of need, partly hatred, partly an hysteria of the imagination, and partly something else struggling to get out. The new book makes this a little clearer. Written at intervals since 1948, the short stories can be read as footnotes to the novels, but this is unfair. Some of them are slight things, hardly more than sketches, unofficial essays prophesying fire next time. But there are two stories, **"Sonny's Blues"** and **"This Morning, This Evening, So Soon,"** which are far better than anything else Mr. Baldwin has done in fiction.

The merits of Mr. Baldwin's work are clear enough. He has, to begin with, a high-pressure rhetoric closely related to old-style preaching. His best essays are sermons. The most vivid pages in *Go Tell It on the Mountain* represent Gabriel's sermon, at the Twenty-Four Elders Revival Meeting, on Isaiah, 6, 5: "Then said I, 'Woe is Me!'—for I am undone; because I am a man of unclean lips, and I dwell in the midst of a people of unclean lips." In one of the new stories, **"The Outing,"** there is a memorable sermon by Father James of the Mount of Olives Pentecostal Assembly. Mr. Baldwin's own performances in this genre are impressive; he is not a gleaming Public Man for nothing. He has something to say and he says it over and over again: an unbeatable formula, given modern methods of communication. When the public style goes flat, it is normally because he has run out of wind: "If we are not able, and quickly, to face and begin to eliminate the sources of this discontent in our own country, we will never be able to do it on the great stage of the world."

There are also the autobiographical pieces. When Mr. Baldwin has an event to record, something to report or remember, the sentences sway to the rhythm of the action and the deed is magnificently "done." In *Notes of a Native Son* there is the essay about his preacher-father, a beautiful piece of work. In *Nobody Knows My Name* I think of the hilarious meeting of the Franco-American Fellowship Club in Paris, with poor Richard Wright, as Auden said of Yeats, "silly like us." And there is the visit to Elijah Muhammad, in *The Fire Next Time.* These things are splendidly written, because Mr. Baldwin has a remarkable sense of "the way it was," and he trusts that sense all the way.

But then there are the novels. They seem to me, when all is said, very bad. "The way it was" is one thing: "the way it might be" is another. Mr. Baldwin is weak on invention. If he has seen or heard or suffered something, he can transcribe it. But if he has to invent a character, imagine a world for him, and devise other characters to live in that world, he is defeated. Worse still if he has to develop the action, complicate the characters, show one thing pressing upon another. Even the best of the short stories are precarious structures, eleventh hour achievements: the novels are poor enough when short, frightful when long. For one thing, Mr. Baldwin's characters, under this pressure of development, all talk like Mr. Baldwin. They have no life apart from his life. In *Another Country* Cass gets into a taxi and starts thinking of Eric. Even as Mr. Baldwin's characters go, Cass is extremely limited in her perception. But her reflections are given thus:

> She would have been glad to know his body, even though the body might be all that she could know. Eric's entrance into her, her fall from—grace?—had left her prey to ambiguities whose power she had never glimpsed before. Richard had been her protection, not only against the evil in the world, but also against the wilderness of herself. And now she would never be protected again.

So Mr. Baldwin makes his feeling serve for all feeling, his intelligence for all intelligence. He cannot imagine things different from his own. In *Giovanni's Room* the first meeting of David and Giovanni sounds like Mr. Baldwin reading one of his essays to himself, aloud, for later transmission on an educational network. So the novels are almost entirely deficient in measure, in scale; for how can you measure things which are all equally you? Mr. Baldwin has only himself to imagine. Presumably this is why he cultivates his own "strangeness"; as in *Nobody Knows My Name* when the Black Boy (Baldwin) looks at the White Boy (Mailer) and finds what Love cannot do: "It could not make me over, for example. It could not undo the journey which had made of me such a strange man and brought me to such a strange place."

Mr. Baldwin may have had trouble in accepting his strangeness, but he has managed it and now would not be seen without it. But Yeats's idiom in "Anima Hominis" comes to mind:

> We make out of the quarrel with others, rhetoric, but of the quarrel with ourselves, poetry. Unlike the rhetoricians, who get a confident voice from remembering the crowd they have won or may win, we sing amid our uncertainty; and, smitten even in the presence of the most high beauty by the knowledge of our solitude, our rhythm shudders.

Mr. Baldwin has a constant quarrel with others, and it is a real and justifiable quarrel, but he gives no sign of quarreling with himself. He uses the word "Love" as if he had a patent on it, and in *Notes of a Native Son* he speaks of his real life being in danger "from the hate I carried in my own heart," but the novels are an interminable quarrel with others, a binge of hatred. ["Going to Meet the Man"] is a sadistic sexual fantasy on the mutilation of a Negro. The detail runs to burning testicles, a can of kerosene, the charred corpse, the joy of the avengers. These images are attributed to Jesse, a local Deputy Sheriff, and the color-scheme is suitably reversed, but the images are Mr. Baldwin's images, rounding out the symmetry of *Another Country*, where Jesse's Gothic scream was first heard.

The new book contains eight stories. Five of them are familiar to readers who keep up with the magazines: **"Previous Condition," "The Outing," "Sonny's Blues," "Come Out the Wilderness,"** and **"This Morning, This Evening, So Soon."** The remaining stories are published now for the first time: **"The Rockpile," "The Man Child,"** and **"Going to Meet the Man."** The themes bear Mr. Baldwin's trademark: hatred between father and mother; young homosexual love; middle-aged homosexual love; Black married to White; how they order these things better in France. In **"Previous Condition"** a Negro actor is thrown out of a white room by a white landlady: the result is a dream of violence which will certainly boost membership of the Klan. The story is a frame-up, though, as the sensitive black plant wilts in the glare of the white man's culture:

> I looked at the ads, unreal women and pink-cheeked men selling cigarettes, candy, shaving cream, nightgowns, chewing gum, movies, sex; sex without organs, drier than sand and more secret than death.

This reminds me of the scene in *Another Country* where Rufus cries his heart out to Vivaldo, accompanied by Bessie Smith singing "Backwater Blues." **"The Man Child"** is a better story, about the murder of a boy by a man who loves the boy's father. **"Sonny's Blues"** is very impressive; especially the long conversation in which the teacher's mother tells him about the white men who killed his uncle, gunning him down with a car. The only serious defect in this story is the old defect that the characters are too often merely Mr. Baldwin's mouthpieces. When Isabel complains about Sonny playing the piano all the time, the complaint comes in the voice of James Baldwin; it is merely a function of his larger, incessant complaint. There is a curious ventriloquism in these reported speeches: we see Isabel making the gestures, but what we hear is the old preacher-prompter, sounding off:

> Isabel finally confessed that it wasn't like living with a person at all, it was like living with sound. And the sound didn't make any sense to her, didn't make any sense to any of them—naturally. They began, in a way, to be afflicted by this presence that was living in their home. It was as though Sonny were some sort of god, or monster. He moved in an atmosphere which wasn't like theirs at all . . . it was as though he were all wrapped up in some cloud, some fire, some vision all his own; and there wasn't any way to reach him.

But where is Isabel? Again, when Sonny talks about the unreality of other people, he fades off into Mr. Baldwin—his voice, his tone, his everything—author of *The Fire Next Time*. Still, the story manages to hold on, surviving, and it lodges in the mind.

The meat of the book is **"This Morning, This Evening, So Soon."** An American Negro singer in Paris is visited by his sister, a schoolteacher from Alabama. He is married to a white girl, Harriet, a Swede, and everything there is fine. Recently, he has made a hit in a film, and fame has come. Now, the night before leaving for the feared U.S.A., he goes out on the town with his French director. They meet a quartet of Southern boys and girls, and a Tunisian ex-prizefighter called Boona, light of finger because life is rugged. So the story proceeds. Ten or fifteen pages later you notice that something is missing. Then you place it: no scream, no hatred, no burning testicles, no grinding axe. We are in yet another country, a place rarely visited by Mr. Baldwin. If France is really like this, there is no excuse for being anywhere else. Anyway, the story brings out the artist in Mr. Baldwin, that suffering thing struggling to escape. It is a short story, so he does not have to strain, pulling and hauling, pumping the prose: there is no recourse to the Public Address System. It is beautifully done. When the American lapses into hate, you catch for a paragraph or two the old familiar venom, blues for Mr. Baldwin, but it passes: other things are acknowledged. The relationship between the singer and his director is sketched with notable tact; there is no attempt to pluck out the heart of every mystery. The incidents are unspectacular: the singer and his party move from one nightplace to another, a girl loses ten dollars, Boona seems to have stolen the money. So the night ends. The singer goes back to his apartment, to his wife, his sister, his son Paul. No more; but enough. Measure, scale, tact: these are the marks of the story. And the writing is at once controlled and free. (pp. 6-7)

> *Denis Donoghue, "Blues for Mr. Baldwin," in The New York Review of Books, Vol. V, No. 9, December 9, 1965, pp. 6-7.*

Stanley Kauffmann (essay date 1965)

[*Kauffmann is one of America's best-known contemporary film and theater critics. A contributor of reviews to several magazines, he has served as the film critic of the* New Republic. *Although the theater and cinema are Kauffmann's primary concerns, he is also a knowledgeable authority on American and world literature. In the following review of* Going to Meet the Man, *Kauffmann asserts that Baldwin's stories are less accomplished than his nonfiction works.*]

[*Going to Meet the Man*] invites little new comment because it contains little new work. Of the eight stories, five were published between 1948 and 1960, and none of the others was, I hope, written subsequently. The first two stories, **"The Rockpile"** and **"The Outing,"** seem to be sketches for his first novel, *Go Tell It on the Mountain,* published in 1953. Freshness from the mint is no test of quality, but neither is quality proved by scraping the past in response to an author's present popularity.

It is widely held that Baldwin's best work is done in nonfiction. His exceptional polemic gifts, as writer and as speaker in the civil rights movement, have helped to fix that view relatively swiftly. That this view is just, that Baldwin is not the ironic artist-victim of the social-political movement in which he is fiercely engaged, is demonstrated again in this book.

Let us look first at the element that strikes the reader first: the prose. It is crusted with cliché. From the very first

paragraph: "Roy felt it to be his right, not to say his duty, to play there."

A glimpse of a barmaid: "When she smiled one saw the little girl, one sensed the doomed, still-struggling woman beneath the battered face of the semi-whore."

A description of jazz: "Creole began to tell us what the blues were all about. They were not about anything very new. He and his boys up there were keeping it new, at the risk of ruin, destruction, madness, and death, in order to find new ways to make us listen."

The triteness of the writing indicates a regard for this prose that is different from that for his essay prose. Would he, in an essay, call a cigarette a "sublimatory tube"? If it is asserted that this is early work and that his fictional prose has improved (which is arguable), then the willingness to publish this book, as is, indicates another difference of regard. Very little of this writing shows the incisiveness of phrase, the rhythmic control, the attractively serpentine and dramatic structure, the simple care, that mark his other writing.

Insofar as the content of fiction can be distinguished from the writing, when we leave Baldwin's prose in these stories to consider their content, we move from the question of sheer workmanship to that of basic talent. He often picks a good locus for a story (it is his best fictional gift), which is often sexual. Saul Bellow wrote of Baldwin's last novel: "All the important questions . . . are translated into sex."

In this collection we have an American Negro with a white Swedish wife, a Negro girl with a white lover, a Southern sheriff who is impotent with his wife until he thinks of Negro girls and racial violence. These are all good blueprints for stories. But when the generally leathery prose allows us to ignore its rivets to see what it contains, we find chunks of material: chosen but not digested, assaulted but not taken: stories that lack the elements of personal truth and personal artifice that move material from concern into art.

"Come Out the Wilderness" has an excellent point of tension: a sensitive Negro girl who lives with a white painter is virtually sentenced to a relationship with her commonplace Negro boss because she feels the futility of her liaison. But as the story moves to its climax, we are principally conscious of the conventional tapering of the spotlight, narrowing on her for a final emotional solo, of the sob that will—inevitably—involuntarily escape her throat.

The force of the subject and the sincerity of the author are swamped in the banalities of method. There is not a stroke in the story that is not stock in characterization or mechanically naked. It would be possible to hypothesize that occasionally Baldwin's intensity of concern paralyzes his art if elsewhere in his book—or in his novels and plays—one had been sufficiently convinced of his power to assimilate observation and experience and to illuminate them, instead of merely relating them to us in compassionate rage, touched up with literary-Freudian veneer.

This inadequacy is underscored in the one story that deals exclusively with white people, **"The Man Child."** It is unimpelled by social anguish and unaided (as others are) by vividness of milieu. "As the sun began preparing for her exit, and he sensed the waiting night," the reader enters an account of a conflict between two farmers seen through the eyes of the 8-year-old son of one of them, who is eventually murdered by his father's friend. The tone of the piece is a throwback to the twenties of O. E. Rölvaag, the stark poetry of the soil that flourished in literary magazines until it collapsed in the Depression. This tone seems a refuge for an author dealing with unfamiliar emotion and environment. The failure of imagination is so thorough that it provides a clear view of the residually small talent in the other stories, there cloaked by social urgency and sexual detail.

All the above only supports my opening statement: there is little new to say about Baldwin's fiction. His strength and value, so far, are in the world of fact, not of art. Speaking of Negro writers, Ralph Ellison said: "What moves a writer to eloquence is less meaningful than what he makes of it." This was not written specifically of Baldwin, but, in my view, it applies to him.

> Stanley Kauffmann, "Another Baldwin," in The New York Times Book Review, December 12, 1965, p. 5.

David Littlejohn   (essay date 1965)

[*An American educator, critic, and fiction writer, Littlejohn is the author of* Black on White: A Critical Survey of Writing by American Negroes *(1966). In the following review of* Going to Meet the Man, *Littlejohn affirms that both negative and positive aspects of Baldwin's short fiction are relevant to an understanding of his novels and nonfiction.*]

There are a number of James Baldwins, who write with varying degrees of honesty, relevance, humility, precision and style. All of them are [apparent in *Going to Meet the Man*]: the autobiographizing lyrist, the taut-strung neurotic, the truth teller of the early essays, the celebrity bully. But the shrill and ugly voices, for our purposes, the inflated and fraudulent selves can be as useful as the eloquent and the honest. For James Baldwin is not just another stylish bestseller, not just the latest and most advertised "Negro" writer; least of all is he only a by-product of and publicist for the Civil Rights episode. He is becoming, if he has not already become, our Exemplary Man. One of his distressing liabilities, I grant, is that he *knows* this, knows it too well, that he wears his robes heavily and with swagger. Nevertheless, to understand him may well be, in many and difficult ways, to understand ourselves, and these stories will help.

Going To Meet the Man should not be read first or alone, since many of its effects depend on interreflections back and forth with the earlier works. Some stories borrow the voice and setting of *Go Tell It on the Mountain;* others the jagged, brittle tones, the Manhattan underground world of *Another Country.* Many echo the essays too, once strong ideas with much of their savor gone. And there are tastes as well as the whining, bullying rant of *The Fire Next Time,* the flip self-importance of the Mailer essay or *Nothing Personal.* But all of it counts, even the dispiritingly

bad. Much of the excitement of reading this collection, in fact, comes from a reader's constant, hovering balance between reassurance and despair, reassurance at what is so right, despair at what is so wrong. It is one of the most full-blooded, alive and anxious books of the year.

Of the weak, or perverse, or even merely dispensable stories—four out of eight, which is probably not bad—two are appendices to *Go Tell It on the Mountain* of 1953, with the same boy hero, the same family and setting, roughly the same manner and tone. **"The Rock Pile"** is a tiny étude, austere and slightly touching; **"The Outing"**—again young John and his family, on a church picnic up the Hudson River—is much more ardently and vigorously bad. It bears the *idea* of a good story, the skeleton of it: the cracking of adolescent tensions within the setting of a Negro Ship of Fools. It even includes a rich, rocking 8-page tour de force of a Negro shipboard service. But we have come a long way down from *Go Tell It on the Mountain.* There, the passional catharsis, the harrowing of emotions, filial, sexual, religious, were worked through, suffered for, honestly earned and attained. Here they are only tiredly told, unconvincingly claimed and remembered.

But there are worse. **"Previous Condition"** and **"This Morning, This Evening, So Soon"**—the latter his *New Yorker* story, his anthology story—represent the worst of the several James Baldwins, the pretentious, near-paranoiac, picked-on Negro, ostentatiously bearing all the sufferings of his race. They recall the worst excesses of *The Fire Next Time.* In both cases, a clue is the total lack of detachment between the author and his heroes, his sniveling, chip-on-the-shoulder narrator heroes. This suffering, self-pitying voice is a sign of James Baldwin's least controlled and least valuable fiction.

It is not easy to be a Negro, a writer, a celebrity and a homosexual in America, and sometimes the strain will show; it is not even easy to be a thinker in America, and this is part of the lesson of Baldwin's weaker work. But at his best, he can move terror and tears, he can do things that need to be done better than anyone else.

"Sonny's Blues" hovers delicately in tone between *Go Tell It on the Mountain* and *Another Country:* it is a small, artless, ambling story, one weak man's memory of his brother. It is the account of his long attempt to understand his brother Sonny, a junkie turned jazz pianist in Harlem, so quietly and uncertainly told that it is almost not a story at all, but just the telling, the trying; a confession that drifts coolly and unhurriedly through digression and reminiscences.

"Come Out of the Wilderness," at the opposite extreme, is a dazzling display of Baldwin's style at its sharpest. Its prose surface has a bristly, electric exactness, its dialogue the bright newness of good talk. Nor is this style mere bravura display; it sparks into life an analysis of mixed emotions, a dramatization of the undercurrents of social intercourse that is diabolically keen. The story, an open and unprejudiced playing through of the *Odi et amo* tensions of an affair, seems a distillate of all that is best in *Another Country.* It has the same crackling Manhattan setting, the same crouching-cat tension. It has something new and

Much of the excitement of reading [*Going to Meet the Man*] comes from a reader's constant, hovering balance between reassurance and despair, reassurance at what is so right, despair at what is so wrong. It is one of the most full-blooded, alive and anxious books of the year.

—David Littlejohn

surprising to say about the races. In its Gallic manipulation of human paradoxes, it offers a cool, cruel analysis of the self-deluding stratagems of lovers, a microscopic plotting of our bitchy little hearts.

"The Man Child" is something entirely new for Baldwin, a highly charged lyrical, pastoral tragedy. Tightened, condensed, closed up, "fired" somehow, it would be as full and classic a piece of pain as a D. H. Lawrence story. Four people—a boy, his father, his father's friend, his mother—are frozen in a mythic isolation. Their story grows, the trap tightens, slowly and expansively, through incremental repetitions, incantatory rhythms, the loving simple cadences of a legend.

The title story, finally, deserves its pre-eminence: it is the most important story here. **"Going To Meet the Man"** is Baldwin's second attempt to imagine sympathetically the mind of a Southern white bigot. I found his picture to be credible, intense and almost hypnotically convincing. It is everything that his first attempt, *Blues for Mister Charlie*, was not.

From a surprising opening in his nuptial bed, we follow the nighttime reverie of a many-ways-frustrated Southern deputy sheriff, a TV newsreel figure come to life. Reflections on his brutal day among the Negroes lead him back, through the device of a remembered song, to where it all began: the pace, the simple river-run structuring are flawless. In a scene worked with exact and almost unbearable crescendo, the reader watches (with the boy Jesse) his first lynch burning, every detail. And as his anticipation turns, with the boy's, to a strange kind of horrified fulfillment, he may find himself forced to admit that there *is* in this barbaric, anti-human rite a genuine primeval satisfaction. Lynchings do really happen, and one comes to understand why. (pp. 478-80)

David Littlejohn, "Exemplary & Other Baldwins," in The Nation, New York, Vol. 201, No. 20, December 13, 1965, pp. 478-80.

Sam Bluefarb (essay date 1969)

[*Bluefarb is an American educator, critic, and novelist. In the essay below, Bluefarb examines themes of alienation and self-identity in Baldwin's story "Previous Condition."*]

In James Baldwin's story **"Previous Condition"** (1948), a young black actor (read artist, intellectual, or both, for actor) attempts to find some form of identification in the white world; but ironically he also fails to find even a place for himself in the black world. He is a not-so-daring young man on a flying trapeze between two unattainable poles.

The opening of the story sets its tone. The first paragraph adumbrates, through its imagery, the plight of the Negro not only in the story but in the United States. Peter the young actor wakes up in a cold sweat, alone in a room, shaking with fear. He may have had a nightmare which, transferred to the waking-up, has him observe: "The [bed] sheet was gray and twisted like a rope." The allusion of this simile should be fairly obvious.

In the second paragraph, Peter tells us: "I couldn't move for the longest while. I just lay on my back, spreadeagled. . . ."—suggesting an earlier form of torture-punishment.

This story of the alienated and invisible man in miniature—it antedated Ralph Ellison's novel *Invisible Man* by some four years—portrays the hero's sensitivity and intellectuality that form the ingredients of his invisibility; it thus reveals the plight of the black artist-intellectual in the white world, but it goes even further to reveal that individual's plight in the black world. In this respect, **"Previous Condition"** is as powerful a piece of writing as any of Baldwin's essays. For it poses a two-fold problem of identification for a certain category of Negro—the Negro intellectual.

That Baldwin makes Peter an actor is interesting, since Baldwin himself has been interested in the theater and has even done a stint of playwriting himself. However, Baldwin, being the pro that he is, makes Peter an actor as a kind of metaphor for the artist-intellectual, which of course permits him to place Peter in "double jeopardy"— his alienation as a Negro, and his alienation as an artist in America, both thoroughly "American" ingredients.

Perhaps Baldwin chose acting for Peter's profession as a kind of provocation to white sensibilities, since for the Negro, being black and being an actor in the mid-'forties (when the story was written) would be an almost impossible combination. As Peter tells us, speaking of a play in which he has recently appeared but which has had a short run:

> I played a kind of intellectual Uncle Tom, a young college student working for his race. The playwright had wanted to prove he was a liberal, I guess. But, as I say, the show had folded and here I was, back in New York and hating it. I knew that I should be getting another job, making the rounds, pounding the pavement. But I didn't. I couldn't face it. It was summer. I seemed to be fagged out. And every day I hated myself more. Acting's a rough life, even if you're white. I'm not tall and I'm not good looking and I can't sing or dance and I'm not white; so even in the best of times I wasn't much in demand.

But Peter's problem is as much his alienation as an intellectual as his alienation as a Negro. He is at once patronized by the white liberals—in the persons of the "Jewboy" Jules Weissman (Whiteman?) and the white Protestant

Ida—and he is not understood by his fellow Negroes; indeed, as we see before the story ends, he is regarded with greater suspicion by them than by his white friends.

There is of course the lack of communication, inevitable in such a situation. Jules and Ida both "know" Peter intellectually, understand his problems intellectually, sympathize with him intellectually—but they cannot *feel* with him. Between Jules and Ida, then, there is little true understanding of Peter's problem—how can there be?— "liberal" as they are.

There are a number of attempts at communication on the part of the white "liberal" world (Jules and Ida)—all unsuccessful. At one point in the story, after Peter has been evicted from his room by his white landlady, Ida attempts to lecture Peter. The lecture, in the face of Peter's virtually insurmountable problems, is a simple-minded "appeal to reason":

> It's no better anywhere else [she tells Peter]. In all of Europe there's famine and disease, in France and England they hate the Jews— nothing's going to change, baby, people are too empty-headed, too empty-hearted—it's always been like that, people always try to destroy what they don't understand—and they hate almost everything because they understand so little—

Jules too attempts to console Peter over the eviction: " 'Cheer up, baby. The world's wide and life—life, she is very long.' " (Curiously, both Ida and Jules address Peter as "baby," a gratuitous familiarity, and Jules's "The world's wide," may have been an ill-concealed "The world's *white!*") Both forms of consolation fail, however, and Peter is left, as he had been all along, alone. His answer to Jules at this point is, quite appropriately, " 'Shut up. I don't want to hear any of your bad philosophy.' "

The white bigot of a landlady tells him that he must leave her rooming house because, " 'I can't have no colored people here. . . . All my tenants are complainin'. Women afraid to come home nights.' " But if these words enrage Peter all the more, he can at least understand them. The landlady who spits them out is at least the tangible enemy, the Ofay. He knows where *she* stands. It is the intangible, and perhaps more insidious, enemy that proves a tougher problem for Peter. This "enemy" is embodied perhaps in such well-meaning but innocent white liberals as Jules and Ida, who in their bumbling ways are ineffective precisely because they try so hard to be effective. Perhaps this is true of many white liberals *vis a vis* "the problem"—they try too hard, and thus turn into what I have called *white Uncle Toms.*

Jules and Ida each lecture Peter—Ida as the "voice of reason"; Jules, as Job's comforter. Yet neither Jules nor Ida can really know (with their entire beings) Peter the Negro, just as his own people cannot know Peter the Artist-Intellectual.

Jules's lectures are gratuitous (though he isn't as vocal as Ida), but they are still the verbal equivalent of Ida's rapping Peter across the knuckles with a piece of silverware in a restaurant for talking himself down. Except that where Jules is the "philosopher," Ida is the "activist" who engages (and enrages) Peter by her brash familiarities (the incident of the knuckle-rapping).

Jules, the sympathetic "Jewboy," as Peter calls him, knows persecution too—though only at a second, or perhaps third remove. Yet Jules in America cannot know, or could not have known, the intense experience of the European Jews under Hitler. As I have said, Jules after all, is a Jew living in *America*—a point that cannot be stressed too much in this context—but Peter is a *Negro* living in America. Therein lies the vast difference. Thus Jules, no matter his "Jewish understanding" as fellow victim, may sympathize with Peter, but he cannot really emphathize with him.

Ida, Peter's girl, though a "liberal," is still the white bitch goddess (that symbol of success and "making it" in the white world) toward whom Peter has ambivalent attitudes. For both guilt and shame are present in Peter, since he could easily be accused of being a sexual Uncle Tom— the "black buck" to satisfy the voracious white nymphomaniac.

While the whites differ from each other—from personal sympathy (Jules Weissman), to "understanding" (Ida), to outright fear and hatred (the bigoted landlady)—in the end it is all one blank white wall that Peter faces. His eventual return to Harlem, to his "previous condition" (really not his *previous* condition) only serves to underline his lack of contact with the white world.

Back in Harlem, Peter sees the sights and the sounds he knows so well, but these give him little comfort either:

> I got off [the subway train] in Harlem and went to a rundown bar on Seventh Avenue. My people, my people. Sharpies stood on the corner, waiting. Women in summer dresses pranced by on wavering heels. . . . There were white mounted policemen in the streets. On every block there was another policeman on foot. I saw a black cop.
>
> God save the American republic.

Peter's journey is no mere journey, then, to Harlem, or back into his "previous condition"; it is a journey to the end of his own personal night. And although he attempts to return to his "previous condition," to "my people," he finds that this too is impossible. It actually is worse than "knowing one's place and keeping it." The title of the story thus reveals its theme, though with intense irony— especially when Peter, after his harsh experiences in the white world ("liberal" or racist) returns to Harlem to find a place for himself there. For even in Harlem he finds himself alone, misunderstood, the object of suspicion.

He is thus a stranger in his "own land" (Harlem, that is); but of course he is an even greater stranger in that greater land of which Harlem is only a part, though still a most significant—and barometric—part.

Peter's inability to identify with either group—black or white—represents of course the true source of his alienation, as a Negro in the white society and as an Artist-Intellectual in the black. He can identify neither with Jules nor with Ida, for a world of time and color separates them from him; yet he cannot identify with his own people, as represented—perhaps unfairly on Baldwin's part—by the old Negro woman he meets in the Harlem bar. For all she can tell him—and she pulls no punches—is " 'Nigger . . . you must think you's somebody' "—which goes unanswered since Peter cannot communicate with her either. "I didn't seem to have a place," Peter tells us after this experience. And, curiously, in these words lies the core of the story. They have become a refrain which is adumbrated when Jules asks Peter, on the occasion of the latter's eviction from the rooming house, how he, Peter, has fared. Peter's answer, as may be recalled, is an ironically wry " 'No room at the inn,' " an answer which has biblical undertones an intellectual—especially a black intellectual—would make in the bitterness of his lot, an answer which has its echoes two thousand years after the incident which inspired it.

With whom, then, can Peter identify? Obviously, at this stage, with no one—unless it be with other black intellectuals, which in itself would become a form of separatism and therefore alienation. Thus, he is too bright and sensitive for the black Harlem milieu of bars and honky-tonks and too black for the white world whether "liberal" or racist. Peter stands between the two, though unable to bridge the gap between them. Thus, like Ellison's invisible man, he can truthfully say:

> . . . there was nothing except my color. A white outsider coming in would have seen a young Negro drinking in a Negro bar, perfectly in his element, in his place, as the saying goes. But the people [in the bar] knew differently, as I did. *I didn't seem to have a place.* [My italics]

In attempting to bridge the gap between the white world and the black, perhaps before those worlds are ready for it, Peter fits in, in neither.

Thus the story ends as it begins, a young black intellectual suspended between two worlds—is it too much to identify Peter with Baldwin himself?—neither of which he feels "at home" in, neither of which really wants him, and perhaps, even more important, neither of which *he* wants.

The story further ends on a note of indecision, as indeed it does today when, most poignantly for both blacks and whites of good will, neither can seem to "join hands" as completely as they would like to. Encapsulated, then, in this story, lies the true dilemma of black and white in the second half of the twentieth century. (pp. 26-9)

> *Sam Bluefarb, "James Baldwin's 'Previous Condition': A Problem of Identification," in* Negro American Literature Forum, *Vol. 3, No. 1, Spring, 1969, pp. 26-9.*

John M. Reilly (essay date 1970)

[*A respected American critic and educator who has served as a contributing editor for* Obsidian/Black Literature in Review *and a continuing reviewer for* Callaloo: Journal of the Black South, *Reilly has published numerous book-length studies on such African-American authors as Richard Wright and Ralph Elli-*

son. In the following essay, which is generally regarded as among the most influential treatments of "Sonny's Blues," Reilly examines Baldwin's sympathetic evocation of black community.]

A critical commonplace holds that James Baldwin writes better essays than he does fiction or drama; nevertheless, his leading theme—the discovery of identity—is nowhere presented more successfully than in the short story **"Sonny's Blues."** Originally published in *Partisan Review* in 1957 and reprinted in the collection of stories **Going to Meet the Man** in 1965, **"Sonny's Blues"** not only states dramatically the motive for Baldwin's famous polemics in the cause of Black freedom, but it also provides an esthetic linking his work, in all literary genres, with the cultures of the Black ghetto.

The fundamental movement of **"Sonny's Blues"** represents the slow accommodation of a first-person narrator's consciousness to the meaning of his younger brother's way of life. The process leads Baldwin's readers to a sympathetic engagement with the young man by providing a knowledge of the human motives of the youths whose lives normally are reported to others only by their inclusion in statistics of school dropout rates, drug usage, and unemployment.

The basis of the story, however, and its relationship to the purpose of Baldwin's writing generally, lies in his use of the Blues as a key metaphor. The unique quality of the Blues is its combination of personal and social significance in a lyric encounter with history. [According to Janheinz Jahn in his *Neo-African Literature,* 1968], "The Blues-singer describes first-person experiences, but only such as are typical of the community and such as each individual in the community might have. The singer never sets himself against the community or raises himself above it." Thus, in the story of Sonny and his brother an intuition of the meaning of the Blues repairs the relationship between the two men who have chosen different ways to cope with the menacing ghetto environment, and their reconciliation through the medium of this Afro-American musical form extends the meaning of the individual's Blues until it becomes a metaphor of Black community.

Sonny's life explodes into his older brother's awareness when the story of his arrest for peddling and using heroin is reported in the newspaper. Significantly the mass medium of the newspaper with the impersonal story in it of a police bust is the only way the brothers have of communicating at the opening of the story. While the narrator says that because of the newspaper report Sonny "became real to me again," their relationship is only vestigially personal, for he "couldn't find any room" for the news "anywhere inside. . . ."

While he had had his suspicions about how Sonny was spending his life, the narrator had put them aside with rationalizations about how Sonny was, after all, a good kid. Nothing to worry about. In short, the storyteller reveals that along with his respectable job as an algebra teacher he had assumed a conventional way of thinking as a defense against recognizing that his own brother ran the risk of "coming to nothing." Provoked by the facts of Sonny's arrest to observe his students, since they are the same age as Sonny must have been when he first had heroin, he no-tices for the first time that their laughter is disenchanted rather than good-humored. In it he hears his brother, and perhaps himself. At this point in the story his opinion is evidently that Sonny and many of the young students are beaten and he, fortunately, is not.

The conventionality of the narrator's attitude becomes clearer when he encounters a nameless friend of Sonny's, a boy from the block who fears he may have touted Sonny onto heroin by telling him, truthfully, how great it made him feel to be high. This man who "still spent hours on the street corner . . . high and raggy" explains what will happen to Sonny because of his arrest. After they send him someplace and try to cure him, they'll let Sonny loose, that's all. Trying to grasp the implication the narrator asks: "You mean he'll never kick the habit. Is that what you mean?" He feels there should be some kind of renew-al, some hope. A man should be able to bring himself up by his will, convention says. Convention also says that be-havior like Sonny's is deliberately self-destructive. "Tell me," he asks the friend, "why does he want to die?" Wrong again. "Don't nobody want to die," says the friend, "ever."

Agitated though he is about Sonny's fate the narrator doesn't want to feel himself involved. His own position on the middle-class ladder of success is not secure, and the supporting patterns of thought in his mind are actually rather weak. Listening to the nameless friend explain about Sonny while they stand together in front of a bar blasting "black and bouncy" music from its door, he senses something that frightens him. "All this was carry-ing me some place I didn't want to go. I certainly didn't want to know how it felt. It filled everything, the people, the houses, the music, the dark, quicksilver barmaid, with menace; and this menace was their reality."

Eventually a great personal pain—the loss of a young daughter—breaks through the narrator's defenses and makes him seek out his brother, more for his own comfort than for Sonny's. "My trouble made his real," he says. In that remark is a prefiguring of the meaning the Blues will develop.

It is only a prefiguring, however, for the time Sonny is re-leased from the state institution where he had been con-fined, the narrator's immediate need for comfort has passed. When he meets Sonny he is in control of himself, but very shortly he is flooded with complex feelings that make him feel again the menace of the 110th Street bar where he had stood with Sonny's friend. There is no escap-ing a feeling of icy dread, so he must try to understand.

As the narrator casts his mind back over his and Sonny's past, he gradually identifies sources of his feelings. First he recalls their parents, especially concentrating on an image of his family on a typical Sunday. The scene is one of security amidst portentousness. The adults sit without talking, "but every face looks darkening, like the sky out-side." The children sit about, maybe one half asleep and another being stroked on the head by an adult. The dark-ness frightens a child and he hopes "that the hand which strokes his forehead will never stop." The child knows,

however, that it will end, and now grown-up he recalls one of the meanings of the darkness is in the story his mother told him of the death of his uncle, run over on a dark coun-try road by a car full of drunken white men. Never had his companion, the boy's father, "seen anything as dark as that road after the lights of the car had gone away." The narrator's mother had attempted to apply her tale of his father's grief at the death of his own brother to the needs of their sons. They can't protect each other, she knows, "but," she says to the narrator about Sonny, "you got to let him know you's *there.*"

Thus, guilt for not fulfilling their mother's request and a sense of shared loneliness partially explain the older broth-er's feeling toward Sonny. Once again, however, Baldwin stresses the place of the conventional set of the narrator's mind in the complex of feelings as he has him recall scenes from the time when Sonny had started to become a jazz musician. The possibility of Sonny's being a jazz rather than a classical musician had "seemed—beneath him, somehow." Trying to understand the ambition, the narra-tor had asked if Sonny meant to play like Louis Arm-strong, only to be told that Charlie Parker was the model. Hard as it is to believe, he had never heard of Bird until Sonny mentioned him. This ignorance reveals more than a gap between fraternal generations. It represents a cultur-al chasm. The narrator's inability to understand Sonny's choice of a musical leader shows his alienation from the mood of the post-war bebop sub-culture. In its hip style of dress, its repudiation of middle-brow norms, and its cel-ebration of esoteric manner the bebop sub-culture made overtly evident its underlying significance as an assertion of Black identity. Building upon a restatement of Afro-American music, bebop became an expression of a new self-awareness in the ghettos by a strategy of elaborate non-conformity. In committing himself to the bebop sub-culture Sonny attempted to make a virtue of the necessity of the isolation imposed upon him by his color. In con-trast, the narrator's failure to understand what Sonny was doing indicates that his response to the conditions im-posed upon him by racial status was to try to assimilate himself as well as he could into the mainstream American culture. For the one, heroin addiction sealed his member-ship in the exclusive group; for the other, adoption of indi-vidualistic attitudes marked his allegiance to the histori-cally familiar ideal of transcending caste distinctions by entering into the middle class.

Following his way Sonny became wrapped in the vision that rose from his piano, stopped attending school, and hung around with a group of musicians in Greenwich Vil-lage. His musical friends became Sonny's family, replacing the brother who had felt that Sonny's choice of his style of life was the same thing as dying, and for all practical purposes the brothers were dead to each other in the ex-tended separation before Sonny's arrest on narcotics charges.

The thoughts revealing the brothers' family history and locating the sources of the narrator's complex feelings about Sonny all occur in the period after Sonny is released from the state institution. Though he has ceased to evade thoughts of their relationship, as he had done in the years when they were separated and had partially continued to do after Sonny's arrest, the narrator has a way to go before he can become reconciled to Sonny. His recollections of the past only provide his consciousness with raw feeling.

The next development—perception—begins with a scene of a revival meeting conducted on the sidewalk of Seventh Avenue, beneath the narrator's window. Everyone on the street has been watching such meetings all his life, but the narrator from his window, passersby on the street, and Sonny from the edge of the crowd all watch again. It isn't because they expect something different this time. Rather it is a familiar moment of communion for them. In basic humanity one of the sanctified sisters resembles the down-and-outer watching her, "a cigarette between her heavy, chapped lips, her hair a cuckoo's nest, her face scarred and swollen from many beatings. . . ."

"Perhaps," the narrator thinks, "they both knew this, which was why, when, as rarely, they addressed each other, they addressed each other as Sister." The point impresses both the narrator and Sonny, men who should call one another "Brother," for the music of the revivalists seems to "soothe a poison" out of them.

The perception of this moment extends nearly to conception in the conversation between the narrator and Sonny that follows it. It isn't a comfortable discussion. The narrator still is inclined to voice moral judgments of the experiences and people Sonny tries to talk about, but he is making an honest effort to relate to his brother now and reminds himself to be quiet and listen. What he hears is that Sonny equates the feeling of hearing the revivalist sister sing with the sensation of heroin in the veins. "It makes you feel—in control. Sometimes you got to have that feeling." It isn't primarily drugs that Sonny is talking about, though, and when the narrator curbs his tongue to let him go on, Sonny explains the real subject of his thoughts.

Again, the facts of Sonny's experience contradict the opinion of "respectable" people. He did not use drugs to escape from suffering, he says. He knows as well as anyone that there's no way to avoid suffering, but what you can do is "try all kinds of ways to keep from drowning in it, to keep on top of it, and to make it seem . . . like *you*." That is, Sonny explains, you can earn your suffering, make it seem "like you did something . . . and now you're suffering for it."

The idea of meriting your suffering is a staggering one. In the face of it the narrator's inclination to talk about "will power and how life could be—well, beautiful," is blunted, because he senses that by directly confronting degradation Sonny has asserted what degree of will was possible to him, and perhaps that kept him alive.

At this point in the story it is clear that there are two themes emerging. The first is the theme of the individualistic narrator's gradual discovery of the significance of his brother's life. This theme moves to a climax in the final scene of the story when Sonny's music impresses the narrator with a sense of the profound feeling it contains. From the perspective of that final scene, however, the significance of the Blues itself becomes a powerful theme.

The insight into suffering that Sonny displays establishes his priority in knowledge. Thus, he reverses the original relationship between the brothers, assumes the role of the elder, and proceeds to lead his brother, by means of the Blues, to a discovery of self in community.

As the brothers enter the jazz club where Sonny is to play, he becomes special. Everyone has been waiting for him, and each greets him familiarly. Equally special is the setting—dark except for a spotlight which the musicians approach as if it were a circle of flame. This is a sanctified spot where Sonny is to testify to the power of souls to commune in the Blues.

Baldwin explicates the formula of the Blues by tracing the narrator's thoughts while Sonny plays. Many people, he thinks, don't really hear music being played except so far as they invest it with "personal, private, vanishing evocations." He might be thinking of himself, referring to his having come to think of Sonny through the suffering of his own personal loss. The man who makes the music engages in a spiritual creation, and when he succeeds, the creation belongs to all present, "his triumph, when he triumphs, is ours."

In the first set Sonny doesn't triumph, but in the second, appropriately begun by "Am I Blue," he takes the lead and begins to form a musical creation. He becomes, in the narrator's words, "part of the family again." What family? First of all that of his fellow musicians. Then, of course, the narrator means to say that their fraternal relationship is at last fulfilled as their mother hoped it to be. But there is yet a broader meaning too. Like the sisters at the Seventh Avenue revival meeting Sonny and the band are not saying anything new. Still they are keeping the Blues alive by expanding it beyond the personal lyric into a statement of the glorious capacity of human beings to take the worst and give it a form of their own choosing.

At this point the narrator synthesizes feelings and perception into a conception of the Blues. He realizes Sonny's Blues can help everyone who listens be free, in his own case free of the conventions that had alienated him from Sonny and that dimension of Black culture represented in Sonny's style of living. Yet at the same time he knows the world outside of the Blues moment remains hostile.

The implicit statement of the esthetics of the Blues in this story throws light upon much of Baldwin's writing. The first proposition of the esthetics that we can infer from **"Sonny's Blues"** is that suffering is the prior necessity. Integrity of expression comes from "paying your dues." This is a point Baldwin previously made in *Giovanni's Room* (1956) and which he elaborated in the novel *Another Country* (1962).

The second implicit proposition of the Blues esthetics is that while the form is what it's all about, the form is transitory. The Blues is an art in process and in that respect alien from any conception of fixed and ideal forms. This will not justify weaknesses in an artist's work, but insofar as Baldwin identifies his writing with the art of the singers of Blues it suggests why he is devoted to representation, in whatever genre, of successive moments of expressive feeling and comparatively less concerned with achieving a consistent overall structure.

The final proposition of the esthetics in the story **"Sonny's Blues"** is that the Blues functions as an art of communion. It is popular rather than elite, worldly rather than otherwise. The Blues is expression in which one uses the skill he has achieved by practice and experience in order to reach toward others. It is this proposition that gives the Blues its metaphoric significance. The fraternal reconciliation brought about through Sonny's music is emblematic of a group's coming together, because the narrator learns to love his brother freely while he discovers the value of a characteristically Afro-American assertion of life-force. Taking Sonny on his own terms he must also abandon the ways of thought identified with middle-class position which historically has signified for Black people the adoption of "white" ways.

An outstanding quality of the Black literary tradition in America is its attention to the interdependence of personal and social experience. Obviously necessity has fostered this virtue. Black authors cannot luxuriate in the assumption that there is such a thing as a purely private life. James Baldwin significantly adds to this aspect of the tradition in **"Sonny's Blues"** by showing that artful expression of personal yet typical experience is one way to freedom. (pp. 56-60)

> *John M. Reilly, " 'Sonny's Blues': James Baldwin's Image of Black Community," in* Negro American Literature Forum, *Vol. 4, No. 2, July, 1970, pp. 56-60.*

Donald C. Murray   (essay date 1977)

[*In the following essay, Murray explores themes of self-identity, escape, loss, and transcendence in "Sonny's Blues."*]

> One boy was whistling a tune, at once very complicated and very simple, it seemed to be pouring out of him as though he were a bird, and it sounded very cool and moving through all that harsh, bright air, only just holding its own through all those other sounds.

In the world of **"Sonny's Blues,"** the short story by James Baldwin, the author deals with man's need to find his identity in a hostile society and, in a social situation which invites fatalistic compliance, his ability to understand himself through artistic creation which is both individual and communal. **"Sonny's Blues"** is the story of a boy's growth to adulthood at a place, the Harlem ghetto, where it's easier to remain a "cunning child," and at a time when black is not beautiful because it's simpler to submerge oneself in middle-class conformity, the modish antics of the hipster set, or else, at the most dismal level, the limbo of drug addiction, rather than to truly find oneself. Sonny's brother, the narrator of the story, opts for the comforts of a respectable profession and his specialty, the teaching of algebra, suggests his desire for standard procedures and elegant, clear-cut solutions. On the other hand, Sonny at first traffics with the hipster world; yet not without imposing "his own halfbeat" on "the way the Harlem hipsters

walk." Eventually, however, as if no longer able to hold his own through all those other sounds of enticement and derision, Sonny is sentenced to a government institution due to his selling and using heroin.

With his brother in a penal establishment and himself a member of the educational establishment, it's fitting that the narrator would learn of Sonny's imprisonment while reading the newspaper, probably an establishment press, and while riding in a subway, an appropriate vehicle for someone who hasn't risen above his origins so far as he hopes. The subway world of roaring darkness is both the outside world of hostile forces and the inner heart of darkness which we encounter at our peril, yet encounter we must. The narrator at first cannot believe that Sonny has gone "down" ("I had kept it outside me for a long time."), but he is forced to realize that it has happened, and, thinking of heroin, he suspects that perhaps "it did more for [Black boys like Sonny] than algebra could." Playing upon the homonym of Sonny, Baldwin writes that, for the narrator's brother, "all the light in [Sonny's] face" had gone out.

Images of light and darkness are used by Baldwin to illustrate his theme of man's painful quest for an identity. Light can represent the harsh glare of reality, the bitter conditions of ghetto existence which harden and brutalize the young. Early in the story the narrator comes upon a boy in the shadow of a doorway, a psychologically stunted creature "looking just like Sonny," "partly like a dog, partly like a cunning child." Shortly thereafter he watches a barmaid in a dingy pub and notes that, "When she smiled one saw the little girl, one sensed the doomed, still-struggling woman beneath the battered face of the semi-whore." Both figures will appear again, in other forms, during the revival meeting later in the story. At this point, however, the narrator turns away and goes on "down the steps" into the subway. He retreats from the light, however dim.

Another kind of light is that of the movie theater, the light which casts celluloid illusions on the screen. It is this light, shrouded in darkness, which allows the ghetto-dwellers' temporary relief from their condition. "All they really knew were two darknesses," Baldwin writes, "the darkness of their lives, which was now closing in on them, and the darkness of the movies, which had blinded them to that other darkness." This image of the movie theater neatly represents the state of people who are at once together and alone, seated side-by-side yet without communication. Baldwin deftly fuses the theater and subway images: "They were growing up with a rush and their heads bumped abruptly against the low ceiling of their actual possibilities." The realities are far different from the idealistic dreams of the cinema; as outside the subway window, so behind the cinema screen there is nothing but roaring darkness.

There is no escape from the darkness for Sonny and his family. Dreams and aspirations are always dispelled, the narrator comments, because someone will always "get up and turn on the light." "And when light fills the room," he continues, "the child is filled with darkness." Grieved by the death of his child, fortuitously named Grace, and aware of the age difference between himself and Sonny, the narrator seems unconsciously to seek out the childlike qualities of everyone he meets. He is not quite the self-satisfied conformist which some critics have made him out to be. He looks back toward a period in the lives of others when they presumably were not tormented by the need to choose between modes of living and to assert themselves. To the extent that he is given to this psychological penchant, the narrator is close in age to Sonny and **"Sonny's Blues"** is the story of the narrator's dawning self-awareness. The revelation of his father's brother's murder and the fact of Grace's death make Sonny's troubles real for the narrator and prompt the latter's growth in awareness.

To be aware of oneself, Baldwin believes, is to feel a sense of loss, to know where we are and what we've left behind. Sonny's presence forces the narrator to examine his own past; that is, the past which he left behind in the ghetto ("the vivid, killing streets of our childhood") and, before that, in the South. "Some escaped the trap," the narrator notes, "most didn't." "Those who got out always left something of themselves behind," he continues, "as some animals amputate a leg and leave it in the trap." The image is violent and is in keeping with the narrator's tendency to see people "encircled by disaster." The violence reminds us of the fate of the narrator's uncle, a kind of black Orpheus who, carrying his guitar, was deliberately run-down by a group of drunken whites. The narrator's father, we are told, was permanently disturbed by the slaughter of his brother. The age difference between the narrator and Sonny, like that between the narrator and his uncle and that between Sonny and his fellow musician Creole, all suggest that the fates of the generations are similar, linked by influences and effects. "The same things happen," the narrator reflects, "[our children will] have the same things to remember."

So, too, the story is cyclical. We begin in the present, move into the immediate past, then into the more remote past of the narrator's family, then forward to the time of the narrator's marriage and his early conversations with Sonny about his proposed career as a musician, thereafter to Sonny's release from prison and his most recent discussion of music ("It makes you feel—in control"), and finally to the night club episode in the immediate present. Similarities in characters and events link the various sections of the story. The barmaid in the opening section, who was "still keeping time to the music," and the boy whose bird-like whistling just holds its own amid the noise, are linked to the revivalists, whose "singing filled the air," and to Sonny, whose culture hero is "Bird" Parker and whose role is to create music rather than merely keep time. The revivalists are singing near the housing project whose "beat-looking grass lying around isn't enough to make [the inhabitants'] lives green." Looking like one of the narrator's schoolboys, Sonny watches the three sisters and brother in black and carries a notebook "with a green cover," emblematic of the creative life he hopes to lead. Unlike his brother's forced payment to the indigent, child-like man, Sonny drops change into the revivalists' tambourine and the instrument, with this gratuitous gift, turns into a "collection plate." The group has been playing "*If*

I could only hear my mother play again!" and Sonny, after "faintly smiling," returns to this brother's home, as if in response to the latter's promise to their mother that he will safeguard Sonny. Recognizing Sonny as both a creative individual and a brother, the narrator is "both relieved and apprehensive."

The narrator's apprehension is justified in that he is about to witness Sonny's torturous rebirth as a creative artist. " 'But I can't forget—where I've been,' " Sonny remarks to his brother and then adds: " 'I don't mean just the physical place I've been, I mean where I've *been*. And *what* I've been'." In terms which might recall Gerard Manley Hopkins' anguished sonnet "I wake and feel the fell of darkness," Sonny goes on to describe his own dark night of the soul: " 'I was all by myself at the bottom of something, stinking and sweating and crying and shaking, and I smelled it, you know? *my* stink, and I thought I'd die'." Because of the enormous energy and dedication involved in his role as Blues musician, Sonny is virtually described as a sacrificial victim as well as an initiate into the mysteries of creativity. Somewhat like the Christ of *noli me tangere*, Sonny's smile is "sorrowful" and he finds it hard to describe his own terrible anguish because he knows that it can come again and he almost wonders whether it's worth it. Yet his anguish is not only personal but representative, for as he looks down from the window of his brother's apartment he sees " 'all that hatred and misery and love,' " and he notes that, " 'It's a wonder it doesn't blow the avenue apart'." As the pressure mounts within Sonny, the author sets the scene for the final episode of the story.

Befitting the special evening which ends **"Sonny's Blues,"** the locale shifts to the "only night club" on a dark downtown street. Sonny and the narrator pass through the narrow bar and enter a large, womblike room where Sonny is greeted with " 'Hello, boy' " by a voice which "erupted out of all that atmospheric lighting." Indeed the atmosphere is almost grandly operatic in its stage quality. The booming voice belongs to the quasi-midwife, Creole, who slaps Sonny "lightly, affectionately," as if performing the birth rite. Creole is assisted by a "coal-black" demiurge, "built close to the ground," with laughter "coming up out of him like the beginning of an earthquake." As if to underscore the portentousness of this evening in Sonny's "kingdom," the narrator thinks that, "Here it was not even a question that [Sonny's] veins bore royal blood." The imagery of light now blends with that of water as the narrator, describing the light which "spilled" from the bandstand and the way in which Sonny seems to be "riding" the waves of applause, relates how Sonny and the other musicians prepare to play. It is as if Sonny were about to undergo another stage in his initiation into mature musicianship, this time a trial by fire. "I had the feeling that they, nevertheless, were being most careful not to step into that circle of light too suddenly," the narrator continues, "that if they moved into the light too suddenly, without thinking, they would perish in flame." Next the imagery suggests that Sonny is embarking upon a sacred and perilous voyage, an approach to the wholly other in the biblical sense of the phrase; for the man who creates music, the narrator observes, is "hearing something else, is dealing with the roar rising from the void and imposing order on it as it hits the air." The roaring darkness of the subway is transformed into something luminous. Appropriately, the lighting turns to indigo and Sonny is transfigured.

Now the focus again shifts to Creole, who seems to hold the musicians on a "short rein": "He wanted Sonny to leave the shore line and strike out for the deep water. He was Sonny's witness that deep water and drowning were not the same thing—he had been there, and he knew." Creole now takes on the dimensions of the traditional father-figure. He is a better teacher than the narrator because he has been in the deep water of life; he is a better witness than Sonny's father because he has not been "burned out" by his experiences in life. Creole's function in the story, to put it prosaically, is to show that only through determination and perseverance, through the taking of a risk, can one find a proper role in life. To fail does not mean to be lost irretrievably, for one can always start again. To go forward, as Sonny did when Creole "let out the reins," is to escape the cycle which, in the ghetto of the mind, stifles so many lives, resulting in mean expectations and stunted aspirations. The narrator makes the point that the essence of Sonny's blues is not new; rather, it's the age-old story of triumph, suffering, and failure. But there is no other tale to tell, he adds, "it's the only light we've got in all this darkness."

Baldwin is no facile optimist. The meaning of **"Sonny's Blues"** is not, to use the glib phrase, the transcendence of the human condition through art. Baldwin is talking about love and joy, tears of joy because of love. As the narrator listens to his brother's blues, he recalls his mother, the moonlit road on which his uncle died, his wife Isabel's tears, and he again sees the face of his dead child, Grace. Love is what life should be about, he realizes; love which is all the more poignant because involved with pain, separation, and death. Nor is the meaning of **"Sonny's Blues"** the belief that music touches the heart without words; or at least the meaning of the story is not just that. His brother responds deeply to Sonny's music because he knows that he is with his black brothers and is watching his own brother, grinning and "soaking wet." This last physiological detail is important, not just imagistically, because Baldwin is not sentimentalizing his case in **"Sonny's Blues."** The narrator is well aware, for example, that his profound response to the blues is a matter of "only a moment, that the world waited outside, as hungry as tiger"—a great cat ready to destroy the birdlike whistling—"and that trouble stretched above us, longer than the sky." The final point of the story is that the narrator, through his own suffering and the example of Sonny, is at last able to find himself in the brotherhood of man. Such an identification is an act of communion and **"Sonny's Blues"** ends, significantly, with the image of the homely Scotch-and-milk glass transformed into "the very cup of trembling," the Grail, the goal of the quest and the emblem of initiation. (pp. 353-57)

Donald C. Murray, "James Baldwin's 'Sonny's Blues': Complicated and Simple," in Studies in Short Fiction, *Vol. 14, No. 4, Fall, 1977, pp. 353-57.*

Peter Freese   (essay date 1977)

[In the essay excerpted below, Freese advances a psycho-analytic reading of Baldwin's story "Going to Meet the Man."]

In 1965, at the height of his fame, Baldwin published his only volume of short stories to date. Of ten stories which had been printed between 1948 and 1962 in magazines as diverse as *Mademoiselle* and *Partisan Review* he selected five for this collection. Four of the other five had been prepublications of parts of novels in progress and thus were no longer available, while the fifth, **"The Death of the Prophet"** (*Commentary,* March 1950), may have been too openly autobiographical for another publication. To these five reprints, one of which was written as far back as 1948, Baldwin added, with **"The Rockpile," "The Man Child,"** and the title story, three hitherto unpublished pieces. This collection, ***Going to Meet the Man,*** became a great success with the general reading public, but it got rather mixed reviews, and, with the possible exception of **"Sonny's Blues,"** so far Baldwin's stories have scarcely attracted any sustained critical commentary. This is regrettable because an early story like **"Previous Condition"** contains nearly all the themes and techniques Baldwin was to unfold in his *oeuvre* and thus serves as a useful introduction to an understanding of his work, an ambiguous parable like **"The Man Child"** merits the closest scrutiny, and the highly controversial **"Going to Meet the Man"** is one of the most brilliant among the rich crop of contemporary Afro-American stories.

It was only in the fall of 1957 that Baldwin, the urban Northerner, visited the South for the first time, and he went there, as he states in his [essay] "Nobody Knows My Name: A Letter from the South," with his mind "filled with the image of a black man, . . . , hanging from a tree, while white men watched him and cut his sex from him with a knife." It is this nightmarish image of the 'strange fruit' of the sexless black man hanging from a tree that lies at the core of **"Going to Meet the Man"** ("GMM") and that puts the story in a group with other narratives about the 'lynching bee' like Faulkner's "Dry September," Caldwell's "Saturday Afternoon," or Wright's "Big Boy Leaves Home." But the story has also a topical significance, as it alludes directly to the events of the sixties in Alabama. In October 1963 Baldwin went South again to help James Forman, the executive secretary of SNCC, to launch a Negro-voter registration drive in Selma, Alabama. There he encountered James Clark, the Dallas County sheriff known as Big Jim Clark and notorious for his violent measures against black demonstrators. It seems quite obvious that this man served as the model for the "Big Jim C." of the story who is also engaged in dispersing a line of demonstrators claiming the right "to register." Even the recurring motif of the lonely car whose lights hit the shutters of a room and frighten the people inside seems to come directly from Baldwin's own experience: telling Fern Marja Eckman about his secret nightly meeting with Forman, he said:

> We were sitting around talking . . . And then you'd realize that a car was coming. And that everyone was listening . . . And the car

would—you'd see the lights of the car pass the
window. In this total silence. And you'd be
aware that everyone, including you, was waiting
for bullets. Or a *bomb*. And the car would pass
and you'd go to the blinds and look out . . .

Thus the story, which must have been written between
1963 and 1965, combines Baldwin's personal experiences
in the South with his almost obsessive concern with the
hidden connexions between racism and sexuality, and it
might be read as a fictional variation upon his earlier statement that the inexorable law that "whoever debases others
is debasing himself " could be "proved by the eyes of any
Alabama sheriff."

The action of **"GMM"** covers about three hours in the life
of a deputy sheriff named Jesse in some nameless Southern
town torn out of its tranquillity by protesting Blacks who
no longer accept 'their place.' But Baldwin, as in all his
work, cannot renounce his conviction "that the past is all
that makes the present coherent," and, in order to convey
this central message, he makes use of his favoured technique, the flashback. Thus the story unfolds in an intricate
sequence of flashbacks within flashbacks within a frame,
and the three hours of the present action are gradually extended through diverse memory fragments until almost
the whole of Jesse's life is compressed into the limited
scope of the story.

The present action, which hardly contains any action,
shows Jesse in bed with his wife Grace, and it reaches from
"two in the morning" to the time of "the first cock crow."
Sleepless, bewildered by the violent events of the preceding day, and deeply disturbed by his sudden sexual impotence, he tosses around beside his sleeping wife, and while
he hovers on the edge between wakefulness and sleep his
thoughts start wandering back into the past. From the incidents of the day they move back to a long forgotten encounter several years ago, and then the "forty-two"-year-
old man suddenly recalls the day when, as a boy of
"eight," he was taken by his parents to participate in the
gory ritual of a lynching. In between Jesse's thoughts always return to the present. . . .

[The] seemingly arbitrary and aimless chain of Jesse's
thoughts is arranged in a symmetrical pattern, both halves
of which begin and end on the level of the present action.
The first part starts the exploration of the past with a return to the immediately preceding day, into which is in-
serted the memory of an event of several years ago. The
second part moves back thirty-four years to the day of the
lynching, which, in accordance with the overall direction
of the narration, is remembered backwards, beginning
with the evening. Such a reconstruction of the story's
movement in time might give the impression that
"GMM" is a rather artless thesis story in which the rigid
patterning of an author intent upon his message becomes
visible behind the supposedly random thoughts of his protagonist. This, however, is not at all the case, for, on the
contrary, the reader never gets the feeling of a manipulating authorial presence, but accepts the flow of Jesse's
thoughts as the reminiscences of a deeply disturbed man
which only follow the relentless logic of an obsessed mind.
To create such an effect Baldwin makes use of the tech-

nique of association, and a closer look at the 'seams' between the different sections will show how naturally
Jesse's mind moves from one level to the next and thus finally and compulsively reaches the traumatic experience
which has determined his future development and formed
his racial and sexual attitudes alike.

When Jesse gives up his fruitless attempts to have sex with
his passive wife, his thoughts run back to the events of the
day, and his wish that he might "never have to enter that
jail house again" triggers off memories of his violent confrontation with the black leader of the registration drive.
His next step further back into the past is convincingly
prompted by his sudden recognition that, several years
ago, he had encountered that very person and that even
then the still boyish Black had dared demand equal treatment. While thus a place of action and a person figure as
associative signals linking different time levels, the next
switch seems to be entirely arbitrary and therefore inexplicable, for the transition is marked by a melody, the first
line of a spiritual, that comes "flying up at" Jesse "out of
nowhere." But whereas the sheriff cannot see the connexion, the attentive reader knows full well that it was the
constant and defiant singing of the black demonstrators
that unnerved Jesse the most. When the sheriff asks himself, "Where had he heard that song?", it is clear that some
hidden and hitherto suppressed nexus will soon come to
light, and it is of an additional, ironic significance that it
is a song from the black man's past of slavery and oppression and a song about the hoped-for rebirth in Christ that
serves as the catalyst of Jesse's self-recognition and the
revelation of his buried past. The final movement back to
the present is brought off by a phrase which Jesse has
taken over from his father, for it is his father's "I reckon"
that is repeated thirty-four years later by the son and that
serves as an indication of the fact that Jesse has inherited
his whole view of life from his father, that the son, as the
pitiable heir of an inhumane tradition, has to pay for the
sins of the father, that the present is nothing but a logical
extension of the past.

It is the very "psychoanalytische Untersuchungsmet-
hode" [or psychoanalytic method of examination] that
Wüstenhagen, from his Marxist point of view, criticized
as one of Baldwin's central shortcomings, that lends a relentless logic and a compelling drive to **"GMM."** The evident parallels between the unfolding of this story and the
standard procedures of the psychoanalytical session that
turn Jesse's marriage bed into the analyst's couch and link
his chain of memories with a patient's process of free association make the story all the more convincing and add a
new level of significance. The obvious temptation, however, to understand Jesse's finally regained potency as the result of a successful act of autotherapy should not be accepted too quickly.

The ominous atmosphere of the story's frame is determined by recurring details, among which three are of special importance: the light of the "full . . . moon," which
has "grown cold as ice" at the end of the story; the two
dogs "barking at each other" in the silent night, which
"begin to bark" again when Jesse comes back out of his
reverie; and the sound of a car "hit[ting] gravel," which

is repeated as "the sound of tires on the gravel road" in the very last sentence. These details, which link beginning and end and create an effect of threat—Jesse is "reaching for his holster" when the car appears—, of loneliness, and of sterility, have another, more important function, for they are also meaningfully connected with the decisive incidents in Jesse's past. The light of the passing car hitting the shutters of the sheriff's bedroom is reminiscent of the return from the lynching when "the car lights picked up their wooden house," and the barking of the dogs in the silence of the night may subconsciously remind Jesse of the night of the lynching when their dog "began to bark" and was "yawning and moaning outside." The icy light of the moon, on the other hand, is contrasted with the burning light of the sun during the lynching; and the singing of the demonstrators which so inexplicably angered and unsettled the sheriff, reminds him, although he does not yet realize it, of "the singing [that] came from far away, across the dark fields" as a dirge for the murdered man on the evening of the lynching.

Thirty-four years have elapsed between the night in which an eight-year-old boy, who had just witnessed the abominable torturing and killing of a black man, was lying sleeplessly in his bed and listening fearfully to the sounds of his parents copulating, and the night in which a forty-two-year-old man, who has cruelly tormented a black prisoner, is tossing sleeplessly in his bed and worrying about his newly discovered impotence. All the carefully but unobtrusively rendered details of the story conspire to create an eerie effect of *deja-vu* and contribute to the brilliant illumination of hitherto hidden connexions between a boy's traumatic experience and a man's pathological behaviour. The missing link between past and present is suddenly brought to light, the behaviour of the brutal racist is exposed as the inevitable result of his socialization, the victimizer revealed as the victim of his diseased mind.

It is obvious that for Jesse racial and sexual attitudes are inextricably linked, and a closer look at the sexual aspects of his behaviour should help to clarify his particular syndrome. When he cannot reach an orgasm, excitement fills him "just like a toothache," and the indistinct image of some black girl whom, in contrast to his wife, he might have asked "to do just a little thing for him" fills him with new excitement, which is, again, "more like pain." When his wife has gone to sleep, Jesse—"one hand between his legs"—is frightened by the sound of a passing car, and fervently wishes—an ironic ambiguity—"to let whatever was in him come out, but it wouldn't come out." Again he reflects that unfortunately he cannot ask Grace to act "the way he would ask a nigger girl to do it," and his recollection that "sometimes . . . he would . . . pick up a black piece or arrest her, it came to the same thing," reveals that he is used to finding his sexual gratification with black women and that he does not mind misusing his official authority in order to make them comply with his wishes. For the Jesse of the present action sexual excitement is closely linked with pain, fear, some indistinct memories, and a belief in the sexual superiority of black people.

When during the first flashback Jesse tortures his black prisoner he suddenly feels "that peculiar excitement which refused to be released" and begins "to hurt all over." When he hits his victim in the testicles he feels "very close to a very peculiar, particular joy," and "something deep in him and deep in his memory was stirred, but whatever was in his memory eluded him." Torturing his prisoner gives Jesse an erection, but he also feels "an icy fear rise in him," and when he beats the black man who appears to him as "a goddamn bull," "for some reason, he grabbed his privates," an instinctive gesture of defense reminiscent of that in the preceding scene. Here, again, the same syndrome can be observed: for Jesse, the sadist, sexual excitement is linked with the notion of black skin, accompanied by fear, released by violence, and related to some indistinct memory.

It is the lynching scene that provides an account of the genesis of this syndrome. Jesse, the eight-year-old boy, is "full of excitement" like all the other spectators. He is "at once very happy and a little afraid," and when he looks at the body of the victim, which for him is "the most beautiful and terrible object," he feels "a joy he had never felt before." When watching the castration "in terror" he feels "his scrotum tighten." Thus the first sexual awakening of the white boy is connected with the violent emasculation of a black man, and the idea of the black man's dangerous and enviable potency is unforgettably implanted in the child's mind. All the grown-up participants in the gruesome ritual are sexually aroused—the radiant eyes and open mouth of Jesse's mother prove this as well as his father's tongue and the light in his eyes—and when Jesse's parents come home, they engage in a lovemaking for which the lynching serves as a kind of stimulating foreplay, while the child in the adjoining room is "terribly afraid," "frightened," and full of "fear" because of what he has seen and is now listening to.

Jesse, the impotent husband in the marriage bed, pays the price for Jesse, the sadistic tormentor in the prison cell, and both act out the pathologically disturbed attitudes once acquired by Jesse, the terrified child at the lynching. The vague and indistinct memories which puzzled the sheriff in the first and second scene can now be located, and the child's feeling "that his father [by taking him to the lynching] had carried him through a mighty test, had revealed to him a great secret which would be the key to his life forever" has come true with a vengeance. What Jesse has acquired in his shocking initiation is an utterly diseased attitude toward sexuality linked with a peculiar mixture of contempt for and envy of black people. For him Negroes are "no better than animals," are "black stinking coons" stigmatized by racial characteristics like strong body odour, "kinky, greasy hair" and "fat lips." But they are also "pretty good at that [i.e. sex]," have testicles that are "the largest thing," and seem to be "goddamn bull[s]." Thus they are objects of scorn and contempt as well as of envy and secret admiration. But one cannot envy and despise the same people at the same time, and so Jesse has to sort out his feelings by destroying the threatening potency of black men and enjoying the sexual prowess of black women, by accepting old and sexually no longer active Blacks as 'good niggers'—of "some of the old women" and "a few of the old men" he knows "that they were singing for mercy for his soul, too"—and by rejecting young and sexually dangerous Blacks as 'bad niggers'—it is the "young people" who have changed the words of the songs and are "singing white people into hell." Such a double standard, however, cannot be emotionally sustained; the peculiar mixture of aggression and suffering, violence and fear, envy and contempt corrupts the mind, and thus finally the victimizer turns out to be the victim of his own obsession, the man who debases others is found to debase himself.

Jesse's contradictory sexual attitudes are paralleled by other, even more obvious contradictions. The man who bears the ironically inappropriate name of the father of King David and ancestor of Jesus, who takes himself to be "a good man, a God-fearing man," and who seriously believes that "God was the same for everyone," daily sins against the basic tenets of Christianity, does not love his neighbour if he is black, rejects the idea of a common brotherhood of man, and jeers at the notion of equality. The man who believes that he is doing nothing but "his duty" in his devoted fight for "law and order" and who feels that he is "fighting to save the civilized world" against the onslaught of black animals—and at the same time being undeservedly criticized by "the bastards from the North"—misuses his official authority in order to act out his sadistic urges upon defenseless prisoners and to degrade black women into the objects of his lust. Jesse has inherited all these contradictions, together with his perverted sexual mores, from "his models," the men of his father's generation, who have taught him "what it meant to be a man." From them, too, he has learned how to treat a white woman, and it fits the overall pattern of the story only too well that his passionless wife, who is so aptly named Grace, appears to him like a "frail sanctuary" covered by the moonlight "like glory." Her he does not dare importune with his sexual desires; she, who talks "gently" to her labouring husband, must not be asked to "help him out," and whenever he wants "a little more spice than Grace could give him" he has to visit some black girl. Grace becomes the embodiment of 'Southern womanhood,' the pure, sexless lady raised upon a pedestal to serve as an object of glorification for Southern chivalric gyneolatry.

It should be obvious by now that Jesse, although convincingly portrayed as an individual, is not so much the single man, but the "Man," the representative of a whole social system, the embodiment of the old order of the South, and that Jesse's plight and his psychically induced impotence stand for the downfall of a social system that has lost its power because of its innate contradictions, its inhumanity, and its moral corruption. Thus, as it were, the ontogenetic process gains a phylogenetic dimension, the story of an individual aberration becomes the paradigm of the pathology of a whole society.

The aspects of this failure are sufficiently familiar from countless sociological studies: Calvin C. Hernton's analysis of the "myth of Negro sexual virility" [in his *Sex and Racism*, 1970] is as relevant to an understanding of **"GMM"** as his interpretation of the ritual of castration, which according to him does not only represent

> . . . the destruction of a mythical monster, but

also the *partaking* of that monster . . . In taking the black man's genitals, the hooded men in white are amputating that portion of themselves which they secretly consider vile, filthy, and most of all inadequate. At the same time, castration is the acting out of the white man's guilt for having sex with Negro women, and of the white man's hate and envy of the Negro male's supposed relations with and appeal to the white woman. And finally, through the castration rite, white men hope to acquire the grotesque powers they have assigned to the Negro phallus, which they symbolically extol by the act of destroying it.

Also appropriate as a comment on Jesse's behaviour is Lillian Smith's observation [in her *Killers of the Dream*, 1949] that "the lynched Negro becomes *not an object that must die* but a receptacle for every man's damned-up hate, and a receptacle for every man's forbidden sex feelings"; equally illuminating with regard to Baldwin's story in general is her ominous image of the *Strange Fruit*. W. C. Cash's discussion of the Southerner's rape complex is as pertinent to an understanding of the disturbed deputy sheriff as his exposition of Southern gyneolatry is to the portraiture of Grace. Thornton Stringfellow's notorious pamphlet "A Scriptural View of Slavery" illustrates why Jesse can take himself to be a God-fearing man and a good Christian and provides the necessary background for a figure like Big Jim C., whose initials, ironically enough, remind the reader of Jesus Christ as well as of Jim Crow. And Eldridge Cleaver's parable about the Omnipotent Administrator who after his pact with the Supermasculine Menial suddenly "discovered that in the fury of his scheming he had blundered and clipped himself of his penis" [in his *Soul on Ice*] reads like a commentary upon Jesse's syndrome. These few references must suffice, for want of space, to prove that the connexion between a perverted sexuality and racism is by no means Baldwin's private invention. Admittedly, Baldwin seems to be obsessed by the discovery "that white men who invented the nigger's big black prick, are still at the mercy of this nightmare, and are still, for the most part, doomed, in one way or another, to attempt to make this prick their own," but whereas the reduction of the complex 'American dilemma' to this aspect only makes his *Blues for Mister Charlie* a heavily biased and only partly convincing play, it should be evident by now that it does not detract from the power of his story.

When, at the end of "GMM," Jesse's uncovering of his suppressed past makes him regain his potency, he can satisfy his wife only by throwing off his deepest inhibitions, giving in to his hitherto repressed fantasies and assuming the role of the over-potent "nigger": "Come on, sugar, I'm going to do you like a nigger, just like a nigger, come on, sugar, and love me just like you'd love a nigger." A reading of this development as a successful act of autotherapy would certainly be wrong. One might argue, however, that self-recognition is a first step towards improvement and that the acting out of one's hidden dreams has a cathartic effect. A prejudiced white racist who indulges in his fantasies in the privacy of his marriage bed might be a lesser risk to society; a man who is "going to meet the man," that is, on the way to discovering himself and confronting his own perversions, might be cured of his disease; a correct diagnosis could lead to a successful therapy.

If seen in this light, Baldwin's story neither "reduce[s] complexity to caricature," as [Daniel] Stern would have it, nor can it be summed up in the flippant statement of [Joseph] Featherstone, "that what all this racial fuss stems from is the white man's inability to get it up." Quite the contrary, **"GMM"** probes deeply into the hidden connexions between distorted sexuality, mindless bigotry, and violent racism; and the very fact that Baldwin, through the choice of his narrative perspective, remains sufficiently detached to stand back completely and to let his protagonist reveal himself as both victimizer and victim makes it a compelling and deeply moving story about the havoc worked by racial prejudice among the oppressed and the oppressors alike. (pp. 172-82)

> Peter Freese, "James Baldwin: 'Going to Meet the Man'," in The Black American Short Story in the 20th Century: A Collection of Critical Essays, edited by Peter Bruck, B. R. Grüner Publishing Co., 1977, pp. 171-86.

Edward Lobb   (essay date 1979)

[*In the essay below, Lobb discusses Baldwin's exploration of the nature and purpose of art.*]

James Baldwin's short story **"Sonny's Blues,"** first published in 1957, has been anthologized several times since its inclusion in Baldwin's *Going to Meet the Man* (1965). It is a fine and immediately appealing story, but it has never received critical treatment adequate to its complexity. The best analysis—an essay by John M. Reilly—rightly asserts the centrality of the blues in the story as a means of personal and social communication. In the last scene, Reilly sees the reconciliation of the narrator and his brother (which certainly does occur) and an affirmation of the blues as "a metaphor of Black community." But the meaning of the blues is, as I hope to show, rather wider than Reilly seems to think, and is part of a larger theme which is conveyed almost wholly through the story's images. **"Sonny's Blues"** is Baldwin's most concise and suggestive statement about the nature and function of art, and is doubly artful in making that statement through life situations.

Throughout most of the story, the narrator is unable to understand his younger brother Sonny, who is a jazz pianist. He feels guilt at not having looked after Sonny, but is really incapable of understanding what has driven Sonny to heroin. Sonny himself is not too articulate on the subject when he writes to his brother from prison: he says "I guess I was afraid of something or I was trying to escape from something and you know I have never been very strong in the head (smile)." This "something" is never precisely defined, but it is always associated with darkness. Sonny writes that he feels "like a man who's been trying to climb up out of some deep, real deep and funky hole and just saw the sun up there, outside," and the temptation is to suppose that the bleak life of Harlem is "the danger he had almost died trying to escape." In part it is: Sonny says that he has to get out of Harlem, and he escapes first to

the navy, then to Greenwich Village. The narrator realizes that Harlem is a place without a future; he sees his students' heads bump "against the low ceiling of their actual possibilities" and thinks that "all they really knew were two darknesses, the darkness of their lives, which was now closing in on them, and the darkness of the movies, which had blinded them to that other darkness, and in which they now, vindictively, dreamed, at once more together than they were at any other time, and more alone." But if the danger were simply the grim facts of life in Harlem—the poverty, the lack of a future, the dope, the seemingly impenetrable wall of white racism—surely the narrator, and Sonny, could be more precise about them.

The fact that they are not is an indication that these things are simply aspects of the larger terror of existence in a universe devoid of meaning. The narrator imagines (and remembers) a child's first awareness of this terror, again employing the metaphor of darkness; ironically, the child's awareness comes after the reassurances of church and a Sunday dinner.

> And the living room would be full of church folks and relatives. There they sit, in chairs all around the living room, and the night is creeping up outside, but nobody knows it yet. You can see the darkness growing against the windowpanes and you hear the street noises every now and again, or maybe the jangling beat of a tambourine from one of the churches close by, but it's real quiet in the room. For a moment nobody's talking, but every face looks darkening, like the sky outside. . . . Everyone is looking at something a child can't see. For a minute they've forgotten the children. . . . Maybe there's a kid, quiet and big-eyed, curled up in a big chair in the corner. The silence, the darkness coming, and the darkness in the faces frighten the child obscurely. He hopes that the hand which strokes his forehead will never stop—will never die. He hopes that there will never come a time when the old folks won't be sitting around the living room, talking about where they've come from, and what they've seen, and what's happened to them and their kinfolk.

> But something deep and watchful in the child knows that this is bound to end, is already ending.

This first sense of the world's darkness—its menace—is soon borne out by experience. The narrator's mother tells him about his uncle's death and its effect on his father: "Your Daddy was like a crazy man that night and for many a night thereafter. He says he never in his life seen anything as dark as that road after the lights of that car had gone away." The "hole" that Sonny is in, then, is a metaphysical one, the result of his sense that the world is a place of meaningless pain. He writes from prison, "I wish I could be like Mama and say the Lord's will be done, but I don't know it seems to me that trouble is the one thing that never does get stopped and I don't know what good it does to blame it on the Lord. But maybe it does some good if you believe it."

There is, of course, no escape from this darkness. The only things that can make it tolerable are human companionship and perhaps some kind of awareness of the truth of our situation. The latter is traditionally associated with light, and it seems natural that light in this story should be the means of saving the characters from the menace of darkness. We know from Sonny's prison letter that he has seen "the sun up there, outside"; but most of the references to light suggest that it is even worse than the darkness. The headlights of the car that kills the narrator's uncle, for example, simply intensify the blackness they leave behind, and the children in the darkening living room are made more apprehensive when the light is turned on.

> In a moment someone will get up and turn on the light. Then the old folks will remember the children and they won't talk any more that day. And when light fills the room, the child is filled with darkness. He knows that every time this happens he's moved just a little closer to that darkness outside. The darkness outside is what the old folks have been talking about. It's what they've come from. It's what they endure. The child knows that they won't talk any more because if he knows too much about what's happened to *them,* he'll know too much too soon, about what's going to happen to *him.*

Sonny for one has learned too much too soon, and has fled to heroin as a result.

The dialectic of the story so far is uncompromisingly bleak. The only thing worse than the pain of existence is full consciousness of that pain; knowledge is presumably desirable but unquestionably dangerous, and there seems to be no way of acquiring it without being annihilated, mentally or physically, by its blinding white light. Even in the last scene of the story the musicians avoid the spotlight, knowing what it means. The narrator describes them as being "most careful not to step into that circle of light too suddenly: . . . if they moved into the light too suddenly, without thinking, they would perish in flame." The resolution of the difficulty is beautifully simple and thematically apt. The lights on the bandstand turn "to a kind of indigo" and in this muted light—a mixture of light and darkness—the musicians begin to play, at first hesitantly, then with growing confidence. "Without an instant's warning, Creole started into something else, it was almost sardonic, it was 'Am I Blue.' And, as though he commanded, Sonny began to play. Something began to happen. And Creole let out the reins." Playing the blues in a blue light, they achieve an equipoise. The darkness of the human situation is there in the light and the music, as is the light of our awareness; but the annihilating power of each is controlled and shaped by art. "Creole began to tell us what the blues were all about. They were not about anything very new. He and his boys up there were keeping it new, at the risk of ruin, destruction, madness, and death, in order to find new ways to make us listen. For, while the tale of how we suffer, and how we are delighted, and how we may triumph is never new, it must always be heard. There isn't any other tale to tell, it's the only light we've got in all this darkness."

In that complex experience comes comfort—the knowledge that others have suffered and endured. The narrator

remembers his uncle's death and his daughter's, but is gladdened: "It [Sonny's performance] was very beautiful because it wasn't hurried and it was no longer a lament. I seemed to hear with what burning he had made it his, with what burning we had yet to make it ours, how we could cease lamenting." What the narrator discovers is the paradox of the blues and of tragedy generally—that melancholy subject matter can be beautifully rendered, without essential distortion, and produce a kind of joy. The experience is not prettified, any more than the white light of knowledge is extinguished by the blue filter; but the *form* of the vision makes it tolerable and saves us from its destructive energy. Nothingness itself assumes a shape; "the man who creates the music is hearing something else, is dealing with the roar rising from the void and imposing order on it as it hits the air. What is evoked in him, then, is of another order, more terrible because it has no words, and triumphant, too, for that same reason. And his triumph, when he triumphs, is ours." In this scene, as Reilly rightly points out, the narrator comes to understand his brother and his own place in the community; the community he acknowledges, however, is not the black community alone but the whole human community of suffering.

The opposed images of darkness and light, and their paradoxical reconciliation in the blue spotlight, outline the essential thematic movement of **"Sonny's Blues,"** the very title of which can now be seen as a punning oxymoron. The theme is reinforced by another pair of images which deserve discussion—those of sound and silence.

Music is traditionally associated with order of one kind or another (the music of the spheres, etc.), and in the last scene of the story music communicates a tragic sense of life. Listening, then, is an attempt to understand the nature of things. Sonny says, "And other times—well, I needed a fix, I needed to find a place to lean, I needed to clear a space to *listen.*" The problem comes when one listens and hears nothing. Silence, like darkness, is a form of absence, a something *not* there, a quality of the void; and when Sonny listens he apparently hears only what Pascal called the terrifying silence of the interstellar spaces. Certainly the narrator has reason to associate silence and horror: the first sign of his daughter's polio is her silence after a fall. "When you have a lot of children you don't always start running when one of them falls, unless they start screaming or something. And, this time, Grace was quiet. Yet, Isabel says that when she heard that *thump* and then that silence, something happened in her to make her afraid. And she ran to the living room and there was little Grace on the floor, all twisted up, and the reason she hadn't screamed was that she couldn't get her breath." And, we recall, the children in the living room are frightened by the adults' silence as well as by the encroaching darkness. It is, then, no mere metaphor when the narrator says that Sonny in his teens "was at that piano playing for his life."

On the metaphysical level, silence is parallel to darkness; on the human level, it is indicative of a surrender to the coldness of the universe, a kind of moral death. Sonny expresses his rage by means of silence. When Isabel's family complains of the noise he makes at the piano, he stops playing, and his brother writes that "the silence of the next few days must have been louder than the sound of all the music ever played since time began." The narrator acknowledges his guilt about Sonny in similar terms: ". . . there stood between us, forever, beyond the power of time or forgiveness, the fact that I had held silence—so long!— when he had needed human speech to help him." After Sonny's release from prison the brothers do talk, but not with any real ease. "I wanted to say more, but I couldn't." It is only in the nightclub that any real communication occurs, and then in wordless ways. Sonny's music breaks the silence that has existed between the brothers, and breaks down the wall of reserve that has removed the narrator, for all practical purposes, from the human community. He teaches algebra—an abstract subject—and lives *above* Harlem in a housing project which "looks like a parody of the good, clean, faceless life." Himself almost faceless, he never reveals his name and says nothing about the effect his daughter's death had upon him: it is only as he listens to Sonny in the nightclub that he remembers the family's troubles and feels his tears begin to rise.

The moment of his redemption is no easy triumph of art, however. He remains aware "that this was only a moment, that the world waited outside, as hungry as a tiger, and that trouble stretched above us, longer than the sky." The music is, as poetry was for Robert Frost, a momentary stay against confusion, not an alternative to the real world. Lest the point be missed, Baldwin has included a guitar in the scene of the uncle's death: no Orphean lyre, it is destroyed along with its owner.

We have established, then, that Baldwin's ideas about the nature and function of art are conveyed more by the images of the story than by its narrative. Even in the last paragraph of **"Sonny's Blues,"** new images appear to deepen the argument. The narrator sends a round of drinks to the band: "There was a long pause, while they talked up there in the indigo light and after a while I saw the girl put a Scotch and milk on top of the piano for Sonny. He didn't seem to notice it, but just before they started playing again, he sipped from it and looked toward me, and nodded. Then he put it back on top of the piano. For me, then, as they began to play again, it glowed and shook above my brother's head like the very cup of trembling." Like many of Baldwin's images, this contains several levels of meaning. The drink is both a Damoclean sword and the cup of the brothers' communion of understanding; Donald Murray sees it as "the Grail, the goal of the quest and the emblem of initiation." It is also "the cup of trembling" referred to in Isaiah (51, 17-23). The passage alluded to suggests, in the context of the story, both despair ("There is none to guide her") and the universality of suffering—a suffering which is momentarily in abeyance, but which can return, like "the trouble stretched above us," at any moment.

Having said that, we have perhaps said enough; but a rereading of the story suggests other and deeper meanings in the image. There are repeated references in the story to trembling and shaking, usually as an appropriately fearful response to the silence and darkness of the world. At the beginning of the story, after reading of Sonny's arrest, the narrator encounters one of Sonny's old high school friends who is coming down from a "high," reentering the world, and "shaking as though he were going to fall apart." Later, when Sonny explains why some jazzmen use heroin, he says "It's not so much to *play*. It's to *stand* it, to be able to make it at all. On any level. . . . In order to keep from shaking to pieces." His own experience has shown him the necessity of facing the abyss: "I can never tell you. I was all by myself at the bottom of something, stinking and sweating and crying and shaking, and I smelled it, you know? *my* stink, and I thought I'd die if I couldn't get away from it and yet, all the same, I knew that everything I was doing was just locking me in with it. . . . I didn't know, I still *don't* know, something kept telling me that maybe it was good to smell your own stink, but I didn't think that *that* was what I'd been trying to do—and—who can stand it?" What Sonny has learned is part of the lesson all tragic heroes learn in their extremity: when Gloucester says to Lear "O, let me kiss that hand," Lear answers, "Let me wipe it first; it smells of mortality."

The wrong way of coping with the trembling is to retreat into illusion, as one does with heroin; the right way is to face the abyss in the manageable form that art gives it. The trembling of the drink is the authentic human trembling in the face of the empty immensity of the universe, but it is controlled by art—by the form of the glass and by the piano which causes the trembling. Once again, we are presented with an image of potentially destructive energy controlled and contained, as the white light is controlled and contained by the blue filter. It would not be going too far, I think, to see in the drink itself another emblem, the Scotch representing the harshness of reality and the milk the smoothness of art.

"Sonny's Blues" is so complete a treatment of the art-theme that it includes bad art as well as good, and suggests its effects. Bad art, like heroin, is merely a refuge from the real world. Early in the story, in a passage cited earlier, the narrator mentions the boys who spend their time in "the darkness of the movies, which had blinded them to that other darkness." Like the blue spotlight, the movie screen is a modulated light; unlike the spotlight, it illuminates nothing, providing only sterile fantasies which feed the boys' rage. The narrator says that they are "at once more together than they were at any other time, and more alone." Their fellowship is as delusory as the version of reality on the screen, for they are united only in frustration and anger; each of them dreams alone, "vindictively." The blues, on the other hand, provide a real sense of community, as does the music of the street revival: ". . . the music seemed to soothe a poison out of them; and time seemed, nearly, to fall away from the sullen, belligerent, battered faces, as though they were fleeing back to their first condition, while dreaming of their last." The singers address each other as "Sister," anticipating the narrator's recognition of brotherhood (literal and figurative) in the last scene.

The other form of false art in the story, though it is mentioned only once, is television, and here again an image is paired with its opposite. At various points in the story the narrator finds himself by a window, and his looking out is obviously analogous in meaning to the act of listening. Sonny, more of a seeker than his brother, is drawn to the window "as though it were the lodestone rock." Most of the inhabitants of the housing project, on the other hand, "don't bother with the windows, they watch the TV screen instead."

Beyond the narrative events of **"Sonny's Blues,"** then, is a level of symbolic discourse on the relation of art and life. Art is distinguished from fantasy by contrast with heroin and the cheap satisfactions of film and television; it is associated with light, sound, and form, and stands against darkness, silence, and "fear and trembling." But if it is to be good art and provide a true picture of experience, it must include the elements it fights against—hence the paradoxical nature of Baldwin's emblems of art: the union of darkness and light, of form and the trembling which shakes things apart, of the roar from the void and the order of music. These and the other pairs of opposites I have mentioned (sound and silence, window and television, tragic matter and joyous form) suggest that the whole story, including the characterization of the brothers, is based on the idea of contrast or paradox—a suspicion borne out by even the most casual details in the story. The narrator, for example, hears a boy whistling a tune which is, like the story itself, "at once very complicated and very simple."

But we should be loath to describe any story as though it were an essay, however fine. Critical paraphrase tends to reduce narrative to a structure of symbols and ideas, and what makes **"Sonny's Blues"** a compelling story is its rendering of life, not its comments on art. It is similar to Baldwin's other fiction in its insistence that people must understand their past if they are to have any future. The narrator must work through his and Sonny's past—as well as his father's and uncle's—if he is to move forward. In the nightclub, with his memories of hard times, he thinks that Sonny "could help us to be free if we would listen, that he would never be free until we did." This theme informs Baldwin's social criticism as well: America, too, must face the reality of its past and clear a space in which to listen. In **"Sonny's Blues,"** the themes of art and life converge, for the chief obstacle to our obtaining a clear view of the past, individually or as a people, is simply our preference for bad art, for the pleasant lies which the media peddle and we in our sadness desire. (pp. 143-48)

Edward Lobb, "James Baldwin's Blues and the Function of Art," in The International Fiction Review, *Vol. 6, No. 2, Summer, 1979, pp. 143-51.*

Michael Clark (essay date 1985)

[*In the following essay, Clark examines Baldwin's use of light and dark imagery and the role of art in "Sonny's Blues."*]

"Sonny's Blues" by James Baldwin is a sensitive story about the reconciliation of two brothers, but it is much more than that. It is, in addition, an examination of the importance of the black heritage and of the central importance of music in that heritage. Finally, the story probes

the central role that art must play in human existence. To examine all of these facets of human existence is a rather formidable undertaking in a short story, even in a longish short story such as this one. Baldwin not only undertakes this task, but he does it superbly. One of the central ways that Baldwin fuses all of these complex elements is by using a metaphor of childhood, which is supported by ancillary images of light and darkness. He does the job so well that the story is a *tour de force,* a penetrating study of American culture.

One of the most important passages in this story is the description of Harlem's stultifying environment, a place where children are "smothered": "Some escaped the trap, most didn't. Those who got out always left something of themselves behind, as some animals amputate a leg and leave it in the trap." The implicit assumption here is that childhood is a holistic state, whereas the process of growing older maims the individual. Indeed, there is frequent evidence throughout the story that Baldwin sees childhood as a touchstone by which to judge the shortcomings of adulthood.

One of the more explicit statements of this same theme occurs in a flashback when the narrator remembers his own childhood home. There seems to be some autobiographical recollection here by Baldwin since he distances this material even from the fictitious narrator: in the course of this passage the boy narrator is transmuted into an autonomous and anonymous "child":

> And the living room would be full of church folks and relatives. There they sit, in chairs all around the living room, and the night is creeping up outside, but nobody knows it yet. You can see the darkness growing against the windowpanes and you hear the street noises every now and again, or maybe the jangling beat of a tambourine from one of the churches close by, but it's real quiet in the room. For a moment nobody's talking, but every face looks darkening, like the sky outside. And my mother rocks a little from the waist, and my father's eyes are closed. Everyone is looking at something a child can't see. For a minute they've forgotten the children. Maybe a kid is lying on the rug, half asleep. Maybe somebody's got a kid in his lap and is absentmindedly stroking the kid's head. Maybe there's a kid, quiet and big-eyed, curled up in a big chair in the corner. The silence, the darkness coming, and the darkness in the faces frightens the child obscurely. He hopes that the hand which strokes his forehead will never stop—will never die. He hopes that there will never come a time when the old folks won't be sitting around the living room, talking about where they've come from, and what they've seen, and what's happened to them and their kinfolk.

> But something deep and watchful in the child knows that this is bound to end, is already ending. In a moment someone will get up and turn on the light. Then the old folks will remember the children and they won't talk any more that day. And when the light fills the room, the child is filled with darkness. He knows that everytime this happens he is moved just a little closer to

that darkness outside. The darkness outside is what the old folks have been talking about. It's what they've come from. It's what they endure. The child knows that they won't talk any more because if he knows too much about what's happened to *them,* he'll know too much too soon, about what's going to happen to *him.*

This passage has much of the same idea—and imagery—of Wordsworth's "Ode: Intimations of Immortality": growing up is an initiation into the trouble of this world. Wordsworth characterizes youth as a time of "light"; adulthood, on the other hand, embraces us like the doors of a prison closing around us, darkening our lives. The imagery that Baldwin uses replicates Wordsworth's, as does in part his theme. In childhood man is in a holistic state, closer to a heavenly condition.

If growing up in general entails the losing of an envied state, then growing up in the ghetto is even worse. The high school kids that the narrator must teach show every evidence—even in their youth—of having already "matured":

> I listened to the boys outside, downstairs, shouting and cursing and laughing. Their laughter struck me for perhaps the first time. It was not the joyous laughter which—God knows why—one associates with children. It was mocking and insular, its intent to denigrate. It was disenchanted, and in this, also, lay the authority of their curses.

These children are not children. Already, the seeds of their destruction are sown. These children are "growing up with a rush and their heads bumped abruptly against the low ceiling of their actual possibilities. They were filled with rage."

It is interesting to note that in the midst of this despair, the narrator's attention is grabbed by a solitary "voice" in the schoolyard: "One boy was whistling a tune, at once very complicated and very simple, it seemed to be pouring out of him as though he were a bird, and it sounded very cool and moving through all that harsh, bright air, only just holding its own through all those other sounds." As Suzy Goldman has astutely observed, this passage foreshadows the concern of the story, for Sonny will be the "one" child who stands out in the otherwise bleak landscape; he is the "singer" in the midst of all the other sounds. And he is the one person through all his hardships who has managed to maintain an unalloyed vision—as vital as a child's—in the midst of complication. For in this story, childhood is the measure of the man.

Baldwin makes good use of the childhood imagery throughout the story. When Sonny's junkie friend comes to tell the narrator of the fate of Sonny, the reader is confronted with a picture of a grotesque child, a person who "though he was a grown-up man, he still hung around that block, still spent hours on the street corners." When he grins, "it made him repulsive and it also brought to mind what he'd looked like as a kid." Here, then, is the adult who has never accepted adult responsibility, a mature man whose "childlike" qualities emphasize his adult deformity. Childhood here serves as the measure of adult shortcomings. And it is not the last time that the image is used in this story.

When the junkie and the narrator are walking towards the subway station, they pass a bar and the narrator spies a barmaid inside: "When she smiled one saw the little girl, one sensed the doomed, still-struggling woman beneath the battered face of the semi-whore." She is just one more example of the trapped animal who has become deformed in order to survive. The "little girl" deserves much better.

It is in the context of such examples as this that the core of this story achieves meaning. This is, after all, a story about a "baby brother." But in order to understand Sonny's position in the world, we might first look at the illustrative example of his father. This story is told by the mother to the narrator. It is meant to be a parallel to the main action.

When the father and his brother (the narrator's uncle) were youths, they were happy-go-lucky spirits. The uncle loved music, as is evidenced by his guitar. One bright, moonlit night, the father and uncle were walking down a hill and the uncle was struck by a car driven by some white men, who did not stop. The "accident" is a blatant example of racism; the people in the vehicle are drunk and "aim the car straight at him." This anecdote, or symbolic tableau, is meant to provide a thematic backdrop to the narrator's own situation. He, too, has a brother that is musically oriented. The mother tells the story so that the narrator might be more diligent in looking after Sonny. The design of this anecdote, however, is further illuminating. This incident in the father's life is parallel to the narrator's description of what took place in the living room of his youth: it is a maturing experience, after which the father's life is never the same. It marks the critical moment when youth gives way to adulthood and responsibility. And this scene partakes of the same imagery that controls the living-room scene, as well as the rest of the story. Before the accident, it was "bright like day," while after the terrible accident, the father "says he never in his life seen anything as dark as that road after the lights of that car had gone away." This accident marks the transmutation of the father's life from youth to adulthood. In addition, the hand of the author is manifest in the controlling imagery, in the change from light to darkness.

So far this essay has shown that the light and dark imagery is pervasive in **"Sonny's Blues"** and that this imagery can be roughly equated with the respective conditions of childhood and adulthood. The question still remains as to how exactly this information can lead us to a better appreciation of Sonny's character. To begin, it might be useful to contrast the narrator and Sonny. There is some evidence for seeing Sonny as a *doppelganger* for the narrator. At least, such lines as the following are susceptible to this interpretation: when the narrator discovers that Sonny has been arrested for heroin possession and use, he notes that "I couldn't believe it: but what I mean by that is that I couldn't find any room for it anywhere inside me. I had kept it outside me for a long time. I hadn't wanted to know." The *lawlessness* of Sonny is something that is excluded from the highly controlled rationality of the narrator, the very kind of split that we find in such classic stories of the "double" as Poe's "William Wilson." Let it suffice for our argument, however, to note only that the narrator possesses qualities that are ambiguous. He is certainly a "success"—he has a college degree and a conventional job teaching high school. He represents middle-class values. But more can be said. He teaches algebra, which suggests his devotion to the scientific and formulaic. When Sonny talks to him about music, he shows no empathy for jazz, especially not for the avant-garde music of players like Charlie "Bird" Parker.

Though the narrator has escaped the most terrible consequences of growing up in the ghetto, then, he still is maimed in some way—and he knows it. When he and Sonny are in a cab on the way to the narrator's apartment, he notes that "it came to me that what we both were seeking through our separate cab windows was that part of ourselves which had been left behind." Both of these characters have been damaged by life. It is significant, then, that the story opens with the narrator looking at a newspaper, reading about Sonny's arrest and then staring at the story "in the faces and bodies of the people, and in my own face, trapped in the darkness which roared outside." The narrator, indeed, is trapped in the darkness. Only the events of the story will show him how to escape.

Sonny's quest is best described by himself when he writes to the narrator: "I feel like a man who's been trying to climb up out of some deep, real deep and funky hole and just saw the sun up there, outside. I got to get outside." Sonny is a person who finds his life a living hell, but he knows enough to strive for the "light." As it is chronicled in this story, his quest is for regaining something from the past—from his own childhood and from the pasts of all who have come before him. The means for doing this is his music, which is consistently portrayed in terms of light imagery. When Sonny has a discussion with the narrator about the future, the narrator describes Sonny's face as a mixture of concern and hope: "[T]he worry, the thoughtfulness, played on it still, the way shadows play on a face which is staring into the fire." This fire image is reinforced shortly afterward when the narrator describes Sonny's aspirations once more in terms of light: "[I]t was as though he were all wrapped up in some cloud, some fire, some vision all his own." To the narrator and to Isabel's family, the music that Sonny plays is simply "weird and disordered," but to Sonny, the music is seen in starkly positive terms: his failure to master the music will mean "death," while success will mean "life."

The light and dark imagery culminates in the final scene, where the narrator, apparently for the first time, listens to Sonny play the piano. The location is a Greenwich Village club. Appropriately enough, the narrator is seated "in a dark corner." In contrast, the stage is dominated by light, which Baldwin reiterates with a succession of images: "light . . . circle of light . . . light . . . flame . . . light." Although Sonny has a false start, he gradually settles into his playing and ends the first set with some intensity: "Everything had been burned out of [Sonny's face], and at the same time, things usually hidden were being burned in, by

the fire and fury of the battle which was occurring in him up there."

The culmination of the set occurs when Creole, the leader of the players, begins to play "Am I Blue." At this point, "something began to happen." Apparently, the narrator at this time realizes that this music *is* important. The music is central to the experience of the black experience, and it is described in terms of light imagery:

> Creole began to tell us what the blues were all about. They were not about anything very new. He and his boys up there were keeping it new, at the risk of ruin, destruction, madness, and death, in order to find new ways to make us listen. For, while the tale of how we suffer, and how we are delighted, and how we may triumph is never new, it always must be heard. There isn't any other tale to tell, it's the only light we've got in all this darkness.

James Baldwin has written [in *A Rap on Race,* 1971] that "[h]istory is the present . . . You and I are history. We carry our history. We act our history." Sonny's "blues" becomes an apt symbol in this story because Sonny has managed to look back at and *use* his own personal life of grief. But from the narrator's perspective, Sonny has looked back even further than that. Undoubtedly, he has looked back to his childhood, to that time before the "amputations" that formed his adult consciousness. This explains what the narrator means when he says that he "seemed to hear with what burning he had made it his." In the context of much of the other light imagery of the story (i.e., the time associated with the light of childhood), this image signifies in practical terms that music taps the very roots of existence, that it puts the artist in touch with the fluid emotions that he has known in perfection only as a child. But Sonny looks back not only to his own past, but also back to *all* the experience that makes up his history—which is the history of his race. Contained in the music that Sonny is playing is the culmination of all the suffering that Sonny and his race have suffered. Consequently, sorrow is transformed into a pure emotion that is not solitary but communal. The music becomes an expression of history: "He had made it his: that long line, of which we knew only Mama and Daddy. And he was giving it back, as everything must be given back, so that, passing through death, it can live forever."

The implication of this story is that art—whether it be the music that Sonny plays or the fiction that Baldwin writes—can give us some temporary relief from brutal reality. The narrator sees Sonny's music as giving him a "moment" though "the world waited outside, as hungry as a tiger, and . . . trouble stretched above us, longer than the sky." Clearly, the moment is worth the effort.

Sonny has succeeded in making his life whole once again. Though he is an adult who has suffered much, who has suffered metaphoric "amputations," he has also through his music managed to recapture the holism that we usually associate with childhood. Baldwin emphasizes this when he has the narrator buy Sonny a drink at the close of the story: "a Scotch and milk." As Sonny began to play again, this drink sat atop the piano and "glowed." It is an apt symbol for the value of Sonny's success: milk, childhood, and light all suggest that this manchild has achieved a reconciliation with reality that is far superior to the narrator's conventional lifestyle. (pp. 197-205)

> *Michael Clark, "James Baldwin's 'Sonny's Blues': Childhood, Light and Art," in* CLA Journal, *Vol. XXIX, No. 2, December, 1985, pp. 197-205.*

FURTHER READING

Biography

Eckman, Fern Marja. *The Furious Passage of James Baldwin.* New York: M. Evans & Co., 1966, 254 p.

Authorized biography of Baldwin.

Criticism

Albert, Richard N. "The Jazz-Blues Motif in James Baldwin's 'Sonny's Blues'." *College Literature* XI, No. 2 (1984): 178-85.

Examines the connotations of jazz and blues images and allusions in "Sonny's Blues" in relation to Baldwin's themes of individualism and alienation.

Bieganowski, Ronald. "James Baldwin's Vision of Otherness in 'Sonny's Blues' and *Giovanni's Room*." *CLA Journal* 32, No. 1 (September 1988): 69-80.

Compares Baldwin's treatment of the theme of alienation in "Sonny's Blues" and his novel *Giovanni's Room.*

Bloom, Harold, ed. *James Baldwin.* New York: Chelsea House, 1986, 164 p.

Collection of critical essays including studies by Marcus Klein and Edward Margolies which focus in part on Baldwin's short fiction.

Byerman, Keith E. "Words and Music: Narrative Ambiguity in 'Sonny's Blues'." *Studies in Short Fiction* 19, No. 4 (Fall 1982): 367-72.

Explicates "Sonny's Blues" as "a study of the nature and relationship of art and language."

Donadio, Stephen. "Looking for the Man." *Partisan Review* XXXIII, No. 1 (Winter 1966): 136-38.

Offers a predominantly negative assessment of *Going to Meet the Man.*

Goldman, Suzy Bernstein. "James Baldwin's 'Sonny's Blues': A Message in Music." *Negro American Literature Forum* 8, No. 3 (Fall 1974): 231-33.

Baldwin's use of musical structure and leitmotifs in the narrative and dialogue of "Sonny's Blues."

Harris, Trudier. "To Be Washed Whiter Than Snow: *Going to Meet the Man*." In her *Black Women in the Fiction of*

James Baldwin, pp. 60-95. Knoxville: University of Tennessee Press, 1985.

Compares Baldwin's treatment of African-American women in *Going to Meet the Man* with those in *Go Tell It on the Mountain.*

Krim, Seymour. "The Troubles He's Seen." *Sunday Herald Tribune Book Week* (7 November 1965): 5, 19-20.

Favorable review of *Going to Meet the Man* in which Krim defends Baldwin as an apt observer of human frailty.

Levensohn, Alan. "The Artist Must Outwit the Celebrity." *The Christian Science Monitor* 57, No. 301 (18 November 1965): 15.

Positive assessment of *Going to Meet the Man,* with particular emphasis on "Sonny's Blues."

Mosher, Marlene. "Baldwin's 'Sonny's Blues'." *Explicator* 40, No. 4 (Summer 1982): 59.

Notes a religious allusion in "Sonny's Blues."

———. "James Baldwin's Blues." *CLA Journal* XXVI, No. 1 (September 1982): 112-24.

Explores the theme of "surviving despite tremendous odds" in "Sonny's Blues."

O'Daniel, Therman B., ed. *James Baldwin: A Critical Evaluation.* Washington, D.C.: Howard University Press, 1977, 273 p.

Collection of new and previously published essays containing five studies on Baldwin's short fiction.

Ognibene, Elaine R. "Black Literature Revisited: 'Sonny's Blues'." *English Journal* 60, No. 1 (January 1971): 36-7.

Examines the relevance of race and communication to social problems in "Sonny's Blues."

Pratt, Louis H. "The Fear and the Fury." In his *James Baldwin,* pp. 31-49. Boston: Twayne, 1978.

Examines Baldwin's role of "the writer as prophet" in his stories in *Going to Meet the Man.*

Stern, Daniel. "A Special Corner on Truth." *Saturday Review* XLVIII, No. 45 (6 November 1965): 32.

Generally favorable review of *Going to Meet the Man,* praising Baldwin's avoidance of sensationalism.

VanDyke, Patricia. "Choosing One's Side with Care: The Liberating Repartee." *Perspectives* 1, No. 1 (May 1975): 105-17.

Examines comic repartee in Bernard Malamud's "The Jewbird" and Baldwin's "Going to Meet the Man."

Whitlow, Roger. "Baldwin's 'Going to Meet the Man': Racial Brutality and Sexual Gratification." *American Imago* 34, No. 4 (Winter 1977): 351-56.

    Explores the relationship between racism and sexuality in "Going to Meet the Man."

Additional coverage of Baldwin's life and career is contained in the following sources published by Gale Research: *Black Literature Criticism,* Vol. 1; *Black Writers; Concise Dictionary of American Literary Biography, 1941-1968; Contemporary Authors,* Vols. 1-4, rev. ed., 124; *Contemporary Authors Bibliographical Series,* Vol. 3; *Contemporary Authors New Revision Series,* Vol. 3; *Contemporary Literary Criticism,* Vols. 1, 2, 3, 4, 5, 8, 13, 15, 17, 42, 50, 67; *Dictionary of Literary Biography,* Vols. 2, 7, 33; *Dictionary of Literary Biography Yearbook: 1987; Drama Criticism,* Vol. 1; *Major 20th-Century Writers;* and *Something about the Author,* Vol. 9.

John Barth

1930-

(Full name John Simmons Barth) American novelist, short story writer, and essayist.

INTRODUCTION

Barth is one of the most important contributors to literary postmodernism, a contemporary movement that comprises works characterized by structural experimentalism, an eclectic mixture of cultural references, incorporation of word games, and a self-conscious examination of fiction writing and the interaction between reader and text. Concerned with transcending the strictures of literary realism, Barth constructs labyrinthine plots and parodies mythical and historical tales. In "The Literature of Exhaustion," the first essay to advance an aesthetics of postmodern fiction, Barth describes the contemporary experimental writer as one who "confronts an intellectual dead end and employs it against itself to accomplish new human work." This essay has been construed as a vital manifesto proposing various keys to fiction's survival in the face of seemingly exhausted possibilities. Barth's only works of short fiction, the short story volume *Lost in the Funhouse: Fiction for Print, Tape, Live Voice* and the collection of novellas *Chimera*, present fictional treatments of his literary theories and are considered among his most experimental and distinguished works.

A series of fourteen pieces, *Lost in the Funhouse* evinces Barth's search for alternatives to conventional writing through his use of diverse styles and his exploration of the creative process. As suggested by the subtitle, "Fiction for Print, Tape, Live Voice," stories in this volume draw on a variety of media sources, with some requiring the reader to listen to tape recordings. Barth also experiments with visual dimensions, as in the first story, "Frame-Tale," which contains only the words "Once upon a time there / was a story that began" printed along the edge of the page with instructions to cut out the words and construct a Möbius strip out of them. Commentators have noted that the resultant structure in which the words twist and loop back upon themselves to repeat the same message is emblematic of ways in which characters and themes are repeated throughout *Lost in the Funhouse*. Stories in the volume may generally be divided into three categories: narratives that focus on the maturation of the protagonist, Ambrose Mensch, from conception through adolescence; metafictional pieces that trace the development of storytelling; and stories based on classical mythology.

Stories in the first category depart from traditional narrative techniques, often parodying literary convention. "Night-Sea Journey," for example, is a mock heroic epic told from the perspective of a sperm on its voyage to a mysterious "Shore," or egg, which upon fertilization will

eventually develop into Ambrose. The elevated tone that the sperm-narrator adopts heightens the artifice and humor of the story. "Lost in the Funhouse," which is frequently interpreted as a parody of James Joyce's *A Portrait of the Artist as a Young Man,* features a third-person omniscient narrator who comments on various literary techniques throughout the exposition of the story. Thirteen-year-old Ambrose goes on a seaside outing with his parents, uncle, older brother, and a teenage girl named Magda to whom both Ambrose and his brother are attracted. Ambrose's attempts to engage in a relationship with Magda are frustrated by self-reflexive thoughts that inhibit his ability to enjoy a sexual encounter. Structured to resemble the disorientation that characterizes a trip through a fun house, the story includes repeated and distorted images that continually draw attention to the self-conscious and, at times, inhibitive nature of storytelling.

Several tales in *Lost in the Funhouse* focus on the process of fiction writing. In "Life-Story" the narrator reflects on the seeming impossibility of writing new, inventive fiction in the late twentieth century and laments that he can only offer "another story about a writer writing a story! Another regressus in infinitum!" Barth urges the reader to assume an active role in his stories, as in "Title," in which the narrator rejects several false starts and ultimately encourages the reader to engage in the narrative: "I'm going to, say it in plain English for once, that's what I'm leading up to, me and my bloody anticlimactic noun, we're pushing each other to fill in the blank." Several commentators regard Barth's unconventional stories as challenging yet coherent experiments. Jack Richardson asserted: "It is [in "Life-Story" and "Title"] that the reader may feel himself bullied into having to attend to the author's professional difficulties and his metaphysical notions of literature, but Barth has enough humor to keep [these stories] from turning into another dark night of a literary stylist's manner."

Barth's method of retelling classical myths is perhaps best displayed in "Menelaiad," which is frequently compared in structure to a set of Chinese nesting boxes—each of which, when opened, reveals another of similar yet smaller appearance. In this story, the Greek hero Menelaus recounts his life story, recalling past events and conversations, which he distinguishes from present circumstances by adding a separate set of quotation marks to the story. Gerhard Joseph has noted that this complicated narrative device represents "the epitome of . . . entrapment within a fabular *regressus in infinitum.*" In "Anonymiad," a story also based on Greek mythology, Barth relates the tale of a minstrel who has been marooned on an island. In his isolation the minstrel writes stories and casts them out to sea, inventing and revising narrative forms until he believes he has exhausted all possibilities. His commitment to writing, however, is renewed when a jar containing a message washes ashore; he realizes that others also need to communicate and that the world "might be astrew with islèd souls," creating a "sea a-clink with literature!"

Barth similarly uses ancient tales in *Chimera,* a collection of three interlinked novellas for which he received the National Book Award in 1973. Written during Barth's middle years when he experienced difficulty writing, the novellas metaphorically represent ways of surpassing the exhausted possibilities of writing. The first novella, "Dunyazadiad," is based on the story of Scheherazade, the heroine of the classical Arabian frame-tale *The Thousand and One Nights.* In the original, Scheherazade is held captive by King Shahryar, who intends to make love to her and then kill her; however, Scheherazade escapes death each night by telling such a compelling story that the king spares her life in order to hear more. Barth combines modern and anachronistic diction in his retelling of the story and also shifts the main point of view away from Scheherazade. "Dunyazadiad" is narrated by Scheherazade's sister, Dunyazade, who witnesses her sister's predicament and is similarly threatened by the king's brother, Shah Zaman. Furthering the story-within-a-story motif, Barth introduces the character of the Genie, a mask for the contemporary figure of Barth himself, who is able to read stories from *The Thousand and One Nights* to Scheherazade and Dunyazade that will provide them with their life-saving narratives.

In the next novella, "Perseid," Barth creates a colloquial version of the story of the Greek hero Perseus. At the midpoint of his life, Perseus wishes he could repeat the heroic

deeds of his past but eventually realizes that to move forward he cannot simply repeat his former actions but must change their pattern to succeed. In the last novella, "Bellerophoniad," the Greek figure Bellerophon confronts middle age and harbors doubts about the significance of his life. Throughout the narrative, he attempts to imitate the actions of previous heroes to secure his own heroic status; yet, unlike Perseus, he never succeeds because he merely repeats the examples of former heroes and, according to at least one critic, lacks individuality. "Bellerophoniad" both exemplifies and parodies the dead end that writers face when they conform to a historic past and fail to assert originality in their retelling of stories.

The extremely complex and metafictional nature of Barth's short fiction has inspired countless exegeses on the direction of contemporary literature. Initially, many critics condemned Barth's focus on the writing process as self-indulgent and charged that his works produced a sense of elitism by appealing only to an academic audience. Numerous other commentators cited Barth's emphasis on the depleted potentialities of narrative forms and his rejection of realism in *Lost in the Funhouse* and *Chimera* as nihilistic. Recent critics, however, have interpreted Barth's exploration of the possibilities of literature as an affirmative message that equally challenges writer and reader. E. P. Walkiewicz asserted that Barth "has given form and substance to a body of work that is traditional, contemporary, and trailblazing, consistent and evolutionary, self-affirming and self-questioning, that acknowledges contradictions and contrarieties and enlists them in the service of art and humanity."

PRINCIPAL WORKS

SHORT FICTION

Lost in the Funhouse: Fiction for Print, Tape, Live Voice
    1968
Chimera   1972

OTHER MAJOR WORKS

The Floating Opera   (novel)   1956; revised edition, 1967
The End of the Road   (novel)   1958; revised edition, 1967
The Sot-Weed Factor   (novel)   1960; revised edition, 1967
Giles Goat-Boy; or, The Revised New Syllabus   (novel)
    1966
LETTERS   (novel)   1979
*The Literature of Exhaustion, and The Literature of Replenishment   (essays)   1982
Sabbatical: A Romance   (novel)   1982
The Friday Book: Essays and Other Nonfiction   1984
The Tidewater Tales   (novel)   1987
The Last Voyage of Somebody the Sailor   (novel)   1991

*These essays were originally published in *The Atlantic Monthly* in 1967 and 1980, respectively.

John Barth   (essay date 1967)

[*In the following essay, which Barth wrote concomitantly with stories that later appeared in the collection* Lost
in the Funhouse *and which is considered a seminal
statement on the subject of postmodern fiction, Barth explicates his literary aesthetics, focusing on what he considers the accomplishments of Argentine writer Jorge
Luis Borges.*]

I want to discuss three things more or less together: first,
some old questions raised by the new intermedia arts; second, some aspects of the Argentine writer Jorge Luis Borges, whom I greatly admire; third, some professional concerns of my own, related to these other matters and having
to do with what I'm calling "the literature of exhausted
possibility"—or, more chicly, "the literature of exhaustion."

By "exhaustion" I don't mean anything so tired as the
subject of physical, moral, or intellectual decadence, only
the used-upness of certain forms or exhaustion of certain
possibilities—by no means necessarily a cause for despair.
That a great many Western artists for a great many years
have quarreled with received definitions of artistic media,
genres, and forms goes without saying: pop art, dramatic
and musical "happenings," the whole range of "intermedia" or "mixed-means" art, bear recentest witness to
the tradition of rebelling against Tradition. A catalogue I
received some time ago in the mail, for example, advertises
such items as Robert Filliou's *Ample Food for Stupid
Thought,* a box full of postcards on which are inscribed
"apparently meaningless questions," to be mailed to
whomever the purchaser judges them suited for; Ray
Johnson's *Paper Snake,* a collection of whimsical writings,
"often pointed," once mailed to various friends (what the
catalogue describes as The New York Correspondence
School of Literature); and Daniel Spoerri's *Anecdoted Typography of Chance,* "on the surface" a description of all
the objects that happen to be on the author's parlor
table—"in fact, however . . . a cosmology of Spoerri's existence."

"On the surface," at least, the document listing these items
is a catalogue of The Something Else Press, a swinging
outfit. "In fact, however," it may be one of their offerings,
for all I know: The New York Direct-Mail Advertising
School of Literature. In any case, their wares are lively to
read about, and make for interesting conversation in fiction-writing classes, for example, where we discuss Some-
body-or-other's unbound, unpaginated, randomly assembled novel-in-a-box and the desirability of printing *Finnegans Wake* on a very long roller-towel. It's easier and so-
ciabler to talk technique than it is to make art, and the
area of "happenings" and their kin is mainly a way of discussing aesthetics, really; illustrating "dramatically" more
or less valid and interesting points about the nature of art
and the definition of its terms and genres.

One conspicuous thing, for example, about the "intermedia" arts is their tendency (noted even by *Life* magazine) to eliminate not only the traditional audience—
"those who apprehend the artist's art" (in "happenings"
the audience is often the "cast," as in "environments," and
some of the new music isn't intended to be performed at

all)—but also the most traditional notion of the artist: the
Aristotelian conscious agent who achieves with technique
and cunning the artistic effect; in other words, one endowed with uncommon talent, who has moreover developed and disciplined that endowment into virtuosity. It's
an aristocratic notion on the face of it, which the democratic West seems eager to have done with; not only the
"omniscient" author of older fiction, but the very idea of
the controlling artist, has been condemned as politically
reactionary, even fascist.

Now, personally, being of the temper that chooses to
"rebel along traditional lines," I'm inclined to prefer the
kind of art that not many people can *do:* the kind that requires expertise and artistry as well as bright aesthetic
ideas and/or inspiration. I enjoy the pop art in the famous
Albright-Knox collection, a few blocks from my house in
Buffalo, like a lively conversation for the most part, but
was on the whole more impressed by the jugglers and acrobats at Baltimore's old Hippodrome, where I used to go
every time they changed shows: genuine *virtuosi* doing
things that anyone can dream up and discuss but almost
no one can do.

I suppose the distinction is between things worth remarking—preferably over beer, if one's of my generation—and
things worth doing. "Somebody ought to make a novel
with scenes that pop up, like the old children's books," one
says, with the implication that one isn't going to bother
doing it oneself.

However, art and its forms and techniques live in history
and certainly do change. I sympathize with a remark attributed to Saul Bellow, that to be technically up to date is
the least important attribute of a writer, though I would
have to add that this least important attribute may be nevertheless essential. In any case, to be technically *out* of
date is likely to be a genuine defect: Beethoven's Sixth
Symphony or the Chartres Cathedral if executed today
would be merely embarrassing. A good many current novelists write turn-of-the-century-type novels, only in more
or less mid-twentieth-century language and about contemporary people and topics; this makes them considerably
less interesting (to me) than excellent writers who are also
technically contemporary: Joyce and Kafka, for instance,
in their time, and in ours, Samuel Beckett and Jorge Luis
Borges. The intermedia arts, I'd say, tend to be intermediary too, between the traditional realms of aesthetics on the
one hand and artistic creation on the other; I think the
wise artist and civilian will regard them with quite the
kind and degree of seriousness with which he regards good
shoptalk: he'll listen carefully, if noncommittally, and
keep an eye on his intermedia colleagues, if only the corner
of his eye. They may very possibly suggest something usable in the making or understanding of genuine works of
contemporary art.

The man I want to discuss a little here, Jorge Luis Borges,
illustrates well the difference between a technically old-
fashioned artist, a technically up-to-date civilian, and a
technically up-to-date artist. In the first category I'd locate all those novelists who for better or worse write not
as if the twentieth century didn't exist, but as if the great
writers of the last sixty years or so hadn't existed (*nota*

bene that our century's more than two-thirds done; it's dismaying to see so many of our writers following Dostoevsky or Tolstoy or Flaubert or Balzac, when the real technical question seems to me to be how to succeed not even Joyce and Kafka, but those who've *succeeded* Joyce and Kafka and are now in the evenings of their own careers). In the second category are such folk as an artist-neighbor of mine in Buffalo who fashions dead Winnies-the-Pooh in sometimes monumental scale out of oilcloth stuffed with sand and impaled on stakes or hung by the neck. In the third belong the few people whose artistic thinking is as hip as any French new-novelist's, but who manage nonetheless to speak eloquently and memorably to our still-human hearts and conditions, as the great artists have always done. Of these, two of the finest living specimens that I know of are Beckett and Borges, just about the only contemporaries of my reading acquaintance mentionable with the "old masters" of twentieth-century fiction. In the unexciting history of literary awards, the 1961 International Publishers' Prize, shared by Beckett and Borges, is a happy exception indeed.

One of the modern things about these two is that in an age of ultimacies and "final solutions"—at least *felt* ultimacies, in everything from weaponry to theology, the celebrated dehumanization of society, and the history of the novel—their work in separate ways reflects and deals with ultimacy, both technically and thematically, as, for example, *Finnegans Wake* does in its different manner. One notices, by the way, for whatever its symptomatic worth, that Joyce was virtually blind at the end, Borges is literally so, and Beckett has become virtually mute, musewise, having progressed from marvelously constructed English sentences through terser and terser French ones to the unsyntactical, unpunctuated prose of *Comment C'est* and "ultimately" to wordless mimes. One might extrapolate a theoretical course for Beckett: language, after all, consists of silence as well as sound, and the mime is still communication—"that nineteenth-century idea," a Yale student once snarled at me—but by the language of action. But the language of action consists of rest as well as movement, and so in the context of Beckett's progress immobile, silent figures still aren't altogether ultimate. How about an empty, silent stage, then, or blank pages—a "happening" where nothing happens, like Cage's *4' 33"* performed in an empty hall? But dramatic communication consists of the absence as well as the presence of the actors; "we have our exits and our entrances"; and so even that would be imperfectly ultimate in Beckett's case. Nothing at all, then, I suppose: but Nothingness is necessarily and inextricably the background against which Being et cetera; for Beckett, at this point in his career, to cease to create altogether would be fairly meaningful: his crowning work, his "last word." What a convenient corner to paint yourself into! "And now I shall finish," the valet Arsene says in *Watt*, "and you will hear my voice no more." Only the silence *Molloy* speaks of, "of which the universe is made."

After which, I add on behalf of the rest of us, it might be conceivable to rediscover validly the artifices of language and literature—such far-out notions as grammar, punctuation . . . even characterization! Even *plot*!—if one

goes about it the right way, aware of what one's predecessors have been up to.

Now J. L. Borges is perfectly aware of all these things. Back in the great decades of literary experimentalism he was associated with *Prisma,* a "muralist" magazine that published its pages on walls and billboards; his later *Labyrinths* and *Ficciones* not only anticipate the farthest-out ideas of The Something-Else Press crowd—not a difficult thing to do—but being marvelous works of art as well, illustrate in a simple way the difference between the *fact* of aesthetic ultimacies and their artistic *use.* What it comes to is that an artist doesn't merely exemplify an ultimacy; he employs it.

Consider Borges' story "Pierre Menard, Author of the *Quixote*": the hero, an utterly sophisticated turn-of-the-century French Symbolist, by an astounding effort of imagination, produces—not *copies* or *imitates,* mind, but *composes*—several chapters of Cervantes' novel.

> It is a revelation [Borges' narrator tells us] to compare Menard's *Don Quixote* with Cervantes'. The latter, for example, wrote (part one, chapter nine):
>
> > . . . truth, whose mother is history, rival of time, depository of deeds, witness of the past, exemplar and adviser to the present, the future's counselor.
>
> Written in the seventeenth century, written by the "lay genius" Cervantes, this enumeration is a mere rhetorical praise of history. Menard, on the other hand, writes:
>
> > . . . truth, whose mother is history, rival of time, depository of deeds, witness of the past, exemplar and adviser to the present, the future's counselor.
>
> History, the *mother* of truth: the idea is astounding. Menard, a contemporary of William James, does not define history as an inquiry into reality but as its origin. . . .

Et cetera. Now, this is an interesting idea, of considerable intellectual validity. I mentioned earlier that if Beethoven's Sixth were composed today, it would be an embarrassment; but clearly it wouldn't be, necessarily, if done with ironic intent by a composer quite aware of where we've been and where we are. It would have then potentially, for better or worse, the kind of significance of Warhol's Campbell's Soup ads, the difference being that in the former case a work of art is being reproduced instead of a work of non-art, and the ironic comment would therefore be more directly on the genre and history of the art than on the state of the culture. In fact, of course, to make the valid intellectual point one needn't even recompose the Sixth Symphony, any more than Menard really needed to re-create the *Quixote.* It would've been sufficient for Menard to have *attributed* the novel to himself in order to have a new work of art, from the intellectual point of view. Indeed, in several stories Borges plays with this very idea, and I can readily imagine Beckett's next novel, for example, as *Tom Jones,* just as Nabokov's last was that multivolume annotated translation of Pushkin. I myself have always aspired to write Burton's version of *The 1001 Nights,* complete with appendices and the like, in twelve volumes, and for intellectual purposes I needn't even write it. What evenings we might spend (over beer) discussing Saarinen's Parthenon, D. H. Lawrence's *Wuthering Heights,* or the Johnson Administration by Robert Rauschenberg!

The idea, I say, is intellectually serious, as are Borges' other characteristic ideas, most of a metaphysical rather than an aesthetic nature. But the important thing to observe is that Borges *doesn't* attribute the *Quixote* to himself, much less recompose it like Pierre Menard; instead, he writes a remarkable and original work of literature, the implicit theme of which is the difficulty, perhaps the unnecessity, of writing original works of literature. His artistic victory, if you like, is that he confronts an intellectual dead end and employs it against itself to accomplish new human work. If this corresponds to what mystics do— "every moment leaping into the infinite," Kierkegaard says, "and every moment falling surely back into the finite"—it's only one more aspect of that old analogy. In homelier terms, it's a matter of every moment throwing out the bath water without for a moment losing the baby.

Another way of describing Borges' accomplishment is in a pair of his own favorite terms, *algebra and fire.* In his most often anthologized story, "Tlön, Uqbar, Orbis Tertius," he imagines an entirely hypothetical world, the invention of a secret society of scholars who elaborate its every aspect in a surreptitious encyclopedia. This *First Encyclopaedia of Tlön* (what fictionist would not wish to have dreamed up the *Britannica?*) describes a coherent alternative to this world complete in every respect from its algebra to its fire, Borges tells us, and of such imaginative power that, once conceived, it begins to obtrude itself into and eventually to supplant our prior reality. My point is that neither the algebra nor the fire, metaphorically speaking, could achieve this result without the other. Borges' algebra is what I'm considering here—algebra is easier to talk about than fire—but any intellectual giant could equal it. The imaginary authors of the *First Encyclopaedia of Tlön* itself are not artists, though their work is in a manner of speaking fictional and would find a ready publisher in New York nowadays. The author of the story "Tlön, Uqbar, Orbis Tertius," who merely *alludes* to the fascinating *Encyclopaedia, is* an artist; what makes him one of the first rank, like Kafka, is the combination of that intellectually profound vision with great human insight, poetic power, and consummate mastery of his means, a definition which would have gone without saying, I suppose, in any century but ours.

Not long ago, incidentally, in a footnote to a scholarly edition of Sir Thomas Browne (*The Urn Burial,* I believe it was), I came upon a perfect Borges datum, reminiscent of Tlön's self-realization: the actual case of a book called *The Three Impostors,* alluded to in Browne's *Religio Medici* among other places. *The Three Impostors* is a non-existent blasphemous treatise against Moses, Christ, and Mohammed, which in the seventeenth century was widely held to exist, or to have once existed. Commentators attributed it variously to Boccaccio, Pietro Aretino, Giordano Bruno, and Tommaso Campanella, and though no one, Browne

included, had ever seen a copy of it, it was frequently cited, refuted, railed against, and generally discussed as if everyone had read it—until, sure enough, in the *eighteenth* century a spurious work appeared with a forged date of 1598 and the title *De Tribus Impostoribus.* It's a wonder that Borges doesn't mention this work, as he seems to have read absolutely everything, including all the books that don't exist, and Browne is a particular favorite of his. In fact, the narrator of "Tlön, Uqbar, Orbis Tertius" declares at the end:

> . . . English and French and mere Spanish will disappear from the globe. The world will be Tlön. I pay no attention to all this and go on revising, in the still days at the Adrogué hotel, an uncertain Quevedian translation (which I do not intend to publish) of Browne's *Urn Burial.*

This "contamination of reality by dream," as Borges calls it, is one of his pet themes, and commenting upon such contaminations is one of his favorite fictional devices. Like many of the best such devices, it turns the artist's mode or form into a metaphor for his concerns, as does the diary-ending of *Portrait of the Artist As a Young Man* or the cyclical construction of *Finnegans Wake.* In Borges' case, the story "Tlön," etc., for example, is a real piece of imagined reality in our world, analogous to those Tlönian artifacts called *hrönir,* which imagine themselves into existence. In short, it's a paradigm of or metaphor for itself; not just the *form* of the story but the *fact* of the story is symbolic; "the medium is the message."

Moreover, like all of Borges' work, it illustrates in other of its aspects my subject: how an artist may paradoxically turn the felt ultimacies of our time into material and means for his work—*paradoxically* because by doing so he transcends what had appeared to be his refutation, in the same way that the mystic who transcends finitude is said to be enabled to live, spiritually and physically, in the finite world. Suppose you're a writer by vocation—a "print-oriented bastard," as the McLuhanites call us—and you feel, for example, that the novel, if not narrative literature generally, if not the printed word altogether, has by this hour of the world just about shot its bolt, as Leslie Fiedler and others maintain. (I'm inclined to agree, with reservations and hedges. Literary forms certainly have histories and historical contingencies, and it may well be that the novel's time as a major art form is up, as the "times" of classical tragedy, grand opera, or the sonnet sequence came to be. No necessary cause for alarm in this at all, except perhaps to certain novelists, and one way to handle such a feeling might be to write a novel about it. Whether historically the novel expires or persists seems immaterial to me; if enough writers and critics *feel* apocalyptical about it, their feeling becomes a considerable cultural fact, like the *feeling* that Western civilization, or the world, is going to end rather soon. If you took a bunch of people out into the desert and the world didn't end, you'd come home shamefaced, I imagine; but the persistence of an art form doesn't invalidate work created in the comparable apocalyptic ambience. That's one of the fringe benefits of being an artist instead of a prophet. There are others.) If you happened to be Vladimir Nabokov you might address that felt ultimacy by writing *Pale Fire:* a fine novel by a learned pedant, in the form of a pedantic commentary on a poem invented for the purpose. If you were Borges you might write *Labyrinths:* fictions by a learned librarian in the form of footnotes, as he describes them, to imaginary or hypothetical books. And I'll add, since I believe Borges' idea is rather more interesting, that if you were the author of this paper, you'd have written something like *The Sot-Weed Factor* or *Giles Goat-Boy:* novels which imitate the form of the Novel, by an author who imitates the role of Author.

If this sort of thing sounds unpleasantly decadent, nevertheless it's about where the genre began, with *Quixote* imitating *Amadis of Gaul,* Cervantes pretending to be the Cid Hamete Benengeli (and Alonso Quijano pretending to be Don Quixote), or Fielding parodying Richardson. "History repeats itself as farce"—meaning, of course, in the form or mode of farce, not that history is farcical. The imitation (like the Dadaist echoes in the work of the "intermedia" types) is something new and *may be* quite serious and passionate despite its farcical aspect. This is the important difference between a proper novel and a deliberate imitation of a novel, or a novel imitative of other sorts of documents. The first attempts (has been historically inclined to attempt) to imitate actions more or less directly, and its conventional devices—cause and effect, linear anecdote, characterization, authorial selection, arrangement, and interpretation—can be and have long since been objected to as obsolete notions, or metaphors for obsolete notions: Robbe-Grillet's essays *For a New Novel* come to mind. There are replies to these objections, not to the point here, but one can see that in any case they're obviated by imitations-of-novels, which attempt to represent not life directly but a representation of life. In fact such works are no more removed from "life" than Richardson's or Goethe's epistolary novels are: both imitate "real" documents, and the subject of both, ultimately, is life, not the documents. A novel is as much a piece of the real world as a letter, and the letters in *The Sorrows of Young Werther* are, after all, fictitious.

One might imaginably compound this imitation, and though Borges doesn't, he's fascinated with the idea: one of his frequenter literary allusions is to the 602nd night of *The 1001 Nights,* when, owing to a copyist's error, Scheherezade begins to tell the King the story of the 1001 nights, from the beginning. Happily, the King interrupts; if he didn't there'd be no 603rd night ever, and while this would solve Scheherezade's problem—which is every storyteller's problem: to publish or perish—it would put the "outside" author in a bind. (I suspect that Borges dreamed this whole thing up: the business he mentions isn't in any edition of *The 1001 Nights* I've been able to consult. Not *yet,* anyhow: after reading "Tlön, Uqbar," etc., one is inclined to recheck every semester or so.)

Now Borges (whom someone once vexedly accused *me* of inventing) is interested in the 602nd Night because it's an instance of the story-within-the-story turned back upon itself, and his interest in such instances is threefold: first, as he himself declares, they disturb us metaphysically: when the characters in a work of fiction become readers or authors of the fiction they're in, we're reminded of the ficti-

tious aspect of our own existence, one of Borges' cardinal themes, as it was of Shakespeare, Calderón, Unamuno, and other folk. Second, the 602nd Night is a literary illustration of the *regressus in infinitum,* as are almost all of Borges' principal images and motifs. Third, Scheherezade's accidental gambit, like Borges' other versions of the *regressus in infinitum,* is an image of the exhaustion, or attempted exhaustion, of possibilities—in this case literary possibilities—and so we return to our main subject.

What makes Borges' stance, if you like, more interesting to me than, say, Nabokov's or Beckett's, is the premise with which he approaches literature; in the words of one of his editors: "For [Borges] no one has claim to originality in literature; all writers are more or less faithful amanuenses of the spirit, translators and annotators of pre-existing archetypes." Thus his inclination to write brief comments on imaginary books: for one to attempt to add overtly to the sum of "original" literature by even so much as a conventional short story, not to mention a novel, would be too presumptuous, too naïve; literature has been done long since. A librarian's point of view! And it would itself be too presumptuous if it weren't part of a lively, passionately relevant metaphysical vision, and slyly employed against itself precisely to make new and original literature. Borges defines the Baroque as "that style which deliberately exhausts (or tries to exhaust) its possibilities and borders upon its own caricature." While his own work is *not* Baroque, except intellectually (the Baroque was never so terse, laconic, economical), it suggests the view that intellectual and literary history has been Baroque, and has pretty well exhausted the possibilities of novelty. His *ficciones* are not only footnotes to imaginary texts, but postscripts to the real corpus of literature.

This premise gives resonance and relation to all his principal images. The facing mirrors that recur in his stories are a dual *regressus.* The doubles that his characters, like Nabokov's, run afoul of suggest dizzying multiples and remind one of Browne's remark that "every man is not only himself . . . men are lived over again." (It would please Borges, and illustrate Browne's point, to call Browne a precursor of Borges. "Every writer," Borges says in his essay on Kafka, "creates his own precursors.") Borges' favorite third-century heretical sect is the Histriones—I think and hope he invented them—who believe that repetition is impossible in history and therefore live viciously in order to purge the future of the vices they commit: in other words, to exhaust the possibilities of the world in order to bring its end nearer.

The writer he most often mentions, after Cervantes, is Shakespeare; in one piece he imagines the playwright on his deathbed asking God to permit him to be one and himself, having been everyone and no one; God replies from the whirlwind that He is no one either; He has dreamed the world like Shakespeare, and including Shakespeare. Homer's story in Book IV of the *Odyssey,* of Menelaus on the beach at Pharos, tackling Proteus, appeals profoundly to Borges: Proteus is he who "exhausts the guises of reality" while Menelaus—who, one recalls, disguised his own identity in order to ambush him—holds fast. Zeno's paradox of Achilles and the Tortoise embodies a *regressus in infinitum* which Borges carries through philosophical history, pointing out that Aristotle uses it to refute Plato's theory of forms, Hume to refute the possibility of cause and effect, Lewis Carroll to refute syllogistic deduction, William James to refute the notion of temporal passage, and Bradley to refute the general possibility of logical relations; Borges himself uses it, citing Schopenhauer, as evidence that the world is our dream, our idea, in which "tenuous and eternal crevices of unreason" can be found to remind us that our creation is false, or at least fictive.

The infinite library of one of his most popular stories is an image particularly pertinent to the literature of exhaustion; the "Library of Babel" houses every possible combination of alphabetical characters and spaces, and thus every possible book and statement, including your and my refutations and vindications, the history of the actual future, the history of every possible future, and, though he doesn't mention it, the encyclopedias not only of Tlön but of every imaginable other world—since, as in Lucretius' universe, the number of elements, and so of combinations, is finite (though very large), and the number of instances of each element and combination of elements is infinite, like the library itself.

That brings us to his favorite image of all, the labyrinth, and to my point. *Labyrinths* is the name of his most substantial translated volume, and the only full-length study of Borges in English, by Ana María Barrenechea, is called *Borges the Labyrinth-Maker*. A labyrinth, after all, is a place in which, ideally, all the possibilities of choice (of direction, in this case) are embodied, and—barring special dispensation like Theseus'—must be exhausted before one reaches the heart. Where, mind, the Minotaur waits with two final possibilities: defeat and death, or victory and freedom. Now, in fact, the legendary Theseus is non-Baroque; thanks to Ariadne's thread he can take a shortcut through the labyrinth at Knossos. But Menelaus on the beach at Pharos, for example, is genuinely Baroque in the Borgesian spirit, and illustrates a positive artistic morality in the literature of exhaustion. He is not there, after all, for kicks (any more than Borges and Beckett are in the fiction racket for their health): Menelaus is *lost,* in the larger labyrinth of the world, and has got to hold fast while the Old Man of the Sea exhausts reality's frightening guises so that he may extort direction from him when Proteus returns to his "true" self. It's a heroic enterprise, with salvation as its object—one recalls that the aim of the Histriones is to get history done with so that Jesus may come again the sooner, and that Shakespeare's heroic metamorphoses culminate not merely in a theophany but in an apotheosis.

Now, not just any old body is equipped for this labor, and Theseus in the Cretan labyrinth becomes in the end the aptest image for Borges after all. Distressing as the fact is to us liberal Democrats, the commonality, alas, will *always* lose their way and their souls: it's the chosen remnant, the virtuoso, the Thesean *hero,* who, confronted with Baroque reality, Baroque history, the Baroque state of his art, need *not* rehearse its possibilities to exhaustion, any more than Borges needs actually to *write* the *Encyclopaedia of Tlön* or the books in the Library of Babel. He need only be

aware of their existence or possibility, acknowledge them, and with the aid of *very special* gifts—as extraordinary as saint- or hero-hood and not likely to be found in The New York Correspondence School of Literature—go straight through the maze to the accomplishment of his work. (pp. 29-34)

*John Barth, "The Literature of Exhaustion,"
in* The Atlantic Monthly, *Vol. 220, No. 2, August, 1967, pp. 29-34.*

Edgar H. Knapp   (essay date 1968-69)

[*In the following essay, which was originally published in* Modern Fiction Studies *(Winter 1968-69), Knapp studies "Lost in the Funhouse," highlighting Barth's use of thematic and structural devices based on myth, masque, cinema, and symposium.*]

After John Barth's **"Lost in the Funhouse"** appeared in *The Atlantic* of November, 1967, common men had a taste of terror, the mad felt a twinge of sympathy, and a faint and tweedy generation of English professors found themselves in the mirror maze of a new fiction.

Warning. You cannot read **"Lost in the Funhouse"** simply for the fun of it. Read it three times: once, to get knocked off your feet; again to regain your balance; and then to be knocked down again. Perhaps a fourth time . . . for the fun of it.

The story adheres to the archetypal pattern of passage through difficult ways, and the hero seems to be a thirteen-year-old boy on a family outing to Ocean City, Maryland, during World War II. The story line is straight. It's the how of the tale that upends one. Its mixture of myth, masque, cinema, and symposium makes **"Lost in the Funhouse"** one of the oldest and freshest of stories.

Myth. The setting of Barth's story is intensely true to the texture of life in tidewater Maryland, 1943. Lucky Strike's green has gone to war; V—— (Vienna) is the halfway point of the trip to the shore; at the end of the boardwalk is an inlet the Hurricane of '33 had cut to Sinepuxent Bay (which the author can't bear to leave as Assawoman). Nevertheless, the setting has another dimension: it is an ironic garden. At the Ocean City amusement park the roller coaster, rumored to be condemned in 1916, still runs; many machines are broken and the prizes are made of pasteboard (in the USA). Everyone except Ambrose M—— and his father exudes and ingests the carnival spirit—on Independence Day in a time of national crisis. Barth ruminates: "In a short-story about Ocean City, Maryland, during World War II the author could make use of the image of sailors on leave in the penny arcades and shooting-galleries, sighting through the cross hairs of toy machine-guns at swastika'd subs, while out in the black Atlantic a U-boat skipper squints through his periscope at real ships outlined by the glow of penny arcades." In a slight variation on the independence theme, Ambrose recalls that, five years before, the kids played "Niggers and Masters" in the backyard. And on the day of the story, even the sensitive hero is uncomfortable to think that a colored boy might help him through the funhouse. The boardwalk is a begrimed paradise to which there is no return: "Already quaint and seedy: the draperied ladies on the frieze of the carousel are his father's father's moon-cheeked dreams; if he thinks of it more he will vomit his apple-on-a-stick."

Ambrose at thirteen suffers from undescended identity. He has experienced two initiation ceremonies which left him cold: one sexual, in a tool shed at the age of eight; another religious, at his own belated baptism during the year of the story. (Each involved kneeling and the forgiveness of a master.) Ideally, such acts as these betoken man's communion with his own kind and with his God, but to the aggravation of his sense of loss, Ambrose "felt nothing." He feigned passion, he feigned tears. From time to time he even pretends to be a real person. And so it is his identity he seeks in a funhouse world where nothing is as it seems.

The dark passageways of the funhouse increase his sense of isolation. Still he must find his way out himself. Peeping through a crack in a plywood wall, Ambrose sees the lonely, old funhouse operator (God?) asleep at the switch. An ironic epiphany. Especially as we interpret the funhouse as world (and the world as funhouse), the mythic structure becomes more visible. Ambrose's adventures are like heroic suffering, death, and resurrection (if indeed one sees him as out of the funhouse at the story's end). The witchlike ticket-seller calls him a marked man. And we recall the tumble of unconscious formulation which follows his brush with life in the raw (*"an astonishing coincidence"*) under the boardwalk: "Magda clung to his trouserleg; he alone knew the maze's secret. 'He gave his life that we might live,' said Uncle Karl with a scowl of pain, as he." These words relate to a subsequent dream scene in the funhouse when a Magda-like assistant operator transcribes the hero's inspirational message, the more beautiful for his "lone dark dying." Mention of the Ambrose Lightship, beacon to lost seafarers, and the meaning of *Ambrose* (divine) and echoes of *ambrosia* (that bee-belabored stuff of immortality) reinforce the mythic overtones of his characterization.

Masque. This Ambrose seems clearly to be the protagonist but in another sense he is not. The "quaint and seedy" sextet may be the hero—each aspects of generalized man. Ambrose and father, both thin, fair-skinned, and bespectacled, combine as soulful tenors; brother Peter and Uncle Karl, both squat and swarthy, thump out a basso counterpoint, with which the two women harmonize as one voice—a sexy alto, limited in range. (They complement each other, appearing to be an at-once-sinister-and-dexterous female unit, the reflections of one another.)

Perceived as aspects of the same personality, Ambrose and his father represent acute awareness of experience and artistic intuition. Unlike his lustful, mesomorphic brother and uncle, Ambrose is seized by "terrifying transports": "The grass was alive! The town, the river, himself, were not imaginary; time roared in his ears like wind; the world was *going on!*" Peter and Uncle Karl represent "the withness of the body," Whitehead's phrase, which Delmore Schwartz uses as an epigraph to his poem "The Heavy Bear."

That heavy bear who sleeps with me,
Howls in his sleep for a world of sugar,
• • • • •
Stretches to embrace the very dear
With whom I would walk without him near,
Touches her grossly, although a word
Would bare my heart and make me clear.

Womankind is the honey that keeps the heavy bear "lumbering." (The women held the syrup-coated popcorn.) Also, the naming within the party of the flesh is symbolic: *Magda* for Mary Magdalene, sinful woman: *Peter,* meaning rock; *Karl,* man of the common people, who is coincidentally a stone mason and an inveterate cigar smoker. (He kept his stone-cutting chisels in an empty cigar box.)

The sextet enacts a masque-like drama symbolic of the inner transactions which result in human behavior. Members of the "heavy bear" quartet communicate by tactile and kinaesthetic means—playful shoves, tugs, punches, and slaps. Prufrock-like, Ambrose recoils from physical contact: the brown hair on his mother's forearms gleams in the sun; he sees perspiration patches at Magda's armpits. (He even gets to play the crab scuttling across the turning funhouse floors.) In the car he removes his hand "in the nick of time," and later in the funhouse he fails to embrace Magda in keeping with his vision.

Additional support to the sextet theory: the two males of each generation, although their actions contrast, share the same woman without deceit or suspicion. Nor is there conflict between corresponding members of the different generations. Although communication is strained between the separate selves, still they gravitate toward one another in artificial ways. For instance, at poolside Ambrose feigns interest in the diving; Magda, disinterest. (" 'He's a *master* diver,' Ambrose said. . . . 'You really have to *slave* away at it to get that good.' " [Italics mine]). These oscillations toward and away from members of the same generation create what may be termed *synchronic resonance.* Given the anachronistic setting, the mirrored manners and adherence to the same routines from one generation to the next have special implications in this Barth story. And particularly the reveries in which Ambrose sees himself, standing before Fat May, with Ambrose the Third. ("Magda would yield a great deal of milk although guilty of occasional solecisms.") By flicking images of generation-to-generation resemblance on the reader's screen, Barth effects a *diachronic resonance.*

Cinema. Whereas the action of the story is mythic and its characterization is related to archetypal masque, its scenic values—its choreography—derive from cinematic techniques. The scenic splicing is suggestive—and not only in a ribald sense. The interstitching of dream and action supports the basic theme of the merging of illusion and reality. Other splices create abrupt switches, with utter absence of transition, from narrative flow to textbook exposition, reminding us that not even the story is real. The action is suspended—reminiscent of the lights dimming and the actors freezing at intervals in Samuel Beckett's play *Waiting for Godot*—and then the motion picture resumes. Another and more conventional sort of juxtaposition is used, as when Fat May's canned laughter sounds ironically over images of war and death.

Perhaps the most intriguing aspect of Barth's scenic art is his use of symbolic ballet. Reinforcing the masque-like characterization, the physical interrelationships in the "blocking" of particular scenes are allegorical. For instance, the story opens and closes with the thematically loaded formation of the older generation in the front seat—the woman between the competing interest of the spirit and the flesh—reflected by the younger generation behind. Barth avoids perfect symmetry by contrasting the arm position of the sexually mature mother with that of the sexually maturing Magda (from B—— Street), who has her arms down, but "at the ready."

The theme is only slightly varied as the *sex*tet swings down the boardwalk to the swimming pool, the heavy bears next to the syrup-coated popcorn. The mirror motif is intensified at the pool: Peter grasps one ankle of the squirming Magda; Uncle Karl goes for the other ankle. Had either looked up he would have seen his reflection! The communion motif, as well, is reflected in the choreography, being subtly varied from the sexual to the religious: first by the child kneeling in sin in the tool shed and later by the fallen woman clutching her savior in supplication in the funhouse.

Not only scenic arrangement but also the varied sensory appeals of Barth's imagery support the illusion-reality theme. Paint peels from the hotels—themselves facades, within which lovers may pretend passion. Not only to do the mirrors within the funhouse distort and confuse but also the sounds of fumbling bees and lapping wavelets re-echo in Amby's ears. He suffers from vertigo, if not labyrinthitis. And "candied apples-on-a-stick, delicious-looking, [were] disappointing to eat."

Symposium. And so we have a significant human experience imaginatively presented in structure and textures organically related to the whole. But the story has one more funhouse dimension which is most puzzling—its point of view. Although Barth's story is spun from the consciousness of the protagonist, a precocious adolescent, in the telling at least six distinct bands of mental formulation seem to be randomly mixed: (1) report of the action proper, (2) recollection of past experience, (3) conscious contrivance of a reasonable future, (4) uncontrolled swings into a fantastic future, (5) consciousness of problems of composition, and (6) recollection of sections from a handbook for creative writers. (After a while the reader can visualize the author seated before a console, gleefully pushing buttons according to the sprung rhythm of his whim.) The first four bands on the list qualify as spritely narrative; the last two, as the conscience of an author not completely free from the shackles of conventional fiction. The relationship which is generated between these technical obtrusions and the rest of the story is that of a symposium. We have a running Platonic dialogue between the experimental Barth and the tradition out of which his work has grown. The dialectic is undeniable, but what is the artistic reason for it? It obtrudes upon the illusion of reality. And it has to be Barth's strategy—similar to Pirandello's and Wilder's experiments in the theatre—to remind the reader continually of the contrivance of literature, the fact that a story is the semblance of lived-experience, not experience. The

frequent italicized phrases are likewise reminders of the artificiality of fiction. One purpose could to be wean us from the particular in time and place so that we will appreciate the universality of Amby's fate, that he is also ourselves, and that we have our opportunities for heroism.

But wait; we're not out of the funhouse yet. Could it be that Barth's story, and not Barth himself, is playing the bright, young heterosexual Phaedrus to a tired, old Socrates, who is in fact the 19*th* century short story? (Peruse Barth's essay "The Literature of Exhaustion" in *The Atlantic* of August, 1967, and you have to believe it.) This doesn't vitiate other interpretations of the story-within-the-story; it is merely an additional crown to the apple-within-an-apple nest of **"Lost in the Funhouse."**

Granted this detachment and accepting the universality of the human experience represented by the M—— family's journey, an allegory of the flesh and the spirit, we are in position to appreciate one more tantalizing suggestion: that one generation of the M—— family is symbolic not only of essential M-a-n but also of essential M-y-t-h—the attempt in story form to help man find his way in the non-human world. The earliest of these fictions portrayed gods as the main strugglers. Hence, the divine characteristics of Ambrose, which set him apart from the common man; his wanderings in a strange dark underworld; his yearning to discover his identity.

When we see a generation of the M—— family as a story, the reappearance of the old structure and dynamics in later generations takes on fresh significance. As every man is like his father, every story bears a likeness to its archetype. The diachronic resonance in the characterization suggests the relationships within literary genres. As Northrop Frye points out, individual works of literature reveal "family likenesses resembling the species, genera, and phyla of biology."

Fiction as we have known it, Barth implies, is at the water's edge. The myth-carrying vehicles have not changed radically (train, car, autogiro), and these recurring outings of the monomyth are distastefully decked with anachronistic trappings. Mention of "the draperied ladies on the frieze of the carousel [seen as] his father's father's mooncheeked dreams" is a comment on "the literature of exhausted possibility," as critic John Barth has labeled it.

And so in a central room of the funhouse, the maze of mirrors, we have the eye. We trust it, as we have learned to, and its imperfect perception goes to a bleary brain: a flickering of self-knowledge (Ambrose did find his name coin there—symbolic of himself.) But with it the *aw*ful chain of reflection cast backward and forward, in space and time. Outside is the funhouse of a lifetime. Beyond that, the history of humanity and the extension of its possibilities. And encompassing that, the marvelous funhouse of imaginative conception, which can project images, construct funhouses, *et cetera et cetera et cetera*. And we can come to the chimerical conclusion that the eye in the funhouse—yours and mind—is at once that of reader, author, character, god, and story. (The hero is amb—— "O brightening glance . . . " Could six characters be in search of an author?) Selfhood is not easy. Best be a common man and not think about it.

But I'm still worried about Ambrose. Did he make it out of the funhouse? If I can still be worried about him after peering down and up these other echoing funhouse corridors, then I consider the story to be a really good one. I tend to believe the dissembling narrator when he says, "The family's going home. Mother sits between Father and Uncle Karl who teases him [Ambrose] . . . " and I say he's out of the Ocean City funhouse, though still in his funhouse world, as much "a place of fear and confusion" as it was. The voice of convention, nevertheless, has reminded us that the climax will be reached when the protagonist is out. But Ambrose doesn't have climaxes and he will expire in his funhouse world. Lost as he is, he can find purpose in life—at least make "a stay against confusion" (and have a fighting chance for one sort of immortality)—through imaginative design. The Whiffenpoofs are lost too, but "the magic of their singing" makes it a joy to be lost with them. And from another angle, we know that when the operator of our funhouse sets the tumbling-barrel turning, struggle for equilibrium does beget fresh intellectual and/or intuitive formulation. And so the funhouse for *man thinking* is a womb of possibility from which he may be reborn. I ruminate: if in one house of fiction we discover that we are lost and toppled and we regain our equilibrium, even to our knees, the author will have found us and so saved himself, according to the terrible and wonderful necessity which only he can know. (pp. 446-51)

> Edgar H. Knapp, "Found in the Barthhouse: Novelist as Savior," in The Process of Fiction: Contemporary Stories and Criticism, *edited by Barbara McKenzie, second edition, Harcourt Brace Jovanovich, Inc., 1974, pp. 582-91.*

Tony Tanner   (essay date 1969)

[Tanner is an English critic and editor whose writings include critical studies of the works of Saul Bellow, Thomas Pynchon, and Joseph Conrad. In the following essay, he laments the excessively self-conscious nature of the stories in Lost in the Funhouse.]

John Barth is what Robert Musil called a "possibilitarian," meaning someone blessed or afflicted with "a sense of possibility."

> Anyone possessing it does not say, for instance, here this or that has happened, will happen, must happen. He uses his imagination and says: Here such and such might, should or ought to happen. And if he is told that something *is* the way it is, then he thinks: Well, it could probably be just as easily some other way. . . . Such possibilitarians live, it is said, within a finer web, a web of haze, imaginings, fantasy and the subjunctive mood [*The Man Without Qualities*].

Obviously without any sense of possibility man would be mindlessly mired in necessity, and the rejection of any one fixed patterning of reality is an effort which American heroes and authors alike are constantly making. But it is possible for the sense of possibility to get out of hand, and here Kierkegaard's comments in *The Sickness Unto Death* are especially pertinent. "Now if possibility outruns necessity, the self runs away from itself, so that it has no necessity whereto it is bound to return—then this is the despair of possibility." Barth has explored precisely this despair in some of his previous novels but it now seems to have touched the author himself. Again from Kierkegaard: "Possibility then appears to the self ever greater and greater, more and more things become possible, because nothing becomes actual. At last it is as if everything were possible—but this is precisely when the abyss has swallowed up the self."

Lacking "the sense of actuality" some people, says Kierkegaard, go "astray in possibility." In his latest book, brilliant as it is, I think that Barth has gone astray in exactly this way. **Lost in the Fun House** sufficiently indicates the impasse to which his sense of the arbitrariness of invention, and the unlimited number of possible fictions, has brought him. "What the hell, reality is a nice place to visit but you wouldn't want to live there, and literature never did, very long. . . . Reality is a drag." So said Barth in an interview. What seems to have happened by the time of **Lost in the Fun House** is that he can no longer get hold of any "reality" at all; everything he touches turns into fictions and yet more fictions. There is no reason for his words to follow in any one direction; as a matter of fact there is no reason why he should go on writing at all except that there seems to be an underlying feeling that identity is coextensive and coterminus with articulation. The "I" is only ascertainable as that which speaks: self is voice, but voice speaking unnecessary and arbitrary and untrue words. The torment of this book is that of a man who cannot really find any sanction for writing either in world or self, yet feels that it is his one distinguishing ability, the one activity which gives him any sense of self. In **"Autobiography,"** intended for tape recording, voice turns on voice in a void. "Now that I reflect I'm not enjoying this life: my link with the world. . . . Are you there? . . . . I hope I'm a fiction without real hope. Where there's a voice there's a speaker. . . . I must compose myself. . . . I'll mutter to the end, one word after another, string the rascals out, mad or not, heard or not, my last words will be my last words." Words floating free in this way never encounter any necessity so they can drift on in self-canceling and self-undermining recessions as long as the voice lasts. If this is what "identity" is, it is surely in a precarious state.

This corrosive doubt about identity and its relation to language reveals itself in Barth's preoccupation with the relationship between self and name. Ambrose, who figures in a number of the stories, knows well "that I and my sign are neither one nor quite two," and I think this sense of the ambiguous relation between "I and my sign" is the focal point of a larger dubiety about the relationship between all names and bodies, between words and world. One rather grotesque story called **"Petition"** takes up the old Mark Twain "joke" about incompatible Siamese twins and gives it a philosophical twist. The petitioning brother is an intelligent almost mandarin figure who is seeking "disjunction" from the coarse brutish appetitive brother to whose back he is stuck. "He's incoherent but vocal; I'm articulate but mute." The incoherent brother is like life itself, constantly shrugging off the attempts of language to circumscribe it within particular definitions. Language, in the form of the articulate brother, would be happy to pursue its inclination to ponder its elegant patternings in pure detachment from the soiling contacts of reality. But they are brothers, divided yet related—neither one nor two. Like Ambrose who cannot work out the relationship between his self and his sign, so Barth seems to have reached a point where he cannot stop troubling himself with his uncertainty about the relationship between the words he invents, and the world he shares.

"Lost in the Fun House" approaches this problem again, with Barth never allowing us to forget the foreground presence of the typing man who, lost in the freedom of his inventions, can put down any words he likes in any order. "This can't go on much longer; it can go on forever." There is no pressure to keep the words in order, and they can start reversing their tracks and dissolving their statements as easily as they can advance to new stages in the account of Ambrose's family and the day they spent at the seaside. "Is there really such a person as Ambrose, or is he a figment of the author's imagination? . . . Are there other errors of fact in this fiction?" In such ways does the story destroy its own sustaining conventions. In addition, Ambrose, the boy who gets lost in the funhouse, is not clear whether what he is experiencing at any one moment is a private fantasy or a public fact, so the uncertainty surrounding any sequence of words is multiplied, leaving us with a sense of fictions within fictions within fictions. At the same time, an anguished sense that meanwhile "the world was *going on!*" just occasionally intrudes into this lexical paralysis: unvexed by reflection and possibility, in dark corners couples wordlessly copulate. One senses Barth's own dissatisfaction with the feelings of exclusion which best the fiction-maker.

The funhouse itself seems to represent a variety of structures—in particular, that pseudo-world which man invents for his own amusement, the edifice of fictions with which we distract ourselves at all levels. Ambrose in the funhouse can imagine various endings to his adventure: Barth at his typewriter can imagine various endings to his story. There is a close connection between the character's situation in the story and the author's position among his words. "The climax of the story must be its protagonist's discovery of a way to get through the funhouse. But he has found none, may have ceased to search." Both Ambrose and Barth may be destined to remain confined in their own fictions. "He died telling stories to himself in the dark." Thinks Ambrose about himself. Writes Barth about Ambrose. Says Barth about Barth. Unfixed in any one frame and unlocated in any one plane, the words float before us—in multiple perspective, in no perspective at all. But the closing narrative statement about Ambrose is clearly a refracted statement about the author. "He dreams of a funhouse vaster by far than any yet constructed . . . he will construct funhouses for others and be their secret operator—though he would rather be among the lovers for whom funhouses are designed." Barth has certainly built some funhouses, but what one notices about *Lost in the*

Fun House is that it is not a funhouse, but a series of depositions about building, or not building, funhouses. It is as though he cannot find any firm foundation on which his architectural abilities can take hold. A sort of plea seems to be contained in the following suggestion: "If one regarded the absence of a ground-situation, more accurately the protagonist's anguish at that absence and his vain endeavours to supply the defect, as itself a sort of ground-situation, did his life story thereby take on a kind of meaning?" But meaning itself is a dissolving notion in a verbal situation in which the narrator thinks that "the word . . . is now evidently nearing the end of its road." One conclusion to all this nonprogressive muttering is that fiction, having acknowledged its fictitiousness, must "establish some other, acceptable relation between itself, its author, its reader." By being exhaustive in making fiction display its own fictitiousness, Barth is perhaps clearing the ground for this new and necessary relationship. Meanwhile no stories get told, no funhouses get built on their ground of no ground. The interest of this in some ways rather oppressive book, is that it suggests that one of the most inventive and prolific of all contemporary American writers has discovered that the freedom provided by what Nabokov called "lexical playfields" may precipitate new kinds of anxiety and incapacity.

Barth has always been fascinated by triangular relationships, and they abound in this book—the Siamese twins, and the one girl they share; Narcissus, Tiresias and Echo who seem to reflect the complicated relations between "teller, tale, told"; and, most interestingly, Menelaus, Proteus and Helen in **"Menelaiad."** Here Barth takes up the image of Menelaus struggling with Proteus which, interestingly enough, Ralph Ellison has used to describe the American artist's relation to American reality. Added to this pair is Helen, "that faultless form," who figures as a contrast to Proteus whose gift for metamorphosis and multiple temporary forms makes him the epitome of fluidity. Menelaus loses Helen because he keeps asking why she loves him instead of being content to accept the mystery of love in a wordless embrace. That loss, brought on by a compulsion to understand and verbalize, is also a loss of substantial reality. From then on, Menelaus can never be sure what he has hold of, if indeed he has hold of anything. His struggles to hold Proteus extend to a more prolonged effort to catch hold of something in his narrative. Menelaus is telling a story which includes within it accounts of himself telling stories, and so on and so on. There are tales within tales, and the narrator can never be sure what he has hold of, just as Menelaus cannot be sure whether when he is trying to hold Proteus he is grappling with dreams. His lament, "When will I reach my goal through its cloaks of story? How many veils to naked Helen?" sounds like a projection of Barth's own despair at ever reaching and holding any authentic formed reality through the multiplying layers of fiction in which he feels entangled—the Hellenic quest is impeded at every turn by the Protean encounter. Even when he does regain his Helen he cannot be sure it is the real Helen or a dream substitute made of cloud. "For all I knew, I roared, what I now gripped was but a further fiction, maybe Proteus himself." The crippling and inhibiting worry that even Helen may be Proteus is a precise analogue of the suspicion that even Reality is a Fiction. At one point Menelaus says, "Menelaus! Proteus! Helen! For all we know, we're but stranded figures in Penelope's web, wove up in light to be unwove in darkness." Again the triangle, again the ever underlying suspicion that all apparent facts may be part of some larger fiction. Penelope's "embroidrous art," Menelaus' "raveled fabrication," Barth's own "cloaks of story"—where does it or can it stop? One hope expressed by the story is that one thing will survive all the changing receding fictions of existence—"the absurd, unending possibility of love." But the story itself is a story of loss, a demonstration of how we lose what we don't believe in, how we can never again be sure of the Helen we called into question. Floundering in fictions, we may never regain a firm hold on reality. This I think is the dread of deprivation which is detectable in these recent pieces by Barth.

It is evident in the last story, **"Anonymiad."** This is the first-person account of a minstrel who was not taken to Troy but left behind in the court of Clytemnestra and subsequently marooned on an island. There he dreams dreams with multiple possible endings, he invents private Mycenae for the real city he has been excluded from, and he invents a new mode of writing—"what I came to call fiction." Although excluded from the Trojan war and all knowledge of it, he amuses himself by imagining various versions of its progress and different possible denouements. Lacking an audience he commits his compositions to the sea in bottles. After running through various genres he finds he has "begun to run out of material" and in a new pessimism he imagines his *"opera* sinking undiscovered"—a neat pun looking back to Barth's own *Floating Opera.* He finds that "as my craft improved, my interest waned, and my earlier zeal seemed hollow as the jugs it filled. Was there any new thing to say, new way to say the old?" He outlines his idea for his next work which would synthesize all genres, merging everything from "grub fact" to "pure senseless music." But of course he does not write it, he only writes about planning to write it. His time is spent in "considering and rejecting forms" (and of course the plurality of available forms and styles can have a paralyzing as well as a liberating effect). He concludes "It was my wish to elevate maroonment into a minstrel masterpiece; instead, I see now, I've spent my last resources contrariwise, reducing the masterpiece to a chronicle of minstrel misery." He then launches the last of his "opera," but foresees the time when it will perish, "with all things deciphered and undeciphered: men and women, stars and sky."

Perhaps in this account of seemingly futile writing in an endless solitude Barth has constructed an analogue for his own situation as he experiences it. But whereas before he distracted himself with stories, he now seems to be tormenting himself with accounts of stories that failed, that cannot be written, that can never be started. The first piece is called **"Frame Tale"** and it invites the reader to make a circular strip out of a page, which will then read "Once upon a time there was a story that began once upon a time . . . " and so on ad infinitum. And inside that verbal circle which moves but does not progress Barth seems temporarily to have trapped himself. At one point in the **"Anonymiad"** he says, "I yearned to be relieved of my-

self. . . . I'd relapse into numbness, as if, having abandoned song for speech, I meant now to give up language altogether and float voiceless in the wash of time like an amphora in the sea, my vision bottled." To abandon the difficulties of language is to leave behind the problems of self: Barth is here giving utterance to a recurring temptation or desire, detectable in much American writing, to give up all forms and definitions and abandon the contours of self and style to dissolution and silence. But this ultimate solution to the torments of identity and narration—torments amply, indeed profoundly, demonstrated in this volume, hovering and limping obsessively around the arbitrariness of all names and naming, all fictions and their telling—is irreversible, a final capitulation to some unselving flow which, along with the dread of getting trapped in fixed patterns, is a nightmare which haunts many contemporary American writers. To float voiceless in the wash of time is effectively to die, and even the self-paralyzing voice in Barth's latest book resists that particular quietus and quietness—"I'll mutter to the end." (pp. 293-95, 297-99)

Tony Tanner, "No Exit," in Partisan Review, *Vol. XXXVI, No. 2, Spring, 1969, pp. 293-95, 297-99.*

Barth on the structure of his writings:

I start every new project saying, "This one's going to be simple, this one's going to be simple." It never turns out to be. My imagination evidently delights in complexity for its own sake. Much of life, after all, and much of what we admire is essentially complex. For a temperament such as mine, the hardest job in the world—the most *complicated* task in the world—is to become simpler. There are writers whose gift is to make terribly complicated things simple. But I know my gift is the reverse: to take relatively simple things and complicate them to the point of madness. But there you are: one learns who one is, and it is at one's peril that one attempts to become someone else.

John Barth, in a interview with George Plimpton in The Paris Review, *1985.*

Robert F. Kiernan (essay date 1973)

[*In the following essay, Kiernan discusses the story sequence of* Lost in the Funhouse *as demonstrative of a* Künstlerroman.]

In the "Author's Note" that prefaces the first American edition of *Lost in the Funhouse,* John Barth maintains with wonderful solemnity that the book is "neither a collection nor a selection, but a series." It is sometimes difficult to know when such instances of Barth's solemnity are to be taken seriously, but this seems to be one of them. At least when reviewers of the book tended to disregard the note and to see the volume as unified only in a loose manner by Barthian humor and by an intermittent concern with literary "exhaustion," the author developed a seven-point addendum to his original note, the first point affirming that his claim for a serial structure "means in good faith exactly what it says." His regnant intention in *Funhouse,* he maintains, is to turn "as many aspects of the fiction as possible . . . into dramatically relevant emblems of the theme." Although the critics have not generally conceded it, Barth's claim for *Funhouse* is not excessive: at the same time that the individual units of the book are generally self-contained, they contribute both conceptually and stylistically to an organic life of the whole. Like Malamud's *Pictures of Fidelman, Funhouse* is a story sequence that approaches the form of a *Künstlerroman,* recording the search of an artist for a viable mode of fiction and shaping that search into a significant and balanced action that is, indeed, emblematic of Barth's theme.

Three stories that concern themselves with a character named Ambrose afford the most immediate key to the sequence, for they are ordered chronologically and trace the growth of a vocation to art. In **"Ambrose His Mark,"** the first story of the three, the title character is an infant for whom an appropriate name has not yet been found. When a swarm of bees settles upon him, he is named for Saint Ambrose, the fourth century bishop to whom a swarm of bees imparted the power of honeyed speech. At the end of the story, we understand that Ambrose has been "marked" by the bees and that he is destined to be a wordman. In **"Water-Message,"** the second story of the three, Ambrose is a fourth grader, alienated already from other people by his special sensibility. He spends his time spinning fictions to impress a younger boy and to rationalize his extreme timidity, for his life outside of the fictions is a constant embarrassment to him. At the climax of the story Ambrose opens a bottle washed up by the sea and finds in it a paper inscribed with an address at the top ("To whom it may concern") and a complimentary close at the bottom ("Yours truly"). Suddenly, we are told, Ambrose's spirit "bore new and subtle burdens," and we understand that it is Ambrose's destiny to write on the blank lines of the paper. His vocation as a word-man, then, is specifically to literature. In **"Lost in the Funhouse,"** the last story of the three, an adolescent Ambrose tries unsuccessfully to mimic the attitudes and passions of ordinary men on a family trip to the Ocean City boardwalk. When he becomes lost in the funhouse, he envisions himself telling stories for the rest of his life, a constructor of funhouses for others, "though he would rather be among the lovers for whom funhouses are designed." The call to literature is heard, then, and accepted reluctantly. Ambrose will become a storyteller.

A stylistic evolution in this set of stories suggests that Ambrose is already developing as a storyteller and that he is consistently, in fact, the teller of his own story. While his personal narration of the first Ambrose story is apparently replaced by more objective modes of narration in **"Water-Message"** and **"Funhouse,"** we note that the ostensibly detached narrators of those stories have an interest in Ambrose's emotional states and difficulties that grows with Ambrose's increasing self-awareness. Furthermore, we note that the later narrators show a passion for phrase-making that keeps pace with Ambrose's developing passion for language. In the second story, for instance, the omniscient narrator is much more interested in Ambrose's point of view than Ambrose is himself in the first story,

and he begins to italicize phrases such as "more weary than exultant," suggesting a delight in verbal postures equal to Ambrose's own delight at that stage of his development. In **"Funhouse,"** the narrator identifies so closely with Ambrose that the narration is almost a stream of consciousness; the narration is thick with italicized, quoted, and pat phrases; and the narrator of the story is so adolescently self-conscious that his identity with Ambrose is almost certain. Ambrose, it seems, is becoming a literary sophisticate and is developing his fictions about himself from a calculatedly detached viewpoint.

The stories with which the three Ambrose stories are alternated both complement and develop this *Künstlerroman* structure. The first story of the sequence, **"Night-Sea Journey,"** is a wonderful tour de force in which an Existential sperm meditates eloquently on the meaning of a strange impulse which drives him on to "Her who summons." Its position at the head of the Ambrose stories suggests that **"Night-Sea Journey"** dramatizes the prenatal period of Ambrose's life, and this impression is reinforced when the voice of the sperm reflects a deeply literary consciousness: the sperm elaborates a whole series of fictions about the night-sea journey, for instance; he is capable of such an elegant accentuation as "my drownéd friend"; and "A poor irony" is the literary sort of observation that comes easily to him. Furthermore, when the sperm declaims *"I am he who abjures and rejects the night-sea journey!"* he postures verbally in the same manner that Ambrose is to develop in **"Funhouse"** and subsequent stories. Thus, it seems natural to understand **"Night-Sea Journey"** as an integral element of the *Künstlerroman,* depicting the storyteller as vocationally determined in his prenatal existence.

The third story of the sequence, **"Autobiography: A Self-Recorded Fiction,"** is another tour de force, capturing a fiction in the process of composing its own autobiography, free for the nonce of both authorial and mechanical manipulation, and yet ironically unable to end itself. "Bear in mind," the fiction has been instructed, and it does exactly that, dramatizing in its very *donnée* that fiction tends necessarily to a life of its own and to an inordinate degree of self-reflection. The dramatization of these tendencies anticipates the self-conscious story telling of **"Funhouse"** and it prepares us for Ambrose's later attempt to become so very mannered that the conventions of storytelling will displace him as both speaker and central subject. Appropriately, the fiction of **"Autobiography"** wonders if it is "still in utero"—still "hung up in delivery," for **"Autobiography"** creates the illusion of Ambrose's autobiography stepping out prolepticly and beginning to tell itself. Although Ambrose does not make an obvious appearance in the fiction, then, the theme of **"Autobiography"** is a structural clue to the developing fictions of his autobiography, and it is an integral part of the total *Künstlerroman* that his fictions become.

"Petition," the fifth story of the sequence, purports to be an unsigned letter from a Siamese twin. In wonderfully formal diction, the author of the letter petitions the king of Siam to arrange for a separation from his brother on the grounds that his brother is trying to kill him and thereby reserve for himself the affection of a female contortionist with whom the twins have established a *ménage a trois*. Following as it does upon **"Water-Message,"** the unsigned letter of **"Petition"** recalls the unsigned letter that Ambrose finds in a bottle and which, we understand, he is to sign himself. Indeed, in a very real sense Ambrose is the ultimate author of **"Petition."** If the twin feels threatened by sexual rivalry with his brother, Ambrose handles sexual matters awkwardly in **"Water-Message"** and **"Funhouse,"** and his older brother Peter is an annoying rival in both of these stories. In **"Water-Message,"** it is Peter's club that embarrasses Ambrose when he naively suggests that Tommy James and Peggy Robbins have been "smooching," and it is Peter who insists that Ambrose leave the clubhouse when a contraceptive is discovered. In **"Funhouse,"** Peter is an overt rival for the affections of Magda G——, and he is annoyingly informed about walking through the funhouse with a girl. Given these similarities of structure and situation, **"Petition"** seems to be a projection of Ambrose's rivalry with his brother into an imaginative and very literary fiction, continuing the tendency in **"Night-Sea Journey"** and **"Autobiography"** for aspects of a *Künstlerroman* to become autonomous fictions. Just as Ambrose soothes his wounded vanity at the end of **"Water-Message"** by the discovery of the blank letter and of all the possibilities that it presents, so, we understand, **"Petition"** is a writing on that blank paper and an integral part of the total *Künstlerroman.* **"Petition"** shows a self-sufficient fiction at one level of Ambrose's consciousness, just as **"Night-Sea Journey"** shows the creation of various fictions by his prenatal consciousness.

"Echo" follows **"Lost in the Funhouse"** in the sequence, and recounts the legend of Tiresias, Echo, and Narcissus from a viewpoint that could belong to any one of the three characters and which flaunts that ambiguity. "Overmuch presence appears to be the storyteller's problem," the narrator remarks midway through the story, and so he withdraws into a Chinese box, announcing cryptically the regnant theme of the story: "None can tell teller from told." As its ambiguous title suggests, the story is itself an "echo," recalling to the reader that the narrators and subjects of the various stories are identical as early as **"Autobiography,"** and that Ambrose as both teller and subject of the stories has created fictions that pretend to be their own teller and subject. **"Echo"** develops, then, a fiction emblematic of the ambiguities of narration in the first six stories of the sequence. It gives dramatic shape and substance to that inversion of the storytelling process upon itself that is suggested by the Moebius strip of the **"Frame-Tale,"** that is metaphorically figured in the title of the sequence, and that is formulated and traced in the stories. In the development of the sequence, it serves to crystallize the vectors of the *Künstlerroman* at the point where the fictions with Ambrose as their explicit subject give way to experimental fictions with Ambrose as their implicit subject.

"Two Meditations," which follows **"Echo"** in the sequence, is composed of two brief fictions subtitled "Niagara Falls" and "Lake Erie." "Niagara Falls" records a series of bizarre correspondences, and "Lake Erie" records a series of equally bizarre consequences. While the inherent interest of these fictions is not great, their position in the sequence makes them richly suggestive. Following upon the dilemma of a narrator's "overmuch presence" in **"Echo,"** they ask to be understood as fictions "stripped down" in an effort to eliminate authorial presence. Interestingly, and importantly, the type of fiction they represent corresponds to a type of fiction already devised by Ambrose. When Ambrose walks on the boardwalk in Ocean City, for instance, he composes a fiction in which soldiers on leave in a penny arcade shoot at miniature German submarines as a German U-boat commander squints through his periscope at American ships silhouetted by the glow of the arcade. The correspondence between Ambrose's fiction and the types of fiction in **"Two Meditations"** helps the reader to appreciate the latter as a further manifestation of Ambrose's *Künstlerroman,* as achieved and self-sufficient fictions with Ambrose as their determinedly effaced author. This understanding of **"Two Meditations"** is the key to understanding all of the subsequent stories of *Lost in the Funhouse.* **"Two Meditations"** inaugurates a series of fictions all of which are properly understood as attempts to write fiction, given the difficulty that fictions tend reductively to *Künstlerroman,* the artist and his conventions always peeping through with "overmuch presence." Because Ambrose is effacing himself so vigorously, it is wholly proper that he make no overt appearance in the remaining stories. Indeed, he has no need to. The blending of **"Autobiography,"** **"Petition"** and **"Echo"** into the series of Ambrose stories has prepared us to understand the last five stories of the sequence according to a similar process of blending.

"Title" (which Barth calls a "triply schizoid monologue") takes as a fiction exactly the opposite tack of **"Meditations."** A type of authorial frenzy is implied by this dialectical arrangement of the two fictions, and the authorial strategy of **"Meditations"** appears retrospectively futile in consequence. Indeed, the strategy of **"Title"** is characterized by an attempt to implement as much self-consciousness as possible and to expel self-consciousness by an inundation of consciousness. "To write this allegedly ultimate story," the narrator says, "is a form of artistic fill in the blank, or artistic form of same, if you like. I don't." By overwhelming us with the narrative processes of which he is a victim, and by continually disparaging them, the narrator attempts to salvage at least a sense of superiority to the processes that betray his presence. As in **"Autobiography,"** however, a strong sense of *taedium vitae* colors the narration; and, in his desperate attempts to call a halt to this mode of fiction, the narrator discredits his own strategy as surely as his turning to this strategy has discredited his tack in **"Meditations."** "O God comma I abhor self-consciousness," the narrator concludes. "I despise what we have come to; I loathe our loathsome loathing. . . ." Clearly, this signifies that the fiction has once again turned back upon itself: sneering at the affectations of fiction is simply another variety of fictive affectation, and Ambrose is still lost in the funhouse.

"Glossolalia," the next fiction of the sequence, represents a new tack in this series of attempts to overcome fiction's betrayal. It consists of six statements by six different speakers (Barth notes that they are Cassandra, Philomela, the man mentioned in I Corinthians 14, the Queen of Sheba's talking bird, an unidentified psalmist, and the author), and the statements are notable primarily for their metrical similarity to The Lord's Prayer. Ecstatic, impersonally shaped speech, then, becomes the next attempt to create acceptable fictions. It is not successful. The metrical gimmick is calculatedly sterile, "more dismaying than delightful" as Barth puts it, and it suggests a merely perverse attempt to impose impersonal form upon language—an attempt so perverse that it reflects actually a highly subjective imposition of form. And again, the authorial voice discredits the method. In the last of the speeches, the "author" suggests that "ill fortune, constraint and terror [all of which apply to his immediate situation] generate guileful art." Again, he remarks apropos of himself that "prophet-birds seem to speak sagely but are shrieking their frustration." The language of ecstasy, like all other modes of speech in *Funhouse,* is formal gimmickery, then; it becomes an aspect of an ultimate *Künstlerroman* inasmuch as the artistic life of the author is inescapably reflected in it, and it is a part of our immediate *Künstlerroman* in that it betrays the continuing need of Ambrose to escape from himself in his fictions.

"Life-Story" follows **"Glossolalia"** in the sequence and attempts a synthetic solution, combining absolute immediacy of reference with a third person distancing. Thus, the immediate act of composing the fiction becomes the subject of the fiction, while the narrator speaks detachedly of what his "author" is doing. As one might expect, the narrator finds himself no more successful with this method of controlling his presence than with the methods of the four previous stories: he addresses the reader impatiently as a "dogged uninsultable, print-oriented bastard" and, disgusted with his fiction, asks, "Can nothing surfeit, saturate you, turn you off? Where's your shame?" Interestingly, the continual attempt of Ambrose to transmute into fiction is now complicated by the narrator's (Ambrose's, and, by clear suggestion, Barth's) uncomfortable suspicion that he is merely a character in the fiction, and "in quite the sort [of fiction] one least prefers." Although Ambrose might be disconcerted, this development is partially what he has struggled for in the four preceding stories, transforming the narrator's presence into a wholly integral part of the fiction. The authorial presence, of course, has not been assimilated into the fiction, and, in fact, it is more delinquent in this story than in any other in the sequence. The narrator acknowledges the authorial presence from within the fiction, but he has little sense of what his author is *doing* with the fiction. For all the narrator knows, he is involved in a *Bildungsroman,* an *Erziehungsroman,* or a *roman fleuve* ("!") Delightfully, Ambrose's frantic attempts to find a proper place in the funhouse by eliminating or integrating the "overmuch presence" that is an embarrassment to him in so many ways has involved him finally in the most familiar order of literary schizophrenia: as the narrator he is reduced to a simple character in the fiction and as the author he finds himself relegated to an unstable, uncontrollable, and eminently visible presence not wholly outside of the fiction. The Moebius strip has brought Ambrose back to approximately the stance of author and narrator in **"Night-Sea Journey,"** and the difficulty of writing a fiction that does not reduce itself to a

Künstlerroman has merely been confused en route. **"Life-Story"** effectively undercuts the narrator's attempts to rid himself of his overmuch presence by ingenious and esoteric strategies, then, and it represents the termination of that effort in Ambrose's *Künstlerroman.*

"Menelaiad," the penultimate story of the sequence, dramatizes Ambrose's attempt to deal with his presence in a more traditional way. His new tack is an Homeric-Conradian effort to obscure authorial presence by an intricate nest of speakers, modulated by an overtone of Joycean myth-grounding. But, as we might expect, the method betrays itself once again. As we listen to Menelaus relate to Telemachus what he had already told Helen he had previously related to Proteus with regard to what he had told Eidothea, our heads quite properly begin to spin, and when these nested speeches involve a quotational knot such as [" ("("(("What?"))')(")'], the narrative method has clearly invalidated itself as a technique for masking authorial presence. As in **"Title"** and **"Glossolalia,"** the effort to write "objective" fiction results in intolerably subjective gimmickry. And so it is that Ambrose steps in at the end of **"Menelaiad"** as, in frustration, he stepped in at the end of **"Glossolalia,"** only to insist with cavalier logic that he is *not* dismayed. Repudiating all that he has struggled for in the previous fictions, he pretends satisfaction that he will survive only as a persona, as "Proteus's terrifying last disguise, Beauty's spouse's odd Elysium: the absurd, unending possibility of love." It is the possibility of love, we are preposterously asked to believe, that narrates the story. Ambrose's desperation has turned momentarily into either self-delusion or chicanery.

"Anonymiad" is the appropriate conclusion to the sequence. Invoking a goatherd as its speaker, it affects a return to the very dawn of written composition and simply refuses to become embroiled in the problems that are the subject of the sequence. Clearly, however, the speaker of **"Anonymiad"** is a sort of composite Ambrose. Like the Ambrose in **"Petition,"** he is in love with a Thalia. Like the Ambrose in **"Water-Message,"** he finds a blank message that might be his own washed up by the sea. Like the Ambrose of **"Funhouse"** and **"Life-Story,"** he is intensely conscious of literary technique and provides a running commentary on his own devices. Like the Ambrose of several stories, he goes through a period of contriving "a precarious integrity by satirizing his own dilemma," only to reject "whimsic fantasy" (**"Petition"**), "grub fact" (**"Two Meditations"**), and "pure senseless music" (**"Glossolalia"**). "Adversity generates guileful art," he comments, playing upon his terminal remarks in **"Glossolalia"** and making evident the continuity of voice in the sequence. The Ambrose of **"Anonymiad"** has a new contempt for the esoteric problems of literature, however, and a new fervor for simply getting the thing done. At the very beginning of the fiction, for instance, the speaker open-mindedly parallels ending his life, commencing his masterpiece, returning to sleep, and invoking his muse. The four understandings of fiction suggested by these processes are neither distinct nor the same, we are given to understand, and we are free to understand this fiction as evidencing any one and any combination of them. Again, the speaker cannot take seriously "the pretension of reality" any more than he can take himself seriously. He is "the contrary of solipsistic," yet he is surprised when the kings and queens of his fiction correspond to actual kings and queens. The real drama of fiction, he insists, "is whether he can trick this tale out at all." Electing henceforth to use the first person anonymous as his point of view, he no longer questions if such a viewpoint is a contradiction in terms and a betrayal of his presence: the only thing that finally matters to him, as he makes clear in the climactic last paragraph, is that the **"Anonymiad"** gets written.

The *Künstlerroman* ends, then, with Ambrose disdaining his earlier attempts to understand and master the funhouse of fiction, and the Moebial involution is complete with his return to a simple making of fiction. The storyteller must remain "lost in the funhouse," continually embarrassed by his suspicion that the real operators are looking at him through peepholes, that old-timers at the entrance have counseled him falsely, and that older brothers and wiry little Seamen who have never contemplated a theory of funhouses are healthier and more expert for their ignorance. Fictions are not the escape from personality that Ambrose (and Eliot before him) would like them to be, for all fictions are finally *Künstlerroman,* things very like funhouses, and no place for the adolescently sensitive. (pp. 373-80)

Robert F. Kiernan, "John Barth's Artist in the Fun House," in Studies in Short Fiction, *Vol. X, No. 4, Fall, 1973, pp. 373-80.*

Peter Ackroyd (essay date 1974)

[*Ackroyd is an English novelist, biographer, poet, and critic. In his fiction Ackroyd concentrates on the interaction between artifice and reality and emphasizes the ways in which contemporary art and life are profoundly influenced by events and creations of the past. In the following review, he censures what he considers to be the jejune nature of the novellas in* Chimera.]

There is nothing particularly ignoble in a novelist being self-conscious about his craft, but when he imposes these trifling concerns upon the poor reader it becomes a matter of public concern. Mr Barth, a Professor of English and winner of the National Book Award, has chosen to do just that in **Chimera,** a tripartite beast, a novel within a novel within something else on the Chinese principle that a great many boxes are better than a hat. It begins well enough, with a sort of highbrow camp as Barth narrates the narrations of Dunyazade narrating the narrations of Scheherazade (known as Sherry to her handmaidens) to Shahryar. But after that I got them all mixed up, mere pips, as Omar Khayyam might say, squeaking in the bowl of night. These particular Orientals come, in fact, from some potpourri known as the *Thousand And One Nights* which Mr Barth thinks of some cross-cultural importance and of which he proceeds to make very heavy weather indeed.

It seems that, behind the seven veils, Sherry is looking for a key. Being something of an Ur-structuralist, she comes to realise that looking for the key is in fact the key itself. Mr Barth then appears in the most inappropriate form of genie, and proceeds to tell her the whole tedious story of

Thousand And One Nights which he has already read in a later existence. It is all an intolerable mish-mash, and should have remained in the misty land of faery, were it not for people like Mr Barth who have an intolerable urge for systems and meanings. The more unintelligent reviewers will no doubt be taken in by the novel's fanciful contemporaneity, and will talk about its "stark presentment of the boundaries of fiction," "medieval simplicity" and such like, and this may well be Barth's intention: there is no doubt that perspectives appear and disappear as if by magic, and that the prose has its glancings and twinklings as it continually evades the issue (whatever the issue may be). But Barth is trying to spin gold out of the pointless questions which pursue formalists and aestheticians, and he does not realise that the pointlessness becomes all the plainer in a fictional guise.

The offence is compounded by Barth's incursions into classical mythology, in the second and third sections of the novel, which are entitled **'Perseid'** and **'Bellerophoniad'.** When an American writer touches upon such matters I feel a *frisson* on behalf of centuries of classical scholarship; Americans, being a poorly educated race, take the Greek myths far too seriously and become either pompous or heavily jocular about them. Professor Barth has naturally gone for the jocular 'angle', and has recounted the unutterably boring mythic lives of Perseus and Bellerophon in a suburban demotic that relives the boredom of the original while increasing its capacity to irritate. In the beginning there is darkness, as Perseus recounts his chequered career to Calyx, who knows the stories already and is thus in the same unfortunate position as the reader. The assiduous handmaiden has actually completed a series of wall-paintings on that very subject, and is clearly reluctant to have her work spoiled by the real thing. This framing device is a pretty conceit (Barth is continually wreaking fantasy upon his fantastics) but it does not save the narrative itself from an intolerable slackness, which became all the more evident when I ceased to wonder who was addressing whom.

The matter is not settled in **'Bellerophoniad',** when Barth becomes even more self-conscious than the conventional experimental novelist and turns his fables into an elaborate apologia for his own apparently miserable and wasted life. At one point he elevates the novelist (i.e. Barth) into a vatic role, and at the next he belabours himself with a dutiful and tedious modesty. Once you mix this sort of thing with a Bellerophon of a more than baroque complexity—he is preparing a career based upon a reading of the preceding **'Perseid,'** setting out a plan for the story he is in fact already telling etcetera—you have a narrative that will not stay still under the reader's gaze. But this complexity is so much a matter of the technical surface of the prose that it takes only a conscious effort of the mind to see through it and, underneath, to find lurking that most fabulous and archaic of mythical beasts, the labyrinth that goes in all directions at once and leads nowhere at all. (p. 86)

Peter Ackroyd, "Chinese Boxes and Other Novels," in The Spectator, *Vol. 233, No. 7621, July 20, 1974, pp. 86-7.*

Jac Tharpe   (essay date 1974)

[*Tharpe was an American critic and educator whose* John Barth: The Comic Sublimity of Paradox *represents the first full-length critical study of Barth's writings. In the following excerpt from that work, he surveys themes, motifs, and narrative techniques in* Lost in the Funhouse *and* Chimera.]

Despite its disconcerting form and its content, *Lost in the Funhouse* generally presents the pattern of the life of the traditional hero. Barth's acknowledged reading of [Joseph] Campbell only helped to crystallize what was forming in his mind in great part as a result of what was occurring in Western culture. As archaeologists and others, such as Lord Raglan and Otto Rank, wrote syntheses of their discoveries about the old myths, novelists of various sorts were dealing with heroism. Joyce may have inspired Barth to his treatment of the artist as a young man, but Western culture was generally interested in defining heroism.

Lost in the Funhouse is a portrait of the artist as hero. The themes are art and love, and the fusion of formula and content promulgates a metaphysics as well as an aesthetics. Though Barth is master of language, he appears to find the mystery of language overpowering. Words accomplish so much that they ought to compose a holy word. Yet something appears to be lacking. Craftsmanship and creativity in perfect union are insufficient to produce the final holy utterance. The result is that something is always left to be said, and everything is to be said all over again. Thus, one seeks for sense in nonsense, as in **"Glossolalia,"** or essence in litany as in **"Help."** *Lost in the Funhouse* is an attempt to see whether the medium can possibly serve as the message.

The floating opera becomes the funhouse, with its labyrinths, distorted mirrors, secret passageways, peepholes, loopholes, and general crazy construction—probably with the author's awareness that even a funhouse that is completely disorganized and chaotic had a deviser—a mind that deliberately created chaos. But the funhouse is also the ivory tower of the artist, including the structure of his own works, the method of his narrative technique, and the relationship between the artist and his works, particularly insofar as the works resulted from the artist's need.

When one does form the Möbius strip of Barth's **"Frame Tale,"** the strip reads continuously in script writ large: "Once upon a time there was a story that began once upon a time. . . ." One begins reading at any point on the strip, and the possible distortion of syntax is unimportant. With the reader's inclination to punctuate and interpret, what he finds will depend on where he begins. And Barth of course articulates the case also of the idiot's sound and fury, telling a story that goes on forever without either end or accomplishment.

The symbol of the Möbius strip allows the numerous distortions of time sequence that occur in the volume. Both Ambrose and the narrator of **"Anonymiad"** can invent fiction. The strip also symbolizes the idea that ontogeny recapitulates phylogeny when someone begins the process of gaining the wisdom of the world over again. Time may be

made so relative, within the context of the time paradox of relativity, that, in the **"Dunyazadiad,"** the author can appear as genie to inspire Scheherazade with her own original stories, just as the original storyteller of the *Thousand and One Nights* began in error to have Scheherazade tell the beginning over again.

The Möbius strip is also a symbol of the labyrinth of the funhouse from which even the extra possibilities of movement allow only cosmopsis, a realization of limited possibilities, whether one deals with the physical universe, the relativity of time, or the house of fiction. One may attempt technique, for example, without ever really being father to oneself or unmoved first cause or the literal deviser and creator of language. The strip perfectly represents the increase in possibilities that relativity theory has provided, while it at the same time shows limitations of the complex maze. The universe is unbounded but finite. Whatever "unbounded" means, "finite" does not mean infinite. If the mind escapes madness in the awareness of the complex paradoxes, it still must shy from the possibility that beyond the finite is a chaos that is both unbounded and infinite. To escape, one goes on with the story.

The speaker of **"Night-Sea Journey"** is a sperm cell on its way to fertilize an ovum, and it is the lone survivor of the millions of its fellows spurted through the canal in the one emission. Barth has ironically set a microscopic spark of life to write the whole account of the mystery of existence. The result is a brilliant summation of the history of philosophical speculation about ontology. Beyond this point, the sketch is so clear an exposition that comment on the content is mere detraction. More pertinent is the observation that Barth confines the content to speculation within a limited set of known conditions. Whatever the state of the sperm's knowledge, the reader knows that since it speaks it lived and met its destined She. The story is an exposition of Spielman's Law, which "showed the 'sphincter's riddle' and the mystery of the University to be the same. *Ontogeny recapitulates cosmogeny*—what is it but to say that proctoscopy repeats hagiography?" (*Giles Goat-Boy*). Among other meanings, Barth may be reversing and punning on Shakespeare's observation that some divinity shapes our ends. But the narrator of **"Night-Sea Journey"** requests his coming self to be heroic and reject the new love and thus break the continuity of eternal recurrence that Spielman's Law states. Though he protests against the instinct that leads him to accept his union with She, the avatars that follow him all feel the instinct helplessly— even Narcissus, who uses the concept of the Möbius strip to turn the instinct upon himself.

The ontogenic articulator must receive a name, a ritual that occurs in **"Ambrose His Mark."** Naming also refers to the knack for calling things by their names, which requires recognition of them. This ability is that of the man of knowledge and especially of the poet. But while others christen babies in the church service, Ambrose derives a name from a secular incident occurring in a black magic ceremony that takes place during the church ceremony. He gets a saint's name in a Protestant community.

Linguistic motifs link the stories and the stages of the youth's development. The phrase "vessel and contents" of

"Night-Sea Journey" suggests the idea of form and content, while also being a sexual metaphor. It also suggests the bottle that Ambrose finds and the jugs of wine that "inspired" the writer of "Anonymiad." The narrator of "Night-Sea Journey" is also "tale-bearer of a generation," that of his immediate companions who perish in their vessel, of the others climbing the alabaster mountains that Ebenezer sees in his recurrent dream and of the generations of storytellers, heroes, and progenitors. "Mid-point" recalls the Möbius strip which had no midpoint, and the numerous other references to beginning, middle and end, whether the references are to history or story. The speaker's feeling that " 'many accounts of our situation seem plausible . . . ' " indicates that he too suffers from cosmopsis.

Andrea's breast in "Ambrose His Mark" ironically anticipates Helen's test of "Anonymiad" and those of the Muses, jugs from which the writer drinks and whose mouths he uses for his Oedipal complexities. Ambrose, "knowing well that I and my sign are neither one nor quite two," recalls Jake's, "In a sense, I am Jacob Horner," and the idea that a name is nothing more than a jumble of strokes in print, as Scheherezade observes, even if one is charged with murder and condemned to death. It also recalls the wish for clarity that ends "Petition." The blank replacing Ambrose's last name anticipates "Title," which also deals with a blank and a name. Ambrose is designed to deal with the spoken, honied word; and he will do so in the "Autobiography" of which his tale of naming is a part.

"Autobiography" shows the child lost in the funhouse of linguistic ambiguity where words express vague intuitions of creativity of both life and story, sex and sublimation. Ambrose of "Water-Message" is lost in the funhouse of adolescence. He is particularly caught between fact and fancy, as he begins to mature. He intuits the knowledge that major secrets exist but does not know the extent of his ignorance. He already prefers fancy, both because he is an imaginative adolescent and because he is a fledgling artist with honied tongue, though the bees that gave him articulation also gave him a complex about bees.

The wealth of facts is in *The Cyclopedia of Facts,* as also in the *Book of Knowledge* of "Ambrose His Mark," the story in which Uncle Konrad persistently gives information. *Facts About Your Diet* tells of the physical organism. But even *Nature's Secrets,* ironically, fails to provide Ambrose with the knowledge he begins to want about both his own nature and the nature of sex.

One of the results is escape to fantasy. The story is a version of the collection of tales, wherein the stream of consciousness that is Ambrose's narrative at the first level includes the series of stories that he imagines. Ambrose is an avatar of the inventor of fiction. His mark is the phylogenic curse, referring to the ambiguity of states and kinds of knowledge. He begins to know of art and love. Thus, he begins to know of knowledge and consequently begins to lose his innocence, like Todd and Ebenezer [protagonists of *The Floating Opera* and *The Sot-Weed Factor*]. At the end of the story, Ambrose discovers a fact about the composition of paper, a bit of wisdom about the nature of secrets and an intuition of more to come. He has begun to feel the wide knowledge of ignorance that his progenitor of "Night-Sea Journey" had. Some of his knowledge came from the sea in a bottle from anonymous, the original goat's hide having turned to paper made of wood.

"Lost in the Funhouse" is a record of awareness. It has two main, disparate, connected themes, art and love. But the point is the point that Barth finds inescapable—awareness of awareness, self-consciousness about roles. The artist-hero who is lost in the funhouse is thoroughly aware of what he does. He knows he is lost. He knows he is in a funhouse with deliberately constructed deception; but he also knows that it is a funhouse. He knows everything that it is possible to know. He knows that he perceives the situation, conceives of the situation, creates the situation, and re-creates the situation in writing an account of it. And, finally, he is aware of his control over some aspects of the account. He may not know the ultimate source of his material, but he can observe himself forming his material. He can observe himself lost, aware of being lost, and aware of the deliberate attempt to discover himself.

He is also aware that, despite all his awareness, he really is lost in something he calls a funhouse. It obviously operates on a principle. Deliberate chaos requires as strict a rationale as any rationalism. But also the operator who appears through the crack is asleep or oblivious. One counts on him for nothing except an absurd floating opera. It is all quite a whirl. Barth should have put his funhouse on a roller coaster, though the distorting mirrors and the uneven floor serve nearly the same purpose.

"Lost in the Funhouse" also deals with the themes of art and love; and if the end is trustworthy, Ambrose, the sensitive youth, chooses to tell stories instead of making love, as Ebenezer also does. The choice is forced on him by his awareness that a choice exists. Peter, interested only in earthly paradise, does not know of the choice. Peter is comparable to the gross twin of "Petition" and is the Peter of "Water-Message," whose name is quite likely a sexual pun; or possibly he is really Ambrose's incarnation of a fantasy about his sexual being.

The funhouse is everything. The term refers to the universe, ramshackle and run-down, fragments of illusions and bad dreams of days past. But the funhouse is also both palace of art and palace of pleasure. One reference is to the tunnel of love of Magda's anatomy, incarnation of the She of "Night-Sea Journey." Ambrose feels the curse of the narrator of that story, who gave him a heritage of urge against the instinctive. Thus, Ambrose is like the twins of "Petition," instinctively ambivalent. His instinct is phylogenically to the tunnel of love and the funhouse, while he also instinctively seeks to prevent that instinct from operating, in consonance with the appeal made by the sperm of "Night-Sea Journey" from which he came. All the dark places are symbols of the cave—the jungle, the hut, the funhouse passageway, the space under the boardwalk. The "little slap slap of thigh on ham" appears to be the only explanation of the principle on which the funhouse operates, as Todd and Jake [protagonist of *The End of the Road*] recognize in their observations on coitus. Possibly even the artist's work is the result of that principle's operation.

"Echo" is also a presentation of an epistemology, even a metaphysics, in parable form. The artistic process is at such a point of importance that the real subject finally is how art works—aesthetic that is a metaphysic. Knowing the shortcomings of language, being obsessed with the need to be accurate, and having a desperately keen awareness of the impossibility of being accurate, one employs elaborate metaphor that turns language back upon itself and makes it work in reverse or like a Möbius strip, or like an unbounded universe that derives its limitlessness from turning back upon itself like a doughnut. The parable is the metaphor, a statement of the case, aesthetic or metaphysical, in a language that deliberately substitutes words for the words that might apply. The point is to escape language through the use of language; instead of getting caught in the attempt to find the exact words to state the case, one deliberately chooses other words to state the case. Then one begins over.

The cave of "Echo" has several meanings. As echo chamber within the context of the phylogenic sea-journey, the cave is chamber of endless cycling and repetition, all occurring in the dark. Echo is symbolically an ultimate—a sound without a voice. The sound is somewhat like Fat May's voice, from an unknown source in a funhouse that is all confusion and secrecy. Notes from underground are echoes from a funhouse. Besides, Echo is the voice of silence. She is also the call to art and possibly just the vague call of the gnostic religions. Only Echo has tempted Narcissus "caveward." The cave and the "dark passage" are echoes of the channel of "Night-Sea Journey" and of the tunnel of love in "Lost in the Funhouse," as well as the hut and the jungle of "Water-Message." Ambrose is both Narcissus and Echo. Because Echo is "afflicted with immortality she turns from life and learns to tell stories with such art . . ."; the words anticipate the choice of art that Ambrose makes at the end of "Lost in the Funhouse."

The motifs here are the rejection of love for art and the concern with finding the self among the possibilities, distortions, avatars. The hint of death may be to Barth's point too: at least unpleasantness is, for at Donacon, Narcissus will discover that self-knowledge is bad news, since "the gift of suicience is a painful present . . . ."

The main significance of "Echo" is that it is placed directly at the midpoint of the volume. Thus, the outer two pieces, both by anonymous narrators, echo into the middle of the volume, deep into the cave, amidst the funhouse wherein they are all lost. Both anonymous narrators are, in their wisdom, types of Tiresias the knowledgeable one, and of Narcissus, the innocent who stumbles about, muddled, in the real world, or somewhere between two worlds. All three reject love—and after this point, one of the main themes is the conflict between art and love, isolation and involvement, themes which are, however, anticipated in the stories immediately preceding, wherein the sexual impulse is troublesome. Narcissus thus represents early manhood, the point where the youthful artist chooses his mistress. "Anonymiad" with the story of Merope echoes the theme of "Echo," the sublimation of sexual energy to produce art.

"Title" indicates the difficulty "To turn ultimacy against itself to make something new and valid, the essence whereof would be the impossibility of making something new." The title of "Title" probably means that the piece has no title but that its title would go where "Title" is placed on the pages. Thus, the story has no title. The title (lack of title) thus suggests the content, as titles traditionally have: for the story deals with "the blank," and with the blank— the blankness—the end, rather than beginning or middle. The story itself, however, making use of its own theory of using paradox to escape contradictions, comes to an end with a sentence requiring "end" that is left unspoken. When words must go on forever, resolving one paradox into another, even when that end is silence, there is neither "end" nor end—only silence, then one again begins; for, paradoxically, when articulation is so necessary because it drives off despair, there is no possibility of silence. "Glossolalia" tells of silences and miscommunication, but uses words, then a nonsense tongue, which, however, utters; and then "Life-Story" begins. Meanwhile, "Everything leads to nothing," as the narrator says at the beginning of the story, which itself begins at some point "waiting for the end."

Barth probably has tried to divide the bulk of his "Menelaiad" into two equal halves, wherein the seventh level ironically is the largest portion, symbolically comparable to the length of the whole tale. That is, if the universe really does turn back upon itself, the utter ideal would be to have a central inner story that has precisely the same length as the frame tale and all its inner tales. Two infinities would overlap. Inner and outer would be the same. And it seems more than likely that Barth does, in fact, intend his narrative technique here to present and symbolize a metaphysics or at least a cosmology.

In the series of tales, "Menelaiad" occurs at a particular point within a collection of tales roughly designed as the autobiography of the artist; which in turn derives in at least some way from an autobiography of the artist who composes the stories. Farther outside this framework is the narrative "frame tale." Outside this circle is the "author's preface," outside which is the devising author, who is a real man in a real world. In this situation, however, the author conceives of the possibility that he is a fictional person in a real world, or a fictional character in a fictional world that may or may not be of his own making. He may be a series of masks like Todd or a series of moods like Jake and thus never consistently anything, either real or fictional, precisely because recognition of a series of changes prevents exact definition. Consistency is never sufficient for definition ever to be complete. No one could ever say what a man is, and this idea is probably one of those that Menelaus has in mind both when he goes through the narrative levels representing earlier stages of his life; and when, in the central story, he chooses a succession of disguises for the purpose of eventually forcing Proteus to provide the information that makes the return voyage possible. Here is an example of regression to silence or a state of exhausted possibilities.

While **"Menelaiad"** is about love, **"Anonymiad"** is about art and the lover of the mistress art. In the interview called "Algebra and Fire," Barth suggests that the narrator is the anonymous inventor of fiction. Anticipating the technique of the **"Dunyazadiad,"** he is, however, also Barth, who presents various details of his own career. The narrator says, for example, that he "sang a sprightly goat-song, fully expecting that the Queen herself would hear and call for me." His singing did bring him a mistress.

These difficulties with love echo other stories, particularly **"Lost in the Funhouse," "Title,"** and **"Life-Story."** The "bee-sweet" name of the girl of his dream recalls Merope and the naming of Ambrose as well as the Genie's friend in **"Dunyazadiad."** The "one tale I knew" recalls **"Echo"** and its idea that the same tale is told again. The "terror of her love" is what drives Menelaus from Helen. The ironic remark "I'm no Narcissus" means he is willing to share his experience with others. The remark is ironic because of course the narcissist is also the egoist who delights in displaying himself. The decision to combine tragedy and satire is to invent tragicomedy or farce as the most realistic genre. The "wish to elevate maroonment into a minstrel masterpiece" is autobiographical in being a statement of Barth's idea that one's performance derives in great part from his isolation in a universe that he cannot understand. All the narrator's work is a "love letter" deriving from sublimation.

"Anonymiad" contains numerous puns connecting sex and art—production and composition. Other technical flourishes include the typographical display that mixes poetry and fiction. The artist works in poetry but thinks in prose and gradually uses prose for expression. Clio "could hold more wine than any of her sisters without growing tipsy" because history is long and full. The "Headpiece" makes the epic's conventional invocation to the Muse. At least one epic simile occurs: the farmboy. As inventor of fiction, the narrator tells the early fables, "of country mouse and city mouse." Part One-and-One-Half quotes from an unfinished Part One; and to compensate, Part Three is omitted, presumably because the artist had nearly run out of space and so put a tailpiece on to the tail of Part One. Thus, Part One-and-One-Half summarizes the uncomposed Part One. Part Two opens with an opening to Part Two about Part Two. The rest of Part Two combines retelling and recounting Part Three, in a hopeless attempt to "get to where I am." Part Three becomes one of the blanks of **"Title"** and of the water message, though already existent in Part Two, which Part One-and-One-Half has replaced. Combining the inspirations of Clio and Thalia—history and comedy—and seeing the overloaded amphora sink are humorous references to his own work. The note "anon I forgot it" in reference to his name, is a half-pun. The idea "to give up language altogether and float voiceless in the wash of time" suggests the technique of earlier pieces as well as Barth's logical conclusion about silence, despite which both he and Anonymous write on. Finally, **"Anonymiad"** is the story of composition of **"Anonymiad,"** and "Wrote it" means the word was spoken down and that the silence came upon him and the waters. The phrase also refers to the epistle of **"Night-Sea Journey"** and to the blank message that Ambrose found.

"Anonymiad" also echoes many of the themes of other pieces in *Lost in the Funhouse.* It begins both the poem and the fiction *in medias res,* as epics conventionally do. **"Middle"** recalls **"Title"** and **"Life-Story,"** both of which are being told over again, in the echo that is **"Anonymiad,"** which also is an echo of **"Echo,"** which pre-echoes the accounts of **"Title"** and **"Life-Story."** Here the "honey" is Merope, as well as the words of love and song. Merope is an avatar of Thalia of **"Petition"** as well as Helen of **"Menelaiad."** The tale also winds on a Möbius strip in and out of illusion and reality. A version of the narrative's origin is interwoven with the narrative that the narrator tells of his past. The minstrel's reply is an ambiguous riddle resembling those of the youthful wit. Ironically, while he gets the position in great part because he sings of love, his art begins to usurp his time for love soon after he arrives at court. The inventor of fiction is a goatherd who sings a goat song of satire and tragedy, rather than a shepherd who sings of Daphnis and Chloe.

"Anonymiad" suggests that the anonymous note of **"Water-Message"** is a message from the self to the self in some recurrence that leads the artist to conceive of himself as a ubiquitous spirit that utters a message in moving over the face of the waters. Perhaps also, the artist who involves himself with his fiction and finds himself fictional, as he does in **"Life-Story,"** is so dispersed—fragmented—as to be merely anonymous. He is no man, no name. The artist's odyssey is over. He is "first person anonymous," a character in his own fiction. To the question "Who are you?" the perfectly audible echo is "I am nobody." The hint of the answer that Odysseus, another wanderer imprisoned in a cave, gave to the Cyclops is probably intentional.

As exemplification of **"Frame-Tale"** (Möbius Strip), **"Anonymiad"** tells of a sea journey just as **"Night-Sea Journey"** does. The book begins and ends with anonymity, and the ending is as insignificant as the beginning. The book throughout has no character except Ambrose, who vanishes in the labyrinthine funhouse of fiction.

Barth exemplifies his concept of the seamless university in his detailed orchestration of *Lost in the Funhouse,* as he does in *Chimera* later. So many linguistic conundrums appear that explication would be far longer than the original, and no discussion of content would be exhaustive. (pp. 91-104)

• • • • •

Barth's *Chimera* is a Chimerid. A Chimerid is a Barthian invention resembling those of Borges, Nabokov, and Joyce. The word also gives a name to an artistic process by means of which the comprehensive Encyclopedia of Tlön and the Library of Babel are fed into a malinoctial computer on perpetual Reset Printout Garble. Barth is dramatizing what would occur if a computer could in fact take all the words in the world and work for an infinite time with infinite capacity to combine. The result would eventually be a quite logical epic—a Chimerid, both a monster and a story of a monster that is the invention of language itself and which records events as they occur.

Thus dramatizing wit and the unconscious by means of computer printout, Barth finds room for hundreds of puns, cross-references to both human motifs and the motif of the printed account, repetitions, double entendres, formulae, keys, secrets, neologisms, and fanciful malapropisms. Barth, in short, has devised a way of communicating through controlled disorder—through jamming, static, and noise, processes that ordinarily disrupt communication. Intelligent confusion and educated guess replace the traditional logic and the traditional symbols of communication. If the universe is chaotic, perhaps a chaotic new tongue will describe it.

Barth says in *Chimera* that the author believes in a fiction capable of unlimited interpretations:

> The general principle, I believe, has no name in our ordinary critical vocabulary; I think of it as the Principle of Metaphoric Means, by which I intend the investiture by the writer of as many of the elements and aspects of his fiction as possible with emblematic as well as dramatic value: not only the "form" of the story, the narrative viewpoint, the tone, and such, but, where manageable, the particular genre, the mode and medium, the very process of narration—even the fact of the artifact itself.

Critics have always read many views into what a man's words mean. Barth is making a cosmophiliac virtue of the ambiguity that illusive language offers to the illusions of private eyes: let any man see all he may in what is writ. There is precedent aplenty in the interpretations of the Bible and other holy books.

Chimera is also autobiography. The hero once more defeats the monster of his own imagining. Now we know where dragons come from. Barth's dragon is the sky-written message Writer's Cramp, which is, symbolically, Bellerophon's affliction. But writer's cramp is far more than a personal aridity in the creative process. It is also cosmopsis, the Lorelei, the Sirens, *la Beauté,* the (self-tormenting) *heautontimeroumenos,* and *l'ennui.* A man who has become a hero is aware of the deficiencies of heroism. He may even have been taken in by his own prescription for cure to the extent that he had briefly forgotten that he had the disease that was incurable. He may have forgotten that nothing has intrinsic value. In any case, he has turned to form because no content has any interest for him.

Chimera is a deliberate account of what has gone before. The artist has become the critic who is artist commenting on his own themes, his own books, and his own performance. Details of public and publishing history keep the theme of the life-story in the forefront of the text in which Barth analogously examines the lives, as he tells the stories, of heroes who are avatars of himself. Like Perseus and Bellerophon, Barth looks at the point midway in his journey when his career has reached a climax—according to Freitag's life-story line. Barth and his avatars live their days nostalgically, examining the question of their heroics—their performances.

One of the major questions is that of immortality—whether they really performed as heroes and whether they will be immortal. Another is the question of personal identity and yet another whether there was any heroism. Was greatness thrust upon them, or were they great in the beginning? A real hero would prefer to be intrinsically great, like a Platonic form, apart from circumstance.

Lost in the Funhouse dealt with the artist as hero. *Chimera* deals with the hero as artist. And Barth gives Scheherezade her due as the one who inspired his storytelling. Throughout his work, Barth has used the *ménage à trois* as a plot device: Todd and the Macks; Jake and the Morgans; Burlingame and the twins. Now that the author is concerned especially with technique, he "houses" a heroine storyteller with two hero storytellers. Since his heroes are Western and his heroine Eastern, he manages to find a symbolic way of devising a seamless ocean of story. Variations of the triangulation theme occur throughout the book.

The triangle, perhaps along with the other mathematical and geometrical figures, is one of the meanings of the "Pattern" that Barth so frequently mentions. Another meaning of the word, of course, is the obvious reference to Barth's version of Campbell's outline of the hero's phylogenic journey. Thus, the word would also refer to the way of the world, thus to the theory of cyclology. Barth is also making fun of the idea, especially when he adds "Salmon-Leaps" to the list of trials and helpers. But Barth's diagram provides some information about what occurs in each story. He makes several of the incidents obvious, when, for example, Bellerophon wanders about asking someone to kick him out of the city. Other uses of motifs may be less obvious. In "Dunyazadiad," the magician helper is the author himself, in his appearance to Scheherezade. The elixir theft of "Bellerophoniad" is one or more of the procurements of the (punning) horsefly (hippomanes) for Pegasus. Bellerophon's fall from Grace is his catapult from Olympus to the Dorchester marshes. Numerous other uses, either straightforward or ironic, may occur. "Dunyazadiad" in some ways jumbles the chronology of the Pattern. It is of course ironic even to apply the Pattern to a heroine, but Barth shows his admiration for Scheherezade's ability to create artistically and heroically under the constant threat of death.

Barth plays with his own mathematical and geometrical symbolism and adds to it—and finds it absurd. He may succumb briefly to the idea that mathematics is the ultimate language or at least the ultimate in the symbolic use of language. He may also be making fun of the idea. The spirals and numbers are Bellerophonics. Certainly, he must associate the various mathematics with the computer as well as with logic and much of human thought. In his latest work, as if by design over the years, he has extended the use of the mere triangle, and the narrative device of the *ménage à trois,* to talk of life, story, love, and art as inventions following the pattern of Golden Triangles, Golden Sections, and Golden Ratios with reference to the Phi value used for centuries as a constant in harmonious and symmetrical design.

The Golden-Triangular Freitag combines the Golden Triangle of mathematics with the literary symbol of narrative action that Barth uses in *Lost in the Funhouse.* He may have used the proportions of the Golden Triangle to arrive at the number of pages in each of the three stories—56,

78, 174—though he has reversed the order. He may even manage to get the climax of the story or the book, or both, at the point of the proportion labeled climax, wherever that point is. And Dunyazad's entire narrative is told, with consummate integration of art and love, while she holds a knife in one hand and her husband's erection in the other, just at the point where the techniques of the two activities approach climax. Finally, the triangle also roughly outlines the round trip that Bellerophon makes in flying toward heaven and then falling into the marshes.

Barth and Scheherezade agree that technique is all one can talk about. One merely tells the story. The rest is silence. Barth has anticipated this idea often, but symbolically he does particularly in the **"Menelaiad,"** where he uses a very elaborate technique to present the single word *Love* at the very heart of the narrative. That is almost silence, in the same way at least that **"Help"** shouts silence. And, as noted elsewhere, Barth's general concerns must logically lead to silence even if the author never stops talking—the silence of The Living Sakhyyan, for example. Of course, the articulate artist can resolve that paradox only by infinite talking.

Or perhaps a tentative way of resolution is omitting the content and concentrating on the form. Technique, therefore, is extremely important. It is the key to the treasure of both art and love. Technique, in fact, represents a Platonic essence. Once one finds the essential technique, he will have no reason to give it content. Or he would not have reason except that of course he still has the problem of informing audiences that he has discovered the essence and wishes to show what it consists in. Both art and love require subtle techniques. Both may offer only pleasure and be otherwise useless. As it happens, however, those pleasures are pure in their uselessness. . . . The value of creative activity derives from its gratuitous uselessness. (pp. 105-10)

> *Jac Tharpe, in his* John Barth: The Comic Sublimity of Paradox, *Southern Illinois University Press, 1974, 133 p.*

Barth on writer's block and the composition of "Bellerophoniad":

I had the experience a couple of years ago of spending, not one whole day or one whole week with a fallow imagination, but nearly a year. What I was trying to write was a story about Bellerophon, the mythical rider of Pegasus, the horse of inspiration, and in my story the problem was that Bellerophon could no longer get Pegasus to fly. As soon as I understood that my writer's block was a precise metaphor for the story I was trying to write, the problem solved itself, the story came out in a burst, and so did the rest of the book in which it's included. Looking back, it seems to me that was as fruitful a year as those jubilee years in the Old Testament when the fields were required to lie fallow so that they'd be more productive.

> *John Barth, in "Complicated Simple Things," The New York Times Book Review, 1972.*

John O. Stark   (essay date 1974)

[*Stark is an American educator and critic whose studies concerning contemporary fiction include* The Literature of Exhaustion: Borges, Nabokov, and Barth *and* Pynchon's Fictions: Thomas Pynchon and the Literature of Information *(1980). In the following excerpt from the former work, he analyzes Barth's fiction as it exemplifies the literary aesthetics expressed in his essay "The Literature of Exhaustion," focusing on themes and techniques in* Lost in the Funhouse *and* Chimera *that illustrate Barth's rejection of realism.*]

John Barth, a generation younger than Borges and Nabokov, has had the great advantage of beginning his writing career after those two older writers had published a considerable body of work from which he could learn. As his essay "The Literature of Exhaustion" demonstrates, he has used this advantage. However, he does not slavishly copy the other two. Unlike Borges and Nabokov, he has explained what they are doing. This evident self-consciousness—part of an infinite regress since it focuses on a self-conscious literature—has helped him to notice and to use in his fiction the most important landmarks in literary history that identify the path leading to the Literature of Exhaustion. He has also codified this kind of literature and even mapped the next steps that fiction can take.

Barth's first two novels, *The Floating Opera* (1956) and *The End of the Road* (1958), are quite conventional and realistic. In them the young Barth—he wrote them both during his twenty-fifth year—looked for his proper mode. He found a mode suitable enough for him to write two reasonably impressive novels, particularly *The Floating Opera*. Despite their intrinsic merit they do not fit into this study because they lie outside the Literature of Exhaustion. I will take some backward glances at them, however, because they lead logically to his later books.

These later works are *The Sot-Weed Factor* (1960), *Giles Goat-Boy* (1966), *Lost in the Funhouse* (1968), and *Chimera* (1972). His four recent works are at first glance very different; colonial American history written in the form of an eighteenth century novel, a mythical account of a hero with various allegorical meanings adhering to it, a collection of bizarre short stories, and a collection of three novellas, two of them rewritten myths. However, the logical development of Barth's career in this phase, the many interrelations among these four works, and his relationships with Borges and Nabokov will soon become clear.

One can most quickly understand Barth's work, too, by looking at his use of Chinese boxes. (pp. 118-19)

Barth accomplishes his purpose of writing a novel, gradually shucking away all his material and leaving only the process of the writing. This sounds like Tony Tanner's notion of entropy, applied not to the world but to a novel. In other words, the subject matter of fiction appears to be exhausted so the narrative impulse must get along by itself, with the aid of the little impetus it gets from demonstrating that its material is used up. Some readers may feel swindled by Barth's negation of his story's significance. Others may admire his ingenuity.

In **"Menelaiad,"** a story in *Lost in the Funhouse,* he surely sets the world record for Chinese boxes. Its tangle of quotation marks indicates the many stories within stories. For example, readers must make sense of punctuation like this:

" ' " ' " ' *Why*?' I repeated," I repeated,'

These are the boxes:

1. Barth
2. **"Menelaiad"**
3. Menelaus' voice
4. Menelaus' story of Telemachus' visit to him
5. Menelaus' story of himself and Helen at sea, told to Telemachus
6. Menelaus' story of Eidothea and Proteus, told to Helen
7. Menelaus' story of himself and Eidothea, told to Proteus
8. Menelaus' story of himself and Helen in Troy, told to Eidothea
9. Menelaus' story about why Helen ran off with Paris, told to her and told by someone in the third-person.

Because the subject of most boxes becomes the auditor of the next one, these boxes interlock, which is a new feature. This sequence stops in the last box because the subject of this box is also its auditor. In the last box the point of view changes to the third person, as if Menelaus fades out of the story. Barth does not identify the narrative voice that replaces him, which makes it seem more like a narrative impulse, trying to keep the story going despite the odds, than like a narrative voice. . . . [The] reader, after he peels off all the layers of the onion, finds in the last layer only the impetus of story-telling.

As he constructs a much less intricate system of boxes in **"Life-Story,"** Barth gives a clue about his purpose in using this technique. The boxes here contain imaginary authors. One of them, "D[,]" is writing a fictional account of this conviction [that he is fictional, so] he has indisputably a fictional existence in his account. . . . E, hero of D's account, is said to be writing a similar account, and so the replication is in both ontological directions." Barth also attacks on ontological grounds, because he denies the existence of the "real" world by showing that it is composed of layers related to each other in a way that makes them inseparable from imaginative constructs.

In **"Dunyazadiad,"** the first novella in *Chimera,* Barth bases his system of boxes on the frame story of *The Thousand and One Nights.* That is, he tries to build a series of seven because an ifrit locked up his girl with seven padlocks. The genie, who represents Barth, admits that "he hoped one day to add to, and conceive a series of say, *seven* concentric stories-within-stories, so arranged that the climax of the innermost would precipitate that of the next tale out, and that of the next, et cetera." He does make seven layers inside the layer of himself: **"The Dunyazadiad,"** Dunyazade's conversation with Shah Zaman, the story of Dunyazade and Scheherazade, the story of the genie, the stories that the genie tells to the girls (which are *The Thousand and One Nights*), the stories that Scheherazade tells to the King (the same stories) and Shah Zaman's story, told to Dunyazade. By the time the last layer appears, the stories from *The Thousand and One Nights* have

been used up; that is, the main story, which has moved more quickly through time, has caught up with the frame story. Barth signals this by shifting to third person and by, at the very end, commenting on the whole process. Because of Barth's veiled appearance and of the Shah's retelling of the frame story of *The Thousand and One Nights,* this last layer does "precipitate that of the next tale out," causing the story line to move in the other direction through the layers. That is, it finishes the stories in previous layers, including **"Dunyazadiad,"** and it reintroduces the genie, this time without his disguise in a form even closer to Barth.

Despite the greater simplicity of the system in **"Perseid,"** the second novella in *Chimera,* Barth makes an interesting point by relating in a curious way two of the levels. He makes the following layers inside the layer of himself: **"Perseid,"** the story Perseus tells to Medusa (after they both have turned into constellations), the story Perseus tells to Calyxa, the story portrayed in the murals, the deeds of Perseus. Again the main story catches the frame story; Perseus leaves at II F 2 to perform further deeds, which the murals have not recorded. The strange relation occurs between the layers that contain the story Perseus tells Calyxa and the murals. Because she has drawn the murals, she already knows the story, at least in broad outline. These two levels intermingle, as in: "Calyxa insisted, and turned away, pouting as it were with her very scapulae, her back's small small, pouting I declare with her lean buttocks. 'No need to go on about small smalls and lean little buttocks.' " Because she knows his thoughts, at this point the layer she creates, the murals, should come before the layer of his story. Also, the murals' aesthetic qualities may cause this phenomenon. "Intermingling" describes this relation less suitable than does "spirals back." That is, the layers spiral back, just like many other things in this story, and thus become "emblematic" as Barth told Israel Shenker he wished all the elements of his works to be.

This emblematic function needs clarification. It appears also in **"Dunyazadiad,"** because the seven concentric circles that comprise the levels of reality in this novella, and comprise the novella itself, echo the seven padlocked boxes in which the ifrit places the girl. Similarly, the spiral effect of the layers in **"Perseid"** echos the spiraled murals, bedspread, Calyxa's navel, Calyxa's final existence as a spiral nebula, the motive of the novella (Barth's examination of, spiraling back over, his career) and the novella's plot (Perseus' ironic repetition of his earlier deeds). In other words, by creating these two works in geometric forms Barth has pushed one step further the Chinese box strategy, recapitulating these works in these figures and making everything in the work emblematic of everything else. Especially, form becomes meanings, and the work because it does not depend for meaning on the "real" world becomes as near to self-enclosed as it can get.

Spirals also control **"Bellerophoniad,"** the third novella in *Chimera,* so again Barth makes the layers spiral. He creates five of them inside his own layer, to fit all the other fives in the novella: **"Bellerophoniad,"** the story Bellerophon tells to Melanippe, the story Bellerophon tells to Philonoë and a layer made up of several parts, like the last layer of [Borges's] "Tlön, Uqbar, Orbis Tertius." This layer begins the spiraling back. It contains the information that Polyeidus wrote *Chimera,* which refers back to the outermost layer. The description of Bellerophon's meeting with Melanippe's mother refers back to the second layer. The quotation of Robert Graves's account of Bellerophon refers back to the fourth layer and also causes the main story line to catch, and begin to pass, the frame because Graves tells more of the story than the part that has happened up to this point of **"Bellerophoniad."** The letters from Polyeides, by equating him with Barth, and Bellerophon's lecture, which contains allusions to Barth, both refer to the layer of the author. Thus, at least one thing in this innermost layer connects with every other layer in the sequence. The last words of this novella, "it's no *Bellerophoniad.* It's a," spiral all the way out of this work to include the whole book. "Chimera" will complete this last sentence, "chimera" in the sense that this word has acquired and, as it names the novel, the three-part entity (like the mythic animal) that Barth at this point of the book has just finished creating. The cross references throughout the book to the other novellas reinforce this point. The spiral continues back over Barth's early work. In *The Sot-Weed Factor* he unconsciously uses the conventions of the mythic hero. In *Giles Goat-Boy* he uses them consciously, and in *Chimera* he uses them consciously to comment on his earlier books.

Barth makes more elaborate Chinese boxes than the ones in Nabokov's and Borges's works. He knows the ontological implications of this device and he uses it to get immediately at these implications, and he develops this technique in an orderly way. In *The Sot-Weed Factor* his use of Chinese boxes typifies the first stage of the Literature of Exhaustion, because it creates and exhausts an infinite set of possibilities. In *Giles Goat-Boy,* **Lost in the Funhouse,** and **Chimera,** however, he is less sanguine about literature and he purports to fear that it has been exhausted already. Therefore, he begins to use this hypothetical fear as his basic premise and to show that all one needs in order to write fiction is a narrative impulse.

Barth also adds his own distinctive twist to the technique of the Literature of Exhaustion that resembles the Chinese boxes, the *regressus in infinitum.* First, he has combined it with the box technique in **"Life-Story,"** since he uses the imaginary authors in this story in both ways. He sometimes makes the elements of the infinite series literary. Gerhard Joseph has noticed this same variation of the technique in *Sot-Weed Factor,* and he identifies Barth's antecedents: "Eben's defense of his virginity which echoes that of Joseph Andrews which in turn parodies that of Pamela, etc., creates the *regressus in infinitum* effect that Barth admires in the fictions of Nabokov and Borges, the literary funhouse in which the reader is invited to amuse himself " [*John Barth,* 1970]. If this technique operating in the imaginary world can keep alive the spark of narrative, operating in the real world it can show that the contents of that world have no reality after all. (pp. 120-25)

Barth attacks the same kinds of literature that Borges and Nabokov have badly scarred, the various kinds of realistic fiction. The novel differentiated itself from other kinds of prose fiction and attained its status as an independent genre because of its realism, so an anti-realist must dispel the belief that novels must perforce be realistic. Barth tries to do this by showing that realism had to be invented, too, that it was not just *there* to be accepted as the natural mode for writers to use. He describes in **"Anonymiad"** a bard inventing a new kind of literature, and claims that "the whole conception of a literature faithful to daily reality is among the innovations of this novel opus." He attacks another disturbing bias in favor of realism by claiming that this mode of literature does not avoid artifice but merely uses another kind of artifice. Among the intercalated comments on the art of fiction in **"Lost in the Funhouse"** is this one: "Initials, blanks, or both were often substituted for proper names in nineteenth-century fiction to enhance the illusion of reality. . . . Interestingly, as with other aspects of realism, it is an *illusion* that is being enhanced, by purely artificial means."

If a reader becomes convinced that realism should not be the criterion by which he can measure modes of literature but only one among many modes, he can calculate its strengths and weaknesses. The problems of opposites and of unity and duality continually foil realists, as Barth shows in the plot of many of his works by having the characters who accept a realistic world view try to deal with opposites. Besides George [in *Giles Goat-Boy*], Eben Cooke in *The Sot-Weed Factor* and the Siamese twin in **"Petition"** cannot cope with this matter. The twin presents the more graphic example, since he has to deal with opposites not only philosophically but also physically. Barth makes sure that these characters try in various ways to make sense of and deal with the world by conceiving of it as a system of opposites. When all of these ways fail, Barth expects the reader to conclude that dividing the world into opposites does not make sense. Opposition, like space and time, is one of the basic constituents of the commonsense notion of the world, so if realism cannot deal with it, realism's claim to superiority among literary modes loses its credibility. Because it cannot make sense of opposites, realism cannot do what it claims, accurately mimic the world. Barth's paradigmatic realist is the nymph for whom **"Echo"** is named. She seems to imitate exactly but she always distorts slightly, usually by omission. A reader who can agree with Barth up to this point will probably concede the next point in his chain of reasoning, that as long as all modes of literature, including realism, are artificial instead of mimetic, writers might just as well revel in their artifice.

The realists have problems not only because of the distortion of the lens they turn on the world, but also because of the world's distortions. The latter does not correct the lens's distortions; it compounds them. As Barth becomes more determined about his anti-realism his characters become more convinced of the world's absurdity. (pp. 126-27)

Like Borges and Nabokov, but less consistently, Barth denies the validity of autobiographical fiction, and he less successfully eliminates traces of autobiography from his works. The events of his life sometimes make their way into his work—for instance, in the descriptions of Todd

Andrews's years at Johns Hopkins in *Floating Opera* and in the academic writer J. B. [in *Giles Goat-Boy*]—though of course neither description is perfectly autobiographical. A story in **Lost in the Funhouse,** although based on his life, is far from accurate autobiography. In **"Ambrose His Mark"** he turns the life of his own German-American family into the fictional equivalent of a Katzenjammer Kids cartoon. These uses of autobiography are all incidental, however. More interesting and less autobiographical in the strict sense, his recreation of the Eastern Shore of Maryland describes the area where he grew up. He writes about it in an essay called "Land-scape: The Eastern Shore" [*Kenyon Review* (Winter 1960)]. This region provides the backdrop for *Floating Opera, End of the Road, The Sot-Weed Factor* and some of the stories in **Lost in the Funhouse. Chimera** contains quite a few references to Barth, both to his literary career and his relations with women. Autobiography serves him mainly as material on which his memory can work to create an ambiance for his fiction. In other words, he uses his life much as Borges uses his, mainly as the source of a setting.

This psychological dimension of his life contributes little to his work. One of his characters, a writer, confesses that in both his art and his life the same things interest him. But he qualifies this confession drastically: "among their other, more serious preoccupations" (**Funhouse**). This description, with the qualification, applies also to Barth's use of autobiography. Barth considers most important the aesthetic themes that lie at the heart of his work and the aesthetic methods that he has developed to turn material, whether autobiographical or not, into art. He understands that he cannot describe his life any more accurately than he can describe the rest of reality. The story which, oddly comprises the narrative voice of **"Autobiography"** agrees that it, and presumably all fiction, distorts its author. An author faced with the impossibility of creating accurate autobiography in fiction should admit from the beginning that supposedly autobiographical material in fiction merely comprises part of the artifice. This admission certainly clarifies one of Barth's stories. In **"Echo"** Narcissus' self-absorption makes him the figure of the autobiographical artist. But appearances are deceiving: "Narcissus would appear to be opposite from Echo: he perishes by denying all except himself; she persists by effacing herself absolutely. Yet they come to the same: it was never himself Narcissus craved, but his reflection, the Echo of his fancy . . . the voice persists." The Echo (the story) and the voice (the artistic means that produced it), and not the autobiographical elements in the story, are the more serious preoccupations that Barth points to here.

In summary, things in fiction that seem to be part of the real world because of their similarity to things one knows about the author actually belong to a fictive world. That is, despite their previous status they become unreal when they appear in the world of art. Furthermore, Barth daringly implies that these same autobiographical facts, like everything else that appears to be part of someone's life, have no inherent reality. The narrator of **"Life-Story"** makes this unnerving claim. Barth's use of autobiography thus leads to a suggestion that at best life is no more real than art, and perhaps it is not real at all. (pp. 128-30)

One of [Barth's] major purposes is to write literature that openly displays its artificiality. He sees no reason to apologize about being nonrealistic. In his *Wisconsin Studies* interview [Winter-Spring 1965] he says, "a different way to come to terms with the discrepancy between art and the Real Thing is to *affirm* the artificial element in art (you can't get rid of it anyhow), and make the artifice part of your point." This strategy can lead to a deadening preciosity. Jack Richardson opens his review of **Lost in the Funhouse** with a list of the flaws that emphasizing artifice can cause, but then claims that Barth's talents have minimized these flaws almost to the point of nonexistence. ["Amusement and Revelation," *New Republic,* 1968]. Barth himself knows about the dangers of this method. In **"Life-Story"** an imaginary author complains about his own work: "Who doesn't prefer art that at least overtly imitates something other than its own processes? That doesn't continually proclaim 'Don't forget I'm artifice!' " Besides talent, which for Richardson justifies this kind of literature, making clear one's purpose in displaying artifice can also allay readers' suspicions about the value of obviously artificial literature. Barth certainly makes clear enough his purpose: to attack realism.

Robert Scholes explains the most striking announcement of artifice in Barth's work [in *The Fabulators,* 1967]. This is the passage in *Giles Goat-Boy* in which the hero comes upon a girl who reveals that she is reading *Giles Goat-Boy* and has got to the precise place in the book where she is described reading. Elsewhere he announces his artifice more conventionally. The apparatus at its beginning and ending also emphasize this novel's artificiality. He includes a publisher's disclaimer and a cover-letter to the editors and publishers at the beginning, and a posttape, a postscript to the posttape and a footnote to the postscript to the posttape at the end. In **Lost in the Funhouse** Barth comments on narrative technique as he tells the title story. His idiosyncratic styles also call attention to themselves and away from his subject matter. He uses this last technique most notably in the imitation eighteenth century style of *The Sot-Weed Factor,* but his style always has a Protean quality, changing magically to suit his purpose.

Barth uses fewer allusions than Borges and Nabokov, and unlike them he alludes more often to history than to literature. However, though he uses other means more often to give his work its literary quality, allusions do play some role in his fiction. Besides its mythological references, **Lost in the Funhouse** contains passing references to other writers. The first story, **"Night-Sea Journey,"** has many literary allusions; one of the most surprising refers to Tertullian—"I can believe them *because* they are absurd"—and a more easily recognized one refers to Ginsberg: "I have seen the best swimmers of my generation go under." (pp. 132-33)

Barth's most interesting use of other literature occurs in **Chimera,** where he frequently mentions his own work. He wrote this book at the probable midpoint of his career, which encouraged him to find out where he was and where he was going by finding out where he had been. He conceived this book as a spiral back over his career. As he gets into the book he begins to refer to the other novellas in it as well and to make the novel a metaphor of his writer's block. He also puts himself into the book, in the thinly disguised figures of the genie in **"Dunyazadiad"** and Polyeidus in **"Bellerophoniad"** and in the only slightly more carefully disguised characters who try simultaneously to solve their narrative and sexual problems. These disguises allow him to write about his own work.

Barth's references to other works matter less than his use of literary history and theory in his fiction. He has been interested in aesthetic themes since the beginning of his career, and they form one of the connections between his first two books and the others. (pp. 134-35)

Lost in the Funhouse is [most] basically about literature. On a superficial level, it contains many statements about narrative technique and sometimes discusses the state of fiction from the perspective of the Literature of Exhaustion. In **"Title"** Barth says that the novel has four possibilities now: rejuvenation, development of new genres, using the impossibility of creating something new as the basis of something new, and silence. More importantly, the organizing principle of this collection of short fictions makes a point about literature. Barth claims in the "Author's Note" that he has carefully organized this book, but it takes some searching to find his principle. It turns out to be the same hypothesis that he uses in *Giles Goat-Boy,* that ontogeny recapitulates phylogeny and cosmogeny. He introduces the three developments in the first story, **"Night-Sea Journey."** The ontogeny is the development of the sperm that narrates the story and of Ambrose, the hero of some of the fictions. The phylogeny is the growth of the human race until it can produce a hero; at first, a conventional hero like those who embark on mythic night sea journeys, and later, artist-heroes. The aspects of the book, like the awakening to sex and language and the vocation scenes, that are modelled on the *Künstlerroman* tradition describe this last development. These last features also form part of the cosmogeny, which is again literary.

In *Lost in the Funhouse* Barth foreshortens the early development of literature in order to trace the development further and describe more fully the Literature of Exhaustion. In the early stories he considers whether literature is possible and if so, whether he can justify spending time creating it. **"Ambrose His Mark"** deals with an essential question, one that needs an affirmative answer before literature can even begin: whether language, and thus literature, can accommodate itself to reality. A family tries hard to name a child and finally decides on "Ambrose" when bees cover him. Their decision suggests that language needs a cultural background; if it did not the child could have been named "bee" instead of being named after a saint associated with bees. Barth mentions many historical and legendary characters in whose lives bees played an important part, but he omits the story that is the paradigm of his book. According to mythology, Aristaeus, trying to find out what angered his bees, learns the story of Orpheus and Eurydice. This story of the archetypal artist and foiled lover is the controlling myth of *Lost in the Funhouse.*

"Autobiography" and **"Water-Message"** also examine the possibility and validity of literature. A story narrates the former, discussing its birth and its parents: an author and

a tape recorder. The narrative voice claims that language can become literature, because the author speaking into a tape recorder has created this story. The latter fiction ends by dramatizing the fact that reality can be transformed into language. A young boy finds a piece of paper with words written on it and, more surprisingly, with a bit of wood pulp visible in it. He then remembers that pulp is physically transformed into paper; symbolically this indicates that reality can become language and literature.

The next section of the book considers realism, especially its weaknesses. **"Petition"** deals with the familiar problems of duality and unity and the relation of opposites, stumbling blocks for rationality and realism. When he describes the distorting mirrors of the funhouse in **"Lost in the Funhouse"** Barth scoffs at realism's claim that it can mirror reality. He suggests a typical alternative to realism when he affirms that mirrors distort and when he uses the funhouse as a symbol of art, which must be nonrealistic.

By the next section of the book literature begins to show signs of exhaustion, and Barth begins to seek remedies. The title character of **"Echo"** must repeat the words of others, just as a novelist late in the history of his genre feels that he can only repeat his predecessors. This story also marks the beginning of Barth's reliance on a strategy that he can use to combat exhaustion: retelling myths. In **"Two Meditations"** he repeats situations: in the first one the straw that broke the camel's back, in the second the belief that pollution leads to knowledge. In **"Title"** he lays out the four possibilities for literature. This story expresses his doubts about nonrealistic writing: "weld iron rods into abstract patterns, say, and you've still got real iron, but arrange words into abstract patterns and you've got nonsense." In **"Glossolalia"** he returns to the technique of repetitions, this time repeating styles.

By the final section of the book authors have developed the Literature of Exhaustion and other postrealistic literature. **"Life-Story"** clearly belongs to the Literature of Exhaustion: involuted, containing Chinese boxes, arguing that life is a fiction. But it also shows some skepticism about this kind of literature, because it charges that turning completely away from the everyday world indicates schizophrenia. **"Menelaiad"** takes this kind of literature about as far as possible, perhaps to the point of self-parody, for it has a very large number of Chinese boxes. In the final story, **"Anonymiad,"** Barth makes a fresh start. He tells the story of a man who creates the novel out of the materials of the epic and invents writing. That is, this imaginary author has successfully dealt with a situation of ultimacy.

Some of Barth's uses of myth should by now be clear, like the function of the Orpheus myth in **"Ambrose His Mark"** and the retelling of myths in other stories in *Lost in the Funhouse.* Also obviously, he depends on the stories of heroes. He claims in his interview that the similarity between Eben and Burlingame [in *The Sot-Weed Factor*], on one hand, and the archetypal hero as described by Lord Raglan, on the other, is accidental, but that he read Raglan's *The Hero* before he wrote *Giles Goat-Boy,* in which he tried to make his hero fulfill all the requirements set down by Raglan. However, one matter relating to myth in his work does need clarification. The mytho-therapy mentioned in *End of the Road* has a misleading name, for it involves not myth-making but arbitrary choosing and then asserting those choices. In other words, it is the same attitude that Burlingame advocates and Eben spurns, except in an opium dream.

Thus, Barth has the same interests in subject matter as Borges and Nabokov. However, his work turns back upon itself more often than theirs does. They seem to have followed their inclinations, whereas he seems to have a keener sense of the state of literature and a stronger feeling that he belongs to a literary advance guard. He does not necessarily have more insight; he has had the advantage of coming to maturity as a writer later than Borges and Nabokov, after more experimental writing has been done. In any case, he neatly recapitulates his work in the Moebius strip he has had printed at the beginning of *Lost in the Funhouse* along with instructions for cutting it out and assembling it. Because the strip is self-enclosed, an infinite number of trips around it is possible, and because of the words printed on it, following the strip and reading the words produces an infinite, self-enclosed story.

Because of his premise that the novel is dying, in his fiction he directs much of the attention to problems of various genres. A writer can comically expose the idiosyncrasies of genres by parodying them. . . . (pp. 138-42)

But if one believes that the novel is dying, parody becomes merely a holding action. One can really nullify death by inventing a new form. First he must mix old forms, hoping that the result will be viable and coherent enough to claim the status of a new genre. The narrator of **"Anonymiad"** does this, for by putting epic materials in prose form he produces a genre that he calls fiction, although that label seems peculiar to modern readers. (p. 142)

Barth has also taken the next step and actually invented a new form of literature, which one day may become an independent genre. Taking his cue from the technological world around him, in *Lost in the Funhouse* he has written pieces intended to be read aloud with part of the narration coming through a tape recorder. Michel Butor's *Niagra* (1965), a novel in the form of a radio play, is perhaps the nearest thing to a predecessor of Barth's book. In public readings from this book he has used tape recorders and shown that his apparently jocular explanation, in the "Author's Note," of the media he intended for each work in *Funhouse* should be taken seriously. This explanation ends with a comment on **"Title"** that shows the scope of his experiments with tape recorded literature: " 'Title' makes somewhat separate but equally valid senses in several media: print, monophonic recorded authorial voice, stereophonic ditto in dialogue with itself, live authorial voice, live ditto in dialogue with monophonic ditto aforementioned, and live ditto interlocutory with stereophonic et cetera, my own preference; it's been 'done' in all six." In short, he has played the bard, not with a lyre but with a tape recorder. He has not created mere stunts, despite the tongue-in-cheek quality of his list of possibilities for **"Title,"** but effective works that mean more with the tape recorder than they do in print.

Borges, Nabokov, and Barth handle in the same ways their most common themes and take nearly the same attitudes toward these themes. Like the other two writers, Barth abhors time, although he uses this theme less often than they do. (p. 143)

Barth . . . succeeds in fending off time, in the usual sense of creating art that will endure, but also in a more original sense. He has created art that seems timeless not only because it is art but also because it is a certain kind of art. As his career has progressed he has managed to create an ever stronger sense of timelessness. As Joseph mentions, Barth's "flight from realism to parodic fable turns out to be a flight from time to timelessness." Barth's device, in all three of the novellas in *Chimera,* of having the main action catch up to the frame story also disputes conventional notions of time. In **"Perseid"** he also scrambles the time sequence when Athene appears. Thus, in this book he shows the arbitrariness of fictional time sequences in order to suggest the arbitrariness of "real" time sequences. Joseph also implicitly points out the basis of the Literature of Exhaustion's attitude toward time: its equations of destructive time with realism, and of blissful timelessness with itself and other forms of nonrealistic literature.

Barth treats rarely but negatively time's acolyte, memory. He associates it, too, with a realistic view of the world, which Eben Cooke defends. He tells Burlingame: "Thy *memory* served as thy credentials, did it not? 'Tis the house of Identity, the Soul's dwelling place: Thy memory, my memory, the memory of the race: 'tis the constant from which we measure change; the sun. Without it, all were Chaos right enough.' " Eben's florid rhetoric bespeaks more conviction than his logic justifies. He reveals his mistake by his failure to recognize that all is indeed chaos. His naive dependence on memory and other tools of the realist causes disaster after disaster for him.

Some other examples of negative themes that appear in Barth's work as well as in Borges's and Nabokov's are the repetition of events in **"Two Meditations,"** the repetition of style in **"Glossolalia"** and the fear expressed by the narrator of **"Life-Story"** that overly-patterned art is schizophrenic. The latter opinion contradicts the position of the other two writers, who approve of artistic patterns and disapprove of imposing patterns on life. Possibly Barth does not completely agree with the others on these issues, but the scarcity of his references to these themes suggests instead that he thinks that the enemies have been routed by Borges and Nabokov, who he claims as allies, so that he need not repeat the attacks but can concentrate on developing positive themes. In short, he recognizes his position in the second generation of the tradition in which he works, and he knows that this can be advantageous.

He agrees with the theory that the domains usually called real and imaginary can be reversed. Sometimes he tries to make this reversal through language, as Campbell Tatham points out. In regard to the scene that describes the "Beist in the buckwheat," Tatham says, "there is the lesser set of abstractions, the poetry reading which suggests that art can in some way replace reality. . . . While the boy who is persistently seducing the girl in the pasture . . . is able to keep straight the distinctions between poems and copulation, between art and reality, George confuses the two"

["John Barth and the Esthetics of Artifice," *Contemporary Literature,* 1971]. Barth embeds this suggestion so deeply in the texture of his work, particularly in *Giles Goat-Boy* and *Lost in the Funhouse,* that it takes this kind of close reading to pry it loose. Examples are numerous, and once a reader learns to look for this technique he can, with attention, discover them for himself.

In *Chimera* the literary realm almost eclipses the "real" realm. He starts slowly in **"Dunyazadiad,"** having Scheherazade repeat "the key to the treasure is the treasure" simultaneously with the genie when she wants him to appear. Thus, language can control part of everyday reality. In **"Perseid"** this controlling force becomes art. The murals in his temple remind Perseus of the early part of his life so that he can tell it to Calyxa and so that he can ironically repeat it. At the end of the story Perseus becomes not only a constellation but also this story being transformed into a work of literature. Similarly, Bellerophon "turned into written words," into "a version of Bellerophon's life." That is, Bellerophon becomes **"Bellerophoniad."** Polyeidus, another character in this novella, also becomes this novella. Bellerophon's killing of the Chimera with a pencil, an instrument of writing, combines with these other things to indicate that "the truth of fiction is that Fact is fantasy; the made-up story is a model of the world."

Unlike Borges, Barth does not frontally attack reality by claiming that it is a dream. He suggests, more moderately, that life is *like* a dream, an opium dream. (pp. 144-46)

To him the world dissolves not into dreams but into language. His theory of the linguistic basis of reality has been related to some of the aspects of his work that have been discussed. The visibility of a bit of wood pulp in a piece of paper in **"Water-Message"** and the equally dramatic invention of writing in **"Anonymiad"** show readers how remarkable it is that men can transmute reality into literature. Also in the naming of Ambrose in **"Ambrose His Mark"** language must be fitted to reality, and this story, too, implies that this process is not automatic but difficult. The relation of this theme to so many others demonstrates its centrality to Barth's vision.

Barth has known for some time that trouble results if someone attaches the wrong word to an object or if he can find no word for an object. Early in his career, in *End of the Road,* he describes the trouble that develops from Rennie Morgan's lack of a word for the combination of love and hate. One of George's assignments in *Giles Goat-Boy* turns out to be purely a linguistic problem. He has failed to fix the clock because he does not understand what he must do, but then he realizes that "fix" can also mean fix in place, in which case he has no problem. This insight, despite Barth's modest disclaimer that he has little philosophical knowledge, sounds very much like one of Wittgenstein's primary contributions to philosophy: his theory that philosophical problems can be reduced to linguistic problems. (pp. 146-47)

Rather than developing some of the other positive themes that interest Borges and Nabokov, Barth expends an inordinate amount of energy on the theme of opposites. In fact, primarily by using this theme he at first examines the validity of realism and later moves beyond it to the Literature of Exhaustion. He works almost obsessively with this theme in *The Sot-Weed Factor* but uses it considerably less in his next three books, in which, oddly, his chosen mode better suits this theme. It took him a bit longer to learn how to apply his new techniques to this theme, so he handled it in the mode of the Literature of Exhaustion only after he had learned to handle other matters in this way. For these reasons the theme of opposites has a central position in these four books, and by tracing it through them one can see his development and, along the way, watch a typical movement toward the Literature of Exhaustion. In this case, ontogeny really does recapitulate phylogeny: Barth's development recapitulates the development of the Literature of Exhaustion.

The importance of this theme lies in the fact that opposites are a category of thought, one of man's most common ways of organizing ideas and therefore one of the most important constituents of this world. Like space and time, realists use them to constitute their ideas of the world, so anti-realists must discredit them. At first Barth chose as a primary target the belief that things exist in simple pairs of opposites. His solution to the problem of opposites later became one of his most important positive themes.

In its simplest aspect the theme of opposites occurs in the characterization in *The Sot-Weed Factor.* The twinship of Eben and Anna permits a display of Barth's erudition in a chapter on the role and meaning of twins, and it also determines a good deal of their personalities. They are opposites by virtue of their difference in sex, yet their twinship suggests that they are also in some ways a unit. Their yearning for union resembles the androgynes' yearning in Aristophanes' myth in *The Symposium,* but it leads to incestuous desires, which occasionally become almost conscious. The union they seek they once had in "the dark identity that twins share in the womb." (pp. 148-49)

In *Lost in the Funhouse* he takes the next and final step toward his solution of the problem of opposites, an artistic solution. In this book he eventually denies this theme in the only completely valid way that a writer can deny a theme, by declining to write about it. However, he begins in his book where he left off in *Giles Goat-Boy.* He returns to the problem of opposites in **"Night-Sea Journey,"** a story published in 1966, the same year as *Giles Goat-Boy.* The tasks of the hero in the mythic plane (or plane of phylogeny) of this story are *"consummation, transfiguration, union of contraries, transcension of categories."* On another plane, ontogeny, opposites unite as they do in the earlier books, sexually, for on this plane the narrator is a sperm. On the plane of cosmogeny, which again equals literature, the goal is to pass beyond realism and its dependence on opposites. Barth does this by writing this book.

Barth's breakthrough comes in **"Petition,"** which first appeared in *Lost in the Funhouse,* two years later than **"Night-Sea Journey."** Here he again uses twins to develop the theme of opposites, but he intensifies the problem by making the twins Siamese. The solution that worked in *Giles Goat-Boy* appears in a reference to the real Siamese twins Chang and Eng, the "veritable Heavenly Twins, sons of the mystical East, whose religions and philosophies . . . have ever minimized distinctions, denying even the difference between Sameness and Difference." The real transcendence, however, comes later when Barth forms another of his characteristic triangles by adding a lady acrobat, Thalia. He underscores the importance of this triangle by making it visual; the three characters form geometric designs as part of their carnival act. The role in mythology of Thalia represents the solution to the problem of opposites; she is the muse of comic and pastoral literature. Pastoral literature plays no part in this story, though it did in the capsule history of literature in *Giles Goat-Boy.* Her identification with comedy, however, does matter, because this identification means that a writer by controlling his tone and also the rest of his techniques can master the problem of opposites, or any other problem.

This happens in **"Petition,"** for Barth there turns a potentially sad story—sad either because of the narrator's personal plight or because of his failure to deal successfully with opposites—into comedy. The addition of Thalia and what she represents thus acts like an exorcism for Barth, and he seems thereby finally to have mastered the problem of opposites. That is, one who has carefully followed Barth's handling of this theme through three books can see that Barth has shown the impossibility of writing literature based on opposites in a peculiar but logical way, by finally not writing that kind of literature. He does not use this theme at all in *Chimera.* This method comes after an early obsession with opposites and a later demonstration that realism cannot work with opposites. Barth thus arrives at the Literature of Exhaustion's position in regard to this theme also. (pp. 155-56)

In his works Barth usually treats positively the theme of sex. Like Nabokov, he considers it not an immersion in the real world but an escape from it. As he does with many of his themes, he develops this one in a logical progression from book to book. In *The Sot-Weed Factor* he presents a wide variety of sex; in fact, Burlingame alone has an almost pansexuality. [Richard] Noland believes that Eben's lack of identity causes part of his sexual innocence. Joseph more convincingly considers the cause and effect relation to be more complicated: "Eben's single-minded devotion to Joan Toast is now a cause, now an effect of his search for selfhood." In any case, Barth connects sex with identity in this novel, using it as a realistic novelist, interested in identity, would use it. In *Giles Goat-Boy,* however, he refers less frequently to sex in order to make a realistic point, or any point at all. Late in the novel it symbolizes the union of opposites, but earlier he merely describes it with great vigor. Scholes forcefully characterizes the effect of this treatment: "Barth's *Revised New Syllabus* comically but seriously reinstates the goatish side of man. George is . . . a saviour who will restore sexuality to an honored place in human existence." In *Lost in the Funhouse* he establishes the main function of sex in the first story, **"Night-Sea Journey,"** in which it is a microcosm. He urges it to argue that the realists mistakenly conceive of the world, because they do not suspect the existence of the kind of order that a microcosm represents.

Barth shares with Borges and Nabokov the technique of

Barth at work.

developing these themes with characteristic, recurring imagery. He rarely uses Borges's favorite image, the labyrinth. It does appear in **"Lost in the Funhouse"** when he mentions the funhouse's labyrinthine corridors. That structure, by the end of the story, symbolizes literature. "Labyrinthine" seems like an appropriate adjective for the intricate structures Barth creates for the reader, who often gropes along trying to follow them. In one of these labyrinthine corridors lies the skeleton of a man who had told himself stories while wandering in the funhouse, and whose stories had been recorded by an eavesdropper. This involution, turning back to describe the production of literature, is aptly represented by the image of the labyrinth, the correct path of which also doubles back on itself.

Like Borges and Nabokov, Barth describes many mirrors, even in his first novel, *The Floating Opera.* . . . In [*Lost in the Funhouse*] the funhouse mirrors dominate and the funhouse itself becomes both the major image and the symbol of literature. Thus one sees from still another angle Barth's progressive disenchantment with realism and his progressive movement toward a classic variety of the Literature of Exhaustion.

This same growing disenchantment influences Barth's characterization. Aside from his self-consciousness as a narrator, Todd Andrews is realistic, as are the other characters in *Floating Opera.* In *End of the Road* the characters begin to lose some of their aura of reality as Barth manipulates them to make intellectual points, as the authors of anatomies manipulate their characters. Throughout his four most recent books Barth uses the same techniques that Borges and Nabokov use to attack the belief that fictional characters should be realistic, and thereby to attack obliquely the notion that actual people have real, consistent identities.

For example, to mount this attack he portrays characters as readers or writers, thereby gently pointing out their fictive nature and their inclusion in the illusory world of the novel. He unmistakably does not imitate actual people. Usually he inserts these points into the plot without jarring the reader. For instance, the list of the books that Eben Cooke likes and his poems that are scattered throughout the text seem to be perfectly natural details. A little more surprising, because it runs counter to the reader's knowledge of history, Barth presents John Smith's diary along with the implication that Smith should be known by what he has allegedly written, not by what historians tell us about him. In *Lost in the Funhouse* Barth cares much less about preserving verisimilitude and about making this point obliquely. Instead he jolts the reader with swift transitions between the real and fictive worlds. An example can be drawn from **"Menelaiad"**:

> " " " " " 'The death-horse dunged the town with Greeks; Menelaus ground his teeth, drew sword, changed point of view . . . '

Barth is even more fond than Borges and Nabokov of tricking his characters out in disguises. Burlingame continually disguises himself, and Barth sometimes does not explain these disguises until later in the novel, so that a reader always wonders whether a character is who he claims to be or just another avatar of Burlingame. Bray in *Giles Goat-Boy* also has mastered the art of disguise, but Barth always makes it clear whether or not Bray is in disguise. At one point George takes his cue from Bray and wears a mask that makes him look like Bray. Proteus in **"Menelaiad"** is the main user of disguises in *Lost in the Funhouse* and the mythological analogue of Burlingame and Bray. In "The Literature of Exhaustion" Barth casts light on the meaning of Proteus, and of the theme of disguise in general, by relating these matters to the tradition in which he is writing: "Homer's story in Book IV of the *Odyssey,* of Menelaus on the beach at Pharos, tackling Proteus, appeals profoundly to Borges: Proteus is he who 'exhausts the guises of reality' while Menelaus—who, one recalls, disguised his own identity in order to ambush him—holds fast." (pp. 156-59)

Little has been written about Barth's style, less than his artistry merits. Most critics who have discussed *The Sot-Weed Factor* have pointed out its obvious imitation of eighteenth century style but have not probed too deeply into the meaning of this tour de force. His style in that book, being anachronistic, calls attention to itself and therefore announces the artifice of literature. Two stylistic analyses, however, provide some help. Robert Scholes, near the beginning of his chapter on *Giles Goat-Boy,* looks at Barth's style, and, though he moves a bit too quickly to analysis of theme, he does provide some insights about the style of this book. Perhaps the best clue to Barth's style appears in Richard Schickel's article on *The Floating*

Opera; he says that Barth writes in "a wayward, quirky, but highly charged style in which the conversational varies with the formal, the flowery with the direct, the vulgar with the sensitive" [*"The Floating Opera," Critique,* Fall 1963].

This mixture of stylistic opposites rings a bell, since the theme of opposites dominates Barth's works. The most interesting feature of Barth's style, then, is that it reinforces a major theme. A reader can most easily see how he does this, and note other important aspects of his style, by carefully analyzing representative passages from his work. The openings of books, because writers usually meticulously fashion them, make good subjects. One must remember that Barth continually changes his style to suit his purpose; for example, the occasionally legalistic prose of *The Floating Opera* fits Todd Andrews. Thus, analysis will often reveal only how his style works at a particular point. After setting aside the introductory matter of *Giles Goat-Boy,* the first paragraph of the First Reel becomes a logical choice for analysis:

> George is my name; my deeds have been heard of in Tower Hall, and my childhood has been chronicled in the *Journal of Experimental Psychology.* I am he that was called in those days Billy Bocksfuss—cruel misnomer. For had I indeed a cloven foot I'd not now hobble upon a stick or need ride pick-a-back to class in humid weather. Aye, it was just for want of a proper hoof that in my fourteenth year I was the kicked instead of the kicker; that I lay crippled in the reeking peat and saw my first love tupped by a brute Angora. Mercy on that buck who butted me from one world to another; whose fell horns turned my sweetheart's fancy, drove me from the pasture, and set me gimping down the road I travel yet. This bare brow, shame of my kidship, he crowned with the shame of men: I bade farewell to my hornless goathood and struck out, a hornèd human student, for Commencement Gate.

Barth's use here of the smallest unit of style, sound, calls attention to itself, as in the jawbreaking combination of hard consonants in "crippled on the reeking peat." Natural in poetry, alliteration often distracts in prose, so it, too, calls attention to itself. He uses it a few times in the paragraph, twice in the last sentence: "bare brow" and "hornèd human." Also, his alliteration lends a sense of energy to his prose by intensifying some of the accents and breaking up the smooth flow. He rarely uses other poetic devices; he writes not poetic prose but unusual prose. (pp. 161-62)

This passage from *Giles Goat-Boy,* though only one paragraph, demonstrates that Schickel's point about the opposites in the style of *The Floating Opera* holds true also for some of Barth's later work. One should not use Schickel's term "quirky" in a pejorative sense. Barth does have an unusual style, but the real issue is its effectiveness. It can serve best by reinforcing the effect created by the other elements of fiction in a given work. This Barth has managed, imposing his vision on his material so completely that he has produced a work whose elements all interact to create a unified effect.

One can double-check the hypothesis that Barth's style reinforces his theme and that it relates particularly to his handling of the theme of opposites by looking at another passage from a story in which Barth develops this theme differently. The best choice is **"Petition,"** the story in which he symbolizes, by means of Thalia, a satisfactory way to handle opposites. Unlike many of the other works in *Lost in the Funhouse,* it does not have so many involuted devices that one finds the prose nearly impossible to analyze. The story takes the form of a letter written by an imaginary character, but this does not diminish its appropriateness as an object of stylistic analysis. Again, the beginning of the work provides the best sample, though the heading and very brief first paragraph of the letter are irrelevant here. This is the second paragraph:

> Though not myself a native of your kingdom, I am and have been most alive to its existence and concerns—unlike the average American, alas, to whose imagination the name of that ancient realm summons only white elephants and blue-eyed cats. I am aware, for example, that it was Queen Rambai's father's joke that he'd been inside the Statue of Liberty but never in the United States, having toured the Paris foundry while that symbol was a-casting; in like manner I may say that I have dwelt in a figurative Bangkok all my life. My brother, with whose presumption and other faults I hope further to acquaint you in the course of this petition, has even claimed (in his cups) descent from the mad King Phaya Takh Sin, whose well-deserved assassination—like the surgical excision of a cataract, if I may be so bold—gave to a benighted land the luminous dynasty of Chakkri, whereof Your Majesty is the latest and brightest son. Here as elsewhere my brother lies or is mistaken: we are Occidental, for better or worse, and while our condition is freakish, our origin is almost certainly commonplace. Yet though my brother's claim is false and (should he press it upon you, as he might) in contemptible taste, it may serve the purpose of introducing to you his character, my wretched situation, and my petition to your magnanimity.

The opposite qualities of style that Schickel finds in *Floating Opera* and that I find in the first paragraph of *Giles Goat-Boy* proper do not exist in this passage from **"Petition."** The style here does call attention to itself, as it did in the other passage, but by its tone, not by devices of sound that are more common in poetry. The sound obtrudes only in the repetition in "latest and brightest," an unstriking example. Rather, this passage's carefully embellished style and its highly civilized tone make it so clearly an artifice. This passage has a Nabokovian dandyism about it. In fact, this quality, in addition to its desperate yet genteel narrator and its building of a fairy kingdom, make it read like an excerpt from one of Nabokov's novels. This dandyism could be balanced by bluntness to form another style built on opposites—after all, this narrator has a tupping of his loved one by his Siamese twin to describe—but it is not.

This dandyism of style appears mainly in the diction: words like "alas," "contemptible," "magnanimity," and "mistaken," all of which could be omitted or replaced by less flowery words. Phrases like "if I may be so bold" and "in his cups" are similar. This fancy diction serves two functions. First, it heightens the comedy by contrasting the narrator's verbal skill with his inept handling of everything else. Nabokov does this also, for example in Humbert's "I have only words to play with." Second, it helps characterize the narrator. Because of his oppression he has developed a protective timidity, which appears in the bathos of "my brother lies or is mistaken." This passage contains many more adjectives than does the passage from *Giles Goat-Boy,* and the ones here are more imaginative. One brief section has two effective adjectives: "gave to a benighted land the luminous dynasty." No blunt words contrast with these fancy ones, and few verbals balance the important adjectives; the style here is contemplative, not active.

Unlike the other passage, this one contains similes and metaphors, including two very effective ones: the comparison of an assassination to a "surgical excision of a cataract" and of the conditions of the narrator's life to a "figurative Bangkok." Also unlike the other passage, this one has no apparent allusions. Yet his sensitive, articulate narrator should occasionally invent apt tropes. Again, regarding this aspect of style, Barth uses no pairs of opposites.

Besides the fancy phrases mentioned earlier, Barth uses some circumlocutions, like "I may say," "the course of," and "serve the purpose of." His sentences are also somewhat baroque. They average about forty-seven words, over half-again as long as the sentences in the other passage. The absence of action causes part, but far from all, of this increase in length. Like the other passage, this one has sentence variety and parallelism. The intricacy of the sentence construction has increased. For example, he puts together the third sentence in real virtuoso fashion, meandering, though with impeccable logic, from the narrator's brother to the King. The clipped, economical phrases that he used in this type of sentence in the other passage rarely occur this time, so once again his style here produces a unified effect.

Both the attention-getting quality of Barth's style and its efficient reinforcement of the other elements of his fiction typify the Literature of Exhaustion. The former quality helps create the artifice of this kind of literature. The latter quality makes a work more unified and self-enclosed, cut off definitely from the real world rather than being a model of it. And of course Barth shares these qualities with Borges and Nabokov.

Barth also combats the realists on the battleground of point of view. Rejecting more sophisticated ways to divide this element of fiction into categories, he uses the common one of first-person and third-person and shows that this can be a false distinction. By doing this he proves that point of view is much more complex than most realists suspect. His most subtle proof of this complexity appears in **"Echo."** Gerhard Joseph has explained it in an intricate discussion that requires extensive quotation:

> **"Echo"** . . . accomplishes the complete amalgamation of the first-and third-person point of view. Narcissus seems to be the speaker, telling

his familiar tale in the third person to Tiresias as an antidote to self-love: "One does well," the story opens, "to speak in the third person, the seer advises, in the manner of Theban Tiresias. A cure for self-absorption is saturation: telling the story over as though it were another's until like a much repeated word it loses sense." As Narcissus explores this perspective, lapsing at one point into the first person within the first person, we are led to suspect that the speaker may be either Tiresias or Echo, in which case the identity of the interlocutor is just as doubtful. While the narrative line is relatively clear because of the myth's familiarity, it becomes impossible to distinguish teller from listener and, ultimately, narrative from narrator.

The reader has even more difficulty making distinctions about this story than Joseph claims, for Narcissus is not the only one who "sees the nymph [Echo] efface herself until she becomes no more than her voice." The reader sees the same thing. In this effacement Barth presents his ultimate quibble with conventional ideas about point of view. He no longer denies only the distinction between first and third persons; he denies the distinction between point of view as a whole and character. He also suggests that everything else in a story can become subservient to a narrative voice. He makes the same suggestion in **"Menelaiad"**: "this isn't the voice of Menelaus; this voice *is* Menelaus." Then he builds so many Chinese boxes in this story that the reader begins to believe this statement by and about the narrative voice.

To pare away the elements of fiction an author can next eliminate the narrative voice, by having the story tell itself. This supposedly happens in **"Autobiography."** Despite the interest, perhaps even the originality of this strategy, executing it does not take much skill, certainly much less than the skill with which Barth handles the point of view in **"Echo."** This idea as it appears in **"Autobiography"** can be visualized as a series of Chinese boxes. The outermost ones are again the author and the work. Then comes the narrative voice, according to Barth the ground of any story, and then the actual content of the story. Lately he has been trying to work outward from this last box, destroying each box as he goes until he leaves only the work and himself. That is, he would like to create a story called **"Autobiography"** that has no content and that would be like a Platonic form of a story. He creates a finite system of boxes in this story, since no other boxes can be built that will encompass the last one. This project sounds like some of Beckett's attempts to make do without various elements of fiction. More generally, to use this strategy a writer of the Literature of Exhaustion must first admit that literature is dead. Then he tries to prove this charge by destroying literature's constituents—while writing stories.

Like Borges and Nabokov, Barth adds a big dose of the leaven of comedy to make his heavy ingredients lighter and more airy. Not by accident, these three writers have in common both a particular kind of literature and great wit. The very nature of their mode requires and encourages a light comic touch. Scholes's term for the writers he analyzes, fabulators, means almost the same thing as the term I am using for these three writers. His statement

about his writers holds also for Borges, Barth and Nabokov (and of course he includes Barth in his group, too): "fabulation . . . seems to partake of the comic." Again at the risk of choosing one that is not funny, a critic can give a sense of an author's comedy only by providing an example. A brief passage in **"Echo"** has several witticisms, some quite subtle, and a neat linguistic mirror that reinforces the visual scene being described: "like the masturbatory adolescent, sooner or later [Narcissus] finds himself. He beholds and salutes his pretty alter ego in the pool; in the pool his ego, altered, prettily salutes: Behold! In vain he reaches to embrace his contrary image; he recognizes what Tiresias couldn't warn him of. Has knowing himself turned him into a pansy?" Barth's comedy does not always occur in such a series or in such subtlety, but it pervades his work.

In many ways, then, Barth is a classic writer of the Literature of Exhaustion, but a tendency in his work, his growing interest in the theme of love, has allowed him to keep in touch with realism. However, he frequently takes an ironic attitude toward this theme. His first two, realistic novels depend quite heavily on the love theme, *The Floating Opera* more heavily than it first appears. (pp. 165-70)

Lost in the Funhouse depends throughout on the love theme and does not subordinate it to other concerns. The cry of " 'love, love, love' " that ends the first story, **"Night-Sea Journey,"** echoes throughout the book. Often the love is unrequited, as in **"Petition,"** or vicarious, as in **"Water-Message,"** but these varieties are no less real. This theme plays an even more important part in two other stories. In **"Menelaiad"** Menelaus learns that he must placate not Athena, the goddess of wisdom, but Aphrodite, the goddess of love. Moreover, after one unpeels all the layers of this story, the core, the love story of Menelaus and Helen, becomes visible. **"Ambrose His Mark"** ends with the main character admitting his attitude toward the experiences he has just had:

> He wishes he had never entered the funhouse. But he has. Then he wishes he were dead. But he's not. Therefore he will construct funhouses for others and be their secret operator—though he would rather be among the lovers for whom funhouses are designed.

This is the subterranean message of *Lost in the Funhouse.*

In *Chimera* Barth treats love ironically. He compares sex so often with narration that the former theme becomes less important in itself than as a metaphor for the latter theme. For example, he says of the genie and Scheherazade " 'this last comparison—a favorite of theirs—would lead them to a dozen others between narrative and sexual art.' " Moreover, Barth's technical experiments so dominate this book that the love relations in it lose their credibility and immediacy. This irony prevails in spite of the autobiographical implications of this theme in *Chimera.* In sum, it looks as if Barth will not use the theme of love to lead him back toward realism, but will instead continue his interest in the aesthetic themes of the Literature of Exhaustion. (p. 171)

Since his seminal essay he has deepened his understanding of the Literature of Exhaustion. He has begun to allude specifically in his fiction to the basic premise of this kind of literature. Dunyazade complains to Shah Zaman that " 'you've had the whole literary tradition transmitted to you.' " Thus, she faces the same predicament as do writers like Barth. Barth, in the guise of the genie in **"Dunyaza-diad"** hopes to solve this problem, "to go beyond [his past works] toward a future they were not attuned to and, by some magic, at the same time go back to the original springs of narrative." He does this in **Chimera** by using myths to communicate the contemporary writer's plight. Specifically, he proposes cryptically that "the key to the treasure is the treasure," that one can write in the face of this condition by writing *about* this condition. He also writes about Scheherazade because she desperately fought against a diminution of narrative possibilities in order to save her own life. The anguish of the contemporary writer took for Barth the form of a writer's block, but he later realized that the same solution would work " 'as soon as I understood that my writer's block was a precise metaphor for the story I was trying to write, the problem solved itself, the story came out in a burst.' " In short, he has publicly demonstrated more awareness than Borges or Nabokov that he belongs to the Literature of Exhaustion, though the lack of statements by the latter two does not mean that they do not know what they are doing.

Until he produces more nonfiction, though, his reputation will rest on his novels and short stories. This work has obvious merits, such as the skill with which he uses words. He also clearly deserves credit for his wit and for his experiments. His detractors usually make the same complaints: that he is dull and that he is bloodless, magisterially and endlessly ruminating on trivial issues and turning his back on the real problems of his era. One cannot argue about dullness, except to say that lack of understanding sometimes causes boredom. Critics also make the second charge against Borges and Nabokov. Defending Barth on these grounds is a bit easier, because of his first two novels. Their realism and the problems they deal with make them the kind of novel admired by detractors of Barth's four most recent works, and this puts those detractors in an awkward position.

The position of these detractors becomes even more awkward when they see the connection between his first two works and his others. He deals with a wide range of interrelated problems in *Floating Opera* and *End of the Road,* but, inevitably, finds the full panoply too complex to admit of any solutions. In his later works he assumes that the aesthetic problems that he considers relevant are paradigmatic of the other problems, and he tries to wage his battle on only one front, giving himself a better chance of success. Both his subsidiary theme of love and his many connections of aesthetic matters with other matters indicate that he has never forgotten the problems that he has temporarily placed in abeyance. He worries about more than aesthetic ultimacy; he writes in **"Title"**: "Everything's finished. Name eight. Story, novel, literature, art, humanism, humanity, the self itself." He also has faith that victory on one front will be decisive, for the next sentence is "Wait: the story's not finished." And it is not, and neither is Barth, and at least for a while neither is humanity.

In other words, Barth chooses reasonable grounds on which to withstand ultimacy. If one grants him his artistic goals and methods—either because of these arguments or because they should be granted to all writers—one can evaluate the products that he makes with them. *Floating Opera* is a first-rate novel, a remarkable work for a twenty-five year old writer. It has both obvious strengths—stylistic and thematic—and latent subtleties, some of which I have made manifest. *End of the Road* is notable mainly for the rapidity with which it followed its predecessor, for both were written during 1955. Otherwise it makes only a very slight advance in technique. It also has some flaws, mainly inconsistencies, like the characterization of Joe as both genius and dunce.

Next Barth switched to his later mode, though he did not completely abandon his earlier mode. *The Sot-Weed Factor,* probably the most enjoyable of his books, perhaps lacks the depth of others, and aside from its stylistic performance, it is not as innovative or technically interesting as some of his other books. *Giles Goat-Boy* brings to fruition the seeds sown in *The Sot-Weed Factor.* It has a certain woodenness but the other aspects of its technique include many genuinely new developments, and it has more philosophical depth than its predecessor. The first appearances of the stories in **Lost in the Funhouse** range over five years, falling both before and after *Giles Goat-Boy.* A few of them seem like five-finger exercises, trying out technical ideas on a small scale. Many of the stories, however, have merit, either technically, like **"Menelaiad,"** or by conventional standards, like **"Ambrose His Mark,"** or on both counts like **"Lost in the Funhouse"** and **"Echo."** Its unity adds strength to it and makes it a collection of carefully interrelated stories in the tradition of *Go Down, Moses* and *Winesburg, Ohio,* a tradition that unfortunately has not been kept up very well lately. In **Chimera** he further refines his techniques, but to do so he repeats aspects of his earlier works. The first two of the novellas deserve high marks, but **"Bellerophoniad"** sometimes drags.

In summary, Barth's fiction earns a high place. His work, especially *Floating Opera,* has found readers, though fewer than it should have. He has too few readers perhaps because he has too few critics: the longest analysis of his work aside from this one is Joseph's forty-page pamphlet, and the essays about him are mainly book reviews and therefore almost inevitably ephemeral. His work bears a great deal of careful explication and merits further attention. (pp. 172-75)

> *John O. Stark, "John Barth," in his* The Literature of Exhaustion: Borges, Nabokov, and Barth, *Duke University Press, 1974, pp. 118-75.*

Jerome Klinkowitz   (essay date 1975)

[Klinkowitz is an American critic and educator who has written extensively on innovative contemporary fiction. In the following excerpt from the prologue to his Literary Disruptions: The Making of a Post-Contemporary American Fiction, *he deplores Barth's short fiction for what he maintains is its uninspired and nihilistic literary aesthetic.]*

Fiction breeds its own continuity. Because it is the most public of the literary arts and the most immediately responsive to social life, developments of form in the American novel have been clear-cut and at times even monumental. The year 1851 marked the publication of *The House of the Seven Gables* and *Moby-Dick;* 1885, the ascendancy of Realism with Howells's *The Rise of Silas Lapham,* Twain's *Adventures of Huckleberry Finn,* and the first collected edition of Henry James. The last commonly accepted milestone in the development of American fiction has been 1925, when F. Scott Fitzgerald's *The Great Gatsby* and Ernest Hemingway's *In Our Time* resolved the dichotomy of Romanticism and Realism in favor of well-crafted fiction and the novel of selection.

Since the Twenties there have been variations in theme of course, but for the most part the American novel has been marked by a conservative stability of form. For nearly fifty years, when in other countries such exotic talents as Gide, Hesse, Beckett, Robbe-Grillet, Cortazar, Borges, and Gombrowicz flourished, American fiction rested content with novels of manners or of social politics, while the innovations of a Patchen, a Hawkes, a Miller, or a Burroughs were kept—in some cases by court order—decisively underground.

By the late 1960's an uneasiness had come to the criticism of fiction. "At the moment," Stephen Koch wrote in 1967, "our literature is idling in a period of hiatus: the few important writers of the earlier generations are dead, silent, or in their decline, while the younger generation has not yet produced a writer of unmistakable importance or even of very great interest" [Stephen Koch, "Premature Speculations on the Perpetual Renaissance," *Tri-Quarterly,* Fall, 1967]. Criticism itself fared no better; by that time no less than four studies of the ranking contemporary novelist, Saul Bellow, had appeared, but a typical review found them "inflated and tiresome exercises in the art of trivia." The novel itself was said to be suffering a "curious death," chroniclers of its demise including Louis Rubin, Leslie Fiedler, Susan Sontag, and Norman Podhoretz. "Even though there is a large body of new work," Koch concluded, "nothing thus far has been heard at the highest levels except an eerie silence."

It must feel strange indeed to be an emerging novelist when the novel has just died. Stranger still to write books which nobody buys, when book companies' stock falls two hundred points in eighteen months; when the returns keep flooding in, when your publisher remainders your first printing. During the 1967-68 publishing season there were many signs to suggest that fiction was in trouble, but Fiedler, Sontag, Podhoretz, and their colleagues were proclaiming the genre's decline even before the review copies were out, which turned out to contain an amazingly rich harvest: Donald Barthelme's *Snow White,* Ronald Sukenick's *Up, In the Heart of the Country* by William H. Gass, *Tales* by LeRoi Jones, major novels by Richard Brautigan, Ishmael Reed, Steve Katz, and others—a season climaxing with the belated discovery of Kurt Vonnegut, Jr., through his retrospective collection *Welcome to the Monkey House,* and the National Book Award for Jerzy Koskinski's *Steps.* The point at issue between this critical

despair and such a flurry of new, substantial work marks another division in the history of the novel, greater than the ones before because of the nature of fiction itself was being challenged in a radical disruption of the genre's development. Ronald Sukenick described the phenomenon in a *Chicago Review* interview with Joe David Bellamy: "One of the reasons people have lost faith in the novel is that they don't believe it tells the truth any more, which is another way of saying that they don't believe in the conventions of the novel. They pick up a novel and they know it's make believe. So, who needs it—go listen to the television news, right? Or read a biography."

"People no longer believe in the novel as a medium that gets at the truth of their lives," Sukenick wrote again in 1973. Conventional novels had presented data, but in terms of fraudulent ideals, and sophisticated readers began despising these works for the lies they presented as real-life stories. Persistent story-tellers would have us believe as fact that life has leading characters, plots, morals to be pointed, lessons to be learned, and most of all beginnings, middles, and ends. In his novel published the same year, *Breakfast of Champions,* Kurt Vonnegut, Jr., played with the cynical farce of all this when he pondered the abominable behavior of his countrymen and concluded that "They were doing their best to live like people invented in story books. This was the reason Americans shot each other so often: It was a convenient literary device for ending short stories and books." Vonnegut added that others suffered disappointing lives which failed to be perfect fictions, as year by year we were learning that still more readers were despairing of the whole mess and abandoning fiction altogether for history, biography, or even television. The more instant and accurate the replay, the more truthful seem the facts, although in the process the organizing and clarifying power of art was forgone, and fiction was at the point of no longer existing.

"The great advantage of fiction over history, journalism, or any supposedly 'factual' kind of writing," Sukenick countered, "is that it is an expressive medium. It transmits feeling, energy, excitement. Television can give us the news, fiction can best express our response to the news. No other medium—especially not film—can so well deal with our strongest and often most intimate responses to the large and small facts of our daily lives. No other medium, in other words, can so well keep track of the reality of our experience." Nevertheless, by the 1960's writers had abandoned the Great American Novel, and had turned fiction instead—like poetry before it—into an elitist, academic diversion. Although several critics had comments on the subject, the key document in defining and endorsing this new aesthetic for the novel was John Barth's essay, "The Literature of Exhaustion." Given prominent publication in the *Atlantic Monthly* of August, 1967, following by a year the wide success of Barth's novel *Giles Goat-Boy* and the prestigious republication of his earlier works, it influenced discussion of fiction in much the same way that social and political essays by LeRoi Jones, Eldridge Cleaver, Julius Lester, and others were affecting their own fields about the same time. Barth's seemingly radical aesthetic was that in the novel writers faced "the used-upness of certain forms of exhaustion of certain possibilities." From then on writers could only parody older stories and earlier forms—but at no great loss, since the crucial matter was "the difference between the *fact* of aesthetic ultimacies and their artistic *use*." Barth's discovery and momentary triumph in his fiction was the issue of "how an artist may paradoxically turn the felt ultimacies of our own time into material and means for his own work."

Three months after his seminal essay, one of the few on literary theory the *Atlantic* had published since the editorship of William Dean Howells, the same magazine featured Barth's contribution, **"Lost in the Funhouse,"** a major story from his forthcoming collection of the same name. "So far there's been no real dialogue, very little sensory detail, and nothing in the way of a *theme*," the narrator admits after the piece is well underway. "And a long time has gone by already without anything happening; it makes a person wonder. We haven't even reached Ocean City yet: we will never get out of the funhouse." And so his protagonist Ambrose admits, never getting into it in the first place. But in *Lost in the Funhouse* (1968) Barth had pushed on into the realm of fiction which his *Atlantic* essay alleged was "new," the Literature of Exhaustion. "The final possibility," his story **"Title"** insists, "is to turn ultimacy, exhaustion, paralyzing self-consciousness and the adjective weight of accumulated history. . . . Go on. Go on. To turn ultimacy against itself to make something new and valid, the essence whereof would be the impossibility of making something new." In some of his stories Barth brought American fiction to the level of innovation and self-conscious artifice practiced by Julio Cortazar in such tales as "Continuity of Parks" and "The Night Face Up" (from *End of the Game and Other Stories*) and by Jorge Luis Borges in "The Circular Ruins" (collected in *Ficciones*). "I try to write simple, straight-forward stories," reported Borges; for his part, Barth confessed to being "less and less interested in working with tapes and graphics and things of that sort—and more and more interested in story telling" ["Algebra and Fire: An Interview with John Barth," *The Falcon*, 1972]. Yet, in comparison with his Argentine models, Barth's attempts were hardly sustained; coming when it did (as he finished *Lost in the Funhouse*), "The Literature of Exhaustion" read as a literary suicide note.

Or else as an equivocation, since for the one story about Ambrose which demands a parody of the conventional (**"Lost in the Funhouse"**), the collection offers two others, **"Ambrose His Mark"** and **"Water-Message,"** which do quite well within the older, apparently unexhausted forms. Moreover, the uses Barth finds in the title story for his new aesthetic are for the most part gratuitous—a musing with italic script, obvious references to unexceptional techniques, and as its principal innovation the simple use of suspense as a structural device: "At this rate our hero, at this rate our protagonist will remain in the funhouse forever." The story's ineffectualness can be seen by contrasting it with Gilbert Sorrentino's "The Moon in Its Flight." In formalistic terms, the latter story is a carefully plotted exercise in literary hysteria, as the author tries to guide his characters through a romance in the historically lost year of 1948, all the time knowing how conventional fiction invites itself to be misread. "Isn't there anyone," he pleads,

"any magazine writer or avant-garde filmmaker, any lover of life or dedicated optimist out there who will move them toward a cottage, already closed for the season, in whose split log exterior they will find an unlocked door? Inside there will be a bed, whiskey, an electric heater. Or better, a fireplace, white lamps, soft lights. Sweet music." Or, "All you modern lovers, freed by Mick Jagger and the orgasm, give them, for Christ's sake, for an hour, the use of your really terrific little apartment. They won't smoke your marijuana nor disturb your Indian graphics. They won't borrow your Fanon or Cleaver or Barthelme or Vonnegut. They'll make the bed before they leave. They whisper good night and dance in the dark." But all of that is impossible, for "This was in America, in 1948. Not even fake art or the wearisome tricks of movies can assist them." Even worse, fears the narrator, how can the contemporary reader of his paperback magazine piece appreciate the meaning of this ancient world? "Who remembers the clarity of Claude Thornhill and Sarah Vaughan, their exquisite irrelevance? They are gone where the useless chrome doughnuts on the buick's hood have gone." Sorrentino uses the same correlative in his novel, *Imaginative Qualities of Actual Things* (1971), as itself one of those imaginative qualities of actual things, when "Leo saw her standing in the sun. Just like Dick Haymes in the old movie. She was something to see, etc." Therefore the narrator tells us at once, to keep the experience one of art and not just history, that "The value of the popular song is that it deals in superficialities that release the emotions. Scratch the veneer of those pedestrian lyrics and you look into a crystal ball of the past." Or as we are asked in the story, "She was crying and stroking his hair. Ah God, the leaves of brown came tumbling down, remember?" Gilbert Sorrentino finds by Barth's own definition a point of true exhaustion in narrative art, and seizes it to more effectively tell his story. Here technique is more than simple discovery—it becomes an integral part of the fiction itself.

But the critical reaction to Sorrentino's work—along with that to a whole artistic generation, including Vonnegut, Barthelme, Sukenick, and others—was for a time aborted, because of the depressing effect of Barth's essay and the even greater impression made by his continuing work. That a newer style of fiction did become popular in the late 1960's was beside the point, since anything designed in the wake of Barth's parody and subversion seemed a hopeless or even reprehensible cause. That right within our dispensation of "the death of the novel" tight, snappy little books by Kurt Vonnegut, Jr., and Richard Brautigan were selling like mad, competing with TV and sometimes winning, was irrelevant. Other writers such as Sorrentino, Barthelme, Sukenick, and Rudolph Wurlitzer were extending these forms, finding a new life for fiction, only to be described by Pearl Kazin Bell (in a review typical of the period) as "celebrants of unreason, chaos, and inexorable decay . . . a horde of mini-Jeremiahs crying havoc in the Western world ["American Fiction: Forgetting Ordinary Truths," *Dissent*, 1973]. The more social and cultural issue, as Nathan Scott let slip in his major essay on contemporary fiction, was that the "inward liberation" of the imagination which these writers used as a counter to transcend Barth "offers us an effective release from the bullying of all the vexations of history"—and, incidentally, that this aesthetic had been so demonstrably adopted "by the hordes of those young long-haired, jean-clad, pot-smoking bohemians who have entered the world of psychedelia" [" 'New Heav'ns, New Earth'—the Landscape of Contemporary Apocalypse," *Journal of Religion,* 1973].

Chimera, John Barth's trilogy of retold classical myths which followed *Lost in the Funhouse* in 1972, stands as an allegory of his own exhaustion. As with **"Autobiography: A Self-Recorded Fiction"** and the funhouse story in the earlier collection, *Chimera* confuses the product of art with the conditions of its inception, a process which obviously fascinates Barth (leading to such pieces as **"Night-Sea Journey"**) but which often results in simple bad writing, as when the story admits "I must compose myself." *Chimera* is even more indulgent, renaming Dunyazade, sister of Scheherazade, "Doony," and in another place allowing a character on the death of a parent to impel herself "dead dadward." Relocating the determinants of race, moment, and milieu from the subject one is writing about to the writing itself, from topic to technique or from ethic to aesthetic, is hardly an innovation; evidence suggests that the same was attempted in the nineteenth century. A figure in most of Barth's work is the writer seeking immortality. "Fair as the country was and the goatboy life my fellow's lot," his narrator of **"Anonymiad"** confesses, "if I could not've imagined my music's one day whisking me Orionlike to the stars, I'd have as well flung myself into the sea." Hence the door closing to new literary activity would be a death sentence: "I had begun to run out of world and material. . . . I imagined my *opera* sinking."

Despite his recourse to technique (in parody, burlesque, and ironic commentary) as a way of sustaining his role as fictionist, Barth has received little attention as a purely formal innovator. Rather, the major studies of his work prefer to discuss his themes. Both Charles B. Harris [in his *Contemporary American Novelists of the Absurd,* 1971] and Raymond Olderman [in his *Beyond the Waste Land: The American Novel in the Nineteen-Sixties,* 1972] find a complete explication within myth and draw neat correlations to the work of Joseph Campbell. Thematically, Barth is read [by Olderman] as an example that "the symbolic affirmation that transcends conflicts without offering a program of action is just about the only affirmative ending the novel of the sixties can have without running into sociology or romanticism." From his own parameters of the decade Olderman excludes consideration of Barthelme, Kosinski, Sukenick, Sorrentino, and most other fictionists who moved formally beyond Barth. So does Harris, who prefers to let that decade close with a facile thematic imperative: "So Barth, like most other absurdist novelists, sees human commitment to other human beings—in short, love—as one of the few relative values available in an otherwise valueless universe."

Barth's narrator in **"Title"** speaks otherwise: "In this dehuman, exhausted, ultimate adjective hour, when every humane value has become untenable, and not only love, decency, and beauty but even compassion and intelligibility are no more than one or two subjective complements to complete the sentence. . . . " Nor can he complete the sentence. In the **"Bellerophoniad"** (published almost coincidentally with Harris's and Olderman's theses) Barth speaks more directly:

> My general interest in the wandering-hero myth dates from my thirtieth year, when reviewers of my novel The Sot-Weed Factor (1960) remarked that the vicissitudes of its hero—Ebenezer Cooke, Gentleman, Poet and Laureate of Maryland—follow in some detail the pattern of mythical heroic adventure as described by Lord Raglan, Joseph Campbell, and other comparative mythologists. The suggestion was that I had used this pattern as the basis for the novel's plot. In fact I had been unaware of the pattern's existence; once appraised of it I was struck enough by the coincidence (which I later came to regard as more inevitable than remarkable) to examine those works by which I'd allegedly been influenced, and my next novel, Giles Goat-Boy (1966), was for better or for worse the conscious and ironic orchestration of the Ur-Myth which its predecessor had been represented as being. Several of my subsequent fictions—the long short-story "Menelaiad" and the novella "Perseid," for example—deal directly with particular manifestations of the myth of the wandering hero and address as well a number of their author's more current thematic concerns: the mortal desire for immortality, for instance, and its ironically qualified fulfillment—especially by the mythic hero's transformation, in the latter stages of his career, into the sound of his own voice, or the story of his life, or both. I am forty.

"He was a writer of tales," a Barth look-alike explains himself to Scheherazade and her sister in the **"Dunyazadiad,"** "anyhow a *former* writer of tales in a land on the other side of the world." He confesses that as a popular vehicle the novel had died, and that

> His own pen (that magic wand, in fact a magic quill with a fountain of ink inside) had just about run dry. . . . His career, too, had reached a hiatus which he would have been pleased to call a turning-point if he could have espied any way to turn: he wished neither to repudiate nor to repeat his past performances; he aspired to go beyond them toward a future they were not attuned to and, by some magic, at the same time go back to the original springs of narrative.

Measuring Barth's work of this period, Robert Scholes has drawn a comparison with the "aesthetic allegories" of Henry James:

> Barth, in *Lost in the Funhouse,* gave us a volume of aesthetic allegory about the nature of fiction which is fully worthy of comparison with James—and the comparison is instructive. For James, in stories like "The Lesson of the Master" and "The Death of the Lion," the career of a dedicated literary artist could be seen comically and the question could be raised as to whether it indeed might compensate for the sacrifice of "life" that it inevitably entailed. But in general James leaves us feeling that the satisfactions of art are sufficient compensation for the sacrifices. While for Barth, it is clear in the *Funhouse* that being an artist is only a poor substitute for being

a lover. ["The Allegory of Exhaustion," *Fiction International,* 1973]

"Imaginative potency is as crucial to the daily life of his spirit as sexual potency," reads the **"Bellerophoniad,"** and it is precisely because Barth has suffered an exhaustion (if not castration) of the imagination that his fiction falters. The last two novellas of *Chimera* are marked with situation-comedy routines of male impotency, as Barth's women shrilly mock his fall from capability. His "own devastating self-analyses in his last two books," concludes Scholes, "say all that can be said" of his successes or failures.

"Nobody had enough imagination," Ambrose muses at the close of **"Lost in the Funhouse."** He envisions a "truly astonishing funhouse, incredibly complex yet utterly controlled from a great control switchboard like the console of a pipe organ." He would be its operator: "Panel lights would show what was up in every cranny of its cunning of its multifarious vastness; a switch-flick would ease this fellow's way, complicate that's, to balance things out; if anyone seemed lost or frightened, all the operator had to do was." Ambrose decides that "he will construct funhouses for others and be their secret operator—though he would rather be among the lovers for whom funhouses are designed." Barth's metaphor for the imagination, as the mechanics of a funhouse, emphasizes its limits above anything else. And there is even less argument for transcendence when it is such a second-best choice.

Throughout Barth's recent work runs an uncomfortable confessional thread: "Somewhere along that way I'd lost something, took a wrong turn, forgot some knack, I don't know; it seemed to me that if I kept going over it carefully enough I might see the pattern, find the key." Again "he felt that a treasure-house of new fiction lay vaguely under his hand, if he could find the key to it." The answer he finds in *Chimera,* however, is no different from and of no greater effect than his suspicions first voiced in 1967. *"The key to the treasure is the treasure,"* he writes, and finds himself back with Dunyazade and her sister, parsing out the thousand and one tales of the Arabian nights. "The narrator has narrated himself into a corner" (***Lost in the Funhouse***), turning "in ever-diminishing circles like a moth around a candle, till I feared we must disappear up our own fundaments" (***Chimera***). Or, "Silence. There's a fourth possibility, I suppose. Silence. General anesthesia. Self-extinction. Silence." Hence the pity for one who was once our most promising fictionist. "Whether he has painted himself into a corner, or is banking into the last turn on his flight to disappearance," writes Robert Scholes, "I want to call out to this great story-teller and say, 'Hey, come out of there. We need you.' But I have neither the right nor the words to make such a plea." (pp. 1-11)

Jerome Klinkowitz, "The Death of the Death of the Novel," in his Literary Disruptions: The Making of a Post-Contemporary American Fiction, *University of Illinois Press, 1975, pp. 1-32.*

Jerry Powell   (essay date 1976)

[In the following essay, Powell studies themes in Chimera, *highlighting Barth's treatment of the "exhausted possibilities" in literature and life.]*

In three years, 1966 to 1968, John Barth published an astounding amount: *Giles Goat-Boy* in 1966, revised editions of his first three novels—*The Floating Opera, The End of the Road,* and *The Sot-Weed Factor*—in 1967, and a collection of some previously published and some unpublished stories—*Lost in the Funhouse*—in 1968. In the middle of an extremely prolific period, Barth also published an article, "The Literature of Exhaustion," setting forth his feeling that all stories have been told—the feeling of exhausted possibilities in the narrative art form. The theoretical considerations of his article are naturally related to his work at the time, for he was publishing furiously at the same time that he was talking about "exhausted possibilities." In his article Barth provides a clue to the apparent discrepancy: in speaking of the artist's ability to comment on his own themes within the art work itself, thereby turning "the artist's mode or form into a metaphor for his concerns," Barth finds that "an artist may paradoxically turn the felt ultimacies of our time into material and means for his work—*paradoxically* because by doing so he transcends what had appeared to be his refutation." Citing Nabokov's *Pale Fire* and Borges' *Labyrinths* as examples, Barth adds, "if you were the author of this paper, you'd have written something like *The Sot-Weed Factor* or *Giles Goat-Boy:* novels which imitate the form of the Novel, by an author who imitates the role of Author."

The problem with linking Barth's theory to his earlier works, such as *The Sot-Weed Factor* and *Giles Goat-Boy,* is that the theory follows the works chronologically. While *Giles Goat-Boy* foreshadows some of Barth's later self-conscious authorial traits—an author imitating the role of Author—as in the framing prefaces and postscripts, the novel is much more of a response to themes that evolved from *The Sot-Weed Factor* and its public reception, such as hero-hood and the quest. *Lost in the Funhouse,* which appeared the year after the article, is more clearly a product of the self-conscious artist who is aware of "exhausted possibilities" in his field, but it is an experiment in format as much as form, for Barth meant the stories to be recorded and played back as well as read, as the complete title suggests: *Fiction for Print, Tape, Live Voice.* One alternative to exhausted possibilities in a printed format is to change the format.

Chimera, unfortunately, has received very little critical attention, mostly focused on Barth's form and technique, as though Barth had discarded "content" in favor of technique, if that is even possible. *Chimera* is far from a mere exercise in technique but an artistic product of the ideas presented in "The Literature of Exhaustion." While some of the narrative techniques were developed in *Lost in the Funhouse,* Barth has returned in *Chimera* to the printed page and to the narrative technique he is best at—"story-telling"—and his achievement is the successful integration into the novel of his ideas concerning the "literature of exhaustion."

In *Chimera* the situation facing an author—the situation

of exhausted possibilities in the narrative art form—is represented by the more general problem of writer's block, which becomes a metaphor for many of the daily problems people face throughout life, such as the difficulties encountered in transitions from one stage of life to another. The idea of exhausted possibilities becomes a central theme of the novel, and the process of writing about writer's block transcends the problem—the paradox is complete. As the Genie and Scheherazade tell us over and over, "the key to the treasure is the treasure."

The problem of writer's block importantly connects the three parts of the novel, for each of the protagonists has to deal with some form of the malady. In the **"Dunyazadiad"** Scheherazade epitomizes the problem: she either tells a convincing story or loses her life. Ironically her "source" for the stories is the Genie, a thinly-disguised version of Barth, who has taken the stories from the treasure-house of literature—specifically, the *Arabian Nights.* The time warp should not be distracting nor should the apparent lapse in logic concerning "authorship" of the stories; the point is that all authors have drawn from the same stories for centuries.

Stories change by shifts in viewpoint. As the Genie says, *"Alf Laylah Wa Laylah,* The Book of the Thousand Nights and a Night, is not the story of Scheherazade, but the story of the story of her stories." In the **"Dunyazadiad"** Scheherazade uses her own stories, in effect, to create her stories, but the story we read—the **"Dunyazadiad"**—belongs to Dunyazade. She tells the story to Shah Zaman in order to make it through "the night that all good mornings come to"—the night being a metaphor for writer's block in the first part. In the second and third parts, **"Perseid"** and **"Bellerophoniad,"** the noon of one's life is compared to writer's block and night becomes more generally a metaphor for death. The shift in emphasis on night as a metaphor is appropriate because the "metaphor" is literal for Scheherazade and Dunyazade: a failure to produce stories *is* death—not a metaphoric one. This distinction is important for it helps clarify the relationship between Part One and Parts Two and Three. The **"Dunyazadiad"** is Barth's source for the solution to *his* writer's block. He learns from Scheherazade that the key to his problem is to write about his problem—that is, to tell Scheherazade's story. Thus Scheherazade's story is both Dunyazade's, in her time, the record of which has not come down to us, and Barth's, in our time: "There (with a kiss, little sister) is the sense of our story, Dunyazade: The key to the treasure is the treasure."

What Barth learns from his writing the **"Dunyazadiad"** is used in writing the **"Perseid"** and **"Bellerophoniad."** The two protagonists—"true and false" mythic heroes, as the Genie respectively calls them—are both afflicted with writer's block, except that writer's block has become a metaphor for middle age, just as writing is so often a metaphor for life in Barth's works. Merely to write about writer's block is not the key; if that were true Barth would have stopped after Part One. Instead, by treating the act of writing as a life-or-death matter in Part One, Barth has gained a new perspective on his own writer's block. As he learned from Dunyazade, a new perspective is all that is

needed to create "new" stories out of old ones. With a new awareness or consciousness, then, Barth creates Parts Two and Three. In Part Two, Perseus, the "true" mythic hero, demonstrates the right way to use that gained awareness. Bellerophon, the "false" mythic hero, demonstrates the wrong way to use that knowledge.

The central question involving these two protagonists seems to be whether a hero is defined by his actions or whether a hero's actions are heroic because a hero has performed them. Barth deals with the problem at length in his other novels, particularly in *The Sot-Weed Factor* and *Giles Goat-Boy.* The solution he comes to is that the question is misleading, or from a different perspective Barth concludes that the solution can only be a relative one. Barth resolves the question into what he calls "rich paradox": a hero acts according to his conception of heroics, based on past actions, yet his present actions redefine what heroics are for the future. A hero is a hero if he acts heroically.

The formulation is part of Barth's solution to the problem of writer's block. One must understand the past in order to comprehend the present, and thus be directed in future actions. Perseus and Bellerophon differ in that Perseus recapitulates his own history in order to progress while Bellerophon tries to conform to the larger historical pattern. Instead of being himself and acting on his awareness of history, Bellerophon tries to relive the pattern of history without changing it and becomes the comic counterpart of Perseus, for he acts with Perseus's consciousness of the past but without an individual consciousness. In the "lecture scroll," Polyeidus/Barth can ironically comment on the origin of the **"Bellerophoniad"**: "I envisioned a comic novella based on the myth [of Pegasus and the Chimera]; a companion-piece to '**Perseid**,' perhaps."

The difference between Perseus and Bellerophon is illustrated by their actions at the various turning points in their lives. Perseus's actions set an example of "true" heroics to which a reader can compare Bellerophon's actions. Before Perseus's major turning point, at the end of his First Flood (to use Bellerophon's categories), Perseus is bored with life. [The critic adds in a footnote: "Bellerophon divides his life, as well as Perseus's, into four "tides"—First Flood, First Ebb, Second Flood, Second Ebb—which roughly correspond to the biological changes of a woman: birth to puberty, puberty to sexual maturity, sexual maturity to menopause, and menopause to death."] He admits his marriage is "on the rocks," he is "twenty kilos overweight," and he "became convinced [he] was petrifying." Prompted by some introspective letters concerning his past (written by Calyxa, it turns out), Perseus decides to recapitulate his "good young days": "but it wasn't *just* vanity; no more were my nightly narratives: . . . it seemed to me that if I kept going over it carefully enough I might see the pattern, find the key." His recapitulation is a false lead, however, for Perseus's attempt to follow "the pattern" eventually leads to his "drowning" in Lake Triton.

The pattern Perseus follows is the one set by himself in his youth, from which he infers that he should "be himself." What he fails to understand is that "being himself" as a middle-aged man is not the same thing as "being himself" as a young man. Athene, representing wisdom, tries to tell Perseus so in the temple: "in general, she concluded, my mode of operation in this second enterprise must be contrary to my first's: on the one hand, direct instead of indirect . . . on the other, rather passive than active." Perseus protests "that direct passivity was not [his] style," yet his actions with the "Gray Ladies" result in an illuminating dip in the lake. As he sinks he spots "not mere folly" but the missing eye in the lake: "Dropped from the high point of my hubris, it winked now from the depths."

Now everything comes together for Perseus. He is saved by Medusa, discovers she is in love with him, and listens to Medusa's story of her life. If one can imagine the various levels of narration as a series of Chinese boxes, to use Barth's simile, then the various narratives converge in the story as follows, starting with the outermost box: Barth writing the **"Perseid"**; Perseus as constellation telling to Medusa as constellation the story of his narration to Calyxa; Perseus telling to Calyxa the story of Medusa's narration to himself by the shore of Lake Triton. Medusa's narration of her own life is interrupted by Calyxa's birthday and Calyxa's story of her life to Perseus, which ends coincidentally with the beginning of Perseus's story to Calyxa and the end of Perseus's First Ebb (the failure at Lake Triton). Such convergences, where all the Chinese boxes are finally collapsed, have different significances in Barth's work. In *Lost in the Funhouse* the boxes collapse around the word "love" or they collapse into silence as with Beckett. In the **"Perseid"** the convergence of narratives indicates the major turning-point in Perseus's life, for he has stopped to analyze and recapitulate his past through the use of Calyxa's murals. The last mural of the spiral gives out onto the desert, art blends into "reality," past turns into present, and Perseus sets out on the second half of his life—which should be, as for Shah Zaman, sweeter than the first half because of the awareness gained in recapitulation.

At the vertex of the turning point in Perseus's life is the unusual set of conditions surrounding Medusa's eyes—her ability to grant either immortality or petrifaction depending on the circumstances. Calyxa, the student of mythology, remarks on the lack of "any analogues for that motif." Perseus, then, finds himself on the shore of Lake Triton in a set of circumstances outside the pattern of mythic history, and he acts on his own impulses, avoiding Medusa's eyes, though he will "face" her eventually. Perseus's instinctive action leads to the above convergences.

Perseus succeeds finally in establishing himself as a hero, for he shows that he is capable of changing a pattern and not merely imitating it. Ultimately, Bellerophon fails as a hero because he lacks individuality—he never acts independently of his consciousness of how a hero should act, reinforced in the **"Bellerophoniad"** by the numerous imitations and repetitions of what has gone before. Bellerophon is both the central imitator and imitation in Part Three. He is constantly looking for the Pattern, but to imitate a pattern is to leave it unchanged. As Zeus reminds Polyeidus, another shapeshifting version of Barth, "By imitating perfectly the Pattern of Mythic Heroism, your

man Bellerophon has become a perfect imitation of a mythic hero." The emphasis in the statement is on the ironic perfection of his imitation.

Bellerophon is always a quarter-step behind Perseus, his actions seeming to parody those of Perseus. Bellerophon's life begins in the middle of Perseus's life; his *story* begins at the turning point of his life, but the transformation is a parody of the equivalent turning point in Perseus's life. Both men are middle-aged at their respective turning points, but in terms of the Pattern, Perseus is between his First Ebb and Second Flow (with Calyxa), whereas Bellerophon is still between his First Flow and First Ebb—which is to say, a quarter-step behind. Ironically, the recapitulation in Bellerophon's life is not of his own life, but a reading of the **"Perseid"**—a review of Perseus's life. In further contrast to Perseus, Bellerophon is still married to his first wife, and she suggests the sea journey instead of Bellerophon. The final irony is revealed at the end, when we learn that Bellerophon himself is only an imitation Bellerophon; he is actually Deliades imitating his dead brother, Bellerus.

The theme, then, of the **"Bellerophoniad"** might be called Recapitulation as Imitation or Parody. Most of the unusual paraphernalia in Part Three illustrate the theme. The actual quotation from Robert Graves' *The Greek Myths,* for example, which tells the story of Bellerophon, gives the reader some useful background information, but its primary function is ironical. Graves' account of Bellerophon is clearly part of the Pattern, an established addition to the corpus of literature, which has formed and ossified the mythological patterns, just as historians order history in their own patterns. Bellerophon, in contrast to Barth's own inclinations, attempts to fulfill the Pattern. All of Polyeidus's shapeshifting, while supposedly helping to direct Bellerophon, is ironically leading him on to that ultimate imitation in which Bellerophon turns into his own story. He becomes literally the printed words of his story, just as he literally "kills" the Chimera by ending the book—or turning into the book, as the last sentence of the novel suggests.

Another form of recapitulation in Part Three is that of Barth's own allusions to his previous works, virtually all of which are incorporated into the text in one way or another. The Polyeidus/Barth lecture scroll contains direct references to *The Sot-Weed Factor* and *Giles Goat-Boy* and indirect references to *Lost in the Funhouse* and *Chimera.* Slightly more concealed allusions to earlier works are the two variant stories of Bellerophon's "rape" of Anteia; the first version comes out of *The Floating Opera,* the second out of *The End of the Road.* At least two stories from *Lost in the Funhouse* are alluded to in a similar fashion: the jug Bellerophon finds with a message inside is taken from **"Water-Message"** (Polyeidus accidentally turns into Peter), and Bellerophon's visit to his childhood haunts recalls a scene taken from **"Lost in the Funhouse."**

The allusions to *The Sot-Weed Factor* and *Giles Goat-Boy* are less explicit, yet these novels are thematically closest to the **"Bellerophoniad."** Bellerophon calls to mind Ebenezer Cooke, and Polyeidus recalls Burlingame in several passages. Bellerophon has many of the same problems that

Ebenezer encounters, such as the problem of self-definition—does essence precede existence or vice-versa? Burlingame struggles with the same question, as does Polyeidus; one suspects Barth himself, the ultimate shapeshifter, has been plagued with similar self-doubts. An encounter between Bellerophon and Proetus raises the question in a slightly different manner. The passage calls to mind Giles, for one of his concerns was whether he was in fact a born hero or whether hero-work was just a result of a "passionate lack of alternatives." Other characters in the **"Bellerophoniad"** suggest *Giles Goat-Boy,* such as the ubiquitous Jerome B. Bray, who resembles Harold Bray in many ways.

As these examples show, Barth has recapitulated Barth in the **"Bellerophoniad,"** even to the point of including himself in various degrees of disguise. The purpose of these self-conscious integrations is to reinforce the theme of imitation and artifact in Part Three. Yet the process of viewing oneself from a distance, as Barth does when he includes himself in the story, has a further purpose, for it exemplifies the process of creating new material out of old material discussed in relation to the Genie and Scheherazade in the **"Dunyazadiad."** Jac Tharpe has described Barth's position this way:

> If he writes of the whole universe, he can think of himself as a powerful linguistic magician in that universe, who is a part of the comedy. If he creates universes, he may as well be a creator, a deity. He can possibly then write fictions about created universes in which the creator appears, as he does in no other universe we know. In this self-enclosed situation, finite but unbounded, the creator of the paradox is the incarnation of the paradox. Barth as-ifs Barth [*John Barth: The Comic Sublimity of Paradox,* 1974].

The same principle is at work in the **"Dunyazadiad,"** where Barth "as-ifs" Dunyazade within the "finite but unbounded" world of Scheherazade.

Chimera, too, is structured on a similar principle. The solution to writer's block is the paradox that both creates **Chimera** and is itself incarnated in the structure of the three parts. In the **"Dunyazadiad"** the "writer" is faced with the age-old problem of having only a limited number of stories to tell—of having exhausted possibilities—and yet he creates new possibilities by telling old stories with a modern consciousness. In the **"Perseid"** the "writer" is at his height. He tells a good story; he is a hero and lives a hero's life; and he becomes immortal, at least as immortal as language and literature or stars and constellations can be said to be. In the **"Bellerophoniad"** the "writer" finds that he may not be a hero; he may not be a storyteller. He suspects his life and stories are mere imitations, and that he himself is only an imitation. He believes the end is in sight, yet it is a chimera, an illusion, for one need only begin again at the beginning as Dunyazade and Barth have done.

Chimera is both a novel about the problem of exhausted possibilities in narrative art and a solution to that problem. The prominent role mythology plays in the novel is as significant as Barth's use of writer's block as a central theme, for the myths also have a double function. On one hand, the mythological tales serve as sources for the stories in **Chimera,** just as writer's block serves as a theme or motif to connect the stories; on the other, in the same way that writing about the problem of writer's block transcends the problem, the process of converting old stories—the myths—into new ones transcends the problem of "exhausted" possibilities.

In order to see exactly how mythology functions in the book, one must understand Barth's interest in myths. From his earlier works, at least as far back as *The Sot-Weed Factor* (1960), Barth has been fascinated with the idea that ontogeny (the development of an individual organism) recapitulates phylogeny (the evolution or development of a species). From this concept Barth's fundamental interest in mythology seems to spring. The concept implies that a man's development repeats the development or history of mankind, a concept which is analogous to Barth's solution to writer's block: to review the past in order to understand the present, which allows one to proceed. What especially interested Barth, however, was the relationship between the life of an individual and the historical life of mankind; the convergence of the two is myth.

In the spurious lecture scroll of Part Three, Barth summarizes some of his personal comments on mythology made in actual interviews: "Since myths themselves are among other things poetic distillations of our ordinary psychic experience and therefore point always to daily reality, to write realistic fictions which point always to mythic archetypes is in my opinion to take the wrong end of the mythopoetic stick, however meritorious such fiction may be in other respects." If one wants to comment on daily reality through the use of fictions, why write realistic fictions that suggest mythical archetypes that point back to reality, when one could write about myths directly as they relate to daily reality? While Jungians regard myths as "original revelations of the preconscious psyche, involuntary statements about unconscious psychic happenings," Robert Graves defines true myth "as the reduction to narrative shorthand of ritual mime performed on public festivals, and in many cases recorded pictorially on temple walls, vases, seals, bowls, mirrors, chests, shields, tapestries, and the like." He further states that "a true science of myth should begin with a study of archaeology, history, and comparative religion." Barth, obviously familiar with Graves, is not interested in a "true science of myth," but he seems to have been intrigued by Graves' conception of true myths. What Graves calls a "reduction to narrative shorthand of ritual mime" becomes for Barth "poetic distillations of our ordinary psychic experience," pointing always towards daily reality. The rituals of mankind, then, which form the common denominators of man's acquired knowledge (epistemology), become our myths. Yet myths are also distillations of ordinary experience, reflecting the individual's confrontations with daily reality—the confrontations that comprise his learning experience. If ontogeny did *not* recapitulate phylogeny, the Greek myths would presumably be of no interest to us.

Barth claims that a certain amount of knowledge is beneficial to a writer, but that too much knowledge is dangerous. Barth apparently follows his own advice, for without delving into too much mythology, he has taken ideas from Graves and rendered them fictionally. Mythology, then, becomes a means to an end instead of the end itself—it is treated symbolically. Graves cites the myth of Chimera as an example of a true myth and explains why the Chimera myth must have originated from various social, political, and religious conditions. What Barth has done by grabbing the "other end" of the mythopoeic stick is to treat myths realistically, instead of treating "reality" in accord with archetypal patterns.

Barth, in his concern with the "reality" of the Chimera myth, uses the elements of the myth that comment on daily experiences of an individual: Perseus awakens one day in a desert, "sea-leveled, forty, parched and plucked . . . and beleaguered by the serpents of [his] past"; Bellerophon, on the eve of his fortieth birthday, finds the **"Perseid"** floating on an ebbing tide and he stops to read it: "By the time he got to its last words he was forty and too tired." Barth has reduced the mythical hero to middle-aged man, so that one recognizes oneself in Scheherazade, Perseus, and Bellerophon.

Apart from the obvious use of myths for his "sources," Barth has integrated a number of aspects of the Chimera myth into his novel—again, apparently using Graves as a source. Graves writes that the Chimera was most likely a common emblem four thousand years ago in the form of a composite beast with a lion's head, goat's body, and serpent's tail. Each component would have represented—among other things—a season of the Queen of Heaven's sacred year—the Queen of Heaven being one of the many titles for the Mother-goddess or Great Goddess. The three parts of the Chimera, then, would be related to a number of calendar divisions: the moon's three phases—new, full, and old; the matriarch's three phases—maiden, nymph (nubile woman), and crone; spring, summer, and winter; and even the upper air, earth, and underworld.

Similarly, each of the three parts of *Chimera* emphasizes the appropriate aspect of the triad, on various levels. Dunyazade is the maiden-figure—her virginity and inexperience are stressed throughout the **"Dunyazadiad."** The stories in Part One take place at night with their conclusions coinciding with the break of day; the final exchange is always "Good morning." In accord with the learning stage of the triad, Dunyazade's experience at the foot of the King's bed is emphasized; just as the Genie and Scheherazade are continually discussing the similarities between storytelling and love-making, Dunyazade's learning experience has encompassed the best of both techniques—though only at a distance until her night with Shah Zaman.

Calyxa, the nymph of the **"Perseid,"** is a woman in the prime of life; she is twenty-five, adept at love-making, and "liberated" in a sense that Scheherazade could only hope for. Medusa is also nymph-like when she meets Perseus and "rescues" him from middle-age. Stories are begun in the evening in Part Two, opening typically with "Good evening" and ending with "Good night." Perseus sets out on his sea-voyage with Andromeda "when spring gave

way to summer." Once the reader is conscious of the allusions to time of day, season, or stage in life, their abundance becomes obvious.

Within the **"Bellerophoniad,"** the third part of the triad is emphasized. Philonoe is the principal crone-figure, but Zeus's wife, Hera, the classic crone of Greek mythology, also makes a brief appearance at the end. The ebbing tide and waning moon are prevalent, just as Bellerophon is past forty and tired. After obtaining an extra-strong shot of Hippomanes from Sibyl the whore—a not unfamiliar character-type in Part Three—Bellerophon is dumped by Pegasus, only to wake up "bruised, headachy, sore." Instead of being attended by nymph-like Calyxa, as Perseus was, Bellerophon ends up in jail under the rule of crone-like Anteia, who has reasserted the matriarchal system. Finally, Bellerophon seems to have "bad nights" all too often, and his story *begins* with the greeting "Good night."

As these examples show, Barth used different aspects of mythology—especially drawing on Graves, and to a large extent the mythical elements reinforce the central theme of writer's block and middle-aged inertia and despair. The result of Barth's use of mythology is an array of details which symbolize the conversion of myth to fictional reality, ritual to daily reality. At the same time, the details enforce the overall structure and unity of the three parts, adding depth to the superstructure of the main theme.

A third way in which Barth integrates the idea of exhausted possibilities into his work is through the analogy of love-making to writing. The analogy sets the tone of the novel in that Barth's attitude towards writing is revealed in *Chimera* through the extended comparison between the two activities. Barth's attitude towards writing and life in general infuses the novel with its tone of half-irony, half-seriousness.

Barth has talent for appropriating material or ideas for his fiction and then both exalting and reducing that material within the context of the work. In *Chimera* mythology is reverenced as the treasure-house of ur-fictions, yet Barth seems to treat myths almost profanely in his modifications of their traditional characterizations and plots. Love, similarly, is both the final sacred mystery of mankind and the most natural, profane act. The tension between these opposing tendencies establishes the tone in Barth's works; the reader is constantly drawn to the optimism and vitality of the characters, but the attraction is countered by Barth's assumption that life is painful and meaningless. One senses Barth's frustration at having to settle for relative values and partial answers; that he feels he does have to is clearly indicated in all of his earlier novels. When Barth speaks of the "felt ultimacies of our time," he includes his sense of the lack of any absolute value system in our society. Such an attitude on Barth's part informs his approach to literature; literature becomes much less a means to an end, containing some message or instruction, and more of an autonomous or self-supporting art form, with references to itself. A few examples of how Barth treats the relationship between art and love will help to illuminate his attitude towards literature.

The most immediate connection between art and love is

the correlation between sexual potency and one's ability to overcome the various stumbling blocks in life—writer's block, middle-age, or whatever. Scheherazade, then, is the most prolific and apparently successful storyteller, and her sexual prowess is at least comparable. Calyxa is adept at love-making, but Perseus is impotent so long as he feels himself a failure. As his story and recapitulation progress, as his vanity and expectation for the future increase, his sexual potency does likewise. Bellerophon, in his various attempts to follow the Pattern, either rejects sex altogether, as with Anteia, or forces it, as in his rape of Melanippe, for the sake of the Pattern. The relatively little sex in Part Three correlates with Bellerophon's failure as a mythic hero.

The relationship between art and love, then, is most explicit in Part One, in the discussions between the Genie and Scheherazade, who both assume that life is going to be painful. Literature, like love, is one of the more pleasant aspects of life, that helps people overcome their difficulties. The Genie calls these "civilized delights," available to anyone capable of "goodwill, attention, and a moderately cultivated sensibility." In particular, the Genie refers to the "treasure of art, which if it could not redeem the barbarities of history or spare us the horrors of living and dying, at least sustained, refreshed, expanded, ennobled, and enriched our spirits along the painful way." The Genie and Shah Zaman both come to a similar conclusion regarding love: although love is a risky enterprise and fraught with the same dangers as life—the pain of disappointment, rejection, and despair—it is still worth the risk. The key to this attitude is the magic phrase "as if," which Barth worked through for himself in his first four novels. One must approach love *as if* it would last forever; one must approach life *as if* it had intrinsic value or *as if* it were not going to be a disappointment.

Finally, the relationship between art and love is based on technique. The success of both is dependent on a polished and varied technique or style, according to Barth. As the Genie points out, however, both activities—storytelling and love-making—are by their very nature erotic. He cites the circumstances framing the tales in the *Decameron* as one example, where storytelling is a "kind of *substitute* for making love—an artifice in keeping with the artificial nature of their little society." The Genie remarks in reference to Scheherazade's situation that "narrative . . . was a love-relation, not a rape: its success depended upon the reader's consent and cooperation, which she could withhold or at any moment withdraw; also upon her own combination of experience and talent for enterprise, and the author's ability to arouse, sustain, and satisfy her interest."

Barth's position, then, is quite similar to that of his contemporary, Nabokov, for whom a novel is a chess game that has the author's moves already programed into it, and that the reader plays by reading. The better the reader, the more demands he places on the author, but the process of reading is the point of the game. Similarly, Barth's main metaphor for writing is the act of love. The metaphor emphasizes the process or act of doing something, as opposed to any specific goal at the end. For both metaphors, chess-

playing and love-making, *what* one says or does is not so important as *how* one says or does it. Now, however, Barth and Nabokov may part company, for Barth seems to take a more pessimistic view of the value of the game itself. They both believe in the playing of the game, but Nabokov seems to believe that the act has some kind of absolute value, while Barth appears to believe he is accepting a relative value for lack of any absolute values in life.

As Barth demonstrates in his earlier novels, any attempt he makes to discover meaning or value in life is going to resolve itself in rich paradox, at best, and despairing contradiction, at worst. Ironically, literature and writing become more important to Barth than they might be if he believed in some kind of absolute value-system in life. Literature may not have any ultimate value, but Barth writes "as if" it were of life-or-death importance in his world. Barth's "as if" attitude prevails throughout his work, whether he is dealing with writer's block or life, love or mythology. A tone of deadly seriousness lies underneath the playful prose associated with Barth's "style." In the process and through the process of working out his own writer's block, the chimeric Genie has certainly "sustained, refreshed, expanded, ennobled, and enriched our spirits along the painful way." (pp. 59-71)

Jerry Powell, "John Barth's 'Chimera': A Creative Response to the Literature of Exhaustion," in Critique: Studies in Modern Fiction, *Vol. XVIII, No. 2, 1976, pp. 59-72.*

Cynthia Davis (essay date 1980)

[*In the following excerpt, Davis examines gender identity in* Chimera *and asserts that Barth upholds a bias toward a male perspective which reduces his female characters to symbols of "non-human aspects of life."*]

John Barth's fictions have always used male-female relationships to explore questions of identity. Barth's characterizations have escaped criticism, however, because his fictions have gradually abandoned the pretense of realism, in favor of parodic and self-conscious techniques. The "self-reflexive" approach allows Barth to explore the deeply traditional structures—the myths—that he finds at the heart of fiction, of experience, and of perception. This pursuit of fundamental form has led him to a mythic definition of male and female identities, one that underlies all the work but becomes most explicit in *Chimera.* The notions of gender identity revealed in Barth's work are important first because they *are* traditional; they reflect the assumptions inherent in a male-centered mythology. But Barth extends the myth, employing it as metaphor for the condition of the artist/perceiver. That "new" myth contains more than the dangers of the old male-female dichotomy; it is a fascinating example of the ways that contemporary subjective relativism can support a myth even more deadening to women. Thus Barth's ideas of gender identity are important not only in illuminating his own fictional views, but also in tracing the emergence of old sex roles in new disguises. (p. 309)

[In *Chimera*] Barth presents . . . varied women characters, many "feminist" in their resentment of male oppression, and heterosexual relations become a central concern. The language makes contemporary references to "raising consciousness" and "male sexist pigs," and all the couples persistently analyze their relations in terms of sex roles and sexual politics. Further, *Chimera*'s development through three novellas, each an elaborate extension of the preceding one, is clearly linked to Barth's larger development by direct allusions to the earlier stories. For example, the description of Rennie Morgan [in *The End of the Road*] "whipping her head from side to side" is transferred to several characters in *Chimera,* and Bellerophon's different versions of his sexual encounter with Anteia repeat language and situations from both [*The Floating Opera* and *The End of the Road*]. Such connections encourage expectations that these stories will further explore some of the problems raised in previous works.

The foundation of *Chimera*'s sex-role patterning is described by the Genie in the **"Dunyazadiad"**: "The teller's role, he felt, regardless of his actual gender, was essentially masculine, the listener's or reader's feminine, and the tale was the medium of their intercourse." After admitting the possibility of (temporary) role-reversal, he adds that such "femininity" need not be "docile or inferior," that one could be a passive "sender" or an active "interpreter." There are two key concepts here: the idea that gender identity is defined by mode of being (receptive, communicative) rather than specific action or relative value, and a kind of Lawrentian idea of balance between equal but opposing polar principles. This view cannot be disposed of as "only" a metaphor, for it is repeatedly supported by situational patterns in these three novellas. The **"Dunyazadiad"** opens with a female narrator, but she describes a more "fitting" situation—Scheherazade receiving "her" tales from the Genie—and Dunyazade's narration is qualified by the two following sections of the novella, one dominated by Shah Zaman's story, and one in the voice of Genie-Barth. In the following novellas, males (Perseus and Bellerophon) tell their life-stories to women. Both, through enfolded narratives, speak to two women at once; that is, Perseus repeats to Medusa almost exactly the tale he told earlier to Calyxa, and Bellerophon goes through the same process with Melanippe and Philonoë. Such double narration directs attention to the contrasts between two types of women. Both types are still defined by reference to the central male, as his "listener" or "interpreter," and his choice between them reflects his choice of identity. The first type, seen in Perseus' nymph Calyxa and Bellerophon's wife Philonoë (and many minor characters), is the devoted worshipper of the man, like Anastasia in *Giles Goat-Boy*. Such women find fulfillment in the man and accept him completely, knowing his weaknesses but needing a hero. They tend to take what Barth calls the "Tragic View of Sex and Temperament," believing that the dream of "perfect equality between men and women," while "the only defensible value in that line," is probably unattainable and even hinders the enjoyment or real, imperfect love. Seeing the gap between ideal and reality, and being "personally unsuited for independence," these women resign themselves to temporal mortal life; not expecting perfection, they accept simple "superiority" to themselves. Despite their love, then, they are reminders of the fall from the ideal, so their admiration cannot sustain the

hero. Perseus' friend Sibyl is another version of this form, restoring him to potency only by introducing him to sex, death, and madness. His wife Andromeda is the worst extreme, devotion gone and only the ugly reminders of mortality left. This type is clearly an extension of Barth's early women, the symbols of external physical reality; once "both the cause of [the hero's] labor and its reward," the demand for choice and consequence, they finally remind him of the arbitrariness and imperfection of the labor. So Jane, Rennie, and Joan [from earlier novels] are the predecessors of Andromeda, Calyxa, and Philonoë—all reminders of consequence and death in temporal life.

But there is a second type of woman, heretofore incompletely developed in characters like Anna Cooke [in *The Sot-Weed Factor*], but now very important, as the likeness of names suggests: Medusa, Melanippe, Melissa. This figure is ultimately the male's "true love" in *Chimera,* and she functions as a Muse rather than discouraging the heroic quest. Melissa, the Genie's absent mistress, is vaguely defined but partially identified with Scheherazade, his "inspiration." Medusa, in the **"Perseid,"** is the purest form of the type; once the petrifying monster, now she can rejuvenate Perseus, though she risks becoming a monster again if he does not love her. In the novella's climax, she gives him the best of both worlds—immortal life as a constellation, mortal life as man. The dual existence is the model for fulfillment in art and love, paralleling the Genie's dictum that nothing is ideal, nothing lasts forever, but "we must live as if it can and will." That "as if" resonates throughout *Chimera,* offering its central paradox. First, the ideal is seen as having its own reality; it is not life, but a distillation or shaping of it. Thus the co-existence of the two Perseuses, the danger that Medusa might petrify her hero, the consistent failure to make woman into the dream, the fiction's repeated separation of idea from reality. But the gap between the two worlds is not all: there is also a relation between them. "Some fictions," says the Genie, are "so much more valuable than fact" that they become "real." The immortal form, in art or love, is not life itself, but is related to it, can affect it, sometimes even transform it. So one can choose to love "as if" the ideal were true, and the force of the attempt might even make it happen. Perseus and Medusa seem to succeed; their faith and love go beyond material fact, and the mortal woman, transformed by the "as if" into an ideal, in turn transforms the hero, and they exist on both the mortal and immortal planes. That possibility may explain the emphasis on commitment in the earlier works, despite the failures of the love relationships; and there is an early version of the double view in Eb's relations with Anna and Joan—the untouchable sister and the all-too-real wife. Now the two are combined in one woman. But Melanippe is a less reassuring version of the Muse, and her story returns *Chimera* to the breakdown seen in the other fictions. Bellerophon sees her as ideal and immortal, but her vociferous denials and his pursuit of perfection lead to their separation and his failure. The "as if," the delicate balance between reality and desire, fails, and Bellerophon admits that he has no talent for loving. By following the dualistic **"Perseid,"** this ending seems to quash any hope for an integration of ideal and real, and casts an ironic light on the earlier story. Given Bellerophon's final failure to reach

Olympus and the absolute disjunction between Perseus' two lives, the nature and power of the Muse become questionable. Her image contradicts the woman's existence in reality, and even her power seems derivative. Medusa's transformation of Perseus depends on his feeling for her; Bellerophon is inspired by an image of Melanippe that she rejects, and her quest is destroyed in his pursuit of his own. Any power the Muse has, then, is a catalyst or vehicle for the hero's imagination, not as independent element. Thus the early paradox of the shapeless and burdensome woman-as-reality is further exaggerated into open conflict by *Chimera*'s female types. The woman can drag a man down to physical mortal life, but cannot elevate him. Ultimately, she can only be a part of his transcendent vision by denying her own reality. Far from having an integrative effect, she becomes the symbol of dualism.

Chimera is not, of course, only "about" love, and it is certainly not intended to offer fully dimensional women characters, any more than its obsessed and flippant men are complex persons. But even allowing for the character typing of self-reflexive fiction, the kinds of limits the author places on his characters can reveal the problems of his position: the only successful relationship in *Chimera* (Perseus and Medusa) is clearly placed outside real life; the women are still extraordinarily passive, by choice or force subjected to male decisions, and they are truly functional only as symbols of the hero's choices. The male-female polarity makes conceptualization a male attribute, and so any sense of self a woman could have would be in imitation of a male model (like the Amazons) or in service of a male goal (as Muse). The only other alternative is to sink into the role of abiding flesh. Melanippe, for example, rejects Bellerophon's image of her to become wife and prolific mother. Over and over bright women, like Philonoë and Melanippe, give up thinking to have babies; magical women, like Medusa, derive identity and power from appearance and from male control; heroic women, like the Amazons, define themselves in imitation of and opposition to men. Outside male concepts, they have no identity but that of the unthinking physical realm. Nowhere do Barth's women have a role equal to men; they neither determine their lives and define themselves as men do, nor exert, in their own distinct way, the irresistible influence on men that they themselves encounter. To call them "interpreters" of men's "stories" is no answer; their "interpretations" are rarely useful to anyone, including themselves. In fact, their "theories" are so often mere echoing of the man's views that they are more recorders than interpreters. (Barth's short story **"Autobiography,"** whose "mother" is a dictaphone and "father" a human being, makes this pattern explicit.)

This identification of woman with external physical world, however powerful, and man with conscious humanity is a dangerous dichotomy that becomes much more than a useful gimmick. Barth does sometimes try to make the division seem "merely" symbolic, by stressing the limits of his narrative; for example, Bellerophon's summary view of his women is modified by a reminder that it is "strictly from [his] viewpoint," and the "impersonal" Melanippe who is "immortal" symbol is distinguished from her "private un-categorizable self." Such elements suggest that the

female-reality connection exists simply because these are male stories; thus the problem is the individual subject-object relationship, not gender identity. So woman is "reality" not as a role definition, but just from a man's point of view. But Barth's general approach belies that kind of justification. Even in Dunyazade's narration, men other than the narrator are not reduced to reality principles, but represent serious alternative views; even her own plan is finally made possible only by consent of her bridegroom. Only women are consistently reduced to vegetative life in Barth's fictions. Women who do long for more are punished; they end up bitter, like Anteia, or settle for non-heroic life after all, like Melanippe. Such is Barth's interweaving of myth and aesthetic that it is hard to tell whether he uses the pattern without clearly seeing its implications or actually attacks feminism by what he thinks are its spokeswomen. At any rate, the assumptions in the fiction are inconsistent, turning on the unnecessary and contradictory identification of individual woman with biological woman, of symbol with reality, of point of view with truth. In work so concerned with the relation of myth and reality, the confusion is especially striking. Barth's obsession with point of view holds the key; he accepts a male-oriented mythic structure, in which the male is human, the female everything else. He does not question those assumptions in the way that he questions others, but accepts a symbolic identification as literally true.

The emphasis on point of view and shaping perceiver, in fact, produces images that are even more reductive to women than the original myth. Having assigned men and women to different poles with distinct philosophical and aesthetic meanings, Barth opts for only one side of the "balance." His protagonists, like himself, prefer myth and abstraction to reality, so they come alive as opposing characters do not. *Chimera* rationalizes the preference: "Since myths themselves are among other things poetic distillations of our ordinary psychic experience and therefore point always to daily reality, to write realistic fictions which point always to mythic archetypes is . . . to take the wrong end of the mythopoeic stick . . . Better to address the archetypes directly." Fiction is "truer" than particular reality, says Shah Zaman; but as both passages suggest, fictions and myths are so important because they "point to" reality, because the ideal shines through concrete circumstance. With Barth's heroes, however, the choice of the archetype does not lead back to daily reality, to combine idea and fact. His characters choose between the two, not acting "as if " the real were ideal, but surrendering one for the other. Even Perseus, who has both mortal and eternal life, finds no visible connection between the two levels, and Bellerophon leaves reality behind for his doomed flight to Olympus. They make the choice that Barth makes with his stylization and reworking of myth: to pursue the fiction and let the fact take care of itself. When such an approach is linked to the symbolic forms Barth uses, it is inevitable that women will be crushed or discarded by men.

In light of the emphasis on balance, such a result might seem a failure; but the real feeling of the novels does center on failure—in love and in other analogous situations. Barth wants to show the paradoxical nature of life, but keeps coming down on one side of the paradox, unable to resolve the polar tensions without surrender of one pole. A perspective so heavily weighted in favor of the "masculine," conceptual, creative pole can hardly celebrate "feminine" principles, particularly when the narrative itself displays the triumph of idea over fact, scheme over ambiguous life. Barth's preference for the "male" side eliminates even the power suggested by the mythic dichotomy, reducing the potent innerness of the Earth Mother to the "vacuum" of the not-self, and reducing the energy of the Muse to the mimicry of the mirror-self. The result is female characters who are always seen from outside, who are reduced to symbols, symbols moreover of the non-human aspects of life, and who are denied power even in that area by narrative insistence on the creative male perceiver. (pp. 315-21)

Cynthia Davis, "Heroes, Earth Mothers and Muses: Gender Identity in Barth's Fiction," in The Centennial Review, *Vol. XXIV, No. 2, Spring, 1980, pp. 309-21.*

My feeling about technique in art is that it has about the same value as technique in love-making. That is to say, heartfelt ineptitude has its appeal and so does heartless skill; but what you want is passionate virtuosity.

—John Barth, on the dust jacket of Lost in the Funhouse, *1968.*

Charles B. Harris   (essay date 1983)

[*Harris is an American educator and critic who specializes in modern American literature. In the following excerpt from his* Passionate Virtuosity: The Fiction of John Barth, *he analyzes the relationship between sex and language in* Lost in the Funhouse.]

One of John Barth's major concerns is the mysterious relationship between sex and other forms of human experience. While implicit in Barth's fiction from the beginning, this relationship receives its first explicit reference in *The End of the Road* when Jacob Horner makes the following observation:

> If one had no other reason for choosing to subscribe to Freud, what could be more charming than to believe that the whole vaudeville of the world, the entire dizzy circus of history, is but a fancy mating dance. . . . Who would not delight in telling some extragalactic tourist, "On our planet, sir, males and females copulate. Moreover, they enjoy copulating. But for various reasons they cannot do this whenever, wherever, and with whomever they choose. Hence all this running around that you observe. Hence the world"?

Ambrose, the narrator/protagonist of *Lost in the Funhouse* (1968), reaches a similar conclusion. Reflecting upon the funhouse tumbling-barrel which upends girls so that "their boyfriends and others could see up their dresses," Ambrose suddenly realizes that such apparent sexual byplay is really "the whole point . . . [of] the entire funhouse!" All that normally shows, he continues, "like restaurants and dance halls and clothing and test-your-strength machines, was merely preparation and intermission." Since the funhouse stands for the universe, Barth's meaning becomes clear. At the center of all human activity lies sex, that "shluppish whisper, continuous as seawash round the globe." At one point Ambrose even goes so far as to wonder whether his story contains any other "sound besides the little slap of thigh on ham, like water sucking at the chine-boards of a skiff."

Observations such as the latter suggest what is perhaps the major concern of *Lost in the Funhouse,* the relationship between sex and language—ultimately, between sex and art. Barth's familiarity with the Freudian notion of language as sublimated sexuality receives specific attention in *Chimera* when Dunyazade comments on the comparisons between narrative and sexual art made by Scheherazade and the Genie:

> The Genie declared that in his time and place there were scientists of the passions who maintained that language itself, on the one hand, originated in "infantile pregenital erotic exuberance, polymorphously perverse," and that conscious attention, on the other, was a "libidinal hypercathexis"—by which magic phrases they seemed to mean that writing and reading, or telling and listening, were literally ways of making love.

A form of substitute gratification, narrative, in Norman O. Brown's phrase, is "made out of love" [*Life against Death: The Psychoanalytical Meaning of History,* 1959].

For Ambrose, however, art fails to gratify. He would much prefer to be among the lovers for whom the funhouse is fun, but the exuberant spontaneity necessary to young love (witness the antics of Peter and Magda) is checked in Ambrose by an almost paralyzing artistic self-consciousness. Even when Magda kneels to initiate the ten-year-old Ambrose into sex, his self-consciousness prevents his full enjoyment: "though he had breathed heavily, groaned as if ecstatic, what he'd really felt throughout was an odd detachment, as though someone else were Master. Strive as he might to be transported, he heard his mind take notes upon the scene: *This is what they call* passion. *I am experiencing it.*" Even at the height of pleasure Ambrose must watch himself react, must convert the experience into language.

Other protagonists in *Funhouse* (each a mask for Ambrose, the true protagonist and "author" of the book) suffer similarly. The narrator's difficulty in composing **"Title,"** for example, comes between him and his understandably frustrated mistress. Words replace deeds in their relationship, and she at one point exclaims, "Is this what we're going to talk about, our obscene verbal problem?" While composing **"Life-Story"** the narrator is interrupted by his mistress, who declares, "The passion of love . . . does not in fact play in your life a role of sufficient importance to sustain my presence here. It plays in fact little role at all outside your imaginative and/or ary life." The commitment to art obstructs even the love of the **"Anonymiad"**'s nameless minstrel for his beloved Merope, as he deserts her for experiences he believes will make him a better storyteller. Tricked by Aegisthus, however, he ends up alone on a desert island, with only imaginary experience left open to him. Each narrator (others could be named) seems destined by artistic temperament to be a partial participant in life. Like Mann's Tonio Kröger, each stands apart from experience, observing and ordering it for others. As Ambrose sadly concludes the title story of **Funhouse,** "he will construct funhouses for others and be their secret operator—though he would rather be among the lovers for whom funhouses are designed."

Unfortunately, the same self-consciousness responsible for Ambrose's failure as a lover also inhibits his success at storytelling. A certain degree of innocent spontaneity, it seems, is necessary for literature as well as for love. Yet Ambrose stands at what he supposes is the end of a long history of narrative literature. And, as the narrator of **"Title"** avers, "Historicity and self-awareness . . . while ineluctable and even greatly to be prized, are always fatal to innocence and spontaneity." Condemned to write, unfit by temperament simply to repeat what has already been written, yet aware that little hope exists for producing something new, Ambrose faces the dreary prospect articulated by the narrator of **"Life-Story"**: "He rather suspected that the medium and genre in which he worked— the only ones for which he felt any vocation—were moribund if not already dead." A paragraph later the same somber observation is applied to Western society. For Ambrose, culture and art, like his personal life, seem bereft of meaningful possibilities.

In "The Literature of Exhaustion," published the year before **Funhouse,** Barth expresses general agreement with this assessment, at least as it applies to narrative. Yet he refuses to let the apocalyptic ambience immobilize him as an artist. "The man or woman whose style I admire most," he has said, "is the one who has a sophisticated awareness of alternatives; who knows the tragic futility of actions, yet doesn't yield to castration by all his sophistication." Barth demonstrates his own sophisticated awareness of alternatives by examining several in **Funhouse.** The one he chooses to employ involves turning "ultimacy, exhaustion, paralyzing self-consciousness and the adjective-weight of accumulated history . . . against itself to make something new and valid, the essence whereof would be the impossibility of making something new," which is of course the alternative explored in "The Literature of Exhaustion." But Barth adopts yet another tactic in confronting the dilemma. While unmentioned though employed in **Funhouse,** this tactic receives specific comment in **Chimera.** The Barth-genie tells Scheherazade and Dunyazade that his literary career "had reached a hiatus which he would have been pleased to call a turning-point if he could have espied any way to turn: he wished neither to repudiate nor to repeat his past performances; he aspired to go beyond them toward a future they were not at-

tuned to and, by some magic, at the same time go back to the original springs of narrative." Barth, that is, wishes to mine the riches of a still usable past without ignoring the present and future, a gesture he has described as "having it both ways."

One method that allows Barth to have it both ways in **Funhouse** is his return to oral narrative via the tape recorder. He slyly suggests the nature and function of this regression by naming his protagonist Ambrose. Ambrose is named after the fourth-century saint because bees swarmed about both their faces while they were infants. But St. Ambrose is significant to Barth's purposes for yet another reason. In *The Gutenberg Galaxy* Marshall McLuhan, with whose theories Barth is familiar, discusses the wonderment described by Augustine when he saw St. Ambrose reading silently. In antiquity through the Middle Ages, McLuhan reminds us, reading necessarily meant reading aloud. The reason for monk's carrels in monasteries was not to insure the reader's privacy but to prevent his oral reading from disturbing others. St. Ambrose's silent reading represented a significant stage in the transition from oral to print-oriented literary cultures. Similarly, Ambrose Mensch's experiments with tape represent a transition from visual media back to the oral and auditory. Thus the bees land on his eyes and ears, rather than on his mouth. Print, according to McLuhan, is an extension of the eyes, the tape recorder an extension of the ear. By landing about Ambrose's eyes and ears, the bees predict his dual use of print and tape.

The naming of Ambrose is significant in yet another sense. It coincides with his weaning, since the bees that inspire his name also sting his mother's breast, an event so painfully traumatic that Andrea will have little more to do with the infant Ambrose. Ambrose's naming, his initiation into a world of words, thus coincides with his forced separation from his mother. Psychologists have often associated weaning with the crisis of differentiation, the infantile trauma at which point the child suddenly becomes aware that he is distinct from others. Barth's association of this crisis with naming—thus with language—suggests the theories of Jacques Lacan, the relationship of whose thought to *Lost in the Funhouse* has been persuasively argued by Christopher D. Morris ["Barth and Lacan: The World of the Moebius Strip," *Critique*, 1975]. According to Lacan, a newborn child exists as an "absolute subject"; his relationship to a world he cannot yet distinguish from himself is purely intransitive. At some point in his early development, presumably around the time of weaning, he becomes aware of a lack, an absence of something (the mother's breast?), which disturbs the state of seamless concord he had previously enjoyed. For the first time the child conceives of himself as a self, an "I" apart from the Other. Language becomes the mode by which he attempts to reappropriate the Other and restore his lost sense of unity. As Anthony Wilden explains, "Lacan views speech as a movement toward something, an attempt to fill the gap, without which speech could not be articulated." Paradoxically, language leads both toward and away from that holistic state man wishes to reattain. It leads to that state because its secret motivation is the desire for annihilation, the end to all distinctions; it leads away because language by its very nature is a spatializing and temporalizing medium, thus is responsible for the very world of distinctions it secretly wishes to dissolve. "Reality," that is, is essentially a linguistic construct of our own creation—a Schopenhauerian as well as Nietzschean notion Barth has called "unexceptionable."

Language, as well as the "reality" it fashions, cuts us off from our lost "authentic" self as surely as it signals that separation. The mythic desire to return to origins is at base the desire to rediscover the authentic self that existed in a state before ego, before language. "Since the discovery of the lack of object is for Lacan the condition and the cause of desire," explains Anthony Wilden, "the adult quest for transcendence, lost time, lost paradise, or any of the myriad forms the lack of object may take . . . can be reduced, if one wishes, to the . . . question asked by Oedipus: 'Who (or what) am I?'" Yet, Wilden continues, the very fact that this question is asked verifies the subject's recognition "that he is neither who he thinks he is nor what he wants to be, since at the level of the *parole vide* he will always find that he is another." The ego, the only "self" we and others acknowledge, is a linguistic category constructed of a medium appropriated from another. As Ambrose muses, "I and my sign are neither one nor quite two." Moreover, not only is our language the "discourse of the other," but our identity is no more than the "internalization of the other through identification." We locate the self in the other; thus our "I", our ego, is another self, fundamentally objective rather than subjective, pure subjectivity lying only in the prenatal state before our fall into language and consciousness.

It is for this reason in **"Echo"** that Narcissus' self-knowledge must remain partial: "it was never himself Narcissus craved, *but his reflection,* the Echo of his fancy" (italics mine). We linger forever "on the autognostic verge" because the self we hope to know is always an *other,* a reflection of the other internalized through identification, just as the language we speak is always ultimately the discourse of the other from which it has been appropriated. The voice which leads Narcissus to the Donaconan spring, while resembling his own, is really another's, Echo's, whose own voice is similarly the appropriation of another's. Both Narcissus and Echo seek self-effacement—yet the self they wish to efface is really a reflection of another. So long as they remain in a world of words, they remain locked into the discourse of the other. Narcissus and Echo, despite their apparent differences, "come to the same."

In his attempt to embrace his reflected self, Narcissus plunges into water. Throughout *Funhouse* water is associated with language, which (like the sea) envelops mankind. Messages are received from the sea in two stories; the sperm cell, himself a message ("both vessel and contents"), journeys a night sea; Ambrose struggles with his story at Ocean City and wonders if that story is nothing more than the "slap slap of thigh on ham, like water sucking at the chine-boards of a skiff"; and bodies of water figure in **"Menelaiad," "Two Meditations,"** even **"Petition"** (Prajadhipok is Supreme Arbiter of the Ebb and Flow of the Tide). But if water in *Funhouse* suggests language, that

autotelic, self-referential medium in which man is awash, it has another significance as well. Archetypally, water signifies the return to the preformal, holistic state before words and world. In this more obvious yet perhaps more basic sense, water reinforces the motif of the return to origins so important to *Funhouse.* Thus water as symbol contains both poles that comprise the essence of language. Language fundamentally seeks to close all subject-object dichotomies and to relocate single, holistic selfhood, yet by its very nature it creates distinctions, confirming the other from which it has been appropriated and with which it would merge.

Narcissism contains a similar ambivalence, which may partially explain Barth's decision to retell the Narcissus-Echo myth. In Norman O. Brown's formulation, narcissism is not restricted to self-love but ultimately represents a desire to recover the state of primal narcissism when the self was indistinguishable from "a world of love and pleasure." The development of the ego forces a departure from this holistic state, which in turn results in "a vigorous attempt to recover it." Self-love, then, like Eros in general, is "fundamentally a desire for union (being one) with objects in the world." What manifests itself as an intensely inner-directed love really conceals a passion to re-collect the world of objects and others into a holistic and prepredicative selfhood.

Barth, then, seems to have chosen the Narcissus-Echo myth because of its relevance to selfhood, language, and the return to origins. But one other implication of the myth appealed to Barth as well. In her various authorial stages, Echo's history parallels the history of narrative literature. As a teller of tales she at first had a body (i.e., an authorial "presence") and her own voice (i.e., she could re-invent "reality" to suit her artistic purposes). After Hera's punishment she retains her body and voice, but now she can only repeat the words of others, a state roughly equivalent to representationalism or realism. In love with Narcissus, she pines away until only her mimetic voice remains, moving into the next state: the "dehumanized" art of the self-effaced narrator. In Barth's story even her voice has ceased to be hers, as it imitates not just the words but the actual voices of others. She has become what Barth calls a "proto-Ampex."

Part of Barth's point seems to be that narrative history represents a progressive movement away from that mythic stage when story, and thus world, was fresh and seemingly inexhaustible. At the cosmogonic moment all "reality" remained to be created; out of the pregnant, primeval condition, poet-magi called the world. Once established, however, the world-become-fact replaced the mythic time of origins. Rather than invent "reality," artists represented an already invented world. Literature relinquished its role as creator of realities, becoming instead a validator of "preexistent," "objective" reality. Objectivity became an esthetic value, as did impersonality. Total absence of authorial presence became a goal. Yet even the super-realism of a Robbe-Grillet, say, still suffers "overmuch presence." As "sharp-eyed Tiresias" espies, "one may yet distinguish narrator from narrative, medium from message. One lesson remains to be learned." Echo learns that lesson as she takes the final step on the long road away from subjectivity. Radically mimetic, she becomes an organic tape recorder. This point having been reached, Tiresias speculates, "perhaps the narrative proper may resume."

Barth's implication seems to be that behind the development of narrative literature lies a desire to exhaust literary possibilities, to extend to the limits the boundaries of objective presentation so narrative can at last collapse back into the subjectivity of the mythic moment. "What the mind finally seeks," writes Carter Wheelock, "is a new arrangement of reality, and to achieve this it must go back to the mythical condition prior to the gods, before language; for out of that pregnancy some more adequate Gods, some better language may come, though it be faceless and wordless" [*The Mythmaker: A Study of Motif and Symbol in the Short Stories of Jorge Luis Borges,* 1969]. Before this radical regress becomes possible, however, the full potential of the present must be depleted. Thus the extreme nature of Echo's final act of self-effacement, like the radically innovative nature of the experimental fictions in *Funhouse,* is fundamentally eschatological. As [Mircea] Eliade maintains, "Eschatology is only the prefiguration of a cosmogony to come. But every eschatology insists on this fact: the New Creation cannot take place before this world is abolished once and for all."

Barth's stories are never seriously eschatological any more than they offer themselves as new cosmogonies. But Barth uses both notions metaphorically; he propels Echo forward toward some eschatological finale while himself moving backward toward origins through his use of ancient myths and an appropriately fabulative mode. Thus he acknowledges both horns of the contemporary writer's dilemma: the inexhaustibility of the narrative impulse on the one hand, and the seeming exhaustion of narrative resources on the other. In the process he constructs an ingenious emblem for the present predicament of narrative art while managing to go "on with the story."

"Echo" is emblematic of the conditions of contemporary fiction in yet another sense. In his "Seven Additional Author's Notes" Barth offers the following description of point of view in **"Echo"**: "Inasmuch as the nymph in her ultimate condition repeats the words of others in their own voices, the words of 'Echo' on the tape or the page may be regarded validly as hers, Narcissus's, Tiresias's, mine, or any combination or series of the four of Us's." In a later interview, however, Barth concedes that "Finally, of course, it's the *author's* voice you're hearing and the author is always all of those things he makes up." The deeper implications of this statement reverberate after its surface meaning registers. Barth often refers to Borges's idea that fictions about fictions disturb us metaphysically because they remind us of the fictitious nature of our lives. Similarly, the realization that all voices in a work of fiction are ultimately a single voice, that of the artificer, resonates in both ontological directions. We are reminded of the Lacanian possibility that we, too, are but the sounds of other people's voices.

This possibility seems to explain the significance of the quotation marks enclosing **"Night-Sea Journey."** The narrator being quoted is a spermatozoan about to impreg-

nate Andrea and become a fetal Ambrose. Not only will it become Ambrose in a literal, physical sense, but what Barth calls its "eschatological and other speculations" will become part of Ambrose's "official Heritage." The sperm cell is the "tale-bearer of a generation." The fictions that comprise the realities of our age, fictions themselves built upon past fictions, the entire construct, as Nietzsche saw, forming the a priori beliefs of our time—these, too, Ambrose inherits. Had the narrator of the story been the fish that early reviewers mistook him to be, his eschatological murmurings, Barth concedes, would indeed have been trite. Given "his actual nature, they are merely correct." Whether the sperm cell is alluding to Ginsberg's *Howl* or to Barth's own *Floating Opera,* or whether he's summarizing "the history of philosophical speculation about ontology," his concerns and formulations are among the pertinent concerns and formulations of our time. Ambrose is an outgrowth of the collected story of his race.

Language does not belong to Ambrose so much as he belongs to it. His utterances are controlled by the limitations of the medium in which he writes, thinks, and lives. Barth quotes one of Borges's editors to the effect that "For [Borges] no one has claim to originality in literature; all writers are more or less faithful amanuenses of the spirit, translators and annotators of pre-existing archetypes." Italo Calvino, whose fiction Barth greatly admires, goes a step further: "I believe that all of literature is implicit in language—that literature itself is merely the permutation of a finite set of elements and functions." Just as the self-recorded fiction of **"Autobiography"** echoes the words of its Father/Creator ("My first words weren't my first words"), so Ambrose, presumably that Father/Creator, echoes the words of Barth, who in turn permutates the elements and functions he has inherited from his precursors. And so on. Yet Ambrose (like Barth) is born at a time when the possible permutations of the finite have apparently been used up. "Everything's been said already, over and over," the artist in **"Title"** complains. Consequently, the desire to squelch the narrative impulse becomes strong. The spermatozoan of **"Night-Sea Journey,"** the self-recorded fiction in **"Autobiography,"** and several other narrators long to stop talking. But all seem to realize, if only implicitly, that to lift the mask of words is to end up like Ahab, lashed to nothingness.

This nothingness, while disturbing enough to Ambrose and his various avatars, is not necessarily viewed by Barth as a Kurtzian horror. Rather, it coincides with that prelinguistic state the separation from which generated language and the return to which all human activity, language included, secretly inclines. Like Borges, however, Barth believes that a complete return to this primal state is impossible (except perhaps for mystics). Man simply cannot leap outside language. Even if he does, the mystic moment of all-in-one, one-in-all inclusiveness is temporary; one must inevitably return to the world of words and men. Once back, as Giles learns, the ineffable remains unspeakable. Thus the admonition "Let go!" that recurs throughout *Giles Goat-Boy* and which demands the abandonment of the world of perceptual and conceptual categories is replaced in *Funhouse* by the imperative "Hold on!" By recasting ancient tales and myths in modern terms, Barth is able to hold onto the demands and concerns of the present while metaphorically returning to literary origins. Barth thus acknowledges the history that contains him, while simultaneously evoking that cosmogonic moment whence all history began.

But if Man's return to origins must be relative rather than radical, Barth remains free to use the idea of radical regression as a controlling metaphor. As Eliade has said, "The return to origins gives the hope of rebirth," and it is artistic rejuvenation Barth seeks. He builds the idea of the radical regress into the structure of many of his stories. Perhaps the best example of this tactic is found in **"Menelaiad."** In constructing his version of the Menelaus-Helen story, Barth has drawn from most existing versions of the myth, including Homer's *Odyssey* and *Iliad*, Stesichorus' *Palinode*, Euripides' *Trojan Women*, even Hugo von Hofmannsthal and Richard Strauss's opera *Die Aegyptische Helena*. These versions are themselves layered within seven different narrative perspectives provided by Menelaus, each perspective indicated by a different number of quotation marks. In his quest for Helen, Menelaus must fight his way through all these layers of "reality." At one point he cries, "When will I reach my goal through its cloaks of story? How many veils to naked Helen?" He learns the answer when, in his innermost story, he asks the Oracle at Delphi the ultimate Oedipal question: "Who am I?" The answer, almost predictable by this point in *Funhouse,* is seven sets of quotation marks enclosing nothing. Neither Menelaus nor Helen exists outside the stories that contain and create them. In a heroic regression, Menelaus has worked his way back through the multiple layers of "reality" to the primordial blank from which issues language and all its categories, "Helen" and "Menelaus" among them. Understandably, Menelaus recoils from the message—retreating like Ambrose and the nameless minstrel, both of whom also receive blank messages, back into story—now "done with questions" and determined to "never let go" of the protean guises of a reality that stands between him and the silence of annihilation.

But though Menelaus "continues to hold on," he "can no longer take the world seriously," for at the point where he realized "that Proteus somewhere on the beach became Menelaus holding the Old Man of the Sea, Menelaus ceased." Previously he had suspected that Helen—indeed, that "all subsequent history"—might be Proteus. But if Proteus is everything, he must also be nothing. "I understood further," says Menelaus, "how Proteus thus also was as such no more, being as possibly Menelaus's attempt to hold him, the tale of that vain attempt, the voice that tells it." Not just Menelaus, but mankind, is the story of its collective story, the sound of its own voice. History, as Barth is fond of saying, is fictive if not false, "our dream, our idea," to which we must cling even when, like Menelaus, we realize its fictiveness.

Without the story there is only the blank. This blank is that sense of absence which propels man to create language, self, and civilization—each a sublimated desire to "fill in the blank." All three are made out of love, since language, which creates self and society, is essentially sexual at base in its Oedipal longing to regain the mother's breast, to fill in the blank separating self from the world. " 'Love is how we call our ignorance of what whips us,' " cries the disgruntled sperm cell of **"Night-Sea Journey,"** as he, too, despite his nihilism, plunges toward the mysterious She and *"consummation, transfiguration, Union of contraries, transcension of categories."* He attains that holistic realm known to mystics and heroes. But of course he will be expunged once again as Ambrose into a world of words and categories, only to return metaphorically through Ambrose's artistic regression to past forms and tales. Love, then, moves us to fill in the blank, to create our history. As Helen tells Menelaus, it is "the senseless answer to our riddle . . . mad history's secret, base-fact and footer to the fiction crazy-house our life." When the teller of Menelaus' tale dies, and then is followed by the tale itself, the tale's motivation and subject, love, will remain.

But if love motivates tale and teller, what of told? Throughout **Funhouse** the importance of an audience—real or implied—to the narrative process is emphasized. Several narrators realize that they must continue speaking as long as they have readers or hearers. "You who listen give me life in a manner of speaking" begins the narrator of **"Autobiography,"** the curious spacing in his utterance making it unclear whether that utterance is indicative or imperative. At least two of the stories actually insult the reader/hearer in an effort to cut off communication. As the author/narrator of **"Life-Story,"** addressing his reader, concludes about the author-audience relationship in the story he is writing: "Don't you think he [the author of the story-within-the-story] knows who gives his creatures their lives and deaths? Do they exist except as he or others read their words? Age except we turn their pages? And can he die until you have no more of him?" Later he answers his own not-quite-rhetorical questions. "That he continues means that he continues, a fortiori you too. Suicide's impossible: he can't kill himself without your help." Not only does the reader give life to the characters and situation in the author's story, but in a real sense the reader gives the author life, since he makes his role possible. By that same token, the writer as well as his story makes possible the reader's role. Tale, teller, and told thus become linked in a reciprocal process. Writing is not a monologue in which a Godlike author creates a world which he then dispenses to a passive auditor; rather, it is—as Heidegger argues all language is—a *conversation*.

"Language is not a mere tool, one of the many which man possesses," writes Heidegger in his essay on Hölderlin; "on the contrary, it is only language that affords the very possibility of standing in the openness of the existent. Only where there is language is there world." But if the "being of man is founded in language . . . this only becomes actual in conversation." (pp. 106-18)

Poetry was the *Ursprache*, the "primitive language of a historical people." In time, of course, the poetic hardened into the vernacular, the mythic into the ritualistic, then the mundane. But the truly original poet's task remains the same: he must return to origins, recapitulating in the moment of creation that primordial creation when the first poet-magi called a world out of darkness. In the words of Eliade,

> All poetry is an effort to *re-create* the language; in other words, to abolish current language, that of every day, and to invent a new, private and personal speech. . . . But poetic creation, like linguistic creation, implies the abolition of time—of the history concentrated in language—and tends toward the recovery of the paradisiac, primordial situation . . . when one could *create spontaneously*. . . . From a certain point of view, we may say that every great poet is *re-making* the world.

[Myths, Dreams, and Mysteries, 1975]

For this crucial reason, despite the reciprocity of the reader-writer process, the reader's need for the writer may be greater than vice versa—far greater perhaps than most readers would be comfortable knowing. The truly serious poet in his various guises continues to invent our universe. In the process he perhaps teaches the reader how to invent his world, which is what Ronald Sukenick calls "the main didactic job of the contemporary novelist" ["The New Tradition in Fiction," in *Surfiction: Fiction Now and Tomorrow,* ed. Raymond Federman, 1975]. The artist keeps the necessary conversation vital by refusing to allow it to harden into meaningless cliché. This is one reason why Barth and his artist-protagonists are so concerned with originality. If language forms our a priori beliefs, if it is the filter through which our "realities" are perceived, then the freshness and significance of those realities depend upon the health of the language. "Where language is corrupted or bastardized," writes George Steiner, "there will be a corresponding decline in the character and fortunes of the body politic" [*After Babel: Aspects of Language and Translation,* 1975]. And when language falls into silence, spiritual if not actual self-extinction follows. "If Sinbad sinks it's Scheherazade who drowns," writes the narrator of **"Life-Story."** "Whose neck one wonders is on her line?" The answer, of course, is our own.

The reader's dependence upon the writer—though often unacknowledged, as Shelley noted—becomes the writer's most pressing obligation. The act of writing, of reaching out to another for understanding and acceptance, is frequently painful since the writer can never be sure he will make contact." Are you there?" asks the self-recorded fiction of **"Autobiography,"** a question echoed by Menelaus' "Anyone there?" and implicitly or explicitly repeated throughout *Funhouse.* More awesome still is the realization that someone may be reaching out to the writer. "To love is easy," speaks Menelaus; "to be loved, as if one were real, on the order of others: fearsome mystery!" This realization confirms the writer's participation in the ontological conversation, thus verifying his existence in the symbolic order that man calls reality. More important, perhaps, it forces the writer to acknowledge his role as poet and the obligations that role entails.

A message from the sea launches Ambrose's role as writer. Similarly, a sea-message resuscitates the moribund narrative impulse of the minstrel in **"Anonymiad."** Marooned on an island, the minstrel invents written narrative, then

muse by muse exhausts its possibilities. Like Echo, he rehearses the various stages of the narrative tradition; having reached its final stage, he faces a depletion of narrative resources: "Was there any new thing to say, new way to say the old?" Just as Ambrose's sea message is blank, the medium forming its sole message, so the minstrel's message is all but blank. But the renewed creativity inspired by the message comes "as much from the lacunae as from the rest." Whereas he had thought himself "the only stranded spirit, and had survived by sending messages to whom they might concern," he now realizes the world "might be astrew with isled souls, *become minstrels perforce,* and the sea a-clink with literature!" The phrase I have italicized suggests a causal relationship between isolation and art, which is precisely the point I have been making. Language issues from the ontogenetic and phylogenic realization of separation. It represents an attempt to fill in the blank sensed by the individual at the point of the infantile trauma and by ancient man at the time of the "catastrophe" or expulsion from paradise. The realization that another is similarly isolated and simultaneously reaching out for understanding and love confirms the existence of a continuing conversation, which Heidegger sees as the ground of being. Thus messaged, the minstrel continues the exchange, realizing now that this **"Anonymiad"** as well as "all its predecessors" are a "continuing, strange love letter."

The minstrel's—thus Ambrose's—realization that art, like language itself, is fundamentally a conversation casts light on a previous statement by the narrator of **"Life-Story."** Concluding that "the old analogy between Author and God, novel and world, can no longer be employed unless deliberately as a false analogy," the narrator lists among the possible fictional responses to this fact the following: fiction must "establish some other, acceptable relation between itself, its author, its reader." This new relation is one of reciprocity. The text is not solely the creation of the author but (to paraphrase **"Autobiography"**) the sum of the author and reader's conjoined efforts. By that same token, the language employed by the author exists prior to its use by that author; thus artistic *parole,* no matter how novel in its permutations, is controlled by the *langue* from which it is selected and which forms the context that gives it sense. Thus all three—teller, tale, and told—are inextricably linked and mutually interdependent.

The artist's obligation to keep the ontological conversation going is manifested in various ways in *Funhouse.* The need to "hold on" to reality's various guises, for example, becomes even more essential when the artist realizes that those forms and guises—our cognitive and perceptual "realities"—depend for their existence on the conversation which actualized them. This conversation, according to Heidegger, is a single one; it has existed continuously since its inception and cannot be interrupted without plunging man and his world back into the void. And while there is throughout *Funhouse* a persistent impulse toward the Baroque, that impulse to get it all said, to exhaust the possible permutations of words and yield at last to the all-encompassing silence, this eschatological tendency is counteracted by a stronger if paradoxically weary desire to continue filling in the blank.

These twin impulses are especially evident in the triptych formed by **"Autobiography," "Title,"** and **"Life-Story."** While all three stories are concerned with the relationship between reader, writer, and story, each story focuses primarily on one element of the relationship: **"Autobiography,"** narrated by itself, focuses obviously on the tale; **"Title,"** concerned with the author-narrator's difficulties in composing his story, focuses on the teller; **"Life-Story,"** particularly the last two sections, focuses primarily on the audience. Each story is radically reflexive, its form not "contentless" (as the narrator of **"Autobiography"** complains) so much as comprising content. The stories discourse, their very processes, form their substance. "You tell me it's self-defeating to talk about it instead of just up and doing it," explains the narrator of **"Title,"** "but to acknowledge what I'm doing while I'm doing it is exactly the point." Yet even this novel approach soon grows hackneyed. "Another story about a writer writing a story!" Complains the narrator of **"Life-Story."** "Another regressus in infinitum! Who doesn't prefer art that at least overtly imitates something other than its own processes?" Despite the curse of exhaustion and apparent meaninglessness, these tales, in the words of **"Autobiography,"** "continue the tale of [their] forebears," refusing (perhaps unable) to end, as indicated by the absence of periods concluding **"Autobiography"** and **"Title."** In this respect these two stories resemble the types of narrative Beckett has described: "It's an unbroken flow of words and tears. . . . it's for ever the same murmur, flowing unbroken, like a single endless word and therefore meaningless, *for it's the end gives the meaning to words*" [Harris's italics].

"Life-Story" does end, however, at least in a relative sense. Indeed, it closes with a pair of periods, the second larger than the first. The narrator of **"Life-Story"** is writing a story about a writer writing a story, both stories concluding almost simultaneously, which may explain the twin periods. But the second, larger period may also apply retroactively to the unconcluded initial stories in the triptych. Significantly, **"Life-Story"** closes when the narrator is led to bed and sex by his playful but determined wife. Narrative, the sexual surrogate, gives way to actual sex. Since this occurs on the narrator's birthday, a regress of sorts also occurs, the act of sex symbolically restoring that harmony interrupted by the birth trauma thirty-six years before. Sex, at its climactic moment, returns us symbolically and perhaps psychologically to Eliade's *illud tempus*, that time before time, before man's fall into consciousness and categories. In the "dizzy instant of coitus," writes Borges, "all men are one man." Moreover, just as the sexual orgy provided ancient man with a ritual for regressing psychically to primal chaos (the mythic state), so do the distractions of modern man, particularly reading, provide the same function. Such is the "mythological function of reading," according to Eliade. "For the modern man it is the supreme 'distraction,' yielding him the illusion of *a mastery of Time* which, we may well suspect, gratifies a secret desire to withdraw from the implacable becoming that leads toward death." Like the act of sex, the acts of reading and writing are forms of love—love in the mythic sense, love as the desire to overcome all dualisms and to heal permanently the primordial breach between man and the other. Thus the narrator of **"Life-Story"** doesn't stop the ontological conversation, even though he does cap his pen. His "ending story" remains "endless by interruption," that interruption causing merely a shift of media, an exchange of the flesh for the word, both of which symbolize the human desire to abolish all distinctions.

Nor does *Funhouse* conclude with the minstrel's affirmative "Wrote it." These words, we understand, apply to the **"Anonymiad"** itself; that realization sends us back to the beginning of that story and, since **"Anonymiad"** forms the final fiction in the series composed by Ambrose, back to the beginning of *Funhouse* as well. The structure of *Funhouse* is therefore cyclic, a fitting shape for a narrative concerned with regressions to origins. But the nature of the cycle, as **"Frame-Tale"** promises, is spiraling, not spheric. **"Anonymiad"** echoes **"Night-Sea Journey"** but with a crucial difference: whereas the spermatozoan is propelled unwillingly by Love, the nameless minstrel, after some recalcitrance, yields enthusiastically. Addressing an absent Merope in terms deliberately reminiscent of **"Night-Sea Journey,"** the minstrel proclaims, "I wish you were here. The water's fine; in the intervals of this composition I've taught myself to swim, and if some night your voice recalls me, by a new name, I'll commit myself to it, paddling and resting, drifting like my amphorae, to attain you or to drown." The new name, of course, will be Ambrose. And the call will be to art, not to physical love. But the subject of Ambrose's fiction will be love, what goes on between men and women remaining "not only the most interesting but the most important thing in the bloody murderous world." And the art Ambrose fashions will demand a reciprocal relationship between reader, writer, and story that resembles love. Moreover, by this point in his narrative Ambrose has perhaps learned that if art is a sexual substitute, the act of sex is itself a substitute, pointing like language to that holistic, primordial state man struggles to reattain. As a record of that struggle, art remains as vitally necessary to the survival of the human race as does sex. "A continuing, strange love letter," it preserves the ontological conversation that is man. (pp. 119-24)

Charles B. Harris, in his Passionate Virtuosity: The Fiction of John Barth, *University of Illinois Press, 1983, 217 p.*

Steven M. Bell   (essay date 1984)

[*In the following excerpt, Bell discusses self-consciousness in* Lost in the Funhouse, *focusing on ways in which language play can assuage existential despair and doubt.*]

Self-consciousness in prose fiction—metafiction—was not invented yesterday. John Barth, one of its champions in America, himself readily concedes its unoriginality, albeit hyperbolically and with tongue-in-cheek, as is his nature. "Self-conscious, vertiginously arch, fashionably solipsistic, unoriginal—in fact a convention of twentieth-century literature. Another story about a writer writing a story!"

What such playful exaggeration does effectively point out is that, while the self-consciousness of much of today's prose fiction does not itself break new ground in the field of literature, in the history of man (which is nothing if not a history of consciousness), self-consciousness, specifically linguistic (and literary) self-consciousness, has never been so prevalent as in the present century: it has engulfed not only literature, but also history, philosophy, and the social or human sciences. (p. 84)

In what follows I discuss Barth's *Lost in the Funhouse* (1968) in the context of this general, twentieth-century heightening of linguistic self-consciousness. As I read it, *Lost in the Funhouse*—Barth's fifth book and only collection of "short stories" to date—affirms "play" as a solution to existential anguish and doubt (a very Nietzschian notion), and posits writing (and indirectly reading) as a possible escape from madness. It seems unwittingly, and so all the more significantly, to embody Derrida's "program" for "the end of the book and the beginning of writing." Seen in this light, *Lost in the Funhouse* reflects the notion of language/written discourse as the play of infinite substitutions within the closure of finite possibilities, and it foregrounds the artist's never-ending search for new and better ways to speak the unspeakable, to write what has already been written, but has somehow never been gotten quite right. I would suggest, furthermore, that the assumptions underlying the trajectory Barth follows through the *Lost in the Funhouse* pieces undercuts his "The Literature of Exhaustion" essay of 1967, their theoretical counterpart. That is the stories as collected *already* embody and in essence anticipate the theoretical formulations only recently recorded by Barth in his 1980 rewriting of the "exhaustion" essay, "The Literature of Replenishment"; it is in the latter that Barth essays the idea of literature as a series of almost repetitions or substitutions, of "virtually infinite" play within a "doubtless finite" system, in Barth's own words, and of the movement of literature—at all levels and in all senses, by allegorical analogy—as thus circuitous, or rather spiral-like. This play, and this spiral-like movement, function not only at the level of the individual book—*Lost in the Funhouse* in this case—but also at the level of Barth's oeuvre to date, and in turn for the whole of Western literature; as such, the play in *Lost in the Funhouse* is as a metaphor or microcosm of the Barthian oeuvre, and ultimately of the history of Western literature itself. (p. 85)

There are of course innumerable ways to categorize or group the various stories. One which deserves some attention is found in the . . . "Author's Note." In it Barth explains that not all of the stories were composed "expressly for print," and he proceeds to elaborate on their different, "ideal media of presentation." These prefatory remarks are clearly, if taken seriously, attempts at radical innovation of the narrative medium and of narrative technique; but as Barth suggests, anticipating his critics, they easily come off as pretentious. It is in fact difficult to decide to what degree Barth wants to be taken seriously in the matter, for the "Author's Note" and the "Seven Additional Author's Notes" represent a virtuoso performance in violating the expectations a particular text induces in its readers, by constantly mocking itself, and frustrating any pos-

sibility of proceeding solemnly. The voice that speaks in the "Note" is just one more of the roles Barth is playing, one more of the masks he dons. Toward the end of his exposition of the different ideal media of presentation, Barth, through exaggeration ad absurdum, pulls the rug out from under himself, parodies himself, and puts everything he has just said in doubt: " 'Title' makes somewhat separate but equally valid senses in several media: print, monophonic recorded authorial voice, stereophonic ditto in dialogue with itself, live authorial voice, live ditto in dialogue with monophonic ditto aforementioned, and live ditto interlocutory with stereophonic et cetera, my own preference; it's been 'done' in all six." After ending the first "Note" with "on with the story," the hyperbole and the undercutting continue: we promptly turn the page and find "Seven Additional Author's Notes"; only to feel deceived still again upon reading that "the 'Note' means in good faith exactly what it says."

There is indeed a certain movement or progression perceived as one moves through the pieces in *Lost in the Funhouse,* and there are indications that it is in some respects circular. But more important, *Lost in the Funhouse* does not come full circle, and it certainly does not represent a closure. Being a collection of autonomous units, and not exclusively (as in the novel) a "whole" which corresponds directly to the covers of a book, *Lost in the Funhouse* exemplifies well Maurice Blanchot's contention that the "work" of a particular writer can never correspond to a single book. Only the author's death, Blanchot insists, can put an end to the serious and truly dedicated writer's work, to a work that continues from one book to the next, and ends due to circumstances generally beyond the writer's control; it is never finished. The "book" as Blanchot would have it, and as *Lost in the Funhouse* demonstrates, fixes or freezes illusorily what is in actuality a continuous and never-ending process.

If we look to certain formal and technical considerations—what Barth at one point calls the "vehicle" of a particular fiction—the various compositions in *Lost in the Funhouse* can be loosely but meaningfully categorized into three groups: allegories, self-referential fictions, and myths rewritten. Allegory predominates toward the beginning of the collection (**"Night-Sea Journey," "Petition," "Lost in the Funhouse"**), self-reference or involution in the middle (**"Autobiography," "Title," "Life-Story"**), and mythical elements in the book's final third (**"Echo," "Glossolalia," "Menelaiad," "Anonymiad"**). These three formal devices are not of course mutually exclusive; all of them are present to some degree in most of the stories, and although the term "formal device" or "vehicle" is not very precise, the generalization is helpful and by and large valid. Such a grouping of the stories leads to insights not only into *Lost in the Funhouse* and its place in Barth's corpus of literary production, but also is significant as an indirect indication of Barth's ideas about literature and fiction in the broader sense—a central concern in all of his work.

The image of the spiral is again called to mind with regard to the arrangement of the pieces: the concluding stories reject in part the purely self-referential mode predominant in the center pieces; at the same time the allegorical elements—present in most of the stories but especially the opening ones—regain some importance, though mythical ones are the central motif and "vehicle" of the final stories. John Stark sees the spiral image as representative of the diachronic trajectory of Barth's entire oeuvre, but does not comment upon its usefulness with regard to *Lost in the Funhouse.* Its spiralling is just one of the ways in which the **"Frame Tale"**'s Möbius strip is emblematic of the work as a whole: *Lost in the Funhouse,* like the Möbius strip, is not just a circle, but rather a circle with a twist; the book does not circle back upon and close itself so much as it is open-ended, or rather open at both ends. From this point of view, if the book could be said to "close" at all, it would be only (paradoxically) at its center, an artificially static moment (as the present is so fleeting as to be practically nonexistent) in an essentially dynamic process. The movement from allegory, through self-referentiality, to myth which is perceived in *Lost in the Funhouse*—undoubtedly a protracted process for Barth—is frozen, made static, recorded for posterity, and documented with the publication of the collection, which then marks a definable moment in the evolution of the whole of Barth's work as it stands (in progress, never finished) at present. The important role of allegorical patterning in *Giles Goat-Boy* (1966), the last Barth novel published before *Lost in the Funhouse,* is picked up right where it left off in the opening stories. Likewise, the rewriting of myth, the predominant mode of the final stories, is continued in *Chimera* (1972), Barth's next book, while hardly missing a beat. The self-referential pieces then, in this arrangement, are at the center of the "funhouse" in more ways than just the literal, physical one might suggest: they are clearly the collection's most distinctive feature, the ones which most clearly differentiate it from Barth's other texts. The center of *Lost in the Funhouse,* in this view, is a pivot, a "twist" in the spiral which is the linear development of the tales, and in that of Barth's entire oeuvre "in progress," for the former are but a moment in and a metaphor for the latter.

The initial use of allegory seeks out and traces parallels between life and literature, in hopes of finding a role or place for literature in life. The subsequent self-referential pieces correspond most closely to Barth's "exhaustion" essay. **"Title,"** the most obvious instance of this, is really a rewriting, a fictionalization of that essay. These central stories mark a vacillation, a certain recognition of and resignation to the supposed exhaustion, and the most truly static moment in the linear, spiralling progression of the book. The rewriting of the myths signals a new direction, a new beginning, an at-least-temporary solution to the crisis, and a leaving behind of pure self-referentiality and self-consciousness, which the voice in **"Title"** comes to "abhor." Most significantly, for my purposes, the turn to myth marks an implicit recognition in Barth of the possibilities for infinite "play," infinite, almost repetitions or substitutions, within a finite system.

The image of the labyrinth, central in the writings of Jorge Luis Borges, is not surprisingly an appropriate metaphor for the path John Barth has followed in his literary labors: he is constantly testing new possible solutions to the maze, retaining what he has found useful, and moving on in new

directions. The self-referential pieces at the center of *Lost in the Funhouse,* as Robert Scholes points out, are at times painfully and paralyzingly involuted, but they are in fact only a turn in the spiral, a pivot and a moving on, both in the context of the *Funhouse* collection and the Barthian oeuvre in progress. In spite of the charges of narcissism leveled against him, Barth's artistic trajectory remains one of the most dynamic and refreshing in literature today. Barth is programmatic in his writing, and extremely conscious of his power to shape literary history, wherein lies the greater part of his energy and vitality. What Barth's most outspoken detractors do see however, which his loyal admirers tend to pass over, is the need to question the deeper implications of the artistic self-consciousness so present in all of his work.

One possible explanation for the new predominance of self-consciousness, in Barth's prose fiction and in the humanistic disciplines in general, is the very polemic notion that we are approaching the end of a significant period of Western culture, the "civilization of the book," whose origins are found in the inception of phonetic writing, and which explodes with the coming of the printing press to Renaissance Europe. The "Author's Note" to *Lost in the Funhouse,* with its pretentions of moving beyond the medium of print into the electronic media, some of the more recently developed "extensions of man," echoes unmistakably Marshall McLuhan's thought. (pp. 86-8)

Another possible explanation for the self-conscious artistry in *Lost in the Funhouse,* the one set forth in this essay, is as an affirmation of the Derridean notion of the "play" of written discourse as an exit from and possible solution to existential doubt. We cannot "know," so why not play? Play, for Derrida, is language itself: "Sign will always lead to sign, one substituting the other (playfully, since 'sign' is 'under erasure') as signifier and signified in turn. Indeed, the notion of play is important here. Knowledge is not a systematic tracking down of a truth that is hidden but may be found. It is rather the field 'of free play, that is to say, a field of infinite substitutions in the closure of a finite ensemble'." Such a conceptualization of language repeats several of the implications I have drawn from *Lost in the Funhouse:* for Barth not only language, but analogously the whole of literature can be depicted as the play of infinite formal and technical substitutions in the closure of a finite (theoretically exhaustible) set of possibilities. "One should, if it's worthwhile, repeat the tale. I'll repeat the tale," Barth's narrator in **"Echo"** says, and Barth proceeds to undertake a recasting of Western myth, the very foundation of Western literature.

Following this Derridean train of thought, what Blanchot says about the writer in a generalized sense applies simultaneously to *Lost in the Funhouse* as an individual work, to Barth's entire oeuvre, and to the whole of our literature: "The writer never knows if the work is done. What he has finished in one book, he begins again or destroys in another. . . . the work—the work of art, the literary work—is neither finished nor unfinished: it is. . . . The writer who experiences this void simply believes that the work is unfinished, and he believes that with a little more effort and the luck of some favorable moments, he—and only he—

81

will be able to finish it. And so he sets back to work. But what he wants to finish by himself, remains something interminable, it ties him to an illusory labor." This notion of the whole of literature as a single, unfinished book constantly being written upon is one we also find in Borges, and it is diverting to speculate that it came to Barth through the Argentine master. *Lost in the Funhouse,* just as the whole of Barth's literary production, is like an open book. It is always pushing forward, and yet constantly circling back, not only upon itself, but upon the entire Barthian oeuvre, and the whole of Western literature. It would seem, then, that it is not so much through his experiments with the recorded media that Barth transcends the printed book, as he may have hoped at one time, but rather a movement away from the closedness and supposed unity of the book in favor of a new concept of literature as "writing" that represents Barth's accomplishment in the *Funhouse.* (p. 89)

> Steven M. Bell, "Literature, Self-Consciousness, and Writing: The Example of Barth's 'Lost in the Funhouse'," in The International Fiction Review, Vol. 11, No. 2, Summer, 1984, pp. 84-9.

Barth on the relationship between writer and reader:

Writing is a tedious vocation, and it takes lots and lots of time. It certainly is a solipsistic and hermit-like thing to do—to close oneself in a room for hours at a stretch, day after day after day, not in human company, listening only to the sound of your own words. Little wonder that one gets interested in stories of people who turn into the sound of their own voices or into their own stories. One of the things that make university teaching valuable to me is that I would simply go buggy if I had nothing else to do but write every day. I think that the absence of other connections with society, with the rest of the world, would be damaging. Students make you listen, you know. There *is* a dialogue between a writer and his readers, Marshall McLuhan to the contrary; it's not a one-way thing. But it's a dialogue in slow-time, between books. You listen to reviewers; you read your mail, and so forth. And your next book may build on some of the reactions to the one before. It's a healthy process, but a very slow dialogue.

> John Barth, in "Algebra and Fire: An Interview with John Barth," The Falcon, 1972.

Deborah A. Woolley (essay date 1985)

[*In the following excerpt, Woolley argues that self-consciousness in* Lost in the Funhouse *presents an affirmative interpretation of narrative reflexivity.*]

In contemporary criticism a myth has emerged, wherein narrative literature, released from its bondage to novelistic convention and mimetic tradition, becomes the freeplay of language speaking to itself, infinitely reflecting and rewriting its own structures. The "text," figured in the critical mythology as "parafiction," "surfiction," "metafiction," *écriture,* "antinovel," *nouveau roman, nouveau nouveau*

roman, and so forth, is envisioned as an "absence" undercutting the sense of presence that language evokes. Thus, according to [Phillippe] Sollers, a text "n'apparaît que pour s'effacer et réciter cette apparition qui s'efface ("appears only in order to erase itself and to recite this apparition which erases itself"). By constantly playing upon the tension between words as signifiers and words as signs, the "text" purportedly denies any dimension beyond language. Drawing upon an ethical vocabulary of oppositions such as pure and impure, free and fixed, new and old, fluid and rigid, the criticism substitutes a heroics of text and language for the older heroics of creative genius and imagination. The "text" heroically foregoes the old securities of presence—signification, thematic unity, totalizing form—and accepts the existentialist challenge to confront the lack of a center at the heart of language and to dwell in that void. Hence, runs the deconstructionist myth, the lack of meaning at the center of a text is a truer and more authentic meaning, the play of language a truer realism. (pp. 460-61)

More importantly for readers of postmodern fiction, the criticism is short-sighted: in its enthusiastic attack on the myth of correct interpretation, and its consequent attention to the play of language, it obscures the double nature of all fiction, including self-reflexive fiction. When postmodern criticism claims that the lack of meaning of the "text" *is* its meaning, that the lack of referential value to language is its truth, it dissolves two types of tension essential to narrative: the linguistic tension between reference and self-reference, and the narrative tension between mimesis and poesis. Self-reflexive fiction certainly does confront us with the fact that language and convention are merely surfaces. Yet the complexity of this type of fiction is due in part to the fact that it simultaneously creates and undermines presences. To turn from the criticism back to the fiction itself is to experience as readers how self-reflexive narrative constantly cultivates this tension.

For instances of this lost tension, we need only look at the many critical studies of John Barth's fiction that cite his work as an example of the "empty" postmodern "text." While one vein of the criticism has focused on Barth's vision of existential absurdity, the dominant critical approach for the past ten years has been a focus on Barth's narrative and linguistic nihilism. James Rother, for instance, sees Barth's fiction as a recurrent demonstration of language's power to "abolish determinisms of beginning and end" ["Parafiction: The Adjacent Universe of Barth, Barthelme, Pynchon, and Nabokov," *boundary 2,* 1976], and Tony Tanner notes the characteristic "nonprogressive mutterings" of a voice wandering through the "lexical playfields" of narrative form ["No Exit," *Partisan Review,* 1969]. For Beverly Gross, Barth's fiction "exists to announce its own inadequacy," and "proclaim[s] . . . the impossibility of narrative" ["The Anti-Novels of John Barth," in *Critical Essays on John Barth,* ed. Joseph J. Waldmeir, 1980]. Even Campbell Tatham, arguing for the relevance of Barth's fictional world to the world outside the text, can grant it only the most limited sort of relevance: "Barth's novels are commentaries on theories of the novel; insofar as novels are a part of life, Barth's novels are a commentary on a part of life" ["John Barth and the

Aesthetics of Artifice," *Contemporary Literature,* 1971]. This is a slim defense indeed against charges of self-reflexive emptiness.

Christopher Morris has attempted to shift the critical discussion away from debate about Barth's affirmations or negations—from concerns with what Morris calls the "inescapable nexus of Barth's nihilism" versus his "grim 'resolutions' of absurdity or tautology"—and to address the problem of language ["Barth and Lacan: The World of the Moebius Strip," *Critique,* 1975]. His deconstructionist reading merely reinforces the argument for Barthian nihilism, however. For Morris, the central motif in *Lost in the Funhouse* is "the rupture between the visual and perceptible world, centered in the self, and the world of language, which exists without a center." Language is "wholly independent of everything outside it, even the speaker who uses it." Consequently the work expresses Lacan's idea of the "loss of the subject . . . at the expense of a discourse which incoherently speaks man rather than the reverse." For Morris, *Lost in the Funhouse* is characterized by the absence of the subject and of signification. "Selfhood in *Lost in the Funhouse* is altogether ignored, except as a farcical or sentimental entity, and the locus of 'narrative' affliction is ultimately reduced to the purely linguistic problem of substitution." The only viable option for the writer, according to Morris's reading of Barth, is to combine and recombine phonemes. The novel thus demonstrates the "collapsible, substitutive nature of language."

I have summarized Morris's argument here at some length because in its sophistication it illustrates the rationale for what is, I believe, a widespread misreading of Barth's fiction and of postmodern fiction in general. It is surely true that this fiction is preoccupied with the deterioration of language in general and of narrative forms in particular. But it does not follow that self-reflexive fiction is nihilistic or devoid of "presence." For while some aspects of self-reflexive narrative lead toward emptiness, others lead toward fullness. By offering an alternate reading of *Lost in the Funhouse* I hope to underline the inadequacy of the deconstructionist reading and to show how Barth deepens our appreciation of the constructive uses of narrative reflexivity.

In *Chimera,* which picks up from *Lost in the Funhouse* the motif of the artist-hero, Barth gives us a model for reflexivity in the form of two documents contained in a jug which Bellerophon finds floating across the marshes. Proposing a "new," "quintessential" fiction, they echo deconstructionist rhetoric and concerns. The first makes a case for an "utterly novel revolution" whose goal will be the "first genuinely scientific model of the genre"; it will "of necessity contain *nothing original whatever.*" The second is Jerome B. Bray's application for a grant to pursue his "Revolutionary Novel NOTES," a scientific fiction which will "represent nothing beyond itself, have no content except its own form, no subject but its own processes." "Language itself it will perhaps eschew," divesting as far as possible the literary sign of its signification: in the maw of Bray's computer, literature is reduced to a list of motifs, plot-structures, and patterns that re-emerge as mathematical formulae and geometrical diagrams.

But the parodic quality of the documents makes it clear that this enthusiasm for *écriture blanche* is to be taken neither at face value nor as Barth's own. For scribbled at the bottoms of Bray's proposal is an editorial response that implies both the triviality of that ultimate reduction of fiction to pattern and the possible danger of such a reduction: *"File. Forget. Throw back in the river. No need to prosecute (or reply)."* However fascinated Scheherazade and the Genie—another of Barth's avatars—may be with questions of fictional technique, with the relations between frame and tale, such questions are for Dunyazade less important than what the stories are about. As the narrator of **"Life-Story"** puts it, "What sort of story is it whose drama lies always in the next frame out?" The question is rhetorical: no kind of story, he implies—at least no story we can care much about. "If Sinbad sinks it's Scheherazade who drowns; whose neck one wonders is on her line?" The problem with "scientific fictions" and postmodern "texts" is that they sacrifice passion for the arid pleasures of technique. In the maze of literature-as-signs, of *écriture blanche,* what Barth refers to as the "felt ultimacies" of our lives are lost. The postmodern writer's sophistication regarding literary form is such that not only must all forms seem derivative, but all statements seem the foregone conclusion of the writer's choice of a given form. As the narrator of the **"Anonymiad,"** having invented writing and made the discovery of fiction, fills jug after jug with (in order of their historical appearance) the various subgenres of narrative and then "run[s] out of world and material," he finds himself in the postmodernist dilemma: "as my craft improved, my interest waned, and my earlier zeal seemed hollow as the jugs it filled. Was there any new thing to say, new way to say the old?"

The answer to that question is "yes," a response proposed by Barth in the *Funhouse* where the narrator of **"Life-Story"** realizes that his lack of "ground-situation" may in fact *be* his "ground-situation," and where the interlocutor in **"Title"** suggests that the narrator try to "turn ultimacy against itself to make something new and valid, the essence whereof would be the impossibility of making something new." It is, of course, a paradoxical "yes," and one that requires us to think of fiction's statements differently from the way in which we ordinarily think of statements. For the writer must address his and our situation; and yet self-consciousness turns all statements ironic, self-negating. Barth's fiction reflects an awareness that the relation between words and what we would have them say is always ironic. That awareness creates a state of self-alienation that renders us unable to complete a statement or a story, to connect with a listener or a lover.

What Barth stages, then, is the drama of the erosions of self-consciousness and the struggle against those erosions. While it is true that he points out the absence at the heart of language, he gives us another sort of presence: namely, our resistance to that absence. The collapsibility of language, the arbitrariness of fictions, the infinite regress of statement, are merely the stage for the drama. Self-reflexivity creates a labyrinth of mirrors that turns fiction into "text"; but the quest in the *Funhouse* is for a context that will enable fiction to resist that reduction and to counter that loss.

Self-consciousness is explored on two planes in *Lost in the Funhouse,* the existential and the linguistic, which come together as problems of narrative voice. Existentially its effects are felt as a loss or dispersal of self, a theme present in Barth's earlier, nonreflexive fiction. In *Chimera* and *Lost in the Funhouse,* self-consciousness becomes an aspect of language as well; and the earlier issues of authenticity and role-playing, power and paralysis, are posed in terms of writing or narrating. Barth's later narrators, typically writers or storytellers, tend by virtue of their self-consciousness to lose personality and pale into mere voice. "The opinions echoed in these speeches aren't necessarily the speaker's"; "this voice persists, whoever it is."

There is a first "felt ultimacy," then, in self-reflexive language—in its tendency to become "shards" independent of speakers and significations. **"Frame-Tale"** situates the *Funhouse* stories in the tension between tale—which bears the marks of a speaker and his or her intentions—and text. For the phrase "once upon a time" conveys a sense of the storyteller's presence, of a person related to us by the act of telling a story; while the following clause, "there was a story that began," tells us that story is a predetermined text. Moreover, by virtue of the instructions for turning the page into a Moebius strip, that second phrase textualizes the first: "there was a story that began, 'Once upon a time' " embeds the tale and storyteller within a text.

As the stories oscillate between tale and text, language's referential function is weakened. Accordingly, Barth's narrators grow increasingly unnerved by the gap between the word and its object. The narrator of **"Night-Sea Journey"** has been reduced to a voice addressing itself and pondering what self-consciousness implies about language's power of reference: " 'Is the journey my invention? Do the night, the sea, exist at all, I ask myself, apart from my experience of them?' "—questions that immediately generate questions regarding narrators: " 'Do I myself exist . . . And if I am, who am I? The Heritage I supposedly transport? But how can I be both vessel and contents?' "

In **"Autobiography"** the autonomy of voice is pushed even further, threatening to overshadow the tale completely:

> I see I see myself as a halt narrative: first person, tiresome. Pronoun sans ante or precedent, warrant or respite. Surrogate for the substantive; contentless form, interestless principle; blind eye blinking at nothing. Who am I. A little *crise d'identité* for you.

Self-reflexivity has advanced another step—"I see I see myself"—as voice admits it is "nothing but talk" and the narrator "a figure of speech." Like the Night-Sea narrator, it tells a story, "the tale of my forebears," the autobiography of a voice born of "a mere novel device" and the paternal hand that "cursed" him. But story has become entirely subject to language: the narrator reminds us that his existence is *literally* "only a manner of speaking" and that the tale exists only as a series of puns—"Dad" begets story with his "pointless pen," "Mother" is "a passing fancy" (Coleridgean, we suppose). The sign has no reference apart from self-reference.

The motif of Ambrose's mark crystallizes this problem of language. Through its range of associations, the sign fans out into a range of signifiers, each with its own range of significations (Ambrose leads to ambrosia, honey, *honig,* mother; or bee, be, B, Barth, being). But this only complicates the problem of what the name signifies, and undermines the principle of reference:

> one feels complexly toward the name he's called by, which too one had no hand in choosing. It was to be my fate to wonder at that moniker, relish and revile it, ignore it, stare it out of countenance into hieroglyph and gibber.

Self-reflexive language slides into "hieroglyph and gibber," enigmatic signs that promise but do not yield significance. His "water-message," which Ambrose reads as emblematic of "that greater vision, vague and splendrous," expresses the double nature of language: empty, yet capable of carrying a message. Thus, at this stage, Ambrose celebrates the emptiness of referential content, as it allows him to envision "currents as yet uncharted," "fishes as yet unnamed."

But elsewhere the emptiness breeds confusion and despair. The ambiguity of the sign infects the narrator's sense of self: "I and my sign are neither one nor quite two," says Ambrose. We are and are not identical to ourselves, since the self is both consciousness and object of consciousness. In **"Petition"** the division is made literal, and it is a burden: "To be one: paradise! To be two: bliss! But to be both and neither is unspeakable"—unspeakable in the sense of agonizing, and literally unspeakable: how can it be expressed? With [**"Lost in the Funhouse"**], doubleness has won out. The hall of mirrors makes literal the effects of reflexivity upon identity. Ambrose wonders, "will he become a regular person?" Personality, he realizes, is a fiction, but a necessary one if "fame, madness, suicide; perhaps all three" are to be avoided.

What makes this well-worn theme compelling in Barth's fiction is that it is posed as a problem of narrative voice. As the **"Night-Sea"** narrator's "both vessel and contents" implies, narrative voice has a double nature: it is both personality and the vehicle by which personality is conveyed—both signified and signifier. The motif of doubleness repeatedly appears in the first half of the *Funhouse,* firmly establishing the problem of identity as a condition of language. As **"Autobiography"** puts it, the "I" is "surrogate for the substantive": a stand-in for a noun, with referential value only by virtue of the noun it replaces. The narrator's "I" is troubled by "absence of presence." Like Ambrose's name, "I" is a linguistic sign without a fixed referent. In **"Petition"** the self has split into an all-too-solid "he" and an empty "I." Ambrose's meditations on his name, the **"Autobiography"** narrator's autonomy from "Mom" and "Dad," the **"Night-Sea"** voice's journey between "Maker" and "She," the Siamese-twin pair of **"Petition"**—all express the tenuous connection between narrative consciousness and narrative person.

In the title story, Ambrose's awareness of language has developed into the capacity to reflect upon his own and others' use of language and to exercise a range of voices. Ambrose's growing awareness of the elusiveness of the self—

"he saw once again, more clearly than ever, how readily he deceived himself into supposing he was a person"—is accompanied by his growing sophistication regarding language. For one thing, he has become skeptical as to the adequacy of linguistic description, particularly its ability to convey passion. "His eyes watered, there aren't enough ways to say that." "Ambrose's throat ached; there aren't enough different ways to say that." Ambrose's insight into the gap between word and object—"Nobody knew how to be what they were right"; "If you knew all the stories behind all the people on the boardwalk, you'd see that *nothing* was what it looked like"—leads to multiple voices. We hear lines that sound like psychology textbooks, instructions on effective writing, histories of fiction, handbooks on grammatical conventions. The story may be read as psychologically representational: Ambrose is trying on a number of voices in an attempt to establish his own voice. We witness Ambrose trying to conform to narrative convention, but not yet comfortable with it—"the smell of Uncle Karl's cigar smoke reminded one of "—or revising a sentence to render its style more conventionally "literary"—"though without the extra fun though without the *comaraderie*"; "who teases him good-naturedly who chuckles over the fact." We can make sense of the repetitions ("unbeknownst unbeknownst to him"; "We would do the latter. We would do the latter. We would do the latter") by reading these as Ambrose's mind dwelling on certain words and phrases that for one reason or another arrest his attention: foreignness, awkwardness, interest. The narrative blanks ("Its principal events . . . would appear to have been *A, B, C,* and *D*") show that Ambrose is aware of what convention requires, but is not yet enough of a storyteller to be able to fill in those blanks; the self-commentary ("What is the story's theme?"; "This can't go on much longer; it can go on forever") is Ambrose reflecting on the story he is in the process of composing.

The above reading casts **"Lost in the Funhouse"** as Barth's *Portrait of the Artist as a Young Man.* Certainly the story encourages us to do so, with its questions regarding the narrative's verisimilitude: "Is it likely . . . that a thirteen-year-old boy could make such a sophisticated observation?" All the commentary on narrative convention, however, might just as plausibly be read as another voice, that of the anonymous narrator of this story, whose difficulties in managing the tale correspond to Ambrose's difficulties in coping with the funhouse of family, sexuality, and identity. Ambrose full of voices, all his, none him; or a narrator full of voices, including Ambrose's. Is Ambrose's voice within the tale, or enclosing it?

Like **"Frame-Tale,"** this story depends upon a tension between impersonal "text" and person, or between convention and voice. At times, the narrative voice is that of Ambrose, therefore personal; at other times, it is that of an impersonal storyteller. But since Ambrose is an apprentice storyteller, the personal merges into the impersonal. There are, in addition, conventionalized impersonal voices within the tale (the "textbook" voices) which can be read as personal (Ambrose trying them out). The twist, of course, is that the storyteller becomes a character within the story, lost in the funhouse with Ambrose, unable to control or foresee the direction of the tale. Thus the narrative voice

is located on the Moebius strip, where outside becomes inside and inside becomes outside. In the hall of mirrors, the reflections and refractions go on infinitely, blurring and distorting Ambrose into not-Ambrose. As the self-reflexive language undermines language's referential function, it undermines our sense of the narrator as person. We have a sense of a mind informing the story, but it is not strictly personal: Ambrose "deceives himself" and us "into supposing he [is] a person," for he exists only as self-consciousness assuming a range of voices, some personal and some conventional. Our sense of narrator-as-person is replaced by narrator-as-voices.

The dilemmas of self-consciousness continue in the second half of **Lost in the Funhouse,** cryptically imaged in the next story as Narcissus's dilemma: self-absorption. What lies behind **"Echo"** is the effort to anchor voice in person, to limit the obsessive chain of self-reflection so that story can begin. **"Title"** and **"Life-Story"** initiate the way out of the labyrinth by expressing the narrative problem as an existential one. Whereas in the title story the tension between voice as person and voice as language is never resolved, here the narrative voice is clearly personal even at the height of self-reflexivity. Even as the language undercuts itself, undermines statement, and creates absences, those processes are made humanly significant through the narrators' personal situations—being "full of voices," self-absorbed, aware of their own "absence of presence," unable to connect with anything but echoes.

In **"Title,"** the sound and fury of self-multiplying voice has come to signify nothing and to state that fact. The story is at once a demonstration of the emptiness of self-reflexive language and a drama of the narrator's efforts to fill that emptiness: "Everything leads to nothing. . . . Can nothing be made meaningful?" The title, **"Title,"** exemplifies the story's basic device: to establish a blank space by supplying a filler that does not carry any content, thus ensuring that the form remains the object of our attention. Some of the blanks are grammatical: "I'll fill in the blank with this noun here in my prepositional object"; "The novel is predicate adjective"; "A person who can't verb adverb ought at least to speak correctly." Others are syntactic or rhetorical elements: "as is the innocent anecdote of bygone days"; "the memorable simile that yields deeper and subtler significances upon reflection, like a memorable simile." Narrative elements become mere slots, named but not filled: "Conventional startling opener"; "A tense moment in the evolution of the story," the narrator says. The tale oscillates between self-reference and reference to an existential situation where men and women are caught in the frustrations of love and communication. The narrative's self-reflexivity is directly suggestive of what has gone wrong in their failing relationship: "Standard conflict. Let's skip particulars. What do you want from me? What'll the story be this time? Same old story." Perceived as convention, as cliché, the relationship has become a blank with nothing to sustain interest. The characters perceive each other in terms of conventional behavior and conventional emotions:

> Why do you suppose it is, she asked, . . . that literate people such as we talk like characters in a story? Even supplying the dialogue-tags, she

added with wry disgust. . . . The same old story, an old-fashioned one at that.

The story simultaneously addresses the state of their relationship and that of contemporary fiction—"Love affairs, literary genres, third item in exemplary series, fourth—everything blossoms and decays, does it not, from the primitive and classical through the mannered and baroque to the abstract, stylized, dehumanized, unintelligible, blank"—denying the possibility of artistic and sexual completion. Fiction and love are on the rocks, and the cause is pinpointed: the narrator's self-consciousness has made it impossible for him to bring the story, and his lover, to a climax and to fill in the blank or the womb—in other words, to create. (This association between technical virtuosity and artistic impotence appears also in the **"Anonymiad,"** where his "professional sophistication, at the expense of his former naïve energy, was to be rendered as a dramatical correlative to the attrition of his potency with Merope . . . or vice versa.")

Thus the story establishes language's tendency to dissolve into emptiness and makes that very tendency its content—a human content, a problem of storytellers and, here, lovers. People and their relationships have become conventions perceived as such, pale shadows, mere pronouns open to infinite substitutions. Yet we sense the possibility of fuller selves, fuller characters and tales than self-conscious fiction allows, a fuller sense of self than self-absorption permits:

> Sometimes it seems as if things could instantly be altogether different and more admirable. The times be damned, one still wants a man vigorous, confident, bold, resourceful, adjective, and adjective. One still wants a woman spirited, spacious of heart, loyal, gentle, adjective, adjective. That man and that woman are as possible as the ones in this miserable story, and a good deal realer. It's as if they live in some room of our house that we can't find the door to, though it's so close we can hear echoes of their voices. Experience has made them wise instead of bitter; knowledge has mellowed instead of souring them; in their forties and fifties, even in their sixties, they're gayer and stronger and more authentic than they were in their twenties; for the twenty-year-olds they have only affectionate sympathy. So? Why aren't the couple in this story that man and woman, so easy to imagine?

If those voices could replace this self-conscious one, if fiction would recognize that people still live their lives "in more or less conventionally dramatic fashion, unfashionable or not"—that is, in a manner resembling fiction's conventions of linear plot, of motive and character—then this love affair and fiction would presumably be saved. But this is wishful thinking, for even as the narrator states, "that my dear is what writers have got to find ways to write about in this adjective adjective hour," he demonstrates its impossibility. Carried away by the force of his assertions, he loses hold on his statement and ends in the same self-reflexive quandary. This *is* the hour of "adjective adjective," of "accursed self-consciousness," of mimetic fiction's bad faith. The force of **"Title"** is in the human implications of the linguistic (and fictional) problem—the real

poignancy of that vision of a couple aging together in the fullness of affection, as set against the abrasive hostility to which these voices are driven by their self-absorption and their frustration with it. The self-consciousness that prevents them from speaking humanly to each other is precisely what makes the story speak humanly to us.

"Life-Story" continues the effort to get beyond reflexivity, first of all by critiquing it. For one thing, self-reflexivity is a convention of twentieth-century literature: "Another story about a writer writing a story! Another regressus in infinitum!" It's dreary, a tiresome mode for both writer and reader: "Who doesn't prefer art that at least overtly imitates something other than its own processes?" The fictiveness of fiction is an obvious truth, hardly enough to sustain even the shortest of tales: "Self-consciousness can be a bloody bore" [Barth, in Joe David Bellamy, *The New Fiction: Interviews with Innovative American Writers,* 1974]. The question, as the narrator of **"Life-Story"** comments, is one regarding the human implications of that truth: "what were to be the consequences of D's . . . disproving or verifying his suspicion [that the world is a fiction and he himself a character in a fiction], and why should a reader be interested?" We evaluate the fiction, and we respond to it, according to the resonances of what is expressed. The suggestion made by Barth in the "Literature of Exhaustion" essay and found in **"Title"** as well—to write of "the impossibility of making something new" and thereby "turn ultimacy against itself"—recurs in **"Life-Story"**: " 'You say you lack a ground-situation. Has it occurred to you that that circumstance may be your ground-situation?' " But this content is too thin; with that tale, Scheherazade's life is on shaky ground.

Various hypotheses are given, in the second section of the story, to account for the persistence of this self-reflexive mode which so plagues the narrator and subverts the story: social decline, physical aging, the metaphysical problem of reality as fiction, his choice of marital love over "a less regular, more glamorous style of life." But these explanations are, of course, neither here nor there. Self-reflexivity persists, interfering—as in the case of every *Funhouse* narrator except the impersonal narrator of the first two Ambrose stories—with the narrator's ability to sustain and complete a story.

And yet he *does* manage to complete it, thanks to two interruptions in his obsessive self-consciousness. First, as he comes to the end of a reflection on narrative structures in general and his life's in particular, he reaches the words "the reader," and they initiate a burst of aggressive energy that begins the third section of the story. It is as though the narrator has suddenly discovered the reader; for the first time he acknowledges the reader: "The reader! You, dogged, uninsultable, print-oriented bastard, it's you I'm addressing, who else." He refuses to let us recede into our accustomed passivity, and pulls us in—"For why do you suppose—you! you!"—taunting us and daring us to stop reading. After this bout of sparring with the reader, the narrator describes three options for how self-conscious fiction may regain the authority of conventional fiction:

> 1) fiction must acknowledge its fictitiousness and metaphoric invalidity or 2) choose to ignore the

question or deny its relevance or 3) establish some other, acceptable relation between itself, its author, its reader.

"Title" has dispensed, as we have seen, with the first option on the grounds of its obviousness and ultimate triviality; the second option is attempted by the **"Life-Story"** narrator as he tries to "tell his tale from start to finish in a conservative, 'realistic,' unself-conscious way"; the entry of the reader signals the third. The way out of the labyrinth of self-consciousness will be found neither by making self-consciousness central nor by denying it. The blank cannot be filled; no statement will hold. Fiction's authority must come from a source other than definitive statement.

What follows this claim, then, is a second interruption, this time by the narrator's wife, who walks into his study unexpectedly. Blocking his view of the page and wishing him a "Happy Birthday," she symbolically puts an end to his self-absorption (and the self-absorbed narrative) and affirms his identity as more than—in fact, as *other* than—self-consciousness. His existence confirmed by her (having just reached that affirmation himself via logical deduction), he is finally able to "cap his pen"—in contrast to the earlier *Funhouse* narrators who end in mid-sentence or otherwise inconclusively.

Filling in the blank, and finding one's way out of the self-reflexive funhouse, means both restoring the capacity of fiction to speak of something other than itself and liberating the narrator from solipsism. Barth finds a solution in the power of voice: the capacity to establish a connection between writer and reader, the capacity to express qualities of the speaker and to address a receiver. As long as we look to statement itself for meaning, self-conscious fiction will seem empty, like the answer Menelaus receives from the oracle or the "message" Ambrose receives from the sea. Ambrose and Bellerophon, questers both, find the same grail—a bottle with a message in it:

TO WHOM IT MAY CONCERN . . .

YOURS TRULY

The lines between were blank, as was the space beneath the complimentary close.

But their reactions are opposite: Ambrose feels the thrill of new knowledge and "other truth"; Bellerophon sees a blank. In terms of statement, Bellerophon is of course right. But for Ambrose, the message consists in the fact of its occurrence. He sees it as an act of address:

Past the river and the Bay, from continents beyond, this messenger had come. Borne by currents as yet uncharted, nosed by fishes as yet unnamed, it had bobbed for ages beneath strange stars. Then out of the oceans it had strayed; past cape and cove, black can, red nun, the word had wandered willy-nilly to his threshold.

It is literally "his truly," a message of concern to one who feels shut off from others and from those mysteries. Bellerophon sees a blank because he looks for a statement; Ambrose finds his meaning in the fact of receiving a message. This explains the curious ending of **"Water-Message,"** where Ambrose, having noticed that the paper on which

the message is written is composed of coarse fibers, now "embraces that fact." Ambrose embraces the medium—not merely the material, the paper, but the letter itself—as evidence of an intentional act of address and as ground on which sender and receiver may meet. The act itself is a message: it says, "I—someone besides yourself—exist, and so do you." The blank is filled by the communicative act itself, by the capacity of voice to "message" someone and thus to establish relationship.

Relationship is, for Barth, a basic condition of narrative. His **"Night-Sea"** narrator tries to deny it: "it is myself I talk to, to keep my reason in this awful darkness. There is no She! There is no You!" But the statement denies its own content, for, as dialogue, it is addressed to someone. Ambrose's adolescent fantasies are based upon an image of himself as independent of others—the lone hero, the lone martyr. But independence is precisely a fantasy, a hysterical claim based on fear or pride. **"Life-Story"** explicitly states the interdependence of narrator and reader: just as the narrator exists by virtue of the reader's attention, the reader exists insofar as the narrator speaks of him. The isolate self easily loses identity: the **"Life-Story"** narrator suspecting that he's a character in a fiction; Menelaus, resisting Helen's love, wondering "Who am I?"; the Anonymous narrator, alone on his beach, forgetting his name. The self-absorbed narrator tends to fade into impersonal or conventional voice. Thus the narrator of the **"Anonymiad,"** having lost his identity along with his zeal for writing, is cheered by the discovery of a water-message of his own. Undecipherable, it nevertheless carries the message of the existence of someone like himself. Perhaps that someone is actually himself: "No matter, the principle was the same: that I could be thus messaged, even by that stranger my former self, whether or not the fact tied me to the world, inspired me to address it once again." Why does it matter little whether the author of that message is himself? Because it is the act of addressing and of being addressed that constitutes the meaning. That is why Ambrose is not disheartened by the conventionalized nature of his message and why the narrator of **"Life-Story"** does not need to finish his sentence in order to complete it. Connection, relationship with an Other, has occurred.

"Messaging" is an inherently meaningful, but also irrational act. Menelaus becomes more and more frustrated as long as he attempts to get a definite answer to his question of why Helen chose *him*. What she asks of him is an act of faith, a belief in a patent absurdity—that she was never in Troy—as absurd as the oracle's answer to his "Why?" and equally definitive. In running from the terrible void of his identity (the oracle's answer to "Who am I" is " " ' " " ' " " ' " ' " ' " ' "), he must affirm a possibility, consent to an improbability. For Menelaus, as for the self-conscious self, to be in relation—as the *Funhouse* presents relation—requires a suspension of disbelief: "To love is easy; to be loved, as if one were real, on the order of others: fearsome mystery! Unbearable responsibility! To her, *Menelaus* signified something recognizable, as *Helen* him. Whatever was it?" To be loved is to be compelled to consent to the fiction of one's own substance and to accept the unknowableness of the Other. Confronted with the oracle's answer to his "Who am I?" Menelaus rushes off, "done with questions," to "re-embrace" Helen (an act that reenacts Ambrose's embrace of the medium that messages him) and "clasp her past speech, never let go, frig understanding." What will fill in the blank is an act of relationship, rather than a fact to be understood. Ambrose earlier had a vision of love as perfect unity: "Somewhere in the world there was a young woman with such splendid understanding that she'd see him entire, like a poem or story." But neither stories nor selves are "entire" in Barth's fiction. They are self-reflexive, complex, and take on meaning only through an act of willing participation.

It is in this sense that love becomes "base-fact and footer to the fiction crazy-house our life." Love demands the same irrational affirmation of the Other and the self that the narrator of the **"Anonymiad"** expresses as he sends out his endless fictions-in-bottles. He imagines his tale drifting past "the unknown man or woman to whose heart, of all hearts in the world, it could speak fluentest, most balmly—but they're too preoccupied to reach out to it." He knows that these projections of himself will likely go unreceived, and consequently that this would-be act of communication is irrational. Nevertheless he continues to send them out, deriving satisfaction from the act emphasized by the eccentric typography of the last line of the story—and the novel: "Wrote it." His affirmation represents a triumph over the despair that the earlier *Funhouse* narrators express at knowing their fundamental isolation.

Barth brings us to the point where writing itself becomes of ultimate value, not because of what is expressed but because of what the act involves: faith, commitment, in the face of absurdity. As Wallace Stevens puts it elsewhere:

> The final belief is to believe in a fiction, which you know to be a fiction, there being nothing else. The exquisite truth is to know that it is a fiction, and that you believe in it willingly

> ["Adagia," in *Opus Posthumous,* ed. Samuel French Morse, 1957]

Knowing that there is no "Menelaus," that the only identity we can know is "first-person anonymous," Menelaus finds the will to cry out to Helen, "Menelaus here!"; for only as Menelaus, a fiction, can he be loved by her. That act of affirmation does not deny his self-consciousness, but it does take him beyond its bounds into relationship.

The personal dilemma and the writerly dilemma as Barth presents them, both products of the mind's and of language's capacity for self-reflection, have the same solution: voice, or rather what voice makes possible—the expression of human qualities and concerns. One of those concerns is the alienation and fragmentation of the self; another is the reduction of language to signs and self-references. Yet another is the need to address an Other and the desire to be "messaged." Voice creates the possibility of relationship and imbues the meaningless word with the mystery of human intentions and human significances, as Ambrose discovers:

> Vanity frets about his name, Pride vaunts it, Knowledge retches at its sound, Understanding sighs; all live outside it, knowing well that I and my sign are neither one nor quite two.

Yet only give it voice: whisper "Ambrose," as at rare times certain people have—see what-all leaves off to answer! Ambrose, Ambrose, Ambrose, Ambrose! Regard that beast, ungraspable, most queer, pricked up in my soul's crannies!

Voiced, the sign takes on personal meaning for Ambrose; it reaches into the soul and evokes a response. At those moments when the name becomes the means of one person "messaging" another—and it is not incidental that the name is whispered: the context is intimate, perhaps erotic—the gap between the self and its sign scarcely matters. So, too, in fiction, where the lack of correspondence between convention and the "real world" pales beside the question of how the writer uses those conventions to stage his own concerns and to speak to us.

Self-reflexivity leads to the awareness that language is fiction-making, that the self and the world are fictions. What, then, can self-reflexive fiction speak of authoritatively? Barth's answer is that it can speak of an existential situation, the dilemma of users of language. Even while Barth disintegrates the tale, the teller, and the medium—superficially *denying* human concerns—he portrays the efforts to make language signify, the desire to speak and be heard, to display oneself and call forth a response. For narrative voice, self-reflexive or not, carries the sense of person and the implication of relationship: "Where there's a voice there's a speaker." As the narrator of **"Title"** fervently hopes for, *Lost in the Funhouse* does manage after all to speak of "what goes on between" people, of how "we grow old and tired, we think of how things used to be or might have been and how they are now" and of how "we get exasperated and desperate and out of expedients and out of words," but not by evading the self-conscious mode as the narrator believes he must, not by any naïve—and impossible—return to purely representational language. By playing at emptying and filling the blanks that self-reflexivity creates, narrative voice dramatizes desire, frustration, love, despair, belief. The gaps between "I" and "he," voice and receiver, word and object, name and self, are still there; but rather than absences, they become what Stevens calls "prolific ellipses" which generate common human concerns.

In *Politics and the Novel,* Irving Howe offers a criterion against which fiction must be judged: "how much of our life does it illuminate? how ample a moral vision does it suggest?" The deconstructionist *mythos* . . . regards self-reflexive fiction as immune from such considerations; it would persuade us that we become heroic readers to the degree that we renounce such concerns. But self-reflexive narrative is still narrative; as such, it is pervaded by voice. Any tendency of postmodern fiction to collapse into linguistic freeplay or mere "text" is counterbalanced by narrative's irrepressible evocation, through voice, of a narrative presence characterized by certain acts, qualities, and intentions—which may even be an intention to purify voice of self. In narrative the very means of negotiating absence is inescapably a mode of presence, pulling self-reflexive language in an opposite direction, towards another kind of alternative to reference. Ignoring this essential narrative tension, the deconstructionist reading reduces narrative to what it contends with, and substitutes its own mythology for the actual complexity of what writing generates. (pp. 463-81)

Deborah A. Woolley, "Empty 'Text,' Fecund Voice: Self-Reflexivity in Barth's 'Lost in the Funhouse'," in Contemporary Literature, *Vol. 26, No. 4, Winter, 1985, pp. 460-81.*

Heide Ziegler   (essay date 1987)

[*In the following excerpt, Ziegler surveys themes and narrative techniques in* Lost in the Funhouse *and* Chimera, *emphasizing the role of the artist and the function of storytelling.*]

[The] German concept of the *Bildungsroman*—the novel of the learning hero, acquiring the education needed to become a useful member of society—is the key to an understanding of *The Sot-Weed Factor* and *Giles Goat-Boy.* The *Bildungsroman,* which ultimately affirms the society that frames it, found its transcendence in the *Künstlerroman,* the novel of the self-reflexive artist. Here the individual whose task it is to acquire *Bildung* is someone who can dictate the premises and the consequences of the learning he receives—at least when he writes about his own development as a writer. (Traditionally, the hero of the *Künstlerroman* is the learning painter or composer.) The German word *bilden,* to educate, is equivalent to the Latin verb *fingere,* to form, to create, whence derives the English word fiction. The hero of the *Bildungsroman,* in acquiring *Bildung,* is called upon to adopt what society offers him in order to form or create himself—that is, to perform on himself the task of the artist. In this sense every *Bildungsroman* is also a *Künstlerroman.* However, by introducing himself as protagonist of his own text, the writer proposes a distance from his former self. The artist, knowing himself to be an artist, devises his own *Bildung* in retrospect. This leads to an autobiographical paradox. There is a former self and a present self; and language has both to define and to relate them. This paradox once again raises the question of origin and authenticity that Barth had seemed to face and resolve in *The Sot-Weed Factor* and *Giles Goat-Boy,* where he both invokes and denounces the validity of origins in order to define himself not as a person—as in *The Floating Opera* and *The End of the Road*—but as an artist. In the book that follows *Giles Goat-Boy,* Barth returns to the dilemma, only now to deal not with a literal but a literary father/author.

Lost in the Funhouse (1968), subtitled a *Fiction for Print, Tape, Live Voice,* contains fourteen pieces which, in his "Author's Note," Barth calls "neither a collection nor a selection, but a series." This situates it structurally somewhere between the novel and the short-story genres. *Lost in the Funhouse* is conceived as a parody of Joyce's *Portrait of the Artist as a Young Man,* James Joyce being the ghost of the father who, in Barth's book, has become his own son. Writing for and yet away from Joyce seemed to imply for Barth a conscious acceptance of his postmodernist condition, dependent on and yet a step beyond the modernism that Joyce had been so influential in shaping. In an interview Barth called *Lost in the Funhouse* "a *Künstlerroman* with a twist" [Evelyn Glaser-Wöhrer's second

interview with John Barth in Evelyn Glaser-Wöhrer, *An Analysis of John Barth's "Weltanschauung": His View of Life and Literature,* 1977], the twist denoting the ironic dialectic between self and other, a state which oscillates between filial obedience and narcissistic rebellion. The subtitle of the book assigns to it another intermediate status somewhere between the spoken and the written word, just as it has an intermediate status between being a series of stories and a novel. And the book proper "starts" with a special device—called **"Frame Tale"**—in the form of a Moebius strip that is intended to be cut out, twisted, and fastened end to end in order for us to read *ad infinitum* the same key phrase: "Once upon a time there was a story that began." Barth's most overtly "experimental" book, *Lost in the Funhouse,* thus calls up an old tradition of story-telling, but it employs it in order to dissolve genre, narrative mode, authorial voice, and consecutive time sequence. Being a form of intermedia, a book where we are given complex instructions as to how each piece should be read or performed, it is thus a paradoxical assertion and dissolution of the whole notion of the artist.

Lost in the Funhouse is a work in which not the artistic process but the development of the artist is constantly questioned, and the author turned round from active creative ego to anonymity and back again. The notion of the evolution of a hero is undercut by a parody of plot development—for the series of fictions claims continuity, even while it disclaims the ideas of gradual moral achievement or of organic self-completion. The "hero," Ambrose Mensch, is created in **"Night-Sea Journey,"** the first fiction after the Moebius strip **"Frame Tale,"** a narrative of how a male sperm and a female egg unite. He gradually grows—interrupted by other fictions—through **"Ambrose His Mark," "Water-Message,"** and **"Lost in the Funhouse"** to be 13 years of age, but disappears or gets lost in the funhouse when he decides to become an artist. Ambrose the artist can no longer function as a character: "Therefore he will construct funhouses *for others* and be their secret operator—though he would rather be among the lovers for whom funhouses are designed" (my italics). Just like lovers, characters may interact with each other; but the decision to become an artist leads to isolation. Yet this is not the isolation of the tragic hero, since for the artist his environment is no longer identical with the real society he happens to live in. His houses are fictions, funhouses which he himself creates. Although being their "secret operator" implies real readers, this relationship between reality and fiction is only indirect. Therefore, in order not to be entirely lost in his own creation, the artist needs to forge alliances with the environments which *are* open to him—the stories that have already been created by the writers of the past.

So, like a Moebius strip, the action of *Lost in the Funhouse* moves on two levels—fiction and reality—and in two different directions—into the future and into the past. The realistically written stories, **"Night-Sea Journey"** in which Ambrose is conceived, **"Ambrose His Mark"** in which Ambrose earns his name, **"Water-Message"** in which Ambrose is initiated into the facts of life, and **"Lost in the Funhouse"** in which Ambrose decides to become an artist, move forward in time. Following the story **"Echo,"** which represents the turning-point of the Moebius strip and of the book, the stories **"Two Meditations," "Glossolalia," "Menelaiad,"** and **"Anonymiad"** move backward into mythical times, the times of oral tradition. **"Two Meditations,"** a reflection upon the relationship between cause and effect, first demonstrates this principle of reversal. It consists of two sections, "Niagara Falls" and "Lake Erie," which subvert the logical sequence of cause and effect just as, geographically, the order of the two sections reverses the fall of the waters of Niagara.

"Glossolalia," six pieces in metrical prose patterned on the Lord's Prayer, attempts to fathom the nature of existential riddles of the past presented through undecipherable "texts" whose mystery derives from the impact of an unknown future: Cassandra's prophecies; tongueless Procne's horrid tale woven into a robe for her sister Philomela to decode; the ravings of Crispus, who has been touched by God and is mentioned by Paul in his First Epistle to the Corinthians; the unheeded warnings of the Queen of Sheba's talking bird; the apparently meaningless song of a psalmist employing—as Barth explains in "Seven Additional Author's Notes" (added to the "Author's Note" in the paperback edition of *Lost in the Funhouse*)—"the tongue of a historical glossolalist." Finally, the sum of all these riddles is reflected upon by the author:

> Ill fortune, constraint and terror, generate guileful art; despair inspires. The laureled clairvoyants tell our doom in riddles. Sewn in our robes are horrid tales, and the speakers-in-tongues enounce atrocious tidings. The prophet-birds seem to speak sagely, but are shrieking their frustration. The senselessest babble, could we ken it, might disclose a dark message, or prayer.

The relationship between the "spoken" texts from the past and the Author's commentary reveals the relationship between oral and written tradition as the difference between original and dependent text. Thus, every later text "frames" every earlier one, paradoxically deferring access more and more to the original text in the process. By reflecting upon the meaning of the preceding five cryptic texts, the author moves into another—ironic or interpretative—frame: into a text that abstracts from, and at the same time incorporates, the preceding texts, changing them into pre-texts in a logical as well as in a temporal sense, yet is meaningless without them. Thus, the framing text implicitly poses the question of the validity of the later as opposed to the earlier word, calling itself into question, yet also affirming its own historical, framing, role. For instance, were Cassandra's prophecies more valid when she first enounced them than when Barth reflects on them? After all, nobody ever heeded Cassandra's warnings anyway; their truth had to be proved by history, which is to say the future. Thus, the later word may rehabilitate the earlier one—this being the reason why the author chose the same metrical pattern for his commentary as for the preceding texts—yet this later word thereby detracts from its own status, replacing meaning with exegesis. At the same time the later word may succeed in disclosing the meaning behind even the "senselessest babble" from the past.

"Menelaiad" attempts to authenticate the method of

framing as substitute for the creation of original meaning. The story consists of seven frames. The story of the innermost frame triggers the next one out, and so on. These seven frames are seven veils, veiling—and in the process of reading, unveiling—the naked beauty of Helen, desired by all men on earth. Yet the seven frames also frame her husband Menelaus's loss of identity as he increasingly has to share Helen's beauty; and as such they tell the story of that loss. Thus the story of Menelaus's loss of self becomes the substitute for that loss.

Menelaus is the legendary cuckold; and Helen is unfaithful to him because his inferiority complex prevents him from believing what Proteus, the seer, tells him: "Helen chose you without reason because she loves you without cause." From his wedding night up to present narrative time, Menelaus wants to know why Helen chose him in preference to all the other much more heroic heroes of Greece. Her love cannot satisfy him, since it defies explanation. Baffled, Menelaus begins to tell his story, searching for the flaw in his life that will render the understanding which beauty fails to offer. Since beauty is self-contained, it cannot be understood; the desire for knowledge develops from a deficiency. Beauty is divine, the search for knowledge human. Demigoddess by birth, Helen wanted Menelaus to overcome the gap between divinity and humanity, eternal beauty and its Platonic reflection, through love. Menelaus fails, since he is nothing but human. Helen avenges herself by remaining eternally beautiful, eternally desirable, and, for Menelaus, eternally unattainable. Yet for Helen to avenge herself eternally, Menelaus too must be made eternal. He becomes immortal through narration, becoming the voice that tells his life-story. Substituting narration for life, Menelaus acquires the role of eternal husband: eternally cuckolded, eternally loved. Yet love, no longer being the substance of life, is consequently transformed into "the absurd, unending *possibility* of love" (my italics); and only as such can it be told. Loss of identity is the price Menelaus pays for existing in a legend and as a legend. For what a legend ultimately wants to trace is the origin, the truth; yet, it owes its very existence to the fact that the truth recedes before it. If it were able to find the origin, its own reason for being would cease. Only the possibility of the truth of the legend of Menelaus and Helen can be affirmed, and this possibility is once more substantiated by Barth's **"Menelaiad"** which frames the original story.

Finally **"Anonymiad,"** the last fiction of *Lost in the Funhouse,* is the culmination of Barth's idea of mythical origin as a riddle about the loss of identity which spawns necessary fictions—as interpretations of, and strategies of compensating for, that loss. **"Anonymiad"** is the story of the nameless minstrel mentioned in Book III of Homer's *Odyssey,* whom Agamemnon left behind to guard Clytemnestra's virtue while he himself went off to fight Troy. Marooned on a desolate island by Clytemnestra's lover Aegisthus, the minstrel is left to himself, not only to lament his fate, brought about by his own false ambition to see the world, but also to transcend the limitations of his ego. He invents the written word and all the literary genres. He then puts his fictions afloat in nine amphorae which Aegisthus has left behind and which, because of the inspiration afforded him by the wine they held, he has named for the nine Muses. At the end of his life the minstrel, who has forgotten his own name during the seven years of his isolation, composes the autobiographical **"Anonymiad,"** a tale not of *an* artist, but of *the* artist:

> Seven parts plus head- and tail-piece: the years of my maroonment framed by its causes and prognosis. The prologue was to've established . . . the ground-conceit and the narrative voice and viewpoint: a minstrel stuck on some Aegean clinker commences his story, in the process characterizing himself and hinting at the circumstances leading to his plight. Parts One through Four were to rehearse those circumstances, Five through Seven the stages of his island life vis-à-vis his minstrelling—innocent garrulity, numb silence, and terse self-knowledge, respectively—and fetch the narrative's present time up to the narrator's. The epilogue's a sort of envoi to whatever eyes, against all odds, may one day read it.

The image of the artist filling the bellies of his beloved muses with fictions and sending them off into the Aegean links up with the opening stories of *Lost in the Funhouse,* in which the sperm that is to generate the future artist is carried towards the shores of love (**"Night-Sea Journey"**) and the future artist receives a message in a bottle revealing to him his calling (**"Water-Message"**). The Moebius strip which frames *Lost in the Funhouse* has come full circle. The sperm bearing the artist becomes the drifting amphorae bearing art. The relationship between the author and his fiction has become as unmediated as that between a father and his sperm. The figure of a narrator has become superfluous, because the narrator has lost his ontological justification as a mediator between reality and fiction. Thus *Lost in the Funhouse* can be called a *Künstlerroman* in the extreme: not only written *by* an artist *about* the artist, but substituting itself *for* the artist.

In *Lost in the Funhouse* life is gradually consumed by art: Ambrose Mensch grows up not acquiring *Bildung* for life, but becoming an artist. While the narrative experiments that provide the themes of the rest of the stories of *Lost in the Funhouse*—**"Autobiography," "Petition," "Title,"** and **"Life-Story"**—constitute an artistic identity, they seem to require the sacrifice of Ambrose as a character. Yet if the artist's development destroys his unquestionable and unquestioning identity, then a conscious regression in time might help to recover that identity. Barth uses Homer's myth of the Mycenaean minstrel to demonstrate that the past, if its exact historical moment and locale are indefinable, dissolves the borderline between reality and fiction, and between identity and anonymity. The anonymous minstrel of the last story in *Lost in the Funhouse* returns story as such to become the watery protoplasm of the first, and artistic solitude bears eventual seed in the drift of time. Here, in new stories generated from old stories in the procreative mystery of love, is the interpretative quality of story which Barth celebrates as essential for life.

If *Lost in the Funhouse* seeks the origin of story and finds it above all in myth, which dissolves the borderline between fiction and reality, then Barth's next book, *Chimera,* suggests that this borderline can be transgressed in both directions; fiction can replace life, life can also replace fiction. *Chimera* consists of three novellas, **"Dunyazadiad," "Perseid,"** and **"Bellerophoniad,"** all drawing on mythic roots of narrative. The impact and arrangement of these three novellas are made to resemble the mythical Chimaera—a fire-breathing monster with a lion's head, goat's body, and serpent's tail. But since this Chimaera is in the Bellerophon myth and only appears in the **"Bellerophoniad"** when Iobates, King of Lycia, sets Bellerophon the task of destroying the monster, this suggests that the stories have a cumulative direction, with the story of the life and death of Bellerophon as the center. And in this story, as in the others, the mythic world of the past is intruded upon from the future world of "reality." The stories of the past do not merely float onward into the future; they can take in a content from that future.

So, at the mid-point of his life, Barth's Bellerophon receives a "water-message" from the future—a letter whose author he supposes to be the seer Polyeidus, the shape-shifter, his mentor, and, as he finally comes to know, his true father. Yet this letter describes the attempt of one Jerome Bonaparte Bray (a descendant of Napoleon's brother Jerome and his American wife Betsy Patterson, and also of Harold Bray, George Giles's adversary in *Giles Goat-Boy*) to compose a "revolutionary" novel called *NOTES* with the aid of a computer. (The reader will learn more of Jerome Bray in Barth's next novel which is called, not quite *NOTES,* but *LETTERS.*) Bellerophon suspects that this computer may be some future version of the seer in his own life. He thus unconsciously foresees Polyeidus's actual relationship to him, for, as a Barth reader would know, the notion of the computer as father has already been established in *Giles Goat-Boy.* As for the concept of the revolutionary novel *NOTES,* it is remarkable in two respects:

> On the one hand, inasmuch as "character," "plot," and for that matter "content," "subject," and "meaning," are attributes of particular novels, the Revolutionary Novel *NOTES* is to dispense with all of them in order to transcend the limitations of particularity; . . . it will represent nothing beyond itself, have no content except its own form, no subject but its own processes. . . . On the other hand, at its *"Phi*-point" . . . there is to occur a single anecdote, a perfect model of a text-within-the-text, a microcosm or paradigm of the work as a whole: . . . "a history of the Greek mythic hero Bellerophon."

Chimera is not, nor does it represent, the revolutionary novel *NOTES.* But it reflects upon the conditions of such a novel. It consists of *notes* towards such a novel. And it demonstrates how the story of the Greek mythic hero Bellerophon can serve as a "perfect model of a text-within-the-text," for the story of Bellerophon is "framed" by the story of his cousin Perseus as recounted in the **"Perseid."** Throughout his life Bellerophon has only copied the heroic life led by his cousin. Perseus has established the pattern on which he feels he must mold himself in order to become a mythic hero; when he leaves Corinth for the world of adventure, he actually asks Polyeidus "for a copy of the Pattern, by way of autobiographical road map."

Perseus, at the mid-point of *his* life, had made up his mind to retrace his steps, to repeat his former heroic deeds—beheading the Medusa, liberating Andromeda, petrifying the inimical wedding-guests with Medusa's head—but he wanted to repeat them self-consciously. Thus, the mode of operation during his second enterprise had to be contrary to the first: he had to permit things to happen to him instead of adventuring to them—in order to be able to reflect upon them. Perseus's ironic but nevertheless heroic endeavor is rewarded by the gods: Athene revives Medusa and even restores her original beauty on condition that she does not show her face to anyone. However, there is one escape clause. Medusa is granted the power to rejuvenate or depetrify, just once, whomever she gazes upon or whoever gazes upon her if this person truly loves her. When Perseus finally decides to lift Medusa's veil, their look of mutual love "estellates" them. They become the constellation of Perseus and Medusa. Immortalized, they tell their story to each other every night—"as long as men and women read the stars."

Bellerophon contrives to make his life follow a similar path, since Polyeidus has indeed provided him with the Barthian Pattern of Mythic Heroism. He also attempts to create a second cycle of his life, like Perseus devising it as a self-conscious repetition of the first. The double irony of *his* ironic endeavor is that the first cycle of Perseus's life was spontaneous, whereas Bellerophon's own has been a self-conscious imitation from the beginning. He leaves behind his gentle wife and family as well as the kingdom of Lycia, which is prosperous and politically stable, for the sole reason that "because mythic heroes at that age and stage should become the opposite of content, my contentment made me wretched." Bellerophon's defect is obvious: he has never been an authentic hero. Since he strives to fulfill the demands of the heroic myth as *story*, his heroism is always belated. This predicament is mirrored in the structure of Barth's book: as Bellerophon's life-story is placed last, it is doomed always to be read *after* that of Perseus—whereas in ancient myth their heroic careers overlapped, Bellerophon thus being granted as much authenticity as Perseus. Thus, all the events in the life of Barth's Bellerophon also have the form of stories; they never appear as a series of heroic deeds that later became the content of a story. Bellerophon's killing of the Chimaera, for instance, is a fiction prescribed for him by Polyeidus. Polyeidus has prepared a special spear which, instead of a sharp bronze point, has a dull lead one, like a pencil. Bellerophon thrusts this spear into the Chimaera's cave. She attacks it and dies when the lead, melted by her fiery breath, burns through her vitals and kills her. Therefore, it is through a trick that the monster dies; it is also a fiction that Bellerophon killed her.

In the same way, the whole life of Barth's Bellerophon is a fiction or lie. Polyeidus, the trickster, manages to make everybody, including Bellerophon himself, believe that Bellerophon is a demigod and that Poseidon is his father, although Polyeidus knows Bellerophon to be supposititious. Bellerophon supposes that he must be a true hero when he is nothing but the hero of Polyeidus's, his father or author's, fiction. Therefore Bellerophon, although he believes he is truly a demigod, does not act like one, but

rather like someone interested in the implications of being a demigod—in other words, rather more like an artist than a hero. When Anteia, the sister of his future wife Philonoë, attempts to seduce him, because she wants to become the mother of a demigod, Bellerophon cautiously points out to her how unlikely it is that she will get what she wants from him. With the help of a Mendel diagram he demonstrates to her that since he is a demigod and she is a mortal, they might indeed produce a demigod together but the chances are two to one against it. The probability is reduced considerably by taking into account that the child may be female, that a demigod's embrace, unlike a god's, may fail to impregnate, and that the equal distribution of divine and human sperm is by no means guaranteed. He further goes on to explain to impatient Anteia that personally he would be much more interested in making love to a demigoddess, because a demigod and a demigoddess can do together something that Zeus himself, with a mortal mate, cannot do: produce a full-blooded deity.

> That's also the only instance of genetical up-breeding in this scheme of possibilities—a child superior by nature to both parents—and the same pairing holds the only possibility of true *down*-breeding. Neither of these hypothetical possibilities, to my knowledge, has been realized in mythic history, but they make the coupling of a demigoddess and myself, for example, a good deal richer in geneticodramatic potential than the coupling of you and me, don't you think?

After this lecture Anteia flees, avenging herself by accusing Bellerophon of the rape which she had hoped for in vain. The comedy here is not superficial; nor is Bellerophon simply trying to avoid making love to Anteia by ruminating on up-breeding and how to create an immortal. Instead he represents the ironic dilemma of the postmodernist author.

This dilemma is implied in the fact that he needs to apply Mendel's nineteenth-century law to the ancient myth of the birth of the hero—that he needs to historicize the mythic time sequence whereby a myth accumulates meaning through mere repetition, in order to justify his claim to heroism. Analogously, the postmodernist author can no longer be an authentic artist; his only claim to originality lies in the reflection upon this dilemma from his own point of view. However, looking backward may yet defy belatedness. As the letter from the future in the **"Bellerophoniad"** illustrates, the method of applying future results of historic or scientific research to ancient myth can shed new light on patterns that seemed to be exhausted long ago: "Neither of these hypothetical possibilities, to my knowledge, has been realized in mythic history," says Bellerophon. This insight is Bellerophon's—and Barth's—original contribution to mythic history.

Being no demigod, Bellerophon cannot *act* like a mythic hero. Yet as an artist he understands that the immortality achieved through heroic deeds—fame—can to some degree be won by procuring an audience for one's *stories*. Consequently, Bellerophon craves audiences: he constantly tells the tale of how he rode Pegasus and killed the Chimaera to his wife and children, who now know it by heart; at the same time he also tells it to his young Amazon lover

Melanippe, who plays to him the role Medusa played to Perseus; finally, it is told to the reader, since at the end of Bellerophon's life Polyeidus changes himself into "you-in-*Bellerophoniad*-form." Since Bellerophon is conscious of his craving for an audience, the effects of his stories upon others become a part of those very stories in the retelling. Thus teller and audience become mutually dependent. Similarly, for Bellerophon Perseus's heroic deeds have already become his own myths; he listens to those myths, and his own imitations of Perseus's deeds represent the writer's adaptation of earlier stories. Forgoing his own identity by willingly identifying with his hero, Bellerophon achieves another identity, paradoxical in that it is neither his nor Perseus's, but that of an artist. Though forgoing the dialogue with others which could have established a substitute identity by constantly telling his story, Bellerophon the unsuccessful hero becomes Bellerophon the successful author, partaking of the precarious immortality of the written word: "Loosed at last from mortal speech, he turned into written words: Bellerophonic letters afloat between two worlds, forever betraying, in combinations and recombinations, the man they forever represent." Bellerophon's immortality is the result of the constant betrayal of the possibility of undivided presence. Thus he no longer remembers to whom he is telling his story at precisely this moment; he often repeats himself, attempting to fill in possible lacunae for a particular audience. This process whereby the author loses himself in the text

Manuscript page showing Barth's revisions to "Dunyazadiad" in Chimera.

could only be brought to a halt if the story were always addressed to the same, ideal audience.

The postmodernist author's need for an ideal reader is the theme of the first novella in *Chimera*, "Dunyazadiad," which retells the story of Scheherazade telling the stories of *The Thousand and One Nights*. Tradition has it that by beguiling King Shahryar with the infolded stories she relates, she saves her life over a thousand and one nights. The King's threatening power denies him the role of ideal audience (Barth has said that Shahryar represents the male-chauvinist extreme of the American academic "publish or perish" principle), but Scheherazade *is* the ideal story-teller, for she translates an existentially suspensive situation into a dramatic suspension of disbelief which, in turn, prevents her death. Moreover, her transfer of continuous peril into narrative resourcefulness intrigues the subsequent reader or listener. The King becomes a secondary figure; the listener or reader who can appreciate this transformation becomes the ideal audience. The ideal listener is represented in Dunyazade, Scheherazade's little sister, who each night initiates her telling of a new story or instigates the continuation of a story-in-progress, each time creating the situation in which story-telling can occur. The ideal reader is represented by John Barth himself, who offers himself as the inspiration of the artist, being able to transport himself back into Scheherazade's times after having accidentally written down the words: "The key to the treasure is the treasure"—the very words Scheherazade speaks when desperate about how to deal with a king who deflowers a virgin each night and kills her in the morning. So she is shown to be overwhelmed when John Barth, "The Genie" from the future, offers to tell her one of the stories collected in *The Thousand and One Nights* every day so that she can then tell it to the King at night. Scheherazade had once had the idea of charming the King with stories herself, but had abandoned it as impractical. She now regains confidence in this device from the proof, provided by The Genie, that it will really work. John Barth, the ideal reader, thus creates the ideal storyteller; but, more importantly, he proves the advantage of the written over the spoken word, since it is the text, preserved through centuries, that unlocks the treasure of the past.

The interpretation of the novella hinges on the words: the key to the treasure *is* the treasure. They are magic words, because it appears as if Barth and Scheherazade were thinking of them at the same time when in fact centuries separate them. Transporting himself back into Scheherazade's time, Barth can meet her as if they were two people alive at the same time. Yet they also meet as author and reader meet—through an act of the imagination. Finally, they meet as potential lovers since they agree "that writing and reading, or telling and listening, were literally ways of making love." What Barth means to demonstrate with the magic tryst between the Author and Scheherazade is the actual value of what he calls heartfelt possibilities. His endeavor in *Chimera* is to present the importance of storytelling (and love) in the face of ultimate extinction—the end of the story (**"Dunyazadiad"**), the end of life (**"Bellerophoniad"**), the end of man (**"Perseid"**).

"The key to the treasure *is* the treasure" means that truth is more likely to be found in possibility than in reality. Just as Bellerophon's life proved to be a lie, Scheherazade's stories prove to be true; or, in Barth's words: "They're too important to be lies. Fictions, maybe—but truer than fact." The importance of her stories or fictions is made manifest through their longevity. If, after centuries, John Barth can still be enchanted by Scheherazade's stories-within-her-story to the degree that he needs to express his "lifelong adoration" of her through a series of written homages like the present novella, then her story as well as her stories have proved to be truer than her possible life and death. The *Künstlerroman* has superseded the artist. Not only has the artist been made superfluous, as in the end of *Lost in the Funhouse,* but in *Chimera* the artist's life-story merely frames the truth which his artistic inspiration has conjured up as if by magic. (pp. 49-63)

> *Heide Ziegler, in her* John Barth, *Methuen, 1987, 95 p.*

John Barth with Loretta M. Lampkin   (interview date 1988)

[In the following excerpt, Barth comments on critical interpretations of his stories in Lost in the Funhouse.*]*

[Lampkin]: *Critics have such conflicting views of your* **Funhouse** *series; some call it nihilistic; others, a tautology. A few like myself find in it one of the most powerful love messages in all of postmodernist fiction. Would you talk about the disparate critical views of that little book and about its "heart of the matter" as metaphor?*

[Barth]: The heart of the matter is or at least includes what you just said. My interest in the self-reflexive aspects of **Funhouse,** for example, is not overwhelming, but it's a very real interest. The formal energy of the stories comes from such concerns as that, which are really of a fairly technical nature. But the juice of the fiction, the heart of the fiction, comes from such other concerns as you just mentioned. Those *are* love stories, no question about it. This is why it distresses me when some critics, whether they're praising or blaming the work, turn their attention only to the technical and somewhat vertiginous aspects of the work's concern with its own processes. A well-constructed, artistically successful work of fiction has its formal interests as well as its substantial interests, and each becomes a metaphor for the other. So which is the term and which is the referent depends on which handle you happen to seize. There isn't any wrong handle; each end of the stick is a proper handle.

That's the Möbius strip, right?

The Möbius is a stick with no ends to it, yes.

You have called **Funhouse** *a series, but the Möbius strip succeeds, I think, in unifying both its technique and its message. In fact, American literature contains a number of such authorially redactive forms—Faulkner's* Go Down, Moses, *for example. Like biblical stories, its parts appear to have been "re-envisioned" by the writer in successive stages, then stitched together and completed, often for a new audience and purpose. Faulkner does not attach his stories to a Möbius strip; still, certain images in* Go Down,

Moses *do link up in a to-and-fro pattern similar to your* **Funhouse** *series.*

Would you talk about why we should call **Funhouse** *a series rather than, say, a process novel, since its form is so unified?*

No doubt it depends on how far you want to stretch the term "novel" or "series." **Lost in the Funhouse** is meant to be more than simply a collection, a miscellany, of short stories whose only common bond is that they came from the same authorial imagination and with maybe a few echoing motifs or even characters among them. It's meant to be a series in that there is an exfoliation and a development, one with a double motion. As the apparent narrator in most of the stories in the series goes through his biographical development, the time of the stories tends to move back from the present into the mythic past, and then at the end, of course, there's a circling back. A difference between the form of *Funhouse*—a cycle with a twist to it—and, say, the form of Joyce's *Wake* (which circles back to its own first sentence) is the difference between a circle and a spiral, or a circle and a Möbius strip. The texts launched by the stranded minstrel at the end of the **"Anonymiad"**—which contain, in addition, his literal sperm—are meant to circle back to the spermatozoan story at the beginning of the book. You go around, but you don't go around in a deadly circle.

And it's more than a matter of mere rhetorical roundness, isn't it? More than the work's closing sentence connecting with the opening sentence as in Joyce's Wake.

That's right. *Finnegans Wake,* of course, is a splendid example of narrative form becoming the ground metaphor, the ground image for the whole world view of the novel. If your view of history is cyclical, as Joyce's at least provisionally was during the composition of the *Wake*—that Viconian principle of eternal recurrence—then, a kind of roller-towel form for the novel is appropriate. I don't know what my view of history is, but insofar as it involves some allowance for repetition and recurrence, reorchestration, and reprise (that *re-* prefix has become a house prefix at the Barth house), I would always want it to be more in the form of a thing circling out and out and becoming more inclusive each time—springing out, to get back to your question, from a heart. If the technics of the fiction aren't part of an impassioned commitment to the enterprise and to the characters involved, then I've no interest in it.

I'm particularly interested in **"Glossolalia,"** *and my students want me to ask whether you ever apprehend in a flash the whole form of a work before working out the details.*

No: my gestalts are slow-motion gestalts. The **"Glossolalia"** piece is in there half as a joke, but a serious joke. In our preliminary conversation you called it a good starting place for anybody who wants to spiral out into the whole fiction. I hadn't thought of it that way, but I see what you mean.

It occurred to me somewhere along the line—a slow-motion gestalt—that in a manner of speaking all of those poor characters in the **Funhouse** stories and probably most of us poor citizens going through our lives—all of us can be seen sometimes as trying to say something actually quite different from what we're apparently saying. It's amusing but also touching to imagine, as every psychiatrist, cabalist, and deconstructionist imagines, that the verbal transactions between us are a kind of code. That the real messages that we're exchanging with one another may be quite a different thing from the actual words we speak and write. We all understand this in a common-sense way: We say, "Gee, it's a nice day today" and "The cotton looks good this year" while what we may really be saying is "Are you all right?" "Are you going to hurt me?" et cetera. Prayer is like that, I presume; prophecy is often like that; in everything from the exchanges between husbands and wives and lovers to the exchanges between nations, this state of affairs exists.

Well, it occurred to me that it would be possible to make a fiction out of literal glossolalia: the speaking in tongues which Saint Paul talks about and which people with country childhoods like yourself and me can just remember hearing. Why not write a fiction, I thought, which consists of several versions of an unspoken text—a text so familiar that you can go through it in nonsense syllables and almost any English-speaking reader will recognize it—and then think of several situations each of which involves a speaker rather desperately trying to give a message to a receiver in some famous historical, mythological, or legendary circumstance. Cassandra, for example. The receiver, perhaps with fatal consequences, never quite gets the message that the speaker is trying to convey. At the same time, there is a third message, that unspoken one (in this case the King James translation of the Lord's Prayer), which is there for some reader to see. Thus, neither the speaker who is trying to say the thing nor the listener for whom it's intended gets the whole message; only the privileged reader does.

For all we know, God's real message in the text of the universe is neither the one we see nor the one that the cabalists decipher, but some other one entirely. If one were to point out that that's a Cassandra-like view of the professional working circumstances of many writers, that's a legitimate inference as well.

"Glossolalia" may not have been what consciously directed the theme or the form of the other stories; still, in "Ambrose His Mark," for example, mark *meaning "name" connects with the grandfather's tombstone-engraving skills, suggesting in* gravestone *Ambrose's wish to make his serious mark as a writer.*

Ah, very good . . .

Hence, the grave accent appearing throughout the series and implied in the Lord's Prayer rhythms of "Glossolalia" provides another qualitative link with "Our Father," "we must forgive them as they forgive us," and similar allusions found elsewhere. This would suggest that "Glossolalia" just might contain the distilled essence of the Funhouse series.

Sounds legit to me. I can't remember the position of "Glossolalia" in the series, but my guess is that it is near the center.

Actually, it's slightly off-center.

Too bad . . .

No, no. That's good, you see. Since the human heart is slightly off-center, the position of "Glossolalia" suggests that you have built a kind of body with these stories whose "heartbeat" is poetic utterance—an influence from your having read Joyce's Ulysses, *perhaps?*

No doubt. There are old memories of *Ulysses* through a lot of my books. That's the most fruitful reading of "Glossolalia" that I've ever heard; I commend it and wish it well. One of the things you've got rightest about it is the appreciation that even a writer who's fairly conscious and programmatic about what he does, as I am—that even such writers as myself work largely by hunch and feel and intuition. We sense that certain things are near the center of our concerns, and we trust intelligent critics to articulate just how that's so. The things you've just said about Ambrose's mark, for example: about two-thirds of them were consciously in my mind and probably exist somewhere in my notes; others are matters of hunch and feel. But your notion of the mark of the hallowèd father and so forth—that's inspired! (pp. 488-92)

John Barth and Loretta M. Lampkin, in an interview in Contemporary Literature, *Vol. 29, No. 4, Winter, 1988, pp. 485-97.*

Max F. Schulz   (essay date 1990)

[*Schulz is an American educator and critic. In the following excerpt from his* The Muses of John Barth, *he appraises* Lost in the Funhouse *and* Chimera *as representative of Barth's attempt to revitalize storytelling conventions of both Western and Eastern cultures.*]

In its brilliant conception and execution *Lost in the Funhouse* dramatizes an early attempt by Barth to fuse into one viable contemporary form the differing novelistic modes of realism, satire, and metafiction, and thereby to rejuvenate the storytelling conventions of Western culture.

That he means the "Poor earthly casket" of a novel pretending to be a book of short stories to carry such an important freight is established by him in the hermeneutical design of "Petition," the sixth of the stories constituting *Lost in the Funhouse,* which has disturbed readers by its apparently incongruous placement, and even inclusion, in the serial sequence. Barth intends it to be obtrusive, I believe, for it typologically prefigures the binary nature of the book as a whole. It combines factual reference to actual person and event and realistic deployment of the epistolary form with self-referential justification for its having been written; and thus as a microcosm of the whole it offers the reader a structure of discourse whose verbal procedure is a model of the overall configuration of *Lost in the Funhouse.*

In "Petition" "a pretty young contortionist" named Thalia precipitates a crisis between para-Siamese brothers joined "front to rear—my belly to the small of his back." Both fall in love with her. But only the front brother is capable of coupling, he salivating and grunting "upon her night after night," while the back brother is left to commune with an imagined "earnest, mute" second Thalia imprisoned within the "feral," "vulgar creature" who welcomes his brother's gross advances. The epistolary story ends with the shadowy rear brother appealing to "His Most Gracious Majesty Prajadhipok" to whom the "Petition" is addressed to bid surgeons to "divide my brother from myself, in a manner such that one of us at least may survive, free of the other"—a plea that ironically runs counter to the ecumenical gesture of the book as a whole.

"Petition" follows **"Water-Message"** and precedes the title story **"Lost in the Funhouse."** In the latter two stories, narrated by the protagonist Ambrose in the first instance, and from his point of view in the second, an older brother Peter figures first as an uncomplicated preteenager and then as a fifteen-year-old successful claimant of fourteen-year-old Magda's budding sensual charms. Given its pivotal place between the two stories, the rivalry of the **"Petition"** brothers resonates allegorically with the sibling tensions joining and separating the Mensch brothers.

This set of erotic involvements remains relatively subliminal, however, not receiving full development until LETTERS.. More germane to the design of *Lost in the Funhouse* is the nature of the Siamese twins' enthrallment with their inamorata. Like them, two in one, Thalia as defined by her name incorporates two perspectives on reality identifiable with literary modes. Her classical guise as muse of comedy accords with the front brother's earthy and gregarious engagement with things of the flesh and of this world. Her avatar as muse of idyllic poetry fits the back brother's introspective and solitary absorption in the artifices of the mind and of the word and song. Thalia suits the differing needs of each brother: the one's body and the other's spirit, the one's consciousness and the other's self-consciousness, the one's id and the other's ego. Other terms are equally applicable—matter and mind, reason and imagination, doer and dreamer, extrovert and introvert. But the apposite reverberations of Thalia do not stop with the Siamese twins, or the Mensch brothers. As a double-jointed "contortionist of good family," she presides over *Lost in the Funhouse* as Barth's muse, the *figura* now of comic Maryland-based realism and now of self-reflexive metafiction.

Despite the persuasive elegance of this typology, critics infatuated with Barth's essay on the exhausted fictional possibilities faced by the contemporary writer have persisted in reading *Lost in the Funhouse* as a sign of the dilemma to which Barth's presumed Borgesian aesthetic has led him. The book is ostensibly the sterile end product of his belief in the "used-upness of . . . forms": the presumed effluvium of writer's block, and tired exercises in the "writing [of] novels in search of a suitable subject." Barth's theoretical interest in fictional form, his academic knowledge of the history of the novel, and his genius for abstract manipulation of plot are mistaken for bankruptcy of subject; and his fascination with the pseudo-nature of history is misinterpreted as a fixation on the fictionality of experience and the indeterminacy of language. Thus, critics buzz like moths around the gnomic and metafictional stories **"Echo"** and **"Glossolalia"** in the belief that they

are the key to *Lost in the Funhouse.* Any number of critics can conclude that Barth's "fictions have gradually abandoned the pretense of realism, in favor of parodic and self-conscious techniques" [Cynthia Davis, "Heroes, Earth Mothers and Muses: Gender Identity in Barth's Fiction," *Centennial Review,* 1980]; and a fine critic like Tony Tanner can read *Lost in the Funhouse* as an analogue of Barth's "own situation as he experiences it," of his "dread of deprivation," "of being just a disembodied voice" floundering in the fictitiousness of words and literary forms, and of being cut off from reality by an irresistible but fatally sterile "verbal circle" [*City of Words,* 1971].

Nobody questions that *Lost in the Funhouse* (1968) is a crucial document in tracing the curve of Barth's oeuvre. The concentration of critical attention on its stories implies as much, without that fact ever quite getting articulated. According to the scenario projected by the critics just cited, *Lost in the Funhouse* encodes in its chronology of fables the evolution of Barth's deterioration as a writer from the spare comic realism of *The Floating Opera* (1956) and *The End of the Road* (1958) to the bloated self-conscious abstractions of *Giles Goat-Boy* (1966). I wish to approach *Lost in the Funhouse* similarly as a paradigm of Barth's fictional quest to date, but to reject the figuration usually assigned its sequence of stories in favor of another equally intrinsic to the sequence: that of a highly self-conscious and sophisticated intra- and intertextual *débat* over conflicting literary intentions and dissimilar narrative modes—which is prolonged through the three novellas of *Chimera* (1972), triumphantly culminated by the metatraditional peroration of LETTERS (1979), that gnomon of Barth's fictional record at mid career, and then extended into the renewed embraces of the self-reflexive intertexts of *Sabbatical* (1982) and *The Tidewater Tales* (1987). To put it in different metaphoric terms: *Lost in the Funhouse* chronicles an interregnum and prologues several grand efforts at postmodern conjugalities, following the monogamously existentialist psychosexual twins *The Floating Opera* and *The End of the Road,* the dual exotic affairs of the parodic *The Sot-Weed Factor* (1960), and the mytho-epic *Giles Goat-Boy.* The years from *Lost in the Funhouse* to *The Tidewater Tales,* in the history of Barth's romance with the age-old tradition of fabulation, are a succession of exploratory generic infidelities, and of climactic miscegenational weddings. It is a time when Barth experiments with a literary *ménage à trois* to see how outrageously far he can manipulate the double-jointed poses of contemporary fiction's muse before her disparate gestures dissolve the old-fashioned unity of storytelling. It is also a time when Barth tries to put his marriage of fictive guises on a more inclusive footing. In love with the existential oral encoding of Scheherazade, and her tale-reciting lineage, he initiates a self-reflexive intertextual flirtation with her feminist story-inventing and recording sister Dunyazade, who watched wide-eyed at the foot of the bed each night while Scheherazade told tales and the Sultan made love, and then, after her marriage to Shah Zaman had staled, wrote out the stories "to be read silently by individuals word for word from the page." The issue of this cross-genre mixed-species affair is *Chimera.* Following its domestication of eastern and classical storytelling, Barth returns in his literary life to the old-fashioned conjuguality of the English and American forms of LET-TERS,, before spicing the wedded amours of *The Tidewater Tales'* shared literate life with an international *Kama Sutra* of metafictional ways to articulate a worldwide frame-"story about story-writing."

No one in American letters today plots a book with more reticulate economy than Barth. David Morrell touches on this controlled intricacy when he notes (unfortunately in words echoing the out-of-focus view of Barth) that the overall structural shift in *Lost in the Funhouse* is "from living in the world to living in the world of fiction" [*John Barth: An Introduction,* 1976]. He adds that in further parallel developments the stories go from the contemporary and realistic to the mythic and fantastic, from young to old narrators, and from the narrators being unselfconscious bodies and masses to their being self-conscious voices and words. Morrell's analysis of the book's movement, while in general unexceptionable, oversimplifies, and in his construct of a single line of development misrepresents, what is a nervous two-way movement and doublestranded configuration. The initial **"Frame-Tale"**—a Möbius strip of unending return to genesis, "Once upon a time there was a story that began Once upon a time there was a story that began . . . "—envelops the narratives that follow in a dual story line continuously "progressing" in reverse directions and alluding simultaneously to origins and closures, progenitors and progeny. The resolve of the author-genie in **"Dunyazadiad"** equally describes the governing conception of *Lost in the Funhouse:* it is "to learn where to go by discovering where I am by reviewing where I've been—where we've *all* been."

Lost in the Funhouse consists of fourteen stories in a skillfully developed sequence—"series" is the word Barth uses in his "Author's Note" to discriminate them from the "collection" or "selection" ordinarily reserved for a volume of short fiction—that climaxes at midpoint with **"Lost in the Funhouse"** and at the end with **"Anonymiad."** In the first half of the book, stories alternate between experimentally self-referential protagonist-narrator forms (**"Night-Sea Journey," "Autobiography,"** and **"Petition"**) and conventionally realistic local-color narratives (**"Ambrose His Mark," "Water-Message,"** and **"Lost in the Funhouse"**). The second half of the book opens with a debate (**"Echo"**) over the place and role of the authorial voice. Should it enclose itself in narcissistic contemplation? Or must it efface the individual self, Echo-like not only in the otherness of a persona's words but also in its voice? The stories that follow alternate between self-reflexive obiter dicta about the processes of their own authoring (**"Title," "Life-Story,"** and **"Anonymiad"**) and disembodied voices dramatically recounting mythencoded truths about human nature (**"Two Meditations," "Glossolalia,"** and **"Menelaiad"**).

So much for the skeletal structure of *Lost in the Funhouse.* Animating it, so to speak, are two topoi, or binary support systems. One duplicates the backwards and forwards infinite regression announced by the Möbius strip of **"Frame-Tale."** The other assumes an elaborate chiasmus. Together they confirm the hold on Barth's imagination of a searching skeptical faith in the central tradition of story-

telling, of "densely circumstantial realisms" that "overtly imitate something" (**"Life-Story"**).

Intrinsic to the thematic development of *Lost in the Funhouse* is an ontological conceit: the unending replication of self as organism, as authorial voice, and as fiction (word and form). The first seven stories mimetically tell the life history of the conception, birth, and growth of a fictional organism, the protagonist Ambrose. At the same time they self-reflexively rehearse the questioning awareness and insistence of this fictional character that he is the progenitor and author of his story. Appropriately, **"Night-Sea Journey,"** whose subject is conception, contains the motifs and language elucidative of the two levels of statement that recur in the subsequent stories. The voice of the sperm uses both biological and aesthetic terms when alluding to his "Father" (and "Maker") and to his engenderment (and "invention"). His transmission of identity at the instant of conceptual encounter with the ovum is motivated and sustained both by genetic "recollection" and by the need to embody himself in literate "expression . . . however garbled . . . a translation, some reflection of these reflections." The stories that follow depict Ambrose's birth and postponed naming (**"Ambrose His Mark"**), his concern about his paternity and lack of identity, particularly of a proper name (**"Autobiography"**), his boyhood (**"Water-Message"**), his sense of a conflict between body/matter and mind/spirit, doing and verbalizing (**"Petition"**), and his emergent adolescent awareness of himself as Ambrose the observer and author (**"Lost in the Funhouse"**). The language also persists in recording the protagonist's organic growth in duplicate aesthetic terms. In **"Autobiography,"** for example, the narrative voice hopes he is "a fiction," calling his "beginning" an "exposition," his "climacteric" a "climax," and his mother "a mere novel device, just in style, soon to become a commonplace, to which Dad resorted one day when he found himself by himself with pointless pen." The sexual (hence biological) dimension of the language here is sufficiently plain to need no belaboring, especially since the pen-penis pun glosses the Barthian text from *Lost in the Funhouse* to LETTERS.. The protagonist similarly is both his father's "creature" and "caricature," and like the sperm of **"Night-Sea Journey"** he identifies "a pair of dads, to match my pair of moms," to account for his felt contradictions of "the vices of their versus."

These two strands of development unite in **"Lost in the Funhouse,"** the keystone story in the series, before proceeding simultaneously forward and backward in time to complete the other half of the chiasmus with **"Menelaiad"** and **"Anonymiad."** Ambrose as observant adolescent at the threshold of learning about life merges with Ambrose as author of his own story at the beginning stage of learning how to construct a narrative. In the latter role he usurps the voice of Barth and muses self-referentially about the technical problems of telling an endlessly recursive story of a young man growing up to become a writer telling the story of a young man growing up to become . . . Thus, the midpoint story presents a variant version of the **"Frame-Tale"** in its reiteration of the Möbius paradigm. In the second half of the book a narrative voice struggles with the problem of writer's block and the question of fictional form, indecisively experimenting with stories mimetically dramatic, archetypally anonymous, and self-reflexively self-conscious. The various regressing and replicating voices climax, and collapse into one, in the great tail pieces **"Menelaiad"** and **"Anonymiad,"** where presumably the narrator-protagonist of **"Life-Story"** manages after many false starts (**"Title," "Glossolalia," "Two Meditations"**) to tell two stories, whose first-person voice is in one wholly dramatic yet relentlessly self-mirroring and in the other insistently self-reflexive yet comically realistic. In the former, the self-conscious sound of Proteus as the voice of Menelaus recalling the past is extended by the accreting utterances of the other participants in the action to become the anonymous archetypal voice of myth narrating the same story over and over. In the latter the epic prose chronicle of an unknown court minstrel's life in Mycenae is reified historically in the written word to become a microcosm of mimetic-metafictional fabulating down through the centuries. Together their two-way movement unites the binary strands of the narrative series into new postmodernist combinations of the linear and the involuted, the realistic and the textual, the generic and the organic-phenomenological.

The filiation of father-son/author-character thus presents a bidirectional regressus. "How do I know" that my father/maker "tried to turn me off," the narrative voice of the "monophonic tape" recording **"Autobiography"** asks, and answers himself, because "I'm his bloody mirror." Even his formulation of thoughts becomes chiastic: "I continue the tale of my forebears. Thus my exposure; thus my escape. This cursed me, turned me out; that, curse him, saved me; right hand slipped me through left's fingers."

The narrative sequence of stories from **"Night-Sea Journey"** and **"Ambrose His Mark"** to **"Menelaiad"** and **"Anonymiad,"** in its crossing of an infinite regression with an equally infinite progression, confirms the narrator-protagonist's bepuzzled perception, in **"Life-Story,"** that his fictive account and his author-creator's are replications "in both ontological directions, et cetera." Frank D. McDonnell describes the **"Menelaiad"** as "a series of framed, inter-connecting, mutually mirroring narratives which is a wildly funny and desperate parody of the movement toward reductive self-consciousness in the previous tales of *Lost in the Funhouse* itself " [*Four Postwar American Novelists: Bellow, Mailer, Barth and Pynchon,* 1977]. It is more than that. The story whose layers Menelaus must thread his way through to reach at their center his account of his wedding night with Helen is structurally and thematically one of two climactic fictive analogues and climacteric conclusions to the biological-aesthetic self-creative drive of the sperm-narrator of **"Night-Sea Journey."** The other is the **"Anonymiad,"** whose "nameless minstrel" echoes the spermatozoon when he ciphers onto his "minstrel masterpiece" a farewell to Merope: "I wish you were here. The water's fine; in the intervals of this composition I've taught myself to swim, and if some night your voice recalls me, by a new name, I'll commit myself to it, paddling and resting, drifting like my amphorae, to attain you or to drown." Thus *Lost in the Funhouse* closes with the primal sounding of the sentiment with which it opens. The single an-swer of " ' " ' " ' " ' "Love!" ' " ' " ' " ' " that Helen gives to Menelaus's question of why she married him is the life force echoing through the ages and surfacing in the dual strands of sexuality and storytelling that comprise the ovum's summons of "Love! Love! Love!" It is also the triumphant culmination of the sperm's genetically conditioned archetypal narrative voice as it grows into Ambrose the late modernist author. Ambrose's is the most recent of self-reflexive fictive voices stretching back to the original Protean mouthpiece whose being is the *mythos* of his narrative; and the anonymous Homeric minstrel at the court of Agamemnon is the first of unending generations of fabulators reaching forward to Barth and beyond. Each will in turn recover the bottled water-message of the unknown original tale-teller with its undesignated greeting, unsigned conclusion, and blank lines between—and each will seriatim fill in the blanks with written words. The final story, **"Anonymiad,"** becomes according to this figuration both the starting point of all fiction and, as the culmination of Ambrose's writing efforts (and Barth's for this volume), the most recent realization of the ongoing fictive venture.

In *Lost in the Funhouse,* seemingly the ultimate instance of metafiction forever adrift in the mirrored reflections of its own and its literary predecessors' words, forever imitating "its own processes" (**"Life-Story"**), there is a pattern discernible that questions and inverts, if it does not outright reject or deny, what critics superficially have taken Barth to represent. The Thalian design of the book paradoxically, paradigmatically, and parodically reaffirms Barth's continuing commitment to the Western literary tradition, its history, conventions, and developing forms.

Take, for instance, the epic strain tonally and structurally underpinning the stories. However banally exalted at one moment and jaded and disillusioned the next, in his perception of his night-sea journey, the sperm-narrator figures as the latest in a long line of quest heroes. He arms his venture with outmoded Victorian slogans of conscience and vainglorious echoes of Tennysonian striving— "Onward! Upward!" "Ours not to stop and think; ours but to swim and sink . . . " "toward a Shore that may not exist and couldn't be reached if it did." In the next breath he sounds like a disillusioned disciple of Ezra Pound, or neoromantic protester of the Allen Ginsberg variety: "I have seen the best swimmers of my generation go under." And he is not above aping the early existential cynicism of Barth: "I find it no meaningfuller to drown myself than to go on swimming." Fueling these sentiments of the heroic and the absurd is the biological destiny of the sperm-narrator to seek, to swim toward, an unknown egg. The shifting allusions and the resultant ambiguity of tone raise a question of Barth's intentions, opening to contrary readings the *figura* he imposes on the sperm-narrator—and on Ambrose. Is the sperm-narrator a latterday Odysseus? or Hugh Selwyn Mauberley? a sixties hippie? or Todd Andrews? How much here is Barthian parodic putdown of premodernist and modernist antecedents? How much is Barth's effort, however tentative and indirect, to persevere in the old generic forms by adapting them to contemporary indeterminacy? How much, in short, is the spermatozoon a genetically programmed culture-bearer of the literary-construct-for-his-time to the fiction-writing Ambrose he is to become?

Interpreted individually (the focus of most of the criticism to date), the stories become self-fulfilling testimony for many critics to what they consider to be Barth's nihilistic point of view. Taken together as a thematic unit, the stories argue for a more fruitful perspective.

That we are to read the self-creative urges of Ambrose's imagination—both his adolescent sexual fantasies and his budding novelistic ambitions—as continuations of the initiatory night-sea journey is confirmed by his repeated identification with Odysseus. Indeed, not just Ambrose but Barth and the anonymous court minstrel as well are reincarnations of the "Immortal" storyteller Borges apotheosizes, all avatars of that first seagoing quester to tell his tale. In **"Water-Message"** Ambrose daydreams that "He was Odysseus steering under anvil clouds like those in *Nature's Secrets*"; and he equates his boyhood crush on the student nurse Peggy Robbins with the "sweetest knowledge" redolent in the "Warm wavelets" of the Chesapeake tidewaters. Just as the sperm-narrator swims "onward and upward will-I nill-I" to impregnate the egg with Ambrose, so the bottle whose words "in deep red ink" "had wandered willy-nilly to his threshold" floats ashore to fecundate Ambrose's mind with its water-message "of Mycenaean red" about the anonymous artist-hero. A few years older, in **"Lost in the Funhouse,"** Ambrose likens lovers wandering hand in hand about the Ocean City funhouse to spermatozoa groping through the "hot, dark windings, past Love's Tunnel's fearsome obstacles"; and he imagines himself with another "lost person in the dark" struggling "like Ulysses past obstacle after obstacle."

Barth has in mind both Homer's tale of Odysseus's epic voyage and James Joyce's adaptation—with the difference that at one level of the story's statement Barth is satirizing his modernist predecessor. Echoes of *Ulysses* abound in the stories of *Lost in the Funhouse.* **"Anonymiad"** epitomizes the parodic comparisons Barth is making. Whereas Joyce and his generation of writers had mistakenly added ancient myth as a layer to their stories in the hopes of thereby ordering and enriching their experience of immediate reality with an overlay of the universal, Barth contends rather that myth is the direct reflection of reality and therefore (a) the ongoing product of the writer's attention to "actual people and events," and (b) the universal stuff of human experience that ever bears direct reexamination and retelling. The crypto-Ambrosian/Barthian minstrel of **"Anonymiad"** accordingly "abandons myth"—that is, stops drawing on the hexametered language of pseudomythic import and the epic verses of *"no particular generation"*—to pattern his "fabrications on [the] actual people and events" of his life—the Trojan War, Agamemnon, Menelaus, Helen, Aegisthus, Clytemnestra—which he ambitiously retells in one final document, from ultimately the "only valid point of view, first person anonymous."

The initial aesthetic plight of the minstrel parallels the misdirected effort of the modernists to make art out of contemporary history by telling it in terms of old epics and myths, and parallels the sterility of their successors the late modernists, who find themselves boxed in by their convoluted language and stale reiteration of used-up forms. The final desperate turn of the ministrel to fictionalizing the "daily reality" of "what was going on at Troy and in Mycenae" mirrors Ambrose's (and Barth's) similar turn to exploring the narrative problem of authorial voice as it was first manifested in the fictive presences who participated in and wrote about the Trojan War. The minstrel's hard-earned development from court singer of second-hand epics to solitary comic chronicler of his own "minstrel misery," furthermore, repeats microcosmically not only the history of literary forms but also the progress of Ambrose through the fictive fashions of his own day in the series of fictions that make up *Lost in the Funhouse.* The "narrative" moves from a self-conscious parody of Joyce to an intertextual tribute to the Borgesian idea of the continuity and singleness of the bardic tradition. The "novel" opens in satire of the chief modernist, clearing away the rubble of the immediate past to make space for rebuilding in the present, and closes emulating the guru of postmodernism. In between, the stories stretch uneasily from realism to extreme self-reflexiveness. Ambrose, at first formalistically tied to the great fictionists of the generations immediately preceding him, writes in the modernist manner. The ostensibly realistic stories, even, yield their tribute to literary fashion, incorporating into their "s[o]ng of innocence" a veneer of *mythos*. Ambrose has a father—both biological and authorial—who limps like Oedipus (**"Water-Message"**), who wishes him "unmade" (**"Night-Sea Journey"**), whom he hates (**"Lost in the Funhouse"**), and whose paternity/authorship he wishes to deny by repeating the cycle in his own "made" son/character. Ambrose then works his way through the metafictional mode to its fruitless *regressus in infinitum* before turning triumphantly to the comic reflexivity of imagining himself anew in the guise of original mythic personalities.

Of equal importance is the Borgesian lesson of **"Anonymiad"** that all narrative modes, including the self-reflexive, lose themselves ultimately in the impersonal storied mimesis of language. To tell of self is to tell of others, which is to include the self again, this time as an anonymous voice. By restating in wholly new narrative terms the ontology of the Ambrose story, **"Anonymiad"** brings full circle (chiasmic and Möbius alike) the endless spiral forward and backward through time of the inky red words (**"Water-Message"**; **"Anonymiad"**) of the artist-hero, and in that fictive act embodying reality the story merges the self-conscious *I* with the omniscient *eye.* The identity of authorship, however insisted upon by the omniscient voice of the authorial *deus artifex* or by the surrogate first-person point of view and self-reflexive agon, is lost in the word, and subsumed by the narrative voice created: "none can tell teller from told" (**"Echo"**). Narcissus disappears into Echo, who duplicates solely the voices of others. Although "The teller's immaterial . . . the tale's the same"; only the anonymous "voice persists" (**"Echo"**). Thus does **"Anonymiad"** answer the self-questionings of author and protagonist-narrator of **"Title"** and **"Life-Story"** about their presence in, and the subject and form of, the story they are trying to write. The intentional artistic reduction of signified to signifier realizes ironically the reverse inclusive encompassing of all but the impersonal assertive self of the life force.

In the narrative of (about and by) Ambrose, *Künstlerroman,* epic, and metafiction merge into a single story told linearly in the present, with a parallel dimension told through time, by an ever-present, Protean, faceless fabulator. *Lost in the Funhouse* is thus more an anatomy of pre- and late modernist modes, and, finally, more a travesty of experimentation, than the last-ditch resort of a bankrupt fictionist. As such it asks us to attend closely to the many ways in which it satirizes its own processes: the trite and worn-out slogans of the sperm-narrator, for one, and the chiastic antithesis of self-reflexive (I) and mimetic (eye) kinds of writing, for another. It is surely significant that the "author" who struggles in **"Title"** and **"Life-Story"** with writer's block is a fictional protagonist-narrator (presumably Ambrose who has been the narrative voice since **"Ambrose His Mark,"** and, arguably, technically since **"Night-Sea Journey,"** and who has been maneuvering at least since **"Lost in the Funhouse"** to take over from the author and direct his own destiny and tell his own story), not Barth, whom unwary readers seek uncritically to identify with the hero of his *Künstlerroman.* There is also the suspicious incidence of a self-reflexive novel taking as its subject the extreme crisis that can afflict a writer—dried up inspiration and depletion of subject matter—and carpentering its middle out of the resultant false starts and failed efforts. Such fictive maneuvers should have alerted us to Barth's larger ends, if the splendidly controlled, formally polar, stories at the beginning and end had not.

The structure and substance of *Lost in the Funhouse* argue that Barth is less an exhausted metafictionist trying to free himself from outmoded and worn-out forms than a postmodernist bent on preserving and combining past fictional practices with the distinctive narrative voices of the present. He is not an errant realist guilty of formalist perversions so much as a radical preservationist looking for ways to conserve old and new storytelling. Metafiction is under the microscope in *Lost in the Funhouse,* with Barth scrutinizing the minute properties of avant-garde forms to ascertain what they share with the Great Tradition, as well as to discover what essential mechanisms, forces, and contours comprise the fictional form regardless of stylistic species or historical allegiance. The progressive styles of the stories—from the realism of **"Ambrose His Mark"** and **"Water-Message"** through the aborted fragments of **"Two Meditations," "Title,"** and **"Life-Story"** to the slangy retelling of the old myths in **"Menelaiad"** and **"Anonymiad"**—record a gestation that is at once an ontogeny of the book and a phylogeny of Western fiction. Such a context gives aesthetic intentionality to the stories. **"Lost in the Funhouse,"** for example, becomes an instance of the self-reflexive technique grafted onto the omniscient narrative of a realistically told story. **"Menelaiad"** and **"Anonymiad"** represent similar, but more subtly complex, fusions of myth, metafiction, and narrative realism. The penultimate story, as an absolute objective narrative (to use Henry James's term, all dramatic scene—nothing but reported conversations), offers an extreme version of the self-referential utterance wedded to the frame-tale, while the final story triumphantly consummates the wedding of Thalia's contrary skills. Ostensibly rendering the world of eleventh-century B.C. Greece in "prose fictions of the realistical" told in "first person anonymous," **"Anonymiad"**

is just as fascinated with disclosing how it came to be told as with actually telling what life was like in Mycenae with Clytemnestra and Aegisthus during the Trojan War.

Barth may be one of that great national resource of writers who grace the history of English and American literature, a novelist, poet, or dramatist who codifies for his contemporaries in definitive essays the literary theory of his time. Like Dryden, Johnson, and Eliot for their respective ages, he has analyzed critically in two articles—"The Literature of Exhaustion" (1967) and "The Literature of Replenishment" (1980)—the crisis in fictional means and matter that the postmodernist novelist faces. Contemporary with his restless imaginative search for a novelistic via media, their titles advertise how thoroughly Barth is bent on corralling, yoking, and driving in tandem the contraries of his literary inheritance.

LETTERS was heralded at its appearance as an extreme example of modernist proclivities mutatis mutandis in its historical feat of self-transcendent parody of the mainstream mimetic forms of the Anglo-American-European fictional tradition. We can discern with hindsight that Barth was aiming in his own fictive renewal at the resuscitation of the novel. It appears, furthermore, that he began this act of literary resuscitation in *Lost in the Funhouse,* where he married regional realism to modernist metafiction, using Greek mythology as the common ancestor. Hence, the book is hardly the "dead end" critics such as Jerome Klinkowitz have recklessly termed it [*Literary Disruptions: The Making of a Post-Contemporary American Fiction,* 1975]. Barth is not so much seeking liberation from the inhibitive presence of literary tradition as he is searching out ways of arousing anew the fecund natures of its alternative worlds. Nor has the rush of fictive promiscuity apparently alarmed him. Neither the threat of conventionality nor that of excess has deflected him from the gestation (and determined legitimization) of additional such historically miscegenated fictions. After he had worked his way through the hetero-literary "glossolalia" that describes much of the loosely combined assemblage of stories of *Lost in the Funhouse* to the formally climactic embraces of the fabular-mythic and the avant-garde of **"Menelaiad"** and **"Anonymiad,"** Barth paused long enough to produce several more of the latter in the Arabian Nights/Hellenic-based sexual dialogues of *Chimera.*

Chimera, however, was not for Barth by any means a repetitive "expense of spirit" and energy. The books from *Lost in the Funhouse* to *Tidewater Tales* are the interlocked parts of an oeuvre unified in its incremental progression. Each book consists of a collection of discrete narrative units, or stories, which coalesce into a skillfully structured plot with a complex, yet single, line of development. Together the books comprise an ambitious attempt by Barth to align his fictions with the great works of the Anglo-European tradition, and with the great frame-tales of world literature, to constitute a modern instance, neither replicative, nor parodic, specifically of *Don Quixote* and *Clarissa,* or of *The Thousand and One Nights* and *The Decameron,* so much, as imitative *natura naturans* of the creative process and of the cumulative word horde of the ur-fictional "Ganges of preexisting fiction," the eleventh-century Sanskrit *Ocean of Stories,* into whose swollen "narrative ocean . . . all streams of fancy flow at last."

Barth confesses, not entirely fancifully, that he owes his sustained creativity from *Lost in the Funhouse* to LETTERS, in part, to "a literary project whose fate" has been "to be put aside for some more pressing work." The enabling work alluded to is an unfinished novel tentatively entitled *The Amateur,* which he began after *The Sot-Weed Factor,* set aside for *Giles Goat-Boy,* rifled for one of the Ambrose stories of *Lost in the Funhouse,* and resurrected as "one of the main lines in the plot of [LETTERS]." The shadowy presence of Ambrose Mensch, in whose fictive architecture Barth "dreams of a funhouse vaster by far than any yet constructed," discloses a thread connecting Barth's novels from *Lost in the Funhouse* to LETTERS. Embedded between these two works is *Chimera,* whose additional enabling "string of allusions" to Jerome Bray, to the spiraling coils of fiction making, to literary and mythological heroes *redivivus,* among others, stretches through LETTERS, and beyond, to *The Tidewater Tales.*

Barth's books sustain even more complex incremental interlocking of narrative strategy than the above observations seemingly allow. The hesitant, exploratory, yet at times excessive concentration on self-reflexive methodology in the discrete narrative of *Lost in the Funhouse* points to the brilliant solution of self-reflexive and authorial voices in LETTERS. At the same time, unexpectedly, dramatically, after the foreplay and "coitus interruptus" of its inhibited middle "stories," *Lost in the Funhouse* climaxes spectacularly in **"Menelaiad"** and, especially, in **"Anonymiad."** These two stories, in turn, whose combination of intertextual reorchestration and self-reflexive narration fruitfully couples ancient bardic and modernist scrivener practices, prelude the triumphant ascendancy of mythic demystification in *Chimera.* Prior to *Lost in the Funhouse,* only the madcap telling of "Taliped Decanus" in *Giles Goat-Boy* hints at the chimerical issue to be born of the free-spirited adultery of Barth's modernist affair with the by-now-matronly muses of classical antiquity.

What laminates Barth's reworking of this classical mythology is his reorientation of it into myths about writing, about the self-conscious concern of the postmodernist writer with his relationship to past writers. The model is the two-way transaction between Ambrose and the anonymous minstrel, which has "the minstrel at the end of *Lost in the Funhouse* [in **"Anonymiad"**] sending out messages that are going to be received by the writer in the beginning [in **"Water-Message"**] of *Lost in the Funhouse,*" who returns the favor by restating the minstrel's story in metafictional terms. This pattern becomes the key narrative device of **"Dunyazadiad"** and **"Bellerophoniad":** "The author in the future is communicating with [Scheherazade and] Bellerophon in the past and telling [them] the story of [Scheherazade and] Bellerophon"; so that they may in turn relay it forward to the present. In its corollary metafictional and personal/human concerns with recycling of classical myths and reprocessing of first chances in life, *Chimera* not only keystones the arch that stretches from *Lost in the Funhouse* to LETTERS, but also adds a span to *The Tidewater Tales,* where such fabulation—this time of

the Nausicaa and Homecoming episodes in *The Odyssey*—achieves stunning results. Of equal importance to *Chimera*'s transitional position is its celebration of conjugal and domestic love, and the emergent presence (thematic and narrational) of women and of a feminist consciousness.

Despite the modest implication to the contrary in the sly infra-dig of the title, *Chimera*'s structurally compatible stories were the logical, and triumphant, next step for Barth after *Lost in the Funhouse*'s loose and motley fictional federation. *Lost in the Funhouse* is a *Künstlerroman* in search of a style, more precisely, of an integral voice, as conventional hero strains to become artist-hero. *Chimera* riots playfully, as if newly discovered, in that style, that voice, actually, a series of narrative voices subsumed arbitrarily by the print medium into the "combinations and recombinations" of Polyeidus's shape-shifting, not unlike the Protean reduction of Menelaus into a succession of voice-echoes that make up the lettered tale **"Menelaiad."** There lurks behind all those voice-echoes, however, as well as behind the Scheherazadian of the Genie, the mytho-historical voice of Barth yarning about his times and about the feints and dodges demanded of the writer in such times. In a complex encoding of old and the new, Barth wields, here, a later twentieth-century muscular prose, which in **"Perseid"** rises often to heights of eloquence. "I could listen all night to the way you talk," Calyxa tells Perseus (as lucky Medusa does every night); and we can only nod assent, especially when bad luck and hard knocks have Perseus confessing honestly in the slangy language of the emergent postmodern artist to his sometimes less-than-heroic mortal nature:

> Nightly, when I wake to think myself beworlded and find myself in heaven, I review the night I woke to think and find myself vice-versa. I'd been long lost, deserted, down and out in Libya; two decades past I'd overflown that country with the bloody Gorgon's head, and every drop that hit the dunes had turned to snake—so I learned later: at twenty years and twenty kilometers high, how could I have known? Now there I was, sea-leveled, forty, parched and plucked, every grain in my molted sandals raising blisters, and beleaguered by the serpents of my past. It must have been that of all the gods in heaven, the two I'd never got along with put it to me: sandy Ammon, my mother-in-law's pet deity, who'd first sent Andromeda over the edge, and Sabazius the beer-god, who'd raised the roof in Argos till I raised him a temple. Just then I'd've swapped Mycenae for a cold draught and a spot of shade to sip it in; I even prayed to the rascals. Nothing doing. Couldn't think where I'd been or where was headed, lost track of me entirely, commenced hallucinating, wow. Somewhere back in my flying youth I'd read how to advertise help wanted when you're brought down: I stamped a shopping PERSEUS in the sand, forgot what I was about, writing sets your mind a-tramp; next thing I knew I'd printed PERSEUS LOVES ANDROMED half a kilometer across the dunes. Wound up in a depression with the three last letters; everything before them slipped my mind; not till I added USA was I high enough again to get the message, how I'd con-

fused what I'd set out to clarify. I fried awhile longer on the dune-top, trying to care; I was a dying man: so what if my Mayday had grown through self-advertisement to an amphisbane graffito? But O I was a born reviser, and would die one: as I looked back on what I'd written, a fresh East breeze sprang from the right margin, behind, where I'd been aiming, and drifted the A I'd come to rest on. I took its cue, erased the whole name, got lost in a vipered space between object and verb, went on erasing, erasing all, talking to myself, crazy man: no more LOVES, no more LOVE, clean the slate altogether—me too, take it off, all of it. But I'd forgot by that time who I was, relost in the second space, my first draft's first; I snaked as far as the subject's final S and, frothing, swooned, made myself after that seventh letter a mad dash.

In *Chimera* Barth worked out one solution to the problem of the divided narrational voice, which had disrupted the narratives of *Lost in the Funhouse.*

The self-reflexive voice in the latter fictions is always striving technically to divorce itself from the author's, to assume narrative control, since the fictional narrator shares with the author a concern about the origin of the tale and about the mechanics of its telling. As protagonist, as well as ostensible narrator, Ambrose is consequently, and curiously, further fragmented. Referred to in the third person singular, he figures as a character with a history as a Chesapeake Bay Eastern Shorer, who transcends the scope, and is the sum, of the individual stories. He also functions in each story as the implied author-narrator, who asserts a storied existence as self-reflexively independent of his fictional creation as of his author creator. Inherent in the metavoice of *Lost in the Funhouse,* then, is the push to fragment, to divide amoebalike, in unending refraction, from Barth the author into Ambrose the neophyte author, who in turn finds his fictional narrator seizing the narrative from him in a regress of fabulators, which does not stop until he ends back at the original nameless bard, whose presence hovers implicitly over all the stories, and emerges in his own right in the final fiction "Anonymiad." This Möbius rondure of narrators' voices coincides with another volatility, that of the autobiographical and the self-reflexive, each vying to be heard. The first group of stories, up to the eponymous title-and-centerpiece, are dominated by the autobiographical; the second half of the book submerges the biographically factual in an overload of self-conscious anxieties about its rendering, until "Anonymiad," where the two expository modes strive for equipoise. Thus, the covert narrative of the artist as hero, which unites the stories and their diverse internal feints and structural thrusts, is ever threatened entropically with dissolution.

In *Chimera* Barth manages to stabilize the narrational voice, paradoxically by division of its narcissistic guises. He adopts, for one, the **"Echo"** and **"Menelaiad"** device (another cross-textual reverberation from *Lost in the Funhouse*) of the autobiographer-protagonist transformed into, and inseparable from his story, teller and tale one; and contrariwise, he revives the *deus artifex* convention, thereby recovering the authorial presence as an independent entity, sometimes slyly implied by the language, sometimes disguised as a character. Barth emphasizes the former with the conceit of the constellated **"Perseid"** and the paginated **"Bellerophoniad."** "I'm content," Perseus says, "to be the tale I tell." Each hero exists in, and by virtue of, the story of his life, indistinguishable and inseparable from it, which is therefore purportedly telling itself. Only purportedly, for in this transformation of the protagonist-narrator into his own biographer/biography sublimely focused in his own life account, Barth finds space to insert the felt presence of a metaformalist. "Polyeidus *is* the story, more or less, in any case its marks and spaces," Bellerophon conjectures; and in that "more or less" lurks an implied author other than Bellerophon or Polyeidus, who, Bellerophon further hypothesizes "could by Antoninus Liberalis, for example, Hesiod, Homer, Hyginus, Ovid, Pindar, Plutarch, the Scholiast on the *Iliad,* Tzetzes, Robert Graves, Edith Hamilton, Lord Raglan, Joseph Campbell, *the author of the* Perseid, *someone imitating that author*" (my italics)—a dizzying Möbius strip of regression and progression endlessly circling from metafictional present to archetypal past, from Homer to Barth. In **"Dunyazadiad,"** Barth employs as his metaformalist conscience a Genie surrogate, remarkably Barthlike, if not twin, who traverses time zones and literary periods (specifically his and Scheherazade's "place and time and order of reality") to participate in the tale. In **"Bellerophoniad"** Barth grants some of his authorial autonomy to the shapeshifter, Polyeidus, who is ostensibly one source (the other is the Genie) of all its documents and "printed pages," as well as of the stories **"Perseid"** and **"Dunyazadiad"** and, by inference at least, the Jerome Bray matter of LETTERS.

This dichotomizing of the narrator's voice into an autobiographer's and a metafictionist's, which Barth experiments within the novellas of *Chimera,* is subsequently, and brilliantly, orchestrated into the primary structural feature of LETTERS. It is then refined out of existence in the self-reflexive fusion of the two roles in the husband-wife writing teams of *Sabbatical* and *The Tidewater Tales,* although in the latter Barth engineers his reentry into the narrative, this time orthographically purified from genie to Djean (jinn), with the reappearance of Scheherazade, an appropriate bit of storytelling logic, which casts him less as "gray eminence" behind the tidewater tales of Peter Sagamore than as collaborator and co-author with Peter and Katherine in a writing chore that involves, along with original composition, the rescoring with new variants of tales already composed, Peter's, Mark Twain's, Homer's, Cervantes's, and Scheherazade's.

At the same time that Barth is reasserting authorial authority, he is carefully, often extravagantly, as the husband-wife autobiographer-narrators of *Sabbatical* and *The Tidewater Tales* indicate, foregrounding the self-reflexive turn of each story. Self-reflexiveness is intrinsically developmental, and in each of the *Chimera* novellas the narrator is an active learner helped toward full expression, which includes parallel growth in person and in self-understanding, as well as in storytelling, with the aid, the "scaffolding" (to use a term current in learning theory), of another person, always of the opposite sex. Dunyazade tells Shah Zaman (in **"Dunyazadiad"**) what has transpired between her and Scheherazade during the thousand and one nights of Sherry's story-spinning; with Shah Zaman, in turn (second half of the story) relating to Dunyazade what had been his and his brother Shahryar's domestic disasters during much of the same time period. Perseus for half of each night "unwind[s] my tale" to Medusa of what he told Calyxa about the first half of his life as a hero and as the husband of Andromeda, and for the second half speaking directly to Medusa about their reencounter ("to where it's ours"), she now "unGorgoned," and their subsequent love life and estellation; as copycat Bellerophon (parodic, if you wish, of Perseus) for much of his story recites "my history aloud, in my own voice, to Melanippe the Amazon" what he told Philonöe about his previous life and its fumbled attempts at herohood.

By means of their autobiographical reflexiveness Dunyazade learns from Shah Zaman to trust the love of males. Perseus learns from Medusa to accept his being "a reasonably healthy, no-longer-heroic mortal with more than half his life behind him" and to treasure an immortal life of "Boundless love" with a woman as a fair trade-off for the middle-aged limitations placed on herohood. And Bellerophon learns from Melanippe to recognize that his "life's a failure," his origins mundane and mortal, his life on equal footing with a woman satisfactory, and his self-less anonymity as a story sufficient immortality. Thus does the complex human relationship governing speaker and listener determine the self-reflexive structure of the novellas, with this cooperative storytelling life process receiving its full realization in the engendering (conceiving/conceptualizing) give-and-take of the married couples in *Sabbatical* and *The Tidewater Tales.*

A corollary development impractically engineered in *Lost in the Funhouse* is Barth's attempt, using modern technological means, to render these narrating voices as heard presences—and, not incidentally, to preserve the oral tradition and to reproduce the ancient scene of the bardic recitation—with monophonic and stereophonic disc and tape recordings. As might be expected from "a print oriented bastard" trying to imagine ways of resurrecting the vocal presentation of a story, the experiments of *Lost in the Funhouse* initiated some bizarre grandstanding, attention-getting platform maneuvers of limited value for a writer of books. Still, in all the wired tomfoolery Barth was signaling the importance for him of the speaking voice.

In *Chimera,* the oral autobiographical voice, epitomized for Barth by the storytelling Scheherazade, commands center stage. Resort to this "oral" transmission of the stories (despite his pretense of delight in the "music of our tongue," Bellerophon's recitation literally, and ironically, takes a paginated form) solves most of the problems inherent in a postmodernist writer's telling anew the ancient stories of classical mythology. The oral convention demands a responsive audience, a talker *and an auditor.* The device of the mythic protagonist telling a mistress/husband/wife what befell her/him in the first half of his/her life introduces the old myths, and familiarizes (or refamiliarizes) the general reader (once removed from the storied auditor) with tales that are still a passive portion

of our cultural heritage but no longer an active part of our daily lives. Behind this immediate retelling lies the original telling, now likewise preserved in documentary form. The first half of each of the *Chimera* novellas reproduces this twofold temporal process as an exercise in postmodernist intertextuality as well as in autobiography. To this public record is appended Barth's twentieth-century extension of the myth (generally freighted with the trials of being a writer in a postmodernist period), which adds to the mythic hero's life subsequent circumstances in the second half of his existence, or, as a variant on that, redreams the old myth from the viewpoint of a peripheral participant.

In their combination of reyarning the old myths and improvising them into postmodern continuations, the *Chimera* novellas manage the incorporation of old into new (or vice versa), of past storytelling with present, which sustains the mythic topos of bardic identity stretching from the anonymous singer at the court of Agamemnon to Barth (and Ambrose of *Lost in the Funhouse,* and Scheherazade/Dunyazade, Perseus, and Bellerophon of *Chimera*). Such recycling of story material replays mythically Barth's narrative fixation on the midlife crises of his heroes and on the human act of reclamation granted everyone to remodel the first half of one's life in the second half. This binary paradigm is central to Barth's philosophy of life, his Tragic View of History, and his idea of the limited, yet open-ended, parameters of art and of being human. Clearly, the notion of repetition, even Barth's "reenactment," misdescribes, actually falsifies, the growth intrinsic to this binary construct, the change, the enlargement, the continuation, which takes place, and is best imaged, in a spiral, and in the Maryland marsh snail Barth celebrates in **"Dunyazadiad,"** which "carries his history on his back, living in it, adding new and larger spirals to it from the present as he grows."

In speech-act transactions what one says to another is determined by the situation, the auditor, and the subject. For a writer to extend and vary the old myths, adding new episodes, carrying the epic heroes into middle age, giving them new lovers, is for him/her to assume the conditions of a speech-act transaction. The original circumstances of the myth prescribe boundaries to the contemporary innovations and variants. Barth acknowledges the terms of this transaction in his responsible summaries of the original story, as prelude to his introduction of fresh incidents, and by his decision to cast the stories in the form of an autobiographical dialogue. With admirable invention he makes substantive capital out of the procedural limitations of his material, correlating the idea of midlife crisis (a cliché of Freud-saturated mid–twentieth-century American bourgeois civilization) with the need to review the major details of the old story before embarking on new, and by that act determining the limits of what the new can comprise. The autobiographical dialogue, at once, allows him to remain true to the contemporary dogma of fiction's self-consciousness, to the second half of the twentieth-century's hang-up about creation and recreation of identity, and to his lifelong adoration of the frame-tale.

The "oral" construct of these stories also efficiently digests the basic situation of courtship/marriage internalized in the English realistic novel of manners. *Chimera* celebrates love, the full spectrum from the comic mechanics of sex to the dogma about the deathless passion of Western civilization's heroes and heroines to the contradictory faiths in the companionship of mutual gender esteem and the boredom of marital familiarity. Being and not being may be the stuff of soliloquies, but lovers prefer to address their feelings directly to a beloved. The revelatory "pillow-talk" of Dunyazade and Shah Zaman, the hearty sexual fellowship of Perseus and Calyxa, the lofty tendernesses of Perseus and Medusa, the Amazonian bonhomie of Melanippe and Bellerophon, the intimate dinner-time give-and-take of Bellerophon and his wife and children—all presuppose an exchange, a transaction, between suitor and wooed, speaker and listener. Ironically, despite Barth's skill in managing these matters, this basic transaction occasionally runs afoul of his penchant for narration constructed on the involuted designs inspired by framing and self-reflexive means. "I told her, honestly" (Perseus is repeating to Medusa a conversation he had with Calyxa about his love for Medusa), "The fact was—no other way to say it in a first-person narrative," Perseus apologizes awkwardly to Medusa about the narrative awkwardness of not addressing her directly, "Medusa really loved me, her first experience of that emotion, and I realized I hadn't been loved since the old days with Andromeda. What's more, she truly was a kindred spirit; we had jolly conversations."

The overview I've been pursuing in this [discussion] illuminates—in a way reading each of the novels individually, without reference to the others, fails to light up—the degree to which Barth has evolved into one of contemporary American fiction's most enlightened limners of love. Not since Henry James has an American male novelist written so well of women, exposed their fears and hatreds, delineated their sexual natures, and championed their independent persons. Whether a case of cause and effect is not certain; yet, contrary to the critics' negative estimate that "the theme of love" will not deflect Barth from "the aesthetic themes of the Literature of Exhaustion" and "lead him back toward realism" [John Stark in his *The Literature of Exhaustion: Borges, Nabokov, and Barth*, 1974], he has swerved in the novels since *Chimera* to ever-more-ecstatic exploration of the joys (and pains and defeats and triumphs) of love and friendship in ever-more-realistic forms without diminishing his "contemporary writer's games and struggles with the medium" [Evelyn Glasser-Wöhrer in her *An Analysis of John Barth's* Weltanschauung: *His View of Life and Literature*, 1977].

Unlike John Updike's male-oriented perceptions of the spritual alienation and sexual tug-of-war of which his protagonists strive to know both their sinfulness and their redemption in the body of a woman (for example, in *Too Far to Go* and *A Month of Sundays*) Barth's gender ruminations positively and zestfully embrace the full range of female matters. No writer has more sympathetically explored from a feminine angle the basic human activities of lovemaking (**"Perseid"**), conception (LETTERS), and gestation (*The Tidewater Tales*). In a world devoid of absolute values and of meaningful existence, the moral responsibility of sexual human beings for one another becomes a precious gift to be treasured and fostered. Since his

youthful flirtation with the absurdities of existential reality in *The Floating Opera* and *The End of the Road*, in which, possibly, the word "love" may never have been used, Barth has inched steadily toward the celebration of male-female companionship. In his most recent novels, the sexes have become a mutual admiration society, sustaining and nurturing one another at all levels of human activity. Each of the autobiographical dialogues of *Chimera* is pitched appropriately as an intimate conversation between spouses and lovers. Of equal importance to this erotic odyssey (which even in the prolonged athletic copulation of Barthian time still leaves many hours in the day and night for other forms of recreational communcation) is friendship. Barth's male protagonists again and again epitomize their beloved as "my best friend."

If the three stories of *Chimera* are read in the order Barth originally intended for them [**"Dunyazadiad"** appearing third rather than first], and read with attention to the subtext of their recreation of the old myths, they reveal a steady exposure of that text to the feminist vision. As one might expect of an over-the-hill jock, and "had-been hero"—epical conqueror of the loathsome castrating-female Medusa and Hairbreadth-Harry rescuer of the ravishing female-in-distress Andromeda—Perseus is a male chauvinist coping with gender consciousness-raising through his encounters with a few free-spirited women in the arenas of marital and extramarital hard knocks. His marriage to Andromeda has deteriorated into endless "squalls and squabbles; flirtations, accusations; relovings and relapses." With typical wounded masculine pride, he charges his wife with "new henpeck[ing] me out of cockhood"; at the same time, he grudgingly credits her nagging insistence on gender parity with having taught him "what few men knew, fewer heroes, and no gods: that a woman's person in her independent right, to be respected therefore by the goldenest hero in heaven." Perseus has not progressed far, though, in liberation from his stereotypical gender thinking. In his "insufferable ego," he still insists on a relationship with his wife weighted "three parts Perseus to one Andromeda." That early militant feminist, understandably, finds unpalliative his (to his mind) conciliatory and magnanimous gesture, with their relationship in shambles, of releasing her from her marriage vows: "You're free, Andromeda." Her spirited rejoinder is "I've *always* been! . . . Despite you!" Mostly impotent at first with his nurse and new girlfriend, the priestess Calyxa, he typically blames his being "psychosexually weak" on his wife: "No man's a mythic hero to his wife," he laments. "No woman remained a dream of nymphhood to her husband either," Calyxa ripostes, and instructs him in the realities of "permanent relationship" however "qualified by comparison, long familiarity, and non-excellence in other particulars . . . fatal to passion." His enlightenment is measured textually by his eventual repression of ego, moved by "a quite miraculous, yes blinding love," to yield himself up to the reciprocal maidenly love of an eager but innocent, tender but incredulous Medusa. That Perseus risks petrification (or in his hardshell ego thinks he does) by opening his eyes to Medusa's love—that he crosses the great divide between herohood and husbandhood to give himself utterly in order to win her irrevocably:

Then (with this last, parenthetical, over-the-shoulder glance at Andromeda and my fond dream of rejuvenation: difficult dead once-darling, fare you well! Farewell! Farewell!) I chucked wise dagger, strode over sill, embraced eyes-shut the compound predications of commitment—hard choice! soft flesh!—slipped back mid-kiss her problematic cowl, opened eyes.

—does not absolutely absolve him of the typical male deficiencies in tenderness, as perceived through the lenses of generations of disillusioned women. "It was brutal of you, darling," Medusa chides from the secure permanence of her estellation with him, "Brutal to jump from my arms into hers [Calyxa's], when I'd just rescued you; brutal again to compare us in bed, as if my awkwardness were anything but innocence, *loving* innocence, which you should have treasured! Don't reply. And brutal finally to dwell on her the way you did and do. Don't you think I have feelings?"

A failure as a martial hero, the phony, but very human, Bellerophon bests his cousin and role model Perseus in the skirmishes of the nursery and the boudoir. On the surface he appears, at first, to fare here, too, no better than the romantic Perseus. We are introduced to Bellerophon in the midst of noisy domestic and messy conjugal matters: on the eve of his fortieth birthday, afflicted with midlife longeurs, and too tired to make love. In dispirited pre-birthday pillow-talk with his long-suffering "never criticiz[ing]" wife Philonöe—who had that evening served him ambrosia "made . . . with her own hands," then "dismissed the servants early [and] donned her best nightie"—he confesses, before rolling over and going to sleep, that he's "over the hill" his "life's a failure," his children bored with "anecdotes of [his] own childhood," and "the citizenry with . . . accounts of [his] later adventures." Bellerophon is a bit of a heel, full of self-pity at his inability to fulfill his grandiose ambitions, tedious, petty, and sourly mean, in turn, in his dealings with family, friends, and womenfolk. Yet, these very human failings also grant him grudging respect for the intimacies and loyalties encumbent upon and accruing in the relationship of the sexes. He values the marital norm of friendly and "gently made love." Beyond the macho comprehension of Perseus is his content, all mixed up with his heroic pretensions, in the quiet satisfactions, the humbling regrets, of parenthood:

"Bellerus and Deliades," I'm saying to the children, back in Lycia; "Deliades and Bellerus. From the day we were born, the country quarreled over which of us should succeed to the throne of Corinth, and my brother and I quarreled over it ourselves, for fun and profit, just as you boys will when you drive me out of town . . .

Twins we were . . . and Polyeidus was our tutor" . . .

"And Polyeidus was your tutor," the children chorused. I'm sending them supperless to bed: Isander has announced that he hates this story because its words are too big and it lasts too long. Hippolochus has kissed him and promised to repeat it all in little words at naptime. My

curly darling Laodamia sleeps in my lap; Philonöe deftly replaces the thumb with a pacifier. Dead now, all of them: dead and dead and dead!

Even more inaccessible to the self-esteem of Perseus is Bellerophon's appreciation of the compromises and the pleasures of growing old with one woman, of the complex amalgam of resentment and gratitude each feels for the other lived in the intimacy of husband and wife:

"It is remarkable," I'd remark to Philonöe in the royal boudoir, as she kindly tried to rouse me, "what a toll pregnancy takes on teeth and muscle tone." Her hand would pause—Melanippe's does, too—for just a moment. Then she'd agree, cheerfully adding varicosity, slacked breast and vaginal sphincter, striation of buttock and thigh, and loss of hair-sheen to the list of her biological expenses in the childbearing way—all of which she counted as nothing, since for three such princelets she'd've died thrice over. But as I was at it I should add, she'd add, the psychological cost of parentage, to ourselves individually and to the marital relationship: fatigue, loss of spontaneity, diminishment of ardor, general heaviness—a kind of accelerated aging, the joint effect of passing years, increased responsibility, and accumulated familiarity—never altogether compensated for by deeper intimacy. For her part (she would go on—what a wife this was!), she took what she was pleased to term the Tragic View of Marriage and Parenthood: reckoning together their joys and griefs must inevitably show a net loss, if only because like life itself their attrition was constant and their term mortal. But one had only different ways of losing, and to eschew matrimony and childbearing for the delights of less serious relations was in her judgment to sustain a net loss even more considerable.

Such sentiments are fitting prelude to the feminist perspective enunciated in **"Dunyazadiad."** In this story Barth sets forth the respective resentments each sex has harbored towards the other: the male suspicion of female inconstancy and the female fear of male incontinence, "the wretched state of affairs between man and womankind that made love a will-o'-the-wisp, jealousy and boredom and resentment the rule." Scheherazade's existential situation—her life is dependent on her ability to tell story after story—has appealed to Barth for more than thirty years. With the sure touch of a storyteller he singles out a correspondence of significance to us in the 1970s and 1980s, translating her tale into a feminist manifesto against centuries of patriarchal "violation, at the hands of fathers, husbands, lovers." In his perception of the intertextual camaraderie binding one writer to another, Barth includes the profounder human interdependence of the sexes—with moving testimony to the loyalty and affection sealing both. Responding to the Genie's hopes that he "have live converse with the storyteller he'd loved best and longest" and that "he might die before his young friend and he ceased to treasure each other as they did currently in their saltmarsh retreat"—Scheherazade offers "if he would supply her with enough of her stories to reach her goal . . . [to be] his in secret whenever he wished after her maiden night with

Shahraryar. Or (if deception truly had no more savor for him), when the slaughter of her sisters had ceased, let him spirit her somehow to his place and time, and she'd be his slave and concubine forever—assuming, as one was after all realistically obligated to assume, that he and his current love would by then have wearied of each other." This elicits an exchange, affirming the ideal of constancy between lovers. As told by Dunyazade:

> "The Genie laughed and kissed her hand. 'No slaves; no concubines. And my friend and I intend to love each other forever.'
>
> " 'That will be a greater wonder than all of Sinbad's together,' Sherry said. 'I pray it may happen, Genie, and your third wish be granted too.' "

Here, of course, is laid the literary groundwork for Scheherazade's reappearance fifteen years later in *The Tidewater Tales,* at Djean's (Barth's) Chesapeake cottage, a not unexpected surprise visit of "his young friend" whom he still treasures, in a sequel testifying aesthetically and emotionally to Barth's unified sensibility.

After the irreal hijinks of the "fictive worlds" of *The Sot-Weed Factor* and *Giles Goat-Boy,* a measure of Barth's re-attention to a "kind of world that reminds us of our own" is that Scheherazade's spirited feminist bill of complaints against males is counterbalanced by Shah Zaman's ardent male apologia for marriage: "to anyone of moral imagination who's known [marriage], no other relation between men and women has true seriousness." Nor is conjugality in the prime of sexual vigor all that Shah Zaman, Shahraryar, and the Genie have in mind when they contemplate wedlock. To the sentimental Genie, whose "experience of love gone sour only made him treasure more highly the notion of a love that time would season and improve," "no sight on earth more pleased his heart, annealed as it was by his own passions and defeats, than that rare one of two white-haired spouses who still cherished each other and their life together."

Shah Zaman's pledge to Dunyazade of "equal fidelity" is a moving indictment of his brother Shahraryar's "equal promiscuity," and of the much-touted open marriages of our times, as is his judgment of his years of joyless one-night stands:

> night after night I brought them to bed, set forth their options, then either glumly stripped and pronged them or spent the night in chaste sleep and conversation. Tall and short, dark and fair, lean and plump, cold and ardent, bold and timid, clever and stupid, comely and plain—I bedded them all, spoke with them all, possessed them all, but was myself possessed by nothing but despair. Though I took many, with their consent, I wanted none of them. Novelty lost its charm, then even its novelty.

A fitting conclusion to the centuries-old "confusion of inequality and difference" between men and women is this mea culpa of Shah Zaman's, speaking for the male perpetrators of sexual tyranny down through the ages, as is his plea and pledge, "Treasure me, Dunyazade, as I'll treasure you!" With his ringing words the narrative cancels the

loathed unfamiliarity of "the foreign body in the dark, the alien touch and voice," in favor of the lifelong companionship of "a loving friend; a loving wife; a treasurable wife; a wife, a wife." It is on these notes of equality and the treasurable that the novella's statement, no less than its structure, rests: the gift of equal time for female and male alike, tellers of tales all, to have their say on the issue, Dunyazade (and Scheherazade) in part 1, Shah Zaman in part 2, and, in a coda, Barth in part 3. (pp. 1-32)

> *Max F. Schulz, in his* The Muses of John Barth: Tradition and Metafiction from *Lost in the Funhouse* to The Tidewater Tales, *The Johns Hopkins University Press, 1990, 220 p.*

FURTHER READING

Bibliography

Vine, Richard Allan. *John Barth: An Annotated Bibliography.* Metuchen, N.J.: Scarecrow Press, 1977, 99 p.
> Annotated bibliography of primary and secondary sources.

Walsh, Thomas P., and Northouse, Cameron. *John Barth, Jerzy Kosinski, and Thomas Pynchon: A Reference Guide.* Boston: G. K. Hall & Co., 1977, 145 p.
> Annotated bibliography of primary and secondary sources arranged chronologically.

Weixlmann, Joseph. *John Barth: A Descriptive Primary and Annotated Secondary Bibliography, Including a Descriptive Catalog of Manuscript Holdings in United States Libraries.* New York: Garland Publishing, 1976, 214 p.
> Extensive compilation of primary sources and annotated secondary materials arranged chronologically.

Criticism

Appel, Alfred, Jr. "The Art of Artifice." *The Nation* 207, No. 14 (28 October 1968): 441-42.
> Review of *Lost in the Funhouse,* praising Barth's use of such stratagems as erudition, parody, and involution.

Barth, John, and Hawkes, John. "A Dialogue: John Barth and John Hawkes." In *Anything Can Happen,* edited by Tom LeClair and Larry McCaffery, pp. 9-19. Urbana: University of Illinois Press, 1983.
> Conversation in which Barth and Hawkes discuss their literary influences and their likes and dislikes concerning contemporary fiction.

Bedetti, Gabriella. "Women's Sense of the Ludicrous in John Barth's 'Dunyazadiad'." *Studies in American Humor* n.s. 4, Nos. 1-2 (Spring-Summer 1985): 74-81.
> Asserts that the novella "Dunyazadiad" "is an exemplary tale of how humor erodes the opposition between the sexes" and concludes that "humor allows woman to control the situation without man losing his sense of maleness."

Bienstock, Beverly Gray. "Lingering on the Autognostic

Verge: John Barth's *Lost in the Funhouse.*" *Modern Fiction Studies* 19, No. 1 (Spring 1973): 69-78.

Studies the relationship between writer, reader, and text in *Lost in the Funhouse,* considering the Möbius strip structure of "Frame-Tale" as emblematic of Barth's collection as a whole in which fiction is "an audience participation medium."

Bryant, Jerry H. "The Novel Looks at Itself—Again." *The Nation* 215, No. 20 (18 December 1972): 631-33.

Review of *Chimera* in which the critic discusses metafictional elements, maintaining that "the process of fiction, appropriate to the classroom, has no place as the subject of fiction."

Cantrill, Dante. " 'It's a Chimera': An Introduction to John Barth's Latest Fiction." *Rendezvous* X, No. 2 (Winter 1975): 17-30.

Provides plot synopses of the three novellas in *Chimera,* examining the works as metafiction and commending their structural complexity.

Davison, Richard Allen. Review of *Lost in the Funhouse. Studies in Short Fiction* VIII, No. 4 (Fall 1971): 659-60.

Praises the challenging and experimental nature of Barth's short fiction.

Farwell, Harold. "John Barth's Tenuous Affirmation: 'The Absurd, Unending Possibility of Love'." *The Georgia Review* XXVIII, No. 2 (Summer 1974): 290-306.

Thematic analysis of Barth's fiction, emphasizing the development of his absurdist worldview and his delineation of the ambiguity of love. Farwell concludes that in his short fiction Barth seems to affirm "the possibility of love—absurd though that may be."

Fogel, Stan, and Slethaug, Gordon. *Understanding John Barth.* Columbia: University of South Carolina Press, 1990, 242 p.

Provides information on Barth's life, novels, and short fiction, as well as a selected bibliography of primary and secondary sources.

Gorak, Jan. "The Nihilist *Deus Artifex*: The Short Fiction of John Barth." In his *God the Artist: American Novelists in a Post-Realist Age,* pp. 145-66. Urbana: University of Illinois Press, 1987.

Analyzes artifice and the storyteller in Barth's novels and short fiction, focusing on a prevailing sense of loss in *Lost in the Funhouse.*

Harris, Charles B. "The New Medusa: Feminism and the Uses of Myth in *Chimera*." In his *Passionate Virtuosity: The Fiction of John Barth,* pp. 127-58. Urbana: University of Illinois Press, 1983.

Discusses feminism and myth in *Chimera,* exploring "the interrelationship of myth and daily reality" and asserting that "*Chimera* is not about the woman's question, but about the larger historical, psychological, and esthetic concerns that the woman's question embodies."

Hicks, Granville. "The Up-to-Date Looking Glass." *Saturday Review* LI, No. 39 (28 September 1968): 31-2.

Positive review of *Lost in the Funhouse,* stressing Barth's experimental narrative techniques.

Hinden, Michael. "*Lost in the Funhouse*: Barth's Use of the Recent Past." *Twentieth Century Literature* 19, No. 2 (April 1973): 107-18.

Compares modernist patterns in *Lost in the Funhouse* to those in James Joyce's *The Portrait of the Artist as a Young Man.*

Jones, D. Allan. "John Barth's 'Anonymiad'." *Studies in Short Fiction* XI, No. 4 (Fall 1974): 361-66.

Analysis of "Anonymiad" in which Jones underscores Barth's depictions of love and literature.

Joseph, Gerhard. *John Barth.* Minneapolis: University of Minnesota Press, 1970, 46 p.

Critical overview of Barth's works up to the publication of *Lost in the Funhouse.*

Klinkowitz, Jerome. "How Fiction Survives the Seventies." *The North American Review* 258, No. 3 (Fall 1973): 69-73.

Reviews works by numerous postmodern fiction writers, including Philip Roth, Donald Barthelme, Thomas Pynchon, Kurt Vonnegut, Jr., and Barth. Of Barth, Klinkowitz writes: "As with [*Lost in the Funhouse*], *Chimera* confuses the product of art with the conditions of its inception, a process which obviously fascinated Barth but often results in bad writing."

Kyle, Carol A. "The Unity of Anatomy: The Structure of Barth's *Lost in the Funhouse.*" *Critique* XIII, No. 3 (1972): 31-43.

Thematic survey of short stories in *Lost in the Funhouse* that emphasizes the "structural unity" of the work.

Mackenzie, Ursula. "John Barth's *Chimera* and the Strictures of Reality." *Journal of American Studies* 10, No. 1 (April 1976): 91-101.

Explores Barth's conception of reality, imagination, and storytelling in *Chimera.*

Morrell, David. *John Barth: An Introduction.* University Park: Pennsylvania State University Press, 1976, 194 p.

Introduction to Barth's fiction in which Morrell divides discussion of each work into three parts: summary of work's inception, survey of initial critical reception, and analysis of the work itself.

Morris, Christopher D. "Barth and Lacan: The World of the Moebius Strip." *Critique* XVII, No. 1 (1975): 69-77.

Interpretation of *Lost in the Funhouse* utilizing the linguistic theory of poststructuralist Jacques Lacan to discern narrative devices in Barth's fiction "which point to the collapsible, substitutive nature of language, to the self-composed signifying chain or Moebius strip within whose confines Barth seeks to establish whatever freedom or respite is available to the contemporary writer."

Raper, Julius Rowan. "John Barth's *Chimera*: Men and Women Under the Myth." *The Southern Literary Journal* XXII, No. 1 (Fall 1989): 17-31.

Studies the contrast between fixed, archetypal characters and those who exhibit variable traits in *Chimera* to examine how Barth "exhausted the familiar heroic myth in order to release the energies of other myths waiting at the periphery of Western consciousness."

Reilly, Charlie. "An Interview with John Barth." *Contemporary Literature* 22, No. 1 (Winter 1981): 1-23.

Interview given on the publication of the epistolary novel *LETTERS* in which Barth discusses his literary theories.

Richardson, Jack. "Amusement and Revelation." *The New Republic* 159, No. 21 (23 November 1968): 30, 34-5.

Contends that Barth transcends the "linguistic excesses" of most experimental metafictionists through well-crafted, amusing, and intelligent stories in *Lost in the Funhouse.*

Sale, Roger. "Enemies, Foreigners, and Friends." *The Hudson Review* XXV, No. 4 (Winter 1972-73): 703-14.

Brief review of *Chimera* in which Sale praises the engaging quality of Barth's narratives.

Scholes, Robert. "Metafiction." *The Iowa Review* 1, No. 4 (Fall 1970): 100-15.

Attempts to define metafiction through a perusal of the experimental works of William H. Gass, Robert Coover, Donald Barthelme, and Barth.

Seymour, Thom. "One Small Joke and a Packed Paragraph in John Barth's 'Lost in the Funhouse'." *Studies in Short Fiction* 16, No. 3 (Summer 1979): 189-94.

Discusses the paragraph that delineates Ambrose and Magda's sexual encounter in "Lost in the Funhouse" as illustrative of four major narrative aspects of the story as a whole: the authorial commentary on the story in progress, the unfinished nature of the story, the illogical sequence of events, and the blurring of the thoughts of the author/narrator with the protagonist.

Slethaug, Gordon E. "Barth's Refutation of the Idea of Progress." *Critique* XIII, No. 3 (1972): 11-29.

Examines *The Sot-Weed Factor, Giles Goat-Boy,* and *Lost in the Funhouse,* concluding that in these works "Barth systematically debunks the idea of progress by showing that life is existentially absurd, by showing that the individual, society, and cosmos are all inherently chaotic."

Tatham, Campbell. "John Barth and the Aesthetics of Artifice." *Contemporary Literature* 12, No. 1 (Winter 1971): 60-73.

Distinguishes Barth from his contemporaries, positing that Barth emphasizes aestheticism over the "romantically oriented existentialism" of socially engaged writers.

Vitanza, Victor J. "The Novelist as Topologist: John Barth's *Lost in the Funhouse.*" *Texas Studies in Literature and Language* XIX, No. 1 (Spring 1977): 83-97.

Assesses narrative structures in *Lost in the Funhouse.*

Waldmeir, Joseph J., ed. *Critical Essays on John Barth.* Boston: G. K. Hall & Co., 1980, 247 p.

Collection of reviews and essays on Barth's novels and short fiction arranged chronologically to survey changes in critical response to Barth's works.

Walkiewicz, E. P. *John Barth.* Boston: Twayne Publishers, 1986, 170 p.

Critical overview of Barth's works up to *Sabbatical: A Romance.*

Warrick, Patricia. "The Circuitous Journey of Consciousness in Barth's *Chimera.*" *Critique* XVIII, No. 2 (1976): 73-85.

Examines the significance of self-consciousness, imagery, and imagination in *Chimera.*

Westervelt, Linda A. "Teller, Tale, Told: Relationships in John Barth's Latest Fiction." *The Journal of Narrative Technique* 8, No. 1 (Winter 1978): 42-55.

Appraises the relationship between reader and author in *Lost in the Funhouse* and *Chimera,* exploring ways in which Barth engages the reader in the self-consciousness and linguistic tricks of these works.

Additional coverage of Barth's life and career is contained in the following sources published by Gale Research: *Contemporary Authors,* Vols. 1-4, rev. ed.; *Contemporary Authors Bibliographical Series,* Vol. 1; *Contemporary Authors New Revision Series,* Vols. 5, 23; *Contemporary Literary Criticism,* Vols. 1, 2, 3, 5, 7, 9, 10, 14, 27, 51; *Dictionary of Literary Biography,* Vol. 2; and *Major 20th-Century Writers.*

H. E. Bates

1905-1974

(Full name Herbert Ernest Bates; also wrote under the pseudonyms Flying Officer X and John Gawsworth) English short story writer, novelist, nonfiction writer, critic, author of children's books, biographer, autobiographer, essayist, dramatist, and scriptwriter.

INTRODUCTION

Bates was a prolific author who enjoyed several phases of popularity during his lifetime. He initially garnered critical attention in the late 1920s with novels and short stories set in the rural English Midlands. In these works Bates employed pastoral imagery and a lush prose style to vividly evoke mood and atmosphere while focusing on ordinary yet significant events in the lives of his characters. During World War II, Bates was commissioned by the Royal Air Force to write about the experiences of fighter pilots, leading to a series of esteemed short stories that examine the effects of war on soldiers and civilians. Later in his career Bates returned to rural settings and themes, frequently depicting poignant incidents in the lives of children or elderly characters. Among his most popular later works are those which feature protagonists who vigorously pursue the sensual pleasures of life and nature. Bates also wrote *The Modern Short Story,* a respected literary study of short fiction.

Bates is perhaps best known for his short stories, particularly those written during the late 1920s and 1930s and collected in several volumes, including *Day's End, and Other Stories* and *Seven Tales and Alexander.* The setting of these early works, noted V. S. Pritchett, "was usually the traditional life of the small farms, cottages and holdings, his people the hedgers, ditchers, thatchers and local carriers—a horse-and-cart England in the main, the England of rural hagglings and feelings which had changed very little for centuries and often sounds Chaucerian and ripe in speech." Critics have frequently compared his early stories to the works of Anton Chekhov, citing their minimal plot lines, thematic emphasis on everyday activities, and lucid evocation of atmosphere and emotions. For example, the story "Alexander" describes a day in the life of a boy who accompanies his uncle to gather apples and visit acquaintances. Bates focuses on the boy's sensual impressions of the lush natural environment and his first intimation of sexual feelings when he encounters a farmgirl. Bates is considered to have reached maturity as a short story writer with *The Woman Who Had Imagination, and Other Stories,* published in 1934. The title story of this volume concerns a young chorale group whose boisterous flirtations are contrasted with the strained relationship between the couple with whom they lodge. Several of Bates's early collections also contain stories that center on Uncle

Silas, a wily, pleasure-seeking elderly man who relates his humorous, fabulistic adventures to his nephew. These stories appear in the volumes *My Uncle Silas* and *Sugar for the Horse.*

During World War II, Bates was commissioned by the British Royal Air Force to chronicle the heroic exploits of fighter pilots in the Allied war effort. Bates received basic officer's training in the fall of 1941 and was assigned to a series of airbases where he gathered accounts from British aviators about their combat experiences. Using the pseudonym Flying Officer X "for service reasons," Bates published short stories based on these anecdotes in the British *News Chronicle* and later collected these pieces in such volumes as *The Greatest People in the World, and Other Stories, There's Something in the Air,* and *How Sleep the Brave, and Other Stories.* Contemporary reviewers lauded Bates's stories as straightforward, unglorified accounts of the sacrifices and extraordinary courage of British fighter pilots and bomber crews. In his critical biography of Bates, Dean R. Baldwin commented: "For conveying an accurate sense of what air warfare was really like [the Flying Officer X stories] will continue to have value, and a few can stand among the outstanding fiction of World War II."

Following World War II, Bates returned to rural concerns with several volumes of short fiction, including *Colonel Julian, and Other Stories, The Watercress Girl, and Other Stories,* and *Now Sleeps the Crimson Petal, and Other Stories.* Set in the English Midlands, the pieces in these collections often focus on children or the elderly and frequently examine the effects of World War II and modernization on their way of life. "Colonel Julian," for example, depicts the disillusionment of a retired British army officer once stationed in colonial India who learns of the horrors of modern warfare from a group of World War II aviators billeted in his mansion. Critics have praised Bates's compassionate portrayal of lonely and isolated individuals in such stories as "Where the Cloud Breaks," which focuses on a retired military officer whose extreme distaste for modern technology alienates him from a woman he admires when she purchases a television set, and "Now Sleeps the Crimson Petal," in which a woman who was emotionally traumatized by an explosion during the Second World War leads an unfulfilling existence as the wife of a butcher. The stories collected in *The Watercress Girl,* published in 1959, feature youthful protagonists whose naiveté is often contrasted with cynicism and emotional disorientation of the adults around them.

In addition to short stories, Bates wrote twenty-two novellas after World War II. Two of his novellas, *The Cruise of "The Breadwinner"* and *The Triple Echo,* are considered among his finest works. Set during the Second World War, the former revolves around the crew of a small vessel who rescue downed fighter pilots and details the cabin-boy's initiation into the glories and horrors of war. *The Triple Echo* concerns the nature of love and the effects of war in its study of the emotional involvement between a troubled soldier and the wife of a prisoner of war. *The Best of H. E. Bates* offers a sampling of his work in a variety of genres, including the short story and novella. In a review of this volume, Valentine Cunningham reflected the opinion of most commentators regarding Bates's work by stating: "What H. E. Bates does best, and what this superb selection aptly shows him best at, is satisfying his characters' and his readers' deep cravings for pastorals. Repeatedly he proves the delights that attend life in the pastoral enclave, the garden enclosed, shut off from discontents and disturbances."

PRINCIPAL WORKS

SHORT FICTION

The Spring Song. In View of the Fact That   1927
Day's End, and Other Stories   1928
Seven Tales and Alexander   1929
The Hessian Prisoner   1930
The Tree   1930
Mrs. Esmond's Life   1931
A Threshing Day   1931
The Black Boxer   1932
A German Idyll   1932
Sally Go Round the Moon   1932

The Story without an End and the Country Doctor   1932
The House with the Apricot, and Two Other Tales   1933
Thirty Tales   1934
The Woman Who Had Imagination, and Other Stories   1934
Cut and Come Again   1935
The Duet   1935
Something Short and Sweet   1937
Country Tales   1938
The Flying Goat   1939
I Am Not Myself   1939
My Uncle Silas   1939
The Beauty of the Dead, and Other Stories   1940
The Greatest People in the World, and Other Stories [as Flying Officer X]   1942
There's Something in the Air   1942
The Bride Comes to Evensford   1943
How Sleep the Brave, and Other Stories [as Flying Officer X]   1943
†*Something in the Air*   1944
The Cruise of "The Breadwinner"   1946
Thirty-One Selected Tales   1947
Colonel Julian, and Other Stories   1951
Selected Short Stories of H. E. Bates   1951
Twenty Tales   1951
‡*The Stories of Flying Officer "X"*   1952
The Nature of Love: Three Short Novels   1953
The Daffodil Sky   1955
Death of a Huntsman   1957; also published as *Summer in Salandar,* 1957
Selected Stories   1957
Sugar for the Horse   1957
The Watercress Girl, and Other Stories   1959
An Aspidistra in Babylon   1960; also published as *The Grapes of Paradise: Four Short Novels,* 1960
Now Sleeps the Crimson Petal, and Other Stories   1961; also published as *The Enchantress, and Other Stories,* 1961
The Golden Oriole   1962
Seven by Five: Stories 1926-61   1963; also published as *The Best of H. E. Bates,* 1963
The Fabulous Mrs. V.   1964
The Wedding Party   1965
The Four Beauties   1968
The Wild Cherry Tree   1968
The Triple Echo   1970
The Good Corn, and Other Stories   1974
H. E. Bates   1975
The Poison Ladies, and Other Stories   1976
The Yellow Meads of Asphodel   1976
The Best of H. E. Bates   (novels and short stories)   1980
A Month by the Lake, and Other Stories   1987
A Party for the Girls   1988
Elephant's Nest in a Rhubarb Tree, and Other Stories   1989

OTHER MAJOR WORKS

The Two Sisters   (novel)   1926
Catherine Foster   (novel)   1929
Charlotte's Row   (novel)   1931
The Fallow Land   (novel)   1932
The Poacher   (novel)   1935

A House of Women (novel) 1936
Spella Ho (novel) 1938
The Modern Short Story: A Critical Survey (criticism)
    1941; revised edition, 1972
Fair Stood the Wind for France (novel) 1944
There's Freedom in the Air (nonfiction pamphlet) 1944
The Purple Plain (novel) 1947
Dear Life (novel) 1949
The Jacaranda Tree (novel) 1949
The Scarlet Sword (novel) 1950
Love for Lydia (novel) 1952
The Feast of July (novel) 1954
A Crown of Wild Myrtle (novel) 1956
The Sleepless Moon (novel) 1956
§*The Darling Buds of May* (novel) 1958
§*A Breath of French Air* (novel) 1959
§*When the Green Woods Laugh* (novel) 1960; also
    published as *Hark, Hark, the Lark!*, 1961
§*Oh! to Be in England* (novel) 1963
A Moment in Time (novel) 1964
The Distant Horns of Summer (novel) 1967
The Vanished World (autobiography) 1969
§*A Little of What You Fancy* (novel) 1970
The Blossoming World (autobiography) 1971
The World in Ripeness (autobiography) 1972

*This volume includes the stories collected in *The Greatest People in the World* and twelve other stories.

†This volume includes the stories collected in *The Greatest People in the World* and *How Sleep the Brave*.

‡This volume includes the stories collected in *The Greatest People in the World* and *How Sleep the Brave* and three other stories.

§These novels were collected as *Perfick, Perfick!: The Story of the Larkin Family* in 1985.

L. P. Hartley (essay date 1928)

[*Hartley was an English novelist and short story writer whose fiction is unified by the theme of the search for individuality and meaning in the post-Christian era. A literary critic as well, Hartley contributed reviews for many years to the* Saturday Review, Time and Tide, *the* Spectator, *and other periodicals. In the following excerpt, Hartley praises the imaginative qualities of the stories collected in* Day's End, *while pronouncing Bates's style unpolished.*]

Day's End, a book of short stories, has some of the qualities of [Mr. Bates's novel, *The Two Sisters*], though without ever quite attaining its intensity. The stories are more literal and more realistic; a shepherd is now recognizably a shepherd, a music-mistress uses the language proper to a music-mistress; a barge is a heavy black wooden boat that moves on the water, not a threatening shape that never was on land or sea. But all the same, Mr. Bates's vision, for all its originality, is still immature; he sees men as trees walking. This constitutes at once his merit and his defect. When his imagination is at its best, one is not troubled by the fact that he lacks a sense of proportion, that

he does not know how to relate the particular phenomenon of life that he is occupied with to life in general. It is a sheer joy to see him striding over, as if they did not exist, the ordinary obstacles that present themselves to the pedestrian novelist. He has a genius for selection and for putting down simply the things that snatch at his interest.

He has no technical resources; he often uses ugly, clumsy words like "soddened," and his sense of humour is very fitful. Describing the shepherd forcing his way through the snow, he says: "With a 'God damn it' he threw himself savagely forward." Mr. Bates's literary manner is akin to the shepherd's method of progress: it is violent and ungainly, but it gets there all the same. He is never deflected by considerations of elegance or through fear of being ridiculous, from saying a thing exactly as he means it. There is no hiatus between thought and expression. His one concession to literary grace is a tendency to strive unduly after strong images. "In the hollows," he says, "the woods tossed and moaned like a pile of wounded bodies thrown into a pit to die." This simile surely goes too far and defeats its object; one cannot see the wood for the bodies. But when Mr. Bates writes well he writes very well; his very lack of affectation, of knowing the way an effect may be obtained, makes him impressive. And he shows, in *Day's End,* an amazing emotional sympathy with a great variety of characters and subjects; he never seems to lead his imagination into paths that are foreign to it, and there is scarcely a story in all the twenty-five that has not some memorable touch of beauty or strangeness. Unlike most novelists, he is utterly unfatigued by the multifarious manifestations of the modern world; they bespeak richness and adventure to him, not ennui and exasperated introspection. His danger is that his imagination, undisciplined by severe acquaintance with the facts of life, may subside, like a kite without a tail. But there is little sign of this, and *Day's End* is a collection of which he may well be proud. (pp. 811-12)

> *L. P. Hartley, in a review of "Day's End, and Other Stories," in* The Saturday Review, *London, Vol. 145, No. 3791, June 23, 1928, pp. 811-12.*

Basil Davenport (essay date 1930)

[*In the following review, Davenport characterizes* Seven Tales and Alexander *as uneven, contending that the stories focusing on youthful narrators are significantly more successful than those featuring adult protagonists.*]

"Alexander" which gives half its title to [*Seven Tales and Alexander*], is a long short-story; the other seven tales are very short; they might almost be called sketches, if that did not imply a shallowness which would do them an injustice. They are stories without plot, vessels made to hold each a moment of emotion and all its overtones. Mr. Bates's method is much like that of Katherine Mansfield: he takes a single incident and so records its implications that it stirs the reader with vague feelings for which there is no name, not quite pity, not quite admiration, not quite recognition, not quite surprise, and yet partaking of all of these. Most of these stories are written from the point of view of a child, and all of them recapture to a remarkable degree the child's directness of view and child's undiscriminating interest in everything, regardless of what other people have decided to be interesting. Those stories written purely from inside a child's mind, such as **"Alexander"** and **"The Barber,"** carry an emotional atmosphere that is only to be expressed by contradictions, a sense of the wonder of everything, which because it is omnipresent the child feels without being aware of it, as one is hardly conscious that one is enjoying fresh air if one has forgotten the feel of indoors. **"Alexander"** also reveals the confident curiosity of the child who has never been hurt and so is not afraid of anything, an illusory boldness which one does not know whether to destroy or protect, but which touches one with a peculiar poignance.

The stories written from a grown person's viewpoint are less strikingly successful. It says much for Mr. Bates that he has been able to take stock of pathetic situations, the death of a gypsy's old mare for instance, and bring to them his own freshness of touch, but still they are less moving than the others. The semi-allegorical fantasies, **"The Peach-Tree"** and **"The King Who Lived on Air,"** are still less successful. In them the author has tried to introduce symbolism and even satire into his fairyland, but the fairyland vanishes at once; it is like putting a burden upon a soap-bubble.

There is however one story, **"The Child,"** in which Mr. Bates has succeeded brilliantly in combining his two worlds. In it a child looks through a window of lemon-colored glass at a bathing beach until, seized by a sudden impulse, she slips off her clothes and runs down naked to join the fat, scandalized bathers. There the falsely golden world seen through the window-glass, the world of ugliness in bathing suits invaded by the direct, naked child, are clear enough symbols, and like all good symbols express much more than can be expressed in any other way, and yet they do not disturb the simplicity of the atmosphere.

This collection is uneven, and it is to be feared that it may not be popular; but the best of the stories have a quality that will greatly commend them to the thoughtful reader: they never indulge themselves in analysis, but they set him at once to analysing their effect.

> *Basil Davenport, "Stories without Plot," in The Saturday Review of Literature, Vol. VII, No. 16, November 8, 1930, p. 305.*

Graham Greene (essay date 1934)

[*Greene is considered one of the most important novelists in modern English literature. In his major works, he explores the problems of spiritually and socially alienated individuals living in the corrupt and corrupting societies of the twentieth century. Greene is also esteemed as a film critic and biographer, as well as a literary critic sensitive to the works of undeservedly neglected authors. In the following excerpt, Greene notes the influence of the Russian writer Anton Chekhov on Bates's works and praises the stories collected in* The Woman Who Had Imagination.]

The short story in England has suffered from the complete absence of any tradition. With the exception of Henry James, no writer of importance, until a few years ago, had given his full time to a consideration of its technique. Certain novelists showed themselves on occasion competent short story writers, generally under foreign influence. Indeed, the English short story became for some years simply an enlargement of Tchehov's themes. Miss Katherine Mansfield is the obvious example: a writer of so little original talent that it is impossible to conceive what form her writing would have taken if she had not come under the Russian influence.

The influence of a great writer is as dangerous as it is valuable: it is valuable in so far as it is a purely technical influence, dangerous if it is a spiritual influence, especially the spiritual influence of a writer of different race. No writer without losing his independence can adopt another's outlook, as Miss Mansfield adopted Tchehov's. There seemed some danger that Mr. Bates might follow the same road. He had mastered Tchehov's technique, in particular that accumulation of objective detail, of which the real importance is that it precedes a sudden abandonment of objectivity. For this was Tchehov's legacy from the conventional *conte;* the point of his story was often contained in the last paragraph, but the point, instead of being the conventional surprise, was a change of tone from the objective to the subjective, a spiritual summing up of the mood which had dictated the story. Here Mr. Bates very closely followed him. To take almost at random two examples. It is impossible not to see the resemblance between these two conclusions, the first of Tchehov's "The Lady with the Dog," the second of Mr. Bates's **"Charlotte Esmond"**:

> "How? How?" he asked, clutching his head. "How?"
>
> And it seemed as though in a little while the solution would be found, and then a new and splendid life would begin; and it was clear to both of them that they had still a long, long way to go, and that the most complicated and difficult part of it was only just beginning.
>
> "Well, and what was it like at the theatre tonight?"
>
> And with the same gentle, ladylike smile she listened to the babble of friendly voices. And while she listened she kept telling herself that perhaps after all it was the Will of God that what was to happen would happen, and that when it was time to change or move or die it would be so. One knew no more.

This is dangerously close; it is impossible to accept so completely another author's technique without accepting his spiritual outlook, for the one was only made to express the other. To learn from an author technically is in part to react from him intelligently, a thing which Miss Mansfield never did, but which Mr. Bates has done in his new volume.

The Woman Who Had Imagination is, to my mind, the first volume of Mr. Bates's complete maturity. In his previous books he has worked out all the superficial aspects of literary influence, and in his new volume he shows himself an artist of magnificent originality with a vitality quite unsuspected hitherto. I cannot enough admire the title story, of which the framework is an excursion to a country house of the Orpheus Male Voice Singers with their wives and sweethearts to take part in a competition. The dresses and slang (which perfectly convey the period of the story), the heat of the afternoon striking up into the crowded brake from the country road, the return at night, the sleepy gossip and the dying away of drowsy flirtations: these frame, in the setting of the country house, an odd romantic episode. But the sureness of Mr. Bates's tact is seen in this: the unusual (of which the treatment is not quite on a level with the rest) is kept in its place and is not allowed to do more than to throw into relief the lovely realism of the choir's outing. This story and at least one other, **"The Wedding,"** containing an excellent character, the bawdy old reprobate Uncle Silas, who figures in three of these tales, seem to me to deserve a place among the finest English short stories.

Occasionally, as in **"The Gleaner,"** Mr. Bates is too purely pictorial; very rarely, in **"A German Idyll"** for example, his sentiment becomes a little lush; and, although the strength of his stories partly lies in his firm sense of a country locality (his pictures of slum life seem by contrast rather literary), his treatment of nature is sometimes over-romantic. His first story is cloyed by an elaboration of flowers and scents and birds, and one remembers Tchehov's advice: "Beauty and expressiveness in nature are attained only by simplicity, by such simple phrases as " 'The sun set,' 'It was dark,' 'It began to rain,' and so on." Sometimes, too, he indulges in a sketch which was hardly worth the while. And yet it is in his trivialities that one can see most clearly Mr. Bates's integrity as an artist. For these trivialities have been studied from the first word: such a sketch as **"Innocence"** has been as carefully designed as a novel; the reader has the satisfying knowledge that he is not being fobbed off with something careless, with something easy, that has occupied only half the author's attention.

Graham Greene, in a review of "The Woman Who Had Imagination," in The Spectator, *Vol. 152, No. 5516, March 16, 1934, p. 424.*

Meyer Berger   (essay date 1943)

[*In the following review, Berger commends the understated tone of the stories collected in* There's Something in the Air.]

Here is sheer beauty in writing. This little volume of short pieces [***There's Something in the Air***] will give the reader a clearer conception of the combat's thinking, fighting, living, than anything that has come before. The little tales are gems cut from purest carbon, handed down so that they spit cold fire.

It is done with quiet little words. Emotion is superbly checked in every passage, yet the full impact flows through the reader. Night scenes that come within the bomber pilot's vision over England, over the Channel, over Brest and Germany are painted so crisply that they crackle:

> The lights of the drome and the lights of the [enemy] bombers were like the lights of a party around a Christmas tree. . . . Then he hit another and he saw it, too, burning among the lights as if something in the Christmas tree had fallen and caught fire. Even then the lights of the drome still kept burning and the bombers circled round like coloured fireflies. It was all so fantastic, with the red and white light shining in the darkness and the coloured lights moving in the sky and the orange fires breaking the darkness, that Anderson could not believe it to be true.

No other book on the British flier—or any other flier for that matter—has the sharp, authentic note Flying Officer Bates has written into this work. Commissioned by the English Government as Flying Officer X, he got all his material first hand, and he has made it come alive. If there were decorations for this sort of thing, H. E. Bates would have the highest.

"The Young Man From Kalgoorlie," the tale of an Australian pilot, is perhaps a little better than some of the rest of these gems. It tells the story of a youth whose farmer parents managed to keep from him, on their remote acres, the news that war had come to Britain and that London and the English countryside were crumbling under Nazi bombs. It tells how he finally learned of it, anyhow, and how he went to England to learn how to pilot a Stirling and how he went out again and again to repay the German pilots for their deadly gifts. It tells how he came to have a "popsy"—a girl—who would wait for him each night when his Stirling was on operations, and of her bitterness one night when he did not come back. "In a week," she says, speaking out of deep pain, "nobody will even remember him":

> For a moment I did not answer. Now I was not thinking of him. I was thinking of the two people who had so bravely and stupidly kept the war from him and then had so bravely and proudly let him go. I was thinking of the farm with the sheep and the eucalyptus trees, the pink and mauve asters and the yellow Spring wattle flaming in the sun. I was thinking of the thousands of farms like it peopled by thousands of people like them: the simple, decent, kindly, immemorial people all over the earth.
>
> "No," I said to her. "There will be many who will remember him."

These are tales told in impressive quiet, tales that are innocent of even the suggestion of flagrant heroism that colors so many stories about combat pilots. The tone is so even and the flow so temperate that the reader is apt to wonder, when he has done with the book, how this effect was achieved. An ordinary writer would have used angry words, words closer to hand. Flying Officer X seems to shun them, yet all the feeling of a magnificent anger and of heroic achievement seems to burn into the reader's soul.

The finest example of this magical literary technique, I think, is **"The Sun Rises Twice."** It is the story of a Stirling pilot who won no medals though he flew faster and farther on most operations than any of his decorated flying mates. It is a model of simplicity—nothing more than a literary hors d'oeuvre—but the taste lingers. In **"Sergeant Carmichael,"** the story of a bomber that comes down in the Channel in early morning dark, suspense is attained by honest writing without once falling back on conventional literary trickery. In this piece there is something of Stephen Crane, but mostly it is Flying Officer X, and no Crane admirer will murmur at the resemblance.

There's something in the air and pretty soon every one must be aware of it. It is something miraculously clean and clear. It is the writing of Flying Officer X.

> Meyer Berger, "British Combat Pilots," in The New York Times Book Review, *May 16, 1943, p. 3.*

Virgilia Sapieha   (essay date 1943)

[*In the review below, Sapieha examines Bates's portrayal of British aviators in* There's Something in the Air.]

Mr. Bates, widely known as an English short-story writer, has used his talent and experience to celebrate, in a new little volume [***There's Something in the Air***], the magnificent few to whom so many owe so much. Here, in these sketches of R. A. F. fliers at a bomber station in England, the author does not so much describe his series of brave young men as introduce them to us with a few rapid clews to their background and then let us fly off with them and judge them for ourselves.

Our whole history is illumined with tales of extraordinary individual courage in the unequal struggles of men against nature and the terrible struggles of men against men. But there has never before been such material for heroic stories as is provided today in the embattled skies.

The story called **"The Greatest People in the World,"** the title under which part of this book was published in England, is about young Lawson, who had never wanted to do anything else but fly. His father had cut hedges and dug ditches in Somerset, while his mother worked at the local rectory and helped in the fields at harvest time, and together they had never earned much more than two pounds a week, yet with endless skimping they had managed to secure for their only child the education he most wanted. Although when he became a flyer Lawson's new life lay far apart from that of his parents, he never forgot what they had done for him. At the flying field Lawson met a stretch of bad luck, beginning with the night when his plane would not take off. Careful and steady as he was, this anticlimax gave him nightmares, and he lost confidence. Another time, when he had flown only a short way, icing began, the plane reeled and Lawson had to jettison his bombs and turn home. The brakes did not work in landing, the under-carriage was smashed. He was afraid he would be grounded. Then Lawson got a telegram. He went home on "compassionate leave" to see the charred ruins where his parents had been killed. After that he never ran into any more bad luck. When he roared over the English fields on his way back from bombing and saw the tiny figures of a man and a woman working, he remembered his parents, the greatest people in the world, and his whole life was clear.

In **"It's Just the Way It Is,"** on a windy November day in the rain, a middle-aged man and a graying woman go into the Wing Commander's office at Squadron Headquarters. "You want to know if everything possible was done to eliminate an accident?" the young officer asks. The man nods his head. "Everything possible was done," says the officer. . . . "But there are things you cannot foresee. . . . You can't be certain." The roar of machines tuning up fills the little room, and over this roar the woman shouts: "Why can't you be certain?" Shaking with grief, she shouts: "You don't care!" She cries violently for a time, then stops exhausted. The Wing Commander stands by the window and looks out. Then he goes back to the man and woman and, very quietly, he tells them how it happened. He tells them how their son brought the crew home safely under the greatest difficulties. When the Wing Commander has finished his story, the elderly man straightened his shoulders, the woman gets up firmly, her eyes quite cleared. "I haven't been able to tell you much," the officer says. "It's just the way it is." "It's everything," the man answers. The Wing Commander watches them go through the window, and then he puts his face in his hands.

There is the story of the girl whose parents do not want her to go out so often with her pilot friend, since there is no future in it; the story of the man from an Australian sheep farm whose parents hid from him for a whole year that England was at war with Germany, and who, when he discovered it, was the angriest young man in the world; and too, the story of Canadian Sergeant Carmichael, who keeps alive his three companions in a storm-tossed dinghy through the night and gets them safely to the shore. Into this little book are crowded the stories of some twenty nerve-taut, daring, infinitely shy young men. At the end of the series there is a short glossary to explain the new words with which these young men cover up their dangers and their deeds.

The root of all these stories of R. A. F. flyers is sacrifice. But Mr. Bates, being a true Anglo-Saxon and a true writer, keeps this root well underground. Sacrifice, implicit in every action, is never mentioned. No high-blown praise mars the account of daily heroism which is beyond words or praise. On the contrary, Mr. Bates writes so reticently, with so much understatement, and his young flyers exchange such brief and almost shame-faced talk about their feats, that only the streamlined modern Anglo-Saxon mind could appreciate the tribute which he pays them.

All stories about flyers are moving. In any book where you read about these flights, these tournaments with death, these solitary endings, you must be filled with fright and wonder. But in this book Mr. Bates makes particularly clear the discipline, the courage and the cost. He makes it particularly clear this what the flyers do is reason enough for an unalterable faith in man.

> Virgilia Sapieha, "The Few to Whom So Many Owe So Much," in New York Herald Tribune Weekly Book Review, *May 30, 1943, p. 3.*

Ben Ray Redman (essay date 1943)

[*Redman was an American journalist, poet, and critic. In the following review of* There's Something in the Air, *Redman, while faulting Bates's style as overly restrained, praises his realistic portrayal of combat pilots.*]

On April 1, 1918, when aerial warfare on the Western Front had reached unprecedented heights of fury, and more than one British squadron was celebrating its fiftieth or umpty-umptieth Hun, the Royal Flying Corps and the Royal Naval Air Service—to the infinite disgust and mutual contempt of the enforcedly contracting parties—were united under the name of the Royal Air Force. Disgust? Contempt? Why, naturally. The R.F.C. and the R.N.A.S. had their traditions, however brief; they had their brave histories. But what pilot, military or naval, could take pride in serving under this newly arranged trio of initials? What naval or military pilot could happily contemplate being lumped, in a common mass, with his opposite number? . . . *Fade Out.*

Fade In. It is twenty-five years later. Those once-despised initials are no longer new; they and that uniform are no longer meaningless. The world knows their meaning. Committed to a struggle against wicked odds, the R.A.F. met the Luftwaffe's full force and grew stronger under fire; grew ever stronger, by day and by night, until the Battle of Britain was won, and with it the probably immortal tribute in which a gifted leader phrased the thought and gratitude of less articulate millions. Now, according to Hitler's own admission, and thanks in great measure to the R.A.F., the Battle of Germany is already on.

What are they like, the men and boys who did and are doing the job? What are their lives like? Articles, short stories, books, and films have tried to tell us; some of them simply and accurately, but far more of them with melodramatic or sentimental distortions. So it is pleasant to be able to report that Flying Officer X (who in private and civilian literary life is H. E. Bates, author of several novels, a play, and ten volumes of short stories) has made a genuine if limited contribution to the cause of simplicity and accuracy [with ***There's Something in the Air***]. His contribution is semi-official, for "In the summer of 1941 he was commissioned Flying Officer X by the British Government and was stationed with the Bomber Command to study the men of the R.A.F. in and out of action." It might even be called a work of propaganda. But there is the propagation of truth as well as of falsehood.

Mr. Bates's limitations are self-imposed. He is more interested in the character behind action than in action itself, and his twenty-one short sketches are predominantly character sketches. Action is there, but it is for the most part subsidiary or illustrative. The result is a quiet book, a designedly quiet book. At times a reader might feel that the author has pushed his design too far; that his reticences are almost exhibitionistic, his under-writing a kind of exaggeration, his silences thunderous. He throws lines away instead of leaning on them, he lowers his voice instead of raising it. But so do most of those of whom he is writing.

For a vivid sense of war-flying, you will, I think, have to

go to another author, or at least to another book. In this one Mr. Bates seldom makes me feel that I am "air-borne" (if the old R.A.F. may use a word that belongs to the new); he never evokes, for me at least, sensations of actual combat. But he knows the men of whom he writes, and because of his knowledge, and his ability to communicate it, you will know and remember many of them. And you will find them good company. They speak a different slang than their fathers did. They are better trained, more scientific, and less expert—one gathers—at serious drinking. Flying from England as they are, from well established stations, the routine of their lives is unlike the expeditionary routines of the last war. Greatest change of all, perhaps, fighter aristocrats and once humble bombers now fly as peers. But, whatever the changes, the faces are familiar. And the thoughts and fears and hopes and hates and determinations behind the faces.

Ben Ray Redman, "The Fighting Faces of the Sky," in The Saturday Review of Literature, *Vol. XXVI, No. 23, June 5, 1943, p. 8.*

William Peden (essay date 1952)

[*Peden is an American critic and educator who has written extensively on the American short story and on such American historical figures as Thomas Jefferson and John Quincy Adams. In the following review of* Colonel Julian, and Other Stories, *he discusses how Bates portrays the loneliness and isolation of his characters through a combination of compassion and humor.*]

This distinguished collection of fifteen short stories [***Colonel Julian, and Other Stories***] by the British author of *Fair Stood the Wind for France* and *The Purple Plain* invites favorable comparison with the best of A. E. Coppard or Elizabeth Bowen or V. S. Pritchett. Indeed, these stories make the work of many of H. E. Bates' contemporaries in England or here in America appear, in comparison, either amateurish or pretentious.

Mr. Bates' primary concern is, like Miss Bowen's, the "problem of human unknowableness," and one might say that collectively his stories constitute an anatomy of loneliness. Though admirably varied in subject matter, they are essentially somber in tone. With the exception of two genuinely humorous sketches involving a robust nonagenarian, they depict with varying degrees of skepticism or compassion the deterioration of the individual ego. Mr. Bates' characters struggle for a kind of unattainable self-realization, if not completely in vain, certainly without success.

With loneliness their destiny, they wander like ghosts through the dry rot of a crumbling manor house or decaying farmhouse, their voices unheard above the sound of the restless sea or lost among the orderly tea rows of an Indian plantation. Some, like the masculine young woman of **"A Girl Named Peter,"** are denied love because of physical or emotional traits over which they can exercise little if any control. Others, like the lovers of **"The Lighthouse,"** are frustrated by custom and tradition and social mores, still others by fear, or stupidity, or by the sheer perversity of things as they are.

Still others struggle to achieve an inevitable defeat. Or, like the protagonist of **"The Frontier,"** they merely give up. "He had been traveling up and down there, in the same way, for twenty years. He had a long lean figure and a pale face, rather dreamy and prematurely gray and in very hot weather blue-lipped, that had become almost Indianized, giving him a look of Asiatic delicacy. He had learned, very early, that in the East time was an immensity that does not matter; that it is better not to get excited; that what does not happen today will happen tomorrow and that death, it is very probable, will come between. His chief concern was not to shout, not to worry, not to get excited, but to grow and manufacture a tolerably excellent grade of tea."

Yet Mr. Bates seldom if ever creates a character to humiliate or destroy him for the sake of the humiliation or destruction. His people are unheroic, to be sure: a sixtyish major with three different sets of false teeth and a shrewish wife; an ignorant farmer who temporarily finds happiness by way of the agony columns; a sensitive young woman badgered in a world of Philistines. They are not, however, ignoble, and long after their fate has been settled, they linger disturbingly in the reader's mind. Mr. Bates avoids the sensational or the melodramatic; through an unerring selection of the exact gesture or thought or act or incident, he reveals the very essence of his characters' thwarted personalities.

William Peden, "At the End Is Loneliness," in The New York Times Book Review, *April 6, 1952, p. 6.*

Milton Rugoff (essay date 1952)

[*In the following review, Rugoff praises the evocative settings and emotional impact of* Colonel Julian, and Other Stories.]

In most of these fifteen stories [in ***Colonel Julian, and Other Stories***] by the British story writer and novelist, H. E. Bates, the main characters are groping for love—in flight from frustration or trapped by it. A few abandon themselves to desire, but rarely without a sense of guilt; the others can find no release and wither in unfulfillment. As through a magnifying glass Mr. Bates focusses light on their lives until they smoulder and burst into flame or curl up and withdraw. He works deliberately, making masterful use of natural surroundings that are mockingly serene and uninhibited: a fine old manor going slowly back to wildness, a tea plantation in the light that falls off Kangchenjunga, a farm at harvest time, an inn on a Swiss lake. In such landscapes his characters reach out to each other, some timidly, some boldly, a few to snatch hasty consummation, most to be thwarted and rejected.

There is in fact almost a polarity between those who indulge their desires freely and those who cannot. The girl in **"The Lighthouse"** and the mother in **"No More the Nightingales"** give themselves so promiscuously and compulsively as to suggest that they have never been and never will be satisfied. In contrast there is the leading character of **"A Girl Called Peter,"** who has been brought up as though she were a boy and when she meets a smooth-mannered young man is agonizingly unable to respond to

him. In much the same pattern, however different the setting, is the story of the girl who runs a music shop in a factory town and, stirred by a stranger who asks for a Schubert air, vainly rebels against going to a rowdy Christmas party. Reversing traditional romance, these tales themselves are tender, their endings harsh.

The male counterparts of these, reminding one of *Of Human Bondage,* are Joe Johnson, who throws his fruit store and gentility to the winds in the pursuit of a mocking little wench, and an aging Major of Hussars, publicly the soul of propriety, privately the fool of his shrewish young wife. But of all these probings of loneliness, tragic, pathetic, comic-pathetic, those which open the volume and close it. **"The Little Farm"** and **"The Frontier,"** respectively, are likely to remain longest with the reader. In the former, the stages by which a young housekeeper brings love and order into the life of a forlorn young farmer are traced in heart-warming detail, which completely disarms the reader and leaves him wide open for an abrupt and stunning ending. In **"The Frontier"** a diffident Welsh plantation owner in India accidentally finds himself host to a young British nurse; as he is excitedly communicating to her his feeling for the beauty of the countryside and his need for a companion, the India he is so enamored of steps between them with fearful violence. It is not only a poignant narrative of a man cruelly cheated but a vivid insight into the drawing apart of empire and colony. The reserve that marks the men in several of these stories (always excepting the two lustily comic tales of "Uncle Silas") will seem British to the point of caricature, but merely underscores the fact that it is generally skin-deep and often pathetic.

The crumbling of the empire figures largely in other stories (that whirring you hear is Tennyson and Kipling spinning in their graves), sometimes adding the note of nostalgia, sometimes of despair. It is the ironic essence of **"The Flag,"** wherein the master of a manor fallen on evil days resigns the manor to decay and himself to drink, and it casts its shadow over the eighty-three-year-old colonel who, in the title story, tries to understand one of the young airmen quartered on his estate, the colonel with his memories of army pomp and form in India in the '80s, and the airman who has come out of the trauma of bomber missions with grafted eyelids, a most casual air and a most bitter slang.

Bates' thematic range may not be great, but he probes deep in a vital emotional salient. His evocation of scene, particularly the English countryside, is heady, and his narrative pace is deliberate and sure, a slow fuse, often exploding only after the last sentence has passed. Short-story anthologists will plunder this little book for years to come.

Milton Rugoff, "Loneliness," in New York Herald Tribune Book Review, *April 27, 1952, p. 9.*

Dunham Curtis (essay date 1952)

[*In the review below, Curtis commends Bates's portrayal of inarticulate, defeated individuals in the short stories of* Colonel Julian, and Other Stories.]

Unfortunately, and not surprisingly, H. E. Bates's popular reputation in [the United States] and, to a somewhat lesser extent, in his native England, is based upon his mediocre later novels in which sex, violence, and exotic background are exploited palatably and unprofoundly. This is regrettable because Mr. Bates is, in such early novels as *Catherine Foster* and in most of the thirteen volumes of short stories he has published since 1926, both a skilled craftsman and a man who presents important experience significantly.

Most of his most recent collection, ***Colonel Julian and Other Stories,*** concerns inarticulate and thwarted men and women who find life more perplexing than pleasurable. The illiterate Tom Richards, who trusts even those who take advantage of him; Joe Johnson, who is unable to understand why his love is unreturned and blames the "caterpillarists"; the girl called Peter, who is treated like a man by her father and the men she would like to be loved by—these are typical Bates characters. Nothing overdramatic happens: Joe Johnson follows a girl around and is cast aside, Peter almost acts like a woman with a man she meets casually. Yet the little that happens suggests whole lifetimes.

Not all the stories are tragic. Those who remember the earlier *My Uncle Silas* will be delighted to meet him again in **"The Bedfordshire Clanger,"** as good a tall tale as Mr. Bates has ever produced. **"Mrs. Vincent"** is a short and mordant satire of a complacent Anglo-Indian while **"The Lighthouse"** and **"No More the Nightingales"** are at least partially happy stories of liberation from sexual repression that recall some of the best work of D. H. Lawrence.

But the best stories bring only the sad cheer that comes from understanding better the unhappy. **"A Christmas Song"** poignantly evokes the life of a sensitive girl forced to live among the vulgar. **"The Major of Hussars,"** about an old army officer with three sets of teeth and a young bitch of a wife, admirably represents the pathos of a situation that appears to be becoming increasingly usual.

Probably the most penetrating of all the stories is **"Colonel Julian."** It consists largely of a conversation between the eighty-three-year-old colonel and a young aviator he tries to understand. Without the interposition of the author or any forcing of the situation, its thirteen pages reveal a great deal about the nature of war, soldiers of the oldest and latest generation, and the disease wartime flying can become. Like all excellent short stories, it is a novel suggested, an epiphany.

Although there are two inferior stories, **"Sugar for the Horse"** and **"Time Expired,"** this is an excellent collection, far more worth reading than most of Mr. Bates's own or of most other writers' novels. By a style that is spare and vivid, through plots that are usually both inevitable and arresting, Mr. Bates deepens our understanding of people we should know more about.

Dunham Curtis, "Reigning Duet," in Saturday Review, *New York, Vol. XXXV, No. 21, May 24, 1952, p. 23.*

Oliver La Farge (essay date 1954)

[*In the following review of the novellas collected in* The Nature of Love, *La Farge extols Bates's narrative style, characterizations, and plotting.*]

The well-written trilogy H. E. Bates is offering under the name of ***The Nature of Love,*** might, perhaps, be better entitled "The Nature of Desire," since there is in it little of love other than the magnetic attraction to each other of male and female, and the principal women of the stories have decidedly round heels. There is a partial exception in the first story, but there the sentiment of love hardly progresses beyond a rudimentary and formless stage. The stories do not constitute an inquiry into the nature of love; but then, if we ever start damning books for ill-fitting titles, what writer would go scot free?

The first story, ***Dulcima,*** is something of a tour de force. Presenting us with an almost repulsive, mean-spirited heroine, having neither virtue nor passion, avaricious on a niggardly scale, it nonetheless convinces the reader that when this woman experiences something approaching real love, her character will change. Dulcima herself, painfully groping towards self-respect, dealing with sensations she cannot verbalize, is a fine study. The influence upon her of a partial release from drab hopelessness is handled well and with fine restraint. The story is a neat, credible triangle with a credible, tragic ending.

The other two stories are also on the tragic side, but less deeply so, since in neither does the central situation contain mutuality of love or equally sustained desire. The protagonists move in a sort of formal dance; the reader does not feel that truly great passion is present. He also knows, and feels that the main character should know, that from the outset the affair has no future.

We do not ask that every writer give us profound tragedy. There is no reason to believe that Mr. Bates was trying to do so, and he writes like a man who knows very well what he is doing. He presents us with intriguing situations in a variety of well-presented settings, builds up his characters with many small, perfectly placed brush-strokes, and tells a smooth, rounded story.

The last of the three is laid in Malaya, but that is not why the writing carries a suggestion of Maugham and back of that a faint reminiscence of Conrad. It is in the technique, the manner in which detail is applied, and the sophistication of the writer himself. The storytelling is in the best of the English tradition, and has a notable quality of neatness.

In this age of brief, hurried stories tailored to the preferences of slick magazine readers, it is a pleasure to settle down once more to full, unhurried narrative underlaid by a good raconteur's development of background. The 4,500-word taboo that afflicts much American short-story writing enforces undernourished tales, notable chiefly for the cleverness of their condensation. Those writers who escape that limitation in the little and special magazines seldom have the technical skill to make good use of their freedom. The art is in the many details every one of which serves a useful purpose and all of which hold the reader's interest. Out of them come real characterization and the priceless illusion of reality.

The Nature of Love is grown-up writing for grown-ups, the work of a real craftsman.

Oliver La Farge, "Male-Female Trouble," in The Saturday Review, *New York, Vol. XXXVII, No. 20, May 15, 1954, p. 13.*

James Stern   (essay date 1954)

[*In the following review, Stern faults the novellas collected in* The Nature of Love *as contrived.*]

Making up *The Nature of Love* are three novellas—"the beautiful and blest *nouvelle*," as Henry James called the long story upon which, until very recently, both English and American editors have cast so scornful an eye. Now, with the assistance of the *New Yorker* and the initiative of Mary Louise Aswell, it looks as though the "short novel" may be about to receive the respectful treatment it has so long enjoyed in France and, in better days, Germany and Russia.

As might be expected from his book's title, H. E. Bates' three stories have a common subject: love—or, to be more correct if more melodramatic, all three are stories of "fatal passions." Two, in fact, end in murder. *The Delicate Nature,* whose scene is laid on a Malay plantation, is so reminiscent of the work of Somerset Maugham that one is not surprised to find this volume dedicated to the author of "Miss Thompson" and "The Casuarina Tree."

The Delicate Nature more than invites, it all but demands comparison with Maugham's earlier short fiction. At his best Mr. Bates can "tell a story" as compellingly as his master. Both men know all the tricks of the trade. But this novella shows that Mr. Bates does not feel quite so at home in the tropics.

Nor does this story of an unloved married woman demanding love from a younger man in order to incite jealousy in her husband, possess that inevitability which carries the reader unquestioning to the climax of a good Maugham story.

Mr. Bates' drama moves too fast; the characters live on the page, but there are moments when one's credulity is strained. Would a woman, however frustrated in her love, throw herself quite so fast and furiously at the feet of a young man she hardly knows? One doubts it.

Mr. Bates is more English, less cosmopolitan than Maugham. The climate of his native land is in his blood. And at describing its fields and flowers, its birds and beechwoods, England in shimmering spring and the heat of summer, he has, since the death of D. H. Lawrence, no living superior. Both *Dulcima* and *The Grass God* are set in this landscape and in both stories the characters are inseparable from the land. The former is a sordid tale of a poor laborer's daughter, the latter of a wealthy landowner, both caught at turning-points in their lives. *The Grass God,* about an unhappily married man whose passion for his acres is interrupted by his meeting an unattached girl,

is the more subtle, more convincing of the two, as well as the only story in the book not to end in violent death.

A more unattractive couple than the brow-beaten Dulcima with her fat legs "hideously knotted with raised blue veins," and the miserly drunken farmer, Parker, with his bundles of money stowed away in biscuit tins in the attic, it would be difficult to imagine. And yet, that these two lonely people could be drawn together by the nature of their lusts (not love) one does not question. What is surely questionable is that a young gamekeeper should suddenly conceive a passion for a painfully ugly girl just because, for the first time in her life, she has brought herself some new clothes and paid a visit to the hairdresser! Likely or not, the consequences are certainly fatal.

James Stern, "With Fatal Results," in The New York Times Book Review, *May 23, 1954, p. 4.*

Edmund Fuller   (essay date 1956)

[*In the following review, Fuller focuses on the impressionistic style Bates used in the short stories of* The Daffodil Sky.]

The reputation of H. E. Bates is growing steadily, both as novelist and writer of short stories. [*The Daffodil Sky*], an importation from England, contains fifteen of his tales, widely divergent in length, scene and theme. They hop about from the English countryside, to France, Switzerland, Italy and India.

Mr. Bates is above all an artist at indirection. As a result, what we suppose to be obvious is revealed as not obvious. His method blends rich detail in portraiture, setting and mood with the most oblique suggestion of event. It is his way to be specific about many things, but, not about meanings, nor always about the outcome of stories crowded with possibilities. Some of the shorter pieces are vignettes—character or mood impressions of rural English scenes and types reminiscent of such of his novels as *The Feast of July.*

There is a cryptic, pent-up tension in the title story, which looks in retrospect upon a crime of passion. It is left to the reader to divine the meaning and anticipate the event at the end when a man out of prison seeks the woman who had betrayed him and finds himself involved with the daughter of uncertain paternity who is so much as her mother used to be, in both appearance and availability.

A woman's passionate, desperate hunger for a child is the heart of **"The Good Corn."** **"Across the Bay"** is in the French setting, which Mr. Bates always handles well. Against a skillfully sketched background of a seacoast resort hotel he projects a summer affair between an Englishman and a Frenchwoman. The relationship is odd and is unfolded in a bitter, post-war mood, leading toward an aching disillusion. Perhaps it is the most ambitious story in the book.

"Country Society" is a dryly satirical account of a wintry afternoon party where the hostess is in an agony of social ambition and her husband is entranced by a pretty girl into a brief vision of liberation from the whole dreary round.

"Roman Figures" strangely blends the dust of archaeology with the double heats of summer and jealousy. **"A Place in the Heart"** is a painful story of subtle nuances involving a crippled girl in India and the double betrayal she suffers.

Graham Greene has compared the short stories of H. E. Bates to those of Chekhov. The collection in *The Daffodil Sky* supports that association.

> Edmund Fuller, "Impressions of Mortality," in The New York Times Book Review, *July 15, 1956, p. 5.*

Robert H. Glauber   (essay date 1957)

[*In the review below, Glauber favorably appraises the novellas in* Summer in Salandar.]

Each succeeding book of H. E. Bates further reveals the extraordinary ability of this writer to control his readers purely through his command of the English language. It has become almost a commonplace for critics to praise him. No longer is it a question of "shall we?" but rather "how?"

[*Summer in Salandar*] offers four novellas which explore four differing aspects of love. Roughly, each has the same theme—the revolutionary manner in which sudden love can affect a life—yet they could not be more dissimilar.

Death of a Huntsman presents a middle-aged, "good old Harry" type suburbanite who disastrously finds himself enamoured of a seventeen-year-old, hypersensitive girl; *Night Run to the West* shows us a brawny truck driver who suddenly discovers through a sex-starved older woman that the line between love and hate can be hardly any line at all; in the title story the agony of needing love yet fearing it is explored with almost frightening clarity; and in *The Queen of Spain Fritillary* the consequences of mixing too long repression, too sudden freedom, and too callous youth are pictured in all their tragic overtones.

In each of these stories Mr. Bates tells us so much more than his words actually say. His crises develop ostensibly through an unexpected flowering of love in apparently loveless people, but he makes us see (always without stating it explicitly) that these people have been preparing all their lives for this particular moment of personal disaster. And with what economy of literary means this is accomplished! In the last story, for instance, no more than twenty or so lines are devoted to Miss Carfax, yet she is able to play a pivotal role in the drama because in so little time Mr. Bates has made us see, feel, and understand this unhappy woman. He offers us only sample comments and leads us empathically to fill in the rest for him. Significantly, as we read we are seldom aware of the exact nature of our participation. That we are involved is all too obvious as he alternately shocks, amuses, frightens, or stirs us, but the subtle means by which this is accomplished offer fresh testimony to his almost unrivaled literary skill.

In one way or another, love is the subject of most fiction just as it is essentially the main pursuit and need of man's life. But love and its corruption often walk ambivalently hand in hand. Mr. Bates has very little to say about this that is new, but he does show us with great artistry the havoc that can be wrought in our lives when we overlook this tendency toward vitiation in man. The stories then become almost variations, one might say, on the particularly frightful odor of festering lilies referred to by Shakespeare. With each of these tales the author makes us aware again that, when sacred, love helps us to be more and more alive, but when profaned traps us into feeling that we might be better off dead. It takes a compassionate understanding of our weaknesses to accomplish this in a reader, and, in addition to all his previously established virtues, the new book demonstrates that Mr. Bates has such perception in abundance.

> Robert H. Glauber, "Four Novellas about Love," in New York Herald Tribune Book Review, *October 13, 1957, p. 5.*

Frederic Morton   (essay date 1957)

[*In the following review of* Summer in Salandar, *Morton praises the "restrained elegance" of Bates's prose style.*]

A few years ago H. E. Bates published a collection of novellas called *The Nature of Love.* He might have used the same title for the present book; it, too, consists of a number of short fictions all of which have man's ways and byways with a maid for their theme. And, like the earlier volume, *Summer in Salandar* leaves one wondering why so much skill adds up to so little—especially when one recalls the impact of so much of Mr. Bates' earlier work, particularly the longer novels.

Mr. Bates can invent resourcefully, then amplify his invention with grace. *Death of a Huntsman,* the first of four novellas, is a melancholy love affair taking place almost exclusively on horseback. *Night Run to the West* traps a truck-driver in a bizarre triangle with a woman and her ancient husband. *Summer in Salandar* finds a travel agent afflicted, excited by a woman's visit during the dead season. And *The Queen of Spain Fritillary* tells of an entomological tragedy staged by an elderly lover of butterflies and a lovely young ignorer of them.

Mr. Bates renders such situations with the reticent elegance to which the English writer is specially privileged. He can summon all the right details with a discreet peck or two on the typewriter. He is incapable of the strained phrase or the clumsy sentence. His landscapes—usually fall or summer—are full of ripe, quiet glories. Yet these virtuosities betray a limitation as well. Page after page brims with pastorals finely but monotonously stroked—always the same, whether seen by the truck-driver of one tale or the gentleman-rider of another. They shimmer, they sway, these vistas; they do everything except breathe. They are the product of a high literary competence, not of a deeper intuition—and, like so many smoothly turned stories of their kind, one is always a trifle too conscious of that competence.

What is true of the settings applies to the people of Mr.

Bates' book. In *The Nature of Love* each protagonist falls in love at first sight. Here in the present volume, every heroine brings about an event that is physically or morally lethal to her lover. Just as in *The Nature of Love,* this imposition of an over-all scheme is not entirely natural. Mr. Bates' people perform deftly devised acts, not inevitable ones.

An exception ought to be made of the travel agent in the title story. The tropical climate of *Summer in Salandar* seems to have inflamed the author into a fiercer sympathy with his characters than he usually cares to summon (one reason, perhaps, why Mr. Bates' exotic fiction is generally his most successful). Therefore, the agent's agony unfolds with steaming, sun-stunned truth.

The other stories are better rounded, prettier even in their baleful tone, more ingeniously decorated, and just a little bit deader than life.

> Frederic Morton, "Man's Ways and By-Ways with a Maid," in The New York Times Book Review, *October 20, 1957, p. 50.*

Patricia Donegan   (essay date 1958)

[*In the following review, Donegan extols the characterizations, settings, and tone of the novellas collected in* Summer in Salandar.]

In his new book, *Summer in Salandar,* H. E. Bates takes a modern theme and treats it with discretion, taste and craftsmanship. Concerned in these four novellas with the problem of loneliness, the author realizes his characters within the richly-textured details and patterns of a particular setting, interlocking characters and surroundings and pulling the reader into the situation with an insinuating yet vivid appeal to his senses.

In *Summer in Salandar,* the title story, Mr. Bates describes the profound isolation of a young travel agent, drenched in the brutal sunlight and glaring boredom of an off season. The tone is set immediately with an initial description of a passing funeral which Manson, the agent, watches indifferently.

> It flashed along the waterfront like a train of cellulose beetles, black and glittering, each of the thirty cars a reflection of the glare of the sun on the sea. He wondered, as the cars leaped away up the avenue of jade and carmine villas, eyeless in the bright evening under closed white shades, why funerals in Salandar were always such races, unpompous and frenzied, as if they were really chasing the dead. He wondered, too, why he never saw them coming back again. They dashed in black undignified weeping haste to somewhere along the seacoast, where blue and yellow fishing boats beat with high, moonlike prows under rocks ashen with burned seaweed, and then vanished forever.

Into this sunburnt sluggishness of rock and sea, the author brings a restless young woman, intruding on Manson's dullness the problems of her eyes, her perfumes and her fears, making herself felt in petty demands. It is as if Manson himself were the off season, as if the brutality of the sunlight had dulled all effort, made him helpless and hopeless, passively defensive against the restless thrusts of the woman. "A smell of oil and hot bullock dung and rotting seaweed seethed in the air. . . . "

More gentle, more poignant, perhaps, is *Death of a Huntsman,* where a "bright yellow break of sunlight" seen through the dense masses of cucumber leaves becomes a young girl, made beautiful by the awareness of her beauty in a gentle, slightly ridiculous, certainly awkward older man. The soft, bright tranquility of an English countryside blankets this story and seems to be part of the communication between the two who love each other. The physical incongruity and awkwardness of the man only intensifies the idyll, and when it is broken it is destroyed with a violence—of which the author is also capable—in a contrast not only of character and action, but of setting, of night and shadows.

Mr. Bates has been compared to Chekov and, in the intense quality of the mood, in the inevitability of the characters' revelations, in depth, his work is reminiscent of the Russian writer. There is unity and meaning to these four novellas, which make a splendid addition to the author's already remarkable achievements.

> Patricia Donegan, "Revelations of the Summer," in The Commonweal, *Vol. LXVII, No. 14, January 3, 1958, p. 364.*

Alice S. Morris   (essay date 1960)

[*In the following review of* The Watercress Girl, and Other Stories, *Morris discusses Bates's vision of childhood.*]

The English short-story writer and novelist, H. E. Bates, has demonstrated in the past that his apprehension of the state of being a child is delicate, penetrating and filled with light. Specifically, in the thirteen stories in his new book [*The Watercress Girl, and Other Stories*], he illuminates the shadowy, indeterminate territory where the reality of the child is confronted by, collides with—or uncannily anticipates—the reality of the adult. Under Mr. Bates' scrutiny, these two realities are revealed as so disparate, of so inherently different an order, that communication between them is fragmentary; except in rare, almost mystical instances of pure divination.

A précis of plots, in the case of "The Watercress Girl" stories, can barely approach the heart of the matter, for the most successful turn on merely transitory situations, or isolated moments of experience. The only story with a plot in the conventional sense—"A Great Day for Bonzo," in which a dramatic conflict between grown-ups is counterpointed by the peripheral involvement of three children—wears an uncharacteristic air of contrivance that invalidates its flashes of literary truth.

Elsewhere, Mr. Bates matches his craft to his vision with sometimes incandescent effect. The first story, "The Cowslip Field," sets the mood. On a summer's day, gathering cowslips with a squat, bespectacled countrywoman, a young boy momentarily discovers in this familiar, homely figure an unfamiliar, mysterious and lovely being unsuspected by the surface-skimming eyes of the world. ("Slowly, like an unrolling blind, the massive coil of her hair fell down across her neck and shoulders and back, until it reached her waist. He had never seen hair so long, or so much of it, and he stared at it with wide eyes as it uncoiled itself, black and shining against the golden cowslip field.")

A little girl who prefers playing house to games of war, in a foretaste of adult betrayal, loses her male playmate to a rival more enthusiastic and able at sudden ambush and playing dead (**"Death and the Cherry Tree"**). Accompanying his father on a visit to a remote, impecunious aunt of whom he has never even heard, a boy has a glimpse into one of the sad outlands of family life and, from the cryptic circumlocutions of their conversation, divines an intimation of the truth (**"The Far Distant Journey"**). Two boys, setting out to find where the world begins, find instead a man who has transformed the necessity for wearing a glass eye into a source of gaiety, and an absolute virtue (**"Source of the World"**).

Mr. Bates' gossamer-textured prose and his lyric passion for the natural world—that often makes his pages *mille-fleurs* tapestries of cowslips, watercresses, birds and butterflies—combine to give his tales a golden sense of eternal summer, only shattered here and there by adumbrations from the wintry purlieus of maturity. Especially in the stories enumerated above, and in a haunting, nostalgic narrative titled **"The Pemberton Thrush,"** Mr. Bates opens an effective and affecting route straight to the heart of childhood: its innocent joys, its uncorrupted vision and its inevitable capitulation to time.

> Alice S. Morris, "Worlds in Collision," in The New York Times Book Review, *January 10, 1960, p. 5.*

Hope Hale   (essay date 1960)

[*In the following review, Hale praises Bates's rendering of his youthful characters in* The Watercress Girl, and Other Stories.]

Though he has written eighteen novels, including *Fair Stood the Wind for France,* an absorbing tale of downed English flyers in enemy-occupied country, H. E. Bates is probably best known for his short stories. The title of an earlier volume of these, **The Nature of Love,** might serve equally well for this latest delightful collection, **The Watercress Girl.** The heroes of these thirteen stories are small boys, genuinely young, equipped with few facts and much misinformation; but most of them are confronted here with the sort of choices which adults must make between intense and conflicting emotional demands.

Except for one sixty-six-page adventure in which three children take decisive action in an imminent tragedy involving three strangers, the stories are brief and lyrical. All are charged with the contradictions inherent in the child's vision, which has a way of magnifying immediate details while viewing larger issues through a mist of myopia. "The larches had little scarlet eyelashes springing from their branches," one child observes. No mole or moustache on an adult face escapes his minute inspection;

no nuance of lower-class speech is missed; no look or taste or smell is lacking. But at the same time we share the child's dark wonder, his sense of mystified loss and foreboding, as the fixed patterns of adult relationships shift and break around him, threatening his world.

In one of his literary studies, *The Modern Short Story,* Bates says that this art form "can be anything the author decides it shall." Among a great many varieties he presents for a writer to choose from, he suggests "the piece which catches like a cobweb the light subtle iridescence of emotions that can never be really captured or measured." For a happily large proportion of his own stories, this is a perfect description.

> Hope Hale, in a review of "The Watercress Girl," in Saturday Review, *Vol. XLIII, No. 3, January 16, 1960, p. 65.*

Rose Feld   (essay date 1960)

[*In the following review of* The Grapes of Paradise, *Feld commends Bates's compassionate portrayal of the fear and loneliness experienced by his characters.*]

After his literary spree with the two novels about Pop Larkin, raffish hero of *The Darling Buds of May* and *A Breath of French Air,* H. E. Bates returns to an earlier love, the novella. Four of them, all interesting, two of them gems of portraiture in depth, comprise his new book, **The Grapes of Paradise.** Here the writer who can laugh at the amoral vagaries of a man who pays no respect to convention turns thoughtful and somber in searching out the bitter core of human fears and loneliness.

Especially is this true of two of the stories in this volume, **"The Grapes of Paradise"** and **"A Prospect of Orchards"**. In the first he tells the tragic tale of a Polynesian girl who gave her heart to a visiting tourist. Thus condensed, the plot sounds worn and trite but as Bates unfolds the story, it holds a freshness of interest and poignancy.

The man, Harry Rockney, came to Tahiti for a three months' stay. Bored with Papeete, he had, after a few weeks, taken a steamer to a nearby island. There, with an enormous lei in her hands, Thérèse greeted him. What struck Rockney, as he relates the story, was the overpowering ugliness of the eighteen or nineteen-year-old girl. Its quality was "exactly that of a primitive idol hacked out of golden-colored wood, and not very well hacked at that." Tall and massively built, laughing and generous, she was at one with the elements, the sea, the rain, the wind.

Aware of her ugliness, the girl made no efforts to seduce the man. She had, as Rockney describes it, "a strange, proud, almost virginal sort of dignity." It is when Rockney, in a mood built up of wine and music and darkness kisses her that the volcanic emotions of the girl burst into flame. With moving understatement, Bates tells the story of this man who sought vainly to escape the consequences of his one, never repeated thoughtless act and the girl who became captive to her need of him.

This compassion of Bates for a human being who feels himself unacceptable to others also informs **"A Prospect** of Orchards." In this, the rejected person is a man, an Englishman. "Templeton was a shortish leaden-footed man with weak brown eyes whose responses (in boxing) were those of a duck with its legs tied. His jaw was babyish, smooth and hairless, like a pale pink egg." This is what he looked like in his youth as remembered by the narrator who used to box with him. This, with the addition of unbecoming flesh, is what he looked like when encountered twenty-five years later.

To rise above his sense of inadequacy, Templeton, married to a woman who despises him, laboriously builds up a myth of devoting himself to growing a new kind of fruit in his orchard. Perhaps the most touching line in the pitiful story of the man's emptiness and loneliness is his response when asked by his former boxing partner why he didn't hit back in their bouts. "I suppose because I rather like you," he replies.

The opening story in the book, **"An Aspidistra in Babylon"** goes back to the year 1921, and plot and character capture the atmosphere of that still gentle period. An English garrison town near the coast, a respectable boarding house run by a stuffy landlady, her lovely innocent young daughter, an officer who is a bounder and a robust, lusty chambermaid are the ingredients of a tale of easy seduction and disillusion.

In **"A Month by the Lake"** Mr. Bates is mildly satiric about a middle-aged Englishman on holiday in Italy who has his eyes opened to the respective charms of youth and maturity.

Unequal in interest, the four novellas nevertheless have a strong kinship of good writing that gives shape and depth to the variety of humanity they portray.

Rose Feld, "H. E. Bates in Familiar, Happy Vein," in New York Herald Tribune Book Review, *October 23, 1960, p. 6.*

James Stern (essay date 1960)

[*In the following review, Stern contends that while the stories of* The Grapes of Paradise *are technically adept, they are ultimately uninteresting.*]

I often wonder what it is that keeps established authors—writers who are neither geniuses nor poor—producing one book after another, year after year. Some of these books are so obviously inferior to their best that one wonders why they have bothered to publish them. Has the act of writing, to these older, usually well-known men and women, become a conditioned reflex? Do they feel ill when divorced from their desks? Or are they simply incapable of judging their own works?

To these questions I once received an answer from one of the kings of the kind of writer I have in mind. Shortly before his tragic death Stefan Zweig, a prolific man of letters and the most translated author then living, was complaining one evening in my presence of "having" to embark on another book. "*Why* do you have to?" I asked him. From his hesitation, the shock in his eyes, I could see that such a question had never occurred to him. "Oh," he muttered

at last, "one owes it to one's public, you know." What a price, I thought, to pay for fame!

Now 55, Mr. H. E. Bates has been writing books for thirty-four years. His publishers give a list of eighteen titles, but the earliest of these appeared as recently as 1938. Even as long ago as the Nineteen Twenties Bates was writing novels and stories on English farm life in the pastoral tradition. Through them all ran a lyrical quality, as well as something both urgent and inevitable. One never hesitated to question their validity. Recently, as his many admirers must know, Bates has completed a hilarious trilogy about the family Larkin, whose members never hesitate to question whether their behavior is right or wrong, amoral or at least anti-social. For the Larkins, in fact, life in the Welfare State is one long lark.

In *The Grapes of Paradise* Bates has returned to what his publishers call his "favorite form of the novella." Of the four here, two are set in the drabber type of English middle-class milieu, a third on the shores of an Italian lake, and the title story in Tahiti. On each of these stories, even on the first page or two, is stamped the Bates signature: a rare gift for camera-quick evocation of scene. When, in this volume's opening paragraph, we read that "in those days the curving line of houses always looked like a freshly starched collar, intensely stiff and respectable, against the strip of biscuit-colored shingle and the sea," we are aware at once, as in the best of Hemingway, of the period, place and sort of people of whom we are about to read.

This tale, which should have been entitled "The Breath of Corruption," is told by a married woman looking back on her first sexual encounter at the age of 18. As old as time, about a girl's innocence lost to a selfish man of 40, it is beautifully executed; yet there crops up not only here but halfway through the other three stories as well a question which, judged by the highest standards, should not have to be asked: "Is this likely?" And in each instance, to this reader at least, came the answer: "No. Not likely. Possible."

Again, though serenely written, it is difficult to know what prompted the author to spend seventy pages on a group of people of so little interest as those in **"A Month by the Lake."** Of the characters in **"A Prospect of Orchards"**, a story which appears to be a study of a male masochist, much the same might be said, except that Arthur Templeton—with whom the narrator used to box when they were young and who tries to delude people into believing that he can grow an apple to taste like a pear—turns out to be not only "an intolerably lonely man" but, like his dreadful wife and her friends, an excruciating bore. Why the narrator should insist on revisiting this couple on their dilapidated farm I simply could not understand.

The natural glory of the Polynesian islands gives Bates, who writes as though from an intimate knowledge of them, full scope for the talent which has earned him the name of master. Yet compared to his superb descriptions of land and reef in mid-Pacific, of approaching storm, of the silence and freshness after rain, of the colorful abundance of tropical fruit and flowers, the story of the relationship between Rockley, the naïve young white visitor from Vancouver and the huge, homely, immensely strong native girl, Thérèse, is unworthy. Suspense is here, but at the expense of violence; the conventional romantic peace of the islands is shattered, but I found the behavior of neither man nor girl convincing. Again one waited in vain for the inevitability of the earlier Bates. (pp. 4-5, 50)

James Stern, "Selfishness Met Was Youthful Innocence Lost," in The New York Times Book Review, *October 23, 1960, pp. 4-5, 50.*

Irving H. Buchen   (essay date 1961)

[*In the following review of* The Enchantress, and Other Stories, *Buchen commends Bates's avoidance of "heavy-handed moralism" in his examination of human behavior.*]

In the Thirties, when H. E. Bates was an angry young Englishman, he proclaimed in a brief essay on Hardy and Conrad: "Morality is virtually a fraud, since there is really no stabilized coinage of morality at all but only the elemental currency of human action and re-action, only human conduct and its consequences." Bates was then fighting for a fiction that would display moral judgments not as something obviously superior to, but as something imperceptibly imbedded in the human condition. Throughout his writing career this has remained his central artistic aim. Happily, [***The Enchantress, and Other Stories***] has the same distinguished focus.

Perhaps the title story, **"The Enchantress,"** best suggests the extent to which the vital relationship between human conduct and morality is contingent upon the reader's own awareness. The "enchantress," Bertha Jackson, born and raised in the slums, marries a fairly wealthy man old enough to be her grandfather. We rapidly conclude that the old man is a fool and that Bertha is a gold-digger. Bates evidently knows his readers well, for he has other characters come to the same hasty, cynical conclusion. Having set the trap, he springs it, catching and embarrassing them and us with this simple observation: "When a man of seventy marries a girl of seventeen . . . it never seems to occur to anyone that all that has possessed him is a firm dose of taste, enterprise and common sense." And, far from being a social climber, Bertha makes her husband happy, and others after him, by her enchanting gift of selfless adoration. Or, as Bates neatly puts it, "Bertha never dispossessed anybody of anything."

At least three other stories, **"Lost Ball," "The Spring Hat,"** and **"An Island Princess,"** also deal with the losses in understanding that often follow upon mechanical and narrowing moral judgments. In fact, all twelve tales in this volume are variations on this theme. Appropriately, those that achieve an unforgettable poignancy have as their central characters individuals who live on the periphery of life. Clara Corbett of **"Now Sleeps the Crimson Petal"** is such a character. A butcher's wife, she enjoys a momentary liberation of soul before she sinks back into the drudgery of delivering neatly wrapped cuts of meat in an old van. Then there is Thelma in the story of the same name, a bedroom maid whose life is measured out, not in coffee spoons, but in cans of hot shaving water which she doles

out every morning to lonely traveling salesmen. She falls in love with one, but when he fails to return she spends the rest of her life giving herself to other salesmen, imagining all the time that it is her beau who is really making love to her.

Significantly, these and the other stories in this volume are moving precisely because they are not pointed with any heavy-handed moralism. In fact, the key to Bates's achievement is his lightness of touch. His characters never crowd or crush the reader. They emerge casually, considerately, as if starting off a long distance away and slowly walking toward us. Their problems and conflicts never thunder or crackle noisily; they are treated by Bates with quiet respect, almost with reverence. And yet, our final impression is of an artistic world surprisingly powerful, rich, and full. Equally as important, we find that Bates has granted the same extended breadth to our understanding of human conduct and its moral consequences.

Irving H. Buchen, "Condition, Conduct, Consequence," in Saturday Review, *Vol. XLIV, No. 41, October 14, 1961, p. 35.*

Colin Murry   (essay date 1962)

[*In the following review of* The Golden Oriole, *Murry attributes a perceived decline in Bates's post–World War II fiction to the loss of his literary mentor, Edward Garnett, a prominent English critic and editor.*]

What has become of H E Bates? Reading his latest collection of five long stories has been a saddening experience. Of the five only the title story might just have found a place in one of his pre-war collections, the others are frankly hack-work. Before coming to this conclusion I made a point of re-reading some of the best of his early stories, an act of homage which not only confirmed my judgment of ***The Golden Oriole*** but also served to remind me what a remarkable talent Bates once had. In those early stories he never once falters. So intense is his spell that the impact is almost physical. At least a dozen of Bates's early stories can withstand comparison with Turgenev's *Sketches From A Sportsman's Notebook.* How then can one reconcile this with ***The Golden Oriole***?

Bate's chief enemy has always been his extreme fluency. Good and bad alike tumbled down the torrent and he needed the guiding hand of his discoverer Edward Garnett to prune his prose and supply the necessary check. Under his tutor's watchful eye Bates matured rapidly. From *The Two Sisters* written in 1925 to *Spella Ho* in 1937 there was a steady upward progression, a growing assurance, a widening of scope. But in 1937 Garnett died and within six years Bates had moved into the bestseller class. Simultaneously his work began the steady downward slide that reached a dismal nadir in *A Breath of French Air* and the rest of the Larkins trilogy. Even the highly competent stories he wrote under the pseudonym of 'Flying Officer "X" ' have a slightly phoney ring that Garnett's fine ear would surely have detected and condemned.

He would have found plenty to condemn in ***The Golden Oriole.*** The keynote to most of these stories is a sort of sleazy sexuality that sounds at times like a vulgar parody of the warm animal passion he once conveyed so powerfully in stories like **'The Mower'**. At a more fundamental level not one of these stories—not even the title one—has been intensely imagined, and the result, inevitably, is that the characters frequently behave in a manner which appears wholly arbitrary. Nor does he help us to suspend our disbelief by passages like this: 'In spite of her quietness she seemed very much like a strongly coiled spring. It seemed likely that some day something or someone would touch her and she would respond like a rampant charge of electricity'. Those clashing similes, that needlessly repeated 'seemed', above all the lack of *freshness* would make Garnett turn in his grave.

Here and there I did detect faint echoes of the old Bates, but nothing substantial enough to persuade me that his next work might be another **'Alexander'**. I hope I may be proved wrong.

Colin Murry, "Without His Tutor," in Time & Tide, *Vol. 43, No. 19, May 10, 1962, p. 34.*

Ernest Buckler   (essay date 1962)

[*In the review below, Buckler emphasizes the entertaining qualities of the novellas collected as* The Golden Oriole.]

"Nobody's fairly ordinary." This rejoinder in **"The Ring of Truth"**, first and best of the five novellas by H. E. Bates [in **The Golden Oriole**], plainly echoes the author's own belief. It is a truth he never tires of demonstrating. A reader might think that after twenty-odd books as varied as *The Jacaranda Tree* and *The Darling Buds of May* his inspiration would show the crow's feet of strain. Not so. Here he is once again, with insight and technique as crisp as before, lodging his effects without a wasted word or irrelevant gesture, the gears never grinding when he makes the lightning shift from serious to bizarre. None of these long (and somewhat tall) stories is a giant. But, from entree to aperitif (the reverse order they come in), they furnish a spanking meal.

Wholly serious, **"The Ring of Truth"** tells of the ironic chance that plunges a son himself into love at the same time it discloses the blistering fact of his dead father's marital tragedy. In each of the next two pieces the blend of pathos and farce makes for a rather uneasy pousse-cafe, but both are accomplished with force and dexterity. **"The Quiet One"**, which deals with Maisie the seamstress and her autumnal affairs, is a study of isolation, proving that one never realizes how stealthily one's outer shell can harden, until the process is irreversible. Prinny Mansfield of **"The Golden Oriole"**, whose obsession it is never to reveal herself but to be "discovered," first makes a coy and habitual game of hiding on the premises from her husband; then, her senses mesmerized by a young lover, finds the perfect hiding place inside herself; then, on his death, discovers there is no place to hide at all.

The final two stories are pure antic. Those who regard that rat-a-tat highjinks and "kipper" jargon so dear to the heart of English humor as a sort of caponized Damon Runyon may not slap their knees at the skullduggery in **"Mr. Featherstone Takes a Ride"**. But I defy them not to chuckle at **"The World Is Too Much With Us"**. It's hard to believe that this three-cornered romance involving a reclusive bachelor, his dipsomaniac hen and the plump shopkeeper widow next door could lay anything but a ponderous egg. But it's actually very funny.

Apart from his astonishing range, Mr. Bates has the gift for making a single phrase double for both definitive description and definitive comment. His dialogue is precisely hand-tooled, without being slick; his action meshes like Swiss watchwork. And if, after all is said and done, the reader has sometimes been treated to little more than a chipper dish of tea, who's to complain? In these days when so many writers are grimly winkling out their psyches with a blunt corkscrew or strangling themselves in their own trailing ambiguities a chipper cuppa now and then is refreshment to be truly grateful for.

Ernest Buckler, "There's Nothing Ordinary about Anybody," in The New York Times Book Review, *September 30, 1962, p. 4.*

Henry Miller   (essay date 1963)

[*Considered among the most controversial and influential of twentieth-century authors, Miller is best remembered for his novel,* Tropic of Cancer *(1934). In this and other autobiographical works of fiction, Miller described his quest for truth and freedom as well as his rejection of conventional social mores. The explicit sexual content of his works and his revolutionary use of scatological humor and obscene language caused his fiction to be censored in many countries, including the United States and Great Britain, until the early 1960s. In his introduction to* The Best of H. E. Bates *excerpted below, Miller discusses significant aspects of Bates's fiction, particularly his descriptions of nature, his portrayals of women, and his humor.*]

It was only a little over a year ago that I came across H. E. Bates' work; up until then I had never even heard his name, strange as this may sound. I blush now when I read that he is the author of forty or more books, has been translated into a dozen or more languages, and that 'his reputation in America, Australia and New Zealand equals, and in some cases surpasses, that in his own country.'

Perhaps I would never have heard of him had I not been laid up with chills and fever in the Hotel Formentor, Mallorca, where I was quartered during the Formentor Conference. Having nothing to read I asked a friend to go to the bookstore in the lobby and select something light, gay, amusing for me. My friend returned with a copy of *A Breath of French Air*. He said nothing about knowing the author until some days later when I told him how much I had enjoyed the book. A little later, at some airport, I picked up *The Darling Buds of May* and *Fair Stood the Wind for France*. The last named impressed me deeply and made me wonder why I had never heard of the author. It struck me as being the only good novel I had read about World War II.

In a way Mr Bates is the very opposite of what I look for in an author. There is certainly little relation between his manner of writing and that of Celine or Blaise Cendrars, my favourites among contemporary writers. (Both dead now, alas.) On the other hand, I do find a kinship between Bates and Jean Giono, whose work I adore. I ought to add—like whom I wish I could write.

One of the great joys for a writer is to find a fellow writer who, because he is so different, captivates and enchants him. To find a writer whose work he will read even if he is warned that it is not one of the author's best.

In general I must confess that I seldom fall for the work of a popular writer. Had I lived in Dickens' time, for example, I doubt that I would have been one of his devoted readers. As for the successful writers of our own time there is hardly one I can think of off hand whom I have any desire to read. It demands an effort for me to read a modern novel, and an even greater one to read a short story. I make exception for the short stories of I. B. Singer, the Yiddish writer. And Mr Bates is supremely a novelist and short-story writer. He is, moreover, a rather conventional one.

After all that has been written about this author it seems rather unimportant that I add my tribute to him. Certainly he needs no further words of praise, and praise, I am afraid, is all I can summon. I assume that the reason I have been requested to write this preface to his collected short stories is because the coupling of our two names will seem highly incongruous both to Mr Bates' readers and my own. I know that I have a reputation for being highly critical of, perhaps even unfair to British authors. On the other hand, it should not be overlooked that the one author (still alive) for whom I have an undying admiration is John Cowper Powys, and that I regard his novel, *A Glastonbury Romance,* as the greatest novel in the English language.

If Mr Bates were a painter I think I could express my views about his work much better. Last night I lay awake trying to pick out the painter with whom I sought to identify his writing. No single painter whose work I know seemed suitable. I thought of Renoir and Bonnard, of Breughel the elder and others. I think that if I were to find one it would be a Flemish painter. The reason is obvious.

Whether it be the short story or the novel, Mr Bates always finds time for lengthy descriptions of nature, descriptions which in the hands of a lesser writer would seem boring or out of place. He dwells long and lovingly on things which years ago would have driven me mad. I mean such things as flowers, plants, trees, birds, sea, sky, everything in short which meets the eye and which the unskilled writer uses as so much window dressing. Indeed, it is not only the unskilled writer who is guilty of mishandling description. Some of the greatest novelists of the past were flagrantly guilty of doing just this, and more particularly British writers. With Mr Bates this fault has been made into a virtue. The reader falls upon these lengthy passages like a man athirst.

There is another virtue which goes hand in hand with the above-mentioned one, and that is the author's feeling for women. His women are always females first and foremost.

That is to say, they are fully sexed: they have all the charm, the loveliness, the attraction of the flowers he knows so well. With a few deft strokes—like a painter again—we are given their peculiar grace, character and utter femininity. Not all of them, naturally, for he can also render the other kind of woman just as tellingly.

And then there is *this* element which crops up again and again, I find—an obsession with pain. Pain stretched to the breaking point, pain prolonged beyond all seeming endurance. This element is usually called forth in connection with heroic behaviour. Perhaps it is the supreme mark of the hero, this ability to endure pain. With Mr Bates I feel that it goes beyond the point of the heroic; it carries us into some other dimension. Pain takes on the aspects of space and time, a continuum or perpetuum which one finally questions no longer.

But no matter how much one is made to suffer, one closes his books with a lasting sensation of beauty. And this sense of beauty, it seems to me, is evoked by the author's unswerving acceptance of life. It is this which makes his flowers, trees, birds, skies, whatever it be, different from those of other writers. They are not merely decorative, they are not showily dramatic: they exist, along with his characters, his thoughts, his observations, in a plenum which is spiritual as well as physical.

There is one other quality which must endear him to every reader and that is his sense of humour. It is a full, robust humour, often bawdy, which I must confess the British writer seems to have lost in the last few centuries. It is never a nasty humour, so common to American writers. It is clean and healthy, and absolutely infectious.

What surprises me most about this man's work is the fact that only one or two of his books have been made into films. Despite the abundance of descriptive passages which I spoke of, there is drama in all his work. Drama and dialogue. Good, natural dialogue which, if transferred to the screen, would need no adaptation.

I realise at this point that I have said little or nothing about the short stories themselves. Aside from a few very short ones I find them all absorbing. Meanwhile I look forward with great relish to eating my way through the thirty odd books of his which I have yet to read, especially those containing his novellas, a form which clearly suits him best, as it did one of my first idols, Knut Hamsun. But I am sure that whatever Mr Bates gives us will always please me. (pp. vii-x)

> *Henry Miller, in a preface to* The Best of H. E. Bates, *Little, Brown and Company, 1963, pp. vii-x.*

Robert Alter   (essay date 1963)

[*In the following review of* The Best of H. E. Bates, *Alter briefly compares Bates's short fiction with that of Polish-born American short story writer Isaac Bashevis Singer.*]

In his enthusiastic introduction to [*The Best of H. E. Bates*], Henry Miller mentions in passing that the only contemporary short-story writer he can read with relish aside from H. E. Bates is Isaac Bashevis Singer. At first glance, it may seem an odd quirk of taste that could select two such different figures out of the whole spectrum of modern short-story writers. Actually, there are some interesting affinities between Bates' lyric but realistic portraits of British provincial life and Singer's imaginative tales of the Yiddish-speaking milieu in Poland.

Both writers have an unusual ability to enter into the suffering of the mute and uncomprehending. Mr. Bates' best stories—like his brilliant piece, **"The Mill"**—generally are those where he gives a voice to mouthless pain. Both writers, moreover, are intensely alive to the presence of sex as a powerful force in human relationships, regenerative when it is associated with love and cruel—in Mr. Singer's fiction, demonic—when it is not. In most of these stories, Mr. Bates employs a conventional rhetoric for sexual arousal (flame, electricity, and the like) which seems to derive from the earlier D. H. Lawrence. He uses this convention, however, with considerably more tact than Lawrence, and he manages to make his men and women as believably full-blooded as Mr. Miller claims they are.

In general, the technical control exercised by Mr. Bates is admirable. His painterly rendering of landscape and scene create atmosphere always intrinsic to the meaning of the story, never merely decorative. The symbols he occasionally uses are artfully worked into the naturalistic flow of the story so that they seem neither contrived nor overly insistent. Admittedly, even this Best of H. E. Bates is not always good enough—some of the stories are curiously abortive, and a few of the later ones are perhaps too personal and merely nostalgic. But there are enough pieces in this selection from the work of 35 years to demonstrate Mr. Bates' mastery of the short story.

> *Robert Alter, in a review of "The Best of H. E. Bates," in* Book Week—New York Herald Tribune, *September 29, 1963, p. 18.*

H. E. Bates   (essay date 1972)

[*In the following preface to the revised edition of* The Modern Short Story, *which was first published in 1941, Bates discusses developments in short fiction since World War II and presents his views on writing short stories.*]

The realm of prophecy and that of betting on racehorses have at least two things in common: whereas both are a mug's game the participants in each are always promising to learn by experience but rarely do.

When at the conclusion of *The Modern Short Story* in 1941 I prophesied that if the war then in progress produced nothing else in the way of literature it would certainly provide a rich crop of short stories, I did not for one moment believe that the statement was by any means a rash one. On the contrary, I felt it to be self-evident that at such a time of dislocation, excitement and widening of experience in all manner of directions and for all manner of people, a vast amount of material, inestimable, as I saw it, in its value for short story writers both established and new, would inevitably be thrown up. The bombing of London,

the war in all its theatres, in the air, on the sea, in the desert, in the jungle: all this offered, or seemed to offer, a rich and exciting vein of experience such as the comparatively humdrum days of peace could never match. Out of it, I consequently thought, must come short stories: my bet being on short stories rather than novels for the good reason that at such a time of crisis the physical effort of producing the shorter form must inevitably make it the more probable and acceptable medium of the two.

In all this I made several mistakes, having forgotten, for example, the fundamental principle that because a short story is short it is not therefore easier to write than a novel, ten, twenty or thirty times its length—the exact reverse being in fact the truth. I had also forgotten another truth, namely, that mere experience of itself cannot automatically create a work of art, since in the last crucial essence all art is a physical act. All the fine dreams, the sublimest excursions of the mind, the most exciting of experiences, the most beautiful of thoughts are as nothing until the act of transmuting them into physical terms has been accomplished. Until the writer has put pen to paper, the artist his paint to canvas, the sculptor his tools to wood, stone and marble, the composer his notes to the score, there is, in fact, nothing.

I had also allowed myself to be misled in yet another direction. I had supposed that the aftermath of war would find expression, after the long dark tragic years, in light and joy. It never occurred to me, even remotely, that it might well express itself in a sourness even darker. Of course the virtues of hindsight are legion. We could not possibly know, in 1941, what course or courses literature would seek out for itself, or be seduced into, in the fifties, sixties, or, Heaven help us, the seventies. We had no way of foreseeing the era of the Angry Young Men, the Permissive Society or the Parade of Pornography.

All this, however, duly came about. The playwrights of the 1950s assailed us and then, for the most part, faded away; various firework novelists followed them in the 1960s and as rapidly fell as damp squibs; there followed the band wagon of *Oh! Calcutta* and its dubious brethren, led for the most part by persons with neither taste nor talent. The gutter took over; the stench was noisome. A new generation of writers sprang up with no other purpose than to tell all, revolting or revoltingly silly though it might be; public copulation, with all the attendant vocabulary, was abroad on stage and screen and no less palpably evident on the printed page. All these things were repeated in America, *ad nauseam,* too.

This, then, was the era of "tell all": the worst possible climate and conditions in which the short story could be expected to flourish. For in the short story, you cannot possibly tell all; this is the road to confusion and negation. In writing the short story, it is essentials that matter. As in a great drawing, so in a great short story: it is the lines that are left out that are of paramount importance. Not that this is all; it is knowing what lines to leave out that is of the greatest importance, too. There is in one of Tchehov's letters a reply of his to a correspondent who wished to have Tchehov's opinion on X, a minor Russian writer of the time. Tchehov's reply is illuminating in its brevity: "I long to rewrite it," he wrote, "*lacily*". Exactly. "Lacily" is the *mot juste,* expressing the very essence of what the short story should be, showing that it must depict more by implication than by statement, more by what is left out than left in. It ought, in fact, to resemble lace: strong but delicate, deviously woven yet full of light and air.

The antithesis of all this is the school of "tell all," which may otherwise be called "the school of stodge," the school where all is offered and nothing left to the imagination, the perception, or the wit of the reader. At the same time, largely due to the war, yet another phenomenon appeared: namely that of the so-called reportage, the factual, or documentary school of writing. The latter was the death-kiss also of many British films before, during, and after the war. An even more bastard form eventually raised its obtuse, ugly head: a creature known as documentary fiction. No such animal can of course exist, since the very definition is a contradiction in terms. What is fiction cannot be documentary, what is documentary cannot be fiction. The business of writing fiction is, in fact, an exercise in the art of telling lies. If the writer tells these lies with all the art and skill he is able to command then he will not only persuade his readers that what he is telling them is the truth but also that it is truer than life itself: all of which brings us back to Thackeray's well-known dictum that "the work of fiction contains more truth in solution than the work which purports to be all true." In other words it is through fidelity to imagination and not fidelity to observation that the truth will be revealed.

My prophecy as to the probability of a new golden age of the short story, such as we had on both sides of the Atlantic in the 1920s and 1930s was, therefore, dismally unfulfilled. There were of course other factors mitigating against it, not the least of them being the economic situation. Even before the war in England the little magazines to which writers of my generation contributed and were very glad to contribute, were already dead or dying. Nor was it merely little magazines that disappeared; in America even a magazine such as Colliers, with a reputed circulation of some millions, was unable to survive; other notable names followed it. Everywhere, therefore, the market for stories dwindled. Young writers, however ardent their desire to write short stories and live by them, found themselves forced, by the sheer economics of the business, into spheres that offered security: novels, plays and some television drama. Nor could they be blamed for this.

This then is the situation of the short story today; if it is not quite one of unmitigated gloom it is certainly not bright. Nor can I myself see it, in a world of rising costs, not only of printing and production but in the very cost of living itself, getting any brighter. It is said that D. H. Lawrence, as a young man, managed on ten shillings a week; another short story writer friend of mine certainly lived on a pound; I, rather more fortunate, scraped along on two pounds. I do not need to point out the ludicrous nature of all this in relation to the literary world of today. Like Somerset Maugham and Joseph Conrad, who firmly rejected the idea of living in a garret, I have no use for starvation as a means of inspiring writers to create masterpieces. They are better done on full bellies.

To this pessimistic picture must be added the fact that the reading public, not only in Britain and America, but also on the continent, shows no disposition to revise its age-old prejudice against reading short stories in volume form. It grants some exceptions to this, of course, as in the case of Maugham, Kipling and some others, but by and large it views volumes of short stories with grave and unwarranted suspicion. The young short story writer, even if able to get his stories published between two covers, need look for no vast fortune in that direction.

Still, paradoxically, great numbers of people yearn to write short stories. A competition for short stories in a national newspaper some few years back is said to have produced the staggering figure of 50,000 entries, of which only the merest handful were publishable. I do not propose to examine here the causes of so lamentable a state of affairs. I will merely repeat what I have said time and time again: that the short story is the most difficult and exacting of all prose forms; it cannot be treated as a spare-time occupation; and above all it must not be allowed to foster the illusion, as I pointed out earlier in this preface, that its very brevity makes it easy to do.

All this brings me to a restatement of what *The Modern Short Story* purports to be and do. It does *not* exist as a manual of instruction for writing short stories; such was never my intention. It examines, instead, the work of many of the most distinguished masters of the form, confiding almost all of its investigations into the form as evolved in the 19th century and as we know it today: an essentially modern art.

Writing a short story may be compared with building a house with match-sticks. There comes a point in its construction when the addition of another stick may well bring down the whole affair in ruins. Thus balance is one of the supreme essentials to its creation and nowhere is this more true than in the very short story, say of one thousand words or less, or in the *novella,* fifteen or twenty times as long.

If it should be thought that one thousand words is really short then I recommend a glance at the Authorized Version of *The Prodigal Son.* This long-renowned and beautiful story contains something just over 130 words and begins with what would at first appear to be an extremely ordinary sentence: "A certain man had two sons". I suggest, on the contrary, that it is a very remarkable sentence, introducing as it does the story's three main characters in exactly six words. Here indeed is true economy.

Balance without stiffness, economy without cramp, essentials that are not merely bare bones, a canvas of scene and character which, though only a quarter or even a tenth of the size of the novel, must nevertheless satisfy the reader just as much and do so, as I have already remarked, perhaps more by what it leaves out than by what it puts in— these are merely a few of the technical challenges that make the *novella* so fascinating to the truly creative artist. It is moreover important not only that the reader should be satisfied but that, as at the end of a perfectly created meal, he should be left wanting a little more—or in other words that his curiosity and interest in the author's characters is still sharp enough to make him want to walk out with them beyond the printed page.

"Fiction," it has been said, "is the natural heir to poetry"; if this is true, and I firmly believe it is, I find it equally true that the short story is to fiction what the lyric is to poetry. In its finest mould the short story is, in fact, a prose poem. If the reader of *The Modern Short Story* absorbs this truth as he reads then the purpose of this book will have been fully justified. (pp. 7-12)

> *H. E. Bates, in a preface to his* The Modern Short Story: A Critical Survey, *The Writer, Inc., 1972, pp. 7-12.*

Walter Allen   (essay date 1981)

[*Allen is an English novelist of working-class life and a distinguished popular historian and critic of the novel form. In the following excerpt from his critical study* The Short Story in English, *he discusses Bates's narrative technique.*]

It was probably due to the dominance of [A. E.] Coppard that during the Twenties the short story in England often appeared as a specifically bucolic form registering a scene and ways of life that had scarcely changed since those depicted in Hardy. Parallels with Georgian poetry abound. At his best, Coppard himself rose above these criticisms and, at his best, his true successor was H. E. Bates. He never, as Coppard does from time to time, surprises with a fine excess but he was an exceedingly careful craftsman who kept up a consistent excellence. In his book, *The Modern Short Story,* he described Stephen Crane's method as that

> by which a story is told not by the carefully engineered plot but by the implication of certain isolated incidents, by the capture and arrangement of casual episodic movements. It is the method by which the surface, however seemingly trivial or unimportant, is recorded in such a way as to interpret the individual emotional life below.

He was describing his own practice, which he had learned from Chekhov. And this careful craftsmanship was infused with a sensitivity to beauty and character that led David Garnett to write that 'his best stories have the extreme delicacy and tenderness of Renoir's paint'. Having been read once, some of his stories exist in the mind as pictures, often as still life, as does **'The Gleaner'**, probably the most famous of his early stories. Movement in it seems arrested almost to the point of having been frozen.

> Her fingers were rustling like quick mice over the stubble, and the red wheat ears were rustling together in her hands before she had taken another step forward. There was no time for looking or listening or resting. To glean, to fill her sack, to travel over that field before the light is lost; she has no other purpose than that and could understand none. . . .
>
> But later, in the heat of the afternoon, with her sack filling up, and the sun-heat and the bright light playing unbrokenly upon her, she begins unconsciously to move more slowly, a little

tired, like a child that has played too long. She will not cover the field, she moves there, always solitary, up and down the stubble, empty except for herself and a rook or two, she begins to look smaller and the field larger and larger about her. . . .

> At last she straightens her back. It is her first conscious sign of weariness. She justifies it by looking into the sky and over the autumn-coloured land sloping away to the town; she takes in the whole soft-lighted world, the effulgence of the wine-yellow light on the trees and the dove-coloured roofs below and a straggling of rooks lifting off the stubble and settling further on again.

The impression he creates of stillness, of stasis, seems at times akin to the rendering of a state of trance, as in the late long short story **'Death of a Huntsman'**, published in 1957, almost a quarter of a century after **'The Gleaner'**. **'Death of a Huntsman'** shows admirably, by the way, Bates's range of social types and scenes, which is considerably wider than one at first thinks. It begins:

> Every week-day evening, watches ready, black umbrellas neatly rolled and put away with neat black homburgs on carriage racks, attaché cases laid aside, newspaper poised, the fellow-travellers of Harry Barnfield, the city gentlemen, waited for him to catch—or rather miss—the five-ten train. . . .
>
> 'Running it pretty fine tonight.'
>
> 'Doomed. Never make it.'
>
> 'Oh! Harry'll make it. Trust Harry. Never fluked it yet. Trust Harry.'
>
> All Harry's friends, like himself, lived in the country, kept farms at a heavy loss and came to London for business every day. J. B. (Punch) Warburton, who was in shipping and every other day or so brought up from his farm little perforated boxes and fresh eggs for less fortunate friends in the city, would get ready, in mockery, to hold open the carriage door.

Barnfield lives for his life in the country and his riding. His wife is gin-soaked, and he falls in love with a girl who habitually rides across his land. She proves to be the daughter of a neighbour, a woman of his own age who was one of the circle he mixed with as a young man. They are sitting, he and the woman, in his stationary car after a hunt ball.

> 'I think she has to be told,' she said, 'that you and I were lovers. Of course it was some time ago. But wouldn't you think that that was only fair?'
>
> He could not speak. He simply made one of his habitual groping gestures with his hands, up towards his face, as if his spectacles had suddenly become completely opaque with the white sickening smoke of her cigarette and he could not see.
>
> 'Not once,' she said, 'but many times. Oh! yes, I think she has to be told. I think so.'

He is so much beside himself at the woman's attempt at blackmail that he loses control of himself and blindly hits out at her. Then he begins furiously to drive away and as she screams and prepares to jump out of the car she has a moment of memory:

> Out of the darkness sprang a remembered figure of a Harry Barnfield in a white straw hat, white flannel trousers and a college blazer, a rather soft Harry Barnfield, simple, easy-going, good-time-loving, defenceless and laughing; one of the vacuous poor fish of her youth, in the days when she kept a tabulation of conquests in a little book, heading it *In Memoriam; to those who fell,* her prettiness enamelled and calculated and as smart as the strip-poker or the midnight swimming parties she went to, with other, even younger lovers, at long weekends.

It is a good example of Bates's ability to dramatize vital information about the past of a character in such a way that the progress of the story is not held up but indeed furthered.

The woman jumps out of the car, having struck out at Barnfield and knocked off his spectacles. Reduced to near-blindness he crashes the car into a telegraph pole and is killed. At his funeral, with which the story ends, everyone joins in to pay tribute to 'a good huntsman, a good sport, a great horse-lover, and a man in whom there was no harm at all'.

'Death of a Huntsman' has a grave and subtle beauty. The relation between Valerie and her mother, who treats her as though she were still a schoolgirl, is very well conveyed and that between her and the business man twenty-five years older than herself is admirably rendered. In the following passage of what I have called stasis, the middle-aged man and young girl appear somehow transfigured:

> 'I think I know every path here now. There's a wonderful one goes down past the holly-trees. You come to a little lake at the bottom with quince trees on an island—at least I think they're quince trees.'
>
> If he had time, she went on, she wanted him to walk down there. Would he? Did he mind?
>
> He tethered his horse to a fence and they started to walk along a path that wound down, steeply in places, through crackling curtains of bracken, old holly trees thick with pink-brown knots of berry and more clumps of birch trees sowing in absolute silence little pennies of leaves.
>
> At the bottom there was, as she had said, a small perfectly circular lake enclosed by rings of elder, willow, and hazel trees. In the still air its surface was thick with floating shoals of leaves. In absolute silence two quince trees, half-bare branches full of ungathered golden lamps of fruit, shone with apparent permanence on a little island in the glow of noon.
>
> 'This is it,' she said.
>
> Neither then, nor later, nor in fact at any other time, did they say a word about her mother. They stood for a long time without a word about

anything, simply watching the little lake soundlessly embalmed in October sunlight, the quince-lamps setting the little island on fire.

> 'I don't think you should go away,' he said.
>
> He answered her in the quiet, totally uncomplex way that, as everyone remarked, was so much part of him, so much the typical Harry Barnfield.

Generally, prose-poetry is a pejorative phrase: that Bates's prose has a genuine relation to poetry is shown by the frequency with which his rendering of nature in its minute particulars especially, as in the description of the quince-trees on the tiny island, reminds us of poets, of Tennyson for example. At the same time, he wrote some splendid heroic stories. This was a development in his talent brought to fruition during the war, when as 'Flying Officer X' he was commissioned in the Royal Air Force to write stories of the war in the air. The finest of these is perhaps *The Cruise of 'The Breadwinner'*, which appeared over his own name in 1946. *The Breadwinner* is a characteristic British wartime improvisation. A small lugsail fishing boat, she patrols the Channel looking for the pilots and crews of shot-down aeroplanes. Her skipper is Gregson who appears to Snowy, the cabin-boy as a 'man of unappeasable frenzy', and Jimmy is the engine-man.

When the story opens, Snowy is still a boy, pining for a pair of binoculars (for he is also the plane-spotter), but when he returns from the day's cruise he is a boy no longer. They have picked up a wounded RAF pilot, who replies to Gregson's 'Summat go wrong?':

> 'One of those low-level sods. . . . Chased him across the Marsh at nought feet. Gave him two squirts and then he started playing tricks. Glycol and muck, pouring out everywhere. Never had a bloody clue and yet kept on, right down the deck, bouncing up and down, foxing like hell. He must have known he'd had it.' The young man paused to look round at the sea. 'He was a brave sod, the bravest sod I ever saw.'
>
> 'Don't you believe it,' Gregson said. 'Coming in and machine-gunning kids at low-level. That ain't brave.'
>
> 'This was brave,' the young man said.
>
> He spoke with the tempered air of the man who has seen the battle, his words transcending for the first time the comedy of the moustache. He carried suddenly an air of cautious defined authority, using words that there was no contesting.

At his behest, *The Breadwinner* turns about to look for the German pilot and in the end finds him and picks him up very badly wounded. 'In a moment of painful and speechless joy' Snowy notices that he carries binoculars. The boy is back in his galley about his never-ending job of brewing tea when *The Breadwinner* is shot up by an enemy fighter, which sheers off, having put the engines out of action and killed Jimmy the engine-man. Engines are a mystery both to Gregson and the boy, and they strive in vain to get her going. A storm gets up rapidly and Gregson unfurls the sail. He orders the boy to go below in order to look after the two wounded men, and Snowy watches them die.

In the late afternoon *The Breadwinner* comes in under the shelter of the dunes. She is safe. Snowy grasps the binoculars in his hands and presses them against his stomach. He goes over his talks with the RAF pilot. He remembers the German pilot in the end mainly as the man who carried the binoculars, 'the only things that had come out of the day that were not sick with the ghastliness of foul and indelible dreams'. Standing beside Gregson, the dead pilots 'became for him, at that moment, all the pilots, all the dead pilots, all over the world'.

> Gregson continued tenderly to hold him by the shoulder, not speaking, and the boy once more looked up at him, seeing the old tired face as if bathed in tears. He did not speak, there rose in him a grave exultation.
>
> He had been out with men to War and had seen the dead. He was alive and *The Breadwinner* had come home.

'The Cruise of *The Breadwinner*' is an austere work in which there are no heroics and no sentimentality. Among other things, it is a story of initiation into manhood. The characters are drawn boldly and simply, and this gives them a representative quality. The British officer partakes of the stereotype of the RAF pilot of the day, and Bates allows for this. He sees the pathos and the paradox of the stereotype: '. . . his words transcending for the first time the comedy of the moustache'. Gregson is beautifully rendered and Snowy is the epitome of boy at that moment in national history: he is defined completely in terms of one or two simple symbols, his prowess as a plane-spotter, his lust after the binoculars, his awe of Gregson. 'The Cruise of *The Breadwinner*' is among the masterpieces of the years it celebrates. (pp. 262-67)

> Walter Allen, "Bates," in his The Short Story in English, *Oxford at the Clarendon Press, 1981, pp. 262-67.*

V. S. Pritchett   (essay date 1984)

[*An English novelist, short story writer, and critic, Pritchett is considered one of the modern masters of the short story and one of the world's most respected literary critics. In the following introduction to Bates's short story collection* My Uncle Silas, *Pritchett discusses the rural settings and characters used in Bates's short fiction, particularly focusing on the character Uncle Silas.*]

The short story is the most *memorable* form of fiction. It is memorable because it has to tell and ring in every line. It has to be as exact as a sonnet or a ballad. It is, in essence, 'poetic' in its impulse. We do not forget it, indeed find more and more in it, whereas even in the greatest novels we easily forget whole chapters. Also, the short story is very suited to the nervous, glancing habits forced upon us by the hurry of contemporary life, which is so unlike the ruminative life of the nineteenth century when the novel was the dominating form of fiction. In the novel we lose ourselves; in the shorter thing we find ourselves. At the

end of the nineteenth century we meet the first outstanding masters of the form in Kipling, Wells, Conrad, James; in artists like Katherine Mansfield, Saki, Liam O'Flaherty, Frank O'Connor, D. H. Lawrence, the Joyce of *Dubliners* and many others. They have read Maupassant, Chekhov and Turgenev. Their special gift is to catch the crucial moments of a life as it passes. We see people who might have been minor characters in great novels, but now enlarged and brought forward.

H. E. Bates was one of the gifted English artists in the genre, especially in what he wrote in the Twenties and Thirties. He was a poet by nature. His setting was usually the traditional life of the small farms, cottages and holdings, his people the hedgers, ditchers, thatchers and local carriers—a horse-and-cart England in the main, the England of rural hagglings and feelings which had changed very little for centuries and often sounds Chaucerian and ripe in speech. We know how his people talk, eat, work, drink, love and die. Their habits had not yet been touched by the industrialization which changed village life after the last war. The people are not the generalized 'Loamshire' folk of radio and television, and for that reason are real in their past. If Bates's temperament was poetic, he was not a prettifier of archaic things. Bates's people and landscape are marvellously seen afresh. In the mere account of a man and boy ploughing or a woman leaning on a gate in fitful spring weather we see not only the day as it passes but how the people, inarticulate as they may be, feel their lives passing. For his evocations of such weathering of men, women and country he has been compared to Hardy; but he is without Hardy's Darwinian melancholy, Hardy's large speculations about class or social tendencies, or his sententious and fateful regard for the pagan and indifferent 'President of the Immortals'. Bates is interested in people for their own curious sakes. In one of his finest stories, 'The Mill,' a tragedy is left to tell itself. It is a tragedy set in motion by the meanness of a country trader in scrap. Bates was often lyrical but here he exposed the sourness and silences of rural poverty and the unprotected sight of innocence abused. The story has remained in my mind for forty years. But Bates was a writer of many kinds of stories. He could be lyrical, dour, even luscious and comic too. In the remarkable 'The Woman who had Imagination' we shall see a vulgar group of cheery villagers boozing, itching and singing on a charabanc trip to give a rural concert in the grounds of a country house; and in the series of stories called *My Uncle Silas* hear a genial rapscallion in his nineties telling extravagant lies about his sinful life to a boy.

Do not mistake the Uncle Silas stories for old-style bucolic farce. Every detail of Silas's unwashed ugliness and of his domestic habits as the village liar and boozer is truthfully put before us, as if we were sitting in his house with him or had been sent down to the cellar to bring up another dreadful bottle of his home-made wine. And Bates has had the art to make us see the villain through the memory of a small boy who is fascinated by the old man, if also, every now and then, sceptical. Silas has the arts of the rural story-teller who drops into long evasive silences and then takes up the tale to add to its enormities, deedily watching his audience. Cats come out of the bag one at a time: that is art and artfulness. He can suggest even more by an un-finished phrase, by a mastery of innocent metaphor or *double entendre*. The boy will believe the old man is, for example, talking to a girl about duck eggs but the old man is insinuating some other attraction. He is a great guzzler, but having a boy before him he is free to boast that in his time there has been nothing he has not eaten—once, out of desperate necessity, iron nails. And not only iron nails, but nails made digestible by a paste of shavings from a rot-ten cellar floor. To prove it he opens his mouth and shows how the enforced diet has left rusty stains on his remaining teeth. But why *enforced?* A girl he was carrying on with shut him in the cellar when she saw her husband about to catch him. Which girl? Ah! Silence; but a glance to the scrawny, hot-tempered old housekeeper who has come in to make the old fellow strip naked so that she can give him something he detests—his weekly bath in a tub by the fire—suggests all.

Is Uncle Silas a preposterous exaggeration? Not entirely, for two reasons. Bates knows how to make silences preg-nant and then the boy is his passive, wondering audience. The listening of the boy makes the stories almost genuine. The second justification is that Uncle Silas is an expert in the techniques of rural story-telling, that is to say he is the villager talking, when an hour will pass while one person and then the next will join in and add some fantasy out of village memory to the tale. He is rumour itself. It will succeed if told in a flat, casually dry passage; until it reach-es an open-ended silence for the next speaker to go one bet-ter, out of village memory. Uncle Silas is in fact the scan-dalizing village memory at work. One is listening to some-thing in the genre of 'The Miller's Tale'; and, in any case, every villager has samples of every kind of man and woman in the world at hand. Well, not every kind, but some very insinuating examples. Like most good short sto-ries from Chekhov onwards, Bates had the art that en-abled him to write many kinds of story. The poet could be the comedian, saved from slapstick by his resources of style and observation. And he was always at his best in the country landscape of his childhood where the hours seemed fuller and longer. (pp. 3-6)

> *V. S. Pritchett, in an introduction to* My Uncle Silas *by H. E. Bates, Oxford University Press, Oxford, 1984, pp. 3-6.*

Dean R. Baldwin (essay date 1984)

[*In the essay below, Baldwin discusses how Bates created and sustained atmosphere through a unity of scenery, characterization, and dialogue.*]

From the early 1930's until his death in 1974, H. E. Bates was considered one of the finest short story writers in En-gland. A prolific author, he published well over two hun-dred stories in seventeen volumes, in addition to novels, novellas, country essays, and an influential study of the short story [*The Modern Short Story*]. An output this large necessarily means that his works are of uneven quality, but as a short story writer he maintains an astonishingly high level of achievement in a wide variety of moods and sub-jects. On the one extreme are stories of harsh naturalism

like **"The Mill"** and **"The Ox,"** while at the other are tales of unabashed romanticism like **"The Cowslip Field"** and **"The Watercress Girl."** Most of his stories are in a tragic or sombre mood, but in two collections of Uncle Silas sto-ries [*My Uncle Silas* and *Sugar for the Horse*] and in oc-casional flights of high spirits like **"A Couple of Fools"** and **"A Party for the Girls"** he shows a rare and genuine comic gift. Considering both the quantity and quality of Bates's output, it is surprising that he is not better known or more highly regarded among academic critics or histo-rians of the genre. Very little has been written about him, though there are signs that his achievement is finally gain-ing recognition. This trend deserves to continue, as Bates is unquestionably a master story-teller whose excellences have thus far been largely overlooked.

On the surface, stories by H. E. Bates seem extremely con-ventional and straightforward. Readers will instantly rec-ognize the influence of Chekhov in his technique of build-ing stories out of trifling events and suggestion rather than through dramatic plot; in the rural stories of the 1930's particularly, the influence of A. E. Coppard is equally ob-vious. But to categorize Bates as a purveyor of rural idylls or Hardyesque studies in pain and endurance is to deny the wealth and variety of his achievement and to miss the individual stamp of his talent. Perhaps it is the surface simplicity which is deceptive. Bates seldom deals in com-plex characters or subtle psychology; his people are drawn from the lower social and economic strata where feeling and impulse dominate, thought has little subtlety, and ideas are few. The young, the inarticulate, and the inno-cent are the usual subjects of his stories. His plots are simi-larly straightforward and direct: a fall from innocence or the eternal love triangle are at the center of a great number of his stories which are spun out with few complications and a minimum of elaboration. Complexities of emotion rather than of plot or character are his trademark, and he almost never ventures into political commentary, social criticism, or abstract ideas. The interactions of people with one another and their immediate, natural environ-ment are the focus of his interest. Yet for all their apparent simplicity, Bates's stories have an intricate structure and a subtle texture that makes them curiously powerful and resonant. By and large their substance derives from his handling of atmosphere; the intricate interplay of mood and scene in relation to character and event is the basis of Bates's considerable art as a short story writer.

One aspect of Bates's romanticism manifests itself in sto-ries of luminous natural beauty, often set on warm spring or summer days. **"The Mower"** is typical of these, depict-ing a hot June day on which a family of three is cutting a field of hay by hand. The physical atmosphere of the story is permeated by images of heat and light:

> In the midday heat of a June day a farm-boy was riding down a deserted meadow-lane, straddling a fat white pony. The blossoms of hawthorn had shrivelled to brown on the tall hedge flanking the lane and wild pink and white roses were begin-ning to open like stars among the thick green leaves. The air was heavy with the scent of early summer, the odour of the dying hawthorn

bloom, the perfume of the dog-roses, the breath of ripening grass.

Throughout the story the colors yellow, white, and green appear and reappear, as do reminders of the sun's relentless heat. Reflecting these motifs are the woman and a hired hand named Ponto, a mower of prodigious skill and strength emanating danger and sexuality. Their illicit passion is joined to the natural scene by the woman's white blouse and green skirt, green being an ancient symbol of fertility.

In addition to this link between the heat of the day and the passion of Ponto and Anna, there is an air of expectancy and tension that permeates the story. At the beginning, this is created by uncertainty over whether Ponto will actually come to help with the mowing. Once he arrives, the question shifts to whether they will be able to complete the mowing that day. These two feelings, expectancy and passion, are joined in the relations between Anna and Ponto, for in spite of the physical attraction that draws them together, they are prevented from consummating their love by the prying eyes of her husband, her boy, and even the sun. At one point they snatch a few moments alone, but that is all. Moreover, Ponto's swaggering confidence in his own sex appeal contrasts sharply with the woman's submissive devotion, adding another layer of tension to the atmosphere. All three are maintained throughout the story, but gradually a fourth emerges, the suggestion of death. The act of cutting hay itself recalls the Biblical proverb, "As for man, his days are as grass; as a flower of the field, so he flourisheth," while the swaggering, carefree Ponto in his skill and power suggests the grim reaper. In the end, none of these tensions is resolved so that the story culminates in a remarkable effect—that on the one hand nothing significant has happened on this hot, lazy summer day, yet everything is quivering with suggestion and possibilities. Thus the story's effect lies not in its characters or incidents so much as in the aura created by the interaction and tension of its various elements.

Another story of illicit passion, **"The Station,"** achieves its effects in quite different ways, though some of the same motifs appear. Like many writers of the 1930's Bates was influenced by film techniques, which are used to good effect in creating the atmosphere of this story. It begins with a still moment, when a delivery truck has pulled up to a small dark cafe on a sultry summer night. As the driver and his mate step down from the cab, the woman inside the cafe turns on a light, illuminating the two men and revealing the mate as "young, but beside the driver he was boyish, his cheeks smooth and shiny as white cherries, his hair yellow and light and constantly ruffled up like the fur of a fox-cub." Thus is introduced a light-dark dichotomy which is maintained throughout: the blond young man and the dark woman, the brightness of the cafe in contrast with its surroundings, the stabbing light of a flashlight as the driver picks plums from a tree behind the building, and finally the garish blinking of a neon sign which the woman had previously neglected to turn on. These dramatic cinematic effects intensify the sudden attraction between the woman and the young man and are in turn heightened by the heat of the kitchen and the odor of ripening fruit and grain, both of which suggest sexuality.

The climax occurs in the garden, with the woman holding the flashlight and the driver in the tree picking plums:

> "Where's your hand?" she was whispering. "Here. It's a beauty." The soft ripe plum was between their hands. Suddenly she pressed it hard against his hand, and the ripe skin broke and juice trickled over his fingers. "Eat it, put it in your mouth," she said. He put the plum into his mouth obediently, and the sweet juice trickled down over his lips and chin as it had already trickled over his hands.

A moment later, the two men are once again on their way, the younger eating plums as the flashing neon light of the station recedes into the darkness. The remarkably erotic moment in the garden is partly the result of the woman's actions, but its effect is made possible by the atmosphere Bates builds out of the contrast between light and dark and the combination of odors and heat that occur in apparently casual descriptions.

Among Bates's best stories are a number which recreate scenes of his boyhood, a time just after the turn of the century when the ancient world of horsepower and manual labor was being replaced by automobile and machinery. In tales like **"The White Pony," "Alexander," "Great Uncle Crow,"** and **"The Cowslip Field,"** the atmosphere is usually as golden and sunny as that of **"The Mower."** In evoking this Eden, Bates calls upon his considerable powers of description and his intimate knowledge of the countryside. **"The Watercress Girl"** joins this sense of innocent beauty to an air of mystery in a tale uniquely evocative of childhood and overlain with a melancholy nostalgia of rare piquancy. The story begins with apparent casualness as the writer recalls traveling by horse and cart to visit his Aunt Sar' Ann. Like most children, the boy cannot keep straight the names and faces of his elderly relatives, but after several wrong guesses and additional hints from his grandfather, he recalls her as a woman with "a voice like a jackdaw's" and her sister as Aunt Prunes (Prudence). The confusion of Prunes and Prudence is part of another mystery in the boy's life: language. His grandfather speaks a strange dialect with words like "quartern," "simly," and "bulls' noon" which his teacher does not use, and there are phrases like "so long," which seem to mean the opposite of what they say. There are additional mysteries in the adult world. Aunt Prunes has a moustache, but grandfather denies this obvious fact with the assertion that, " 'Females don't have moustaches—you know that.' " He is accused of eating too much and of having eyes bigger than his stomach, though he is still hungry; and he can only wonder at why adults sleep in the afternoon when night is the time for rest. Later, there is yet another mystery when Sar' Ann calls the girl he met at the brook nothing but a "Gyppo," someone who "nicks" things, when he has found her friendly and generous. The eventual point of the story is the contrast between the golden world of his childhood and the jagged, faded modern world of television and pre-fab bungalows, but an important element in developing this theme is the atmosphere of childhood confusion which Bates creates essentially by focusing on the perplexities a child feels in trying to fathom the ways of adults. In fact, that atmosphere carries over into the theme of regret, suggesting that the "prog-ress" of the last several decades is as mysterious and con-tradictory as the confusions of childhood. Thus once again there is an interaction of atmospheres: the golden glow of summer, mingled with the child's sense of the world's wonder and mystery, combined with the adult's feelings of nostalgia and loss.

"Love in a Wych Elm" is a story similar in theme to **"The Watercress Girl"** but entirely different in construction and atmosphere. Here, the first two paragraphs establish a tone of carefree casualness by describing the house lived in by the Candleton family and sketching the background of Mr. Candleton. This is achieved largely by the indolent rhythms of the prose, which appears almost haphazard in its syntax, lazy in its perceptions. The verbs are condition-al—"gave the impression," "felt," "seemed"—and these reinforce the feeling that the writer is taking no more pains over his story than the Candletons did over their erratic lives. The story progresses through a series of loosely con-nected episodes and observations so that in structure it re-flects the atmosphere established by the opening para-graphs, and this in turn is mirrored in the Candleton way of life, typified by Mrs. Candleton whom the author de-scribes as "looking like the jaded mistress of a rag-and-bone man." Bates's purpose is not to depict his subjects as slovenly misfits, however, for their casual way of life stems from a fundamental innocence. This is symbolized by the family's physical traits: pale violet blue eyes and hair the color of yellow oat straw. It is also seen in their casual attitude toward sex. For example, when the eldest daughter elopes with a soldier who turns out to be mar-ried, she returns home as if from a delightful adventure, showing not the slightest sense of shame. Similarly, the narrator at the age of nine is one day received by one of the daughters, at that time about twelve years old, wearing only her petticoat. She invites him to her room for "a man's opinion" of her dress. The title of the story refers to the fact that the author and Stella were "married" at the age of nine or ten in a Wych elm, where he was then informed that it was his duty to make love to his bride, though neither of them knew why or how. This family in-nocence is eventually destroyed through financial ruin, and the author learns that the Candletons were not aristo-crats as Stella had claimed, but rose from the worst street in town through Mrs. Candleton's money. Thus the theme of lost innocence is joined to and reinforced by the atmo-sphere of casual living and uncomplicated sexuality inher-ent in the style and structure of the story itself.

In the sharpest possible contrast to the sunny romanticism of these stories is **"The Mill,"** one of Bates's undisputed masterpieces of naturalism. From first to last it maintains a relentlessly grim atmosphere which Bates himself once described as "emotionless negativity." At the center of the story is Alice Hartop, an adolescent girl so browbeaten by her father that she has literally no personality or will of her own. To supplement the family income, she is sent to care for Mrs. Holland, suffering from dropsy and living in a disused mill. Bates's description of Alice's arrival typi-fies the story's mood of static nullity:

> Beyond the piles of rusted iron a sluice tore
> down past the mill-wall on a glacier of green

slime. She stopped and peered down over the stone parapet at the water. Beyond the sluice a line of willows were shedding their last leaves, and the leaves came floating down the current like little yellow fish. She watched them come and surge through the grating, and then vanish under the waterarch. Then, watching the fish-like leaves, she saw a real fish, dead, caught in the rusted grating, thrown there by the force of descending water. Then she saw another, and another. Her eyes registered no surprise. She walked round the parapet, and then, leaning over and stretching, she picked up one of the fish. It was cold, and very stiff, like a fish of cellu-loid, and its eyes were like her own, round and glassy.

This is typical of the story, with Bates narrowly avoiding excessive cruelty in depicting the characters and the set-ting in which they move. The comparison between Alice and the fish is perfectly apt, for throughout she is a passive victim, being sexually used by Mr. Holland and then jeal-ously abused by his wife. She is also described as having a face "moulded in clay" and an expressionless counte-nance; her movements are mechanical and automatic. The rushing water of the mill and the pervading damp of the house represent an inexorable, Hardyesque fate over which she has no control, and the cold and barren mill with its surrounding junk yard and rank weeds is linked to the general atmosphere of chill indifference. The weath-er itself reinforces the atmosphere of gloom: at the begin-ning of the story, the Hartops are driving through a lash-ing rain storm, and later much of the action occurs during dull Midlands winter:

> Darkness began to settle over the river and the valley in the middle afternoon: damp, still No-vember darkness preceded by an hour of watery halflight. From Mrs. Holland's bedroom Alice watched the willow trees, dark and skeleton-like, the only objects raised up above the flat fields, standing half-dissolved by the winter mist, then utterly dissolved by the winter darkness. The af-ternoon was very still; the mist moved and thick-ened without wind. She could hear nothing but the mill-race, the everlasting almost mournful machine-like roar of perpetual water, and then, high above it, shrieking, the solitary cries of sea-gulls, more mournful even than the monotone of water.

Taken together, the rushing water of the mill, the pervad-ing chill of the house, and the flat, spiritless landscape create a mood of universal indifference. There is only mo-mentary release from this feeling when the Hollands' son returns from the army and takes a friendly interest in Alice, but this only serves to heighten the tragedy when she must finally return to her parents—pregnant—and for the first time breaks into tears.

Equally severe is the atmosphere of plodding futility that surrounds every human activity in **"The Ox."** The mood is set at the beginning in the description of the Thurlows' house:

> The Thurlows lived on a small hill. As though
> it were not high enough, the house was raised

up, as on invisible stilts, with a wooden flight of
steps to the front door. Exposed and isolated, the
wind striking at it from all quarters, it seemed
to have no part with the surrounding landscape.
Empty ploughed lands, in winter-time, stretched
away on all sides in wet steel curves.

Here the loneliness and exposed situation of the house suggest the condition of the Thurlows themselves, particularly Mrs. Thurlow who exists in an endless round of cleaning and washing for other people, daily pushing her bicycle laden with laundry and other burdens from house to
house. "Her relationship to it was that of a beast to a cart."
Her husband is equally alienated, having suffered a head
wound on the Marne which left him with a silver plate in
his head and periodically excruciating headaches. The
Thurlows are not even a family but a collection of isolated
individuals with no affection for one another. The only
bond is Mrs. Thurlow's mindless dedication to the future
welfare of her sons as she slaves at her cleaning and laundry, hoarding her money under a mattress. This is the environment in which the rest of the story takes place: Thurlow's murder of a man who doubts the existence of the silver plate, his theft of his wife's money, his capture, trial,
and conviction. In the process, Mrs. Thurlow loses even
her sons, for they prefer living with their prosperous
uncle. In the end, she is left with her bicycle, her work,
and the dull Midlands mud, which "seemed to suck at her
great boots and hold her down."

Between these extremes of romanticism and naturalism
are a great number of stories, usually involving love triangles, which combine elements from both approaches. Atmosphere in these stories is less obvious but no less important in determining the overall effect. Of these, **"Across
the Bay"** is typical in building up an atmosphere from a
series of repeated images and objects. The story takes
place at a seaside hotel in France just after World War II
and focuses on an Englishman named Harris who is vacationing for as long as his money lasts; after that, he has no
plans and no prospects. This setting and Harris's situation
create at the outset a tension between expectation and vacuity, hope and nothingness. These are mirrored in two
patterns of imagery, the first of which centers on references to light and sun. "Sealight from the wide hot bay
sparkled on Madame Dupont's spectacles as she lifted her
face," and "An afternoon of indigo and snow-white brilliance blew in exhilarating bursts of wind that flowered
into occasional running whirlwinds of sand," are but two
of many examples. Related to these numerous references
to food, particularly small pink lobsters called langous-
tines, and fruit, especially grapes and peaches. As the story
develops, Harris's relationship to the food and the light
signify his moods and suggest the state of his love-affair
with Yvonne, a young woman staying at the hotel alone
during the week, but on weekends occupied with a man
claiming to be her father, but who is eventually revealed
to be her lover. The other pattern of images relates to corruption and vulnerability, seen in the repeated instances
of maggots in the peaches and in references to Harris's
scar, described at one point as "tight and dead." The repetition of these two groups of images maintains an atmosphere of tension throughout the story. In this atmosphere
the love affair between Harris and Yvonne alternates between periods of happiness and pain caused by separation.
The other motifs in the story, particularly Harris's repeated allusions to taking a trip across the bay, support this
overall feeling. In the end, the tension is resolved tragically, with Yvonne returning to Paris with the man who
keeps her, and the story concludes by repeating the two
groups of images in singular fashion:

Harris looked away from the sea to where Jean-
Pierre, splitting a gold-pink peach in halves, was
prodding with the point of his fruit knife a trun-
dling fat maggot that had fattened on the blood-
brown shining heart of flesh.

"Kill it! Kill it!" Madame Dupont said. "Put it
away! Take it out of my sight. I can't bear it! For
God's sake put it out of my sight!"

Across the bay the sea flashed with its deep noon
beauty and in the dining-room Madame
Dupont, quite pale behind her golden spectacles,
buried her face in her hands.

It would be wrong to suggest that Bates's talent as a short
story writer lay solely in his ability to create and manipulate atmosphere, for he possessed complete technical mastery, including a flexible and lucid style, a rare gift for natural description, and the ability to draw convincing characters with great economy. However, his use of atmosphere distinguishes many of his stories and marks them
as among the best produced by any British writer in this
century. (pp. 215-22)

> *Dean R. Baldwin, "Atmosphere in the Stories
> of H. E. Bates," in* Studies in Short Fiction,
> *Vol. 21, No. 3, Summer, 1984, pp. 215-22.*

Dean R. Baldwin   (essay date 1987)

[*In the following excerpt from his biographical study*
H. E. Bates: A Literary Life, *Baldwin discusses Bates's
involvement with British propaganda efforts during
World War II and assesses his short fiction of the era.*]

Victory in the Battle of Britain assured that Germany
would not invade, but beyond this single fact the only certainty was Churchill's promise of "blood, toil, tears, and
sweat." Britain was perilously underarmed and overex-
tended. With a far-flung empire to defend, shipping lanes
to keep open, supplies to obtain, munitions to manufacture, armies and navies to raise, civilian populations to organize, and cities to repair and rebuild while bombs continued to fall, Britain seemed in danger of internal collapse. The state of the publishing industry is typical of the
country as a whole. Early in the war it looked as though
people were going to forgo reading altogether, and during
1939-40, magazines fell as quickly as German bombs, with
such venerable edifices as *Cornhill, Criterion, Fact, London Mercury,* and *New Verse* toppling into ruins. On 29
December 1940 London's publishing area of Paternoster
Row was heavily bombed, virtually wiping out the stocks
of several publishers, including Hutchinsons, Blackwoods,
Longmans, and Collins, losses totalling approximately
twenty million volumes. Cape was among the luckiest of
London's firms, suffering virtually no damage, managing
even to hang on to its ornamental railings in spite of a fe-

verish metal drive, but all lines of production and distribution were fouled by reductions in staff, bombing losses, interruptions of supplies, and transportation difficulties. Slowly, however, publishers learned to cope with these difficulties, and by 1941 sales were beginning to improve as people realized that the end of civilization was not at hand.

For writers in general and Bates in particular, time seemed suspended, unreal. At best the war was an interruption of their careers; many had already joined or shortly would attach themselves to some branch of service: William Sansom was in the London fire brigade; Graham Greene was on fire-watch before joining the secret service; David Garnett, a conscientious objector during the first war, was already in the Air Ministry; Somerset Maugham was assigned to public relations work in the United States. Bates, apart from membership in the Little Chart Home Guard, was not yet directly involved, having been granted a temporary exemption as a man of thirty-five with a family of four children. Soon, however, this would expire, and H. E. would be pressed into some kind of war service. He was not reluctant to serve, but like every other professional he wanted to put his talent to good use. One appeal he sent to the Society of Authors:

> Osbert Sitwell suggests that the Society of Authors may be able to help me get some sort of national service work in which I shall be able to use my particular qualifications. I don't want a job for the sake of having a job or, of course, for the sake of avoiding national service. But I am after all a writer of some reputation and I'd like to do my service as a writer if possible. I could fit in well with anything to do with agriculture, rural administration and such things; but I have also just done (for the M. O. I.) the preface to the new volume of R. A. F. war pictures, and the M. O. I. was pleased with it, and I've also been asked by the Bobbs Merrill company in New York if I'll do a book on the Eagle Squadron. I've done a little administrative work; I've no end of important contacts—personal ones—in America; and I'll go abroad if necessary. But I'm convinced I can do something useful in my own line, and if you can help it would be a very good thing and I should be very grateful.

While he waited for something to materialize, he spent his time compiling *The Modern Short Story,* and he still had the weekly "Country Life" column in *The Spectator* and reviews to write for *Life and Letters,* but apart from these projects he was at loose ends, with little to do but wait.

Bates's work on *The Modern Short Story* suggests that like many of his countrymen at the time, he was in a reflective mood. His interest in the subject dated back to his very earliest days as a writer, to the hours of leisure in the warehouse when he was reading Chekhov, Maupassant, and Turgenev, looking for models and studying his craft. His first substantial piece of criticism was an article on Stephen Crane for *The Bookman* in 1931. From that time on he produced a steady stream of articles and reviews, particularly in *John o' London's Weekly,* on individual writers and topics like "The British Short Story" and "The Short Story Today." Working on the staff of *New Stories* brought

him into contact with a great many younger writers as well. Thus, *The Modern Short Story* was more than ten years in the making, though the work had been unsystematic and essentially unconscious. Had he been so inclined, H. E. could have supplemented his considerable knowledge of the short story with a methodical inquiry into the genre, but he was a professional writer, not a scholar. It is, therefore, an insider's view of the history, development, and accomplishments of the form that he produced. As a work of history and criticism, it is fluently and engagingly written, with acute and telling observations on the nature of the form, its foremost practitioners, and the quality of their achievements. There is nothing stodgy or dull about it. On the other hand, its lack of system is a defect. There is no unifying theme holding together the various ideas and observations that Bates tends to drop casually; it is a book without a thesis and essentially without a plan, save for its basically chronological outline. There are also considerable gaps in the book's coverage: Hawthorne and Melville are barely mentioned; Twain is ignored. Henry James, whose writing Bates could never abide, is glanced at but never discussed. Among his countrymen, Elizabeth Bowen, William Plomer, G. K. Chesterton, E. M. Forster, Graham Greene, Saki, Sylvia Townsend Warner, and V. S. Pritchett are omitted or barely mentioned, while Kipling receives some hard (and not always fair) knocks. There are times, as in the discussion of James Joyce, when the reader would appreciate fuller treatment. Nevertheless, within its limits, *The Modern Short Story* is an illuminating and stimulating survey. It gives rightful attention to writers often ignored by critics and anthologists—A. E. Coppard, Liam O'Flaherty, George Moore. Its emphasis on the international character of the short story, its Continental and American contributions, is exactly right. Above all, its individual observations and judgments, whether one agrees with them or not, show the critical eye of one who practices the form. Reviewers were quite positive about the book and its endurance is unquestionable. It went through several printings immediately and continued to sell steadily, so much so that in 1971 a revised edition was called for. Though it has been superseded in some respects by T. O. Beachcroft's *The Modest Art* and Walter Allen's *The Short Story in English,* it remains a standard text and reference for students of the short story.

Publication of *The Modern Short Story* by Nelson and Sons did not, however, please Cape. When he saw it announced in a trade journal, Wren Howard wrote to Bates inquiring about the book and reminding him of his agreement to do a country book for Cape. It was a month later when Bates responded with his side of the story:

> Many thanks for your two letters.
>
> I have delayed answering the first because I felt that you seemed rather anxious to jump to erroneous conclusions about me. Your impression appears to be that I am writing books right and left for other people and am offering none to you. In your second letter for example you say that THE SATURDAY BOOK appears to be a collaboration between Agnes Miller Parker and myself. This is quite wrong. THE SATURDAY BOOK as its title suggests, is a new book-magazine, and I

have a short essay in it which is illustrated by Miss Parker. As to the book for Nelson, this is quite true; but on the other hand there is nothing in our contract which governs a book of criticism of me.

Perhaps I might set out my side of things? Since the war began I have been asked by various publishers to write no fewer than twelve books. The total advance offered by these publishers was £1200. Obviously it was out of the question to do them all, but I mention it merely to show that my reputation is going higher. You, on the other hand, so far from suggesting I should do a book, have turned down several. My last novel, for example, still lies in the drawer—and it lies there not because it is entirely bad but simply because I was never offered the slightest encouragement to revise it. I then offered you a collected volume of my *Spectator* notes. This would have made a nice volume, but you refused it. Two other publishers made offers for it. Then I offered you a country book on some rather topical lines, but you were very luke-warm about it. Yet when I offered Chapter I of it to *The Field* they were so impressed that they offered to serialize it all. This they are going to do. Now if you had accepted these suggestions my debt to you would probably have been wiped off by now.

I don't want you to misunderstand me. There are no publishers anywhere that I want to write more for than yourselves. But I can't live on air, and I can't write without just a little encouragement. Everyone else seems to give me that encouragement except you. Moreover, on the financial side, I must point out that I have taken out a large insurance policy, involving a premium that scares me stiff every time I have to find it, and have given you the necessary interest in it to cover any possible loss to you. Also you have the advantage of setting my total debt to you against all my books, which is, as you know, not a common procedure.

I shall say nothing about the fact that war-time, with four children, has been financially a very trying time for me. My income has been hopelessly reduced and I am, of course, waiting to be called up. In fact but for the Nelson book I should have been called up by now and I should have been in the financial doldrums. From this you will see why I am naturally a little discouraged by your attitude.

It took Wren Howard some weeks to plow through back correspondence so that he could reply to Bates's complaints. *The Saturday Book,* of course, was no problem; but Howard did point out that Bates's account with Cape was £300 in arrears and that the life insurance policy was not of much comfort. He went on to say that Bates had agreed in 1940 always to consult with Cape before publishing a book with anyone else, and as to "encouragement," he was sorry if Bates felt neglected, but he had done his best, particularly as regards the country book. There the matter rested for two years, with nothing having been resolved.

Meantime, Bates was still looking for a way to lend his tal-

ents to the war. Knowing that he was scheduled to enter the RAF in some capacity, he wrote to David Garnett at the Air Ministry, asking if some work could be found before October when his exemption expired. What he wanted to avoid above all was being shunted into some bureaucratic rabbit warren where he would be reduced to writing official reports or petty journalism and where his talents would receive no exercise. He had already seen in his futile efforts to do the book on the Eagle Squadron how easy it was to get lost in the shuffle.

As it turned out, David Garnett was exactly the right person to write. He had been associated with the intelligence branch of the Air Ministry since 1939, writing material to entertain and boost morale among the troops, but at the time of Bates's letter, the RAF was looking beyond its ranks to the need for publicity among civilians. Garnett persuaded John Nerney that Bates was the right man for the job they had in mind. On 5 September Bates had an interview with Nerney, who suggested that he apply for a commission in the reserves, and then Nerney would do what he could to get Bates into the Air Ministry. This Bates did, and true to his word, Nerney arranged another interview, this one with Harold Peake and Hilary St. George Saunders as well. These three offered H. E. a most original and daring proposition, that he would be commissioned by the RAF to write not dreary propaganda but short stories about the men of the air force. Moreover, within certain very flexible limits, Bates would be free to write what he wanted in his own way. He would, in other words, be an artist first and a propagandist second. Garnett would later say [in *Great Friends*], "Getting Bates that job was the most valuable service I did while I was in the Air Ministry."

From this distance it is difficult to recall that in 1941 the RAF's need for good public relations was acute. As the youngest of Britain's services, the RAF had suddenly emerged as the "glamour" branch, and as the most important so far in the war. The army had suffered only defeat and humiliation in France, ending in the near-disaster of Dunkirk. The navy, for all its tradition and in spite of its deterrent force in helping to prevent an Axis invasion, had seen relatively little action. It was the Battle of Britain pilots who had forestalled Hitler's invasion plans; it was their heroics that had captured the public imagination. On the other hand, in the fall of 1940, German tactics had changed from preparing for invasion to saturation bombing of cities, and urban dwellers were reeling from bombs, incendiaries, and UXB's—unexploded bombs. As the blitz continued and more and more people were made homeless and/or jobless, resentment against the inability of the RAF to prevent destruction could grow. It was necessary to tell the populace what the RAF was really doing and interpret its mission to the public in a way that would keep morale high but not raise unrealistic expectations. Some indication of popular feeling can be gauged by recalling Lord Beaverbrook's success in involving the public personally in the RAF's effort through his largely spurious but nevertheless successful "aluminum drives," by which housewives from the lowliest Cockney to the Queen herself donated aluminum cooking utensils that were to be turned into Spitfires and Wellingtons. Later came the idea of raising money to "buy" a Spitfire in the name of a working group, municipality, or even individual—a scheme by which £ 13,000,000 was raised by April 1941 for the construction of planes. Activities like these, plus the newspapers' tendency to speak of pilots as "knights of the air" and to lionize those of particular skill or bravery, embarrassed young men unused to any sort of attention. What was needed, then, was someone to humanize the pilot and explain the air war without histrionics or slogans.

To meet the need for realistic propaganda (if it is possible to coin such a term), the RAF decided that it required trained writers who could function from the *inside.* Thus, from 1939 on, journalists and writers were recruited for the service, given officers' training, and posted to various units. As officers and members of the RAF, they could move freely among the airmen and crews and actually take part in or at least observe firsthand what was going on. Moreover, everything they wrote would be subject to military censorship, and of course, they could be assigned to cover whatever aspect of the war the RAF wanted publicized at the moment. In all of these ways, such writers were from the military's point of view superior to civilian correspondents. The only disadvantage would be that their material might have to be published at military expense, but even this problem was solved by the simple expedient of using civilian outlets such as newspapers for much of it.

Over the next month, H. E. went to Rushen to be kitted out; then final arrangements were made, and he was inducted into the RAF. *The Spectator* announced his departure on 24 October 1941 with a brief note at the foot of his last "Country Life" column. When that note appeared, Bates was already involved in basic officers' training at Uxbridge, where the most useful thing he learned was the fine art of goldbricking. From there he joined his unit briefly, which consisted of only four other men, and then it was on to Oakington air base near Cambridge for a posting that lasted three months. Here he was expected to pick up ideas and material for short stories about the pilots and their missions, but it was no easy task. For one thing, at the advanced age of thirty-six, H. E. was ten years older than the oldest pilot, and nearly twice the age of many. Moreover, Air Force men were suspicious of anyone from the outside, and though Bates wore the rank of flying officer, he knew no more about flying than pilots did of storywriting. Not only were these men given to silence or understatement but also when they did talk it was in a strange slang, full of terms like "bind," "brassed off," "u.s.," "prange," "bought it," and "tore off a strip"—designed, as all slang is, to exclude anyone not already part of the group. At first Bates tried to listen without asking questions and to join activities like card playing, billiards, and casual drinking where, for an instant of two, the men would let down their guard and reveal something significant. When this failed to work, he took to buying the fellows drinks, which did loosen their tongues a bit. The trouble was, it became so expensive that he finally had to appeal for an expense account to keep from going broke. Amazingly, the appeal was granted. Beyond this there were opportunities simply to observe and absorb—in briefings, in landings and takeoffs, in the mess, above all

in the eyes of men returning from missions. From such incidentals he could infer quite a lot. What he waited for chiefly was the unguarded remark, the chance phrase, a brief bit of irrelevant home-life detail that would illuminate a man or an incident and provide the peg on which to hang a story. The first of these came from a wing commander who confessed that the most difficult part of his job was dealing with loved ones who came to him asking for details of a young man who had been reported killed or missing. From this came the first story, **"It's Just the Way It Is."** This he hastily wrote and submitted to Hilary Saunders, who was enthusiastic. He was on the right track.

Landing a good assignment in the RAF was an important accomplishment for Bates, and a step that had profound effects on the rest of his life. It did not solve, however, many of the pressing problems of the moment. His family was now fatherless and would remain so for much of the next four years, leaving Madge to cope as best she could with two small boys (the girls were in Rushden), a largish house, a huge garden, and a miniscule budget. So strapped were the family's finances that Bates had to ask Jonathan Cape for a personal loan to cover his insurance premiums. Just before joining the RAF, Bates had high hopes that a new play, *The Day of Glory,* would end the creative impasse he had been in for some time and also go some way toward reducing his debt with Cape. The play was produced at Salisbury on 31 October and broadcast over the BBC on 5 November, but it was not the success Bates had hoped for. *The Day of Glory* did not receive a London production until after the war, by which time its topical appeal had been lost; its literary quality was not high, and once again his hopes for the stage were dashed.

During Bates's first three months at Oakington (November 1941 through January 1942) he wrote several stories that were released beginning on 2 February as weekly features in the *News Chronicle,* the first being **"It's Just the Way it Is,"** followed by eight others. The accompanying headline was a bit breathless: "First Short Story by Flying Officer X" and beneath this, "One of the most famous of British short story writers is now in the R. A. F. For service reasons he writes under a pen-name." Each story was given a prominent place on page two and an eye-catching illustration of fighter or bomber action. The "service reasons" cited by the *News Chronicle* for H. E.'s pseudonym could hardly have been security precautions; more likely, Bates's identity needed to be shielded so that he could move freely among the airmen. Had they known he would turn their exploits into fiction, they would have avoided him completely. This would also explain why he returned only briefly to Oakington before being reassigned to Tangmere, near Chichester in Sussex. In a new location he could again mingle freely and gather information for more stories.

While the last of H. E.'s stories was appearing in the *News Chronicle,* the war marked its one thousandth day (29 May 1942). In those one thousand days, publishing and the book-buying public had changed dramatically, in some ways unalterably. For publishers, the problem was no longer how to sell books but how to obtain enough paper to print them. At the beginning of the war, they were restricted to 60 percent of their 1938 consumption, but as supplies grew ever more scarce, they were gradually reduced to a miserly 37.5 percent. Children's books were hardest hit, but even newspapers were reduced in length. To start a new magazine was illegal. By carefully conserving their rations, however, some publishers were able to get 60 percent of their prewar production from just over a third of the paper. A number of writers were less irritated by rationing than by the government's consumption. Of the 250,000 tons available, the government took 100,000 to issue White Papers, and 25,000 tons were given to the army. Only 20,000 tons were reserved for books. Especially frustrating was the fact that after 1941, demand for books rose astronomically, for reasons that can be only partly explained. Certainly the nightly blackout convinced many people to stay home rather than risk the perils of navigating lightless streets. Many not confined indoors spent long, tedious hours in shelters, on fire-watch, or in a similar duty where there was nothing much to do. Traveling by rail or coach could take hours—hence the need for something to read. The gravity of the crisis convinced many people to take stock of themselves and their civilization; there was an unprecedented interest in serious reading, including the literary classics. Whatever the causes, reading increased markedly, and with supplies down, publishers found themselves in the enviable position of being able to sell anything they printed, including stocks that had long lain unwanted in warehouses. Choosing books to publish became, as Lovat Dickson complained, too easy, as the public bought whatever was available.

All these facts relate to the story surrounding the publication of the Flying Officer X books. When the first series came to an end in May 1941, Bates suggested Cape as publisher for the collected stories. When Cape heard the offer, he was less than enthusiastic, as the firms' publishing commitments would use all its available paper. Moreover, the cool relations between Cape and Bates, plus the fact that nothing of his since *Spella Ho* had sold very well, made the prospects look mediocre at best. All this changed, of course, when the Air Ministry offered to supply the necessary paper. On his side, Bates regarded the Flying Officer X contract as a favor to Cape. It demonstrated his loyalty, and judging from the reception the stories had received, he had cause to think they would sell. What he could not have foreseen was the size of the printing the Ministry would order: 100,000 copies at first, later raised to 250,000. Here, H. E. reasoned, was his chance to erase his debt to Cape; the only problem was that, having written the stories as a Crown employee, he was not entitled to royalties—a fact that Cape saw immediately. Always a stickler for the letter of an agreement and never generous with authors, all he could see was that Bates was still £200 in arrears on royalties and that he had lately shown considerable disloyalty. Nevertheless, he was prepared to offer H. E. £100 in consideration for the stories. In his reply, Bates pointed out that a £100 gratuity on each of two books would leave him nothing whatever. He went on to say:

> It needs only a very simple calculation to see that this is a modest suggestion. At the Penguin

rate of £1 per thousand for sixpennies, you would have already owed me, under ordinary circumstances, £200. But the Penguin rate for a 1/—book is £2 per thousand, which equals £400. But even then, leaving out entirely the 2/6 edition, I calculate that the two books could have not earned less than £1000 for me. This must, of course, argue a handsome profit for yourselves.

> These are my suggestions, and I am sorry to have to write at such length about them. But the only reason our relations during the war have been unsatisfactory is simply that you at Bedford Square don't seem to regard me in anything the same light as other people. I am constantly being told that I am the finest short story writer in England and so on and so forth, but I don't seem to engender the same confidence in you. I wish I could. I have never believed that money is the whole of writing; still less that it is the whole of publishing.

It is difficult to say whether the financial or the personal issue was the more important, but it is significant that once again the question of "confidence" arose. With his close friends now gone from Cape (Rupert Hart-Davis was in the Coldstream Guards; Edward Garnett of course was dead), there was no one at the firm to encourage him, to praise the stories as stories or to offer hope that before long his luck would change and he would write a really profitable book. To H. E., Cape seemed a soulless firm, interested only in profit. On his side, Jonathan Cape could rightly argue that he owed Bates nothing in return for these books and that fifteen years of encouragement had not made him a profitable author. H. E. was sent £100 for the stories, and there the matter rested—still not fully resolved.

When ***The Greatest People in the World*** was released in September [of 1942], the *News Chronicle* revealed Bates as its author and hailed the stories as capturing the "spirit and character of the R. A. F." Indeed, the collection met with almost unanimous praise from reviewers, nor was it surprising it should do so. On nearly every battlefront there was more bad news than good, while at home, rationing was becoming increasingly strict. In a war fought mostly by machines, involving masses of people and casualties in the tens of thousands, Bates's stories told people things they needed to hear, that an offensive war was being waged bravely and effectively, that there were heroes of whom they could be proud, and above all that there were people and values worth fighting for and preserving. The papers had been proclaiming these things for months, of course, but these stories were written by someone on the inside, and they did not appear to be ground out by a propaganda mill; in fact, they were the opposite of strident sloganeering. With their quiet understatement and matter-of-fact tone, they sounded deeply honest and trustworthy. Reviewer after reviewer hailed the truth and beauty of these little sketches. As Battle of Britain ace J. H. "Ginger" Lacey said, "Bates got it just right."

Forty years later, the artistry of the two Flying Officer X collections (***How Sleep the Brave*** appeared in 1943, and the two were collected into one in 1952) is still impressive. All the tension, fear, monotony, heroism, brilliance, bad luck, determination, and escapism of the pilots is brought colorfully alive. This Bates accomplished by his customary devices of simple language, vivid description, and understatement; there is no straining after effects, no exaggeration, no rhetoric. His method perfectly matched the stoicism and tight-lipped endurance of the men he portrayed. By catching the idiosyncratic gesture, the trick of speech, the barroom chatter, and the grim humor of his subjects, Bates made his airmen convincing people, whatever their background or nationality. Much is conveyed by the skillful rendering of dialogue. There are moments, like the fire in **"How Sleep the Brave,"** of intense excitement narrated in racy and vivid prose. Through it all, Bates also manages to indicate relations between people and between man and machine. This is particularly so in **"The Young Man from Kalgoorie,"** where the central figure is an Australian lad whose parents kept him ignorant of the war for a year, fearing to lose him, or again in **"There's No Future in It,"** focusing on the precarious love of a pilot and his "popsy." In the best of the stories, **"How Sleep the Brave,"** exciting action, quiet heroism, and perfect construction produce a story reminiscent of Crane's "The Open Boat," on which it is partially modeled. But what makes these stories work is not just their timely subject matter or quiet tone. Through them Bates finds a vehicle for one of his most deeply felt beliefs—that the real heroes of the war, as of life generally, are the ordinary people whose heroism is unseen. A returning pilot, flying his disabled plane a bare hundred feet above the treetops, sees an old couple in the fields below and thinks of his parents who sacrificed everything so that he could get an education, "and he saw them alive again in the arrested figures of the two people in the fields below: as if they were the same people, the same simple people, the same humble, faithful, eternal people, giving always and giving everything: the greatest people in the world."

Time has also revealed weaknesses in these tales. Because of the conditions under which they were written, they appear formulaic in construction and occasionally shallow in characterization. Most begin with a description of a person or situation, then provide a few illustrative incidents, and close with a "clincher" ending, usually a restatement of the story's title. The characters, individual as they are, are sometimes airmen first, people second, adding up to a collection of types. Having noted these deficiencies we must admit that as fiction written to order, these stories are of surprisingly high quality. They are certainly more accomplished than John Macadam's similar stories, *The Reluctant Erk,* and more revealing about war than Alun Lewis's *The Last Inspection.* Their closest rivals are William Sansom's gripping descriptions of life in a London fire brigade. They demonstrate at the very least Bates's professionalism and certainly cannot be dismissed as hack-work. For conveying an accurate sense of what air warfare was really like they will continue to have value, and a few can stand among the outstanding fiction of World War II. (pp. 145-55)

> *Dean R. Baldwin, in his* H. E. Bates: A Literary Life, *Susquehanna University Press, 1987, 267 p.*

Brock Baker   (essay date 1988)

[*In the excerpt below, Baker reviews Bates's achievements in the short story genre as he discusses the retrospective collection,* A Month by the Lake, and Other Stories.]

[*A Month by the Lake, and Other Stories*] is a selection of short works by the English short-story writer and novelist H. E. Bates, who died in 1974. Chronologically, they range from his first published work, **"The Flame,"** which appeared in 1926, to the title story of his last collection, **"The Song of the Wren"** (1972). Included are two stories by "Flying Officer X," the pseudonym adopted by Bates while serving in the British Army during World War II.

What an extraordinary writer H. E. Bates could be! One first notes his exuberant power of physicality, of evoking settings with delicate intensity: the look and feel of early fall by an Italian lake in the title story, or the summer fields throughout **"The Cowslip Field"**; the bleak cold of a military airfield in **"It's Just the Way It Is,"** or the hollow bonhomie of an inexpensive London restaurant on a Saturday night (**"The Flame"**). Then there are the plots. In **"A Month By the Lake"**, he is able to dangle before us the destinies of two unattached and unspectacular persons until our engrossment takes on the status of a personal investment in a happy ending which, at the same time, we don't dare anticipate in case we are disappointed. In **"Cowslip,"** told in the first person by a very young boy who is being taken on an expedition to find "the cowslip field," the sadnesses of his companion, a plain young rural woman, are gradually disclosed—yet by the child's affection for her and their shared delight in the flowering countryside they are made almost sacred. And in **"Where the Cloud Breaks,"** perhaps my favorite of this remarkable group of stories, a retired colonel living alone in a picturesque country cottage and already getting a little daffy as a result has only one friend, a spinster lady a few years younger, with whom he communicates by semaphore since he is in perpetual warfare with "progress" and eschews as many modern conveniences as he possibly can, including the telephone. One day she gives him a nasty shock: a television set has been installed in a corner of her living room, and she invites him to watch it with her in the evenings. His friendly feelings for her, that have often almost but not quite welled over into expressions of love, are crushed. He is bitterly disappointed at her betrayal of all the values he thought they held in common, that made him feel close to her. He rushes back to his lonely, disorderly cottage, thoroughly shaken. I will leave the reader there, only adding that in its non-horrified or patronizing exploration of the yearnings, emotional and sexual, of the no longer young, **"Where"** is remarkable, if not unique, in modern Anglo-American literature.

But all the stories have a great deal to recommend them. **"It's Just the Way It Is,"** by "Flying Officer X," locates the bravery or enterprise that the horrors of wars can bring out in those who fight them in an unexpected place, in the officer who meets with the angry, grieving parents of a young pilot killed while under his command. **"The Chords of Youth"** is an elaborate, brilliantly sustained spoof of postwar small-town politicking between self-serving representatives of opposing powers; in this case, officials of small towns in Germany and England, who get drunk together at a dinner given in their honor by an elderly English lady who is certain she knew, and was a little bit in love with, the fat, gluttonous German mayor when he was a dashing young mountaineer before the war.

H. E. Bates's reputation is no longer what it was, and all of his story collections and most of his novels have fallen out of print. While he had and continues to have many distinguished admirers, especially of his stories—Graham Greene has compared his "best tales" to those of Chekhov, as quoted in the jacket copy—to most readers born since World War II, contemporaries such as Evelyn Waugh, or Greene himself, are much better known, perhaps because their works seemed better suited to the times. But starting with this artful selection, American readers at least can begin to appreciate him (or appreciate him anew) at his true worth. These are "tales" full of strong, active, fructifying feelings, and their author has a capacity for imaginative sympathy that is almost miraculous; for instance, his portrait of a complicated and dignified woman character like Miss Bentley in **"A Month By the Lake"** is as satisfying as, say, Anita Brookner's in the best of her recent highly acclaimed novels.

All in all, a very fine book. . . . (pp. 72-3)

Brock Baker, "H. E. Bates, Storyteller," in The New Criterion, Vol. 6, No. 7, March, 1988, pp. 72-3.

FURTHER READING

Bibliography

Eads, Peter. *H. E. Bates: A Bibliographical Study.* Twentieth Century Writers Series, no. 6. Detroit: Omnigraphics, 1990, 224 p.

Bibliography of published works by Bates. A section on Bates's short stories and novellas includes a comprehensive list of periodicals and books in which each of these works was published or collected, as well as indexing commentary on each title mentioned in Bates's autobiography.

Biography

Baldwin, Dean R. *H. E. Bates: A Literary Life.* Selinsgrove, Penn.: Susquehanna University Press, 1987, 267 p.

Critical biography of Bates that includes commentary on his short fiction and a chapter on his work as Flying Officer X.

Criticism

Burgess, Anthony. Introduction to *A Month by the Lake, and Other Stories,* by H.E. Bates, pp. vii-x. New York: New Directions, 1987.

Discusses Bates's career and reputation as a short story writer.

Gindin, James. "A. E. Coppard and H. E. Bates." In *The English Short Story, 1880-1945: A Critical History,* edited by Joseph M. Flora, pp. 113-41. Boston: Twayne, 1985.

Comparative study of Bates and the English short story writer A. E. Coppard.

Vannatta, Dennis. *H. E. Bates.* Boston: Twayne, 1983, 147 p.

Critical and biographical overview of Bates's life and career.

Stephen Vincent Benét

1898-1943

American poet, short story writer, essayist, dramatist, librettist, scriptwriter, and critic.

INTRODUCTION

Best known as a poet who sought to document, explicate, and celebrate the American experience, Benét also wrote a number of classic short stories with nationalistic themes. With "The Devil and Daniel Webster" and "Johnny Pye and the Fool-Killer," Benét created archetypal works of distinctively American fiction that have become part of national myth.

While a student at Yale Benét published his first three books of poetry, *The Drug-Shop; or, Endymion in Edmonstoun, Young Adventure,* and *Heavens and Earth,* the latter of which was accepted in place of his master's thesis. After graduation he studied for a year in Paris and published two novels, *The Beginning of Wisdom* and *Young People's Pride.* Although he preferred poetry to fiction, Benét out of necessity focused his efforts on the more lucrative market of short stories tailored for mass circulation magazines. Beginning in the 1920s, he wrote and published numerous mawkish, contrived romances and slick, quasi-sophisticated accounts of high society. Despite his distaste for this kind of formulaic fiction, Benét was able to secure a reasonably steady income. In 1925, however, Benét decided that he wanted "to have some fun doing these things." He therefore began in prose to explore themes that he had exploited to good effect in his poetry, nostalgically evoking the American past and presenting a noble conception of the American national character. An early successful story of this kind, "The Sobbin' Women," is derived from the Roman legend of the Sabine women and transplanted to the American West of the nineteenth century. The narrative is presented as the reminiscence of a village raconteur identified as "the Oldest Inhabitant." This framing device proved successful and many subsequent "Oldest Inhabitant" stories followed, including "The Fool-Killer," "True Thomas," and "The Lucksmith." Benét never entirely abandoned formulaic magazine fiction; as Charles A. Fenton noted, "he had to break his concentration repeatedly in order to write something immediately salable." During World War II Benét wrote a number of allegorical stories condemning fascism and totalitarianism, as well as patriotic radio plays, speeches, and propaganda broadcasts.

The 1936 publication of "The Devil and Daniel Webster" represents Benét's greatest success with archetypally American settings, characters, and themes. Benét based his characterization of the revered statesman on historical accounts but invented and extrapolated details about Webster's personality and accomplishments. Many read-

ers received Benét's account of Webster's oratorical contest with Mr. Scratch as a retelling of existing myth, but in fact the conception was wholly original. In this story Benét successfully combined regional humor with a serious moral by suggesting that the best representative of humanity, a true American hero, can overcome even an infernal adversary. "The Devil and Daniel Webster" won the 1936 O. Henry award for the best American short story and has been widely anthologized and adapted for radio, stage, and film. Commentators also highly regard "Johnny Pye and the Fool-Killer" as one of Benét's most technically accomplished and contemplative stories. The eponymous protagonist is a familiar literary type—a naïve youth who slowly acquires knowledge and understanding through the commonplace hardships of a long life. Pye repeatedly encounters the Fool-Killer, a legendary bogeyman who is finally revealed as the personification of Time and thus an avatar of human mortality. "Johnny Pye" combines fantasy, humor, and such timeless themes as human folly, the acquisition of wisdom, and the evanescence of life.

Critics commonly dismiss much of Benét's popular magazine fiction, concurring with Joseph Wood Krutch that these "mildly moralized stories of the jazz age" are "good enough and quite competent, but scarcely distinguishable from hundreds written by dozens of other writers." Often commended, however, are a number of stories that skillfully utilize elements of the fantastic. In particular, "By the Waters of Babylon" presents a grim, yet ultimately hopeful, vision of human life after a catastrophic war has decimated the population and technology and science have been forgotten. Regarded as the prototype of the post-apocalypse story in modern science fiction, "By the Waters of Babylon" introduced themes that remain current in that genre. Greatest acclaim is reserved for Benét's distinctively American tales that transcend folklore and local color fiction, investing characteristically American subject matter with qualities of timelessness and universality. Krutch has commended Benét's use of "American material in a way which is not only interesting but tending at the same time to make the American past more dignified, more meaningful and more comprehensible to the imagination."

PRINCIPAL WORKS

SHORT FICTION

The Devil and Daniel Webster   1937
Thirteen O'Clock: Stories of Several Worlds   1937
Johnny Pye and the Fool-Killer   1938
Tales before Midnight   1939
Selected Works of Stephen Vincent Benét.   2 vols. (poetry and short stories)   1942
Twenty-Five Short Stories by Stephen Vincent Benét   1943
The Last Circle   (poetry and short stories)   1946

OTHER MAJOR WORKS

The Drug-Shop; or, Endymion in Edmonstoun   (poetry) 1917
Young Adventure   (poetry)   1918
Heavens and Earth   (poetry)   1920
The Beginning of Wisdom   (novel)   1921
Young People's Pride   (novel)   1922
The Ballad of William Sycamore, 1790-1880   (poetry) 1923
Jean Huguenot   (novel)   1923
Tiger Joy   (poetry)   1925
Spanish Bayonet   (novel)   1926
John Brown's Body   (poetry)   1928
Ballads and Poems, 1915-1930   (poetry)   1931
Litter of the Rose Leaves   (poetry)   1931
James Shore's Daughter   (novel)   1934
Burning City   (poetry)   1936
Nightmare at Noon   (poetry)   1940
Western Star   (poetry)   1943

*This work was originally published in the magazine the *Saturday Evening Post,* 24 October 1936.

E. B. C. Jones   (essay date 1938)

[*In the following excerpt, Jones offers a guardedly favorable review of* Thirteen O'Clock: Stories of Several Worlds, *mentioning strengths and weaknesses of several stories in the collection.*]

Provided that the reader is not misled by the blurb into expecting "greatness" from Mr. Vincent Benét, he will find much to enjoy in this American writer's stories [in ***Thirteen O'Clock: Stories of Several Worlds***]. They belong to the leisurely kind less frequently found today, and are even sometimes rather too long-drawn out for their subject-matter. This is true of **"Glamour,"** which a man tells in the first person about a period when his life was entangled with a family of Southerners less feckless than they seemed. **"Everybody Was Very Nice"** is also a man's own story, this time of a broken marriage; the moral climate of well-to-do suburban society, "enlightened" in the sense that the couples marry on the understanding that they shall be free—that "if you meet a handsomer fellow it's all off "—is extremely well rendered. **"The Blood of the Martyrs"** has topical interest: an eminent biologist, utterly aloof from politics, finds himself in the brutal clutches of a totalitarian State because he refuses to make science subserve political aims. **"A Death in the Country,"** in which a man revisits the scene of his childhood, is marred by that slight sentimentality which makes some writers exalt the old at the expense of the young and middle-aged. Aunt Emmy, who had bullied Tom when he was a child, has somehow become a perfectly wise, mellow and beneficent person in the intervening years. It is significant that here Mr. Benét's prose tends to the rhythms of verse:

> Then suddenly the earth had begun to crumble.
> A wind blew, a bell sounded, and they were dispersed.
> There were shrunken old people, timorous and pettish,
> And a small, heart-stifling town.
> These and the grown-up children, more strange than strangers;
> But Hessian Street was over—the great tree was down.

As an antidote to this sweetness, I recommend the story called **"A Story by Angela Poe,"** which, though a little too long, has an agreeably astringent quality, and may have been partly suggested by an actual murder.

> *E. B. C. Jones, in a review of "Thirteen O'Clock," in* The Spectator, *Vol. 160, No. 5722, February 25, 1938, p. 332.*

Forum and Century   (essay date 1938)

[*In the following essay, the critic commends the folktale qualities of Benét's* Johnny Pye and the Fool-Killer.]

Stephen Vincent Benét's distinction . . . is in his ability to create characters that have the fundamental human qualities and the fixed destinies of people in a folk tale. His ***Johnny Pye and the Fool Killer*** reads as if it had come out of that folk America that so few know and that only a writer of consummate literary ability, like this author or Thornton Wilder in *Our Town,* can reveal—the America whose art was the sampler, whose verse was the tombstone rhyme, and whose recreations centered around the church socials, the village store, and the horse-and-buggy drive.

Johnny Pye and the Fool Killer is a story of life and death where the humor never becomes facetious and the fantasy never forced; it has a spareness like a New England landscape and the tang of a grape growing over a Connecticut fence. It is nothing but the story of an orphan boy, his life, his marriage, his few excitements—such as shaking hands with two presidents—his old age, and his end. But it is that rare thing in literature, a story that reads as if it were made not by a single writer but out of folk experience. The making of such a story calls for a combination of rare qualities, those that Oliver Goldsmith showed in *Goody Two-shoes,* fantasy and common sense, qualities only in a poet, a balance between a mystic wisdom and a common literalness, the use of usual words in a way that gives an aroma to the talk.

If a prize existed for the most characteristic American book of the year, it should be divided between Kay Boyle's *Monday Night* and Stephen Vincent Benét's *Johnny Pye and the Fool Killer,* for in both the American mind reveals itself as different from any other mind that has yet expressed itself in literature.

The praise that Stephen Vincent Benét's *Johnny Pye and the Fool Killer* is likely to receive should not be regarded as a challenge to American writers to go in earnestly for the production of "folk" literature. The American destiny in literature, it could be claimed, is more on the lines of the Henry Jameses, the Ernest Hemingways, and the Kay Boyles: in short, a line that is toward the internationalizing of literature. Anyhow, the self-conscious efforts at producing a "folk" literature that some contemporary American writers have dedicated themselves to has resulted in something that seems a synthetic concoction when compared with the folk literature of older countries. The American attempt, when self-conscious, has been only a phase in that interest in building up a past which has a parallel in colonial houses, blanket chests, shoemakers' benches, and corner cupboards. American "folk" literature is too often a confection, although minds like Stephen Vincent Benét's or Thornton Wilder's can produce it authentically. They have a real sense of the past and need not be misled by the idea that all literature has to be a revelation of the contemporary.

> *"Authentic Folk Imagination," in* Forum and Century, *Vol. C, No. 4, October, 1938, p. 167.*

Joseph Wood Krutch   (essay date 1942)

[*Krutch is one of America's most respected literary and drama critics. A conservative and idealistic thinker, he was a proponent of human dignity and the preeminence of literary art; his literary criticism is characterized by such concerns. In the following excerpt from a retrospective analysis, he assesses Benét's short stories that incorporate local color and folklore as his best work and pronounces them a distinctive contribution to American literature.*]

The best of Mr. Benét's work, or at least those of his pieces which most completely come off and reach nearest to perfection, are those short prose pieces collected [in *Selected Works of Stephen Vincent Benét*] under the general title "Stories of American History." They are not merely local color stories and they are not merely pieces of folklore, or at least they are not at all examples of that sort of writing, at once precious and condescending, which literary folklorists are most likely to produce. For one thing the stories are, I assume, mostly created rather than merely retold. What is more important they seem to me to achieve exactly the effect which they are intended to achieve; they take American scenes and American men out of the realm of mere history or mere folklore and naturalize them in the world of the imagination. Or to put it concretely, they make it evident that Daniel Webster has as much right as Dr. Faustus ever had to hold converse with the devil.

One volume of the [*Selected Works*] is devoted to prose tales of which by no means all are in the manner just described. Eight of them, called "Tales of Our Time," seem strangely out of place for they are mildly moralized stories of the jazz age, good enough and quite competent, but scarcely distinguishable from hundreds written by dozens of other writers. The seven classified as "Fantasies and Prophecies" range all the way from the, to me, rather obvious **"Doc Mellhorn and the Pearly Gates"** to **"The Last of the Legions,"** which is almost as good as the best of the American stories, and **"The King of the Cats,"** which is probably one of the three best stories about a feline ever written—the other two being Wodehouse's tale of the missionary-bishop's Tom who went Bohemian in Chelsea and the other Saki's breath-taking anecdote about the cat who was unfortunately taught to talk. But the best are certainly in the "Stories of American History," among which should be singled out not only **"The Devil and Daniel Webster,"** but also **"Jacob and the Indians,"** as well as the finest of them all, **"Johnny Pye and the Fool-Killer." "A Tooth for Paul Revere"** is just a shade too quaint; **"Freedom's a Hard-Bought Thing"** just a shade too consciously heroic.

Mr. Benét has written a considerable body of interesting prose and verse and he has succeeded in interesting a great many people in it. Is *John Brown's Body* the American epic, or at least the nearest thing to it so far? Is Mr. Benét genuinely inspired by the strong American muse whose diverse heart so many have tried to understand? How much has he done to make it clear not only that enough men have died here, but that their deaths are memorable?

The safest answer as well as probably the justest is to refuse any reply to questions put in such grandiose terms. But if, instead, one asks simply whether this is solid work and whether it uses American material in a way which is not only interesting but tending at the same time to make the American past more dignified, more meaningful and more comprehensible to the imagination, then the answer is unmistakably affirmative. Our contemporary literature and our national consciousness are both very much the better for Mr. Benét's *Selected Works.*

Joseph Wood Krutch, "Stephen V. Benet and the American Past," in New York Herald Tribune Books, *June 21, 1942, p. 1.*

R. L. Duffus (essay date 1943)

[*In the following excerpt, Duffus commends the insight, imagination, narrative skill, and timeless quality evident in Benét's best short stories, legends, and fantasy tales.*]

Even those who never set eyes on Stephen Vincent Benét must feel a pang of loss at the knowledge that there will be no more of the sort of prose that is in these stories, written at intervals between 1925 and 1939 and [collected in *Twenty-Five Short Stories by Stephen Vincent Benét*].

William Rose Benét said in 1941 (in an article that now appears as an introduction) that he had watched his brother "become a first-rate writing man, support a wife and three children, and at the same time save his soul." Unlike Jabez Stone, Steve Benét didn't have to call in Daniel Webster or any other high-priced lawyer to save his soul. He did it himself. The evidence is here. A man without a soul couldn't have written these stories.

The reading public, to be sure, may not worry much about a writer's soul. It may feel that something is wrong if he hasn't got one, but it will not buy his books merely for his soul's sake. A writer with a strong, honest soul may be dull, or deficient in a sense of structure, or lacking in humor, or unobservant, or not possessed of a sense of character, or indifferent to the sound and meaning of words. Steve Benét had none of these deficiencies. Whether he wrote in solid prose or in measured lines he was a poet. He had the kind of imagination that sees meaning in things that most people pass over and relations between things that to most of us do not seem to be related.

He was a born story-teller, with the power to make strange events seem natural (see **"The King of the Cats"**) and natural events (mark the slow building up of terror out of the commonplace in **"A Story by Angela Poe"**) seem strange. He could create a legend that one might think would require a lot of people and several generations—witness the famous tale of **"The Devil and Daniel Webster"** and **"The Sobbin' Women."** And he had a style with a strong, masculine cadence to it, as though it were made to be read aloud.

He worked some veins that produced little gold. **"Daniel Webster and the Sea Serpent"** may have been written because so many people liked the other Daniel Webster story. It creaks with the author's inventive effort. One usually believes Mr. Benét, but this time one doesn't. There is a personal devil; an orchestral conductor may have a tail like a cat and even conduct with it; New York City may well become a Dead Place and a Place of the Gods; no doubt there are leprechauns, such as the one Tim O'Halloran found in the prairie, that had come to America "just for the love of Clonmelly folk"—but there isn't and never was, any sea serpent named Samanthy.

But this slip points up the fact that one usually does believe Steve Benét. What he says goes—and it goes especially well at that most trying hour for any writer and any book, when one reads in bed and the dull and improbable are slung across the room with a bang.

There are stories here that nobody but Steve Benét could have done, and stories that a number of other people might have done. For a time Mr. Benét seems to have been disturbed by persons who drank too much, talked too much and didn't get on with their wives or husbands. This must have been chiefly in the late Nineteen Twenties. In **"Everybody Was Very Nice"** a man who didn't really want to was bullied by the customs of the time into switching wives. In **"A Life at Angelo's"** a man sits drinking a couple of little ones before dinner, some wine at dinner, a little touch after the coffee and a couple of long ones and a nightcap before going home; he thinks he is "being modern," and perhaps, as of that date, he is. In **"Schooner Fairchild's Class"** the successful graduate wonders if the man who never cared much for money and couldn't take stocks and bonds seriously but can do imitations on the piano hadn't really had the best of it. Mr. Benét did things like this excellently. Still, other writers could have done them.

What other writers couldn't do, at least in a comparable way, was to get inside of the consciousness of Professor Malzius, who is about to be shot because he doesn't care to betray the young men who trusted him; or to build up the strange fantasy of the Napoleon Buonaparte, who died, a frustrated man, at St. Philippe-des-Bains on May 5, 1789; or think up the Pontipees and their Sabine wives; or catch the pathos of the broken dream in **"Glamour"** and **"Too Early Spring"**; or suggest a more robust Hawthorne in **"Johnny Pye"** and **"Jacob and the Indians."**

The resemblance to Hawthorne is not accidental. There is a kind of timelessness about the Benét legends. Steve Benét loved his country with a rich and creative affection. He didn't wish it to be commonplace and mean. He wanted the goings and comings of men, their loyalties and betrayals, their struggles for power and love to have significance. He wrote of Daniel Webster's plea to the infernal jury:

> There was sadness in being a man, but it was a proud thing, too. . . . And he wasn't pleading for any one person any more, though his voice rang like an organ. He was telling the story and the failures and the endless journey of mankind. They got tricked and trapped and bamboozled, but it was a great journey.

This was what Steve Benét seemed mostly to want to get said. He was nowhere near finished with it when he died, not even with the last lines he wrote.

R. L. Duffus, "A Benét Anthology, and Three Novels," in The New York Times, *November 28, 1943, p. 6.*

Charles A. Fenton (essay date 1958)

[*Fenton's* Stephen Vincent Benét: The Life and Times of an American Man of Letters, 1898-1943, *is a chronologically arranged, anecdotal critical biography. In the following excerpt from that work, he provides an overview of Benét's career as a short story writer.*]

An excerpt from *"The Devil and Daniel Webster"*

Yes, Dan'l Webster's dead—or, at least, they buried him. But every time there's a thunderstorm around Marshfield, they say you can hear his rolling voice in the hollows of the sky. And they say that if you go to his grave and speak loud and clear, "Dan'l Webster—Dan'l Webster!" the ground'll begin to shiver and the trees begin to shake. And after a while you'll hear a deep voice saying, "Neighbor, how stands the Union?" Then you better answer the Union stands as she stood, rock-bottomed and copper-sheathed, one and indivisible, or he's liable to rear right out of the ground. At least, that's what I was told when I was a youngster.

You see, for a while, he was the biggest man in the country. He never got to be President, but he was the biggest man. There were thousands that trusted in him right next to God Almighty, and they told stories about him that were like the stories of patriarchs and such. They said, when he stood up to speak, stars and stripes came right out in the sky, and once he spoke against a river and made it sink into the ground. They said, when he walked the woods with his fishing rod, Killall, the trout would jump out of the streams right into his pockets, for they knew it was no use putting up a fight against him; and, when he argued a case, he could turn on the harps of the blessed and the shaking of the earth underground. That was the kind of man he was, and his big farm up at Marshfield was suitable to him. The chickens he raised were all white meat down through the drumsticks, the cows were tended like children, and the big ram he called Goliath had horns with a curl like a morning-glory vine and could butt through an iron door. But Dan'l wasn't one of your gentlemen farmers; he knew all the ways of the land, and he'd be up by candlelight to see that the chores got done. A man with a mouth like a mastiff, a brow like a mountain and eyes like burning anthracite—that was Dan'l Webster in his prime. And the biggest case he argued never got written down in the books, for he argued it against the devil, nip and tuck and no holds barred.

Stephen Vincent Benét, in his Thirteen O'Clock: Stories of Several Worlds, *Farrar & Rinehart, 1937.*

[Early in his career, Benét's literary agent Carl Brandt] assured him that he would earn between five thousand and seventy-five hundred dollars during the coming year. All he had to do was [write] . . . short stories. It sounded easy but Benét already knew different. "The short story," he confessed to [his wife] Rosemary, "was never exactly my forte." He was an instinctive poet, knowing and possessing the form since childhood, relishing its richness of scope, fascinated always by its technical abundance and problems. He had to discipline himself to the short story.

"Finished another short story today," he told Rosemary in September 1921, "a very short one, thank God, only 4000 words. I tried to copy Millay-Boyd in it and rather produced the effect of an elephant trying to walk the tightrope—I am not at my best in the flippant sentimental." Even now, in mid-1922, his work sought after by editors,

he made discouraging false starts in some instances and in other cases he laboriously finished stories that proved thoroughly unsalable.

"I am writing a silly story for the Cosmo," he told Rosemary in June 1922, "about a doctor who created a lady out of dirt. I do not think much of it, but it may bring us GOLD." He sketched a heaping mound of moneybags on the margin of the letter, but the story brought not gold but rejection. Brandt phoned the next day, Benét told his wife, "& said he didn't like my 'Dr. Faustus' at *all*." But it took as long to write a silly story as a good one. Even the good ones were by no means automatic sales. His Cabell-like parable, **"The Barefoot Saint,"** had traveled from desk to desk. "Carl has for the nineteenth time nearly sold it," Benét wrote his wife, "this time to Frank of the *Century,* but don't breathe or it will probably pop open again. That tale has worn more editorial praise and less cash than anything I ever did."

Benét's problem, as with most magazine writers, was always plot. He had an inventive and ingenious mind, but the demands he was making on it were large. More and more, as he had done unsuccessfully with the Faust legend, he began to improvise the central situation from his vast reading. He blended the Restoration period and classical mythology into a tale called **"The Golden Bessie,"** about the seventeenth-century daughter of a miser, who was dipped—nearly—in gold paint, and he returned to his favorite Spanish Main for a first-class story, **"Snake and Hawk,"** which N. C. Wyeth illustrated for the *Ladies' Home Journal.* In another story he freshened a conventional love story by reviving the legend that lovers once prayed before the Venus de Medici. In some cases Brandt relayed to him the specific needs of a certain editor.

"C. wants a love-story—modern," he told Rosemary in July. "Says Ray Long is howling for them." Again Benét renovated a timeless legend, this one the tale of the maiden who bade her three suitors compete for her hand by act of prowess. The trivial plot was redeemed by freshness of style, some effective comment on the American rich, and intriguing incidents. The story did not appeal to Long after all, however; it finally went to *Redbook* instead of *Cosmopolitan.* The blurb made recognition of Benét's growing status, describing him as "an author whom people are talking a lot about these days."

Cosmopolitan did, however, buy several of his stories during this period. Ray Long was at the height of his success, commanding with enormous prices the most proficient magazine writers of England and America. He featured Benét's ingenious and melodramatic **"Elementals"** in the April 1922 issue; Benét received a number of letters from rather simple-minded readers who wanted to put themselves to the same elaborate test he had devised for his fictional lovers. Long was generally indifferent, however, to the kind of fresh, occasionally satiric characterizations which continually and exasperatingly thrust their way into Benét's short stories.

"She considered him," Benét wrote that summer of one of his heroines. "He Faced Facts so firmly. An enemy might have said that those facts lay always somehow on the fringes of sex and that he had not only Faced them continually but even dragged them out when nobody else would have found them there to Face—a slick, blond collie never weary of exhuming the same disreputable bone." It had a prose vitality which compensated for the winded plot, but it had to be sold to the poorer-paying *Harper's Bazaar.* Benét did his best to harness these troublesome instincts.

"This damn man in my story is strapped on an operating table," he wrote Rosemary. "I must leap and either save or kill him. I'd much prefer the latter, but I'm afraid he's worth more money living than dead." Brandt had become thoroughly aware of his client's wayward humors. He reversed the earlier prescription, now advising Benét to postpone any new serial for the time being and stick to short stories; their comparative brevity would allow him less room for license. (pp. 123-25)

Most of the short stories he wrote in 1923 and 1924 were mechanical and superficial; the freshness that had disguised **"The Golden Bessie"** and **"Snake and Hawk"** was lost to the trivialities of the synthetically sophisticated. *Redbook* became the principal market for the least commonplace of his stories. The rest trickled down to such less demanding magazines as *Metropolitan* and *Liberty.*

As his work became increasingly stereotyped, his editorial value rose, from $200 a story to $250, to $400, now to $500. Only once during those eighteen months was he able to cheat a meaningful story from the formula. **"Uriah's Son,"** published in the May 1924 issue of *Redbook,* was an effective piece of work. It was an indulgence, however, and Benét even doubted that it would sell. "I've just finished a story that you won't care to publish," he told the *Redbook* editor, "for it's not my usual sort."

To his surprise they bought it immediately. It was a reminder that it was not the taste of magazine editors but the natural inability of writers to constantly freshen the formula which accounted for the drabness of the popular magazines. **"Uriah's Son"** was included in the O. Henry Memorial Award volume that year, the first of a number of such awards to his magazine fiction. He was gradually taking his place with such craftsmen of the genre as Wilbur Daniel Steele, Booth Tarkington, and Richard Connell. (pp. 133-34)

[In 1925 Benét told his agent] that he wanted to write some stories he could be interested in. "I've got to have some fun doing these things," he told Brandt. If he were going to do modern stories, they had to have something more than just sentiment. He didn't propose to violate the various taboos, but what he wanted to work with, Benét said, was material that would be outside the conventional situations. He didn't know exactly what they'd be; he knew what they wouldn't be.

"Why not," said Brandt, who by now had considerable confidence in Benét's capacity and persistence. "The love stories aren't selling, and you're sick of writing them anyway. Why not. Let's try it."

Benét put aside the contrived romances of office girls and Long Island heiresses, and the mannered toughness of Manhattan sophistication. He wrote during the late winter of 1925 and the first four months of 1926 a group of short stories in a new mood and idiom. He abandoned the flippancy on which he had made most of his magazine reputation. He turned back, in much of the work he did during these months, to the American past, to the towns he had known as the nomadic child of an army family, and to those earlier periods he had possessed through his reading and his imagination. He began to give to his stories, freed from the jargon of the falsely contemporary, some of the poetic prose which fifteen years later became his singular voice in magazine fiction.

"He was the only one of us," John Marquand said many years later, "who could write a story for the *Saturday Evening Post* and make it read like literature."

Benét's objective with these 1925 and 1926 stories, though he did not thoroughly clarify his intentions, even privately, for several years, was no less a mission than to break to his individual talent the mold of American mass audience fiction. "We have our own folk-gods and giants and figures of earth in this country," Benét said once. "I wanted to write something about them."

Two ingredients were essential if Benét was to reproduce in marketable prose the success he'd already had with some of his verse. He must work with the American past, which would permit him nostalgic evocation as well as the display of his moving convictions about the national character. He must also—even more difficult—somehow inject into commercial fiction the fantasy so important to what was best in his poetic imagination.

The short story was never exactly my forte.

—*Stephen Vincent Benét*

It was not an easy assignment. The renaissance in American letters which was then occurring—primarily in Europe, but with important native and New York aspects— had no connections with the large circulation magazines. The bulk of the thoroughly mechanical material which was later siphoned off into radio soap opera, or its successor the TV situation comedy, was in 1925 and 1926 the fixed diet of the big slicks and their lesser competitors. There is an air of outrage and disbelief in those introductions which Edward O'Brien wrote during the 1920's for his annual collections of the best American short stories. O'Brien's target was always the popular journals. What O'Brien had been unable to effect through persistent attempts to establish higher standards, Benét was undertaking as a single, vulnerable, commercial writer.

The first indication of his restless experiment emerged in a *Collier's* story, in late January 1926. The story was called **"The Odor of Sanctity."** As was natural at the beginning of a complex revision, the story was little more than a sketch, a kind of uneasy scenario of what was to follow. Only two thousand words long—a structure thoroughly uncharacteristic of his work either then or later—it was closer to fable or essay than genuine narrative. It ended with a clumsy final paragraph in which Benét sought the fantasy he was anxious to introduce into his fiction. The sketch as a whole was damaged by conflicting strains of satire and bathos. The protagonist was a caricature; he couldn't possibly serve as the folk hero whom Benét had to create if the elements of reality and fantasy were to be effectively joined.

He had, nevertheless, attempted the fantasy. He had taken a tentative step into the post-Civil War America of small towns and national serenity. Gradually he began to get his footing. The May 1926 issues of two very different magazines carried stories in Benét's new, still partially blurred voice. Brandt, whose efforts for Benét consistently went beyond his 10 per cent reward, had with prophetic insight placed one of the stories with *Country Gentleman.* Benét's first sale to what was in effect the rural edition of the *Saturday Evening Post,* with a circulation of one and a half million, was an important step.

The association did more than raise Benét's story price and bring him into the outer orbit of the *Post.* It gave him an audience and editorial staff which were more friendly to his new treatments than the subscribers and editors of, say, *Cosmopolitan* and *Redbook.* Two of the magazine's young associate editors in particular were immediately responsive to Benét's work. Ben Hibbs and Robert Reed later became senior editors in the Curtis hierarchy, Hibbs as editor of the *Post,* Reed of *Country Gentleman.* Hibbs, according to Brandt, was in 1926 "like Benét in having an eagle on his shoulder."

Brandt's labors were even more vividly dramatized by the nature of the second magazine in which he placed Benét's other May story. Unable to dispose of **"The Shadowy Crown"** to any of his regular buyers, but mindful that Benét ought to be encouraged at this point, Brandt refused to give up on the story. He sold it—in certain respects at a distinct loss to himself—to the *Elks' Magazine.* Here again, though in this case the magazine was of little consequence, and its national circulation small, the audience would be a sympathetic one. If worse came to worst, the *Elks' Magazine* could also be counted on for further sales during this difficult transition period.

"The Shadowy Crown," like **"The Odor of Sanctity,"** was another piece of retrospection. Benét, discarding the awkward, omniscient point of view, used the town doctor as narrator. This gave him an opportunity for literate comment on the characters and situation, and for intimate knowledge of the town's habits and values. That the form was resolving itself was shown by Benét's introduction of a specific name for the town, a name he retained in subsequent stories. He called the town Freestone. The name was symptomatic of what he was seeking. It included in its source-words both liberty and permanence. It also permitted his ironic examination of the reverse of these qualities as exhibited in the semi-rural America of a generation earlier.

The story itself, with its theme of the exceptional individual in an unexceptional environment, was a fresh one. Benét, on the other hand, had not yet mastered the problem of a situation for his material. **"The Shadowy Crown"** had a bookish quality, an inevitable excess of the literary as he ducked away from the stereotypes of magazine plots. Some of the dialogue was overquaint—what Benét later condemned in another of his stories as "too damn itsy-bitsy"—and he had to resort to desperate breaks in the time sequence to squeeze out the necessary wordage.

Country Gentleman, on the other hand, very definitely had the best of the May bargain. **"The Sobbin' Women"** was the first of these new stories in which Benét demonstrated consistent grace and confidence. The story represented the completion of tentative experiment. Benét would write better stories than **"The Sobbin' Women"**—and many, from necessity or weariness or haste, that were inferior to it—but this one would never shame its superiors. Years later both Hibbs and Reed remembered the story distinctly, even recalling it as the first they bought from Benét. "I wish," said Reed in 1954, "we could have paid him what it was worth." **"The Sobbin' Women,"** above all, inaugurated a satisfactory solution to the troublesome problem of a narrator. Benét created what he called a "frame"— the story was told by a village sage whom the author termed the Oldest Inhabitant—and he preserved this frame for some time in his later stories of nineteenth-century America.

There was a clarity of story line and a localized stability that had been missing in **"The Shadowy Crown."** The bookish quality remained—the legend of the Sabine women, after all, was a Roman one—but the nature of the heroine and the circumstances of local terrain made this credible. The types whom Benét would use with vigorous national pride emerged for the first time. Here were the bound girl, the hedge parson, the fabulous pioneer. The folk-hero quality was developing, blurred because it was shared by seven brothers, but nevertheless taking shape.

Benét was sufficiently at ease now—and sufficiently liberated from the vulgarity of magazine wit—so that his own sly, tart humor began to flow into the material. It was as if **"The Sobbin' Women"** had fully released the flow of fresh prose that had been inhibited by an act of will since 1921. His plots were still the ones that would meet the rigorous requirements of editorial buyers. Boy still met girl, and eventually boy would get girl, but in the five to ten thousand words that lay between these two unalterable events Benét continued to unbend his style and strengthen his narrator.

"They say growing up in a small place makes for a limited view of things in general," said the Oldest Inhabitant in **"The Lucky Fist,"** published in *Collier's* in late June 1926. "Maybe so, but it seems to me that where you haven't so many things to look at you're apt to get more juice out of what you do see." As the title indicated, Benét was exploring in this story what would become one of his favorite themes. He wrote of Luck and its nature with vivid force.

> Ham's fist was something to look at. It was big and blunt and strong, but there was more to it than that—a sort of driving force like the force

you imagine in the head of a hammer combined
with a curious quality that was almost grace.
The little red-blond hairs on the back of it shone
in the light as he flexed the fingers slowly and
shut them up again in a hard stone clump . . .
For an instant, in the shimmer of the lamp as I
watched it, it seemed to change to something incredible and a little dreadful, a lump, a hard,
shining ball of solid, actual gold.

As had happened in all the earlier stories, here too, in
"The Lucky Fist," Benét showed that he was still marked
by the five years of servitude to standard plot and one-
dimensional character. The symbol of the lucky fist was
almost submerged in the maneuvers of boy separated from
girl. The necessities of fast-moving narrative corrupted
similarly his second *Country Gentleman* story, **"Miss Willie Lou and the Swan,"** but there were glimpses of his informed sense of the period.

[They] came from England . . . and settled in
Virginia a while. But then they got the itch to be
movin' west—and when families moved then
they moved like the children of Israel. The
Faithfuls took cuttin's from their garden and
wines from their cellar and barrels of leather-
bound books. They brought their slaves and
huntin' dogs and their blood horses . . . to that
wild, raw border country, and they settled down
to make a place that'd be the spittin' image of the
place they'd left in Virginia . . .

This had been Benét's most productive period since the
first weeks he spent on *Spanish Bayonet* in the spring of
1925. He had written almost a dozen short stories; one,
"The Sobbin' Women," was the best work he had yet done
in the medium. Four of the stories were cited in both the
O'Brien and O. Henry annual rolls of honor. In this mood
of speculation—his hopes riding, after all, on a small foundation grant intended to underwrite a project as unlikely
of success as an epic poem—Benét attempted a story that
was recklessly counter to a basic prohibition of the editorial mystique. He used a biblical situation in which one of
the disciples was the hero and Christ a subsidiary character.

"Eleven leaderless men," he began the story **"True Thomas"** in the April *Good Housekeeping,* "without wealth or
rank or power, who had followed a carpenter and now
found themselves, since his death, suddenly set at war
with the greatest and most able civilization in the world."

Benét was beginning to give his talent for fiction its first
real airing. He had the storyteller's traditional power, in
the overworked but meaningful phrase, of bringing the
past to life, of vivifying a commonly held legend. "So
Judas was dead already. And He was dead. Utter good
and utter evil had finished together and left only human
flesh to take up the burden that had broken a god." The
ultimate theme of the story was characteristic of Benét's
profound confidence in mankind.

"He is God—He is very God!" cried James in an
ecstasy.

"He is man," said Thomas to himself. "Thank
God, He could be man as well."

But, loving the others suddenly, he did not say
it so they could hear.

It was an extraordinary performance for a writer who six
months earlier had seemed creatively spent and perhaps
fit for no more than a long period of literary journalism.
The O. Henry judges placed **"True Thomas"** among those
American stories of 1926 "ranking highest." O'Brien gave
it his three asterisks of distinction. (pp. 168-76)

The success of such stories as **"The Sobbin' Women"** and
"True Thomas," not only in terms of his own satisfaction
with them but also as promises of further editorial acceptance, did not reconcile Benét to magazine fiction.
Throughout his career he objected to the extremes of editorial perversity which during his lifetime controlled the
American short story. "I think [Edward O'Brien] is just
as prejudiced in favor of the formula formless story,"
Benét said later, "as the big-magazine-editor of 1925 was
prejudiced against it." Brandt, he knew, found it much
harder to sell these less conventional situations. He himself chafed that they took so much longer to write than the
more trivial ones. (p. 176)

. . . . .

[Benét] spent most of the late fall of 1927 . . . on several
new short stories, "for a little of that cash," he told his
brother, "that we all of us need." . . . Benét picked up as
if without interruption the narrative frame of the Oldest
Inhabitant, which he had last used eighteen months before, and the material of American history. Brandt sold
the first new story to *Country Gentleman* almost as soon
as it reached New York. Hibbs and Reed were delighted
to get **"The Fool-Killer,"** postponing a scheduled story to
make room for it in the November issue. The story contained more stretches of effective prose than even **"The
Sobbin' Women"** or **"True Thomas."** It was crammed—
over-crammed, in fact—with passages that confirmed
Benét's absorption in native American types. Still writing
in the loose, full style of *John Brown's Body,* he virtually
overpowered the story with the abundance of his exposition and reflection. But there were neat lines of satire, and
a realistic evocation of the period. "It was a bad time for
fools and wildcats, and a good time for huskin' bees and
pride in the land you'd cleared. And the men and women,
for the most part, was hearty and strong and fool-
despisin', like the time."

Lem Burdick, the fool-killer, was a part of Benét's creative
extension of American folklore, a variation of Bunyan and
Fink and Davy Crockett. Peter Vane, the story's hero-
inventor, was similarly related to the Lincolnesque legend.
Benét was again freshening the standard components of
historical fiction. "He'd had two wives in his time," says
the Oldest Inhabitant of the fool-killer, "but wives didn't
last long with him, though he took good care of his stock."
(pp. 195-96)

[In **"The Lucksmith"**] Benét explored the intangibility
which was permitting him a degree of fantasy in his magazine fiction.

"Luck's like gold," said the Oldest Inhabitant
dreamily. "It's where you find it. And it's like
gold another way too. One man'll walk over a

piece of lucky ground and never so much as pick up an old safety-razor blade. And another'll go to sleep there, some dark night, and when he wakes up in the mornin' he's turned into John D. Rockefeller. Yes, luck's a curious thing."

In **"The Giant's House,"** on the other hand, his memories of Army garrisons still stirred by the work on the long poem, Benét created his situation from the traditions of Ordinance and gun-making. He gave the narrative additional strength by his imaginative use of a young boy's memories. "The world grows smaller as you grow up in the world. Mind and all that—but the mere matter of height has something to do with it. That's one reason children are apt to be fond of small people—and why stories like 'Jack the Giant Killer' have lasted so. Because children actually do live in a giant's house—a house not built for them. And the giants may be friendly or unfriendly—but a certain gulf remains."

All three were good stories, their quality again verified by the various asterisks and citations of the O'Brien and O. Henry rolls of honor. They would provide a few months' income to replace the Guggenheim quarterly check. Brandt also wrote him that **"Bon Voyage,"** one of the worst of the stories he had done in the spring of 1925, had finally been sold to *College Humor.* Benét himself was still not fully comfortable with the form, preferring, so long as he had to write prose, the more fluid structure of the novel, and hopeful always of the secondary profits of serialization. (pp. 196-97)

[Throughout late spring and early summer of 1928 Benét] produced seven stories that were all immediately marketable. One of them—**"The Story about the Anteater"**—was a moving account of a happy marriage which represented not only therapy but testimonial. (p. 202)

From unused fragments of his *John Brown's Body* research he . . . composed two short stories with the Reconstruction as their setting. "Let me recall as I can," the narrator of **"Candleshine"** begins, "that old, drowned South of my youth, where I was born and ran wild as a rabbit in a lost brier-patch. It was a strange place and strange time, that South of the first decades after the Civil War. A time of bitter memories . . . "

He even managed from this same block of material the vexing editorial delight of a seasonal story. **"Green Christmas"** had as its theme, in the holiday season of 1877, Benét's profound convictions about the Union. "Yes, we followed the state," says a former Confederate major who had served with Wade Hampton. "But we must all live under one roof now—the best man we ever had said so." Benét was particularly pleased by the sale of **"Green Christmas"** to the *Ladies' Home Journal,* for it raised his story price to a new high of $700. Brandt sold the *Journal* two other stories, both contemporary trivialities which Benét provided as ballast for the historical material.

The last story he did in mid-1928 was a compromise between these two areas of his magazine fiction. **"Two White Beans,"** in part as a consequence of the attempted compromise, was poorly constructed, its narrative awkwardly broken between an effective account of Caribbean filibus-

tering and the small town to which one of the survivors escaped. The reader was jerked from one character to another—each of them well drawn—so that his interest was scattered without control. The vivid portraiture and the topical quality—this was a decade, after all, which seemed always to have Marines in Nicaragua—made it nevertheless acceptable to *Country Gentleman,* partial as they were to the freshness and vigor of Benét's work. (pp. 203-04)

. . . . .

In April [of 1930 Benét] finished the first short story he had written in more than a year. **"American Honeymoon"** was a crisp, satiric portrait of contemporary manners; Benét was not surprised when it was rejected by the circulation magazines. . . . He set to work on material and situations which he hoped he could keep within the taboos.

"Here's some light summer reading for the chewing-gum trade," he told Brandt in June 1931, enclosing a new story. "Try and get it swallowed by some large editor."

It was a bitter period, as his tone indicated, for it meant a return to the fictional trivialities he had fled five years before. Such stories were now all the more distasteful to manufacture because in the interval he had enjoyed the eighteen-month security of the Guggenheim Fellowship, the creative satisfaction of *John Brown's Body,* and the brief financial prosperity of 1929 and 1930. "I have cut about 800 words of this story," he wrote Brandt in December 1931, about a story which had been questioned by an editor, "and that is all I can or will do. If Hartman isn't satisfied with that, tell him to send it back. There has to be a certain development and progression in fiction whether editors like it or not. The last story they almost took, they thought was too short. In fact, they're all crazy."

His bitterness was apparent even in the most stereotyped of his fiction itself. "Nobody ever looked unhappy in snapshots," reflected the central figure of his **"Days of Sunshine,"** which Maclean's published in January 1932, "nobody ever looked regretful. The people were always about to do something interesting." One of the stories he wrote during the summer of 1931, **"The Crime of Professor Sandwich,"** Brandt was unable to sell anywhere; another, **"A Death in the Country,"** made all the familiar editorial stops before finally being sold to *Harper's.* It was one of the best stories he had yet written, a moving and adult account of growth through pain, and *Harper's* paid it the editorial compliment of printing it immediately, ahead of material that had been bought earlier, but it became a symbol to Brandt and Benét of the hazards of writing fiction that was too good for the market.

"I am busy," he kidded Brandt, at a time when the agent was urging him to come up with something salable, "on my plans for turning **'A Death in the Country'** into a five-act drama in blank verse to be produced by the Associated Morticians of America."

Benét was nevertheless a thoroughly professional writer. He did not often produce work that was unmarketable or limited to the quality magazines. The rest of the stories which he wrote during . . . 1931 and 1932 were harshly tailored for the trade; they were sold readily to *Pictorial*

Review, the *American Magazine,* the *Saturday Evening Post*— his first sale there—and *Delineator.* "Here is a story," he wrote Brandt, enclosing a new one, "with, at least, a worthy moral." (pp. 244-46)

He spent the late spring and all of the summer of 1932 on a short story which turned into a novelette. As always his problem was the disorder which invariably developed whenever his imagination was aroused by a situation originally designed to be formula fiction.

"This is merely to let you know that I am not dead," he wrote Brandt in a brief note in July, "and have been working on the long story. It's taken more time than I expected for I rewrote the second section completely and, I think, improved it a good deal. I think I have something, if I can get it the way I want, and do it right. At least I feel I want to more or less shoot the moon with it, and that takes time. I'm in the third section now. It will certainly run 30,000 words, maybe 40,000. If I could, I'd get it about the size of Willa Cather's *The Professor's House.* But I don't know whether that will be feasible."

The note betrayed the pressures under which he worked. There could never be any true structural or thematic compatibility between a conception that was part magazine serial and part something as sensitive as *The Professor's House.* "It was a pleasant and healthy summer," he told Bob McClure in October, "though I have had more trouble with this stinking novelette than I've ever had in my life. I now think I've done it from the wrong point of view and ought to do it over again from another, which is always a help when you've written The End and sighed. The trouble with it is that one character in it is too good to throw away, and so are some of the scenes, but the whole thing isn't baked right. Writing is sometimes as enjoyable as prickly heat."

He had to break his concentration repeatedly in order to write something immediately salable. "Here's a vapid little short story you might be able to work off," he told Brandt. "I have been trying to work [the] long one but it hasn't quite jelled." It never did jell; four months of hard work was gone, with very little money earned during that period and none to come in later as its fruit. (pp. 247-49)

He went back to the American material, and he was particularly pleased with **"The Yankee Fox,"** which he finished in December 1931. It was turned down not only by *Country Gentleman* but also by the regular buyers of his contemporary stories. Again he talked his situation over with Carl Brandt.

"I should like you to think over the possibility of getting a new market for this variety of story," he wrote the agent. "It is much more my kind of story than a story like **'Serenade,'** and, if it were possible to make some sort of profitable connection, I could do a series on the line of an American *Puck of Pook's Hill*—though hardly, as you will agree, with the same ability. Nevertheless, it seems to me that a series of rather simple, romantic stories, American in background, with a certain fairytale quality might have a chance of appealing to the larger market in this particular time, when nobody very much wants to read about the depression any more. Would the *Post,* with its new colorwork, be interested in such a series?"

Brandt, as always, was tireless in his efforts, but 1932 came and went without any editorial response to the idea. (pp. 249-50)

The short stories that [Benét] valued continued to receive awards and honors in the annual O. Henry and O'Brien selections, but, as he told Brandt, "I usually have to pay the rent about the time somebody gives me a medal or a testimonial." (p. 250)

. . . . .

Gradually things began to get better. Just as 1932 had seemed to close out one period for himself and the nation, so 1933 was slowly launching a new one. (p. 253)

The change was signaled in a small way by the sale of an Oldest Inhabitant story to *Pictorial Review.* **"Young Lochinvar"** was not one of the best of his American tales, but it was a gay and lively sketch of the meeting between the Oldest Inhabitant and aviation. He was even more encouraged when **"The Yankee Fox,"** the excellent story he had written in December 1931, was finally bought by *Woman's Home Companion* and published in June. The *Saturday Evening Post* had brooded long over **"The Yankee Fox,"** and Benét amiably made several changes for them before legitimately snarling a bit when they finally turned it down.

"The other comment," he wrote Brandt when the latter passed the *Post*'s note on to him, "seems to me a little foolish. I have already specifically stated that it was the sort of country where people went out with their hounds whatever errand they happened to be doing. Naturally they'd take the hounds with them, when they went on a lynching-party. And, in this case, they'd certainly take them not because they didn't know where the hero was—but specifically to humiliate him by chasing him out of his house with the descendants of the hounds his grandfather had brought from England. Hasn't anybody on the *Post* ever seen a Southern possum hunt or a Southern mob? What a lot they've missed."

It was heartening to have the story sold, however, and in the summer of 1933 the *Post* did buy his new **"The Bagpipes of Spring."** This was a contemporary story of Park Avenue, better than the worst of his magazine fiction but not comparable to the American material. Even here the *Post* was skittish. Brandt urged Benét to keep his temper with them; it would be worth it, the agent reminded him, to get established there. "Thanks for your nice letter," Benét wrote back from Peace Dale, "and also for the good news about **'The Bagpipes of Spring.'** Why does the *Post* always fuss about prices so—however, you're perfectly right and I'll be glad to have the money. Can you get it for me as soon as possible as I have to pay the rent."

He finished an article for *Fortune* on the United Press, though now he had to row with Ralph Ingersoll, the managing editor, when the latter seemed to be fiddling a research assistant out of his pay. Two other new stories were sold to the *Delineator.* . . . He was heartened by the President's inaugural address, his earlier mistrust of Roosevelt

Benét and his publishers, John Farrar and Stanley Rinehart, examine the 24 October 1936 publication of "The Devil and Daniel Webster" in the Saturday Evening Post.

lessened now like that of most American liberals. (pp. 253-55)

. . . . .

The state of the nation became more and more [Benét's] primary concern. "Try to write after dinner," he noted in his diary, "but waste time in idle thought about political situation instead." What he hoped for, and this was the appeal for him of the New Deal, was simply an America of more genuine opportunity. (p. 282)

Now, too, his short stories had additional comment on the current political and social scene. For the first time he began to give to his stories of the American past a sustained contemporary relevance.

He wrote, in **"A Man from Fort Necessity,"** a good story about the young Washington. It was published in the *Saturday Evening Post.* The parallel between the hatred of Roosevelt and Washington was apparent. "You can say that he wants to make himself a king or a dictator, if you like," says the innkeeper who had served with Washington in the French and Indian Wars. "Every man to his own brand of politics. But you'll have to say it outside; not in my house. He's a man that likes his way; yes, I'll grant you that. I don't give a shinplaster for a man that don't, myself; other people may be otherwise minded. But as for that New York newsletter and what it says about him, you can put that right back in your pocket while you're drinking my liquor."

In the spring of 1935, his mind preoccupied with the native fascism of Huey Long, Benét wrote an even more detailed parable for the times. In **"Silver Jemmy"** he drew the parallel between Jefferson and Aaron Burr on the one hand and Roosevelt and Long on the other. The contemporary implications were harsh and telling. "He talked to me for some time," says the New Orleans aristocrat after an audience with Jefferson, "of his belief in 'the common man' and 'democracy'—beliefs which we know to be both subversive and impossible of realization . . . his influence is rapidly waning and his doctrine of 'the common man' has roused much resentment among the better educated. It seems likely that he will be the last President of this present confederation—and that the nation will then either fall apart of its own weight or give rise to some dictator."

These were the months, after all, in which the Liberty League was born; these were months in which some of the hostility toward Roosevelt, and particularly among the class of whom Benét saw so much socially, became pathological. Many Americans in 1935 were questioning the utility of a democracy, weighing various alternatives. One of his friends announced emphatically that she would move to England—she didn't—if Roosevelt won in 1936. Benét listened to the tirades at Manhattan dinners and on Rhode Island beaches. Now, in **"Silver Jemmy,"** he translated them into an historical perspective.

"It is the first time *you* have known them," the old creole tells his son, "the cries and the wild voices, the prophets of calamity. And yet they come not once in the life of a nation but many times. Your sons in their turn will know them, and their sons also."

Cosmopolitan, which eventually bought the story and finally published it in May 1936, was fearful of its theme and tone. They argued first that it needed more romance and a lighter touch. Benét made cheerful concessions to their anxiety about the love interest, but he refused to tamper with its basic statement. When a *Cosmopolitan* editor protested to Brandt that the story was too intellectual, Benét became thoroughly exasperated.

"If patriotism is intellectual," Benét wrote his agent, "so is the banking system—and Father Coughlin can fill Madison Square Garden by talking about the banking system, not about cuties. In other words, this happens to be a time when people are interested in things which might have been considered intellectual in '28. And any editor with brains can tie this story into the present with a ten word blurb. Doesn't the Cosmo think that a few men might like to read the magazine once in a while? This is a man's story, as I see it—but I'm damned if I think that's a defect, in principle."

The editorial timidity was chronic; it was not confined to *Cosmopolitan.* The *Saturday Evening Post* bought his notable antitotalitarian story, **"The Blood of the Martyrs,"** but Benét was irritated by their attempts to soften its indictment. "Illustrator has done his best," he noted, "to portray all possible European types & thus avoid damages." Wesley Stout, successor to George Lorimer as editor of the *Post,* aroused Benét in memorable fashion when he objected to the opening paragraphs of **"Schooner Fairchild's Class."** Stout's prose, as he denounced Benét's characterization of the story's central character in a letter to Brandt, was more oratorical than editorial.

Benét, Stout told Brandt, had created in Lane Parrington "not an individual but a stuffed shirt, an effigy of the conservative cause. It is a tract worthy of the immaculately conceived Harry Hopkins. I care not how ridiculous he may make his Parrington, as long as he does not offer him as a symbol of the blasphemy of opposing those selfless, consecrated knights of the Holy Grail." Stout thereupon suggested that the *Post,* which was then paying Benét $1250 a story, would nevertheless buy **"Schooner Fairchild's Class"** if the characterization of Lane Parrington was altered. Benét would have no part of it.

"I can't make any revisions," he wrote Brandt. "I wouldn't know where to begin if I wanted to. . . . The whole thing is pretty surprising to me—and pretty disappointing. Because if the *Post* is going to want the opinions of its editorial page stuck willy-nilly into its fiction—if you have to class-angle a story for the *Post* as you'd have to for the *New Masses,* only in reverse—there's no point in my trying to write for them. I can't work that way. Any magazine can make its own rules—but that seems to me a stupid policy for a general magazine. Where does Stout think he gets his three million circulation? From the Union League Club?"

Some of this kind of editorial pressure was removed when Ben Hibbs became fiction editor of *Country Gentleman* in 1934. Now Benét's Oldest Inhabitant stories were again welcomed there; his price rose gradually during the rest of the decade to $1500, and in 1934 and 1935 *Country Gentleman* bought and published four of his American tales. The most interesting characteristic of these new stories was the confirmation they gave that Benét could not be labeled a merely regional or period writer. Beyond their common quality of a recurrent narrator they resembled each other only in their imaginative evocation of the American past. They might deal with the antebellum South or post-Appomattox bitterness, with the flatboat legends of the Mississippi or the covered-wagon caravans pressing across the mountains. He would write a clippership story and a hunting story, a trotting story, a steamboat story, and a story about Yankee peddlers. Benét was roaming unrestricted through a hundred years of American history, the first genuinely national American storyteller since Washington Irving, more richly talented than the latter and thoroughly free of Irving's uneasy sense of American inadequacies.

Benét varied the historical fiction, as always, with a coating of trivialities, most of them published in *Redbook* and the *Delineator.* "This is the Xmas story to Mr. Vetluguin's specifications for *Redbook,*" he wrote Brandt in August 1935. "If he likes it, stick him for it." Here too, however, as with the more substantial material of the American past, there was editorial perversity. *Redbook* also craved revisions and simplification.

"I think that is a little whimsical on Mr. Balmer's part," Benét told Brandt, when the agent sent him the *Redbook* suggestions, "[but] Vetluguin is a good egg, I'd like to please him, and if you consider it absolutely necessary, I'll make the revision. But I would like to point out to him or to Mr. Balmer that I have to have a little fun writing a story of this sort or it isn't going to be any good. I'm perfectly willing to work to any sort of specifications, but I think I ought to be allowed to put in my own doors and windows. If you revise and revise, and put in this and take out that, it gets to be like the movies and the thing goes dead and flat." (pp. 282-87)

"The Devil and Daniel Webster" consolidated the national role which had been slowly materializing for Benét ever since the publication of the ballads of 1922 and 1923. Though he wrote the story in ten days, it was in a very real sense the product of ten years of labor. Its realistic fantasy and extraordinary plausibility came from a decade's drafts and revisions of those fifteen Oldest Inhabitant stories which preceded it. In Daniel Webster he had found an ideal folk-hero. Webster was ambiguous enough for productive characterization, less remotely sacred and frozen than Lincoln, majestic in his strengths and weaknesses, national in his values. Just as Longfellow rehabilitated Paul Revere, so too had Benét revitalized another tarnished hero.

Americans responded to the story in a way that astonished the *Post,* who published it in the issue of October 24. Soon the magazine wooed Benét and Brandt with an attractive contract that pledged four stories a year for $1750 for each story. When Benét stopped off at Brandt's office he found himself, he said, "quite the white-headed boy. *Post* depending on me, etc." His publishers brought out the story in hard covers; it went through eleven editions during the next twenty years and was still in print in 1957. There were deluxe editions from fancy presses, with elaborate illustrations. It was precisely the kind of permanent classic which Benét had once denied **"The Barefoot Saint"** to be, "a story you can read in an hour but which you keep remembering for a long time."

When it was given the O. Henry Memorial Award as the best American short story of the year, Harry Hansen, the editor of the series, reported that it was one of the rare occasions when all the judges were unanimously of the same opinion. "Second and third readings," said one of them, "convince me of its fine chance for as near an approach to immortality as a short story can attain." It was as widely anthologized as any single American tale by an American writer. It reached continuous and additional audiences as operetta, one-act play, and full-length movie.

Benét had begun with no more than a title, taken from the work sheet on which he listed phrases that seemed to have the promise of a good story in them. Not until several months later did he read Irving's "The Devil and Tom Walker," which was often supposed to have been his inspiration. All he had was a title, "The Devil in New England." His initial conception . . . was to have the Devil come to a modern small town. "Then I tried shifting it back into the past," Benét explained later. "It seemed a good idea but I didn't know what I'd have him do when he got there." It was at this point that he first visualized Webster as the Devil's antagonist.

"I had always thought of him," Benét said in 1941, "as an orator with one hand stuck in the bosom of his frock coat, till I read of him in Van Wyck Brooks' *The Flowering of New England.* Then he began to come alive and I read more about him."

He did a good deal of research on Webster in late June of 1936, as was indicated not only by this story but also by its successors in the *Post,* **"Daniel Webster and the Sea Serpent"** and **"Daniel Webster and the Ides of March."** Once he had fixed on Webster, the rest, he said, was easy. "Webster's strong point was oratory," he explained, "so naturally he'd have to meet the Devil in an oratorical contest and win." The enormous success of the story required Benét to discuss it publicly in a way that he rarely did with his work.

"It's always seemed to me," he said later, "that legends

and yarns and folk-tales are as much a part of the real history of a country as proclamations and provisos and constitutional amendments. . . . **'The Devil and Daniel Webster'** is an attempt at telling such a legend . . . I couldn't help trying to show him in terms of American legend; I couldn't help wondering what would happen if a man like that ever came to grips with the Devil—and not an imported Devil, either, but a genuine, homegrown product, Mr. Scratch."

After the publication of **"The Devil and Daniel Webster"** Benét became a story-teller to the nation. He could now write for the largest magazine in the United States stories about leprechauns and sea serpents, and about Nazi tyranny and American responsibilities. He wrote for the biggest audience that any American writer of his stature had ever possessed. For many of his readers his political and moral values were their only encounter with this particular set of national convictions.

His personal as well as his professional status was consolidated by **"The Devil and Daniel Webster."** The early summer of 1936 was the last period of truly desperate financial pressure which he had to endure. It ended dramatically in August, when, Jabez Stone-like, he found temporary prosperity: two more stories were sold to the *Post;* one of the studios unexpectedly bought the movie rights to a story called **"Everybody Was Very Nice"** for twenty-five hundred dollars; and Rosemary inherited a thousand dollars from an aunt whom she scarcely knew. "Thus ends," Benét wrote in his diary, "one of the strangest weeks in our lives." Thereafter his income rose rapidly on the strength of the Daniel Webster success; it leveled off at between twelve and fifteen thousand dollars a year for the rest of his life. (pp. 293-96)

He had discovered and disciplined his fiction talent in the big slicks, though he'd had to escape the prison first. "[Writing]," Benét told the short story writer Pauli Murray in 1939, "is a job to be done, like any job—it's a profession to be learned, like any profession. It isn't learned in a month or a year—it takes time. But it can be learned." For evidence—though he was without that kind of vanity—Benét could have referred Miss Murray to back issues of *Country Gentleman* and the *Elks' Magazine* and *Cosmopolitan.* More particularly, however, the story was public verification that now he was what could not have been anticipated on the basis of his earlier work for *Metropolitan* and *Redbook* and *Liberty.* He had become an important and revered American man of letters. (p. 296)

. . . . .

The rewards of being a man of letters were largely in the form of influence and prestige, neither of which Benét valued particularly. His joint earnings from lecturing and editing and reviewing barely paid the New York and Rhode Island rents. "Academy of Poets started. Wish they'd give *me* $5,000," he noted in his diary after reading of the newly established grant. He still continued to depend on short stories for the major part of his income. During the second half of the 1930's, however, there was a profound alteration in his relationship with the circulation magazines.

Not once during the last three years of the decade did Brandt have to rely on the second-line magazines for sales. Benét's work no longer appeared in *Liberty* or *Redbook* or *Woman's Home Companion.* Eighteen of his new stories were published during 1937, 1938, and 1939. Thirteen appeared in the *Saturday Evening Post,* two in *Country Gentleman,* one in *Collier's,* one in the *Ladies' Home Journal,* and one in the *Atlantic Monthly.* The purchase of **"A Tooth for Paul Revere"** by the *Atlantic* was the single forced sale at a loss; all his regular buyers turned it down as too much of a fantasy. Each of the other seventeen stories, with the exception of **"Schooner's Class"** and **"Into Egypt,"** was bought by the magazine of Brandt's choice, for prices—including the two that were rejected by the *Post*—which ranged from $1250 to $1750.

It was even more significant that only one of the eighteen stories was in the stereotyped formula Benét had formerly employed in at least two-thirds of his magazine fiction. **"A Cat Named Dempsey,"** which the *Post* bought without hesitation, was a facsimile of the trivialities he had once written so regularly for *Metropolitan* and *Everybody's.* The other seventeen were divided among four significant categories; each was a notable example of magazine fiction at its most expert and adult.

The majority—**"A Tooth for Paul Revere," "O'Halloran's Luck," "Oh, My Name Is William Kidd,"** the two new Webster stories, **"Johnny Pye and the Fool-Killer," "Jacob and the Indians," "The Die-Hard,"** and **"A Man from Fort Necessity"**—were folk-tales of the American past. Two of the stories—**"Doc Mellhorn and the Pearly Gates"** and **"Henry and the Golden Mine"**—were modern fantasies. **"Among Those Present"** was contemporary satire, a vivid characterization done in the first person and reminiscent of Dorothy Parker and Ring Lardner; it was an excellent statement of Benét's complex feeling about New York and its effect upon the young men and women whose talent drew them to it. The remaining four stories were in certain respects the most important, overshadowing the charm of the American material, the richness of the fantasies, the bite of contemporary satire.

In this final group he extended the contemporary comment he had initiated in 1936 with **"The Blood of the Martyrs."** Two—**"Greatness"** and **"The Last of the Legions"**—were parables of the times in which he used episodes from the European past to illuminate the European present. "I thought of my man at the villa," reflects the Roman centurion as he and the legion prepare to leave Britain, "and how he might die in peace, even as Agathocles had said. But all the time, the moss would be creeping on the stone and the rain beating at the door. Till, finally, the naked people gathered there, without knowledge—they would have forgotten the use of the furnace that kept the house warm in winter and the baths that made men clean."

"Into Egypt," on the other hand, was a direct and moving indictment of totalitarian persecution, made plausible by the realistic portrait of a young fascist officer. The fourth story was a triumphant blend of all of them, in which he projected successfully the tempting, difficult fantasy of a future civilization. **"The Place of the Gods"** rose above the level of tour de force where most such stories remain; the new, postwar wilderness of America had its origins, as it were, in Benét's imaginative sense of the precolonist America of the sixteenth century.

Even Benét granted these stories some merit. For the first time he consented to the publication of a handful of them in book form. ***Thirteen O'Clock*** was published in 1937, ***Tales before Midnight*** in 1939. Of the twenty-five stories in the two collections, fourteen had originally been published in 1936 or later; several of the earlier ones had first appeared in such quality magazines as *Harper's* and the *Century.* "I have been trying to write the kind of short stories I like to write," he told an interviewer in 1939. It was characteristic of him that when he talked about his magazine fiction he said nothing of the editorial resistance which had been the prelude to this new level of achievement. "Fortunately," he said instead, "magazine editors are giving me considerable liberty."

The publication of ***Thirteen O'Clock*** and ***Tales Before Midnight*** was the first formal literary presentation of Benét in the storyteller role by which he had made his living since 1922 and with which most of his working time had been occupied. The reviews were both respectable and respectful; there were a number of warm acknowledgments of his achievement and some critical surprise at the high level of his performance. Everybody, however—the reviewers, Farrar who encouraged him to allow the collections, Rosemary who read the galleys and congratulated him, the public who bought more copies than was customary with short story volumes—everybody was more pleased than Benét.

He eliminated stories ruthlessly when he made the selections for ***Thirteen O'Clock,*** leaving out a number from *Country Gentleman* that might have been included and several from *Harper's Bazaar* and the *Elks' Magazine.* He spent several weeks revising the token selection which he did tolerate; he made additional changes in the proofs. He altered the title of **"The Place of the Gods"** to **"By the Waters of Babylon."** The only three he really approved of in ***Thirteen O'Clock,*** he said, were **"The Devil and Daniel Webster," "Glamour,"** and **"The Curfew Tolls."**

He was more pleased with ***Tales before Midnight,*** all but two of whose stories had been published in 1937 or later. Even here he was diffident and scrupulous. "Look over old stories & discover I wrote a good many bad ones." It was his eighteenth book, however, and something of a milestone; the hard core of political creed and contemporary indignation gave the group an impressive unity. "I think they made a handsome book of it," he wrote his mother, "and I am glad to have the collection together."

Even the inevitable reviews by fastidious critics who deplored his tendency to write for money did not discourage him. When Robert Nathan told him how much he admired the stories, Benét answered with a cheerful reference to a bad notice he'd received. "I had just read a review of myself by an able young man," he told Nathan, "and was wondering whether I couldn't write because of (a) native incapacity or (b) because the machine was running down."

In point of fact his fertility and competence had been joined for the most propitious use of the medium of his career. His sensitivity to the past was now put to the even richer purpose of clarifying the present. He wrote these tales of totalitarian denunciation rapidly, once he conceived the situation, but always there was a period of blocked ferment which might last anywhere from ten days to a month. All kinds of factors and individuals contributed to his creative process during those preludes.

In the middle of November 1939, "money getting low," he struggled typically for a new story. "Try to think of story," he noted on November 15. "Try to work on story," two days later, "don't get anywhere." And on November 18, the same four or five hours of wrestling at his notes. "Try to work—no ideas." The exhausting germination continued on into the last days of the month, a kind of dry heaves of composition. "Try to work—get nowhere. Money running very low. . . . Try very hard to think of story, but don't. Money extremely low. . . . Cold. Don't get anywhere."

Then, abruptly and with splendid relief, the whole painful ordeal ended. A kind of sweet fruitfulness began. "Start idea for story **'Into Egypt,'** " he noted on December 1. He finished the initial draft—10,000 words—the next day, and on the third day he typed it. Rosemary read it with pleasure and approval, though Benét simply noted that "she seems to think O.K."

The exhausting labor had been attended, however, by other elements than the need for money and his own resolve to sweat dryly until an idea came. On November 14, one day before he began work, he had read in the *Times* the appalling dispatches from Berlin. "Killing Jews in Germany," he wrote in his diary. On November 18, during the fourth day of his search for an idea, his mother telephoned him from Pennsylvania. She, too, was thoroughly upset by the Nazi genocide and anxious to discuss it in detail with her son. On November 25, the ninth day of his sterile gestation, he walked downtown and back. On the way he stopped at Louis Cohn's House of Books, to see if the dealer had any new Americana for him. Cohn, worldly and cosmopolitan, as familiar with Paris and Berlin as with New York, was in a terrible state. He and Benét discussed the new Nazi horrors. For ten more days these three encounters sat in his subconscious, along the still unlubricated tract of his indignation. Then on December 1 the various forces were freed. "Start idea for story, **'Into Egypt.'** "

On December 5 Brandt telephoned him. He liked the story very much. Five days later, on a Friday afternoon, the agent's secretary called. Would he please come to the office some time on Monday, at his convenience, and talk to Mr. Brandt. Benét gloomily read the signs. "Damnfool *Post* probably doesn't like story." He stewed through the week end. On Monday his suspicions were confirmed. The *Post* had rejected **"Into Egypt"** because, they explained to Brandt, they had been getting so much material on Jews. "This is pretty silly," Benét concluded in his diary, knowing perfectly well that the magazine's fundamental objection had been to the story's unequivocal and controversial position and theme.

Benét at work.

The painful travail of November was now prolonged in different form. Ten more days went by, the bills continued to come in; at last Brandt telephoned once more. He had sold the story to the *Ladies' Home Journal* for $1500. "Get check," Benét noted on December 29, "and pay school-bills." A process which began on November 14, when he read the morning *Times,* ended almost seven weeks later when he spent the payment. The sequence of frustration, labor, and fulfillment was reproduced each time Benét began and completed a major short story from 1937 through 1942; he wrote at least half a dozen each year and sometimes eight or nine. (pp. 333-39)

. . . . .

Of the nineteen stories which Benét published between 1940 and early 1943 . . . four had been written some years before. They were bought now, appropriately, by the very magazines for which they had originally been intended. Thus, incongruously, at a time when his new short stories were being cited as classics, he was simultaneously appearing in *Redbook* and *Harper's Bazaar* and the *American* with these culls from what Brandt called the B-file.

Several of his new stories, on the other hand—**"The Captives"** and **"The Minister's Books"** in particular—were effectively constructed from the frontier research he was doing for *Western Star*. Others, like **"The Great Swingle-field Derby"** and **"The Angel Was a Yankee,"** were hasty and inferior fragments of Americana. A small group of these final stories of his career, however, were among his major achievements. In them he somehow matched, despite the full-time obligations of his war work, the noble themes and expert craft of **"Into Egypt"** and **"The Blood of the Martyrs."** Such a story was **"Freedom's a Hard-Bought Thing,"** published in the *Saturday Evening Post* in May 1940. Like everything he was writing now, it brought the same extraordinary flood of letters; descendents of Negroes who had escaped on the underground, and relatives of those who operated it, wrote to thank him for it. The grandson of a slave wrote to describe how the bells in his grandfather's collar had been packed with mud as he dodged his pursuers. Once again, as so often in the past, Benét was given the O. Henry Memorial Award for the best American short story of the year.

He had less and less time, however, for new work that required the concentration of such major short stories of this period as **"The Bishop's Beggar,"** **"A Judgment in the Mountains,"** **"The Prodigal Children,"** and **"Freedom's a Hard-Bought Thing."** He was kept financially solvent only by Brandt's tireless ingenuity, his own dogged and profitable labor during 1941 on a skillful movie version of **"The Devil and Daniel Webster"**—Hollywood provided the title, *All That Money Can Buy*—and the unexpected bonanza of a new two-volume collection of his poetry and fiction which was chosen as a Book-of-the-Month Club selection in 1942. "Absolutely no money," he noted in his diary, "so borrow $1000 from B&B. Then JF phones to say I will get $3000 from BofM for advance on collected works."

The *Selected Works* was heavily subscribed by the book club members, in large part as a result of his new status as America's most widely heard poetic voice. He continued to get these improbable riches from work which had in most cases been written years before. "Stan [Rinehart] stuns me," he noted in 1942, "by saying B of M has paid further on set and I will get about $6000 more." He insisted on omitting some of the material which Basil Davenport, its editor, had chosen, including five short stories and some verse from *Heavens and Earth*. He also argued against Farrar and Rinehart's tendency to make the volumes overelaborate. "My only other criticism," he wrote Farrar, "is on the hand-lettered 'Benét' on the title-page, which seems to me unnecessarily fussy."

On the whole, however, he was comforted by the quality of what he had written in the past, republished as it was in the midst of his wartime propaganda. "I am pleased and impressed by having this sort of edition," he told Farrar, "and, thinking of my latter end, feel I probably don't deserve it." He was amused by the grudging respect which the critics gave the two volumes when they were published in June 1942. "The boys are always surprised that in spite of the fact that I am read, I show craftsmanship. If I had blown up like Bromfield then they could have written an article on how I used to have promise. But I haven't blown up."

And yet as he read the galleys of *Selected Works* he also felt a profound melancholy. He had done most of this work in the twenty-three fruitful years between his seventeenth and fortieth birthdays. Now he was forty-three and the conviction was growing within him that his major work was done. "Will I ever do good work again?" he wondered in the diary. (pp. 364-67)

There were times when he could not be inwardly tranquil, though he could still be philosophical. "Get dummy for collected edition," he wrote in his diary. "A very handsome tombstone." (p. 368)

> *Charles A. Fenton, in his* Stephen Vincent Benét: The Life and Times of an American Man of Letters, 1898-1943, *Yale University Press, 1958, 436 p.*

William J. Harris   (essay date 1976)

[*In the following excerpt, Harris comments on Benét's critical standing and assesses the short stories "The Devil and Daniel Webster" and "Johnny Pye and the Fool-Killer."*]

> *John Brown's Body* has merit enough; it has hair-raising defects; and yet it deserves to be widely read and, within reason, praised.
>
> Allen Tate, *The Nation*, September 19, 1928

Stephen Vincent Benét, a winner of two Pulitzer Prizes for poetry, an author who was one of the most popular of serious writers in America, a man of letters who wielded a great deal of literary power, has been forgotten by the American literary world. He is no longer attacked for his "hair-raising defects" by some stern and serious critic but, rather, is simply ignored. He is not included in Richard Ellman's 1973 edition of *The Norton Anthology of Modern Poetry* (somehow Masters, Sandburg and Lindsay have survived him) nor is he included in Albert Gelpi's *The Poet in America* (1973), and, perhaps even more significantly, he is excluded from Louis Untermeyer's *50 Modern American and British Poets* (1973). Benét was included in Untermeyer's earlier anthology *Modern American Poetry* (1962). Not only the anthologists ignore Benét but the critics do also: Roy Harvey Pearce (*The Continuity of American Poetry*, 1961), Hyatt H. Waggoner (*American Poets*, 1968), and Walter Sutton (*American Free Verse*, 1973) never mention Benét.

I would not be very troubled about Benét's literary misfortunes if he had only written *John Brown's Body* and **"The Devil and Daniel Webster,"** his most famous works. I would not care that he has been damned to the high schools if he still even occupies that circle of Hell. Yet he has written a few short stories that should not be forgotten—**"Johnny Pye and the Fool-Killer"** and **"A Death in the Country,"** in particular—and written an important and successful epic poem, *Western Star*. (pp. 172-73)

"The Devil and Daniel Webster" is not a product of a "cheap" imagination but it is too fragile a vehicle to handle its profound message about the brotherhood of man whether he be damned or saved. Benét's imagination becomes profounder in both prose and poetry as the poet grows older. *Western Star,* his last poem, published posthumously and unfinished, is a serious epic which presents a humane and peopled history of America's first years. (p. 173)

"The Devil and Daniel Webster" contains Benét's vision as completely as any of his works: damned or not men are brothers and there is the possibility of decency in every man. It is the liberal vision of man. I believe the message but though Daniel Webster may be able to melt the hearts of the jury from hell Benét does not manage to melt my heart with his tale. The telling of the story is too cute. In the first two paragraphs of "The Devil and Daniel Webster" we can see its almost arty folksiness:

> It's a story they tell in the border country where Massachusetts joins Vermont and New Hampshire.
>
> Yes, Dan'l Webster's dead—or, at least, they buried him. But every time there's a thunderstorm around Marshfield, they say you can hear his rolling voice in the hollows of the sky. And they say that if you go to his grave and speak loud and clear, "Dan'l Webster—Dan'l Webster!" the ground'll begin to shiver and the trees begin to shake. And after a while you'll hear a deep voice saying, "Neighbor, how stands the Union?" Then you better answer the Union stands as she stood, rock-bottomed and copper-sheathed, one and indivisible, or he's liable to rear right out of the ground. At least, that's what I was told when I was a youngster.

It's too self-consciously an American folk tale with its "Dan'l," "Union stands as she stood, rock-bottomed and copper-sheathed," and "he's liable to rear right out of the ground"; it's too preciously colorful; the paragraphs are too contrived with their opening and closing lines, shouting this is a gen-u-ine American Tall Story.

"Johnny Pye and the Fool-Killer" says all men are fools because they must die. We have another seeker after the truth to add to our list, Johnny Pye. Johnny Pye spends his life trying to escape the Fool-Killer, a supernatural agent of death. At the age of eleven he runs away from home and over the years apprentices himself to a variety of "wise" men: a con man, a businessman, a congressman and others. He hopes that one of them will give him wisdom. Eventually he discovers that all men are fools and there is no way to escape death. In fact, in his early nineties he welcomes the Fool-Killer.

"Johnny Pye and the Fool-Killer" has a resonance that "The Devil and Daniel Webster" does not. The Fool-Killer is authentic. I gather from reading "A Death in the Country," one of Benét's best stories, that the Fool-Killer is a "real" boogieman from his childhood. Grown-ups told their children that they better watch out for the Fool-Killer. Benet has taken this childhood boogieman and has transformed him into an excellent personification of death. There is nothing arch about him. As LeRoi Jones says: "The most powerful way to deal with an image is to make sure it goes deeper than literature. That it is actually 'out there' " (*Home*). The Fool-Killer is more "out there"

than "Daniel Webster." Yet by the time of *Western Star* Benét is able to make history "out there," to make history as living as his personal experience.

Allen Tate, in *The Nation,* said of *John Brown's Body* shortly after its first appearance that "it has hair-raising defects" and I agree with Mr. Tate. Earlier I spoke of what a poor story *John Brown's Body* told and as a poem it is almost as bad. There are good individual sections, like the "Invocation," but there is much flat language in it. But to dismiss *John Brown's Body* should not mean the dismissal of Benét. I do not find very many hair-raising defects in *Western Star* and "Johnny Pye and the Fool-Killer": they are moving and effective works. (pp. 177-78)

I cannot truly say how highly Benét should be ranked in comparison with other modern American writers—it has been an incredibly rich century for literature—but I think Benét has written at least a very good poem and a few stories that deserve to survive. His work is an excellent expression of the liberal imagination. *The Waste Land* must make room for *Western Star.* The world of the religious and the spiritual must make room for the world of the political and social. The Anglo-Catholic church is one solution for modern man's problems but another is the community of man, Benét's answer. We are all brothers faced with the Fool-Killer and we have the potential if not of an "earthly paradise" at least of a workable democracy. But we need new Daniel Websters in order to find this democratic decency in our hearts. (pp. 179-80)

> *William J. Harris, "Stephen Vincent Benét's 'Hair-Raising Defects'?" in* A Question of Quality: Popularity and Value in Modern Creative Writing, *edited by Louis Filler, Bowling Green University Popular Press, 1976, pp. 172-80.*

W. Warren Wagar (essay date 1982)

[*In the following excerpt, Wagar notes that Benét's story "By the Waters of Babylon" established archetypal post-Apocalypse themes in American speculative fiction.*]

In American speculative fiction, the prototypical [post-apocalypse story] is Stephen Vincent Benét's much acclaimed "By the Waters of Babylon," first published in 1937 as "The Place of the Gods." The hero is a young man, a priest's son, who is slated to become a priest himself some day, in a tribal society of upstate New York after "the Great Burning and the Destruction." Somewhere to the east of the tribe, across the Hudson, lies the Place of the Gods, now a forbidden city of the dead. The young man defies the death penalty prescribed for such visits, and goes there to see it for himself. He learns that the "gods" were only men, like those of the tribe. His father spares his life, but warns him not to speak to the folk of his expedition. "Truth is a hard deer to hunt," he tells his son. "If you eat too much truth at once, you may die of the truth. It was not idly that our fathers forbade the Dead Places." But the spell is broken for the young man. Although he agrees with his father that the ancients may have eaten knowledge "too fast," he vows that when he becomes chief priest, "we shall go beyond the great river.

We shall go to the Place of the Gods—the place new-york—not one man but a company. . . . We must build again."

Benét's influence on postwar American speculative fiction was considerable. Many American examples of the post-holocaust tale reinforce the positivist side with a secret organization of scientist-survivors who aid the rebels in their struggle against unreason. (pp. 163-64)

> W. Warren Wagar, "Prometheus Unbound," in his Terminal Visions: The Literature of Last Things, *Indiana University Press, 1982, pp. 155-68.*

Robin Bromley   (essay date 1985)

[*In the following excerpt Bromley discusses the fantastic and supernatural themes in Benét's short fiction.*]

The demise of Stephen Vincent Benét's literary reputation is a stark reminder of how fleeting fame can be. Heralded after the publication of *John Brown's Body* in 1928 as "the national poet" and certainly one of the most popular short story writers of his day, Benét now is largely forgotten, having been relegated to the nether ring of minor poets by such influential critics as F. O. Matthiessen and remembered by others only as the author of **"The Devil and Daniel Webster."** With his relentless concern for the glories of the American past and with his often folksy diction, Benét is deemed old-fashioned, an upholder of overblown patriotism and outgrown values. This is unfortunate, for by writing ordinary people into his historical poems, he brought a new immediacy to the Civil War and the Western frontier and discovered a medley of regional dialects. Furthermore, although certainly not in the mainstream of supernatural writers, Benét worked some wonderful experiments with the fantastic folktale, infusing the genre with a peculiarly modern spirit by suggesting that while the supernatural is more pervasive than we generally acknowledge, it is also much more banal. (p. 797)

The titles of Stephen Vincent Benét's first two collections of short stories, *Thirteen O'Clock* (1937) and *Tales Before Midnight* (1939), can be misleading. Only seven of these twenty-five stories (published posthumously in 1943 in a volume called *Twenty-five Short Stories*) employ the supernatural, and then primarily as a vehicle for Benét's chief concern—defining a distinctly American culture that has grown out of a uniquely American past.

The most famous of these, **"The Devil and Daniel Webster,"** is a case in point. Benét was quite direct about what he considered the thrust of this story:

> It's always seemed to me that legends and yarns and folk-tales are as much a part of the real history of a country as proclamations and provisos and constitutional amendments. . . . **"The Devil and Daniel Webster"** is an attempt at telling such a legend. . . . I couldn't help wondering what would happen if a man like that ever came to grips with the Devil—and not an imported Devil, either, but a genuine, homegrown product, Mr. Scratch.

Interestingly enough, Benét makes his "homegrown Mr. Scratch" a dapper American businessman, quick to leap on the oath that Jabez Stone utters when he runs into financial trouble on his farm, and equally eager to get the soul of Daniel Webster when the orator comes to the farmer's aid. More mincing than menacing, Benét's Satan is too stylized to be truly frightening. But he is a droll symbol of the greed that threatens our country's values and a welcome foil for the somewhat overblown Webster, who is convinced that "if two New Hampshire men aren't a match for the devil, we might as well give the country back to the Indians."

The collection of butchers, witch burners, and pirates called from the dead to sit on the trial for Stone's soul, on the other hand, is genuinely ghastly. And, in addition to raising the awful possibility that the final arbiters of life are consummately evil, they neatly undercut the sentimentality of the tale. When they are finally moved by Webster's speech, it is out of respect for what Webster calls "the failures and the endless journey of mankind," and not only because of Webster's power. This seems to suggest that the story is as much about the obdurate pioneering spirit as it is about an American Faust or a New World Job, as some critics claim. In any case, it has proved to be a popular story, having been produced as an opera in 1939 (with libretto by Benét), a film (*All That Money Can Buy*, 1941), and several stage and television plays, as well as having been reprinted in many anthologies.

After the success of **"The Devil and Daniel Webster,"** Benét wrote two more Webster tales for the *Saturday Evening Post*: **"Daniel Webster and the Sea Serpent"** and **"Daniel Webster and the Ides of March."** Only **"Daniel Webster and the Sea Serpent"** has been reprinted (*Thirteen O'Clock*).

A comic folktale in the tradition of the Paul Bunyan stories, the **"Sea Serpent"** purports to explain how Daniel Webster, secretary of state, got himself out of an awkward social predicament at the same time he got the United States out of a war. This time "Dan'l" is up against Samanthy, a leviathan of no ordinary intelligence who falls madly in love with him. Following him to Washington, she stirs up a ruckus, threatening his negotiations with England and demanding the return of her affections. It is not long, however, before Dan'l, with his mythological wit, comes up with a solution: he makes Samanthy part of the American navy, which has the double effect of scaring off the British ambassador and of consigning the enamored fish to the South Seas.

The implication seems to be that more went into the making of this country than we usually imagine. But this is a theme Benét handles better in a later story such as **"O'Halloran's Luck."** In **"Daniel Webster and the Sea Serpent"** the heavy-handed paean to Webster's ingenuity is only barely buoyed up by the narrator's winking good humor and by amusing details like Samanthy's predilection for Italian sardines.

Set in contemporary New York and somewhat critical of the people it finds there, **"The King of the Cats"** is a completely different kind of story. It is based on a European folktale that reflects a very primitive way of regarding animals as the possessors of hidden supernatural powers and institutions. In Benét's hands, the story gets not only an American setting but also a comic touch.

Here the supernatural feline comes in the shape of Monsieur Tibault, a European conductor human in every respect except for his extraordinary tail—an appendage he uses to conduct the orchestra and to captivate New York society. Only Tommy Brooks, a thoroughly shallow Princetonian, remains immune. It seems his almond-eyed girlfriend—a descendant of Siamese royalty—has also fallen for Tibault. Jealousy, of course, whets suspicion, and it is not long before Tommy finds out exactly why Tibault likes to curl up on the couch. But even after he learns the magic of the famous legend and sends Tibault up in a cloud of smoke, Tommy hardly triumphs. He loses his princess and winds up with a pedestrian wife from Chicago.

While this tale lacks the liquid elegance of, say, Algernon Blackwood's otherworldly cat story "Ancient Sorceries," it has plenty of comic bite. One can only surmise that the supernatural cats are far too elegant for the superficial Tommy, who is incapable of appreciating any world but his own.

For the stories collected in *Tales Before Midnight,* Benét turns from legendary to commonplace characters and sends them on great American journeys, the goal of which is usually work.

In **"Johnny Pye and the Fool-killer,"** the journey begins when Johnny's harsh foster parents, a miller and his wife, threaten him once too often with their image of death—the demon who destroys all fools. A smart boy, Johnny suspects that "the Fool-killer got you wherever you went." Nevertheless, he decides to "give him a run for his money," and, leaving home, the boy begins his search for work that might help him escape the folly of ordinary mortals.

The story then catalogs the men Johnny meets along the way, everyone from a quack selling "Old Doctor Waldo's Unparalleled Universal Remedy" to the president of the United States. Although one is clever and another rich or brave, they all make some mistake that sets Johnny to hearing the approach of the Fool-killer, so eventually Johnny acknowledges the futility of his quest and decides to return home. This is a decision the Fool-killer seems to respect; when the scissors-grinder finally comes for Johnny, he offers to let Johnny live if he can solve this riddle: "How can a man be a human being and not be a fool?" In an amusing twist, Johnny's answer, "When he's dead and gone and buried," and his subsequent refusal to accept immortality without immortal youth, make a fool of the Fool-killer; he has to take Johnny even though the man is not a fool.

Benét reappraises the stature of death again in **"Doc Mellhorn and the Pearly Gates,"** a matter-of-fact fantasy about the afterlife of a crusty old country doctor. What gives the story its crispness is the narrator's droll omnipotence and indulgent patience with skeptics like the good doctor and us. It also offers one of Benét's best opening lines: "Doc

Mellhorn had never expected to go anywhere at all when he died. So, when he found himself on the road again, it surprised him."

Once past the Pearly Gates, Mellhorn, of course, has to accept the existence of heaven. But, he reasons, he does not have to stay there; he elects to go to hell instead, where people need him. The problem is that his clinic there is such a success it plays "merry Hades with the whole system," and Mellhorn is kicked upstairs once again. En route, he falls into a deep depression, until he finds that he is not necessarily doomed in heaven to eternal rest.

"O'Halloran's Luck" is another tale told to correct popular misconceptions, especially those which maintain that leprechauns are confined to Ireland or that the supernatural life of America is not as rich as that of the old country. In this story, such spirits are fundamental to the strength of this nation. O'Halloran's luck is only one example.

The title refers to the leprechaun that Tim O'Halloran rescues from wolves on the Western prairie. After exchanging stories about old times in County Clonmelly and about how hard it is for Irishmen, no matter what size, to make their way in this country, Tim and the leprechaun decide to throw in their lot together on the railroad. Posing as a nephew of Tim's named Rory, the leprechaun proves more than a little mischievous around camp. But with his second sight, he also proves extremely useful. Giving Tim prescient tips on how to build the railroad, he helps the Irishman first to a promotion and then to a girl. In return, Tim's kindness helps Rory to leprechaun liberty. At times, swelling lessons about hard work, happenstance, and freedom threaten to engulf this story, but in the end, irascible characters and rolling dialect lend it a salutary charm.

A fantastic truth about the birth of the nation is also the subject of **"A Tooth for Paul Revere,"** the only fantastic folktale in Benét's *Selected Works* that did not appear in earlier collections. First published in the *Atlantic Monthly,* the story posits that the American Revolution began not with Paul Revere or the Founding Fathers, but with an apolitical Lexington farmer in search of a cure for his aching tooth. Having been told that Paul Revere is as good at forging artificial teeth as he is at silver, Lige Butterwick travels to Boston, where he cannot help noticing the tension between Redcoats and colonists. Meeting Paul Revere raises his patriotic consciousness still further, so when he accidentally takes the magic box that Revere has filled with "gunpowder and war and the makings of a new nation," he knows that he must take his own ride to join Revere on the road between Lexington and Concord.

In his critical study [*Stephen Vincent Benét*], Parry Stroud says that with this story Benét makes "in fresh fashion the point that the American Revolution began when the common man, through whatever homely circumstances, joined the leaders in becoming involved in political issues." But contemporary readers may find that freshness marred by the quaintness of the characters and the cuteness of the supernatural machinery, which seem to work against each other and the theme.

As a rule, Benét is much more successful when he reverses the formula and exposes the homeliness of the not-necessarily-supernatural. This is what he does with such wit in **"Doc Mellhorn"** and **"Johnny Pye"** and what he does again, with equal drollery, in **"The Angel Was a Yankee."**

A wry little story about "the biggest attraction" P. T. Barnum "never got," **"The Angel Was a Yankee"** recalls how, after winning the angel from a recalcitrant farmer, the circus owner suffers a pang of conscience and lets the little fellow go. It seems that he cannot quite bring himself to hold a fellow Yankee. He does, however, manage to ask the angel if death will afford him "the opportunities to meet celebrities—er—such as George Washington, for instance." But the New England angel, a captain in his lifetime and a captain now, only gives this unsatisfying reply, "Ain't seen 'em. I'm telling you—Coast Guard duty. Far as the Grand Banks. Can't tell you I've seen 'em when I ain't."

Crackling dialogue and salty characters form the comic soul of this story. Especially good are the sketches of Barnum, the wily Yankee who is ultimately outwitted, and the laconic little angel who confesses that he just cannot believe the circus midget is real.

Benét took a darker view of beings from the otherworld and their earthly counterparts in the stories he wrote after 1940. Although it occasionally strains against his optimism, most of the stories published in *The Last Circle* reflect a growing sense that human life might not amount to much and that the afterlife cannot comfortably be mocked. **"The Danger of Shadows,"** for instance, questions the value of both work and family and gives harrowing form to the spirit that would have life another way.

Tired of the dull routine of Harbison's job and marriage, Harbison's shadow grows defiant, tugging him toward his young secretary and resisting him on the walk home. At first, Harbison puts up a struggle. But as the winter wears on, he grows weary, while his shadow seems "to grow more corporeal everyday." Once the shadow convinces him to leave his wife and children, however, Harbison realizes that he has to get rid of his shadow; suicide seems the only way.

An unfortunate domestic denouement flattens the ending of the story. But before that, the threatening figure on the wall and the suggestion that our shadows may lead very active lives of their own are as unsettling as the image of Harbison's drab existence.

Work also fails to bring salvation in **"The Minister's Books"**; in fact, ambition to succeed contributes to the main character's demise.

Set in the late nineteenth century, the story traces a young minister's seduction into a coven of ghostly witches. Alone in a new town and struggling with his ministry, Hugh McRidden finds himself strangely drawn to the books in his library. Each marked with a bookplate picturing a stern-looking group of Puritans gathered "for what appears to be prayer" in an open glade, the tomes seem at first to be religious histories. But *An Examen into the Invisible* soon opens his eyes, and it is not long before he succumbs to the magic. Although ridden with guilt, the min-

ister relishes the "fearsome joy in crossing to the other side" and his miraculous ability to save the town from a deadly epidemic. When the time comes to pay for these favors with a human sacrifice, however, McRidden's original ministry wins out, and he chooses to kill himself instead.

Although once again the suicide is aborted, this time the character's salvation is far from secure. The warlock from the eighteenth-century bookplate catches up with McRidden, and Benét provides no clue as to whether the meeting is the product of madness or not. Full of dark hints about the evil done in the guise of Christianity and about the villagers' chilling indifference, this is one of Benét's bleakest and deepest tales.

"William Riley and the Fates" is also about the intrusion of the extraordinary in ordinary American life, but this time the story is weighed down by heavy-handed homilies and the implausible prospect of the Fates picnicking in a public park.

Benét's portrait of William Riley—a young man eager for the achievements he is sure he is going to attain—is wonderful. But the Fates—three women who seem "to be knitting all the time" and a wizened old man spinning a wheel of fortune—are an obvious crew, sent in to warn him against taking the future for granted. The trouble is that the story, published barely two months before the attack on Pearl Harbor, dissolves into propaganda, and Benét's best devices, like the Fates's futuristic newsreel of a war-torn Europe, are undermined by William's facile conversion from isolationism and his glib pronouncement that "fate's Fate, but a country's what you make it."

"The Gold Dress" works much better. Eschewing broad statements about the national character, Benét explores the yearnings of a repressed old maid and brings a touch of comic poignancy to the ghost tale.

The mechanism is standard: never having gotten what she wanted in life, Louella Weedon comes back to demand her due—love, merriment, and the young banker she had hoped to marry. The sad twist is that even as a ghost Louella is bound by propriety. All she can do is sit primly in her parlor and ask her young man to help with the sewing. Only under the hilariously understated threat of exorcism can Louella blurt out what she really wants—one of the fine dresses that have lain hidden in her closet for twenty years. Clearly, it is difficult to fulfill even the simplest desires.

Even the most optimistic story in this group, **"The Land Where There Is No Death,"** contains a strain of uncertainty. On the surface a comforting allegory about the inseparability of life and death, the tale also suggests that the best of stories can lead us astray.

The title refers to the land that young John invents to console his childhood companion Hilda, distraught over her first experience with death. As the two children grow older, they elaborate upon the myth and then forget it until, under the pressure of taking his clerical exams, John resurrects and begins to believe in the fantasy. Reasoning that death cannot exist if God is truly good, he leaves school to travel "into strange lands, among strange folk" only to end, not surprisingly, where he began. An old man, with nothing but the stories he has told along the way to show for his life, John tries to frame one last tale to warn others against such delusions. But his story of death turns into a story of life as he realizes that without death there could be no life, that people would not know "what it was to be safe if they knew not danger." The implication is that death is not an end but a beginning. Still, it does not squelch the possibility that, near death himself, Benét was seriously questioning the worth of a lifetime spent telling stories.

One might question the significance of Benét's fantastic fiction with the same misgiving, and first because it was not his primary medium. Benét was a poet who turned to short stories only under financial duress and then with some contempt. Fenton reports that Benét went into the business with some reluctance, confessing, "The short story is not my forte," and Benét himself was in the habit of deriding his "bright, gay stories about gay, bright, young dumb people." Of one he said, "It is a dear little candy laxative of a tale. . . . I do not see how it can fail to sell—it is so cheap." Second, even when, in the mid-1930's, he began to take the form seriously, he was more interested in writing folktales that would enrich our literary heritage than he was in the possibilities and implications of the fantastic itself. But as he worked with the form—fitting otherworldly beings with contemporary concerns and re-imagining the spiritual life of the past—he did add a new dimension to the genre that might still be exploited. One wonders what a Doc Mellhorn would find en route to heaven today, or how a contemporary writer would handle Daniel Webster's confrontation with the devil. (pp. 798-802)

> *Robin Bromley, "Stephen Vincent Benét," in* Supernatural Fiction Writers: Fantasy and Horror, Vol. 2, *edited by E. F. Bleiler, Charles Scribner's Sons, 1985, pp. 797-803.*

FURTHER READING

Bibliography

Maddocks, Gladys Louise. "Stephen Vincent Benét: A Bibliography, Parts I and II." *Bulletin of Bibliography* 20, Nos. 6-7 (September-December 1951; January-April 1952): 142-46; 158-60.
  Lists primary and secondary sources.

Biography

Benét, William Rose. "S. V. B.: 1898-1943." *The Saturday Review of Literature* 26, No. 13 (27 March 1943): 4.
  Poem written in tribute on Benét's death.

———. "My Brother Steve." In *Stephen Vincent Benét,* by William Rose Benét and John Farrar, pp. 1-11. New York: Farrar and Rinehart, 1943.
  Reminiscence that includes anecdotes about Benét's family life and professional career.

Farrar, John. "For the Record." In *Stephen Vincent Benét,* by William Rose Benét and John Farrar, pp. 12-36. New York: Farrar and Rinehart, 1943.
  Essay by a longtime publisher of Benét commending his character and discussing disparate aspects of his career, including his writing of librettos, radio broadcasts, and stage adaptations of his own works and those of others.

La Farge, Christopher. "S. V. B." *The Saturday Review of Literature* 26, No. 13 (27 March 1943): 11.
  Elegiac poem.

"As We Remember Him." *The Saturday Review of Literature* 26, No. 13 (27 March 1943): 7-11.
  Tributes and reminiscences by Leonard Bacon, Philip Barry, John Berdan, Carl Carmer, Archibald MacLeish, Christopher Morley, William Lyon Phelps, Muriel Rukeyser, and Thornton Wilder.

Wylie, Elinor. "Love to Stephen." *The Saturday Review of Literature* 26, No. 13 (27 March 1943): 6.
  Poem by Benét's sister-in-law.

Criticism

Bailey, Robeson. "From an Expert Craftsman." *The Saturday Review of Literature* 30, No. 1 (4 January 1947): 16.
  Assesses *The Last Circle* as a collection of minor works more suggestive than representative of Benét's talents.

Bartel, Roland. "Brief Comments on Other Works of Fiction with Biblical Allusions." In *Biblical Images in Literature,* edited by Roland Bartel, James S. Ackerman, and Thayer S. Warshaw, pp. 179-94. Nashville, Tenn.: Abingdon Press, 1975.
  Maintains that Benét's allusion to Psalm 137 in the title of "By the Waters of Babylon" imparts a mood of apprehension to the story.

Carmer, Carl. "Worthy of a Nation's Hosannas." *The New York Herald Tribune Books* 16, No. 12 (19 November 1939): 3.
  Enthusiastic review of *Tales before Midnight* commending especially such "American fantasies" as "Johnny Pye and the Fool-Killer."

Maxwell, William. "No Two Alike." *The Saturday Review of Literature* 16, No. 26 (23 October 1937): 11.
  Commends the various styles and memorable plots of the stories collected in *Thirteen O'Clock: Stories of Several Worlds.*

———. "Fool-Killers and Others." *The Saturday Review of Literature* XXI, No. 3 (11 November 1939): 14.
  Assesses the short stories collected in *Tales before Midnight* as competent and entertaining but unremarkable as literature.

Mayo, Lawrence Shaw. Review of *The Devil and Daniel Webster. The New England Quarterly* X, No. 4 (December 1937): 822.
  Commends this short story as exceptionally entertaining and original.

McPeek, James A. S. "Benét and Monroe's Fourth Reader." *College English* 20, No. 3 (December 1958): 132-33.
  Suggests that a story included in a standard primary-

school textbook of the 1800s inspired a section of "The Devil and Daniel Webster".

Starke, Catherine Juanita. "Black Individuals." In her *Black Portraiture in American Fiction: Stock Characters, Archetypes, and Individuals,* pp. 171-248. New York: Basic Books, 1971.

Notes that Cue in the story "Freedom's a Hard-Bought Thing" and Spade in the poem *John Brown's Body* are among the first fully individuated black characters created by a white American author.

Stroud, Parry. "The Short Stories: From Wholesaling to Artistry." In his *Stephen Vincent Benét,* pp. 114-36. New York: Twayne, 1962.

Provides an overview of Benét's short stories in the context of his life and career. The volume includes primary and secondary bibliographies and a chronology.

Walsh, Thomas F. "The 'Noon Wine' Devils." *The Georgia Review* 22, No. 1 (Spring 1968): 90-6.

Derives a Faustian pattern of "deals with the devil" from "The Devil and Daniel Webster" and applies this pattern to an examination of Katherine Anne Porter's short story "Noon Wine."

Additional coverage of Benét's life and career is contained in the following sources published by Gale Research: *Contemporary Authors,* Vol. 104; *Dictionary of Literary Biography,* Vols. 4, 48; *Twentieth-Century Literary Criticism,* Vol. 7; and *Yesterday's Authors of Books for Children,* Vol. 1.

Giovanni Boccaccio

The *Decameron*

Boccaccio (1313-1375) was an Italian short story and novella writer, poet, essayist, novelist, nonfiction writer, and
critic. The following entry presents criticism of his best-
known work, the *Decameron* (1370).

INTRODUCTION

The *Decameron* is a collection of one hundred novellas
widely recognized as a masterpiece of world literature.
Praised for its narrative unity and tenable character delineation, the *Decameron* has been deemed paramount to the
development of short fiction. Although most literary
works of the Middle Ages were composed in Latin, the
Decameron was written in Italian vernacular, thus elevat-
ing the language of the middle-class, and by implication,
their values and concerns, to classical importance. The
Decameron is also recognized for its synthesis of comic,
tragic, and erotic subject matter and its dialectical investigations into morality and human behavior. Often described as one of the first works of medieval literature to
explore secular rather than theological issues, the *Decameron* is generally classified as a transitional work that both
reflects the spiritualism of the Middle Ages and anticipates the humanism and rationalism of the Renaissance.

The *Decameron* centers on seven women and three men
who, hoping to escape the Black Plague of 1348, retreat
to the hills of Fiesole above the city of Florence, Italy.
After meeting one another for the first time in the church
of Santa Maria Novella, the group is persuaded by Pampinea, the oldest woman, to flee to the mountains where
they can alternately stay at their respective country estates. While Pampinea chastises those who have long ago
abandoned Florence, she realizes that because the city has
been so severely stricken, their decision is ultimately a
matter of self-preservation: "[No] one can reproach us for
taking the course I have advocated, whereas if we do nothing we shall be confronted with distress and mourning,
and possibly forfeit our lives in the bargain." Once in the
mountains, the group members decide they will occupy
their afternoons with storytelling. In order to avoid dis-
agreements, Pampinea proposes that they tell ten stories
per day and that each day a different member of the group
guide the speakers by choosing a particular subject or
theme to address. After ten days of candidly discussing
such topics as love, intelligence, and human will, Panfilo,
the leader of the tenth day, suggests the group return to
Florence "[lest] tedium should arise from a custom too
long established, and lest, by protracting our stay, we
should cause evil tongues to start wagging."

Although the *Decameron* comprises numerous themes,
characters, and topics, critics note that Boccaccio's masterly use of framing structures—narrative devices used by

IOANNES · BOCCATIVS

an author to reveal his intentions and provide a coherent
format—lends a sense of thematic and stylistic unity to a
work which otherwise might have appeared disordered
and fragmented. Vittore Branca, a leading Boccaccio
scholar, asserted: "In comparison with the structure of episodic clusters of tales which characterizes the collections
of novellas which preceded it, the *Decameron* appears as
a unified work, firmly governed by a plan based on ideas,
a work grounded in a precise moral structure of which the
so-called 'frame' is an essential element." Primary framing
structures in the *Decameron* include Boccaccio's proem,
or preface, his introductions to the first and fourth days,
and his epilogue. In the proem, for example, the frame
which is most often cited by critics, the narrator explains
that he has recently suffered from the "pains of love" and
had it not been for the support of his friends and family
he never would have recovered. In order to return the
favor, the narrator maintains he will attempt, through his
stories, to offer comfort and entertainment to those who
most need it: lovesick women who—due to the social restrictions of the time—are forced to "conceal the flames

of passion within their fragile breasts." Most critics concur that it is in the proem that Boccaccio identifies his intended audience and imparts the underlying character
motivations inherent throughout the *Decameron*—namely
compassion, generosity, and gratitude.

Boccaccio also incorporates into the *Decameron* a logical,
tightly structured progression of themes, a framing technique often referred to as the "Wheel of the Decameron,"
or the "Fortune's Wheel." Boccaccio's storytellers begin
by offering tales in which wit or ingenuity prevail over
what the narrator calls the forces of fate. For example, Ser
Cepperello, the subject of the first story of Day 1, is an evil
man who, on his death bed, deliberately deceives a friar
with a false confession in order to protect his associates
who are still involved in illicit activities. When Cepperello
dies, the friar reveals the extent of Cepperello's alleged
goodness and thereafter "there was hardly anyone who
did not pray for his assistance in time of trouble, and they
called him . . . Saint Ciappelletto." In Days 2 through 4,
the storytellers continue to discuss what can occur when
human will, love, and divine intervention come into direct
conflict. The stories of Day 2, for instance, present characters who lack the means to control their futures, while the
narratives of Day 4 focus on men and women "whose love
ended unhappily." As the group continues to reflect on the
hardships of love on Day 5, the stories, because they center on "lovers who survived calamities or misfortunes and
attained a state of happiness," emphasize triumph and recovery.

Most critics believe that Day 6 of the *Decameron* signifies
a shift in the tone and content of the novellas. After principally addressing theoretical concerns, the group members
decide to immerse themselves in the tangible pleasures of
real life. Consequently, the manner of the storytelling becomes much more relaxed and playful and the subject
matter more sexually explicit. Suggesting in Days 6
through 8 that repartee and quick-wittedness are necessary to survival, Boccaccio presents protagonists who are
able to endure disastrous situations through their clever
use of the *beffa,* or the practical joke. On Day 9, generally
considered to contain the most plainspoken and crass stories of the *Decameron,* the storytellers are given the opportunity to introduce whatever topic they choose with the
result that most of the stories involve love triangles and
unfaithful spouses. The bawdy tales come to an abrupt
halt, however, when on Day 10 Panfilo announces that
they will discuss "those who have performed liberal or
munificent deeds, whether in the cause of love or otherwise." By ending the *Decameron* with stories about renunciation, heroism, and magnanimity, Boccaccio returns to
the virtues of compassion and generosity that he introduced in his proem. Therefore, while the individual novellas illustrate numerous circumstances and represent a
wide variety of viewpoints, most critics agree that the
work as a whole possesses a distinct thematic pattern.

Although it is generally recognized that many of the stories in the *Decameron* are based on *fabliaux*—humorous
French tales popular throughout the Middle Ages—and
Oriental fables, most scholars concur that the collection
is both formally and ideologically distinctive. In addition

to its use of innovative framing structures, the *Decameron*
is one of the first works of medieval literature to advocate
that people develop individualized codes of morality instead of blindly following the dictates of religious dogma.
For example, in the last novella of the *Decameron,* commonly known as the story of Griselda, a woman remains
with her husband despite his brutally abusive behavior.
Rather than offering any ecumenical absolutes to justify
the husband's actions, Boccaccio suggests that readers
must draw their own conclusions. Teodolinda Barolini has
emphasized the secular values inherent in the *Decameron*
and has summarized the work's contribution to the development of humanistic thought: "[The *Decameron*] is a
world without answers. We are—in matters of adultery as
in matters of fate and Providence—on our own. It is this
programmatic and deliberate openness of the *Decameron*
that makes it such a revolutionary text, such a harbinger
of things to come."

The *Decameron* attained enormous popularity among literate middle-class merchants when it first appeared in
manuscript form in 1370, but Boccaccio's own feelings toward his work appear to have been ambivalent. In a letter
dated 1372, Boccaccio referred to the *Decameron* as
domesticas nugas, or "domestic trifles," that he wrote "as
a young man . . . impelled by the command of a superi-
or." Writers and scholars belonging to higher literary circles also seemed indifferent to the *Decameron,* and the
work was rarely included in aristocratic and scholarly libraries. The *Decameron* did not receive serious critical attention until 1870, when Francesco De Sanctis, in his
Storia della letteratura italiana (*History of Italian Literature*), described it as the "Human Comedy," thus suggesting it worthy of comparison to Dante's *Divine Comedy.*
Since De Sanctis's study, criticism on the *Decameron* has
been voluminous, with much of it centering on Boccaccio's use of allegory and irony, his attitudes toward
women, and the significance of metaphors, symbols, and
allusions in the individual novellas. In contrast to the intelligentsia who once shunned the book, modern scholars
now recognize that the *Decameron* is a multifarious collection that in addition to addressing the most complex, fundamental, and eternal questions facing humankind, remains one of the world's most popular and enduring
works of literature.

* PRINCIPAL WORKS

SHORT FICTION

†*Decameron*   1470
  [*Decameron,*   1620]

OTHER MAJOR WORKS

Elegia di Madonna Fiammetta   (novel)   1472
  [*Amorous Fiammetta,* 1587]
Filocolo. 5 vols.   (prose)   1472
  [*Thirteen Most Pleasant and Delectable Questions of
    Love,* 1566]
Genealogia deorum gentilium. 15 vols.   (myths and histo-
    ry)   1472
  [*Boccaccio on Poetry, Being the Preface and Fourteenth*

and Fifteenth Books of Boccaccio's Genealogia Deorum Gentilium, 1930]

De Montibus, Silvis, Fontibus, Lacubus, Fluminibus, Stagnis seu Paludibus et de Nominibus Maris Liber (nonfiction) 1473

De mulieribus claris (biographies) 1473
   [*Forty-six Lives Translated from Boccaccio's De Mulieribus Claris,* 1943]

De casibus virorum illustrium. 9 vols. (meditations and history) 1475
   [*Falls of Princes,* 1494; also published as *The Fates of Illustrious Men,* 1965]

Teseida (poetry) 1475

Ninfale fiesolano (poetry) 1477
   [*The Nymph of Fiesole,* 1960]

Trattatello in laude di Dante (criticism) 1477
   [*Life of Dante,* 1898]

Comedia delle ninfe fiorentine (poetry and prose) 1478

Filostrato (poetry) 1480-83
   [*The Filostrato,* 1873]

Corbaccio (prose) 1487
   [*Corbaccio,* 1975]

Buccolicum Carmen (poetry) 1504
   [*Boccaccio's Olympia,* 1913]

Amorosa visione (poetry) 1521

Rime (collected poetry) 1802

Caccia di Diana (poetry) 1832

Opere latine minori (poetry, prose, and letters) 1928

Tutte le opere di Giovanni Boccaccio. 12 vols. [edited by Vittore Branca] (poetry, prose, and letters) 1964

---

*The dates given are of the first dated editions of Boccaccio's works and do not reflect time or order of composition.

†First dated edition based on the manuscript of Francesco Mannelli (1384). Most modern editions of the *Decameron* trace their origins to Mannelli's manuscript or the Berlin, Hamilton 90 manuscript (1370).

Giovanni Boccaccio   (essay date ca. 1370)

[*In the following excerpt, taken from the epilogue to the* Decameron, *Boccaccio, anticipating negative critical reaction to the work, justifies his use of common Italian vernacular, his focus on women characters, and his interjection of eroticism and irony.*]

Noble young ladies, for whose solace I undertook this protracted labour, I believe that with the assistance of divine grace (the bestowal of which I impute to your compassionate prayers rather than to any merit of my own) those objectives which I set forth at the beginning of the present work have now been fully achieved. And so, after giving thanks, firstly to God and then to yourselves, the time has come for me to rest my pen and weary hand. Before conceding this repose, however, since I am fully aware that these tales of mine are no less immune from criticism than any of the other things of this world, and indeed I recall having shown this to be so at the beginning of the Fourth

Day, I propose briefly to reply to certain trifling objections which, though remaining unspoken, may possibly have arisen in the minds of my readers, including one or two of yourselves.

There will perhaps be those among you who will say that in writing these stories I have taken too many liberties, in that I have sometimes caused ladies to say, and very often to hear, things which are not very suitable to be heard or said by virtuous women. This I deny, for no story is so unseemly as to prevent anyone from telling it, provided it is told in seemly language; and this I believe I may reasonably claim to have done.

But supposing you are right (for I have no wish to start a dispute with you, knowing I shall finish on the losing side), I still maintain, when you ask me why I did it, that many reasons spring readily to mind. In the first place, if any of the stories is lacking in restraint, this is because of the nature of the story itself, which, as any well-informed and dispassionate observer will readily acknowledge, I could not have related in any other way without distorting it out of all recognition. And even if the stories do, perhaps, contain one or two trifling expressions that are too unbridled for the liking of those prudish ladies who attach more weight to words than to deeds, and are more anxious to seem virtuous than to be virtuous, I assert that it was no more improper for me to have written them than for men and women at large, in their everyday speech, to use such words as *hole,* and *rod,* and *mortar,* and *pestle,* and *crumpet,* and *stuffing,* and any number of others. Besides, no less latitude should be granted to my pen than to the brush of the painter, who without incurring censure, of a justified kind at least, depicts St Michael striking the serpent with his sword or his lance, and St George transfixing the dragon wherever he pleases; but that is not all, for he makes Christ male and Eve female, and fixes to the cross, sometimes with a single nail, sometimes with two, the feet of Him who resolved to die thereon for the salvation of mankind.

Furthermore it is made perfectly clear that these stories were told neither in a church, of whose affairs one must speak with a chaste mind and a pure tongue (albeit you will find that many of her chronicles are far more scandalous than any writings of mine), nor in the schools of philosophers, in which, no less than anywhere else, a sense of decorum is required, nor in any place where either churchmen or philosophers were present. They were told in gardens, in a place designed for pleasure, among people who, though young in years, were nonetheless fully mature and not to be led astray by stories, at a time when even the most respectable people saw nothing unseemly in wearing their breeches over their heads if they thought their lives might thereby be preserved.

Like all other things in this world, stories, whatever their nature, may be harmful or useful, depending upon the listener. Who will deny that wine, as Tosspot and Bibber and a great many others affirm, is an excellent thing for those who are hale and hearty, but harmful to people suffering from a fever? Are we to conclude, because it does harm to the feverish, that therefore it is pernicious? Who will deny that fire is exceedingly useful, not to say vital, to man? Are we to conclude, because it burns down houses and villages and whole cities, that therefore it is pernicious? And in the same way, weapons defend the liberty of those who desire to live peaceably, and very often they kill people, not because they are evil in themselves, but because of the evil intentions of those who make use of them.

No word, however pure, was ever wholesomely construed by a mind that was corrupt. And just as seemly language leaves no mark upon a mind that is corrupt, language that is less than seemly cannot sully a mind that is well ordered, any more than mud will contaminate the rays of the sun, or earthly filth the beauties of the heavens.

What other books, what other words, what other letters, are more sacred, more reputable, more worthy of reverence, than those of the Holy Scriptures? And yet there have been many who, by perversely construing them, have led themselves and others to perdition. All things have their own special purpose, but when they are wrongly used a great deal of harm may result, and the same applies to my stories. If anyone should want to extract evil counsel from these tales, or fashion an evil design, there is nothing to prevent him, provided he twists and distorts them sufficiently to find the thing he is seeking. And if anyone should study them for the usefulness and profit they may bring him, he will not be disappointed. Nor will they ever be thought of or described as anything but useful and seemly, if they are read at the proper time by the people for whom they were written. The lady who is forever saying her prayers, or baking pies and cakes for her father confessor, may leave my stories alone: they will not run after anyone demanding to be read, albeit they are no more improper than some of the trifles that self-righteous ladies recite, or even engage in, if the occasion arises.

There will likewise be those among you who will say that some of the stories included here would far better have been omitted. That is as may be: but I could only transcribe the stories as they were actually told, which means that if the ladies who told them had told them better, I should have written them better. But even if one could assume that I was the inventor as well as the scribe of these stories (which was not the case), I still insist that I would not feel ashamed if some fell short of perfection, for there is no craftsman other than God whose work is whole and faultless in every respect. Even Charlemagne, who first created the Paladins, was unable to produce them in numbers sufficient to form a whole army.

Whenever you have a multitude of things you are bound to find differences of quality. No field was ever so carefully tended that neither nettles nor brambles nor thistles were found in it, along with all the better grass. Besides, in addressing an audience of unaffected young ladies, such as most of you are, it would have been foolish of me to go to the trouble of searching high and low for exquisite tales to relate, and take excessive pains in weighing my words. And the fact remains that anyone perusing these tales is free to ignore the ones that give offence, and read only those that are pleasing. For in order that none of you may be misled, each of the stories bears on its brow the gist of that which it hides in its bosom.

I suppose it will also be said that some of the tales are too long. To which I can only reply that if you have better things to do, it would be foolish to read these tales, even if they were short. Although much time has elapsed from the day I started to write until this moment, in which I am nearing the end of my labours, it has not escaped my memory that I offered these exertions of mine to ladies with time on their hands, not to any others; and for those who read in order to pass the time, nothing can be too long if it serves the purpose for which it is used.

Brevity is all very well for students, who endeavour to use their time profitably rather than while it away, but not for you, ladies, who have as much time to spare as you fail to consume in the pleasures of love. And besides, since none of you goes to study in Athens, or Bologna, or Paris, you have need of a lengthier form of address than those who have sharpened their wits with the aid of their studies.

Doubtless there are also those among you who will say that the matters I have related are overfilled with jests and quips, of a sort that no man of weight and gravity should have committed to paper. Inasmuch as these ladies, prompted by well-intentioned zeal, show a touching concern for my good name, it behoves me to thank them, and I do so.

But I would answer their objection as follows: I confess that I do have weight, and in my time I have been weighed on numerous occasions; but I assure those ladies who have never weighed me that I have little gravity. On the contrary, I am so light that I float on the surface of water. And considering that the sermons preached by friars to chastise the faults of men are nowadays filled, for the most part, with jests and quips and raillery, I concluded that the same sort of thing would be not out of place in my stories, written to dispel the woes of ladies. But if it should cause them to laugh too much, they can easily cure themselves by turning to the Lament of Jeremiah, the Passion of Our Lord, and the Plaint of the Magdalen.

There may also be those among you who will say that I have an evil and venomous tongue, because in certain places I write the truth about the friars. But who cares? I can readily forgive you for saying such things, for doubtless you are prompted by the purest of motives, friars being decent fellows, who forsake a life of discomfort for the love of God, who do their grinding when the millpond's full, and say no more about it. Except for the fact that they all smell a little of the billy-goat, their company would offer the greatest of pleasure.

I will grant you, however, that the things of this world have no stability, but are subject to constant change, and this may well have happened to my tongue. But not long ago, distrusting my own opinion (which in matters concerning myself I trust as little as possible), I was told by a lady, a neighbour of mine, that I had the finest and sweetest tongue in the world; and this, to tell the truth, was at a time when few of these tales remained to be written. So because the aforementioned ladies are saying these things in order to spite me, I intend that what I have said shall suffice for my answer.

And now I shall leave each lady to say and believe whatever she pleases, for the time has come for me to bring all words to an end, and offer my humble thanks to Him who assisted me in my protracted labour and conveyed me to the goal I desired. May His grace and peace, sweet ladies, remain with you always, and if perchance these stories should bring you any profit, remember me. (pp. 829-33)

> *Giovanni Boccaccio, "Author's Epilogue," in his* The Decameron, *translated by G. H. Mc-William, Penguin Books, 1972, pp. 829-33.*

Petrarch   (letter date 1373)

[*An Italian poet and scholar, Petrarch is regarded as one of the greatest literary figures of the Renaissance. An ardent humanist and Latinist, he is primarily known for the lyric expressiveness, passion, and psychological power of his poems, collected in the* Canzoniere (1374), *which exerted a tremendous influence on European literature. In the following excerpt from a letter to Boccaccio dated 1373, Petrarch defends the unscholarly subject matter and relaxed narrative style in the* Decameron, *stating: "It is important to know for whom we are writing, and a difference in the character of one's listeners justifies a difference in style." This letter also originally contained Petrarch's Latin translation of the story of Griselda, the last narrative in the* Decameron.]

Your [**Decameron**], written in our mother tongue and published, I presume, during your early years, has fallen into my hands, I know not whence or how. If I told you that I had read it, I should deceive you. It is a very big volume, written in prose and for the multitude. I have been, moreover, occupied with more serious business, and much pressed for time. You can easily imagine the unrest caused by the warlike stir about me, for, far as I have been from actual participation in the disturbances, I could not but be affected by the critical condition of the state. What I did was to run through your book, like a traveller who, while hastening forward, looks about him here and there, without pausing. I have heard somewhere that your volume was attacked by the teeth of certain hounds, but that you defended it valiantly with staff and voice. This did not surprise me, for not only do I well know your ability, but I have learned from experience of the existence of an insolent and cowardly class who attack in the work of others everything which they do not happen to fancy or be familiar with, or which they cannot themselves accomplish. Their insight and capabilities extend no farther; on all other themes they are silent.

My hasty perusal afforded me much pleasure. If the humour is a little too free at times, this may be excused in view of the age at which you wrote, the style and language which you employ, and the frivolity of the subjects, and of the persons who are likely to read such tales. It is important to know for whom we are writing, and a difference in the character of one's listeners justifies a difference in style. Along with much that was light and amusing, I discovered some serious and edifying things as well, but I can pass no definite judgment upon them, since I have not examined the work thoroughly.

As usual, when one looks hastily through a book, I read

somewhat more carefully at the beginning and at the end. At the beginning you have, it seems to me, accurately described and eloquently lamented the condition of our country during that siege of pestilence which forms so dark and melancholy a period in our century. At the close you have placed a story which differs entirely from most that precede it, and which so delighted and fascinated me that, in spite of cares which made me almost oblivious of myself, I was seized with a desire to learn it by heart, so that I might have the pleasure of recalling it for my own benefit, and of relating it to my friends in conversation. When an opportunity for telling it offered itself shortly after, I found that my auditors were delighted. Later it suddenly occurred to me that others, perhaps, who were unacquainted with our tongue, might be pleased with so charming a story, as it had delighted me ever since I first heard it some years ago, and as you had not considered it unworthy of presentation in the mother tongue, and had placed it, moreover, at the end of your book, where, according to the principles of rhetoric, the most effective part of the composition belongs. So one fine day when, as usual, my mind was distracted by a variety of occupations, discontented with myself and my surroundings. I suddenly sent everything flying, and, snatching my pen, I attacked this story of yours. I sincerely trust that it will gratify you that I have of my own free-will undertaken to translate your work, something I should certainly never think of doing for anyone else, but which I was induced to do in this instance by my partiality for you and for the story. Not neglecting the precept of Horace in his *Art of Poetry,* that the careful translator should not attempt to render word for word, I have told your tale in my own language, in some places changing or even adding a few words, for I felt that you would not only permit, but would approve, such alterations.

Although many have admired and wished for my version, it seemed to me fitting that your work should be dedicated to you rather than to anyone else; and it is for you to judge whether I have, by this change of dress, injured or embellished the original. The story returns whence it came; it knows its judge, its home, and the way thither. As you and everyone who reads this knows, it is you and not I who must render account for what is essentially yours. If anyone asks me whether this is all true, whether it is a history or a story, I reply in the words of Sallust, "I refer you to the author"—to wit, my friend Giovanni. (pp. 191-94)

My object in thus re-writing your tale was not to induce the women of our time to imitate the patience of this wife, which seems to me almost beyond imitation, but to lead my readers to emulate the example of feminine constancy, and to submit themselves to God with the same courage as did this woman to her husband. Although, as the Apostle James tells us, "God cannot be tempted with evil, and he himself tempteth no man," he still may prove us, and often permits us to be beset with many and grievous trials, not that he may know our character, which he knew before we were created, but in order that our weakness should be made plain to ourselves by obvious and familiar proofs. Anyone, it seems to me, amply deserves to be reckoned among the heroes of mankind who suffers without a murmur for God, what this poor peasant woman bore for her mortal husband.

My affection for you has induced me to write at an advanced age what I should hardly have undertaken even as a young man. Whether what I have narrated be true or false I do not know, but the fact that you wrote it would seem sufficient to justify the inference that it is but a tale. Foreseeing this question, I have prefaced my translation with the statement that the responsibility for the story rests with the author; that is, with you. And now let me tell you my experiences with this narrative, or tale, as I prefer to call it.

In the first place, I gave it to one of our mutual friends in Padua to read, a man of excellent parts and wide attainments. When scarcely half-way through the composition, he was suddenly arrested by a burst of tears. When again, after a short pause, he made a manful attempt to continue, he was again interrupted by a sob. He then realised that he could go no farther himself, and handed the story to one of his companions, a man of education, to finish. How others may view this occurrence I cannot, of course, say; for myself, I put a most favourable construction upon it, believing that I recognise the indications of a most compassionate disposition; a more kindly nature, indeed, I never remember to have met. As I saw him weep as he read, the words of the Satirist [Juvenal] came back to me:

> Nature, who gave us tears, by that alone
> Proclaims she made the feeling heart our own;
> And 't is our noblest sense.

Some time after, another friend of ours, from Verona (for all is common between us, even our friends), having heard of the effect produced by the story in the first instance, wished to read it for himself. I readily complied, as he was not only a good friend, but a man of ability. He read the narrative from beginning to end without stopping once. Neither his face nor his voice betrayed the least emotion, not a tear or a sob escaped him. "I too," he said at the end, "would have wept, for the subject certainly excites pity, and the style is well adapted to call forth tears, and I am not hard-hearted; but I believed, and still believe, that this is all an invention. If it were true, what woman, whether of Rome or any other nation, could be compared with this Griselda? Where do we find the equal of this conjugal devotion, where such faith, such extraordinary patience and constancy?" I made no reply to this reasoning, for I did not wish to run the risk of a bitter debate in the midst of our good-humoured and friendly discussion. But I had a reply ready. There are some who think that whatever is difficult for them must be impossible for others; they must measure others by themselves, in order to maintain their superiority. Yet there have been many, and there may still be many, to whom acts are easy which are commonly held to be impossible. Who is there who would not, for example, regard a Curtius, a Mucius, or the Decii, among our own people, as pure fictions; or, among foreign nations, Codrus and the Philæni; or, since we are speaking of woman, Portia, or Hypsicratia, or Alcestis, and others like them? But these are actual historical persons. And indeed I do not see why one who can face death for another,

should not be capable of encountering any trial or form of suffering. . . . (pp. 194-96)

Petrarch, in a letter to Boccaccio in 1373, in Petrarch: The First Modern Scholar and Man of Letters *by James Harvey Robinson with Henry Winchester Rolfe, 1898. Reprint by Haskell House Publishers Ltd., 1970, pp. 191-96.*

Boccaccio, on his intentions in the *Decameron:*

[In] order that I may to some extent repair the omissions of Fortune, which (as we may see in the case of the more delicate sex) was always more sparing of support wherever natural strength was more deficient, I intend to provide succour and diversion for the ladies, but only for those who are in love, since the others can make do with their needles, their reels and their spindles. I shall narrate a hundred stories or fables or parables or histories or whatever you choose to call them, recited in ten days by a worthy band of seven ladies and three young men, who assembled together during the plague which recently took such heavy toll of life. And I shall also include some songs, which these seven ladies sang for their mutual amusement.

Giovanni Boccaccio, in his preface to the De-cameron, *translated by G. H. McWilliam, Penguin, 1972.*

Francesco De Sanctis   (essay date 1870-71)

[*De Sanctis was a nineteenth-century Italian critic who is regarded as the founder of modern Italian literary criticism. He is best known for his* Storia della letteratura italiana (1870), *a collection widely viewed as a classic in Italian literary history. In the following excerpt, taken from the English translation of this work, De Sanctis provides one of the first scholarly analyses of the* Decameron *and explains how it profoundly influenced subsequent Italian literature.*]

[If] we open the ***Decameron,*** hardly have we read the first tale when we seem to have fallen from the clouds and be asking with Petrarch, "How came I here, and when?" It is not an evolution; it is a cataclysm, a revolution—one of those sudden revolutions that from one day to another show us a changed world. Here we have the Middle Ages not only denied, but made fun of.

[The character] Ser Cepperello is a Tartuffe some centuries before his time, with the difference, however, that where Molière aims at rousing us to hatred and disgust for the hypocrisy of Tartuffe, Boccaccio gets fun out of Cepperello's, and is less concerned with our feelings towards the hypocrite than with making us laugh at the expense of his good confessor and the credulous friars and the credulous people. So the weapon of Molière is sarcastic irony, whereas the weapon of Boccaccio is merry caricature. To meet again with Boccaccio's forms and aims we must go as far as Voltaire; Giovanni Boccaccio, in certain aspects, is the Voltaire of the fourteenth century.

Many people complain of Boccaccio, saying that he spoiled the Italian spirit. And he himself, in his old age, was overcome with remorse and ended his life as a cleric, inveighing against his own book. But it is evident that his book would never have been possible if the Italian spirit had not already begun to be spoiled—if "spoiled" is the correct word for it. If the things Boccaccio laughed at had been venerated (granting for the sake of argument that then he could have laughed at them) the people of his day would have been indignant. But the very opposite was the case. The book seemed to respond to something in people's souls that for a long time had been wanting to come out, and to be saying boldly what all were saying in their secret hearts. It was applauded so loudly, and met with such great success, that the good Passavanti took fright at it and set up his *Specchio di vera penitenza* as an antidote. Boccaccio, then, was the literary voice of a world that men were already confusedly aware of. A secret was about: Boccaccio guessed this secret, and every one applauded him. This fact, instead of being cursed, deserves to be studied.

The character of the Middle Ages was transcendence: an ultra-human and ultra-natural "beyond" of Nature and man, the genus and the species outside of the individual, matter and form outside of their unity, the intellect outside of the soul, perfection and virtue outside of life, the law outside of the consciousness, the spirit outside of the body, and the aim of life outside of the world. This philosophical theology was based on the existence of universals. The world was populated by beings or intelligences, and there were endless disputes over their nature. Were they divine? Were they real genera and real species? Were they intelligible species? But the structure was already shaking under the blows of the Nominalists, the people who denied the existence of the genera and the species and declared that only the single, the individual, existed. Theirs was the motto which was afterwards to become so familiar, "Entities should not be multiplied unnecessarily."

The natural result of this exaggerated world of theocracy was asceticism. Earthly life had lost its seriousness and its value. Man lived on the earth with his spirit in the next life. And the acme of perfection was set in ecstasies, prayers, and contemplation. So literature too was theocratic, and the mysteries, visions, and allegories arose, so [Dante's] *Divine Comedy* was born, the poem of the other world. (pp. 290-91)

[In the *Decameron* Boccaccio turns his back] on allegory and chivalry and mythology, on the world of Dante and the world of the classics, shuts himself up in his own society, and lives in it, and is happy, for at last he has found himself: the life he depicts is his own life. And we wonder that he took so long to find his genre and recognize that his strength as a writer lay precisely in the depiction of his own society, directly and naturally, as he knew and saw it at first hand. And yet . . . what a long gestation and difficult labour were necessary before that world of his spirit could come to birth.

But Boccaccio's world of the *Decameron* was not a new world: it had existed long before Boccaccio. The whole of Italy was filled with romances and stories and Latin can-

zoni, licentious songs. Women . . . were in the habit of reading these books to each other in the privacy of their rooms, and a continuous stream of amusing and licentious tales was provided for them by the writers of *novelle*. The romances as a rule were connected with the adventures of the knights of the Round Table and of Charlemagne. The *Amorosa visione* mentions a large number of these heroes and heroines of chivalry: Arthur, Lancelot, Galahad, Iseult the Fair, Chedino, Palomides, Lionel, Tristan, Orlando, Rinaldo, Guttifre, Robert Guiscard, Frederick Barbarossa, Frederick II. Boccaccio, like the others, wrote his romances for women. Having written a new version of the romance of Florio and Biancofiore, he had turned to the heroic and primitive times of Greek tradition as more compatible with his studies of the ancients. But of all the types of literature of that day the one that was to spread the quickest and be the most enjoyed was the *novella*, the tale or short story, for this was the type which was most in keeping with the spirit of the times. And the writers of tales furbished up or invented every sort and kind of them, serious and comic, moral and obscene, decking them out and varying them to suit their public. So the short story was alive—was a type of literature that was swayed and changed by the imagination. Men of culture despised the legend equally with the tale, and kept to their own sphere, high above both of them, leaving *The Little Flowers of St. Francis* and the *Life of the Blessed Columbine* to the friars, and the story of the simpleton Calandrino and the gallant adventures of Alatiel to the ordinary man who liked an amusing story.

And here is Boccaccio, walking into the middle of this profane and frivolous world of *novelle*, with no other aim than to turn out pleasant tales to suit the women who were his public. And lo! from that rough and illiterate and unformed material he created the harmonious world of art.

Learned researches have been made into the sources of Boccaccio's tales. And there are many people who are under the strange impression that one is taking away from Boccaccio's glory by proving that the greater number of them were not invented by himself—as though the duty of an artist were to invent rather than to shape. As a matter of fact, the material of the *Decameron*, like the material of the *Divine Comedy* and of [Petrarch's] *Canzoniere*, was not the creation of a single brain, but was the growth of numberless minds in unconscious collaboration, and had passed through many and various forms before Boccaccio with his genius fixed it and made it eternal.

Tales under different names were extremely common among all the Latin peoples; there had been stories and story-tellers, but never as yet *the* story and *the* story-teller, especially not the latter. There had never yet been the single author in whom the separate tales had been brought together, unified, and made into an organic world. It was reserved for Boccaccio to take these separate stories, of different times, of different customs, of different tendencies, and fuse them into a single and complete picture of the living world of his time, of his own contemporary society, of which he himself had all the tendencies whether for good or for evil.

Boccaccio is not a superior soul, a writer who looks at society from a lofty height, sees the good and the bad in it, exposes it impartially, and is perfectly conscious of it all; he is an artist who feels himself one with the society in which he lives, and he writes with that sort of semi-consciousness of men who are swayed by the shifting impressions of life without stopping to analyze them. And this really is the quality that divides him substantially from the ecstatic Dante and the ecstatic Petrarch. Boccaccio is all on the surface of life, among the pleasures and idlenesses and vicissitudes of everyday existence, and these are enough for him, he is busy and satisfied. He is not the type to turn his soul into himself and think deeply with knitted brow and pensive gaze; it was not for nothing that they called him "Giovanni the Tranquil." Intimacy, raptness, ecstasy, the unquiet deeps of thought, the living in one's own spirit with phantasms and mysteries, disappear from Italian literature when Boccaccio enters it. Life rises to the surface, and is smoothed down, made attractive. The world of the spirit makes its exit; the world of Nature comes in.

This world of Nature, empty and superficial, devoid of all the inner powers of the spirit, has no seriousness at all of means or of end. The thing that moves it is instinct— natural inclination; no longer God nor science, and no longer the unifying love of intellect and act, the great basis of the Middle Ages: it is a real and violent reaction against mysticism. The author introduces us to a merry gathering of men and women who are trying to forget the ills and tedium of life by passing the warm hours of the day in pleasant story-telling. It was the time of the plague, and men faced by death on every side felt that all the restraints of life were loosened, and gave themselves up to the carnival of the imagination. Boccaccio had had experience of carnivals at the court where the happiest days of his life were spent, and his imagination had taken its colour from that dungheap on which the Muses and the Graces had lavished so many flowers. In the *Ameto,* the pastoral **Decameron,** we have a similar gathering of people. But the stories in the *Ameto* are allegorical, so are preordained to an abstract ending. Though the poem has nothing of the spirit of the *Divine Comedy,* it is built on its skeleton. Here, on the contrary, the sole aim of the stories is to make the time pass pleasantly; they are real panders to pleasure and to love, the Greek title of the book being only a modest veil of the author's Italian title, which was that of the Prince Galeotto. And the characters, evoked from so many different people and so many different epochs, here are all of the same world, the external world of tranquil thoughtlessness.

In this care-free world of the **Decameron** events are left to take care of themselves, the results being decided by chance. God and Providence are acknowledged by name, almost by a sort of tacit agreement, in the words of people who have sunk into complete religious, political, and moral indifference. Nor is there even that intimate force of things which endows the events with a sort of logic and necessity; the book, indeed, is charming for exactly the opposite quality; it is charming for its completely unexpected dénouements, which are utterly different from anything we could reasonably have foreseen, and this by the whim of chance. It is a new form of the marvellous, no longer

caused by the penetration into human life of ultra-natural forces, such as visions and miracles, but by a curious conflux of fortuitous events that no one could possibly have foreseen or controlled. We are left with the feeling that the ruler of the world, the *deus ex machina,* is chance; we see it in the varied play of the inclinations of these people, all of them ruled by the changing chances of life.

Since the machinery, the moving force of the stories, is the marvellous, the fortuitous, the unexpected, it follows that their interest does not lie in the morality of the actions, but in the strangeness of their causes and effects. Not that Boccaccio rejects morality or alters the ordinary ideas of right and wrong; it is only that questions of morality do not happen to be the questions that interest him. But the thing that does interest him is his power to stimulate his readers' interest by strangeness of character and events. Virtue is used as a means of impressing the imagination, an instrument of the marvellous like the rest, so ceases to be simple and proportionate; in fact, it is exaggerated to such a degree as to show clearly the emptiness of the author's conscience and his want of moral feeling. A famous instance is the story of the patient Griselda, the most virtuous of all the characters of the book. To prove that she is a good and faithful wife she suffocates every natural feeling of a woman, and her own personality, and her free will. The author, in trying to show an extraordinary example of virtue that will strike the imagination of his readers, has fallen into the very mysticism he dislikes, and makes use of it by placing the ideal of feminine virtue in the abnegation of self, exactly like the theologians, who teach that flesh is absorbed by spirit, and spirit by God. It is a sort of sacrifice of Abraham, except that here it is the husband who puts Nature so cruelly to the test. And the virtue in the stories of Tito and of Gisippo is proved by such strange and out-of-the-way happenings that instead of charming us as an example it only amazes us as a miracle. But extraordinary and spectacular virtue is rare in the tales; the virtue is generally the traditional virtue of chivalric and feudal times—a certain generosity and kindliness of kings and princes and marquises, reminiscences of chivalric and heroic tales in bourgeois times. A prince's virtue lies in his using his power to protect the people below him, and especially to protect the men of high intelligence and culture who happen to be poor, as did the Abbot of Cluny and Can Grande della Scala, who treated Primasso and Bergamino with magnificence. A much-praised person is Charles I of Anjou, who instead of seizing and raping two beautiful girls, daughters of a Ghibelline, who had fallen into his power, preferred to dower them magnificently and find them husbands. These powerful nobles were virtuous because they did not misuse their power, but behaved instead in a liberal and courteous manner. And already a class of literati was arising who lived at the expense of this virtue, feeding on its bounty and extolling it in fair exchange. The lofty soul of Dante had bent itself with difficulty to this patronage; not the least of his causes of bitterness was the begging of bread from strangers, crust by crust, and the treading of other people's stairs. But the heroic age was past. Petrarch allowed his Maecenas to provide for him and support him, and Boccaccio lived on the refuse of the court of Naples, comically enraged when the provision struck him as not up to standard, and disposed to panegyric or satire according to whether the food was good or bad. In Boccaccio's world "virtue" as a rule means liberality or courtesy of soul, which had spread from the castle to the city, and even into the woods where the outlaws had taken refuge—men like Natan, and Saladino, and Alfonso, and Ghino di Tacco, and the wizard of Ansaldo. Strictly speaking, of course this virtue is not morality; but at least it is a sense of nice behaviour, which makes the habits of the day more agreeable, takes from virtue that theological and mystical character connected with abstinence and suffering, and gives it a pleasing appearance, in keeping with a cultured and gay society. It is true that the chance which ruled the lives of these people played them many a trick, and the pervading gaiety, the charming serenity, were often disturbed by some sad event. But the clouds came suddenly, without warning, were soon scattered, and gave an added value to the sun when it shone again; in Fiammetta's words, sorrow was "a fine material for tempering gladness."

If we look more deeply into these questions of joy and sorrow, we shall see that the joy has very few chords; the joy would be level and dull, and no longer joyous (as is often the case with idyllic poems), except that pain pierces into it—pain with its richer and more varied harmonies, and its living passions of love, jealousy, contempt, indignation. Pain is here not for its own sake, but as a seasoner of joy; it is here to enliven the spirit, to keep it in suspense, to excite it—until kindly fortune, or chance, shall suddenly make the sun to shine again. And even when the story has a sad ending (as in all of the tales of the third day) the sadness is only superficial; it is relieved and softened by descriptions, dissertations, and musings, and is never so strong as to be torment, like Dante's proud suffering. In that world of Nature and love pain is a tragic apparition that flits past. It is not caused by a moral purpose, but by the "point of honour," the chivalric virtue—by honour in collusion with Nature and love. A case in point is the lovely story of Gerbino; and also the story of Tancredi, who is a witness to his daughter's shame, and kills the lover, and sends the lover's heart to his daughter in a golden cup; his daughter puts poison in the cup, and drinks it, and dies. The tragedy turns on the point of honour. Tancredi feels more dishonoured by his daughter's having loved a man beneath her in rank than by the fact that she has loved illicitly. But his daughter justifies her love by quoting the laws of Nature, and saying that true nobility comes from worth and not from blood. When we take leave of the father weeping vainly and remorsefully over his daughter's body, we see him not as a man who has avenged his tarnished honour, but as a traitor to the laws of Nature and of love. But indeed we pity the father and daughter equally—the high-souled father and the human and tender-hearted daughter; both are victims of the society they belong to, and neither has sinned. Our last impression is that Nature and Love have taken their revenge. So the tragic motive is in keeping with Boccaccio's world; and the fugitive, vanishing pain is shown most tenderly and gently, almost with compassion. Pain gives a flavour to joy, for joy would end by being insipid if pain were not there to season it. Tragedy is changed at its root. There is no longer the terror of a mysterious fate, shown in catastrophe, as with the Greeks, nor of a punishment falling on

man for breaking the laws of a higher justice, as in Dante; tragedy here is the fact that the world is at the mercy of its own blind and natural forces, and the higher law in this struggle is love—whoever opposes love is in the wrong. With Dante Nature was sin; with Boccaccio Nature is law. And it is not opposed by religion or morality (of which nothing remains at all, though both are believed in theoretically, and quoted), but by society as arranged in that complex system of laws and customs called "honour." But the struggle is all external; it is shown in the events that arise from these various forces brought into conflict, and is ended by the kindness or the spite of chance or fortune. And the struggle stops short at that inner conflict which leads to passion and makes character. Boccaccio has no idea of rebelling against society, and certainly is nothing of a reformer; he takes life as he finds it. And though his sympathies are entirely with the victims of love, he is not biased for that reason against the characters who are driven to cruel actions through love; they too are worthy of respect, for they are victims of love like the others. Though he glorifies Gerbino, who breaks his pledge to the King, his grandfather, rather than break the laws of love and be thought a coward, he has no word of blame for the King, who orders the death of his grandson, "choosing to be without a grandson rather than be thought a king wanting in honour." In the midst of the outer conflict of events an inner calm, a sort of equilibrium, is born, an inner calm quite empty of emotion, except the degree of emotion that is necessary for varying its life. And so this bourgeois, indifferent world of tragedy, whose only ruler is Nature, is external and superficial, is a piece of wreckage adrift on the immensity of the ocean. The action is developed from strong passions provoked by the conflict of events, not by conscious thought; and it melts away into a game of the imagination, becomes an artistic contemplation of the different events of life that arrest our attention and surprise us. Virtue and vice are meaningless except in so far as they lead to "adventures," to strange events governed by the caprices of chance. To the audience they are only a means for making the time pass pleasantly; virtue and pain are procurers of pleasure.

A world ruled by pleasure and guided by chance is heedless and gay, but is comic too. This taking of events without seriousness, this capricious interweaving of chance happenings, this inner equilibrium undisturbed by the most cruel vicissitudes, are the natural breeding-ground of the comic. When laughter is empty and meaningless it is nothing but the mirth of fools; laughter to be intelligent and malicious must have a point and a meaning, must be comic. And the comic gives this world its physiognomy and its seriousness.

Boccaccio's world is material for comedy by its very nature; for nothing is more comic than a thoughtless and sensual society, which gives rise to types like Don Juan and Sancho Panza. But it represented the extreme of culture and intellect that was known at that time, and was aware of the fact. It had the advantage of being taken seriously by all the world, and at the same time of being able to make fun of the world. In fact, these tales have two sides to them that are serious: the glorification of intelligence (the most powerful nobles are shown as respecting it) and a certain pride of the burgher who is taking his due position in the world and is setting himself up as the equal of the barons and the counts. This bourgeois class was Boccaccio's own; it was a class of educated, intelligent people, who thought that they were the only people who were civilized, and that all the others were barbarians. And the comedy springs from the caricature by the intelligent man of the things and people in a lower stratum of intellectual life than his own. Side by side with cultured society were the friars and priests, or, in Boccaccio's words, "the Catholic things"—prayers, confessions, sermons, fasts, mortifications of the flesh, visions, and miracles. And behind the Catholic things were the people, with their stupidity and their credulity. These are the two orders of things and people round whom he cracks his whip.

Prayers like the Lord's Prayer of St. Julian, the serving of God in the desert, the everyday life of the friars and priests and nuns, which belied their teachings, the art of sanctification taught to Fra Puccio, the miracles of saints and their visions, such as the apparition of the Angel Gabriel; and the stupidity of the people made game of by the clever—these are comic material. Most clear of all in the *Decameron* is the reaction of the flesh against the inordinate rigour of the clergy, who had forbidden the theatres and romances, and had preached that Paradise was only to be won through fasting and the wearing of hair shirts. The natural form of expression of the reaction is licence and cynicism. The flesh avenges its curse, turns on its enemies, and calls them "merchanists"—meaning people who judge stupidly, who follow vulgar opinion. So the exaggerated world of the spirit has become "vulgar." We can well picture all the voluptuousness of the flesh as it stretches itself after its long subjection; with what relish it unfolds its joys one by one, choosing just those ways and expressions which of all others have been most forbidden, and often giving obscene double meanings to holy words and sayings. The profane world is in open rebellion, has broken its bonds, and is mocking its former master. This is the basis of the comedy; a great variety of intertwined chance events are built on it. We have the two eternal protagonists of all comedies: the person who makes fun and the person made fun of, the clever man and the simpleton; and of all the simpletons the most cruelly treated and the most innocent, are the husbands. And amid the many fortuitous events are born a great variety of comic characters, of which some have remained as real types, such as the *cattivello,* the naughty one, of Calandrino and the revengeful scholar who knows where the Devil keeps his tail. The serious characters are rather singularities than types; individuals lost in the minute description and the eccentricity of their natures, like Griselda, Tito, the Count of Anguersa, Madama Beritola, Ginevra, Salvestra, Isabetta, and Tancredi's daughter. But the poignant and intimate part of the book is in the comic characters; these are the universal types which we meet with every day, like Compar Pietro, and Maestro Simone, and Fra Puccio, the friar who was sheep-like, and the judge who was *squasimodeo* (of no account), and Monna Belcolore, and Tofano, and Gianni Lotteringhi, and all the others, for "the number of the stupid is infinite." And this gay and thoughtless world unfolds itself, gains an outline and a character, and becomes the "human comedy."

And so, within a short distance of each other we get the comedy and the anti-comedy—we get the "divine comedy" and its parody, the "human comedy." On the same threshold and in the same times we have Passavanti, Cavalca, Catherine of Siena—voices of the other world—and Giovanni Boccaccio drowning them with his loud and profane laugh. The Gay Science has arisen from its grave with its laughter as fresh as ever; the troubadours and the story-tellers, whom the priests had silenced, have come back to life and are dancing as merrily as before and are singing their profane canzoni in the Florence of the Guelfs. The forbidden tale and romance are ruling in the realm of literature; they forbid in their turn, and are the absolute masters of literature. Naturally the change is not quite unannounced, does not come like an earthquake. As we have seen, the lay spirit has kept an unbroken tradition through the whole of literature, until in the *Divine Comedy* it takes its place with boldness, and declares that it too is sacred and of divine right, and Dante, a layman, speaks like a priest and an apostle. But Dante is so careful that his building shall stand, that its foundation shall be firm. Dante's *Divine Comedy* is a reformation; Boccaccio's is a revolution, which throws the whole edifice to the ground and erects another on its ruins.

The *Divine Comedy* ceased to be a living book; it was expounded as a classical work, but was little read or understood or enjoyed, though it was always admired. It was divine, but no longer alive. And sinking into its grave it drew along with it all those kinds of literature whose germs appear so strongly and vigorously in its immortal sketches: tragedy, drama, the hymn, the laud, the legend, the mystery. There feeling died with them for the family, for Nature, for country, the belief in a better world, rapture and ecstasy and inwardness, the pure joys of friendship and love, the seriousness of life, and ideality. Of all this immense world which collapsed before it came to fruition, all that remained was Malebolge, the realm of malice, the seat of the "human comedy"; Malebolge, which Dante had thrown into filth, the place where laughter was choked by disgust and indignation. Here is Malebolge, but on the earth, laughing infernally, adorned by the Graces, and announcing that it alone is truly Paradise—as Don Felice understood very well, but not poor Fra Puccio. The world in fact is upside down. To Dante the *Divine Comedy* is heavenly bliss; to Boccaccio the "comedy" is earthly bliss, and one of the pleasures of this earthly bliss is the driving away of sadness by making jokes about Heaven. The flesh is out to enjoy itself; the spirit is paying the bill.

The flesh was reacting against a spirituality that was overstrained and out of touch with real life. And if the reaction had taken the form of an active struggle in the lofty regions of the spirit, as happened in other countries, the change would have come more gradually or have been more opposed, but would have borne more fruit. Faith and conviction would have been strengthened by the struggle, and would have generated a literature full of vigour and substance, with something of the passion of Luther, the eloquence of Bossuet, the doubts of Pascal, and with those literary forms which are found only when the inner life is strong and healthy. The movement would have been at the same time negative and positive, destructive and constructive. But audacity of thought had been punished without mercy, the Ghibelline faction had been crushed with bloodshed, and the papacy was near at hand, watchful and suspicious. The world of religion, as corrupt in its habits as it was absolute in its doctrine and grotesque in its forms, collided with the new culture that had grown so fast, with the spirit that was so adult and so matured by the study of the classics. These cultured people were unable to take the religious world seriously, and so were cut off from the rest of society, from the greater part of the people, who remained as they were, passive and inert in the hands of the priest of Varlungo, of Donno Gianni, of Frate Rinaldo, of Frate Cipolla. Educated people came to look on that world as stupid and mechanical, and to laugh at it became the hallmark of a cultured person; even the priests themselves laughed at it, those priests who aspired to being cultured.

And so there were two separate and distinct societies, living side by side, and on the whole without bothering each other too much. Men were forbidden to think for themselves, or to question abstract doctrines, but their everyday lives were another thing entirely—they lived and let live, squeezed amusement out of everything, and eased their feelings by calling on the names of God and Mary. Even the preachers amused their congregations with mottoes, jokes, bantering, a habit which Dante thought obnoxious in the highest degree, but which drew a laugh from Boccaccio. At the end of his *Novelliere* he says: "If the sermons of the friars, preached to make men remorseful for their sins, are full of jokes and nonsense and mockery, it seemed to me that these same things would not be unbecoming in my tales, which are written to drive away melancholy from women." Dante's indignation has gone, and in its place has come laughter, as though at the expense of things become common. Anger is the sign of saints and of men of conscience everywhere; to be angry a man must first believe, must feel his beliefs to be outraged. But the cultured society of that day had no notion of losing its temper over the sinfulness of mankind. In the **Decameron** the "unblushing dames of Florence" are charmers and seducers of men and are grouped into "living pictures," as they would be called today. The traffic in holy things, which drove believing Germany to schism, which Dante in his noble wrath called "adultery," here is only a matter for amiable quibbling, without rancour or malice. The confessional is the centre of ambiguities that are very amusing; the laity, both men and women, play tricks on the priests—on "the round and fat men"—as we see from the confessor of Ser Ciappelletto and from Frate Bestia, excellent comic characters. Sham miracles, like that of Masetto, the market-gardener, or of Martellino in difficulty, or of Frate Alberto, or of Frate Cipolla, and the faking of saints and making them into miracle-workers, as in the tale of Ser Ciappelletto—these are shown with the gay sense of the comic of a cultured and sceptical people. Profanations like these make people laugh, because the things profaned no longer inspire any reverence.

This society was taken bodily, just as it was, warm, palpitating, vividly alive, and was put into the **Decameron.** The book is an immense picture of life in all its variety of the characters and the events most calculated to make people

marvel. Here is Malebolge, the sensual and profligate world of cunning and ignorance, taken out of Hell and staged on the earth; and within Malebolge, but not amalgamating with it, is the cultured and civilized world, the world of courtesy, the echo of chivalric times—just a trifle bourgeois, perhaps, but witty, elegant, clever, pleasing; its finest type is Federigo degli Alberighi. The priests and friars and peasants and artisans and lowly burghers and small merchants, with their women, are the natives of the country; and the loud plebeian laughter of these people in their perpetual carnival is all around the ladies and the knights of the world of spirit, culture, wit, and elegance, with its courtesies and habits of chivalry—a world gay like the other, but with a polite and measured gaiety, with a large way of doing things, pleasant modes of speaking, and decorum in its customs. These two worlds, different, but living cheek by jowl, are fused together in the background of the picture, producing an effect of harmony that is unique; they are fused into a single world that is thoughtless and superficial, living externally in the enjoyments of life, and led hither and thither just as fortune decrees.

This twofold world, whose varied notes are so excellently harmonized, takes its tone from the author and from the merry company he puts on the stage. The author and the characters who tell the tales belong to the cultured class: the name of God is often in their mouths, they speak respectfully of the Church, conform to the customs of religion, take a holiday on Friday, because Friday was the day on which Our Lord "died that we might live," sing allegorical and Platonic canzoni, and live a life of gaiety, but one arranged in a manner befitting civilized persons. This society had culture, wit, elegance, poetry, to make it pleasant—was, in fact, like the high society of today. It reflected the feudal world of courtesy, which the cultured and wealthy burgher-class was taking as its model, but dressing up with a new adornment of culture and wit. Just as the feudal world had had its buffoons and jugglers, this society had the people who made it merry; its buffoons and jugglers were the people about it—that numberless crowd of priests, friars, peasants, and artisans; amusement was drawn from everything, from the stupid as well as from the clever. The comedy is utterly lacking in any high or serious intention, either to break down prejudice, or to attack institutions, or to fight ignorance, or to moralize, or to reform—as was true with Rabelais or Montaigne, whose comic art is a reaction of good sense from the artificial and the conventional. The laughter of those writers is serious because it leaves something behind it in the consciousness. But Boccaccio's laughter is an end in itself. Its aim is to drive away melancholy and prevent tedium, and that is all. Boccaccio looks at that plebeian world with the eye of an artist studying his model; he is bent on mastering its curves and features and placing it in the light best calculated to please his noble company. From all the immense shipwreck of conscience there still survives a sense of literary integrity, of artistic feeling, strengthened by wit and culture. The masterpieces of the **Decameron** are the fruit of this literary conscience; types are idealized to suit and please the intelligent and sensual society of our genial artist, the idol of the young women to whom he dedicates his stories.

The special quality that makes these models immortal is the comic ideal of showing that society at close quarters and exactly as it is, with all its ignorance and malice, and as seen through the eyes of intelligent people who are there merely to enjoy the spectacle and clap their hands. The motive of the comedy does not come from the mortal world, but from the intellectual world; the intelligent people are making fun of the ignorant, who are much more numerous. What makes the picture so lively is chiefly a certain simplicity of mind that we find in uncultured people, thrown into relief by that cunning which is the basis of a fool's character; besides being stupid, the fool is often credulous, vain, boastful, vulgarly ambitious. So cunning gives vanity to character and throws its ridiculous side into relief. But cunning is comic too—not, of course, to the fool himself, but to the clever people who understand him. So the two types of actor play into each other's hands, each doing his best towards getting the laughs. And here we have the foundation of Boccaccio's "comedy": culture blossoming for the first time, and conscious of itself, and turning the ignorance and malice of the lower classes into a joke. And the comic element is most highly flavoured of all when it happens that the people made game of are those who have the habit of victimizing others—the cunning people who victimize the simpletons made game of in their turn by the intelligent, as when women make game of their confessors.

Then the comedy leaps out with a sudden movement that illumines the whole situation, and laughter breaks out, spontaneous, irresistible. The stories are short, and their flavour is all in their tail, as with the sonnet. Such, for example, is the story of the Jew who is converted to Christianity on seeing how corrupt the Christians are. The ending is so utterly unexpected, so surprising, in view of what has gone before, that the effect produced is very great. There are several stories of this type that are not so effective, because the author was working on a material that was already known, for instance, the tales of the Marchesana di Monferrato, of Guglielmo Borsiere, and of Maestro Alberto. These cross-fires of mottoes and subtleties, which shine so splendidly in high circles, and win for the author the title of a man of wit, are after all the most elementary part of his wit; these mottoes, jokes, epigrams, subtleties, belong to the school of the troubadours and the Gay Science. A great number had already passed into the Florentine dialect, among the many others invented by the acute and wide-awake Florentines. The **Decameron** is sprinkled with these sayings. But they had already passed into the language and had ceased to be anything but phrases and words. Burchiello's work of collecting and arranging them is unworthy of a man of intelligence. They are only the colouring of the comic, not the comic itself; they are already a national patrimony and so have lost the freshness and spontaneity that are needed for wit; they are only effective if the writer adds some new and unsuspected association. Burchiello's work is dull and uninteresting because to Boccaccio these mottoes were not ends in themselves, but were only methods of style, only colouring.

Wit, in its higher meaning, is an artistic faculty; it may be said to take the place in the comic that sentiment takes in the serious. And wit, like emotion, is a great condenser;

The frontispiece of the 1492 Venice edition of the Decameron.

it quickens our perceptions and gives us like and unlike in the same breath under contrary appearances. Cleverness travels to its goal by the road of thought, but wit makes a leap straight to the same goal by intuition. Ugolino's sons in their exaltation of emotion say, "Thou didst put upon us this miserable flesh, and do thou strip it off." Here emotion takes the place in drama that wit takes in comedy; it joins different ideas and images unexpectedly in one sentence. But wit must be feeling too, the feeling of the ridiculous. The writer must stand in the middle of his world feeling all its emotions, must live inside of it, be amused by it, and must take the same interest in it that others take in the more serious things of life. But at the same time his emotion must be that of an intelligent onlooker, rather than that of an actor taking part in the piece. He must have that calm and quickness of mind which hold him aloof from the events of the play. The man who is really witty does not laugh himself, but makes others laugh. He dominates his world by reason of the calm that makes him superior to it; and so he can fashion it as he chooses, can tie up the threads and develop the plot and describe the personages and distribute the colouring.

Wit in Boccaccio is more imagination than intellect; it shows itself more in producing comic forms than in looking for far-fetched connections. Where his predecessors had tried to spiritualize, Boccaccio tries to incorporate. And he makes his effects not through this or that characteristic, but through the whole, through the details taken together in a mass. His predecessors wrote sketches; he writes descriptions. They looked for impressions rather than for things; Boccaccio shuts himself up and entrenches himself in the thing itself and gets to know it inside out. So often we are given the thing rather than the impression it produces, its sensation rather than its emotion, imagination rather than fantasy, sensuality rather than voluptuousness. Too much density and repetition make his work opaque. This manner is intolerable when the subject is serious, as in the *Filocolo* and the *Ameto* with their endless orations, which make us feel that we are stuck fast in the mud and unable to budge. And even the ***Decameron*** is irritating at times, for instance, when Tito and the daughter of Tancredi make speeches according to all the rules of rhetoric and logic. But the comic form is one of the most natural in the whole of art, and was the first form to appear after the elementary eruption of mottoes and proverbs. Comedy is the realm of the finite and the senses, and its first impressions are centred in minute observation of habits, whereas in serious literature the first impressions give us the forms of allegories and personifications, forms generalized in the intellect. The first form of the comic is caricature.

Caricature means depicting the object directly in such a way as to put its defective and ridiculous side into evidence. No doubt it would have been enough just to show us the defect and leave us to guess the rest: a single ray is enough to light up the whole and show it to our imagination. But Boccaccio aims at more than this; he is like a painter who depicts the entire figure, choosing and distributing the accessories in such a way that more light is thrown on the defective parts than on the others. Therefore the element of the ridiculous is not isolated, but spreads to the whole picture; each part contributes to the effect produced; there is a kind of crescendo in the comic scale. He so prepares us and puts us in the right mood for the laugh that it rarely breaks out unexpectedly and irresistibly, as in those short passages which give us unexpected connections; instead of laughter we more often get a feeling of equable pleasure, are kept gently satisfied. We are appeased, not excited. Though we do not actually laugh, our faces are serene and happy; the laugh is there, but is latent; it is not an irresistible laugh that breaks out in spite of ourselves. And the reason is this: the author does not give us a series of related thoughts, the fruit of his intellect, but a series of forms made by his imagination. And the forms he gives us are ample, solid, fully clothed, and minutely described. He seems to be sunk in that world of the imagination, and at the same time to be its creator; he has the air of adding nothing at all of his own. And we look at it as though enchanted. His attention never strays, and he never turns his head with a grimace to make us laugh. He never treats his subject lightly, laying it down, going back to it; his mind is fixed on it, and his subject pursues him, catches hold of him, pins him down, and gives him no rest till it has all come out. And our minds do not wander any more than his; we seem to be rocked deliciously in our contemplation; though we laugh from time to

time, we are still attentive, and plunge back at once into the subject and run with it; and when the race is finished we are still running, gently exhausted. It is not the Eastern world, in which the opium-drugged imagination springs tremblingly from the branch of love to fly away into the vast infinitude, giving us that feeling called voluptuousness, the infinite of the senses—that something which is vague, indefinite, and musical, which enfolds us and uplifts us and reveals God to us. Boccaccio's world is purely sensual, enclosed in precise, well-defined forms; there is nothing here to detach us and carry us off into exalted regions. And for the very reason that these flowers have no scent and these lights no rays, we get sensation instead of feeling, imagination instead of fantasy, sensuality instead of voluptuousness. Our eyes are no longer fixed on the sky in ecstasy; we have found our Paradise—in that full and delightful reality. The flesh, making its reappearance in the world, seems to have stripped itself naked for our enjoyment, and fills our Paradise with allurement and caresses. And so we get cynicism, more especially when an ironical sense of modesty is used to stir up the senses.

As the form of Boccaccio's world is caricature, the fruit of a rich imagination, we are shown the whole object complete in its finest shades—not merely its peaks and elevations. The author has very few preliminaries and sets about his work quickly; the curtain is raised, and the action already in full swing, with the characters moving and speaking. From the very first we get comedy, which develops little by little, step by step, each comic motive dovetailing into the others with increasing effect. Boccaccio develops that special quality which the French call *verve* when they try to imitate his force and facility, and the Italians call *brio* when they aim at lively wit. The tale of Alibech and that of Ser Ciappelletto are wonderful examples of this quality. To add pungency to the caricature he mixes it with irony, and irony here is not a primary form but an accessory. It is an apparent good-nature, an air of ingenuousness; the person telling the tale has an assumed air of being easily shocked and full of scruples, says a thing hesitatingly, but says it all the same, hesitates to believe a thing but believes it all the same, and crosses himself with a half-smile. This irony is like a kind of comic salt that gives pungency to laughter at the expense of the paternoster of St. Julian and the miracles of Ser Ciappelletto.

The ***Decameron,*** being based entirely on description—that is, the object not with its rays of light and its scent, but isolated and individualized—requires a full and rich form of expression. And so we get the two forms of the new literature: in poetry the *ottava rima,* and in prose the "period."

We have already seen the *nona rima* developed with Eastern magnificence in the poem of the *Intelligenzia.* The *ottava rima* was not invented by Boccaccio, any more than the period was his discovery. What he did was to give to both body and resonance. The *ottava rima* before his day had been a detached medley of objects thrown together at random, objects that could very well have stood separately—mere objects, not developed nor clothed: it was a mechanism, not yet an organism. Boccaccio in the ***Decameron*** made it into an organic whole, the thing developed little by little in all its shades. It is true that we find some very successful octaves in his poems, but as a rule they are complicated, badly put together, and falling away suddenly in their best moments. In his heroic poems they are forced and stretched; in the idyllic they are commonplace and redundant. The fact is, the *ottava rima* is the highest form in poetry, and requires a bright activity of the spirit that is wanting in Boccaccio, who wanders in artificialities and conventions. His fault is within him, in his very soul; whatever is coldly conceived comes to birth as a weakly and badly formed creature; and artifice does not help it.

But in the **Decameron** Boccaccio is at home, he is painting his own world, in which he lives with the greatest enjoyment, and as he is right in the very middle of it, he throws aside all artificial wrappings. He is more than a literato, he is the man who sinks into his world and swims in it, is proud of it, and revels in it like an epicure. The result is a form which is that very world itself, that world which excites our flesh and our imagination. And this is how the form arose that is known as the "Boccaccian period."

The great literary movement centred in Florence had of late been spreading beyond Tuscany. The rediscovery of antiquity had opened new horizons to the imagination; the world of Greece was just dawning, wrapped in those vague half-lights which heighten illusions; men were beginning to be aware of it. The language of Dante was not yet the Italian tongue; it was called the "Florentine idiom"; Latin was still the language of Italy, and the opinion still held good that only frivolous and amorous stories could be treated in *latino volgare,* as they called the dialect. Boccaccio says of himself that he wrote in the "Florentine idiom," and the writers who used the vulgar tongue said that they wrote in *latino volgare.* Latin was still the ideal, the perfect, language, and the erudite classes aimed at a vulgar tongue that would be noble and illustrious, modelled on Latin, and raised to the Latin perfection of form. This is what Dante aimed at in the *Convivio;* he was fully convinced that the most serious speculations of science could be expressed in the vulgar tongue as successfully as in Latin; he took the scholastic *latino volgare* or *volgare latino,* naked, all nerve and bone, and wrapped it magnificently, for the first time, in the large folds of the Roman toga. But the vice of scholasticism was rooted even in Dante, and these scholastic barbarians, dressed out in their rich clothes, seem ill at ease, like the villager out for a holiday dressed in his Sunday garments. There is no fusion, but only points and contrasts.

Boccaccio had not passed through the schools, and later in life, when he studied philosophy and a little theology, his spirit had already been formed in the experiences of ordinary life, in the use of the vulgar tongue, and in the study of the classics. Like Petrarch, he abominates the scholastics; he sees them as the very contrary of that elegant Greek and Roman culture; to him they are simply roughness and barbarism. His mind is ruled by Virgil, Ovid, Livy, and Cicero, and not by the Bible, and St. Thomas. When he wants to paint some serious side, moral or scientific, of his world, his imitation is an outer and mechanical artifice, since he has more imagination than feeling, more intellect than reasoning. His form is noble, decorous, often

easy, but too equable and placid—and now and then he makes us sleepy. His period is like the monotonous sound of a wave, moved laboriously by a tired and sleepy sea. In the place of inspiration he gives us rhetoric and logic; for Boccaccio when separated from images and thrown into the vagueness of feeling loses his footing and goes under. He treats ideas as though they were solid things, analyzes them and dissects them to the point of exhaustion. The ideas are commonplace and diluted by a coming and going of little useless accessories with "ifs" and "buts" and "thoughs" and "becauses." He strives so much for exactness, and anatomizes every smallest thought so minutely, that he makes the emptiness and commonplaceness of the idea show all the more plainly. The form stands out visibly from the thing, and shows itself as an ingenious mechanism, accurately worked out, and always mechanical. What is underneath? The commonplace. This was later called "literary form." And there is nothing more contrary to science, which is word and not phrase, and is hardly recognizable amid the circumlocutions, the periphrases, the pleonasms. This artifice is certainly a progress in literature; we find in it an art of connections and shadings that was new to prose, and it shows a matured spirit educated in the classics. But there is the opposite fault— the wish to make every idea into a chain beginning and ending in itself; which is more like a puddle of stagnant water than a running stream. Though Boccaccio hates the scholastics, his period is nothing more than a disguised syllogism, or a generalized phrase, such as, "It is human to pity the afflicted." His formulae are well constructed, but the old foundation is still there; the scholastic has a new dress and one more fashionable. And if the "period" of Boccaccio in its ample circuit is an artificial chain in which science loses its simplicity and elasticity and freedom of movement, it is quite as absurd when it tries to express feeling, to show the freer and uncontrollable forces of the spirit, which break the ties of logic and leap out impetuously. The sudden and tragic movements of the soul seem here to be crystallized between conjunctions and parentheses and reasonings. There is nothing of the subjective and it is difficult to get into the inner life. The events are extraordinary, the action is interesting, and the situations are dramatic, but our tears refuse to come, because the soul is revealed in commonplace and contorted sentences. Take for instance the tale of Madonna Beritola and that other of the Count of Anguersa, where the form never changes, but stays in its ceremonial dress and neatly gloved through all the most piteous calamities and changes of fortune. Yet here and there we do feel a certain—not excitement, exactly—but a certain emotion of warm imagination, and now and then there are movements of feeling, as in the last words of Tancredi's daughter, and in places in the story of Griselda.

This form of the "period," so little suited to science and feeling, in which it seems like a mere bit of machinery pretending to be Latin, takes a meaning and movement of its own when staged in the imagination, that is to say, when the author is in the midst of it, dealing with living actors, not with ideas and feelings, and is faced by well-determined objects. Take for instance the description of the plague or the fight of Gerbino. The action is no longer single and simple, like an idea, but is an aggregate of circumstances and accessories. This is the "period," which in its evolution has become in literature what in painting is called a picture. To group circumstances, grade them, and coördinate them around a centre, is the supreme art of Boccaccio. When description stands alone, abstract and separated from action, it does not sufficiently warm the imagination, and it becomes overloaded, as often happens in the introductions. But when it contains something that moves and walks, and resembles an action, the imagination gets going too, joins in the action, and paints pictures, in those large forms which are called "periods." This way of telling a story by means of pictures is certainly not the natural gait of action, which loves impetus and attrition; the rapid movements of action are arrested by the quiet eye of the imagination that is painting it. So this manner is unsuited to history. Nor is it exactly prose: it is art in a prose form with poetical narration. These paintings and periods do not give us the successive movements, the order of the action, nor its connections, nor its meaning, but its movements and attitudes and degrees: the result is a form called "physiognomy" or "expression."

But where Boccaccio's period becomes a creation *sui generis,* a living and breathing thing, is when he is treating of the comic and sensual side of his world; and not because his art or finesse is greater, but for the reason that here he is the very soul of his world—which means that he gives us a whole subjective train of malice, sensuality, mordacity, the true feeling of comic and sensual art. And this is the only sentimentality that Nature had given to Boccaccio; it penetrates into these flexible turnings of the form, and makes of them its chords. This period curves and winds and glides and twists most wantonly, with sudden shrinkings and breakings off and languishings and swellings, with digressions and graces and coquetries of style, which show us not only the spectacle in its prosaic clearness, but also its sentimental and musical motive. Those resounding waves, those ample Latin folds, grave and decorous, that embodied the majesty and pomp of public life, have been removed from the Forum and put within the walls of an idle and sensuous private life, have become the lewd transports of pleasure, tickled by malice. In the mouth of Tito or of Gisippo, we feel the rhetorical imitation of a world that had ceased to exist in the consciousness; the tune was the same, but it was sung by a bourgeois class that did not feel it, and often missed its meaning. But here, on the contrary, in this erotic and malicious world, we have the same air with a different motive, one that conquers and assimilates it; those magniloquent forms which puffed out the orators' cheeks are used here to soften vice, to adorn it, and to provide its finishing touch of allurement. As a rule, when Latin authors want to express the comic they discard their heavy weapons and arm themselves lightly. Boccaccio conceives like Plautus and writes like Cicero, yet so alive and so true is his imagination that it turns Cicero into an enticing siren who bends and moves her body alluringly. But often when he is deep in his subject he throws away the wrappings and coverings and jumps out of it, alert, swift, direct, incisive; he is a master of shortcuts and the jumping of fences. When his imagination is warmed by true feeling, he roams like a master among ancient and modern forms and melts them into one; of them he makes his own world, and stamps it with his own personality. If it were not for the art that pervades it, this world would be unbearable, would be deeply disgusting, but art clothes its nudity in these ample Latin forms as in a veil blown by lascivious winds. Art is the only thing in life that Boccaccio feels seriously, the only thing that makes him pause in the orgies of his fancy, in his moments of greatest licence, and knit his brows in thought—as happened with Dante and Petrarch in their highest and purest inspirations. Boccaccio's style is a reflection of the different men who lived in him: the literato, the man of erudition, the artist, the courtier, the man of the study, and the man of the world. It is a style so personal, so intimately one with his nature, that no imitation of it is possible: it stands alone, a stupendous monument, among many counterfeits.

What is it that we miss in Boccaccio? What we miss in this world of Nature and the senses is that feeling for Nature and that voluptuous perfume which later were found in Politian. What we miss in this world of comedy is that other feeling for the comic in its humorous and capricious forms which later was found in Ariosto.

And what is this world? It is the cynical and malicious world of the flesh, left in the low regions of sensuality; it is caricature that is often buffoonery, charmingly clothed in the graces and allurements of a form full of coquetry. It is a plebeian world that snaps its fingers at spiritual things; a world that is gross in its feelings, but polished and adorned by the imagination. And within it moves elegantly the bourgeois world of wit and culture, with echoes of the chivalric life.

It is the new comedy—not the divine comedy but the earthly one. Dante wraps his Florentine robe around him and vanishes; and the period of the Middle Ages, with its visions, its legends, its terrors, its shadows, and its ecstasies, is banished from the temple of art. And into the temple Boccaccio comes with a clatter, drawing after him the whole of Italy for many years to come. (pp. 333-59)

Francesco De Sanctis, "The 'Decameron',", in his History of Italian Literature, Vol. 1, *translated by Joan Redfern, Harcourt Brace Jovanovich, 1931, pp. 290-359.*

John Addington Symonds   (essay date 1895)

[*Symonds was an English poet, historian, and critic who wrote extensively on Greek and Italian culture. In the essay excerpted below, he depicts the* Decameron *as a transitional work that incorporates the spiritualism of the Middle Ages and the intellectualism of the Renaissance.*]

Great pains have been taken to investigate the sources used by Boccaccio in the composition of his tales [in the *Decameron*]. Men like Landau in Germany and Bartoli in Italy have ransacked the stores of Indian, Arabic, Byzantine, French, Provençal, Hebrew, and Spanish fables, with the view of tracing resemblances between the *Decameron* and pre-existing literature of various sorts. It has been shown by these researches that very few of Boccaccio's stories are original, in the sense of having been invented by himself. Like Shakespeare, he used materials ready to his hand, wherever he found something to the purpose of his art. But scholarship of this sort has introduced a somewhat false note into our criticism of the subject. We are, as it were, invited to believe that Boccaccio possessed a polyglot library of fiction, which he consulted in the course of composition. The truth is that story-telling was a favourite pastime in the Middle Ages, and that very few good stories are new. From Hindostan, from Baghdad, from Greek and Roman books on history, from the folklore of Teutonic and Celtic races, from a thousand-and-one sources, anecdotes were freely taken up, which passed into the common substance of the mediæval mind. They circulated from lip to lip between the Ganges and the Seine. They were the property of everybody. Thus the learned investigations to which I have referred, are interesting, because they show how large and various a stock of stories were current in the days before Boccaccio wrote. But such researches have small importance for the criticism of the *Decameron* as a work of art. They only prove his wide acquaintance with the tales of many lands, as these formed elements of social culture common to his race.

The same line of treatment might be adopted with regard to the charge of plagiarism from North French tale-tellers, which has been brought against Boccaccio by sensitive French patriots. It is true that he borrowed largely from the *fabliaux;* and what is more to the purpose, he adopted the style of narration in use among Trouvères, Ménestrels and Jongleurs. Such professors of the arts of entertainment pervaded Europe, and undoubtedly haunted the Angevine Court at Naples. An artist of Boccaccio's stamp, born to excellence, appreciative of the slightest hints of mastery in the trade he had adopted, certainly learned much from these men. He learned from them in the same way as Mozart learned from fashionable composers of Italian opera. But when we compare their work with his, the charge of plagiarism becomes almost comic. Comic indeed is not the word for it. I would rather say that the man who makes such charges, writes himself down thereby a dullard in the art of criticism. He is incapable of perceiving the bottomless gulf which yawns between old French *fabliaux,* humorous, obscene, disconnected, with blunt native glimpses into human character, and that stately artwork which we call *Decameron,* completely finished, fair in all its parts, appropriately framed, subordinated to one principle of style, with the master's Shakespearian grasp on all heights and depths, on the kernel and the superficies, the pomp and misery, the pleasures and the pangs of mortal life.

Where Boccaccio found his stories, matters little. How he formed his style of narrative, matters equally little. These questions have their antiquarian interest indeed; and at leisure moments readers of the *Decameron* would do well to consider them. But the critic has to avoid such side-issues, after mastering their points and giving them due weight. He must remind people that the real question is, not where Boccaccio found his stories, nor how he acquired his style, but whether he used those stories and employed that style in a way to distinguish him from all his predecessors, and

to make the *Decameron* a monumental work of modern art.

Comparing Boccaccio, not with previous mediæval storytellers, who are nowhere in the reckoning, but with himself as literary craftsman, we pronounce that in the *Decameron* he accomplished that to which his earlier writings of every sort in Italian poetry and prose had been but preludes. These essays of his immaturity were marked by misdirected energy, by euphuism sprung from a mixed literary impulse, by want of proportion, by declamatory monologue directed towards the author's self as audience. The *Decameron* emerges into the clear atmosphere of perfected objective art. We do not feel the author's subjectivity, his longings and his disappointments. He paints actual men and women, dealing with them humorously or sympathetically, exhibiting their nobleness, bringing their foibles and deformities into relief, even as light falling round an object does. He has ceased to declaim. There is no haste, no disproportion in the work. Each tale is told in its appropriate manner; and all the tales are built into a stately palace-house, wherein the mind of man may walk for solace or instruction through well-planned and spacious chambers. The style, though artificial, has disengaged itself from pedantries and hesitations. Handled as it is handled here, Boccaccio's Italian prose proclaims its fitness to be used for every purpose, serious or gay, coarse or sentimental, elegiac or satirical, descriptive or analytical, rhetorical or epigrammatic. Changing, according to the master's mood, within the bounds of equable and polished diction, it is suited to every whim or exigency of stylistic utterance.

The *Decameron* has been called the "Commedia Umana." This title is appropriate, not merely because the book portrays human life from a comic rather than a serious point of view, but also because it forms the direct antithesis of Dante's *Commedia Divina.* The great poem and the great prose fiction of the fourteenth century are opposed to each other as Masque and Anti-masque. The world of the *Decameron* is not an inverted world, like that of Aristophanes. It does not antithesise Dante's world by turning it upside down. It is simply the same world surveyed from another side, unaltered, uninverted, but viewed in the superficies, presented in the concrete. Dante, in the *Divine Comedy,* attempted a revelation of what underlies appearances and gives them their eternal value. He treated of human nature in relation to God, of life upon this earth in relation to life beyond the grave. Boccaccio deals with appearances, and does not seek to penetrate below experience. He paints the world as world, the flesh as flesh, nature as nature, without suggesting the question whether there be a spiritual order. Human life is regarded by him as the plaything of fortune, humour, appetite, caprice. Dante saw the world in the mirror of his soul. Boccaccio looked upon it with his naked eyes; yet poet and novelist dealt with the same stuff of humanity, and displayed equal comprehensiveness in treating it.

The description of the Plague at Florence which introduces the *Decameron,* has more than a merely artistic appropriateness. Boccaccio's taste might be questioned for bringing that group of pleasure-seeking men and maidens into contrast with the horrors of the stricken city. Florence crowded with corpses, echoing to the shrieks of delirium and the hoarse cries of body-buriers, forms a background to the blooming garden, where birds sing, and lovers sit by fountains in the shade, laughing or weeping as the spirit of each tale constrains their sympathy. Remembering that these glad people have shunned the miseries which weigh upon their fellow-creatures, our first impulse is to shrink with loathing from their callousness. But the reflection follows, that black Death is hovering near them too, and may descend with sweeping scythe at any moment on their paradise. This introduction, therefore, suggests a moral for Boccaccio's "Human Comedy." The brilliant masquerade of earthly life which he has painted with such inexhaustible variety, has the grave behind it and before it, and Death is ever passing to and fro among the dancers. Meanwhile men eat and drink, sing and play, sleep at nightfall and rise refreshed in dewy morning, for new pleasures, unmindful of the hospital, the battlefield, the charnel-house. Boccaccio was too great an artist to point this moral in a work of mirth and relaxation. There it is, however, like the grinning skeleton who threads the mazes of a *Danse Macabre.*

The description of the Plague has another undesigned significance. A Florentine chronicler of those times, Matteo Villani, dates the progressive deterioration of manners and the political anarchy which followed from the Black Death of 1348. The Plague was, therefore, an outward sign, if not the efficient cause, of those moral and social changes which the *Decameron* immortalised in literature. It was the historical landmark between two ages, dividing mediæval from Renaissance Italy. The cynicism, liberated in that period of terror, lawlessness and sudden death, assumed in Boccaccio's romance a beautiful and graceful aspect. His art softened its harsh and vulgar outlines, giving it that air of genial indulgence which distinguished Italian society throughout the heyday of the Renaissance.

Boccaccio selects seven ladies of ages varying from eighteen to twenty-eight, and three men, the youngest of whom is twenty-five. Having formed this company, he transports them to a villa two miles from the city, where he provides them with a train of serving-men and waiting-women, and surrounds them with the delicacies of mediæval luxury. Their daily doings form the framework in which the stories of the *Decameron* are set. He is careful to remind us that, though there were lovers in that band of friends, "no stain defiled the honour of the company;" yet these unblemished maidens listen with laughter and a passing blush to words and things which outrage our present sense of decency. Nothing is more striking in the *Decameron* than the refinement of the framework contrasted with the coarseness of the pictures which it frames. I do not think that Boccaccio violated the truth of fact for the purpose of his art. Plenty of proof exists that the best society of the period found entertainment in discussing themes which would now be scarcely tolerated in a barrack.

The light but remorseless satire of the *Decameron* spares none of the ideals of the age. All the mediæval enthusiasms are reviewed and criticised in the spirit of a Florentine citizen. It is as though the *bourgeois,* not content with

having made nobility a crime, were bent upon extinguishing its essence. Indeed, the advent of the *bourgeois* is the most significant note of the times to which Boccaccio belonged. Agilulf vulgarises the chivalrous conception of love ennobling men of low estate, by showing how a groom, whose heart is set upon a queen, avails himself of opportunity. Tancredi burlesques the knightly reverence for stainless scutcheons by the extravagance of his revenge. The sanctity of the "Thebaid," that ascetic dream of purity and self-renunciation, is made ridiculous by Alibech. Ser Ciapelletto casts contempt upon the canonisation of saints. The confessional, the adoration of reliques, the priesthood, the monastic orders, are derided with the deadliest persiflage. Christ himself is scoffed at in a jest which points the most indecent of these tales. Matrimony affords a never-ending theme for scorn; and when, by way of contrast, the novelist paints an ideal wife, he runs into such hyperboles that the very patience of Griselda is a satire on the dignity of marriage. It must not be thought that Boccaccio was a bad Churchman because he unsparingly attacked the vices of the clergy and the superstitions of his age. The contrary is amply proved. In those times, when there was no thought of schism from the Mother Church of Christendom, a man might speak his mind out freely without being arraigned for heresy. Not until the Reformation created a panic, and pushed Rome to extremities in the Catholic reaction, was the *Decameron* condemned to expurgation and placed upon the "Index."

This is not the place to discuss in detail the stories of the *Decameron.* The book lies open to English readers, who ought to take it as its author meant it to be taken—to look upon it mainly as a source of pleasure for all times. It would be easy to fill many learned pages with disquisitions on its potency in modern literature, to show how imaginative art of every sort in Italy was penetrated with its spirit, how Chaucer felt its influence in England, and how a princess of the House of Valois reproduced it in the French Renaissance. I am inclined to think that such disquisitions impair the satisfaction which we have in finding out those obvious relations for ourselves. There is a certain charm in exploring rivulets of literature, tracing them to their source in some large lake like the *Decameron,* noticing their divergence, detecting their specific quality, and testing as a final effort of analysis the meeting of many old-world waters in the reservoir itself. (pp. 79-92)

John Addington Symonds, in his Giovanni Boccaccio as Man and Author, *1895. Reprint by AMS Press, Inc., 1968, 101 p.*

Hermann Hesse   (essay date 1904)

[Recipient of the Nobel Prize for literature in 1946, Hesse is considered one of the most important German novelists of the twentieth century. In the following essay, which first appeared in German in 1904, Hesse speculates whether Boccaccio "left behind specific traces of his personality, his life, and his character in the Decameron.*"]*

Because of the biased conception that the Italian Renaissance was a reawakening of classical antiquity, Boccaccio, together with Petrarch, possesses the somewhat dubious historico-scholarly reputation of being one of the harbingers of this reawakening. He zealously read and collected the Roman authors and performed some not very impressive services in encouraging the reading of the Greek philosophers. Boccaccio himself took no little pride in his philological and historical labors, whereas he seems to have attributed scant importance to his *Decameron,* and in his later years would have preferred to disown it. Until recent times scholarship too has concerned itself with his Latin works, preferring primly to avoid the *Decameron.*

So one might think that in the end the Florentine was proved right in having preferred his numerous Latin writings to the book that in reality is his principal work and also one of the most important and valuable books of the fourteenth century. Well, fortunately the longevity and fame of outstanding writings have never been dependent on scholarly judgment and, thank God, what is good and viable has constantly sustained itself, whereas even the most determined attempts to galvanize dead greatness into life have seldom or never succeeded. Thus the collected scholarly writings and the youthful poetry of Boccaccio have long since almost completely disappeared, and for us today they belong among the bric-a-brac and curiosities of the past, while his splendid book of stories is still read by thousands and continues to have all its old richness, power, and freshness. Anyone to whom the word "Renaissance" is not a scholarly abstraction but a living picture of the culture of Italian cities in the fifteenth and sixteenth centuries could, if necessary, quite easily omit from this picture the *De genealogiis deorum gentilium* and the *De claris mulieribus* but not possibly the immortal *Decameron.*

It seems unnecessary to say much about the nature and character of this famous book. Everyone knows it at least by name and everyone knows that inside a simple narrative framework it contains a collection of a hundred stories, the content of which was at that time (around 1350) especially admired in society and among the common folk in Italy. It is also known that this delightful book for hundreds of years has enjoyed a bad reputation on account of its free and occasionally coarse tone. This evil reputation, at all events, is primarily responsible for the book's great success and its enormous distribution throughout all of Europe, for without this it would never have occurred to anyone to heap so much slander on a work whose coarsest improprieties were far exceeded by numerous contemporary literary works in every country (especially Germany and France). The suppression and persecution of the *Decameron* proceeded primarily from the clergy, and in the first instance was not concerned with the sensual coarseness and vividness of the novellas but with the daring independence with which Boccaccio loved to talk about the lives and characters of the priests and monks of his time. So, for example, it is amusing to see in what direction the many editions of the *Decameron* in the fifteenth and sixteenth centuries, revised for the worse by ecclesiastical censors, were actually changed. A novella in which perhaps a beggar or nobleman seduces a woman or is betrayed by his wife remains unaltered; if, however, a priest or monk is guilty of a similar disgraceful action, the novella is not, to be sure, suppressed, nor is the language modified, but *in majoram ecclesiae gloriam,* the priest is simply turned into a knight, the monk into a duke, the nun into a burgher's daughter, and everything is now fine and unexceptionable.

This, however, is not our subject here. Of the countless questions that must arise in the mind of every attentive reader of the *Decameron,* let us choose just one: To what extent is the author of this most famous of all story collections an original writer and creator and how much of his own life and personality has he included in the book?

The hundred novellas in the *Decameron,* simply in respect to subject matter, may contain little or almost nothing truly invented by Giovanni Boccaccio. They consist of anecdotes, fables, jokes, *bons mots,* remarkable life histories, and other little stories which, having originated in all countries and centuries, belonged to the literary treasury of the people and the nobility and were retold by the collector partly from oral tradition, partly from older written sources. Many of them are to be found in Oriental storybooks, in the French *fabliaux,* and elsewhere. However, as soon as we examine not the content but the form of presentation, the book proves to be a completely self-sufficient personal work of literature in which the collector and author welded the variegated mass of material into a new book unified in spirit and execution. The powerful instrument that made possible this melting down and reshaping of old treasures was first of all Boccaccio's language. This long work, from its introduction to the last word of the hundredth novella, speaks consistently in a lively, elegant, vigorous language whose magic enchants the reader and holds him spellbound. Whether the style swells in long sonorous speeches or the narrative proceeds simply and with apparent carelessness, or takes on a graceful roguish tone, joking as it goes, it always has the same bubbling freshness, cleanliness, and vigor, never limping, never flagging, but at every instant supplely youthful, but for all its delicacy gritty and original. In many places there is no mistaking the fact that the author was a quite conscious student of the Latin classics, especially of Cicero; for example, he loves the well-constructed long, balanced period, often with almost coquettishly interlarded clauses. But if Cicero was his master in the architecture of the sentences, Boccaccio drew the language itself, the words and images, directly from the *lingua parlata* of society, the streets and the market place. Best of all in this combination was his native delicacy of feeling, a gift that alone makes an author into a poet: the secret rhythm, the sovereign personal freedom from convention and pedantry, the animation and shading of the words, the pregnant new expressions, the beautiful, self-confident style amid all the variety.

Along with the language is the transformation of unorganized and chance collections into a new, unified work of literature. The hundred novellas are not presented as narrated by Boccaccio himself. He lets each one of the ten young people of Florence—seven young women and three young men—speak; these have fled from the dying city in the year of the great plague, 1348, and are spending some time in rural sociability, their favorite pastime being the telling of interesting and witty stories. Each day one of the company is chosen king, is responsible for the entertainment of the others, and usually dictates the general theme for the stories to be told that day. This framing and arrangement of the multifarious material is masterfully carried out and constitutes not only a delicate stylistically pure idyl in mood and language, but also an authentic and outstanding description of Florentine rural and social life in the trecento. And beyond this each novella gains greatly in color and charm because it is related by a particular person and in a particular connection. Between stories there is conversation in which the company sometimes discusses the last story told; or there are banter, joking, and song. The round of storytelling is interrupted in a lively and attractive fashion that never outweighs or disturbs it.

Thus in the detail of the overall narrative, as well as in its total composition, the *Decameron* proves to be the masterpiece of a writer of genius, though the mass of his material may have been brought to him by every wind. Now it is natural to inquire whether the poet, in addition to the conception, arrangement, and language, has left behind specific traces of his personality, his life, and his character in the *Decameron.*

In older times there was much dispute as to whether the whole account of the merry country outing of the ten young people was pure invention or whether these characters were perhaps real portraits. In fact, between Florence and San Domenico, the Villa Palmieri situated on a hill above the valley of Mugnone is pointed out to travelers as the probable scene of this idyl. But however tempting it would be to identify this scene with certainty and however seriously and credibly Boccaccio describes the flight of the young people from the plague as a fact, very little can actually be established with certainty about these matters. For the author cautiously avoids describing a recognizable place near Florence. What he has to say about the position of his villa and the landscape around it fits almost any estate near Florence and simply allows no certain conclusions to be drawn.

Moreover, it is certain that Boccaccio was not in Florence during the time of the plague. His famous and detailed description of the *Pestilenza mortifera* does not therefore lose its value as an authentic account, for the plague, which came across from the Orient, raged no less horribly in Naples in the year 1348 when the author was probably living there. Now if we think we can recognize Boccaccio himself in one of those three Florentine youths who accompany the seven young ladies into the country, then the assumption that an actual occurrence is being dealt with loses much of its probability. And it is natural to be inclined to see in young Dioneo, who is king on the Seventh Day, characteristics of the author himself. Not only is this Dioneo drawn with much more affection and care and provided with many more individual characteristics than any of the other persons in the group, but he also plays the role of funmaker, entertainer, cheerer, which Boccaccio himself as author of the *Decameron* had undertaken and to which he expressly admits in the Foreword. Furthermore, it seems, vague though the indications are, that Dioneo was meant to be the lover of Fiammetta, the queen

on the Fifth Day, and if this is so many doubts would be banished. For we know with a good deal of certainty who Fiammetta was.

That one of the charming ladies of the *Decameron* bears that name goes back to one of the profoundest experiences of the poet's youth. Boccaccio had spent the greater or, at all events, the more important part of his younger years in Naples. Against his inclination and natural bent he had been destined by his father to be a merchant, and it was as a merchant, after long apprentice years in Florence, that he finally came to Naples, where he soon changed horses and took up the study of canonical law, in which, however, he made no striking progress. Through his influential countryman Niccolo Acciajuoli he was introduced at the luxurious Neapolitan court, fell in love with Maria, a natural daughter of King Robert, whom he saw for the first time at Easter Sunday service in San Lorenzo (1334?). She was known officially as the Countess Aquino and was married to a prominent courtier. The young poet's not unrequited love completely filled the first part of his stay in Naples and is the subject of almost all his youthful poems. He celebrated his noble beloved, whose real name he obviously dared not mention publicly, always under the name Fiammetta, and *Fiammetta* is also the title of a novel written by him even before the *novellino.* Boccaccio left a final memorial to this love, rich in happy and bitter experiences, by giving the name of his beloved to one of the young ladies in the *Decameron,* whose beauty and amiable ways he praises in beautiful language (at the end of the Fourth Day). Even though when he wrote this his relationship with Maria had ended and the former passion had expired, nevertheless the memory of it remained the most powerful one of his life. Also this late praise may signify a final melancholy, forgiving obituary, for in all likelihood Maria-Fiammetta died during the year of the plague in Naples.

Whoever wishes to follow this thread further will find many little hints and allusions to that experience in the apparently so impersonally written work. Essential revelations about the character, inclinations, and views of the author are also to be found in his Introduction, under whose gallant and delicately playful tone unmistakable seriousness is often evident. His descriptions of the country estate near Florence are a good mirror of his way of life and his way of seeing and enjoying nature. However similar they are on occasion to the Roman pastoral writers and to some of Pliny's letters, nevertheless a subtle personal flavor is unmistakable in these enchanting pictures of nature and at times an almost modern appreciation of nature. The Third Day of the *Decameron* begins with a description of the beautiful country estate which is now popularly identified with the Villa Palmieri and its surroundings. The garden adjoining the palace is painted with particular love, enthusiasm, and great detail: the paths lined by roses and jasmine, the lawns surrounded by lemon trees and pomegranates, with grass deep green in color (*quasi nera perea*) and embroidered with bright-colored flowers, the springs, the canals, the birds in the trees and in the air. All this is presented with a love for natural beauty which the painting of that time had found no adequate means to express. Nor is the fragrance of the lemon trees forgotten, or the fine spicy sweet smell of the vineyard blossoms that deliciously fills the whole garden. Whoever has rested on a fair early-summer morning in the valley of the Mugnone, the Greve, or the Elsa can conceive of no more enchanting and fragrant description of this fruitful, rich, garden landscape, and there is nothing more delicious than to read that description in the shadows of the lemons or cypresses between the orchards and the Tuscan hillside meadows, sown with huge bright-colored anemones.

And so the introductory and encircling narrative of the ten storytellers presents itself entirely as a free and beautiful creation of Boccaccio's in which he had no hesitation in weaving unobtrusive references to emotions and memories from his own life. It is otherwise with the hundred novellas themselves; at least, the author emphasizes in his remarkable introduction to the Fourth Day that he has been at pains to keep from any alteration and is reporting all the histories exactly "as they happened," that is, as he heard them from trustworthy reporters. And yet without doubt he has given here, too, much of himself. He may have altered nothing or almost nothing in the factual content of the stories, but he surrounds them with alluring descriptions, adds long speeches, begins or ends them with general observations from his own experience and knowledge of life. In oral repetition, every story has something anecdotal about it, does not linger over descriptions, does not quote long speeches, holds to its point or resolution. This is how Boccaccio must have heard his novellas. In writing them down at leisure, however, in rounding them out, bringing them into proper proportion, and carefully stylizing them, necessarily much of his own experience was added in the agreeable elaboration of details; by no means to the disadvantage of the novellas.

When the stories tell about the business, journeys, and adventures of Florentine merchants, the author is certainly indebted in great part to his own experience for the accuracy and vividness of his descriptions. Thus in the tenth novella of the Eighth Day there is a detailed description of the practices and duties of harbor traffic. We are told how and where the foreign merchant stores and insures his wares, how the middleman learns the nature and price of the imported goods from the ledgers in the customs house, how these goods are sold and traded, etc. Similar descriptions can be found in many other places in the book.

Less frequent and less clear are the references to Boccaccio's political views and experiences. In the numerous novellas that have their scene at court, his fanatical republicanism could only have had a disturbing effect. On the other hand, his enthusiasm for the time and character of the ancient Romans is frequently and clearly evident. And least of all does he restrain his contempt for the clergy on the other side of the mountain. It is striking in itself that he shows such fondness for stories in which priests, abbots, monks, and nuns play despicable or ridiculous roles. Yet it may well be true that with the decline of monastic life and of the clergy (this was the period of the papal exile in Avignon) and with the increasing freedom of thought and life in the cities, anecdotes of this sort were especially relished and hawked about in all quarters. Nevertheless Boccaccio is not content with that. He weaves into his no-

vellas and repeats in his introductions with visible satisfaction indignant and detailed denunciations, especially of the monks (the most characteristic one being in the seventh novella of the Third Day).

Nevertheless it is in a story about a monk (Sixth Day, tenth novella) that we come to know the author in his most attractive aspect. This is the amusing story of Brother Zippolla and his sermon on relics, one of the pearls of the ***Decameron.*** Boccaccio is never lacking in sparkling jokes, sharp-witted or burlesque inspirations, but in this masterly narrative he reaches the heights of a true, penetrating, pure humor such as we search for in vain among the countless later Italian story writers. The way in which the sly beggar monk, traveling about with his fake relics, outwits his outwitter, the way in which he is able to rescue himself from a highly painful embarrassment, the way he obviously derives more satisfaction from his own cleverness than from the money gained by swindling, and finally the way he comes out of the ticklish situation as an unmasked evildoer, to be sure, but unpunished, and almost with a small diabolical halo, all this was not to be found in Boccaccio's sources or in Cicero but is a product of his very own creativity. Because of its genuine Tuscan wit and grace, this particular novella has always been the favorite of the Florentines and is still so today. When around 1570 another "purified," that is, an unrecognizably mutilated edition was proposed under ecclesiastical supervision, the Florentines of their own accord insisted that at least this one story of Brother Zippolla should remain word for word unchanged in its original form.

A single novella, although here too there may be an older model, is said by a number of witnesses to represent an experience of the writer. It is the seventh novella of the Eighth Day. A student is tricked and shamefully derided by a widow and for this he takes a savage revenge.

Now we know from Boccaccio's own mouth that at the age of somewhat over forty he once fell in love with a widow. For a time she behaved encouragingly, although she had long had another lover. She spurred Boccaccio on to a fiery exchange of letters, and behind his back with her young friend made no little fun over him and his letters. That was the author's last, bitter love affair.

In the novella mentioned he tells about a student whom a lady kept waiting all one winter's night in the snow in a windy courtyard while she and her young lover laughed and made fun of her freezing admirer to their hearts' content behind the locked doors of the house. The student, however, decided to have a proper revenge. He waited for summer and then found an opportunity to lure the widow alone onto a tower far outside the city, ostensibly to perform certain magic ceremonies with her. Then he left her locked on the top platform of the tower without clothes or a place to lie down, without food or drink and without any protection against the sun, languishing and roasting for a whole blazing day, an experience that very nearly cost her her life from exposure and mosquito bites.

It might seem as though the particularly unfeeling brutality of this ignoble revenge indicated that the story was an old one and not an invention of Boccaccio's. And if he had written nothing after the **Decameron** one would certainly support this interpretation. But unfortunately we have every reason to assume that he is morally responsible for this repulsive scene and intended through it to express his impotent thirst for revenge against the beautiful and wanton widow.

For it was Boccaccio's tragicomic fate that he who spent his youth on a passionate love, who in the **Decameron** calls himself explicitly an ardent honorer, friend, and servant of women and whose earlier poems have hardly any subject but the love of women—that this same author in his later days was to become a pitiless, spiteful woman-hater. In this novella we find an isolated early expression of his contempt.

The sobering experience with the widow seems to have given him the decisive push. And soon thereafter he, the author of so many love poems and novellas about love, wrote his dreadful *Corbaccio,* one of the meanest and most contemptible books ever written against women. It seethes with the most unqualified and filthiest abuse. Its vulgar and repulsively scathing tone, however, gives us the right to laugh at the author's later disapproval of his masterwork and to take the younger Boccaccio's part against the old one.

After this change for the worse, all that was needed to make the author repent of and disown his **Decameron** was supplied in the year 1361, about five years after the completion of *Corbaccio,* by the Carthusian monk Ciani. Though Boccaccio had regretted his early esteem for women and had recanted his hymns in their honor, nevertheless he had continued to be a bitter mocker of priests and monks. But then in 1361 there appeared at his house this monk Giovachino Ciani, who succeeded—presumably beyond his own expectation—in tricking the sly, inventive, experienced rogue and enemy of monks into conversion by means of a very transparent, crude, and violent bit of practical trickery. Boccaccio was terrified and thought his end was at hand, he crept to the cross and there laid down forever his last and heaviest sin.

Boccaccio, on the purpose of the *Decameron*:

In these tales will be found a variety of love adventures, bitter as well as pleasing, and other exciting incidents, which took place in both ancient and modern times. In reading them, the . . . ladies will be able to derive, not only pleasure from the entertaining matters therein set forth, but also some useful advice. For they will learn to recognize what should be avoided and likewise what should be pursued, and these things can only lead, in my opinion, to the removal of their affliction. If this should happen (and may God grant that it should), let them give thanks to Love, which, in freeing me from its bonds, has granted me the power of making provision for their pleasures.

Giovanni Boccaccio, in his preface to the Decameron, *translated by G. H. McWilliams, Penguin, 1972.*

All that, fortunately, is now more than five centuries in the past. The *Corbaccio* has disappeared, the monk Ciani is forgotten, the picture of the aging Boccaccio has grown pale and has faded into the distance. The **Decameron,** however, and its author, *Vir juvenis Boccatius Certaldensis,* are as young and blithe and lively today as they ever were, and the delicious book provides no less pleasure now to countless young and old than it once did to the Florentines of the trecento. (pp. 294-304)

Hermann Hesse, "Giovanni Boccaccio," in his My Belief: Essays on Life and Art, *edited by Theodore Ziolkowski, translated by Denver Lindley, Farrar, Straus and Giroux, 1974, pp. 294-304.*

Alberto Moravia (essay date 1953)

[*Moravia is one of the foremost Italian literary figures of the twentieth century. His depiction of existential themes in his novels and short stories anticipates the writings of French authors Jean-Paul Sartre and Albert Camus. Deeply informed by the theories of Karl Marx and Sigmund Freud, Moravia's work commonly focuses on such subjects as politics, sexuality, psychology, and art. In the following essay, originally published in Italian in 1953, Moravia asserts that the eroticism that pervades the* Decameron *is not of primary importance, but rather only a means through which Boccaccio advances his characters' actions.*]

It has been remarked before now that while true men of action are usually embittered if reduced to impotence, inertia and incapacity, placid and dreamy men find that these things enrich and enhance the very real pleasure they derive from their imagination. It is surely not an accident that writers of adventure stories are mostly sedentary people.

Moreover these imaginative yet lazy men, these insatiable yet stationary pursuers of action, are by nature and necessity very far removed from any form of moral reflection. It is peculiar to the moralist that he cuts down the number of possible alternatives and acts resolutely and consistently within them. The moralist defends himself from the imagination as from the most dangerous of mirages, above all when the imagination plays on action that is entirely governed by the caprices of chance, action for action's sake. In fact action for action's sake, whether dreamed up or practised, requires a flexibility, a flightiness, an indifference, that do not harmonise with moral conscience.

I have always thought that Boccaccio—that placid and comfort-loving 'Giovanni of tranquillity' as he is usually portrayed to us—was in the depths of his soul, by way of compensation and perhaps of sublimation, a great lover of action. Surely he was the kind of man who cannot enjoy ease and comfort unless he imagines himself in danger and discomfort, who needs to conjure up a fantastically active life so as to be able to pursue his quiet existence in peace. One thinks of a man like Sacchetti, the pleasing domestic and provincial story-teller, as the exact opposite of Boccaccio. Sacchetti finds complete fulfilment in shrewd and effective representation. His imagination does not take him outside the confines of his own narrow world. All he wants as a story-teller is to give pleasure—his work, like his life, is calm. But consider the voluptuous delight with which Boccaccio's episodes are elaborated, enriched and decorated; the liveliness with which he presents his characters, as though jealous of them. Consider the enormous variety of his settings: at sea, in cities, woods, rooms, caves, and deserts; and the way his characters comprise all conditions, nationalities, and periods—facts which go to show that the important thing for Boccaccio was less to give pleasure and surprise than greedily to feel himself living within the widest variety of people, situations, places, and periods. His cosmopolitanism is made up of extent and quantity rather than of civilisation and education. Florence and its surroundings were too small to satisfy his thirst for action. He needed the East, France, Naples, Venice, Rome and Sicily, the ancient world and the high Middle Ages, and not only places and periods familiar to him, but those he knew of by hearsay. Most writers move within a given space and time. Where this does not happen, as with Boccaccio, it means that the process of liberation and consequent widening of vision has reached fruition. Boccaccio's uprootedness and freedom, which seem so extraordinary to anyone who knows how rare such conditions are, are the primary reason for his universality.

There have been various ways of explaining the amorality and callousness that many believe they can detect in Boccaccio's work. He has been called a sensualist, as if sensuality necessarily excluded moral conscience. His lack of severity of spirit has been ascribed to the decadence of customs, the death of medieval chivalry, the transition to the modern middle-class age, and the change from the ancient ideas of transcendentalism to the immanence of the Renaissance.

But I for my part am convinced that morality is not a thing—like fashions or other superficial characteristics—that follows in the wake of historical change. Unquestionably Boccaccio was as moral a man as Dante or Manzoni. We should not let ourselves be misled by the fact that his stories contain so many adulteries and deceptions as well as a kind of superficiality and indifference. A careful reading of the **Decameron** reveals it as a book of only moderate sensuality, and it is never, or hardly ever, that sensuality is the main subject of a story. And as for superficiality and indifference, they are only a defect when viewed extrinsically; to carry through a work of this kind they are a necessity.

Let us try to compare [Gustave] Flaubert and Boccaccio for a moment. Flaubert's problem was quite different. He was concerned with providing in each of his books a more or less disguised portrait of himself and hence with knowing and judging himself. Knowing and judging himself led logically to knowing and judging the world around him. In this sense moralism was for Flaubert as necessary as amoralism was for Boccaccio, as we shall see in due course. The fact that he described ordinary, normal, common things was simply a result of this undertaking. Only ordinary, normal, common things can provide the moralist with material that does not frustrate him or disperse his cohesion. The moralist needs to believe in the existence of

a stable social set-up, of interests and passions that cannot evade judgement, of a serious and concrete world in which human beings bear full responsibility for their actions. The play of fortune, adventure and chance are excluded from his world, or if they find their way into it they are inexorably drawn into the framework of moral judgement. A hare-brained and adventurous fellow in a Boccaccio story would be turned by the moralist into a swindler and a criminal; adventure becomes error, sin, a trick or crime. Moreover variety serves no purpose, for one single fact scrutinised with attention is quite enough for the moralist's ambition. He does not wish to live many lives, but only one—his own. Flaubert felt the tyranny of this situation, and more than once deluded himself into thinking he could escape it. *Salammbô* is the result of one such attempt at escape. But Flaubert's spirit was not to be set free merely by being transferred into distant and mythical ages. *Salammbô* is just as heavy and narrow as *Madame Bovary*. The monstrous coherence of Flaubert's path ends up in the blind alley of *Bouvard et Pécuchet*.

Boccaccio's task was quite different. He wanted neither to judge himself nor to know himself, and still less to condemn or reform. The corruption and decadence of customs left him indifferent not because he shared in them but because they were factors that were of no use to him. Moralists are praised too often for pillorying certain vices. When we reflect that, given their temperaments, they desperately need those vices then we can see that their merit is not all that great. On the other hand Boccaccio, with his thirst for adventure, needed quite different things. First of all he needed not to be weighed down and impeded by serious or strict moral concepts, not to have continually to establish a relationship of moral judgement between himself and his characters, between himself and the world. So much for the negative side; as for the positive side, what Boccaccio needed was action pure and simple. Action of any kind, for the value of action lay in its being action, not in its being good or bad, sad or gay, imaginary or real. And when we think how infinitely beautiful and various and in all things enjoyable and desirable the world appeared to the enchanted Boccaccio, we see what a deprivation it would have seemed to him, amid such variety and wealth, to choose a little corner in which he could grow roots, to sacrifice so many possibilities to a concern for only one.

For these reasons it is vain to blame Boccaccio for not being moral, for being sceptical and superficial. It is contradictory to admire, say, the story of Andreuccio da Perugia and then blame Boccaccio for superficiality. What would have remained of Andreuccio's adventure if Boccaccio had probed into what lay behind his fecklessness and dash? The play, the lightness, the charm of those pages would have evaporated. It is useless to dwell on Boccaccio's flaw which to readers of today is a black separating gulf—the flaw of seeming to give absolution to his crime-prone and dishonest characters. We must realise that this absolution is the price paid for countless poetic events and curious magical details. Boccaccio seems to be saying to the reader: 'Let's agree once and for all that my characters are doing what they're doing for their own good reasons which it would be boring to pinpoint and evaluate. So relax; let them carry (, and let us enjoy ourselves.' A love of action that tends to precipitate action so as to enjoy it as soon as possible is, in my view, the mechanism with which Boccaccio's world operates. Notice how Boccaccio's way of telling a story is exactly the opposite to that of modern novelists. If we look at the first page of *Madame Bovary,* for instance, we certainly shall not find a statement of the book's main theme, nor the premises from which the development logically stems, set down with conventional clarity. We shall not find, 'Madame Bovary, born in such and such a place, married to such and such a man, had such and such ambitions', and so on. Flaubert, like nearly all modern writers, does not set out to make his characters act, but to create them; and his attention is set on a reality of whose developments he himself is ignorant. This is the reason why books like his almost give us the impression of living through the events that we are reading; and, as happens in life, we do not know today what may happen tomorrow.

On the other hand Boccaccio, whose main concern is to make his characters act and act wholeheartedly without hesitation, provides us headlong at the beginning of each story with the characters and data essential to the intrigue. Then once he has cleared the ground of these, he can devote himself body and soul to the development of the action. It is this convention, this preliminary liberation of the author from the burden of the characters and their motives, that enables Boccaccio to ornament his action with such magic, sensuality and light-heartedness.

For this reason it is mistaken in my view to see Boccaccio as an erotic writer. The truth is that though most of the stories in the **Decameron** pass for love stories, Boccaccio is not very interested in love. The role of love here, as in reality, is as a mainspring of human action and once the spring has been released Boccaccio turns his attention exclusively to action. In other words love is a sub-heading for one kind of action and no more desirable as such than many other sub-headings. This becomes plain when we observe Boccaccio's ignorance about normal, emotional, psychological love; for him love has no savour unless it is adventurous, difficult, full of vicissitudes and equivocations. And Boccaccio hurries through love as he does through so many other emotions, giving it a few words at the beginning of his stories.

> Lorenzo . . . who was goodly in person and gallant . . . when Isabetta bestowed many a glance upon him and began to regard him with extraordinary favour . . . Which Lorenzo marking, he began to affect her . . . and 'twas not long before . . . they did that which each most desired . . .

This handful of words relates Isabetta's love for Lorenzo in the most exemplary love story Boccaccio has written. Boccaccio hurries through love, its birth, the people, the facts, so as to get, we feel, to what concerns him most, the famous passage about the 'pot' in which Isabetta, after burying the head of her dead lover, plants 'some roots of the goodliest basil of Salerno'. And about this pot, and the beauty of the plant and the way the brothers get to know that the pot contains the lover's head, Boccaccio spreads himself with a kind of tender cruelty. Once he has cleared the ground of the psychological and emotional data, he

can, as usual, sit back and lavish all his care on the action and the objects on which it depends.

We have already said that Boccaccio's passion for action gave a subtler, keener edge to his enjoyment of his comforts as a peaceful man, a humanist and an honoured and solid citizen. And we have, in the structure of the **Decameron** itself, a reflection of a peaceful life rendered more delightful through the continual conjuring-up of exciting adventures and outlandish escapades. Indeed, the whole idea of the plague and the happy group of young people retiring to the country villa to tell stories, is significant, for the young people's safe withdrawal to the country, while the plague works havoc in the city, reflects Boccaccio's love of danger and his fascinated contemplation of the harsher, crueller things of life while safely basking in his own immunity. Moreover, we must not let ourselves be deceived by the seemingly 'historical' and 'pitiful' character of Boccaccio's plague. The plague—which he describes almost voluptuously and from a literary and æsthetic point of view, with obvious references to other plagues in books, and especially the vivid and detailed one in Thucydides— might well not have existed except as a foil to the delightful and reassuring description of the happy group in their *buen retiro*. As regards historical accuracy and pity, we should compare Boccaccio's plague with the one in [Alessandro] Manzoni, which really is historically accurate and deeply pitiful in spite of its morbid and decadent overtones. Compare, for instance, the famous passage from Manzoni: 'A woman came down from the doorstep of one of those exits and approached the convoy . . . ' with Boccaccio's cold and externalised exclamations which seem to betray not only the complacency of someone who has escaped death, but even a touch of irony:

> How many grand palaces, how many stately homes, how many splendid residences, once full of retainers, of lords, of ladies, were now left desolate of all, even to the meanest servant! How many families of historic fame, of vast ancestral domains, and wealth proverbial, found now no scion to continue the succession! How many brave men, how many fair ladies, how many gallant youths! . . .

With Manzoni, the sadistic taste for death, destruction and chastisement is genuinely outmatched by Christian compassion, whereas in Boccaccio we sense the thrill of someone far away in a pleasant place, removed from all danger, who contemplates a great calamity and speculates in a waking dream as to its details. And, in smug contrast, we have 'the little hill on the summit of which was a palace, with galleries, halls and chambers disposed around a fair and spacious court, each very fair in itself and the goodlier to see for the handsome pictures with which it was adorned'. We have the 'meadow where the grass grew green and luxuriant, nowhere being scorched by the sun'. We have the garden with its paths 'each very wide and straight as an arrow and roofed in with trellis of vines', and walled in with roses 'white and red, and jasmine'. We have the 'basin of whitest marble' rising in the middle of a lawn 'so green that it seemed almost black' and 'tables being already set and fragrant herbs and fair flowers strewn all about'. And there is the 'little lake' where 'the fish darted to and fro in multitudinous shoals', and the 'vale' where there were beds 'equipped within and without with stores of French coverlets and other bed-gear'. There is the 'little church nearby' where the group goes for 'divine service'; and the 'copse' full of 'roebucks and stags and other wild creatures as if witting that in this time of pestilence they had nought to fear from the hunter' and, indeed, all the other pleasing and peaceful things which, in the introductions, serve to offset the plague and the stirring events of the stories. In fact the calm and tranquil passages about peaceful occupations far removed from passion reflect life as Boccaccio lived it, for he was a frequenter of courts and côteries whereas the plague and the events of the stories are the longings of his imagination which helped him to luxuriate yet more in the quiet serenity of his life. That this is so is proved by the way in which he relegated the pleasures of country life to a marginal role in the book—not where they would be if they were the true source of his inspiration. Whereas Tasso, for instance, two centuries later, set such pleasures at the heart of his *Aminta,* for his life was neither calm nor pleasant and he had every reason to long for an idyllic life of luxury. If Boccaccio had confined himself to describing the calm, light-hearted life at the villa, he would have been a mere Arcadian; if he had confined himself to adventure he would have been a romantic yarn-spinner. But the combination of the villa and the stories reveals the dualism in the depths of his soul. The plague, with its horror, enhances the pleasures of the villa, just as corpses in a cemetery enrich the earth and thus nourish the flowers that grow in it. So it was a welcome, delightful plague, as contrasted with Manzoni's Christian plague, [Daniel] Defoe's demoralising plague, Thucydides's historical plague, and [Edgar Allan] Poe's grotesque plague. But inventories of plagues in literature have been made before now, so let us return to Boccaccio.

We have no intention here of analysing all Boccaccio's stories so as to illustrate our point as to the mainspring of his inspiration. Such an analysis would be tedious and mechanical. Think of Bonaparte's book on Poe where the same procedure is applied to every story, and the same discoveries made, until near-boredom sets in. Nevertheless the first story in the *Decameron,* the one about Ser Ciapelletto, seems to me highly important and typical of a whole vein of Boccaccio's kind of narrative, so I would like to discuss it—the more so as many readers may find that that story, lacking in action and real events as it is, contradicts what has been said so far.

The tale of Ser Ciapelletto is well known and has no need to be retold. Boccaccio establishes at the outset, in his usual conventional and brisk way, the criminal and impious character of Ser Ciapelletto who is given to every form of corruption; and thence, with the help of a complicated and rather improbable sleight of hand, he puts him in a situation where he can play the saint and, from his death-bed, carry out a long and blasphemous joke at the expense of his confessor. At first sight this might seem to be a satire on the rites and credulity of priests, a highly irreverent satire and, in last analysis, an unwarranted one. But on closer inspection Boccaccio's main concern is seen to be not the satire itself but the mechanism by which it is obtained. In

other words his interest is not in the things themselves but in their interplay when thrown violently together. His interest is not in priests or the Christian religion any more than in Ser Ciapelletto, it is in the development of the joke, and perhaps even more in the interplay of force and action that sets the joke in motion.

The theatre, whether classical or modern, is full of deceits and jokes. Moreover the theatre comes nearer to action than any other literary *genre.* Where there is deceit, the deceiver finds himself in a peculiar position of freedom and power in relation to the deceived. He knows he is deceiving, whereas his victim does not know he is being deceived. His freedom is unlimited so long as the deception lasts and his action, based as it is on contemplative satisfaction, is entirely gratuitous and an end in itself. Deceiving, moreover, means acting without danger, escaping the immediate consequences of action, acting from the cosy and perfectly safe ground of make-believe. It is precisely that kind of action that the lazy and easy-going Boccaccio must have enjoyed. Deception is a dream of action which has recourse to secrecy because it cannot be developed in an open way. They enjoy deceit who feel that the demands of open and brutal action are beyond their scope. In deceit cleverness has its revenge on force and all other irrational factors. Now Boccaccio's pages are full of deceits of this kind.

But we do not mean to imply that Boccaccio's own nature had leanings towards dissimulation and fraud. Indeed, if we realise that action pure and simple almost always lacks bite, and that deceit is intimately linked with the type of bourgeois and conventional lives that Boccaccio wanted to depict, then we shall see why nothing can be deduced from the frequency of the ***Decameron***'s deceits as to similar characteristics in the author. Boccaccio's taste for deceit reveals, if anything, something akin to that constant longing of mankind: the longing for invisibility. Who has not dreamt at least once that he had a wand, or a powder, or some other device for making himself invisible, and, once invisible, that he had gone off to the ends of the earth to play practical jokes on important people, to escape punishment, and generally behave with perfect immunity in the most dangerous circumstance? Now the situation of the deceiver is equivalent to a kind of invisibility. The deceived does not see the deceiver as he really is, so the deceiver can act with all the freedom and consistency that he would have if he were invisible. As can be seen, it is a dream of power and action if ever there was one.

Boccaccio must often have thought about such very human kinds of revenge. In the story of the scholar and the widow, Boccaccio's description ends with a smirk of complacency as he concludes: 'Wherefore, my ladies, have a care how you mock men, and especially scholars.' Here we don't know which to admire most, the extremely self-interested admonishment or the bland way in which the writer first takes pleasure in a detailed description of one of the cruellest pranks that could ever be thought up, and then all unknowingly reproves the very vice in which he revelled only a short while before. The story itself is often marred by long-winded passages, above all in the dialogue between the scholar at the foot of the tower and the wretched, weeping widow at the top. We get a feeling that a more powerful ending would not have spoilt the tale. But once he has devised his prank, Boccaccio wants to make us wallow in it. He wants to squeeze it of its last drop of honey—in other words he wants action beyond the bounds of what is either possible or æsthetic. The tortures inflicted on the tender and lovely body of the widow are described with an excessive and cruel delight, just as the prank previously played by the widow on the scholar was excessive and cruel. Both cases, but especially the second, suggest a not entirely unconscious sadism. And what are their prolonged conversations if not moral tortures drawn out with voluptuous care? The deceit is shown up in its true colours, as action dreamed up by someone who has experienced a serious disillusion in real life, yet would be incapable of taking his revenge in such a cruel way even if the occasion presented itself. We have mentioned sadism but we certainly do not mean to imply that Boccaccio's art is sadistic. The frequent traces of sadism in Boccaccio bear witness not to a more or less decadent perversion but to the chance coming-together of his thirst for action and a healthy and normal sensuality. Such sadism is no more than an active, though excessive and uncontrolled, male instinct. Every action, by the fact that it is carried through from a given premiss to its logical conclusion and without regard for the consequences, always involves a certain degree of sadism. The premiss in the story of the scholar is revenge. And in fact the scholar is not satisfied until the woman's beautiful body is reduced to a 'half-burnt stump', and the same goes for Boccaccio. Or better, there is an air of disillusion and discontent in the story, as if Boccaccio had suddenly noticed the inadequacy of the dream and felt bitter about it, or noticed that he had indeed just been dreaming and nothing more.

The story of the scholar and the widow is really Boccaccio's autobiographical expression of his passion for action. And it is because the autobiography is ill-disguised that the revenge is so improbable and far-fetched and the story carried through with such angry determination with little regard to its absurdity or its very obvious retouches. The part about necromancy is touched up, for instance, for halfway through the story Boccaccio realises that the widow could easily make the experiment in magic in one of her villas or some other place where she could thwart the scholar's plans, so he quickly assures us that the lady's 'estate and the tower' are 'very well known' to the scholar. Then, later, good fortune sees to it that the place is not only isolated but, at that hour, 'the husbandmen had all gone from the fields by reason of the heat'. Finally, Boccaccio suddenly remembers that the maid, who is every bit as guilty from his point of view as her mistress, is emerging from the adventure unscathed, so he promptly makes her break her thigh when coming down from the fateful tower with her mistress. This is a typically sadistic forcing of effect, though entirely lacking the sensuality that usually goes with sadism. I have already said that Boccaccio betrays his feelings at the end. But even halfway through the story we have him exclaiming, 'Ah! poor woman! poor woman! she little knew, my ladies, how rash it is to try conclusions with scholars' and he is clearly referring to himself.

But action free from any ulterior motive, action as an end in itself, action for action's sake, in a word adventure, always lies at the heart of Boccaccio's most secret aspirations. But as we have already said, this kind of action runs the risk of seeming unwarranted and hence unreal. [Ludovico] Ariosto, another contemplative writer in love with action, remedies this drawback by means of irony; Boccaccio, less disillusioned than Ariosto, counters it with what we could call (to use an overworked term) a kind of magic realism. That is, a visionary yet concrete precision of detail, combined—within a rarefied and ineffable atmosphere—with an extraordinary sense of the coincidences offered by reality itself at the moment of narration. I have said that this magic realism enables Boccaccio to avoid the pitfall of unreality peculiar to adventure. But perhaps it would be more accurate to say that this magic derives precisely from his indifference to the ethical factor, from the scepticism which people still insist on seeing as one of the defects of Boccaccio's art. For what is a dream, where magic seems at home, if not a reality from which all rational, practical, moral and intellectual elements have been banished, and in which the fantasies of the unconscious are expressed? For moralists reality tends to demand a judgement and thus it harmonises realistically with characters and events. But for adventure-dreamers reality is just as ineffable and mysterious as the places, objects and people that we caress with our deepest instincts when we are asleep. The surrealists, in their researches, have sometimes isolated and blown up details in old pictures and thereby revealed the magical and metaphysical character of many of these details—which have a lucid incoherence unknown to the modern impressionists and realists. This is because, like Boccaccio, the old masters often dreamed and dreams are fertile ground for analogies and enigmas. When seen through a magnifying glass, some of Boccaccio's backgrounds, places and notations become arcane and suggestive, like the tiny *natures mortes,* corners of landscapes, and background-figures of some of our fourteenth-, fifteenth- and sixteenth-century painters. Action, pure action, without intended meaning or ethics, gains depth, lucidity and mystery from those details that no amount of serious moral intention could give it.

An outstanding example of this blending of magic detail with passion for action is provided by the story of Andreuccio of Perugia. Here, moreover, the thirst for adventure is overt and total. There are none of those erotic elements that at first sight may seem to be inseparable from Boccaccio's art. Andreuccio is a young man, nothing else; we know nothing about him except that he came to Naples to buy horses. In a word, Andreuccio lies entirely within the action, and from the action he derives if not his character, at least his consistency; apart from the action he has no features, no character, no psychology. The starting-point of the tale is the intrigue initiated by the Neapolitan prostitute for Andreuccio's undoing. Without involving himself too far in the probability of the story of a sister lost and found, Boccaccio immediately enters into a compulsive, dreamy atmosphere which is truly magical. We have the 'curtained bed', with 'dresses in plenty, hanging on pegs' in the prostitute's house; we have 'the narrow blind alley' into which the unfortunate Andreuccio falls; we have the 'fellow with the black and matted beard . . .

yawning and rubbing his eyes as if he had just been roused from his bed, or at any rate from deep sleep'; we have those two thieves who, on hearing Andreuccio's story, exclaim, 'Of a surety, 'twas in the house of Scarabone Buttafuoco'; and, finally, we have the cathedral in which the archbishop has been buried, the cathedral where—though not described—we seem to see the tall shadowy nave, the vast paved floor dimly shining, the massive brown groups of pillars and columns and, at the end, all twinkling with candles, the altar with the prelate's sarcophagus. Andreuccio enters the tomb and there the thieves leave him. Shut up in the tomb with a dead man, he is in an anguishing situation almost worthy of Poe. But the church echoes with footsteps, other thieves come along (and, incidentally, how many thieves there are in Boccaccio!—but in a world of humanists, merchants and courtiers, the criminal world is the only one that *acts*), the lid is raised from the tomb and the anguish evaporates. And now the point is, what does it matter if Andreuccio, the honest merchant, becomes a thief and a desecrator of tombs; what does it matter if later (as Boccaccio tells us, not without ingenuousness) his companions congratulate him and help him make away with the stolen goods—granted that the writer has borne us through the adventure in one breath?

A passion for adventure in quantity—like someone who wants to appease his hunger at all costs and to whom eating the same food matters little—can be found in the story of the Sultan of Babylonia's daughter. Here, too, the magic of the detail makes up for the monotony of the series of rapes. The ship, with only women aboard, that 'swiftly sails the sea before the storm' and then runs aground on the sand, and Pericone riding on horseback along the devastated beach after the storm, are like pictures from Ariosto. But the subsequent murder of the Prince of Morea takes place in surroundings and circumstances suggestive of Elizabethan drama.

> The palace was close by the sea, but at a considerable altitude above it, and the window through which the prince's body was thrown looked over some houses which, being sapped by the sea, had become ruinous, and were rarely or never visited by a soul.

From that window the prince looks out, 'bare to the skin', to 'enjoy a light breeze' and, as we would add, to contemplate those melancholy surfbeaten ruins under the moonlight. The murderer, Ciuriaci, comes up behind him, stabs him, and throws his body into the ruins. Ciuriaci is strangled in his turn by one of his companions, 'with a halter brought with him for the purpose', and then is thrown down onto the prince's body. This is behaviour of Machiavellian and Renaissance atrocity. Meanwhile the lovely woman sleeps on unawares and half-naked in her bed before the open window. The Duke of Athens, having strangled Ciuriaci, takes a light and

> gently uncovered her person as she lay fast asleep; and surveyed her from head to foot to his no small satisfaction . . . his passion waxed beyond measure, and reckless of his recent crime and of the blood which still stained his hands, he got forthwith into bed.

The crime is discovered in a strange and terrifying way. 'An idiot roaming about the ruins where lay the corpses of the prince and Ciuriaci drew the latter by the halter and went off dragging it after him . . . ' This is only one episode of the story but quite sufficient to provide material for a tragedy by Webster or Marlowe.

Or we have the tale of Riccardo de Chinzica, with the great Mediterranean sea, scoured by gallant pirates such as Paganino da Monaco; with those two boats plying along the coast in the heat of the day, one bearing the unfortunate judge, the other the beautiful wife and her maids. Paganino's castle is not described; but like Andreuccio's cathedral we seem to see it high on that rocky and beflowered coast. Paganino and Riccardo's wife send the poor judge back in disgrace. If Boccaccio had been the middle-class townee writer that he has often been called, this simple turn of events could well have happened within the four walls of a house. But Boccaccio, with his passion for adventure, and perhaps to counterbalance the dry-as-dust judge with his sedentary life, brings in Pisa and Monaco, the sea and the corsair—things that introduce a distant and legendary atmosphere to a not very unusual plot. In passing it is worth noting that the sea always evokes a deep and passionate response in Boccaccio, as if its huge vastness and eternal variety alone could satisfy his greed for freedom and action.

But it was not only in space that Boccaccio sought scope for his passion for action; he sought it also in time. I have always considered historical novels and stories an absurdity unless history, instead of presenting itself to the author as a kind of *place d'armes* in which time (to take the words of the imaginary seventeenth-century writer of the Introduction to *The Betrothed*) passes the years in review and draws them up in battle array, unless history brings the years back to the surface of memory like some ancestral recollection, or poetic longing, or nostalgia. Boccaccio, though he lived in a time that no one could suspect of historicism—between the Middle Ages which rejected history in the name of theological immobility, and the Renaissance which was equally foreign to the spirit of history owing to its Plutarchian cult of the personality—Boccaccio must nevertheless have had a mythical and obscure sense of the almost legendary past of the high Middle Ages and the Lombard invaders, if only transmitted by oral tradition and family memories. Apart from other stories where the period is uncertain and wrapped, as it were, in the darkness of a magic long-ago (such as the ones about Tancredi, Prince of Salerno; Nastagio degli Onesti, and Alibech in the desert of the Thebaid), we find a sense of a Lombardic and barbarous Middle Ages in King Agilulf and Queen Teodolinda, told out as it is in the stained glass of a cathedral, and there is also some kind of prenatal memory present as if someone were recounting things neither invented nor heard but experienced in another life. The Italian groom belonging to the oppressed race who is in love with the Lombard Queen, risks death to lie with her and, this achieved, spends his life remembering those minutes of royal love, is a very complex figure in whom are blended the passion for action and a sort of nostalgia for a dark barbaric era that lacked the light of art or culture yet fostered strong wholehearted passions, like the protagonist's for King Agilulf's wife. There are plenty of kings and queens in Boccaccio, but these two are the only ones that achieve social relief and concreteness, contrasted as they are with the low-born groom. Agilulf and Teodolinda, we feel, reign barbarously by right of conquest over an enslaved people. The groom has no hope and is content just to be near the queen, tending the horses. But this timid fetishism does not satisfy his passion indefinitely. When desire gains over prudence, he decides to risk his life and try to possess the queen. As usual, once the decision is taken, and the plot formulated, Boccaccio hurtles into the action—which, as he proceeds, is deepened and enriched by the background details.

The attentive reader is sure to remember the place in which the groom's adventure occurs. This is King Agilulf's palace, probably a rough castle of wood with square palisaded towers like the ones Agilulf's ancestors built in the clearings of the northern forests, a fitting setting for a king who at night goes to seek his wife wrapped in a great mantle and carrying a 'lighted torch' in one hand and a wand in the other. It is also a fitting setting for the groom who disguises himself as the king and, making the 'drowsy' chambermaid open the doors to him, lies down silently beside the queen in the darkness. Basically it is the same kind of deception as in many another licentious story, but the remote period, the place, the palace that seems to have emerged from a Germanic saga and the royal atmosphere, confer a poetic quality on what elsewhere might be a mere diversion or joke. Once the deception is discovered, the king makes straight for the place where he imagines his unknown rival to be.

This is the 'long dormitory' above the horses' stables—words charged with evocations of feudal servitude. Here in different beds 'well-nigh all' the kings' household sleeps. 'Well-nigh all', for the Lombard kings had no courts, the king being a feudal man like everyone else. His peers were not in the palace but in other castles scattered across Italy; in the royal palace there dwelt only the members of the royal family, and the family's servants. We imagine the 'long dormitory' as narrow and low with pallets for all (or 'well-nigh all') the servants stretching as far as the eye can see under a beamed ceiling. The king enters the corridor, walks slowly along the row of beds, and feels the heart of each sleeper with his hand. Note how this deep deathlike sleep of all the servants, worn out by the day's toil, is in accord with the image of the long dormitory. The king cuts a tuft of hair from the head of the one whose heart seems to him agitated. But the groom, outwitting the king, cuts a similar tuft from the heads of all his companions. So the next day, when the king sees all the family servants partially shorn, he has to admit defeat from his unknown rival.

I have gone into this story at length because it seems to me one of the best in the *Decameron* and one in which the passion for action seems to attain the highest level of articulation and depth. Moreover, with its homely human tone and gay deceit, it marks the transition of Boccaccio's art from the stories we might call 'lucky' (that is those in which the vicissitudes lead to a happy ending in a clear and light-hearted atmosphere) to stories we might call 'un-lucky', where the adventures have a tragic ending. Our traditional image of Boccaccio depends mainly on the first type, and especially on those stories with erotic and comic plots. But it is a partial image and takes less than half Boccaccio into account. In fact Boccaccio felt equally deeply about happiness and unhappiness, and this because they are the two faces of Chance, the only god who survives the disappearance of all others and still shines brightly in the serene sky of the *Decameron.* For Boccaccio chance plays the part of fate in Greek tragedies but we owe his love of chance not to cynicism but, like everything else, to his taste for action and adventure. For what is chance in Boccaccio's stories but the expression of a devoted passion for the manifold in life? All who put their trust in chance put their trust in life as in a river with multiple currents to which we should abandon ourselves in the knowledge that they will ultimately lead somewhere. Chance, moreover, allows every action to be its own self-justification as it occurs. Hence the freedom, the variety, the beauty of all actions without exception, their grafting not onto a dull and limited moral world but onto the most charming and colourful of æsthetic worlds. Chance and mischance are beautiful alike, to be caressed and wondered at with feelings of lascivious desire. All ends up in beauty.

It is perhaps this æstheticism of adventure over which the two faces of chance preside that lies behind the beauty of the stories we have called 'unlucky' for they are among the most beautiful and the most characteristic of his art (contrary to the tradition about Boccaccio as a typical licentious story-teller). They are scattered throughout the book, but one whole day is devoted to those whose loves have unhappy endings. Boccaccio participates in these sad stories with the feelings we detected in him in his treatment of the plague—with the voluptuous, dreamy caressing of tragic action by someone far removed from any such situation in fact. This may not be much, but it is enough to prevent Boccaccio from falling into the flatness and grossness of many writers who have ventured on similar themes, such as Giraldi and Bandello. It is this attitude that gives the 'unlucky' stories their enchanted air of dark immovable fate and at the same time their flavour of legend. They are stories from which, owing to the remoteness of the matter treated, all pity has vanished, and all that remains is naked action charged with mystery.

We have already spoken of Isabetta and the pot of basil. But consider the ruthlessness with which Boccaccio drags the two lovers to death in the story of Tancredi, Prince of Salerno. The grotto with an opening 'all but choked with the brambles and plants that grew about it', the room in the princely palace communicating with the grotto—these closely recall the window and the ruins by the sea in the murder of the Prince of Morea: a secret, melodramatic, melancholy place, a setting well suited to ill-starred loves. Tancredi's 'tender love' for his daughter whom he cannot bring himself to give in marriage, has the odour of incest, and his words to her when he discovers the affair with the page, his lamentations and the revenge he carries out on young Guiscardo, suggest a lover rather than a father. Ghismonda's long speeches remind us of the widow and the scholar: a complacent drawing-out of a situation already decided.

At first we expect Friar Alberto (in the next story) to be the protagonist of a tale that is all laughter. But that unfortunate lover, having taken flight into the Grand Canal without wings, and been dragged into the Piazza San Marco disguised as a 'wild man' and exposed to the mockery of the crowd, is punished for his sensuality not according to some moral concept, as the conclusion 'God grant that so it may betide all his likes; might suggest, but simply because Boccaccio enjoys the improbable and picturesque prank.

> Today we hold a revel, wherein folk lead others about in various disguises; as, one man will present a bear, another a wild man, and so forth; and then in the piazza of San Marco there is a hunt, which done, the revel is ended.

It is an animated and detailed picture, worthy of Bellini or Carpaccio. The same sought-out cruelty is apparent in the story where the King of Tunisia's daughter, after a naval battle, is bled to death and slaughtered before her lover's eyes in spite of all her tears and entreaties. Then there is the story of Girolamo, Salvestra's lover, who, in his sorrow at not being able to possess her, 'gathering up into one thought the love he had so long borne her, and the harshness with which she now requited it, and his ruined hopes, resolved to live no longer and in a convulsion, without a word, and with fists clenched, expired by her side.' Here, first, is the admirable invention of a suicide both highly unusual and well suited for producing the effects that follow: the husband getting up in the night and carrying the young lover's body into the doorway of the house; the wife, at her husband's instigation, going to church for the young man's funeral and dying in the same surprising and mysterious way. Boccaccio shows an equally inventive spirit and taste for unusual situations in the story of Pasquino who, in an extraordinary garden on a trip to the country, eats and drinks and chats happily, then rubs his teeth with a leaf from the fatal sage bush and dies. Extraordinary garden, I said; and indeed, like Agilulf's palace and Andreuccio's cathedral, it is one of those Boccaccian settings that evoke a whole vision by virtue of a single detail, in this case the sage bush. The young man who takes the sage leaf and rubs his teeth with it, 'saying that sage was an excellent cleanser', evokes the laziness and languid wellbeing that come with a successful outing. But in addition the sage bush conjures up the whole garden, a place we imagine to be outside the walls, uncultivated yet full of trees, flowers and grass while the 'toad of prodigious dimensions' discovered beneath the bush adds a note of horror and latent threat.

We have not mentioned the many other stories in no way inferior to these, and perhaps more typically Boccaccian—erotic stories, country ones, ones about nuns and priests, and simple anecdotes. This is because they are too well known to need quotation and also because of our conviction that the comic and licentious vein which has made Boccaccio famous is spectacular rather than characteristic, typical rather than deep. Though Boccaccio had a gay, carnal sense of life, the heart of his inspiration lay elsewhere, in his passion for action, in the delight he derived from imagining he was active, in his taste for adventure. As proof of this, note how, when this taste is absent, Boc-

caccio runs the risk of becoming no more than an inventor of piquant and witty anecdotes.

The fact that it is chance that lies behind the vicissitudes of the stories and not a high moral consciousness or system of thought, in no way proves that Boccaccio was a lazy or frivolous writer. Chance, that deceptive and enigmatic goddess, puts the more lovable and younger human faculties to the test first and foremost. Faith in chance is a prerogative of the young, of all those whose vitality has not yet been stultified and put at the service of some idea or interest. Boccaccio, who was young in spirit, trusted in chance out of excess of imagination and vitality rather than scepticism and frivolity. And after all, to oust all the dull ghosts from heaven and put in their place the blindfold goddess at her wheel means removing the grey monochrome of normality from the world and acknowledging its boundless richness and variety. Such chance, such interplay of agile and free forces is unknown to us, alas, and what we often mistake for dull and sinister chance is a destiny that is inscrutable but no less logical and pitiless for that. (pp. 134-55)

> *Alberto Moravia, "Boccaccio," in his* Man as an End: A Defense of Humanism, *translated by Bernard Wall, 1965. Reprint by Farrar, Straus and Giroux, 1966, pp. 134-55.*

Vittore Branca (essay date 1976)

[*A noted Italian literary critic, Branca has written numerous studies on Francesco Petrarch, Alessandro Manzoni, and Boccaccio. In the following excerpt, taken from* Boccaccio: The Man and His Works *(1976), Branca explains how the* Decameron *is representative of middle-class medieval society and was influenced by medieval literary tradition.*]

The **Decameron** could not have become known for many years to the cultural and commercial societies of Italy, when Francesco Buondelmonti, the nephew and most faithful agent of the great seneschal Niccolò Acciaiuoli, wrote to Niccolò's cousin Giovanni Acciaiuoli in Florence (at that time archbishop-elect of Patras) in July 1360. The letter indicated the anxious eagerness with which the first copies of the **Decameron** were read and passed around and, sometimes, hungrily purloined:

> Reverend Domine, here is Monte Bellandi writing to his wife that she is to give you the book of the tales of messer Giovanni Boccacci, belonging to me; wherefore I beseech you *quantum possum* that you have it delivered to you; and if the Archbishop of Naples has not left I beg that you send it by him—by his servitors, that is— and he is not to give it to Messere (Niccolò Acciaiuoli) nor to any other person than myself. And if the Archbishop has departed, have it given on my behalf to Cenni Bardella: let him send it to me at L'Aquila or Sulmona; otherwise, do you send it to me yourself by one who you believe will deliver it to my hand; and do be most careful that messer Neri shall not get hold of it, for then never would I have it. I am having it delivered to you because I trust you more than anyone else and I hold it most dear; and do be

careful not to lend it to anyone because there are many who would be dishonest. . . .

The same enthusiasm, the same trepidation, the same joy derived from making a discovery, enlivens the prologue, with which in those same years, an anonymous admirer praised writers on love. . . . He then continued:

> . . . among others whom I recall at present, who are deserving of fulsome praise and celebrity, there is the worthy Messer Giovanni di Boccaccio, to whom God give a long and prosperous life as he himself may wish. Not so very long ago he has written beautiful and delightful books, in prose and in verse, in honor of those gracious ladies whose high-souled noblemindedness takes pleasure in occupying itself with pleasant and virtuous matters; they take great pleasure and delight in books and beautiful tales, whether by reading them or in hearing them read, whereby for him fame increases, and for you, your delight. And among these books he composed one especially beautiful and pleasurable, entitled *Decameron:* which, you must know if you have heard it read, treats of a gay company of seven young women and three young men. . . .

Insofar as it is possible to deduce from his writing characteristics, the writer of those lines belonged to the Florentine merchant society, in all probability to that gravitating around the company of the Bardi family. That is to say, he belonged, as did the Buondelmonti and the Acciaiuoli, to that upper middle-class society which had founded the great fortunes of the Florentine Commune in the thirteenth and fourteenth centuries.

This upper middle class very promptly disseminated through its thousand channels those works for which its men showed preference. For this reason, the Buondelmonti, the Acciaiuoli, the Bardi, the Cavalcanti (Boccaccio's epistle XXI) immediately spread the news of the *Decameron,* which became popular with the middle class because it clearly reflects the enthusiasm and the activity of that society. As is intimated above, this was nothing new, for copies of more than two-thirds of the manuscripts written between the late Trecento and early Quattrocento—so far as my researches have been able to ascertain—were possessed by those families, while, on the contrary, there seem to be no copies that belonged to famous libraries or to have come from the more esteemed copyists' shops. As the descriptions of the codices reveal, copies of the *Decameron* were owned by the most eminent merchant families of Florence. . . . Indeed, copies of the *Decameron* physically were involved in the complex finances that constituted the adventurous life of that society. We repeatedly come upon traces of accounts, rentals, or loans noted on the margins of codices . . . Sometimes we find modifications of the text, which reveal mercantile interests or tendencies.

The names of unusual amanuenses are related to the same mercantile environment. They were persons of the most varied stations and professions who had turned copyist, who had adapted themselves to the long, patient work in order to satisfy a personal desire to have that fashionable text always at hand. (pp. 197-99)

In contrast to the extraordinary popularity of the *Decam-*

eron in the middle classes, the more properly literary circles remained indifferent to it. That is, even after several years, even after the most official recognition of Boccaccio's fame, one seeks in vain for any evidence in the world of culture corresponding to that explosion of middle-class enthusiasm. The famous judgment of Petrarch in the last of the *Seniles* contains his Latin translation of the Griselda story ("Librum tuum quem nostro materno eloquio, ut opinor, olim iuvenis edidisti nescio quidem unde vel qualiter ad me delatum, vidi: nam si dicam legi, mentiar . . . "). Perhaps, . . . Petrarch's criticism is strictly literary . . . , remote from any implied disinterest. His judgment seems, however, to set the tone for the attitude of reserve and almost wilful disregard manifested by that first Humanistic circle. Indeed, the entire following generation seemed to be disinterested in the *Decameron,* although it praised and glorified Boccaccio's erudite output. Filippo Villani, Benvenuto da Imola, Coluccio Salutati, Leonardo Bruni shared this attitude and if they quoted the *Decameron,* it was only marginal and often not even explicit. Certainly it is not merely the question of the language which caused this negative position, for Petrarch himself in another of the *Seniles* appears much more warmly interested in the vernacular poetry of his great friend; at the end of the century those men of letters allude to that same poetry with great interest.

But middle-class enthusiasm remained undiminished in the face of this prolonged cultural diffidence. There is evidence of this in the increased number of copies of the *Decameron,* the ever-more diligent imitation of Boccaccio by others, the repetition of the tales from the lips of the jugglers and the story-tellers in the public squares, to which the public listened eagerly. Sacchetti's *Paradiso degli Alberti* was inspired by the *Decameron,* as was a whole series of songs and of illustrations on wedding chests, which relate tales and themes of the *Decameron.*

This contrast of enthusiasm and of interest is not merely the result of the cultural atmosphere of its time. Instead, it originates from elements characteristic of the work of Boccaccio, which are reflected in its fortunes preceding its full recognition as a literary masterpiece.

This is to say, the *Decameron* appeared during the last decades of the Trecento, not as a work adhering to literary tradition but as a book for agreeable, pleasant reading, as a work created not for the savoring of the refined men of letters but for the joy of less-cultured readers. The merchants of the circle of the Acciaiuoli or the women of the house of Cavalcanti, whom Boccaccio had advised not to read his book, were the first readers we find poring over the *Decameron,* and they are indicative of this episode in the life of fourteenth century Italy.

The *Decameron* was not written following the style of the classical manner, highly venerated by Italian protohumanists, as it had been earlier by Italian prehumanists; it was not even influenced by the more aristocratic medieval tradition, which imitated the great classical examples, that is, it did not come down from the lyrical tradition. Its antecedents were to be sought, if anywhere, in the exuberant and woodsy narrative production of a middle-class and popular character. Boccaccio wrote the *Decameron* on a lower level, without literary pretensions, in a style which the middle-class society of the preceding centuries preferred to read for entertainment. The **Decameron** was disseminated by word of mouth as well as by the written word. To those readers the **Decameron** appeared as the masterpiece of its type, as the clever systemization of a material beloved but still raw and in a fluid state (although it might have needed a harmonious and stable arrangement). It did not exact the respect and the admiration owed to literary masterpieces but, as the manuscripts show, it evoked a happy and familiar confidence which encouraged alterations and omissions and insertions of new tales, as well as coupling with other narrations. That is, it produced a confidence in the reader so that he would feel free to tailor the book most particularly to *his own* tastes, needs, and preference. That means the **Decameron** appeared as a completely extraliterary work. Boccaccio himself stressed the idea in the introduction (". . . I mean to relate a hundred tales, or fables, or parables or stories, however they may be called, . . . as a help and refuge for ladies in love.").

Indeed, to that protohumanistic society which already dominated the Italian culture of the second half of the fourteenth century, the work probably appeared to be not only extraliterary but almost antiliterary. Those men, after the "darkening" which followed the great medieval classicism, were laboriously rediscovering the highly venerated classical culture. They entertained the supreme ambition of reuniting themselves to the Latins, while skipping over—as nearly as possible—medieval culture. With passionate trepidation they felt the supreme "dignities" and "reasons" of the spirit entrusted to literature. Such a work as the **Decameron,** on the contrary, tended entirely toward medieval and Romance culture and its world. Boccaccio was intent on collecting and studiously arranging the fancies beloved by the populace. It is this, perhaps, which shows through in the feeling and emotion of the epitaph which Salutati composed for Boccaccio, in the elegant lines of which it is possible to distinguish an implied reproof: "te *vulgo . . .* percelebrem."

Perhaps these interpretations or rather, these attitudes, are only the result of an episodic cultural situation. However, the diverse reactions to the **Decameron** reflect its certain, if not exclusive, reliance on the medieval and Romance tradition.

As has been said, in the extremely varied and complex material of the **Decameron** the classical influence is almost completely absent. The sole tale of a Greco-Roman type, that of Titus and Gisippus (X, 8), is only a conventional setting illuminated by the most characteristic deforming lights of medieval literature. It is but an ornate transcription of one of the most celebrated works of that age, the *Disciplina Clericalis,* enriched with elements derived from a little poem by Alessandro di Bernay. The only two novellas in which some classical influence may be detected, that is, the tenth story of the fifth day (V, 10) and the second of the seventh day (VII, 2), come straight from a Latin writer, Apuleius. Boccaccio himself admitted that one of his inspirations for the two novellas was Apuleius—an author who, like Boccaccio, had lent an ear to the narratives

of the people and had deemed them worthy of a literary consecration.

Story-tellers of the Renaissance drew their material from the classical world, even as much as certain narrators of the thirteenth and fourteenth centuries did. They all repeated and adapted the ancient epical or historical exploits. Boccaccio did this as well, but he also decided to yield to his natural inclination for the imaginative. Boccaccio had vast knowledge of classical literature, and, more than any of his contemporaries, was able to draw from that source ample material for narration. Indeed he drew on classical sources for such works as the *Epistole* and the *Teseida,* the *Amorosa Visione* and the *Ninfale Fiesolano.*

In the **Decameron,** on the contrary, even when classical models are available, natural and impressive, Boccaccio seems to avoid them deliberately. Instead he turned to the medieval texts he admired. We have already mentioned this influence in the novellas, V, 10 and VII, 2. Also, Boccaccio's preference for medieval sources over the classics is indicated in the novella of Chynon (Cimone, V, 1), which is much closer to an episode in the story of Barlaam and Josaphat than to the Greek romances proposed by

Boccaccio's image appears on part of a Florentine fresco by Andrea dal Castagno.

Rohde, and which Boccaccio must have known. In the novella of Andreuccio of Perugia (II, 5) Boccaccio eliminates almost every trace of an episode of the *History of Antheia and Habrocome* by Xenophon of Ephesus (which was known to him). In his version the influence of a *fabliau, Boivin de Provins* is apparent. In the novella of the Angel Gabriel (IV,2) the possible Ovidian references are blurred by the narration of the pseudo-Hegesippus. It would not be difficult to give many other examples, but one of them marks the *Decameron* beyond any possibility of doubt. This is the famous evocation of the plague in the sombre "overture" of the *Decameron.* Acquainted indirectly with the tragic Lucretian description as found in Macrobius and other annotators of the *Georgics,* Boccaccio modelled his grandiose and terrible pages on those in which Paulus Diaconus—a writer he used frequently—had described the pestilence which tormented various provinces of Italy in the last months of the empire of Justinian. . . . (pp. 200-04)

Even if Boccaccio's use of medieval traditions did not completely overshadow classical influences in his work, his tendency to "contaminate" the latter would suffice to characterize as medieval both his artistic technique and his poetical imagination itself. Moreover, Boccaccio was quite willing to fuse very diverse texts and examples. . . . In his youthful minor poems Boccaccio merged the traditions of the great Latin epic of Virgil and of Statius with the newer and popular tradition of the *cantari,* as he did again in his later works, from the *De Genealogia* to the *Esposizioni.*

Boccaccio's sensibility, his clinging to the literature and the traditions of the immediately preceding centuries—so different from the disdainful coldness of Petrarch and his friends—is indicated by the sympathetically open and frank way with which he adopts the popular art of story-telling in the *Decameron.* Almost two-thirds of the antecedents which can be traced for the tales of the *Decameron* belong to this literature. The very poetry of the people of those centuries—from the *cantari* to the *lamenti,* from the *canzoni a ballo* (ballads) to the *rispetti*—is given its most illustrious recall and reflection in the *Decameron.* In many cases this has saved it from the oblivion of the centuries.

But even more than in the recapture of the content, the preoccupation of Boccaccio's imagination with this world is revealed in the intonation and the coloring of the narration. The amorous adventures and the salacious jests are related with the carefree and mirthful sprightliness of the *fabliaux.* The sad and sorrowful stories are patterned after the anguished pity of the *lamenti.* The lofty tragedies of love and death are scanned to the doleful and stately rhythms of the adaptations of French romances. The eventful and risky adventures in far-off places across the Mediterranean or in western Europe have the rapid and straightforward movement of the reports of the Florentine merchants, the real "conquistadores" of that age. The marvellous and fabulous episodes glitter with the fairy-tale lights and the choral enchantment of the *cantari.*

Boccaccio put together and in a certain sense, ennobled, this material, these modes, this complex tradition by means of a technique and style of harmonious writing ab-

solutely congenial to the world in which they were written. He avoids any of the classical drapery or complacent classical starching used by Petrarch and story-tellers of the following age, even for figures and episodes extraneous to the Greco-Roman world.

Boccaccio achieves a dignity of style, a superior harmony . . . from his medieval technique based on the *cursus* and rhymed prose. Also, for ornament he drew from the style of the *De Vulgari Eloquentia.* From the treatises on style and rhetoric of the preceding centuries Boccaccio evolved the literary preciosities which he seems to enjoy scattering through his work like little gems: reference to the canonical numbers, three and ten, the flashing use of names, either allusive to or in rapid correspondence with imaginative periphrases; and the employment of *senhal,* the calculated and scrupulous topographical distribution of the novellas according to a completely literary and medieval geography. . . . In addition, Boccaccio followed medieval literary precepts when, in outlining his tales, he gave each one a moral-didactic premise. Boccaccio uses symbolic colors (white, green, red, and perse) to indicate the dowries or the sentimental situation of the ladies. He relies on "styles" following the precepts of the most authoritative rhetorical science for writing treatises, from Alberico da Montecassino to John of Garland.

But Boccaccio's objective in the *Decameron* was not merely literary. Unlike later novella writers, he did not organize the diversified material for his novella purely with regard to literary structure. Nor was his intention clearly allegorical. Instead, Boccaccio wished to give his material a coherent development in a rhetorical and moral sense. The *tesserae* (pieces put together to form a mosaic) from the medieval tradition are carefully placed in accordance with the esthetic convictions of that age and of Boccaccio himself, and the precision of the design imparts a metaphysically valid meaning to the work. Likewise in the *Filocolo* and the *Comedia,* the most direct anticipations of the *Decameron,* the "questions of love" and the narrations of the Nymphs were developed with a clear conception of ideas and morality.

The design of the *Decameron,* then, makes it a structurally organic work and not merely a collection of a hundred novellas. As Ferdinando Neri has shown, the structural framework of the tales is the ideal itinerary, which goes from the harsh reprehension of vice (Day I) to a carefully planned eulogy of virtue (Day X).

During the narration, Boccaccio unfolds his version of the "comedy of man." He shows how man can make himself worthy of entrance to the "splendid kingdom of virtue," overcoming the great forces that, like instruments of Providence, seem to govern the world: Fortune, Love, Ingenuity. In orderly succession, Boccaccio presents varied and agitated pictures of mankind; man the plaything of Fortune (Day II); then man victorious over Fortune "by his industry" (Day III). He describes man undergoing the highest ordeals of human joy and sorrow, enduring the rule of Love, the sovereign of the world (Days IV and V). And then, with poignant mirth, he portrays men who use their Ingenuity to distinction (Day VI). He pictures this either in the rapid skirmishes of witty sayings (Day VI) or in deceits and practical jokes which, in accord with the accidents of Fortune and the entire medieval literature, develop and persist in the overwhelming amorous material (Days VII and VIII). Thus, from the initial censure of human vices, through contemplation of the measure which men give of their intellectual and moral endowment under the hazards of Fortune, Love, and Ingenuity, after the pause of the ninth day, Boccaccio presents the magnificent and fabulous epilogue on the tenth day, which describes the most lofty virtues. In the solemn laudatory atmosphere of the epilogue, Boccaccio seems to propose the establishment of the highest motives, the great force-ideas which had governed the unfolding of the magnificent and eternal human comedy. He seems to consecrate them in an almost metaphysical fixity. Thus the epilogue presents Fortune (novellas 1, 2, 3), Love (novellas 4, 5, 6, 7), and Ingenuity (novellas 8, 9) in a new light. In it they are the touchstones of the nobility of man, which are overwhelmed and surpassed by Virtue. Through Griselda, representative of Virtue in the Epilogue, these three great forces find their noblest expression. Fortune turns a poor shepherdess into a splendid lady of the manor; Love transforms Gualtieri and makes Griselda heroic; and Ingenuity is used by Gualtieri to test his wife. Griselda's virtue is portrayed as almost hallowed and stylized, drawn from the traditional concept of the lady "humble and lofty more than any creature." (The echo of the prophecy of Simeone and of the "Ecce ancilla" is clear, for example in the phrases: "Although these words were like dagger-thrusts in Griselda's heart, . . . she answered: 'My Lord, I am ready and prepared.' ")

Thus, Boccaccio wrote the *Decameron* in the form of an itinerary, "a principio horriblis et fetidus, in fine prosperus desiderabilis et gratus." That is, he evolved a plan which "inchoat asperitatem alicuius rei sed eius materia prospere terminatur"; a gallery of figures from Ser Ciappelletto, the new Judas (I, 1, 15) to Griselda the new Mary (X, 10, 28 and 51). He designed and wrote the *Decameron* according to the structure of a "comedy" in the most authoritative medieval tradition, present under Uguccione da Pisa and John of Garland to Dante. This was not only a tradition that Boccaccio revered and loved, but followed exactly as in the *Esposizioni* after approximating it in the *Comedia,* an artistic exigency later theorized in Book IV of the *Genealogia* (especially in chapters 9-13).

Boccaccio gave more clearness and solidity to his design, to his setting forth of ideas, by placing it in a framework that somehow emphasizes the important moments, even beyond and independently of the explicit statement of the themes of the various days. This framework, even though it is almost an obligatory poetical scheme for Boccaccio's imagination, is also characteristic of medieval literature and rhetoric and almost inconceivable outside it. It is not necessary to give examples nor to stress this fact, so constantly has it been brought out by the best criticism of Boccaccio's work. But if any further proof were needed, it would suffice to consider how Boccaccio's design becomes lifeless and loses even its eminent decorative value when it is repeated by the novella writers of the next two centuries. It becomes merely a literary device, a more-or-less

wearied homage to the first great example in the literary tradition of the Italian art of novella writing.

Beyond the purely medieval meaning that Boccaccio has instilled in the *Decameron,* he has indicated the rhetorical ideals of that age by the manner in which he realizes his design. Midway between the developments of the "frame," Boccaccio placed the very charming episode in the Valley of the Fair Ladies. The series of the "reigns" of the girls is symmetrically interrupted by those of the young men. The reign of the first day is chivalrously bestowed on the eldest of the girls, Pampinea, just as rule over the last day is allotted to Pamphilus, the senior of the youths. Boccaccio writes the ballads for each day on the paradigm 3:4:3, beginning with an allegorical treatment in the first three, tarrying in a lofty lament of love in the central four, resolving finally in a spacious song of exultation in the final three. Contrary to the more formal and pragmatic manner of the episodes themselves, Boccaccio becomes more imaginative in the "frame, showing the influence of medieval tradition. For example, descriptions of nature fill a large part of the frame" [E. G. Kern, in *Publications of the Modern Language Association of America* LXVI, 1951]. They are always composed with a decorative elegance, in a stylization of precious arabesque. They never have a value taken by themselves; they do not present at all the Panic vitality of landscapes after the example of a Poliziano, although in content they anticipate the elements of his descriptions.

Likewise, the refined and aristocratic humanity of the storytellers in the "frame" is revealed within fairy-tale atmosphere created essentially by the use of an elegant eurhythmy of all the action. This rhythm seems to be controlled by the soft sound of music and performed to a dance step, as in the ideal courtly social groups which serve as a background to the subtle discussions of Andreas Cappellanus, or as in the representations of the chivalric circles of the kings, Arthur and Charles, especially in certain Italian compilations. That is, the action in the "frame" does not represent a human world psychologically alive and real, but only a felicitous visualization of those ideal, longed-for, conditions of life, weightless and remote from any daily concern. This idealized world is both the necessary justification of the art of the *Decameron* and the atmosphere most in harmony with its very exceptional development.

In a way more intimately connected with the philosophical basis of the work, the "frame" clearly reveals the medieval structure of the *Decameron.* Besides providing an organizational principle for the work, the "frame" also discloses the theoretical reasons and ideals which inspire the very diverse and splendid tales.

For example, Fortune and Love are presented as the highest measures and tests of man's capacity. They are also, however, the great themes that link the tales and provide structural and ideological unity; each tale has a theoretical interpretation relevant to its function in the "frame." This structural formulation is firmly rooted in scholastic and medieval traditions.

Pampinea, "the wise," the young woman most gifted with

astute human prudence, in the prologues to the third novella of the second day and the second novella of the sixth day, outlines the Thomist and Dantean concept of Fortune. Fortune is not a blind distributor of good or bad luck but is a general dispenser of Providence and of Divine justice. As I have shown elsewhere, Boccaccio conceived of Fortune in the introductions to the *Filostrato* and the *Teseida,* and in *Epistles* IV and V, in a purely fatalistic sense, dwelling upon autobiographical laments. However, he developed a more rigorous and scholastic concept, which is implicit in the whole ***Decameron,*** and in cantos XXXI-XXXVI of the *Amorosa Visione.* It is a concept which remained a basic idea in Boccaccio's whole work. It was adhered to explicitly in the *Corbaccio,* the *Esposizioni,* and particularly in *De casibus.* It is a concept absolutely opposed to the humanistic-Renaissance idea which was to be developed from Pico della Mirandola to Machiavelli.

The medieval influence on Boccaccio is also easily discerned in his representation of Love. From the Introduction to the defense (of love) on the fourth day and on to the very end, aside from the merry, facile, carefree, or mundane remarks on Love (always isolated in an atmosphere of middle-class common sense), we get a constant sense of astonishment and almost of dismay in the interventions of the author, who is faced with the total and dazzling power of Love: a dismay which bears the echo of the whole impassioned debate carried on during those centuries. Also, it may bring to mind the anguished astonishment of Dante in the fifth canto of the *Inferno,* which Boccaccio himself stressed. Even Boccaccio's youthful works reflected a human experience dominated almost exclusively by Love. But in it throbbed such a feeling of suspense, such a moral preoccupation with regard to the power of this force, that Boccaccio felt the need to clarify the problem for his own sake. He took recourse . . . in the attitudes and scholastic schemata reflected in the essay writing of Andreas Cappellanus and of Boncompagno da Signa and in the meditative lyric poetry of Guittone d' Arezzo. In cantos XXXVIII-XLV of the *Amorosa Visione* he makes an attempt to compose his thoughts into a more rigorous formulation, in line with those theoretical schemata. Boccaccio does not hesitate to accept the suggestions and more severe distinctions of St. Thomas and Richard of St. Victor.

Boccaccio derived his most compelling declarations concerning the nature and the force of love from his rigorous theoretical formulation, which succeeded in infiltrating even the strictly narrative and imaginative tissue of the ***Decameron.*** Apart from the interruptions the author makes to comment on love, mentioned above (in Introduction, prologue to the fourth day, conclusion), Boccaccio has Emilia theorize in the prologue to the seventh novella of the fourth day on the contrast between the love of nobles and that of commoners, just as Andreas Cappellanus does in his *De Amore.* In the introduction to the sixth novella of the third day and in the conclusion of the sixth of the tenth day, Fiammetta points out the paradigm of the degrees of love, also according to the example of Andreas Cappellanus as revised by Guittone. Pampinea, by proclaiming the duty of "always loving a lady of higher lin-

eage" (I, 5) and Emilia by her lengthy anticonjugal argument in III, 7, attain the casuistry of the *De Amore.* It would be easy to continue to demonstrate how the epilogue is influenced by the discussion on love and charity of Richard of St. Victor; how the subtle allegory of the first three ballads is based on elements of treatise writing which were continued in the lyrical poetry of Guittone; how Boccaccio's particularly frequent references in the fifth and seventh days to the relationship between the rational faculties and love reflect principles expounded by Saint Thomas *(Commentary on the Nichomachean Ethics)* and repeated by Dante *(Convivio)* and so on.

Boccaccio would accept as key themes only those truths that were central and essential to all medieval thought, only convictions that were rationally arrived at, and only problems that were sedulously debated and then victoriously resolved in his own conscience. Also, he used only themes that could symbolize human striving and virtue, tested and measured continually by those higher and almost semidivine forces of Fortune, of Love, of Ingenuity. So, also, although to a lesser degree, had the authors of works dating from the *Golden Legend* to the *Mirror of True Repentance* written examples and narratives devoted to the higher forces; in such a way the authors of the books of virtue and the books of examples arranged complex story-telling material behind a studied theoretical and moral façade. The Aesopic collections were also adapted and slanted toward exemplification in this way. Finally, Dante himself had continually brought the moral and prophetic message of his sacred poem down to the level of human episodes and human examples. Precisely in this manner Boccaccio himself theorized in the middle of his most compelling poetry, thinking perhaps of the novellas of his masterpiece: "Fabula est exemplaris seu demonstrativa sub figmento locutio, cuius amoto cortice, patet intentio fabulantis: et sic, si sub velamento fabuloso sapidum comperiatur aliquid, non erit supervacaneum fabulas edidisse. . . . " He added that this "species tertia [fabularum] potius historiae quam fabule similis est" *(Genealogia).*

Boccaccio's need to present his narratives in the guise of historical testimonies, with a very particular meaning and value (which is illustrated in Chapter IV), is due to this broad and implied "exemplary" inspiration. It is clearly reflected also by the ideal design of the ***Decameron.*** This requirement, too, like all the other more elemental requirements of the ***Decameron,*** is presented in an explicit theoretical declaration in the prologue to the fourth day and in the conclusion; and it is also confirmed from the lips of Fiammetta in the novella IX, 5: " . . . if I had wished or might I wish to wander from the factual truth, I would have been able or would be able indeed to compose and relate it [this tale]; but because departure from the truth of past events, in story-telling, inflicts great loss of pleasure to the listeners, I shall relate it to you in its proper form and aided by the aforesaid reason."

The most active, effective, ideal, and imaginative premises of the ***Decameron*** also determine the chronological limits of the narrated actions, which were almost without exception (only three in a hundred novellas) the period immediately preceding Boccaccio's own time—that is, the stormy but splendid age of the last Crusades, the struggles of the communes against the Hohenstaufens, the adventurous events in southern Italy, and those decades of chivalry of the thirteenth and fourteenth centuries which witnessed the apogee of the Italian, but especially the Florentine, mercantile power. If the latter period formed part of the more personal experiences of Boccaccio, the former had influenced him through the recollections and the memories of those of his friends who were richest in human experience, such as Marino Bulgaro, Coppo di Borghese Domenichi, Pietro Canigiani (to mention three names as oral sources of the *Decameron:* V, 6; V, 9; VIII, 10). Also, perhaps, he was influenced by some bit of popular poetry, works dating from the time of the *cantari del Barbarossa* to the "laments" of the Anonimo Fiorentino (The Anonymous Florentine) and to the historical ballads of Pieraccio Tedaldi. . . . (pp. 204-12)

It was the earlier age which had witnessed the formation of a more typically Italian civilization. It had marked the detachment and the differentiation of the political and civil life of the peninsula from that of the rest of the Empire. It was the time when the foundations of the greatest Italian Kingdom were laid, that of Naples (which was particularly dear to Boccaccio on account of his youthful experiences). That time had seen the rise of a new culture and a new literature, which, finally, had firmly established the hegemony of Italian merchants on the Mediterranean and in western Europe. That is, it represented the fabulous and heroic past of a splendid and adventurous present. It seemed to be the refulgent and blazing noon which had prepared the warm lights of an opulent afternoon, of that golden "autumn of the Middle Ages" which Boccaccio lives and pictures with such warm sentiment.

Indeed the history of Italy and of Europe between the eleventh and fourteenth centuries is the background, noble and majestic, of the loftier and more impassioned novellas. The epic deeds, the Crusades in the East, create a more amazing and fabulous framework for the novellas of the Marchesa of Monferrato and of Messer Torello. The great internal and external wars which led to the firm foundation of the kingdoms of France and of England inspired the tragic and surprising tales of the Conte of Aguersa, of Giletta of Narbonne, of Alessandro Agolanti. The fierce struggles between the communes which characterize the Italian history of those centuries come alive again in the burnings and sackings which glow with a sinister light in the novellas of Guidotto of Cremona and of Madonna Francesca. The selfish interventions of foreign kings in the struggles are considered in the tales of Ser Ciappelletto and of Martellino; the feelings of terror which weighed on the life of the coastal towns, threatened by the Corsairs, are echoed in the novellas of Landolfo Ruffolo, of Gostanza, of Restituta. The sadness of a Rome abandoned to the bitter struggles of the Colonna and Orsini families lends its own color to the whole courtly novella of Pietro Boccamazza. The long series of wars and the vicissitudes of the kingdom of Naples and Sicily under the Normans, the Angevins, and the Aragonese—which characterize the history of Italy between the twelfth and fourteenth centuries— live again in the novellas of Gerbino, of Ghismonda, of

Teodoro of Madonna Beritola, of Gianni of Procida, of Andreuccio of Perugia, of Nonna de 'Pulci, of Re Carlo, of Re Pietro, and so on.

In the course of these novellas, idealized portraits of the protagonists of the history of those centuries are also presented: Tancred and Guglielmo the Good, the two Fredericks of Swabia, and Manfred, the two Charleses, and Robert of Anjou, Pietro and Federico of Aragon and Ruggiero of Lauria, Guy de Monfort and Gianni of Procida; and also Can Grande della Scala and Currado Malaspina, Filippo il Bornio and the "Young King"; Pope Alexander III and the king of Scotland, Pope Boniface and Saladin; the king of Jerusalem, Guy de Lusignan; and Guillaume de Monferrat, Azzo d'Este and Guinigi da Camino. . . . These are figures which always are portrayed in a heroic atmosphere, against backgrounds made precious by a whole throng of admirers; figures which speak their lofty words or perform their noble feats before astonished onlookers, without whom it seems as though those words and those generous deeds could not have come to be. They are epic figures, figures of song and romance, to whom the precious and laudatory atmosphere of the last day is particularly suited.

Boccaccio also includes some notable contemporaries in the novellas: Guglielmo Borsieri and Master Albert of Bologna, Cecco Angiolieri and Guido Cavalcanti, Cimabue and Giotto, not to mention other minor figures of artists, such as Mico of Siena and Carlo Figiovanni. Also, we feel the continual, but implicit, presence of Dante.

The reader of the *Decameron* gradually forms an imposing and very human picture of a decisive period of the history and the civilization of Italy. It is a picture painted in heroic and dazzling colors. It is an epic (that is, an interpretation beyond the events) of that age in which the chivalric and feudal life coincided splendidly with the pulsating and fervid life of the "companies" and the "arts" (trades). The stately structure of the empire was breaking up into many kingdoms, principalities, and communes.

Boccaccio's warm recollection of the immediate past, notwithstanding its fabulous and heroic colors, notwithstanding its gallant figures caught in always nobly statuesque attitudes, is not composed along the nostalgic lines of the Dantean evocations of Guido Guerra or Marco Lombardo or Cacciaguida. Beside the eminent and gilded world of the kings and the knights, Boccaccio sets the industrious and adventurous society of his own age. Federico degli Alberighi and Lisabetta of Messina have a human nobility not inferior to that of Carlo Vecchio or Ghismonda. They wear no crown, but they possess a humanity perhaps deeper and closer to our own sensibilities; they possess a generosity, simpler but more inward and decorous. Gentile de' Carisendi is no less chivalrous than Re Pietro. Cisti Fornaio is a no less shrewd and elegant jester than Guido Cavalcanti. Andreuola has an aristocratic pride not inferior to that of the Marchioness of Monferrato. The adventures and the conquests of the Florentines are set against broad backgrounds (the vast stormy Mediterranean with its pirate fleets; France, jealous and distrustful of the enterprising Florentines; England cold, and a little mysterious, like an *ultima Thule*).

Boccaccio was deeply attuned to the spirit and culture of the Middle Ages, as has been said. For this reason, he instinctively feels and succeeds in portraying in the *Decameron* the wonderful and ideal continuity between the age of the knights of the sword and the world of the knights of human ingenuity and industry; between those regal figures, solitary and shining with gems, and the heroes of the Italian middle class. Boccaccio linked the age of the Crusades with that of the formation of the free republics and the free communes, the establishment in Naples of a kingdom intermediary between East and West, the great wars of France and England.

In its themes, its structure, and in its imagination the *Decameron* stands as a monument to the highest style of the Middle Ages. But as with epics and literary testaments in general, the *Decameron* glorified an age that was coming to an end.

The massive critical tradition that sees the *Decameron* as the manifest of a new era has erred as the result of two important influences. The first, expounded by Olympia Morata and Pope Blount, was anti-clerical and anti-Roman. Based upon Lutheran polemics, it flourished from the sixteenth century on. The second is a nineteenth-century concept which contrasted the "darkness" of the Middle Ages with the "light" of Humanism. According to this tradition, Dante was the poet of transcendental realities, while Boccaccio was the champion of a new civilization which exalted the earthly life. The divine comedy had bowed to the human comedy.

The critics failed to notice that this theory destroyed the whole design of the *Decameron*—the color and symbolization, the gallant and vibrant humanity. Compared to the new Renaissance poetry, the *Decameron* appeared only crude and violent, its development too tumultuous.

Actually, the *Decameron* does not stand in opposition to the *Divina Commedia;* rather it seems to complement it. That is, each presents an aspect of Italian medieval society, and together they portray the harmony of the eagerness for the real and the quest for the transcendent which characterized that age. The poem of Dante summarizes the intellectual and moral speculation of Italian society and in a way is an intimation and prophecy of the age to come, while the *Decameron* is the representation, or rather the consecration, artistic and, in a sense, metaphysical, of the history of every man and the daily reality of that very human world. It too is a *summa;* the *summa* of the toilsome life, rich in adventures and in snares, in which, every day, man measured his abilities and his strength; it is the *summa* of a world which, according to its own scholastic thought, is no less real and no less sturdy than that which was dominated by the transcendence sung by Dante. (pp. 212-16)

> *Vittore Branca, in his* Boccaccio: The Man and His Works, *edited by Dennis J. McAuliffe, translated by Richard Monges, New York University Press, 1976, 341 p.*

Shirley S. Allen   (essay date 1977)

[*Allen is an American educator and critic who has written about women during the Renaissance. In the essay below, she analyzes varying interpretations of Boccaccio's story of Griselda.*]

Ever since Dioneo finished telling the hundredth tale in the *Decameron,* his story of patient Griselda has provoked controversy, not only among members of predominantly female audiences like his own and among those, like the Canterbury Pilgrims, engaged in arguments about marriage, but also among scholars in the unfeminine world of literary criticism. Like Dioneo himself, male as well as female readers have often objected to the uncomplaining and even cheerful acquiescence of the virtuous peasant girl to her high-born husband's cruelty. Like the medieval Clerk who tells the tale to Chaucer's pilgrims, even male chauvinists deplore Gualtieri's actions in taking away her children to be murdered, in sending her almost naked back to her father after thirteen years of perfect wifely behavior, and in recalling her as a servant to prepare the house for his new bride. And to most readers Griselda's joyful satisfaction with the restoration of her children and her wifely status as the sole reward for her patience and humility is both psychologically unconvincing and a violation of poetic justice. Such an extreme example of female submission embarrassed men even in the fourteenth century; to post-Freudian readers it suggests a diagnosis of masochism.

More than one scholar has wished to dismiss the tale as unimportant to an interpretation of the *Decameron* as a whole, but its position as the last tale gives it special importance. Moreover, in the *Decameron* Boccaccio has used the medieval device of numerical structuring to organize his material, so that the Griselda story is not merely the last, but also the tenth tale of the tenth day. And certainly Boccaccio was aware of the importance of the number ten as a classical and Christian symbol for completeness and perfection. Furthermore, in the frame of the *Decameron,* the Tenth Day is presented as a climax to the action and culmination of themes introduced on the previous days. Within the Tenth Day itself the narrators suggest a rising action by their introductory comments, each claiming to cap the previous story. We can hardly avoid the conclusion that Boccaccio intended the Griselda story to be the climax of his work. And we must not forget that it became the best known of all the tales, even if chiefly through the agency of Petrarch's Latin revision.

Yet no interpretation of the Griselda tale has been quite satisfactory. Petrarch's translation of it into a moral exemplum in which the husband's cruelty is explained as a providential plan for testing Christian patience did not satisfy Chaucer, whose Clerk objects in specific contradiction:

> He hadde assayed hire ynogh bifore,
> And foond hire evere good; what needed it
> Hire for to tempte, and alwey moore and moore,
> *Though som men preise it for a subtil wit?*
> But as for me, I seye that yvele it sit
> To assaye a wyf whan that it is no nede.
> And putten hire in angwyssh and in drede.

[critic's italics]

Nor did Petrarch's interpretation stick, for despite his denial (echoed by Chaucer) that the tale was intended to teach wifely behavior, Griselda was widely used as an example for wives in sermons and treatises; in 1396, Philippe de Mézières included it as a true story in a letter to King Richard II urging him to marry. Although a number of recent scholars, most notably Vittore Branca, have reasserted Petrarch's interpretation, the Christian allegory remains unconvincing because of the inevitable ascription of Gualtieri's cruelty to God—a problem that troubled Petrarch as well as Chaucer. On the other hand, those who read the *Decameron* on a purely human level, rejecting Branca's allegorical reading and claiming it as a Renaissance work that celebrates doctrines of love and nature directly opposed to the medieval Christian "sufferance of life," find the Griselda tale disturbingly incongruent with the spirit of the whole.

The most serious charge against Boccaccio's artistry arising from the Griselda tale is that of dramatic impropriety in assigning it to Dioneo, since either a Christian exemplum or a tale of wifely virtue accords ill with his personality. Characterized from the beginning as gay, amusing, and full of witticism, Dioneo displays throughout the *Decameron* a licentiousness and unruliness often associated with the deified force his name suggests (for Dionaea is a classical metronymic for Aphrodite). In his first tale he introduces the subject of sexual pleasure to the group, and he develops it in his subsequent tales, which are the most explicitly sexual of any in the *Decameron.* In conversation and in comments on other tales, he insists on the universality and irresistibility of sexual desire, consistently deriding female chastity, clerical celibacy, and church doctrines about the sinfulness of sexual pleasure. When he is king, he chooses as the topic for the day's stories "tricks played by wives on their husbands." His objections to his own tale of Griselda and the tone of those objections are in keeping with his character; any intention of a Christian moral exemplum is not. Nor is a purely human story of wifely submission. Indeed, Chaucerian scholars, although equally engaged in controversy over interpretation of the Clerk's Tale, have praised Chaucer's superior dramatic sense in using the Griselda story as part of a discussion about marriage and in assigning the tale to a medieval cleric instead of a young lover like Dioneo.

Although we may deplore the patronizing attitude toward Boccaccio revealed by scholars who look at his work chiefly as a source for Chaucer, we should do well in this case if we used some Chaucerian approaches to the Griselda problem that have not been sufficiently explored in *Decameron* studies: investigation of the relationship between tale and teller, of the interactions between the teller and his companions, and of the ironic implications in both.

Boccaccio's careful development of Dioneo's character and his use of that character in the structure of the *Decameron* suggest that his assignment of the last tale is not a lapse in dramatic propriety but intentionally significant. Dioneo's character is full of complexity, ambiguity, and irony. He is the first to acknowledge the leadership of the ladies, praising their foresight and wisdom in leaving Flor-

ence, but in the same speech he usurps the leadership by threatening to go back if they do not accept his prescription of amusement as the party's sole purpose; and the next day he begs to be excused from following their rules for the story telling. Moreover, when granted the privilege of departing from the chosen subject—with the attached penalty, proposed by himself, of telling the last tale each day—he exercises it in surprising ways that suggest ironic comment upon the preceding tales. When he professes to be adhering to the proper subject, he tells a tale that uses it ironically. So on the Third Day, as an example of one who gains something greatly desired, he tells of Alibech's search for God's grace, which ends in her learning "to put the devil in hell"—thus equating sexual pleasure with God's grace. During the ten days of story telling, he explicitly exercises his privilege only twice, but one of these is the day of his own rule when he condemns himself elaborately for not being able to think of a story on the subject he commanded, which he has shown to be his favorite subject.

In his remarks and in his tales Dioneo often achieves a result that is the opposite of his apparent purpose. While he seems to be echoing the sentiments of medieval misogynists on female lust, he is actually encouraging women's sexual freedom and their equality with men in its enjoyment. Even in the most obscene of all his tales, V, 10, which leaves the ladies too shocked to laugh, he justifies the wife's adultery as the proper course for a woman married to a sodomist. In commenting on Filomena's tale of Zinevra (II, 9)—source of the wager subplot of Shakespeare's *Cymbeline*—he calls Bernabò (Posthumus) stupid for trusting his wife, a perverse insistence on the conventional male view that results in increasing the audience's sympathy with the wronged heroine. Then, pretending that this opinion has moved him to discard his intended story for one that will prove the universal faithlessness of wives, he tells the tale of Ricciardo di Chinzica, in which he makes the adulterous wife a totally sympathetic heroine.

There is wiliness in Dioneo's clowning. He teases the ladies with his bawdy remarks and tales for the purpose of exposing any latent hypocrisy. When they object to his chosen topic for the Seventh Day, he suggests that their reluctance to speak of wifely unchastity lays them open to the suspicion of guilty acts. When he finds that they have spent that afternoon swimming nude in a hidden lake, he taunts them with the question, "Are you beginning to act in deeds before you'll say it in words?" At the end of the Fifth Day when he is asked to sing for the group, he proposes one outrageously bawdy title after another until the queen's anger forces him to choose "una bella;" but the song he gives them expresses such pious adoration of an unnamed lady that one suspects satire of the *dolce stil nuovo.*

Dioneo's personality is remarkably similar to that of the author of the *Decameron* as revealed by his fictional devices and by the persona speaking in Boccaccio's name as narrator. Boccaccio, like Dioneo, appears to offer with one hand what he takes away with the other. In the Proem, proposing to comfort women in love by telling a hundred tales, he orders them, if his effort is successful, to give thanks to Love "who, by freeing me from its bonds, granted me the power to serve their pleasure." In the Epilogue, he pretends to retract his harsh treatment of friars while he gives them new insults. Like Dioneo, he often achieves results opposite to his expressed purpose. He offers his book as the consolation of amusement to divert the ladies from their suffering in the flames of love, but the effect of the hundred tales is an incitement to concupiscence (as Panfilo suggests after the last one is told) and to action that will help them achieve a more palpable consolation in their lovers' embraces. His arrangement of the tales shows a similar kind of irony, the announced subject for the day often being a blind for the real subject that emerges as the tales unfold. For example, he introduces the story telling with an assertion that all undertakings should begin with praise of God and then presents the first four tales, which indirectly cast doubt upon the canonization of saints, the righteousness of the Roman hierarchy, the Christian claim to absolute truth, and the celibacy of the clergy. Like Dioneo, he is wily in argument against those who criticize him and quick to point out hypocrisy. Like Dioneo, who calls himself a crow among doves and a "witless fellow" to excuse his telling an obscene story (IX, 10), Boccaccio assumes a self-depreciatory attitude in the Proem to the Fourth Day, where he defends his book.

Indeed there is a congruence between Dioneo's attitudes and the overall effect of the *Decameron* that has led many readers to see Dioneo as Boccaccio's *portavoce* or even his self portrait. We can therefore assume that Dioneo's authorship of the Griselda tale must emphasize rather than diminish its significance and that the character of the teller is a clue to its meaning.

Dioneo's tale of Griselda is the ironic culmination of his argument that sexual desire is an important aspect of human (female as well as male) nature and that no institution, neither marriage nor the church, can or should suppress nature. Since the ladies have objected to his implication that wives play tricks on their husbands, he shows them their ideal wife, who obeys her marriage vows against every natural inclination. The absolute submission of the wife to her husband, promised in the marriage vows, preached in the churches, and demanded by men in a feudal society, is carried to its logical extreme in the tale of patient Griselda. Must a woman set her promise to love, honor, and obey her husband above the lives of her children by submitting without demur to his destruction of them? Must she set it above her own rights as a wife by continuing to keep her vow after he has dissolved the marriage? Must she set it above her human dignity by serving as a scullery maid to his new wife? Even a medieval bachelor clergyman like Chaucer's Clerk would have to answer no. So would the little band of Florentines, who have spent ten days telling stories that celebrate the power of human intelligence over brute force, that proclaim the value of human love, and that teach women how to outwit despotic husbands and priests.

But Dioneo's *reductio ad absurdum* of the traditional concept of marriage undermines absolute standards and provides the opening wedge for relative morality, as he em-

phasizes with his bawdy suggestion of what Griselda should have done when her husband sent her home in a shift. For this reason his tale provokes a long argument among his listeners. Readers who have failed to see Boccaccio's intention have perhaps been less ready than they to entertain the shocking suggestion that a woman ought not always to submit to her husband. Among these we may class Petrarch, who appears to have been insensitive to Boccaccio's irony in what admittedly was a hasty perusal of the *Decameron* and who asserted that the last tale did not at all resemble the rest. More cogent than these reasons for doubting Petrarch's interpretation of the Griselda story is the conviction that his ambivalent view of women as either heavenly goddesses or hellish temptations blinded him to the whole message of the *Decameron,* in which Boccaccio asserts that women are neither angels nor devils but human beings, like men. [Aldo] Scaglione puts it this way [in his *Nature and Love in the Late Middle Ages,* 1963]:

> His women characters are both, and even simultaneously, interested and disinterested, loving in order to give and loving in order to take, safe and dangerous, self-centered and generous, in brief "good" and "bad." They are *real* according to *nature,* not to a superimposed schema of manmade, mentally construed and idolized, supraworldly, suprahuman, and supranatural perfection. From them can come happiness, as for Federigo, or extreme suffering, as for the scholar.

But even this is not the whole truth. Precisely because Boccaccio regards women as persons in their own right and not just as sources of happiness or suffering to men, the *Decameron* expresses a new attitude, too different from medieval thought to be accepted by his contemporaries (and, as Scaglione shows in his Epilogue, soon afterward eclipsed by the rise of humanistic idealism, which again set women apart from the human race).

Interpreting the hundredth tale as an ironic argument for women's liberation suggests a new unity of theme and structure in the *Decameron.* Beginning with his dedication of the work to young ladies, not in the hope of receiving favors from them, but for their amusement and instruction, Boccaccio expresses concern for the problems of women and sympathizes with them as persons whom Fortune has wronged through society's restrictions on their lives. They have to hide the flames of love; they are bound by the authority of fathers, mothers, brothers, and husbands; they must spend their time in idleness, shut up in the narrow circuit of their rooms; they are not allowed the diversions of hawking, hunting, fishing, riding, gambling, or engaging in the world of trade. Therefore, he will give them a book not only to divert them from their sufferings, but to offer useful advice by showing them what to seek and what to avoid in a world that (he implies) is dominated by men. His attitude is further defined in the Proem to the Fourth Day, where he speaks of himself as one who fights in the service of women and where he addresses them as comrades in a war against his detractors, who are presumably their detractors. His argument bears traces of the medieval tradition of the *querelle des femmes;* and with typically Boccaccian irony, he uses the medieval ex-emplum of the hermit and the goslings, with its inherent identification of women as devils, for the opposite purpose: to show that women are naturally admirable.

Boccaccio sets up as a frame for his tales an idyllic world in which his ladies have been freed from the restrictions of medieval society. Choosing "as guides and servants" three young men, who acknowledge their leadership, they plan and govern the sojourn in the country, where they are as free as the men, not only within the grounds of the es-tate, but even in the countryside. It is the ladies who find a hidden valley where they can take off their clothes and swim—a symbolic shedding of social restraints. Surely such an unrestricted life, where women are pictured as at least the equals of men, was intended to suggest something to the oppressed women readers described in the Proem.

The tales themselves carry out Boccaccio's doctrinal in-tention. Many are introduced with comments about the proper behavior of women in certain situations, and al-though such remarks are often ironic, a number of stories give seriously appropriate advice about what to seek and what to avoid. For the ladies of a society in which a social-ly superior man could rape a woman with impunity, Boc-caccio relates tales that show how a marchioness politely dissuaded the King of France from such intentions (I, 5), how a gentleman's daughter escaped a magistrate's sexual attack (IV, 6), how a raped woman obtained justice (I, 9), and how a Sultan's daughter victimized by many men avoided disgrace (II, 7). For the ladies of a society in which husbands often became jailors, Boccaccio relates tales that describe methods of outwitting a cruel, jealous, or unworthy husband (II, 9; III, 9; V, 10; VII, 5, 8). Sever-al tales show women how to use their wits to defeat their traditional enemies, the clergy (III, 3; VI, 3; VIII, 4). Oth-ers show how to get rid of unwelcome admirers or boring companions (VI, 1; IX, 1). A number contain traditional advice often given to women: avoid jealousy (III, 6), vani-ty (IV, 2; VI, 8), coyness (V, 8), and any taint of prostitu-tion (VIII, 1, 2); and never torture an admirer (I, 10; VIII, 7). Women are pointedly praised for a number of virtues, but especially for wit. On the Seventh Day each tale tops the preceding in displaying a woman's skill in winning love on her own terms despite the superior power of men.

Underlying many tales is a basic assumption that a woman has the same right as a man to satisfy her sexual needs and the same right to choose, win, and enjoy one she loves. A score of tales, including nearly all of the Seventh Day, pic-ture a woman's pleasure in extra-marital sex; and in sever-al others a woman's love, as distinguished from merely physical sexual pleasure, is given precedence in a conflict with marital fidelity (III, 7; IV, 8, 9; VI, 7; VII, 7, 9). In two stories young girls succeed in choosing their own hus-bands in defiance of their parents (II, 3; V, 2). In the tragic stories of the Fourth Day, women who choose their own lovers and defy authority even to the point of suicide are presented as heroines (Ghismonda, Isabetta, Andreuola, Simona, Salvestra, and Madonna Rossiglione). But these tragic endings are unusual; the whole thrust of the *Decam-eron* is an assertion of the individual's capacity to achieve his own well being in spite of obstacles imposed by human

agency or by fortune—a doctrine that marks the change from the medieval to the modern world. More revolution-ary than this doctrine, perhaps, is Boccaccio's extension of it to include women. In his tales women are shown to be as capable as men of using wit to gain their own ends, sometimes well outside the domestic sphere; Giletta learns her father's medical skill, and Zinevra becomes a sultan's captain of the guard (III, 9; II, 9). Madonna Filippa, caught in adultery and facing burning at the stake, be-comes her own lawyer and successfully presents a feminist position six centuries ahead of her time when she asserts that the law should not treat women differently from men, that women should not be subject to laws made without their consent, and that a wife should be allowed to have a lover if she also fulfills her obligation to her husband (VI, 7).

Such explicit doctrine, however, is rare in the *Decameron,* since Boccaccio achieves his ends more subtly—by irony, by arrangement and structure, and by what [Howard C.] Cole has termed "whimsical cross-referencing." An excel-lent example of his subtlety is the ninth tale of the Ninth Day, which seems to assert a medieval view of marriage and is introduced by Emilia's sermon on the necessity of beating wives into submission. Boccaccio ironically con-tradicts the story's surface meaning by his juxtaposition of two pieces of Solomon's wisdom. A young man who asks Solomon what he must do to be loved is told to love, and another who wants to reform a shrewish wife is told to go to the Bridge of Geese. Although the tale appears to end happily when the husband, by watching a mule driver on the bridge, learns to beat his wife into subjec-tion, Emilia's vivid description of the brutal wife-beating dis-gusts the reader and leads him to look for irony. A first level of irony can be found in the mule-driver incident, where the epithet "goose" might well be applied to a man who beats his mule nearly to death to get it across the bridge in spite of the young men's pleading with him to lead it gently. A second level of irony can be found by re-versing the two pieces of advice: a man who worries about not being loved is a goose, and a man who has a shrewish wife should love her. This irony is prepared for in Emilia's prefatory sermon, where she suggests a bawdy play on the word "stick" and thus gives a Boccaccian twist to the kind of love a shrewish wife is lacking.

Such ironic reversal of the surface meaning of a tale is one of many ways in which Boccaccio prepares the reader for his ironic intention in the hundredth tale. In his own Proem to the Fourth Day he anticipates ironic use of the Griselda tale by introducing a similarly medieval exem-plum, which also has folk-tale and mythic elements, for a purpose opposite to its traditional use. In his careful de-velopment of Dioneo's character, he prepares for his giv-ing an ironic twist to the Tenth Day's theme of liberality and generosity. The ascending order of tales on the Tenth Day, each capping the previous one, is anticipated on the Seventh Day, where Boccaccio deliberately wrenches the tenth tale out of the cycle, calling the reader's attention to Dioneo's privilege, already used ironically on earlier days.

More important than any of these is Boccaccio's careful

construction, through many tales, of a new concept of the relationship between man and woman. Beginning with his first heroine, the Marchioness of Monferrato, who wittily shames the King of France out of his intended sexual possession of her, Boccaccio suggests the superiority of a reciprocal relationship, in which there is mutual respect and trust, no matter what the social class of either partner, and physical love without coercion. He shows that such a partnership demands intelligence and initiative from the woman as well as the man. Zinevra, for example, must escape her husband's hired assassin, forge a new life for herself, and prove her innocence before she can enjoy such a marriage. Although in most tales this kind of love can exist only outside the lord-vassal relationship of feudal marriages, on the Tenth Day, where other major themes of the *Decameron* also reach their climax, Boccaccio shows the basic conditions for his concept of marriage: physical love (X, 4), trust and personal integrity (X, 5), self-control and social sanction (X, 6, 7), and deep, abiding passion (X, 8).

Then in the penultimate tale he shows us such a marriage in Messer Torello, a gentleman who unawares shows the greatest Christian virtue—*caritas*—to the most powerful enemy of Christendom, and his wife, Madonna Adalieta, who is described in terms that recall other heroines of the *Decameron,* especially Ghismonda. She is "savissima" and "di grandissimo animo," and her spirit is [according to Richard Aldington] "rather regal than feminine." Her character is demonstrated by her own initiative and independent actions that accord perfectly with her husband's because of an equally noble spirit rather than an intuition bred from submissiveness.

The climax of the marriage theme comes in the contrast to this couple presented by Gualtieri, a misogamist persuaded by his subjects to marry, and Griselda, who is virtuous according to the traditional Christian and medieval criteria, but who lacks the *virtù* and *ingegno*, the unfeminine self-reliance, found in the *Decameron*'s heroines. The contrast between the two marriages is pointed up by parallel scenes: Griselda receiving on her unkempt hair a marriage crown from the Marquis, who takes possession of her by the act, reminds us of Adalieta putting on the magnificent crown sent by the Sultan in recognition of her hospitality to him given independently from her husband. Griselda's meek faithfulness in carrying out her husband's order to prepare his house for his new bride contrasts with Adalieta's iniative in preparing entertainment for the foreign travelers with assured anticipation of her husband's wishes. The pitiful scene in which Griselda, bereft of her children and dressed as a peasant, serves the wedding guests under her lord's watchful eye recalls the scene in Messer Torello's house when Adalieta, richly dressed and accompanied by her two children, is left by her husband with their guests so that she can entertain them in her own right. Thus the story telling ends with a pair of stories intended to comment upon each other, a device used frequently in the *Decameron* and just previously called to our attention by the matched pair of stories about two famous adversaries known to every Florentine, King Carlo and King Pietro (X, 6, 7).

Boccaccio's final address to his readers as "simple young women," who have not sharpened their wits by study, ironically suggests his confidence in their ability to see beneath the surface meaning his real intention in the *Decameron.* But a more powerful irony, the irony of fortune, prevented Boccaccio's portrayal of women from reaching a wide audience of female readers. Petrarch's obtuseness stripped Griselda of the fine clothes in which Boccaccio's had dressed her and sent her out in a medieval shift through the countries of Europe, where she did incalculable harm to the cause of female equality. And the *Decameron,* labeled as a low and comic book, was enjoyed by men clandestinely, lest it endanger the innocent hearts and weak minds of simple young women. (pp. 1-11)

> *Shirley S. Allen, "The Griselda Tale and the Portrayal of Women in the 'Decameron',"* in Philological Quarterly, *Vol. 56, No. 1, Winter, 1977, pp. 1-13.*

Giuseppe Mazzotta   (essay date 1978)

[*Mazzotta is an Italian-born American educator and critic who has written extensively on Dante and Petrarch. In the following essay, he examines how Boccaccio used comedy, irony, and laughter in the* Decameron *to question traditional perceptions of reality.*]

The fifth *novella* of the eighth day [in the *Decameron*] features Masetto del Saggio who goes to the local law court in the belief that a friend he is looking for may be idling his hours away watching the lawyers' performances and squabbles. As soon as Masetto catches a glimpse of the judge who appeared "più tosto un magnano che altro a vedere," he abandons the search for his friend and decides to play a trick on the judge. He feigns a complaint against an imaginary thief and vociferously pleads his case in order to fix upon himself the general attention. In the meantime, an accomplice of his who has secretly crawled beneath the bench where the judge sits, pulls his pants off.

By these simple touches Boccaccio has drawn the classic pattern of the "beffa"—literally a joke, a comic situation—to which we shall repeatedly return. The foolish magistrate, like all fools in the *Decameron,* is mercilessly flouted by the trickster, and by the mockery the very principle of inviolability of the law is subverted. But what on the surface may seem to be merely a somewhat anarchic pleasure of undermining pretenses, of literally divesting the figurehead of his semblance of authority, hides important implications for some comic motifs in the *Decameron.* The oblique target of the *beffa* is the notion that there can ever be a detached perspective snugly sheltering the judge: Masetto's trick actually shatters that distance and, through the resulting inversion, the man who sits ostensibly outside the events to judge them is turned into a principal while the spectators take his place. The comical shifts of focus are constant in the *beffa* and because of them any fresh attempt on the part of the critic to want to fix the comedy of the *Decameron* within stable definitions may turn out to be a hazard, a way of falling into the author's unconscionable trap and being caught, like the judge, in the spirals of laughter.

But critics have traditionally practiced a calculated prudence when engaged in a definition of Boccaccio's laughter. They have generally eluded the problem or, which amounts to the same thing, have reduced the comical sense of the *Decameron* to a caricature of the social order. [Erich] Auerbach, to mention a critic who has [in his *Mimesis: The Representation of Reality in Western Literature*] most powerfully probed the ideological subversiveness of this text, echoes De Sanctis' detached Hegelian stance in his view of Boccaccio's "light entertainment" as the radical perspective from which he is enabled to dismantle the moral relics of medieval Christianity.

Auerbach's critical statement is certainly not wrong; if anything, it is partial or, more precisely, evasive. The evasiveness may be the proper response to the problem of laughter, which, according to an age-old commonplace, eludes all definitions. In any discussion on laughter the obvious point of reference is tragedy, and it, by comparison, seems all too accountable. We acknowledge rather clearly, for instance, the grief and terror which shape the tragic vision, or at least accept their mystery as the inevitable ingredient of a dangerously alien world. But laughter, for all our familiarity with it, remains impenetrable and as soon as we ask the question "why do we laugh" we reach a deadlock.

De Sanctis, to be sure, knows why we do not laugh with the *Decameron*. To him, the *Decameron* represents "un mondo della commedia (cui) nanca quell'alto sentimento del comico che nelle sue forme umanistiche e capricciose gli darà l'Ariosto" [*Stora della letteraturo italiana*]. Its precise meaning notwithstanding, De Sanctis' insight is capital for it captures, as we plan to show, Boccaccio's singular impasse. The *Decameron* is a book of consolation for impending death; but it is also an elegy for comedy and a systematic retrenching into the production of games, *beffe,* which might be called emblematic of the loss if the emblem were not in itself a problem for Boccaccio.

Masetto's trick on the judge seems to originate spontaneously and irrupt unpremeditated into the ordinary business of life, transforming its texture into a playground, a theatrical space where he impersonates both the role of the defendant and the lawyer's cavils. By so doing, Masetto brings into the open the inherent theatricality of the situation, in which a crowd was already idly watching the debates and the judge was as deceptive as the thieves whose cases he tried. In effect, Masetto's own trick (and the implication of this statement will be evident later on) is a weapon in that it appropriates the spectacle; more cogently to our concern, it discloses the mimetic quality of the text. Mimesis is conventionally seen as the rational, Aristotelean principle of imitating the fragmentation of reality. This traditional definition is encompassed, in a fundamental way, within a view of mimesis as impersonation,—the actor's specific craft, the deceptive emblem of the play which sustains the world of the *Decameron.*

It is through this shifty metaphor that Boccaccio persistently and obliquely raises the question "why do we laugh" every time that the *brigata* will laugh at each funny story. For there is a sense in which the *brigata's* laughter is willed just as the choice of the comical perspective in the

Laurent le Premierfait's interpretation of the ladies and youths of the Decameron *leaving Florence, 1414.*

Decameron is deliberate. The general introduction to the tales bears an unmistakable tragic focus: the city of Florence is infected by the plague; laws and familial bonds are shattered; medical science cannot purge the city of its evil. No sooner, however, has Boccaccio conjured this tragic horror than he turns his back to it. The catharsis can occur by moving to a *locus amoenus,* the playground where the burdens of life are lifted by the *brigata's* indulgence in dances, games and storytelling. Here they even tell tragic stories which possibly betray the symbolic hold that death has over their imagination and suggest that laughter is flanked by a fear of death. How the thought of death and comedy will encroach upon each other's borders remains to be seen. The *brigata,* nonetheless, seems untroubled by darker visions and their somber stories, untypical of the mood of the *Decameron* are part and parcel of the world of play.

Their play cannot be dismissed apriori as a simple experience of non-sense: it aspires, rather, to be a utopia, a totally inverted image of the chaotic world they leave behind. And ostensibly, by moving to a marginal rest spot, they construct a realm of phantasy which suspends the purposive structure of ordinary life and envelops it within the form of the ritual. The conclusion to the seventh day and the brief introduction to the eighth day—a day on which this paper largely focuses—emphasizes this point.

The *brigata,* we are told, resumes storytelling on a Sunday after observing a suspension of two days in memory of Christ's death. As Boccaccio specifies the Sunday, he seems to stress the sense of time off, the holyday spirit which shapes the *Decameron.* The juxtaposition of religious ritual and storytelling, however, deserves a special comment. It may be taken to be a sign of Boccaccio's confused morality, the surd coherence of piety and worldliness. But in their contiguity the two experiences stand in an ironic self reflection: as each is cut loose from the other, the ritual purification is emptied of any content, and storytelling, in turn, is drawn within the boundaries of pure ritual. Yet the characters' own sense of utopia, of the imagination entirely self enclosed, is not very sure of itself. As they tell stories of *beffe*, symbolically sitting by the fountain, they are, in effect, engaged in an act of self-reflexiveness in which their desire for an imaginative utopia is asserted and its possibility is questioned. It is as if by the *beffe*, to anticipate, they localize their imagination and in the process utopia is lost.

Fundamental to the motif of the *beffa*, a prank by which a schemer is unmasked and repaid in kind, is a paradigm of exchange, the *quid pro quo;* and as such it mimes both the law of the market, a recurrent motif in the *Decameron* and the narrative structure of the text. Stories are recalled and exchanged by the *brigata* and this circuit of exchange simultaneously depends on and constitutes the bond of community between narrators and listeners.

The law of exchange and its mobile structure is the explicit theme of the *beffa* in the first story of the eighth day. Gulfardo, a German mercenary soldier, falls in love with Ambrogia, a merchant's wife, and asks her to be "del suo amore cortese." Ambrogia will comply with his request on two conditions; first that secrecy, a basic requirement of the courtly love transparently evoked in the story, be maintained; secondly, that he pay her two hundred florins. If the point of departure of the *novella* is the metaphoric exchange, conventional in medieval love literature, from *ars bellandi* to *ars amandi*, the metaphoric movement is undermined by the very emblem of exchange, money.

Ambrogia's demand transgresses the code of "courtly" love: what for Gulfardo is a purely gratuitous giving is to her a transaction, an occasion of barter. Deeply humiliated by her commerce (meretricious love can find no place in Andreas Capellanus' system) Gulfardo turns his love to hatred and contrives his *beffa*. He borrows the two hundred florins from her husband, gives it to her but later tells her husband that, having had no need of the money, he handed it back to Ambrogia.

From the point of view of Neifile, the storyteller, Gulfardo's *beffa* is an expedient of retributive justice, the just counterpart for Ambrogia's greed. Her demand, it would seem, violates the free exchange of love, draws it within the law of the marketplace, while the *beffa* punishes her wrongdoing. Neifile's pattern, however, is at odds with a more fundamental motif of the *novella*. What Gulfardo reacts against is precisely a threat to his very identity. The price which has been fixed gives a fixed value to him and his desire; more importantly, as Ambrogia asks for money she turns into a mercenary, deals with him on his own terms. The *beffa* Gulfardo devises is the weapon by which he establishes a difference: he casts Ambrogia as a worthless item and himself as her intellectual superior.

There are, thus, two perspectives on the *beffa*: on the one hand, the storyteller assigns to it a value of retributive justice against the law of the market which has disrupted the fairyland of courtly love. On the other hand, Gulfardo sees in it the means by which a hierarchy of intelligence is asserted. The double perspective designates the interest, the movement of appropriation which is inherent to the *beffa*. The very notion of free entertainment that underlies the *brigata*'s escape is undercut by the investment that each character and the storyteller have at stake and because of this the *beffa* enters the world of commerce.

This motif carries thematic weight throughout the *Decameron,* where money lenders and crafty merchants are the characters that to some extent eclipse the medieval romances of lovers and heroes. The merchants are the true tricksters who manipulate events and are in full possession of rationality. Critics, unsurprisingly, have always noted how keenly Boccaccio looks into men's affairs and their ability to deal with the dangers that lurk behind all transactions. It would be easy to remark that the critics, flattered in their own sense of intellectual self importance, are like merchants fixing a value on their own superior wisdom. Yet, by the *beffa* the world of rationality and self-possession, ostensibly celebrated in the *Decameron*, is subjected to a fierce critique and Boccaccio has a way of insinuating that the fool, dispossessed of value, is always somehow right. We must turn to the story of Calandrino's quest for the heliotrope in order to explore this structure.

The primary trait of Calandrino is to be forever the same, unchanged by his experiences and, like the masks of the *Commedia dell'Arte*, eminently predictable. By the quest of the heliotrope, he seeks an absolute autonomy and pursues his own fantasy to become transcendent and invisible, and gain the invulnerable standpoint from which he can govern and control the world. His steady reappearance as a fool in the *Decameron,* however, shows that he is doomed to be visible and that his desire is shattered. His recurrence, no doubt, is the core of the comical: as the two painters Bruno and Buffalmacco endlessly contrive plots by which Calandrino is forced into his space of self identity, we know that nothing irrevocable happens to him. At the same time, Bruno's and Buffalmacco's repeated *beffe* at his expense bespeak the pleasure inherent in the impulse to repeat: the *beffa* is the weapon to master even if it may betray the masters' insecurity in the presence of Calandrino's foolishness.

For he is very much a fool: not the fool in motley who cloaks himself in simulated inferiority to best ridicule his masters, the clown such as those one finds on the Elizabethan stage. Calandrino's foolishness is banal and his banality is profoundly disturbing. For in the measure in which he is a fool, he asserts the value of the imagination and at the same time sanctions its inevitable failure to create vital resemblances.

As the *novella* opens, Calandrino—himself a painter—is watching the paintings and *bas-relief* of the tabernacle which had recently been erected above the high altar in the church of San Giovanni. While he is enthralled by the artifice, Masetto contrives a trick against him. He pretends to confide to a friend, loudly enough so that Calandrino might hear, the secret of the land of Cockayne, the place where vines are tied with sausages and mountains are made of Parmesan cheese. Calandrino, the maker of images to which he is provisionally bound, is quickly ensnared by the tale and takes Masetto at his word. But he is not a don Quixote who will wander over the vastness of the world to test and find the reality of his fiction. The horn of plenty Masetto evokes is distant and out of reach and Calandrino will settle on the heliotrope, the fabulous stone which, according to the lapidaries, gives the bearer invisibility and which he thinks he can find along the banks of the Mugnone river. The heliotrope, as the wise Masetto of course knows, does not exist: it is only a name, literally the "utopian" center of gravity of the *novella* and around this absence, this word without content, the vault of the story is built.

It could be argued that in the measure in which Calandrino believes he can find the magic stone along the local river, the myth of Utopia has already collapsed. Yet the implied contraction of his vision also suggests that Calandrino lives in a world of confused unreality where all that is familiar is at the same time strange, the near at hand mysterious. He is, after all, a foreigner displaced in Florence, and to him Florence is the realm of the marvelous where the impossible quest can occur.

In its occurrence, it marks both a logical extension and a radical departure from the world of painting. If painting is the fictional space of semblances, the quester seeks reality and sheer invisibility. But there is a special dramatic force in Boccaccio's detail at the beginning of the story where Calandrino is gazing at the "dipinture e gl'intagli del tabernacolo." In the liturgy of the Church the tabernacle is God's dwelling, the place where the invisible Godhead is given a sacramental visibility. In patristic exegesis, more cogently, the tabernacle is uniformly glossed as "aedificatio terrenae felicitatis" because it symbolizes the promise of the messianic millennium. At the same time, the tabernacle is the typological sign of the transfiguration, the event of the manifestation of the Messiah and the prophecy that like Moses and Christ on Mount Tabor the faithful will experience the glory of divinity and attain to the knowledge of the invisible realm.

From one point of view, Calandrino's adventure is a brilliant parody of the traditional spiritual associations with which the emblem of the tabernacle is burdened. The promise of the millennium is inverted into the quest for earthly pleasures; the mystery of the transfiguration is comically turned into a mad desire to be invisible so that he can rob the banks of their riches. But above and beyond these parodic reversals of the biblical and Christian motif, something very serious takes place. Calandrino, in effect, attempts to charge with an immediate reality both the world of symbolic constructs and Masetto's fable. Whatever is just a pure image is valueless to him, and as he tries to seduce both Bruno and Buffalmacco to join him in his search for the heliotrope he trivializes the import of their paintings: "Compagni . . . ho inteso da uomo degno di fede che in Mugnone si truova una pietra, la quale chi la porta sopra non è veduto da niun'altra persona; . . . noi la troveremo di certo . . . e cosi' potremo arricchire sub-

itamente, *senza aver tutto di' a schiccherare le mura a modo che fa la lumaca.*"

It is at this point that the *beffa* reaches its climax. On a Sunday before sunrise, Bruno and Buffalmacco pretend to join him on his venture but secretly engineer a spectacle whereby the city of Florence is a stage on which Calandrino, believing himself unseen, is the visible occasion for general laughter. Calandrino never reaches the object of his search for the point where the word and its reality coincide is non-existent, truly utopian. Nevertheless, the illusion that he has found the stone is to him an exhilarating experience: he is provisionally freed from the tyranny of the others' gaze, unaware that his illusion of being autonomous, to put it in the terms of the profound insight of the *Commedia dell'Arte,* masks the fact that he is more than ever an automaton.

Nor does the final fall from his fantasy, when on reaching home he is seen by his wife, bring any sobering self awareness to him. In the best misogynistic tradition, he attributes the loss of the stone's virtue to his wife and fiercely beats her. This is possibly for Boccaccio a way of saying that there is no deception which is ever quite as powerful as self deception; more cogently, this is his expedient for releasing Bruno's and Buffalmacco's hoax into the domain of the inessential.

For their trick is dwarfed by Calandrino. Ostensibly, they occupy a world of sense, of orderly and meaningful patterns. They are makers of images who can tell fiction from reality and reason from unreason, and who know that the heliotrope is an arbitrary sign without any reference outside of itself. Calandrino, by contrast, is involved in a quest over the trails of the imagination. This imagination is not to be understood as the esthetic faculty that duplicates the world or funnels its experience into a stable picture. It marks, rather, a purely visionary venture which blurs the line of separation between illusion and reality. On Sunday, the *dies solis,* he seeks the heliotrope, literally the conjunction with the sun.

This impossible hope depends on his act of faith that objects must exist because words for them exist and this, in a real sense, is his madness to which the text twice has oblique but certain allusions. The first time, when the two friends feign not to see Calandrino, Buffalmacco says: "Chi sarebbe stato *sì stolto* che avesse creduto che in Mugnone si dovesse trovare una così virtuosa pietra, altri che noi?" The second time madness is Calandino's direct attribute: as he is seen by his wife, "*niquitoso* corse verso la moglie, e presala per le treccie la si gittò a' piedi." As a madman, he lives in a world of pure exchange in the sense that everything can be mistaken for everything else, and a word, literally nothing, can give access to the whole world. By mistaking what are only words for reality, Calandrino ultimately obliterates the value of words. Asked by Buffalmacco the name of the stone they would be looking for, he simply replies: "che abbiam noi a far del nome, poi che sappiamo la virtù? a me parrebbe che noi andassimo a cercare senza star più."

Calandrino's madness is his chief liability but also his strongest asset. As he is visible, he opens our eyes to a world which is too small, to a vision which is too narrow; and his story is a veritable romance of which he is the mad hero. He travels the distance that separates words from things, trying to fill that gap and knowing that the value of fictions is not sanctioned by their self-enclosures; as such, he is the boundary line within which Bruno and Buffalmacco are contained. He is the threat to the artists who give up the possibility of finding utopia and accept its irrevocable absence within the world.

The storytellers join Bruno and Buffalmacco and the Florentine public in laughing at Calandrino. But as they laugh with "gran piacere," they betray their uneasiness over their own utopian quest, over their belief that by moving to the *locus amoenus* they have found the hiding place from the convulsion of the times. Their laughter seems to draw attention to the fact that their own utopia—far from being a self enclosed totality—is a play, a put-on like Bruno's and Buffalmacco's trick; and for all their frivolity, the games of laughter are a necessary retrenching from madness.

Madness, to be sure, constantly menaces the stability of the world in the ***Decameron.*** Witness, for instance, the story of Cimone (fifth day, 1). Cast as an epyllion, the tale focuses on Cimone's redemption from beast (the significance given his name by Boccaccio) to man through the love for Ifigenia. Cimone sees Ifigenia asleep—discovers, that is to say, his own spiritual lethargy—and inflamed by love for her, wakes up to virtue. The stilnovistic dream that love ennobles man is flagrantly parodied as Cimone's newly acquired virtue turns into a veritable madness of love. The narrative (one is reminded of *Othello*) takes place in Cyprus, the island of the mad Venus, and Cimone's love succeeds only after generating mighty wars. This story of madness is controlled by the frame of order, is part of the experience of storytelling; yet, as an object of persistent fascination, madness is the border line of fiction, the temptation that threatens to erode the edifice of order and occasions, just as Calandrino does to Bruno and Buffalmacco, the world of representation.

We must turn to another *novella* (eighth day, 9) where Bruno and Buffalmacco once again come forth as the zany fabricators of the *beffa* in order to probe further the question of the value of the trick. The joke this time is contrived against a foolish physician, Master Simon, with the ostensible purpose of unmasking his pretenses of learning: from the outset, in fact, Simon is introduced as dressed in scarlet robes and "con un gran batalo, dottor di medicine, secondo che egli medesimo diceva."

The carefree life of both Bruno and Buffalmacco arouses his curiosity and he decides to befriend them to find out the reason for their merry lives. Bruno pretends to share with him an imaginary secret and weaves the fiction that they are members of a society founded by the necromancer Michael Scott which assembles twice a month and by magic practices they enjoy the pleasures of banquets, music, and midnight revels.

Simon, like Calandrino earlier, is unable to decipher the transparent lie and is wistfully seduced by it. He believes that the world of appearances pulsates with occult life,

that a mythic bond exists between appearances and the beyond. Eager to experience those imaginary pleasures, he begs to join what Bruno defines as a "paradiso a vedere," so that he might enjoy "la più bella fante del mondo." In this sense, the story comically conjures the motif of the Saturnalia, the golden age of revelry where restraints are abolished and one's fantasies are realized. When finally the night appointed for the meeting arrives, Simon is instructed to wear his most sumptuous robe and go to the cemetery of Santa Maria Novella. Of course, neither otherworldly prodigies nor erotic fulfillments take place. The tale actually turns into a masque, a literal carnival which, as its etymology suggests, is the ironic counterpoint of the erotic expectations. While Simon waits in fear, Buffalmacco disguised as a bear and wearing the mask of a devil comes to take the physician to share in the delights of the magic paradise but, after a few moments, throws him into a ditch of excrement. Bruno and Buffalmacco are hardly able to contain their laughter at their own trick. The morning after, with their bodies painted to simulate tortures received on account of Simon's cowardice, they visit him to complain for the troubles he had caused them. Fearful of becoming a public laughing stock, the doctor from that day forth pampered the two friends more than ever before.

Simon's fall into the mire marks a symbolic degradation, the manipulations by which he is sanctioned as an inferior to the two tricksters. Above and beyond this apparent pretext, the degradation implies that laughter is linked with a fall from Paradise. But for Boccaccio the fall has no theological focus: Paradise is an illusory misnomer and what is really lost by the fall is Hell.

The *novella,* I submit, features a deliberate dantesque design as if Boccaccio were directly involved in a parody of Dante's Hell. The allusion to Michael Scott is an overt recall of *Inferno* XX, the canto of contorted shades where divination and necromancy are expiated; the ensuing description of the assembly's entertainment, "costoro adunque servivano i predetti gentili uomini di certi loro innamoramenti e d'altre cosette liberamente . . . poi preserci di grandi e di strette amistà con alcuni, più gentili che non gentili," is a paraphrase of Iacopo della Lana's commentary on that canto. The painted bodies of Bruno and Buffalmacco to simulate the tortures echo the description of the hypocrites as "gente dipinta" in *Inferno.* And just as in Dante between the world of the sorcerers in *Inferno* XIX (the canto of *Simon magus*) and the world of the simulators there stands the so-called *commedia dei diavoli,* in Boccaccio's text we find its playful reenactment.

By staging the *commedia dei diavoli,* Dante primarily dramatizes the common medieval conception of Hell as the place of tricks and frauds. At the same time, he implies that laughter has a demonic property and is in touch with the dark powers. Like the Christian apologists, Tertullian, Cyprian and Boccaccio himself in the *Genealogy of the Gods,* Dante sees mimes and spectacles as arts of the devil, distracting man from his heavenward ascent. He even goes further than this: the devils' comedy enacts a steady danger of spiritual degradation of self. Unsurprisingly the pilgrim, at this stage of the poem, is directly threatened by the devils. Commentators have tried to explain the impasse by resorting to raw autobiography, the suspicion that Dante in his own life may have been guilty of barratry. In effect, the world of comedy is seen as black magic, a fraudulent game in this area where "Michele Scotto, fu, che veramente / de le magiche frode seppe 'l gioco." Dante dismisses this ludic moment because it is an illusory instrument by which the world can be shaped and radically juxtaposes to it his own *Commedia.*

What for Dante is an experience of moral terror, Boccaccio displaces into sheer buffoonery. Part of the fun, no doubt, lies in the fact that Boccaccio, a serious commentator of *Inferno,* is here involved in a deliberate misreading of it. Historically it will be left to Pico and the hermetic tradition to reverse altogether Dante's perspective and regain magic as a high wisdom, the imaginative realm of man's autonomy whereby the possibilities of angelic perfection or descent into matter are made available to him.

For Boccaccio, Simon literally falls into matter in what seems to be an overt mockery of spiritual falls. In this context there is a further detail that deserves comment: the front wall of Simon's hospital bears the emblem of Lucifer. By the detail, Boccaccio casts the physician as an ineffectual sorcerer and releases medicine as a practice of black magic. At the same time he exposes the lunacy in his belief both in the uncanny marvels of the Saturnalia and in mysterious bonds between symbolic representations and hidden essences.

Nor are the tricksters molders of worlds: to fashion themselves is simply a travesty, the wearing of a mask to make fun of and gain ascendancy over the gullible Simon. In the *Genealogy of the Gods,* Boccaccio still vindicates the value of the poet as a creature who forges and wields the illusion of new worlds. But in this story the imagination, the power by which man is the chameleon, is parodied. Bruno and Buffalmacco are the wizards who conjure the other world, who bring fictions into life and change life into fiction; but the process is contracted into play, a frivolous exercise which has renounced any claim to be vital.

By so doing, Boccaccio silences Dante's tragic sense of laughter and is far removed from Pico's belief in mythmaking through the arcana of magic. In a sense, he purifies the ground, as it were, of the supernatural and valorizes the world of play and *beffe.* The masque is the hub of play and we must look closely at it. For both Bruno and Buffalmacco, the mask is the sign of their superiority, the means of unmasking Simon's own self deceit. By wearing the mask and simulating tortures they appear, however, as actors. Isidore of Seville gives a definition of the hypocrite which is cogent to our point: hypocrisy, he writes, is the practice of actors who paint themselves in order to deceive. If Simon's appearance is false and hides an essential vacuity, Buffalmacco's impersonation of the devil is a pure fiction, a figure of substitution for nothing. As he wears the mask, he slips into Simon's very world of false appearance; more paradoxically, as he manages to frighten Simon he vindicates his belief that the world of appearance veils occult realities. Not one of them steps out of the bounds of illusion.

The *brigata,* gratified by the story, laugh at Simon just as they laughed at Calandrino and empathize with the tricksters. We surely understand why the physician is the object of laughter. After all, the introduction to the **Decameron** makes explicit the point that the art of Hippocrates is superfluous, has no restorative power from the threat of death. The masque, which is significantly acted out in the cemetery—the place of death—can hardly conquer death and is, in this sense, equally redundant. Yet, it seems to be a necessary alternative to mad visionaries, a style of mediocrity by which the tricksters always gain a superiority and the storytellers find temporary relief from their anxieties.

But can the game really be such a comforting fiction? Can we really make the world our own at the expense of fools or believe that nobody is ever laughing at us? We must turn back to the second day of the **Decameron** to find some possible answers to these questions.

The thematic burden of the day is the world of Fortune, which, in the introduction to the third story, appears as the Intelligence of God, the rational order that subtends and presides over the chaos of the fallen world of change. This view of Fortune as the providential agency governing the economy of the world recalls explicitly, as has often been remarked, Dante's digression in the canto of the avaricious and prodigals. Dante's discourse casts human rationality as a precarious construct, beset on the one hand by the unintelligibility of Pluto, the god of wealth, and on the other by Fortune's providential but inscrutable designs. The sinners who in their lives transgressed the economy of exchange by overvaluing or dissipating common goods now ironically exchange insults and move in a gloomy circle that parodies the perfect circularity of Fortune's wheel. From man's temporal standpoint, Fortune's movement does not follow any discernible plan: man, however, can still conquer Fortune by the exercise of virtue and by the acknowledgement that she reigns over the things of the world and that there is nothing which really belongs to us.

Boccaccio's extensive rephrasing of Dante's view of Fortune is comically altered later on in the day when the adventures of Andreuccio da Perugia (Second day, 5) are recounted. This story, in fact, is a parody of the spiritual allegory of man's confrontation and binding of Fortune. Andreuccio, as the etymology of the name implies, is the little man caught in the world of change. He is a merchant, a horse dealer who on a Monday (a detail that suggests that his destiny is linked to the phases of the moon and that he belongs to the sublunary world of change and corruption) appears in the marketplace of Naples to strike his deals. While he uncautiously shows off his money he is seen by Fiordalisi, a woman who, in flagrant inversion of her name, is a prostitute. She invites him to her house in Malpertugio which means, in Boccaccio's own etymologizing, a place of ill affair. Andreuccio has no *virtue* and actually mistakes his manhood for *vir*ility. He accepts her invitation only to have his erotic fantasies deluded. Fiordalisi tells him that she is his natural sister, entertains him for the whole evening in a room which suggests the garden of love, and finally robs him of his money. Only when Andreuccio has fallen into the excrement does he seem to realize that he has been tricked.

As he is fallen, he is involved in what is a transparent parody of the spiritual dark night: the city of Naples is a ghostly labyrinth from which there seems to be no exit. Andreuccio falls once again into a well where he cleanses himself and finally with two thieves he goes to the church to steal the ring off the Archbishop who has been buried that day. The church, far from being the place of moral regeneration, is literally transformed into den of thieves. Yet here he finds him conversion, a figurative death and resurrection comically inverted. He steals the ring and gets caught in the crypt; but then, by an unexpected reversal of the wheel of Fortune and an acquired virtue to exploit the coincidence, he gets out of the crypt, gaining both a new lease on life and the Archbishop's ring.

The name of the Archbishop, we are told, is Filippo, literally a lover of horses. By this etymological resonance and the fact that the ring is worth more than the florins he lost, the movement of the story both mimes the circulation of Fortune and suggests that there is a gain for Andreuccio. Whereas for Dante, Fortune is conquered by not clinging to earthly goods, Boccaccio inverts Dante's moral paradigm by showing how the very opposite takes place. These reversals are not simply techniques of Boccaccio's art; they are, as we shall now see, the very core of the story.

Far from being the order of a providential agency, the world is the empire of *alea,* a veritable *regio dissimilitudinis* where things are not ever what they seem to be. This view of Fortune sustains the ambiguities, constant inversions, falls and reversals of the *novella:* three times does Andreuccio fall and rise; by the extensive use of etymologies, Boccaccio seems to suggest that there are names which are "proper," stable receptacles of a univocal sense and identity. But the names appear as deceptive masks: Fiordalisi, regardless of her name, is a prostitute; Andreuccio's own name wavers between virtue and virility. More generally, he possesses, loses, and regains; there is a sister who turns out not to be a sister; the city of Naples is ironically twisted into a disorienting space where all directions are confused.

This land of unlikeness is triggered by Andreuccio's vainglory, concupiscence of the eyes, and concupiscence of the flesh. But as this conventional moral scheme is hinted at, it is quickly discarded. In this perspective, allegory-voided of its moral structure and parodied—is the poetics of dissemblance, for it represents a condition whereby things are not what they mean. By parodying the allegory, Boccaccio seems to be on the side of Bruno and Buffalmacco in showing that the gap between the semblance of things and their meaning can never be bridged.

The only order in such a world of dissemblance and instability is the regularity of Fortune's shifts. If the marketplace is the metaphor of traffic, the space where goods are brought to be exchanged and assessed at their proper value, the wheel of Fortune mocks the merchant's efforts. It is Fortune who is the true trickster of the world. For Dante she is the distant spectator of the "corta buffa" who "beata si gode"; for Boethius she behaves dissemblingly

like a play actor, "sic illa ludit . . . hunc continuum ludum ludimus." She teases man's power to dispose of goods and assigns them in a constant and irrational exchange. In this sense, she enacts Caldandrino's very madness in his changing one order of reality for another and in his desire to rob the bank, the place where exchange occurs. This view of Fortune tells us that human mastery, gain and hierarchy—that which is embodied by the *beffa*—are always provisional and contingent, just as the identity between the proper name of Filippo and its sense for Andreuccio is sheer chance, an ironic undercutting of any notion of providentiality.

When Andreuccio's adventure ends happily, the *brigata* laugh, pleasantly relieved at the last twist and turn of the wheel of Fortune. But in spite of the happy ending of the story, there is no real closure: the steady rotation of the wheel asserts the open-endedness of events. Andreuccio wins, but we are asked to extend the trajectory and realize that his fall may happen all over again because even as he is at the top of the wheel he is always on its shifty curve. The virtue by which he wins over chance, more importantly, is an act of thievery: the diamond into which his money was metamorphosed may have permanence, but, ironically because of its permanence, it is the more coveted and its possession ever endangered by other thieves.

Both Andreuccio's constant predicament and the *brigata*'s relief disclose the central oddness of the games of laughter—the comical tendency, that is, to mistake provisional appearances for the whole reality. This ambiguity informs the *novella genre* in the **Decameron.** The *novella* is a deliberate fragment, a cross section of a totality which, if it exists at all, can never be fully grasped. Boccaccio repeatedly tries to impose on his kaleidoscopic range of stories a unified design and cohesion: the frame; the thematic movement of the text from the chaos of the plague to the difficult order in Griselda's tale; the transitional passages; the topics by which stories are duly placed within given fields of signification; the symbolic numbers of totality (ten days and one hundred *novelle*). All are expedients which suggest how the sequence can be constructed as a unified totality.

Much like Petrarch's *Canzoniere,* the **Decameron** aspires to be a whole of parts but, at the same time, denounces the impossibility to be arranged as a total and coherent pattern. In the *Canzoniere,* the principle of repetition—as each poem begins anew it inexorably ends up echoing what has already been said—shows that totality is an illusory mirage. Nonetheless, the *Canzoniere,* has had and continues to have readers who are taken in by the esthetic simulation of order; the **Decameron,** I might add, has had exactly the same destiny. Auerbach's close analysis of a passage of a tale, for instance, depends on the assumption that each part reflects the totality and by the synecdoche one knows a fragment and, thus, one can grasp the whole. In a real sense, Auerbach is like the *brigata* in the garden who seize on the provisional and the partial and wistfully extend it to cover the whole.

Wistfulness is the heart of laughter. It betrays the desire for sense and relief which governs the life of the characters and, for that matter, of the critics. For Boccaccio the metaphor of totality, the project of both Calandrino and Simone, is madness and hence unspeakable. Dissolving their pretenses and borrowing from them there is the world of *beffe,* the play which discloses the illusoriness of the metaphor and which has laughter as its proper response.

In the wake of Aristotle, Thomas Aquinas speaks of laughter as precisely the activity proper to man. "Pratum ridet," as an exchange of properties, is a metaphor to describe the coming of spring. "Homo ridet," instead, has a proper sense, for laughter is man's distinctive and inalienable quality. Boccaccio shows both how laughter is a hollow mask which deceives, blinds us to what we lose, and how it is produced by a mask behind which the tricksters try to appropriate the world and, like the *brigata,* enjoy it.

The *Decameron* constantly moves between the dream of utopia and the pleasure of the representation: laughter is the precarious point where these polarities intersect and at the same time pull apart. This constant movement discloses laughter as the domain of the imaginary which seeks pretexts and occasions to become "real" and is always a put-on. The rhetorical name for this movement is catachresis, the figure of a borrowed property, the elusive borderland of madness where all efforts at sense are defied. (pp. 115-31)

> *Giuseppe Mazzotta, "Games of Laughter in the 'Decameron',"* in *The Romanic Review, Vol. LXIX, Nos. 1-2, January-March, 1978, pp. 115-31.*

Joan M. Ferrante   (essay date 1978)

[*Ferrante, an American educator and critic, has written numerous works on medieval literature, including* The Conflict of Love and Honor: The Medieval Tristan Legend in France, Germany and Italy *(1973) and* Woman as Image in Medieval Literature: From the Twelfth Century to Dante *(1975). In the excerpt below, in which she provides a formalistic analysis of the* Decameron, *Ferrante explains how Boccaccio's complex narrative patterns advance his themes.*]

Now that structuralists are looking closely at plot and theme variations in the *Decameron,* Boccaccio's "disegno ideale" is beginning to receive the attention it deserves. Larger patterns had been discerned, and the numerical frame has always been suggestive, but it is only recently that the concept of narrative patterns in the *Decameron* has been treated seriously. The more aware we are of such patterns, the better we can appreciate not only Boccaccio's technical skill, but his meaning as well. Boccaccio himself alerts us to his technique by the comments he has the frame characters make about their own and others' tales and about the art of story-telling. As Almansi remarks, the message of VI,1—art is the enjoyment of forms, not things—is an implicit invitation to conduct a formalist reading of the *Decameron.* I propose to trace here the themes and patterns that suggest themselves to me within each day, taken both as a separate unit and as a part of the whole, in relation to the overall design. These comments are intended to be complementary not antagonistic

---

> **Boccaccio, on envy:**
>
> Dearest ladies, both from what I have heard on the lips of the wise, and from what I have frequently read and observed for myself, I always assumed that only lofty towers and the tallest of trees could be assailed by envy's fiery and impetuous blast; but I find that I was mistaken. In the course of my lifelong efforts to escape the fierce onslaught of those turbulent winds, I have always made a point of going quietly and unseen about my affairs, not only keeping to the lowlands but occasionally directing my steps through the deepest of deep valleys. This can very easily be confirmed by anyone casting an eye over these little stories of mine, which bear no title and which I have written, not only in the Florentine vernacular and in prose, but in the most homely and unassuming style it is possible to imagine. Yet in spite of all this, I have been unable to avoid being violently shaken and almost uprooted by those very winds, and was nearly torn to pieces by envy. And thus I can most readily appreciate the truth of the wise men's saying, that in the affairs of this world, poverty alone is without envy.
>
> *Giovanni Boccaccio, in his introduction to the Fourth Day of the* Decameron, *translated by G. H. McWilliam, Penguin, 1972.*

to other studies of Boccaccio's style; since I am attempting to survey the whole work in a brief space, I will touch only on what seem to me to be the most obvious points, which should be put together with the work others have done and may yet do in this area.

The frame of the *Decameron* begins with the chaos and horror of the plague in Florence, the state of sin in the midst of corruption in which we all find ourselves and from which we would flee, and ends with the harmony and order of the brigata's life in exile, whose influence will presumably be felt even after the return to Florence. In the stories we move from corruption on the first day to virtue and generosity on the last, with the dangers of selfishness exposed in-between. The work falls naturally into two parts. As Neri pointed out some time ago, the first half of the *Decameron* is concerned with fortune, the second with wit or virtue; Branca discerned a similar pattern (fortune, II and III; love, IV and V; ingenuity, VI-VIII). One might say that in the first half God's providence, through fortune, governs; in the second, man determines actions by his wit, whether for ill, by vice, which is punished, or for good, by virtue, which can bend even fortune, as the tenth day demonstrates. On the first day, we are shown the mysterious ways in which God works, and the not-so-mysterious acts of his regents in church and state, the orders established by God for man's guidance; on the second day, the operations of fortune or providence, and on the third, fortune with the aid of the human subject, man working with providence. On the fourth, we see love thwarted, man working against providence; on the fifth, love accepted—here love replaces fortune as the dominant force. The success of love on this day makes possible the operation of justice through the ensuing days: On the sixth, the failures of human judgment (social conventions and customs) are exposed; from the seventh to the ninth, human faults are punished (VII, the guilty is tricked by his victim; VIII, he is tricked and exposed by his weakness; IX, he is tricked into enacting the essence of his fault, the normal world is turned inside-out). On the tenth day, which in many ways answers and parallels the first, powerful virtues overcome the evils of previous stories. The whole corrupt situation described in I has to be turned around; it must be replaced by X. In a sense, the two halves of the **Decameron** parallel each other in an inverted order, with V and VI serving as the turning point. . . . (pp. 585-86)

Further correspondences between days, the third playing variations on the second, the fifth on the fourth, etc. I shall return to later. There are other kinds of narrative patterns which I will not discuss, but which contribute to one's sense of an underlying design, e.g., core structures repeated with variations. The existence of such patterns does not prove that Boccaccio had a tightly worked-out scheme for all the stories of the **Decameron** but certainly that he had definite ideas in his mind, which he was consciously playing with.

I will concentrate here on the structure and themes of the ten days and their relations to each other. On the first day, there is no stated subject, but one recognizes very clear themes: corruption in high places, where good examples are called for, the failure to carry out one's social function (whether one is a priest, a statesman, or a woman), and, because action fails, the need to use words (exemplary stories or clever remarks) to correct the wrongs, a theme which will recur and dominate the sixth day. The first three stories are concerned primarily with the mysterious ways of God, though they also contribute to the picture of corruption in church and state (the ability of usurers and murderers to hoodwink innocent clergy in 1, the corruption of the papal curia in 2, and the guile and stinginess of a king in 3). In the first story, which describes the false confession of Ciappelletto that results in apparently real miracles, we are left uncertain: Did he die a shockingly unrepentant villain, or was he a death-bed convert at the last moment? The latter seems unlikely but we are asked to consider the possibility. Should we be more disturbed by his abuse of the sacrament or by the confesser's naïveté which allows such evil to go unpunished, indeed rewards it? Or should we simply praise God's mercy to us, as Panfilo does, for looking not at our errors but at the purity of our faith? The second story, the conversion of Abraham, illustrates that very point, that God can use the evil, even the very fact of their corruption, to good ends, as Boccaccio does in the **Decameron.** And the third, the tale of the three rings, makes the intriguing point that man cannot be sure, on his own, which religion is the true one, but must presumably trust to God and accept the one he has, at least if he is a Christian. All three stories make the point that man cannot, by his own powers, comprehend the ways of God. He must, as the next several days show, accept providence and learn to work with it. God has ordained certain organs, church and state, to guide man in his search and the bulk of the first day is given over to showing, or showing up, their functions. We see the hypocrisy of the clergy in 2, 4, and 6, combined with lust in

4, and avarice in 6 and 7; a king's avarice in 3, lust in 5, and sloth in 9. Woman's function seems to be to inspire to proper action (she arrests the king's lust in 5 and goads him to action in 9), and to value true worth (10). Boccaccio's main narrative device for dealing with the abuse of office is, fittingly, the reversal of expectations: In 1, a holy man confesses to a sinner and miracles are done in the name of a false saint; in 2, corrupt priests turn a man to the faith; in 4, an abbot follows the example of a monk into sin, and commits it in an unexpected position; in 5 and 9, a king is taught a lesson by a subject; in 6, an inquisitor is corrected in his fault by a layman's interpretation of scripture; and 7 begins with the unexpected, sudden stinginess in men known for their generosity.

In the first two stories, bad actions lead to good results; in the next four, clever words halt bad actions; and in the last four, words move to good actions. Words, another central theme, are the key means of correction on this day: In 1 and 2 they are abused, in the false confession of Ciappelletto, and in the churchmen's attempt to deceive God by changing the names of their sins—as if God, like man, could be misled by words; in 3 and 7, the fault is corrected by a story within the story; in 5 by a simple statement linked to a symbolic object, the chickens; in 8, by one word; and in 10, by a metaphor. In 4 and 6, criticism disguised as praise reveals awareness of the fault, and in 9, criticism disguised as a question corrects it.

On the first day, we have all the possible versions of abuse of position or function: in kings (one tries to use his position to get money, 3, another to get a woman, 5, and a third fails to use it, 9); in the clergy (an innocent friar becomes the tool of evil, 1, corrupt cardinals convert a sinner, 2, an abbot follows the bad example of a monk, 4, and an abbot's bad example corrects a nobleman, 7); and in women, who are meant to inspire and honor good men (one is a victim of lust, who enjoys it, 4, another successfully defends herself from seduction, 5, a third, a victim of rape, uses her plight to rouse a king to uphold justice, 9, and a fourth, the object of proper love, learns to accept and value it, 10). And, somewhat more subtly, Boccaccio also indicates the function of the writer by using words as the means of correction, as he will do again on the sixth day, where he brings in the larger subject of audience response to art, as if to remind us what he is about in the **Decameron.** If all other guides to morality fail, the artist can still move men.

On the second day, we are made to acknowledge the workings of fortune in men's lives: Since men have been led by fortune from the beginning of the world and always will be, the stories, Filomena decrees, will be about those who, hindered by various obstacles, reach a happy conclusion beyond their hopes. The day falls into two parts, perhaps to reflect the operation of the wheel of fortune, down and up: In the first five stories, the hero, a man, falls to the bottom of fortune's wheel through his own fault; in the last five, the central figure, a woman in all but one case, is the innocent victim of fate or the malice of others. There is a progression within the first five of the hero's capacity to deal with his fate: In 1, he gets in trouble for no purpose, simply out of exuberance, or mischievousness, and is saved through no action of his own; in the second, a man's foolish trust in prayers is punished with losses, but his faith in his saint is rewarded by unexpected gains, and recovery of lost goods; in 3, the prodigality and usury of a young man's family (here he pays for the sins of his relatives) cause the loss, but his own courtesy is rewarded; in 4, a man loses everything through greed and accident, but learns caution; and in 5, a fool who is conned by an expert learns to take advantage of the weakness of others in his turn.

The stories of this day also seem to be arranged in contrasting pairs: The first two have a religious center, 1 deals with a blasphemous act, a fake miracle that mocks a saint, 2 with an excessive trust in prayers to a saint; in 1, false robbers are saved, in 2, real ones are hanged. The third and fourth stories are concerned with riches, one with wasting, the other with hoarding: In 3, poverty turns men to usury, in 4 to piracy; the prodigals in 3 never learn, the greedy man in 4 does. The fifth story contains the opposing parts in itself: First Andreuccio acts like a fool and suffers, then he begins to act with cunning and makes up his losses. The pairing in the last five stories is more complex, 6 with 7, 8 with 9, but also, to a lesser extent, 7 and 8, 9 and 10. These all deal with innocent victims: In the sixth, Beritola is not only innocent, but essentially a passive onlooker at the political and personal events that occur to her husband and her children, whereas in 7, Alatiel is the catalyst that causes all events—she is at the center of rapes, kidnappings, murders, and wars. Alatiel is the victim of the lust of numerous men, while the hero of 8, the Count of Aguersa, is the victim of the lust and revenge of a single woman. The count is exiled wrongly for a rape he did not commit; in contrast, the heroine of 9 is forced to flee for a seduction she did not submit to. In both, a rape is claimed but not committed: In 8, the man is exiled, the guilty woman dies unpunished; in 9, the woman flees, the guilty man is punished severely. In 9, the husband's pride and lack of faith is contrasted with his wife's chastity, and she is forced to flee but returns to him; in 10, the husband's hypocrisy and impotence are in conflict with his wife's desires, and she is carried off, but chooses to stay with her captor.

In the early stories of the second day, a woman, a stranger, often appears as the arm of fortune: In 2, she takes the hero in for the night, offering him love and hospitality; in 3, she makes the hero her companion, then her husband, and restores the losses of his family; in 4, she fishes the hero out of the sea and nurses him back to health; in 5, where the situation is reversed, she pretends to be his sister and offers him hospitality, but then robs him. It does not seem far-fetched to see the woman in these stories as the figure of fortune, who is usually portrayed as a woman, raising or dropping men on her wheel.

There are a number of themes which run through the stories of this day and underline the lessons of fortune. All the stories involve a journey, or several, often a voyage by sea; travel forces an encounter with fortune, a change in one's life. This aspect is further carried out in the acquisition of new clothes, which represent a new identity and the hero's acceptance of what fortune gives him. In many of these cases, the new clothes involve a disguise, an assumed rôle, a temporary change of identity which is forced on the characters by fate or chosen by them in order to combat their fates. The opening story is about mummers, who play first a cripple cured by a false miracle and then victims of a robbery; in 2, thieves pretend to be merchants, and the hero plays the part of the lady's husband; in 3, a woman pretends to be a man and an abbot; in 4, a man is mistaken for a chest; in 5, a crook pretends to be a man's sister; in 6, 8, and 9, nobles assume the identities of servants; in 7, a woman who has slept with numerous men pretends to be a virgin; in 8, a woman pretends to be the victim of rape, and in 9, a man claims to have played a successful seducer; in 10, the judge assumes a rôle which he is ill-equipped to play, that of husband, and then substitutes one he can handle, that of religious devotee.

Another and more violent way of tinkering with the workings of fortune, is the taking of something one does not possess, either through theft, piracy, or rape. Theft occurs or is claimed in 1, 2, 5, and 9; piracy in 4, 6, 10; and rape in 7, 8, and 9. This kind of grasping action is usually contrasted with the free giving of self, as the woman does in 2 and 3, the chest in 4 (he tries to push it away, but it forces itself on him); in 5, the woman offers herself for bad motives; in 6, the woman, whose baby has been carried off, offers her milk to baby goats; in 8, the woman offers herself but is rejected; in 9, she is accused of having given herself, though she did not; and in 10, she gives herself freely to the pirate who kidnapped her. Alatiel, the victim of several kidnappings, in 7, gives herself after some hesitation to most of the men who take her, but although the story purports to be about lust for beauty and the violence that results, it is difficult not to see another meaning in it. Alatiel might well represent any earthly goods, the gifts of fortune, which men desire, steal, kill for, and which pass from one to another virtually unharmed, while the men who held them are destroyed. Although the stories of the first half of this day seem to be about greed, and those of the second half about lust, they all, in fact, are concerned with possessiveness, with man's or woman's desire to have what fortune has NOT destined for him.

At the end of the second day, Neifile decrees a respite for two days, during which time the brigata will observe Friday and Saturday in prayer and washing, renewing themselves spiritually and physically, like the heroes of the second day who assumed the new rôles fate had cast them in with their new clothes. The subject she sets for the third day is still connected with fortune, but aided by man's efforts: those who, with their own industry, acquire something very much desired, or recover something lost. Although the story-telling of the third day takes place in a new location, the connections between it and the previous day are strong. In fact, to a great extent, the third day parallels the second, although the emphasis in the third is on the gains made, whereas in the second it was on the recovery of loss. . . .

[On] the third day people get what they want, although sometimes it is more than they bargained for (1, 2), either through their own cleverness (1, 2) and another's simplicity (3, 4), or despite another's trick (5, 6), and often with added benefits (1, health and children, 7, the life of the husband, 8, a son, 9, two sons, 10, a needed fortune to the husband, sexual satisfaction to the wife).

This increase of benefits, which is particularly true of the second half of the third day (6-10), is emphasized by the structure of that day, again essentially binary. . . . The first and tenth stories are connected by the subject of sex with religious figures: In the first, the gardener cuckolds Christ by making love to a convent of nuns; in the last, a girl thinks she is serving God by putting the devil in Hell for a hermit. Both end with wealth, but the gardener has to give up his sex life eventually, and the girl keeps both. The second and sixth stories tell of a wife tricked into sleeping with another man; in 2, it happens only once and the husband foregoes revenge to avoid public disgrace; in 6, the wife accepts the situation to avoid shame, but gets to like it, and the affair continues. In 3 and 7, a confession is the hinge of the plot: In 3, it is used to establish the affair, in 7, a real confession destroys the affair, and a fake one offers the means to reestablish it. In 4 and 8, a husband's religious credulity is used by a cleric to get at the wife, with a fake penance in 4, and a sojourn in a fake Purgatory in 8. In the latter, the husband's jealousy is cured and his wife bears a son. In 5 and 9, the husband imposes unfair conditions in order to avoid meeting his obligations; in 5, the lover gets his rendezvous with the lady nonetheless, and in 9, the lady not only achieves one with her reluctant husband, but produces twin sons as a result. In 5, the lover uses the husband's avarice, despite his guile; in 9, the woman uses her husband's lust, despite his scorn for her.

As he did on the second day, Boccaccio pairs stories on the third, contrasting them with each other: In 1, a servant (gardener) takes what is offered and usurps the place of Christ as the husband of the nuns; in 2, a servant (groom) takes what is not offered and usurps the place of the king in the queen's bed. In 3, a friar acts unwittingly as go-between for lovers; in 4, a husband acts unwittingly as go-between for his wife and a monk. In 5, the lover uses the husband's avarice to arrange a meeting with the wife; in 6, he uses the wife's jealousy of her husband to achieve the rendezvous with her; in 7, one confession ends an affair and another renews it; in 8, a confession offers the means to the confessor to begin an affair. The ninth story, in which a wife takes the place of her husband's mistress, breaks the pattern, but is paired with the sixth story, in which a wife thought she was taking the place of her husband's mistress.

Deception is obviously the most successful means of achieving the desired end on this day, since the object of desire is not, for whatever reason, ready to give freely. Some sort of trick or deception is practiced in each of the ten stories, replacing the theme of theft and rape, the violent acquisition of the object on the second day. The theme of disguise, or assumption of a new identity, is carried over but more sharply focused, becoming an exchange or reversal of rôles, usually between the lover and the husband (occasionally the wife and the mistress), or the husband and the priest, who becomes the lover: In 1, the gardener plays the rôle of the nuns' husband, Christ; in 2, a groom takes

the place of the king; in 4, the husband takes minor orders and devotes himself to religion, leaving the monk to make love to his wife; in 5, the lover must play the wife's rôle along with his own, because the husband forbids her to speak; in 6, the lover pretends to be the husband, while the wife is pretending to be the husband's mistress; in 7, a variation on the theme, the husband is condemned for killing the missing lover, and the lover takes the place of the friar who had ended the affair, to visit the wife; in 8, an abbot takes the place of the supposedly dead husband; in 9, a wife substitutes herself for her husband's mistress; and in 10, another variation, a husband replaces the sexually exhausted hermit.

Since deception and the exchange of rôles necessitate discretion on the part of the conscious participants, silence is a recurrent theme through the day: The gardener in 1 pretends to be a mute and the abbess maintains a discreet silence when she learns he is not; the groom in 2 must not speak when he visits the queen in the dark, and the king chooses not to speak about the affair; the lady in 3 tells no one but her confessor what is supposedly going on; the husband in 4 is enjoined to keep his special penance a secret; the wife in 5 is forbidden by her husband to speak; the wife in 6 cannot talk without revealing her identity, and the lover disguises his voice for the same reason; in 7, the dangers of speaking are disclosed—the wife says too much in her confession, and the murderers are discovered when they are overheard discussing the need to keep quiet about what they have done; in 8, the wife is told to keep her husband's trip to Purgatory a secret; in 9, as in 6, the wife must be silent to conceal her identity.

Love or sex—one rarely has the sense of anything more than physical satisfaction—is the object of the hero or heroine's effort in every story on the third day, and the point is clearly made that if one tries hard enough one can attain it. But on the fourth and fifth days, we are, for the most part, dealing with a much stronger emotion: the disruptive effects of love thwarted on the fourth, and the unifying power of successful love on the fifth. The two days are mirror images of each other, in their themes and in their plots. What is wrong on the fourth day is right on the fifth. . . . (pp. 586-94)

Generally, on the fourth day, the lovers start out together, but are separated, while on the fifth they are apart at the beginning, but come together at the end. The main obstacle to love on the fourth day is one lover's family (a possessive father in 1, watchful cousins in 2, a grandfather in 4, brothers in 5, a mother in 8, a jealous husband in 9). On the fifth day, in contrast, the love is the means by which separated families are reunited: A father exiles his son for his boorishness in 1, but love cures him; the attempt to seize the girl in 5 leads to the discovery of her father and brother and to the family's reunion after many years; the public punishment of the lover in 7 provokes his recognition by the father from whom he had been taken as a child. Some families are initially pleased with the marriage (4, 8), others become reconciled to it (3, 9); none remains hostile. Love is thus shown to be a force for harmony and social order on the fifth day—all but the last story end in marriage, and that one ends with an extended marriage, a *ménage à trois*. In contrast, on the fourth day, all but the last story end in death, and in the last there is an apparent death, when the lover is accidentally drugged. In six of the stories both lovers die (IV, 1, 4, 5, 7, 8, 9), but they are buried together in only four (1, 4, 8, 9), so most of them are kept apart even in death. The destructive forces at work on the fourth day are emphasized in the physical dismemberment of the lover which occurs in several stories: The heart is cut out in 1 and 9, the head cut off in 4 and 5, the heart torn out in the prophetic dream in 6, and, a kind of physical disfigurement, the body swollen in 7. In the tenth story, the theme is parodied: The husband, a surgeon, has to cut a bone from the leg of a patient, and prepares an opiate which is administered to the lover by accident. The theme of dismemberment recurs on the fifth day, but only metaphorically: The lover in 4 feels as if his heart had been torn from his body when they are discovered; the heart and entrails are cut out of a woman's body in the vision in 8; and in the ninth story, the lover kills his falcon, which is like a part of himself, for his lady, and her child, who is like a part of her, dies. But in each case, the horror is simply a prelude to the happy solution of the love problem.

With the fifth day, Boccaccio strikes the most positive note yet in the **Decameron.** He has love bringing together not only the two principals, but their families as well, so that it is contained within the social structure. He will rise to a similarly positive view on the tenth day, but, before reaching that point, he must bring us through a series of days concerned with human faults, corrected or punished by means of words, *motti,* on the sixth day (as on the first), and of actions, *beffe,* on the seventh, eighth, and ninth. On the first day of the **Decameron,** Boccaccio pointed to corruption in figures responsible for guiding society; on the sixth he questions the validity of many accepted conventions of birth and class, beauty and law. He shows how the divine forces of fortune (which dominated the first five days) and of nature often hide their valued possessions (the noble nature in the baker, Cisti, 2; the brilliant mind and artistic genius in the ugly bodies of Giotto and his lawyer friend, 5; conversely, Ciesca's beautiful body hides an arrogant and stupid soul, 8). We are asked, by the brief tales of this day, to rethink our own perceptions and, at the same time, to reconsider our response to the **Decameron,** because these stories are concerned with art and the audience response to it, and we would have to be obtuse, like Ciesca, not to apply the lessons to ourselves. Art holds the mirror up to life, as the uncle attempts to do in 8, but if we fail to recognize ourselves it will do us no good.

Most of the actors in the stories of the sixth day are artists of one kind or another: a story-teller in 1, the painter Giotto in 5, the poet Guido Cavalcanti in 9, the religious con-man, Fra Cipolla, in 10 and, on a lower level, the baker Cisti in 2 and the cook Chichibio in 4; even God himself is facetiously described in the sixth story as a beginning painter, in the early stages of creation, who did not yet have the features or proportions right. Humorous or not, the story makes the connection between artist and creator. All these figures have lessons to teach about the function of art and the audience's response to it: The artist must be in control of his material (1), it is not enough for him to

have a good story, he must tell it well; he must suit the quality of his material to the audience (2)—special wine is not for servants is how Cisti sees it; the tone must match the occasion—a sharp observation is countered by a sharper rebuke in 3, while a master's anger is turned to laughter by a servant's wit in 4. From Chichibio's case, it is clear that one may need inspiration and a certain amount of luck, as well as artistry. The artist sees things as they really are and makes us see ourselves more clearly: Giotto, who can paint likenesses almost more real than his subjects, reminds his companion how HE appears to others (5); the uncle in 8, when he warns his niece to stay away from the mirror if she would avoid unpleasantness, is telling her that beneath her surface beauty, there is ugliness, but she misses his point. The audience, which can be manipulated, persuaded, corrected, amused, or deceived by the artist, must be able to see what he is showing them, as the niece does not, and as only one of Cavalcanti's companions does (9). The message of that story is apparently that, to be alive, we must not only understand but question and think. The tenth story shows what happens when we do not, how easy it is for a resourceful man, like Fra Cipolla, even when he has been tricked himself, to keep one step ahead of a credulous and unthinking audience. The husbands of the seventh day will serve as precisely such an audience.

The clever remarks that correct faults on the sixth day only work on intelligent subjects. On fools or people rendered vulnerable by their weaknesses they have no effect; against such, the only weapon is action, hence the tricks that are described in the stories of the next three days. Previously, particularly in II, III, and V, the audience has been encouraged to good behavior by the hope of reward. From now until the last day, we are shown what awaits us if we are too stubborn to mend our ways. The seventh day is given over to the tricks women play on their husbands, but the husbands fall prey to the deceptions because of their jealousy and foolish credulity. Indeed what wives do to jealous husbands, Fiammetta tells us, should not be condemned but commended, since jealous husbands seek the death of young wives (5); their very possessiveness drives their spouses to sin. The general attitude toward husbands that prevails on this day is revealed in the first story, where the ass head is used to signal the husband's presence or absence; in other words, to represent him. (The crack in the wall through which another wife communicates with her lover [5], also represents the husband's weakness, the jealousy which she takes advantage of.)

The seventh day, like the second and third, seems to fall into two parts: The first five stories focus on the husband's foolishness and jealousy which the wife turns against him; 6 to 9 center about the wife's cleverness, her manipulation of husband and lover. In the first story, the husband represented by the ass head is persuaded by his wife that her lover is a ghost; in 2, he is told that the lover has come to buy a tub, and he climbs into the tub to clean it while the visitor makes love to his wife; in 3, the husband believes that the lover, a friar, is exorcising worms from his child, and even rewards him; in 4 and 5, the husband's jealousy instills in his wife the idea and determination, and in 5 the means as well, to give him a reason for it. In the second group of stories, we see that there is no point to a husband's jealousy, since a woman can, in any case, manage whatever she wishes. The ninth story serves as a kind of allegory for the day's message: The wife offers the lover three tokens of her devotion, which are in fact proofs of her domination over her husband, and then, for the final blow, lets the husband watch them make love and convinces him he never saw it. It is not a coincidence that the *brigata* has moved to the Valle delle Donne for this day. Throughout these stories, the wife is the clever author manipulating characters and creating lies and illusions, while the husband is the foolish audience, and sometimes the fool of the piece for an audience of her relatives (4, 8). His folly is underlined by the numerous references to magic and superstition, one of the themes of the day—indeed he gives himself over to the woman's powers as if they were magic: the exorcizing of ghosts, 1; spells to cast out worms, 3, or to put husbands to sleep, 5; the whole experience of discovering the lover made to seem an illusion in 8. In 9, the husband is convinced that his pear tree has the power to make anyone in it imagine a sexual act occurring beneath it; in 10, one lover returns from the dead to tell another which sins are punished in the next world. The lover, or lovers, in these stories is a pale figure, usually a tool of the woman (although in some cases he makes the first advances). He is a kind of ghost (pretended in 1, real in 10), a servant of the husband (7, 9) or a stand-in for him, a godfather, a spiritual father, considered too close a relative to engage in sexual relations with the wife (3, 10).

On the eighth day, of unrestricted tricks, the scope of attack is extended beyond jealousy and foolish credulity to the more general vices of greed, lust, vanity, and cruelty (the greed of women in 1, 2, 10, their cruelty and vanity in 7; the folly and vanity of men in 3, 6, 9, their greed in 5 and 6, their lust in 4 and 8), which Boccaccio had described on the first day. Here he shows us what can happen to us if we give in to them. In the cast of characters, too, the author moves back toward the first day (and looks ahead to the tenth), with a variety of public figures, a doctor, a scholar, and a judge, as well as churchmen. And he introduces the emblematic fool of the *Decameron,* Calandrino, who is everything Boccaccio deplores: vain, greedy, and stupid. He is persistently tormented by Bruno and Buffalmacco whose function, like Boccaccio's—and it is no mere coincidence that their names also begin with B—, seems to consist in showing up the folly of others, the learnèd doctor, the bad judge, and the stingy governor, as well as Calandrino. Because the same tricksters are involved with the obvious fool and with the doctor, we are invited to equate the two, to see that the learnèd fool is no better, perhaps even worse, than the ignorant fool.

The early stories parallel those of the seventh day, to some extent, but with broader connotations, moving gradually beyond the essentially private sphere of adultery into a more social one. The first two stories are still concerned with an adulterous situation: In VII,1 and 2, the husband is deceived by his wife because he is a fool; in VIII,1 and 2, the wife is deceived by her lover because she is greedy. In what may be a comment on the preceding day, Neifile remarks that a woman who indulges in illicit sex may be pardoned if she submits for love, but should be burned if she does it for money (1). In VIII,3, although the wife is the innocent victim of her husband's foolishness, the focus is on his greed and credulity, his belief in a magic stone—to preserve which he allows himself to be pelted with stones (in VII,3, the husband's belief in religious magic was used to conceal the wife's affair from him). In VIII,4, an old, ugly, but vain, canon courts a young widow who manages to get rid of him only by pretending to accept him: She puts a deformed servant in her place and then summons the bishop and her brothers to witness his shame. In VII,4, a drunken husband, jealous without cause, drove his wife to give him cause, and was publicly exposed as a drunk and beaten up by her relatives. The introduction of the bishop in VIII,4, points up the public concern: It is not only the man's ill-suited lust which is criticized, but the fact that he indulges it, although he is a canon. In the next story, the stinginess of a governor in putting unqualified people on the bench and the inadequacy of his chosen judge are even more publicly exposed. (In VII,5, a husband who had taken on a rôle he had no right to play, that of a priest in the confessional, was shown up by his wife.)

In each of the first six stories of the eighth day, the character who is at fault gets his comeuppance, usually, though not always, through someone who has suffered at his hands. Then in the seventh and eighth, the victim specifically seeks and gets revenge, the scholar on the widow who so cruelly abused his love, and the wronged husband on his neighbor's wife. Interestingly, the revenge in the latter case is so mild, a simple exchange of partners, compared to the fierceness of the seventh story, presumably because in 8 the revenge is for an act of love, whereas in 7 it is for the lack of it. The two concluding stories of the day show up people who live by their wits, the learnèd doctor and the confidence woman—all the other characters have thought highly of their own cleverness, but these two make careers out of it. The doctor who, for all his learning, cannot understand the simple happiness of Bruno and Buffalmacco, and covets the wealth and orgies they describe, is exposed for the coward he is and ends covered with dung. The confidence woman is done out of her gains and much more, by one of her victims; as Dioneo comments, she discovered that other people knew as much as she did. This is a variation on the Andreuccio story (II,5), but there the victim simply learned enough from his experience to take in someone else; here the perpetrator becomes the victim. The trick turned against the trickster will be the basic situation on the ninth day. Lauretta comments, in VIII,9, that we should not condemn those who play tricks on people who ask for it, as in 8, or who deserve it, as in 9. This remark calls attention to the sense of justice which underlies this day's tales of retribution.

Since the eighth day is concerned to a great extent with folly, focused particularly on those who think themselves clever, belief in magic is again a theme, as it was on the seventh (e.g., 3, 6, 7, 9), but there is a new motif of exposure. On the seventh day, the wife might make a fool of her husband and deceive him, but she had a great deal to lose by public disclosure of her action, so the audience for her deception was usually restricted to her lover, and sometimes her husband. On the eighth day, however, public revelation is part of the point. The canon in 4 is found naked in bed with a deformed woman, the judge in 5 loses his pants in public; the widow in 7 is left naked on a tower. They are stripped of their pretenses and seen for what they are; Calandrino, on the other hand, well known for what he is but incapable of seeing himself, believes that he can be invisible to others.

The subject of retribution continues on the ninth day, in that the faults, particularly certain people's obstinate refusal to recognize shortcomings which make them vulnerable, become the means of their punishment. But the presentation is more grotesque, the situation is turned upside-down, in complete reversal of what it should be: In 1, a widow forces her unwanted suitors to take the place of a dead man and rob a tomb, an allusion presumably to the fact that in paying court to her they have been trying to take what belongs to the dead; in 2, an abbess appears with a priest's pants on her head; in 3, Calandrino is made to think he is pregnant, which he blames on the unnatural position his wife assumes in their love-making; in 4, two men are drawn together by their hatred of their fathers, the servant abuses his master, the robber accuses his victim of robbery; in 5, Calandrino pays court to a prostitute as if she were a lady; in 6, a false dream is accepted as true; in 7, a true one is rejected as false; and in 10, a man tries to turn his wife into a horse.

The main concern of the day seems to be the necessity for people to recognize, or to be made to recognize, their own faults. Like several others, the day falls into two parts, with the second half picking up motifs from the first. In 1, a woman catches in time her own fault (accepting the attention of two suitors) and corrects it; in 6, a woman quickly sees her error (getting into the wrong bed), makes the best of it, and ends thinking it was all a dream. In 2, the abbess tries to correct her fault in someone else, but is made to acknowledge it in herself and then condone it in the other person; the woman of the seventh story, like the abbess, looks for her faults in others—suspicious and petty, she projects evil motives on her innocent husband—and fails to see them in herself, but unlike the abbess she ignores a warning when it is given to her and suffers badly for this neglect. Calandrino, in 3, blames another for his predicament, refusing to see any fault in himself, and he pays through the nose for his folly in both money and disgrace. 8, like 3, begins with a trick played on a character whose weakness (gluttony) makes him vulnerable; unlike 3, however, it ends with the trick returned with interest to the player, who is also a parasite but who failed to see that he was vulnerable in the same way; this experience permanently cures him of playing such tricks. The difference between him and Bruno and Buffalmacco, who always get away with their tricks, is that they are not guilty of the faults they ridicule in others. Both the fourth and the ninth stories present two modes of behavior, two solutions, love and punishment: In 4, one man is rescued by the father he hated, the other is punished for his crimes; the ninth story teaches us to love if we would be loved and to correct vices, but its scope extends over the whole ***Decameron***. As the ninth story of the ninth day, it is in a significant position, and its lessons, delivered by the ultimate

figure of human wisdom, Solomon, are the positive and negative lessons of the book; they are conveyed by the two modes employed in all the stories, one by words (the exhortation to love), the other by action (the mule beaten at the bridge). The negative lesson is the one that has been taught in the last three days (VII to IX)), the positive one will be embodied in the tenth day.

The tenth day teaches that lesson in an extended form, and goes much further. The day begins with stories of virtue rewarded or recognized, and moves on to ever more impressive and selfless displays. The stories seem to be grouped in threes, rather than twos: The first set tells of men who act out of a desire to win glory or repay debts, but who are limited by worldly values. In the first story, a knight eventually receives what his valor has earned, but only after he has learned that he has no right to demand it, because fortune has denied him. In the second, an abbot gives what he owes, having learned that man's view of right and wrong is narrow, that injustice can be caused by fortune as well as by men. In the third, the hero becomes what he wanted to be thought, generous, when he learns that real generosity does not consist in dispensing wealth. In the next trio, fortune gives the hero what he wants, but he sacrifices it out of noble motives. In 4, a man rescues the woman he loves, restores her and her unborn child to life, but returns them to the husband, having first established that he has a legal claim to them. In the fifth, the lover wins the woman he wants with perseverance, money, and magic, so that even the husband acknowledges his claim and insists that his wife make it good rather than betray her word, but the lover is moved by the husband's integrity and relinquishes his right, which in turn moves the magician to decline his pay, an example of the snowballing effect of virtue, which recurs in 8. In the sixth story, a king who is attracted by the two daughters of one of his knights is not only dissuaded from taking advantage of his position, but bestows dowries on them so they can be married to others. (Their names, Ginevra and Isotta, evoke the Vulgate-Cycle story of the destruction of Arthur's world because of the indulgence of personal desires.) These three examples of self-denial are followed by three of selfless giving: first, a king who saves a girl from a romantic death (she is dying of love for him) with an equally romantic solution (he offers to be her knight and carry her token). In the previous story, a king gave up for political reasons a love he should not, but could, have indulged and offered material support; here a king takes on a love for which he bears no immediate responsibility, out of pure compassion, and offers personal service as well as a dowry. In the next story, 8, a young noble gives up his fiancée to his friend, who later confesses to a murder the first is accused of, offering his life in order to save the other's; this display of devotion so moves the real murderer that he admits his guilt, a striking example of virtue begetting virtue. The ninth story describes the kingly generosity of an ordinary man (wealthy, but not noble), who gives lavishly simply because he recognizes true worth even when it is disguised.

Finally, the last story presents the highest display of virtue in the ***Decameron,*** the total denial of self in a peasant woman's devotion to her husband. (We have come down the social ladder from kings through nobles and merchants to a peasant, whose class disguises the highest nobility of soul—cf. the sixth day—, as merchant clothes disguised a king in the previous story.) Her love is so strong that she can bear all the wrongs of fortune, all the trials her husband imposes on her, not only with patience but with magnanimity. Fortune, in the guise of the husband, Gualtieri, gives and takes without any apparent justification, but virtue, in Griselda, bears it all without ever bending. Thus, in the end, virtue proves to be a greater force than fortune.

Fortune, as I mentioned earlier, is an important force in the first half of the **Decameron,** but is more or less neglected thenceforth until the last day. Here it is treated as a mysterious force which can be hostile (it does not always reward virtue [1], and makes good men suffer [2]), or benevolent, or both at once. Yet good men are able to overcome it, as the king and the knight do in 1, the abbot and the outlaw in 2, the lover in 4, the king in 7 (who first curses fortune for making the girl the daughter of an apothecary, but then improves her fate with his attention and gifts), Saladin by means of magic in 9, and Griselda by pure virtue in 10. If one compares the two chests in the first story with the three rings in the third story of the first day, which initially make the same sort of point (man cannot tell which is the true or valuable one, only God can), one readily sees how subtly Boccaccio has modified his presentation of fortune. The knight in X,1, not knowing which chest contains the treasure, makes the wrong choice, but the king knows and the king can give him the one he failed to choose. One could, of course, see the king as a figure for God, and take the point of the two stories to be the same, but I prefer to think that Boccaccio wants to leave us with the sense that virtue has the power to bend fortune.

In many ways the stories of the tenth day bring us back to the very first day by reintroducing the mysterious workings of providence, by showing virtues in those figures in whom vices had formerly been exposed (kings, clergymen, nobles, in two cases the same men), and by countering the vices of the first day, lust and greed, with their opposite virtues. The tenth day also parallels the first, virtually story by story. . . . (pp. 595-603)

[Boccaccio] clearly countered the faults, greed and lust, that he criticized on the first day and thereafter, with examples of generosity, in money and in action, of self-denial, and of charity. The corruption in high places is answered by virtue in the same figures. Kings and clergy teach by their example on the tenth day as they were meant to. Two figures, an abbot and a king, appear on both days, as if to force us to make the connection, Saladin and the Abbot of Cluny. On the first day they were caught out in small faults, on the tenth they demonstrate big virtues. Saladin's virtue is greater than the abbot's but, as Elissa remarks (X,2), munificence is more exceptional in a cleric than in a king. Women, whose function, we were taught on the first day, is to inspire men to good action, and to value the love of good men, have little importance on the last day except as the objects of men's desires, but Boccaccio chooses a woman as the culmination of the **De-**

cameron, the figure of perfect virtue, tempting to interpret, as readers have done from the fourteenth century on, as an allegory of the human soul, tested repeatedly like Job, but never failing. In any case, she is no more "real" than the figure of complete vice at the beginning of the **Decameron,** Ciappelletto. Both represent the extremes of vice and virtue between which man moves in life, hopeful of some success if he is capable of love and uses his wits, with the aid of providence, threatened with harm or disgrace if he gives in to his selfish impulses. The world is filled with people ready to take advantage of his weaknesses, and there are few who will attempt, like the author of the tales, to set him in the right direction. (p. 604)

> *Joan M. Ferrante, "Narrative Patterns in the 'Decameron',"* in *Romance Philology, Vol. XXXI, No. 4, May, 1978, pp. 585-604.*

Alfredo Bonadeo (essay date 1981)

[*In the essay below, Bonadeo examines Boccaccio's portrayal of marriage and adultery in the* Decameron.]

What is the sentimental and rational basis supporting marriage in the **Decameron**? How persuasively do the conditions and plot development in any given novella lead to marriage, the conclusion of most love stories in the masterpiece? Some critics have noted that love does not play a leading role and that the psychic and moral reality of the relationships is considerably weak. The inception of love, for example, seldom embodies the interplay of emotional and mental forces or the intensity and complexity of passion. It is described by some laconic remarks concerning the identity of the lovers and the time and space dimensions within which any given relationship develops. It can be added that the causes of love are usually represented by stock expressions which produce something less than poetical and emotional impact. Thus, a monk sees a country girl, and "fieramente assalito fu dalla concupiscenza carnale"; Ricciardo Minutolo "s'innamorò d'una la quale . . . passava di bellezza tutte l'altre" (III, 6); Guiscardo "più che altro le piacque, e di lui . . . fieramente s'accese" Ghismonda (IV, 1); Lorenzo, "essendo assai bello della persona e leggiadro molto . . . 'ncominciò stranamente a piacere." to Lisabetta (IV, 5); Andreuola "per ventura d'un suo vicino che aveva nome Gabriotto s'innamoro" (IV, 6); Martuccio Gomito, "assai leggiadro e costumato . . . s'innamoro" of Gostanza, and the latter "di lui similmente s'accese" (V, 2); and Nastagio degli Onesti "s'innamorò d'una figliuola di messer Paolo Traversaro" (V, 8).

But in the **Decameron** marriage is not the triumph of love for reasons more important than the initial weakness of sentimental bonds. It has been speculated that in matters of love, noble and moral ideals often overcome sensual and economic considerations. Such conjecture postulates a sentimental freedom and a power to make decisions that in fact the lovers in the masterpiece do not possess. Textual evidence suggests that marriage is often the victim of coercion because the love impulses are suppressed by external circumstances, such as social impositions and compulsion exercised by the family. One does not have to agree entirely with [Robert] Briffault's opinion that in the Middle Ages marriage was a "matter of pure economic convenience," or with the view of a recent critic that "there was no place in medieval society . . . for passion to lead to marriage." Nevertheless, the "and they lived happily together thereafter" formula concluding the stories of love and marriage appears to be very much at odds with the situations that precede it, and the incongruity does not exactly make marriage a perfect match of hearts and wills, for very little is left to the lovers' emotion and freedom of choice. For instance, in view of Beltramo di Rossiglione's repeated rejection of Giletta di Narbona, a physician, the reader finds it singularly hard to believe at the conclusion that he accepts her as his legitimate wife and will love her forever (III, 9). Early in the novella, urged by the king of France to marry her, the proud nobleman offers spirited resistance. "Conoscendo lei [Giletta] non esser di legnaggio che alla sua nobiltà bene stesse," Beltramo regards such a marriage as a kind of violation of social as well as divine laws: "Già a Dio non piaccia che io si fatta femina prenda giammai." Eventually forced by the sovereign to do what his own will and sentiment would never have consented to, Beltramo goes through the formality of the ceremony, but immediately thereafter abandons his newly wed wife. Pressed by Giletta to honor the marriage, he proclaims he will do so only when she wears a ring, which he knows well he never takes off his finger, and when she will procreate his child. Beltramo poses these terms because he is positive that the conditions, being "impossibili cose," will never be met. When Giletta manages through an ingenious design and execution to win the wager, Beltramo cannot believe it, and "tutto misvenne" that is, he is extremely surprised and upset by the wholly unexpected outcome. But *noblesse oblige,* and he joins Giletta in normal matrimonial life.

Beltramo's final move has nothing to do with a change in his views and disposition. He is neither overwhelmed by a sudden wave of love for his wife, nor has he changed his opinions concerning the social incompatibility between a nobleman and a physician. He merely goes through the motions of a dutiful husband because he is forced to do so by the outcome of the wager, totally independent of his desire and will. He is forced to live with her by circumstances he wishes had never materialized. The conclusion of the story, the reconstitution of the family, may certainly be regarded as a victory for Giletta, but from Beltramo's standpoint it is a defeat.

Elements extraneous to the interplay of sentimental and rational forces have the power to determine the conclusion of some love stories in a particularly dramatic way. The impasse between the luckless Nastagio degli Onesti and the obstinate daughter of Paolo Traversaro is broken by a supernatural and terrifying event, the vision of a lady in the pinewoods of Chiassi chased and dismembered by ravenous dogs as a punishment for her being obdurate in love (V, 8). Originally his beloved's "singular bellezza o . . . la sua nobiltà" make her so "altiera e disdegnosa" that Nastagio is driven to the brink of suicide. But as soon as she witnesses the ghastly vision (conveniently reenacted every Friday), and she grasps its meaning (ruthless punishment for recalcitrance in love), she is apparently so

blinded by terror ("e tanta fu la paura che di questo le nacque") that her attitude dramatically alters: her arrogant antagonism is quickly replaced by abject subservience. Having "l'odio tramutato in amore," without consultation and without hesitation, she sends word to Nastagio that she is ready to do his pleasure, "ch'ella era presta di far tutto ciò che fosse piacer di lui." Asked by Nastagio to marry, she promptly "gli fece risponder che le piacea." She finally tells her parents "che era contenta d'esser sposa di Nastagio," and they too "furon contenti molto." The anxious compliance underscored by the insistence on the verb "piacere" and the adjective "contento" points to the hurried, irrational and coercive nature of the decision that brings the novella to a close, a decision that remains unexplained and unexplainable in terms of a modification of the sentimental or class attitude of Paolo Traversaro's daughter toward Nastagio. There is no attempt on her part to disavow her earlier animosity, nor to repudiate her haughty social stand. The change of hatred into love ("l'odio in amore tramutato"), her eagerness to submit to Nastagio, and her unqualified consent to a marriage once tenaciously opposed, depend exclusively upon the fear of, and desire to guard against, violence ("paura . . . che questo a lei non avvenisse"). Violence or fear of violence may indeed have the power to force certain actions, but it can hardly engender good feelings; least of all can it engender love and become the stable foundation of a marriage.

Critics admire greatly the novella of Cimone and Efigenia (V, 1) mainly because of the description of the effect of love upon the uncouth young man; possibly because of this admiration they overlook the real determinant of the marriage, Cimone's irrational and brutal pursuit. At the end of the novella Efigenia is said to begin a long blissful existence with her husband, but as a victim of her lover's doings she may not be as happy as Boccaccio pictures her. "Io son per te divenuto uomo," at one point Cimone tells her, and by the fourth year of his love for the charismatic girl he has become "il più leggiadro e il meglio costumato . . . giovane." Where will this uncommon virtue lead him? There are two problems with Efigenia: she has already been promised in marriage to someone else, and unlike other female personages of the *Decameron* who repudiate a marriage arranged for them by the family, she has no mind to play the rebellious daughter. The other problem is that she just does not care for Cimone. But Cimone is not discouraged. When he learns that she is leaving for Rodi to be married, he readies a vessel "con ogni cosa opportuna a battaglia navale," and engages in a royal battle to retrieve her. Boarding her ship, Cimone "fiero come un leone . . . fra' nimici con un coltello in mano si mise, e quasi pecore gli abbattea." But his bloody triumph is no cause for Efigenia to rejoice. She cries as she is handed over to him, and as a dangerous storm breaks out soon after her "liberation," she interprets the hostility of the elements as a divine sign directed against Cimone's love and violence, and she curses his passion: "Forte piangendo . . . nel suo pianto aspramente maladiceva l'amor di Cimone e biasimava il suo ardire, affermando . . . quella tempestosa fortuna esser nata se non perchè gl'iddii non volevano he colui, il quale lei contra li lor piaceri voleva aver per isposa, potesse del suo presuntuoso disiderio godere." Recaptured by her betrothed, Efigenia has to be liberated again, and success is insured by another massacre, performed by Cimone in the home of Efigenia's intended husband, Pasimunda. The killing done, "lasciata piena la casa di sangue, di romore, e di pianto e di tristizia . . . stretti insieme con la lor rapina," Cimone and his companions in slaughter safely reach a waiting ship and "lieti della loro rapina goderono." Cimone celebrates the marriage with Efigenia, who, now passive and her will stunned, is only his "rapina," his loot, a conquest made by violence not by love.

A less overt form of coercion may govern love and marriage, as in the noble and gentle novella of Federigo degli Alberighi (V, 9), a story structured around a distinct pattern of economic and psychic destruction. Love induces the gallant nobleman to give exceptionally extravagant and costly performances which reduce him to such a state of deprivation that, "divenuto allo stremo," he withdraws in poverty and shame to a small country farm. Even the falcon, his only remaining beautiful and precious property, has to be sacrificed. It is only at this point, when he has used violence against his possessions down to his last and most cherished one, and his soul has thereby qualified for future residence in a well-known Dantean wood, that the cold and indifferent heart of Monna Giovanna begins to warm up. She realizes then "la grandezza dello animo suo [Federigo]," acknowledges his "valore," and regards his final act of self-denial, the killing of the falcon, as a "magnificienzia ultima." And it is also at this point that Monna Giovanna decides to remarry and chooses Federigo (who by now has lost not only his property but the power to take initiative and make decisions), once an exuberant, active nobleman, rich in spirit and money, now only the shadow of a man. The motive for the marriage is something other than love; it is the spirit of pity and charity, the impulse to reward one for an exceptional deed, to compensate for loss and for a life of misery. The matter of compensation is aired by Monna Giovanna herself first when she approaches Federigo about the falcon. "Io son venuta a ristorarti [to compensate you] de' danni li quali tu hai già avuti per me." Later again she replies to her brother's objection to marriage that it is indeed her intention to marry a poor man, someone who may need and use her wealth: "Io voglio avanti uomo che abbia bisogno di ricchezza, che ricchezza che abbia bisogno d'uomo."

In the last of the Hundred Tales marriage is made to depend not merely upon economic impoverishment and subsequent rescue from misery through compassion, but also upon the utter destruction of one party's human dignity. Gualtieri and Griselda are a terribly ill-matched couple: he is a feudal lord, "marchese di Saluzzo," but she is a plebeian, "guardiana di pecore," and a social disparity of this kind in the *Decameron* can only be a source of antagonism, not of mutual understanding and happiness. The aristocratic husband inflicts upon Griselda trials and tribulations that would normally shatter any woman's equilibrium: the first and then the second of her two children are taken away from her to be murdered, so she is told; Gualtieri repudiates her and throws her out of his house naked; finally he takes her back as a servant. These physical and mental tortures last thirteen years. Even though

Boccaccio himself styles the treatment as cruel, as "agre e intollerabili . . . esperinze," "rigide e mai più non udite prove," he then writes that the couple settled down to a prolonged happy existence, and some critics think indeed that the image of a perfect bourgeois family finally emerges from the sordid tale of sadistic abuse and abjection. This is all very doubtful, for what really makes the marriage supposedly normal and happy is Griselda's endurance of excruciating mental and physical suffering without a gesture of rebellion. But in the process of the unusual and cruel punishment her dignity, her conviction, her sense of good and evil, and her will, in sum, her whole human personality is violated and destroyed.

Constraints and violations of the lovers' sentimental choice are often imposed by the intervention of their families, and sometimes this causes the couples to undertake perilous adventures. Critics have noted Boccaccio's penchant for venturesome plots and have labeled them gratuitous and unreal. But the harrowing experiences the lovers undergo in the course of their adventures do become determining elements in the development and outcome of a number of love stories, while the original love impulse loses any meaning and function. Martuccio Gomito is poor, and therefore his love for Gostanza cannot be crowned by marriage. Gostanza's father "rispose lui [Martuccio] essere povero e per ciò non volergliele [Gostanza] dare" (V, 2). The initial situation of the novella reflects a well established social convention in the *Decameron,* the interdiction of marriage between rich and poor. Martuccio submits and conforms to the will of Gostanza's family. He renounces marriage temporarily, but he endeavors to modify his social condition in order to overcome the opposition to it. He leaves his native Lipari swearing not to return "se non ricco." To become rich he makes himself the head of a gang of pirates. Martuccio and his henchmen in fact "divenuti ricchissimi," are so carried away by their extraordinary success that "di trasricchire cercavano." At this point, Boccaccio could have sent Martuccio, now wealthy, back home to marry Gostanza. But he cannot do it because Martuccio is now so glaringly implicated in crime that he hardly is a candidate for Christian marriage. Martuccio must first expiate his sins, and thus he is captured by a band of cruel Saracens. As false word of Martuccio's death comes to Gostanza, she resolves to die, and attempts suicide by abandoning herself in a small boat to the violent capriciousness of a stormy sea.

To meet the demands of the family, and indirectly those of society, Martuccio must turn into a robber and Gostanza into a desperate woman driven to suicide. Their love affair must be indelibly marked by the scorching experience of suffering, death and survival; it must turn into a near tragedy. Perils and risks, not love, make the marriage possible and meet the basic requisite, wealth; Martuccio "venne . . . in grande e ricco stato," and can marry Gostanza in Lipari.

The situation into which Pietro Boccamazza and Agnolella Saullo (V, 3) are cast is similar to that prevailing for Martuccio and Gostanza except that, unlike Martuccio, Agnolella, a plebeian, lacks the resources to modify her condition and so qualify for marriage to Pietro, the scion of a Roman aristocratic family. As soon as opposition is raised by Pietro's family, the couple elopes but goes off in the wrong direction. Pietro is captured by a party of Colonna's soldiers who intend to hang him as an Orsini partisan. Miraculously he escapes, wanders a whole day through the wood, crying, exhausted, fearing the wolves and watching terrified as they devour his horse, "forte sbigotti e immaginossi di non dover mai di quella selva poter uscire." Agnolella escapes another armed party, hides in a haystack into which a spear is cast, "e assai vicin fu ad uccidere la nascosa giovane . . . per ciò che la lancia le venne alato alla sinistra poppa." Rejoined, the lovers come to the friendly castle of Lillo di Campo di Fiore where a "bonissima e santa donna" learns all about their vicissitudes, and agrees to arrange for the celebration of their marriage because she believes that the sufferings they incurred in the course of their perilous adventures make marriage an act expressly willed by God: "Credo che egli [marriage] piaccia a Dio, poi che l'uno dalle forche ha campato e l'altro dalla lancia, e amenduni dalle fiere selvatiche; e però facciasi [marriage]."

Not all lovers are enterprising and determined like Martuccio, ready to pay for marriage the high price exacted by society; nor are they all intrepid like Pietro and Agnolella, willing to take high risks to bring about marriage. Some of them are weak and powerless, unable to face perils and the unknown in the name of their love. Then parental and societal intransigency overcome them by ruthlessly destroying their love or their marriage. Girolamo Sighieri, of a very wealthy family, falls in love with Salvestra, the daughter of a tailor (IV, 8); his mother perceiving this and fearing the possibility of a secret marriage, sends Girolamo to Paris to prevent unpleasant surprises. When Girolamo returns to find Salvestra married to someone else and his love dream shattered, he dies a silent, desperate death at the side of his lost beloved. Andreuola, a nobleman's daughter, makes love to Gabriotto, "uomo di bassa condizione" (IV, 6). Realizing the gravity of their moral violation and the hopelessness for a normal matrimonial life, they secretly marry to continue furtively "gli lor congiungimenti." Sidestepping the scrutiny and approval of family and society by a secret marriage may be considered one of the most offensive breaches that can occur in the world of the *Decameron,* where nobody can circumvent conventional standards with impunity. The lovers' dream, "una cosa oscura e terribile," and "una veltra nera . . . affamala e spaventevole" robbing Gabriotto of his life, is a warning about the horrible transgression they are perpetrating and also the revelation of their deep-seated sense of guilt. The breach of convention is not even sufficiently repaired by Gabriotto's sudden demise and the consequent destruction of the marriage. The atonement must go as far as the imperious assertion of social and moral standards through the humiliation of the surviving lover who reneges her sentimental choice and marriage, meekly proclaims herself an obedient daughter, and "cosi piagnendo . . . cadde a'piedi" of her father.

Gostanza and Pietro Boccamazza's families simply express disapproval and opposition and then disappear into the background of the novellas, while the lovers attempt various types of adjustment. But other families are very active in denying the sentimental preferences of their offspring and in taking control of marriage. This parental role produces sometimes unexpected results, such as a mother acting as a procuress ("a guisa d'un ruffiana") between her son and the latter's beloved. This is a "gran dama," wife of one of the king of England's marshals, whose son "si forte . . . s'innamoro" of a beautiful foundling, Giannetta, that he becomes very seriously sick (II, 8). Once the cause of his illness is diagnosed as unrequited love, the concerned mother insinuates first that Giannetta should have a lover, and then proposes the lover should be her son. The noble lady is so sure that Giannetta will not dare refuse to have sexual intercourse with the young knight, that she is incredulous of a negative reply: "Negherestigliele tu?" Since the girl wants to preserve her chastity, the woman finally suggests that her son rape Giannetta: "Metterla con lui in una camera e ch'egli s'ingegnasse d'avere di lei il suo piacere." Marriage is finally approved because all else fails and because the family, "amando meglio il figliuol vivo con moglie non convenevole a lui che morto senza alcuna," has no choice.

The extent that coercion through parental intrusion determines marriage in the *Decameron* is illustrated in V, 5 where Ricciardo Manardi, whether he likes it or not, must marry without delay Lizio da Valbona's daughter when the couple is caught in bed at sunrise in an especially compromising posture. Fortunately for Messer Lizio, his daughter's lover, like himself, belongs to the nobility. The cool, calculating father sees marriage then as an advantageous reparation to be exacted from the improvident seducer. "Noi," he confides to his wife, "non possiamo aver di lui [Ricciardo] altro che buon parentado." Accordingly, while the lovers are still in bed, Lizio imposes marriage on Ricciardo, threatening him with death: "Acciò che tu tolga a te la morte e a me la vergogna, prima che tu ti muova, sposa per tua legittima moglie la Caterina . . . e in questa guisa puoi e la mia pace e la tua salvezza acquistare; e ove tu non vogli cosi fare, raccomanda a Dio l'anima tua." Under the pressing circumstances Ricciardo's choices are obviously very limited, and he meekly submits to a hastily celebrated wedding.

In two stories the family comes one step closer to exercising actual violence over the offspring, and ultimately it imperiously asserts its will upon the lovers. Giannotto, a servant, and Spina, daughter of the noble Currado Malaspina (II, 6), Violante, daughter of the noble Amerigo Abbate, and the ex-slave Pietro (V, 7), are brought near death because their irreconcilable social status at first rules out marriage. Currado Malaspina was "disposto di fargli [lovers] vituperosamente morire," and Amerigo Abbate, "salito in furore, con la spada ignuda in mano sopra la figliuola corse." But when it is eventually recognized that both Giannotto and Pietro are of noble lineage, then marriage is eagerly and brutally imposed upon them. Perceiving that he could "e la sua vergogna e quella della figliuola tor via, dandola per moglie a costui [Giannotto]," Currado Malaspina peremptorily tells him: "Dove ella [Spina] disonestamente amica ti fu ch'ella onestamente tua moglie divenga." And upon discovering Pietro's true identity, Messer Amerigo feels that "si potea molto bene ogni cosa . . . emendare." Pietro's father, the noble Armenian Fineo, firmly reassures Messer Amerigo that his son will not escape the marriage trap: "Io intendo che mio figliuolo la vostra figliuola prenda; e dove egli non volesse, vada innanzi la sentenzia [death sentence] data di lui."

Finally, if a marriage satisfactory to the family is impossible, then parental authority may endanger and even destroy the lives of the lovers. Ghismonda, forbidden by her father, Prince Tancredi, to remarry, takes a lover, Guiscardo, but unlike many couples in the *Decameron* engaged in intimate relations, she is unique in that she experiences no apprehension. She displays no sense of guilt and treasures her lover and her sinful experience immensely, as she will defiantly tell her father. The more intense the passion of the lovers, the harsher will be the reaction of the family. Prince Tancredi orders the plebeian Guiscardo strangled, and Ghismonda boldly defends him and their love before her father. Even the rebellious voice, heard only after paternal authority has already asserted itself, has to be muted, and Boccaccio suppresses it by consigning the unconventional lady to a romantic death and a posthumous apotheosis. If it is true that for Boccaccio carnal love is "blessed" only in matrimony, then the substitution effected by Ghismonda, illicit, pleasurable love for the sanctity of marital communion, is the gravest moral infraction present in the Hundred Tales. With the tale of Ghismonda, the exercise of force over the sentimental choice of the individual reaches its ghastly height.

Forced conformity to conventional social standards, submission to parental will and authority, and the impersonal effects of adventures and ordeals not only combine to rob lovers of their sentimental freedom, but no less importantly, undermine the stability of marriage and set a crippling block to the happiness of husbands and wives. Boccaccio's narrative usually abandons the lovers at the time of their marriage, and consigns them to an unverifiable blissful existence through a fable-like epilogue. Therefore the reader will never know the outcome of those marriages created under strained and unnatural circumstances. But those couples who live united by the holy bond of marriage reveal a good deal about the quality of matrimonial life in the Hundred Tales.

A good many marriages that are not terminated are nevertheless so spectacularly ridden by dissensions and infidelities that the reader's faith in marriage Boccaccio style is likely to be shaken rather than fortified, making it hard to share the view of some critics that the *Decameron* bears witness to Boccaccio's "faith in marriage" because there are only a few broken matrimonies in his work. What is the meaning of this extraordinary frequency of adultery in the *Decameron*? It is not a deliberate repudiation of marriage as an institution, or wanton glorification of fornication. Adultery is the manifestation of sentimental freedom, and implicitly the repudiation of the coercion that went into marriage; it is the outlet for those elementary but powerful individual emotional forces that, Boccaccio the humanist knows well, cannot be eradicated from human nature. Those feelings may be checked but cannot be eliminated; sometime, somehow, they will assert themselves, and in the *Decameron* they prevail through adultery.

Adultery in the masterpiece plays a vital role, for it evokes none of the reprobation which fornication among unmarried lovers does, nor is it treated comically by Boccaccio, as [Thomas Greene] would have it. It often helps to solve some of the problems of the protagonists' existence, such as freeing wives from unbearable husbands. Adultery is never the result of coercion, is not a subterfuge or an escapade, nor is it represented as an evil act; on the contrary, it is quite often an eminently successful and fulfilling experience. No lover in the *Decameron* is punished because of a commission of adultery, but most fornicators enjoy indefinitely their extra-marital bliss, even when their affairs are uncovered. The representation of adultery is in fact so forceful and impressive that it has led one critic [Erich Auerbach] to build a case for a "doctrine of free love" upon a relationship (Frate Alberto and Madonna Lisetta, IV, 2), which, given the disreputable character of the protagonists, can hardly be made to support the weight of any "doctrine," let alone one of free love. In sum, adultery in the *Decameron* exhibits those characteristics one would look for in marriage, but in vain: spontaneity, free play of wills and emotions, and freedom from social and moral constraints. From a realistic point of view, rather than from that of literary conventions, the irresistible attraction the wife of Guglielmo Rossiglione experiences for Guiglielmo Guardastagno, and their love affair, can only be explained by a deficient marriage. If the lady were happily married to the noble Rossiglione, her adultery would not make any sense. There must also have been something wrong with the couple represented in IV, 2, a busy, indifferent merchant and Madonna Lisetta, a woman whose concern with her own beauty is evidently affecting her mental balance. And though one of the lovers is "uomo di scelerata vita e di corrotta," and the other "sentia dello scemo," there is a concrete, albeit negative, element of self determination that has universal significance that lends a degree of plausibility to Madonna Lisetta's adultery, female vanity. Asked by the lecherous friar about her love life, she extols her beauty thus: "Paionvi le mie bellezze fatte come quelle di queste altre? . . . Ma non sono le mie bellezze da lasciare amare ne da tale ne da quale. Quante ce ne vedete voi, le cui bellezze sien fatte come le mie, che sarei bella nel Paradiso." Failures in married life provide more specific reasons for adultery in the *Decameron.* Capellanus theorized that husbands' jealousy is unnatural, a distinct peril to married life, and that, therefore, it is "condemned throughout the world." Jealousy originates from the thought that one's wife is capable of some shameful act, and this thought alone irremediably undermines marriage. In the wake of this opinion Boccaccio depicts husbands' jealousy (and in the *Decameron* those affected by jealousy are exclusively husbands), as strongly unsettling the existence of the wives concerned, as a problem real and serious enough to amply justify their infidelity. Thus a rich peasant, "fuori d'ogni misura geloso," forces his wife into the arms of her confessor, for only through relations with another man can she save herself from a life of utter misery. "Cosi matto . . . geloso di me . . . altro che in tribulazione e in mala ventura con lui viver non posso," she acknowledges in desperation (III, 8). The jealousy of

Monna Ghita's husband, a "villan matto," is so offensive to her that she "prese sdegno," and punishes him by committing adultery (VII, 4). And a very rich businessman, without any cause "oltre misura geloso" of his wife, keeps her like a prisoner, treating her like those "che a capital pena son dannati"; because "la sua vita era pessima," she seeks and finds relief in a young and understanding lover (VII, 5).

Boccaccio did not have to resort to esoteric theories to visualize sexual failure (on husbands' part) as a major disruptive element of marriage. Monna Isabetta, young, attractive and vigorous, finds herself married to a man endowed with qualities exactly opposite to her own. And "per la santità del marito, e forse per la vecchiezza, faceva molto spesso troppo più lunghe diete che voluto non avrebbe." Thus, she becomes an adulteress, and "con discrezione lungamente" enjoys her lover (III, 4). Because Mazzeo della Montagna's wife "il più del tempo stava infreddata, si come colei che nel letto era mal . . . tenuta coperta . . . viveva pessimamente contenta," chooses a lover, and their love and pleasure continue "sempre . . . di bene in meglio" (IV, 10). Monna Teresa, "savia e avveduta molto," betrays the husband negligent of his marital duties (VII, 1), and in VII 6, "non soddisfacendo a Madonna Isabella molto il suo marito," she has an affair with Leonetto.

Impotence and homosexuality are obvious and compelling reasons for adultery. The resentment of a "bella e fresca" wife who unknowingly marries a pederast, Pietro di Vinciolo, is the perfect expression of a marriage undermined at the very beginning by a choice that neither the man nor the woman had possibly made: "Io ero femmina, perchè per moglie mi prendeva se le femmine contro all'animo gli erano? Questo non e da sofferire. . . . Se io aspetterò diletto o piacere di costui, io potrò per avventura invano aspettando invecchiare; e quando io sarò vecchia, . . . indarno mi dorrò d'avere la mia giovinezza perduta" (V, 10). Her husband's irrational choice, the realization that she has been cheated, her awareness of the ineluctable passage of time that deprives her of the joy of sex, her rage and desperation, admirably support her decision to betray Pietro, making adultery a legitimate, "moral" act. A vibrant apology of adultery in the name of sexual conventions comes from the young and attractive wife of the Pisan judge Ricciardo da Chinzica. Bartolomea's "grave malinconia" arising from forced sexual abstinence is suddenly lifted by a virile corsair with whom she becomes indissolubly bound. Urged by her husband to abandon the pirate and return to Pisa to live as an honored wife, she defends and praises her kidnapper as "pietoso ragguardatore della sua giovinezza," condemns the society that forced her to marry a decrepit man, and repudiates her married life as immoral. The adulteress does not hesitate to spurn moral and social conventions in the name of her own belief, inclination and sexual life. Her lover, she relates with exhilaration, "tutta la notte mi tiene in braccio e strignemi e mordemi, e come egli mi conci, Dio ve 'l dica per me" (II, 10). Adultery to meet the pressing demands of youth is also central to VII, 9 (Lidia and Pirro). A considerable part of the narration is devoted to the details of the plans and efforts directed to bringing about the illicit

union. Adultery is the supreme goal of a young girl evidently sacrificed by the family to money and social status. Its achievement constitutes an engaging and sometimes strenuous experience, especially for Lidia, who employs the services and the skillful oratory of a go-between, and must provide her prospective lover with some unique proofs of the sincerity of her passion, such as yanking one of her husband's good teeth. In another instance unsatisfactory sex life leads to adultery, and simultaneously to its legal sanction: Madonna Filippa's defense of her exuberant sexuality causes a statute advocating death for adulteresses to be abrogated in Prato (VI, 7).

Disparity in social status, deliberately ignored by the family when it decides upon the marriage of the offspring, may create an intolerable situation for husband and wife. A "gentil donna . . . d'alto lignaggio" obviously forced by the family to marry for money to a very wealthy artisan, "estimava niuno uomo di bassa condizione . . . esser di gentil donna degno." Extremely unhappy, and "non potendo lo sdegno dell'animo porre in terra," she decides to grant her husband as little sexual favor as possible, "ma di volere a soddisfazione di se medesima trovare alcuno, il quale più di ciò che il lanaiuolo le paresse che fosse degno." And through an ingenious plan and perseverance of efforts she succeeds in establishing an adulterous relationship with a "valoroso uomo" (III, 3). Even more enterprising and vindictive is the wife of Arriguccio Berlinghieri, a very rich merchant who thought, wrongly, "di voler ingentilire per moglie." Caught in flagrant adultery, she manages to convince her mother and brothers that Arriguccio was mistaken in accusing her of infidelity. "Egli non ne fu degno d'avere una figliuola fatta come se' tu," the mother-in-law berates Arriguccio, "mercantuzzo di feccia d'asino . . . che, dove tu se' la miglior figliuola di Firenze e la più onesta, egli non s'è vergognato di mezzanotte di dir che tu sii puttana" (VII, 8). A whole family indirectly endorses the adultery of one of its members.

Whereas premarital love in the *Decameron* rarely bears traces of development, or rational and passional conflicts, and is poorly individualized, among adulterous lovers love appears as a real force with a visible origin and development, and whereas premarital love exists in a vacuum, adultery oftentimes finds its origins and justification in a genuine sentimental texture. It is true that Ricciardo Minutolo succeeds in making love to Catella (III, 6) by means of deception, but his motives and intentions are more serious than his trick would let one suppose, and are different from those of a casual seducer. Desperate, and "da amore . . . non potendo disciogliersi," he plans and executes the ruse. There was no choice, for, as the frustrated lover says, "quello che io semplicemente amando non potei, Amor con inganno m'ha insegnato avere." And it is precisely the tension of love, Ricciardo's "soverchio amore," that finally overcomes Catella's reluctance and conquers her: Catella, "voltata la sua durezza in dolce amore verso Ricciardo, tenerissimamente . . . l'amò, e . . . goderono del loro amore."

It is Zima's lengthy and elaborate declaration subtly analyzing the causes and effects of love, and concluding with images and language of distinctly "stilnovista" tenor that induces Francesco Vergellesi's wife to commit adultery. Because "le affettuose parole dette dal ferventissimo amante, . . . [the lady] cominciò a sentire ciò che prima mai non aveva sentito, cioè che amor si fosse" (III, 5). The use of traditional elevated modes of expression in connection with matrimonial infidelity, a use peculiar to Boccaccio's prose, lends adultery considerable moral distinction. It occurs in an even more significant manner in VII, 7, where Madonna Beatrice's adultery with Lodovico (who is drawn by the lady's beauty to Bologna from Paris to live as a servant in her home) is prepared and preceded by a detailed representation of the stages of the lover's passion, again after dantesque and stilnovistic pattern ("cominzo," "fiore," "sospirare," "pietà," "arra," "effetto"), and a formal declaration of love. Madonna Beatrice is apparently so impressed by Lodovico's tactful and elaborate advances that she instantly surrenders. "Tu m' hai fatta," she replies, "come le tue parole durate sono, troppo più tua divenir che io non son mia. Io guidico che tu ottimamente abbi il mio amor guadagnato, e per ciò io il ti dono." The two stories exhibit features absent in the premarital love relationships, the progression of passion and the conquest of the lady by love.

Adultery is an erotic exploit that meaningfully engages the sentimental energies of the lovers in a climate of moral and social freedom, and all stigma must be lifted from it. Boccaccio does this explicitly in III, 7, where Monna Ermellina suddenly and inexplicably cuts off her adulterous relationship with Tedaldo degli Elisei throwing him into a "fiera malinconia e spiacevole" that leads him "a doversi dileguar del mondo." Having returned to Florence in disguise and learning directly from his ex-lover that the interruption of their affair was caused by a monk's threats of eternal punishment, he delivers a vehement, bitter diatribe against certain church commandments. The denunciation that occupies several pages of the novella is interspersed with a thorough-going defense and justification of their adultery based on the idea that its interruption was sinful, that it was indeed "ruberia e sconvenevole cosa." "L'usare la dimestichezza d'uno uomo una donna è peccato naturale: il rubarlo o l'ucciderlo o il discacciarlo da malvagità di mente procede," insists the disguised Tedaldo. He adds that the suspension of the love affair was a sin and that Ermellina is paying for it now through the imprisonment of her husband unjustly accused of a serious crime. When Tedaldo appears in his true identity shortly after the stern and impassioned discourse, Monna Ermellina throws herself into his arms, "e andatisene insieme a letto, di buon volere fecero graziosa e lieta pace, l'un dell'altro prendendo dilettosa gioia." It is finally through Tingoccio, less ponderously and more humorously than through Tedaldo, that Boccaccio endeavors to extricate adultery from the tentacles of conventional morality, with the authority of a verdict issued from the other world. An impenitent and reckless adulterer ("io mi giaceva con una mia comare, e giacquivi tanto che io me ne scorticai") after a premature death appears to his friend Meuccio. The surviving friend anxiously inquires about the punishment for his adultery with Monna Mita, and Tinguccio replies that he was indeed trembling with fear while waiting for the sentence. But, he continues, the infernal custodian having heard of Tinguccio's "gran peccato" blurted out: "Va

sciocco, non dubitare, che di quà non si tiene ragione alcuna delle comari!" (VII, 10).

In the **Decameron** the existence of both lovers made prisoners of social conventions and deprived of their sentimental choice and, at the same time, numerous married couples engaged freely and spontaneously in adultery is no mere chance. And if today critics write of common "toleration" and of "idealization" of adultery in the Middle Ages, one can understand why: extra-marital relationships were the manifestation of suppressed but inextinguishable inner forces. From this point of view, adultery may be said to embody a doctrine of free love, not, however, in the sense of a thing "opposed to medieval-Christian ethics," but as an expression of individual sentimental freedom. (pp. 287-301)

Alfredo Bonadeo, "Marriage and Adultery in the 'Decameron'," in Philological Quarterly, *Vol. 60, No. 3, Summer, 1981, pp. 287-303.*

Boccaccio, on the plague:

It is a remarkable story that I have to relate. And were it not for the fact that I am one of many people who saw it with their own eyes, I would scarcely dare to believe it, let alone commit it to paper, even though I had heard it from a person whose word I could trust. The plague I have been describing was of so contagious a nature that very often it visibly did more than simply pass from one person to another. In other words, whenever an animal other than a human being touched anything belonging to a person who had been stricken or exterminated by the disease, it not only caught the sickness, but died from it almost at once. To all of this, as I have just said, my own eyes bore witness on more than one occasion. One day, for instance, the rags of a pauper who had died from the disease were thrown into the street, where they attracted the attention of two pigs. In their wonted fashion, the pigs first of all gave the rags a thorough mauling with their snouts after which they took them between their teeth and shook them against their cheeks. And within a short time they began to writhe as though they had been poisoned, then they both dropped dead to the ground, spreadeagled upon the rags that had brought about their undoing.

Giovanni Boccaccio, in his introduction to the First Day in the Decameron, *translated by G. H. McWilliam, Penguin, 1972.*

Teodolinda Barolini   (essay date 1983)

[*In the essay below, Barolini surveys the books of the* Decameron, *touching on Boccaccio's themes of loss, moral degeneracy, and the necessity of compassion.*]

From its first clause, indeed from its first word, the **Decameron** signals its nontranscendence: "Umana cosa è aver compassione degli afflitti", begins the author, locating us in a rigorously secular context and defining its parameters. At this point, *compassione degli afflitti* belongs to an amorous register, referring to Boccaccio's past affliction as a lover for whom his friends felt pity; thus, he claims that he is writing the **Decameron** to repay their kindness, since "la gratitudine, secondo che io credo, trall'altre virtù è sommamente da commendare" (Proemio, 7). Here again, the Proem continues to insist on a human set of values, for gratitude is technically not a virtue at all, but a social grace, a virtue only in that it makes life more livable. And, because he wants to make their lives more livable, Boccaccio writes for the ladies, shattering their enforced contemplation with *novelle,* news of life, life-surrogates.

Beginning as it does with the author's gratitude for the generosity of his friends, which encourages him in turn to show generosity to the ladies, the **Decameron** comes full circle by ending with the generosity—*liberalità*—of the characters of Day X. Generosity, like gratitude, is a social virtue, one which palliates and civilizes the experience of living, and in fact the stories of the last Day are the final step in a process which has made the *brigata* fit to re-enter society, to embark once more on the business of life. Generosity is generated by compassion; this *compassione,* which motivates the author in his Proem at one end of the book and the characters of Day X at the other, is not only the social glue which holds together the fabric of human society, which literally humanizes that society, but is also the textual glue linking the several levels of the **Decameron.** The transition from the courtly atmosphere of the Proem to the onslaught of the great plague is mediated by compassion, either present (in the Proem) or absent (in the Florentine society afflicted by the plague as described in the Introduction to Day I), but always the irreducible standard by which human affairs are measured.

The Introduction to the First Day is the catalyst of the rest of the **Decameron** in that it defines the text's negative pole, the level of loss from which the *brigata* must recover. The reduction of Florentine society to grade zero is accomplished rhetorically through the Introduction's portrayal of two discrete stages of loss which together bring about total collapse; the narrator concentrates first on the loss of *ingegno* and secondly on the loss of *compassione.* The first part of the plague narrative emphasizes intellectual failure: "in quella [la peste] non valendo alcuno senno nè umano provedimento" (I, Intro.). The qualification of "provedimento" with the adjective "umano" underscores the fact that the intellect is, with compassion, the essential ingredient of human society; but here, as society crumbles, the intellect is powerless, human ingenuity is unavailing. Failure in one quintessentially human sphere leads, predictably, to failure in the other; thus the narrator passes in linear fashion from depicting the loss of *ingegno* to depicting the loss of *compassione;* since *compassione* is the "umana cosa" par excellence, its disappearance signals the final breakdown. The process of decay, once initiated, is as inevitable as the disease itself, progressing from the incapacitation of the intellect to the denial of all ethical commitment; this chain effect is indicated by the narrative sequence, which moves from the symptoms of the plague, the horrid *gavoccioli* which the doctors are unable to treat (Boccaccio stresses the "ignoranza de' medicanti," to its powers of contamination. The fact that the disease is contagious leads to a widespread callousness toward the suf-

ferings of others, a lack of compassion marked in narrative terms by the use of the adj. *crudele:* "e tutti quasi a un fine tiravano assai crudele, ciò era di schifare e di fuggire gl'infermi e le lor cose."

Crudele, the word contrasted with *compassione* throughout the plague description, signifies for Boccaccio a destructive autonomy, an inhuman desire to preserve the self at all costs; by abandoning the sick, many believe that they will save themselves: "e così faccendo, si credeva ciascuno a se medesimo salute acquistare." The author outlines four types of popular reaction to the plague: There are the introverted extremists, who lock themselves in their houses; the extroverted extremists, who pursue a policy of "eat, drink, and be merry"; the moderates, who do not greatly alter their behavior; finally, the group Boccaccio labels, significantly, "di più crudel sentimento." These are the ones who, caring for nothing but themselves, abandon "la propia città, le proprie case, i lor luoghi e i lor parenti e le lor cose," the ones by whom the most sacrosanct bonds of human life (stressed by the repetition of the possessive adjective) are broken: "l'un fratello l'altro abbandonava e il zio il nepote e la sorella il fratello e spesse volte la donna il suo marito; e, che maggior cosa è e quasi non credibile, li padri e le madri i figliuoli, quasi loro non fossero, di visitare e di servire schifavano." The dissolution of the parental bond is the last step in the society's achievement of a non-human, negative, status; the city's descent into noncivility is complete.

It is in the wake of this analysis of its citizens' behavior that Boccaccio outlines the city's moral degeneracy: the women who allow themselves to be tended by male servants, the forming of a class of profiteers who for a sum will take bodies to burial, and so forth. Running throughout is the motif of indifference to others, the lack of compassion, a moral flaw with relentlessly practical consequences; as the narrator emphasizes, many were left to die unaided because they had previously set just this example: "avendo essi stessi, quando sani erano, essemplo dato a coloro che sani rimanevano, quasi abbandonati per tutto languieno." Their previous cruel behavior thus guarantees not their preservation but their ruin, since there is no one who will care for them when they in turn fall victims to the scourge. The moral code implicit in this passage is practical, civic, social; far from promising rewards to the servants who tend the sick for a fee, the author does not hide the fact that such actions often bring about their deaths: "sé molte volte col guadagno perdeano." Compassion is not so much a good as it is a necessity, a *sine qua non* of our identities, as stated in the text's opening sentence and repeatedly underscored by the narrator's animal analogies, his insistence that bestiality is the inevitable outcome of indifference: "non come uomini ma quasi come bestie morieno." Ultimately, therefore, compassion is a *sine qua non* for human survival.

The Introduction to Day I is divisible into two distinct parts roughly equal in length: The first recounts the events surrounding the plague's arrival in Florence, detailing the loss of *ingegno* and *compassione;* the second recounts the gathering of a group of young people in Santa Maria Novella and their decision to leave Florence for their salvation. If the purpose of the first part is, in narrative terms, to create a *tabula rasa* on which the *brigata* and the text can build (in fact, before introducing the ladies, the narrator claims that the city is "quasi vota," the second part initiates the process of construction. The change in tone is signaled by Pampinea's speech on their inalienable right to life; the change in atmosphere is palpable as the moral turpitude of the pestilential city gives way to the "leggiadra onestà" of the *brigata*. We note, however, that the *brigata*'s behavior is rigidly premised on what came before; they must establish their difference precisely with respect to the prevailing norm. Therefore Pampinea stresses not only their right to survival, but also the fact that, in leaving the city, they will be abandoning no one, since all their kin is dead. It is paramount for Boccaccio to establish that the *onesta brigata* does not behave like any of the groups described in the first part of the Introduction; although their program shares features with some—like the introverts, they isolate themselves and refuse to entertain news from the outside; like the cruel ones, they leave the city—the crucial difference is that they do these things only now, when there is nothing else left to do. As Pampinea declares: "noi non abbandoniam persona, anzi ne possiamo con verità dire molto più tosto abbandonate."

The rest of the **Decameron** constitutes the gradual recreation, through recreation, of the *brigata*, whose chief characters represent not only facets of the author, but also basic aspects of human nature. Pampinea, whose name means 'vigorous', is the force of order; the instigator of their flight from the city, she takes immediate steps to organize their idyll, remarking that "le cose che sono senza modo non possono lungamente durare." She proposes a form of government, with rotating rulers, to regulate their otherwise potentially anarchic existences, and assigns specific tasks to the servants who have accompanied them. Her last words to these, her most significant commandment, is that, whatever they see or hear, they are to bring no unhappy news from the outside world: "niuna novella altra che lieta ci rechi di fuori." Again, there is a deliberate echo of the introverts' program for survival, since they too refused all news of death or sickness, closing themselves inside "senza lasciarsi parlare a alcuno o volere *di fuori*, di morte o d'infermi, *alcuna novella* sentire" (italics mine here and later). The use in both instances of *novella* in the sense of 'news', along with the fact that the isolationists are the only previous group to be called a "brigata" by the author, underscores their role as precursors of the *onesta brigata*. In demanding complete protection from external events, Pampinea is acceding to Dioneo, who had stipulated, as the necessary condition determining his stay with the others, that there be a total severance of their ties to the city. Establishing two distinct spheres of existence, according to the binary opposition "in" vs. "out", he states that he has left his cares in the city, "li miei [pensieri] lasciai to *dentro* dalla porta della città allora che io con voi poco fa me ne usci' *fuori*," and that they must either join with him in amusement, laughter, and singing, or give him leave to return to the "città tribolata." We know Dioneo's hallmarks: his etymological sensuality (his name derives from Dione, Venus' mother); his defense of women's rights (a defense which goes beyond feminism in the narrow sense if we consider that, in the Proem, the women

seem tantamount to all those deprived of the opportunity to live their lives); his privileged status as the storyteller who always has the last word. Dioneo and Pampinea are the *brigata*'s ideologues: While she is in charge of the details of their daily existence, he is concerned with outlining the essential prerequisites for new life. Thus, it is he who delivers the ultimatum insisting on their quarantine from unhappiness and, essentially, from reality.

Although Pampinea, ruler of the First Day, leaves the subject of the Day nominally open, critics have long noted that the stories of Day I are characterized by the triumph of the intellect, which succeeds through a brilliant use of language in reversing a given situation, sometimes effecting a return to the status quo, otherwise simply improving conditions for the story's protagonist: The Marchesana di Monferrato rids herself of the King of France's dangerous importunities by staging a clever joke; the courtier Bergamino embarrasses Cangrande della Scala into showing his accustomed generosity (I 7); the rebuke by a lady from Gascony transforms the King of Cyprus from a weak man into a brave one who will redress her wrongs (I 9). Day II, dealing as it does with lucky resolutions to unlucky situations, introduces the problematic of Fortune into the **Decameron;** here Fortune has the upper hand. Nonetheless, most of the happy endings of Day II are achieved by dint of some coöperation on the part of the protagonist's intellect: In his final predicament, it occurs to Andreuccio to grab the priest by the leg (II 5); even Alatiel, the **Decameron**'s most buffetted heroine, has the wit required to convince her father that she has been in a nunnery, rather than the consort of eight different men (II 7). Day III alters the balance by adding our efforts, "industria", to the equation. Here man is no longer Fortune's plaything, but is able to overcome through use of intelligence: Ricciardo wins Catella by deceiving her, commenting in words that aptly represent Day III, "quello che io semplicemente amando aver non potei, Amor con inganno m'ha insegnato avere" (III 6,); in the same way Giletta, with a display of deceptive wit surely intended to contrast with Griselda's brute patience, wins back her reluctant husband (III 9).

As Days I-III effect the *brigata*'s recovery of *ingegno*, so the tragic love of Day IV, offset by the happy love of Day V, effects their recovery of *compassione*. Before beginning the first *novella* of Day IV, the tale of Tancredi and Ghismunda, Fiammetta comments on the nature of the king's assignment; she considers Filostrato's topic particularly cruel, "Fiera materia di ragionare n'ha oggi il nostro re data", because they have come here to be cheered, "per rallegrarci venuti siamo", and instead are forced to recount the sorrows of others: "ci convenga raccontar l'altrui lagrime, le quali dir non si possono che chi le dice e chi l'ode non abbia *compassione*" (IV 1). It is thus established from the outset of Day IV that the effect of the Day's stories is to elicit the compassion of the storytellers, a notion stressed throughout the Day in the narrator's accounts of the *brigata*'s reactions: Filomena is "tutta piena di compassione del misero Gerbino e della sua donna" (IV 5); Neifile concludes her story of Girolamo and Salvestra's thwarted love "non senza aver gran compassion messa in tutte le sue compagne" (IV 9); Filostrato follows Neifile by assuring his audience that in their reaction to his bloody tale "vi converrà non meno di compassione avere che alla passata" (IV 9). Only Pampinea refuses to obey Filostrato, insisting instead on the necessity of counteracting *compassione* with *ricreazione*. Thus, her story of Frate Alberto complies with the letter of Filostrato's order, but not with the spirit, for although the *novella*'s protagonist comes to a miserable end, the story itself is amusing. Her inclination is not to please the king but to restore her companions from the sorrow aroused in them by the previous *novella*; she is "disposta a dovere alquanto recrear loro" (IV 2). Precisely because she finds them "pieni di compassione per la morte di Ghismunda", she hopes that her story will have the effect of enlivening them: "forse con risa e con piacer rilevare" (IV 2).

Telling the tragic tales of Day IV has moved the *brigata* to pity; as Filostrato remarks (with respect to himself, but the comment seems applicable to all), the effect of the stories is to allow the dew of compassion to put out the fire within (he praises Fiammetta's *novella,* and exhorts Pampinea to tell a similar one, because "senza dubbio alcuna rugiada cadere sopra il mio fuoco comincerò a sentire" [IV 2]). We may assume that a story that so moves Filostrato will have an even greater impact on his comrades, since Filostrato is more immune to compassion than the others, assuming a "rigido viso" at the end of the first *novella* while the ladies weep (IV 2), and showing "nulla compassion" to Andreuola (IV 7). If the stories of Day IV are intended to elicit compassion and thereby, as Fiammetta remarks, to temper the *brigata*'s gaiety ("Forse per temperare alquanto la letizia avuta li giorni passati l'ha fatto" [IV 1]), Pampinea, as chief executrix of that gaiety, is concerned lest the cathartic effect of Day IV be too pronounced. The words she uses to counteract Filostrato— *recreare, rilevare*— are references to the *brigata*'s primary mission. Dioneo's story, IV 10, picks up on Pampinea's concern and marks the shift from a "così dolorosa materia" to one which is "alquanto più lieta e migliore" (IV 10). The happier *materia* introduced by Dioneo, the only other member of the *brigata* who, like Pampinea, has the stature and authority to counter Filostrato, will be developed on the following Day, which, as the mirror image of Day IV, rewards lovers with a happy ending. While Day IV elicits compassion from the members of the *brigata,* Day V takes compassion on them; this transition is underlined by the narrator himself, who remarks that, whereas the first stories of Day IV had saddened the ladies, Dioneo's has made them laugh, and restored their spirits: "questa ultima di Dioneo le fece ben tanto ridere . . .che esse si poterono della *compassione* avuta dell'altre *ristorare*" (IV, Concl.). The role of the tragic tales as generators of compassion is thus underscored at the Day's end.

The recovery of *compassione* is a necessary step in the *brigata*'s journey back to their starting-point, but it is also a step which must be superseded, placed into proper perspective with respect to their ultimate goal as stated by the author above: *ristorare*/restoration. Renewed in the basic human faculties of *ingegno* and *compassione*, they must now be prepared more specifically for the return to Florence and reality. Day VI marks the new beginning, and is not coincidentally therefore likened by the author to

Day I. Similarities between the two Days have been noted by critics, who have pointed to thematic parallels: Day VI, like Day I, stresses reversal through repartee. A marker of the link existing between the two Days is Filomena's verbatim repetition, in the first story of Day VI, of Pampinea's words from the last story of Day I; both ladies agree that brief witticisms, "leggiadri motti", are to all pleasant discourse "come ne' lucidi sereni sono le stelle ornamento del cielo e nella primavera i fiori ne' verdi prati" (I, 10 and VI 1). Nor can this repetition be considered a simple authorial lapse, since Filomena explicitly calls attention to the fact that she is treading on familiar textual territory: "Ma per ciò che già sopra questa materia assai da Pampinea fu detto, più oltre non intendo di dirne" (VI 1). Filomena's prologue therefore constitutes a deliberate link between I 10 and VI 1, implying that Day VI picks up where Day I leaves off. Even more important is the Introduction to Day VI, which exactly parallels in its function its counterpart in Day I; as the Introduction to the First Day (which is not, technically, a general Introduction, but the preface to a particular Day) starts the *brigata* moving away from Florence, so the Introduction to the Sixth Day starts them moving back again. The preface to Day VI is therefore marked by an event which is, as the narrator takes care to point out, unique in the **Decameron**'s frame: "avvenne cosa che ancora adivenuta non v'era" (VI, Intro.). He is referring to the quarrel among the servants, an outbreak which erupts into the staid world of the frame characters with profound consequences. Licisca, a maid, maintains that women do not go to their wedding-beds virgins; Dioneo not only supports her contention but will later decide to use her observation in formulating the topic of his Day, thus allowing the world of the servants to have direct repercussions on that of their masters.

If Licisca operates as a kind of reality principle, whose function it is to introduce aperture where there was closure, reversing the *brigata*'s isolationism and turning them back toward Florence, her effect should be felt at once, even before her argument inspires the theme for the following Day. And, indeed, there are immediate indications of a significant shift. Whereas the stories of the previous five Days have ranged geographically from Babylon and Alexandria to London and Paris, those of Day VI are situated in Tuscany, for the most part in Florence. The only *novelle* not explicitly located in or around the Tuscan capital are Story 7, which takes place in Prato; Story 8, whose location is unspecified; and—in the ultimate Boccaccesque figure for homecoming—Story 10, which is located in Certaldo. But the most dramatic indication of a change is in VI 3, where Dioneo's rule is broken, and the plague is allowed to enter the world of the stories for the first time in the **Decameron.** In presenting the protagonist of her story, Lauretta inserts a subordinate clause of great importance, specifiying that she was a young woman killed by the plague, "la quale questa pistolenzia presente ci ha tolta" (VI 3). Because they are set in Florence, the stories of Day VI involve characters whose lives and histories are known to the *brigata,* with the result that the plague—and reality—must finally intrude. Nor is this insertion of an alien element into the narrative accomplished casually; the deliberateness of Boccaccio's reference to the "pistolenzia presente" in the third *novella* is evidenced by the Conclusion to this Day, where Dioneo himself, the original drafter of their isolationism, invokes the "perversità di questa stagione" (VI, Concl.) as an inducement to the ladies to comply with his risqué theme for Day VII.

Ready now for immersion into life at its most real, a vicarious dip into the complete amorality of existence, the *brigata* tells the coarse and at times brutal stories of Days VII, VIII, and IX. Day VII is ruled by Dioneo, who as early as the Conclusion to Day V had foreshadowed the change in tone of the second half of the *Decameron,* attempting to sing bawdy popular songs instead of the courtly material favored by the ladies; the Day's theme is provided by Licisca, who has helped to dispel the courtly atmosphere further by insisting that "messer Mazza" entered "Monte Nero" not "per forza e con ispargimento di sangue", but "paceficamente e con gran piacer di quei d'entro" (VI, Intro.). Not surprisingly, therefore, on this Day the floodgates of sensuality are opened. One could trace a crescendo in sexual explicitness, beginning with Peronella in VII 2, continuing through the scholar's reaction to the widow's nudity (VIII 7), and culminating in Day IX's final *novella,* in which Father Gianni attempts to transform his neighbor's wife into a mare. Although (as Dioneo had foreseen while defending his topic) the *brigata*'s own behavior remains circumspect, a gradual relaxation overcomes them during these Days; the stories, not for nothing the *Decameron*'s most concentrated tribute to the *fabliaux,* mark the high point of the *brigata*'s verbal indecency. Another factor stressing the turn toward reality is the continued insistence on Florence; in the opening story of Day VII, Santa Maria Novella is mentioned for the first time since the *brigata* met there in the Introduction to Day I. The church, originally the scene of their departure, thereafter appears only in the half of the *Decameron* devoted to their return: After serving as headquarters for the cuckolded laud-singer Gianni Lotteringhi (VII 1), it is mentioned twice as a rendezvous in the Rabelaisian course of Maestro Simone's induction into Florentine life (VIII 9). Finally, Santa Maria Novella figures in the final sentence of the Conclusion to the last Day, to mark the end of the cycle which was initiated within it:

> E come il nuovo giorno apparve, levati, avendo già il siniscalco via ogni lor cosa mandata, dietro alla guida del discreto re *verso Firenze si ritornarono;* e i tre giovani, lasciate le sette donne *in Santa Maria Novella, donde con loro partiti s'erano,* da esse accommiatatosi, a'loro altri piaceri attesero, e esse, quando tempo lor parve, se ne tornarono alle lor case. (X, Concl.)

Another marker of the turn toward reality / Florentinity is the emergence of a local folk hero, Calandrino, and of a group of characters, all Florentines, who recur from story to story. Kinship and friendship bonds begin to dominate the *novelle:* Nello, who in IX 3 is presented as a friend of Bruno and Buffalmacco, in IX 5 turns out to be related to Calandrino's wife, Tessa. The incidence of characters who appear in more than one story is high: besides Bruno, Buffalmacco, Calandrino, and Tessa, there are also Nello, Maestro Simone, and Maso del Saggio, who like Calandrino becomes the center of his own cycle of *novelle.*

These developments are reflected in an overt intertextuality; the *brigata* becomes extremely concerned with referring one story to another, making links between the *novelle,* and between characters in the *novelle,* explicit. One story thus leads to another, as Filomena explains: "come Filostrato fu dal nome di Maso tirato a dover dire la novella la quale da lui udita avete, così né più né men son tirata io da quello di Calandrino e de'compagni suoi a dirne un'altra di loro" (VIII 6). Because of their common urban setting, these *novelle* are particularly interchangeable: Filostrato announces, in the beginning of VIII 5, that he is discarding the story he had intended to tell in order to tell one about Maso del Saggio, prompted by Elissa's previous tale about Maso (VIII 3); when Filostrato later decides, on Day IX, to return to the *novella* he had discarded on Day VIII, it turns out to be a Calandrino story (IX 3). Not only are the members of the *brigata* preoccupied with establishing relations between their stories, but the *novelle* themselves develop a memory, articulated by the characters within them: In the second Calandrino story, VIII 6, Bruno and Buffalmacco bludgeon their friend into surrendering his capons, recalling that he had already fooled them once, on the occasion of their search for the heliotrope in the first Calandrino story, VIII 3; in IX 5 Nello stirs up Tessa against her husband by reminding her too of the events recounted in VIII 3, which for her took the form of an undeserved beating.

All of these narrative devices underscore the basic fact that the *brigata* is now, in narrative terms, on home ground; "Io non so se voi vi conosceste Talano d'Imolese", says Pampinea in her preface to IX 7, thus underlining the possibility and likelihood that her companions might personally know her neighbor, the protagonist of her story. This sense of a shared social identity pervading Days VII-IX is further evidenced by the stories which refer to Florentines known not only to contemporaries, like Calandrino, but also to posterity. Here too Day VI initiates the trend: VI 2, where Cisti is introduced as "nostro cittadino," contains Geri Spina, one of the leaders of the Black Guelphs in Florence c. 1300; Giotto is present in VI 5, returning from his property in the Mugello region to Florence; Guido Cavalcanti is the hero of VI 9. The other stories replete with famous Tuscans are both in Day IX, which—although technically an open Day—is in fact a continuation, thematically, of Days VII and VIII. IX 4 contains the Sienese poet Cecco Angiolieri; IX 8 is perhaps the most quintessentially municipal story of the *Decameron,* crowded with figures from the *Comedy,* the text which more than any other has immortalized Florentines, albeit often negatively: It contains the glutton Ciacco, the wrathful Filippo Argenti, as well as the leaders of both the White and the Black factions, respectively Vieri de' Cerchi and Corso Donati. Ciacco's existence, unlike Calandrino's, is thus confirmed by an extra layer of textuality, provided by Dante. Moreover, the narrative employs various techniques to embed these real people into the flux of real—municipal—life; although IX 4 recounts the deception played by Cecco Fortarrigo on Cecco Angiolieri, the story ends by preparing us for another story, not presently forthcoming, that of Angiolieri's later reprisals. This has the effect of opening up the text to the "real life" of the characters: "E così la malizia del Fortarrigo turbò il buono avviso dell'Angiolieri, quantunque da lui non fosse a luogo e a tempo lasciata impunita." Likewise, IX 8 ends by letting us know that Biondello took care never to trick Ciacco again, thereby inserting the story into a chain of events operating outside, and independently of, the text. All of these developments, by creating an atmosphere of dense municipality in which the *brigata* is seen to participate, belong to the thematics of the return.

For all that the stories of Days VII, VIII, and IX are remembered primarily as amusing *beffe*, there is a serious theme as well, best stated by the topic of Day VII, where the wives are motivated to trick their husbands "per salvamento di loro". Self-preservation is the name of the game, first through the *pronta risposta*—the word—in Day VI, and then through the practical joke or *beffa*—the deed—in Days VII-IX. Only when the *brigata* is fully coached in the lessons of survival does it complete its turn toward Florence, with Day X, which shows men and women practicing generosity and renunciation, the very social virtues required for the *brigata*'s reintegration into society. The amoral vagaries of Days VII, VIII, and IX—summed up in the ultimate Dionean story, IX 10—come to an abrupt halt when Panfilo announces the topic for the Tenth Day.

The subject of Day X is proposed by Panfilo with an explicitly exemplary goal; he says, in the Conclusion to Day IX, that the discussion of munificent and liberal deeds will kindle in the members of the *brigata* a desire to emulate such behavior in their own actions: "Queste cose e dicendo e faccendo senza alcun dubbio gli animi vostri ben disposti a valorosamente adoperare accenderà" (IX, Concl.). And what must the *brigata* seek to incorporate into their lives? From the fourth *novella*, in which Messer Gentile returns the lady he has raised from the dead to her husband, to the eighth, in which Gisippo gives Sofronia to Tito, all the stories of Day X are concerned with sexual renunciation; thus, the central portion of the Day presents generosity in a particularly aggravated form. Within this kernel of *novelle*, moreover, the key stories are numbers 6 and 7, in which we witness the renunciation not of commoners but of kings, that is, of those responsible for the well-being of the social order. Especially important is the story of King Charles the Old, who foregoes the delightful Ghibelline sisters, Ginevra and Isotta. In setting the king on the right path, his friend advises him that true glory lies less in the ability to overcome one's enemies than in the ability to overcome oneself, especially when one is in the position of setting an example for others: "Io vi ricordo, re, che grandissima gloria v'è aver vinto Manfredi, ma molto maggiore è *se medesimo vincere;* e per ciò voi, che avete gli altri a correggere, *vincete voi medesimo e questo appetito raffrenate*" (X 6). This principle is echoed verbatim by the narrator, Fiammetta, who, in the *novella*'s conclusion, reëmphasizes the connection between self-discipline and social responsibility: "Così adunque il magnifico re operò, il nobile cavaliere altamente premiando, l'amate giovinette laudevolmente onorando *e se medesimo fortemente vincendo*" (X 6). The following story, X 7, reconfirms the principle by reversing the plot structure: Lisa, the apothecary's daughter, falls in love with King Peter of Aragon, who re-

sponds not by taking advantage of her but by arranging her marriage to a young nobleman.

Not only does Day X advocate self-discipline for the characters in its stories, but in fact the Day constitutes a form of self-discipline for the *brigata* telling the stories. In justifying his return to a defined theme for Day X, Panfilo comments on the invigorating effect of the narrative freedom allowed by his predecessor: "la discrezion d'Emilia, nostra reina stata questo giorno, per dare *alcun riposo* alle vostre forze arbitrio vi diè di ragionare *ciò che più vi piacesse*" (IX, Concl.). The result of the open Day is that now, refreshed, they are able to return to the "accustomed law": "per che, *già riposati essendo,* giudico che sia bene *il ritornare alla legge usata*" (IX, Concl.). Indeed, the very act of telling stories is itself presented as a form of discipline from the beginning of the *Decameron;* although amusing, *novellare* is nonetheless a restraint, a limitation imposed on the total self-indulgence which would otherwise engulf the *brigata*. Thus, Pampinea tells her companions that, if they do not care for her suggestion, they should amuse themselves however they please, "e dove non vi piacesse, ciascuno infino all'ora del vespro quello faccia che più gli piace" (I, Intro.), using a variant of the expression later adopted for the theme of the two free Days (where they discuss "quello che più aggrada a ciascheduno" [I] and "secondo che gli piace e di quello che più gli agrada" [IX]), an expression which recurs throughout the *Decameron:* Whenever the *brigata* is not telling stories, they are doing "whatever they please". Within this context—whereby the ordered telling of a story, its form, imposes a "law" which justifies its content, whatever it may be—Day X can be viewed as exacting a more contentually rigorous application. In fact, Day X imposes a law with respect to ALL the rest of the *Decameron,* and not only, as Panfilo says, with respect to Day IX; or rather, Day IX, described by Emilia as affording the opportunity "di vagare alquanto e vagando riprender forze a rientrar sotto il giogo" (VIII, Concl.), stands paradigmatically for all the previous Days. While usually the *novelle* have encouraged following one's instincts and have exposed the pathology of repression—as, for instance, in Tancredi's incestuous relationship with his daughter in IV 1, in Day X the positive aspects of repression are stressed. While sexual renunciation has previously been viewed negatively—as, for instance, in VIII 7 where the scholar deflects his carnal desires to exasperate his appetite for vengeance—Day X presents renunciation as a socializing force, required for the preservation of a civilized society. In a larger sense, then, the *riposo* has been all the *Decameron,* and the *legge usata* is civilization, society, Florence.

The *Decameron* could be pictured as a wheel—Fortune's wheel, the wheel of life—on which the *brigata* turns, coming back transformed to the point of departure. In Days I through V they move steadily away from the city as they are renewed in *ingegno* and *compassione*, i.e., intellectually and ethically. The outward turn of the wheel is completed with their arrival at the Valley of the Ladies in the Conclusion to Day VI. Geographically, they are now at their farthest remove from the city; here the ladies relax to an unparalleled degree, taking off their clothes for a swim (an action anticipated at the end of Day I, where, however, they merely step barefoot and with naked arms into the water): "tutte e sette si spogliarono e entrarono in esso, il quale non altramenti li lor corpi candidi nascondeva che farebbe una vermiglia rosa un sottil vetro" (VI, Concl.). The *Valle delle Donne* is the **Decameron**'s *locus amoenus* par excellence, an even more perfect conflation of the natural with the artificial than the garden they reach at the beginning of the Third Day. Here, where the ladies finally unveil their "corpi candidi", the *brigata* convenes to tell the sensual stories of Day VII. However, just as they locate the epitome of the ideal, the place most distanced from reality, the wheel reaches its zenith and begins its inevitable descent, back toward Florence and back toward reality.

Diagramming this wheel, one notes that there are four Days which are equidistant from and parallel to each other: Days I, IV, VII, and X are all separated by two intervening Days (see chart). In other words, these Days seem to initiate precisely marked legs of the *brigata*'s spiritual journey, a hypothesis which is supported by the fact that the rulers of these Days are the four characters whose physiognomies are most clearly delineated: Pampinea, Filostrato, Dioneo, and Panfilo. The **Decameron** depicts human beings in a moment of crisis; the *brigata*'s handling of this crisis can serve as a model for human deportment, and for the sage deployment of the various facets of our natures. First, Pampinea takes over, and there is an attempt to impose unity where there was fragmentation: the structure of the frame, the order of art. The second stage is marked by the governance of Filostrato, the despairing defeatist, under whose aegis the *brigata* is forced to dwell again on the tragic aspect of existence, to readmit the possibility of death (a very real possibility, we recall, since there is no indication that the *brigata*'s return to Florence coincides with the end of the plague). The third major stage is initiated by Dioneo, the life-affirmer, and it is on this leg of their journey that the plague is reintegrated into the *brigata*'s lives and their cure is pronounced complete. Death holds no more power over them; were anyone to witness their morning walk through the forest, comments the author in the Introduction to the Ninth Day, he would be forced to say " 'O costor non saranno dalla morte vinti o ella gli ucciderà lieti' " (IX, Intro.). They bend their thoughts now for the first time to the future: Panfilo exhorts them to perpetuate their lives in laudable deeds ("ché la vita nostra, che altro che brieve esser non può nel mortal corpo, si perpetuerà nella laudevole fama" [IX, Concl.]); in the opening to Day X we find them "molte cose della loro *futura vita* insieme parlando e dicendo e rispondendo" (X, Intro.). As Dioneo balances Filostrato and life balances death (Day VII paralleling Day IV), so Panfilo—the only one of the male frame characters never to make even verbal assaults on the propriety of the ladies—completes Pampinea (Day X parallelling Day I), ensuring that the order she institutes will be grounded in a clearly defined secular morality.

Some conclusions may be drawn also regarding the alliances of the lesser frame characters. Fiammetta, the only member of the *brigata* to be "physically" described, is depicted in strict accordance with the prevailing literary and amatory codes, and seems to represent a courtly and artistic ideal; she is the one of the company best able, says

Filostrato, to restore the spirits of the ladies after Day IV, the "aspra giornata d'oggi" (IV, Concl.; immediately after being thus distinguished from her peers, Fiammetta is further isolated by means of the unique *descriptio*). Dioneo, who is "life" to Filostrato's "death", is also the "real" to Fiammetta's "ideal"; the two play music together before the storytelling of Day I begins, thus prefiguring the contamination of reality with ideality throughout the **Decameron,** and they sing a courtly song derived from the thirteenth-century French poem, *La Chastelaine de Vergi,* in the Conclusion to Day III. It is therefore interesting that in the Introduction to Day VI, a moment whose importance to the text cannot be stressed enough, Dioneo should sing not with Fiammetta but with Lauretta. Their material is still courtly and literary; in fact, they sing of Troilus and Criseida (one wonders if the location of such tragic material immediately before Licisca's comic entrance is not a means of further defusing Filostrato, whose name is the doomed Troilo's sobriquet in Boccaccio's homonymous early text). Dioneo's shift in companions is further emphasized by the fact that Fiammetta sings alone in the Conclusion to Day VI; Dioneo will not sing with her again until after the crucial moment has passed, in the Conclusion to Day VII, where the parallel between the couples Dioneo-Lauretta and Dioneo-Fiammetta is made explicit by the fact that the subject is again drawn from one of the author's own earlier works, in this case the *Teseida.* Why then does Dioneo choose Lauretta in the Introduction to Day VI? Lauretta, it turns out, is associated with Dioneo and reality in a number of ways: She anticipates his reference to the plague in the Conclusion to Day VI by being the first to mention it, in VI 3; she is chosen by him as the queen of Day VIII, an opportunity she uses to confirm Dioneo's approach to storytelling, enlarging his topic from the tricks played by wives on their husbands to the tricks which "tutto il giorno o donna a uomo o uomo a donna o l'uno uomo all'altro si fanno"—i.e., her topic is, as her language itself makes clear, the open-ended bedlam and chaos of unexpurgated life.

If Lauretta is associated with Dioneo, Elissa is linked with Filostrato. She too is connected by her name to tragic love and to death: As Filostrato is related to Troilus, so is Elissa to Dido, whose alternate name she bears. Elissa's song, like Filostrato's, tells of unhappy, indeed cruel, love; moreover, she is the only other one of the frame characters to be asked, like Filostrato, to sing her song on the Day she rules (Fiammetta asks Filostrato to sing on his own Day so as to make him unable to extend his morbid influence beyond it, "acciò che più giorni che questo non sien turbati de'tuoi infortunii" [IV, Concl.]). Most importantly, Elissa is at odds with Dioneo, as a number of critics have noticed. She is the queen whose composure he upsets by attempting to introduce vulgar and plebeian material into the *brigata*'s courtly repertoire. Her rebuke in the Conclusion to Day V constitutes the severest confrontation between members of the *brigata* in the course of the frame story: She is "un poco turbata", and warns him to desist lest he discover "come io mi so adirare" (V, Concl.); she also threatens Licisca with a whipping in the Introduction to Day VI. Finally, in the Conclusion to that Day, after Licisca's presence has been registered and Dioneo has announced that the maid has inspired him with a new topic (in what is surely the **Decameron**'s most explicit and extravagant application of the author's dictum from the Introduction to Day IV, that "le Muse son donne", and after the ladies have surreptitiously sneaked away to the *Valle delle Donne,* prompting Dioneo to ask them if they are doing first in their deeds what they will later recount in words, thus associating the ladies of the *brigata* with the independent adulteresses of Day VII—after all this has happened to change the tone of the **Decameron,** Elissa sings her unhappy song, which she follows with "un sospiro assai pietoso" (VI, Concl.). But the tide has definitively turned, a fact marked by the adversative "Ma" and Dioneo's peremptory reaction: "Ma il re, *che in buona tempera era,* fatto chiamar Tindaro, gli comandò che fuori traesse la sua cornamusa, al suono della quale *esso fece fare molte danze*" (VI, Concl.). Dioneo, who is in a good mood, refuses to allow the company's spirits to be dampened by Elissa's song, and so he calls out Tindaro, the same servant who had that morning with Licisca disrupted their peace, and whose bagpipes will entertain them again under Lauretta's auspices, in the Conclusion to Day VII.

We remember that the *brigata*'s key rule for their new life was that no news, "niuna novella", may penetrate to them from outside, "di fuori". But, although they take refuge in an ideal world, the *brigata* passes its time telling stories that are for the most part taken from the real world. In other words, the *novelle*—or news—from the real world of Florence are replaced by the *novelle*—or stories—of the **Decameron.** Thus, the **Decameron**'s most perfected *locus amoenus,* the Valley of the Ladies, is the scene for the telling of some of its least perfect tales; thus, the Proem's lovesick ladies are offered not an opportunity to withdraw from love, but the chance to engage in it vicariously. Connected to this insistence on *engagement* is the author's disapproval, also registered in the Introduction to Day I, of living each day with the fear of death; he sees indifference to death not as wise and stoic resignation but, ultimately, as indifference to life:

> anzi tutti, quasi quel giorno nel quale si vedevano esser venuti la morte aspettassero, non

d'aiutare i futuri frutti delle bestie e delle terre e delle loro passate fatiche ma di consumare quegli che si trovavano presenti si sforzavano con ogni ingegno.

Here we see the psychological ills brought about by the plague, which has succeeded in making the feeblest minds accept death in a way previously not attained by the wise, and has therefore forced an entire populace to become "scorti e non curanti," more knowledgeable than is good for them. These ills—characterized by a nonchalance toward the "futuri frutti" and a mad consumption of the "presenti"—result in a kind of spiritual sickness, from which the *brigata* is cured: hence their talk of the future, their freedom from indifference and from the paralysis of the *non curanti.* They are freed, however, by precisely what they initially reject, by the *novelle,* which become increasingly less fabulous and increasingly more newsworthy as the arc of the *brigata*'s journey declines toward its end, until in Day X the two threads are interwoven and the magical is incorporated into the real, which is revealed to possess a luster the plague had all but obliterated: Messer Gentile rescues his beloved, a new Eurydice, in Bologna; a spring garden blossoms in the dead of winter, in the province of Friuli; Messer Torello is whisked home on Saladin's bed, to Pavia; Griselda's extra-ordinary trials take place in ordinary Saluzzo. The point of the *novelle,* which are not "stories" but "news", carriers of the real, is what the ladies of the Proem knew all along, that life is the only antidote for life. (pp. 521-39)

> Teodolinda Barolini, "The Wheel of the 'Decameron'," in Romance Philology, Vol. XXXVI, No. 4, May, 1983, pp. 521-39.

Giuseppe Mazzotta   (essay date 1986)

[*In the following essay, Mazzotta expounds on his theory that Boccaccio's use of allegory in the* Decameron *could be deemed pornographic. Mazzotta also examines the moral tone of the* Decameron, *concluding that its juxtaposition with the tales' erotic nature leaves Boccaccio's intent ambiguous.*]

An illustration by Pesellino depicting the story of Griselda.

Several tales of the *Decameron* feature an allegorical structure which, though essential to Boccaccio's narrative, has been somewhat neglected by critical commentaries. This is possibly due to the belief that the importance of the *Decameron* lies precisely both in Boccaccio's act of rescuing his stories from the ponderous allegorical mechanisms which figure in other medieval texts and in his attempt to recover the texture of reality in its rich and random literalness. Within this perspective, allegorical structures, much like other codes that formalize experience, such as courtly love and stilnovism, are stressed only in so far as they are subverted by Boccaccio's mimetic art and are held up as objects of ridicule.

But Boccaccio's literary subversiveness is much more radical than is commonly recognized, and my aim here is to map the ruses of his strategy. The primary focus is the allegory of the Earthly Paradise as it is dramatized in the Introduction to the third day and the tales of Masetto (III, I) and Griselda (X, 10). In the tale of Griselda, Boccaccio brings to bear on the literal plot the weight of allegory, its moral and doctrinal implications. In the tale of Masetto, he places in the narrative foreground an allegorical construct and shows how it dissolves as it comes into contact with the domain of worldliness. In both cases, the procedure, taken at its simplest, issues into a corrosive burlesque of medieval techniques of allegorization. The allegory is crushed by the exigencies of the literal sense, but there is more at stake than a simple ironic process of demystification from the standpoint of "reality." The realistic impulse is only a stage, albeit a crucial one, in the endlessly ironic movement of Boccaccio's narrative: ultimately, the notion of "reality" and its mimesis—apodictic canons in recent critical endeavors—are questioned and their dangerous illusoriness is exposed. The text is unveiled as what could be called pornography, in a sense that demands some clarification.

In his essay on pornography, which he defines etymologically as the "graph of the harlot," D. H. Lawrence sets Boccaccio apart from what he takes to be the neurotic practices of nineteenth-century writing. Pornography, in Lawrence's view, is the symptom of the diseased state of the body politic or more generally, "the attempt to insult sex, to do dirt on it." In this fierce polemic against the self-appointed moral guardians of society, who censor the plain representation of sex, Boccaccio's "natural fresh openness about sex" figures as the best antidote to the circle of vice and secrecy on which the worm of pornography feeds.

There is probably little doubt, as will be shown, that Boccaccio would share Lawrence's own passionate moral convictions about the need to unmask, in the name of irrepressible natural instincts, all sexual hypocrisies. But Boccaccio moves well beyond the naive myth of spontaneity that Lawrence attributes to him. He is aware . . . of the constitutive temptation of all love literature to turn into pornography, to be a "galeotto" with powers to give and arouse erotic pleasures. The *Decameron* effectively provides a view to the mechanism and poetics of pornography, and allegory plays a prominent role in it.

The point of departure for this critical-textual analysis is the Introduction to the third day. We are imaginatively located in a garden, which is a veritable *hortus conclusus,* "un giardino che tutto era da torno murato" (a garden that was walled all around) where the storytellers retreat. Described as a space where all elements are given fixed boundaries and symmetrical arrangement, the landscape comes forth as a harmonious cluster of flowers, birds' songs, brooks and other paraphernalia of the pastoral storehouse. The overriding strain of the description is the bounty of a generous Nature, for the place swarms with the infinite variety of living things. But the natural cycle of the seasons, with its inherent hint of death and impermanence, is suspended: in this eternal springtime, the trees "(hanno) i vecchi frutti e' nuovi e i fiori ancora . . . " (have the old and the new fruits as well as their blossoms). By the detail, Boccaccio insinuates that in spite of the natural abundance, this order of nature is wrought, that nature is an artifice miming the order of eternity. The palace that walls in the scenery, the marble fountain at the center of the lawn and the brooks which "*artificiosamente* fatti fuor di quello divenuta palese" (artifically constructed came into view out of there) move in the direction of translating the organic and wondrous world of nature into an imaginative compression of illusion and reality, the pictorial artifice whereby substances and appearances are indistinguishable.

The enclosure, fashioned with stylized elements, resembles many other literary *loci amoeni:* it recalls, for instance, other gardens that Boccaccio had described in the *Teseida, Amorosa visione* and, more fundamentally, the garden in the general Introduction to the *Decameron.* In a sense, this garden is the generic repertory of all gardens for it contains "tutta la spezieria che mai nacque in Oriente" (all the spices ever grown in the East). For all its commonplace quality, however, there is a specific *hortus conclusus* that with ironic insistence Boccaccio is recalling: the garden of *Deduit* in Guillaume de Lorris' *Roman de la Rose.* After seeing the allegorical carvings on the wall, and drawn by the music that comes from within, Amant is introduced by idleness to the enclosed garden of Love. The textual parallelisms between Guillaume's and Boccaccio's descriptions are so conspicuous that they suggest more than a mere coincidence of conventional pastoral motifs. The occurrences hint, in effect, that Boccaccio is involved in a critical reading of Guillaume's poem. Let me first point out the verbal analogues.

In Boccaccio's garden, the paths are hedged by "*rosa bianchi e vermigli* e di gelsomini erano quasi chiuse" (white and red roses and jasmine), a description that is an almost exact replica of Guillaume's phrase "videte i avoit trop bele e parvenche fresche e novele, / s'i ot *flors blanches e vermeilles.*" Boccaccio's own suggestion that the lawn seems artfully decorated—"un prato di minutissima erba e verde tanto, che quasi nera parea, *dipinto* tutto *forse di mille varietà di fiori*" (a lawn of exceedingly fine grass, so green as to seem almost black, all dotted with perhaps a thousand kind of flowers"—closely echoes Guillaume's metaphor that the garden is *"pointe / de flors de diverses colors / don mout estoit bone l'olors."* The tame animals that populate the garden in the **Decameron** (rabbits, hares, does and roe-deer) roughly correspond to the list enumerated in the *Roman*. More cogently, Boccaccio's underlined phrase, *"d'una parte uscir conigli, d'altra parte correr lepri . . . "* (From one side rabbits emerging, hares from the other side running) recalls *verbatim* the underlined words in Giullaume's description of the rabbits coming out of their burrows *"Conins i avoit, qui issoient / Toute jor hors de lor tesnieres."* Further, Amant's astonished impression that he is in the Earthly Paradise, *"Lors entrai, senz plus dire mot, / Par l'uis que Oiseuse overt m'ot, / Ou vergier, e quant je fui enz . . . sachiez que je cuidai estre / Por voir en parevis terrestre"* is picked up by Boccaccio, who also shows his characters spellbound by the vision and believing that if *"Paradiso si potesse in terra fare"* (if Paradise were constructed on earth), it would have the enchantment of the garden they behold. Even the "trente manières", a phrase by which Giullaume summarily encompasses the variety of animals, become "venti maniere" (twenty kinds) as Boccaccio refers to the birds singing.

I readily grant that no single textual parallel, taken in isolation, is particularly compelling, for each element is uniformly part of stock material. Yet, taken cumulatively, they suggest a deliberate pattern of allusions; the case is strengthened by the fact that Boccaccio adapts the conceptual frame of Giullaume's garden in order to establish some vital counterpoints to, and to argue against, the broader implications of the *Roman*. For Giullaume, the artfulness of the garden is a sign of the perversity of the place where rationality is befuddled by cupidinous love. Amant's quest for the rose is a sexual quest and as such it mocks the allegory of the spiritual pilgrimage for, like Adam in the Earthly Paradise, Amant fails. The fountain of Narcissus to which he comes reveals his erotic quest to be an experience of self-love and makes the garden the place where, as the story of Narcissus' self-fascination exemplifies, love and death mingle.

Boccaccio's introduction to the third day is, like Giullaume's poem, a subtle mockery of the religious quest for Eden. The opening sentence of the description 'L'aurora già di vermiglia cominciava, appressandosi il sole, a divenir rancia, quando la domenica . . . " (Dawn was already beginning to change from vermilion to orange with the approach of the sun, when on Sunday . . .) is a poignant paraphrase of Dante's *Purgatorio*. The leisurely journey of the *brigata* alludes to and mocks Dante's painful askesis from Purgatory to the Garden of Eden. But for the *brigata* this is not, as it is for Dante, Easter Sunday, nor will there be for it a stern moral voice—as there is for the pilgrim—to dissipate the esthetic relief provided by Casella's song. Boccaccio's mockery, actually, is twofold. He spoofs Dante's allegory of the spiritual pilgrimage, his ascent to Eden, and, in so doing, he follows Giullaume's own parody of the Earthly Paradise. But Boccaccio also mocks the naturalistic thrust of Giullaume's poem. Far from being Amant's erotic quest, the *brigata*'s journey aims at a gratuitous, purely esthetic evasion into the artifice of nature. If Giullaume exposes the deceptive lures of

the garden and obliquely denounces the fallacy of art because art—like the ambiguous mirror of Narcissus—makes things appear both as they are and are not, Boccaccio capitalizes on this very ambiguity. His garden is neither Dante's allegory of Eden nor is it Amant's garden of literal, fleshly delights. It is the imaginative domain where the allegory and the letter are alluded to and equally superseded, where the young people of the *brigata* indulge in esthetic pastimes and are drawn into the artifice: they dance, play, read romances and tell stories. Within this illusory context, their stories evoke a world of sexuality which superficially appears to be an ironic counterpoint to the garden of the introduction but, in a real sense, they end up by exposing the dangers of the esthetic imagination.

The explicit impulse of the tale of Masetto (III, I), which immediately follows this contrived picture of nature, is to shed without compunction all artifices. Filostrato, the narrator, seems to make merry wreckage of artificial morality as he upbraids both the false belief that nuns by taking a vow have renounced their sexual appetites and the pious assumption that to love them is to perpetrate a sin against nature. Filostrato objects that nature is not a fixed moral order; he buoyantly asserts that everyone is free to live as he pleases and justifies the love of nuns on account of their idleness and solitude. Solitude, as the circumstance favorable to love, is one of the many pointed allusions, as we shall see shortly, to the *De arte honeste amandi*. Idleness, a crucial category in Boccaccio's fiction, is not the *otium* which allows the humanists to indulge in scholarly pursuits. It leads, rather—as in the case of Amant—to the garden of sexual delights.

The tale of Masetto begins, cogently enough, as a parody of the allegory of Eden. The monastery where Masetto enters, ostensibly as a gardener but with the secret purpose of seducing the nuns, is conveniently glossed as the *hortus deliciarum* where the mystical marriage of Christ and the Virgins is celebrated. Christ is the "virginum Sponsus" according to the mystical exegesis that Bernard of Clairvaux gives of the *Canticle of Canticles*. The allegory of marriage is obliquely suggested in the text and becomes the object of overt fun. In the closing lines, Masetto's sexual feat is viewed as cuckolding Christ: "così trattava Cristo chi gli poneva le corna sopra 'l cappello" (. . . so did Christ treat anybody who placed a pair of horns on his crown). Boccaccio clearly reverses the conventional exegeses of the *Canticle of Canticles*. While the allegorists spiritualize the literal erotics of the biblical garden, he takes the allegory literally and weaves on it a series of comical equivocations and double entendres. Thus, the sexual allusion in Masetto's aside "io vi lavorerò sì l'orto, che mai non vi fu così lavorato" (I will tend your garden better than it's ever been tended before) exploits the allegorical resonance from the interpretation of the *Canticle* by St. Bernard who speaks of "virginitas flos horti." And even Masetto's own role as a husbandman is the parodic literal inversion of the allegory of Christ as the spiritual husbandman who redeems and changes the wilderness into a paradise. In this process of reducing the allegory to its literal counterpart, Masetto, as he puts his devilish plan to work, acts as the metaphorical serpent of Eden corrupting the mystical garden of the *Canticle*—itself a typological reenactment of prelapsarian innocence—into the garden of the fall.

The allegory of the fall is in turn questioned by another subtle reference. The sexuality of the monastery, we are told, is not barren and, actually, Masetto and the nuns are "blessed" with a large number of children. By the detail, Boccaccio seems to exploit the potential whimsicality of the casuistic debate in which the Fathers of the Church were long engaged. Discussing the morality of sexual intercourse, the fathers distinguished between the prelapsarian and postlapsarian sexuality. In the Garden of Eden—they surmised—sexuality must have been carried out without the lustful shame which accompanies the act in the fallen world. Procreation, they concluded, is the moral end which redeems sexuality as it is practiced since the fall. But Masetto's lovemaking is not directly *causa prolis* and his sexual aim is unencumbered by moral sophistries. Masetto acts as if he were in the Garden of Eden, and as Boccaccio alludes to the fertility of the union, he flagrantly pokes fun at—and dismisses—the pertinence of the patristic distinctions.

The metaphor of the mystical marriage in the garden—though extensively mocked—provides the rationale for the articulation of the tale and binds together its disparate dramatic elements. Boccaccio, in effect, grafts onto it a series of verbal allusions drawn from the *De arte honeste amandi*. Andreas' system of adulterous love, of course, depends on marriage and is unimaginable outside of it. As Boccaccio casts Masetto cuckolding Christ, he signals that this story is to be read within the bounds of the courtly love system. Masetto's feigned muteness, as has been remarked, observes a basic requirement of courtly love. Secrecy, the injunction that love cannot be divulged—as the nuns quickly realize—is seemingly assured by Masetto's muteness: "costui perché egli pur volesse, egli nol potrebbe né saprebbe ridire" (if he wanted to, he wouldn't be able to tell anybody about it). At the same time, by highlighting Masetto's trick, Boccaccio parodies still another principle of Andreas' doctrine. For Andreas, a successful way of acquiring love is "copiosa sermonis facundia." He ostensibly dismisses this means of gaining love, yet his own text is, ironically, a repository of speeches which the lover should use to seduce the woman. By Masetto's muteness, Boccaccio implies that sexual seduction needs no language. This ironic twist is effected on another requirement of the art of love. Andreas rebukes readiness in granting what the lover seeks. Masetto does precisely the opposite: "senza farsi troppo invitare quel fece che ella volle" (without needing too much coaxing, he did what she wanted him to do).

The ironic inversion of Andreas' doctrine is paramount in the tale. In the chapter on the love of nuns, the chaplain suggests that he who indulges in their love "ab omnibus meretur contemni et est tanquam *detestabilis belua fugiendus*" or, as a fourteenth-century Italian adaptation of *De arte* renders it "come *odievole bestia è da fuggire*." In Boccaccio's novella, Masetto sets out deliberately to seek the nuns' love and it is the nuns who approach Masetto in order to "provare che *bestia fosse l'uomo*" (find out what kind of animal man is). Under the same rubric "de amore monacharum," Andreas enjoins Walter "unquam poteris opera Veneris evitare nefanda scelera sinistra committens." Boccaccio picks up the precept and turns it against the moralists who object to the love of nuns "come se contra natura un grandissimo e *scelerato male fosse stato commesso*" (as if some enormous and evil crime against nature had been committed). Further, under the heading of "de amore rusticorum," Andreas vetoes their love and as the Italian version has it "adunque basti loro la continua fatica di *lavorare i campi* e gli sollazzi della zappa e del marrone." The proposition is given a pointed refutation by the very experience of Masetto and, more precisely, by a phrase that seems to be a calculated polemic against Andreas' veto and those who believe that "*la zappa et la vanga . . . tolgano del tutto a' lavoratori della terra* i concupiscibili appetiti" (digging and hoeing . . . remove from those who work on the land all lustful desires).

It would appear from this sustained parody of *De arte honeste amandi* either that Boccaccio writes against the subtle ironies that punctuate Andreas' handbook of love or that, blind to these ironies, he mistakes the chaplain's pornographic text for a moralistic construction which he sets out to dismantle. If this were the case, it could be argued that Andreas' system of courtly love, much like the allegory of the mystical marriage in the garden, is decried by an all too urgent sense of the power of sexuality. Within this perspective, it could also be argued that the tale of Masetto serves as a deliberate shattering of the esthetic garden of the Introduction to the third day. But Boccaccio creates a vastly more complex irony through the juxtaposition. As the two gardens stand in sharp contrast to each other, they mirror and parody each other. Masetto's "edenic" delights debunk the artifices of the introductory garden; the tale of Masetto, however, is a *story told* within the bounds of that artifice; it is drawn within an illusory frame. The fictional frame undercuts the substantiality of the literal sense in Masetto's story and it is for Boccaccio a way of bringing into the open the imaginary quality of the sexual experience. Significantly enough, Masetto's tale is told by Filostrato, the emblem of the frustrated lover as he defines himself at the close of the third day. Masetto's successful adventures jar with the narrator's unhappy loves and the ensuing disparity makes the story a pure fantasy, Filostrato's imaginary self-projection. This narcissistic underpinning belies the notion that the tale is simply a mimesis of reality; it emerges, on the contrary, as a reflection on the constitutive properties of pornographic literature, the literature, that is, in which sexuality is suspended as a self-contained vagary of the imagination. But why would Boccaccio indulge in a polemic gesture against *De arte honeste amandi* which is a veritable specimen of pornographic literature? Can it be that he is deliberately misreading this text as an ironic means of hiding a more profound complicity with it?

The explicit burden of *De arte* is to expose the techniques of erotic seduction so that Walter may know how to avoid them. The moralistic caveat and the retraction by which Andreas disavows the erotic thrust of his book are too bland to be taken seriously—as some critics have done—or to dispel the lingering suspicion that the very palinode is the target of the chaplain's irony. The critical debate directed to establish whether Andreas' overall "intentions" are moralistic or not is doomed to be fruitless if it must end up by choosing one such reading to the exclusion of the other. In effect, there is no antagonism between the moral and the erotic elements in the treatise. It is actually the moral cover that, by veiling the directly lewd statements, makes Andreas' text pornographic. The moral justification is essential to pornography because it provides a necessary alibi, an obliqueness which is pleasurable in so far as it obscures what it seeks to reveal.

The pornographic quality of *De arte* is sharply suggested by Dante. In the canto of the lecherous sinners in *Inferno*, Francesca's speech is replete with allusions from Andreas Capellanus: for Dante, this text is as much a "galeotto," a dangerous erotic mediator, as is the romance of Lancelot which muddles Francesca's imagination, leads her into narcissistic identification with the love heroine and engenders her fall into sinfulness. Boccaccio, however, does not share Dante's hard indictment of pornographic literature: he even twists Dante's *ethos* as he subtitles the *Decameron*—echoing the same canto V of *Inferno*—"galeotto" and overtly acknowledges it to be a surrogate of love, a book written to be enjoyed.

Like Andreas who obscures the eroticism of his manual with moralizations, Boccaccio shrouds the sexual facts with verbal puns which allude to sexuality and at the same time elude it. Thus, Masetto is said to plan cultivating the nuns' "orto;" Filippo Balducci's son is strongly attracted by "papere." Dioneo's novella at the close of the third day, more poignantly, exploits the ambiguities which inhere in the language of sexuality and that of the practice of spiritual askesis. The story, as every reader of the *Decameron* remembers, takes place in the desolation of the "diserto di Tebaida" (the desert of Thebaid,) and it involves Alibech, a very young woman who wants to learn how God can best be served, and Rustico who lives as a hermit in the desert. Alibech's youth and beauty act on Rustico as the hermit's steady obsession and thereby defeat his monastic discipline.

There is a subtle irony in Boccaccio's use of the word "discipline." Etymologically the word suggests the monk's ascetic exercise, the stiff spiritual training he daily subjects himself to in order to repel the temptations in what is a fierce *psychomachia*. By an ironic reversal, Rustico (one wonders if this is not a faint echo of Andreas' *de amore rusticorum*) takes on the role of a "migliore maestro" (a more capable teacher), one who is thought of as fit to guide Alibech in her apprenticeship. The reversal is not an isolated occurrence. Even the detail, for instance, that the makeshift bed, on which Alibech will spend her first night in Rustico's cell, is made of "frondi di palma" (palm leaves) belongs to the same rhetorical scheme. The seemingly offhand specification of the foliage is primarily, no doubt, an element of local color, a reference to the vegetation in the quasi-tropical region where the action develops. But the palm leaf is also a symbol of triumph: in a context in which Rustico first surrenders to the urgings of the flesh and later gives up when he cannot satisfy Alibech's abundant sexual appetite, the irony of the emblem is transpar-

ent. The irony is heightened, one might add, by another symbolic value with which the palm tree is invested. In patristic exegesis, the process by which the Christian *viator* moves from the realm of fleshly delights to the pleasures of the Heavenly Jerusalem is figured through the palm tree. In the novella, by a pointed reversal, the palm leaves are the bed on which Rustico moves from prayer to carnal pleasures. To complicate the pattern further, by the end what seemed for the monk to be carnal delights become for him a veritable hellish punishment.

These reversals turn out to be the playful center of the narrative and are even part of the special structural role the novella occupies in the economy of the day. It is quite clear, to begin with, that Dioneo, by telling at the end of the day the story of an anchorite in the desert who is unable to satisfy the sexual advance of a novice, pokes fun at Filostrato's first story of one man, Masetto, who in the garden manages to look after the needs of nine nuns. More specifically, key phrases in Dioneo's tale such as "la resurrezion della carne" (the resurrection of the flesh), "la superbia del capo" (the pride of the head), and "rimettere il diavolo in inferno" (put the devil back into Hell) rhetorically organize the text by their overt movement from their original spiritual sense to a physical context, as well as by their concealing the sexual act in the guise of moral allegory. The humor of the story issues from the strident and close union of the spiritual and physical activities, from the ease with which the two registers are "exchanged." The humor, which is a cardinal ingredient of the narrative, stems from the confusion of the two semantic fields, a confusion which humor, paradoxically, also sanctions.

The technique of indirection—the strategy of *not* naming sexuality directly—is deployed systematically in the *Decameron* and not just to observe a principle of esthetic decorum. In the *Conclusione dell'autore*, Boccaccio attempts to rescue his novelle from the charges of immorality by claiming that the objectionable words he uses such as " 'foro' e 'caviglia' e 'mortaio' e 'pestello' e 'salsiccia' . . ." ('hole' and 'rat' and 'mortar' and 'pestle' and 'crumpet' . . .) are not obscene in themselves and that his tales are no more harmful than the Scriptures have been to some readers.

The apology implies that all writings, sacred and profane alike, are morally neutral allegories and openly claims that the responsibility for interpreting the stories lies with the reader. The notion that Scripture and the *Decameron* have in common a dangerous ambiguity—they can edify or corrupt the reader—retrospectively illuminates the perverse poetics at work in the tale of Masetto. Pornography in the story parodies the allegory. But the allegorization of the *Canticle of Canticles* or Andreas' allegory of education, far from being simply dismissed as abstract moralizations, are implicitly unveiled as pornography because the erotic story they tell is contrabanded as a moral myth. By the same token, the opposite is also true: pornography is an allegory for like allegory it needs a cover. In allegory, the ambiguities are provided by the husk that envelops the moral kernel; in the present figuration of pornography, morality is the chaff hiding the erotic fruit. This bold view is the precise reversal of the theory of allegory Boccaccio elaborates and underwrites in his *Genealogy of the Gentile Gods.* In this mythographic encyclopedia the allegorical veil which clothes the naked truth is said to challenge the subtle reader to exercise his understanding, whereas the unskilled one is captivated by the pleasures of the surface. Pornography, instead, makes the pleasure of the surface the narrative's own aim, while the naked truth is always bypassed.

By this unusual complicity between allegory and pornography, Boccaccio lays open the esthetic basis of pornography. Like the garden to which the storytellers retreat, pornography is a locus where the distinction between reality and imagination is blurred, the metaphor whereby literature is in the process of becoming sexuality and sexuality becomes a book. In this steady movement of dislocation pornography is always irreducibly "other," a version of formal allegory, one which in effect is devoid of any substantial, intrinsic moral content and by which sexuality is dodged even as it is at the same time kept as an alluring mirage. This constant oscillation suggests, further, that the imaginary pleasures engendered by the reading of the "galeotto" are essentially hollow: there is always a split at the heart of the pornographic text, for desires are aroused and are simultaneously frustrated. Filostrato, in a real sense, is the true pornographer.

But does Boccaccio ever break out of this bind? Does he ever gain an undistorted perspective of moral order in the ***Decameron***? To answer these questions we must turn to the novella of Griselda which ostensibly presents itself as an allegory of order. In the tales of the tenth day, actually, there seems to be a radical shift away from the dramatic substance of the previous days. The jests and bawdiness commonly associated with the *Decameron* give way now to exemplary moral tales. It is as if Boccaccio were intent on sealing his narrative with the reassuring intimation that all contrasts are resolved and a desirable moral order is finally established. In this sense, the ***Decameron*** mimes, at least on the surface, the trajectory of the comical plot as it moves from its bleak beginnings (the plague) to its climax with the cathartic vision of a happy ending.

The specific moral substance of the last tales, however, is somewhat ambiguous. The sixth story, for instance, dramatizes a process of moral conversion. Within the framework of the chivalric tradition, it features the *fol amor* of the old King Charles of Anjou for the young Guinivere and for her twin sister Iseult. The king ultimately acknowledges the madness of his desire and turns into the girls' benefactor. But the bulk of the story lies in the account of how the king, who has just experienced a victory on the battlefield, is in turn defeated by love. The time is one of leisure in Neri's delightful garden, where food and delicate wines are served according to a model of "ordine"—which is to be understood here as Boccaccio's own ideal of elegant ritual and gracious living. The pleasant conviviality is interrupted by the arrival of two young girls, the sight of whom causes astonishment in the king. The girls enter a pond to catch fish, some of which they throw on the table where the king is seated.

For all its playfulness, the fishing scene is a metaphoric displacement of the king's erotic fascination with the two young women, whom he cannot distinguish from each other. As the text moves to recount the king's passion, Boccaccio gives an arresting dramatization of Andreas' etymological definition of love. "Love," Andreas writes, "gets its name (*amor*) from the word for hook (*amus*), which means 'to capture' or 'to be captured,' for he who is in love is captured in the chains of desire and wishes to capture someone else with his hook. Just as a skillful fisherman tries to attract fishes by his bait and to capture them on his crooked hook, so the man who is a captive of love tries to attract another person by his allurements and exerts all his efforts to unite two different hearts with an intangible bond, or if they are already united he tries to keep them so forever."

Captive of this passion, the king is tempted to take the two girls away from their father, but is persuaded not to do so by Count Guido. His arguments span the morality of courtly love (it does not become an old man to fall in love with young women); the questions of political self-interest (Manfredi's defeat was a consequence of the violence his soldiers perpetrated on women); and finally, what could be called the king's own narcissism: the reasoning is that it is a great glory to defeat Manfredi, it is a greater one to triumph over one's own baser appetites.

The count's words effect the king's moral conversion, and his generosity in supplying the girls with splendid dowries is unequivocal. The reference to Guinivere's and Iseult's marriages supplants the picture of sexual temptation; it further suggests that marriage, by which most of the last novelle are brought to a close, is the exemplary metaphor of order and reconciliation in the ***Decameron.*** In this view of marriage Boccaccio is of course exploiting a standard Christian motif. If the fall is the sin by which man has lost the order of Eden (and the delightful garden here is its faint echo), marriage is the sacrament that reflects and reenacts the plenitude of the prelapsarian condition. The final tale of Griselda, which we shall examine in some detail, tests directly the allegory of order and plots the incongruities within it.

Readers of the story have traditionally been baffled and frankly disappointed by what they have taken to be its exaggerated moralism and lack of verisimilitude. Luigi Russo is an exception, however, to this general view. He interprets the novella as a case of "oratorical" literature in the sense that in it Boccaccio willfully contemplates an ideal world which he superimposes on his genuinely comical vein. Instead of pursuing further this central intuition, Russo ultimately shares the general opinion that the narrative is uninspired and impaired by the abstract idealizations. By and large, the critical reaction has been such that one is led to infer that modern critics have hardly departed from Petrarch's reading of the story. In his celebrated translation, it will be remembered, Petrarch makes of the ordeals of Griselda and the cruel arbitrariness of Gualtieri the allegory of the soul tested by God. Petrarch recounts it, as he says, not to arouse the ladies to imitate Griselda but to urge all men to be steadfast to God when he tries us just as this poor woman was steadfast to her temporal lord. Petrarch's allegory is a veritable "translation" because it deliberately transforms into a pietistic tract and considerably simplifies the ironic complexities of Boccaccio's story. The allegory which Petrarch explicitly brings out has as its paradigm the biblical account of God testing the patience of Job. This paradigm, in fact, is already present in Boccaccio's version.

The ordeals of Griselda, to begin with, are symmetrically encompassed between two correlated actions. As she emerges from her father's hut to be introduced to Gualtieri's retainers, she is stripped of her clothes: "(Gualtieri) la fece spogliare ignuda; e fattisi quegli vestimenti che fatti aveva fare, prestamente la fece vestire e calzare e sopra i suoi capelli . . . le fece mettere una corona" (Gualtieri caused her to be stripped naked: and calling for those clothes which he had had specially made, and quickly got her to put them on and made her put a crown . . . on her hair). Toward the end of the novella, Gualtieri humiliates Griselda by sending her back to her father stripped of all ornaments: "scalza e senza alcuna cosa in capo" (barefoot and without anything on her head). We might point out that in formal terms the language of clothing and nakedness, traditionally charged with allegorical resonances, heightens the allegorical thrust of the events narrated. More to the point, the two actions broadly hint at Paul, man holds sway over the woman. Gualtieri's madness, however, forfeits the Pauline notion of the hierarchy to be enacted by marriage and from the point of view of Griselda this sacramental Eden is literally a hell.

Unlike Petrarch, who exploits the story for a univocal fable of moral edification, Boccaccio delineates the allegory and at the same time undercuts it. He does not aim, by so doing, at a simple mockery of allegorical abstractions in order to vindicate the value of the reality of experience. By the strategy of contradictions and inversions, Boccaccio actually represents the radical rupture between the allegory of order and its human, literal counterpart. By showing the contradiction within the metaphor of marriage, he splits open the very rock upon which the possibilities of order are founded and recognizes that human existence and its allegorical formulations collide with and contradict each other; what may be fully significant in God's plan appears as a mass of unaccountable and senseless quirks in the world of man. In this rupture, the allegory and the letter function each as a critical perspective on the other and both together map out the rift at the core of the myth of order.

The doubleness in the midst of the sacrament of unity is consciously deployed in the novella. From one point of view, the novella is structured as a veritable *psychomachia,* a moral battle of vice and virtue. Boccaccio's gloss on "bestialità" as "vizio dell'anima," on the one hand, and Griselda's continuously acknowledged virtue, on the other, strongly hint that the spiritual battle is a real, though somewhat submerged, motif. The conflict is introduced in Dioneo's opening remark as he addresses the "mansuete mie donne" (my gentle women), an epithet which obliquely alludes to Griselda's *mansuetudo,* and announces that he is about to recount a story of "matta bestialità." The primary battle is between *mansuetudo* and *bestialitas* and the moral link between them was formulated by Thomas Aquinas.

In the seventh book of the *Nichomachean Ethics,* Aristotle identifies *bestialitas* as a kind of madness, the occurrence of cruelty, folly, and tyranny in exaggerated forms. In his commentary on the *Ethics,* Thomas Aquinas links bestiality to intemperance ("Et inde est quod vitia intemperantiae maximam turpitudinem habent, quia per ea homo bestiis assimilatur"). But it is in the *Summa theologiae* that he explicitly classifies *bestialitas* as a sin against the virtue of temperance. In answer to the question whether or not temperance is a virtue, St. Thomas writes that man naturally seeks a delight which is appropriate to him and that ["Clearly this is to agree and not to clash with the burden of human nature. Which is not to deny that temperance is against the grain for merely animal nature uncomplying with reason"]. And in the definition of the virtues in the *secunda secundae* of his *Summa,* more cogently, Aquinas proposes a scheme by which *mansuetudo* is a part of temperance, the quality of bridling one's own excesses ["Clemency and gentleness likewise imply a certain restraint: as we have seen the one reduces punishment, the other softens anger. For this reason they are classified with the principal or cardinal virtue of temperance, and in this respect are treated as parts of temperance"].

Even Griselda's endurance of her misfortunes is explainable within the framework of the *psychomachia:* as she bears her afflictions "con fermo viso" and "con forte animo" (with a show of bravery and strength of mind, she displays a spiritual fortitude which consists, as Aquinas says, in the possession of firmness, ["Secondly, courage can be taken as meaning firmness of mind in enduring or repulsing whatever makes steadfastness outstandingly difficult; . . . "]. As a virtue of the irascible appetite, fortitude is opposed to fear (*timor*): unsurprisingly, as Gualtieri takes Griselda back, he confesses that he tested her because he felt "gran paura" that she might fail him.

The *psychomachia* ends with Griselda's victory. In the moral that Dioneo draws from the narrative, Griselda's patience is praised and Gualtieri's fitness to rule over other men is doubted: "che si potrà dir qui? se non che anche nelle povere case piovono dal cielo de' divini spiriti, come nelle reali di quegli che sarien più degni di guardar porci che d'avere sopra uomini signoria" (What more needs to be said here, except that celestial spirits come from Heaven even in the houses of the poor, just as there are those in royal places who would be better employed as swineherds than as rulers of men?). The rhetorical question suggests Dioneo's uneasiness over his conclusion. In the final paragraph the uneasiness becomes outright disruption of the moral lesson he has so tentatively voiced: "[Gualtieri] non sarebbe forse stato male investito d'essersi abbattuto a una che quando, fuor di casa, l'avesse fuori in camiscia cacciata, s'avesse sì a un altro fatto scuotere il pilliccione che riuscito ne fosse una bella roba" (For perhaps it would have served Gualtieri right if he had chanced upon a wife, who, being driven from her house in her shirt, had found some other man to shake her skin-coat for her, earning herself a new dress in the process). By the comment, which is marked by a stylistic shift to a coarse *aequivocatio,* Dioneo opens a breach in the moral statement of the story and, as he alludes to a different turn that the story might have taken, he unmakes the story he has just told.

The experience of obstinate domestic violence we have witnessed could have been replaced by Griselda's sweet revenge had she sought, to counter her ordeal, sexual pleasures. Understood in this sense, Dioneo's last comment points to the proximity between violence and libertine pleasures, an issue fully dramatized in the seventh day of the *Decameron,* the day which is under Dioneo's rule.

But the phrase "scuotere il pilliccione" echoes "il pilliccion ti scotesse," which appears in another tale (IV, 10) told by Dioneo. This is the account of a surgeon from Salerno, Mazzeo della Montagna, whose marital inadequacies parallel those of Riccardo di Chinzica (II, 10). The wife's unhappiness, which is cast in unmistakable Dantesque language of the *tenzone* with Forese, prompts her to choose as a lover a young libertine. One night, while the doctor is off to Amalfi, the woman arranges a rendezvous with Ruggiero, who, feeling thirsty, drinks a potion the surgeon had prepared for an operation he had to perform the next day. In a way the novella is a parody of the magic philter of romances, for the potion simply deadens Ruggiero's body. From this point the plot takes many complicated twists till the maid, to save her lady's reputation, pretends, first to the doctor and later to the judge in the courtroom, that Ruggiero was her lover and had entered her room by stealth to sleep with her. Her lie brings to a happy resolution Ruggiero's ordeal, who, finally freed, gives himself to even greater pleasure with his mistress. Their pleasures are probably intensified by the awareness of the body's fragility (the patient's leg has a gangrenous bone; Ruggiero's drowsiness is provisionally mistaken for death) or, more generally, by the relief at the dangers the two lovers avoided. More to our concern, Dioneo's phrase plunges us back to the heart of the *Decameron*'s comedy, to a story which evokes the confusion of social estates (the libertine patrician, the surgeon, the magistrate, moneylenders, maid and lady).

In a way, Dioneo's comment at the end of the last tale of the *Decameron* suggests that nothing is definitive and final in this narrative universe: the very end, conventionally seen as the privileged perspective from which the moral coherence and order of the text are constituted, is disclosed as a contingent and purely formal closure. By this expedient Dioneo implies that storytelling is an endless activity and that the "right" finale lies elsewhere. When the novella of Torello is over and his turn to speak comes, Dioneo dismisses the praises showered on Messer Torello as worthless from the point of view of the "buon uomo, che aspettava la seguente notte di fare abbassare la coda ritta della fantasima" (the good man, who was looking forward to lowering the erect tail of the werewolf). Much as he has done at the exordium of Griselda's story, he hints, as a way of closing, at a frankly erotic tale which would displace the moral sententiousness which could be extrapolated from the tale.

There is no doubt that Dioneo's comment is an ironic perversion of the traditional technique of appending a palinode to a morally ambiguous account: his comment, actually, lets the pornographic dimension of the *Decameron* resurface at the point where its morality is bland and the literal and the allegorical are cut off from each other. But the erotic allusion is not simply the residue, the pleasurable alternative to the breakdown of the allegory of order. We must stress that we catch only a glimpse of the pornographic alternative, just as in the story of King Charles, when the two sisters emerge from the pool, we are allowed to see their thin white dresses clinging to their bodies as to conceal "quasi"-almost-nothing. Pornography, as has been argued, is the convergence of imagination and desire, an ever elusive mirage whose pleasures are displaced, always somewhere else. The alibi is the constitutive property of pornographic literature: its "otherness" suspends the very notion of its becoming a literal, real experience; it subverts the possibility of coercing the literal within an allegorical structure; and, more importantly, it lays open the radical instability of figurative language in the *Decameron.* (pp. 105-30)

> *Giuseppe Mazzotta, in his* The World at Play in Boccaccio's "Decameron," *Princeton University Press, 1986, 281 p.*

Victoria Kirkham   (essay date 1987)

[*In the following essay, Kirkham explores various modes of communication in the* Decameron *and analyzes their effect on human expression. She further outlines parallels between passages in the* Decameron *and the writings of Aristotle, Cicero, and Augustine, which, she contends, underscore the importance of ethics in Boccaccio's tale.*]

The most appealing characters in Boccaccio's *Decameron* are memorable less for what they do than for what they say. A remarkable talent for talking distinguishes two of them in particular. One is Ser Cepparello, arch sinner of the opening tale, who wins the title of sainthood with a blasphemously mendacious confession. His peer in inventive loquacity is Frate Cipolla, that oratorical rival to Tully and Quintilian, whose brilliantly improvised sermon at the end of Day Six metamorphoses an ordinary stroll through Florence into a fabulous mid-eastern pilgrimage, and enables him to display for the awed peasants of Certaldo not "la penna dell'agnolo Gabriello," as he had planned, but "benedetti carboni" from the grate of St. Lawrence's martyrdom. This roguish pair of gifted performers is strategically teamed in the *Decameron.* Its first day of storytelling is a Wednesday, where, after Cepparello's bravura recital, all of the tales revolve in one way or another around well-spoken words. The art of knowing how to speak re-emerges on Day Six, the following Wednesday, which culminates with Cipolla's Ciceronian preaching under a diurnal rubric calling for quick, witty retorts. Calendrically mated, the Wednesdays of Days I and VI are architectural portals leading into both the anthology as a whole and its second half. Their shared theme, implicit the first time around and explicit the second, is symbolically appropriate to "mercoledi," because for medieval mythographers and astrologers alike Mercury was the god of eloquence.

Mercury's rule at the threshold of each narrative week raises the medium of language itself to high-ranking status in the system of values that informs the author's message. Although he claims to be writing mainly about love, what Mercury fosters must somehow, on a less superficial regis-

Boccaccio, on why he wrote about the plague in the *Decameron:*

Whenever, fairest ladies, I pause to consider how compassionate you all are by nature, I invariably become aware that the present work will seem to you to possess an irksome and ponderous opening. For it carries at its head the painful memory of the deadly havoc wrought by the recent plague, which brought so much heartache and misery to those who witnessed, or had experience of it. But I do not want you to be deterred, for this reason, from reading any further, on the assumption that you are to be subjected, as you read, to an endless torrent of tears and sobbing. You will be affected no differently by this grim beginning than walkers confronted by a steep and rugged hill, beyond which there lies a beautiful and delectable plain. The degree of pleasure they derive from the latter will correspond directly to the difficulty of the climb and the descent. And just as the end of mirth is heaviness, so sorrows are dispersed by the advent of joy.

This brief unpleasantness (I call it brief, inasmuch as it is contained within few words) is quickly followed by the sweetness and the pleasure which I have already promised you, and which, unless you were told in advance, you would not perhaps be expecting to find after such a beginning as this. Believe me, if I could decently have taken you whither I desire by some other route, rather than along a path so difficult as this, I would gladly have done so. But since it is impossible without this memoir to show the origin of the events you will read about later, I really have no alternative but to address myself to its composition.

Giovanni Boccaccio, in his introduction to the First Day in the Decameron, *translated by G. H. McWilliam, Penguin, 1972.*

ter, take precedence over the pervading activities prompted in the tales by his planetary neighbor Venus, since no storytelling at all is permitted during her two days. "Venerdì" is reserved instead for turning away from the flesh to the spirit with penitential meditation on Christ's crucifixion. Readers have long admired the dialogue and direct discourse in the *novelle,* unusual in its frequency, as evidence of Boccaccio's consummate ability to achieve, in alternating rhythms of humor and seriousness, realistic character portrayal. Not until recently has the initial and central structural emphasis on discourse been noticed, leading Almansi (1975), Mazzotta (1972; 1975), and Marcus (1979) to argue that the *Decameron* is in essence a meta-linguistic text. But these studies, while rightly stressing Boccaccio's mimetic skill and alerting us to the anthology's self-conscious literary nature, have evaded the ethical coordinates of its 14th-c. rhetorical matrix.

Assuming that communication is indeed a capital topic in Boccaccio's collection of tales, I propose to sound the range of expression it takes there with reference to the philosophical teachings on human locution inherited by the later Middle Ages. This will involve constructing two grids, both necessarily general, given the broad lines of my inquiry. The first will present an overview of speech pat-

terns in the *Decameron,* which run the gamut from mute gesticulation to perfect linguistic decorum. For the second, a survey of classical and Christian writings on rhetoric, I shall take as primary authorities Aristotle, Cicero, and Augustine. Their reasoning reveals that the words Boccaccio put into the mouths of his characters were not chosen simply for verisimilar, humorous, or esthetic effect. He also knew that speech, the intellectual instrument by which man is distinguished from the beasts, comports a powerful ethical valence. What we say and how we say it is the measure of our humanity. Proper speech mirrors the well-ordered soul and makes possible a harmonious social life; its failure accompanies morally defective behavior and works against the interests of the political community in which all men, like Boccaccio's emblematic frame narrators, must rationally participate to achieve their ontological perfection.

Let us begin by sampling the possibilities of discourse presented in the *Decameron.* On Day One, if deception is the key note in Cepparello's confession, the third tale describes linguistic entrapment eluded, as Melchisedech the Jew answers the Sultan's tricky question on true religion by telling his own *novella;* and in the seventh, an appositely told story within the story similarly assists the professional raconteur Bergamino. Pithy replies are the rule for the rest, except 1.2, but even there words count. A Parisian Jew named Abraam is converted in spite of the utter corruption he observes in the Roman clergy through the proselytizing efforts of his friend Giannotto, an uneducated merchant whose words are pleasingly persuasive because the Holy Ghost had put them on his tongue. Formally announced in its governing rubric, the anecdotally brief tales of Day Six, counterpart to One, generate quintessential models of how people should—and should not—speak: "Si ragiona di chi con alcun leggiadro motto, tentato, si riscotesse, o con pronta risposta o avvedimento fuggì perdita o pericolo o scorno."

Elsewhere in the *Decameron* speech is otherwise conspicuous, sometimes by its absence. This is strikingly the case for the Sultan's daughter Alatiel (2.7), whom Mediterranean language barriers reduce to verbal silence as the vicissitudes of maritime violence send her through the hands and beds of many foreign lovers before final reunion with her long-promised husband, felicitously in the guise of *virgo intacta.* A rich sex life also results from taciturnity for Masetto da Lamporecchio (3.1), the enterprising youth who penetrates a convent as the nuns' gardener by pretending to be a deaf mute.

Alatiel and Masetto are, however, exceptions in the *Decameron*'s panoramic range of discursive possibilities, from which, as I have already suggested, readers are most likely to recall the characters more inclined toward loquacity. Their utterances frequently create humorous distortions of speech, which may be dictated on the one hand by naive ignorance, on the other by calculated ingenuity. So the simple-minded Ferondo (3.8) reports, after his presumed resurrection from close on to a year "in Purgatory," divinely imparted news of the son that will be born to him, an annunciation he has heard straight from the "Ragnolo Braghiello." Again, Monna Belcolore, partner in the materialistic little country-bumpkinish romance with the priest of Varlungo (8.2), has a rustic husband, Bentivegna del Mazzo, who one day conveniently departs for the city, explaining in nonsensically confused legalese that he is going there "per alcuna mia vicenda . . .per una comparigione del parentorio per lo pericolator suo il giudice del dificio." Conversely, Maso del Saggio, whose name signals his sagacity, can knowingly manipulate language. His double talk on the magical qualities of the heliotrope, aimed at gullible, thick-headed Calandrino (8.3), conveys the astonishing fact that whoever possesses on his person the fabulous stone will become invisible, "wherever he isn't."

But Boccaccio's undisputed master of dazzling linguistic legerdemain is the brilliant orator Frate Cipolla. His talent shines in a parodic inventory of precious relics: "Il dito dello Spirito Santo così intero e saldo come fu mai, e il ciuffetto del serafino che apparve a san Francesco, e una dell'unghie de' gherubini, e una delle coste del Verbum-caro-fatti-alle-finestre e de'vestimenti della santa Fé catolica . . . " Notable on the list is the first item, the finger of the Holy Ghost, true author of sacred writ, celestial power of the Pentecostal gift of tongues, and, within the *Decameron,* source of the inspired words that helped simple Giannotto convert his friend Abraam. The relic that was to have been the centerpiece of Cipolla's sermon, "la penna," receives repeated mention in the story, nineteen times by concordance count. Such insistence on the word invites us to associate it with the story's thematic verbal nexus in an alternate application as "quill" and "pen." This exotic feather actually came from a parrot, of course, a non-human creature known for its capacity merely to mimic human pronouncements. Propping the friar's kerystic *tour-de-force,* with its sesquipedalian mockery of the incarnational mystery central to the "santa Fé catolica," are underlying layers of authorial word play, concentrated on communicational media in this climatic tale of the *Decameron*'s second "mercoledì."

Other markedly rhetorical moments in the anthology are more seriously cast. This is true, for instance, of the solemn, self-exculpatory declamation delivered by widowed Ghismunda (4.1) to her jealous father, Prince Tancredi, in defense of her love affair with a page in his household. An even more powerful speech in the high style—and one of the two longest rhetorical displays within the tales—is the diatribe that bursts from Tedaldo (3.7), who inveighs against hypocrisy in the clergy to justify his own hidden romantic liaison. The longest single speech made by any character in the *Decameron* is that of Tito Quinzio Fulvio (10.8), student of philosophy from ancient Rome and eloquent advocate of perfect human friendship.

Finally, at an opposite pole, the matter at stake is simple abecedarian literacy. Significantly, the alphabet first surfaces at the center of the day whose theme is language itself as distilled in the quick retort. In 6.5 we meet the foremost jurist of the time, that "armory of civil law" Messer Forese da Rabatta, together with Giotto, its leading painter. Both are sights to behold in the ragged, mudspattered peasant garb that a sudden summer thundershower has forced them to borrow while returning from their country

houses to Florence. Eying his companion, Forese asks, "Giotto, a che ora venendo di qua alla 'ncontro di noi un forestiere che mai veduto non t'avesse, credi tu che egli credesse che tu fossi il migliore dipintore del mondo, come tu se'?" With antiphonal word play on the verb "believe," the artist retorts in the anecdote's punchline, "Messere, credo che egli il crederebbe allora che, guardando voi, egli crederebbe che voi sapeste l'abicì." While their sublime wisdom is masked by coarse, bedraggled clothing, even the finest fur-lined gowns of another man cannot hide the sheer idiocy of his babbling. He is Maestro Simone, Boccaccio's dim-witted doctor from Bologna, said to have learned his abc's "in sul mellone." The phrase punningly contrasts the physician's brainless, gourd-like head with the "mela" on which parents were accustomed to carve for their children letters of the alphabet before allowing them to eat the fruit. The message in these two stories is evident: don't believe what you see; people are to be judged by what they say and how they say it, not by the appearance of external trappings.

Sometimes in the *Decameron,* then, the tongue is silenced altogether to be replaced, as in the stories of Alatiel and Masetto, by sign language and mute gesticulation. But facility with speech, starting with one's abc's, is a skill of fundamental value. The ignorant who lack it, unless guided like Abraam's friend by the Holy Ghost, produce amusingly garbled words and can run off at the mouth about miraculous whisperings from the "Arse-Angel Bagriel." They in turn are naturally vulnerable to gulling by those who do possess an enviable gift of gab, even if without benefit of formal education. Frate Cipolla fits this description: "Niuna scienza avendo, sì ottimo parlatore e pronto era, che chi conosciuto non l'avesse, non solamente un gran rettorico l'avrebbe estimato, ma avrebbe detto esser Tulio medesimo o forse Quintiliano."

Ranging from dumb reticence to polished eloquence, the widely diverse verbal options within the tales of the *Decameron* stand in contrast to the constant propriety and ideal speech of its ten Florentine frame characters. Although Dioneo threatens their rigorously honest code with a bawdy song at the end of Day Five, the *brigata* will not allow him to sing any of the risqué musical ditties he teasingly proposes. As if to reinforce the dignity of the register on which the group converses, their servants cause a clamorous disruption in the next frame episode, which opens the second Wednesday. Quarreling in broad language, Licisca loudly berates Tindaro for being a "bestia d'uom" if he is foolish enough to believe that women are virgins when they marry, and that on a certain Sicofante's wedding night, "Messer Mazza entrasse in Montenero per forza e con ispargimento di sangue." Such farcical, erotic double-entendres fall beneath the elevated linguistic norm maintained by their masters and mistresses during conversational interludes between the tales. That high standard will also extend to the world of the stories for precisely the day on which successful speaking is the enunciated theme, the sixth, when narrators and *novelle* come into closest expressive proximity.

To be sure, a certain license is permitted in storytelling on other days, and this becomes an issue under the irrepressible Dioneo's rule, where piquant cases of cuckolding are the order (7). But as he submits on receiving the crown at the end of Day Six, the exceptional nature of the times can justify some elasticity in subject matter, all the more so because their group seeks only honorable enjoyment. True throughout their sojourn to verbal and behavioral rectitude, the circle will in the end earn praise for it from Panfilo at the close of his concluding reign:

> Quantunque liete novelle e forse attrattive a concupiscenzia dette ci sieno e del continuo mangiato e bevuto bene e sonato e cantato (cose tutte da incitare le deboli menti a cose meno oneste), niuno atto, niuna parola, niuna cosa né dalla vostra parte né dalla nostra ci ho conosciuta da biasimare: continua onestà, continua concordia, continua fraternal dimestichezza mi ci è paruta vedere e sentire. (10, Concl.)

Consequently, just as the storytellers' actions remain within the bounds of virtue, so within the confines of the frame does their talk. What they do and what they say are in perfect harmony.

This is an indispensable consonance in the *Decameron*'s ethical system. To see why, we must now turn to the Classical and early Christian rhetorical tradition that had passed into Boccaccio's cultural milieu. It will be appropriate to begin with Aristotle. Although he did author a treatise on rhetoric, Cicero's *De inventione* and the pseudo-Ciceronian *Rhetorica ad Herennium* supplanted it, so the Philosopher's views on language for the Middle Ages are to be sought elsewhere. Linguistic concepts as basic as they were influential receive prominent consideration in both the *Nicomachean Ethics* and the *Politics*.

In the *Ethics,* of which Boccaccio's copy survives together with his own transcription of the *Commentary* by Thomas Aquinas, Aristotle defines moral virtue as a mean between extremes of excess and deficiency. His three-step scale with its ideal happy medium applies not only to what people do, but just as logically to what we say, that is, to intercourse in words. Such intercourse, he affirms, is of two sorts. One is truth, whose mean is truthfulness; its excessive form is boastfulness, and its defective manifestation is false modesty. The second kind of verbal intercourse relates to "pleasantness." It is, in turn, two-fold; either friendship, or more to the point for our purposes, the ability to amuse and entertain others: "In the giving of amusement the intermediate person is ready-witted and the disposition ready wit, the excess is buffoonery and the person characterized by it a buffoon, while the man who falls short is a sort of boor and his state is boorishness."

Returning to his assertions about buffoonery and boorishness later in the *Ethics,* Aristotle will offer a variant statement on their mean. Called "tasteful intercourse," it is "saying—and again listening—to what one should and as one should." Representative of such conversational ability is polite joking, through which a person reveals virtuous character with ready wit and sallies tactfully tailored to the audience. Witty humor does not admit vulgarity or indecent language, but rather conveys its fun in pleasant innuendo.

From the remarks on these passages appended by St.

Thomas we learn that in playful conversation the exaggerator is termed a buffoon or *bomolochus* ("altar plunderer") after those birds of prey that steal entrails from the sacrificial *bomos,* because he comically misappropriates words and actions to himself. On boorishness Aquinas does not expand. The man who observes the mean, however, "vocatur eutrapelus, quasi bene se vertens ad omnia, et dispositio vocatur eutrapelia." Only a reasonable man who possesses a soul free from slavish passions can enjoy the habit of this virtue, which reveals his internal rational disposition and depends on his education: "Qui scilicet instructus est qualiter debeat ludere, differt a ludo hominis indisciplinati, qui nulla disciplina in ludo refrenatur. Unde manifestum est quod ad medium habitum virtutis pertinet decentia in ludo dicere et audire."

These Aristotelian-Thomistic ideals of tasteful intercourse may serve as a touchstone for judging some of the talk in the *Decameron.* A "bomolochus" 'buffoon' surfaces, for example, in melon-headed Maestro Simone. He is a boastful fool who yaks cacophonously about student-day conquest by fisticuffs of a puny female in Bologna and his current wenching in "Cacavincigli." These risible vaunts are meant to prove his qualifications for admission into a secret orgiastic club that necromantically steals exotic queens for its members' nocturnal gatherings, which al-

An 1873 interpretation of Boccaccio's storytellers in the garden by T. Stothard.

ways feature first a lavish banquet supplied with fare spirited from others' tables. Boorishness finds its match in niggardly Calandrino's bizarre manners, perfect bait and butt
for Maso del Saggio's lapidary joke, or again, in the unpleasant, hypercritical Cesca (6.8), who doesn't understand that to spare herself disagreeable sights, she should
never again face a looking glass. But *eutrapelia,* the desirable mean in playful conversation, initially appears, and
probably not by accident, at the center of Day 1, when in
tale five the Marchioness of Monferrato tactfully cools her
royal French houseguest's "folle amore." Adept as well at
artfully turning a phrase is the Marchioness's Mercurian
and structural 'second' in the *Decameron,* Giotto, who
presides at the center of Day Six. But surpassing all in eu-
trapelian subtlety is the brilliant philosopher-poet Guido
Cavalcanti (6.9), recalled by Elissa, queen for that day,
with a story that shows him as deft in deed as he is in
word. His vault over a sarcophagus at the San Giovanni
door symbolizes the difference between well-mannered,
well-spoken "uomini scienziati" like him, and the others,
who are "idioti e non litterati."

Boccaccio's *brigata,* too, admirably mirrors the Aristotelian mean, one that underlies Elissa's choice of the witty
retort as theme for the Sixth Day. Its initial tale directly
recalls the last on Day 1. Pampinea, who tells 1.10, had
prefaced it with words of praise for fair speech and with
biting remarks on the sad degeneration of conversational
ability among women. Hardly any are left, she complains,
who can understand or respond to a clever saying. Nowadays they merely chatter with their laundresses and baker-
esses instead of engaging in true verbal congress with worthy men. To illustrate the need for pitching one's words
to suit time, place, and audience, she then recounts an anecdote about Madonna Malgherida's embarrassing misas-
sessment of her interlocutor, Maestro Alberto, a mature
gentleman of youthful spirit who nippingly bests her in
banter.

When Filomena presents the first story on Day Six, she repeats Pampinea's lament, echoing almost verbatim her assertions about the special beauty of graceful sallies. These,
she says, crown beautiful speech, itself partner to proper
moral habits:

> Giovani donne, come ne' lucidi sereni sono le
> stelle ornamento del cielo e nella primavera i
> fiori de' verdi prati e de' colli i rivestiti albuscelli
> così de' laudevoli costumi e de' ragionamenti
> belli sono i leggiadri motti; li quali, per ciò che
> brievi sono, tanto stanno meglio alle donne che
> agli uomini quanto più alle donne che agli
> uomini il molto parlar si disdice.

A reversal of Pampinea's tale, Filomena's significantly situated "meta-novella" relates the courteous conversational
coup of Madonna Oretta, who knew just what to say and
when to a knight who did not. Unlike the tale of the scat-
ter-brained cook, Chichibio, whose blurted retort, three
stories later, can compensate for the drumstick snatched
from a crane, Madonna Oretta's speech-act is not a fluke
of one-time luck. Rather it is typical of an aristocratic culture that has taught her the habit of pleasant talk, a conversational mean called *eutrapelia.* Intelligently shaped,
pithy remarks and prompt replies, distillations of speech

at its most beautiful, have in this venerable Aristotelian
context a value that is more than esthetic. They display excellence of character. Tasteful intercourse holds a place in
the *Ethics* on a par with such qualities of self-mastery as
chastity, truthfulness, friendliness, liberality, courage, and
temperance—moral virtues requisite for human happiness.

Why, though, should restraint in speaking be a particularly female virtue? For the unequal measure of speech alot-
ted men and women Aristotle again can offer explanation,
provided we turn to his *Politics.* Political order, he asserts,
requires the same kind of power hierarchy that should obtain in the soul and individual household. Thus, the head
of state, endowed with perfect virtue, must rule his subjects as reason rules our appetites and man his wife. Like
their leader, the other members of the state should cultivate virtues suitable to each one's station and sex. So a
man displays courage in commanding, but a woman in
obeying. Obedience belongs to the human female no less
than silence, "a woman's glory." Thus, continues Aristotle, "a man would be thought a coward if he had no more
courage than a courageous woman, and a woman would
be thought loquacious if she imposed no more restraint on
her conversation than a good man." Given Aristotle's assumption of woman's natural inferiority, her virtues will
lie in her submissiveness. It is through wifely obedience
and verbal restraint that she fulfills her role in the well-
ordered household and, by the same token, in the larger
community as well. Boccaccio's vain Venetian blabber-
mouth Madonna Lisetta, chosen as mistress by the "Angel
Gabriel" in his second Decameronian descent (4.2), fool-
ishly violates this social code. Patient Griselda (10.10)
wisely observes it. Disruptive violence results in the first
case, reaffirmation and continuity of community in the
second, with the reconvergence of Gualtieri's family members.

These ideals of wit and discretion, inherited by the later
Middle Ages, depend logically on Aristotle's more famous, primary linguistic enunciation. It stands at the start
of the *Politics:*

> Nature, as we often say, makes nothing in vain,
> and man is the only animal whom she has en-
> dowed with the gift of speech. And whereas
> mere voice is but an indication of pleasure or
> pain, and is therefore in other animals (for their
> nature attains to the perception of pleasure and
> pain and the intimation of them to one another,
> and no further), the power of speech is intended
> to set forth the expedient and the inexpedient,
> and therefore likewise the just and the unjust.
> And it is a characteristic of man that he alone
> has any sense of good and evil, of just and unjust,
> and the like, and the association of living beings
> who have this sense makes a family and a state.

Language and its proper use belong to the heart of human
behavior, rational and political by definition. Beasts and
gods need not speak because they can live in self-reliant
isolation, but man achieves perfection only when living
communally. Essential to his bonding in the body politic
is speech, which, as Thomas Aquinas would later put it,
"manifests to another what lies hidden in the mind."

Expanding on the Aristotelian axiom with Thomistic commentary in mind, Dante reiterates in his *De vulgari eloquentia:* "Nam eorumque sunt omnium soli homini datum est loqui" (1.2.1). Animal behavior, says Dante, is instinctive and consistent, while human behavior is intelligent and unpredictable. Consequently, to communicate our intentions to others, we must enunciate orally the ideas silently formulated in our rational soul. Locution, a divine gift for the good of man, he says in the *Convivio,* is an operation proceeding from and proper to the rational soul, man's highest attribute. Indicative of the natural connection between human reason and speech is Isidore of Seville's (early 7th-c.) derivation of *oratio* from *oris ratio,* "the reasoning of the mouth" (1.5.3; 12.1.5). Boccaccio's Trecento Italian is rooted in the same equation, for "ragionare" means 'to speak'. The absence of speech, by contrast, is a defining characteristic of brute animals, unreasoning creatures moved by the lower sensitive appetite. Isidore, for example, could say, "*Pecus* dicimus omne quod humana lingua et effigie caret" (emphasis added). Creatures of sense only, beasts, unlike man, need no words to express themselves, as Boccaccio himself will later write in a polemical chapter of his *De casibus virorum illustrium* (c. 1360): "cum igitur nutu, sibilo vel mugitu animalia cetera suas affectiones ostendant, verbis intentum exprimere homini solo concessum est nec immerito. Quid prudentius potuit fecisse natura quam actu tali hominem, celesti anima preditum, a beluis, quibus sola sensualitas dux est, separasse?"

In the **Decameron,** failure to communicate articulately often accompanies animal-like behavior. Alatiel remains inhumanly mute through a chain of passive, indiscriminate sexual couplings in dark, silent places; the sensual appetites of nuns and peasants bring to Filostrato's mind Masetto da Lamporecchio, who feigned muteness to lie with the sisters in a convent—nine in all, the same number of lovers through whose 'hands' Fortune passed Alatiel. Silence and beastliness most obviously go together in Cimone (5.1) before love inspires him to learn the alphabet and join ranks with the philosophers in a suspiciously precipitate turnabout. His pejorative nickname is a consequence of his earlier, primitive nature: "Per ciò che mai né per fatica di maestro né per lusinga o battitura del padre o ingegno d'alcuno altro gli s'era potuto metter nel capo né lettera né costume alcuno, anzi con la voce grossa e deforme e con modi più convenienti a bestia che a uomo, quasi per ischerno da tutti era chiamato Cimone, il che nella lor lingua sonava quanto nella nostra 'bestione'." Cimone relates in turn by name to Doctor Simone, alias "maestro Scimmione" (9.3), whose cranial pumpkin scarcely contains even the most elementary letters (8.9). Beneath the vair that decorates his academic robes, there lurks a pecorine beast that goes about asking silly, senseless questions and singing "artagoticamente." If he ends up wallowing in a hole full of excrement, it is just where such "pecoraggine" belongs.

Absence of mental acumen also logically produces garbled speech like Ferondo's annunciation from the "Ragnolo Braghiello" or Bentivegna del Mazzo's "errancies" in the city. Both peasants, they point to a telling line of associations connecting rusticity, illiteracy, and animal sexuality.

The "mazzo" in Bentivegna's last name signals his loutishness. It is an implement related to the "bastone" on which Cimone leans while gazing at Efigenia, the "scure" that the country laborer Masetto bears on his shoulder into the nunnery, and finally, the punning "messer Mazza" in the servants' quarrel over brides' maidenheads. A cluster of coitional symbols, hammers, sticks, axes, and clubs are country tools typifying life at the rudimentary level of the beast and denoting detachment from the sphere of influence of intelligent speech, the linguistic medium that unites men in rational, political community.

To promote social welfare, however, it is not enough that language spring from rational intelligence. Philosophical knowledge is also indispensable to the civilized art of speaking well. This additional qualification finds expression in the Roman tradition on rhetoric. Its primary authority for the Middle Ages was Cicero, whose *De inventione* is posited on the view that "sapientiam sine eloquentia parum prodesse civitatibus, eloquentiam vero sine sapienta nimium obesse plerumque, prodesse numquam" (1.1). Whoever wishes to speak well and usefully for the community must complement his study of eloquence with solid grounding in philosophy and ethics. Such a speaker will surpass all other men in excellence: "Ac mihi quidem videntur homines, cum multis rebus humiliores et infirmiores sint, hac re maxime bestiis praestare, quod loqui possunt. Quare praeclarum mihi quiddam videtur adeptus is qui qua re homines bestiis praestent ea in re hominibus ipsis antecellat" (1.4).

Among Cicero's many medieval commentators and translators was Dante's teacher Brunetto Latini, who elaborates in his *Rettorica* (c. 1260) on the above passage. Elephants are bigger than men, lions more powerful, he says; the five senses, too, are stronger in animals, as in the boar hearing, the lynx seeing, the monkey tasting, the vulture smelling, and the spider's touch. In speech, however, man is always superior to the animals. Even more influential than the *De inventione* was the *Rhetorica ad Herennium,* mistakenly believed to be Cicero's as well, and often distinguished from the master's slightly earlier treatise by the title *Rhetorica nova.* (Boccaccio's library contained both the "ars nova et vetus Ciceronis.") A student of philosophy, which he reads with the pupil of oratory addressed in the title of his manual, the wise pseudo-Cicero prefaces his lessons with the injunction that "non enim in se parum fructus habet copia dicendi et commoditas orationis, si recta intelligentia et definita animi moderatione gubernetur" (1.1). Such concepts were refined by the second great luminary of rhetorical wisdom in antiquity, Quintilian. As set forth in the proem of his *Institutio oratoria,* he undertook to describe the perfect orator, "qui esse nisi vir bonus non potest, ideoque non dicendi modo eximiam in eo facultatem, sed omnis animi virtutes exigimus . . .vir talis, qualis uere sapiens appellari possit, nec moribus modo perfectus . . .sed etiam scientia et omni facultate dicendi."

Now Boccaccio's convivial Brother Onion, who seemed "Tulio medesimo o forse Quintiliano," becomes a rather less congenial character than commonly thought when weighed against the standards of what his classical archetypes had taught. Although a superlative speaker, Cipolla lacks "scienza" absolutely. This intellectual, ethical defect is externalized and epitomized in his Doppelgänger, the animalistic servant Guccio Balena/Imbratta/Porco, whom the friar proudly credits with traits horrible enough to wreck all the virtue, wisdom, and moral sense in Solomon, Aristotle, and Seneca. The noble, human qualities of his counter-paragons are quite absent in this bloated, grease-caked lackey, around whom only filth, stench, and creatures clump. His emphatic, final piggish surname may tag him historically as one Guccio Porcellana, so known from employment at the trecento hospital of San Filippo in Via del Porcellana. He is about as mean a man, according to his master, as ever was painted by the notorious canvas-spatterer Lippo Topo ("Phil the Mouse"). An inveterate womanizer, Guccio appears at his best zeroing in for the pickup on a repulsive scullery lass laden with breasts "che parean due ceston da letame." Perched perspiring by the hearth in August heat, he sets out to con her with scrambled lingo on the high station in life that he has "on credit" and his currently huge fortune, "de' fiorini più di millantanove." Clever in a style copied from the friar, he belongs to that apish clan of the *bomolochi,* who on Thomistic authority get their names from plundering birds. So when Boccaccio envisions him pressing his suit with terms metaphorically avian, he parodies amorous pursuit couched in the courtly mode, and at the same time shows us the big black predator diving for his steal. Happier in kitchens that "sopra i verdi rami l'usignuolo," Guccio swoops down upon fat little Nuta "non altramente che si gitta l'avoltoio alla carogna."

Figuratively speaking, Cipolla himself has less of the man than the beast, and he literally bears a name that lowers him even further, down into the domain of the plants. It is, for example, his wont to collect alms in Certaldo, because "buona pastura vi trovava"—fields fertile with reference to Isidorian etymology for eleemosynary peculation. A member of the mendicant order of St. Anthony, whose iconographic attribute is the pig, he facetiously claims to have embarked on his far flung pilgrimage in search of "i privilegi del Porcellana." The phrase has porcine odor that replicates Guccio's third moniker and complements Cipolla's sodomistic bent, a tendency announced in the goatish "capitoli del Caprezio" generously given by him to the Patriarch of Jerusalem. This verbal counterfeiter, who descends from the evil family of Antonine "pigs" excoriated by Dante for distorting Holy Scripture and chattering buffooneries from the pulpit, is named after a lowly vegetative item of agrarian produce and travels the countryside armed with the feather of a bird that just parrots human speech, as the poet's *Convivio* reminds us:

> E se alcuno volesse dire . . . che alcuno uccello parli, sì come pare di certi, massimamente de la gazza e del pappagallo, e che alcuna bestia fa atti o vero reggimenti, sì come pare de la scimia e d'alcuno altro, rispondo che non è vero che parlino nè che abbiano reggimenti, però che non hanno ragione, da la quale queste cose convengnono procedere. (3.7)

In view of these associations with subhuman subsistence levels symbolic of his lack of "scienza," it is not surprising that Cipolla's discourse, spun around a prank made into a "miracle," should turn on twisted words.

No doubt the real miracle in this tale is Boccaccio's comic prestidigitation of the word on the page, for it is brilliant humor with a sobering latent thrust. Spellbinding, pointless oratory like Brother Cipolla's, while harmlessly amusing for the undeceived, signals serious trouble when those beguiled by it belong to the community of the Lord's faithful, in whatever pastures they may dwell. So we learn from Saint Augustine, whose *De doctrina christiana* can grant approval to Ciceronian rhetoric, provided it is for the good in the service of the truth:

> Qui vero affluit insipienti eloquentia, tanto magis cavendus est, quanto magis ab eo in iis quae audire inutile est, delectatur auditor, et eum quoniam diserte dicere audit, etiam vere dicere existimat. Haec autem sententia nec illos fugit, qui artem rhetoricam docendam putarunt: fassi sunt enim sapientiam sine eloquentia parum prodesse civitatibus; eloquentiam vero sine sapientia nimium obesse plerumque, prodesse nunquam. (4.5)

Christian orators, above all, bear a solemn responsibility for addressing their flocks in clearly understandable, truthful terms, for what they say is of the greatest import to the eternal welfare of their listeners.

In the bon vivant Cipolla, Boccaccio brings to life a peddlar of nonsense utterly nonchalant toward salvation. An incomplete orator by both classical and Christian standards, he specifically answers Dante's description of those degenerate evangelists who fatten on the spoils of "fables"—hot air, really, which is all they feed their flocks: "Per apparer ciascun s'ingegna e face/sue invenzioni; e quelle son trascorse/da' predicanti e 'l Vangelio si tace." Sermons made of ingenious inventions, but silent on the Gospel, puff up the cowl with self-satisfaction, but for greedy shepherd and gullible lambs alike, the devil lies in wait: "Ora si va con motti e con iscede/a predicare, e pur che ben si rida,/gonfia il cappuccio e più non si richiede./Ma tale uccel nel becchetto s'annida,/che se 'l vulgo il vedesse, vederebbe/la perdonanza di ch'el si confida."

If Cipolla ignores sacred verse in his homily, he has a confrere of sorts who does, so to speak, preach on the Gospel and successfully convert an audience. With Tedaldo Elisei (3.7), castigator of clerical corruption, Boccaccio brings to open, heated attack criticism veiled by humor in his portrayal of the Antonine Onion. Tedaldo has appealed to readers, not only as the author's spokesman against the scourge of the friars, but also a perfect courtly lover, the intellectual hero of an old-fashioned, bittersweet romance. Appearances in the **Decameron,** though, are often ambiguous. Here we see how eloquence, even from the mouth of a cultured man, can take a dangerously misleading turn.

Grief drove Tedaldo from Florence after sudden rejection by the married lady whose love he had secretly won. During seven years' absence he makes his fortune in business on Cyprus and then, hopeful of regaining his lady, returns home disguised as a pilgrim from the Holy Sepulcher, only to discover that Ermellina's husband has just been accused of his murder. The error causes him to ponder "la cieca severità delle leggi e de' rettori, le quali assai volte, quasi solleciti investigatori delli errori, incrudelendo fanno il falso provare." Identity still concealed beneath the palmer's cap and cloak, he proves to his lady with sophistry in oratory that she should not have abandoned him just because "un maladetto frate" threatened her with damnation if she persisted in the affair. Those who call themselves friars today, lashes out Tedaldo, ensnare the faithful masses with lies to cultivate their own temporal comfort: "E quale col giacchio il pescatore d'occupar ne' fiumi molti pesci a un tratto, così costoro, colle *fimbrie ampissime* avvolgendosi, molte pinzochere, molte vedove, molte altre sciocche femine e uomini d'avilupparvi sotto s'ingegnano" (4.2, italics mine). To critics these brothers merely reply, "Fate quello che noi diciamo e non quello che noi facciamo." Why, fulminates Tedaldo, do they not follow the holy word of the Gospel, "Incominciò Cristo a fare e ad insegnare"?

Tedaldo's diatribe mines Matthew 23, where Christ heaps woe on the Scribes and Pharisees. It is the Gospel on hypocrisy:

> Tunc Iesus locutus est ad turbas et ad discipulos suos dicens: Super cathedram Moysi sederunt scribae et pharisaei: omnia ergo quaecumque dixerint vobis servate et facite, secumdum opera vero eorum nolite facere: dicunt enim et non faciunt. . . .Omnia vero opera sua faciunt ut videantur ab hominibus: dilatant enim phylacteria sua et *magnificant fimbrias.* (4.28-29)

Tedaldo may be right about the clergy, but since all he says is aimed at persuading the lady to resume their affair, he speaks the truth neither for good nor "in truth." When he advocates doing what the clergy does, not what it says, he turns Christ's words inside-out, ergotizing all the worse because it evades any reference to the commandment on adultery. Infidelity in marriage, he says, is only a sin of the body, "peccato naturale," trivial compared to her "malvagità di mente" in ending their affair and causing his exile. Ironically, Tedaldo rivals his city's leaders' treacherous ability to contend diabolically for wrong and "prove the false." As Augustine had put it:

> Sunt etiam quaedam praecepta uberioris disputationis, quae jam eloquentia nominatur, quae nihilominus vera sunt, quamvis eis possint etiam falsa persuaderi: sed quia et vera possunt, non est facultas ipsa culpabilis, sed ea male utentium perversitas. (2.36)

Tedaldo is arguing the wrong side of the case. Still, in the story his perversity passes for sanctity because he pretends to be a holy man who has visited the Sepulcher. Then he reassures Ermellina: "Voi dovete sapere che io son frate, e per ciò li loro costumi io conosco tutti." Were the content of his scathing invective not enough to make us distrust the sincerity of anyone in fraternal garb, this tale's allusions to the hypocrites in Dante's Hell should make it clear that all is not right with "sepulchral" Tedaldo.

Dante's hypocrites have scriptural ancestors in the scribes and Pharisees of Matthew 23, "whited sepulchers" literalized in the lost souls of *Inferno* 23. All friars, they stoop under gilded lead "cappe con capucci bassi/dinanzi a li occhi." Himself in pious disguise, Tedaldo duplicates the hypocrisy of the clergy he denounces. Friars today, he says, "niuna altra cosa hanno di frate se non la cappa"; yet he himself has nothing of the Christian pilgrim except "la schiavina e 'l cappello." Throughout the story there is always a discrepancy between what Tedaldo seems and is, what he says and does, one that parallels the disjunction between Ermellina's behavior and her name (ermine is a symbol of chastity). Whether as incognito exile or citizen, he is a master of the mask; secrecy and concealment are the hallmarks of his actions. Beneath this onus of duplicity, his romantic glow dims: model lover and enterprising, intelligent citizen, he is also a perfect hypocrite.

If the clerical representatives of Christ should teach like Him by deed and word, so must all right-minded Christians. Boccaccio's deed and word is, of course, the ***Decameron,*** whose enunciatory registers are a widely ranging, instructive profile of man, the talking animal. When he speaks for himself, as in his prefatory evocation of the plague, he has full rights to the classical precepts of Ciceronian eloquence. His frame narrators, too, can enjoy the privilege, but not so the majority of characters whose stories they tell. Among the latter, the more "copious" the discourse, the more socially injurious its potential usually seems to be—at least, until we come to the exemplary protagonists of the Tenth Day.

Before then, though, Tedaldo's specious reasoning does not stand alone. We should also by now see a darker side to Ghismunda's allegedly admirable, feminist declamation (4.1). Since her father, Tancredi, all too humanly, could not divine her motivations for taking a lover, she must manifest them to him with words, whose necessity Augustine recognizes in Christian parallel to Aristotle:

> Quomodo venit, nisi quod Verbum caro factum est, et habitavit in nobis? Sicuti enim loquimur, et id quod animo gerimus, in audientis animum per aures carneas illabitur, fit sonus verbum quod corde gestamus, et locutio vocatur. (1.13)

Although Ghismunda's translation of thought to speech is no doubt perfectly accurate, a problem lies in her thinking itself. It is dictated not by the rational intellect, but "concupiscibile disiderio," as she expressly states, and it claims justification from ideas canonical to the truancy of courtly love. Externalized in stylistically impeccable form, her self-counsel rests on unvoiced premises as morally fallacious as those of Dante's Francesca: the pull of my flesh was an irresistible force.

Tedaldo's and Ghismunda's copious discourse is not a sign of noble character. On the contrary, it argues their preference for cupidinous over Christian love. As advocates of pleasure, not virtue, they perversely ill-use eloquence. Nevertheless, full-blown rhetoric need not always betoken suspiciously smooth talking. It can express goodness that speaks in the service of good, the ideal both ancient and medieval.

Boccaccio's most accomplished orator, therefore, is the most admirable man he could conceive. He is Tito Quinzio Fulvo (10.8), a Roman student of philosophy in Athens who becomes fast friends with his classmate, Greek Gisippo. Gisippo saves Tito's life (he was dying from lovesickness) by secretly giving him his bride, Sofronia; later, back home, Tito reciprocates by offering to die in place of Gisippo, who has been wrongly accused of murder. Matters are set straight, and the story ends as Tito gives Gisippo his sister's hand. Tito's splendid speech—longer than any other in the *Decameron*—justifies his *de facto* marriage before the angered parents of Gisippo and Sofronia, and publicly persuades them that he did what was right in every possible respect.

Striking length likens Tedaldo's to Tito's oratory, inviting us to compare the tales. In the former, Fortune is blamed for bizarrely painful events; the logic of divine Providence comfortingly rules the latter. The Florentine is a courtly poet who has sojourned on Cyprus, island of Venus, and who takes his pleasure in physical possession of Monna Ermellina; the Roman is a philosopher who truly falls in love with wisdom (Sofronia is cognate with the Greek *sophrosyne*, wisdom). Tedaldo argues for adultery, Tito for marriage. Tedaldo serves himself above all, while Tito is selflessly magnanimous.

Tito epitomizes Stoic prudence, the highest virtue attainable in his pre-Christian world. His "scientia" in turn makes him a perfect orator, one whose eloquence is coupled with wisdom. First in the book's closing trio of tales, themselves a fictional "peroration" on virtue, this story spotlights language at an ideal pitch. Rhetoric is the *novella*'s real protagonist, appropriately so, at the *Decameron*'s finale.

As talk goes within the hundred tales, Tito is a paragon. Touchstones outside the text—Aristotelian, Ciceronian, and Augustinian—help us better understand that talk. Speech suppressed (Alatiel, Masetto, Cimone), misused (Ferondo, Maestro Simone), or abused (Cipolla, Tedaldo, Ghismunda) denotes moral deficiency and sometimes unreasoning behavior akin to the ways of the brute animals. But proper speech (Madonna Oretta, Tito, the frame narrators) reveals man at his highest. In the Classical and Christian traditions alike the better we speak, the better we are as human beings. Rational, social animals, our perfection requires us to live in groups whose cohesion is made possible by our ability to communicate what we are thinking. Speech at its most quintessentially urbane thus becomes a motif well-fitted to rule the days with which each half of the *Decameron* begins, calendrical mates given to the astrological family of the ancient god of eloquence. Finally, the narrators' linguistic decorum is itself politically and morally emblematic. Prompted by reason, they have fled for their lives from a diseased, infernal city of anarchy to reconsitute the community through hierarchically ordered, harmonious daily living, a retreat shaped by virtuous words and deeds in ideal ethical consonance. (pp. 127-46)

Victoria Kirkham, "The Word, the Flesh, and the 'Decameron'," in Romance Philology, *Vol. XLI, No. 2, November, 1987, pp. 127-49.*

Christopher Nissen (essay date 1989)

[*In the following excerpt, Nissen provides a framework for apprehending Boccaccio's presentation of ethics in the* Decameron *by which readers may discern patterns among the diverse "moral moods" he creates.*]

The *Decameron* is generally seen to put forth a totalized worldview, a picture made large of man and society—if this is so, then what is the key helping us pinpoint a unified ethics within the text? What moral system does it set forth and how does the reader, now or at any other time in history, "read" it ethically? I hope, in this study, to contribute something toward a resolution of these problems. Although I agree with the prevailing consensus that the *Decameron* presents us with a broad portrait, on an almost epic scale, of the human experience, I do not intend to present yet another totalized overview, nor make my interpretation of Boccaccio's ethics part of any single definition for the work as a whole, in part because hindsight seems to show that such a definition will rarely hold the field unchallenged for long, and in part because I do not think a work as richly complex as the *Decameron* is easily or profitably reduced to facile labels. What I do intend to do is to propose a system for reading and appreciating the way Boccaccio presents ethics in his *novelle,* a way which sorts out patterns amidst the diversity of moral moods created by Boccaccio without pretending to be a single, exclusive approach.

Analysis of ethics necessitates analysis of culture: culture is the matrix within which ethical systems are formulated, and cultural considerations, as manifested in the text, must lie at the root any examination of *Decameron* ethics. The hundred tales present a particularly intricate picture in this regard: within the forest of individual narratives two different cultural worlds, the ideal and the real, have long been distinguished. Vittore Branca is among those critics who have sought to delineate this central cultural and stylistic dichotomy in the *Decameron:* in his article "Registri narrativi e stilistici nel *Decameron*" he recognizes Boccaccio's shifts in style as he presents these worlds in different *novelle.* Some *Decameron novelle* reflect the idealized past of aristocratic virtues, the then fading world of knightly magnanimity and self-sacrifice, while others are more oriented toward the bourgeois mercantile values of Trecento Florence, a world more "real" and immediate for the bulk of Boccaccio's audience. Branca outlines Boccaccio's stylistic shifts between these two worlds with their varying presentations of character type, setting and plot development; in effect he is noting that Boccaccio can switch his stylistic key, or "registro", in the presentation of each world, reflecting the rich mingling of values and the coexistence of the ideals of past and present that characterize the autumn of the Italian Middle Ages. Branca does discuss ethics in this regard and acknowledges that shifts of ethical tone accompany the depiction of these two worlds with their different moral values; what he does is to hint, in effect, of the presence of ethical "registri" in the *Decameron* as well as cultural and stylistic ones.

I propose to carry that hint a step further and present a system of ethical modes for the *Decameron,* an outline of the tendency for diversity of moral mood and tone which

Boccaccio's work continually presents us. I hope to demonstrate how Boccaccio employs his various ethical modes within the context of his appreciation of the ideal/real dichotomy mentioned above, the dichotomy which pervades his *novella* collection and allows him to create so rich a portrait of the cultural flux and diversity of his time.

The dichotomy of values and cultural settings which we have acknowledged in Boccaccio's work, the clear distinction between "mondo aristocratico" and "mondo comunale," must lie at the base of any system of ethical modes for the **Decameron.** Ethics in its most fundamental sense constitutes the potential for an individual to make correct choices of action in a social context. In the **Decameron** *novelle* characters are continually presented as making clear-cut choices for right action; these are the protagonists with whom the reader is expected to identify, whose moral choices are defensible according to a moral system fully understood and accessible in terms of reader expectations. The peculiarity of the **Decameron** is that it has more than one such system; previous tale collections typically did not present so much variety in this regard. The **Decameron,** as we have had occasion to note, is the product of a 14th century Italian *comune,* a society in a state of flux and social change, exhibiting a merging of values. With the **Decameron** it becomes necessary to talk of opposing ethical systems, opposing modes of ethical discourse which, on the level of the text, embrace a wide variety of factors: elements of style mingle with presentation of character type and sociological references to create an overall tone of "propriety" for a given *novella.* Recognition of the ethical mode which predominates in each *novella* involves awareness of the most fundamental goals of the protagonist, of which basic choices of action result in the presentation of the moral good, of how a just end is achieved. These factors are presented not only within the *novelle* themselves, but also in the tale teller's pronouncements in the introduction preceding each *novella,* which are pre-textual with respect to the *novella* and are not part of the story narrative, but all the same have an integral role to play in the exposition of ethical and exemplaristic features.

If we examine the *novelle* and their introductions individually according to these criteria of goals of the protagonist and choices of action, a few basic patterns of characters' moral behavior emerge, three broad modes of ethical discourse to be exact, to which we may assign variously each of the hundred tales. In one such mode characters may be seen to gain materially or hedonistically while remaining praiseworthy; the example they set is one upholding the propriety of gain. This ethical mode is most readily associated with the bourgeois and mercantile "mondo comunale", with what Branca calls the "mondo reale" or "mondo comico": for the purposes of this study I call this mode Ethics of Acquisition. Opposite it, naturally enough, stands a contrary mode in which material or hedonistic gains are foregone according to another system of values: this is the mode corresponding to the "mondo ideale", to be associated with adherence to aristocratic or feudal values of magnanimity, largesse and self-sacrifice. This mode I will call Ethics of Renunciation. Ethics of Acquisition (which would seem to predominate slightly in the **Decameron**) and Ethics of Renunciation are the twin moralistic

poles of the *novella* characters; their correct choices in society frequently reflect clear identification with one or the other of these modes. Yet these two are not sufficient in themselves to describe all motivation for right behavior in Boccaccio's characters, and indeed one more mode remains to be described. This is Ethics of Retribution wherein "right" characters deliberately (or at times, instead, almost unwittingly) set out to correct or punish the behavior of "wrong" ones who are usually clearly labelled as such.

These modes reflect, in the most direct way, the primary goals and choices of action of ethically correct characters. Seen in these terms, characters are either acquiring, relinquishing, or punishing in the name of moral good: in their actions lies the essence of whatever moral message the reader may extract from the tale. A specific ethical mode pervades each *novella,* as an integral part of its individual makeup; it is essential that we examine closely certain tales, to determine how each ethical mode manifests itself. The first two *novelle* I have chosen for analysis show us both traits of Acquisition (the tale of Agilulf and his groom, III, 2) and those of Renunciation (the tale of Federigo degli Alberighi and the falcon, V, 9).

The *novella* of Agilulf, in which a king discovers his groom has impersonated him in the queen's darkened bedchamber, provides us with some intriguing moral material because its presentation of didactic content is not simplistic or linear: the king and his groom each present different, parallel moral lessons. It is a *novella* about which a great deal can be said with regard to the subject of ethics.

The first line of approach in determining the ethical content of this *novella* (or indeed that of any **Decameron** *novella*) is to take note of certain external factors belonging more properly to the outward frame story than to the text of the *novella* itself, but which provide the initial orientation for the study of *novella* ethics. Of primary importance is awareness of the day in which the story is recounted: here we are in the Third Day, wherein we read of *novella* protagonists who gain things they want or regain lost things through their own cleverness, through human intelligence which can defeat the machinations of Fortune. Given this awareness, we can readily identify the protagonist of this tale and recognize in him those qualities of wit which, in the context of this day's theme, are set forth for our admiration. He is the *pallafreniere,* the groom, and the choices he makes are those which are ethically correct for this particular narrative moment in the **Decameron.** We are clearly expected to find him praiseworthy, for he gains something he has long desired, and gains it cleverly, losing nothing thereby. Nontheless, in the tale's introduction, we find Boccaccio speaking as much of the king's choices as of those of the groom: so many indiscreet men, finding themselves in Agilulf 's position, would have raised a public outcry in their efforts to find the miscreant even though such an action would only serve to make their shame known to everybody. There is a sort of contradiction here, which makes this story so interesting. Boccaccio means the protagonist to be the groom but a major part of the story's moral lesson will derive from the right actions of the king, his antagonist. Boccaccio stresses the king's discretion and wisdom in the tale's introduction, and as it turns out, these are things which apply as well to the groom, so careful to hide his love and act discreetly. Boccaccio's language tells us about his characters' motivations—they act in their own best interests, for personal gain. The two main characters stand in conflict, but each has a reward of sorts. The groom outwits the king but the king makes the best of things by displaying a discretion uncommon to men in his position: his "senno", or wisdom, provides a contrast for the groom's "astuzia", or craftiness. In the wider context of the *Decameron*, wit and discretion emerge as main components of Ethics of Acquisition—they recur constantly when characters are to be praised for gain. Traditional "high" virtue, as it appears in Boccaccio's world, is exemplified best by acts of renunciation and liberality, and can frequently be a public act designed to attract attention and general praise. On the other hand acquisition, for all that it may be a good thing and an ethically correct goal in so many *Decameron* tales, is best sought away from the public eye, in the margins of social awareness. In this *novella* all is done in secret: the king discovers something it behooves men facing exposure as cuckolds never to know, (" . . . che per loro non fa di sapere."). Having discovered it he shows great wisdom in staying discreet and maintaining appearances, gaining thereby the avoidance of shame and tarnished honor. Likewise the groom acts secretly and to his consistent advantage, first in assuaging his love desire, second in employing his *astuzia* to outwit the king. He reflects the shrewdness of the realist, as befits a protagonist of the Third Day. He is intelligent enough to know that revelation of his desire will gain him nothing, so he says nothing and makes no gesture that might betray him. After he has satisfied his desire without having been seen, or even identified as a stranger by the queen, he resolves not to lose the bliss he has acquired, so he discreetly withdraws and preserves his life.

Both men make the best of a bad situation and each is content with the outcome. The king acts not only to preserve his own honor but also that of his queen, whose innocence he is shrewd enough (and merciful enough) to recognize. The portraits of the deeds and natures of these men stress both their intelligence and competence in acting in their own best interests. The groom gained as much as fortune would ever concede him, and as he is wise enough to recognize this fact, he never again will so tempt fate (" . . .nè più la sua vita in sì fatto atto commise alla fortuna."). Ethics of Acquisition is the ethics of rational choice, of the intellect and the process of intellection, of the wise recognition of the scope and limits of the gifts of Fortune. All these characteristics are well reflected in this *novella*, and recur frequently in many others throughout the *Decameron*.

The *novella* of Federigo, who unwittingly serves his prize falcon to his beloved, shall be our model for the mode of Renunciation. It is told in the Fifth Day, wherein love stories have happy endings. For most of the tales of this day the predominant mode tends to be Acquisition, so Federigo's stands as something of an exception. And indeed, the tale teller makes this plain from the start, as she refers to the power of women's beauty over noble hearts, and to the need for women to consciously choose the persons on whom they should bestow their largesse. Acquisition has been temporarily dethroned by another, loftier moral power, manifesting itself in references to "cuor gentili" and magnanimity; of particular importance to us in our identification of ethical modes is the explicit reference to characters' choices of action. As we go on to further explore this new moral ground in terms of the tale's presentation of characters and their deeds, we see right away that the spirit of renunciation inspires not only a lady, but most notably Federigo. Of Federigo we hear that he is a nobleman distinguished in arms and *cortesia*. The word *cortesia*, referring to that elusive medieval concept of courtly, aristocratic moral virtue, immediately channels us into a moral atmosphere that differs significantly from that of the tale of Agilulf, despite Agilulf's regality. Specific mention of *cortesia* evokes an ideal, in which desire for gain is submerged by the need for magnanimity and self-sacrifice; avarice has no place in the *Corte d'Amore*, in the poetic realm of the courtly lover. We have shifted ethical worlds and expectations. Throughout this *novella* Boccaccio sounds the note of *cortesia* with the kinds of characters he presents, their activities (jousting, falconry), their humble and decorous ways of addressing one another, etc. In tales of this sort, Boccaccio tempers his characters' naked desire for gain with the solemnity of aristocratic ritual (as we see in Federigo's dedication to knightly service for love) or with the stylized and quasi-surreal *topoi* of the romance tradition (as in the case of the boy who falls grievously ill and can only be cured by gaining the object of his desire). Humility, honorable deeds and self-sacrifice predominate over the gross motivations of acquisition. Boccaccio balances his portrait of the gentle nobleman Federigo with those of the other characters who, nontheless, belong to the class of the *borghesia*. Giovanna has the principal qualities of faithful devotion to her husband and tender love for her son, while the husband himself is honorable and generous.

Boccaccio builds his tale around a central act of pathetically ironic renunciation: the confused Federigo, challenged to commit a great act of self-sacrifice in the name of hospitality and courtly largesse, unwittingly eliminates his chance to earn his lady's favor through bestowing the falcon to her alive—in effect, one act of renunciation precludes the other, leaving him deeply distressed. This tragic sense of irony is heightened by the lady's grief at what she has brought about and by the eventual death of the boy. But sacrifice, for the faithful knight no less than for the pious Christian, has its reward in final acquisition, and Federigo gains both the woman and material wealth at the tale's conclusion. This resolution in marriage and material gain shows how completely Boccaccio allows his tale to be pervaded by elements of the *borghese-comunale* world, and yet we must still note that Federigo is motivated not so much by *borghese* intelligence as by dogged adherence, in the face of all rejection and adversity, to the ideals of *cortesia*. His moral lesson is one of the value of renunciation.

In both of these *novelle*, the prime substance of plot lies in the protagonist's central choice of action. The groom chooses his secret conquest of the queen, and Federigo chooses to sacrifice his falcon. Each choice reflects a completely separate moral ideal. Character choice combines with lesser factors such as style, character type, *topoi*, etc., to produce varying moral moods, which is to say (in terms of the present study) varying ethical modes. These modes reflect patterns of character behavior and plot which in time become familiar to the reader as he progresses through the *Decameron novelle*, resolving themselves into predictable and recurring conclusions for the different tales. Exposition of the system of ethical modes helps us analyze and systematize the varying moral atmospheres that infuse different *novelle* in turn, allowing us to understand characteristics which otherwise can appear vague and even contradictory.

Modes of Acquisition and Renunciation ought not to be difficult for a reader to grasp as concepts, since *Decameron* criticism has long been accustomed to the idea of a sociostylistic dichotomy between real and ideal worlds; recognition of these two modes springs ultimately from continued awareness of at least the bare outlines of this dichotomy. Retribution, my third ethical mode of correct punishment, is another matter, I believe, less likely to suggest itself as a cohesive unit in the scheme of the *Decameron*'s ethical structure. Most would readily admit that punishment is a common resolution for many plots of *Decameron novelle*, or indeed that punishment may often be seen as a sort of moral imperative, without wishing to postulate an Ethics of Retribution within a triform scheme of ethical modes. But the *Decameron* is a thematically rich work and it is easy to forget how much of a polemicist Boccaccio is: as fond as he may appear of tales of love and adultery, of practical jokes and the quirks of fortune, he also sets out numerous targets for wrath and punishment. The key to recognizing the role of retribution in the *Decameron*'s ethical system lies in remembering the structural and thematic elements in the work which, as we have noted, tend to portray right behavior within individual *novelle*. Characters' choices of action, statements made within the tale's preamble, variations of style all come into play, to present a *novella* oriented toward a conclusion of just retribution in the name of one of Boccaccio's pet polemics, just as others may reveal the virtues of acquisition and renunciation. Punishment prevails most apparently perhaps in the famous tales of *beffa* or pranks, but is no less a feature of the many tales of *motti* or sharp retorts spoken by righteous characters in order to put offenders of good manners in their place. Taking all of its manifestations into consideration, the theme of retribution occurs in no fewer than twenty-seven of the 100 *novelle*, to be found primarily in Days I, III, VI, VII, VIII, and IX. In these *novelle* Ethics of Retribution predominates. That is to say, we can reduce the prime ethical substance in them to an attempt on the part of certain characters to act rightly through punishment, just as we can reduce the basic motivation to do right in the *novella* of Agilulf to desire for acquisition and in the *novella* of Federico to desire to renounce. Earlier I described Acquisition and Renunciation as the twin moral poles of the *Decameron,* corresponding roughly to the wider thematic scheme of the real/ideal. Ethics of Retribution likewise has a place in this scheme, but its role is more ambiguous, linked to both the real and ideal worlds and serving to some extent as an essential reconciliation between the two. Ethics of Retribution has a pivotal posi-

tion in the grand scheme of the *Decameron*'s ethical modes. The need to punish in Boccaccio's stories comes as a response to a variety of situations in which ethically correct characters may find themselves. Punishment may serve as a vehicle of revenge for wrongdoing or as a means to humiliate fools or the pompous: as such, it functions within the scheme of realism, the comic stylistic mode. It may serve instead as a vehicle of illumination or correction for those who perpetrate unvirtuous, discourteous acts: as such it functions as an accessory to the *Decameron*'s idealistic world. Branca has described the *Decameron* as a "human comedy" constructed out of a progression of the grand themes of Fortune, Love, Ingenuity, and ultimately in the sublime Tenth Day, high Virtue; seen thus, Acquisition functions within the confluence of Fortune and Ingenuity (characters get what they want through manipulation of these two forces) while Renunciation functions within the confluence of Fortune and Virtue (Fortune creates a situation compelling a virtuous character to act magnanimously, seen most consistently as a feature of the Tenth Day but apparent also in Federigo's story). Retribution operates within the margins of both sharply delineated and contrary moral realms, those of Ingenuity and Virtue. A character chooses retributive action at the service of either desire for revenge or entertainment (which has value in the real world) or desire for correction of wrong attitudes (which has value in the ideal world).

The nature of the ethical mode of Retribution is therefore far more problematic than those of Acquisition or Renunciation. It becomes a linking factor between the twin realms of the real world (as it exists) and the ideal world (as it ought to exist). This factor is ultimately indispensable to our comprehension of the work as a cohesive whole. Punishment is a conscious response to injustice or offensive behavior: a *novella* protagonist chooses castigation when confronted by a character who offends the established norms of the moral world of the *Decameron.* Boccaccio carefully constructs these norms out of his subtle play of reader expectations, deriving his moral consciousness from a host of pre-existing literary traditions. Thus, in this work, under certain circumstances the reader can expect a husband to merit castigation from his justifiably adulterous wife, or a traitor to the ideals of *cortesia* to merit a stinging rebuke. Boccaccio's presentation of the function and mechanisms of Ethics of Retribution follows circumscribed patterns which he establishes as the work progresses. Retribution in the *Decameron* responds to certain kinds of offensive behavior, which we can break down thus: lack of virtue, hypocrisy, jealousy, unjustified perpetration of *beffa* (the "beffatore beffato" theme, when a trickster finds himself tricked) or any combinations of all these. The analysis of Boccaccio's application of Ethics of Retribution becomes in effect a study of all the attitudes he finds wrong and wishes to condemn in his book; his technique for such condemnation is the depiction of punished characters. When Boccaccio shows us punishment for lack of virtue, most consistently in Days I and VI, the form he gives it is that of *mordere*, a verbal "biting" meant to put offenders of aristocratic manners in their place: this is retribution within the context of the ideal world, which often includes the offender's ashamed recognition of wrongdoing and potential rehabilitation into proper society. A fine example of this, akin to tale LI in the late 13th century *Novellino* and generally representing older patterns in medieval narrative, is the ninth tale of the first day, in which the oafish king of Cyprus, indifferent to his subjects' welfare, is shamed into proper behavior by a sarcastic and biting comment from a woman who is sexually assaulted within his kingdom. Such rehabilitation is not a characteristic of castigation for hypocrisy, seen usually in clerics, or jealousy, seen in the hordes of thick-headed husbands who keep unreasonably close guard over their wives, to the point that the wives commit adultery for revenge. These are tales in which retribution is pursued in the context of the desires and motivations of the real, middle class "comic" world.

I will give one brief example of a *novella* of this type to round out my illustrations. In the Seventh Day, in which tricks are played by wives on husbands, we find the tale of Tofano and Ghita (*novella* 4), a prime example of the discreet correction of a jealous husband by a wife intent on maintaining social appearances. Tofano's senseless jealousy of his wife Ghita, which he himself cannot even explain, is enough to cause him to be condemned and punished by Boccaccio's righteous instrument of *Decameron* style justice, who is fittingly Ghita herself: she chooses, as a justified course of action for a woman so mistreated, to take a lover and make Tofano suffer the very thing which he fears most (". . . cadde nell'animo alla donna di farlo morire del male del quale senza cagione aveva paura."). In these words the ethical tone of the tale is firmly established. Boccaccio's portrait of Tofano clearly sets him up for his fate; he is a drinker, and worst of all in Boccaccio's eyes (if we remember the wise discretion of Agilulf and others like him), he is a fool, bent on revealing his cuckolded state to all as a means of dealing with his wife, once he suspects her affair. When he has caught her on an assignation and trapped her outside the house at night, he announces his plan to raise hue and cry and vituperate her before their neighbors and her relatives; an extremely hazardous and even potentially fatal situation for a medieval woman. Boccaccio bestows the gift of intelligence on his protagonists in the context of all three ethical modes: righteous choices are generally also intelligent ones, and Ghita has sufficient wit to not only save herself but also to achieve everything she desires. Once she has turned the tables on Tofano and locked him out she can raise a mighty outcry, awaken the neighbors, and accuse him of forever returning home late after drunken binges: the bewildered Tofano finds himself cursed by the town and beaten severely by Ghita's outraged relatives, hot to defend her honor. The public defamation which Tofano, the cuckolded fool, was about to bring down on his own head in an attempt to punish Ghita now is the very tool of castigation which Ghita puts to use at his expense. Ghita's revenge moves on two planes: first she clandestinely means to seek private satisfaction through a love affair in order to make Tofano's absurd jealousy real, and now she triumphs by turning the entire town against him. Her actions pay off with real gains: Tofano is reduced to asking her forgiveness and promising to never again mistreat her or be jealous. Tofano's reformation is complete, for he corrects every sin, including that of lack of discretion; he now realizes the value, already known to Agilulf, of keeping adul-

tery quiet and discreet: ". . . le diè licenzia che ogni suo piacer facesse, ma sì saviamente, che egli non se ne avedesse". The woman has gained a reformed, tolerant husband as well as freedom to pursue her extra-marital affair, on condition that she live according to the *Decameron*'s cardinal virtue of social discretion. Punishment is the central element of plot, her correct ethical choice given the circumstances, which has led her to this happy outcome. We may also note that Tofano's reformation is not so much the sort that allows him to rejoin proper society, as in the virtuous tales of Days I and VI, as much as it is a means to allow Ghita to gain her personal desires: this is punishment in the context of the real, comic world, not the world of sublime social ideals. (pp. 191-96)

[My] system of ethical modes is not meant to provide the ultimate key to appreciating and interpreting the essence of the *Decameron,* for there is far more to the work than Boccaccio's concepts of ethics, and too often critics have tried to pin such all-inclusive labels on it, to its detriment. But as long as we are prepared to recognize how important a role ethics plays, and yet how diverse and even confused is Boccaccio's presentation of it, we ought to appreciate any sort of system which helps us sort out and make sense of it. The *Decameron,* woven as it is out of the stylistic and cultural nexus of the ideal and real worlds, must accommodate its elaborate sense of ethics within this nexus: we have also seen how it may even allow one of its subdivisions a role as a linking element, to join the disparate parts of this grand dichotomy of worlds. (p. 196)

Christopher Nissen, "Ethical Modes in Boccaccio's 'Decameron'," in Romance Languages Annual, *Vol. 1, 1989, pp. 191-96.*

FURTHER READING

Biography

Carswell, Catherine. *The Tranquil Heart: Portrait of Giovanni Boccaccio.* New York: Harcourt, Brace and Company, 1937, 352 p.
> Traces Boccaccio's life within a cultural and political context. Includes brief critical bibliography.

Chubb, Thomas Caldecot. *The Life of Giovanni Boccaccio.*
Port Washington, New York: Kennikat Press, 1930, 286 p.
> Traditional biography in which Chubb attempts to accurately portray fourteenth-century Florentine society and to recreate the "complex personality of an extremely interesting and extremely human man."

MacManus, Francis. *Great Writers of the World: Boccaccio.*
New York: Sheed & Ward, 1947, 306 p.
> Depicts Boccaccio as a transitional figure between the Middle Ages and the Renaissance. Contains illustrations and brief critical bibliography.

Criticism

Almansi, Guido. *The Writer as Liar: Narrative Technique in* the "*Decameron.*" London: Routledge & Kegan Paul, 1975, 157 p.

Formalistic analysis of the *Decameron* in which Almansi states: "[My] purpose is to set this suggested reading of the text alongside the other more traditional interpretations which lay emphasis on the psychological and realist current of the stories, in order to offer an alternative critical viewpoint."

Bergin, Thomas G. "The Decameron." In his *Boccaccio,* pp. 286-336. New York: Viking Press, 1981.

Surveys Boccaccio's tales and offers background information on their composition.

Bonadeo, A. "Some Aspects of Love and Nobility in the Society of the *Decameron.*" *Philological Quarterly* 47, No. 4 (October 1968): 513-25.

Discusses the respective roles of the aristocratic and merchant classes in fourteenth-century Florentine society and speculates how the social and cultural differences between these two groups are reflected in the *Decameron.*

Brownlee, Marina Scordilis. "Wolves and Sheep: Symmetrical Undermining in Day III of the *Decameron.*" *Romance Notes* XXIV, No. 3 (Spring 1984): 262-66.

Examines the breakdown of gender differentiation in Day III of the *Decameron* and describes the intended audience of the collection as "generalized, non-gender-specific inscribed human [readers] with base sexual inclinations."

Chandler, S. Bernard. "Man, Emotion and Intellect in the *Decameron.*" *Philological Quarterly* XXXIX, No. 4 (October 1960): 400-12.

Asserts that the *Decameron* is emotionally subjective despite its focus on human intelligence and cognition. Chandler explains: "For [Boccaccio] there can be no question of an 'objective representation of reality,' or of 'detachment' from his subject matter. Such concepts . . .have bedevilled criticism of the *Decameron* for too long."

Cole, Howard C. "Dramatic Interplay in the *Decameron:* Boccaccio, Neifile and Giletta Di Nerbona." *Modern Language Notes* 90, No. 1 (January 1975): 38-57.

Comparative analysis of Boccaccio's story of Giletta and William Shakespeare's *All's Well That Ends Well.*

Cottino-Jones, Marga. *Order from Chaos: Social and Aesthetic Harmonies in Boccaccio's "Decameron."* Washington, D.C.: University Press of America, 1982, 200 p.

Maintains that Boccaccio's tales are representative of society's progression from chaos to order. Cottino-Jones links the narrative complexity of the *Decameron* to the tumultuous environment in which it was written, suggesting that Boccaccio offered the *Decameron* as a solution to the societal problems of his time.

Davis, Walter R. "Boccaccio's *Decameron:* The Implications of Binary Form." *Modern Language Quarterly* 42, No. 1 (March 1981): 3-20.

Argues that many of the tales in the *Decameron* are written in two distinct parts, beginning with realism and ending in absurdity.

Deligiorgis, Stavros. *Narrative Intellection in the "Decameron."* Iowa City: University of Iowa Press, 1975, 233 p.

Examines the "patterns of internal dependence" in the *Decameron* in order to identify the work's major and minor themes.

Dombroski, Robert S., ed. *Critical Perspectives on the "Decameron."* London: Hodder and Stoughton, 1976, 148 p.

Collection of notable critical essays by such prominent Boccaccio scholars as Francesco De Sanctis, Vittore Branca, and Erich Auerbach.

Durling, Robert. "Boccaccio on Interpretation: Guido's Escape (*Decameron* VI.9)." In *Dante, Petrarch, Boccaccio: Studies in the Italian Trecento in Honor of Charles S. Singleton,* edited by Aldo S. Bernardo and Anthony L. Pellegrini, pp. 273-304. Binghamton, N.Y.: Medieval and Renaissance Texts and Studies, 1983.

Studies the allegorical implications of the story of Guido Cavalcanti in the *Decameron* and identifies allusions from the Bible and Dante's *Commedia.* Durling further hypothesizes that Guido's story is a reflection of Boccaccio's life.

Farnham, William. "England's Discovery of the *Decameron.*" *PMLA* XXXIX, No. 1 (March 1924): 123-39.

Traces the history of the *Decameron*'s English translations and speculates how Boccaccio influenced Geoffrey Chaucer and William Shakespeare.

Ferrante, Joan M. "The Frame Characters of the *Decameron:* A Progression of Virtues." *Romance Philology* XIX, No. 2 (November 1965): 212-26.

Provides a moral interpretation of the *Decameron* through an examination of its characters and unifying narrative structures.

Hastings, R. *Nature and Reason in the "Decameron."* Manchester, England: University Press, 1975, 116 p.

Maintains that Boccaccio incorporated traditional medieval notions of nature and reason into the *Decameron.*

Heffernan, Carol F. "Chaucer's *Shipman's Tale* and Boccaccio's *Decameron,* VIII, i: Retelling a Story." In *Courtly Literature: Culture and Context, Selected Papers from the 5th Triennial Congress of the International Courtly Literature Society—Dalfsen, The Netherlands, 9-16 August 1986,* edited by Keith Busby and Erik Kooper, pp. 261-70. Philadelphia: John Benjamins Publishing Co., 1990.

Explores links between Chaucer's and Boccaccio's tales.

Hollander, Robert. "Boccaccio's Dante: Imitative Distance (*Decameron* I,1 and VI,10)." *Studi Sul Boccaccio,* 13 (1981-82): 169-98.

Parallels segments of the *Decameron* with Dante's *Commedia* and *Inferno,* claiming that Boccaccio not only alluded to Dante's work but also asserted his philosophical differences with Dante within the context of the *Decameron.*

Jones, Barry. "Romeo and Juliet: Boccaccio and the Novella Tradition." *Stanford Italian Review* 1, No. 1 (Spring 1979): 75-99.

Compares Luigi da Porto and Mattea Bandello's versions of the Romeo and Juliet story to the *Decameron.* Jones asserts: "It is hoped that . . .it will become apparent that the *Decameron* is a possible major source and point of diffusion for the various narrative elements of which the story of Romeo and Juliet is composed."

Kirkham, Victoria. "An Allegorically Tempered *Decameron*." *Italica* 62, No. 1 (Spring 1985): 1-23.
Analyzes the actions of several characters in the *Decameron* as representative of a moral code of conduct.

———. "The Last Tale in the Decameron." *Mediaevalia: A Journal of Medieval Studies,* 12 (1989): 205-23.
Contends that humility and obedience are the major themes of the story of Griselda. Kirkham further discusses Griselda as a symbol representing Christ and Job.

———. "The Classic Bond of Friendship in Boccaccio's Tito and Gisippo (*Decameron* 10.8)." In *The Classics in the Middle Ages: Papers of the Twentieth Annual Conference of the Center for Medieval and Early Renaissance Studies,* edited by Aldo S. Bernardo and Saul Levin, pp. 223-35. Binghamton, New York: Medieval and Renaissance Texts and Studies, 1990.
Depicts Tito and Gisippo's friendship as representative of a bond on which societies are based.

Kirkpatrick, Robin. "The Wake of the *Commedia:* Chaucer's *Canterbury Tales* and Boccaccio's *Decameron*." In *Chaucer and the Italian Trecento,* edited by Piero Boitani, pp. 201-30. Cambridge: Cambridge University Press, 1983.
Underscores the structural and thematic differences between the *Canterbury Tales* and the *Decameron.*

Lee, A. C. The *"Decameron": Its Sources and Analogues.* London: David Nutt, 1909, 363 p.
Analyzes various stories in the *Decameron* in order to identify their historical and literary sources.

Levarie Smarr, Janet. "Rewriting One's Precursors: Notes on the *Decameron*." *Mediaevalia: A Journal of Medieval Studies,* 5 (1979): 205-16.
Examines how Boccaccio incorporated elements of Vergil's *Georgics,* Ovid's *Metamorphoses,* and Dante's *Commedia* into the *Decameron.*

Lipari, Angelo. "The Structure and Real Significance of the *Decameron.*" In *Essays in Honor of Albert Feuillerat,* edited by Henri M. Peyre, pp. 43-83. New Haven, Conn.: Yale University Press, 1943.
Opposes the traditional critical view that the stories in the *Decameron* are primarily literal. Lipari concludes: "[It is] fair to assume [Boccaccio's novellas] were meant to be allegorical in character."

Marcus, Millicent. "Misogyny as Misreading: A Gloss on *Decameron* VIII, 7." *Stanford Italian Review* 4, No. 1 (Spring 1984): 23-40.
Examines Boccaccio's tale of the scholar and the widow as representative of antifeminist thought. Marcus claims that the misogyny contained in this tale is a departure from Boccaccio's overall stance espousing love of women.

———. "Cross-Fertilizations: Folklore and Literature in the *Decameron* 4,5." *Italica* 66, No. 4 (Winter 1989): 383-98.
Argues that Boccaccio sought to transform folklore to a highly regarded literary form.

Markulin, Joseph. "Emilia and the Case for Openness in the *Decameron*." *Stanford Italian Review* 3, No. 2 (Fall 1983): 183-99.
Explores the function of the narrator in relation to the *Decameron*'s "literary function" and views the structure of the tale as significantly different from traditional four-

teenth-century fiction. Centering on the character of Emilia, Markulin explains how she, as a storyteller, is linked to the reader's reorientation to a new literary discourse.

McGrady, Donald. "Chaucer and the *Decameron* Reconsidered." *The Chaucer Review: A Journal of Medieval Studies* 12, No. 1 (Summer 1977): 1-26.
Refutes several critical studies that conclude Geoffrey Chaucer did not imitate the *Decameron* in his *Canterbury Tales.*

de'Negri, Enrico. "The Legendary Style of the *Decameron.*" *Romanic Review* XLIII, No. 3 (October 1952): 166-89.
Maintains that Jacopa da Varazze's *Legenda aurea,* a compilation of numerous medieval fantasies and legends, greatly influenced Boccaccio's narrative technique in the *Decameron.*

Ó Cuilleanáin, Cormac. "Man and Beast in the *Decameron.*" *Modern Language Review* 75, No. 1 (January 1980): 86-93.
Studies the narrative, allegorical, and metaphorical functions of animals in the *Decameron.* Ó Cuilleanáin claims that Boccaccio used animals to represent human social interactions and that, as symbols, the animals lead to a better understanding of Boccaccio's imaginative scope.

———. "Boccaccio's *Decameron:* The Plot Thickens." In *Italian Storytellers: Essays on Italian Narrative Literature,* edited by Eric Haywood and Cormac Ó Cuilleanáin, pp. 78-110. Dublin: Irish Academic Press, 1989.
Compares the narrative techniques of Boccaccio and Dante, using examples from the *Decameron* and the *Inferno.*

Olson, Glending. "Petrarch's View of the *Decameron.*" *Modern Language Notes* 9, No. 1 (January 1976): 69-79.
Examines Francesco Petrarch's critical perspective of the *Decameron* as evidenced in a letter the Italian scholar wrote to Boccaccio in 1373.

Potter, Joy Hambuechen. *Five Frames for the "Decameron": Communication and Social Systems in the "Cornice".* Princeton, N.J.: Princeton University Press, 1982, 231 p.
Theorizes that the *Decameron* was written in five different frames, all of which highlight specific elements of society, most notably communication, religion, and morality. Potter further explores the ambiguities of the text, claiming that Boccaccio's enigmatic narrative style lends depth to his tales.

Selig, Karl-Ludwig. "Boccaccio's *Decameron* (VIII/10): The Devices and Strategies of Deceit." *Teaching Language Through Literature* XIV, No. 1 (December 1984): 26-9.
Focuses on trickery in the story of Jancofiore and Salabaetto and claims that the tale is one of learning and experience. Selig notes that money is a central feature of the *Decameron* and argues that its use in VIII.10 as a source of stability adds irony to a story about the fragile structure of society.

———. "*Decameron* I/7: The Literary Space of a Text." In *Florilegium Columbianum: Essays in Honor of Paul Oskar Kristeller,* edited by Karl-Ludwig Selig and Robert Somerville, pp. 107-12. New York: Italica Press, 1987.
Claims that although Boccaccio builds on traditional narrative techniques in this tale, the *Decameron* "presses

the world of the narrative to new possibilities, to new dimensions and frontiers, to new spheres of the literary and artistic imagination."

———. *"Decameron* IX/7 and X/4 and the Text Within." *Teaching Language Through Literature* XXVII, No. 2 (April 1988): 34-9.
   Contrasts the "inter-texts" of two novellas in the *Decameron.*

Serafini-Sauli, Judith Powers. "The *Decameron.*" In her *Giovanni Boccaccio,* pp. 58-94. Boston: Twayne Publishers, 1982.
   General thematic and formalistic overview of the *Decameron* as well as an introduction to "some of the most valid and compelling interpretations" of this work.

Toscano, Antonio. *"Decameron:* Cimone's Metamorphosis." *Italian Quarterly* XXIX, No. 114 (Fall 1988): 25-35.
   Addresses the dichotomy of style and content in the story of Cimone. Toscano claims that the first part of the story appeals to knowledge and reason, while the second part appeals to base sexual desire.

Usher, Jonathan. "Boccaccio's *Ars Moriendi* in the *Decameron.*" *Modern Language Review* 81, No. 3 (October 1986): 621-32.
   Examines the role of death in the *Decameron,* claiming

that perceptions of death undergo transformations over the course of the tales.

———. "Gardens in the *Decameron.*" *Medium Ævum* LVIII, No. 2 (1989): 274-85.
   Discusses the symbolic implications of Boccaccio's use of gardens in the *Decameron.*

Wallace, David. *Giovanni Boccaccio: "Decameron"—Landmarks of World Literature,* edited by J. P. Stern. Cambridge: Cambridge University Press, 1989, 117 p.
   Offers a contemporary, chronological overview of Boccaccio's tales.

Wright, Herbert G. "How Did Shakespeare Come to Know the *Decameron.*" *Modern Language Review* L, No. 1 (January 1955): 45-8.
   Examines the similarities between the *Decameron* and Shakespeare's plays *All's Well That Ends Well* and *Cymbeline,* speculating that Shakespeare may have been introduced to Boccaccio's work through Antoine le Maçon's French translation.

Yudkin, Jeremy. "The *Ballate* of the *Decameron* in the Musical Context of the Trecento." *Stanford Italian Review* 2, No. 1 (Spring 1981): 49-58.
   Explores the musical aspects of the *Decameron.*

Colette
1873-1954

(Full name Sidonie-Gabrielle Colette; also wrote under the pseudonyms Colette Willy and Willy) French short story writer, novelist, and journalist.

INTRODUCTION

Colette is regarded as one of the leading writers of short fiction in twentieth-century French literature. Lauded for her insightful observations on love relationships and for her precise, evocative, and sensual prose style, Colette is best remembered for her characterizations of women, which many critics regard as the first genuine presentations of feminine perspectives in French fiction. Drawing upon autobiographical influences, her stories often focus on the personal and domestic aspects of life. Although many of Colette's writings were originally published as novels, critics generally regard them as novellas or short novels and observe that much of her fiction defies generic categorization.

Colette began writing under the direction of her first husband, Henry Gouthier-Villars, an ostensibly prominent journalist and novelist whose works were frequently ghostwritten. Following her husband's rigid editorial guidelines, Colette produced a series of novels based on memories of her school days which featured a heroine named Claudine. Published under her husband's pen name, "Willy," the Claudine novels achieved immense popularity, and Colette and Gouthier-Villars became national celebrities.

In 1904 Colette attempted to establish herself as a writer independent of her husband by publishing *Dialogues de bêtes* (*Animal Dialogues*), a series of poetic conversations between a cat and a dog who make observations concerning male and female characteristics and the wonders of nature. Colette's exceptional empathy for animals and her love for the outdoors was expressed in many stories throughout her career.

Disturbed by her husband's exploitation of her talent and his chronic infidelity, Colette divorced Gouthier-Villars in 1906 and found work as a music hall dancer and mime. Her experiences in the theater during the next six years inspired her short story collection *L'envers du music-hall* (*Music-Hall Sidelights*), in which she portrays performers who maintain determination and generosity in the face of illness and extreme poverty. Colette's knowledge of the theater influenced her stories throughout her literary career; dramatic structure and an emphasis on performance are manifested in her presentation of dialogue, action, and role-playing. While Colette's stage career was frequently surrounded by controversy due to the risqué nature of many of her dramatic roles, her personal life was also the

source of scandal resulting from several lesbian affairs, most notably her liaison with Missy de Belbeuf, the Marquise de Morny. Colette's bisexuality was the basis for the novella *Ces plaisirs* (*The Pure and the Impure*), in which she emphasizes the juxtaposition of both masculine and feminine characteristics in all individuals, blurring conventional notions of gender, sexuality, and morality.

Most of Colette's works explore the intricate patterns and nuances of love relationships. Married life in particular is the subject of *La femme cachée* (*The Other Woman*), in which she portrays men and women who feel confined within their marriages. In "The Hand," a newlywed woman, while lying next to her sleeping husband, is disturbed by conflicting feelings of attraction and revulsion as she contemplates her husband's hand. The story describes her resignation to the duplicity of emotions she experiences in her marriage. Colette frequently reversed traditional gender roles in her stories, dismissing them as limiting stereotypes. In "The Tender Shoot," for example, a middle-aged man named Albin feels that he has been victimized and seduced by Louisette, an adolescent girl with whom he has had an affair. While Louisette encourages physical intimacy, she refuses to play the submissive role in their relationship by rejecting Albin's expensive gifts and various attempts to dominate her.

Many of Colette's works focus on strong, emotionally independent women who achieve self-knowledge and fulfillment outside the supposed security of marriage or love relationships. For instance, in her short novel *La vagabonde* (*The Vagabond*), a writer named Renée, who is working as a mime, feels attracted to the warmth and security offered by a suitor named Max, but is reluctant to relinquish the freedom of her independent life-style. Renée ultimately decides to embrace her autonomy, finding satisfaction in her experience of the outside world and through writing. Critics have noted that Colette's female characters also acquire strength and self-knowledge through their renunciation of love and resultant feelings of loneliness and unhappiness. Several of the short reflective pieces collected in *Les vrilles de la vigne* (*The Tendrils of the Vine*) focus on a divorced woman who achieves a sense of inner peace after she retreats to the country with only her pets and the occasional company of several female friends. Similarly, a divorced woman's struggle to maintain emotional independence, courage, and dignity is the focus of the novella *Julie de Carneilhan,* in which the eponymous heroine's newfound independence is undermined by feelings of weakness, disillusionment, and loss when she agrees to visit her former husband who has fallen ill.

Another highly praised trait of Colette's short fiction is her sensitive characterizations of older women. In *Chéri* and its sequel *La fin de Chéri* (*The Last of Chéri*), widely considered to be her most memorable works, she depicts the love affair between an aging courtesan named Léa de Lonval and a young and remarkably beautiful man she nicknames Chéri. *Chéri* describes Léa's maternal yet passionate relationship with Chéri and the gradual and painful realization that her advanced age will force her to end their affair. A relationship between an older woman and a younger man is also the subject of her short novel *La naissance du jour* (*Break of Day*). Unlike the emptiness and sorrow Léa experiences with her loss of youth, the elderly female narrator of *Break of Day* accepts her aging as a natural process. Many critics have suggested that Colette's mother, Sidonie Colette, provided the model for the positive qualities Colette admired in older women. Colette revered her mother throughout her life, portraying her as an idealized, almost mythic figure in such semiautobiographical works of short fiction as *Sido* and *La maison de Claudine* (*My Mother's House*). In both of these works, Sidonie is depicted as independent and generous, possessing an instinctive understanding of nature, and loved by her children, spouse, neighbors, and animals.

Several of Colette's short works portray characters whose nostalgia for their lost childhood prevents them from fully participating in their present lives. For example, *The Last of Chéri* and *La chatte* (*Saha the Cat*) focus on young men who resist the responsibilities of adulthood and marriage by retreating into fantasy and their idealized memories of the past. In *The Last of Chéri,* Chéri returns several years later to Léa, his former lover and the maternal source of security and warmth during his youth. Chéri's attempt to reclaim the past only intensifies his sense of despair when

he finds that Léa has aged nearly beyond recognition, and he ultimately commits suicide. *Saha the Cat* similarly expresses a young man's attempt to return to a womblike source of comfort. Increasingly alienated from his practical, robust wife and their modern apartment, Alain escapes with his beloved cat to the beauty and peace of his maternal house. Critics have asserted that Alain's cat represents his idealized vision of a mysterious world of love, security, and fantasy.

Highly respected by her contemporaries, Colette was elected to the prestigious Académie Royale Belge and Académie Goncourt during her lifetime. She remains an esteemed figure in French literature, admired for the stylistic excellence and intensity of feeling conveyed in her fiction, as well as for her adventurous life-style.

PRINCIPAL WORKS

SHORT FICTION

Dialogues de bêtes [as Colette Willy] 1904; also published as *Douze dialogues de bêtes* [enlarged edition], 1930
Les vrilles de la vigne [as Colette Willy] 1908
La vagabonde [as Colette Willy] 1910
   [*The Vagabond,* 1954]
L'entrave [as Colette Willy] 1913
   [*Recaptured,* 1931; also published as *The Shackle,* 1964]
L'envers du music-hall 1913
   [*Music-Hall Sidelights* published with *Mes Apprentissages,* 1957]
Mitsou; ou, Comment l'esprit vient aux filles 1919
   [*Mitsou, or, How Girls Grow Wise,* 1930]
Chéri 1920
   [*Chéri,* 1929]
La maison de Claudine 1922
   [*My Mother's House,* 1953]
La femme cachée 1924
   [*The Other Woman,* 1971]
La fin de Chéri 1926
   [*The Last of Chéri,* 1932]
La naissance du jour 1928
   [*Break of Day,* 1961]
La seconde 1929
   [*The Other One,* 1931]
Sido 1929
   [*Sido,* 1953]
Ces plaisirs 1932; also published as *Le pur et l'impur,* 1941
   [*The Pure and the Impure,* 1933; also published as *These Pleasures,* 1934]
La chatte 1933
   [*Saha the Cat,* 1936]
Duo 1934
   [*Duo,* 1935; also published as *The Married Lover,* 1935]
Julie de Carneilhan 1941
   [*Julie de Carneilhan* published with *Chambre d'hôtel,* 1952]
Le képi 1943
Gigi 1944
   [*Gigi,* 1952]
Short Novels of Colette 1951

The Collected Stories of Colette 1983

OTHER MAJOR WORKS

Claudine à l'école [as Willy] (novel) 1900
   [*Claudine at School*, 1930]
Claudine à Paris [as Willy] (novel) 1901
   [*Claudine in Paris*, 1958]
Claudine en ménage [as Willy] (novel) 1902
   [*The Indulgent Husband*, 1935; also published as *Claudine Married*, 1960]
Claudine s'en va: Journal d'Annie [as Willy] (novel) 1903
   [*The Innocent Wife*, 1934; also published as *Claudine and Annie*, 1962]
Le fanal bleu (diaries) 1949
   [*The Blue Lantern*, 1963]
Oeuvres complètes. 15 vols. (novellas and short stories) 1949-1950
Colette: Oeuvres (novellas and short stories) 1960
Earthly Paradise (autobiographical writings) 1966
Oeuvres complètes de Colette. 16 vols. (novellas and short stories) 1973
Letters from Colette (letters) 1980

Lloyd Morris (essay date 1929)

[*Morris was an American biographer, critic, social historian, essayist, and pioneering educator, who is credited with introducing contemporary literature courses to the American university system in the 1920s. In the following essay, he praises Colette's short novels for their presentation of a feminine perspective and focuses on* Chéri, *asserting that the work reveals her characteristic depiction of intense emotions.*]

It is easier, as French critics long since discovered, to account for the popularity than to estimate the merit of Madame Colette's novels. All but unknown to American readers, she has for many years delighted an enormous audience in France. She has a flair for sophistication and has written vivaciously of a Paris that seems, even to Parisians, somewhat sensational. In other books she has written with considerable felicity of animals and children and the provincial countryside, and with these she has captivated readers who find her Parisian novels competent but trivial. Whatever her subject, Madame Colette very seldom commits the indiscretion of writing badly, so that the consistent excellence of her prose has often led critics to wonder whether she may not be a very distinguished writer indeed.

She is, perhaps, more significant than distinguished. Unlike most women novelists, who have either consciously or unconsciously imitated men, Madame Colette has chosen to write as a woman, to suppress any perception of life which does not have its origin in her femininity. Since literary tradition is largely man-made, she has chosen to ignore it; since conventional literary psychology is chiefly masculine, she has chosen to discard it. Her work therefore seems uniquely original, but the penalty laid upon extreme originality is that it shall always seem a little mad. The world to which the novels of Madame Colette introduces us is more like an hallucination than a counterfeit of the world we inhabit and know. It is a world perceived exclusively by sensibility and instinct; whatever does not reveal itself to these is either absent or, if present, is incomprehensible. In that world people have a species of animal wisdom, but lack intelligence. Desire and feeling are the only motives of behavior. Physical passion is the only source of ecstasy. Frustration is the only cause of misery. Sentimentality is the principle of its moral order. In that world men are hostile and eccentric creatures until they fall in love, after which they become indistinguishable from women except by the physiological peculiarity which makes them desirable. Because Madame Colette writes convincingly the hallucination is complete, until one becomes aware of the absence from her world of most of the values, most of the activities, most of the ends which contribute to our existence the illusion of a meaning. It is the world of a voluptous, complex and acutely sensitive animal; it is deficient only in relevance to our common experience of life.

Chéri is a characteristic example of Madame Colette's work. More than a decade has passed since its publication; enough time to make it seem less sensational and more substantial than it seemed when first published. It won a certain notoriety as a daring book; it now seems less daring than artfully contrived. It is woman's version of one of the oldest fables in literature, the fable which men have written as *Manon Leacaut*, *La Dame aux Camellias*, and *Sappho*. *Chéri* deals with the love affair of a courtesan aged fifty, and a gigolo some thirty years her junior. The traditional literary values are transposed: in this story it is the young man who is the actual harlot, and all the emotions usually suffered by jilted lovers are handed over to the middle-aged heroine. This transposition of values has, however, one very strange result; Madame Colette never succeeds in making even the physiological masculinity of her gigolo convincing. As he emerges from the story, beautiful, sensual and thoroughly effeminate, the despair which he produces becomes less and less credible; in the end one feels for the aging and unfortunate heroine the sympathy which one might feel for one who has lost the companionship of a pet cat. Actually, he is the occasion rather than the cause of emotion; the cause, as Madame Colette implies, is that we are seldom as old as our bodies, and this may have consequences that are both ludicrous and pitiable.

The substantial merit which *Chéri* shares with Madame Colette's best work is an absolute fidelity to the data of sensibility and instinct. Few writers of our time have translated with greater subtlety and precision that portion of human experience which takes place on the purely animal level. This is by no means a negligible achievement. Many years ago William Butler Yeats wrote that "art bids us touch and taste and hear and see the world, and shrinks from what Blake calls mathematic form, from all that is of the brain only, from all that is not a fountain jetting from the entire hopes, memories, and sensations of the body." Some such injunction as this is fulfilled in the work of Madame Colette. For the rest, *Chéri* is a book which proves that although woman is naturally a voluptuary, she is normally incapable of being a libertine. If this is true, it may perhaps be significant.

Lloyd Morris, "Mme. Colette," in New York Herald Tribune Books, *August 25, 1929, p. 4.*

Arthur H. Samuels (essay date 1931)

[*In the following review, Samuels discusses the plot of* The Other One, *emphasizing the work's tragic quality, and asserting that it falls short of the realistic and subtle characterizations presented in Colette's previous works.*]

Unusual among Colette's books, both in theme and treatment, is this subtle and penetrating study of a woman forced to watch her husband's endless and rather vulgar infidelities [entitled **The Other One**]. It is not often that Colette has chosen to handle the material of tragedy. She deals often with strong emotions, but with strong emotions which are nevertheless a necessary part of daily living, and which may be subordinated almost at will to the claims of egotism or self-interest, which may even be laughed at because they are distorted or out of proportion. Colette's habitual attitude is both very feminine and very Gallic. Without touching great depths of emotion, she contrives to give a charmingly ingenious and, in its way, a perfect representation of life, recognizably real and lighted by a wit which is daring but never offensive.

Colette is usually subtle, moreover, without appearing to strive for subtlety, without resorting to deliberate obliqueness of thought or phrase. Her touch is light but sure. The outlines of her pictures are fine almost to the point of painful minuteness, but they are as unmistakably clear as the lines of a steel engraving. In the present novel, however, Colette has somehow violated this impression of clarity. In approaching a subject which, in its implications, is rather larger and deeper than the topics she usually prefers, she has fallen somewhere short of her accustomed grasp.

The complexities of Fanny Farou's nature escape the confines of this slight portrait. She was not strong enough to break the bonds of her attachment to the playwright Farou, even if she had wanted to, and she was aware that he knew it. Through storms of jealousy at his numerous affairs she had come to a kind of unwillingly blind acceptance of his rather Mohammedan ideal of happiness. She had learned to regard herself as the permanent fact in an existence dotted with casual attractions, as Farou's most cherished possession and his greatest encumbrance, in short, as his wife. His infidelities, at any rate, had always been characterized by a reasonable discretion. Now, however, when she discovers that his latest affair involves his secretary, Jane Aubaret, for four years her own cherished friend and companion, the problem which confronts her is infinitely complex. If she interferes, Farou will have lost nothing he cannot easily replace. Indeed, Fanny's long knowledge of his habits leads her to suspect that the affair is already waning by the time she discovers it. But she will have lost not only a friend, but the indispensable companion who protects her from solitude with Farou. She feels herself somehow no longer young enough, or rich enough,

or brave enough, to stay alone with Farou, or to stay far from him either.

The final and disillusioning scene of the book, in which Fanny confronts Jane and Farou with her knowledge of their guilt, is a strange one and inconclusive. In the end Fanny reflects upon the other steadfast couples of her acquaintance—how the women displayed their possession by complaining of their men, by boasting of them, by waiting for them.

> But everything that they set up might be done just as well without the actual presence or existence of the man. . . . She realized that she was blackening the remains of a pure religion, whose faithful lived only in expectation of the god and the childishness of the cult. And she retraced her steps on that road toward a security which could come to her only for loyalty, be it wavering or sometimes treacherous, a woman's loyalty, constantly undermined by the man, constantly built up again at the man's expense.

Arthur H. Samuels, "A Pitiful Wife," in The New York Times Book Review, *October 4, 1931, p. 6.*

New York Herald Tribune (essay date 1932)

[*The review excerpted below discusses Colette's willingness to explore taboo subjects throughout her literary career and praises the poignant depiction of emotional suffering she presents in* The Last of Chéri.]

Colette, bulky of body and crowding sixty now, but as robust and indiscriminate in her personal habits, apparently, as she ever was—and as fecund in her writing—is an extraordinary phenomenon in contemporary French letters. Critics eulogize her now; young writers imitate her, and her output, certain of a tremendous sale, is bargained for far in advance by reputable publishers. The rosette of the Legion of Honor adorns the buttonhole of her sturdy tailleur, and she is regarded by large numbers of her discriminating countrymen as France's premier novelist.

Most of these happy facts have been true, however, only since 1920, when **Chéri** was first published in *La Vie Parisienne*—though Colette had been turning out novels industriously and selling them most profitably for twenty years before that. Way back in the 1900's a sophisticated French public had been swift to claim Colette for its own. There were "Claudine" lotions, glacés, perfumes and hats for sale on the boulevards in honor of the heroine of Colette's tremendously popular series. But respectable critics and the conventionally minded of the public found not only Colette's subject matter, to which they were naturally averse, but her own way of life difficult to swallow. Her books were famous—or, more accurately, notorious—for almost a generation before the correct world of letters took her to its heart.

In the long run, however, Colette's career has come to represent the almost extravagant triumph of the forbidden. Her shield, if she had one, would most certainly carry the emblem Virtue Recumbent. For almost without exception her novels have involved the nonchalant blazoning forth of subjects which had hitherto been regarded as indecent and unacceptable. Writing with the rapier-like thrust, the lightness and immaculate grace of a superb fencer, Colette was both the exponent and defender of a taboo world—the world of the cocotte, the elegant courtesan, the gigolo, the homosexual. She not only wrote of sex with a candidness that was startling, but she presented, generally, those phases which most of the unblushing moderns still avoided—the nethermost world of sex, its animalistic and unwholesomer fringes, its shoddier, crueler sides. And she wrote—and this also delayed her fame—realistically of the world which she herself knew best. "*Claudine* un roman?" exclaimed her friend and biographer, Jean Larnac. "Non! Trop de personnages sont reconnaissables!"

It is a limited world, this world in which Colette's remarkable talent functions, but she portrays it brilliantly. She has a prodigious capacity for observation, a tireless memory for significant detail. She writes . . . of unhealthy matters, with no distaste and very little malice. And with neither pity nor condescension.

The Last of Chéri, published in Paris in 1926 and just now brought out here, is, of course, a sequel to the unique *Chéri,* [a] story of a gigolo. Despite its title, the original novel was really Lea's: it dealt with the tragic decline of the aging courtesan involved in her last love affair. Chéri was, at the most, merely a highly enamelled lay figure. Now, in *The Last of Chéri,* we have the precise and final word on that "rich young man with too little heart," Chéri, the essential boulevardier, Lea is of the past; he is married now to Edmée, rich, beautiful and characterless, herself the daughter of a courtesan. Edmée is a business woman and financial go-getter in a rather large way. Her capacity to make money and to keep herself occupied without him definitely deprives her husband of something intangible yet essential to his sense of marital well being. And throws him back, forlorn, upon his past—a past which the physical change that age has brought about in Lea has utterly destroyed. So it is with Chéri, left by adverse circumstance, a solitary, despairing, small figure in a world to which he can contribute nothing and from which he can draw little. He suffers poignantly, as people often do, for want of the fiber and character which he never, even potentially, had.

The Last of Chéri is so slight in plot as to seem almost structureless: it is a study of the slow decline and dissolution of a man's soul. For Chéri, the descent to Avernus is not a swift toboggan slide: the grade and the distance are both too slight. A sad little book, and a beautiful one, it demonstrates once more the capacity of a genuine artist to create, out of apparently unworthy materials, something indisputably worth any man's cherishing.

> *A review of "The Last of Chéri," in* New York Herald Tribune Books, *November 6, 1932, p. 10.*

Margaret Wallace   (essay date 1936)

[*In the following review, Wallace describes the plot and characters of Colette's* The Cat, *characterizing the short novel as a sensitive but insubstantial work.*]

I don't like to write. I like to live, but I have no ambition. Talent and an inclination to write are two different things. Perhaps I possess literary talent, but I certainly have no inclination. How amazed I am at those people, most of them without any literary gifts, who are always glad to get a chance to write.

—Colette, from "Conversation with Colette," in The Living Age, *May 1931.*

The title of this fragile little novel [*The Cat*] was well chosen. There are actually only three characters in the story. And of the three, Saha, the dainty little Chartreuse cat with her lady-like ruff and her golden eyes, is by far the most real. Even that half of the reading public which prefers Scotties will find it difficult to resist the aloof charm of this little animal upon whom Colette has expended some of her most subtle literary gifts. Alain had bought her when she was a little five months' old kitten at a cat show, because of "her perfectly formed face, her precocious self-possession, her hopeless timidity behind the bars of a cage."

"But why didn't you buy an Angora?" Camille asked.

"It wasn't just a little cat I was carrying at that moment," Alain mused. "It was the incarnate nobility of the whole cat race, her limitless indifference, her tact, her bond of union with the human aristocrat."

Camille was Alain's fiancée, a very handsome and rather expensive young woman of 19. The marriage pleased every one, save for some possible mental reservations on the part of Alain himself. He had known Camille for several years and rated her at her own valuation as a modern girl. He admired her beauty and her grooming. He knew that she drove a car a little too fast and a little too well. He realized that she lied unblushingly, as do children and very young people. But he found in her, on the whole, a beauty less satisfying and a tact less perfect than Saha displayed to him daily.

The course of this engagement and the honeymoon which follows is the novel's whole theme. Perhaps it would be too much to say that Saha is responsible for the discords which threaten to dissolve this very modern young marriage. Colette manages to imply to us, nevertheless, that this is the case. Alain, a slightly neurotic only child, handicapped by the psychological effects of a prolonged illness in his youth, pampered by his mother, accustomed to a dreamy solitude and the society of his cat, is peculiarly ill-fitted to undertake the responsibilities and adjustments of marriage. Nor is the brittle and empty-headed little Camille apt to prove of much help to him. What gives the novel its air of slightness is the fact that it does not seem to matter very much. The marriage, such as it is, does not seem particularly important or worthy of preservation.

There is some writing in this novel which would be hard to match for delicacy and exactness, and there are dozens of delightful pictures of Saha. No one who is fond of cats can afford to miss the acquaintance of this one. Equally, no one who is fond of Colette will want to miss it. But it must be admitted that **The Cat** does not provide the most desirable introduction to Colette's more complex and substantial work. It is definitely one of her minor masterpieces—not only because of its brevity but because its very substance slips through one's fingers like fine dry sand. She has woven for us a spell out of nothing, and little will remain after the book has been laid aside but some pictures of Saha in an assortment of engaging moods and postures.

> *Margaret Wallace, "Colette and a Cat," in* The New York Times Book Review, *August 9, 1936, p. 7.*

Mark Van Doren   (essay date 1936)

[*Van Doren, the younger brother of the poet Carl Van Doren, was one of America's most prolific and diverse twentieth-century writers. Like his poetry and fiction, his criticism consistently examines the inner, idealistic life of the individual. Below, he provides a descriptive review of plot and characterization in* The Cat *and questions the work's meaning, asserting that it presents an essentially trivial situation.*]

Surely it is only in France that a novel [**The Cat**] could be written whose hero at the age of twenty-four looked at himself one night in the mirror and exclaimed: "But get to bed . . . you're all to pieces . . . it's disgraceful. . . . They think I'm beautiful just because I'm blond; dark, I'd be hideous." He stood there nevertheless and smiled "so that he might admire his teeth again; affectionately stroked the natural part in his too thick blond hair; and was pleased with the tints in his eyes, gray, shading into green near the dark lashes; the eye itself surrounded by a purplish circle." Alain was to be married in a day or two, and he had just been going over some of his old things in the charming, ugly house where he lived with his indulgent Mama. There was one box which contained his absolutely personal treasures:

> a gold dollar; a signet ring; an agate charm from his father's chain; a few red seeds from a rare East Indian plant; a mother-of-pearl rosary; a broken bracelet, souvenir of a young, hot-tempered mistress who had remained in his life briefly and left it tempestuously. . . . Dreamily he fingered these small relics, shining and worthless like the bits of broken stones found in the nests of plundering birds. "I must throw away all this . . . or leave it here. I don't care about it . . . or can it be that I do?"

He did. He cared about everything that he could finger in this dreamy way; everything, in fact, about his mother's charming old ugly house with its wonderful walled garden where even when he shut his gray-green-purple eyes he could be sure that the expensive fertilizer about the base of every flower was exhaling a miraculous moisture. Moisture. That was it. This twenty-fourth summer was hot in

Neuilly, and there was a disappointing dryness in the thoughts he was able to have from time to time concerning the rather commonplace modern girl he was going to marry. Camille was dark and lovely, and there could be no doubt of her passion for Alain. But she was hard; drove a roadster in the regulation way of pampered maidens; and was something of an intrusion, really, in this hothouse of his little memories and of his daily pleasures which after all were so difficult to disentangle from the entire secret jungle where his dreams had root. It was not easy for him in his dreams to know whether he was four or twenty-four; though it was easy to dream. He simply had to drop down on the fresh sheets which Emile would of course have spread for him in the room where nothing else must ever change; run his hands skilfully over the fur of Saha, his blue Chartreuse cat who at such a time crept silently to the breast of his pajamas; and be off at once among the great rings of light and the tropical vines of fancy which writhed together in patterns quite indescribable later on when he woke up and went with a certain unwillingness to keep some eleven o'clock engagement with the immaculately dressed Camille. Occasionally, to be sure, he dropped languidly down to the business his father had left him, and talked for an hour or two with old M. Veuillet. But that was as he chose; and more frequently he chose to remain all morning in the garden where Saha conducted her fierce little hunts after butterflies and moths, and where the two of them knew the significance of every gesture and every small cry that either of them might make.

Alain didn't know how well he would get on without Saha after his marriage. The separation was to be brief; only until the new house was ready next to this one of his mother's, which somehow seemed to him violated whenever he glanced over at the piles of wood and plaster beyond the familiar horizon of honeysuckle. But it was to be a separation. He and Camille were to spend their honeymoon in Patrick's apartment, nine stories up; and this was no place for Saha. Temporarily, as things turned out, it was the place for Alain and Camille, who learned how to forget everything else in each other's daily and nightly arms. Yet, rather to Camille's chagrin, Alain did eventually remember his cat and go to see her—and what was worse for a woman capable of French jealousy, bring her back with him. What happened afterwards is something that no reviewer should tell. But it was terrible and tragic, and on the last page it looked as if it would be a long time before either lover—if such a term was applicable now—studied again the down, black or gold as the case might be, on the other's outstretched anatomy.

Surely it is only in France that such a novel could be written and not be wholly preposterous. And probably it is only Colette who could contrive to write it in a hundred and sixty pages. In as little space as that she definitely establishes the existence of her offensive young man, his fiancée and his bride, his mother, his servants, his private world of poetry, and of course his cat. I must confess that I do not know what should be written in the heavy English hand about so able a piece of—perhaps—triviality. If every other people is slightly ridiculous to us, and if the French certainly cannot be excluded from the compliment, at least it is true that no other people manages to go on being itself so purely, so intelligently, and with such a fantastic self-possession. How well Colette understands her story I do not know, any more than I know whether I understand it at all; or whether there is anything to understand. As to its importance in the universe of books— well, that must be left to someone wise beyond the present year, and wise beyond nationality. (pp. 216-17)

> *Mark Van Doren, "Blue Chartreuse," in* The Nation, *New York, Vol. 143, No. 8, August 22, 1936, pp. 216-17.*

Glenway Wescott   (essay date 1951)

[*Wescott was an American novelist, poet, and short story writer who often focused on the nature of freedom and the perception of reality in his fiction. In the following essay excerpted from his introduction to* Short Novels of Colette, *he comments on each of the novellas included in the collection, providing an overview of their plots and examining the nuances of the various love relationships depicted in each work. Wescott considered Colette "the greatest living French fiction-writer," and he attributed her greatness to the authenticity of her characterizations, the sensual quality of her prose, and her exquisite use of detail.*]

Upon publication of her love story of World War I, *Mitsou,* Colette received a letter from Proust. "I wept a little this evening, which I have not done for a long while . . . " *Mitsou* concludes with a passionate communication from a little musical comedy star to her lieutenant in the trenches; and this impressed Proust especially, but he quibbled. "It is so beautiful, it even verges on prettiness here and there, and amid so much admirable simplicity and depth, perhaps there is a trace of preciosity." He could not quite believe in the sudden elevation and refinement of *Mitsou*'s style, educated only by love. And, how characteristic of the very neurotic great man! the chapter of the lovers' dining in a restaurant reminded him dolefully of an engagement to dine with Colette which he had been compelled to break, it unfortunately having coincided with one of his illnesses.

Upon publication of *Chéri* she received a letter from Gide. He expected her to be surprised to hear from him; and perhaps she was. While Proust was a great complimenter Gide was known to be somewhat chary of endorsements. He had read the tragical tale of the youngster in love with the aging courtesan at one sitting, breathlessly, he said. "Not one weakness, not one redundancy, nothing commonplace!" Why in the world, he wondered, had none of the critics compared her young hero or villain with Benjamin Constant's "insupportable" Adolphe? "It's the same subject in reverse, almost." On the whole this was higher praise than Proust's, and deservedly higher; for in the three intervening years Colette had extended and intensified her art. Gide quibbled also, or rather, he suggested that with his natural uneasiness and malicious humor, if he took a little more trouble, in all probability he would find something quibble-worthy. "I'd like to re-read it but I'm afraid to. What if it were to disappoint me, upon second reading? Oh, quick, let me mail this letter before I consign it to the waste-basket!"

It is pleasant and, I think, appropriate to begin with a glance at these two little documents of literary history. For, now that the inditers are both dead and gone, Colette is the greatest living French fiction-writer. (pp. vii-viii)

. . . . .

It was *Chéri* (1920) which made Colette famous. Though she did not get around to writing *The Last of Chéri* until six years later, they really constitute one and the same work. It requires an unusual ability to hold a theme in mind for so long a time, ripening it, resolving it, perhaps depending for some of its elements on one's further experience as well as developing artistry.

Colette's first pairing off of novels, *Minne* followed by *les Égarements de Minne,* was just upon order from Willy; and as soon as they became her property she combined them rather imperfectly in one volume, *l'Ingénue Libertine* (1909). But perhaps this effort of reconstruction inspired her serious interest in binary form. The connection between *la Vagabonde* and *l'Entrave* is more than just the further developments in the life of Renée Néré. Over and above the explicit continuity there are recurrences of emotion, like echoes in the transepts of a large building, back and forth.

In *Chéri* and *The Last of Chéri* the double construction is handled much more decisively and strongly. There is an entire shifting of key and change of tempo from one to the other, and a somewhat different proposition in morals and psychology; yet the reader feels that all this was a part of the writer's knowledge and plan in the first place. A sweeping and agitated, sensual, humorous love-story ending in farewell, then a concentrated and solemnly instructive account of psychopathology, they are structurally perfect together, with an effect of not simply chiming echoes but of polyphonic music; with clear perspectives both in the passage of time and in the way the mind of each protagonist focuses on the characters of the other protagonists, and all according to human nature and fatality from start to finish.

Said Lawrence Sterne, of all men of genius perhaps the least masterly, "I begin with writing the first sentence, trusting to Almighty God for the second." Do you observe and compare the odd little beginnings of the various great novels? It is pleasant to do so, and it often illumines the deep-laid aesthetic and particular nature of the novelist in question. Both of Sterne's own first sentences are famous. There is a thrilling solemnity about the four and a half syllables of *Moby Dick,* "Call me Ishmael"; and the rest of the paragraph meandering along, "the watery part of the world" and so forth. The dozen words of *Anna Karénina,* thoughtful, universal, and yet simple, give an instant impression of narrative genius: "All happy families resemble one another; every unhappy family is unhappy in its own way." In due course there was struck the new note of American literary art, in Hemingway's first book, for instance, "Everybody was drunk . . . "

Now turn to the opening page of *Chéri;* the voice of the spoiled youngster addressing his aging mistress, an absurd outcry:—"Léa! Let me have your pearls!" Do you see? it is rather like theatre, sudden, in order to prevail over the incredulity and metropolitan nervousness of the audience; and poetical in the way of the stage, with more paradox than sentiment.

It is not unlike the fine opening scene of *Der Rosenkavalier,* first thing in the morning, with the dramatic soprano in or on her grandiose eighteenth-century bed, and the mezzo-soprano uttering the clarion notes of the pledge of everlasting devotion which in fact only lasts out that act. If I were in Paris, and the pleasure and privilege of a call on Colette were accorded to me, this is a question I should be tempted to ask:—Had she seen the music drama of Strauss and Hofmannsthal (1911) before writing **Chéri** (1920)? She has always been appreciative of music, and indeed in Willy's day helped with his music-criticism, and went along to Bayreuth.

No matter. The theme of an oldish woman in love with a very young man or a boy, and vice versa, is an old and fairly familiar theme; natural, insoluble, therefore persistent—except perhaps in the United States. We seem to take our matriarchy straight, in the proper context of family relationship, and more often analytically than for the expression of heartache or heartbreak.

"Léa, Léa, you're not listening to me!" the heartbreaking French youngster continues. "Let me have your string of pearls, Léa! It's as becoming to me as it is to you. Are you afraid of my stealing it?" And there, swiftly and simply, you have the three or four moral factors upon which the entire sad story turns: Chéri's childishness; and his exceeding good looks and corresponding self-admiration; and that constant concern with cash value, which was practically all the education he had been given, prior to this love-affair; and his resigning himself to having a bad reputation, not so much cynicism as defeatism.

Mauriac, a strictly Roman Catholic writer, having written a biography of Racine, situating the glorious dramatic poet in relation to baroque theology as well as classical theatre, emphasizing his profoundly troubled Christianity, inscribed a copy of it somewhat surprisingly: "To Colette, nearer than she thinks to this periwigged man."

If we give it a second thought, even in the opera-like or operetta-like first part of **Chéri** we find something of Mauriac's meaning: the suggestion that mere human nature, natural human happiness, is hopeless, that there is original sin, *et seq.* None of Colette's unhappy mortals, whether like puppets jerked to their death by pride and error, or just drawn to it by time in the ordinary way, seems to have the least sense of the eternal life, or any feeling of having to choose between salvation and perdition. But often their undeluded, unreconciled attitude as to the condition of human kind here below is quite Catholic. In the mentality of Chéri, in his plight of psyche if not within his will-power, is a readiness for religion.

Interviewed by someone, in the *Nouvelles Littéraires* if I remember correctly, Colette stated the subject of this pair of novels in plain terms without a hint of religion or even of philosophy, as follows:—When a woman of a certain age enters into a relationship with a much younger man, she risks less than he. His character is still in a formative stage, and therefore the more likely to be spoiled by their

love, deformed by the failure of it. After they have parted he may be haunted by her, held back by her, forever.

This of course is what reminded Gide of Benjamin Constant's *Adolphe.* I am tempted to quote from the famous commentary which Constant added by way of preface to the third edition: as to those degrees of passionateness which a young man may think that he can arouse in his mistress without feeling them himself; which nevertheless little by little take root in him also, and injure him terribly in the uprooting. No, it would require lengthy quotation and perhaps new translation.

Chéri is younger than Adolphe, Léa is older than Ellénore. Shall I tell you the plot? It is simple: the life and love and death of one Frédéric Peloux. Chéri is his pet name, as we should say darling or dearie—the French word is not quite so belittling; we have a derivation from it in cherished. The protagonists of the older generation are all courtesans, or so near as makes no matter; and all rather superannuated and retired. The cleverest and least pleasant of them, Charlotte Peloux, Chéri's mother, has contrived, no, only facilitated his attachment to her old friend, Léa, born Léonie Vallon, known as Baroness de Lonval. Léa was in her forties; in all walks of life women were expected to retire early then. Chéri was nineteen. It suited Mme. Peloux to have him kept out of mischief, and schooled and exercised for his future marriage, and at someone else's expense the while.

It worked like a charm. It continued for six years, quite peaceably and dignifiedly, in good understanding and good health and powerful enjoyment of sex. You may look down at it, as a kind of mutuality of the commonplace and the materialistic—bourgeoisie gone wrong—in its way it was love. At any given moment it must have seemed to everyone that Chéri was playing the inferior part. He would always take that wrongly suggestive tone; his requirement of the pearls, for example. Oh, probably his love never attained any particular height or powerfulness, except in intercourse. On the other hand, it never really diminished or altered, until the day of his death. Only his young body detached itself from Léa's old body, and only when ordered to do so.

How remarkably Colette makes us see and feel Léa's physical, sexual attractiveness, despite the emphasis on the fact of her aging rapidly: blue-eyed and rosily blond, with long legs, and that very flat back which you may also observe in Italian Renaissance sculpture, with dimpled buttocks and with somewhat exceptionally elevated breasts, long-lasting.

Colette lets her do most of the emphasizing on age herself. With one eye always on the mirror—as a normal and necessary part of the discipline of courtesanship—evidently, a good while before her intimacy with Chéri started, she had learned always to think of herself as gradually growing older. That was what the passage of time, every day, every hour, every minute, meant to her. She had accustomed herself to the prospect of finding herself, one fine day, really old, disgracefully and decisively old; and she had resolved to call a halt to love-life and sex-life before that happened. Thus, in her sorrow when it came time to lose Chéri, to let him go, indeed to help him go, there was a factor of submissiveness to fate; long-prepared, philosophical.

The gerontophilic devotion—the feeling of a young person for someone definitely not young—is a very genuine, earnest, and passionate devotion. Who has not experienced it or observed it? Only as a rule it is not to be depended on; it is short-lived, subject to sudden coldness and indeed sexual incapability; it is a fire in straw. It was not exactly like that in Chéri's case. The elder person, beloved in that way, very naturally skeptical to begin with, nevertheless as a rule is almost certain to get enthralled little by little. But if you have any common sense, good education, or worldly wisdom, you will keep your skepticism in mind even after it has ceased to have any currency in your heart. For you must be prepared to yield your young person to some other young person or persons one fine day, upon a moment's notice. Was this not what happened between Léa and Chéri, when young Edmée came on the scene? Not exactly.

For we feel quite certain that Chéri would never have decided upon, nor lifted a hand to procure himself, that pulchritudinous well-schooled impeccable creature; not in a thousand years. It was all managed by the matriarch, more managerial than anyone, and more mercenary. Edmée was the daughter of the courtesan noted among them for having put away the most respectable amount of money. It was a case of gerontocracy's having prevailed over gerontophily. And in the essentials Léa functioned as one of the gerontocracy. She cooperated in the transfer of her darling back home, back under his mother's control, and into that holy state of matrimony which, as the French conceive and practise it, certainly is a mother's province.

Miserable young man! his emotions are pathetic and profound, as we see terribly by the outcome. His heart is in the right place but he has scarcely any head. Whether in happiness or unhappiness he has not even observed exactly what his emotions were until too late; until someone else has decided things. To all intents and purposes he is inarticulate. His talk—his explanation of what is so beautiful about his eyelids, for example—is a kind of play-acting, like that of infants at a certain age; sound rather than sense. In more ways than one he is a kind of infant. In the very first instance, his passage from his mother's malicious and avaricious salon to Léa's bed and board, oh, blissful bed and sumptuous board! was but a bewitchment—and now back again, as it were the dream of an infant not yet born, from one part of the womb to another!

The comedy of the aging courtesans is as well developed, and perhaps as important, as Chéri's misery. And in their scenes together the malicious, almost joyous tone and brisk pace of the first volume continue into the second: satirical *vivace* even amid the funeral march. Once in a while we laugh at them, but more often with them, in appreciation of the fun they make of one another. It is not all unkindness. In this class of womanhood one has to be careful of old friends, in view of the difficulty of replacing them. Their main objective in their youth and in their prime having been to please men, now it is rather to find various

ways of conciliating other women; talking amusingly is one way. Sense of humor keeps up their courage, and serves another mutual purpose also: helps them pretend that those compulsions which constitute their morality—competitiveness, avarice, cruelty—are not really heavy upon them; that a part of their evil is not evil at all, but only a convention, affectation and clowning.

Léa is the least amusing, but partly in consequence of that, keeps our sympathy from beginning to end. Note especially her first encounter with Mme. Peloux after the marriage of Chéri and Edmée. Upon previous readings I seem to have missed this passage; now it delights me. After absenting herself in the South of France for a season, by way of discipline and therapy, Léa has returned to town with her heartbreak not remedied, but anaesthetized, scarred over. She has reached that decision so long meditated: farewell to men, once and for all, and at once. Naturally she has been feeling dull and nervous, listless and slack.

Then, without warning, she is called upon by Chéri's mother, Edmée's mother-in-law; triumphant, and infernally inquisitive, and, yes, at the same time, sincerely friendly. For an hour Léa sits and gazes at that all too familiar face and form, the short and tight and tirelessly bestirring body, the large inhumane eyes and the glib lips; sits and listens to that lifelong chatter, petty but savage, detail after detail of the skilful, almost mechanical futility of her existence, the organized heartlessness. All of this, Léa reflects, with self-commiseration for a moment, visited upon her as a test of her strength of character . . .

And the next moment, exultantly, she realizes that in fact her character is strong enough. In the time to come as in the time gone by, she will be able to strike back. She knows, or can soon figure out, what well-turned phrase will hurt, what practised and well-timed smile will worry. And upon the instant she feels less discouraged about herself. From her dreaming of love, and nightmare of the end of love, and sloth of sorrow, now animadversion and contempt and resentment have waked her up. She feels her heavy-heartedness, her sense of having nothing to live for, lifting and dispelling. What she will have to live for is simply self-defense. Her terrible old friend, old enemy, will keep her on her marks. In the strain of losing Chéri, and in the spirit of general renunciation, she has been living at a somewhat higher level and greater tension than was good for her. Mme. Peloux has brought her down to earth. She is grateful.

Here in a small way we have a philosophic mystery: the vision of evil as giving opportunity for an exercise of virtuousness of a sort . . . I realize that my comment upon this is longer than Colette's telling. In incident as in aphorism, along with the stimulation of our senses, acceleration of our sentiments, she has the power to set our brains to work. Even as in the maxim of Montesquieu: "A great thought is one that puts us in mind of a number of other thoughts."

Meanwhile the process of Chéri's death has started, though it does not happen until 1919. Noted above, a certain lack of intellect has been ominous in him all along, predisposing him to demoralization. Stupid! or if you like, innocent! apparently he has taken it for granted that he will be able to resume amorous intimacy with his old beloved after the necessary term of concentration on his young wife. He attempts it one night; and perhaps, if he had not then noticed certain new ravages of her age, devastated nape of neck, weightiness or weightedness of cheek—he pretends to be asleep, and peeps at her with only the narrowest beam of morning light between his beautiful eyelids, through his thick eyelashes—and if she had not noticed his noticing, perhaps . . . !

Indeed they are tempted by one another even after that; later that morning. For just a moment there glimmers between them a further hope of the recommencement of love, a lunatic hope, "such as may be entertained by persons falling down out of a tower, for the time it takes them to reach the ground . . . " That is the conclusion of the first novel; a thrilling chapter. What difference would it have made if they had recommenced? Only the difference of a few more months of enjoyment, or perhaps a year, perhaps two years; downhill enjoyment of course. But is that not the best that is ever offered anyone on this earth: prolongation, with deterioration? Also, for Chéri, the difference between suicide and a gradual ordinary death . . .

As it happens his suicide is gradual too. The entire second novel, *The Last of Chéri,* is devoted to it. No suspense; the very first page indicates to us, with many tiny touches—I count seven suggestive words, set in odd cadences—that he feels condemned to death, or has condemned himself. But he finds it a strange hard task to carry out the sentence. Even his self-absorbed wife senses something wrong with him: "white shirt-front and white face hanging in a darkness." One thing he has to overcome is his self-esteem, his narcissism; that more than anything might have inclined him to spare himself. Every time anything

Colette and Willy, her first husband.

or anyone reminds him of his good looks, the prospect seems to brighten.

The outbreak of World War I is wonderfully timely for him, just two years after his marriage; and as long as it goes on, his morbidity does deviate into heroism. And when peace has been restored, will that not, we ask ourselves, serve as at least an acceptable substitute for happiness? No, it is the ignobility of the post-war life which strikes him; ignoblest of all, his own parent and his own spouse. Of course the real trouble, or perhaps I should say, the true pretext for the real trouble, is just his inoperative and irremediable feeling about Léa. Not infrequently, I believe, great love gets one in a habit of procrastination; so that one's grief at the failure or loss of it also rather maunders, loiters, creeps.

Notwithstanding Colette's deftness and forward-moving rhythm, she has allowed *The Last of Chéri* to be, doubtless wanted it to be, her slowest book. It has called to my mind the catchphrase of a comedian in old-fashioned burlesque years ago, one of those endlessly patient, absolutely pessimistic types prone to more or less comic accidents: "No hope, no hurry." Nothing that really deserves to be called accident happens to Chéri, scarcely even incident. We are given a fantastic feeling of being with him morning, noon, and night, while all his life is in a kind of quiet decomposition, unravelling and discoloring. We watch him as he seems to be deliberately experimenting with himself, with singular little techniques, little exercises, to turn his mind backward, to deaden himself to the present, to withhold himself from the future. It is all quite harmless behavior, only entirely unenjoyable and motivationless.

At the last he spends most of his time with an awful little old woman, the oldest of all the courtesans, called la Copine, that is, the chum or pal, who knew Léa well in her heyday. Comedy again, but this time it is not *vivace* or even *allegro;* la Copine is like a death's head wearing a wig, reminiscing all through the night, *largo.* She has a great collection of photographs of Léa, studio portraits framed and snapshots just thumbtacked up. In one of the snapshots she is escorted by one of her young lovers; not the one before Chéri, but the one before that. In another snapshot there appears in the background an elbow which la Copine declares must have been Chéri's own elbow; but he knows better, and it is only a blur anyway.

And then suddenly, when it has become almost a bore—in the scenes with la Copine Colette has lulled our minds along with a soft, almost listless humorousness—suddenly we have reached the end. Chéri has reached the point of real readiness for the little flat revolver which he has had in his pocket a long time. He bolsters it up between two pillows so that he can stretch out at ease, his ear pressed to the barrel. In his freakish fatigue of life, at the last minute he seems almost unwilling or unable to make the effort of dying. We have a feeling that his laziness might almost have saved him. The worst and most rudimentary of the forms of will-power, stubbornness, has destroyed him. We mourn over him very little.

Instead our minds run on ahead to what might possibly furnish a third volume: the reactions of those who have loved him. It is a gauge of the verity of Colette's characterizations that we can conceive their suffering in a circumstance she has not written—series of thunderclaps in their several minds, especially punishment of Mme. Peloux, and ghastly bafflement of Léa, realizing how stupid she was ever to let him go, how conventional, how lazy; and of course for them both, for all the courtesans, fear! The sudden needless passing of one so young sounding the knell of everyone older, deafeningly!

. . . . .

Glancing back at all the above synopsis and commentary, I have a troubling impression of having imposed on the story of Chéri an extra sordidness somehow; accentuation of the immorality, diminution of the charm. No wonder! For what, in fact, have I had to offer? Only some of its bones, no flesh and blood, nothing in the skin of the language in which it was written—none of the beauty of the way Colette writes, which is often like a conferring of her own personal physical beauty upon the fictitious creatures she writes about, even unfortunate old satirized macabre creatures like la Copine. By means of diction, syntax, cadence, she gives them all something like complexion, milkiness and snowiness, rosiness and amber, and something like sheen of hair, sometimes raven and sometimes golden, and sinew in one place and bosom softness in another, and every single lineament of things in accord with every other, according to all five senses; that is, verbal equivalents . . .

Style! that is what Colette is most celebrated for, in France, in French; or perhaps I should say, what first brought about her celebrity. Even in the early volumes, perhaps not in the *Claudines,* but surely in the ***Dialogues des Bêtes*** (1904) and *les Vrilles de la Vigne* (1908), she wrote like an angel; handled the language to perfection, or almost to perfection, in an inimitable though influential way.

And of course the sensuousness which I have tried to suggest is only one aspect of it. Elegance, brevity, and clarity are other aspects; and those turns of phrase, speedy and forceful and neat, and with a sense of fun, for which the French have the word *esprit.* Expressiveness above all! In the first place, the expression or at least implication of the mentality of the author, in passages where the nature of the work requires this to be rather reserved, held back— the moral temper, idealism, philosophy, and perhaps religion—unifying the lifework as a whole, that is, the mature and post-mature work; giving an effect of a peculiar or unique balance of emotions. I seem unable to think of a way of defining this in Colette's case. Will half a dozen loosely balancing words serve? As follows: an odd form of pride, which I call gloriousness; and serenity; and thankfulness; and stoicism; and a certain sharpness or asperity . . .

And in the second place, more important for the novelist as such, the rendering of nuances of the particular subject-matter, minutiae of characterization, instantaneities of the plot, with almost imperceptible touches, subtle selections of vocabulary, small patterns of syntax, even little calculated disorders. When a manner is as fine and intensive as

Colette's it can hardly be distinguished from the action or emotion or thought it has to convey. On many a page her meaning really resides in the mode of utterance rather than in the terms of statement; the nuance is all-signifying, as in poetry; and it loses heartbreakingly in translation as poetry does.

Having mentioned in passing certain subtleties of this kind in *The Last of Chéri* I wish that I could examine passages in the other novels with the like or even closer application. But I know that, alas, writing about the detail and texture of writing is a mug's game, especially in English. English and American literature never having been as painstakingly wrought and self-conscious as the French, we are short of technical terms of the art. Academic critics of course invent technicalities and teach them to their pupils, but neither the general reader nor, indeed, the creative writer, understands them very well. Perhaps on the whole the best way is just to express enthusiasm simply, as one would any other feeling, rejoicing in the artistry in question, marvelling at it, pondering, with imagery more or less in the manner of the artist under consideration, and with borrowings from the phraseology of the other arts if they seem to suit.

In this way, for my part, I often compare Colette's prose to dancing. That was at the back of my mind when I declared that her years on the stage had been helpful to her in the development of her greatness as a writer. I borrow an exquisitely apt term, not, to be sure, from the kind of dancing Colette did, but from the old Italian-Russian-French tradition: absoluteness, as applied to the perfectly trained and entirely experienced female ballet dancer, *assoluta.* A discipline and indeed muscularity altogether disguised by gracefulness, so that the eye of the beholder is deceived, the sense of reality set aside—for a split second, she is emancipated from gravity; she pauses and reposes in mid-air, stops to think in mid-air! Does this seem altogether far-fetched, as an analogy of literary style? Believe me, I could prove it, with plentiful and suitable citations, with perfect phrases suspended in mid-paragraph, and never for a split second failing to keep time to a general music. . . .

. . . . .

Twice, a quarter of a century apart, Colette has undertaken a most difficult or delicate theme: triangularity in marriage, by which term I mean something more than chance infidelity, something different from the regular sinfulness of adultery; some involvement of the marriage partner sinned against, condonation or acceptance for whatever reason, or perhaps inclusion somehow—in *The Indulgent Husband* (1902) which is the third in the *Claudine* series, and in *The Other One* (1929).

In the very early work the involving element, connecting link, is some measure of homosexual responsiveness between young Claudine and a strange young woman named Rézi, who presently turns out to be Claudine's husband's mistress. He encourages their attachment, with intermingled amusement, kindness, and lustfulness. To be a good novel, with this oddity and criss-crossed compounded feeling, it would have had to be very good. It is only pleasant and interesting.

For one thing, there is the dubious, perhaps illegitimate, but irresistible biographical interest: the mirroring of Colette's own youth in the immature and surely distortive creation. In those days when *Claudine* was not only a best-selling book but a successful play, played by Polaire, Willy persuaded Colette to bob her wonderful long hair to match the bizarre and entrancing little actress's. In a recent edition of *Mes Apprentissages* Colette has let us see a photograph of them, out of doors somewhere, at the races or at a garden-party: unhappy young host-writer and moody young matinée idol in strikingly similar white ruffles, like twins, escorted by their notorious elderly employer. Perhaps Willy intended only a bit of good publicity. We certainly cannot come now to the conclusion to which an excitable Parisian public undoubtedly jumped. In one of her most beautiful miniature narratives, [*Mes Apprentissages*], Colette has made her feeling about Polaire quite clear, as of great importance in her life then, in another way; no triangle. Possibly it was public misapprehension, wrong gossip, which provided her with that part of the plot of *The Indulgent Husband* in the first place. Inspiration may be the merest accident.

But in spite of her great lifelong use of experience of her own in her work of fiction, on the whole she has been less inspired by the turn of personal events, the impulse to explain or to justify her conduct, than most authors. Her life has provided her with knowledge, but in the handling of it she has been extraordinarily objective, with pride of aesthetics rather than of reputation, and with unusual educability and severe critical sense. I am inclined to think that even in her early work, when any self-indulgence or frivolity appears in it, it is because, at that time, she could do no better; she had not learned how to write those pages more seriously. *Le Blé en Herbe* (1923), her masterly novel of young love, youngest love, initiation and defloration—the modern *Daphnis and Chloe*—recapitulates one of the themes of the not quite successful *Ingénue Libertine*. I think that dissatisfaction with *The Indulgent Husband* may have been one thing that moved her to write *The Other One.* Alas, once more she somewhat missed the mark. If she were to live long enough, she might try it again, in still another volume, perhaps a masterpiece . . .

Certainly the autobiographical factor has ceased to amount to much in *The Other One.* Farou, the husband in it, bears not the slightest resemblance to Willy. He is a playwright but rather, if I may say so, just for fun, like Henri Bernstein. He is a great bull-like, hard-working, tireless and tiring creature. He loves his wife Fanny very well, though he has been unfaithful to her in the way of a little relaxation now and then, as it has happened to come in handy. She has always forgiven him and relaxed about it; and now relaxation, even laxness, laziness, is a part of her nature. She seems just not capable of not forgiving, though this time it is under her own roof, under her nose. The mistress this time, Jane, Farou's secretary, has become her good friend and comfortable companion. Fanny is not young; neither is Farou, but he still seems rather excessive in her life, too much for her. All things considered she feels the need of Jane; and Farou needs her, rather more in the secretarial capacity than the amorous capacity. Fanny gets to thinking of Jane no longer conven-

tionally as interloping mistress, rather as assistant wife; and the book comes to a close in this way, which is a kind of happy ending.

As a whole *The Other One* lacks vitality. Perhaps this subject-matter lay fallow in her mind too long. It does not lack plausibility or function or general human interest; only it is not intensely interesting. It lacks *chiaroscuro;* no brilliance anywhere in it, no deep sort of obscurity either. Or perhaps I should say, the lights and shades, the several contrastable elements, are not arranged to set each other off to best advantage. The date of it puzzles and fascinates me: 1929, the year after the avowedly autobiographical *Naissance du Jour,* sumptuous with landscape-writing, grievous with frustrated and stoical amorous feeling, haunted by Sido's ghost. Perhaps wearied by that, she went to the other extreme in the story of the Farou family; overdid the objectivity. And after it, not another volume for three years—then a spate again, the most remarkable sequence of all: *le Pur et l'Impur* (1932), the boldest of her reminiscences, all about various singularities of sex, then *The Cat* (1933), and then *Duo* (1934) . . . When we consider *The Other One* in its place, in relation to the life-work, it is mysterious. In seemingly shallow, limpid, even glassy waters we discern greenish and bluish tones; something sunken perhaps, wreckage or treasure.

. . . . .

Duo (1934) is also a story of marital irregularity, but not condoned at all, quite the contrary; and it has an unhappy ending, as unhappy as *Chéri,* except that the dénouement comes about more promptly. The marriage of Michel and Alice has lasted a decade; a good marriage, with no lack of sexual responsiveness thus far, a happy hard-working life, working more or less in double harness in various theatrical enterprises. But, recently while he was absent in the South of France on some business venture, she gave herself to one Ambrogio, a business associate; a silliness, a mistake, to which she called a halt after about two weeks. And, indiscreetly, she has kept some improper letters from him, in a purple letter-case; and she carelessly lets Michel catch a glimpse of this, then tries to persuade him that there is not, never has been, any such object; and thus the deadly trouble starts; jealousy, the unpleasantest conceivable subject, the shame and disgrace of humankind, from the beginning of human history. No, not from the beginning, but ever since Dante or ever since Catullus . . .

"I do not believe in dénouements," Balzac made one of his highbrow great ladies say. Literature can do as well as chance, if the literary man tries hard enough. "But," she concluded, "if we re-read a book it is for the details." Colette's details are a marvel. For example, turn to Michel and Alice's breakfast on the terrace. It is the morning after the first evening of his wild jealousy and her evasiveness and defiance; after a night of extra-deep sleep, in avoidance of intercourse. Our concern about them has been well worked up, in behalf of them both: the justifiably but exorbitantly aggrieved husband, the culpable but regretful and well-meaning wife. "Man and woman, close together, disunited, languishing for one another . . . " We hope that they may soon make peace.

Wifely, there on the terrace, to make him as comfortable as possible, she reaches across and turns the coffee pot and the cream pitcher, so that he shall have the handles on his side. Without comment! A good part of matrimony is in that gesture. Then a still slumberous bee comes clumsily to the honey pot, and she will not let him swat it with his napkin. "No, let it go," she cries, "it's hungry, it's working." And the mention of those two fundamentals, work, hunger, bulking so much larger in her womanly mind than jealousy—that male mania, negative form of eroticism, which is tormenting him, destroying their marriage, destroying him—brings tears to her eyes.

Note Colette's probity in this particular. Thus she informs us of Alice's being the healthier-minded of the two, having the more constructive purpose. Michel is the sympathetic one, we suffer for him; but she is rather to be approved, less disapproved. And beyond probity, subtlety . . . Writing as a woman, with wisdom explicitly womanly always, Colette enters farther into Alice's mind and motivation than Michel's. She seems to hint at various extenuating circumstances, excuses for her infidelity. Also, I think, she makes it quite clear that, if asked, as one woman moralizing with another, she would agree with Alice that infidelity was no such terrible thing, *per se.*

In due course, remembering and understanding everything about Alice, her background, family, upbringing, and all, Colette also added a sequel to *Duo, le Toutounier* (1939)—Alice widowed, back in the family studio-apartment in Paris; a conversation-piece with two of her sisters, Colombe and Hermine, somewhat woebegone bachelor girls, career-women. Their fond curiosity brings out Alice's defects, inadequacies; their psychology mirrors hers with the greatest animation of little lights and colors. And here we note that those characters Colette knows best, and perhaps loves best, put her under no particular obligation of indulgence. Here we learn why we did not like Alice better in the former novel; what it was about her that, almost more than the fact of her infidelity, contributed to her husband's desperation. For example, a certain conceit not unusual in women, but especially brought out by tactlessness in her case; and a kind of bravery that is not real courage, only false pride and defiance. Think back! how she frittered away Michel's patience and good will by changing her story every little while: admixture of truth and falsehood, unkinder than either. . . . How self-indulgent she is, doubtless always was; therein she trespassed in the first place. Worst of all, her lack of imagination; therefore she fails to say the things that might possibly have consoled the poor creature trespassed against; therefore at last she lets him have it, the entire documentary truth, crude and exciting.

Note how I have mingled tenses in all these sentences, turning from the one book to the other; years apart in the writing, only months in the chronology of Alice's life. Here once more the binary form is impeccable; the division of the material very precise and meaningful. For one thing, at the end of *Duo,* we are alone with Michel when he is planning to drown himself; whereas in *le Toutounier,* Alice allows herself to believe, and convinces her sisters

(and the insurance company), that it was an accidental death.

Nevertheless she blames him, even for misadventure—hah, the fool! stumbling into the flood-water, forgetting the slipperiness of the red-clay river bank—because she loved him, still loves him, and terribly misses him. There is often a factor of anger in great bereavement. Do you remember Schumann's song cycle, *Frauenliebe und Leben?*—"Now for the first time you have hurt me, hard unmerciful man, by dying, and that struck home!" She also blames him for his proneness to tragical feeling, darkening those last few days before the so-called accident; much ado about nothing, a trait of maleness . . .

But thus she does not blame him as Colette blames him, and as we blame him. Colette shows us his abysmal pessimism, his self-destructive ardor, from the first word of the trouble. And at the end, Alice's impatient stupid entire revelation, with documentary evidence, which maddens him: he himself insisted on it; he would not take no for an answer. Neither to the right nor the left would he turn or even look; nothing else touched or excited him, only his determination to know more than he could bear knowing. The sign of Psyche! he would commit it if it killed him, and it did.

Let me also call attention to the pages about the singing of the nightingales, once to each of these miserable mortals whose love is failing. The nightingale is a bird very dear and personal to Colette. *Les Vrilles de la Vigne* (1908), one of the first works of her own sole devising, without Willy, begins with a sort of allegory or fairy tale, two or three pretty pages. A nightingale falls asleep in a vineyard in the burgeoning spring-time, and when it wakes up, has a bad fright; for the tendrils of grave grapevine have begun to wind around its feet and wings. Therefore, thereafter, it sings and teaches its young to sing, "While the grapevine is growing, growing, growing, I'll stay awake." In French this is a near enough approximation of nightingale-rhythm . . . It expresses her feeling of escape from marriage—thirteen years of tendrils!—and of blessedly finding that she had voice and song of her own; that is, literary talent and something to express by means of it.

Here in *Duo,* in the prime of that talent, we have nightingales once more. The poor adulteress leaves the room, and the poor cuckold, sitting there by himself, begins to pay attention to a number of them, singing their hearts out, but softly, remotely; and then to a soloist, a much greater voice than the others, or perhaps only proximity makes it seem so. But how sad! how sick! Michel is not able to take any pleasure in any of it. It is as though his thoughts partly deafened him. How can a man so sad and sick partake of glorious nocturne? Only by withholding his breath, then trying to breathe in time to the music, which suffocates him a little and keeps him from thinking for a minute or two. And afterward—one of Colette's characteristic touches, with her sense of physiology keener than anyone's!—he feels a burning thirst.

A couple of pages further on, he goes out of the room; Alice comes back. It is her turn to listen, especially to that one loud tenor voice seemingly wasting itself away in brilliance, in repetitions so insistent and variations so far-fetched that it scarcely suits her troubled heart; it seems to hinder all emotion, except its own emotion, if it can be called emotion. But, but, when the soloist pauses for a moment to catch its breath, there arises the soft chorus of the far-away singers, each for himself, each at the same time in harmony with the others—*accordés* is Colette's word, which means reconciled as well as harmonized; which also means matched, mated, betrothed. And unhappy Alice is reminded of the great spring labor going on along with the spring concert: assembling and weaving the nests, laying and hovering and hatching the eggs, feeding the fledglings; labor of the females for the most part. But not lonely; as long as they have to labor the males will not fail to serenade them!

It is one of those metaphors, extended and, as you might say dramatized—bearing as great a portion of the author's thought as her dialogue or her action—for which I love her. Do you not? Do you see what it signifies, suggests? The woman listening to those male birds, thinking of those dutiful female birds inarticulately nesting, is childless. In her joint life with Michel now stricken suddenly, in their hapless marriage unbalanced, toppling, hopeless, that important corner-stone of civilized heterosexuality is lacking: no egg, no fledgling, no real nest! Therefore, perhaps she thought of herself as free to lead a little double life for a fortnight, entitled to partake of modern single-standard morality; thus she erred in idleness, with not even watchful conscience, not even sufficiently troubling to keep it secret. Therefore . . . Go farther with this theme if you wish. Colette always knows when to stop; here she has stopped with the metaphor.

A bad thing about jealousy is the element of pornography in it: the stimulation of visioning one's darling in someone else's arms, with the consequence of desiring somewhat more than usual just when one is expected to content oneself with somewhat less—or as in extreme and morbid instances, as in Michel's case, looking backward, crying over spilt milk, desiring the past. How clearly Colette has marked this, though with no stress or scabrousness! Michel himself admits it, in a single painful exclamation, after Alice has let him read all Ambrogio's letters: one of the games of love played by those two happened to be, ah, something the miserable husband has especially delighted in, more than anything, more than life.

Another detail: whereas Alice is Parisian, Michel is a Southerner, meridional—even as Sidonie, née Landoy, and Jules-Joseph Colette. Make no more of this parallel than it is worth; it doubtless furnished their daughter with observations of the contrast of temperaments. From the first page of *Duo* it is suggested that Alice is somewhat the more intelligent or more civilized—or rather, the other way around: Michel is the more instinctive, primitive. I over-simplify. . . . The point is that he is not at all the type of man for whom it is normal or natural to forgive a breach of the marriage vow. But for the grace of God, but for a generation or so, and a veneer of twentieth century morals, this story might have ended in murder instead of suicide. It would have done Michel good to give Alice a beating, would it not? Yes, but perhaps he would not

have known when to stop. Indeed, this might quite plausibly be given as his excuse for committing suicide: to prevent murder, or to punish himself for murderousness.

As representations of suicide, a subject most important to us, important in the symbolical or anagogical way especially: psychologists having shown us how frequently misdemeanors and misfortunes partake of the same dark frenzy, only a little less dark—the same desire to die but less determined, the same unwillingness to live, dilatory—see how the case of Michel compares, contrasts, with the case of Chéri! This is but a momentary violence, though the result is forever; an act almost of aggression, though the point of departure is true uxorious devotedness.

Whereas Chéri is bemused and benumbed, torpid, unmotivated. Would that he had been capable of a bit of violence! Colette has given us, as one of the gravest indications of his state, the fact that he feels no jealousy of Edmée. That might have waked him up and saved him. Or, alas, he might have relapsed into his slumberousness again, gone sleepwalking away in some other realm no less lonely. For there is a curse upon him; and we feel that if he had not turned it into the channel of death it would have developed in another direction: imbecility or worse.

The Last of Chéri, from the first page to the last, is a representation of that famous so-called sin of the middle ages, rampant again in this century in more ways than one: acedia, that is, horrible languor, malignant listlessness, irremediable boredom, paralysis of soul; the intolerable sorrowfulness when the specific sorrow keeps slipping one's mind. And this is the greatest portrayal of it in modern literature. Michel is not in this classification at all. If the enraging circumstance of Alice's infidelity had not befallen him, or if Alice had kept him in blessed ignorance of it, he would have been all right.

See the mystery of morals! Although Chéri's background is so bad, all those old courtesans constituting so gross and mean and base a society—and Michel and Alice and even Ambrogio are just average inoffensive humanity—the opprobrium upon him is slighter; for the most part we think of it as sickness. Michel is the wickeder. In cases of suicide we cannot moralize upon the act itself—we do not know enough—only upon the attitude of mind, heart, and soul, just prior to it. What was in Michel's mind, heart, soul? Possessiveness, punitiveness, intermingling of lust and prudery, deafness and blindness to all the signs of Alice's love, rejection of her. In Chéri's? Only disappointment, disappointment in himself and in the crazy bad sick world—many a saint has felt as much—and fatigue and loneliness and stupor; nothing very bad, nothing unfair.

And see the indivisibility of morals and psychology! in *Duo* Alice is the healthy one. In so far as Michel's wicked intention is to make her suffer, he miscalculates, it miscarries, she is too strong for him. Wherein lies her strength? In her dullness of mind as well as her robustness, lack of imagination as well as good nature. Her salvation and Chéri's perdition correlative in some way, but impossible to correlate . . . The fact is that neither of the two sets of values by itself—neither right versus wrong, nor sickness versus health—will serve to explain or to save humanity.

We have to try first one, and then the other. And in the last analysis of course there is no salvation: everyone is deathward bound, the road has no turning, God is not mocked.

. . . . .

It occurs to me that I have taken *Duo* out of chronology, for no particular reason; not far out. *The Cat* (1933) is another of Colette's masterpieces, made of rather similar materials of middle-class humanity, matrimony again; matrimonial misunderstanding and mischance and fiasco. Approximately of the same length, the same shortness, I think you will agree that because it is more poetical, it tells more and signifies more per page. It has no sequel, needs no sequel.

The marriage of Alain and Camille scarcely deserves to be called a marriage; it lasts only a few months, a trial and a failure. We first see Alain still living at home with fond parents. He has a most cherished, most beautiful cat named Saha, a thoroughbred Carthurian, greyish-bluish. After the honeymoon he takes it to live with them. Marriage does not make him any the happier; neither does he make his wife happy. He lets her realize his vague sense of having made a mistake, vague longing to be back home again, infidelity of spirit. The cat seems to Camille emblematic of all that. She tries to kill it, does not succeed. But Alain cannot forgive her, nor she him.

Do you observe how this constitutes a sort of diptych with the story of Michel and Alice? And here also, how strong and sure Colette's sense of justice is; how deft her communication of it, though never passing specific judgment! Is it by instinct, or with intellect like a precision instrument? I think it is a part of her femininity, and an attractive part, to seem to set aside claims of mere cerebration. As in *Duo* she has presented the wife somewhat more understandingly than the husband, that is, more explanatorily, with an extra perspective, a brighter light. But, thus, all the more critically! We are not in the least obliged to love the female; we are allowed to love, and to feel that Colette herself loves, the male.

Indeed, peering a little more profoundly into creative coincidence than it is proper to do, we may remark that we have heard of only one other person on earth as devoted to cats or to a cat as this young Alain; that person is old Colette herself. And as she conceived this story she may well have arrived at a part of the tension between him and his bride by asking herself, What if I had to choose between my cat and some such vain, disrespectful, disturbing new young person?

Alain's young person really is a terrible girl, a type that may sometimes incline one to despair of the epoch: so very nearly in the right about almost everything, but just missing the point; so self-righteous but so lacking in self-assurance; possessive without strength, destructive without deadliness. She has energy to burn but somehow very little warmth except perhaps in the specific conjugal connection. With a certain fatuity, as to her importance to her husband, which gradually gives way to sadness and bitterness, in the realization of her unimportance, she seems to have nothing else to live for.

Indeed we sympathize with her as to her resentment of the cat. We see that it is less exorbitant and less abstract than Michel's jealousy in *Duo*. The trespassing of Ambrogio against him was a thing of the past; and even at the time of its happening he felt no injury, not the slightest pang, no deprivation. Whereas Saha is an ever-present rival, lauded by Alain with every other breath, and established by him as a permanent feature of their married life. But why, we wish to know, why could she not somehow gradually vitiate and exorcise the childish magic it has for her dear husband? Is there ever any point in a vain, violent iconoclasm, loudly denying the tabu and pushing down the sacred image? And if it came to the point of violence against her will, if her husband in his ailurophily suddenly maddened her, why so inefficient about it? Why defenestration, instead of poisoning or drowning? The very idea of just giving it a push, hurting it, and arousing its hatred, paroxysm of hissing and explosive yellowish eyes, which is what betrays her to Alain!

The worst of this kind of female character, we say to ourselves, is that even in violence it falls between two stools. It results not even in disaster but in muddle and mess and absurdity. But, beware! this kind of objection is valid in aesthetics, if you really prefer tragedy to comedy; but in morals it is evil nonsense. Falling between two stools is better than successfully killing cats. The reason for Camille's weakness and coarseness and confusion, and even loss of husband, is fundamental and creditable. To express it in the sentimental style, she is on the side of life. It not only enables us to forgive her, it necessitates our forgiveness.

Her dear husband really is a maddening youth, though attractive. He is as fatuous in his feeling of unimpeachable male supremacy as she in her feeling of absolute female desirability; as self-indulgent in his daydreaming and voluptuous frivolity with his pet as she in her vain commotion and pursuit of pastime. We can never feel quite happy about him, even when he is perfectly happy himself, even when he gets back home where perhaps he belongs. In the very first chapter we observed how recklessly his parents have spoiled him; marriage to Camille seemed the only hope for him. At the end of the story we cannot see into his future at all; it seems all beclouded and scarcely even tragic, just harrowing. A type that may sometimes incline one to despair of France. . . .

Two thousand years ago St. Paul decided that it is better to marry than to burn; a way of stating the case which seems to start marital relations off on the wrong foot. Psychologists nowadays, scarcely less severe, have added that it is better to be infantile—better to disappoint a wife and concentrate on a cat and give up marriage altogether, as Alain did—than to commit suicide. If we agree, we are constrained to admire this young man more than the poor hero of *Duo*. Colette seems not to have reached any absolute decision upon this point; no aphorism that I can recall. But certainly she expects us to take Alain's cat as an emblem of child-life, home-life, childish home-life, and of its compromise and consolation in secret: autoeroticism. No pettiness about this; nothing belittled or made sordid or left sordid—not ever, in the writing of this good woman and liberal writer!

Let me call your attention to her description of Saha at night, at the beginning of the story: one night just before Alain's marriage, on his bed, thrusting her claws through his pyjamas just enough to worry him, with a pleasurable worrisomeness; then giving him one of her infrequent quick kisses with her chilly nose; then seating herself on his chest while he fell asleep; and until morning, vigilant perfect superhuman creature! seeming to fix with her hard eyes, and to follow around and around in the darkness, the fateful zodiacal signs, lucky and unlucky stars, which in unknowable time and space dance to and fro over sleeping humanity. Two things at once—it is that manifoldness which I have mentioned, as of the time of her nervous breakdown—the littlest instance, Alain's mere inconsequential self-provided soporific pleasure, and at the same time, the greatest concept, great eternality and destiny even as personified by the cat-goddess of the Egyptians.

Toward the close of the story there is another little picture of Alain and Saha together. He holds her in his arms, rejoicing in her entire contentedness and entire confidence in him. With the peril of Camille's rivalry happily averted, Saha has, Alain reflects, a life-expectancy of perhaps another decade; and he winces at the thought of the brevity of life, the brevity of love. In the decade after that decade, he promises himself, probably he will want a woman or women in his life again. He does not specify Camille; he is not such a cad as to expect her to wait for him. In any event, he promises Saha, he will never love another cat.

Yes, this love-scene of childish man and almost womanly cat seems almost too good to be true, too pretty and tender and humorous. It is a kind of happy ending. Any valid commentary upon a work of narrative art has to be in some measure a re-telling. Now suddenly I realize how much less cheerful my re-telling of this has been than the text itself. The loveliest of love-stories; at the same time a serious study of modern matrimony, yes, indeed! But the true love in question is that between Alain and Saha; the true marriage is theirs. Camille is the trouble-maker, the interloper, who makes a fool of herself and is successfully driven back out of the way. It is almost an allegory or a fairy-tale; and what truth there is in it I certainly cannot state, in the way of either ethics or psychotherapeutics.

Suddenly I am ashamed of all my stating and interpreting topsy-turvy and wrong end to. For the little pure narrative itself is preferable to any meaning one can read into it or moral one may attach to it. Is not this the profound thing about narration, the almost mystic belief of the true narrator? Its incident, description, characterization, dialogue, are the means of expression of truths that are greater, more affecting, truer, than anything that can be put in general or theoretical form. Perhaps a great narrator like Colette only pretends to be thinking about her characters, coming to conclusions about them, pointing morals—the supreme narrative device, to convince us of their reality! We are able to moralize about them; *ergo* they exist . . . (pp. xxiii-l)

Glenway Wescott, in an introduction to Short Novels of Colette, *The Dial Press, 1951, pp. vii-lvii.*

Katherine Anne Porter (essay date 1951)

[*Porter was an American short story writer, essayist, critic, and educator whose fiction is often closely linked with her personal experiences and often focuses on human motives and feelings. In the following review of* Short Novels of Colette, *she asserts that Colette's greatness is attributable in part to the light-hearted realism and capacity for genuine feeling revealed in her art.*]

The important thing to read in this collection [*Short Novels of Colette*] is Glenway Wescott's introduction. It is a labor of love, affectionate but unblinded; a deserved tribute to a most lively genius, full of Wescott's wry judgments—all well seated in a long knowledge of all the works, in French—possibly the only language that can ever really contain them—and a true introduction. This long study, or meditation, on the life and writings of Colette does his dear author the justice to tell the new reader who is depending on translations that these short novels, for all their varying brilliancy, are not her best work.

He re-tells from her own autobiographical writings, and with more reserve than she, the highlights of that long, difficult, complicated life of hers, much more absorbing, much deeper and more truthful, than any of her fictions. He relates this life, headlong, willful, full of gaiety and suffering, "almost scandalous," as he says, yet strangely disciplined and austere in sum, to her work; in the end she could absorb, survive, re-see and re-make almost everything. To an astonishing degree she could use her experience as an artist and yet not lose her memory of what it cost her as a living, growing human being; so that her later writings, especially about her disastrous, perverse first marriage, have a strange daylight, morning freshness on them that her earlier work did not have.

It was hardly fair to American readers to have kept Colette from them for so long; nor fair to Colette, either, who should have been the fashion here at least twenty-five years ago—when we think how her lessers were being brought in all that time with fanfares, from every direction. In France she has been known and loved and read from the beginning, and though one always heard of her as "a light writer," that was no term of disrespect—quite the contrary. The French above all know how much strength and discipline and even sheer genius it takes to write lightly of serious things; they never called her frivolous, far from it.

Yet there was always that tone of particular indulgence, reserved for gifted women who make no pretentions and know how to keep their place in the arts: a modest second-best, no matter how good, to the next ranking male. Wescott, mentioning that both Proust and Gide wrote her letters of praise, says, flatly: "For, now that the inditers are both dead and gone, Colette is the greatest living French fiction writer."

I agree to this extent: that she is the greatest living French writer of fiction; and that she was while Gide and Proust still lived; that these two preposterously afflicted self-adoring, frankly career-geniuses certainly got in Colette's light; they certainly diminished her standing, though not her own kind of genius. She lived in the same world, more or less in the same time—without their money or their leisure. Where they could choose their occasions, she lived on a treadmill of sheer labor. Compared to their easy road of acknowledged great literary figures, her life path was a granite cliff sown with cactus and barbed wire.

But she had the immense daylight sense of reality they both lacked and, beyond that, something that Gide tried all his life to have, or to appear to have, and which he lacked to the end: a genuine moral sense founded on a genuine capacity for human feeling. She never attempts to haul God into criminal collusion with the spiritual deformities of her characters. Being a generous woman born to be exploited by men, she has for some of them the abject tenderness and indulgence which is so terribly womanly. Yet she knows this; she does not deceive herself. And her women, if possible less attractive even than the men, are still women, which Proust's never were.

The beings who people these six short novels are all of the race of the half-born, the incomplete, turning each one in his narrow space. They have no minds to speak of, they are in a limbo of physical indulgences, and they live and die their desolate lives in the longest waking dream. In the end, it is middle-classness, incapacity for tragedy—or comedy either—for faith, for any steadfastness except in delusion and obsession. It is stupidity—which the introduction once charitably tries to interpret as innocence.

The two must not be confounded, ever; innocence is a not-knowing of childhood, or inexperience. Stupidity is the inability to learn in spite of experience. Innocence can lead the innocent into evil; stupidity is itself an evil. Colette is the wisest kind of artist; the light of her quick intelligence plays over this Limbo, in her warmth of emotion she cannot reject or condemn them, and here is the strangest thing—the stories are full of light, and air, and greenery and freshness, the gayest sparkle of laughter, all in a way misleading, if you like; for there is a satire of the sharpest kind in this contrast between the sordidness, the obstinate dreariness, of human conduct and motive, and the disregarded, the ignored, the unused possibilities for human happiness.

Colette conceals her aim, her end, in her method. Without setting her up in rivalry with her great jealous, dubious male colleagues and contemporaries, let us just be glad of such a good, sound, honest artist, a hard-working one; we could really do nicely with more "light writers" like her. The really light-weight ones weigh a ton beside her. (pp. 5, 52)

> *Katherine Anne Porter, "A Most Lively Genius," in* The New York Times Book Review, *November 18, 1951, pp. 5, 52.*

Maeve Brennan   (essay date 1952)

[*Brennan is an Irish-born American short story writer who is best known as a regular contributor to the* New Yorker. *In the following essay, she discusses* Short Novels of Colette, *focusing on Colette's insightful portrayal of weaknesses and needs manifested in love relationships.*]

Colette, that inhumanly gifted Frenchwoman, writes about lovers, but not as pairs. She gives her attention to those most in love, the more needy ones, and traces in her stories the concessions they have to make, and keep on making, in order to be loved. She writes of the destructiveness of love, of the gradual erosion of the spirit through need, and of the simple truth that in the world of sexual love ordinary strengths count for almost nothing and the thought of equality, or even of fairness, is ridiculous. Equality is not a notion that interests her, as a writer, anyway. Her world contains only two people, one of them struggling to be allowed to stay; this is the only struggle that counts. Outside matters—causes, promises, competitions, and rights—go by the board. She is concerned only with the bed, as it is shared, betrayed, deserted, and adored. No matter where the public sees them, her lovers remain, to all intents and purposes, right beside the bed from which they have just risen, before the maid (there is always a maid—no time for housework in this world) has even had time to come in and air the sheets. The atmosphere of their world, obsessed as they are by themselves and by each other, is at once subhuman and profoundly spiritual, and charged with a villainous awareness that sometimes lags but that never lets up. Usual obligations, like work and children, almost never interfere with them.

Colette's writing is ripe, open, and without shame, and it is self-intoxicated in a way that is sometimes disconcerting, because it is humorless. She has plenty of humor, but of the deadly, malicious, witty sort that flourishes best in society, or against society. Her women meet, for luncheon or tea, to lay each other waste, but their eyes grow faint, turning inward, and they never laugh at themselves. This is just as well, for laughter might make them shy, and then we would not find out so much. Another novelist could stumble and become ludicrous writing in such a manner, but Colette transfigures every page with her genius, and she is always, under all circumstances, entertaining.

It is a pity that the people who put together the new collection called *Short Novels of Colette* were content to do such a haphazard job, because, although they have included *Chéri* and *The Other One,* both among her best novels, they have also given space to some much less important stories, which could well have waited till a later date. *Chéri,* told in two parts—*Chéri* and *The Last of Chéri*—is a cold, hard, brilliantly polished parable of human love, lightly disguised as a love affair between an aging courtesan, Léa, and a decorative young man, Frédéric Peloux, nicknamed Chéri. Chéri, himself the son of a courtesan, is born, in the eighteen-eighties, into the society and ways of his mother's friends, most of them women of her own profession. Léa, the most beautiful and envied, takes him to live with her when he is a boy, rears him, loves him, and finally releases him to a suitable young woman, for marriage. By then, Chéri is twenty-five and Léa is fifty. She suffers from the separation, but it is only what she expected would happen, and that is that. The first part of the story ends with their separation.

The Last of Chéri begins shortly after the First World War. Chéri, now thirty and a veteran of the war, can find nothing familiar in his home or outside it, and he instinctively seeks reassurance in Léa. He finds her unrecognizable, for she has grown not simply old but indifferent to him and to herself. They part for the last time, saying goodbye as strangers. During this fatal meeting, as Chéri stands face to face with the stony, hostile woman Léa has become, he himself alters, and he goes away from her no longer an elegant, self-centered young man but a human being so chilled by rejection that he will never be able to get warm again. Still, he is not yet aware of what has happened to him. Of his departure from Léa's house, Colette writes:

> Under Chéri's feet the stairs were like the bridge of sleep between two dreams, and he found himself in the street, not knowing how he had reached it. He saw the sunset sky mirrored in the stream, still swollen by the rain, and on the blue backs of the swallows, flying low, and because the dusk was cool and the memory he had brought away with him hid itself, treacherously, in some deep recess of his spirit, there to gather strength and assume its final shape, he believed he had forgotten everything, and he was happy.

It is Léa who is assuming her final, gigantic, complex shape in Chéri's spirit, for in denying him she has revealed his need, and the need is all for her. She has been not merely his mistress but his mother and teacher, the container of his childhood, and the source of all his confidence. If Chéri, bewildered by time and self, is human love, Léa is everything that human creatures love. She is warmth, strength, protection, pleasure, and certainty. Now, unloving, her power is malignant. In his astonishment, Chéri turns for reassurance to a new dream. He dreams that he is not yet born, and he tries to reach back across the years to the time when Léa was young, because he must believe that the kind, natural woman of those days might still love him. A despairing jealousy excites him as he studies ancient snapshots of Léa with her first lovers, but the jealousy is only a last illusion that he still shares life, and he kills himself. Léa, in the earlier story, dies another way, by cutting Chéri off from her. By this act she assures his doom, although she could not have understood that. She herself, a middle-aged woman, after all, with a life behind her, continues to live in her other enjoyments—food, gossip, and the manipulation of money.

Colette often has her people, in their moments of worst crisis, behave as they are obliged to but at the same time lets them imagine themselves behaving quite differently. For instance, Chéri, in his last interview with Léa, talks politely and with control, while he imagines himself on his knees before her, beseeching her to save him. This double exposure is a favorite device of Colette's, and it is natural to her, and natural to the people she writes about, because they watch themselves incessantly and are all perfectly aware, always, of the effect they are creating.

In the next novel in this collection, *The Other One,* she has, perhaps, gone farther in this direction, and permitted the second, imaginary self—the complaining, weak one—

> [Colette] writes of the destructiveness of love, of the gradual erosion of the spirit through need, and of the simple truth that in the world of sexual love ordinary strengths count for almost nothing and the thought of equality, or even of fairness, is ridiculous.
>
> —*Maeve Brennan*

---

to assume a name and an identity. *The Other One* is the story of a marriage. Fanny, the wife, a beautiful young woman, has lulled herself into a lethargy, a kind of amiable sleepiness, as a result of trying not to care about the habitual unfaithfulnesses of her husband, Farou. Farou is a successful man of the theatre, who knows many women and sleeps with most of them at one time or another. There is a third character, named Jane, a shaky, shadowy creature, who appears to have a real presence but, behind it all, seems actually to be a personification of Fanny's smothered jealousy. Jane is Fanny's personal maid, her housekeeper, and her companion. She is Farou's secretary as well. She is pretty, but she is also hysterical, servile, voluble, and irrevocably in the wrong when she tries to assert herself. She is given to sudden tears, to pathetic outbursts of affection, and to equally pathetic shows of self-confidence. She is all that Fanny despises, fears to be.

As the story opens, Fanny realizes that her husband has a new mistress, an actress, and shortly afterward she discovers that he is also sleeping with Jane. Unhappy herself, she gets relief and a mean satisfaction from watching Jane's unconcealed jealousy of the actress. The crisis arrives when she accuses Jane, and then follows a reluctant, frightened scene that sounds more like one outraged woman trying to calm herself than like two arguing. Farou walks in on this, and walks out when he sees what is going on. He goes off alone to a party, and the crisis collapses, leaving the two much as they were before but quite exhausted, and a little deeper in defeat, since they have betrayed their weakness to him. During the unlikely final scene, in which the two women sit timidly together, listening to Farou's stealthy return, we cannot help feeling that we are seeing only one woman, the wife, who regrets having given way to her weakness and is now anxious to be allowed to make amends. Of course, Fanny must make peace with her jealousy, because she knows that if it masters her, it will separate her from Farou. Fanny's need of her husband is so intense that she would seem abject if it were not that her desire to please is matched by her determination to be pleased by him. This determination, which she shares with all of Colette's women, and which alone compels their concessions and their compromises, is what makes the stories work. But it must be admitted that Farou seems much too busy a man to be able to make even the vaguest anguish worth while.

This is as good a place as any to remark that, except when they end in a death, Colette's stories do not have endings.

We finish each story with the feeling that the people in there have been granted a breathing spell—no more than that. Their natures will continue alternately to feed and to suffocate each other until indifference sets in, unless jealousy becomes strong enough to drive them apart. This is true whether she writes of love in marriage or out of it. Indifference, the fading of recognition, the death of love, is the chill wind that blows about all her stories, the threat it holds giving them their steady perspective. These people are never permitted to forget that their time is short and their time together perhaps very short. This intimation of change comes to them naturally, not from outside but from their doubt of themselves and of each other, and from reminders and encounters that rise up out of the past to harass them. There is nothing unreasonable about Colette, even in her most heightened moments. She says only that we love as we can, and she is as matter of fact about the course of sexual love as she is romantic about its extravagances.

Duo is a much slighter story of jealousy in marriage. *The Cat* is a grotesque, somewhat playful retelling of the story of Chéri. It is a fancy little novel, full of handsome young people and pretty sights and sounds. The most remarkable person in it is an older woman, an echo of all Colette's subtle, powerful older women, every one of them a born mother-in-law. *The Indulgent Husband* is a very early novel. It is a highly sensuous, even sensational story about an extremely young girl married to a much older man, who condones and oversees her love affairs. This complacent young-old husband could be taken for a caricature of Colette's first husband, Willy, the one she is reported to have described as "worse than mature."

The editors of this book might well have attempted a chronological collection of novels, or several chronological collections, instead of assembling a hodgepodge from Colette's whole writing life. Most of her novels are very short. None of them is very long. Many of them are far better than the three just named. Glenway Wescott has written an introduction to this volume, and he makes several interesting remarks about the fierce bond of love, understanding, and mutual respect that existed between Colette and her mother. (pp. 69-73)

Maeve Brennan, "The Need of Love," in The New Yorker, *Vol. XXVII, No. 47, January 5, 1952, pp. 69-73.*

Sonya Rudikoff (essay date 1953)

[*In the following essay, Rudikoff discusses Colette's writing style in terms of its professionalism, autobiographical influences, strong sense of physical reality, and effective portrayal of passionate emotions.*]

Madame Sidonie-Gabrielle Colette is one of the great members of the generation of Proust and Gide; and, with the ranks of that group so depleted—and of later generations, too—Colette is likely to seem a little lonely in her eminence. We can hardly help thinking of her as a noble curiosity against the background of wars, disease, politics, neurosis, social changes, and the other problems of life since 1870. What a feat for anyone to survive, and so mag-

nificently! But Matisse is one of that generation also, and there is more than the arthritis they share to suggest a resemblance between them; for, neither the grand old literary woman nor the venerable painter have receded into the dimness of the recent past; they refuse to be only historical, and, as if to prove it, they continue to live and work in the full consciousness of their illustrious careers. Not only their great age is impressive: an ancient peasant living on yogurt commands respect, but we pay a different tribute to these two exquisitely complex and refined artists who have actively survived in the midst of the civilized world, in a country that may be the most civilized of all.

Perhaps these pictures of serene complex old age communicate little to Americans, for in our country we have no very great interest in the old; we have, instead, geriatrics, which suggests old age as a disease to be healed, and maturity is still a great American *problem*. We have made much of Fitzgerald's remark that American lives have no second acts, because it seems to express something very noticeable about ourselves. In no other civilized country are children so important and the new generation so insistent; early and quick success characterizes our life, and the values of youth displace the values of maturity. Even that useful corrective, traditionalism, made much of its impression through novelty. The commonplaces of our competitive life show up in cultural matters as well, although the famous spirit of the times can obscure rapid changes in preference. Thus, we have always taken the Fitzgerald remark to mean that the force of American lives fades too quickly, but, for a greater truth, we should notice how often the audience leaves at the end of the first act. Perhaps the French, with their declining population, can afford to remain in their seats.

It is hard not to think of these things when we contemplate Colette in the fullness of her eighty years, her life and career so different from our American performances. For fifty-three years—ever since her first husband, "Willy," published her *Claudine à l'Ecole* under his own name—Colette has figured in the French literary scene. She has no American counterpart; literature has a different place in France, and Colette is different from the writers our country produces and provokes. Our serious writers are not usually so prolific; but the space she takes up on a bookshelf is not the only thing that interests us, for she may be rivaled in that. In other respects, too, Colette can be surpassed, and it is true that she has written no long, large novels, and nothing with an explicit cultural intention. In spite of her professed seriousness, which we have no reason to doubt, there is about her relation to literature something cavalier, almost careless, or frivolous—we may not be able to define it more precisely. Faulkner and Hemingway among our own writers come to mind as having something of the same attitude, yet Colette is still different from them, for they show a desperate kind of withdrawal that she does not.

The difference may be seen in Colette's choice of characters and situations, and these two collections [*The Short Novels of Colette* and *Gigi, Chance Acquaintances, Julie de Carneilhan*] offer good examples of her choice— theatrical people (*The Other One, Duo*), or journalists

(*The Indulgent Husband*), music-hall dancers or business-men (*Chance Acquaintances*), children of the bourgeoisie (*The Cat*), or courtesans (*Chéri*), or the children of courte-sans (*Gigi, The Last of Chéri*), or divorcees (*Julie de Car-neilhan*). The lives of such people may touch upon politics or large affairs, but they are not involved in problems of the intellect, or conscious of the implications of their actions and desires; yet they are not primitive or simple. Colette's world is not one that can be mapped out, shown in its ideology or the massing of its forces, in the steadiness of its legend or the angle of its vision. The characters do not represent points of view, their situations do not stand in any very clear relation to the crisis of French society or of European culture; their lives are not symbolic nor are their figures mythic, and it is a question whether their values or manners can satisfy the prevailing American hunger. Colette is really as different as a writer can be from the image our demands create.

The strong physical sense we have of [Colette's] characters is immediate and substantial; the physical exists on its own terms, not as symbolic of something more inward; the men and women have real bodies, the cats have fur we can feel.

—Sonya Rudikoff

Perhaps there was something fortuitous about her birth in 1873. Had she been born a decade or a generation later, we may feel everything would have been different and more difficult, and yet that doesn't account for our interest in her. Nor does it explain her achievement; we may still wonder how it was done, what strength was required to be as she is and was, what faith, what standards, what resilience. Although it might be hard to think so, Colette was probably fortunate in the beginning of her career, when writing was something of a duty or trade, a matter of being locked in a room for four hours to write at Willy's command. Her literary career did not begin in a turmoil of expression and rebellion and sensitivity from which she might not have escaped; not that she remained aloof from the stresses of the creative life, or ignorant of them—but only perhaps that she learned early to separate problems of sensitivity and problems of literature. Colette's later, more capable work—rather than the Claudine books—is the ambiguous tribute to that apprenticeship, grim and shabby though it may have been in other ways. Its perversities, however, should not lead us to a wrong view of its value for Colette. Given the circumstances of her marriage, the work she did for Willy, and especially the fact that he passed off her first work as his, writing was probably more restrictive and anonymous than it was personal or liberating; it was not likely to suffer in the same degree that Colette herself suffered. Life provided sufficient human complications, but she never found it necessary to renounce writing in order to regain her personality, as

Katherine Mansfield did. It was not only Colette's good fortune to precede that generation and to be exempt from the problems of its women writers, for by the time she found herself in their situations, she was already a professional writer whose craft was distinct and separate from herself.

Of course, Colette was not "ruined" by her professional beginnings; and, if it seems strange that she needs such apologies, we must remember the unattractive image of the professional writer, whose work—in our day, at least—being so mechanical, seems to preclude the qualities of good imaginative literature. Perhaps because things are extreme in America, we see this problem, too, in its most lurid light, although it is not only an American problem. Naturally, no final solution of it can be found in Colette's career—the problem is too large and complex—but her example may be instructive. The relation she contrived between herself and her writing does not suggest the sterile automatism of professional virtuosity, from which the person and the personality have been removed. We cannot speak of Colette's work in terms of privation or failure or deadness. Although her literary life may not have begun in the urgency of personal expression, it can hardly be called impersonal. Her standards have been high, her dedication great, her pride and delight in literature intense; and her dissatisfactions and criticisms were no less scrupulous than if she had begun and worked differently.

Nor has Colette's fiction been marked by a want of feeling. In fact, the very opposite is so, for, when Colette writes of love, of animals, of what people want and how they get it, we respond to a great depth of feeling even as we are struck by its clarity. These are not the qualities we usually find in a professional writer, although, of course, a lucid depth of feeling is the quality of all very good fiction. Colette uses her own feelings and her own experience as all writers do, but even when she is being most personal, her subject is related to her own feeling, not equivalent to it. Unfortunately, these two collections contain none of her autobiographical writing which—especially the writing about her mother—shows most clearly Colette's relation to her subject. In her fiction, however, we can see evidence of that relation in the way she describes and realizes her characters; they exist for us without handicaps, without privilege. Her relation to them is not directly personal; they do not express her feelings only, nor is she too easily or finally identified with them. We may observe that she is closest to Claudine, the first of her characters and the least satisfactory. Claudine controlled too much of the world and never met with enough real opposition; she scored her triumphs so easily that we can't be more than amused at her. But, when Colette's characters make a deeper impression on us—as Léa, the lovely courtesan, does in her love for Chéri—they move in a more crowded field: at a distance from their author, unprotected by her watchfulness, although created out of her own sympathy. Neither manipulated nor destroyed, they become real when they are vulnerable, and they affect us especially when Colette shows them as mean or stupid, grasping or selfish, defiant or childish. If Léa smiles to see Chéri "as she loved him most—mutinous but amenable, insufficiently chained and yet incapable of being free," Colette is not provoked to denounce or defend her; Léa doesn't suffer from having her feelings revealed and analyzed, nor does Colette preen herself on the acuity of her insights. Her freedom to observe and to communicate a variety of feelings arises out of the distance from which she views her characters: at this close distance, no one is really indulged and no one sacrificed. Thus, it is not merely an unrelated aspect of Colette's skill that her characters have so tangible a physical existence and so distinct a physical awareness of themselves; nor is it only Colette's sensitivity and her famous style that make her animals and her natural descriptions so vivid. The strong physical sense we have of her characters is immediate and substantial; the physical exists on its own terms, not as symbolic of something more inward; the men and women have real bodies, the cats have fur we can feel. The same sense for the physical reality of hair and fur and skin is used to evoke and specify the emotional reality of discrete feelings. Just as the animals, the flowers, the storms Colette writes about do not derive their existence from the displaced feelings of the characters, so the characters are not swollen into life by Colette's own feelings about them. Her emotional distance from Léa, from Chéri, from Gigi, from Julie de Carneilhan, instead of stunting them is exactly what gives them life.

Colette's style and her sensitivity are unusual, but rarer still is the way she uses them. Some writers, when they are "sensitive," can alienate us by demanding too much of a sacrifice for sensitivity. The intense vision that attempts to appraise human life can often be deficient in the degree to which it is intense in representing its own completeness. Colette's success with her sensitivity is not of this sort because her insight claims only a partial not a universal truth. She writes about many kinds of love and sexual situations, some of them rather unusual, but we are never exhorted by a willful sensitivity to accept the situations as final or complete; although the characters involved may have this attitude, Colette herself does not. If we think, for example, of how *The Cat* might have been handled by other writers, we can see Colette's grace and skill clearly: a beautiful cat is so important to a young man named Alain that he gives up his new young wife, Camille, and returns with the cat to his mother's house (think of Katherine Mansfield with such an idea, or of other "sensitive" writers). Our feelings about Saha, the magnificent cat, and about the intricate situations of the marriage she disrupts, are maneuvered into a very complex understanding. Alain's love for Saha is serious and tangible: we can sense all of its qualities and appreciate them even as Alain does. Colette never pretends that it is only a mild crotchet; she recognizes its deeply emotional, sexual, childish nature, and she also notices its part in the sexual situation of that new marriage. Her perceptions evoke Alain's love sufficiently; she doesn't need to see an *exclusive* poetry in it. We should note, too, how little symbolism the cat carries, how much she is substantial, palpable, independently motivated, yet not anthropomorphic; nor does she destroy the story by an overwhelming surrealist "presence." Camille is cruel and tries to kill the cat; but the oddly moving love of Alain and Saha is not used to denounce Camille's coarseness and cruelty, and Camille is not presented as so

healthy and strong that her crudity is justified by the decadence around her. Colette keeps all the emotions distinct by her precise and sure discriminations among the various voices; it is no part of her purpose to unite her own voice with any one of the characters or in any one of the situations.

The emotional *ambiance* of Colette's work has been of great interest to American readers, perhaps because Colette writes more completely about passion than is usual or possible in America. Not only is it the subject of much of her fiction, but, also, the novels themselves are often modeled on the shape of a passion. (And Colette may not satisfy the reader who expects more resolution or awareness than the shapes of these passions provide.) In our cultural climate, the quality of Colette's emotional and sexual insight might have an interesting and salutary effect. For Colette does not write from the distance of a child's desires, and her tones are not those of despair and wounded bewilderment and horror, which, in America, are often found more congenial for the treatment of emotional life and of specific sexual situations. (I am not speaking of the conscious, explicit use of a child-observer, but of an underlying attitude; the presence of children is irrelevant.) The tone Colette uses is compelling and comprehensive. It is Chéri's tone, especially in *The Last of Chéri,* when he tries to find the beautiful Léa again and finds instead a fat, gray-haired woman. He can feel only his own despair; Léa seems a grotesque creature who has grown old on purpose to spite him, and his rage makes him see all the world as useless, cruel, and terrible. But this is not Colette's rage, and when Chéri declines, it is not Colette's decline. Although Chéri must finally put a pistol to his ear in despair over his irrecoverable past, he has not been invested with so much of her feeling that he puts an end to feeling. Colette does "finish him off," but she doesn't end with him; her writing goes beyond this one emotional situation. As we think of Colette's great production, we can even see this not so much as an aspect of cultural difference alone, but as a clue to her talent and her remarkable endurance; for it is a question how long the material of fiction can resist the demands of the secret images of a single feeling. (pp. 332-38)

Sonya Rudikoff, "Colette at Eighty," in Partisan Review, *Vol. XX, No. 3, May-June, 1953, pp. 332-38.*

Elaine Marks   (essay date 1960)

[*Marks is an American editor and critic. Excerpted below are two chapters from her critical study* Colette. *In the first, she compares Colette's early writing style with that revealed in her later works by analyzing the themes and characters of the short novels* Mitsou *and* Gigi. *In the second, Marks analyzes the similarities and differences between Colette's short stories and novellas, focusing on writing techniques, characterizations, and the recurring theme of psychological revelation.*]

The year 1919-1920 marks a new and important development in Colette's work. Until this date Colette, almost exclusively, had used a first-person narrator in her writings. With the publication of *Mitsou,* in 1919, the barely disguised confessions which characterize her novels from the *Claudines* to *L'Entrave* are apparently abandoned.

In the years immediately preceding the first World War, Colette began her career as a journalist. Although many of her articles are written in a very imaginative, impressionistic style, and although the first-person narrator often dominates them, newspaper writing, both of articles and serialized stories, forced Colette to a degree of objectivity and economy which her writings had hitherto lacked. This perhaps partially explains the fact that *Mitsou,* the first short novel she wrote after her initial years as a journalist, and all the novels which were written after *Mitsou* are more objective, more condensed, than her early writings.

The change from a first-person to a third-person narrator was to influence Colette's style and the form her novels took, rather than the novels' characterizations. Indeed, the word "novel" hardly applies to Colette's fictional writings from *Mitsou* to *Gigi,* particularly if one considers a novel to be a work of a certain length. The longest novel of this period, *La Seconde,* has only one hundred and fifty pages. However, since Colette herself referred to these works as novels, rather than novelettes or long short stories, the present study will employ the same term.

As these novels become progressively shorter, they tend also to be more and more devoid of any description which does not bear directly on the action. The landscapes of which Colette was so fond disappear almost completely. The long, lyrical passages so frequent in the early novels are totally absent. Colette concentrates on dialogue, on the unspoken thoughts of her characters and on descriptions of their gestures, their facial expressions, their physical and their mental states. The constraint imposed on Colette by her effort to conceive and organize a sequence of events which do not necessarily stem directly from her own experience is reflected in a change in her prose; it becomes less verbose, more disciplined, a vehicle both for irony and humor.

Mitsou and *Gigi* were written in time of war, *Mitsou* toward the end of the first World War and *Gigi* toward the end of the second. The twenty-five years that separate the two novels enable us to see some of the changes that took place in Colette's approach to the craft of fiction.

The time at which the novel was written and the time depicted in it coincide in *Mitsou.* Although *Mitsou* can hardly be considered a "war" story, the war plays a part in creating the atmosphere and situations of the novel: the excitement engendered in Mitsou's music-hall colleague, Petite Chose, by the presence of so many uniformed young men, the conditions under which Mitsou meets her "blue" lieutenant, the fact that they have only one night together, the importance of their correspondence. But the war, like the music hall, is merely the background for the main theme, which is, as Colette herself has defined it in the subtitle, "How intelligence comes to young girls."

Gigi was written when Colette was turning seventy; it is her last work of fiction and her adieu to a bygone age. The source of this short novel was an anecdote related to Colette in 1926. The most significant change made by Colette in her transformation of the anecdote into fiction was a time change. The events related in 1926 had taken place in 1918; the action of *Gigi* takes place in 1899, at the time when Colette, guided by Willy, had come to know the demimondaine world. It is the period of the early *Claudines;* Colette has returned to her point of departure.

In writing *Gigi,* Colette reduced to a minimum the necessity of inventing and imagining. For the characters given in the anecdote, Colette easily found models from her own fictional world and from her past acquaintance. That this past should have remained so vivid is proof of the influence it exerted on Colette and its fusion in her mind with the even more remote past of her childhood. Despite her age, her arthritis and her concern for her husband's safety, Colette was able to evoke this past as if it were present. The distance between Colette and her characters is considerably smaller in *Gigi* than in *Mitsou,* and this is an important factor in the superiority of *Gigi.*

Mitsou is Colette's only experimental novel. It is obviously an attempt at integrating into one novel certain techniques which Colette had already used in *Les Dialogues de Bêtes* and in *La Vagabonde. Mitsou* is a half-dramatic, half-epistolary novel. The alternation of stage settings and dialogue with letters allows Colette to describe quickly and to present humorously Mitsou and her world and also to show the changes that occur in Mitsou and her "blue" lieutenant through their correspondence. Thus the characters are presented objectively, as the author sees them and as they speak, and subjectively, as they see and understand themselves. The subjective, first-person presentation is much less successful than the objective. Colette herself was undoubtedly aware of this, since *Mitsou* is the last of her novels in which she includes a subjective presentation of character.

Gigi is a very simply narrated story in which, as always in Colette's fiction, the largest share of the writing is given over to dialogue. The double surprise ending, Gigi's acceptance of Gaston's proposal on his terms and Gaston's final acceptance of Gigi on very different terms, seems to be an anomaly in Colette's usual presentation of the game of love. But the happy, Cinderella ending was in the anecdote and Colette faithfully kept to her source.

The names "Mitsou" and "Gigi" evoke a certain milieu and a certain kind of snub-nosed young girl or woman. Mitsou and Gigi are lucid and romantic, simple and proud. They share with the other "Colette-Claudines" uncanny intuition and common sense, coupled with great naïveté and piquant beauty. The adjectives that best fit them, "cute," "pretty" and "nice," have, in the past years, been so abused as to be almost useless. They are, however, admirably suited to a general description of Colette's young ladies.

Because of their sincerity and their innate refusal to accept conventional or unconventional norms of behavior, Mitsou and Gigi are rather amusing characters. A rich source of humor, particularly for the American and British reader, is that neither Mitsou nor Gigi does what is expected of her. Neither of them conforms to preconceived and often literary notions of how a show girl and the offspring of an unwed mother should act. Both emerge morally un-

Colette in her dressing room during her years as a music hall performer.

tainted from a demimondaine environment, and both are saved, or rather save themselves, by love.

Mitsou, at twenty-four, is a music-hall dancer at the Empyrée theater in Paris. The established mistress of an elderly "respectable man," Mitsou has never been in love until she accidentally meets the "blue" lieutenant. Her life is the routine, dull life of which Renée speaks in *La Vagabonde.* Like Renée, like Colette herself, Mitsou, the music-hall star, has more good will than talent; her success is due to her personal appeal rather than to her art. Indeed, in all she does, Mitsou is disarmingly artless. On stage and off, she is very simply and irreducibly Mitsou. Hence her charm.

Gigi, at fifteen, looks "like Robin Hood, like a stiff angel, like a boy in skirts, she seldom resembled a young girl." Although Gigi is definitely female, she is unself-consciously female, she is still at an ambiguous, equivocal age and, like so many of Colette's adolescents, combines the physical graces of both sexes. The comparisons chosen by Colette to describe Gigi acquire an added force by the very fact that they are the only images in the novel which refer to a world not limited to the demimonde. Thus, from the beginning, Colette is attempting to portray Gigi as a general type of adolescent as well as a product of a very particular social group.

The daughter of an unimportant singer at the Opéra-Comique, the granddaughter and grandniece of two retired courtesans, Gigi is receiving from her exclusively female entourage the training necessary for her future career as the mistress of wealthy men. Gigi is taught by her grandmother, Madame Alvarez, to keep her knees close to each other when she is seated, to keep her legs together when she is standing. She is told not to wear stays because they spoil the figure, not to get to know the fathers of her school friends. She is taught by her great-aunt Alicia how to select cigars, how to distinguish between precious stones, how to eat lobster, American style. Aside from her restricted contacts with her school friends, Gigi's relation to the world outside the family is limited to the mundane gossip in the newspaper *Gil Blas*—real news referring to real people, like Polaire and Liane de Pougy—and the erratic visits of Gaston Lachaille, the bored and very wealthy son of one of Madame Alvarez's former lovers.

These highly readable, unpretentious stories contain a wealth of subtle details and moral implications which become particularly significant when seen in relation to the rest of Colette's writing. By themselves, they are more or less delightful, slice-of-life, period tales. As parts of a whole, they are chapters illustrating varied aspects and styles of the game of love.

Both *Mitsou* and *Gigi* are concerned with the problem of education. For Mitsou, the education is accomplished through love, and as the progress in style in Mitsou's letters over an eight-month period shows, it is a very rapid education, a very painful but tangible gain in awareness. Whether or not Mitsou will ever win back her disillusioned "blue" lieutenant she is, in any case, victorious, because she has had the experience of love, because she has acquired a "private life," be it happy or sad, because this experience has "brought intelligence to a young girl. . . . " This notion of the acceptance of experience for its own sake, one of Colette's major themes in her nonfiction, is developed much more fully by the narrator "Colette" in *La Naissance du Jour.*

Gigi's education, presided over with great care and seriousness by her doting grandmother and her great-aunt, involves a series of concrete things that one must know, that one must do or not do. Gigi's scepticism in regard to this education is evident from the sarcastic tone in which she enumerates to Gaston some of the "Do's" and "Don't's." Above all, the principle is impressed on Gigi that the women in her family do not marry.

Gigi, the victim of a plot, triumphs over the conspirators. This plot, first conceived by Aunt Alicia when Gigi arrives at her apartment in Gaston's car, later carefully thought out by Alicia and Madame Alvarez and finally Gaston himself, is predestined to fail. Madame Alvarez has already failed with Gigi's mother, Andrée, who finds it less tiring to sing than to sleep for a living. What, of course, no one really took into account during the transaction was that Gaston loved Gigi and Gigi loved Gaston. The double surprise ending is the proof of this love and of the inadequacy of any rigorous principle in the guidance of someone else's life.

It would indeed be rare today to find someone who would cry, as did Marcel Proust, while reading Mitsou's final letters to her lieutenant. The modern reader, on the other hand, would heartily agree with Proust in his criticism of the too pretty, too contrived, too affected passages which are found in Mitsou's often impossibly honest letters, and in his praise of the incomparable restaurant scene between Mitsou and her about-to-be lover. The lieutenant, like Gaston in *Gigi,* is an amusing, slightly ridiculous character, and it is in great part due to the way in which Colette portrays him that the novel escapes being oversentimental. His increasing uneasiness, as Mitsou candidly horrifies the waiter and the wine steward by her lack of sophistication and taste, becomes physical, to the extent indeed that the lieutenant begins to doubt whether he will be able to execute the ritual duties of a lover. This unexpected concern on the part of a bourgeois, rather stilted young man is an amusing and, at the same time, acute commentary on the elusive whys and wherefores of desire. Presented in some of their more comic aspects, these whys and wherefores relieve the heaviness that often accompanies the exaggeratedly serious statements of the not too bright, but sincere Mitsou.

Gigi is certainly the most humorous of Colette's fictional writings. All the characters in the novel participate in a bubbling comedy of manners. *Gigi* contains none of the contrived sentences, the sentimental outbursts, that occur in *Mitsou.* Since Colette did not have to worry about inventing a story, she was able to concentrate most of her attention on her characters. The result, within a deliberately limited medium, is close to perfection.

Although Madame Alvarez and Alicia are very definitely ladies of the demimonde, they take from "Colette-Sido" their enthusiasm and their attachment to the real. Madame Alvarez, who "retained from her past life the honor-

able habits of women who have lost their honor," is almost as wise in her domain as Sido in hers. If she miscalculates in her judgment of Gigi, there is no malice in her plotting, and the lessons and advice she gives Gigi could be useful in almost any situation. Alicia, undoubtedly a more successful courtesan than her younger sister, to judge by the opulence of her apartment and the variety of her jewels, is also more calculating, more sophisticated and perhaps a bit less genuine. But she, too, has been modeled after "Colette-Sido," and the two sisters, together, are a formidable team. While they are amusing because of the intensity which they display in their pedagogic roles, their double link to the demimonde and to "Colette-Sido" gives them a naturalness and a solidity which neither Mitsou nor even Gigi quite achieves. The affection bestowed on them by their creator is second only to the affection bestowed on "Sido." This affection is, in Colette's world, a baptism which leads if not to immortality, almost inevitably to success.

When the "blue" lieutenant discovers Mitsou's crime is that "She makes you have to think about her just when you are tempted to say, 'You are only a little anxiety, you aren't big enough to be a real torment,' " he has discovered a truth that applies, not only to Mitsou, but to all the "Colette-Claudines" and, by extension, to all the novels in which they appear. One is seduced without really wanting to be, without ever being quite sure of one's feelings, and, trying to escape, again seduced by an unexpected charm in author, in character or in style. But one is always aware of the fact that it is a seduction and not a deep love. (pp. 99-108)

. . . . .

The *nouvelle,* or short story, was originally an anecdote based on a real event, purportedly related by someone who was present at the time the event took place. Today, the short story is usually defined as a brief work of fiction, rigorously composed, concerned, as a rule, with a single episode and sustained by a unity of mood. Those of Colette's short stories in which "Colette" is the narrator, and they constitute by far the largest group, are all *nouvelles* in the original sense. Only eighteen of the twenty-two stories in *La Femme cachée,* five of the eleven stories in *La Fleur de l'Age,* "Le rendez-vous" in *Bella-Vista,* "Armande" in *Le Képi* and "L'Enfant malade" in *Gigi* are short stories in the current sense of the term.

The title, *La Femme cachée,* is to some extent misleading, for in these stories it is a question, not only of the "hidden woman," but also of the "hidden man," unless, of course, the title is to be read as implying that "to hide" is essentially a female trait. It is unsafe to think of the title which Colette gives to a group of stories as applying to them all. Almost always the book takes its name from the first story, but although this is the case in *La Femme cachée,* the word "hidden" is nevertheless pertinent, not only to the theme of all the stories in this particular collection, but to Colette's other short stories as well. In a very unpretentious and concrete manner, Colette is dealing with the problem of reality and appearances.

The differences, as well as the similarities, between Colette's short stories and her novels are striking. On the whole, the short stories are much less subjective. The characters do not fall into the family groups that exist in the novels, nor does the action in which they are involved follow the patterns established in the novels. Of course, as may be expected, most of the short stories deal with aspects of love, but even here there is greater variety in the age, the background and the situation of the characters. In general, too, the men in Colette's short stories are infinitely more sympathetic and stronger than their novelistic counterparts.

The reader will recognize immediately, however, that he is still well within the bounds of Colette's fictional universe. The tendency to move from a particular incident to a general conclusion or implication, the tremendous importance given to a certain kind of detail and, above all, the concision and density of the style reveal the hand and eye of Colette. The short stories, indeed, because of their often minuscule size, are an excellent means to study some of Colette's techniques of composition.

Most of the stories in *La Femme cachée* range from three to four pages in length. Of these, seven are concerned with conjugal love, six with other forms of love, two with the lost paradise of childhood, one with the triumph of life over death as shown in the day of a painter, one with the relation between a woman and her critical butler and one with the semi-crazy people who haunt the offices of daily newspapers.

> Colette is deliberately attempting an anti-romantic portrayal of human beings. She refuses to over-dramatize murder, suicide, love, memory, to make of them anything but "facts."
>
> —*Elaine Marks*

In each case, the story is a revelation, through an often trivial detail or incident, of what makes people love, fall out of love, go on living, kill, become jealous or heroic. A new hairdo, the constant movement of a thumb over lips, a hand lying on a sheet, a familiar whistle, an anniversary bracelet, an unknown song, a mildewed picture, an omelette, these are some of the seemingly unimportant details from which Colette produces her revelations.

As in the novels, though less often through dialogue, the reader is brought immediately into the action with only the vaguest suggestion of an introductory statement.

> "For a long time he had been watching the movement of the masked figures. . . ."
>
> "The surgical suddenness of their rupture left him dumb."
>
> "He had fallen asleep on his young wife's shoulder. . . ."

"He had taken her from another man. . . ."

(pp. 151-53)

The factual, undramatic tone of these first sentences, whether they refer to a very ordinary or a very startling situation, sets the mood, and illustrates Colette's very particular, ironic point of view. In using the same tone for all the stories, Colette reduces the extraordinary to the ordinary and raises the ordinary to the extraordinary. Whether the principal character is a murderer, a widow, a bored married man, a newlywed wife, a robber, a lesbian or a painter on the verge of suicide, becomes of little importance, and this in itself is a sufficient element of surprise to arrest the attention. The contrast between the unconventional status and role of some of the characters and the extreme situations in which some of them are found, and the rather conventional status, role and situation of others, is an all-important key to an understanding of these short stories.

Colette persistently forces acceptance of the fact that there may be no significant difference between the reactions of a perpetually irritated wife and the reactions of an unsuccessful robber. They are both victims of the annoying consequences of their actions, in one case marriage, in the other attempted theft, and they are both capable of a final, heroic silence in which they reveal a sense of compromise and propriety. Everything and anything human beings do is only a source of small vexations and small pleasures, which, depending on the angle of vision, may seem either very unimportant or very important. Colette is deliberately attempting an anti-romantic portrayal of human beings. She refuses to over-dramatize murder, suicide, love, memory, to make of them anything but "facts." Aside from the very positive value she gives to silence, Colette is totally unconcerned with demonstrating anything other than the general notion that all lives are conditioned by details and that there is no relation between the apparent insignificance of the detail and the gigantic meaning it may assume as an instrument of revelation. Just as the novels explore variations on the theme of love, the short stories explore variations on the theme of the revealing detail. In the novels there is essentially one love, and in these short stories, because of the all-pervading unity of tone, there is essentially one human being, involved in a variety of situations, revealed by a variety of details.

In the title story of *La Femme cachée* and in Colette's longer short stories, the theme of revelation is more fully developed. Irène in "La Femme cachée," Bernard in "Le rendez-vous," Armande in "Armande" and Jean in "L'Enfant malade" reveal themselves as being very different either from the image they attempt to impose on others (Irène, Armande and Jean) or from the image they have of themselves (Bernard). Irène, Armande and Bernard momentarily find a means of escaping from their false apparent selves to their true selves. Irène, at a masked ball, protected by her disguise, tastes for an instant "the monstrous pleasure of being alone, free, truthful in her native animality, of being the unknown woman, forever solitary and without shame, that a small mask and a hermetic costume have restored to her irremediable solitude and to her dishonest innocence." Armande, ordinarily prudish, becomes loving and caressing in gesture, intimate and vulgar in language, when her timid would-be lover, Maxime, is knocked unconscious by a falling chandelier while leaving her home. Bernard regains a sense of dignity when he helps a wounded Arab boy discovered at the place he and his mistress had chosen for a nocturnal meeting: "Poor Rose. . . . She was my woman, but he is my equal. It is curious that I had to come to Tangiers to meet my equal, the only one who can make me proud of him and proud of me. With a woman, one is easily a little ashamed, of her or of oneself."

Ten-year-old Jean, in **"L'Enfant malade,"** escapes through fever from the real world of his sickbed and the solicitous questions of Madame Maman to a fantastic, poetic world, composed of familiar objects metamorphosed, the existence of which he keeps hidden from those around him. Jean's recovery means the death of this world of perpetual revelation.

In each of these stories, and to a lesser degree in all the short stories of *La Femme cachée* and *La Fleur de l'Age,* the characters are playing a game of hide-and-seek, alone and with others. In general, those who seek find something unexpected, and those who hide are discovered.

Irène's husband, who has deliberately not told his hitherto faithful wife that he is going to the masked ball and who in turn has been similarly deceived, finds her wandering from man to man, taking her fill of kisses. Although she does not recognize him, he recognizes her and allows her to betray herself. Maxime, who has failed miserably in his attempt at controlling his shyness in what he considers to be Armande's forbidding presence, pretends to be unconscious so as to enjoy the revelation of a sensual, affectionate Armande. Bernard, who is prepared for an evening of love, discovers that his mistress is essentially vulgar and that in binding Ahmed's wound with strips torn from his own jacket, he has given and received much more than that which he sought with Rose.

Jean is always beginning to play a game of hide-and-seek with Madame Maman and she with him, but neither of them can be trusted to close his eyes and count to twenty. "She thinks I'm asleep. . . . He thinks that I think he's asleep. . . . She thinks I'm not suffering. . . . How well he knows how to imitate a child who isn't suffering. . . ."

Jean's important game of hide-and-seek is played with death. The further Jean goes in his exploration of a world in which he can fly on a paper knife or ride on a lavender smell, a world in which applesauce is transformed into "an acid young provincial girl of fifteen who, like other girls of the same age, had only disdain and arrogance for the ten-year-old boy," the further he moves from the real world, the closer he comes to death, which is what he is really seeking. Colette refuses Jean what might have been an empty revelation, the very unsatisfactory ending of a dangerous game. She brings him back to a world in which a paper knife cuts, lavender smells and applesauce is an often unattractive food. In abandoning, with Jean, her brief excursion into the world of imaginative revelation, Colette deliberately casts her choice for a world in which revelation is limited to that of the "hidden man" or the "hidden woman." (pp. 154-58)

Elaine Marks, in her Colette, *Rutgers University Press, 1960, 265 p.*

Sylvie Romanowski   (essay date 1981)

[*In the following essay, Romanowski considers the female characters in Colette's short novels, categorizing them as either "adolescent" characters who are newly initiated into adulthood, or "mature" women, who are in a process of relinquishing the experiences of youth.*]

This study takes the novels of Colette as constituting a totality, and assumes that each character can be properly understood only if she is situated within a typology, in a structure of the types of women in the novels. The scope of the study is limited in two important ways: it will deal only with women, and it will not attempt a description at the level of each individual work. Furthermore, it will not attempt to discuss all the women in all the novels, but will focus rather on the ones that have been found to be more complex and richer illustrations of the types. The reader is free to take this study as a hypothesis and test it in relation to the other women in Colette's works. A complete exposition of Colette's woman population will not be attempted, but only suggested by means of some of her outstanding creations.

One critic, Elaine Marks, notes [in her critical study *Colette,* 1960] that "Colette's female characters may be divided into two family groups: the 'Colette-Claudine' branch and the 'Colette-Sido' branch." But she goes on to link these characters with the author, as her choice of labels clearly indicates, a practice which will be avoided in this essay. I would propose, in basic agreement with E. Marks' analysis, that there are indeed two major types of women in Colette's writings, which can be called, very simply, the adolescent and the mature woman. Each of these types can in turn be subdivided into two variants, which can be called the positive and the negative variant. It should be stated here first that these are relative terms indicating a position that the characters occupy in a structure. Second, these types and subtypes are not realized absolutely in any one novel; in addition, there are nuances and shadings. After analyzing Colette's women in terms of these types, certain questions can be asked concerning her understanding of woman in general.

The young adolescent woman is the type that is the most clearly divided into the two subtypes. The best, least ambiguous examples are Vinca (*The Ripening Seed*) for the positive variant and Camille (*The Cat*) for the negative one, and this analysis will concentrate on these two characters. Colette delineates and suggests the values of each character through the accumulation of numerous details of description and associated imagery as well as through the contrast within the novel between characters belonging to another type or subtype.

Thus descriptions of Camille are punctuated with reference to her nouveau-riche background, her slight vulgarity, her obvious make-up, and her lack of both finesse and modesty. In the very first paragraphs the colors of her face appear too clear-cut to be natural: "she would . . . look pale again, her chin white, tired little lines under her ochre-tinted powder." The portrait continues in the chapter with mention of her "white fingers and lacquered nails" and her "wiping with her pointed nail two little clots of red saliva from the corners of her mouth." The impression, almost that of a collage of flat painted surfaces, is enhanced by a reference to her solid black hair, "brilliantined, and the color of a new piano."

Moreover, references to her habits of driving a bit too fast, her swearing at cab drivers, and the unevenness of her temperament continue to give a somewhat pejorative coloring to her, which is not compensated for by Alain's reflections on her beauty. And surely her family's recent wealth, acquired in the modern business of washing machines, contrasts with the old, slightly declining but still aristocratic making of silk, a cloth of time-honored noble and distinguished connotations.

In this novel, the most obvious and persistent contrast is drawn between Camille and Saha, the Chartreuse cat who seems to be everything that Camille is not. The contrast between the loves of Alain, particularly well-explained by Mieke Bal, is clarified by an examination of the positive subtype of the adolescent woman, Vinca.

Vinca also moves from girlhood to womanhood in the *The Ripening Seed,* though not in an official manner through marriage, and with a slower, more reluctant pace than Camille. Just as the opening portrait of Camille inclined the reader toward a somewhat pejorative judgment, so the opening portrait of Vinca sets the tone for the remainder of the book. Her tomboyish dress and attitude is mixed with young-girlish clothes and grace. No make-up or artifice here: her eyes are "the color of Spring rain," her legs are deeply tanned by the sun to a "color of terra-cotta," her hair is "golden like straw," her neck "milk-white." Though she too seems a collage of colors, unlike Camille she derives her colors only from nature and not from self-consciously applied make-up. The association with nature of both positive subtypes, the adolescent and the mature woman, is opposed to the negative subtypes' association with civilized, manufactured articles, artificial beauty, and urban life. Camille likes to go to casinos and drive fast cars, whereas Vinca likes to go fishing and walking in sand dunes.

Saha the cat is also a creature of nature, not merely because she is a cat, but because she lives by nature's rules, by instinct, and in nature's place, the garden, her favorite location. While Camille remains on the porch, Alain "sought safer refuge in the lawn" where Saha hides; "a silvery flash leapt out from the hedge and glided around Alain's legs like a fish." This sentence describes Saha only in nature images, ending a poetic evocation of the garden illuminated by moonlight. Her aristocratic, delicate manner of being contrasts with the nouveau-riche and less-than-subtle Camille. This clash is one of the principal themes of the novel, as the two females vie for one man's attention and devotion.

The method of contrast between the two female characters in *The Cat* is also used in *The Ripening Seed,* with the brief apparition of the somewhat mysterious and elusive Madame Dalleray. Always dressed in white and visibly (though rather discreetly) made up, she lives in a house closed off from the outside world by a high wall, isolated from the sun's light and heat by heavy curtains of red, white, black, and gold. She lacks all of Vinca's natural colors, and Vinca's openness and sincerity as well. For when Madame Dalleray seduces Phil, she does so out of calculated selfishness and acquisitiveness, "entirely for her own pleasure and with little thought for him."

Vinca gives herself, hesitatingly and awkwardly, in an outdoor setting of recently beaten buckwheat. Significantly, Colette does describe fairly directly the first sexual encounter of Phil and Vinca, which, though clumsy, might be "perfectible," while the encounter of Phil with Madame Dalleray is not described, but only indicated in terms of symbolic images of falling.

The positive subtype of the young woman is delineated in terms of union not only with nature, but also with the loved partner. Both Vinca and Saha, at the end of the novels, find the most intimate kind of rapport with their men. Vinca is able to make love to Phil, and the union of Saha and Alain is represented in the vision of the final paragraph by an exchange of human and feline characteristics: Saha "was following Camille's departure with the expression of a human being," while Alain "played deftly, making the palm of his hand hollow like a paw, with the rough green chestnuts of early August." The negatively valued women (such as Madame Dalleray, who leaves abruptly and has a little boy say good-bye to Phil in her stead), on the other hand, experience loss of love, deprivation, and separation not only from nature, which they never truly appreciated, but from human companionship as well.

Many of the same associations and nuances can be found in the depictions of the older woman, although the positive and negative subtypes might be slightly less differentiated at times; or, more precisely, while there is clearly a positive subtype, the negative variants are not so clearly set off and often possess some positive connotations and attributes.

Apart from the obviously antipathetic and ridiculous old women that abound as minor background figures, the clearest example of a relatively negative variant of the older woman is Léa in *Chéri.*

The initial impression the reader has of Léa is of "two magnificent thin-wristed arms, lifting on high two lovely lazy hands." The voice is "soft, deep," and her common sense, her gentle and tolerant attitude toward the boy-man Chéri complete a rather sympathetic picture of the forty-nine-year-old Léa. Yet, immediately, mention is also made that her "throat had thickened and was not nearly so white, with the muscles under its skin growing slack." And she acknowledges the subtle aging process by noting that she takes off the necklace so as not to attract Chéri's attention to her aging neck, which presumably she did not do at the beginning of her six-year liaison with him ("she put it away at night now"). The delusion of Chéri becomes self-delusion in the next chapter, as she blames the heat for her swollen legs, an excuse that does not even fool the servant.

During the course of the novel, the aging process seems

to accelerate. After an absence of only six months during Chéri's marriage, Léa has acquired a "nervous twitch of the jaw" and the beauty of her tanned complexion is offset by the fact that her neck "had shrunk and was encircled with wrinkles that had been inaccessible to sunburn." The subtle, beneath-the-skin sagging has become an all-too-evident degradation. Like Camille, she too has harsh colors: "careless henna-shampooing had left too orange a glint in her hair." The dreaded adjective is finally said aloud, " 'What lovely handles for so old a vase!',' " as she contemplates her raised arms in the ever-present and truthful mirror.

Aging, itself a natural phenomenon, is nevertheless given a pejorative connotation in the description of Léa; there is a further factor that contributes to the negativity of Léa, the disproportion of age between her and her young lover. She becomes aware of this, as her growing older moves her ever further away from Chéri's youthfulness and beauty: " 'It serves me right. At my age, one can't afford to keep a lover six years. Six years! he has ruined all that was left of me'." The aging process seems to reach a climax by the end of the novel, when Colette uses the strongest possible terms: "An old woman, out of breath, repeated her movements in the long pier-glass, and Léa wondered what she could have in common with that crazy creature."

The jolt of seeing her unflattering image in the mirror might be, however, a crucial experience that will lead her to a new understanding of herself, just as the mirror stage ("le stade du miroir") is crucial to the child's development of his identity in Jacques Lacan's analysis. The child's experience is one of recognition, accompanied by jubilation and playfulness, whereas Léa's experience is one of bewilderment and shock. Both the child's and the adult woman's experience have a positive, founding aspect that can propel them into a new self-understanding and identity, but for Léa the text remains silent on the outcome, in the interrogative mode ("she wondered . . .").

Léa's life, though filled with so many men that she herself loses count, ends in solitude; Chéri, she remarks in the novel's final sentence, seems to be happy to be leaving her: she sees him, from inside her room, "fill his lungs with the fresh air, like a man escaping from prison." Society seems to have no place for the woman who had lived in defiance of many of its norms. Solitude, separation, resignation—such is the lot of Léa, and of others in her category.

The acknowledgment of separation underlies the stories of *Chéri* and *Break of Day.* Both novels describe an older woman who has a relationship with a considerably younger man. Both men are loved by younger women but do not return that love in equal measure. In the end, both older women decide to give up their young admirers. Though the plots resemble each other, the similarities end there. The feelings and attitudes of the older women, on whom the novels concentrate their attention, are so different that, though both experience the same kind of loss, the results are quite dissimilar. Colette takes the same plot, the same problem, and seems to be saying that the same experience can be lived in two very different ways, one resulting in emptiness, solitude, and sorrow, as with Léa, the other resulting in a much more positive outcome, as with the narrator of *Break of Day.*

Like the positive variant of the younger women, the positive type of the mature woman such as the narrator of *Break of Day* lives a simple life close to nature, surrounded by the sea, her garden, her animals, in a non-urban setting. Her friends are not ridiculous, catty old women as in *Chéri,* but healthy young men and women who tan on the beach and eat the simple foods grown in the country. Though she realizes that she is much older than they, that does not prevent her from enjoying their company, and she is much less self-conscious about her age than they are. Unlike Léa, she is not obsessed with growing older, and she accepts the signs of age with good grace: "He [her young friend, Vial] looked at my hand, which proclaims my age—in fact it looks several years older— . . . It is a good little hand, burnt dark brown, and the skin is getting rather loose round the joints and on the back." Aging is seen as the natural process that it is, and accepted with ease and cheerfulness.

Neither does aging seem to be the threat to love and passion that it was for Léa—perhaps because the nature of the sensuality and sexuality in *Break of Day* is quite different from that in *Chéri.* In the latter novel, Léa's relationship with Chéri is unambiguous from the very beginning where Léa is shown in her bed, with Chéri nearby in his pyjamas. The focus of Léa's and Chéri's relationship is narrowly sexual, as had indeed been most of Léa's previous encounters with men. In *Break of Day* the relationship is never clearly defined, only hinted at; it is not so much sexual as sensual, consisting of a diffused sensuality that does not exclude friendship with the total person and is not completely dependent on physical attractiveness.

Moreover, unlike Léa, the narrator of *Break of Day* does not live by love alone: she has much to fill her day, such as other friends, gardening, and, chiefly, her writing. When she realizes that she would "incur ridicule" by continuing her attachment to Vial, especially since a young woman is in love with him, she accepts that, before Vial leaves her, she must leave him: " . . . it's a question of beginning something I have never done. So understand, Vial, that this is the first time since I was sixteen that I'm going to have to live—or even die—without my life or death depending on love. It's so extraordinary. You can't know. You have time."

She shares with Léa some feelings of regret and even anguish at the coming separation, not only from Vial, but from being in love. Her life style and her acceptance of herself mitigate powerfully the grief and possible loneliness, so that the novel is able to end on a very positive note of openness to the whole universe. There is another factor, however, in the narrator's generally positive experience of aging and loss of love, and that is the ever-present figure of her mother. Together with the other semi-autobiographical books *Sido* and *My Mother's House,* *Break of Day* portrays the most unambiguously positive subtype of the older woman. That Sido, the mother, represents "an ideal, a woman living in harmony with nature, and who has given, as she says, only a limited place to love" is unquestionable and has long been recognized by

Colette and critics alike. In *Break of Day* Colette calls her "my model," with the difficulty that the word implies of ever being her equal.

As would be expected, Sido shares all of the characteristics that make up Colette's positive women, in particular the older women. Sido does not care for life in the big city which she visits very infrequently, preferring to stay in the provinces, close to her animals and plants which she understands better than anyone else in her family. Like the narrator of *Break of Day,* she accepts growing older, though the harsh limitations caused by her last illnesses and extreme old age are hard for her to bear because of her strong and independent nature. She does not suffer from loneliness. For a long time she had a devoted, passionate husband still as in love with her as when they were newly wed. Her life is full in many ways: full of love of children, spouse, neighbors, animals, because she is full of love for them, generously giving and sustaining life in all its forms.

Sido's superior knowledge and wisdom give her an added dimension compared to Colette's other women. This knowledge is rooted in her understanding of nature, but goes far beyond that. When she wanted to know the time, "she consulted, not her watch, but the height of the sun above the horizon, the tobacco flowers or the datura that drowse all day until the evening wakes them" (*Sido*). This is only a small symbolic example of her insight into plants, animals, and people that reaches deep below the surface, as she gazes with "those deeply divining and completely undeceived grey eyes" (*My Mother's House*). Not only does she seem to be gifted with "infallibility" with regard to understanding plants or forecasting the severity of the coming winter, but she also seems to possess some kind of special power: "I am sure she still is, with her head thrown back and her inspired look, summoning and gathering to her the sounds and whispers and omens that speed faithfully toward her down the eight paths of the Mariner's Chart" (*Sido*).

It is noteworthy that it is only with respect to Sido that Colette brings any metaphysical or religious dimensions into her writings, a dimension which is hinted at by the use of such words as "divining" and "omens." Although Sido follows the rituals and precepts of her church quite exactly, at least in outward appearance, she does treat them somewhat lightly, seeing no objection to taking her dog to the service or to reading Corneille's plays hidden in her prayer book. This attitude cannot be explained only by her strong individualism; it stems from a deeper conviction that the divine is not to be found only, or primarily, in churches. When her daughter brings back from church a flower bouquet that has been blessed by lying on the altar, her mother "laughed her irreverent laugh, and looking at my bunch of flowers, which was bringing the maybugs into the sitting-room right under the lamp, she said, 'Don't you think that it was already blessed before?'" (*Sido*). Irreverent perhaps, but only with regard to religious observances. Relating another incident, Colette says significantly that "I found my mother beneath the tree . . . her head turned towards the heavens in which she would allow human religions no place." Her superior

understanding of nature and people does not come from some mysterious or magical power, but from her instincts, her intuitive participation in nature, her reverent respect towards the holiness of all life.

Sido is in fact portrayed as being so superior to all other human beings that even the narrator of *Break of Day,* herself a much more positive character than Léa, sometimes takes on a negative connotation. An excellent example of this ambiguity caused by Sido's presence is the letter that is quoted at length in *Break of Day* concerning Sido's discovery that a wool-seller, an "ugly little fat man . . plays a subtle game of chess." She continues: "We play and I think of what is imprisoned in that fat little man." The narrator reflects: "Flair, instinct for hidden treasure. Like a diviner she went straight to what shines only in secret" and she contrasts this with her own unsubtle behavior: "She would never have asked brutally: 'So, Vial, you've become attached to me?' Such words wither everything."

That Sido is idealized from childhood perceptions that persist into adult memory is quite possible; yet in the novels she appears not to be overly idealized or made into a totally unreal person. She remains a woman of flesh and blood with her own shortcomings and idiosyncrasies that make her a very concrete person on a par with other women in Colette's writings. Both an ideal figure and real person, Sido is the least ambiguous woman among the four types: her presence leads to some questions that can be raised about the constellation of women outlined in this essay.

The principal types of women that Colette focuses on are the young adolescent and the mature older woman: the inexperienced girl turning into a woman through love, and the older woman who is at the threshold of giving up youthful passion. One kind of woman is opening up to new experiences of adulthood, the other is leaving them behind. It seems that Colette is focusing of moments of passage, of change from childhood innocence into adult awareness and responsibility, or from the adult fullness of life into the renunciation of old age. Colette does not often dwell on the woman between the beginning and the end of life.

In short, with the possible and partial exception of Sido, the position of the principal kinds of women in Colette's writings is that of desire, of change, of wanting something that is not fully known, or of leaving something that is no longer rightfully possessed. It seems that the writer, then, is best able to portray womanhood in moments of lack, of movement toward or away from the essence of woman. Sido, as suggested earlier, is only a partial exception: although she enjoys plentitude of being, in harmony with herself and with the universe, she is so much an ideal that she too creates a desire, a lack in others who can never measure up to her. In the void of desire is born the work of the writer: truth, says Gérard Genette, "inhabits the work, as it inhabits every word, not by showing itself, but only in hiding." Or, in the words of Paul de Man, the writer discovers "desire as a fundamental pattern of being that discards any possibility of satisfaction." The essence of woman is unsayable, and constantly calls forth words to bespeak its ever-absent reality. (pp. 66-73)

Sylvie Romanowski, "A Typology of Women in Colette's Novels," in Colette: The Woman, The Writer, *edited by Erica Mendelson Eisinger and Mari Ward McCarty, The Pennsylvania State University Press, 1981, pp. 66-74.*

V. S. Pritchett   (essay date 1983)

[*Pritchett is a highly esteemed English novelist, short story writer, and critic. Considered one of the modern masters of the short story, he is also one of the world's most respected and well-read literary critics. Pritchett writes in the conversational tone of the familiar essay, a method by which he approaches literature from the viewpoint of a lettered but not overly scholarly reader. A twentieth-century successor to such early nineteenth-century essayist-critics as William Hazlitt and Charles Lamb, Pritchett employs much the same critical method: his own experience, judgment, and sense of literary art are emphasized, rather than a codified critical doctrine derived from a school of psychological or philosophical speculation. His criticism is often described as fair, reliable, and insightful. In the following excerpt from his review of* The Collected Stories of Colette, *he discusses Colette's role as an observer in her fiction. Pritchett also notes the sensuous detail of the descriptive passages in her stories.*]

"Look for a long time at what pleases you, and longer still at what pains you"—Colette's advice to a young writer defines her as a born watcher, not only of men, women, children, animals, and landscapes but of herself. She was very much an autobiographer, as a portrait painter, novelist, and storyteller. She watched with the candor of a child and a poet, and watched herself watching. Her work has also the apparent spontaneity of one who revised continuously—sometimes to sharpen, at other times to elaborate. In elaboration and in her own presence in a story, she was Proustian, and rarely the invisible narrator. (In some of her short stories, she seems to hark back to a master like Mérimée when she openly intrudes in her tale and distributes her own personality.) The role of the privileged observer may strike us today as being old-fashioned or too easygoing, and close to the vice of explanation, but in his introduction to **The Collected Stories of Colette** Robert Phelps makes an interesting defense of Colette's habit of being "there." In a well-known story like **"Bella-Vista,"** when we see her pretty well camped in the middle of it—and with one of those favorite, uncannily responsive dogs of hers, too—she is there, he says, not to explain but, like a good neighbor, to experience her changing judgments of the people. She is there as the traditional French day-to-day moralist, with more on her hands than she realizes. This has the virtue of taking out the trickery of the surprise ending, which would otherwise be a mere fooling of the reader. Mr. Phelps supports the view by quoting a remark of Glenway Wescott's that Colette was "a kind of female Montaigne," who alights on other natures as she explores her own. The volume contains a hundred of her sketches, portraits, and fuller stories, a third of which have never before appeared in English translation. Among the distinguished translators are Antonia White, Herma Briffault, Anne-Marie Callimachi, and Matthew Ward. The last is not always apt with French colloquialisms—the translator's nightmare. It is jarring, for example, to find the phrase "You must be kidding" uttered in *la belle époque.*

In the early "Chéri" stories, Colette was not there in person. She is almost anonymous in the early tales of the rundown music-hall companies in which, as a hungry young actress, she went through the mill, but here she is imbued with the comradeship of the theatre, though she has to put up with some isolation. She is bourgeoise! What she does share with the company is a passion for attire, costume, the inborn fantasies of the actors and actresses. One says "inborn" because as a country child she saw nature not raw but arraying itself. If she is a sensual pagan realist and has a peasant's eye for the object, she is, like all French novelists, a moralist who formulates her *précisions* at once when her emotions and imagination are shamelessly aroused. She sees nature, and lives in its modes and seasons. She is at once moralist and *couturière:* in the spring landscapes the plum blossom appears, shines, and blows away, but it is she who notices that it changes color at first light, changes to pink at sunrise, and becomes pinker until, in the last hours, it flies away like snow. A cycle. So people, too, in their moods and feelings have their frills and style, their *maquillage,* their scents and fashions. She is one for the comedies, tragedies, and vanities of appearance, for the sight of the body dressed in temperament. (Young girls are dangerous in their torpor. Women are fastidious in their dress; but in rage they are not fastidious.) She is detached and exact about both. In an early "Chéri" story, that perfect Narcissus is by turns vain, tender, charming, greedy, pettish, arrogant, violent, cruel as a child. We see him returning to Léa, his middle-aged mistress, to tell her he's about to marry someone else. He "leans his naughty chin over Léa, and the same pink spark, from the window, dances in his dark eyes, on his teeth, and on the pearls of the necklace." Preposterously thinking of his plumage, he has cadged her pearls from her. Why shouldn't a beautiful male wear pearls and be astounding and demanding? In many portraits or stories, we shall see other "pink sparks" from some object lighting up teeth, lips, chins, skin; hear asides on the formation, even the language, of noses long, straight, or squashed. We shall see necks Roman or stringy, skin smooth or coarse or wrinkled, and scores of pairs of eyes—the blue, one must say, to the point of surfeit and idolatry, but also brown, brown turning to orange, and coffee. Some blondes have chestnut eyelashes. In nature, flowers, trees, insects, dogs, cats, birds will have the same emotive examination. The facts and fantasies of appearance belong to the paganism of *la belle époque*—Proust himself lived for them. As with the body, so with the emotions: the passion of love—whether it is by nature heterosexual, homosexual, lesbian, narcissistic, or maternal—enlarges and remakes everyone even when it turns to agony, disillusion, and sorrow. Do not lose your sorrow too soon, a woman advises her miserable friend. In it lies the indispensable therapy; suddenly she will find herself set free, and rediscover the affections of her neglected friends, the easy norms of society, work, and living which keep us sane. In **"The Cure,"** we shall find this unrepentant analysis. Unrepentantly, Colette had "lived." But what she called living was working hard day and night.

Colette is rarely frivolous in her detachment. She is sustained by stoicism; she is compassionate but tough. Her continuing subject is illusion.

—*V. S. Pritchett*

Her second husband, Henry de Jouvenel, the journalist and politician, was angered by her preoccupation with love and personal relationships, her total lack of interest in politics and social commitment—perhaps *his*? It is useless to ask an artist to be other than he or she is. Colette was clearly a shrewd rebel in her time. What never bored her was "ordinary" life, and earning a living. In her theatre stories, she knew all about poverty, hunger, the almost debonair human will to survive and live out one's life. She knew the dark side of the music halls, and the dressing up that gives the actors a double life and sustains their iron will. I think of Gonzalez, the actor in **"The Starveling,"** who at mealtimes did not stay to eat but left the company on the pretext that he was going to "have a look at the neighborhood." His clothes were wretched, his bilious face—especially his awful nose—was a disaster. His aim in life? Not to spend his earnings on the tour, so that he would be able to eat for the two months when he would be looking for a new job. "Once again," Colette writes, "I am confronted by real poverty. When, if ever, shall I cease to find it?" And not only poverty but cheating and exploitation—*la belle époque* not all that *belle*. Yet **"The Starveling"** is not a sob story: "The stage bell started to ring above our heads, and Gonzalez, incurably late, fluttered off to his dressing room with all the lightness of a dead leaf, with the airy macabre grace of a young skeleton, dancing."

Colette is rarely frivolous in her detachment. She is sustained by stoicism; she is compassionate but tough. Her continuing subject is illusion. Although these theatre stories are presented through the veil of reminiscence, they break out into realism, partly because of her visual flashes and her genius for real dialogue. **"The Starveling"** is a story; others are portraits of acrobats, conjurers, and knife-throwers, but the "acts" and the risks of each one are precise. The girl who plays the sinister scenes in sketches about The Hall of Poisons, Satan, The Paradise of Forbidden Pleasures, The Beheaded Woman, and Messalina has a superb neck but a meagre body; offstage she picks up her velvet robe and cheerfully reveals that she has bowlegs. (One of Colette's first roles was in the sketch Miaou-Ouah-Ouah; she was hired to mew and bark in this animal routine.) The backstage scurryings, head-tossings, and shouting are excellent. In the long story **"Gribiche,"** a scream breaks out—a girl has caught her shoe in the iron staircase and falls headlong, bleeding. The other girls rush to help, and they guess at once what has happened: the girl

has had a back-street abortion. She is carried off to the miserable room where her sly, frightened mother looks after her. Colette is excellent at drawing wary old women—indeed, all women when they are on the defensive. The members of the cast club together on the girl's behalf, out of their miserable pay. The scene of awkward politeness is extraordinary. The girls guess Gribiche will die. She does. The story ends with Colette rather too studiously seeking an "emblematic" phrase that will define the tragedy. In fact, the story has a far better end in an earlier paragraph, when we see the whispering of the girls, nature being the better artist:

> The next evening little Impéria came hobbling hurriedly up to us. I saw her whispering anxiously into Lise's ear. Balanced on one leg, she was clutching the foot that hurt her most with both hands. Lise listened to her, wearing her whitest, most statuesque mask and holding one hand over her mouth. She removed her hand and furtively made the sign of the cross.

These observations of body attitudes are astonishing and, I suppose, have the instinctive feminine preoccupation. Even a comic moment earlier in the story has this: "La Toutou gave her colleague a blue glance, equally sublime in its stupidity, its indignation, and its deceitfulness. The anguish of her indigestion made it even more impressive."

There are a number of slight, witty sketches of husbands pursuing wives, confrontations of mistresses, the ironies of adultery and concealed jealousy. The sketches are briefly piquant, but today the genre seems faded. Also, one cannot guess the backgrounds of these smooth sinners. Where Colette is strongest is in stories into which she brings the working life. In the famous **"The Kepi,"** for example, we are in the seedy world of ghostwriters who turn out romances to order—Colette's early world. A plain, ill-dressed, aging lady in this business, one who has never had a lover, answers a lonely hearts advertisement from a young army officer. The parties meet and are both transformed by instant sexual victory; indeed, this is one of Colette's rare overtly sexual scenes. The officer is hardly in the room before he is throwing off his uniform at the foot of the bed. His cap—the kepi—somehow gets lost in the bedclothes. The unwise, intoxicated lady grabs it, puts it on her head, and sings a soldiers' marching song. The officer is appalled. End of the affair. A Maupassant story: but, after that, rather spoiled by a knowing chat about the phases of love between Colette and a too ironical friend.

In a long story, **"The Rainy Moon,"** Colette makes a more sophisticated use of her role as the watcher inside the tale. She becomes elaborate, and every incident makes the mystery more intricate and edgy. She is seen delivering a manuscript to her slaving typist, who supports a sister called Délia, who is ill and will soon appear to be on the verge of insanity. Délia's husband, one Eugène, has left her, and, listening to the typist's lamentations and complaints, Colette guesses that she, too, had been in love with the missing husband and was jealous. Quite wrong: superstition and relics of popular magic and witchcraft haunt the minds of the sisters. Délia is plotting a murder: she is engaged in "convoking" spirits, by the ancient routine of unceasingly, silently pronouncing and cursing the name of the husband, hundreds of times a day, willing his death. (Dear old animal magnetism, in short!) Even the sane sister believes in the possibility, and, rather snobbishly, says that Délia is possessed by nothing so commonplace as the Devil but something far more powerful. How can such a tale be made tolerable or credible? By what seems to me a stroke of genius. Colette herself, the rational narrator, catches the infection of murderous passion:

> I kept relapsing into a nightmare in which I was now my real self, now identified with Délia. Half reclining like her on *our* divan-bed, in the dark part of our room, I "convoked" with a powerful summons, with a thousand repetitions of his name, a man who was not called Eugène.

She has remembered that she, too, had someone to hate. Of course, the next day the rational Colette comes to her senses. But—second turn of the screw—months later she will see Délia outside a stall in the street eating from a bag of chips and wearing the white crêpe band of a widow. Grand Guignol, of course. But—as Henry James once showed—there is a probable third turn: a concealed neurotic history inhabits the implausible. Colette has prepared us for this, without our noticing it much, at the beginning of the story. Rereading it, one notices how much she stresses that the flat the two sisters live in was one in which she had once lived. The room that Délia slept in had been Colette's room. The impossible story is perhaps, like *The Turn of the Screw,* the narrator's own fantasy. Mr. Phelps' reference to Colette's neighborliness as she settles among her people here takes a haunting turn. Our fantasies are a wardrobe containing borrowed attire. Yes, a Mérimée might have contrived this imbroglio and convinced us because he, too, was in his tale. And Colette's beloved Balzac—whom she read avidly when she was a child—had taught her to pack in the furniture, even the wallpaper, when you elect to chill. It is noticeable that the two sinister things in the story are, first, "something to wear" and, second, physical allure: that band of white crêpe and Délia's "little Roman chin." (pp. 137-40)

V. S. Pritchett, "Colette," in The New Yorker, *Vol. LIX, No. 44, December 19, 1983, pp. 137-40.*

Sonja G. Stary   (essay date 1984)

[In the following essay, Stary considers Colette's theme of memory and its destructive potential in Chéri.*]*

Personal memories were basic source material used by Sidonie-Gabrielle Colette in writing her fiction. Elaine Marks aptly remarks that in Colette's novels 'the adolescents, the women, the men, the animals, the flowers . . . are never completely invented. They reflect the tendencies and attitudes of Colette herself or they are the composite images of the real people, the real animals, the real flowers that she observed.' Since Colette transposed many of her own attitudes and experiences into her novels, one may be tempted to see her goal in writing as being somewhat similar to Marcel Proust's recapturing of past time. Colette's fictional portrayal of memory—which very likely reflects her own attitude towards it—leads us, however, to inter-

pret her aim in writing quite differently. In one of her most important novels, *Chéri* (published in 1920), Colette reveals that, for her protagonists, memory is incapable of recapturing the past. Indeed, when her characters indulge in thoughts of past happiness, Colette shows that their minds only fabricate illusions. This fictional depiction of memory and the novelist's own use of memory in writing is an interesting comparison which deserves greater attention. First, however, let us examine in more detail the way in which Colette portrays memory in her novel.

In *Chéri,* Colette describes the association, separation and shortlived reunion of two lovers who discover, only in retrospect, the greatest happiness of their lives. Léa Lonval, Colette's middle-aged courtesan, and Fred Peloux, the handsome young son of Léa's female companion and rival, Charlotte Peloux, form a liaison which not only surprises others but themselves as well. Although twenty-four years scandalously separate them in age, Léa and Fred, whose nickname is 'Chéri,' stay together for six long years. If they are unaware during their liaison of their happiness together, this relationship later will be considered by them both to have been a dream-come-true. And yet, as shall be seen more clearly in their attempt to reunite, the happiness they discover through memory is not based upon mutual love so much as upon an illusory image they have, each one, of themselves.

Léa is already at the end of her career of being a carefree mistress of handsome young men when her relationship with Chéri unexpectedly begins. During their liaison, which spans the time between Léa's 43rd and her 49th years, Colette portrays the thoughts and feelings of her heroine as being contradictory. At one moment, Léa sees her deteriorating beauty lucidly as a sign that her life as a courtesan cannot continue. But, in the next instant, Léa is totally convinced, as she examines herself in the full-length mirrors of her pink and white bedroom, that she is still young enough to maintain her immoderate lifestyle, telling herself, 'un corps de bonne qualité dure longtemps.' Certain colors, clothes and jewelry help Léa to disguise—albeit from herself—the tell-tale signs of aging; but far more important to Colette's heroine is the mere presence of Chéri. With this good-looking young man in her arms, Léa can tell herself not only that she is still the courtesan she has always been, but also that her feminine charms and beauty are as good as ever. Because of Chéri, Léa's life has not changed, and its continuance seems assured. Chéri is, after all, only one of the many lovers Léa has had, and she permits herself to compare him to the others in her past: 'Des nourrissons méchants, j'en ai eu de plus drôles que Chéri. De plus aimables aussi et de plus intelligents. Mais tout de même, je n'en ai pas eu comme celui-là.' Furthermore, Léa has persuaded herself that Chéri will not be her last lover either, as is implied in the remark she makes to her friend, Patron: 'Je le changerais bien pour un autre.' There is, nonetheless, an interesting ambiguity to be found in this attitude because, although Léa tells herself that her liaison with Chéri is only temporary and claims it will last only until his marriage, she does not really believe that any young girl will ever agree to marry him. Indeed, to prevent his marriage from ever occurring, it can be said that Léa cultivates Chéri's devilishness and spoils him excessively, exhibiting more joy and more tenderness for him when she can call him 'méchant nourrisson.' For this reason, Léa thinks Chéri's marriage is out of the question: 'Ce n'est pas possible,—ce n'est pas . . . humain . . . Donner une jeune fille à Chéri,—pourquoi pas jeter une biche aux chiens?'

As for Colette's hero, between his 19th and his 25th years, that is, long after what would be judged to be his chronological childhood, Chéri finds in Léa a maternal figure who cares for and adores him no matter how wildly he behaves. Clearly, Léa is much more to Chéri than just an avid admirer. It is significant that he affectionately calls her 'Nounoune,' a name that a child might use to refer to his nursemaid, or *nourrice*. The analogy between Léa and a nursemaid is revealing because it pinpoints her role in Chéri's life. Léa is not a replacement for Chéri's real mother, but rather a woman who performs a function his mother has neglected or ignored. Léa brings Chéri up. To be sure, Charlotte Peloux gave him birth, but Léa, even though it may appear to be too late, initiates and brings her young lover into adulthood. In particular Colette shows that Léa takes charge of Chéri's physical wellbeing. That is, she sets about to build up his body and beautify him. From the start of their liaison, Léa models Chéri's physical appearance, feeding him better than his mother used to do and having him develop his muscles in workouts with Patron, the boxer. Relentlessly, Léa seems to prepare her fledgling for adulthood, as though the six years of their liaison occurred in his infancy. There is no doubt that this nursemaid's activity is a means for Léa to justify and sanction, to others as well as to herself, her keeping Chéri with her so long. Nevertheless, when Chéri himself sees the dramatic metamorphosis of his own physique, it is only natural that he should think about leaving the nest, that is, about finally reaching the goal toward which he believes Léa to have been maternally directing him all along.

In short, Chéri is perhaps best understood if one takes him strictly for an adolescent despite his actual age. His life had no direction before his liaison with Léa; and, after six years of being nurtured by his mistress, Chéri is naively eager to conquer the world. Léa has demonstrated to him that growing up is a process marked by the acquisition of greater beauty, power and resources. This is what his marriage to Edmée obviously means to him. When he tells Léa about his forthcoming wedding, Chéri explains that he will benefit from wedlock in two ways. First, although his fiancée is not as rich as he, she will add to his wealth: 'La petite a une fortune personnelle.' Second, her presence, like a material acquisition, testifies to Chéri's increasing authority: 'Elle m'aime. Elle m'admire. Elle ne dit rien.' As for Léa, Chéri realizes he must leave her; but, in a way, he does not see their separation as being absolute. Chéri tells Léa something which a bride might tell her mother: 'Il y aura toujours toi, Nounoune . . . dés que j'aurai besoin que tu me rendes un service.'

This marriage, however, brings the liaison between Colette's protagonists to an end. While their relationship lasted, neither of them thought it would represent the happiest moments of their lives. Rather, when they were togeth-

er, Léa and Chéri frequently argued about messy bathrooms and lost socks, threatening to leave one another forever. Only, separation makes them see their liaison differently. Although Léa and Chéri both appear haunted by the absence of each other, the key loss they suffer is the identity each one enjoyed when they were together. Chéri is no longer an adolescent. Now considered an adult, he suddenly has new responsibilities. He must not only conduct his own life without Nounoune, but he is expected to watch over his wife as well. The world without warning has turned upside down. Chéri cannot be the growing young man any more. In fact, he is shocked to find out he is *older* than his wife!

Léa, without Chéri, loses her courtesan identity. Suddenly, she is an old woman—a fate which she alternately denies or accepts, but always fears. Thus, after returning home from her trip to the south of France where she had fled in order to forget Chéri, Léa's thoughts go from changing her hair and buying herself a fashionable wardrobe to finding in her old companion, Charlotte Peloux, an unchanged ally with whom to share old age. Permeating these contrary reactions, however, is Léa's anxiety upon seeing the way she looks. Recent photos must be torn up and thrown away, as Léa tells herself, 'Ca ne mérite pas de vivre!' Bedroom mirrors that reflect an old woman will have to be removed: 'Elle projetait de remplacer tous les grands miroirs par des toiles anciennes, peintes de fleurs et de balustres.'

In their memory of the time they spent together, Léa and Chéri identify in retrospect a paradise from which they are now banished. Could their happiness ever be reconstructed? This is what Colette's characters try to do when they fly into each other's arms near the end of the novel. The experiment they undertake may appear to be all the more feasible when one considers that the continuation of Chéri's childhood growth and the extension of Léa's life as a courtesan were both, as has been seen, merely illusions to begin with. That is, during their liaison, Léa was actually too old to be the siren she had been when younger, just as Chéri was too old to be a child. Superficially, then, it would seem that their reunion could generate mutual illusions of happiness once again. Certainly, the needs of both of Colette's protagonists, in this respect, are unchanged. Colette reveals, however, that her characters' memory of the happiness they had together only six months earlier has not become embellished in their minds to such an extent that their conceptions of it clash tragically, one with the other.

When Chéri first rushes into Léa's bedroom and slams the door, Colette hints at the primary reason for his return when she writes: 'Il ne regardait pas particulièrement Léa mais toute la chambre.' Léa's bedroom was the earthly heaven where Chéri was nourished and cared for. Hoping nothing has changed, Colette's hero examines everything in it carefully, and at first decides with gratitude and delight that this ideal environment is still intact. Léa's brass bed, her pearls and her perfume are still the same. And yet, one soon realizes that Chéri does not wish to go backwards in time to relive his postponed childhood with Léa. Rather, he wants the conditions of the past to remain in

Cover of the May 21, 1910, issue of La Vie Parisienne, *in which serialization of* La vagabonde *began.*

existence in the present where he himself resides. Now an adult in an insecure world—which also includes a wife—Léa's former lover feels he still needs to be nurtured and beautified by her. In this way, Chéri's memory has singled out what is for him the most ideal element of their former liaison, namely, his own well-being. By returning to his former mistress, Chéri wishes not only to recapture this well-being, but also to develop it further in an atmosphere which must remain constant.

On the other hand, Léa's memory of her liaison with Chéri has glorified the youth and beauty she believes she had at that time. Chéri's return causes Léa's mind to construct bigger and certainly more shamefully false illusions about herself and her situation. Now that they have finally confessed their undying love for each other openly, Léa is convinced she has not only seized upon 'l'amour qu'on n'a qu'une fois,' but also found the key to her own rejuvenation. Blinded by happiness and gratitude, she slips back into her dual role of beloved courtesan and nursemaid again, yielding to her young lover's amorous passion and ordering her maid to prepare him his favorite breakfast of hot chocolate and *brioches*. Time and space no longer exist in the lie Léa creates for herself. Her *nourrisson méchant* will stay with her forever—'Il est là pour toujours'—and they will live together in an exotic place, Léa telling her-self, 'Il me faut un pays où nous aurons assez de place pour ses caprices et mes volontés.'

Colette brings out the fundamental opposition between her two protagonists in their dialogue at breakfast the next day. Because Léa's memory has enhanced her youth and beauty, now that Chéri has returned to her, she sees herself and her lover as younger than ever. This misconception becomes evident when Léa begins to treat Chéri like a twelve-year-old. At breakfast, she criticizes her adolescent lover for not eating enough, and then appears alarmed by his mannerism of pulling off the skin around his toenail. Léa, without realizing it, stunts Chéri's physical growth in order to become younger herself. This shocks Colette's hero somewhat, but, finally, when Léa jealously ridicules Chéri's wife, Edmée, because she considers herself to be Edmée's rival, she goes too far. She completely destroys Chéri's illusion that she is the same 'Nounoune' he remembers. Denouncing her behaviour, Chéri asks her accusingly: 'Est-ce ainsi que Nounoune doit parler?' Of course, Chéri's conception of Nounoune has become highly idealized in his mind even though he has been separated from her only six months. In thinking about Léa, Colette's nostalgic male character does not see the middle-aged courtesan who used to provide for his *physical* needs with an excess of zeal. Rather, somewhat ironically, he sees her to have been his unselfish *moral* guide and counselor. This is because, as he now explains to Léa, Nounoune used to tell him not to be 'méchant' and not to 'faire souffrir.' This, according to Chéri, was 'ma Nounoune, chic type je t'ai connue.'

In her possessiveness, Léa the courtesan had forgotten about Nounoune who, while lavishly ministering to her adolescent lover or sharply criticizing him, never used to show him her private emotions. Once Léa realizes what has happened, she desperately attempts to make reparations by becoming the 'Nounoune' which Chéri has described her to have been. At the end of the novel, however, Léa—as Nounoune—cannot finally do otherwise except bless her naughty baby and send him back to his wife. It is too late to return to their former paradise because the self-identities of both characters have been shattered. Now, Léa knows Chéri is not really her 'lover' and that she is not his eternally young 'mistress.' By the same token, Chéri understands that he is now completely alone. Neither Léa nor anyone else will be his physical and moral guide in the future.

In her novel, Colette shows that memory propagates a tragic lie when it enhances past happiness. While, even in the present, the lives of her characters are portrayed as being fraught with illusions concerning their own identities, Colette perceives their remembrance of past happiness to be so fanciful that it has no basis in reality. Because Léa's and Chéri's memory of the liaison they had is nothing more than a figment of each one's imagination, their hopes of recapturing what they had in their relationship together are impossible to achieve. Indeed, their indulgence in memory can be seen as a destructive force which tears both of their lives asunder.

It is interesting that a writer like Colette who relies so heavily upon personal recollections in composing her books should portray memory in such pessimistic terms. It is true that in many of her narratives, Colette engages in reminiscing. For example, in *La Maison de Claudine* and in *Sido,* published in 1922 and 1929, respectively, the writer attempts to recapture in the Proustian manner the way her mother, Sido, used to act and talk when Colette herself was a child. If Colette returns to her childhood in these narratives, however, it is important to note that she does not do so to examine herself. Rather, in both of these works, the principal aim of the writer is to make a tribute to her dear mother. Colette's novel, *Chéri,* must be distinguished from such works because, in it, the writer strives to look at herself through her fiction.

Although *Chéri* may appear at first glance to be one of Colette's least autobiographical works of fiction, one can find in both protagonists of the novel fundamental links to the writer herself. For example, it is not difficult to see that Colette had much in common with her heroine, Léa. When she wrote the novel at about 47 years of age, Colette, like Léa, was undoubtedly becoming aware of her loss of youth and experiencing the terrifying advance of old age. And yet, the novelist can also be identified with her hero, Chéri, in the sense that Colette gives her male protagonist a blissful, carefree childhood reminiscent of her own in which she was cared for and cherished by Sido. Moreover, it is probably no coincidence that when Colette was a child, her mother affectionately would call her 'Minet-Chéri,' a nickname which closely parallels that of the hero of her novel. Of course, it then follows that the figure of Léa is not only a reflection of Colette herself in the present, i.e. in middle age, but also—especially in her instinctively maternal mannerisms—a fictionalized caricature of Colette's mother. These correlations between the author and her characters are too striking to be merely coincidental.

In writing *Chéri,* Colette appears to sum up her own life— the past in her young hero and the present in her aging heroine. The novelist infuses into her two main characters fears and passions which were conceivably her own, namely, the desire to have her footsteps guided and her existence lovingly developed as when she was a child, coupled with the fear of old age. However, when in her novel Colette's protagonists are distraught to discover that their conceptions of past happiness are only illusions, Colette the author moves herself an objective and critical distance away from these mirrors of herself. As the writer harshly delineates her two protagonists' blindness to reality, her self-criticism is razor-sharp. This is no more evident than in the conclusion to the novel where both characters, despite what has happened, engage in 'make-believe' one final time. Chéri leaves Léa's apartment but, for an instant, he pauses, undecided, in the middle of the courtyard before continuing on his way. Likewise, Léa appears willing to revert back to her illusions, for when Chéri hesitates for a moment, Colette's heroine, who has been watching him from her window, cries out madly to herself: 'Il remonte! il remonte!' The final irony, assuredly, is that when Léa sees her reflection in the mirror at this precise moment, this causes her to wonder 'ce qu'elle pouvait avoir de commun avec cette folle.'

The indecisiveness on the part of both of Colette's characters leaves the novel open-ended and implies that the emotional dilemma which Colette describes in her two characters remains unresolved. It is possibly for this reason that Colette returned to her characters again six years later, in 1926. In the sequel to *Chéri,* entitled *La Fin de Chéri,* Colette's male protagonist, after four years of fighting in the war and one more year of morbid depression with his married life, decides—rather illogically—to look once again for his former mistress. Hardly able to recognize her in the fat old woman he encounters, Chéri finally kills himself with a revolver, saying just before pulling the trigger, 'Nounoune—my Nounoune.' In contrast, Léa, although now severely disfigured by old age, continues to live on in apparent indifference. In an interview with André Parinaud, Colette explained that she had to kill off her male protagonist because she wanted to keep Chéri pure. He was incapable of ever growing up—something Colette implies when she asks her interviewer rhetorically: 'Que vouliez-vous qu'il fît dans la vie? Le voyèz-vous grand industriel, installé derrière un bureau avec plusieurs téléphones?' We surmise that the death of Chéri as well as the grotesque disfigurement of Léa's appearance were necessary in *La Fin de Chéri,* because they bring Colette's emotional dilemma to an end. By ridiculously exaggerating her hero's hopeless nostalgia and her heroine's deformed features, Colette effectively dissociates herself from them both. The overly-dramatic demise of her male character signals the writer's personal rejection of the concept of recapturing, or living in, the past. By means of the hideous corpulence and egocentric arrogance of her aged heroine, Colette derides the monstrous ego that was once afraid to grow old. In *La Fin de Chéri,* then, Colette liberates herself from these past echoes of herself because, no longer a victim of their illusions, she is ready to accept the realities of her life in the present.

In *Chéri* and *La Fin de Chéri,* the transposition of the writer's thoughts and memories into fiction causes her to see herself with more objectivity. Colette uses her fiction in these two novels as a means of self-discovery. Her primary goal must, therefore, be viewed as an exercise in self-examination, and not as an attempt to recapture past time. When the subject of her narrative is herself, Colette denounces the past which, no matter how happy it might have been, cannot become a sanctuary from reality. It is perhaps to this salutory goal of her writing that Colette refers when, two years after the publication of *La Fin de Chéri,* she states in *La Naissance du jour:* 'Pourquoi suspendre la course de ma main sur ce papier que recueille, depuis tant d'années, ce que je sais de moi, ce que j'essaie d'en cacher, ce que j'en invente et ce que j'en devine?' (pp. 114-22)

Sonja G. Stary, "Memory in Colette's 'Chéri'," in Orbis Litterarum, *Vol. 39, No. 2, 1984, pp. 114-22.*

Ann Leone Philbrick   (essay date 1984)

[*In the following discussion of* Chéri *and* The Last of Chéri, *Philbrick analyzes the characters Léa and Chéri in terms of their relationship to their physical surroundings.*]

When critics judge and defend Colette's work, they frequently settle on her journals and the novels that are most nearly autobiographical. These choices imply that what is finest about her writing is her own highly charged and spiced life, and that her most authentic characters speak directly for her. It is true that people in her world generally feel rather than think their way to clear and telling perceptions: Yannick Resch observes eloquently that they "discover the world and others through their bodies." There is, however, a rich and complex communication among characters who seem at first to exist only to bemuse us. When we find that sensations and the objects or spaces that evoke them may replace language—spoken and thought—then these fantastical figures take on shades of force and pathos and become Colette's most vital creatures.

In *Chéri* and *La Fin de Chéri,* which together form arguably Colette's most ambitious and finely worked novel, living spaces assume a compelling role as voice and catalyst of people's experience. It is essential to discuss these works as one: A separation of Chéri and his mistress Léa and its repercussions in their lives is central to both novels; furthermore, each aspect of their relations to their world and to each other that is introduced in *Chéri* is resolved in *La Fin de Chéri.*

In *Chéri,* Léa, a twentieth-century courtesan, chooses to conduct her last affair with the son of her friend. Chéri is an adored princeling in his mother's demi-mondain circle. After five years with Chéri, during which Léa teaches him about love and indeed grows to love him, she relinquishes him to a marriage with the young and colorless Edmée; she then flees to the Midi to recover from the loneliness that is witness to a deeper love than she had suspected. Chéri rushes to her after a six-month separation, but, suddenly aware of her aging, leaves her again.

La Fin de Chéri picks up the story of these two lives after the First World War. Chéri is a hero, but finds himself a passive and ignored figure, lost in the excitement and vulgar bustle of his wife's post-war social causes. He returns again to Léa, seeking the rich, closed world he had once created around them both; however, in the meantime she has become an old woman, resigned to a jolly asexuality. Chéri, left with no place to hide or nurture a new life, tries desperately to recreate life with Léa in a mouldy room plastered with photographs of her golden days. When this imagined world fails to conjure up his lost Léa, he shoots himself.

Chéri and Léa have radically different understandings and reactions to their places in society. While Chéri, as passive center of his world, waits for people and sensations to act upon him, Léa attends to her living spaces as extensions of her identity. In his book *Colette and Chéri,* André Joubert assigns to places—and specifically the "privileged place" of Léa's bedroom—a catalytic role in the defining and dissolution of people's relations with one another: " . . . in the framework of privileged places, the ballet of the characters in relation to each other is reflected in the play of alternating distancing and rapprochement of their mutual living spaces."

Colette's world is an anthropocentric one; she, in her autobiographical writing, and her "survivor" characters in fiction find themselves at the living center of a world they must master—by self-isolation or by direct challenge—in order to survive. People who have no clear apprehension of this active and independent role of space in their lives are seen as victims of their surroundings.

If, as Georges Poulet maintains in *Les Métamorphoses du cercle,* "The human being is a center where outside reality converges and synthesizes itself," then Chéri's sense of reality is an insubstantial creation, based on his muddy perceptions of the world as a series of stage sets arranged in deference to his beauty and his needs. We see him posed in a series of spaces: Léa's pink boudoir, his bizarre and luxurious house, moonlit gardens. It is clear that he is defined by the way he responds to and chooses spaces and by others' perceptions of him within those settings. Once chosen, a space becomes an active element of Chéri's life; he responds continuously to his surroundings, happy and secure only when they seem to be unassailable, unchanging sets. He is a passive occupant of space, animated by his violent and inarticulate reactions to changes in his world, especially Léa's body and her gloriously ego-reflecting apartment.

Joubert claims that Léa's room tells nothing of her inner life or identity: " . . . this dwelling is limited in its evocations almost to the exterior signs of the demi-mondaine's success and to the setting of amorous intimacies. Léa's moral personality doesn't divulge itself there." Léa is, however, sensually, even morally, aware of her living space. She perceives her apartment, bedroom, and body as an intricately constructed and maintained series of containers for her self. She is continuously examining the surfaces, textures and lighting of these spaces, calculating their strengths and losses. Each layer of space—her skin, lingerie, the apartment walls and draperies—reflects the metamorphosis of its center. There is a continuous reciprocal activity between her self and her spaces.

Léa's room is her setting and her second skin, an old-fashioned nest of rosy clouds of gauze, veils and shades that glows in response to her body, "white tinted with rose": "The noontime sun entered the pink room, gay, over-decorated and dated in its luxury, doubled laces at the windows, rose-petal silk on the walls, gilded wood, electric lights veiled in pink and white, and antiques upholstered in modern silks." This hermetic space of reflecting, enveloping colors and lights seems to lend life to Chéri by its mere evocation. About to return to Edmée after a three-month desertion, he finds himself dreaming of lovers' trysts "chez Léa":

> He tried to evoke the morning games, at Léa's, certain afternoons of long and perfectly silent pleasure, at Léa's,—the delicious sleep of winter in the warm bed, and the cool room, at Léa's . . . But he could see in Léa's arms, in that daylight the color of cherries that flamed behind Léa's curtains, in the afternoon, only one lover: Chéri.

Fortified by this identification of himself with that Léa-world, he returns to Edmée in triumph; he is confident of regaining at will that nurturing, identifiable space in Léa's arms.

Chéri makes no effort to alter his world; space is for him an unapprehended force. He perceives place as a strangely animated and self-willed entity that acts upon him and so propels him through life. When life and society move independently and randomly by him, he is overcome by that unregimented and chaotic force. In *La Fin de Chéri,* he confides this sense of alienation to Edmée, who is determinedly nursing wounded veterans and adorning her own salon with post-war *arrivistes:*

> For you, it's obvious, you are accomplishing a sacred mission. But for me? . . . If you were forced to spend every day in the upper rotunda of the Opéra, I wouldn't see any difference. That would leave me just as . . . just as apart. And the ones I call your remnants, well, they're wounded, too. Invalids a little luckier than some others, by chance. I've got nothing to do with them, either. With them, too, I am . . . apart.

When Chéri returns to Léa after his marriage, he announces, "I'm home!" This is his home, his place, in far more significant ways than the gaudy palace he shares with Edmée. He takes possession of Léa's bedroom with an urgency that tells of his need of it. The next morning, he wakes in Léa's bed, filled with a sensation of joy and plentitude that is transmitted by light, and represented by it:

> He didn't move. He was afraid that his stirring would crumble a remaining joy, an optical pleasure that he tasted in the ember pink of the curtains, in the steel and copper scrolls of the bed sparkling in the colored air of the room. His great happiness of the night before seemed to him hidden, melted and very small, in a reflection, in the rainbow that danced on the side of a crystal decanter filled with water.

Léa's created world represents her to Chéri in a more satisfying and "real" form than she herself can now muster. One is given to understand that Chéri would willingly spend his life in that womb, sensing Léa in the colors and perfumed air around him. Indeed, in *La Fin de Chéri,* he attempts—and fails—to replace Léa with a room that evokes her presence by old photographs peeling from its dingy walls. His imagination is not rich enough to fulfill him without sensual enhancement of the objects, colors and textures of her apartment.

For Chéri, Léa's place and body come to be one being. At the beginning of *La Fin de Chéri,* he has not seen his mistress during the five years of the war, and appears to be absorbed in his life with Edmée. Edmée casually mentions one day that they should purchase a country house, and Chéri suddenly sees in his mind's eye Normandy as Léa had shared it with him during their first summer together. He actually faints, as he struggles to "re-read" that space that she had created for them, redolent of ripe fruits, exotic color and light:

> . . . he didn't hurry to regain full conscious-

ness. He retreated, behind his eyelids and lashes, to the heart of the green domain that he evoked at the moment of his seizure, a flat land, rich with strawberry plants and bees, with white water-lilies hemmed by warm stone. . . . When his strength returned he kept his eyes closed, thinking: "If I open my eyes, Edmée will read in them all that I see . . . ".

Just as this marvelous re-creation of a country idyll resuscitates a specific place shared with—and indeed created by Léa—the evocation of Léa's apartment revives for Chéri the image of his own Léa, his "Nounoune." He hears one day during idle conversation that Léa has a new apartment, "small, but it's charming." His reaction is instantaneous, almost instinctive: "Chéri clung to these two words. . . . When invention failed him, he painfully constructed a rosy decor, threw in the vast ship of gold and steel, the great bed rigged in laces . . . ". The new apartment is hereby transformed into a dreamed version of the old.

Chéri cannot conceive of any alteration in Léa and her apartment because together they form the womb-like center and container of his own identity; he himself has remained an unaltered figure amid the post-war upheavals around him. Since his world has no meaning or form without Léa, he expresses his despair at losing her through an effort to find her in every aspect of his surroundings: "A door that opens, it was Nounoune; the telephone, it was Nounoune; a letter in the garden box: perhaps Nounoune . . . Even in the wine I drank, I looked for you . . . ". It is important to note that he searches for Nounoune, his private creature, rather than the real woman Léa, distinct and independent.

His immense sensitivity to all that surrounds her is balanced by the lifeless and repelling spaces of his own house. The garish and opulent colors there reflect only themselves, and seem to flatten people rather than define or orient them:

> Of weak invention and banal proportions, the dining room owed its luxuriousness to a yellow paper sprinkled with purple and green. The white and gray stucco-work of the walls threw too much light on the guests, already stripped of all shadow by the light that fell on them, unshaded, from the ceiling.

Chéri's mother describes the house to Léa: "Sinister . . . Sinister! Violet carpets! Violet! A black and gold bathroom. A salon without furniture, full of Chinese vases as big as me!" As she speaks, she and Léa are sitting in Léa's salon, a calm and welcoming space that reflects and enhances Léa's own charm: "A normal, familiar light bathed the salon and played in the draperies."

The bedroom Chéri shares with Edmée is at the heart of this collection of elegant but impersonal spaces. The room is Chéri's creation: "It was as he wanted it, blue, fragrant, consecrated to repose." This "repose" is an escape from sensation, Chéri's fumbling attempt to deaden the pain of losing Léa. He retreats here as to a lair, a blind and blinding hole in the midst of a world that will not offer him a stable and identifying place. It is a set piece, artificially lit, "blue and somber like night on a stage." The room evokes the vital forces that are absent in his marriage:

> . . . he drew back with an inexpressible repugnance before the idea of living, paired off, in a domain [marriage to Edmée] that wasn't governed by love. . . . And as he walked beside Edmée toward the room that would witness neither reproaches nor kisses, he felt himself to be penetrated by shame, and he blushed at their monstrous "understanding."

Chéri sees that the places in the world shared with Edmée are deadening elements, which absorb and flatten his sense of identity, his apprehension of his place and function in society. In one pitiable effort to be a part of the bustle of Edmée's life, he visits "her" hospital to see the wounded veterans:

> Too much white fell from the ceilings, glanced back from the floors, erased the angles, and he pitied the recumbent men to whom no one offered the charity of shadow. . . . "Give them shadow, give them a color that isn't this white, always this white . . . ".

Here is the threatening force of space that erases people, allowing no contour, no intimate or secret facets in daily existence. Chéri fears these destructive aspects of space, without either defining or defying them.

Chéri's and Léa's places in the world are created from two fundamental and opposing reactions to their surroundings: flight in Chéri's case, and ultimately, penetration in Léa's. He flees any space that doesn't envelop and protect him in an immobilizing and dependable security. His constant movement away from the places of his world—whether a physical flight through the streets, his three-month desertion of Edmée, or a dreamy evasion of surrounding activities—produces a progressive loss of consciousness of his relation to the events and people around him. He has found no person or inner resource to replace the welcoming and healing refuge created by Léa before the war, and he is increasingly portrayed as a disoriented, disinherited figure in a rapidly changing, oblivious world.

Society assaults his sense of stability and identity. He faces every day as a long wait in which each event recedes without significance into an undefined distance: "Each day, awake early or late, he began a day of waiting." Unable either to captivate Edmée by his glamorous languor or to join her in her buzzing social activity, he subsides into the role of still observer, disconnected from all around him:

> He got into the habit of sitting in the garden in a wicker armchair, as though he'd arrived at a hotel garden from a trip, and he watched, astonished, the approaching night annihilate the blue of the aconites, and substitute instead a blue in which the flowers' form melted, while the green of the foliage persisted in distinct masses.

He sees these transformations without responding to them; indeed, his own still figure seems to be an element of an impressionist painting. He takes pleasure from this sensation of floating in time and space: "On his own property he tasted the pleasure of a passerby seated in a square,

and he didn't wonder how long he rested there, leaning back, his hands dangling."

Léa never allows herself to relinquish her living spaces. She knows—as Chéri never will—the value of an equilibrium sought and carefully maintained: between flight from failure or disillusion, and between acceptance or penetration to the heart of such difficulties. What release she seeks always replenishes her energies and perceptions. Public spaces, such as the fresh air and the view from a window, streets, or long voyages, clear her head and reinforce her will to know and to affirm herself.

Enmeshed as they are in their private world, Léa and Chéri turn to the outside, at least momentarily, when faced with drastic changes in their lives. Yannick Resch remarks incisively that windows open onto a space that breaks the too-intimate bond between a woman, her inner life, and—usually—her lover. The window provides respite from illusion: "The link between two universes, it is the privileged object that attaches the person to the exterior world and thereby symbolizes in moments of crisis, evasion, liberty." Whereas Léa makes use of the spiritual hiatus gained from turning to an open window, in order to strengthen her perception and control of a situation, each of Chéri's "flights" takes him further from any mastery of people and events.

Resch points out that Léa finds no fantasy escape from her involvement with Chéri. An open window allows her rather to recover her pride and equilibrium in the world existing beyond their affair. In the last, violent scene of *Chéri,* she realizes that he has discovered her age. Almost frantic with a desire to reach out to him before he can leave her forever, she turns instead to her window, to hide a lust that would seem grotesque to his young eyes. This evasion is itself the result of a profound understanding of herself. When Chéri leaves, Léa's world closes in about her, leaving her alone at its center, solely responsible for her own sanity and survival. Space has been her accomplice in this parting, offering a way to hide her aging face, disguise her despair, and invent the shade of the admirer who may arrive at any moment in the courtyard.

Chéri, too, seeks refuge through open space from the crises of his marriage and Léa's aging, but his energy and self-image are dissipated rather than reaffirmed by the distracting activity of the outside world. In the midst of an unproductive and querulous exchange with Edmée, he turns to a window open to the night air in order to marshal his arguments before confronting her with their marital failure. He finds the strength to speak, but never to argue or resolve their difficulties.

When Chéri and Léa venture outdoors, they are disconnected from their private spaces and thrown into confrontation with an oblivious—and thereby treacherous—world. Outside, we see how little Chéri knows of himself, and how much Léa is forced to confront. Chéri often plunges into the night, to walk aimlessly, savoring his detachment from others' concerns. In *Chéri,* he finds himself walking to Léa's apartment after six months of marriage. As he approaches, he feels a sensual quickening:

> At the end of the avenue, he deliberately inhaled

the vegetal odor that came from the Bois on the heavy moist wings of the west wind, and hurried toward the Dauphine entrance. . . . "I walked too fast," he told himself.

Léa's concierge reports that she has not returned, and Chéri retreats into the dark, exhausted by the disappointment of his anticipation:

> He stumbled twice and almost fell, like people who feel eyes staring at them from behind. At the metro railing, he leaned on his elbows, over the black and pink shadow of the underground, and felt crushed with fatigue. When he straightened up, he saw that they were lighting the streetlamps on the square and that night was turning everything blue. "No, it isn't possible? . . . I am ill!"

Typically, he makes no conscious attempt to link this ominous change in his evening stroll with Léa's absence; he simply allows the fatigue of his long walk to obliterate that real source of his misery.

After a longer absence—the duration of the war—Chéri again escapes into the night, now fleeing Edmée's new and unrelenting social activity that seems to exclude him. He fades into the dark, walking like a cat: "All of his senses quickened, freed from thought." Sound translates into image for him, as for a cat: He passes invisibly by two murmuring forms, and imagines the amorous soldier as he hears and identifies the soft clink of a swordbelt.

These night walks reinforce Chéri's alienation from his established place in the world. On a humid, luminous fall night, he again stalks away from one of Edmée's blaring dinner parties. He is absorbed by the dark, metamorphosing into a shadowy, cat-like figure. In this half-world of fading identity, he feels himself accompanied by another lost soul, the new, aged Léa. He longs for a familiar and sheltering space, but even Chéri has finally come to feel that no space can hold static the life he requires for himself, and he is haunted by the image of Léa as she has become:

> "Ah, a good hotel room; a good, pink room, nice and ordinary, nice and pink. . . ." But wouldn't it lose its banality at the moment when, with the light out, total night would allow the weighty and teasing entrance of that long, impersonal jacket and that thick gray hair?

A rose-colored room can never be neutral for Chéri; it evokes Léa-Nounoune, his cradled existence with her, and their loss.

Faced with so overwhelming a sense of his loss of place, Chéri must consciously consider his plight, but never for long or deeply. In one dramatic instance, as he walks toward the Bois de Boulogne, the forces of nature and the sensations they elicit do stir his sense of dissolution:

> A blurred light over regions that had been stagnant and hardly perceptible until that moment, began to show him that purity and solitude are a single and identical misfortune. . . . He stopped to watch a herd of low clouds above the Bois, of an elusive pink, that a gust of wind buf-

feted, grabbed by their misty hair, twisted, dragged over the lawns, before carrying them off to the moon. . . . Chéri contemplated familiarly these luminous enchantments of a night that those who sleep believe to be black.

Here his union with natural forces is so strong that he confronts Léa's disappearance almost consciously. The pathetic fallacy has a savagely ironic function here. Jolted by the strange wildness of that moment, Chéri is for once forced into an insight brutal in its pragmatic finality: " 'For me,' concluded Chéri, 'I really think that everything has been said'."

Not all of Chéri's flights from crises—or Léa's confrontations with them—are figurative. Each flees Paris when life seems to reach an impasse, and each returns with a new course of action revealed. Chéri's resolution will again follow from a passive, sensual apprehension of the world; Léa's provides her with the energy for both a new assault on Chéri's love, and a response to the demands of old age.

Soon after Chéri's marriage, Léa joins her old circle of friends in Chéri's mother's salon. She escapes the gathering, horrified by those spectres of her own future self when her age will finally begin to betray her: "Which one of the three will I resemble, in six years?" She decides at once to reaffirm her independence and vigor by a triumphant trip to the Riviera, in full regalia, with car, chauffeur and mountains of luggage. Her trip is no idyll, however, but a confirmation of realities that can no longer be sealed off by her apartment walls. Visions and intimations of aging women surround her as she unpacks in Paris:

> It's horrible. And after those [women encountered during her trip], as before them, others, others who will resemble them. There's nothing to be done about it. It just is that way. Maybe everywhere there's a Léa, those Charlotte Peloux types, those LaBerche and d'Aldonza types, will spring from the earth, old horrors who used to be beautiful young things, people, impossible people, impossible, impossible . . . [.]

These phantoms are "impossible" because they have been young and beautiful, seemingly indestructibly so, and are no more; and furthermore, they are as real as Léa. It follows that she will soon be one of them.

Armed with that sure knowledge of both her present and future resources, Léa prepares to face Chéri and his world once more as a desirable and independent woman. She and Chéri have one final night of passion and renunciation; Léa's voyage has readied her for both aspects of that encounter.

Chéri's flight is in troubling contrast to Léa's—an aimless and sterile circling of the outskirts of Paris, where the hot August air offers no replenishing sensation or revelation. He begins to bring the aged and frightful Baronne de La Berche, "virile companion," on these nighttime escapes, because she is silent and because he feels that she is as alone as he. On a particularly blazing evening she suggests that they spend the night in the country, and return to Paris in the cool dawn. Chéri refuses, too quickly; is he subconsciously wary of playing a travestied love scene with the crone—a shade of what Léa must become? La Baronne responds immediately with as brutal and penetrating an analysis of Chéri as any that Léa supplies for herself: "Yes, yes. You will run around all day, but you return to the pen every night. Ah! you are well-kept!" His home is no castle, but an increasingly solitary prison. He abandons any illusions of a real married life and slides into a reflective, inner world: ". . . he existed, innocent, walking, tranquil inside of his freedom like a prisoner in the depths of his cell, and chaste as an animal brought from the Antipodes, who doesn't even search for a female in our hemisphere."

After he sees Léa for the last time, an aged, jolly hulk in her stolid old lady's world, he seems to move almost joyfully in a space that holds no place for him:

> He went toward a Paris that he had forgotten. The crowd jostled his paradoxical equilibrium that required a crystal emptiness and the routine of suffering. . . . He thought that a certain interior floating, which he compared to a grain of lead bouncing in a celluloid ball, was provoked by hunger, and he took refuge in a restaurant.

That "floating" is more than hunger; it is the sensation of being washed away from any enduring or definable contact with people in the outside world.

That feeling of floating signals danger to Léa, a weakening of her control and consciousness of her world. After the Riviera trip, she deliberately chooses a new persona that will separate her from Chéri. Wearing a new costume, bulky tweeds and sturdy walking shoes, she strides out to take her first walk as an elderly lady. The outside world does not adapt itself to her act, which springs from no authentic self-perception. Léa is caught off balance, out of a framework that could enhance this new image of herself. Twice, she hears a footstep, recognizes a gesture that must be Chéri's, and panics: "If I must meet him, I'd prefer that he see me otherwise, he who could never stand brown, first. . . . No . . . no, I'm going home, I . . . ". The young man—who resembles Chéri not at all—steps into a taxi and disappears.

Léa's new persona is crumbling around her, and she responds with brutal lucidity: ". . . Léa did not smile and had no further sigh of relief, she turned on her heels and went home." Her own world—one that she now knows she is not yet prepared to relinquish—is quickly put to rights: "A whim, Rose. . . . Give me my peach-blossom tea gown, the new one, and that big embroidered stole without sleeves. I'm smothering in this wool."

Back at the ordered center of her life, Léa can afford now to examine her momentary loss of stability. She has retreated from an inevitable metamorphosis, but only until she sees how to fashion her world to frame that new self. When she does re-make her surroundings, Chéri finds himself in a nightmare. Change signals deformation for him. His conception of space and its elements—color, odor, light, boundaries—extends to even more literal perceptions of the world. He associates the perfumes and rose tints of Léa's old apartment with her as though she were a world and the apartment a fixed atmosphere unique to her, "like the sea carries with it, when it recedes, the terrestrial fragrance of hay and flocks."

Chéri cannot imagine that a new Léa exists quite independently of—and grotesquely mismatched with—this rosy atmosphere. When he arrives at her new apartment, he is first shocked by the absence of her perfume in a blue and empty vestibule. The familiar rose-colored light floods over him as the maid opens the salon door, and he anticipates a miraculous resumption of his old existence in their shared, womb-like world. There stands, of course, the fat and elderly Léa, an alien in his cherished space, and a devastating trauma to his conception of how people and their surroundings are linked.

Chéri feels himself collapse into a hallucinatory world. Léa and her aged friend, interrupted in their gossipy tea, boisterously examine him as they would a show animal:

> "I grant you the chin, which will fatten up soon. And the feet are too little, the most ridiculous thing for a boy who's so tall."
>
> —There, I don't agree with you. But I *have* noticed that the thigh is too long in relation to the back of the leg, from here to there.
>
> They argued calmly, weighing and detailing the high and low points of the beast of luxury.

So Léa reduces Chéri from bijou to beef, resisting any pitiable flirtation on her part, and thoroughly disorienting his tenuous perceptions of self and place. The room becomes for him a container of dreadful spaces and surfaces, each changing and threatening beyond his control. He feels his identity fragment, and watches with amazement one Chéri sitting arrogantly and even boorishly relaxed, while another kneels on the floor wailing incoherently at the destruction of his world.

In an effort to pull himself back into the comforting ritual of teatime, he reaches for a cake. It, too, has become a distorted version of itself, the sugared surface hiding a poisonously transformed interior: "He chose from a plate a cake shaped like a curved tile, then put it down, convinced that if he bit, a silent cinder of rose brick would fill his mouth." Surfaces betray him, hiding or destroying the sweet rosy interiors that had defined his and Léa's world.

Finally, Léa's body itself plays a spatial role, as victim and witness of the monstrous instability of life. The delicately nurtured, cracking shell of an aging courtesan becomes a wide and sturdy container for her new self. Chéri imagines this bulky lady to be a diabolical creation, a grotesque envelope in which his sleek Léa must be captive. Indeed, he catches glimpses of his own Léa:

> The gray-haired lady turned, and Chéri received straight on the shock of her blue eyes. . . .
>
> The great innocent laugh rang out again, and Chéri searched for the source of this laugh, here, there, everywhere except in the throat of the gray-haired woman . . . [H]e told himself to be patient, with the half-formed hope that this first image would give way to a luminous remission.

He has a hallucinatory urge to shriek at this "placid disaster," to force his Léa to reappear and to exist for him.

The woman named Léa is therefore split in two by Chéri's refusal to recognize her. This dreadfully healthy, cheery old woman betrays a certain unease and shame for her new self, as she attempts to hide her huge neck under a wispy silk scarf. But Léa really has accepted her new body and values its bulk as a refuge when she must confront Chéri's horror and incredulity. He asks if he is keeping her from dressing for the evening, in a distracted effort to remain on the surface of convention, and she responds by laughingly asserting her new place in life: "Dress? And in what, in God's name, do you expect me to dress? I am dressed, definitively!" The black skirt and stern white jabot are her new skin and they herald her new world. Color and texture simply encase Léa and signal her age; there is no further need for the play of surface color and texture to bemuse a lover.

Chéri has refused to acknowledge the altered frame for himself and his life. He is left one final space for retreat, where he can try to reconstruct—through confused daydreams—the life that Léa had given them both. An aged and impoverished courtesan, La Copine, offers him the use of her room, a veritable hole, "narrow, secret and black." Its walls are covered with portraits and photographs of a past, goddess-like Léa, frozen in a series of poses, luminous, smooth and young. Here is a wall of Léas, each image a bit of the facade that obliterates a certain stout old woman and confirms Chéri's fading vision of his "Nounoune." Daily, La Copine croons through anecdotes of Léa's past, peopling and furnishing Chéri's dream world as she describes lovers, toilettes, the material of her dresses and the luxurious events of her days.

This act of re-creation does force Chéri into some understanding of his role in Léa's life; he realizes that he was, after all, one in a string of lovers. He doesn't grasp, however, that, as the last of that series, he was the most important of all. The resulting state of mind is a greater sense of alienation from this world. He nurtures this feeling of loss of place, aware that once emptied of memory and evocations of Léa's world, he will be left without the resources or will to construct a life for himself:

> Indistinct, that force that comes from dissimulation and resistance formed itself painfully, in the deepest part of him, and he tasted the excess of his detachment, with the vague foreknowledge that a paroxysm can be used and exploited as a tranquilizer, and that one can find in it counsel that serenity cannot offer.

The young Léa is irrevocably lost, and with her the youthful, perfect Chéri, the only self he can imagine. The wall of pictures eventually begins to fail him; his reveries cannot recreate and repeople that womb-like past: "Already the like image inspired in him only a rancour, an ecstasy, a palpitation all diminished." It is after this last glimpse of his ruined world that Chéri shoots himself.

Space as Colette exploits it is not a stage or setting where people may act out their lives freely and independently. It is rather a continually shifting reflector and container of individual lives; a shelter from external shocks at times, but also, ultimately, a witness to the struggle for identity and equilibrium against the shocks of age and disillusion. Colette's creatures struggle simply for a balance between possession and alienation of self, on a brutal, even visceral level.

Colette's protagonists find little occasion for transcendence of their world. Chéri's defeat ends in his suicide, Léa's in the loss of her gorgeously constructed world and—to Chéri—a grotesque compromise with age. In this world there is no explosion of creativity in the acceptance or forging of a space, but rather a simple, cruel and rare salvation: an acceptance of the incapacity to control one's living space, and the strength to apprehend the exterior world in accordance with the relentless exigencies of the inner one. (pp. 249-63)

> Ann Leone Philbrick, "Space and Salvation in Colette's 'Cheri' and 'La Fin de Chéri'," in Studies in Twentieth Century Literature, *Vol. 8, No. 2, Spring, 1984, pp. 249-64.*

Donna Rifkind   (essay date 1984)

[*In the following essay, Rifkind focuses on characterization in* The Collected Stories of Colette, *praising the work's sensitive use of detail and suggesting that Colette's originality is enhanced by her conflicting feelings of sympathy and detachment from her characters.*]

"I want to tell, tell, tell everything I know, all my thoughts, all my surmises," Colette wrote in her little fable, **"The Tendrils of the Vine."** That impulse is clear throughout this large new collection of stories [*The Collected Stories of Colette*]: Colette is eager to present us not just with a world, but with *her* world, her voice, her experience. In each of these sketches, whether or not she appears directly as a character, Colette's presence dominates the scene; and as she narrates she expresses her intention to propel herself into the action and to own it. Although not exclusively autobiographical, the stories read like specifically located fragments of recollection whose author has missed no detail in the act of remembering.

Most of the facts of Colette's life are by now well known, and again this is to a large extent because of her eagerness to tell us everything she knows. She became an international celebrity before her death and something of a French institution after it, but it was primarily Colette, rather than her admirers, who made her own image into a publicly recognized fact; certainly, no one wrote as exhaustively about her life as Colette herself did. Her first "Claudine" novels are transposed journals of her schoolgirl days in Burgundy. *La Vagabonde* (1911) and *L'Envers du music-hall* (1913) chronicle Colette's life as a pantomime artist after her separation from her first husband, Henri Gauthier-Villars (the famous "Willy"). Her later work as a journalist for *Le Matin* is less strictly objective reportage than a personal record of Colette's activities in the years before and after World War I.

It is the more subtle ways in which Colette projects her life onto her work, however, that make both her personality and her writing interesting. Always impulsive, always intimate, Colette's fiction blurs the boundaries between memoir, journalism, dramatic dialogue, and standard fictional techniques in order to concentrate on what she considered more important: the workings of the female mind. Colette's women are all as engaging as their keenly observant creator, and as eager to display their sophistication in matters of fashion and gossip, beauty and sexuality. "When you've been all around the world, you'll think like me," a pantomime artist declares in **"The Circus Horse."** "Over and above that, there are nasty people everywhere, so one has to learn to keep one's distance; and one can count oneself lucky when one comes into contact, like today, with people who are good company and have class."

Every story in this collection contains a character who knows what Colette knows, who is indeed some aspect of Colette herself, delivering large and confident insights, most of which carry a similar tone and subject matter:

> There is hardly a woman who feels threatened by her age who does not know, after a period of trial and error, how first to try on, then how to give her face a characteristic look, a style which will defy the work of time for ten, fifteen years
>
> **("Alix's Refusal")**

> For even if she is fond of her, a woman always judges another woman harshly.
>
> **("The Kepi")**

> Isn't a woman entirely in what she doesn't say? . . . for a woman forgives a man—even a reporter—everything but insight
>
> **("An Interview")**

After imposing such rigid specifications for character types upon her women, Colette goes on to endow them with a rich, spontaneous variety of details. She elaborately describes brilliant costumes, showing how they disguise women who are plain or aging, "combative and desperate." Friends in the stories offer long, excessive compliments to one another, but each takes "pitying and ironic pleasure" in silently calculating the other's imperfections. With all of these details heaped on so little surface, we can begin to feel rather like the women wearing these costumes, confined and a little breathless.

Colette also uses stagecraft in her fiction, designing her stories so that each achieves an elegantly planned mood. No matter how various the situations, we always detect the mind creating them: the clairvoyant again looms larger than the vision she has summoned. Colette is quite aware of this fact and uses it to her advantage, making her characters' most thoughtless gestures seem deliberate, thereby displaying her own control over the scene. In **"The Kepi,"** which describes an older woman as "all too tiresomely like every woman in love," Colette shows us how familiar she is with this kind of woman and how monotonous her love affair seems to her now. Even vehemence is boring for Colette, who, writing about the woman's impassioned young lover, remarks that "impetuosity has its own particular ritual."

This habit of highlighting her authority over her characters comes dangerously close to ruining our pleasure in them. If we read too many of these stories at a sitting, each can become "all too tiresomely" like every other, despite the variations of setting and detail. It is of course difficult to write wearily without wearying one's readers, but, fortunately, Colette's failure to remain altogether dominant over her characters saves us from giving up in exhaustion. André Gide, noting that Colette, "despite all her superiority," seems to have been tainted by her milieu, points to this same tension in Colette between wishing to remain superior to her situation and wishing to be included as a part of it.

All the poignancy of these stories comes from this condition of feeling simultaneously outside and inside a predicament. "I belong to a country which I have left," Colette writes in **"Gray Days,"** and because she is still attached to this country (which represents both her first home in Burgundy and her abandoned state of childhood innocence), she is still vulnerable to the loss she feels in leaving it. Outside the country where Colette belongs, all desire is unrequited and is therefore certain to result in pain; yet neither she nor her characters can shake free from that desire. Love keeps leaving and returning to the people in Colette's world and is as familiar a burden as their poverty or their ennui. "I don't believe I'd know what to do with myself if I didn't have my sorrow," a young actress says in **"Gitanette."** "It keeps me company." Colette here is no longer cool or detached; she shares completely in the woman's sorrow—keeping Gitanette company.

So Colette struggles between sympathy with and detachment from her characters, and she tries to offer us an entire world despite the limitations of her strongly subjective vision. Generous in her intention if not usually in her execution, Colette wants to give us Paris in all of its fin de siècle color and variety; what we receive, however, is Colette's Paris, which is something quite different. Again, more like memoir than fiction, these stories strictly limit themselves to Colette's experience. We can never quite approach any character's mind other than the one onto which Colette projects herself; the other people she writes about are "mannequins," "dolls," figures in a dream. Here Paris is almost entirely a feminine city, where men are conspicuous by their absence, serving as mere occasions for the women's actions and preoccupations. In this Paris, almost every woman, regardless of her position, is a survivor, struggling through her day, exhibiting "le gout de durer"—the will to survive in confrontation with poverty, obligation, loss of love.

However limited this world of Colette's is, it nevertheless is as rich as a series of memoirs could hope to be. George Eliot has written that memory has as many moods as temper, and here within Colette's memory we are given every mood, every detail of gesture and impulse possible. All of the nostalgia that accompanies memoir enriches Colette's stories, making them moving but not sentimental; the characters here are aware of a better, less fractioned world, a world they have left, and the memory of that world, along with the hope for its return, keeps them going. Somehow we share this nostalgia with the characters who speak for Colette, and we share her conflicting desires to approach and retreat from the preoccupations of her characters. The tension between these impulses remains as unresolved as dreams, as sustained as music, and the moods of the stories, like dreams, stay with us even after we have forgotten their details.

By traveling the distance between cognition and recognition, between imagination and memory, Colette has placed herself in a unique position as a writer. Her insights, spread loosely throughout these brief sketches and stories, become a bit diluted, just as memory becomes experience-once-removed in the act of recollection, with details applied thickly in some places and obscured or ignored in others. Despite this weakness, Colette's work demands to be taken seriously. The mind that remembers these dreams for us and makes us nostalgic for a time we did not know is extraordinary, for it allows us to gain from the mixture of memory and fiction something akin to the rich immediacy of an intense experience. The shared longing for it to stay, and to stay whole, remains. (pp. 549-50, 552)

> Donna Rifkind, "Herself," in The American Scholar, *Vol. 53, No. 4, Autumn, 1984, pp. 549-50, 552.*

Anne Duhamel Ketchum   (essay date 1985)

[*In the following essay, Ketchum discusses the reversal of gender roles depicted in "The Tender Shoot."*]

The work of Colette, encompassing more than half a century of French bourgeois life, brings more than the fragrant realm of gardens and the complicity of friendly pets; more than the racy pranks of tomboy Claudine or the love rebuffs of courtesans, music-hall dancers and gigolos, in the Gay Paris before World War I. Sensitive, like Proust, her contemporary, to the deep changes French society was undergoing during the first half of the century, Colette promoted a truly feminine ethics, a fact which is not always clearly perceived. An ethics that is not only for women, but one facing openly the needs and concerns of women in a rapidly changing society.

Because, Colette chose her characters from the lowest strata of society—aging courtesans, spoiled children of the "flaming youth," and the then despised "show business" people and homosexuals—the general consensus is that she had few concerns other than advocating easy-going morals and emphasizing a most frenzied sexual liberation, above all for women. Not only is this, of course, an oversimplification, but it can lead to gross misconceptions. Our purpose here, however, is not to re-evaluate all of Colette's attitudes throughout her work; we propose instead to examine the positions she had arrived at in one short story, **"The Tender-shoot,"** written when Colette had sufficiently weathered and pondered the past to give form to her own set of values. We will not try in the least to "rehabilitate" Colette as we feel, with Jean Cocteau, that "Colette does not need to be rehabilitated, for she is sterling."

The Képi is a collection of four short stories: the **"Képi"** itself, **"The Tender-shoot," "The Green Wax"** and **"Armande."** We are concerned only with the second one. The volume is the work of a seventy-year-old Colette, during the terrible year of 1943, in occupied Paris. She feels the greatest anxiety about her husband, Maurice Goudeket, who had been arrested by the Germans in 1941.

France is cut in two "zones" and governed by an eighty-five-year-old soldier. More than one and a half million Frenchmen are prisoners of war in Germany, and the entire cost of the German occupation is levied on the French.

The Pétain government, with its motto "work, family, fatherland," is openly challenging the views of the third Republic: Catholic instruction is offered again in French schools; "return to the land" is praised, in a Barresian attempt to help the nation recover its "true roots." A beaten France submits to the idea that she needs workers rather than scholars, and measures are taken by the Vichy government to limit the number of young university graduates, an unprecedented measure.

Yet liberty is more than ever on the mind of the French people, and central to major works being published: *The Flies* by Sartre, *The Stranger* by Camus, *Poésie et Vérité* by Eluard. In such bleak context, tales and legends from the past bring the enchantment of a lost paradise, helping to soothe the pain of an intolerable present. It is the magic of the past which [Colette] tries again to recapture during World War II in publishing *Looking Backwards* in 1941, *The Képi* in 1943 and *Gigi* in 1944.

The date of **"The Tender-shoot"** is very precise: May 1940, a time when the French, taken by surprise by the invader, were "all like animals without a sense of smell." Albin Chaveriat, around seventy, with the natural distinction of a true Basque, oddly never married. In his spare time, he enjoys roaming around the woods and the countryside with a shotgun slung on his shoulder; for there is nothing he would like better than to become a hunter. But somehow he always returns with nothing more than "a handkerchief full of mushrooms," picked on his way. In his teens he experienced one of those "adolescent friendships to which a normal boy is more faithful at heart than to a mistress." What Chaveriat calls a "beautiful sentimental solidarity" between the two boys became so important to him as to overshadow all other relationships. This exclusivity of feelings between two young males is by no means rare; it is at the root of all associations and clubs reserved for men so common in England, for instance. They have their counterpart in all the "sociétés," "mutuelles," "amicales" and veterans associations so active in France. They attest to the strong links tying men together in western societies. Officially justified by the necessities of business, their total exclusion of women elicits the belief that all matters of importance—business or other—can be dealt with only between men, another way to imply that only relationships between men count for much.

Very few of Colette's contemporaries had her insight regarding the crippling consequences an exclusive friendship between boys might have for later life, tarnishing all relations with the other sex. Consider the very common practice of ancillary sex and, more generally, of holding all women simply as sex objects, of which Chaveriat is clearly a good illustration.

His friend's ultimate marriage was taken as "the first treason," and a terrible blow. Out of spite, he turns, at thirty, to eighteen-year-old beauties, delighted by their "sincere abruptness," their "beauty in the rough." Soon he discovers, "terrified," his preference for those "champions of the risk" who approach danger with surprising serenity; this was a trait particularly attractive to Chaveriat who, in spite of his visions of conquest, actually was shunning danger. But he defends himself against the common opinion that any man approaching young girls is a coward: Chaveriat insists on the contrary, that it takes a "special kind of self-control to resist them." Since the rest of the story shows how little he resists such temptations, Colette's conclusion is very clear.

It is in 1923 that a fifty-year-old Chaveriat is invited to the country house of a friend. There he discovers a lovely, ancient house which he compares to a woman, "in négligé," "with a great coat of Virginia creeper, rose in places, covering one shoulder." His contemplation is interrupted by a devilish black goat chasing him downhill, followed by a girl of fifteen—a strawberry-blonde peasant child, with freckles.

Louisette is nothing but a symphony in russet and rose. Responding to such beguiling signals, an enchanted Chaveriat compares the Renoir-like girl, significantly enough, not to a painting by that master, but to one by Boucher, giving from the start a licentious dimension to his interest. He describes the little "country girl" as "plump" with a "flawless set of teeth," as though he were a horse-dealer examining a filly. The young girl stiffens, haughtily retreating to her "castle" as she calls the dismantled old house, guarded by two imposing stone lions sporting only "lambsnouts."

Terms of hunting are used in **"The Tender-shoot"** in the preparation for the conquest, but all Chaveriat gives of himself is his money, to buy a cheap little coral necklace. On several occasions will he thus attempt to buy the girl he calls "the prettiest little servant in France." "Bait in hand," the next day Chaveriat "lies in ambush . . . waiting for the game." The story takes an unexpected turn when Louisette "red with anger" throws the necklace at his face, not out of fear of her mother, but of "what her mother might think." The abrupt change in tone coincides with the discovery on Louisette's property of a magnificent spring of water, quite unexpected in the arid area. Its appearance at this point in the text, along with the great thirst of Chaveriat for its water, deserves our attention: in previous works, Colette at times has evoked such spontaneous thirst for an irresistibly pure water. One such occasion can be found, for instance, in *Retreat from Love* the last volume of the Claudine series. To regain her balance, a disenchanted Claudine has fled from Paris to the very same Franche-Comté where **"The Tender-shoot"** takes

place. Part of the volume is concerned with opposing the vanity of facile pleasures to the goodness of all things natural; as they are revealed to Claudine, she evokes a sudden, quasi-mystical thirst from her childhood, one of the most beautifully poetical passages of the book. "I am thirsty. But only for the water colored with an ordinary and colorful wine which Mélie poured for me, in the cool, slightly musty diningroom. Give me a drink, Mélie, quick!."

A very determined girl, then, and a "wild pony," she shows her lover very little "affection." Chaveriat feels that "it was not asking too much to hope that, softened and satisfied, she would come to treat her unselfish lover as a friend." This comic yearning for affection from the old goat should be taken for what it is: The suspicion, and the fear, of being used as a stud, a mere sex object by a girl who indeed, "treated sensual pleasure as her lawful right."

"Shocked" by Louisette's aloofness, Chaveriat reassures himself that her lack of feeling for him, the "mutism" of an "adorable idiot" are only marks of her "want of intelligence." But he cannot fool himself much longer. Finally, the truth dawns on him, for only a brief instant: "It seems . . . not to have been such a gay adventure as I thought." "Louisette was nothing more than a girl I was relieving of her boredom. . . . At the time, I used to wonder, now and then, whether Louisette were not exploiting me like a lecherous man who's found a willing girl."

The reversal by Louisette of traditional roles completely upsets Chaveriat's comfortable male standards. In a game where he longs to impose his undisputed rule (the "hunter"), he finds in a fifteen-year-old goose, a master. We have understood, by now, that ever since "the first treason," when he reproached a young wife for taking away his best friend, Chaveriat deeply resents women. It is his need to assert his supremacy as a man and a master that makes him turn exclusively to immature, defenseless girls who can best satisfy his senses without presenting any threat to his ego.

Louisette, however, becomes his ruin. Growing up in a remote corner of the French countryside, far away from the maleficence of urban civilization, Louisette is a child of Nature. Early aware of the needs of her senses, she sets about, with simplicity, to gratify them. When her choice falls on Chaveriat, it expresses itself with passion and with a directness of purpose which startles him a bit when she unhesitantly surrenders her body. But nothing else. Her own life, her person remain totally private, and entirely in her control. The only opinion she clearly cares for is not Chaveriat's, but her mother's, a fact which puts him off a good deal. Behind her silence and what Chaveriat takes for simple-mindedness, Louisette is a strongwilled, self-possessed person; alone with her widowed mother, she has learned early enough the harsh fight for survival. She is concerned about maintaining her integrity as a person in a hostile world, and about building up her self-confidence and respect. She easily relinquishes her virginity, simply because it is not the important thing to preserve. But in all circumstances she retains her dignity, sets when and where they meet, and is in control of the situation at all times.

It is also in the name of female dignity that Louisette's mother, descending regally the stairs of their "castle" with the lamp of justice in her hand, swoops down on the lovers, and puts them to shame. To Chaveriat's attempt to drape himself in whatever pride he has left and to bluff his way out, Louisette puts an unexpected stop: "I forbid you to talk to my mother in that tone." This leaves no doubt as to who is now in command. The question of Louisette's mother, "Monsieur, may one know your age?" shatters Chaveriat, definitely throwing him off balance: "I found myself making a series of idiotic gestures such as running my hand through my hair, pulling my leather belt down over my loins, and drawing myself up to my full height." He lies about his age.

Louisette's spontaneous reaction brings about the totally unorthodox dénouement, though the only *natural* one: "Do you want me to go for him, Mother? Us two, we'll chase him, shall we?" "I had shot out of the house," admits Chaveriat, "and the Devil himself could not have stopped me." He flees, then, as fast as he can! Just as he feels out of danger, he is literally stoned by both angry women, standing on top of a wall, above him! He feels sure that they would have stoned him to death if he had not had the sense to pass to the attack. Then, "they too recovered their reason and the conscience of their female condition, for after hesitating, they fled and disappeared." For Chaveriat then, both women had lost their reason in attacking the seducer, and "the conscience of their female condition" dictated that they consent to being seduced, humiliated and otherwise submissive to the male master. Colette's statement here is very strong, and Chaveriat is presented by her as the epitome of phallocratism. The end of the story stresses even more Chaveriat's vileness with his resigned admission that, for him henceforth, remains "the practice of the chambermaid."

Colette had no hesitation in ridiculing and punishing him severely. Mother and daughter, then, have succeeded in giving the old lecherous man a masterful lesson. Praising in both women the old basic sense of measure of the French peasant, Colette allows them to give to an otherwise poetical tale a twist reminiscent of the medieval farces, of picaresque adventures, of Rabelais, Molière and Beaumarchais to name a few, making lavish use of ridicule to shame the aggressor, and even of violence to chastise him.

All her life, Colette has had a very high idea of womanhood. But through the years, this idea has evolved a great deal. She was brought up, in a rather traditional way, by an exceptional woman who remained her constant model. Coming to Paris upset all the fundamental values Colette had learned and which were no longer in play in the big, ruthless city. It was a tremendous shock, from which she never fully recovered.

But she took, first, all the indispensable measures: she divorced, fought to conquer independence and respect, and decided that she would write about "things pure." Frus-

trated with the utter difficulty for a divorced woman to make her place in the world, she rebelled, with *The Vagabond,* against the double standard, against male possessiveness. She discovered also the duplicity women resort to, in order to outsmart men's treacherous ways.

In a second stage, we find Colette looking for models she could emulate: they are Mitsou, Léa first, Julie de Carneilhan later. Searching desperately for some measure of integrity in the human world, she thinks she had found it in *Chéri,* ultimately to realize that she had only found it in Sido.

Late in her life, Colette remembers Sido's maternal vigilance. Both in **"The Tender-shoot"** and in **"The Green Wax"** of *The Képi* does Colette proclaim the need for young girls—that choice prey in a male world—for the protection of their mother. She praises valiant mothers, such as Louisette's, as the last defenders in our corrupt society of truly human values against men's constant aggressions.

But the greatest need of women reaches beyond the liberation of their senses. For Colette, it remains the awareness of their priceless value in a world which uses them, abuses them as another priced commodity, the better to deny them equality.

Colette's ideas of women have changed greatly through the years. From the heroic, self-sacrificing archetypes of the early works, her heroines have evolved into stronger, more secure women, supported by the idea of their value as the creators but also the defenders of life and all which makes it worth living, against mercantilism, crime and war. (pp. 71-6)

> *Anne Duhamel Ketchum, "Defining an Ethics from a Later Short Story by Colette," in* Continental, Latin-American and Francophone Women Writers, *edited by Eunice Myers and Ginette Adamson, University Press of America, 1987, pp. 71-7.*

FURTHER READING

Biography

Cottrell, Robert D. *Colette.* New York: Frederick Ungar Publishing Co., 1974, 150 p.
    A biographically based discussion of Colette's major novels.

Phelps, Robert. *Belles Saisons: A Colette Scrapbook.* New York: Farrar, Straus and Giroux, 1978, 302 p.
    Pictorial account of Colette highlighting interesting details of her personal and professional life with commentary by Phelps and numerous quotes by Colette.

Richardson, Joanna. *Colette.* New York: Dell, 1983, 258 p.
    Considered a clear and sympathetic portrait of Colette.

Sarde, Michèle. *Colette: Free and Fettered,* translated by Richard Miller. New York: Morrow, 1980, 479 p.

Regarded by some critics to be the most comprehensive biography on Colette. Strongly feminist in tone.

Criticism

Annan, Gabriele. "Not So Close to Colette." *The New York Review of Books* XXXI, No. 7 (26 April 1984): 12, 14-16.

Discusses strengths and weaknesses of several stories in *The Collected Stories of Colette,* criticizing Colette's ever-present personality and undiscriminating inclusion of subjective impressions in her fiction.

Blake, Patricia. "Cornucopia." *Time* CXXIII, No. 2 (9 January 1984): 70, 73.

Favorable review of *The Collected Stories of Colette.*

Cohen, Susan D. "An Onomastic Double Bind: Colette's *Gigi* and the Politics of Naming." *PMLA* 100, No. 5 (October 1985): 793-809.

Highly academic feminist analysis of *Gigi,* arguing that a central theme of the work is the relationship between language and power.

Davies, Margaret. *Colette.* New York: Grove Press, Inc., 1961, 120 p.

Considered an effective and engaging general introduction to Colette's literary career and major works.

Dick, Kay. "Under the Blue Lamp." *The Spectator* 253, No. 8143 (4 August 1984): 20-1.

Praises the selection and arrangement of *The Collected Stories of Colette* and asserts that the stories based on Colette's music hall experiences lend valuable insight into her seldom-considered work ethic.

Dranch, Sherry A. "Reading through the Veiled Text: Colette's *The Pure and the Impure.*" *Contemporary Literature* XXIV, No. 2 (Summer 1983): 176-89.

Structuralist discussion of the implications of the unwritten subtext in Colette's loosely-connected series of stories centered around the theme of homosexuality.

Duchêne, Anne. "From Sequins to *monstre sacré.*" *The Times Literary Supplement,* No. 4357 (2 November 1984): 1238.

Faults *The Collected Stories* for several inaccuracies.

Eisinger, Erica Mendelson, and McCarty, Mari Ward, eds. *Colette: The Woman, The Writer.* University Park: The Pennsylvania State University Press, 1981, 200 p.

Selected critical essays focusing on three general areas of discussion: the evolution of Colette's literary career, themes concerning gender roles in her fiction, and literary theory and techniques revealed in her writing.

Ford, Marianna. "Spatial Structures in *La Chatte.*" *The French Review* 58, No. 3 (February 1985): 360-67.

Argues that "the spatial structures in [*La Chatte*] inform the action, provide a complex organizing element, and are an essential factor in the interpretation of the story."

Kapp, Isa. "Mistress of Tristess." *The New Republic* 190, No. 3620 (4 June 1984): 38-42.

Favorable review of *The Collected Stories of Colette* including many quotes from the text to illustrate the reviewer's arguments.

Owen, Peter. "Mere Moments." *The Times Literary Supplement,* No. 3625 (20 August 1971): 986.

Praises Colette's characterizations of women in the collection *The Other Woman* and criticizes the self-indulgent tone of *My Friend Valentine,* a posthumously published novella included in the volume.

Phelps, Robert. Introduction to *The Collected Stories of Colette,* edited by Robert Phelps, translated by Matthew Ward and others, pp. xi-xiii. New York: Farrar, Straus and Giroux, 1983.

States that Colette's primary interest as a writer was the joy and pain found in the private lives of individuals and maintains that it was her personal observations and perceptions of life that she strove to share with her readers.

Rose, Phyllis. "Having the Best of Both Worlds." *The New York Times Book Review* (25 December 1983): 3, 14.

Review of *The Collected Stories of Colette* discussing Colette's theme of "the heroism of women," and the difficulty of placing her fiction into specific genre categories, and criticizing the selection and arrangement of stories in the collection.

Ryan, Nancy. Review of *The Other Woman,* by Colette. *Saturday Review* 55 (1 April 1972): 74-5.

Discusses Colette's honest examination of married life in several stories in *The Other Woman.*

Sackett, Victoria. Review of *The Collected Stories of Colette. The American Spectator* XVII, No. 6 (June 1984): 43-4.

Favorable review praising the variety of the editor's selection.

Stewart, Joan Hinde. "Chance Acquaintances." In her *Colette,* pp. 110-34. Boston: Twayne Publishers, 1983.

Discusses the salient features of Colette's short fiction, paying particular attention to the narrator's ambivalent attitude toward involvement with the characters whose stories she both relates and participates in.

Stockinger, Jacob. "Impurity and Sexual Politics in the Provinces: Colette's Anti-Idyll in *The Patriarch.*" *Women's Studies* 8, No. 3 (1981): 359-66.

Examines the short story "The Patriarch," and asserts that Colette's focus on incest and male dominance is an expression of social criticism, refuting critics who view Colette as an apolitical libertine.

Sutherland, Donald. "Small Lasting Virtues." *The New Republic* 129, No. 17 (23 November 1953): 17-18.

Positive review of *My Mother's House* and *Sido,* asserting that "[the] sketches are exquisitely composed, full of a delicious combination of pastoral poetry and Parisian irony, of an intimate but lucid sympathy for all creatures within its range."

Additional coverage of Colette's life and career is contained in the following sources published by Gale Research: *Contemporary Authors,* Vols. 104, 131; *Dictionary of Literary Biography,* Vol. 65; *Major 20th-Century Writers;* and *Twentieth-Century Literary Criticism,* Vols. 1, 5, 16.

Anaïs Nin

1903-1977

French-born American novelist, diarist, short story writer, and critic.

INTRODUCTION

Nin is considered an important figure in twentieth-century literature, most often recognized for her association with the Surrealist movement of the 1920s. Strongly influenced by tenets of psychoanalysis, her short fiction is praised for its insight into intimate relationships between women and men and its emphasis on female characters of exceptional depth and complexity. Many of her stories are autobiographical, presenting characters who strive to gain self-knowledge and a sense of completeness, and reflecting the introspective analysis of emotions and experiences Nin recorded in seven volumes of diaries published from 1966 through 1981. Often likening her writings to the works of D. H. Lawrence and Virginia Woolf, critics have praised the poetic imagery and lyrical structure of Nin's short stories.

In her short fiction, Nin frequently depicts female characters whose emotional and psychological growth has been impeded by troubled or severed childhood relationships with their fathers. Critics have consistently noted the autobiographical source for Nin's father-daughter theme, observing that the trauma of her father's abandonment of her family when she was eleven years old greatly affected Nin's writing. In the story "Stella," for example, a movie star whose father abandoned her as a child is unable to reconcile her glamorous stage image with her deep feelings of self-doubt and insecurity. Tormented by a sense of incompleteness, Stella becomes possessive and jealous and ultimately destroys her current love relationship. In "Winter of Artifice" (originally published as "Lilith"), Nin describes the reunion of a father and his daughter Lilith after twenty years of separation. Having idolized her father ever since he abandoned her when she was ten years old, Lilith enjoys an initial idyllic reunion; however, she is soon disappointed by her father's childishness and narcissism. Critics have observed that many of the characters in Nin's short stories are burdened by neuroses and delusions associated with their pasts. The potential for transcending this kind of traumatic personal history is examined in "The Voice," in which Nin depicts the healing relationship between a psychoanalyst and his patients, each of whom is inhibited by memories of some person or event from his or her past.

Many critics have deemed Nin's short story collection *Under a Glass Bell* her most significant artistic achievement, praising its sensitive delineation of character and

emotion and its hauntingly beautiful surrealist images. Fantasy and dreams recur throughout the collection, often presented as the means to achieving artistic discovery and spiritual growth. "Houseboat," for example, which is often described as a prose poem, depicts the narrator's voyages through a dream world on a boat which Nin characterized as the ideal setting for life and art. While fantasy is frequently associated with artistic transcendence in *Under a Glass Bell,* most of the characters in the stories are artists who ultimately fail to emerge from the confinements of the self, remaining entrapped within their obsessions, illusions, dreams, and the past. In "The Eye's Journey," a painter becomes increasingly debilitated by feelings of persecution until he is confined to an asylum. The crippling effects of obsessive and deluded thinking are also the focus of "The All-Seeing," which reviewers have praised as an example of Nin's most beautiful writing. The story describes a man's agonized preoccupation with his mother's discouragement concerning his playing the violin as a child and the grief he suffers because of his stifled creativity.

Critics have praised Nin's short fiction for its insightful representation of the complex nuances of human relationships and highly effective characterizations of women. While her works emphasize the importance of mutual understanding, balance, and generosity between men and women, her stories also exhibit an acute sensitivity to the potential for victimization and entrapment within relationships. In "Hejda," Nin presents the doomed partnership between the painters Hejda and Molnar; Molnar is a highly critical man who gradually erodes Hejda's individuality through his weakness, dependence, and excessive control, until she finally loses interest in her own painting and becomes absorbed in his. Many critics have observed that "Hejda" reveals Nin's preoccupation with love limited by narcissism and selfishness, which is also a motif of the father-daughter relationship depicted in *Winter of Artifice.* Women's opposing experiences of imprisonment and growth are also vividly portrayed in *Under a Glass Bell* in such pieces as "The Mouse," which relates the trauma concerning a pregnant maidservant who is refused medical help after she attempts an abortion on herself. "Birth," considered one of Nin's most successful works, similarly chronicles a woman's experience of intense physical and psychological anguish. The story describes a painful and prolonged labor and birth of a stillborn child and has been interpreted by some critics as symbolizing a woman's struggle to achieve personal rebirth through releasing a dead part of herself.

Much of Nin's fame is also attributable to the short erotic pieces she wrote for a patron while living in Paris during the early 1940s. Although Nin valued her erotica less than her other writing, she first became a best-selling author during the 1970s with the posthumous publication of these collected episodes in *Delta of Venus* and *Little Birds.* Like her other short fiction, Nin's erotica emphasizes sensitivity, desire, and personal freedom from a woman's perspective.

PRINCIPAL WORKS

SHORT FICTION

Winter of Artifice   1939; also published as *Winter of Artifice: Three Novelettes* [enlarged edition], 1974
Under a Glass Bell   1944; also published as *Under a Glass Bell, and Other Stories* [enlarged edition], 1947
This Hunger . . .   1945
Collages   1964
Waste of Timelessness, and Other Early Stories   1977
Delta of Venus   1977
Little Birds   1979

OTHER MAJOR WORKS

House of Incest   (novel)   1936
Ladders to Fire   (novel)   1946
Children of the Albatross   (novel)   1947
Four Chambered Heart   (novel)   1950
A Spy in the House of Love   (novel)   1954
Solar Barque   (novel) 1958; also published as *Seduction of the Minotaur* [enlarged edition], 1961
The Diary of Anaïs Nin. 7 vols. 1966-81

Edmund Wilson   (essay date 1944)

[*Wilson was a prolific reviewer, creative writer, and social and literary critic who exercised his greatest literary influence as the author of* Axel's Castle *(1931), a seminal study of literary symbolism, and with widely read reviews and essays in which he introduced the best works of modern literature to the reading public. In the following excerpt from the first significant critical commentary on Nin's work, Wilson commends the poetic language, realistic observations, and evocative imagery of the stories in* Under a Glass Bell.]

The unpublished diary of Anaïs Nin has long been a legend of the literary world, but a project to have it published by subscription seems never to have come to anything, and the books that she has brought out, rather fragmentary examples of a kind of autobiographical fantasy, have been a little disappointing. She has now, however, published a small volume called *Under a Glass Bell,* which gives a better impression of her talent.

The pieces in this collection belong to a peculiar genre sometimes cultivated by the late Virginia Woolf. They are half short stories, half dreams, and they mix a sometimes exquisite poetry with a homely realistic observation. They take place in a special world, a world of feminine perception and fancy, which is all the more curious and charming for being innocently international. Miss Nin is the daughter of a Spanish musician, but has spent much of her life in France and in the United States. She writes English, but mostly about Paris, though you occasionally find yourself in other countries. There are passages in her prose which may perhaps suffer a little from an hallucinatory vein of writing which the Surrealists have overdone: a mere reeling-out of images, each of which is designed to be surprising but which, strung together, simply fatigue. In Miss Nin's case, however, the imagery does convey something and is always appropriate. The spun glass is also alive: it is the abode of a secret creature. Half woman, half childlike spirit, she shops, employs servants, wears dresses, suffers the pains of childbirth, yet is likely at any moment to be volatilized into a superterrestrial being who feels things that we cannot feel.

But perhaps the main thing to say is that Miss Nin is a very good artist, as perhaps none of the literary Surrealists is. **"The Mouse," "Under a Glass Bell," "Rag Time,"** and **"Birth"** are really beautiful little pieces. "These stories," says Miss Nin in a foreword, "represent the moment when many like myself had found only one answer to the suffering of the world: to dream, to tell fairy tales, to elaborate and to follow the labyrinth of fantasy. All this I see now was the passive poet's only answer to the torments he witnessed. . . . I am in the difficult position of presenting stories which are dreams and of having to say: but now, although I give you these, I am awake!" Yet this poet has no need to apologize: her dreams reflect the torment, too. (pp. 73-4)

Edmund Wilson, "Doubts and Dreams: 'Dangling Man' and 'Under a Glass Bell'," in The New Yorker, *Vol. XX, No. 7, April 1, 1944, pp. 70, 73-4.*

The New York Times Book Review   (essay date 1948)

[*The following essay notes that the early stories collected in* Under a Glass Bell *benefit from a greater degree of realism than do Nin's later works of "dream literature."*]

The thirteen short stories and the novelette **Winter of Artifice,** now brought together in a single volume, have been previously available before in this country only in the limited private editions hand-set by Miss Nin herself, and decorated with spidery anatomical, subaqueous copper engravings by Ian Hugo, in a technique copied after one revealed to the poet William Blake "by his brother in a dream." The engravings and typographical errors are gone, and the present book looks like any other.

The first part, **"Djuna,"** of **Winter of Artifice,** tells of a girl who had waited twenty years, from the time she was 10 to the time she was 30, for her father, a celebrated musician, to return to her, and of the life they had together after his return. During those twenty years she kept a voluminous diary which "described every phase of their life in detail, minute, childish details which seem ridiculous and absurd now, but which were intended to convey to her father the need that she felt for his presence."

This is the famous diary in fifty volumes which brought Anais Nin to the attention of the literary world about ten years ago when Henry Miller described it in a long, enthusiastic tribute in T. S. Eliot's *Criterion.* In the second part of **Winter of Artifice** everything is significant because it is told to a psychiatrist, **"The Voice."** Such experience, together with the entirely harmful and fantastically adulatory letters which Henry Miller wrote to her and which may be found in his printed essays, do much to explain the egotistical self-absorption of the shadowy and unrealized characters in Miss Nin's later work, and the attribution of profound, esoteric significance to the most trivial and whimsical behavior.

In Miss Nin's early stories, however, preoccupation with dreams and the interior life is coupled with healthy realism, as in the story **"Birth";** with a satirist's eye for human self-deception, as in the portrait of her father after his return; in **Winter of Artifice,** and above all with unselfish human sympathy, as in the story of the pregnant servant girl in **"Mouse."** In this early work the characters' dreams illumine and are illumined by a real life as vivid, fantastic and dramatic as the dreams. But in Miss Nin's later work real life is seen dimly beyond the dreams, and fades as quickly as they do.

This is a reversal of the direction in which the author at one time planned to go. At the end of **"Djuna"** Miss Nin wrote, "At last she was entering the Chinese theatre of her drama and could see the trappings of the play as well as the play itself, see that the settings were made of the cardboard of illusion . . . She was coming out of the ether of the past." And in the original preface to **Under a Glass Bell,** Anais Nin described dream literature as opium.

> The Spanish war awakened me. I passed out of romanticism, mysticism and neuroticism into reality. . . . But it is necessary to understand, to be aware of what caused the suffering which made such an opium essential . . . And to this task I will devote the rest of my writing.

This was obviously a passing mood, but a mood whose return Miss Nin's admirers might well wish to see.

> R. G. D., "The Fantastic World of Anais Nin," in The New York Times Book Review, *March 28, 1948, p. 24.*

Vernon Young   (essay date 1948)

[*Young is an American critic who has written extensively on drama and film. In the review of* Under a Glass Bell *excerpted below, he praises Nin's sensitive depiction of women, but criticizes her unskillful use of surrealist principles and her portrayal of male characters as overly negative.*]

Decadence, sometimes of style, mostly of viewpoint . . . prevails in the fiction of Anais Nin; the critical vocabulary balks at the very concept, fiction, for has one not been told that Nin's work is drawn from a massive and unending diary? One is morally blackmailed at the start, since, by this entangling alliance, strictly *literary* criticism is almost proscribed. Yet willing publication obviously betokens a measure of artistic objectivity, and republication of Miss Nin's [**Under a Glass Bell**] by E. P. Dutton (formerly it was directed at the cognoscenti in limited editions) removes it from the kindness of the private circle and places it where it is obliged to meet the challenge of a more public analysis.

I believe there is little question that when Anais Nin is writing on her master subject, the interior stresses of the female personality, she has no equal in minute analysis, in conveying the nuances of expectation and withdrawal, the ambivalences of possession and surrender, the delicacies and gaucheries of contact. Better than anyone writing today, she can reveal the psychic essence of the feminine polarity and her revelation, as a consequence of being acutely implicated, arrives at the anxiety proportional to obsessive neurosis. The Female as Female is embraced with such tenderness, such solicitation of her particularity, such a ferocity of defense, that man is necessarily, to the morbid guardian of the woman veiled, the natural enemy—man's inhumanity toward woman is, therefore, the special injustice in the world of Nin. Under this pressure and told with an exquisitely deceptive simplicity is the story **"Hejda"** in this volume, the purest example of Nin's clairvoyant talent for divulging the tensional forces of incompatibility. This vignette of the Oriental Hejda's unveiling, or rather of her husband's incapacity for making that unveiling fruitful, is the symbol for the heart of Nin's work, around which, if it represented her most passionate conviction, all her finest art would be clustered.

Reading outward from this center, however, one discovers that the agonized privacy of the Nin heroine is endemic and does not indisputably follow upon the violation, by incomprehension, of the male. The objective honesty of **"Hejda"** and **"Djuna"** is cancelled (this is to say that the protestation of passivity is cancelled) by the confessional in **"The Voice"** and by various passages in the other stories, many of which emit a distinctly Sapphic odor. Nin's woman does not want man; again and again this decision is ratified by Nin's inability to set in believable motion any male who is not pompous, vain, ill or mad. Nin's Amazons are pursuing themselves: they are sick with their own preciousness, infatuated with their own proportions; writhing together like undulating snakes in a barrel, they attempt to cover their nakedness with the cry, "Woman Agonistes!" They flatter themselves that their breasted uniqueness has been cheated of its natural rights in the reciprocal flow, but in truth their predicament is simply that of infantile regression. With all their tremulous need for the perfect union, for the mutuality that will not rape their integrities, they are moral cowards who have poeticized their limitations; at their best they are autotrophic; at their simplest they are appallingly vain and their hearts belong to Daddy!

I believe there is little question that when Anais Nin is writing on her master subject, the interior stresses of the female personality, she has no equal in minute analysis, in conveying the nuances of expectation and withdrawal, the ambivalences of possession and surrender, the delicacies and gaucheries of contact.

—*Vernon Young*

Not that Nin's art is solely conscripted to justify the third sex. It is wonderfully deployed to seize the fragmentation of modern city life (**"Ragtime"** and **"The Voice"**), to note with compassion in a style that savors and respects its own music the lives broken by fear, by the multitude and by nature (**"The Mouse," "The Child Born out of the Fog," "Birth"**). Nin's poetic voice, when not choked in the vortex of self-delirium, is plastic and saltatory, lyrically able to define without *explaining;* it constructs a character by evoking his compulsions, the objects of his affection and reference, his attitudes and possessions, as in the masterfully *gestalt* study of the father in the **"Djuna"** section of *Winter of Artifice.* There, and elsewhere at her strongest, working with her eye on the score, her instrument at full diapason, so to speak, she is unequalled by anyone in this range since D. H. Lawrence and we know we are in the presence of literary genius; when the instrument falters, it squeals like an abused piccolo.

The drastic limitations of her method are explained in this admission of over-compensation:

> His paternal role could be summed up in the one word: criticism. Never an elan of joy, of contentment, of approval. Always sad, exacting, critical, blue eyes. Out of this came her love of ugliness, her effort to see beyond ugliness, always treating the flesh as a mask, as something which never possessed the same shape, color and features as thought. . . . People were made of crystal for her. She could see right through their

flesh, through and beyond the structure of their bones. Her eyes stripped them of their defects, their awkwardness, their stuttering. She overlooked the big ears, the frame too small, the hunched back, the wet hands, the web-footed walk. . . . she forgave. . . .

This is a manifesto of falsification as well as of sympathy—my statement may flush a covey of aesthetic treatises—and in it Nin's dual character as an artist is more than rationalized. She herself (I cannot summon the tact to distinguish her from her Seeing-Eye), clarifies the difficulty she has controlling the exfoliation asserted above:

> Her feelings never deceived her. It was only her imagination which deceived her. Her imagination could give a color, a smell, a beauty to things, even a warmth which her body knew very well to be unreal.
>
> In her head there could be a great deal of acting and many strange things could happen in there. But her emotions were sincere and they revolted, they prevented her from getting lost down the deep corridors of her inventions.

Down these corridors she is all too frequently lost; one turns from passages of emotional fidelity to those in which the imagination has obviously betrayed her. " 'When I went to Lapland,' said Jean, holding an empty opium pipe, 'I found the country of silence. . . .' " (S. J. Perelman slept here!) Jean is a tedious and affected homosexual who has been sulking for years because his mother made him stop playing the violin; but in Nin's transliteration he is an archeologist of the soul, a spiritually autocratic lover, a ship without moorings—"Just before he talked he seemed like a very soft animal, sensitive and porous." In another of these "corridors" she finds a lunatic named Pierre whose introductory challenge goes like this: "You are Beatrice Cenci. Your eyes are too large for a human being." She is apparently noncommittal, and later on: "he leaped away from my eyes and walked into the hothouse. . . . When he reappeared there was the scum of veronal on his lips, and his gestures were slower." Two pages farther, though he hasn't been near that hothouse, the edges of his mouth "were blackened with laudanum."

The unarguable merits of Miss Nin's technique are localized when her phenomena graduate into art with no divorce of judgment from intuition or, as she says herself, feeling from imagination. Failing to retain the correspondence, she parodies the valid principle of surrealism (illogical placement of logical objects) and is ludicrous except to the Pierres, Jeans and Djunas who invariably prefer charades to art, anyway. Her equipment is forever at the mercy of her temperament. Ruthlessly undercutting conventional form with all the compositional daring of Picasso, she risks losing herself down tunnels of artifice in which, lightless and without air, she can envisage those shapes born only of opiate, hallucination and death. (pp. 427-29)

Vernon Young, "Five Novels, Three Sexes, and Death," in The Hudson Review, *Vol. I, No. 3, Autumn, 1948, pp. 421-32.*

Kent Ekberg   (essay date 1977)

[*In the following essay, Ekberg analyzes unifying themes in the short stories in* Under a Glass Bell.]

Under a Glass Bell (1944) represents a turning point in the life and career of Anais Nin. It deserves the recognition of the literary world on a broader scale than it has yet received. Edmund Wilson was the first critic to hint at this in his reviews of Nin in *The New Yorker* in 1944 and 1945. Nin's work, he said, was endangered by becoming the property of a cult, and today this danger is still present. Bound by the circle of her coterie, covered by the epithet "feminine writer," and obscured by the brighter light of her more highly regarded *Diary,* her fiction too often remains not understood or ignored by the academic community. Richard R. Centing, the editor of Anais Nin newsletter, *Under the Sign of Pisces,* is correct when he says that "the only element lacking in Nin's recognition is serious criticism; understanding." In the hopes of facilitating this process, and perhaps providing this missing element, I begin here in examination of *Under a Glass Bell*'s place in modern fiction and a look at its themes, techniques, and structures which are often characteristic of Nin's fiction generally. For *Under a Glass Bell* is an important work in Nin's canon that completes her metamorphosis from apprentice writer to mature artist, and as a single volume of fiction in itself it perhaps has no equal in her work.

Nin came to regard *Under a Glass Bell* as perhaps her best work. It is the one she recommends to new readers and would like to be remembered by. Although *Under a Glass Bell* does not have the fluid style and humorous tone of *Collages* (1964), and it is not nearly as ambitious as *Cities of the Interior* (1974), *Under a Glass Bell* is very much her most finished book, gemlike and polished. One of the reasons it is such a success, in her opinion, is that she lived with the book day in and day out as she hand-set the stories page by page and revised for economy of expression over and over again in a Greenwich Village loft. Nin has called *Under a Glass Bell* a "dream" from which she is now "awake." Oliver Evans has interpreted this to be an implicit apology for the book's non-political tone. But *Under a Glass Bell* is dreamlike in another respect as well. Here Nin is able to use the subjective dream for the first time as a blueprint for discovery. Nin's early work was influenced by the realm of the dream through psychoanalysis and surrealism. *House of Incest* (1936) was composed from a written record of Nin's dreams. *Winter of Artifice* (1939) was a deliberate fictional exploration and escape from the nightmarish influence of Nin's father on her life. With *Under a Glass Bell* Nin's fiction becomes less ethereal and disjointed in technique. She has, it seems, conquered both some of her emotional and artistic problems with this book. After *Under a Glass Bell* her fiction will become less somber and less subjective, and her characters will more often be composites rather than simply autobiographical heroines or portraits from life.

Nin also refers to *Under a Glass Bell* as "a second birth" in the *Diary.* With this work, her naturalization as an American writer begins. Although the stories in *Under a Glass Bell* usually take place in Europe and not in America, in the books that follow this situation will reverse itself.

Collages, for example, in an early draft at the Northwestern University Library is called "Under a Glass Bell U.S.A.," and the stories in that book usually take place in or around Los Angeles or New York. *Under a Glass Bell* also represents a second birth in the psychological sense of the term. As Nin explains in the *Diary,* according to Jung, everyone is responsible for pursuing his own individuation as a human being, and at this second birth of the personality we have only ourselves as midwife. *Under a Glass Bell* is the partial record of such critical experience. It is a deeply personal book. Here Nin relives in fictional form some of the most profound traumas of her life, and as a work that relives and refinishes these traumas *Under a Glass Bell* constitutes a transcendence over them.

If we are to see *Under a Glass Bell* at once and as a whole, it is better to think of the work as a novel and not as a mere collection of short stories. Like Joyce's *Dubliners,* Anderson's *Winesburg, Ohio,* and Hemingway's *In Our Time,* the stories in Nin's *Under a Glass Bell* achieve unity and force through accretion. But unlike the novel-collections of Joyce, Anderson, and Hemingway, Nin's work is not unified by place or time as much as it is by form and feeling, common themes, techniques, and structures of thought. There is a discernible line in modern short fiction from Joyce through Anderson to Hemingway that depends on realism, colloquial speech patterns, and high but understated moments of life to depict a person and his place. Joseph Warren Beach once called this line and these writers a cult—"the cult of the simple." With Nin's stories there is no such hankering after concrete universals or hunting for plain fact absolutes. There is only the systolic and diastolic rhythm of the heart and the wavelike flow of life through crests and troughs.

In stories like Joyce's "A Little Cloud," Anderson's "Hands," and Hemingway's "Indian Camp," these authors take a single experience and use it as an image of a character's life in a moment of time which he must soon go beyond or be forever imprisoned in. The short story form itself encourages such vignettes and still lifes. Joyce's Little Chandler, Anderson's Wing Biddlebaum, and Hemingway's Nick Adams, the protagonists in these stories, are all paralyzed, grotesque, or innocent but unaware characters who are trapped by life. Nick Adams, for example, in "Indian Camp" witnesses an Indian woman in painful labor during a breach birth while her husband turns his face to the wall in the same room and cuts his own throat in agony at hearing his wife's screams. Young Nick is left to ask some childlike questions before he sinks back into the world of his own innocent nature, but he is not able to integrate this experience into his life. Often in Nin's stories—such as **"The Mouse"**—the protagonist is in a similar situation; here a pregnant servant-girl is caught in a "gesture of panic, that of falling into a trap." But in many of Nin's stories, such as **"Birth,"** that have autobiographical heroines, the protagonist goes beyond herself, gives up a part of herself, not without struggle and not without grief, to make a new beginning, a second birth. Such an effort at understanding is a survival technique for many of Nin's characters.

The great theme of *Under a Glass Bell,* and of all of Nin's fiction, is self-realization through spontaneous expression of emotions in relationships with other human beings. This is as much true of the *Diary* as of her novels. As the successive volumes of Nin's *Diary* have come out, it quickly becomes apparent that the published volumes are not haphazard or arbitrarily conceived books, but that each volume has its own integrity and helps to develop a progression from subjectivity to objectivity as they advance the story of a shy girl who comes to America with a notebook in a straw basket and who becomes a recognized author, lecturer and public figure some fifty years later. A part of this same story is told in *Under a Glass Bell* where a similar process of revelation takes place. Many of the characters and incidents in the stories can be found in the *Diary* also.

There are whole groups of stories in *Under a Glass Bell* with similar themes and situations. **"The Mouse," "Under a Glass Bell," "The Child Born Out of the Fog,"** and **"Hejda"** are all stories of two or more people thrust together, trying to understand each other, and at the same time needing their freedom to seek their own individuality by themselves. In **"The Mouse,"** it is the narrator and her servant-girl, the fearful, furtive "Mouse," who go through the ordeal of the girl's abortion in Paris. In **"Under a Glass Bell,"** the sister and brothers Jeanne, Jean and Paul are caught in a strange symbiosis like flies in amber. Don and Sarah, a black man and a white woman, come together from completely different and dislocated pasts to have a child, Pony, in **"The Child Born Out of the Fog."** And in much the same way, Hejda and Molnar, two painters of quite different styles, together try to satisfy but finally only frustrate each other's efforts to become successful artists in the story **"Hejda."** All of these stories are unfinished in the sense that the main characters in each have goals or aspirations that are only partially realized.

There are also a number of stories in *Under a Glass Bell* where the individual is left alone to his own devices for sustenance and survival. Sometimes he fails and falls into madness and paranoia. **"The Mohican"** is a bizarre astrologer who does research on esoteric writings in the Bibliotheque Nationale so that he can predict the future, but all his predictions are colored by disaster and he remains obscure and distant to those around him. In **"Je Suis Le Plus Malade Des Surrealistes,"** Pierre has original theories of drama and feels a reciprocity with the narrator, but the narrator cannot fully enter the world of laudanum and hallucination that he inhabits. Eventually, Pierre goes mad and is brought in a straight jacket to a hospital, raving his incomprehensible fantasies and finally falling in a heap on the floor. In **"The Eye's Journey,"** Hans, a painter, meets a similar fate; he dies in a fire in an insane asylum, too impassive to move and escape the flames. There are other stories of the individual alone that are not so tragic, but remain inconclusive nonetheless. The companion stories **"The Labyrinth"** and **"Through the Streets of My Own Labyrinth"** are about an eleven year-old girl who walks confusedly through the pages of her life like a wanderer might walk through the maze like streets of New York or Fez. Jean, also, "the archaeologist of his own soul" is list in his past and the prison of unfulfilled dreams in **"The All-Seeing."**

A third group of stories—**"The Houseboat," "Ragtime,"** and **"Birth"**—are very different because here the protagonist is neither frustrated by dependence on another person nor hopelessly lost and alone in an exclusive inner world. These stories have a different feeling about them because the "I" of the story has found her bearings and is in the flow of things again. They continue the theme of self-discovery which was touched upon in **"The Labyrinth"** and **"Through the Streets of My Own Labyrinth,"** but they also go beyond these two stories into a new and open realm of unexplored beginnings. In fact, **"Houseboat," "Ragtime,"** and **"Birth"** frame and illustrate Nin's program for self-realization which demands complete immersion in life, a careful consideration of experience, and a renewed estimate of the importance of the past.

"Houseboat" is an evenly balanced, almost symmetrical, story of four parts. Like the tramps who live under the bridges of the Seine, the narrator has broken away from the carefully regulated life of Paris and has come to live in a houseboat and to flow with the current of the river. In part two of the story the houseboat begins to travel through the "landscape of despair" and a series of events and images reflect the tumultuous inner world of the narrator: a drowning woman grasps the anchor chain, flotsam surrounds the barge, tramps quarrel, and an orphan cries. Finally, in part three the houseboat sails beyond this climate to the "island of joy," and sunlight and a holiday atmosphere fill the scene. In the last part of the story, the houseboats of the Seine are forced to move in order to clear the river for a visit from the King of England. Not without dignity, the houseboat is pushed into exile by a tugboat. This little allegory, with its landscape of despair and island of joy, makes clear what the ebb tide and flow of life feel like when the narrator is self-contained and in harmony with its currents. The story is remarkable for its imagery and its measured movement which parallels the narrator's own emotions.

"Ragtime" is a central story in the volume because it depicts the process of loss and recovery, an important theme in *Under a Glass Bell.* The ragpicker walks at night through the streets of the city searching for "the broken, the worn, the faded, the fragmented. . . . Fragments, incompleted worlds, rags, detritus, the end of objects, and the beginning of transmutations." He collects these objects in his ragpicker's bag and saves them. While making his rounds, the ragpicker gives back to the narrator lost objects that cause her to remember her dead past and to ask, "Where are all the other things . . . I thought dead?" And, "Can't one throw away anything forever?" The ragpicker answers her with a laugh and a song: "Nothing is lost but it changes. . . ." Finally, the narrator falls asleep and the ragpicker puts her in his bag for transformation. Although the story is cryptic and surreal in style, it is clear that **"Ragtime"** emphasizes recollection and renewal as its theme.

The story **"Birth,"** the last story in the book, is also the best one in *Under a Glass Bell* and a key to the work. Although the extraordinary emotional intensity of the story cannot be reproduced by summarizing the plot, the situation in **"Birth"** is really quite simple. The narrator, six

[*Under a Glass Bell*] is a deeply personal
book. Here Nin relives in fictional form
some of the most profound traumas of her
life, and as a work that relives and
refinishes these traumas *Under a Glass
Bell* constitutes a transcendence over
them.

—*Kent Ekberg*

months pregnant, is confined to a hospital. The child inside of her is dead and she must go through an arduous
and painful ordeal. Although the doctor and nurse try to
help the woman, they are unable to ease the birth. Finally,
they become almost violent in their efforts, and the narrator in a rage and in great pain demands that they stop.
Suddenly, and quite mysteriously, the woman relaxes her
will and is able to give birth to her dead daughter unassist-
ed.

This is not the first time this story has been told. In *Ladders to Fire,* Lillian confesses to Jay that she is pregnant
and also has a stillborn child. Nin includes a passage at
the end of Volume I of her *Diary* that is nearly identical
to the story **"Birth"** and to the passage from *Ladders to
Fire.* There is also an interesting draft of the birth story
in the Anais Nin Collection at the Northwestern University Library. Nin did some later pencil work on this typescript, but for the most part this is the source for both the
passage in *Ladders to Fire* and **"Birth."** There are whole
paragraphs in the typescript that might have halted action
in a story, novel, or diary. They were later omitted from
published work, but these omissions provide an interesting
gloss on the author. In these deleted paragraphs Nin emphasizes the point she makes in the *Diary:* the trauma of
the stillbirth was an important event in her life that forced
her to take stock of herself and to make changes that
would enable her to grow. **"Birth"** then is a doubly ironic
story, not only because it is about the *death* of a child, but
also because it is about the second *birth* of the narrator.

Although Nin is a writer who often eschews technique, the
changes she makes in the draft of her birth story show her
to be an artist who has control over her materials here. By
separating the first part of the draft (an apostrophe to the
unborn infant) and the second part (a narrative about the
stillbirth itself), Nin makes **"Birth"** a more vivid and intense work. She also eliminates passages about the father
of the unborn child, the narrator's own father, and the infant's birthright of suffering which would have blurred the
point of view and effect of the story. Her editorial work
on the typescript—the elimination of words, phrases, and
sentences—also heightens the climax of the story, the stillbirth, and brings about a more sudden denouement.

In *Under a Glass Bell* as a whole the hand of the artist is
at work through technique also, although perhaps not
quite so consciously. The most pervasive device used
throughout these stories is the dream image or motif that

occurs regularly but is open ended and can never be fully
explicated. Ian Hugo's cover engraving for the Swallow
edition suggests the hypnagogic images one might see in
a river of dreams. The dream in these stories is often present, and frequently the narrative proceeds "at a dream
pace," as events are slowed down, speeded up, or fused
into each other to create the desired effect. As in much of
her fiction, the dream sometimes serves as a dead end but
more importantly it can also represent a possible way out
of an impossible situation in these stories. As the narrator
says in **"Houseboat,"** "When I lie down to dream, it is not
merely a dust flower born like a rose of the desert sands
and destroyed by a gust of wind. When I lie down to
dream it is to plant the seed for the miracle and the fulfillment."

The glass bell of [**"Under a Glass Bell"**] governs the entire
work; it is a symbol of suffocation and separation, much
like Sylvia Plath's bell jar. Mazes and labyrinths as symbols of confusion or paths to self-knowledge appear frequently throughout the book, as do mirrors and keys
which reflect back on the self or promise to unlock the
protagonist's spirit. Nin's characters in *Under a Glass Bell*
are often actors who try on different roles for the self, like
Jean who is always in disguise to suit some new mood or
personality. They are often on obsessive odysseys for the
absolute, like Pierre. There is also a fascination with madness and frustration in these stories. For example, **"The
Unknown Woman of the Seine,"** who drowns herself but
is so beautiful the coroners make a death mask of her face,
makes appearances in several stories. So does Jean's cruci-
fied violin, which is nailed to the wall as a symbol of frustrated creativity.

Twin situations of reciprocity and doubleness are everywhere apparent in the stories of *Under a Glass Bell.* In
"Houseboat," "The Unknown Woman of the Seine" has
a counterpart in "the phantom lover" of "all women."
They are twins of each other, ghostly projections of unfulfilled human needs. The narrator and the servant in **"The
Mouse"** share similarities of outlook, although in the servant fear and dependency are more pronounced. The sister and brothers of **"Under a Glass Bell,"** who are so much
alike there is no room in their lives for anyone else, have
interchangeable personalities. Pierre and the narrator in
the story **"Je Suis Le Plus Malade Des Surrealists"** are
spiritually brother and sister and are nearly brought together by a common imagination, although the narrator
finally realizes their differences and shrinks away from
him. Don and Sarah, and Hejda and Molnar, and the narrator and Jean are also paired opposites. Like all of the uneasy couplings in *Under a Glass Bell,* Hejda's relationship
with Molnar is ruined by what she calls "the dream of
every maternal love": Hedja hopes that by fortifying Molnar he will in turn support her, but this is like holding up
a chair with no legs and trying to sit on it. The narrator
in **"The All-Seeing"** makes clear the difficulty of twinship
in love: "People who are twins, . . . there is a curse upon
their love. Love is made of differences and suffering and
apartness, and of struggle to overcome this apartness. Two
people who love the dream above all else would soon both
vanish together." This, in fact, is what happens to Jean
and the narrator in this story, as they drift apart.

What is not nearly as apparent is that twins, doubles, and parallel situations appear repeatedly in different stories also and help give *Under a Glass Bell* further unity. The narrator's relationship with the Mouse and the doctor at the servant's abortion anticipates the narrator's situation with doctor and nurse later on in **"Birth,"** except the Mouse is "trapped" and the narrator in **"Birth"** is freed. The Mohican, Pierre, and Hans all suffer from isolation and eventually become insane. The Mohican cannot distinguish "between the dream and the actuality." Pierre becomes lost in his "constant obsessional quest for the irretrievable." And Hans, too, travels in his imagination "to reach this other side of the world," never to return. The only character in *Under a Glass Bell* who is able to cross back and forth between the world of the dream and the world of actuality is Nin's autobiographical narrator in the stories of *Under a Glass Bell*. She is able to travel through despair and joy in **"Houseboat,"** the realm of the fixed past and the constantly changing present in **"Ragtime,"** and death and renewal in **"Birth."**

The structures of these three stories—fluid, open, continuing—provide a marked contrast to the forms of the other stories in the book that are often claustrophobic and shut in. (Hans in **"The Eye's Journey"** even thought that his room "was growing tighter around him, growing smaller, emptier, and the solitude would strangle him." In **"Houseboat," "Ragtime,"** and **"Birth"** there is a feeling of movement through the knot of the story and movement out of its fictional world into a new realm. This is why I like to think of the first and last stories of the work as a rather fluid frame for *Under a Glass Bell;* they are the stories in the collection that lead the reader into and out of the closed world of art under glass.

Under a Glass Bell is an important work in Nin's canon because it brings together subjective and objective points of view, closed and open forms, in various short stories for the first time in her fiction. Although she does not concentrate on *Under a Glass Bell* specifically, Evelyn Hinz sees a "canonical form" in Nin's work that moves from inner to outer vision during the course of her career. This is the general movement of *Under a Glass Bell* and the whole enterprise of Nin's writings. Although, in Nin's opinion, it is true that one cannot be objective until one knows the depths and distortions of one's own subjectivity (this is why *House of Incest* and *Winter of Artifice* were necessary books for her), with *Under a Glass Bell* Nin reaches a new plateau of self-knowledge and understanding. With this work we can see the abiding identifications and similarities that connect the autobiographical narrator with her characters—the Mouse, Jean, the Mohican, Pierre, Hans, et al.—and, more importantly, we can see the differences in her personality that will allow her to develop her full individuality as a woman in her later works, especially in the still continuing *Diary* of a still unfinished woman. (pp. 4-17)

Kent Ekberg, "The Importance of 'Under a Glass Bell'," in Under the Sign of Pisces, *Vol. 8, No. 2, Spring, 1977, pp. 4-18.*

Kent Ekberg   (essay date 1977)

[*In the following essay, Ekberg discusses* Waste of Timelessness, and Other Early Stories, *a late publication of Nin's early works that provides indications of themes she developed in later volumes.*]

In the brief "Preface" to **Waste of Timelessness, and Other Early Stories** Anais Nin explains that the stories collected in the volume were never intended to be published and that she still tends to judge these stories harshly as the work of an immature writer. But she goes on to explain that she has been persuaded that they have value "for those who understand and love my work and are interested in the progression." Nin's apprehension that her readers would be severe judges of these early stories will be unfounded; the same themes, situations, and concerns that pervade her early published works of fiction, including *House of Incest*, **Winter of Artifice,** and *Under a Glass Bell* are present here, and readers who have been pleased by these books will most certainly enjoy the new collection. In fact, the publication of **Waste of Timelessness, and Other Early Stories** is a minor historical event because this volume (along with her erotica, **Delta of Venus,** also published this year) is the first new fiction by Nin to appear in print since **Collages** (1964).

"Two elements appear here which were to be affirmed in later work: Irony and the first hints of feminism," Nin says in her "Preface." There is also the same concern with nuance of expression, the rhythm of relationship, the liberating influence of love, the confines imposed by convention, and the need to examine life deeply lived in these stories. Most of them take place in Paris and have for their principal characters writers, artists, dancers, and romantic visionary women as their heroines. The search for brilliance, exoticism, imaginative "other worlds" is also quite pronounced. Most of the stories are very short—the complete collection of sixteen numbers only 105 pages—sometimes they appear to be sketches that are not always fully developed. Although they are frequently shot through with wit and humor (something many critics have not been able to find in Nin's later fiction), there is also more of the "upholstery" that Nin was later to remove from her fiction. In contrast to Nin's other fiction, the characters in **Waste of Timelessness** often have last names (Roussel, Farinole, Breman, Harney, Lunn, Stellam, Foraine); the reader often sees them behind the scenes (getting dressed, putting on make-up, shaving); they frequently engage in conversation and extensive dialogue is used; sometimes they have dreary occupations (businessman, "Head of the Rubber Stamp Company," landlady). Nin has not yet fully learned the art of abstraction and condensation that she will use so effectively in the novels of Cities of the Interior. The young author must also struggle with the heavy burden of literary influence: [D. H.] Lawrence, and to a lesser degree [James] Joyce and the Surrealists, sometimes can be heard along with the quiet feminine voice that Anais Nin is struggling to find here.

But the tone and atmosphere of the dream—the characteristic mode of Nin's fiction—is here in these first efforts. Evidence that Nin was aware of this all along can be found in the second volume of the Diary where in August, 1936 she describes a dream she had of "spending the night in the fishing boat at the bottom of the garden." The dream occurred years before when she had visited a house that had once been occupied by [Guy de] Maupassant. The image of the boat re-occurred in Nin's dreams, her fiction, and in her life; but in *The Novel of the Future* Nin indicates that the title story of the volume *Waste of Timelessness* was the first result of the dream of the boat in the garden that she had so many years before. **"Waste of Timelessness"** is, therefore, the most important story in the volume—a seed work from which others will grow. In *House of Incest,* **Winter of Artifice, Under a Glass Bell,** *Cities of the Interior,* and *Collages* the image of the boat is again picked-up and developed as either a symbol of aimlessness and paralysis or as a symbol of freedom and flowing change.

In **"Waste of Timelessness"** Nin's attitude toward the dream of the boat seems ambivalent. The story is about a circuitous journey that is less than miraculous here. In the first part of **"Waste of Timelessness"** we are at a houseparty given by the Farinoles. The protagonist and her husband are the guests of Mr. and Mrs. Henry Farinole, the neighbors of the famous writer Alain Roussel. The protagonist seems to be more interested in Roussel than her conventional and insipid hosts. The only other item of interest at the Farinoles' is an old fishing boat that has been washed up in the garden and is now used as a tool house. The narrator finds relief from the dense atmosphere of the Farinoles' library in her thoughts of the boat in the garden and how she would like to escape in it. So in section three she does, by sleeping alone in the boat and thinking to herself:

> There must be a trip one can take and come back from changed forever. There must be many ways of beginning life anew if one has made a bad beginning. No, I do not want to begin again. I want to stay away from all I have seen so far. I know that it is no good, that I am no good, that there is a gigantic error somewhere. I am tired of trying to find a philosophy which will fit me and my world. I want to find a world which fits me and my philosophy. Certainly on this boat I could drift away from this world down some strange wise river into strange wise places.

In the morning the boat is gone, and in the afternoon her husband takes the train home to discuss business problems with his associates. Then the narrator's trip on the river is described. She meets Roussel during her journey, and he encourages her to go on. The narrator encounters her husband, but she is still bored with the mundane life on shore and continues to drift toward "something big." Again she passes Roussel's house, and it is apparent that she has travelled in a circle; now Roussel encourages her to go back to her life. When she finally does discover that there is no other world beyond the high civility of the Farinoles' garden, she instantly returns to the point from where the journey began twenty years before and concludes ambiguously: "I have been wasting a lot of time."

There are other stories in the volume that are noteworthy for their simple beauty and their similarity to works of fiction that Nin was yet to write when the stories in *Waste*

of Timelessness had already been completed. **"The Song in the Garden"** tells of a sensitive young girl who cries when she hears the melody of her mother's song. By this sign she knows that she is different from her other playmates, and she tries to find out how this difference came about. Like **"The Labyrinth"** in *Under a Glass Bell,* **"The Song in the Garden"** is a young "unborn" artist's search for self-definition. **"The Russian Who Did Not Believe In Miracles and Why"** is the story of a Montparnasse *poseur* who haunts cafes in the hopes of having others buy his drinks. Like Pierre, in **"Je Suis Le Plus Malade Des Surrealistes,"** he finds a sympatic female follower who he tries to seduce and whom he depends on for both financial and emotional sustenance. Lolita (**"The Gypsy Feeling"**), Chantal (**"The Idealist"**), and Lyndall (**"A Dangerous Perfume"**)—all unconventional women—might be thought of as the prototypes for Lillian, Djuna, and Sabina of *Cities of the Interior.* What is most noticeable about the stories of *Waste of Timelessness* is that many of them (**"The Fear of Nice," "Faithfullness,"** and **"A Slippery Floor"**) have characters who are involved in love triangles and the themes of fidelity in marriage and its alternatives are explored.

Finally, the significance of *Waste of Timelessness and Other Early Stories* will not rest with the volume's historical importance nor in the embryonic similarities it shares with Nin's more mature fiction. Nor are the autobiographical parallels between the heroines of the stories and particular aspects of Nin's own life (which readers of the *Diary* will quickly see) be of paramount importance. These are merely some critical tools for understanding the work. The significance of *Waste of Timelessness* is that it leads us into the world of art where, to quote Henry Miller on the first page of *Tropic of Cancer,* "the hero . . . is not Time, but Timelessness." This is an enduring book—and like Miller's, it is a "song," a "spot of time," a fragment from the vast stretches of eternity. (pp. 13-17)

Kent Ekberg, in a review of "Waste of Timelessness and Other Early Stories," in Under the Sign of Pisces, *Vol. 8, No. 3, Summer, 1977, pp. 12-17.*

Alice Walker on the introspective nature of Nin's works:

Anaïs's apolitical nature was self-indulgent and escapist; her analysis of poverty, struggle, and political realities, mere romantic constructions useful to very few (ghetto children, she is reported to have said, should "write" as she had done, thus escaping their wretched existence).

But throughout her life she believed in her right to record what *she* saw and what *she* felt, and to be serious enough about it to do it *exhaustively.* She made of her own mind and body a perpetually *new* frontier, enlarging our consciousness by exploring and presenting the many and varied exposures of the same Anaïs Nin. Her readers travel with less fear through those strange countries inside ourselves which she, in herself, was unafraid to explore.

Alice Walker, in her "Anais Nin: 1903—1977," Ms., April 1977.

Harriet Zinnes (essay date 1977)

[*In the following essay, Zinnes discusses Nin's use of poetic language and feminine perspective in* Delta of Venus, *a collection of erotica that represents "the first American stories to celebrate sexuality with complete and open abandon."*]

Anais Nin's famous erotica (only brief excerpts of which appeared in *Diary III*), written in the early 1940's for a private collector, have now become public under the suggestive title of **Delta of Venus.**

At first, it seemed very simple for the diarist: erotica for much needed money. Henry Miller, who discovered the book collector, the man who supposedly purchased the stories for a "friend," was the first to pull out. Erotica interfered with his more serious writing. Nin continued, became what she jokingly called "the madam of this literary, snobbish house of prostitution . . . " a "house" that included such friends as poets Harvey Breit, Robert Duncan, George Barker. Soon, however, Nin began to hate the collector who wanted her to "Concentrate on sex," and to "Leave out the poetry." At one point, Nin wrote him an angry letter, denouncing sex without love. Suddenly, however, she had an illumination: focusing "only on sensuality, we had violent explosions of poetry. Writing erotica became a road to sainthood rather than to debauchery."

What is the impact of these erotica today? Are the stories obscene? Do they divorce sex from feeling? Begun, as Nin writes in *Diary III,* "tongue-in-cheek," the stories that Nin then thought were "exaggerated" and "caricaturing sexuality" can be read as original contributions to a slowly emerging American tradition of literary erotic writing. They are, furthermore, the first American stories by a woman to celebrate sexuality with complete and open abandonment.

In a postscript to **Delta of Venus,** written in September 1976, a few months before her death, Nin noted that in the erotica she was "intuitively using a woman's language, seeing sexual experience from a woman's point of view." She had already noted in *Diary III* that the "language of sex has yet to be invented, the language of the senses has yet to be explored." Anaïs Nin became the inventor of such a language: the language in **Delta of Venus** is delicate, sinuous, precise and sensual; it is a language that is astonishing as much for its "purity," its freedom from prurience and from the usual "dirty" language of erotica written by men as for its spirited, unsqueamish sexuality. Though Nin concentrated on "sex," as her collector demanded (all the usual mandatory scenes of erotica are here: masochism, sadism, flagellation, incest, homosexuality, lesbianism, group sex, interracial sex, necrophilia, nymphomania, seduction by parents), what she emphasized in her best stories was not exploitative aggression (common to male erotica) but the pleasures of sexual surrender. The result is what Peter Michelson in his excellent book, *The Aesthetics of Pornography,* has called an "artistic or complex pornography" where a "mythos of love . . . poetically complex" is created. Even as Nin, therefore, yielded to her collector's demand to leave out

the poetry, she was still able to "concentrate on sex," and write the poem!

The characters in these stories, though occasionally caricatures, as Nin realized, are similar to the Parisian artists and Bohemians of the 1940's that appear in her other fiction. But whereas in *House of Incest,* for example, she depicts these characters in a language that is elusive and dreamlike, in her erotica she writes more directly, using language that becomes more poetic for its very precision, even for its naturalism.

Sex, as Nin describes it, is a creative human pleasure where nothing of mutual joy is "abnormal." The only abnormality, as Nin has written in a recent essay, is the "incapacity to love."

"Pleasure," therefore, is a word that occurs frequently in these stories. The young girl who lives among the ragpickers of Paris has her "pleasure" as she fantasizes on a canopied bed with a meticulous floorwalker in a department store. Leila, the lesbian, has her pleasure; the heterosexual or homosexual his; or Leila, Elena and Bijou find themselves enjoying a kind of double pleasure when as women they suddenly understand a male's desire for them. The brothel or the opium den, the studio or the Swiss chalet become *mythic* settings in **Delta of Venus,** not only for the fulfillment of love or its failure but for a quest for knowledge through the body. When the young homosexual Donald cries out because Manuel wants to take him as a woman not as a man, his humiliation is more than sexual. Elena, a central character, is symbolically woman in love, who, because of her biology, her all-over bodily hungers, is different from man seeking sexual pleasure.

Delta of Venus is a joyous display of the erotic imagination. (pp. 11, 26)

Harriet Zinnes, "Collector's Item," in *The New York Times Book Review, July 10, 1977, pp. 11, 26.*

Sharon Spencer (essay date 1977)

[*Spencer is an American novelist, short story writer, critic, and educator. In the following excerpt from her critical study* Collage of Dreams: The Writings of Anaïs Nin, *she discusses the themes of motion and dreams as they are illustrated in the story "The Voice."*]

The position of the dream at the center of Nin's art may be wonderfully illustrated by looking at one of her most brilliant pieces, **"The Voice."** Here the dream is truly a vehicle of mobility. **"The Voice"** is a virtuoso piece that spins off from contrasting motions: soaring, plummeting, floating, sinking, spiraling, rushing, or flowing, along a horizontal or lying quietly on a bed to daydream. This thoughtful work is neither a story nor a sketch, but an animated essay or exposition of ideas through a seemingly random selection of characters and incidents. The center is a psychoanalyst's office located in a skyscraper (suggestive of the Empire State Building or one of the structures at Rockefeller Center). Most of the characters are presented to the reader through the compassionate vision of Djuna, who analyzes the analyst himself, The Voice. Tortured New Yorkers all, The Voice's patients include, besides Djuna herself: a young violinist who wishes to be released from her lesbianism; Mischa, a cellist whose childhood experiences have paralyzed his emotions; Lilith, who suffers from frigidity; The Voice himself who, appealingly, falls in love with Lilith, the only one of his patients who can see beyond her own needs to the hungers of the man whose voice is so comforting to the others. As in later works, Djuna plays the role of confidante to both parties in this unwise and ultimately impossible dream of romantic love between analyst and patient.

The portraits of the patients and their progress with The Voice are enclosed or framed by opening and closing meditations that unite the concept of motion with the idea of the dream. Like *Collages,* "The Voice" is composed of many short sections; there are fifteen. The first and second comprise Djuna's meditations on movement and growth, while the third, fourth, and fifth depict The Voice working with his patients. In the sixth the focus is returned to Djuna, who after an initial ascent to the top of the building now finds herself in an underground drugstore with others whom the city has "swallowed." A more terrifying descent still is reported: the suicide of a woman pregnant with a five-month child but without anyone to love her. The seventh, eighth, and ninth episodes are concerned with Lilith's overly intense relationship with her brother (another appearance of the incest theme in Nin's work) and her immature dream that love for The Voice may free her from this past entanglement. The tenth passage is again Djuna's. It is a rhapsody, a vision of identification with the moon which since time immemorial has been thought to control the cyclic life of woman through her physiology. "Djuna was one with the moon, thrusting hands made of roots into the storm, while her heart beat like a drum through the orgy of the moonstorm." By contrast, Lilith still struggles, suffering from a headache, finding that "the seed would not burst; the body left the earth, pulled upward by a string of nerves and spilled its pollen only in space . . . " Lilith cannot release herself into storms of emotion as Djuna has done in her vision.

The twelfth and thirteenth portions of **"The Voice"** explore Lilith's frigidity and her sorrow. Like other characters to follow, Lilith seeks refuge in Djuna. Between women there is not the tension of polarity that troubles relationships between men and women, the more so as they are individuals burdened with emotional problems. Lilith understands, finally, that it is self-defeating to be in love with The Voice. Knowing that she must free herself from him as a doctor, for this is part of her treatment, Lilith has fantasized a love for the healer as a man, imagining that this would enable her to hold onto him. "But when he was not being the doctor, she discovered, he was not a man but a child." Growth means discarding illusions about others as well as reaching for independence. Lilith accepts the fact that "neither her powers of illusion nor her dreams had worked the miracle. He remained nothing but A VOICE." In this relationship Nin has traced the well-known process of transference, but the sensitivity, the fineness of perception, and gentle humor with which she has

done it altogether transform the clinical situation into a skillfully fictionalized one. She has made the parties to a therapeutic relationship sympathetic, vulnerable human beings.

Though there are references in **"The Voice"** to the identification of the dream with flowing motion, this piece emphasizes the contrasting rhythms of rising and falling, or ascending and descending. In the Hotel Chaotica, Djuna envisions "hysteria and darkness, wells, prisons, tombs." "Lying down in a cell-shaped room," she imagines the rapid movements of the elevators whose passengers are trapped between the top and bottom floors of the hotel. "The people riding up and down the elevators are never permitted to crash through the last ceiling into pure space and never allowed to pierce through the ground floor to enter the demonic regions below the crust of the earth." They are trapped in the reality of the hotel, a mundane reality that reaches neither toward the heavens nor toward the lower infernal regions. Djuna alone is able to navigate these regions through the forceful propulsion of her imagination.

Counterpointed against the constant rising and falling of the elevator is the horizontal rush of pedestrians along New York's crowded streets. After each patient leaves the analyst, he experiences a charge of liberation, a great release that enables him to do or to feel something that was formerly impossible because of the inhibitions of neurosis. Djuna, for example, has been fighting a desire to remain

Anais Nin with her diary.

still, to refuse motion and change, but "suddenly she began walking faster than whoever was walking beside her, to feel the exultation of passing them. The one who does not move feels abandoned, and the one who loves and weeps and yields feels he is living so fast the debris cannot catch up with him." The young woman violinist drops to the sidewalk to pray. Mischa is flooded with warmth and fire that cause him to burst out in song. Lilith comes upon a rare sense of harmony: "She was breathing with the day, moving with the wind, in accord with it, with the sky, undulating like water, flowing and stirring to the life about her, opening like the night."

These moments of spontaneous expression balance the terrifying descent that occurs near the middle of **"The Voice,"** the suicide of the pregnant woman who jumps from the roof of the hotel. Perhaps she could have saved herself if she had allowed her dreams to carry her beyond this roof, or ceiling, in transcendence. Immediately after the dull thud of her falling body there is a renewal of motion and activity. Since the characters in **"The Voice"** are patients in analysis, the woman's suicide is especially ominous. To reassure themselves they immediately begin to move in countermotion horizontally. "One must get dizzy. One must move. Move." This theme is underscored when Lilith goes to the harbor to meet her brother whom she has not seen since childhood. Their meeting draws her back into the past toward an encounter with the origin of her neurosis. She and her brother are said to "sail inside the static sea of their fantasies." Neurosis is a fixation on some person or situation from the past. The cure is to step inside the dream, allowing it to carry one downward toward self-discovery or upward toward release, exhilaration, toward the freedom of soaring into space. But this rising and falling motion must be balanced with the horizontal stream or flow of life in which one lets oneself be carried along with others, mixing with them, taking part in the communal as well as in the private and purely personal life. (pp. 58-61)

Sharon Spencer, in her Collage of Dreams: The Writings of Anaïs Nin, *The Swallow Press Inc., 1977, 188 p.*

Bettina L. Knapp   (essay date 1978)

[*Knapp is an American critic, educator, and biographer. The following excerpt from her critical study* Anaïs Nin *discusses "Winter of Artifice" and "The Voice," as antinovelettes that explore such themes as the past, fragmentation of the self, father-daughter relationships, and dreams.*]

"Winter of Artifice" and **"The Voice"** do not adhere to the conventional techniques of the short novel and its structured characters and linear plots. As antinovelettes, they feature clusters of pastiches with little or no story line and no progressive character delineations. Nin uses the literary devices of repetitions, omissions, ellipses, dream sequences, and stream-of-consciousness insertions that interrupt the free-flowing atmosphere, jarring the reader into a new state of awareness and plunging him into the penumbral void. Juxtapositions of images occur and recur

with differing nuances, and like painful and joyous litanies that distort the atmosphere, they heighten tension and pave the way for what have been called nonverbal zones: wordless images articulated via musical tonalities and associations.

"Winter of Artifice" is the story of Djuna, who idolizes her father. She has not seen him for twenty years and, as the story opens, awaits his visit. Valescure in the South of France is the idyllic setting for their meeting. In her father's company she experiences a range of emotions: from ecstasy, when she looks upon herself as her father's "mystical bride," to depression, when she realizes that her Prince Charming father is an illusion, a figment of her imagination. In reality her father is a superficial, luxury-loving, and rigid man who lives for externals only. The love they feel for one another, Djuna now understands, is narcissistic; each projects aspects of himself or herself onto the other. Their stultifying passions are expressed in circular imagery and in musical tonalities. Djuna soon grows aware of the dichotomy existing between her father's outer countenance and the weakly structured inner man, and concomitantly she realizes the schism existing within her own psyche. Important too is her growing understanding of the fact that her father is as much her creation as she is his. The illusion she has been harboring concerning her father's "perfectibility" vanishes and she sees him for what he is. When she leaves Valescure, she is no longer bound to her father, but has grown detached. "Today she held the coat of a dead love."

In **"The Voice,"** Djuna is a lay analyst residing at the Hotel Chaotica in New York. The Voice, whom she consults to heal the breach within her, is a psychoanalyst. He tells her that her detachment, aloofness, and introversion prevent her from participating in life. Case histories are related in the narrative about a lesbian violinist corroded with guilt; about a cellist, Mischa, whose hand is paralyzed and foot crippled; and about a sensual *femme fatale*, Lilith, who is not in love with her husband. Each patient is a facet of Djuna's personality, incarnated, vibrant, weighty. As Djuna's understanding of the roles she is portraying increases, she becomes less and less dependent on the Voice, a kind of father confessor, healer, shaman, and priest image. He, on the other hand, yearns to be accepted by her not merely as a spiritual guide but as a man as well; consequently he loses his authority over Djuna. The volume concludes with a dream Djuna has: she attempts to push a landlocked boat back into the sea.

In both **"Winter of Artifice"** and **"The Voice,"** dream and reverie and the stream-of-consciousness technique are fused, no longer with the surrealistic spontaneity and automatism as in *House of Incest,* but rather in the style of Virginia Woolf and James Joyce. The question now is not merely how to enter the protagonists' unconscious and create another inner dimension and logic; the question is now how to use the discerning power of the artist as an instrument capable of sorting out the flow of emerging images and sensations and of sifting and cutting and polishing them in order to create a finished work of art.

Also important here is Nin's preoccupation with the space/time continuum. In the manner of Proust she examines the conflicts that emerge from her struggle between linear and cyclical time schemes as well as between subject and object. Like Proust also, acting as the demiurge throughout, she includes in her antinovelettes hypnopompic and hypnagogic dream sequences that further break up the narration, disrupt the protagonists' dialogues and moods, and uproot their dependency on other individuals and their identifications.

Stylistically speaking, Nin's prose is straightforward. "Conscious order. Excision of irrelevant details" is necessary, she wrote in her *Diary.* Her eidetic imagery is condensed, decanted, and bone hard: "I hate stuffing." What remains is the Giacometti-like statue, the "pure essence of the personality . . . the deepest self."

. . . . .

> The dream taught me not only the delight of sensory images, but the fact, far more vital, that they led directly into this realm of the unconscious which Joyce, Woolf, Proust attained in various ways—Joyce by free association with words, play on words, Proust by trusting the free associative process of memory and staying lingeringly in the realm between sleep and waking which resembles the waking dream, Virginia Woolf by accepting the vision of the poet as reality.

Like Woolf, Nin used poetic and symbolic means to penetrate the inner being, to evoke mood, and to arouse sensations of pain, joy, of love. Both women drew almost exclusively from their own experiences to create the substance for their novels and antinovelettes. Woolf's childhood delineates for the most part the intellectual and leisured upper-middle class. Her descriptions of these people are ambiguous and impressionistic, and her characters are never whole; rather, they live through the actions and reactions of others. The same is true of the characters in **"Winter of Artifice"** and **"The Voice."** Djuna and her father merge and separate as entities, each projecting on the other, each concretizing his or her illusions, phantasmagoria, tensions, and inhibitions. The philosopher George Berkeley suggested "to be perceived is to be." Such a view could be applied to the creatures of Woolf and Nin. Djuna's Don Juan father, with his stiff, unbending outer image and strong, virile countenance, existed for Djuna as an incarnated abstraction throughout her childhood and adolescence. In **"The Voice,"** though disembodied for the most part, her father is equally present, haunting, absorbing, and wistful.

Woolf was said to have used the Pointillist technique in *The Waves,* which enabled her to add another dimension to her peceptions: a *niveau océanique.* She explored the unknown through clusters of dots. Impressions thus became a conglomerate of separate identities, individual sensations, atomized feelings that took on objective reality when gathered into a cohesive whole. Like Seurat in his painting *La grande jatte,* where masses of intensely colored dots were set out like impersonal "building blocks" in the construction of a unified picture, Nin built up her characters in a series of mobile atoms. Her father, as opposed to the Voice, and Djuna, as contrasted to Lilith,

were single entities, disparate forces molded together in an integrated and rigorously planned harmony of personalities. Each was a blending of many clusters of particles, like figures and objects featured in the Pointillist paintings of Seurat, Pissarro, and Signac.

The stream-of-consciousness technique is used to convey each character's psychic life and allows for the presentation of thoughts, impressions, and feelings on a pre-verbal level, the author remaining aloof, not commending or judging the actions. Woolf used the stream-of-consciousness technique to articulate an entire chemistry of impressions and sensations, from the acidulous to the melliflous. In **"Winter of Artifice"** and **"The Voice"** father and daughter, as well as psychoanalyst and patient, present their fluid and shifting feelings and reactions in free association, symbol motifs, repetition of words, and rhythmic devices. Facts and situations are not as significant as are the notions of *becoming,* of creation, and the flux of being. By using the stream-of-consciousness technique, Nin gives the reader the impression of experiencing two worlds concomitantly: linear time in the conscious frame of reference and the cyclical time scheme as the unconscious pursues its lucid course. The protagonists—as well as the reader—know that time is passing, that moods and feelings must be apprehended instantly if life in all of its fullness is to emerge. Important too is the complex set of relationships that comes into being when using the stream-of-consciousness technique: the past, present, and future of each of the protagonists is fluid and as such flows into an eternal time scheme. Characters are presented as sharply delineated impressions that then become reflected and refracted, thus interacting upon one another; each penetrating the other's world, diffused, disparate; each a luminosity with its own aerial transparency, its own earthly yearnings.

Neither Woolf's nor Nin's protagonists are active in the sense that they seek exterior adventure like Sterne's Tristram Shandy does or Fielding's Tom Jones. Woolf and Nin prefer introverted beings who probe, think, meditate, reflect. Their characters use interior monologues to convey their visions in ordered sequences; that is, they use their own logic, which may set up mysterious resonances and correspondences in the reader. In Woolf's *To the Lighthouse,* the warmth of the protagonists as they indulge in their human relations is achieved through the repetition of a phrase that resonates like a refrain throughout the work, each time pointing up the tenderness and delicacy of the mood. The same may be said of **"Winter of Artifice"** and **"The Voice"**; for example, the words "mask," "rhythm," "time," and "circular" are repeated in many different ways, each time underscoring the artificiality, the hypocrisy, the struggle involved. The mystery of mood and of beings is incubated and its secrets revealed in droplets, particles, aromas, liquid experiences, a blend of visual and sensual motifs.

Joyce used the stream-of-consciousness technique and free association in depicting the thoughts and feelings of his characters. Rather than recounting linear events, which he considered artificial and unlike life, he follows his characters' unconscious yearnings and emotions, allowing some to reveal their multiple points of view and conflicts. In *Ulysses,* Molly Bloom expresses her thoughts helter-skelter at night when serene after having made love. The unconscious flow of memories and reveries that emerges portrays her better and more realistically than any kind of expressionistic description. She takes on life: an undifferentiated woman who lives on an instinctual dimension where tactile forces predominate and sensuality reigns supreme. Similarly, Nin allows Djuna to speak out from subliminal spheres, either in a state of repose or in a frenzied state of anguish, and each time emotions bubble forth uninhibited and uninterrupted until the power energizing her articulations slackens. Every time Djuna allows free association or stream-of-consciousness to take hold, the reader is better able to understand her torment and her feelings of incarceration or paralysis.

Proust's influence on Nin was as significant as Woolf's and Joyce's, perhaps more so with regard to the concept of time. **"Winter of Artifice,"** Nin wrote, "was a struggle with shadows," that is, a fight against time, its shifting relationships, its harmonizations and discords. In both of Nin's antinovelettes the protagonists recapture and relive ideal relationships that existed only in their fantasy worlds—in imagined Edenic periods. Proust's intent was, of course, different. He resurrected a past he had loved and without which he could no longer live. In *Remembrance of Things Past* he tried to restore a period when he had been the focal point of his mother's life. Until her death, Proust had known only perfect maternal love: a doting mother who hovered over her son's needs and desires, who tried to alleviate the severity of his asthmatic attacks, but who might have been unwittingly their cause. When she died, Proust wrote (at the age of 34), "She takes my life away with her."

Unlike Proust's past, Djuna's was not wonderful. Yet, in her mind's eye, there were moments of ecstasy during those early years when she and her family traveled together from one exciting experience to another: concerts, hotels, fame, fortune, luxury, parties. There were other moments, however, and these grew more prolonged, when recriminations, insults, anger, and war invaded the household. Also her father denigrated her intellectually and physically. She felt shattered. Djuna did not want to recreate the past; she wanted to create one.

The past, Henri Bergson once said, lives in every individual, conserved in its every detail, such as feelings, thoughts, longings. Frequently, the individual may be unaware of the storehouse of treasures that lives within him, which Bergson called "captured duration." Proust used Bergson's concepts of time and space as a literary device that he related to memory. Memory is divided into two categories: voluntary and involuntary. Voluntary memory when associated with time, destroys everything in the world including civilizations. Man is powerless to stop the present from transforming itself into the past and the future into the present. When the subject, who is no longer young, returns to his childhood home, he finds that everything has changed. People erode as do material objects; they age, disintegrate, and die—and so do feelings of love and hate. Relationships are not static entities. A person may be viewed in one way at one point in life, and in another way years later. The "I" is always shifting; soul states alter; needs and interests transform. (pp. 69-75)

In her own way Nin . . . recaptured segments of the past in **"Winter of Artifice"** and in **"The Voice."** Simultaneity of sensations enabled her to re-create an atmosphere and a mood she had experienced twenty years previously, in a hotel room at Valescure, when her father's cold and arrogant air dazzled and terrified her. Nin's analysts also helped her bring up her past, which she incarnated in the various protagonists that filled the Hotel Chaotica. In **"The Voice"** it is the "friction of the words" that arouses Djuna's involuntary memory sequences, bringing turmoil and pain, mystery and yearning. Like her mentor Proust, Nin captured secret relationships through subtle metaphors or through suggestion, revealing all the while hidden analogies, clusters of intuitions, and conduits leading to various levels of existence. And like Proust, Nin not only experienced the feelings resurrected but also analyzed, dissected, and objectified them in turn, as though observing specimens through a microscope—generating and regenerating creatures in an endless death-rebirth ritual.

. . . . .

Although the patriarchal world order dominates in **"Winter of Artifice,"** as it does in *House of Incest,* a new note is sounded: Djuna is not helpless and passive. She is aware of her fantasies and illusions, the world she has created, and seeks a new orientation. But first she must be certain of the existing state of affairs. She must experience her father's presence again, his world, as an adult. Only then will she be able to understand the distorted picture of her father she bears within her since childhood.

The symbol used to depict the narrator's soul states—her progressive detachment from her father and the creation of her own destiny—is encapsulated in an image delineated at the outset of **"Winter of Artifice;"** the bowl and the glass fish within, which may have been inspired by Matisse's series of paintings of goldfish in a bowl (1915). "This glass bowl with the glass fish and the glass ship—it has been the sea for her and the ship which carries her away from him after he had abandoned her."

Nin was playing with an optical illusion; goldfish in water, and particularly when made of glass, reflect and refract light, and thus twist the objects out of shape. The curved bowl further distorts the original image of the fish within. Forms, then, although distinct, become misshapen; although clear, become blurred.

Such are Djuna's sensations when seeing her father after many years of absence. The fishbowl contains its objects: they are incarcerated, yet protected from breakage or other malevolent forces; that the fish are of glass indicates their hardness and brittleness as well as their immobility. Although glass is transparent, it acts as a separation: the fine wall existing between father and daughter, between outer and inner worlds. Djuna at times experiences her father as a glass object—an unbending and brittle entity. For this reason, perhaps, she can see through him and perceive him in a variety of poses, circumstances, moods, and reflections. "People were made of crystal for her. She could see right through their flesh, through and beyond the structure of their bones."

Fish represent psychic life, nourishment, and a potential world. Pisces, the last sign of the zodiac before rebirth, symbolizes the world of the spirit existing beyond the world of appearances. Fish and ships flow through waters and have been associated in this regard with mystic entities: "ship of life," or the Egyptian sun god's "night sea journey," which is undertaken in a boat.

During the confrontation with her father, Djuna on one occasion leans backward and inadvertently pushes "the crystal bowl against the wall." It cracked and the "water gushed forth as from a fountain, spilling all over the floor." Disruption and disorientation. A breakage has taken place. "The glass ship could no longer sail away—it was lying on its side, on the rock-crystal stones." The narrator bemoans the fact that the fish-ship (now the image is fused) cannot budge: the ship lies on its side, dying for lack of water, starving for nutrients. What Djuna does not know yet is that the fish heretofore enclosed in the bowl are also dying, unable to flow or float—unable to shape events, to function in life, to orient destiny.

The shattered bowl is a step forward and can be looked upon as a step in Djuna's evolution. Her energy is no longer imprisoned in the glass bowl. It has been shattered and scattered. Should another image not be forthcoming, however, such a dispersion of being and evaporation of water and spirit could lead to death.

Glass, as we have seen, acts as a division, a compartmentalization of inner and outer personalities. Djuna's father has a dual personality: his persona, or mask, functions as a mediating complex and is visible in company, during concert tours, or when he wants to seduce women. By donning the mask he effects a compromise personality that enables him to mediate between himself (the individual) and the society (collective) whose admiration he needs. The mask allows him to stand above others, particularly above members of his family. But with the mask he rejects the individual world in favor of the collective. It strengthens the breach between the outer and inner man. His persona, with which his ego identifies at times, leads to a state of inflation. Imbued with self-admiration, he speaks on occasion in lofty tones with pride at being the great concert virtuoso and the handsome, elegant Don Juan. "When he was not smiling, his face was a Greek mask, his blue eyes enigmatic, the features sharp and wilful." At other times, his weak inner self protrudes. His self-esteem deflated, he complains and indulges in self-pity. Arriving at the hotel with Djuna, for instance, he complains of excruciating pain. "He was cursing his lumbago." He can hardly move; yet he will not allow his daughter to help him unpack his valise. He wants no intimacy; people must be kept at a distance so he can hide the weakly structured Don Juan he really is. There he is in all his glory—unable to bend or stand, looking grotesque, ridiculous, pusillanimous.

The man behind the mask is constantly struggling with his outer self. This conflict is manifested in various ways: his obsessive cleanliness, his orderliness, the rigidity of his attitudes. "His clothes were never wrinkled, he wore clean linen every day and his fur collar on his coat was wonderful to caress. He was always immaculate, elegant, sweet smelling, strong, handsome." The inner man is fearful, timid, almost feminine—a pitiful aging Don Juan. Because of his inability to adapt to society—to reveal himself as he is instead of hiding behind his persona—he is a solitary figure divested of everything that is real, alive, and moving. He opts for an imaginary and abstract realm: a fantasy world he has created. What remains behind the impenetrable mask is a feeble and unrelated being.

Djuna's father never analyzes himself and never attempts to know himself. He functions as an automaton hiding behind his mask. For Djuna, at times he is cold and unreachable, a remote figure who has refused to acknowledge her as an individual and considers her only as a love object or as someone from whom he seeks to escape. "His face wore a mask. The skin did not match the skin of his wrists," Djuna notes as she begins to see her father more objectively. Neither guilt nor self-hate plague him. His centroversion is such that nothing matters except the gratification of his desires.

Djuna begins to notice the severe split that exists within him: the outer being that tries to live up to the image people have created of him, and the inner being that is flabby, weak, effeminate. The greater the breach between the inner and outer man and the more emotional and quixotic his behavior becomes, the more tragic a figure he is. Djuna has experienced him in many of his roles. When she was a child, he represented perfection, but he could also be insulting, belittling, or terrifying. The only time calm existed was when guests arrived. Then the persona dominated. Djuna experienced her father as a destructive force: a negative god image with mythological ramifications.

> Her father was standing behind a window, watching. There was never a smile on his face except when there were visitors, except when there was music and talk. When they were alone in the house there was always war: great explosions of anger, hatred, revolt. War. . . . A life rippled with dissension.
>
> Her father's eyes were always cold, critical, unbelieving. Because he was so critical, so severe, so suspicious of her, she became secretive and lying. . . .

On the other hand, he was also a positive god figure. "Her true God was her father. At communion it was her father she received, and not God."

The father-daughter identification is close. Each projects contents of his unconscious onto the other. He becomes an extension of her personality and she of his. She is his anima figure (inner woman), and he her animus (inner man). In both cases the attitudes are unconscious; images encapsulate characteristics the conscious attitude lacks. Proust once suggested that love is a projection; what is of import, however, is the depth of such a projection.

At the outset of **"Winter of Artifice,"** Djuna lives in a state of virtual identification with her father, as the initial image of the fishbowl indicates. She is imprisoned in her father's vision of her and hers of him. But as long as she experiences her father as a judge or critic whose persistent eye observes her every action, she will not be free to live her own life. "It was as if behind her there stood a judge, a tall judge he alone could see, and to this judge her father addressed a beautiful polished speech. . . . " At other moments, the animus offers her delight. "But she was so happy to have found a father, a father with a strong will, a wisdom, an infallible judgment, that she forgot for the moment everything she knew, surrendered her own certainties." To have a father who is seer and God answers, at least for the moment, her needs. Yet, when functioning in the real world, she realizes that his overly critical demeanor hounds her (his voice constantly reverberates in her ear drum), cuts her off from her own feminine nature, and shatters her—symbolized in the fishbowl image.

As long as Djuna does not create some kind of connection or real relationship with a positive animus figure, she will not be able to experience an authentic rapport with a man. When feeling harassed or defeated, she would escape; if surfeited with attention, she would grow bored; reviled by a man, she would feel ugly and lacking in harmony. She would blame herself for being unable to fulfill her role as woman. The animus acts upon her like a *daemon.*

In time Djuna begins to evaluate her situation. She sees other aspects of her father that allow her to wrench herself away from him. The identification or *participation mystique,* that made of her a dependent nature, is now being severed. When, for example, her father reads her diary and discovers that she has had a life of her own and made friends of her own and has not spent twenty years mourning a father who deserted the family, his jealousy and anger are aroused. He feels Djuna is leaving him as other women in his life, including his second wife, have left him. The aging Don Juan that becomes visible is to her pitiful, and she does not see herself any more as the "mystical bride of her father" or as floating about blindly in the nebulous area between illusion and reality.

Beneath the handsome countenance, the romantic and glittering concert pianist who played in every capital in Europe before captivated audiences, another individual is exposed: a man in the prime of life, who has not yet awakened to the realities of the world. Because he cannot understand or face himself, he is unable to develop a higher consciousness and is caught off balance by Djuna. Not able to accept his limitations, he is given to outbursts of rage in situations with which he cannot cope. The overly immaculate and rigid man is his own antagonist, his own destroyer.

Djuna's awakening ego causes her to begin paying attention to her own needs and desires, to fulfill herself and not live any more as a reflection or projection. Thus she finds it unnecessary to play the role she had thought would please her father and which he expects of her.

The musical image interwoven into the narrative at this juncture in a stream-of-consciousness sequence acts as a conclusion to the first step of Djuna's separation process. To choose music as a demarcation line indicates that music, and the feeling associated with it, is the vehicle re-quired to pass onto another stage of Djuna's development. Her father tells her that, just as music remains indefinable and amorphous, so the women in his life are "incognito." When he thinks about his women, he says, "it comes out a *do* or a *la,* and who could recognize them in a sonata?" It is this inability to see women as individuals that prevents him from coming to terms with them or with himself. Interesting in this work is the fact that a musician makes analogies in a way similar to alchemists, who associate metals with planets and personalities. *Fa, do, sol* are considered masculine elements and associated with fire and air; *la, mi, ti* are feminine and pertain to water and earth. It is significant, then, that the father explains, "it comes out a do or a *la,*" which indicates an unconscious yearning to perform a marriage between opposites—that is, between fire and air (symbolized by *do*) and earth and water (symbolized by *la*). This points up the feminine and masculine components within his personality: the inner and outer man, or strength and weakness.

For Nin, as well as Proust, musical tones had a literary equivalent. As emotions can be articulated and translated into another language, so melody can be formulated into the word. Proust used to go to the Salle Pleyel in Paris and listen to Beethoven quartets; or he would ask his friend Reynaldo Hahn to play and sing for him; and sometimes he hired musicians to come to his house. Proust felt it was not sufficient to convey sensations through analogy; they had to be materialized and explicated for the reader. Like Plato's "Allegory of the Cave," music may be looked upon as a series of constructs, clusters of shadows, and resonances that the composer intuits, interprets, and then recaptures in fleeting tones and shifting rhythms. Art preserves the sense experience.

For both Nin and Proust, music represents an emotional involvement. They each associate melodies, harmonies, and rhythms with some situation, relationship, or feeling. Djuna experiences an orchestrated interlude with her father, "as if they were listening to music . . . inside both their heads . . . there was a concert going on." The image is grandiose: an orchestra composed of a hundred instruments. The violin is singled out for scrutiny and compared to nerves: "and she passing the violin bow gently between her legs; drawing music out of her body. . . . " For Djuna, the violin represents the heart: gentle, tender, and suffering. Other instruments express the personalities of father and daughter: the vibrating drums with their rhythms, tone, timbre, and serial patterns incorporate the syncopated beats of the soul, the mystical correspondences between the individual and the universe at large. Pythagorean "music of the spheres," dependent upon meter and number, also represents a melodic hierarchy of emotions. The high-pitched tones of the violin represent a leap of anguish; the brass, strings, and timpani express in loud and subdued vibrations the moods of repose and terror.

Music has been called "the science of modulations." In many civilizations, during traumatic periods, music is used as a mediating force between God and man. When Orpheus played his harmonies, he hypnotized his listeners (inanimate as well as animate) into submission. Djuna, a disciple of Orpheus, sought out her master's way: she drank from the waters of Mnemosyne (memory) in the underworld, or inner world; not from the waters of Lethe, which lead to forgetfulness. In the land of memory she is able to conjure up a past that helps her distinguish truth from fiction and so pass onto the next stage of her development. "No music could come from the orchestra" when her father conducted it, she now realizes. He was too rigid, submerged in detail and structure—in outer, not inner tonalities.

The glass bowl and the musical interlude enable Djuna to understand and successfully pass to the third step of her growth process. As she and her father are driving south, he takes off his shoe because it is too tight. When he

> pulled off his sock she saw the foot of a woman. It was delicate and perfectly made, sensitive and small. She felt as if he had stolen it from her: it was her foot she was looking at, her foot he was holding in his hand. She had the feeling that she knew this foot completely. It was her foot—the very same size and the very same color, the same blue veins showing and the same air of never having walked at all.

The foot is a catalyst. It forces her to regress. She looks upon it as hers, a double. The identification is so great that she loses all ability to differentiate. What is hers? Her self-estrangement is apparent, her facelessness disconcerting. Father and daughter are now pathologically linked. Had such a condition continued, Djuna would never have been born into womanhood. Her task, she knows, is to dissociate herself from her father. That the foot should be the instrument to effect such a severing is significant. Feet represent one's relationship with the earth principle: the foot contacts the earth physically. It is at opposite poles with the head, spirit, and soul. Yet, it is linked to the so-called higher being. One without the other cannot function harmoniously. The foot is also a phallic symbol, and the removal of the shoe a feminine element. Thus is the mask removed from both father and daughter.

Djuna singles out the foot for observation because she is ready to step out of her old existence as her father's reflection and appendage. She is beginning to adapt—naked—to the world at large. No mask is necessary. Certainly her father has wronged her by his egotism and negativity. But the daughter likewise prolonged this infantile and unfortunate rapport. She could not yet extricate herself from her dependency on the patriarchal image. At times she attempts to be what she thinks he wanted her to be: beautiful, charming, delectable—an anima figure. At other times, she rebels. She resents not being herself and is determined to cast him off. Like the shoe, he cramped her style, restricted her movement, the pain became unbearable.

At the conclusion of **"Winter of Artifice,"** Djuna "held the coat of a dead love" before her and the nightmare as she has known it is over. She refuses to be the little girl, the cripple suffering from remorse and guilt. She seeks to transform herself into a mature woman. As such, she does not need a father. The patriarchal society she has experienced, with its negative father image, could not help her find fulfillment.

. . . . .

Just as the bowl of goldfish contains the germ of **"Winter of Artifice,"** so the early image of Djuna lying in her "cell-shaped room" in the Hotel Chaotica reveals the underlying themes of **"The Voice."** The Hotel Chaotica, like the fishbowl, is a microcosm. It is filled with living beings that struggle, love, and hate in an attempt to keep alive amid insurmountable difficulties. Because the action takes place in New York, Nin chose to dramatize the events in *crescendo* and at a *prestissimo* pace. The condition created by people disgorging from the elevators, messengers rushing about, telegrams and mail being delivered, and phones ringing is one of turmoil and disquietude. The rhythms and cacophonies are high-powered, frenetic, and act like clusters of catalysts.

At first the Voice, which is the psychoanalyst, is disembodied. Djuna therefore is no longer talking with her flesh-and-blood father but rather with a sublimated, spiritual being—a collective figure, healer, shaman—who is helping Djuna to "be born again." His method requires regression. He wants Djuna to turn back to her childhood so that through her talk he will be able to pinpoint her trauma and understand the split corroding her psyche. "I want to reconcile you to yourself," he says.

As in the case of spiritual figures such as oracles, deities, and heroes in ancient times, the Voice emerges from a cavelike, or cell-like, area clothed in darkness. The containing factor of the room gives Djuna a feeling of protection and security resembling the warm and understanding uterine inner world. She begins to feel at ease. Far from the crowd and the masks she has to don, removed from the lies of life's experience and the hurt that has caused her such pain, Djuna is able to withdraw into herself and experience her "dark night of the soul"—her Orphic descent. Within these quiet inner recesses she listens to the Voice and experiences the patriarchal force as a saving spirit, a kind of God, as in the Gospel of St. John (1): "In the beginning was the Word, and the Word was with God, and the Word was God." The Voice is her God, an impersonal force and a positive spirit that brings her torment, to be sure, but also innundates her world with energy sufficiently powerful to disentangle the knots that paralyze her existence. Like the mystic, she reaches out to the Voice in articulate terms and expresses her moments of ecstatic joy in a past that surges forth to become a present reality. Past and present weave their way throughout the narrative in syncopated rhythms and energetic patterns, clearing and cleansing an encumbered existence.

The visual image is that of a series of instantaneous snapshots. Emotions and sensations are caught and fixed in a unique instant, each harboring secret selves, each revealing countless treasures and arcana. Djuna still shuns the outside world. She seeks to remain in the darkness of her cell-like room of the hotel that is an integrated image of her baroque inner world. Like an animal that has been maligned and hurt throughout life, she slinks into her introspective world. The Voice seeks her out and assuages her pain. He commands her to look outward to the stream of people in the hall and into the world beyond the hotel.

As in Samuel Beckett's play *Not I,* which features a mouth as a protagonist, so the Voice narrates his diagnosis: Djuna does not participate in life; she stands still and has cut herself off from the mainstream. Djuna remonstrates. She observes the outside world, the stream of people being "carried away," not one master of his or her destiny. Chance, automatism, flux. Obsessed with the fleeting nature of time, she comments, people are like "debris." Destruction is implicit in the human as well as in the organic object. Djuna has not yet adapted to life, nor has she been transformed by it. Time is experienced as eschatological, not as a cyclical force; therefore clock time pervades. She feels the fleeting nature of past, present, and future; anguish pervades her being: her fear of getting old, of dying without having made one's imprint on the world. She articulates her mistakes, pains, and suffering in a series of fragmented phrases that float about in contradictory and antithetical images as elements in space. Each phrase when uttered seems to be caught up in another network of abrasive, searing visualizations. Time is experienced as destructive. It is as devisive a force as Djuna herself. Each aspect of her personality tears at the other; nothing works in harmony. Djuna knows only temporal consciousness but not the feeling of eternity. Her life is as cut up as time divided into seconds, minutes, days, weeks, months, years.

Along with her emotional fragmentation as envisaged through time, Djuna is bombarded by rhythms and floating forms that invade her cell-shaped room. She finally takes the Voice's advice and forces her way out of her room into the street and thus into collective existence. A reduction of distance between herself and the world at large takes place—a confrontation. She feels compelled to deal with reality now that she is beyond the safety of her walled room and hotel. She must fight for survival: "moving, moving. Flowing, flowing, flowing." The repetition of words and phrases is caught up in a network of fleeting images. Djuna remains powerless and immovable, as if experiencing a nonverbal zone: wordless visualizations are reproduced as if in a dream. Contrapuntal beats intrude and project themselves onto objects around her, radiating outward into some distant area, some future time-space continuum. Music interweaves its tonalities into the instant, resuscitates past moods. "No days without music. She is like an instrument so tuned up, so exacerbated, that without hands, without players, without leadership, it responds, it breathes, it omits the continuous melody of sensibility. Never knew silence."

Speed increases, dilates, and intensifies. As in a Futurist painting, Djuna portrays her inner dynamism in successive stages of motion and emotion, movement and life. Like the canvases of Severini and Boccioni, which suggest motion by cutting up heretofore single forms, so Djuna attempts to cope with her feelings of frustration by an inner dismemberment. Then, as she examines each aspect of her inner being, she projects frequently on the world outside of herself; she fuses with the beings on the crowded and cluttered street, with the machines speeding by; with objects of all types. Like a sculpture, she becomes a prolongation of space. She feels energized and transformed by the speeding forces at work. As in Marcel Duchamp's painting *Nude Descending a Staircase,* she experiences an inner destruction and the loss of her ego amid the stifling and crushing collective forces.

> I have the fear that everyone is leaving, moving away, that love dies in an instant. I look at the people walking in the street, just walking, and I feel this: they are walking, *but* they are also being *carried away.* They are part of a current. . . . I confuse the moods which change and pass with the people themselves. I see them carried into eddies, always moving out of some state they will never return to. I see them lost.

Parallel images surface. With slight alterations Nin created a link between **"Winter of Artifice"** and **"The Voice"**: musical tonalities emerge and inject a sense of liberation, an unheard-of freedom. The shoe-and-foot image in **"Winter of Artifice"** is recaptured in **"The Voice,"** but viewed in a different way. When Djuna, for example, is speaking to the Voice, she removes her shoes to "uncover her very small and delicate feet." The atmosphere is now feminized. She knows that she is alluding to *her* foot and to no one else's. No longer a projection, a fantasy image, or a fetish, the foot stands for her rapport with reality. But minutes later a nebulous world imposes its presence and contradictory images abound; a series of isolated visualizations, as if suspended in space, come into being in the conversation between Djuna and the Voice.

A succession of characters comes into focus: Hazel, Georgia, Lilith, Mischa—each a projection of Djuna. Scenes catapult forth and these incarnations impress their personalities onto the proceedings; recognition and cognition come into being. Lilith, a lesbian violinist, feels the weight of her guilt to such an extent that she cannot play any more. The Voice heals her. Mischa, the cripple who cannot play his cello because his hand has grown stiff, after consulting the Voice begins to accept his problems and adapt to them.

Djuna returns to the lobby of the Hotel Chaotica. Her foray into the external world, the street, has seared her. "Her throat tightened." Yet, each time she has to face life within the hotel, she is equally terror stricken. She fears that *"someone out of the past"* will emerge and she will be unable to cope with the instincts and emotions that may surge forth. She fears to be reminded of her youth and her adolescence. Her inner world, ablaze and cut open by conflicting instincts and emotions, is expressed by discordant metaphors that now haunt the narrative. Spatial and temporal incongruities seem to sever what should have been whole and seem to disorder what should have been channeled. Unlike Proust's narrator, who enjoyed the upsurging of past sensations, Djuna dreads it. She thought she had thrown out her past "with the broken toys, but they sat there, threatening to sweep her back." They stand undaunted within her mind's eye like broken-faced gargoyles: "stuffed, with glass eyes, from a slower world, they look at her on this other level of swifter rhythms until they reach with dead arms around her." Djuna feels suspended in some airy sphere and contemplates the world about her: its tangled emotions, its discarded feelings. The drama unfolds: from the window in her room she sees a woman committing suicide by jumping out of a window. Although the psychological implication of such an image implies that an aspect of Djuna seeks suicide, we know that she seeks desperately to maintain some kind of balance amid the disruptive instincts invading her. The crippling effects of the images that emerge helter-skelter from the inner world are taking their toll as they vibrate, titillate, and shock her into a new state of awareness. Djuna does not wish to escape any more. Slowly, ploddingly, she goes on to the next step of *gnosis:* her own development.

That Lilith should play a role in **"Winter of Artifice"** is significant. The original Lilith as introduced in Talmudic literature was Adam's first wife. She was a harlot, adamant in her desire to captivate and hold men within her grasp. Unable to bear children and with no milk in her breasts, her aim was to divest other mothers of their newborns. Slim and beautiful with wings and the feet of an owl, Lilith was forever seducing men, revenging herself upon them for her own deficiencies. Lilith is an aspect of Djuna. She is that part of Djuna that seeks to dominate the patriarchal world. She is Lilith the demon, the nymphomaniac who seeks to attract, seduce, and then destroy her victim. She is the female Don Juan.

Lilith works her magic on the Voice. But as long as he remains remote—the seer, the God, the father—he holds dominion over her. When at the end of the story he becomes humanized and incorporates the frailties incumbent on a corporeal man, that is, when he longs to be loved as a man rather than as a deity, her idealization of him vanishes. "In the Voice she felt the ugliness of tree roots, of the earth, and this terrific dark, mute knowing of the animal." She wants spirit, but he seeks the flesh.

> What she read in his eyes was the immense pleading of a man, imprisoned inside a seer, calling out for the life in her, and at the very moment when every cell inside her body closed to the desire of the man she saw a mirage before her . . . a figure taller than other men, a type of savior, the man nearest to God, whose human face she could no longer see except for the immense hunger in the eyes.

The real man, whether father or psychoanalyst, could not capture her being. Only the sublimated, spiritual force could invade her soul.

"Winter of Artifice" concludes with a premonitory dream. It reveals in images Djuna's inability to cope with her still fragmented world, her longing for orientation, her desire to escape into the ineffable world of reverie where she can experience her narcissism to her heart's content. It also shows her feverish desire to face herself, to succeed as woman and artist.

"When I entered the dream I stepped on stage." She is actress and observer. She prepares for her exciting venture into the fourth dimension—time. The vertical and the horizontal mark her course: "a tower of layers without end, rising upward and closing themselves in the infinite, or layers, coiling downward, losing themselves in the bowels of the earth." The dreamer explodes, bursts, shatters. She loses her course as she traverses spatial domains. She experiences the void in which potential creation lives. She experiences empty fields, a one-way course. She needs to expand and experience the fullness of life—the mystic's All.

The inability to let go and feel her identity, to find her way amid the whirling and spiraling waters and rocking rhythms, terrorizes her. The beats lull the sleeper into a semiconscious state.

A *participation mystique* again comes over Djuna. She begins feeling one with organic form. She feels herself breathing in the "life of plants" in a flower. She becomes a biomorphic form, a fish, living inorganically, as Lautréamont's character Maldoror. Individuality vanishes. She embraces the cosmos. The collective dominates. She longs for a loss of memory. Her personalities flake and erode as time is measured by the hourglass. She longs for cyclical time—the mystic's celestial sphere. Daybreak and consciousness enter the dream. "The soul then lost its power to breathe, lost its space." Weighed down with the pain of life, divested of her nightly vision, of her anterior existences that had encrusted pain on her braised skin, yet allowed her to know grandiose heights, she clings desperately to some stable force as night descends. Details are blurred. Delineations grow unclear. Individual existences blend into multiple worlds. Oscillation and vibration radiate their ambivalent sensations, multiply and generate excitement, energize her being, arouse her flights of fancy and intensify her need for liberation. "The pressure of time ceased." The most important section of the dream, an image that will be repeated in many of Nin's works, is related:

> The boat I was pushing with all my strength because it could not float, it was passing through land. It was chokingly struggling to pass along the streets, it could not find its way to the ocean. It was pushed along the streets of the city, touching the walls of houses, and I was pushing it against the resistance of the earth. So many nights against the obstacles of mud, marshes, garden paths through which the boat labored painfully . . .
>
> The boat was passing through the city unable to find the ocean that transmitted its life voyages. The light cut into the bones with bony words that could not commune or change substance for communion.

Conceived as a microcosm, the ship is associated with maritime and spatial navigation. It is the earthly counterpart of an astral vehicle. In Djuna's dream the ship is not directed by divinity, but by her. As a receptacle and containing device, the boat is associated with the womb, the inner woman. Djuna's ship is landlocked. No matter how hard she tries to push it, to guide it through the cluttered city streets, the marshes, the insurmountable convolutions and involutions of life, it is too heavy for her. Djuna seeks the free-flowing water, the preformal state before birth, without obstacles and difficulties, just floating about without orientation or disorientation. She is impeded in her wish. She must push the boat and she does. Now she relies on no one but herself to find her direction. Neither her father in **"Winter of Artifice"** nor the Voice are called to participate. Search, struggle, and pain, Djuna is prepared for these eventualities. The artist within her has the will and strength to succeed. (pp. 76-94)

Bettina L. Knapp, in her Anaïs Nin, *Frederick Ungar Publishing Co., 1978, 168 p.*

An excerpt from *Delta of Venus:*

He wanted to know when she had experienced her first sensual tremor. It was while reading, said Elena, and then while coasting on a sled with a boy lying full length over her, and then when she fell in love with men she only knew at a distance, for as soon as they came near her, she discovered some defect that estranged her. She needed strangers, a man seen at a window, a man seen once a day in the street, a man she had seen once in a concert hall. After such encounters, Elena let her hair fall wild, was negligent in her dress, slightly wrinkled, and sat like some Chinese woman concerned with small events and delicate sadnesses.

Then, lying at her side, holding only her hand, Pierre talked about his life, offering her images of himself as a boy, to match those of the little girl she brought him. It was as if in each the older shells of their mature personalities had dissolved, like some added structure, a superimposition, revealing the cores.

As a child, Elena had been what she had suddenly become again for him—an actress, a simulator, someone who lived in her fantasies and roles and never knew what she truly felt.

Anaïs Nin, in her Delta of Venus, *Harcourt Brace Jovanovich, 1977.*

Benjamin Franklin V and Duane Schneider (essay date 1979)

[*Franklin, an American educator and critic, edited a primary bibliography of Nin in 1973. Schneider is an American educator and critic and coauthor, with Franklin, of* Anais Nin: An Introduction. *In the following excerpt from that work, the critics contrast structure and themes of Nin's second book, the novella collection* Winter of Artifice, *with those of her first, the prose poem* House of Incest.]

An author's second book has traditionally been the most difficult to write because something approaching all that he knows has been spent in his first effort. Nin states as much at the outset of *House of Incest,* and she was never able to match the artistry of that first work of fiction. Her second, *Winter of Artifice* (1939), contains many of the themes of the prose-poem, but this collection of novelettes is not as tightly or convincingly written as its predecessor. Of all of her works she seems to have had the most difficulty with this one: she signed a contract for it as early as 1935, she decided upon its final contents only after two decades and five editions, she permanently cast aside one novelette and completely rewrote two others after the 1939 edition, and she evidently felt so strongly that the contents of the first edition were inadequate that a revised *Winter of Artifice* was the first volume she published under the imprint of her own Gemor Press in New York in 1942. Further, in 1939, the year of the first edition, World War II was beginning, Nin misplaced numerous

copies of what must have been a small press run, copies sent to America were impounded by the postal authorities (this according to Nin, without documentation), and she and her friends were in the process of fleeing Paris and Europe for New York and America. With this turmoil surrounding its writing and publication it is surprising that *Winter of Artifice* is as good as it is.

As originally published, *Winter of Artifice* contained three sections. The first, **"Djuna,"** has never been reprinted, although there are analogues and parallel episodes in the first volume of the *Diary.* **"Lilith,"** the second section, eventually became entitled **"Winter of Artifice."** The third part, **"The Voice,"** has always been retained in later editions, although it, like **"Lilith,"** went through a number of substantial alterations in text, stylistics, and tone. (pp. 20-1)

. . . . .

Stella [protagonist of **"Stella"**] is a movie star (this is implicit in her name) who is unable to reconcile her image on the screen with her real self. On the screen she is glamorous, larger than life, graceful, and perfectly able to satisfy the fantasies of the audience; in the reality of existence off the screen she is, to her own way of thinking, a small, mousy individual who is filled with doubt and insecurity. In her attempt to overcome the disparity between the two Stellas, she surrounds herself with glamorous accoutrements: a "Movie Star bed of white satin," rows of shoes, a closet full of hats, and a room of mirrors. All of these, of course, are ineffectual because it is Stella herself who impedes her growth into wholeness. The real Stella is, in fact, jealous of her image on film and so imitates that; it is the screen Stella who earns the love and responses of the people; it is the screen Stella whom the people come near and touch and love. More importantly, it is the screen Stella who is free; it is this woman whom the people court. The neurosis of the real-life Stella exists partly because of this disparity between the reality and the image, but it is also nurtured by her own inner obstacles that keep her stature small in her own eyes. The irony of her situation becomes clear: she is not so limited as she thinks she is; also, it is her image on the screen that is able to bring happiness (love) to the movie audience, whose limitations are her own; and, finally, the ideal to which she actually aspires (the fantasy life of glamour) is not only unattainable but also undesirable. Every one of Nin's women is haunted to one degree or another by this problem of incompleteness.

What Stella wants is joy, especially joy as love, for this is what she had taken away from her in her youth. Yet, instead of explaining fully the circumstances of Stella's painful childhood, Nin takes the reader to the time when, later in life, she has a lover Bruno, who is a married man with whom she is destined to be unhappy. His qualities oppose her own. Although it is the yoking together of opposites rather than similarities that is consistently encouraged in Nin's work, here it produces nothing because of Stella's jealousy and her inability to function maturely. When she does move in rhythm with Bruno, she immediately moves into a vast world where the joy she attains is so intense that Bruno is unable to share in it. Consequently, what she thereby achieves is a split between reality (human love) and an unattainable ideal (her exuberance), which is a dichotomy similar to the separation of the real self and her screen image. This is one of the themes that is basic to Nin's work.

The love of Stella and Bruno is doomed when Stella goes outside the realm of humanity (always a dangerous direction in Nin's fiction), but it is also doomed by her inability to love Bruno on a human level. She is possessive; she needs continual assurance of his love (as she tries to reassure herself by gathering luxurious objects about her). But when she suspects him of neglecting her (as when he arrives at the hotel without his valise) she feels betrayed and withdraws from him. The love she offers is a love of doubt and suspicion, a love that is unsatisfactory because it is less than an absolute, ideal love. Neither Bruno nor anyone else can meet her demands.

Bruno's own life with his wife and children has become routine; certainly he has found a new vitality in his relationship with Stella, but, unlike her, he will not take his love outside human bounds because he cannot give all to love. Bruno needs moorings (contacts with reality, one might call them) in order for his love to be sincere and to survive. If he were to lose himself in love, as Stella does, it would be counterfeit because it would be rootless. So when Stella finds his love limited, she feels a sense of frustration that is understandable but that stands as a more important symptom of the deeper frustration that has been hers since childhood. No man can fulfill her needs.

After this focus on Stella's involvement with him, Bruno appears only once more in the story, but their relationship is summarized symbolically in the sixth of the twelve sections that comprise the novelette. Immediately prior to this section Stella has fled from him and has experienced real human emotion (exemplified in the tangibility of the tears she shed). Soon thereafter Bruno calls her on the telephone at a pre-arranged time, but instead of answering it, she plays a recording of a concerto and ascends the small stairway leading to her bedroom. She is unable to answer his call because she has lost the feeling that she felt when she cried, and she has now thrown her vision "back into seclusion again, into the wall of the self " as she enters "the solitary cell of the neurotic." Throughout this section Stella is confused, altering the natural qualities of music and the telephone. Music, which usually serves as a unifying device in Nin's work, is used here by Stella to move her toward isolation. The telephone, being mechanical and cold, yet bearing the warm voice of Bruno, is disregarded, though it ought to function as a medium for connecting the two lovers. Stella further simplifies and distorts the nature of the music she hears when she perceives in the trombone a caricature of men and in the flutes the essence of women, so that she takes great pride in hearing the flutes (of Stella) emerge victorious over the trombones (of Bruno): "And as for the flute, it was so easily victimized and overpowered. But it triumphed ultimately because it left an echo. Long after the trombone had had its say, the flute continued its mischievous, insistent tremolos." When the telephone rings again, Stella moves farther up the stairs, away from the caller: "Fortunate for her that the

trombone was a caricature of masculinity, that it was an inflated trombone, drowning the sound of the telephone. So she smiled one of her eerie smiles, pixen and vixen too, at the masculine pretensions. Fortunate for her that the flute persisted in its delicate undulations, and that not once in the concerto did they marry but played in constant opposition to each other throughout." Aloft in her solitary cell, the music that helped her gain that isolated height is "without the power to suck her back into the life with Bruno and into the undertows of suffering." Here, as elsewhere, the ideal is untenable; isolation is self-defeating; and in order to experience love and life, one must accept pain and imperfection. In this way, Stella's performance not on the screen, but in real life with Bruno (especially in the sixth section), serves symbolically as a vivid example of this recurring truth in Nin's fiction. It is an idea similar to the one that Hawthorne wrote about so persistently. When Aylmer eradicates his wife Georgiana's birthmark so that she will be perfect, she can only die. Perfection is not of this world, and to approach attaining it is a kind of imperfection because one is necessarily dehumanized. Conversely, to accept imperfection is a form of perfection because it is accepting the realities of the human condition. Hawthorne's narrator states this position effectively; Georgiana's birthmark is "the fatal flaw of humanity, which Nature, in one shape or another, stamps ineffaceably on all her productions, either to imply that they are temporary and finite, or that their perfection must be wrought by toil and pain. The Crimson Hand [the birthmark] expressed the ineludible grip, in which mortality clutches the highest and purest of earthly mould, degrading them into kindred with the lowest, and even with the very brutes, like whom their visible frames return to dust."

The sixth section is a symbolic portrait of Stella's relationship with Bruno; the next symbolizes the origin of her trouble. After the concerto scene, Stella goes to her bedroom in which she keeps her movie-star accoutrements, the objects that nurture her own false view of herself. Although she is feeling lighthearted from having ascended the staircase, she is also feeling considerable pain. The irony is clear. She is suffering from having cut herself off from a human relationship, but the relationship itself brought her anguish. She frightens herself by discovering that she has been seeking pain all along; she brands herself a masochist. This kind of self-analysis is, in Stella's case, neither whimsical nor casual, for she is attempting to learn the source of the suffering that has been hers for so long. But she is unable to discover the true cause of her psychological difficulty. Shortly after this point in the narrative, Stella views a movie about Atlantis that is accompanied by Stravinsky's music. On the screen she sees images that take her back to the painless and rhythmic prebirth of Atlantis and the world (her own prenatal life); she dissolves into the "paradise of water and softness," just as the narrator does at the beginning of *House of Incest*. The peace of the prebirth is short-lived, however, for an explosion causes a new continent to be born above the old, submerged one. Atlantis and Stella disappear; earth reforms itself after multiple explosions; and in the new world that develops, Stella views a small and insignificant figure that is obviously herself. She has now arrived, in her own subconsciousness, at the cause of her years of suffering: as the world began with an explosion, so did her own life, but the result was the fragmentation of herself into many separate parts and lives that did not cohere, that were not linked, that did not form a whole. She recalls several incidents from her childhood that caused her considerable pain and embarrassment. A child is normally at one with himself, but as she reflects upon her past, she realizes that by the time she was eleven no image of herself had evolved; but more importantly, perhaps, she recognizes that by the time she was fourteen she had begun to disguise herself as an "actress multiplied into many personages." More astonishing is her conviction that she could possibly regain her lost vision of herself only by *acting* herself, thus recreating herself into a whole and single being. This self-prescribed remedy will not do, however. Although one "can look back upon a certain scene of life and see only a part of the truth," later

> a deeper insight, a deeper experience will add the missing aspects to the past scene, to the lost character only partially seen and felt. Still later another will appear. So that with time, and with time and awareness only, the scene and the person become complete, fully heard and fully seen.

> Inside of the being there is a defective mirror, a mirror distorted by the fog of solitude, of shyness, by the climate inside of this particular being. It is a personal mirror, lodged in every subjective, interiorized form of life.

As unsatisfactory as Stella's state is, she is in a better condition than the narrator at the outset of *House of Incest* who yearns for the state of prebirth and nonlife of the Atlantide and finally becomes entrapped in an incestuous house. Stella laments the loss of a painless life, but she is able to function, though less than totally, in reality and in society.

Most of the remainder of the novelette concerns her father, who was the real culprit in her life. He is an actor who left his family and destroyed their ability to love. This man, who is central to most of *Winter of Artifice,* is now married to a girl-woman named Laura who is described in terms similar to those used to characterize the titular figure in **"The Mouse."** The father's treatment of Laura parallels his behavior with Stella's mother; in all relationships he seems to function as one who is detached, not as a person with human sympathies. He wears sterile clothes; he keeps people at a distance and considers them to be intruders in his life. It was he, of course, who caused Stella's suffering. When she had been twelve years old and living in a state of want and need, her father would occasionally entertain her in a grand and opulent fashion, but then he would return her to a life of poverty with her mother. This recurring disparity between the real and the ideal evolved into her psychological problem and explains why she—functioning, actually, in a manner similar to her father—is unable to sustain a relationship with Bruno. There is a key difference, however, between the father and the daughter: he pretends to be something he is not (an ideal), while she aspires to regain a reality that truly exists within her. Her father functions as a cold and impersonal human being who is directly responsible for the unhappy plight of his daughter, but he also kills the love of his former wife (Stel-

la's mother) and of Laura. When he suffers a heart attack, he is acting out in reality a physical death that mirrors the psychological distance he has maintained from mankind. When his heart falters he must die, for he draws his sustenance from women; and yet he kills the love of the three women closest to him. At what must be his death, only Stella of the three is there to comfort him, not because she loves him, but because she feels a closeness to him as a fellow human being. His death then, is, in a sense, a suicide.

The remainder of the story unwinds quickly as Stella becomes enamored of Philip, a Don Juan who represents joy and happiness to her. One day he asks her to wait for him in his apartment, and while she is there she examines the articles in his bedroom and discovers a set of silver toilet articles similar to those of her father. Her father thus reappears in Philip so that she concludes her story with a future resembling her past: she anticipates that once his glamorous appeal has subsided, he will treat her as her father has treated her. She recalls, simultaneously, the past and future loss of love and recognizes that the "people who fall in love with the performers are like those who fall in love with magicians; they are the ones who cannot create the illusion or magic with the love—the mise-en-scene, the producer, the music, the role, which surrounds the personage with all that desire requires." At the end Stella has no one, not Bruno, Philip, her father, nor any other human being. She was strangled in her childhood and youth by her father, and she has not yet learned to breathe again: "How could joy have vanished with the father?" she asks. The answer is inexplicable, but it happened, and part of the answer may lie in the fact that "human beings have a million little doorways of communication. When they feel threatened they close them, barricade themselves. Stella closed them all. Suffocation set in. Asphyxiation of the feelings." Her image, "the outer shell of Stella," continues to appear on the screen. But she recognizes that the rare bouquets sent by her fans are more appropriately to be labeled as flowers for the dead, for Stella is as close to life-in-death as any person can be.

. . . . .

"Winter of Artifice" was published originally in the 1939 collection under the title **"Lilith,"** though the text came to be greatly altered. For example, in its earlier version Lilith narrates the story, but later Nin recast it into the third-person point of view. One cannot help but recognize that in some ways the first-person point of view is strikingly more effective in a story that recounts the events of a daughter's reunion with her father after twenty years' absence. One might consider, for example, the different effects of the two following passages, the first from the 1939 version, the second from the revised text.

> I am waiting for him. I have waited for him for twenty years. He is coming to-day.

> She is waiting for him. She was waiting for him for twenty years. He is coming today.

The first passage is immediate and engaging; the second is much more ordinary and flat. At any rate, this change of perspective is one of many substantial textual alterations that Nin made, and it may stand as an example of the care that she took in revising her works through the years. Nin's decision to place **"Winter of Artifice"** after **"Stella"** was logical; it demonstrates as well her care in organizing materials. Although **"Stella"** was published six years after the original version of **"Winter of Artifice,"** it is well to have it precede the second novelette. Stella's story is only partly concerned with her father, but his importance is so great to her that the reader may wish to know more about this man who deserted his family, thereby leaving indelible emotional scars on his only daughter. His full portrait is revealed in **"Winter of Artifice"** after having been introduced to the reader in **"Stella."**

In **"Winter of Artifice"** neither the father nor the daughter is named, but this fact does not detract from the sense of continuity that extends from the first novelette to the second, because the basic nature of the two is the same: the daughter is devoted to the superficial father, and in both stories the father is married to a woman named Laura. Instead of an actor the father is now a pianist.

For the twenty years since he had abandoned her when she was eleven, this daughter, whom we shall call Stella, has yearned to be reunited with her father, a man who has been her ideal for those two decades. The present events in the story depict their reunion and their new life together, though the reader is frequently taken into the daughter's youth and the intervening years so that one might see the effect of the father's absence upon her. A key cluster of symbols informs the daughter's existence during these years of waiting: "This glass bowl with the glass fish and the glass ship—it has been the sea for her and the ship which carried her away from him after he had abandoned her. Why has she loved ships so deeply, why has she always wanted to sail away from this world? Why has she always dreamed of flight, of departure?" An abandoned child would understandably love or hate (or love and hate) a delinquent parent, and perhaps especially one of the opposite sex, but the effect on Stella is to isolate her from humanity, just as the characters from *House of Incest* are isolated, and just as Stella cannot find authentic relationships with Bruno and Philip. Ever since her father left her, Stella has tried to flee from the past and from real life by means of the glass ship in the glass bowl. This necessarily fragile mode of transportation may be linked to one of her chief memories of her father, his standing isolated behind a window, showing obvious disgust at being bothered by his family. She has taken this glass window, transformed it into a boat, and, embracing her father psychologically, has sought refuge from this world. But when she is actually reunited with him and he promises to take her with him to the south of France, "she leaned backwards, pushing the crystal bowl against the wall. It cracked and the water gushed forth as from a fountain, splashing all over the floor. The glass ship could no longer sail away—it was lying on its side, on the rock-crystal stones." Her father has returned, the lost love has supposedly been recaptured, and their future together appears promising; so her fragile evasions of life no longer seem necessary. At the end of the story, however, the "rock-crystal stones" that demolished her insular life have turned into a destructive force that not only destroys fragile ships but also substantial loves. When the bowl breaks, the daughter observes,

"Perhaps I've arrived at my port at last. . . . Perhaps I've come to the end of my wanderings." But this is not to be the case, because only the illusion of a better future lies before her upon her father's return.

Only infrequently in Nin's work is a male character developed in such detail as Stella's father is in **"Winter of Artifice."** Usually men—husbands and lovers—are present to help point up certain characteristics of the women with whom they are associated. This is an artistically sound device, for it is the women who function as the chief characters. In this story the man is neither a husband nor a lover to Stella, although there are suggestions and impulses of these relationships; here, rather, the father is a highly symbolic character who is presented fully because he is at the core of Stella's problems. In a sense he may stand for the father image that is so important to Nin herself in the *Diary*. Stella's father is a musician of some reputation who, ironically, is unable to transfer to life any of the sensitivity he displays in his art. He walks out of step with the rest of humanity. He has been loved by women and he has fathered children, but he is unsuccessful as a husband, lover, and father because he is unable to give of himself in a human relationship. He views women as sexual conveniences and has little regard for them as human beings; he views his own children as casually and impersonally as he does women and other human beings. He tends to be cold, superficial, and insensitive to the feelings of others; a man who is elegant in his gloves and filter-tipped cigarettes, but one whose elegance betrays a goodness basic to people (love, compassion, feeling) and so leads ultimately to his isolation from others. He is a man of the mind and not of the heart; he is reminiscent of many other characters in literature, including Hawthorne's Chillingworth, Aylmer, and Ethan Brand; Joyce's James Duffy; as well as a number of Henry James's characters.

Stella, in contrast, is a woman of feelings and of the heart, but she has not been able to love as she ought because of the destructive impact upon her of the father's desertion. The natural love of the daughter for the father was violently crushed, and the vividness with which Nin portrays the entire desertion scene is powerful, thereby providing heightened expectations from the daughter (and consequently from the reader) when the father is about to return. "Since that day she had not seen her father. Twenty years have passed. He is coming today." But during these past twenty years she has been an unfulfilled woman, incapable of loving others fully (as she herself was unloved). Even though he treated her coldly and critically—sometimes cruelly so—when he was part of the family, at least then he was accessible to her; it is his absence rather than his typical inhumaneness that has oppressed her for so long.

As a youth Stella wanted to be an artist because her father was one; but rather than pursue her desires and talents, she established a barrier between herself and life. When her father left, she tied herself to him emotionally in a lengthy letter that became her diary and that "was a monologue, or dialogue, dedicated to him, inspired by the superabundance of thoughts and feelings caused by the pain of leaving him." The letter becomes more than she had intended; although it had been meant to be an avenue for the revelation of her love for her father, by accident it became a place for seclusion, a wall behind which she could escape pains and frustrations, and so she was shut off from the explorations that are a part of a normal childhood. At that time her mother had great difficulty keeping her family together in the United States, which was a new country to them, and therefore the mother was not as sensitive to the needs of her daughter as she might otherwise have been. And so, with both parents absent, as it were, Stella found it necessary to pursue at least one of them rather than to face alone the alien world of New York City. This pursuit took the form of writing and living in the diary, the letter to her father, where increasingly she found happiness and security in her solitude. Her love for him flourished because he remained an ideal in her mind, and for twenty years he was to be one of the most important persons in her life and perhaps the most important one of all. She began to realize the dangers of her insular existence in the diary as she grew into womanhood, and indeed it had become to some extent her shadow, or her double, functioning in the same way that the concepts of incest and narcissism operate in *House of Incest*. She awaits her father in Paris at the age of thirty-one, hoping he will become once again her real father and thus permit her to cease writing and living in her diary.

As one might expect, she is totally disappointed. Just as her father could not accept the responsibility of parenthood years before, so is he no more capable of responsible fatherhood now. When he and his daughter are reunited, he is the possessive, jealous lover (like the dancer in *House of Incest*) who wants his daughter's love exclusively for himself. At long last, in a scene of heightened intensity, she is able to present to him the diary that had been intended to be "a revelation of her love for him." His reaction is precisely the opposite of what she had intended and hoped for.

> Her father's jealousy began with the reading of her diary. He observed that after two years of obsessional yearning for him she had finally exhausted her suffering and obtained serenity. After serenity she had fallen in love with an Irish boy and then with a violinist. He was offended that she had not died completely, that she had not spent the rest of her life yearning for him. He did not understand that she had continued to love him better by living than by dying for him. She had loved him in life, lived for him and created for him. She had written the diary for him. . . . She had loved him in life creatively by writing about him.

There is no response of affection or love from him. And Stella responds predictably to this criticism, disavowing her love of others and subordinating her real self to him. This possessiveness further suggests the father's cruelty and insensitivity: he wants her entirely for himself, but he seems to want to give her nothing. If he could have his wish, she would be something like an Amazon who could care for herself and not need to depend upon him for anything. But Stella is now a woman and responds much differently to her father and his attitudes than the way she had reacted as a child; she now sees that the father she has

loved and yearned for is neither a father nor a man; he is a child who tries to evade all human contact and adult responsibilities. She finally understands his shortcomings: "He was now as incapable of an impulse as his body was incapable of moving, incapable of abandoning himself to the great uneven flow of life with its *necessary* disorder and ugliness." [critics' italics] After looking for the father and loving his every symbol, she had awaited him and had found a child.

The climax of the story is a four-page section describing the union of the father and the daughter, which takes place while a mistral is blowing. Normally cold, this mistral is hot, suggesting perhaps the confusion or tumult of their relationship. A sexual union may be suggested, but it is a mystical rather than a physical relationship that is consummated in the form of symbolic orchestration. Trembling violins, pounding drums, and mocking flutes fuse in rhythm for an instant and elevate father and daughter from the pain of the earth to a place *"where pain is a long, smooth song that does not cut through the flesh."* They are seeking serenity through music as Stella sought to find it in order to avoid the pain of Bruno; but the answer to the final set of questions (*"Can we live in rhythm, my father? Can we feel in rhythm, my father? Can we think in rhythm, my father? Rhythm—rhythm—rhythm"*) is no. They may unite temporarily in the mystical dream state or through emotional elevation, but not in reality. She now sees him too clearly to love him humanly. She can tell herself intellectually that she loves him, but her heart will not permit her to live that lie. She finally comes to understand fully her former yearning for him at a point in the narrative when she slips into a mood between sleep and dream, discovering that what she loved all along was not her father but herself mirrored in him. Her attraction to him was the same as that of the narrator's to Sabina in *House of Incest;* it was narcissistic, inhuman, and therefore sterile. Falsity has characterized her father and her love for him, and together they constitute a winter of artifice. Just as the glass bell functions as an image of sealing off human beings from each other, an artificiality keeps the father safely sealed from the distasteful or undesirable, and while the unpleasant aspects of life are conveniently lost, "with the bad was lost the human warmth, the nearness." She rejects the pattern of his artificial life. She rejects his fear of emotion, of closeness, and sees him as a very sick man. And although she regrets having loved him and trusted him again, she feels ambivalent about the reunion and recognizes that she had to obey the need to join him once more. But Stella comes to realize still more that together they were "slaves of a pattern," for as the story moves quickly to its ending after the climax, she completes "the fatal circle of desertion" by reversing their roles. When she leaves on a trip, he accuses her of desertion, and Stella now understands her earlier difficulties to the degree that she is able to gain some distance from them and to reflect upon their significance for her. She sees clearly that her former love of her father was manifested to satisfy a myth, not life, and she absolves herself of any guilt by believing that "the feelings they had begun with twenty years back, he of guilt and she of love, had been like railroad tracks on which they had been launched at full speed by their obsessions." Her emotional development had been preordained, determined by the same force, the iron rails, that sent Ahab on his monomaniacal quest for the white whale. Now she has emerged out of the unreflecting "ether of the past," has gained maturity, and is able to stand alone as a woman. Truth finally is possible. Her father was able to see their relationship when he recognized in himself a truth: "Now I see that all these women I pursued are all in you, and you are my daughter, and I can't marry you! You are the synthesis of all the women I loved."

The ether of the past envelopes them both; they are seeking the self in the other, and they enter a dream state where they fuse. But the ether—and the dream—must wear off, and the daughter in her maturity and understanding is able to cope with it. The father is not. Their separation is to him what it had been to the daughter in her childhood. She had needed him and he left; now he (emotionally a child) needs her, who is very much as a mother to him. She had given herself to him, he had hurt her, and she no longer has any faith in him. She soon recognizes that she would be happy only when separated from him. He reacts predictably: " 'Go on,' he said. 'Now tell me, tell me I have no talent, tell me I don't know how to love, tell me *all that your mother used to tell me*'." When the daughter replies, "I have never thought any of these things," she suddenly realizes that he has, in fact, failed to achieve the fatherhood she had idealized; he is still the judge. If she has risen in status to the level of her mother, she is also explicitly now his antagonist as well.

In the final lines of the story, Stella is depicted as coming out of that ether of the past that had fogged her mind.

> The last time she had come out of the ether it was to look at her dead child, a little girl with long eyelashes and slender hands. She was dead.

> The little girl in her was dead too. The woman was saved. And with the little girl died the need of a father.

Although Nin uses the death of a child more powerfully elsewhere, here the implication is clearly that the symbolic child in Stella has gone, that the emotional child at the core of the woman Stella has now ceased to be as she has outgrown her need of the father and has transcended, finally, the arrested emotional development visited upon her by her father in her childhood. The natural process in which Stella can now participate—and which the artificialities of her father precluded—is "the process of growth, fruition, decay, disintegration, which is organic and inevitable." It is the process of the living, of life itself.

· · · · ·

"The Voice," the third section of the volume, has always been a part of *Winter of Artifice,* just as the second section has been, and it, too, was rewritten subsequent to its appearance in that 1939 volume. It has always been placed last in the collection with good reason: it is an attempt to show several troubled characters solving their problems with the aid of a modern priest (the Voice, a psychiatrist) and finding wholeness and relative peace of mind. The focus is no longer directed on one or two chief characters; the narration presents the difficulties of all four of the Voice's patients, as well as the difficulties of the Voice him-

self, for the possibility of a modern tragedy lies in the tragic aspects of the healer himself who needs help more desperately than do his patients. The title and the thrust of the narrative both point toward this tragedy, but, as we shall see, Nin pursues it to only a limited degree, letting his story lie under the surface, to be inferred by the reader rather than developing it as a primary element. This is not to say that the story is a failure; the four patients are fairly well drawn and fully presented, and two of them (Djuna and Lillian) will become central to Nin's lengthy continuous novel. Also, Lillian emerges at the end of *Seduction of the Minotaur* as the one woman examined in depth in Nin's fiction who achieves a permanent wholeness and true contentment in life.

Djuna is the first character to be introduced. Unable to exist comfortably in a middle position between extremes, she is compared to the elevator that explodes through the ceiling and plummets through the bottom floor into the hysteria of tombs. She lives in a hotel, in a cell-shaped room; her existence there is insular. The hotel itself (appropriately designated as Hotel Chaotica) is like the Tower of Babel in which communication between people is not possible and confusion consequently results. As the hotel contains all this inner confusion, so too does Djuna with her inner conflicts and her inability to fuse into a whole woman. She stands outside of life. She observes others caught in life's current and ferment, but what obsesses her is the residue and debris of real life: dead flowers, punctured broken dolls, wilted vegetables, dead cats. She concludes that human effort and movement lead only to waste. Fortunately, Djuna is aware that she is ill at ease with herself, and she seeks the Voice through whom she understands that the waste and death that interest her are really symbolic of the immobility and detachment from life that she sees in herself. The Voice counsels, "If you were in the current, in love, in ecstasy, the motion would not show just its death aspect. You see what life throws out because you stand outside, shut out from the ferment itself." In every instance in which stasis occurs in Nin's work, it is tantamount to death. With the Voice's aid, however, Djuna learns that she is dependent on other people, and she begins to move, to flow: "She was moving faster than the slowly flowing rivers carrying detritus. Moving, moving. Flowing, flowing, flowing. When she was watching, everything that moved seemed to be moving away, but when moving, this was only a tide, and the self turning, rotating, was feeding the rotation of desire." She is now filled with music (Nin's symbol of unification) and is able to ride the elevator, attaining fullness and satisfaction at the top floor rather than bursting through it in a quest of some unattainable absolute as she had done before.

Djuna is not left in this state of completion for long. Before her story resumes, however, the short tale of Lillian and her relationship to the Voice is told. Lillian thinks that she is perverse because she is at least superficially masculine and has had such women as Hazel and Georgia as lovers. Since youth she has acted like a male and has had an aversion to feminine accoutrements, and yet she feels guilty for these feelings and for believing that she killed a woman to keep her from marrying a man, for all men are harsh in her eyes. She feels guilty for being caught passing a violin bow between her legs and for thinking that she caused the death of a boy by giving him an enema with a straw. But her seeming masculinity becomes more than just a psychological quirk when she is deprived of her reproductive organs; as she says about her operation, "I was told it was for appendicitis, and when I got well I found out I had no more woman's parts." She then feels that no man would want her because she is incapable of bearing children. In order to simulate the sexual act she uses a toothbrush. Lillian is uncertain about herself, but like Djuna she becomes a patient of the Voice and appears to be cured by him: "I have something now which you can't take from me [;] ever since I came here I have [*sic*] a feeling so warm and sweet and life-giving which belongs to me, I know you gave it to me, but it is inside of me now, and you can't take it away." Although the reader does not see Lillian interacting with people or performing sexually with men, the warmth she feels after her experience with the Voice suggests that even if she is not completely healed she is at least well on her way to becoming a psychologically whole woman who is content with herself.

Lillian interacts with none of the Voice's other patients, and her tale is a set piece that could as easily be deleted as included; but although the next patient, Mischa, is presented in only a few pages, he functions as the introducer of the fourth patient, Lilith, and thus introduces the remainder of the tale to the reader. Mischa is necessary to *"The Voice"*; Lillian is not, and yet they share several characteristics. Both are musicians (Lillian is a violinist, Mischa is a cellist) whose discipline teaches harmony and rhythm but who, like Stella's father, cannot function harmoniously with life. Both have confused notions of their own sexual identities. (Lillian likes to act as men do, Mischa likes to hide in women.) Mischa is much like the paralytic who introduces the modern Christ and the lame Jeanne in *House of Incest:* all three are kept from movement and human interaction by physical disabilities that are probably psychosomatic in nature. Mischa was a child prodigy who was unable to continue his musical artistry past youth (and therefore was unable to develop into manhood), because his hand became stiff, preventing him from manipulating the instrument. Like most physical ailments in Nin's works, Mischa's was a result of a psychological injury, in this case one he had incurred from what he perceived to be a hostile relationship, with sexual overtones, between his parents. Shortly after he had viewed his father bloodied by the animals he had killed, he awakened in the night to see his mother in a white robe stained with blood. Believing that the stain was caused violently by his father, Mischa struck him with a riding whip to keep him from her. As a result of this impetuous act, the arm used to strike the father became stiff and useless.

One can understand why Mischa's hand should become paralyzed, but the true cause of the ailment is more difficult to discern. His stiffness developed to take attention away from his lame leg that contains a fragment of death because it is incapable of functioning naturally. It is the crippled leg that leads women to treat him dispassionately. And so he grows to hate them. It is this deadness of emotion (suggested by the deadness of the leg) that is the cause of his inability to love, and it is this that he wishes to conceal. The lameness, Mischa feels, is the cause of the rejection he perceives, and so he shows his hand "so no one would notice the lameness." Once the Voice helps him to understand the cause of his physical difficulties, Mischa is liberated, walks with confidence, and sings as he walks into the street and into the flow of life. Psychological awareness has brought understanding that in turn has freed Mischa from his internal turmoil.

One woman who feels tenderness toward Mischa and exhibits a need to protect him is Lilith Pellan, the last of the Voice's patients to be presented. Tenderness and protection are, of course, precisely what Mischa does not want, and, for that matter, they are also not what Lilith herself wants to provide. Her actions toward Mischa and all people are dictated by the experiences of her youth, the most vivid of which was her wandering with her father who came to destroy her childhood by deserting his family. This is exactly what happens to Stella in **"Winter of Artifice,"** but Lilith grows, from the time of the desertion, to detest change, and she comes to live life very conservatively; she becomes an island, a fixed center, a person mistrusting pain and loss. And so she becomes unable to depend on others and to interact with them. The tenor of her relationship with Mischa and her brother Eric is thus established. Djuna, Lillian, and Mischa all are aware of their incomplete selves and go to the Voice for assistance; so does Lilith. It does not take him long to bring her to see the cause of her problems, and she is soon "breathing with the day, moving with the wind, in accord with it, with the sky, undulating like water, flowing and stirring to the life about her, opening like the night." She is now able to cope with life maturely, but she continues to fear the Voice and Djuna, because they do not permit her to lean on them for assistance as much as she would like; she is therefore no longer able to love herself in them as she has done and can do with others. A result of this is that she begins to love the Voice for himself; she becomes interested in his needs and deficiencies; his detective work in making all the discoveries in her lead her to become sensitive to his feelings as well. He

> took her back, with his questions and his probings, back to the beginning. She told him all she could remember about her father, ending with: "the need of a father is over."
>
> The Voice said: "I am not entirely sure that the little girl in you ever died, or her need of a father. What am I to you?"
>
> "The other night I dreamed you were immense, towering over everyone. You carried me in your arms and I felt no harm could come to me. I have no more fears since I talk to you like this every day. But lately I have become aware that it is you who are not happy."

Consequently he begins to confess to her, for no one prior to Lilith had been concerned with him as a person, and the stage is set for his tragic tale.

The Voice not only confides in and confesses to Lilith, but also to Djuna as he tells her of his problems (jealousy and fear) and of his love for Lilith. Instead of pursuing his inner turmoil, the narrative shifts again to Djuna and Lilith, both of whom have slipped back from their new wholeness (acquired through the help of the Voice) into a regression that may be associated with their increasing closeness to the Voice. Djuna becomes associated with the moon, loses her identity, and is alone within herself as she drinks in "the jungle of desire." Lilith has experienced similar difficulties. She is unable to sleep because "she lived in the myth," in the dream, and "found the absolute only in fragments, in multiplicity." She yearns for the absolute as Djuna had earlier and so is unable to spend the passion that has accumulated within her. Djuna is in greater control of herself, however, and is able to counsel the anguished Lilith; she loves only a mirage in the Voice. The qualities that she, Lilith, loves in Djuna are only the qualities that she possesses in herself, and so they ought not to be sought: "But none of this is love, Lilith. We are the same woman. There is always the moment when all the outlines, the differences between women disappear, and we enter a world where all feelings, yours and mine, seem to issue from the same source. We lose our separate identities. What happens to you is the same as what happens to me. Listening to you is not entering a world different from my own, it's a kind of communion." Lilith does not heed Djuna's advice about the Voice, and she therefore helps to cause what passes for his tragedy in the antepenultimate section of the story. There he and Lilith try to love each other, but their attempt is unsuccessful because each wants what the other person no longer is willing or able to offer. Lilith continues to transcend reality in human relationships as she searches for a god, some ideal to fill the void created by her father's desertion many years before. Although the Voice can offer her fatherly impulses (for he can be paternalistic, oracular, and supportive), by this time he is weary of being loved for those qualities; he wants to be loved as a man, as an individual, as a human being. Lilith finally eludes the Voice, and when he loses the power that he has been able to maintain as a doctor, he is unable to function and becomes a virtual nonentity, a child, merely a voice.

One sympathizes with the Voice. He is able to cure, or help to cure, the emotional ills of his patients, but he never is able to achieve wholeness or fullness himself. When he attempts to live his own life, he fails and desperately needs another Voice to aid him. One wants to know what his weakness is, what flaw in the construction of his personality enables him to be a helper but never to be the rich, fulfilled person toward whom he can at least help others incline. The novelette does not supply information on this point. Though ironic as well as tragic possibilities abound in the very nature and fabric of the tale, Nin avoids examining him fully, shifts away from his relationship with Lilith, and fixes upon Djuna instead. She, like most of Nin's characters, has been hurt by life and discovers that dreams are not painful. Her dream is revealed in the final six pages of the story, where she finds that the dream, though painless, is nonetheless dangerous. She learns the lesson promulgated in *House of Incest:* the dream state is a necessary part of one's life, but exclusive residence in it forces one out of life's current and into isolation and sterility. Fortunately for Djuna she is not lost in the dream; she finds that life begins there *"behind the curtain of closed eyelashes,"*

and that *"to catch up, to live for a moment in unison with it, that was the miracle. The life on the stage, the life of the legend dovetailed with the daylight, and out of this marriage sparked the great birds of divinity, the eternal moments."* This is an orthodox statement about the nature of the relationship between the dream and reality, but **"The Voice"** is not much concerned with that problem. One is gratified that Djuna reaches this awareness, and perhaps it symbolizes the fusion of all of her parts; but it leaves one with the feeling that the author did not wish to pursue the Voice's story. Perhaps she wanted to emphasize the other characters and wished to heighten their own dramas for the reader.

The three parts of **Winter of Artifice** concern women attempting to understand themselves and to make themselves complete human beings after having had their emotional and psychological growth stunted early in life. This is the subject of *House of Incest,* and it was to remain Nin's primary concern throughout all of her other works. (pp. 21-39)

Benjamin Franklin V and Duane Schneider, in their Anaïs Nin: An Introduction, *Ohio University Press, 1979, 309 p.*

Rosalind Thomas   (essay date 1982)

[*Thomas is an English educator and critic. In the following essay, she discusses Nin's erotic literature, focusing on its feminine perspective and themes of imagination, fantasy, creativity, and psychological exploration.*]

Although she felt that the inclusion of eroticism in literature was "like life itself," Anaïs Nin personally was opposed to focusing one's whole literary attention on the sexual life. Her main work, *Cities of the Interior,* embraces the sexual experiences of her central characters, but only as such experiences, like all other vital experiences, afford some understanding of the deeper, interior self. Most of all, Nin was concerned with the psychic development and full integration of her characters. Inasmuch as most of them were women and Nin's poetic language was particularly adept at revealing the feminine psyche, her fiction, though written primarily in the thirties, offers a female perspective toward sexual experience.

Had she lived, Nin probably would not have been surprised that her explicitly erotic work, which she valued less than her other writing, would finally make her a bestselling author. **Delta of Venus** (1977) and **Little Birds** (1979), her two collections of erotic work, though written long before, met the sexually-liberated tastes of the 1970s and gained attention, too, because these erotic stories were written from a woman's point of view. Although they were written at a dollar a page for a male patron and can, therefore, be set apart from Nin's more serious fiction, they are not really that divorced from her other work. Principally, that is because of a wholeness in Nin, as both a writer and a person. Though she called the deliberate writing of erotica "unnatural," she could not altogether deny to her own erotic writings the qualities of style and perception that distinguished her other work. As a person, she believed that the sensual and the spiritual were inseparable. She embraced sexual expression as a means of transcendence. Critic Wayne McEvilly, in his introduction to *Seduction of the Minotaur,* states that Nin's work belongs to the "literature of bread," that is, those works that affirm and sustain life. In this respect, her erotic work is at one with her life-affirming aims. She was personally opposed to focusing one's whole literary attention on the sexual life. "It becomes something like the life of a prostitute," she wrote in her *Diary.* The total concentration of either prostitute or literature on the sexual act denies the fullness and richness of sexual experience. Concerned, however, that sexual experience as described from a woman's point of view had been little represented in American literature, she decided to publish her own erotica at whatever risk it might entail to her being taken seriously as a writer. (pp. 57-8)

Nin wrote erotica while living in Paris in the early forties. Without her friendship with Henry Miller, she might never have considered doing such a thing. A book collector first offered Miller a hundred dollars a month to write erotic stories for a wealthy patron. Miller found after a brief period, however, that his interest in writing with "a voyeur at the keyhole [took] all the spontaneity and pleasure out of his fanciful adventures." He suggested that Nin write the stories instead. Like other of her artist friends who needed money, she accepted the offer. She became what she called the "Madame" of an unusual house of literary prostitution. She was the person who negotiated the sale of other hungry artists' erotic writings, as well as her own, protecting their identity and collaborating on the work in progress.

Nin never considered her erotic writing her "real work," which she temporarily put aside for what she referred to as "that world of prostitution." She recognized that, although she wrote only for the money and felt that her own natural style of expression was stifled by her "client," her own feminine point of view was still detectable, and for this reason she valued her erotic work to a certain extent. Like Miller, however, who did not want to use any of the material he was planning to use in his fictional work, Nin did not want to give the collector "anything genuine, and decided to create a mixture of stories [she had] heard, inventions, pretending they were from the diary of a woman." (p. 59)

Despite Nin's own personal denigration of her erotic work for its limited focus, it has been at least as successful as her other fiction. For one thing, her writing style lends itself rather naturally to this form of writing. In fact, while many might regard it as only vaguely related to her more general subject of the feminine spiritual and emotional life, the erotica contains many overlapping elements with her other fiction. The events in her erotic stories, for example, are simple, as they are in her other writings. She gives little background about characters' lives, and she suggests environments more than describes them. In both kinds of fiction, she emphasizes feeling, desire, and personal freedom. Most important in Nin's fiction is her characters' regard for dreams, fantasy, and the marvelous. As she defined it, dreams meant "ideas and images in the mind *not under the command of reason.*" Dreams, Nin felt, could help one transcend ordinary life. Like the nineteenth-century tran-

scendentalists, she believed that the self had deeper rich layers of being which, with effort, could be perceived and assimilated into life as a whole. Where the earlier writers had turned to nature for their model, Nin turned to the creative life and to dreams. The relationship between dreams and reality is present in the erotica, although developed primarily in sexual rather than in the psychological terms of the rest of her fiction.

Despite prodigious efforts, Nin always had difficulty communicating her literary intentions. In part, because of its novelty and because it functions on a simpler plane, the erotica did not suffer the same abounding critical abuse as her other fiction. The criticism leveled at her for her other writing—that it was too narrow, emotional, and feminine—is the point of her erotic writing. The nature of the genre requires that it be accessible and focused. That it was written from a woman's perspective has simply enhanced its interest. For the first time, Nin's fictional style was not criticized for being "unconventional." In fact, critics and the reading public alike were more receptive to her writing than they had ever been before. With the publication of **Delta of Venus,** Nin made the *New York Times* list of best-selling fiction for the first and only time in her writing career.

No one has suggested that Nin's erotica is great art. Its interest resides primarily in its feminine perspective and in its unmistakable poetical quality. When she reviewed the erotica many years after writing it, Nin recognized that, in spite of the collector's demands, her feminine voice was not altogether stopped. "I was intuitively using a woman's language, seeing sexual experience from a woman's point of view."

In *Cities of the Interior,* Nin's women characters struggle for satisfying relationships with men and usually fail, while in the erotic writings their need for mutual desire and fulfillment, at least on one level, is reciprocated. The female characters in both genres search for the unknown, are exceptionally curious, artistic and feminine, and seek sexual fulfillment—but with particular men. Present in all of Nin's fiction is the unwavering conviction that individual initiative and creativity are positive solutions to life's ills. By living expansively one can change external circumstances to fit personal needs. "Transformation" is a term Nin uses frequently to describe the turning of a negative situation into a positive experience. In her work she points out some of the psychological obstacles which must be overcome in order to achieve harmony in one's personal life. In *Cities of the Interior* she is concerned with the dichotomy between the trained impulse to please, serve and nurture others, and the simultaneous need to fulfill oneself. This conflict is present in the erotica as well, but where, in *Cities of the Interior* Nin's women characters are paralyzed by this situation, in the erotica they frequently move ahead to take their pleasure. The immediate resolution, the gratification or fulfillment of one's desire explains, in part, the success of Nin's erotica.

Nin's erotic stories are quite obviously told by a woman. Her intention, despite orders from the collector, is not simply to titillate, but to describe the nuances, curiosity and passion which surround sexual experience. She writes of the impact of a man's perfume, of the sound of his belt being unbuckled, or particular clothes and certain gestures which arouse a woman's interest. She also delves into the emotional complexity of sexual relationships by writing of sensitive issues that could cause discomfort and alarm to the reader, but which accurately reflect the full range of sexual expression. Included in this discussion are such topics as impotence, violence and exhibitionism in men, and frigidity and manipulation in women. Still, one would not accuse Nin of writing in a "realistic" manner in her erotic stories. Although she deals with problems of sexual involvement, they are secondary to the experience itself, and often, the means of overcoming them is the real point of interest in the stories.

According to Nin, men and women are attracted to one another often for specific reasons which have little or nothing to do with the things we have been trained to believe. In one story, for example, a man convinces a prostitute to wear the clothes of a woman he has always desired, but loses interest when he discovers that she does not have a little mole on the inside of her thigh as the other woman had. Another story, about the death of passion, tells about a woman's lover coming to her without his customary exotic perfume and of her resulting indifference to him.

Throughout the erotica, personal desire and fulfillment are often very closely aligned with another's pleasure. Sometimes, in fact, much effort is made solely in the giving of pleasure to another person, and in this way the giver is simultaneously gratified. (pp. 61-3)

The only sadistic or violent moments in all of Nin's writing occur in the erotica, and they happen when one character takes pleasure at the expense of another. The characters in Nin's work who sexually abuse each other are doomed to separate, predictably with bitterness on both sides. Nin makes it clear that she does not object to domination *per se* in sexual activity, and even depicts ways in which it briefly can contribute to sexual fulfillment, primarily when it occurs with mutual consent. But in a story entitled **"The Basque and Bijou,"** she shows the inevitable frustration and resentment which comes from prolonged emotional and sexual domination. In the story, the Basque takes Bijou from a whorehouse to live with him as his model and sexual companion. Although Bijou is anxious to distinguish between her former life and her present circumstances as the model and companion of a respected painter, the Basque takes pleasure only in subjugating, humilating, and exposing her in the presence of his friends. . . . The impact of Bijou's relationship with the Basque is that she has become "so accustomed to his fantasies and cruel games, particularly the way he always managed to have her bound and helpless while all kinds of things were done to her, that for months she could not enjoy her newfound liberty or have a relationship with any other man."

The relationship between the Basque and Bijou is exceptional in Nin's erotic work because elsewhere she stresses male tenderness and reciprocity in sexual relationships. Although the story cannot be ignored, it might best be perceived as an example of those aspects of sexual experience which Nin regards as powerful in a purely destructive way. It is also typical of her work that no sudden event or illumination changes the behaviour of a character for the purpose of a tidy conclusion. Only after much reflection, and usually emotional pain, too, does a character in Nin's fiction become aware in significant ways. In the erotica such character development does not take place.

Nin's erotic stories do go beyond the obvious depiction of two people simply getting together for the purpose of lovemaking. In particular, she focuses on women who have the faculty of arousing passion through illusion and curiosity, as well as through desire, which she frequently terms as "hunger." By creating a poetic veil around sex, Nin believes, one can orchestrate the senses while maintaining or heightening the mystery and power of the sexual experience. Much of what gives her erotic writing its feminine flavour is the examination of the "minor senses," as Nin refers to the fuel which "ignites" sexual interest. (pp. 64-5)

No one has suggested that Nin's erotica is great art. Its interest resides primarily in its feminine perspective and in its unmistakable poetical quality.

—*Rosalind Thomas*

The imaginative role is not always shared by both lovers in Nin's work. Sometimes the male is forced to create a sexually vital experience without his partner. For example, in the story **"The Maja,"** the painter Novalis marries Maria, a Spanish woman, who is Catholic and bourgeois in her attitude about sex. To his regret, she refuses to pose for his paintings or even to let him see her naked body. When she becomes ill and the doctor prescribes pills which cause her to fall asleep, Novalis takes advantage of her drugged state by drawing back the covers and sketching her naked body for his paintings. After a time he loses all interest in Maria while she is awake, and waits to respond to her when she is abandoned and soft in sleep. Upon returning from a brief vacation, Maria fears she has lost Novalis when she discovers him on the floor of his studio making love to a painting of her. "He lay against it as he never had against her. He seemed driven into a frenzy, and all around him were the other paintings of her, nude, voluptuous, beautiful. He threw a passionate glance at them and continued his imaginary embrace." Maria responds to this scene by removing her clothes and, for the first time, offering herself "without hesitation to all his embraces."

Nin explores other forms of sexual fantasy in her stories, such as when one person allows or encourages a partner to project his or her own personal fantasies onto their sexual experience. Mutual enjoyment results from shared imaginative experimentation in Nin's world. Perhaps the most obviously autobiographical story, entitled **"The Model,"** describes the sexual awakening of a young woman who has become an artist's model. When an artist invites the model to go to the country where many artists are working for the summer, she accepts, thinking she can make some money there. But after she arrives, the artist insists on her having sex with him, and, when she refuses, he successfully prevents her from getting work with the other artists in the small town. She leaves the town and goes for a walk in the woods. There she comes upon a painter who agrees to hire her as his model. Draping her in a white sheet, he props her against a wooden box and tells her to go to sleep while he paints her. When she awakes, he is leaning over her, touching her very lightly. He tells her he once saw a woman in Fez asleep as she was, and that he had dreamed many times of awakening that woman just as he has awakened her. Then he asks her permission to live out the rest of his sexual fantasy from the past, which she allows him to do.

Regardless of the form the imagination takes in lovemaking, Nin consistently asserts the conjunction of sex and feeling. She explains, for example, how sex can generate maternal feelings towards a man: "She felt herself as a mother receiving a child into herself, drawing him in to lull him, to protect him." She also writes about a woman who wants to lose her virginity in order "to be made a woman." In order to be a "woman," she suggests, one must first feel like one. In most of the erotic stories, Nin hints that these feminine urges which make a woman more specifically aware of herself as a female derive from the combined effects of sex and feeling for a man. The character who wants to become a "woman" is seeking someone with whom to fall in love in order to fulfill her dream of womanhood. The woman who has maternal feelings for her lover also cares deeply for him in other ways. At one point her lover tells her that he knows: "you are capable of many loves, that I will be the first one, that from now on nothing will stop you from expanding. You're sensual, so sensual." She makes it clear to him, however, that she distinguishes between capacity and real desire stemming from feeling. " 'You can't love so many times,' she answered. 'I want my eroticism mixed with love. And deep love one does not often experience.' " In a different story Nin reminds the reader that this need for emotion in sexual relationships is not exclusive to women. In contemplating the enthusiastic response of her lover, the female narrator of the story muses: "Women very often pursue him, but he is like a woman and needs to believe himself in love. Although a beautiful woman can excite him, if he does not feel some kind of love, he is impotent."

Along with the emotional ties that accompany sex, Nin is interested in the specific form and impact of women's desire for men. Although she is capable of exaggeration at times, she acknowledges in the "Preface" to **Delta of Venus** that her occasional caricatures of sexuality are deliberate and are prompted by anger toward her clinical patron. A noteworthy example is: "There was a picture of a tortured woman, impaled on a thin stick which ran into her sex and out of her mouth. It had the appearance of ultimate sexual possession and aroused in Elena a feeling of pleasure." On the other hand, Nin can use overstatement in a positive way and with humour to describe a woman's passion. At these times she is at her best; her short staccato sentences combine with her rather formal use of the lan-

guages to produce a comic effect. An example concerns the "Madam" of a house of prostitution who takes seriously her job of appraising men:

> All day Maman had nourished herself with the expeditions of her eyes, which never traveled above or below the middle of a man's body. They were always on a level with the trouser opening. . . . At times, in great crowds, she had the courage to reach out and touch. Her hand moved like a thief's, with an incredible agility. She never fumbled or touched the wrong place, but went straight to the place below the belt where soft rolling prominences lay, and sometimes, unexpectedly, an insolent baton.

Nin describes a feminine interest in men in more serious terms when she attaches a psychological dimension. Ironically, her psychological probing could surprise the reader who has followed traditional sexual myths about women. The reader learns, for example, that a female character's prolific sex life is due to numbness, that the reason for all her activity is based not on desire, but on her need to feel anything at all:

> She is always smiling, gay, but underneath she feels unreal, remote, detached from experience. She acts as if she were asleep. She is trying to awaken by falling into bed with anyone who invites her. . . . I have never once heard of her resisting—this, coupled with frigidity! She deceives everybody, including herself. She looks so wet and open that men think she is continuously in a state of near orgasm. But it is not true. The actress in her appears cheerful and calm, and inside she is going to pieces.

The outcome of this story is that the narrator manages to awaken the frigid woman. In this particular case, the psychological dimension contributes to the interest and drama of the story. Often it is more of an aside or diversion from the events than central to them; sometimes it is even an intrusion. (pp. 66-9)

Nin's repeated psychological journeys into her characters in a genre which essentially, as she acknowledges, is one-dimensional, perhaps testifies to the struggle she had confining herself to this level. One gathers that she was a sensual woman, as she suggests herself in the "Preface" to **Delta of Venus:** "If the unexpurgated version of the *Diary* is ever published, this [erotic] feminine point of view will be established more clearly," thus hinting that her own personal sex life was important enough to her to record in her daily journal, and perhaps, one day, even publish.

Sexuality to her was a positive experience in its ability to affirm, nourish and inspire. It was an authentic human expression which, when combined with caring, could be as transcendent and creative a form of expression as any other. Through the wisdom and fulfillment gained from personal experience, including sensual expression, she argues throughout her writing, one learns about the true nature of the self. (p. 69)

Rosalind Thomas, "Anaïs Nin's Erotica: A Feminine Perspective," in Room of One's Own, *Vol. 7, No. 4, 1982, pp. 57-69.*

FURTHER READING

Bibliography

Cutting, Rose Marie. *Anaïs Nin: A Reference Guide.* Boston: G. K. Hall & Co., 1978, 218 p.

Includes an introduction discussing Nin's life and career and the critical reception of her *Diary* and fiction, followed by selected primary and secondary bibliographies.

Franklin, Benjamin V. *Anaïs Nin: A Bibliography.* Kent, Ohio: Kent State University Press, 1973, 115 p.

Bibliography of Nin's books and pamphlets, her contributions to books and periodicals, recordings of her work, and her editorship of periodicals.

Biography

Fancher, Edwin. "Anaïs Nin: Avant-Gardist With a Loyal Underground." *The Village Voice* IV, No. 31 (27 May 1959): 4-5.

Relates a conversation in which Nin discussed her ventures in self-publishing, her experiences in Paris, and the influence of her friendships with several prominent writers.

Nin, Anaïs. *A Woman Speaks: The Lectures, Seminars, and Interviews of Anaïs Nin,* edited by Evelyn J. Hinz. Chicago: Swallow Press, 1975, 270 p.

Collection of Nin's lectures and interviews in which she discusses the role of women in society and as artists, the importance of the development of an authentic self, and her philosophies on art and writing.

Criticism

Evans, Oliver. "The Figure of the Father: *Winter of Artifice.*" In his *Anaïs Nin,* pp. 44-62. Carbondale and Edwardsville: Southern Illinois University Press, 1968.

Provides a thorough analysis of characterization and the father-daughter relationship depicted in *Winter of Artifice.*

Scholar, Nancy. "*Under a Glass Bell:* Into the Labyrinth." In her *Anaïs Nin,* pp. 90-7. Boston: G. K. Hall & Co., 1984.

Examines characters in *Under a Glass Bell* who fail to transcend the confinements of the self, and relates several stories to Nin's experiences as recorded in her *Diary.*

Tindall, Gillian. "Doldrums." *New Statesman* 76, No. 1956 (6 September 1968): 292.

Review of *Under a Glass Bell* contending that Nin's work is limited by egoism and that it is not highly innovative.

Additional coverage of Nin's life and career is contained in the following sources published by Gale Research: *Contemporary Authors* Vols. 13-16, rev. ed., Vols. 69-72 [obituary]; *Contemporary Authors New Revision Series,* Vol. 22; *Contemporary Literary Criticism,* Vols. 1, 4, 8, 11, 14, 60; *Dictionary of Literary Biography,* Vols. 2, 4; and *Major 20th-Century Writers.*

Edna O'Brien

1932-

Irish novelist, short story writer, dramatist, scriptwriter, poet, and essayist.

INTRODUCTION

O'Brien is best known for such novels as *The Country Girls, The Lonely Girl,* and *Girls in Their Married Bliss,* a trilogy that portrays young Irish women chafing under the constraints of a conservative culture and seeking emotional and sexual freedom. She is also the author of several volumes of short stories, including *A Scandalous Woman, and Other Stories, Returning,* and *A Fanatic Heart.* Her short fiction commonly explores the emotional lives of women dealing with complex and often contradictory aspects of family and love relationships.

Shortly after *The Country Girls* was published in 1960, O'Brien moved to London to escape what she perceived as the oppressiveness of Irish culture. In fact, many of O'Brien's stories are banned in her native Ireland because of the frankness with which O'Brien writes about women's sexuality. Much of her short fiction first appeared in the *New Yorker;* her first collection, *The Love Object,* was published in 1968. Subsequent collections include *Mrs. Reinhardt, and Other Stories* and *Lantern Slides,* which won the 1990 *Los Angeles Times* Book Award. O'Brien often draws on the scenes of her childhood—Irish village life during the 1940s and 1950s—as well as contemporary urban life in her short fiction. Although her stories depict characters from different social classes and backgrounds, her protagonists are usually women who are involved in problematic love and family relationships.

O'Brien's Irish stories are characterized by vivid descriptions of the Irish countryside and by her skillful evocation of the hidden turmoil that can be present beneath the seemingly placid surface of village life. They often depict young protagonists who yearn for love and attention or for a greater measure of freedom than the circumscribed nature of village life affords them. In "My Mother's Mother," for example, a lonely girl craves her absent mother's affection while being raised by relatives. She constructs elaborate, and ultimately futile, plans to rejoin her mother. In many stories young women attempt to reconcile their sexual desires with the strictures of Catholicism. O'Brien's realistic and compassionate handling of this struggle has received much critical favor as well as controversy. As the title suggests, the 1982 collection *Returning* focuses on the Ireland of O'Brien's childhood and features women who either physically return to their homeland or who are immersed in childhood reminiscences. Characters from earlier novels appear in stories throughout the collection; for example, the central figure from *The Country Girls* appears as a schoolgirl in "Sister Imelda."

O'Brien's urban stories often involve more sophisticated women whose experiences with men and sex have left them disappointed. "Over" and "Forgetting," from the collection *The Love Object,* present women trying to overcome the emotional consequences of broken love affairs. The protagonist in the title story of the collection is unable to relinquish the memories of her former lover, and she laments: "If I let go of him now . . . all our happiness and my subsequent pain . . . will have been nothing and nothing is a dreadful thing to hold on to." *Mrs. Reinhardt, and Other Stories* continues the theme of feminine adversity, but it portrays women who attain some degree of peace and happiness in their lives. "Mrs Reinhardt" focuses on the reunion of an estranged couple, and in "Ways" a woman forgoes a sexual encounter with a man to whom she is attracted out of respect for his wife.

O'Brien's portrayal of character has been the focus of much critical attention. Although she is generally commended for her insights into female psychology, some critics, noting that her women characters are concerned with sex and love relationships to the exclusion of other interests, accuse O'Brien of perpetuating stereotypes of women as emotional and subservient. Furthermore, with few exceptions, men in O'Brien's stories are portrayed as selfish, drunk, violent, libidinous, or incompetent. While acknowledging certain limitations in her characterizations, however, most critics agree that O'Brien's depiction of women responding to disappointment and betrayal are realistic and insightful.

PRINCIPAL WORKS

SHORT FICTION

The Love Object   1968
A Scandalous Woman, and Other Stories   1974
Mrs. Reinhardt, and Other Stories   1978; also published as *A Rose in the Heart, and Other Stories,* 1979
Returning   1982
A Fanatic Heart: Selected Stories of Edna O'Brien   1984
Lantern Slides   1990

OTHER MAJOR WORKS

*The Country Girls   (novel)   1960
*The Lonely Girl   (novel)   1962; also published as *The Girl with Green Eyes,* 1970
†Girl with Green Eyes   (screenplay)   1964
*Girls in Their Married Bliss   (novel)   1964
August Is a Wicked Month   (novel)   1965
Casualties of Peace   (novel)   1966
Three into Two Won't Go   (screenplay)   1969
Zee & Co.   (novel)   1971
Night   (novel)   1972
‡X Y and Zee   (screenplay)   1972
The Gathering   (drama)   1974
Mother Ireland   [with Fergus Bourke]   (nonfiction) 1976
Arabian Days   [with Gerard Klijn]   (nonfiction)   1977
Johnny I Hardly Knew You   (novel)   1977; also published as *I Hardly Knew You,* 1978
Virginia   (drama)   1980
Vanishing Ireland   (nonfiction)   1987
The High Road   (novel)   1988
On the Bone   (poetry)   1989

*These works were published as *The Country Girls Trilogy and Epilogue* in 1986.

†This screenplay is an adaptation of the novel *The Lonely Girl.*

‡This screenplay is an adaptation of the novel *Zee & Co.*

The Times Literary Supplement   (essay date 1968)

[*The following is a review of* The Love Object.]

There must be many people who, in discussing all the heated and often tedious words written and spoken about the Problem of being a Woman in modern society, would instance Miss Edna O'Brien as a traitor to both sides. No sooner does she make us laugh with some cunning evocation of the perfidy of the male than she compels sympathy for the desperate female left to fend for herself. Woman

continues to torment herself with longing for the man whom she knows to be unworthy of her love; pride and desire are never to be reconciled in her pursuit of satisfaction: fulfilment never fails to bring a bitter and lonely reaction in which the desired becomes suddenly contemptible and distant. Perhaps one might say that these stories [in *The Love Object*], in which such themes constantly obtrude, crystallize the talent and also the limited territory which belong to any novelist so determinedly feminine as Miss O'Brien.

It is, for instance, remarkable that not one of the men who figure as objects of love or fantasy or fear or contempt in these stories ever comes across as worthy of inspiring such emotions. They are seen entirely as objects—Miss O'Brien is under no illusion in selecting her title—caparisoned as rich, distinguished, drunken, dictatorial—their lives outside the central sexual situation entirely blurred and irrelevant. In the title story, the lover happens to be a married man, eminent and therefore preoccupied with secrecy; he cannot concentrate on making love while his dress suit, complete with medals, hangs accusingly from the wardrobe; he asks for a clothes brush after their first night together; he feels it wrong to continue the affair when she admits to being in love; he will never be allowed to know the intensified love that the end of the affair has aroused in her. The pattern is almost laughably commonplace—almost, the impassioned self-indulgence of any girl consoling her first heartbreak by reliving every detail on paper. And yet, because Miss O'Brien is never prepared to forget or forgive the injustice or the humiliation to which women so ridiculously subject themselves, this is neither a sad nor a sentimental tale.

Five out of the eight stories in this volume have been previously published in the *New Yorker,* so it is perhaps not surprising that they should span much of the material Miss O'Brien has used in her novels. The girl from the hill farm in Ireland who bicycles so excitedly into town for her first party at the Commercial Hotel, only to find that shifting the furniture is her least frightful role for the evening, comes straight from those early naive country girl days, when sex was guiltier and pleasure simpler. **"How to Grow a Wisteria"**, the most self-conscious parable in the book, enlarges on the strange Svengali husband who appeared at the end of *Casualties of Peace.* **"Paradise"** is almost a blueprint for the South of France nightmare in *August is a Wicked Month;* the millionaire charmer, villa peopled with tough insiders, leisure and pleasure pursued with ruthless abandon, is moved by the shy clumsy girl who cannot even swim; he is recognizably recalled and fleetingly seductive—yet seen with extraordinary callousness, simply as the provider of security and secret sex, and, even as she marvels at the new excitements, his mistress recognizes him as someone who refuses involvement and fears her kind of truth.

Miss O'Brien is a writer on whom the tamer, less scandalous moments of experience might seem hardly to impinge; yet here again she can surprise by the accuracy of her observation and the skill with which she uses some very tangible detail to emphasize the poignancy of a relationship; the country mother, over from Ireland to visit her daughter in London, comments that Green Park would make very good grazing, and fills a small liqueur bottle with holy water as a bashful hint that sophisticates need a protective talisman. Just as one begins to suspect that the artlessness is concealing not art but merely an alert memory, Miss O'Brien will twist a phrase, introduce an image, or sneak in a quiet sardonic comment, and force one to recognize how considerable is the skill and care needed to make it all seem so simple.

> *"The Girl Can't Help It," in* The Times Literary Supplement, *No. 3462, July 4, 1968, p. 697.*

The Times Literary Supplement (essay date 1974)

[*In the following excerpt, the critic discusses O'Brien's portrayal of women in* A Scandalous Woman.]

Miss O'Brien opens [*A Scandalous Woman, and Other Stories*] with the title story. . . . Its beautiful, blighted heroine—the daredevil country girl Eily who is always a little out of breath, plays at surgical operations and meets the local bank-clerk in the woods—is perhaps not a very novel gift to literature; and our narrator, looking back to her dateless days in the cornfield and on Eily's "operating table" with the standard Celtic tendency to harp on innocence, treads an even better-beaten path through the Irish countryside. But something in the restraint of the writing, perhaps the reassuring lightness of touch with the Irish accents in the prose, made momentarily startling once in a while by some odd rural term suddenly remembered, keeps the reader well enough rewarded to continue. It is often a matter of the tiniest nuances. When Eily's father, for instance, hears that the bank clerk's attentions have had the worst possible effects on his daughter, he comes stumping around in a neatly delineated rage: "When we opened the door to him the first thing I saw was the slash hook in his hand, and then the condition of his hair which was upstanding and wild." The shock of the well-named murderous implement and the suddenly very Irish "condition" and "upstanding" are nicely matched. And then the narrator, filled with sympathetic dread, feels as she thinks of Eily that she too is having a baby, "and that if I were to move or part my legs some terrible thing would come ushering out". This strange intransitive use of "usher", no doubt connected by more or less ancient linguistic ties with *uscire,* makes the emotion distinct and appropriate.

At the end of this opening piece, Eily is glimpsed again, "years later", serving in the shop her bank-boy-turned-grocer has taken to keeping. As she remembers the occasion, the narrator sighs: "I thought that ours indeed was a land of shame, a land of murder and a land of strange sacrificial women." It is a thoughtful conclusion—almost a debating-society motion, in fact—but one which would reverberate more lastingly in the mind if the rest of the book did not tease it out so repetitively. Miss O'Brien's "strange sacrificial women", whether explicitly Irish or not, seldom liberate themselves from the repressed-child/lost-adult formula, and soon an atmosphere of defeatism begins to spread forward through the book.

"Over", the second item, is a peculiarly abject plaint ut-

tered by an abandoned woman half-mad with humiliation ("Oh my dear I would like to be something else, anything else, an albatross"). So when **"The Favourite"** tells of a girl universally blessed and cosseted, it is no great surprise or revelation to find her later life turning suddenly bad, on a whim of nature ("Oh Jesus", she uttered aloud. "Is this how it is when one begins to be unhappy"). By the time we get to **"Honeymoon"**, however strange the events recorded therein, we are in no doubt that the new wife will come to realize, all too soon, that "her own husband was a man she had loved, but that she had been mistaken, and . . . she cried from the very depth of her young, and about to be chastised, being".

What the promised chastisement will consist of we know from **"Over"**, and will learn anew from **"The House of My Dreams"**, the last story, where another distraught ex-wife—described in the third person this time, though it seems to matter remarkably little—makes a memory-torturing tour of her stripped and dusty ex-home: "She saw the sad world that she had invented for herself, but of the future she saw nothing, not even one little godsend." Altogether, this seems to be a book destined to appeal most deeply to those in a like case. Its different angles and ranges all aim in the end at the same distress: that nameless area of despair which grandmothers used to identify, with a shake of the head, as "what every woman knows". Miss O'Brien's mood announces itself with an undeniable force, but one is powerless to respond to it constructively as one is when faced, for example, with a woman who detests the influence of her own hormones over her behaviour. In other words, the problem expresses itself best in extra-literary terms; none of Miss O'Brien's reiterations of what her blurb-writer calls her "hopelessly vulnerable" personages is likely, on the present evidence, to exorcize whatever demons render them, and their creator, helpless. Indeed, Miss O'Brien's work marks her out as an awkwardly unfashionable case: a person for whom the twin businesses of being a full-time author and a full-time woman do not exactly clash, but, more seriously, feed all too destructively one off the other.

> *"What Women Know," in* The Times Literary Supplement, *No. 3783, September 6, 1974, p. 945.*

Agnes McNeill Donohue (essay date 1975)

[*Donohue is an American educator and critic. In the following excerpt, she praises the lyrical prose in* A Scandalous Woman.]

Since her first novel, *The Country Girls,* (1960) Edna O'Brien has grown as an artist. Like Mrs. Lessing she writes short stories, novels and plays; recently she has written three screenplays. Unlike Doris Lessing, Edna O'Brien seems to have no overweening political or social conscience. Her focus, as Lessing's, is on women, but women in heat, betrayed and abandoned not by capitalist pigs, middle-class morality, or hunger for food, but by their own too-hungry, too-generous, too-undiscriminating hearts.

The social critic could and would submit that O'Brien's

insulted and injured women are in reaction against the repressive religious and superstitious simplistic morality of rural West Country Ireland. Early and enforced abnegation and denial of natural instincts leads to later violent and insatiable longing for love and pitiful gratitude for husks dropped by older married men or professional playboys. However I don't think this is what O'Brien is saying. She is at her best when she writes of the Irish countryside and her lyrical lilting prose (totally unlike Lessing's) is of a deeper mythic disquiet. The banshee wail is soft but omnipresent under the rattle and clatter of Dublin and London; the Irish cow dung stinks through the cheap French perfume worn defiantly by her country girls, and the taste of the peat bog is in the gin and orange.

Her language is a miracle of evocation: the crooning and keening and melancholy of Synge—"She began to cry quietly and unobtrusively, and yet she cried from the very depth of her young and about to be chastised being," the vulgarity of Behan—"Hickey picked him up, threw him over a paling, and told the world at large that such a twit had for a backside two eggs tied up in a handkerchief;" the fatalism and gloom of O'Casey—"It is not good to repudiate the dead because they do not leave you alone, they are like dogs that bark intermittently at night;" There is not the Joycean rage at the old sow who eats her young but a few of the epiphanies are there: "There are times when the thing we are seeing changes before our very eyes, and if it is a landscape we praise nature, and if it is celestial we invoke God, but if it is a loved one who defects, we excuse ourselves and say we have to be somewhere and are already late for our next appointment. We do not stay to put pennies over the half-dead eyes."

But most of all O'Brien is herself with the lyric short story form which she manipulates now in the first person, now in the third, with skill and mastery. **"The Favorite"** is a minor triumph in sixteen pages of a young country girl for whom everything goes right. She is everyone's favorite, her father's, the nuns' at the convent school, and the delight of the husband of her choice. But after forty, her children away at school, her husband beefily snoring by her side, her smugness is suddenly punctured by her realization of the monotony of her life, and she exclaims: "Oh Jesus . . . Is this how it is when one begins to be unhappy?"

"The Creature" tells of a woman turned out of her house by her son and daughter-in-law, dreaming always of the possibility of a loving reunion. A schoolteacher trying to get over an unhappy love affair insists that the son visit his mother. Everything goes wrong and the busybody teacher realizes too late—"Whereas for twenty years she had lived on that last high tightrope of hope, it had been taken away from her, leaving her without anyone, without anything. . . ."

Mostly, though, O'Brien writes of the scandalous women forever *giving* to married men, or men with mistresses, or to men who are defiantly uninvolved, and they get heart-scalded when they are left, as they invariably are. Here O'Brien sometimes chokes on the old Kinsey report and we are given not erotic but rather clinical Lessing-like descriptions of what she calls "inventive" love-making.

Somehow these details of the private parts of the aging gentleman lovers and the demands made on them by the hungry women may explain why all her women get left. Sheer exhaustion and near apoplexy may be the simpler reason for male defection. Not every man—Irish, English, or Lower-Slobovian—is a trapeze artist.

An encounter with Doris Lessing and Edna O'Brien is to be inundated with women, women, women, and a few vague, pale men, and like the old joke says—it's hard to tell the screwer from the screwee. (pp. 60-1)

    Agnes McNeill Donohue, in a review of "A Scandalous Woman, and Other Stories," in The Critic, *Chicago, Vol. 33, No. 2, January-February, 1975, pp. 58-61.*

Eugene Kraft   (essay date 1975)

[*In the following excerpt, Kraft explores reasons for the popularity of O'Brien's short stories and characterizes O'Brien as a writer of "little versatility."*]

Edna O'Brien is one of the contemporary Irish-English writers apparently able to be translated into American. One of the greatest enigmas facing the critic of contemporary fiction is why certain English writers of unquestioned merit (V. S. Pritchett, Elizabeth Bowen, H. E. Bates) have never really attained much popularity in this country among the reading public, while other writers (Muriel Spark, Iris Murdoch, Edna O'Brien) seem to have bridged the Atlantic with relative ease. It is certainly an important question, and occasionally a distressing one. There would seem on the face of it to be absolutely no reason why A. E. Coppard is the forgotten writer he is today in this country.

Edna O'Brien's [*A Scandalous Woman, and Other Stories*] augurs well for her in this respect. . . . One reason for her popularity is the fabulistic tone to her stories, particularly in the title story in this collection. **"A Scandalous Woman"** might have been written fifty years ago; O'Brien has remained unaffected by the technical advances of Joyce, Beckett, or Miller. She has remained uninfluenced by the recognized necessity for extreme condensation in the short story. When she does not write fables, she writes the easiest sort of conversational prose. These facts, together with the fact of her ability to infuse a strong sense of genuineness into her writing probably account for her popularity.

This sense of genuineness is what makes **"A Scandalous Woman"** the very fine short story it is. Rural Ireland is the setting and the morally hysterical, male-dominated culture of Ireland is, as always in O'Brien's fiction, the villain. Nevertheless, it is as impossible to call O'Brien an Irish writer as it is to call Elizabeth Bowen an Irish writer. From the passion with which O'Brien hates Irish Catholicism and the anguish with which she remembers her own Irish childhood one is certain that had she never left Ireland her writing career would never have gotten off the ground.

It is in those stories in which the sense of genuineness is not really worked at that O'Brien's efforts do not amount to much. **"The Creature"** and **"Honeymoon"** are two such stories. As far as these stories go, they are believable enough. But the author does not really have a story to tell, she does not really feel what she is saying, and all the reader is left with are bits of "local color." She reminds one, in this respect, of John Updike; both writers are intelligent enough to write interestingly when they cannot write genuinely.

"The House of My Dreams" is another well-written story in the collection, once again because the sense of genuineness is very strong. The reader is as sure that Edna O'Brien has had nervous collapses as he is sure that Anne Sexton had them. In fact, O'Brien has rather too many nervous collapses; she has rewritten the same story of the deserted, neurotic woman many times. Her art is cyclic; the woman never escapes from the horror of desertion or the sterility of her life alone. In **"Over"** we have another deserted woman and in **"A Journey"** though the desertion has not yet occurred, it probably will very soon. There is not much hope, and the woman in all these stories is not liberated. She sits passively, waiting for the telephone to ring.

O'Brien is a good writer in the one area of life she has chosen to depict, but she has little versatility. She is not interested in experimentation, and if she has made any attempts to broaden her scope as a writer, there is no evidence of it in this book. Thus, the irony of her greater popularity than that of more serious artists remains. (pp. 291-92)

> *Eugene Kraft, in a review of "A Scandalous Woman, and Other Stories," in* Studies in Short Fiction, *Vol. XII, No. 3, Summer, 1975, pp. 291-92.*

O'Brien on the influence of environment on her writing:

If I had grown up on the steppes of Russia, or in Brooklyn— my parents lived there when they were first married—my material would have been different but my apprehension might be just the same. I happened to grow up in a country that was and is breathlessly beautiful so the feeling for nature, for verdure and for the soil was instilled into me. Secondly, there was no truck with culture or literature so that my longing to write, sprung up of its own accord, was spontaneous. The only books in our house were prayer books, cookery books and blood-stock reports. I was privy to the world around me, was aware of everyone's little history, the stuff from which stories and novels are made. On the personal level, it was pretty drastic. So all these things combined to make me what I am.

> *O'Brien, in an interview with Philip Roth in* The New York Times, *18 November 1984.*

Frank Tuohy (essay date 1978)

[*Tuohy is an English novelist, short story writer, and travel writer. His work focuses on the influence of social customs and physical surroundings on his characters. In*

the following review, he examines the varied settings and shared themes of the short stories in Mrs. Reinhardt.]

The stories in Edna O'Brien's third collection [**Mrs. Reinhardt, and Other Stories**] are varied in setting, in style and in execution, though the theme of feminine adversity remains fairly constant. They retain the odd, stubborn energy, the baffled resilience that triumphs over humiliation of spirit and circumstance, which characterized the early novels. A certain decorousness seems, however, to have set in—attributable perhaps to the chastening influence of the editors of *The New Yorker*.

Five stories have Ireland as their setting. There is a sure and unobtrusive touch in scenery and atmosphere, the blue hills, burned-out houses, the desolate seashore towns with shops full of hand-knitting. Though the circumstances are grim, the effect is not as depressive as it is in other Irish writers. **"The Small Town Lovers"** and **"A Rose in the Heart"** celebrate a strong will to survive. The latter story traces a girl's relationship with her mother from horrific childbirth to near-farcical funeral, taking in on its way a drunken hatchet-wielding father, a lesbian nun, a marriage to a man "as odd as two left shoes", a failed reconciliation in an expensive hotel, and then the mother's death, leading to the discovery of a packet of savings for the daughter, but no message. Communication never takes place: "A new wall had arisen, stronger and sturdier." Another long Irish story, **"Clara"**, is less successful, an attempt at objectivity by a writer engrossed in the personal life. It is odd that the narrator, full of native wit, should turn out to be a Dutch oil-man—and one called Herema, too—and the story itself, as an exercise in Irish-Gothic, owes something to Sheridan Le Fanu, but lacks the structure that would make it other than a somewhat arbitrary succession of events.

Away from Ireland, the physical world is described with comparable exactness, but there is some loss of definition in the people that inhabit it. Men, particularly beautiful young men, tend to be threatening; the young American in **"Mrs Reinhardt"** is nearly as nasty as a Patricia Highsmith hero. Such characters seem now to be taking over the role that seducing females had in earlier popular fiction; and there is a sense of moral gain whenever the heroine resists them. In the story—nowadays nearly obligatory among our far-flung writers—which is set on an American campus, the onset of a Vermont winter is marvellously evoked; but the narrative weakens when the protagonist, standing in for the author, righteously eludes the young seducer. **"In the Hours of Darkness"** is set in Cambridge, England. After uneatable grouse at a dons' dinner-party (Edna O'Brien excels at describing food) there is an appalling night spent alone at a ghastly hotel. Here again, the male characters have been found wanting: the don is self-confessedly inadequate and the protagonist's freshman son disappears promptly into a masculine world. O'Brien characters always spend much of their time as casualties of peace, convalescing from affairs but nowadays they are fortunate in that they can suffer in comfort in expensive French hotels. It is unusual, indeed, to find a writer who can describe being rich with as much conviction as being poor—an absence of social curiosity leaves the perceptions uncluttered.

The procedure comes unstuck only when the scene is London, and the world as portrayed in glossy magazines. This world exists, and so do the classless people like Mr and Mrs Reinhardt who inhabit it. But irony and speculation are needed to bring it and them to life. Elsewhere, in spite of some clumsy writing, there is no lack of the bruised awareness which is Miss O'Brien's speciality, nor of the sensuous perception which brings such pleasure to her readers.

> Frank Tuohy, "Suffering in Comfort," in The Times Literary Supplement, No. 3972, May 19, 1978, p. 545.

Victoria Glendinning   (essay date 1982)

[Glendinning is an English educator, journalist, and biographer. Her studies of Edith Sitwell and Elizabeth Bowen have been praised for their shrewd observations, sympathy, and liveliness. In the following excerpt, she lauds O'Brien's realistic and nostalgic portrayal of childhood in Returning.]

In [**Returning,** a] collection of nine stories, some of which first appeared in the *New Yorker,* Edna O'Brien returns, as her title suggests, to the Ireland of her childhood. There is no connecting narrative link between the "tales", but the child is the same child throughout, a small farmer's daughter in a frugal, narrow community where nothing happened except ploughing, planting and harvesting, where "none of the women wore cosmetics and in the local chemist shop the jars of cold cream and vanishing cream used to go dry because of no demand".

Other shops did better; in **"Courtship",** handsome Michael and his brothers run the grocery shop, which also stocked "animal feed, serge for suits, winceyette, cotton, paraffin, cakes, confectionery, boots, wellingtons, and cable-knit sweaters that were made by spinsters and lonely women in the mountains". Also pink corsets and, in the back, pints of porter. Not many of the local boys were as desirable as Michael; a new curate or bank clerk or creamery manager had an inflated sexual value in this shut-off rural world where Gort and Limerick were big places and Dublin a metropolis only to be dreamed of.

Because of the cooling discipline of the child's-eye view, **Returning** is stripped of the over-fluent lyric keening that has sometimes made Edna O'Brien's writing dangerously like a parody of itself. But even in this tauter version, there is much to be learnt from her language by anyone interested in Irish-English, which, intonation apart, has its own vocabulary and sentence structures—presumably deriving in part from long-ago adaptations of Gaelic, and in part (which sometimes gives an odd impression of stilted gentility) from English words or phrases that have fallen out of common usage in England.

Edna O'Brien also has words for country things and everyday gestures that are unfamiliar to English ears, and some that sound zanily exotic—whimsical Mrs Morgan "had a figari to buy an egg-timer", for example. Is a figari an Irish vagary? It has to be said that sometimes the syntax is a little awkward by anybody's standards, and that

one of the best of the exotic words—pretty Nancy puts a lock of the new curate's hair into "a little lavallièu that she wore round her neck"—turns out to be a misprint for *lavallière.*

There is a double vision in these tales: the adult that the child will become says from time to time what she can see from her greater distance. In **"The Connor Girls"**, about a family whose proud but faded Protestantism makes them alien, the narrator flashes forward to show how the child-self, when she marries out of the community, will become equally alien. "I realized that by choosing his world I had said good-bye to my own and to those in it. By such choices we gradually become exiles, until at last we are quite alone." Elsewhere she describes the way childhood infiltrates the rest of life:

> The years go by and everything and everyone gets replaced. Those we knew, though absent, are yet merged inextricably into new folk so that each person is to us a sum of many others and the effect is of opening box after box in which the original is forever hidden.

The "original", in **Returning,** is as likely to be malicious or sinister as to be loved or loving. With all the people from her past forever "entangled" in her, the child already knows she will, in the end, go away. She never loses "the desire to escape or the strenuous habit of hoping". Having escaped, there is the desire for return—only possible in imagination—to that "far-off region of childhood, where nothing ever dies, not even oneself ".

The authenticity of her return seems proven by the way this book reminds you of aspects of childhood that are instantly recognizable, though hitherto forgotten: for example, the little subterfuges made to conceal illicit intentions. In **"My Mother's Mother"** the child, staying with her grandparents and aunt, plans secretly to run away back to her home. "I told my aunt I was going on a picnic and affected to be very happy by humming and doing little reels." This has a pathetic ring of remembered truth. This story is also good on the passionate way a child focuses on food, in this case fresh home-made bread "dolloped with butter and greengage jam". In the same story the child is given a present of a toy watch on a bead bracelet, and in describing it, Edna O'Brien again establishes the attentive close-up focus peculiar to children.

There are some childish spyings on adult sex, and a few predictably depressing gropings from desperate country bachelors; but in the last story, a story of first love, the loved one is a nun in the convent where the girl is now a boarder. This is the best shaped of all the pieces here, not overwritten, told with an air of slight bewilderment and no overtones of adult knowingness.

The rebellious schoolfriend Baba is in **"Sister Imelda"** too, thus linking the end of this book with the earliest of Edna O'Brien's novels. In the years between, her fiction has, on the evidence of this volume, gained in hardness and truthfulness, which generally means saying less rather than more; for as she writes at the end of **"Sister Imelda"**, "in our deepest moments we say the most inadequate things". Oddly, this book about childhood is probably the least childlike fiction that Edna O'Brien has written.

Victoria Glendinning, "In the Far-Off Region," in The Times Literary Supplement, No. 4125, April 23, 1982, p. 456.

Edna O'Brien with Shusha Guppy   (interview date 1984)

[*In the following interview with Guppy, a Persian-born journalist and critic, O'Brien discusses the inception and course of her literary career and her principal literary influences and themes.*]

[Guppy]: *You once said that as far back as you can remember you have been a writer. At what point did you actually start writing literature?*

[O'Brien]: When I say I have written from the beginning, I mean that all real writers write from the beginning, that the vocation, the obsession, is already there, and that the obsession derives from an intensity of feeling which normal life cannot accommodate. I started writing snippets when I was eight or nine, but I wrote my first novel when I left Ireland and came to live in London. I had never been outside Ireland and it was November when I arrived in England. I found everything so different, so *alien*. Waterloo Station was full of people who were nameless, faceless. There were wreaths on the Cenotaph for Remembrance Sunday, and I felt bewildered and lost—an outsider. So in a sense *The Country Girls,* which I wrote in those first few weeks after my arrival, was my experience of Ireland and my farewell to it. But something happened to my style which I will tell you about. I had been trying to write short bits, and these were always flowery and over-lyrical. Shortly after I arrived in London I saw an advertisement for a lecture given by Arthur Mizener [author of a book on F. Scott Fitzgerald, *The Far Side Of Paradise*] on Hemingway and Fitzgerald. You must remember that I had no literary education, but a fervid religious one. So I went to the lecture and it was like a thunderbolt—Saul of Tarsus on his horse! Mizener read out the first paragraph of *Farewell to Arms* and I couldn't believe it—this totally uncluttered, precise, true prose, which was *also* very moving and lyrical. I can say that the two things came together then: my being ready for the revelation and my urgency to write. The novel *wrote itself,* so to speak, in a few weeks. All the time I was writing it I couldn't stop crying, although it is a fairly buoyant, funny book. But it was the separation from Ireland which brought me to the point where I *had* to write, though I had always been in love with literature.

If you had always loved literature, why did you study chemistry at university rather than English?

The usual reason, family. My family was radically opposed to anything to do with literature. Although Ireland has produced so many great writers, there is a deep suspicion about writing there. Somehow they know that writing is dangerous, seditious, as if "In the beginning was the Word and the Word was with God and the Word *was* God." I was an obedient little girl—though I hate to admit it now!—and went along with my family's wishes. I

worked in a chemist's shop and then studied at the Pharmaceutical College at night.

The protagonist of The Country Girls *also works in a shop. Is the novel autobiographical?*

The novel is autobiographical in so far as I was born and bred in the west of Ireland, educated at a convent, and was full of romantic yearnings, coupled with a sense of outrage. But any book that is any good must be, to some extent, autobiographical, because one cannot and should not fabricate emotions; and although style and narrative are crucial, the bulwark, emotion is what finally matters. With luck, talent, and studiousness, one manages to make a little pearl, or egg, or something. . . . But what gives birth to it is what happens inside the soul and the mind, and that has almost always to do with *conflict*. And loss—an innate sense of tragedy.

What Thomas Hardy called "the sadness of things," and Unamuno "el sentimiento tragico de la vida"?

Precisely. Not just subjective sadness, though you have to experience it in order to know it, but also objective. And the more I read about writers, their letters—say Flaubert's—the more I realize it. Flaubert was in a way like a *woman*. There he was, in Rouen, yearning for the bright lights of Paris and hectic affairs, yet deliberately keeping away from all that, isolating himself, in order to burn and luxuriate in the affliction of his own emotions. So writing, I think, is an interestingly perverse occupation. It is quite sick in the sense of normal human enjoyment of life, because the writer is always *removed,* the way an actor never is. An actor is with the audience, a writer is not with his readers, and by the time the work appears, he or she is again incarcerated in the next book—or in barrenness. So for both men and women writers, writing is an eminently masochistic exercise—though I wonder what Norman Mailer would say to that! (pp. 25-7)

So the catalyst for your own work was that lecture on Fitzgerald and Hemingway. Before that you said that you read a great deal in Ireland, partly to escape. What sort of books did you read? And which ones influenced you most?

Looking back on it, it was not so much escape as nourishment. Of course there is an element of escape as well, that entering temporarily into a different world. But I think literature is food for the soul and the heart. There are books that are pure escapism: thrillers, detective and spy novels, but I can't read them, because they don't *deliver* to me. Whereas from one page of Dostoyevsky I feel renewed, however depressing the subject. The first book I ever *bought*—I've still got it—was called *Introducing James Joyce,* by T. S. Eliot. It contained a short story, a piece from *Portrait of the Artist,* some other pieces, and an introduction by Eliot. I read a scene from *Portrait* which is the Christmas dinner when everything begins pleasantly: a fire, largesse, the blue flame of light on the dark plum pudding, the revelry before the flare-up ensues between people who were for Parnell and those who were against him. Parnell had been dead for a long time, but the Irish being Irish persist with history. Reading that book made me realize that I wanted literature for the rest of my life.

And you became a ferocious reader, first of Joyce then of others. Who else did you read in those early days?

I am a slow reader, because I want to savor and recall what I read. The excitement and sense of discovery is not the same as in those days when I would get thoroughly wrapped up in *Vanity Fair* or *War and Peace.* Now I set myself a task of reading one great book each year. Last year I read *Bleak House,* which I think is the greatest English novel—I read a few pages a day. But one's taste changes so much. I mentioned Scott Fitzgerald, whom I read, oh, so lovingly and thoroughly! I loved *Tender Is The Night* and *The Great Gatsby,* which is a flawless novel. So I can say that he was one of my early influences. But now I know that fundamentally I respond to European literature in all its dark ramifications. I think the Russians are unsurpassable. Of course Joyce did something extraordinary: He threw out the entire heritage of English literature—language, story, structure, everything—and created a new and stupendous work. But for emotional gravity, no one can compare with the Russians. When I first read Chekhov's short stories, before I saw his plays, I knew I had heard the *voice* that I loved most in the whole world. I wrote to my sister, "Read Chekhov—he does not write, he *breathes* life off the page." And he was, and still is, my greatest influence, especially in short-story writing.

Later on, when you tried your hand at drama, did Chekhov come to your rescue there as well?

I think so, though it is very dangerous to take Chekhov as a model. His dramatic genius is so mysterious; he does what seems to be the impossible, in that he makes dramatic something that is desultory. And of course it is not desultory—indeed, it is as tightly knit as that Persian carpet. Shakespeare is God. He knows everything and expresses it with such a density of poetry and humor and power that the mind boggles. But then he had *great* themes—*Othello, Hamlet,* the history plays. Chekhov, on the other hand, tells you, or seems to tell you, of a profligate family that is losing an orchard, or some sisters who yearn for Moscow, and inside it is a whole web of life and love and failure. I think that despite his emphasis on wanting to be funny, he was a tragic man. In a letter to his wife, actress Olga Knipper, he says, "It is nine o'clock in the evening, you are going to play act three of my play, and I am as lonely as a coffin!" (pp. 28-30)

What about women writers? You haven't mentioned any as a major influence so far.

Every woman novelist has been influenced by the Brontës. *Wuthering Heights* and *Jane Eyre.* The poetry of Emily Dickinson, the early books of Elizabeth Bowen—especially the one she wrote about her home in Ireland, *Bowen's Court.* My admiration for Jane Austen came much later, and I also love the Russian poet Anna Akhmatova. Nowadays there are too many writers, and I think one of the reasons for the deterioration of language and literature in the last forty years has been the spawning of inferior novels. Everybody writes novels—journalists, broadcasters, T.V. announcers . . . it is a free-for-all! But writing is a vocation, like being a nun or a priest. I work at my writing as an athlete does at his training, taking it

very seriously. Whether a novel is autobiographical or not does not matter. What is important is the truth in it and the way that truth is expressed. I think a casual or frivolous attitude is pernicious.

Is there any area of fiction that you find women are better equipped to explore?

Yes. Women are better at emotions and the havoc those emotions wreak. But it must be said that Anna Karenina is the most believable heroine. The last scene where she goes to the station and looks down at the rails and thinks of Vronski's rejection is terrible in its depiction of despair. Women, on the whole, are better at plumbing the depths. A woman artist can produce a perfect gem, as opposed to a huge piece of rock carving a man might produce. It is not a limitation of talent or intelligence, it is just a different way of looking at the world.

So you don't believe in the feminist argument that the differences between men and women are a question of nurture and not of nature; that women look at the world differently because they have been conditioned to do so?

Not in the least! I believe that we are fundamentally, biologically, and therefore psychologically different. I am not like any man I have met, ever, and that divide is what both interests me and baffles me. A lot of things have been said by feminists about equality, about liberation, but not all of these things are gospel truth. They are opinions the way my books are opinions, nothing more. Of course I would like women to have a better time but I don't see it happening, and for a very simple and primal reason: people are pretty savage towards each other, be they men or women.

Yet your own success is, to a certain degree, due to the fact that your writing coincided with the rise of the feminist movement, because invariably it portrayed loving, sensitive, good women, being victimized by hard, callous men, and it hit the right note at the right time. Would you agree with that?

I would think so. However, I am not the darling of the feminists. They think I am too preoccupied with old-fashioned themes like love and longing. Though one woman in *Ms.* magazine pointed out that I send bulletins from battle fronts where other women do not go. I think I do. The reason why I resent being lectured at is that my psyche is so weighed down with its own paraphernalia! No man or woman from outside could prescribe to me what to do. I have enough trouble keeping madness at bay.

Your description of small towns and their enclosed communities reminds me of some of America's Southern writers, like Faulkner. Did they influence you?

Faulkner is an important writer though an imperfect one. I did go through a stage when I read a lot of Southern writers: Carson McCullers, Eudora Welty, Flannery O'Connor. . . . Any small, claustrophobic, in-grown community resembles another. The passion and ignorance in the Deep South of America and the west of Ireland are the same.

This is the opposite of the high society and the aristocratic world of Proust's À la recherche du temps perdu, *which has also been a major source of inspiration to you.*

Proust's influence on me, along with his genius, was his preoccupation with memory and his obsession with the past. His concentration on even the simplest detail—like one petal of a flower, or the design on a dinner plate—has unique, manic intensity. Also, when I read his biography by George Painter I felt the tenderness of his soul and wished I could have met him as a human being. You see, Joyce and Proust, although very different, broke the old mold by recognizing the importance of the rambling, disjointed nature of what goes on in the head, the interior monologue. I wonder how they would fare now. These are more careless times. Literature is no longer sacred, it is a business. There is an invisible umbilical cord between the writer and his potential reader, and I fear that the time has gone when readers could sink into a book the way they did in the past, for the *pace* of life is fast and frenetic. The world is cynical: the dwelling on emotions, the perfection of style, the intensity of a Flaubert is wasted on modern sensibility. I have a feeling that there is a *dying,* if not a *death,* of great literature. Some blame the television for it. Perhaps. There is hardly any distinction between a writer and a journalist—indeed, most writers *are* journalists. Nothing wrong with journalism any more than with dentistry, but they are worlds apart! Whenever I read the English Sunday papers I notice that the standard of literacy is high—all very clever and hollow—but no dues to literature. They care about their own egos. They synopsize the book, tell the plot. Well, fuck the plot! That is for precocious schoolboys. What matters is the imaginative *truth,* and the perfection and care with which it has been rendered. After all, you don't say of a ballet dancer, "He jumped in the air, then he twirled around, etc . . . " You are just *carried away* by his dancing. The nicest readers are—and I know by the letters I receive—youngish people who are still eager and uncontaminated, who approach a book without hostility. But when I read Anita Brookner's novel *Look At Me,* I feel I am in the grip of a most wonderful, imaginative writer. The same is true of Margaret Atwood. Also, great literature is dying because young people, although they don't talk about it much, feel and fear a holocaust.

What about your own relationship with critics? Do you feel misunderstood and neglected by them, or have they been kind to you? Have you ever been savaged by them?

Oh yes! I have been savaged all right! I believe one reviewer lost her job on the *New Statesman* because her review of my book, *A Pagan Place,* was too personal. She went on and on about my illiterate background. On the whole I have had more serious consideration in the United States than in Britain or Ireland. Perhaps because I am not known there as a "personality"! I do not despair though, for the real test of writing is not in the reading but in the rereading. I am not ashamed of my books being reread. The misunderstanding may be due just to geography, and to race. The Irish and the English are poles apart in thought and disposition.

It may also be due to a certain—and very un-British—

démesure in your writing; I mean they find you too sentimental.

I am glad to say that Dickens was accused of sentimentality and, by God, he lives on!

You were brought up as a devout Catholic and had a convent education. At one point you even contemplated becoming a nun. What made you give up religion?

I married a divorcé, and that was my first "Fall." Add to that the hounding nature of Irish Catholicism and you can dimly understand. We had a daily admonition which went:

> You have but one soul to save
> One God to love and serve
> One Eternity to prepare for
> Death will come soon
> Judgement will follow, and then
> Heaven—or Hell—*For Ever*!

In your novel A Pagan Place, *the heroine does become a nun. Was that a vicarious fulfillment of a subconscious wish?*

Perhaps. I did think of becoming a nun when I was very young, but it went out of my mind later, chased away by sexual desire!

Another interesting aspect of that novel is that it is written in the second person singular, like a soliloquy. It is somewhat reminiscent of Molly Bloom's soliloquy in Ulysses; *were you conscious of the influence?*

I didn't take Molly's as a model. The reason was psychological. As a child you are both your secret self and the "you" that your parents think you are. So the use of the second person was a way of combining the two identities. But I tend not to examine these things too closely—they just happen.

Religion has played such a crucial part in your life and evolution, yet you have not dealt with it on any philosophical or moral level, as have Graham Greene or George Bernanos; you haven't made religion the central theme of any of your novels. Why?

That is perhaps one of the differences between men and women who go through the same experiences. I flee from my persecutors. I have not confronted religion.

Do you think you ever will?

I hope so—when I have got rid of the terror and the anxiety. Or perhaps when I know exactly what I believe or don't believe.

Let's talk about the subjects that are dealt with in your work, its central themes, which are romantic love and Ireland. Some people—and not only feminists!—think that your preoccupation with romance verges at times on the sentimental and the "Romantic Novel" formula. You quoted Aragon in answer: "Love is your last chance, there is really nothing else to keep you there."

Other people have said it too, even the Beatles! Emily Dickinson wrote, "And is there more than love and death, then tell me its name?" But my work is concerned with *loss* as much as with love. Loss is every child's theme because by necessity the child loses its mother and its bearings. And writers, however mature and wise and eminent, are children at heart. So my central theme is loss—loss of love, loss of self, loss of God. I have just finished a play, my third, which is about my family. In it for the first time I have allowed my father, who is always the ogre figure in my work, to weep for the loss of *his* child. Therefore, I might, if the Gods are good to me, find that my understanding of love has become richer and stronger than my dread of loss. You see, my own father was what you might call the "archetypal" Irishman—a gambler, drinker, a man totally unequipped to be a husband or a father. And of course that colored my views, distorted them, and made me seek out demons.

Is that why, in nearly all your novels, women are longing to establish a simple, loving, harmonious relationship with men, but are unable to do so?

My experience was pretty extreme, so that it is hard for me to imagine harmony, or even affinity, between men and women. I would need to be reborn.

The other central theme of your work is Ireland. It seems to me that you have the same love-hate relationship with Ireland that most exiles have with their native country: on the one hand an incurable nostalgia and longing, and on the other the fact that one cannot go back, because the reasons that made one leave in the first place are still there. There is a constant conflict in the soul.

My relationship with Ireland is very complex. I could not live there for a variety of reasons. I felt oppressed and strangulated from an early age. That was partly to do with my parents who were themselves products and victims of their history and culture. That is to say, alas, they were superstitious, fanatical, engulfing. At the same time they were bursting with talent—I know this from my mother's letters, as she wrote to me almost every day. So I have to thank them for a heritage that includes talent, despair, and permanent fury. When I was a student in Dublin my mother found a book of Sean O'Casey in my suitcase and wanted to *burn* it! *But without reading it!* So they hated literature without knowing it. We know that the effect of our parents is indelible, because we internalize as a child and it remains inside us forever. Even when the parents die, you dream of them as if they were still there. Everything was an occasion for fear, religion was force-fed the way they feed the geese of Strasbourg for paté! I feel I am a cripple with a craving for wings. So much for the personal aspect. As for the country itself, it is no accident that almost all Irish writers leave the country. You know why? Ireland, as Joyce said, eats her writers the way a sow eats her farrow. He also called it a warren of "prelates and kinechites." Of course there's the beauty of the landscape, the poetry, the fairy tales, the vividness. I have shown my love and my entanglement with the place as much as I have shown my hatred. But they think that I have shown only my hatred.

> [My] work is concerned with *loss* as much as with love. Loss is every child's theme because by necessity the child loses its mother and its bearings. And writers, however mature and wise and eminent, are children at heart. So my central theme is loss—loss of love, loss of self, loss of God.
>
> —Edna O'Brien

Is that why they had an auto-da-fé of your first novel in your native village?

It was a humble event, as befits a backward place. Two or three people had gone to Limerick and bought *The Country Girls*. The parish priest asked them to hand in the books, which they did, and he burnt them on the grounds of the church. Nevertheless, a lot of people read it. My mother was very harsh about it; she thought I was a disgrace. That is the sadness—it takes you half a life to get out of the pits of darkness and stupidity. It fills me with anger, and with pity.

Do you think that after all these years and through your books you have exorcised the demon and can let it rest?

I hope not, because one needs one's demons to create.

After that small auto-da-fé, did anything else of that kind happen?

They used to ban my books, but now when I go there, people are courteous to my face, though rather slanderous behind my back. Then again, Ireland has changed. There are a lot of young people who are irreligious, or less religious. Ironically, they wouldn't be interested in my early books—they would think them gauche. They are aping English and American mores. If I went to a dance hall in Dublin now I would feel as alien as in a disco in Oklahoma.

You are not a political writer because as you say politics are concerned with the social and the external, while your preoccupations are with the inner, psychological life. Nonetheless, considering your emotional involvement with Ireland, how have you kept away from the situation in Northern Ireland—terrorism, the IRA, etc . . . ?

I have written one long piece on Northern Ireland for the German magazine *Stern*. My feelings about it are so manifold. I think it is mad, a so-called religious war, in this day and age. At the same time, I can't bear the rhetoric of the Unionists; I mean Ireland is *one small* island, and those six counties do not belong to Britain. Equally I abhor terrorism, whoever does it, the IRA, the Arabs, the Israelis. But when I stayed in Northern Ireland to research and write the article, I realized that the Catholics are second-class citizens. They live in terrible slums, in poverty, and know no way of improving their conditions. I have not set a novel in Northern Ireland simply because I do not know enough about it. I dislike cant—you get that from politicians. Writers have to dig deep for experience. I might go and live there for a while, in order to discover and later write about it. But so far I have refrained from bringing the topic into a book merely as a voyeur. (pp. 32-41)

Having been successful at novels and short stories, you tried your hand at drama—plays and screenplays. How did that come about?

I was asked to adapt my own novel, *A Pagan Place,* for the stage and it opened a new vista for me. Then with some experience I tackled [Virginia] Woolf. Now I have written a third play which for the time being is called *Home Sweet Home,* or *Family Butchers.* I feel drama is more direct, more suitable for expressing passions. Confrontation is the stuff of drama. It happens rather than is described. The play starts in the early morning, the voice of an Irish tenor comes over the gramophone—John McCormmack is singing "Bless This House, Oh Lord We Pray," then he's interrupted by a gunshot followed by another gunshot. The lights come on, a man and a woman appear, and you know that this is a play about passion and violence. You go straight for the jugular.

When you start a play, or a novel, or a short story, do you have a basic idea? Or a sentence? Something that triggers off the process of creating the work?

I always have the first line. Even with my very first book, *The Country Girls,* I went around with this first sentence in my head long before I sat down to write it.

Once you have started, do you have the whole scheme in your mind or do characters and plot take their own course and lead you, as some novelists say they do. I mean, Balzac was so surprised and moved by Old Goriot's death that he opened his window and shouted, "Le Père Goriot est mort! Le Père Goriot est mort!"

I know more or less, but I don't discuss it with myself. It is like sleepwalking; I don't know exactly where I am going but I know I will get there. When I am writing, I am so glad to be doing it that whatever form it takes— play, novel, etc.—I am thankful to the Fates. I keep dozens of pens by me, and exercise books.

When success came and you began to be famous and lionized, did it affect your life, work, and outlook in any way? Is success good for an artist, or does it limit his field of experience?

It depends on the degree of success and on the disposition of the artist. It was very nice for me to be published, as I had longed for it. But my success has been rather modest. It hasn't been meteoric. Nor was it financially shattering—just enough to carry me along.

But you have had a great deal of social success: fame, publicity, so on . . .

I am not conscious of it. I go to functions more as a duty than for pleasure, and I am always *outside* looking in, not the other way round. But I am grateful to have had enough success not to feel a disaster—it has allayed my hopelessness. Undoubtedly success contributed to the break-up of my marriage. I had married very young. My husband was an attractive father figure—a Professor Higgins. When my book was published and well-received, it altered things between us. The break would have come anyway, but my success sped it up. Then began a hard life; but when you are young, you have boundless energy—you run the house, mind the children, *and* write your despair. I don't know if I could do it all now. Looking back I realize that I am one of the luckiest people in the world, since no matter how down I go something brings me back. Is it God's grace or just peasant resilience?

Perhaps it is the creative act of writing. John Updike once said that the minute he puts an unhappiness down on paper, it metamorphoses into a lump of sugar!

I think he was simplifying. The original pain that prompted the writing does not lessen, but it is gratifying to give it form and shape.

Did money ever act as a spur? You were very prolific in the sixties, and still are.

I have never written anything in order to make money. A story comes to me, is given me, as it were, and I write it. But perhaps the need to earn a living and my need to write coincided. I know that I would still write if tomorrow I was given a huge legacy, and I will always be profligate.

How do you organize your time? Do you write regularly, every day? Philip Roth has said that he writes eight hours a day three hundred and sixty-five days a year! Do you work as compulsively?

He is a man, you see. Women have the glorious excuse of having to shop, cook, clean! When I am working I write in a kind of trance, long hand, in these several copybooks. I meant to tidy up before you came! I write in the morning because one is nearer to the unconscious, the source of inspiration. I never work at night because by then the shackles of the day are around me, what James Stephens (author of *The Crock of Gold*) called, "That flat, dull catalogue of dreary things that fasten themselves to my wings," and I don't sit down three hundred and sixty-five days a year because I'm not that kind of writer. I wish I were! Perhaps I don't take myself that seriously. Another reason why I don't write constantly is that I feel I have written all I had wanted to say about love and loss and loneliness and being a victim and all that. I have finished with that territory. And I have not yet embraced another one. It may be that I'm going towards it—I hope and pray that this is the case.

When you are writing, are you disciplined? Do you keep regular hours, turn down invitations, and hibernate?

Yes, but discipline doesn't come into it. It is what one has to do. The impulse is stronger than anything. I don't like too much social life any way. It is gossip and bad white wine. It's a waste. Writing is like carrying a fetus. I get up in the morning, have a cup of tea, and come into this room to work. I never go out to lunch, never, but I stop around one or two and spend the rest of the afternoon attending to mundane things. In the evening I might read or go out to a play or a film, or see my sons. Did I tell you that I spend a lot of time moping? Did Philip Roth say that he moped? (pp. 42-6)

If someone had time to read only one of your books, which one would you recommend?

A Pagan Place.

Do you feel that your best book, the one that every writer aspires to, is yet to come?

It had better be! I need to develop, to enlarge my spheres of experience.

When you say you are changing your life, do you also mean that the subject matter of your fiction will change with it?

I think so. I am giving a lecture in Boston next month about women in literature. I had to come to the forlorn conclusion that all the great heroines have been created by men. I had an anthology of women's writing called *Bold New Women* in which the editor, Barbara Alson, very wisely says that all women writers have written about sex, because sex is their biological life, their environment, and that for a woman a sexual encounter is not just the mechanical thing it can be for a man but—and she uses this wonderful phrase—"a clutch on the universe." I have written quite a lot of love stories; I don't think I want to write those anymore. I even find them hard to read! It doesn't mean that I am not interested in love anymore—that goes on as long as there is breath. I mean I am not going to *write* about it in the same way.

Could it have something to do with age?

Bound to have something to do with age. The attitude toward sex changes in two ways. Sexual love becomes deeper and one realizes how fundamental it is and how rich. At the same time, one sees that it is a sort of mutual game and that attraction makes one resort to all sorts of ruses and strategies. To an outsider it is all patent, even laughable. Shakespeare saw through this glorious delusion better than anyone and *As You Like It* is the funniest play about love, yet it is steeped in love.

What about the new cult of chastity? Germaine Greer's new book advocates restraint—a backlash against a decade or so of permissiveness. Have you been influenced by the changing mood?

I have always espoused chastity except when one can no longer resist the temptation. I know promiscuity is boring, much more than fish-and-chips, which is comforting.

Do you find sex scenes difficult to write, considering your puritanical background?

Not really. When you are writing you are not conscious of the reader, so that you don't feel embarrassed. I'm sure Joyce had a most heady and wonderful time writing the last fifty pages of *Ulysses*—glorious Molly Bloom. He must have written it in one bout, thinking: I'll show the women of the world that I am omniscient!

What do you think the future has in store for literature? You have been very pessimistic so far. For example, last year nearly three hundred novels were published in France, and few except the ones that won the big prizes were read. Will we go on endlessly writing novels with so few making a mark?

As you know the future itself is perilous. But as regards books, there is first the financial aspect of publishing. Already books are very expensive, so that a first novel of quality will have less of a chance of being picked up. Say

a new Djuna Barnes, or indeed Nathalie Sarraute, might not get published. If Woolf's *The Waves* were to be published today it would have pitiful sales. Of course, "how-to" books, spy stories, thrillers, and science-fiction all sell by the millions. What would be wonderful—what we *need* just now—is some astonishing fairy tale. I read somewhere the other day that the cavemen did not paint what they saw, but what they *wished* they had seen. We need that, in these lonely, lunatic times.

So if we manage to save the planet, is there hope for literature as well?

Oh yes! At this very moment, some imagination is spawning something wonderful that might make us tremble. Let's say there will always be literature because the imagination is boundless. We just need to care more for the imagination than for the trivia and the commerce of life. Literature is the next best thing to God. Joyce would disagree. He would say literature *is,* in essence, God. (pp. 47-50)

Edna O'Brien with Shusha Guppy, in an interview in The Paris Review, *Vol. 26, No. 92, Summer, 1984, pp. 22-50.*

Dean Flower (essay date 1985)

[*Flower is an American educator and short story writer. In the following review of* A Fanatic Heart, *he admires O'Brien's narrative voice and eye for detail.*]

Edna O'Brien is always happiest when the story she has to tell begins and ends in wretchedness. That is her home territory, and as [*A Fanatic Heart*] attests, she has long travelled it with authority. O'Brien's is a distinctive kind of wretchedness, compounded of the Irish exile's bitterness and the divorced woman's disillusionment, where the experience of being betrayed is always countered by feeling oneself as the betrayer. O'Brien's title is drawn from Yeats's "Remorse for Intemperate Speech," with the relevant passage given in an epigraph: "Out of Ireland have we come. / Great hatred, little room, / Maimed us at the start. / I carry from my mother's womb / A fanatic heart." Like many another exile O'Brien seems to have learned that the intemperate anger was a type of love, and that the place and its people were not easily left behind. As one of her more recent characters recalls, "Only one thing was uppermost in me and it was flight, and in my fancies I had no idea that no matter how distant the flight or how high I soared, those people were entrenched in me."

In almost every story the autobiographic mode prevails. Whether O'Brien tells of a loony bachelor or a beautiful nun or a hoydenish Australian, there is always a narrator to remember and reflect them through her own experience of growing up in the villages and farms of western Ireland. Something ballad-like is felt: whole lives are encompassed, often a novel's worth of experience, in a summary narrative that leaps and lingers over the years. **"The Rose of New York"** spans the history of a woman's love for her mother, from birth agonies through fierce dependencies to final alienations and death. **"A Scandalous Woman"** treats the history of the narrator's friendship with a girl who experiments disastrously in love, charting the successive stages of distancing between them. O'Brien does not favor epiphanies, the lethal close or quick ironic twist so commonly found in shorter stories. Her recollective manner is always ready to conjure up more, letting one thing lead to another, and another. The onrushing rhythm of this is often wonderful:

> I used to go over there to play, and though they were older than me, they used to beg me to come and bribe me with empty spools or scraps of cloth for my dolls. Sometimes we played hide-and-seek, sometimes we played families and gave ourselves posh names and posh jobs, and we used to paint each other with the dye from plants or blue bags and treat one another's faces as if they were palettes, and then laugh and marvel at the blues and indigos and pretend to be natives and do hula-hula and eat dock leaves.

Style is never allowed to be decorative or ingenious or obtrusive with O'Brien. If her precisely-noted details sometimes become metaphoric or symbolic, that is made to seem only natural, inherent in the material. In this she resembles Frank O'Connor more than any other Irish writer. They both labor to achieve an unaffectedly clear speaking voice, and would persuade you there's no trick to it at all. "We had all returned from our long summer holiday and we were all wretched," she writes in **"Sister Imelda,"** a fine story of a teaching nun who has chosen against a promising career. The narrator remembers her own intense longings for intimacy with the affectionate but elusive sister, and in the process—as if incidentally—conveys the abysmal loneliness of the nun. As a mere afterthought the narrator mentions "her nun's silver ring slipped easily and sometimes unavoidably off her marriage finger. It occurred to me that she was having a nervous breakdown."

There are more richly evocative moments than these, of course, but they are still underplayed. In **"A Scandalous Woman"** we find an exquisite moment of youthful friendship, dramatized by the gift of a bottle of perfume and an exchange of kisses, all treated with a fine leisurely sensuousness and then expertly drawn to a close: "That moment had an air of mystery and sanctity about it, what with the surprise and our speechlessness, and a realization somewhere in the back of my mind that we were engaged in murky business indeed and that our larking days were over."

In recent years O'Brien has acquired an unfortunate reputation as A Woman's Writer. Friendly female critics praise her for championing their cause; hostile male critics categorize her as "an expert in female passivity" or as "narrow" and "obsessive." Now it cannot be denied that the sufferings of women figure everywhere in O'Brien's work, and occasionally a direct comment surfaces. One story concludes (atypically), "ours indeed was a land of shame, a land of murder, and a land of strange, throttled, sacrificial women." But O'Brien never coerces her subject into a cause. Expert at figuring the lives of women who are wretched, she does not address the Wretchedness of Woman. Her weaker stories tend to be about dissociated modern women out of touch with themselves and the past.

"The Love Object" and **"Paradise"** are about such women, and the narrative turns in upon itself in a way that collapses perspective. O'Brien gets too close to the present here perhaps, too close to the way she lives now, and the details fail to reverberate. But in the recollective mode her whole world opens up: the anguish of fending off an unwanted Romeo (**"Courtship"**), the anti-climax of a drunken party (**"Irish Revel"**), the illusions of worldly life (**"The Connor Girls"**), the return of the unwanted native (**"Savages"**). Here the voice seems unerring and all the details count. (pp. 302-04)

> *Dean Flower, in a review of, "A Fanatic Heart," in* The Hudson Review, *Vol. XXXVIII, No. 2, Summer, 1985, pp. 302-04.*

Peggy O'Brien   (essay date 1987)

[*In the following excerpt from an overview of O'Brien's literary career and critical reception, the critic assesses general characteristics of O'Brien's prose and discusses thematic concerns in her short fiction.*]

An intriguing fact about the past reception of Edna O'Brien's work is that American and Irish audiences have been largely at odds, her compatriots tending to be harsh while critics here have lavished praise. . . . Much of the disapproval from home has been directed at O'Brien's persona, an outrageous concoction of what foreigners expect an Irish person to be—mellifluous, volatile, wanton, irrational. But more serious artistic reservations underlie this carping. The American criticism . . . discloses many of the deep reasons why discerning readers of whatever nationality might find O'Brien flawed. Some American critics repeat the error of endorsing O'Brien's stage-Irishness, but many incisive observations about her art push the process of just evaluation further along. Using these readings as a starting point, I will explore the ways in which the inadequacies of her prose are bound to less visible strengths. My interest is double: to understand rather than judge an author's psychology that avoids certain opportunities and embraces others, and to broach those questions of literary evaluation which these choices raise.

Mary Gordon's review of **A Fanatic Heart** [in *The New York Times Book Review,* 18 November 1984] epitomizes the rapt response one has come to expect outside of Ireland. Gordon is seduced by O'Brien's voice, enthralled by the Irish writer's use of language: "All the words are fitting; none of them shocks. . . . It is the emblem of her genius: the genuinely surprising word, not in itself exotic but conjuring in the reader a response inexorably physical." This leads Gordon to praise O'Brien's undoubted descriptive powers, the way she evokes the physical world through sensuous language. Recalling O'Brien's description of a young woman, Gordon comments, "The physical detail burrows into the mind; how clearly one sees Eily." What limits Gordon's judgment is the way she elevates linguistic richness and vividness over other qualities of good prose, such as narrative control. Moreover, Gordon invites suspicion, if not derision, from Irish skeptics when she betrays that she views O'Brien through green-tinted glasses. She is beguiled quite simply by the author's Irishness. This, along with her gender, goes a long way toward establishing O'Brien's credentials with Gordon: "Edna O'Brien tells the Irish woman's inside story . . . she speaks with a voice identifiably and only hers. No voice could be less androgynous or more rooted in a land." It is worrying to the Irish, especially Irish women, that O'Brien is viewed as their representative and voice. But there is a contradiction in Gordon's statement that must be noted. Does O'Brien present herself as an individual, speaking "with a voice identifiably and only hers," or as a type of her sex and nationality? O'Brien herself is only too willing to exploit the potential for universal acceptance in such confusion.

Whereas sometimes she puts herself forward as the essential woman and other times as the voice of Ireland, in the short essay, "Why Irish Heroines Don't Have to be Good Anymore," she conflates the two stereotypes to define Irish womanhood. In a transparent effort at pandering to transatlantic taste, she assumes a susceptibility on the part of Americans for Celtic charm and trades blatantly on her origins. So open and roguish is she in weaving her obvious spell, however, that it is not so much this manipulation which seems reprehensible as her misappropriation of a native tradition. Hers are sins of presumption and reduction. Sprinkling tidbits of Yeats and Synge and snippets from legend and history throughout the essay, unabashed, she aligns her own persona with the great women of Ireland's past. Her egoism robs other characters and events of their individuality and usually their stature. She transforms the seering story of Deirdre into a maudlin, melodramatic tale of woman's woe. No self-ironic tone indicates an authorial awareness of how her penny-romance summary robs a great tragedy of passion. Characteristically, she touts intensity but presents risible soap opera: "When Deirdre of the Sorrows saw her husband slain, she tore her golden hair out, became distraught, uttered the most rending lament and then fell down beside him and died." The busy syntax, piling verb upon verb, creates a flurry of excitement rather than a solemn procession toward death. An austere heroine becomes an hysterical exhibitionist.

The essay, however, contains a clue to the serious shortcoming of O'Brien's imagination and, ironically, its interest. After she gives a cursory and specious account of two types of Irish heroine, robust and meek, she places her own Baba and Kate in this double line: "Realizing that the earlier heroines were bawdy and the later ones lyrical I decided to have two, one who would conform to both my own and my country's view of what an Irish woman should be and one who would undermine every piece of protocol and religion and hypocrisy that there was." She places calculating Baba in line with heroines such as Deirdre and the Old Woman of Beare who have been justly celebrated for their passion and spontaneity. The telling and dangerous opinion divulged as the basis for her thinking is that being strong means having no emotion. Defending her decision to kill off vulnerable Kate in the epilogue and allow crass Baba to survive she explains, "lyricism had to go, just as emotion had to be purged." The question of vigor and invulnerability is alarming, for this repudiation of emotion points to an evasion in O'Brien's work, which

is nearly disguised by sexual and ethnic antics. It is the paradoxical birthplace of both the silly and the serious in her. More, it is the source from which her imagination springs and continues to be generated.

In an interview with her [in *The New York Times Book Review*, 18 November 1984], Philip Roth asks some penetrating questions which, overall, demonstrate an enviable balance between indicating the impressive and hinting at the defective in her. Paying tribute to her prodigious memory and the part it plays in her descriptive ability—"the ability to reconstruct with passionate exactness an Irish world"—he also wonders if a tenacious clinging to the past, especially an obsession with her mother and father, hasn't blocked O'Brien emotionally. He asks, "I wonder if you haven't chosen the way you live—living by yourself—to prevent anything emotionally too powerful from separating you from that past?" O'Brien answers, "I'm sure I have. I rail against my loneliness but it is as dear to me as the thought of unity with a man." In this same interview O'Brien speaks of a continuing battle with her father that has only abated slightly with his death but that still would make it intolerable to be reincarnated as his daughter. The dream of unity, therefore, is in direct proportion to the reality of alienation. A stalemate exists because the emotion which creates this tension hasn't been released. In the same interview she also speaks of loving her mother overmuch and having "a sense of her over my shoulder judging." Then, in another section she talks of what seems at first an unrelated subject, her need to leave Ireland: "I do not think I would have written anything if I had stayed. I feel I would have been watched, would have been judged (even more) and would have lost that priceless commodity called freedom." It seems that the need to recover Ireland imaginatively and from a distance is more deeply a need for union with her mother. The great poignancy and artistic success of a story like "**A Rose in the Heart**" is that it meets this estrangement head-on and records with unflinching honesty an emotional ambivalence that doesn't take recourse in any of the diverting extremes of sex or country which are so common in O'Brien and are nothing but red herrings for the critic.

In his interview Roth also makes the important connection between O'Brien's descriptive acumen and these unresolved emotions, seeing description as a strategy to contain what are otherwise anarchic feelings: "You seem to remember the shape, texture, color and dimension of every object your eye may have landed upon while you were growing up—not to mention the human significance of all you saw, heard, smelled, tasted and touched. The result is prose like a fine piece of meshwork, a net of perfectly observed sensuous details that enables you to contain all the longing and pain and remorse that surge through the fiction." O'Brien's descriptive skill does, indeed, enable her to deal with emotional tumult, but it also encourages an avoidance of emotional honesty that places the value of her work in question. Her psychology as an author is revealed more by certain decisions she makes, especially with regard to how much she will indulge a narrator. There is a peril in using an interview, however, as evidence for this argument, since doing so can imply that my appeal is to certain biographical truths about Edna

O'Brien, but, given her irrepressible, perverse humanity, the voice that we hear in her interviews is even more fictional than that of her fiction.

One could be forgiven for seeing O'Brien's work as autobiographical, for she is a writer who sounds most affected speaking in ordinary life and most candid narrating prose fiction. (pp. 474-77)

The abiding problem for critics of O'Brien's work is to explain the constant blend of powerful and weak writing in her. So often she creates chilling evocations of confused and chaotic existence by means of an art which fails to distance itself from this cogent material. More often than not it enacts the same confusions. Her practice as a fiction writer raises proverbial questions about the craft, such as whether authorial detachment and objectivity are necessary virtues or whether to demand them is to be outmoded and unfair. A perfect example of this dilemma is raised by the story **"Paradise,"** a terrifying representation of a needy woman's insecurity and self-loathing in a loveless relationship. The prose itself is brittle with the anxiety and panic felt by the protagonist; however, she is also a relentlessly whining, self-pitying person who is never thrown into ironic relief by authorial interpositions. The author seems complicitous in the self-destructive behavior, and this can prompt reader disapproval as much as intense reader identification. If we disapprove, the problem arises of whether we reject the personality of the author, that of the character or some elusive entity that we call the art itself. The fact remains, however, that the story leaves an indelible impression as the recreation of an extreme mental state. (pp. 477-78)

Much of O'Brien's descriptive writing is not the product of deliberate looking at something but distracted movement away from one thing, usually an acute feeling, toward another, an object, a transition essentially from emotion to sensation. A moment in the story **"Paradise"** demonstrates this involuntary response. When a conversation among people she fears comes to a subject that provokes anxiety in the protagonist, the dialogue abruptly stops and the next words are, "The sun, filtered by the green needles, fell and made play on the dense clusters of brown nuts. They never ridicule nature, she thought, they never dare." This is more than description and a more radical outcome is intended than finding self-affirmation through recreating nature imaginatively. Here we witness an empathic flow into the object itself. Invulnerability from excruciating pain comes from a Keatsian entry into an object which the senses have intensely perceived. This particular imaginative act blurs the boundaries of genre and we enter the territory of lyric poetry. We also come to the crux where strength and weakness combine in O'Brien, for at such moments she fails to distance herself from the narrator to enable us to see the gesture of escape for what it is. We fail to receive an emotional profile of the character, achieved through irony, gaining instead, through our own unaided extrapolations, a profile of the author, who participates in both the romanticism and escapism.

O'Brien's penchant and capacity for descriptive writing does more for her prose than lend it texture and warmth. Even Roth's image of containment, the fine meshwork through which feeling surges, doesn't do justice to the subtle interaction of emotion and description that takes place. (p. 482)

The preeminent attraction of descriptive writing for O'Brien is that its overt focus is the non-human world, one safely outside the emotional melee of human relationships. The descriptive act becomes anodyne when it mingles the unbearable feelings produced by intimacy with the innocence and inertness of objects. If one reads O'Brien for the extreme effect those first intimates, mother and father, have had on her authorial psyche, then various aspects of her fictional practice become comprehensible, indeed seem necessary in the light of these psychological exigencies. The collusion between author and character is essentially a blurring of the boundaries between individual and parental identities; and the unresolved nature of these primary relationships accounts for O'Brien's overall obsessiveness. It is this quality of her imagination which provides the energy both to explore unfamiliar psychological recesses and to repeat the same hackneyed experiences over and over again, without apparent control. The former makes reading her works exciting, the latter makes it wearying. The reader is torn between interest and impatience.

O'Brien admits baldly to Roth, "I am obsessive, also I am industrious. Besides, the time when you are most alive and most aware is in childhood and one is trying to recapture that heightened awareness." A telescopic look down the length of her works reveals this quality of obsessiveness in a simple, direct way: the repetition of the same characters in only slightly different guises. Kate and Baba appear in the three early novels, then become Willa and Patsy in *Casualties of Peace,* Stella and Zee in *Zee & Co.,* Emma and Caithleen in *A Pagan Place.* The procession of pairs within the stories is too long to relate. The passive-aggressive husband figure enjoys minor mutations in the different fictional embodiments of Eugene in the trilogy, Robert in *Zee,* a malevolent presence in *August is a Wicked Month,* Dr. Flaggler in *Night,* Herod in *Casualties.* The recurrence of stock characters and incidents articulates the psychological law that early crises dictate the content, in the form of psychological projection, of later experience. No wonder adult life seems tepid compared to childhood, when the only immediate experiences, if they are not subsequently relinquished, take place. It is intriguing to ask why evidence of obsessiveness mounts in the works directly after *Country Girls.* The answer may be that sex comes into her fiction after this point and physical intimacy unleashes primitive feelings that induce a regression back into the triangle of the parent-child relationship. (pp. 483-84)

The story **"Forgetting,"** a chronicle of the bland, recuperative days after the end of an affair, contains instances of an extreme, in fact bogus, realism prevalent in the later works, where Baba's cynicism eclipses Kate's naïveté. The truth is more that the two converge but with the hard, protective armor of Baba on the surface. The realism is only apparent. A soft center lies within the stark perimeters a jaded eye perceives. It is apt, therefore, that the scene is a Mediterranean resort where a glaring sun gives objects their clinical outline and the heavy scent of holiday sex provides the required, lurid aura. The opening words contain an unsettling blend of apparent naturalism and obvious metaphor. It begins with a studied neutrality—"Then the foliage is wet, the sun shining on it, while all the umbrellas and parasols are already dry and people hurrying down on their pop-pop bicycles or on foot, down to the sea"—but quickly abandons this antiseptic vision to observe, "By evening the yellow flower of the marrow tops will have wilted to an unrecognizable shred, holiday couples will have quarrelled, will have made love and half-built castles will be like forlorn forts on the vistas of dark sands." Once the metaphorical intention has been made explicit, we endow retrospectively what has come before with an implicit content. The initial coldness is seen with hindsight as a pitiable denial of feelings that seem crushed by circumstance. The flat surface of images is a barrier to keep down a pain derived through sexual involvement with men. O'Brien gives us no pointers by which to perceive this irony.

The feelings associated with the father are so engulfing they make distancing impossible. It is his introjected image which makes O'Brien ceaselessly portray sexually insatiable women, like the father, in disastrous relationships with hurtful men, also like the father. When one of her protagonists complains that "one man is the same as another," we read a profound truth beneath the cliché: when each man is a projection of an original father figure and each romance a replaying of an original trauma, sameness is the result. The promiscuity which has become a hall-mark of O'Brien's writing is the result of a serious authorial need to realize the full content of the intense feelings associated with a father figure. As though still relying on an unreliable father to validate their relationship as an intimate one, she seeks one male spectre after another in futile quest of this elusive conclusion to years of waiting. The sexual partners become more apparitional and allegorical as her fiction evolves because they become mere representatives of an inherently remote figure from the past. However painful and inaccessible the father has been, however, he is idealized in direct proportion to the degree he has removed himself and caused hurt. (pp. 485-86)

Much of the tedium that comes with reading O'Brien is the result of the melodramas constructed around men, while the struggle with female identity produces a hidden content which is more subtle—so too the artistic rendering of it. If the lack of objectivity about the father results in a lack of ironic distance from her female characters; masochism in relation to men, the basic collusion between the author and these characters, the continuous nature of their composite identity, is the consequence of a failure in differentiation from the mother. An unhealthy fusion is responsible for that blurring of boundaries between author and protagonists which creates so many evaluative doubts. But the search for identity involved also creates an interaction between author and characters which is the essential but covert story O'Brien is telling. A dimension beyond conventionally defined content, this struggle for self-objectification gained through the process of narrating gives a psychological immediacy and urgency to the prose that compels our attention and respect.

Much of her best writing occurs when O'Brien confronts directly the implications of fusion with the mother. The sustained honesty of **"A Rose in the Heart"** stems from her finding the courage to admit and articulate a paradoxical truth, one half of which is alienation from the mother, the other half an intense fusion:

> The food was what united them, eating off the same plate, using the same spoon, watching one another's chews, feeling the food as it went down the other's gullet . . . when it ate blancmange or junket it was eating part of the lovely substance of its mother. . . . Her mother's veins were her veins, her mother's lap was a second heaven . . . her mother's body was a recess that she would wander inside forever and ever . . . a sepulchre growing deeper and deeper. . . . She would not budge, would not be lured out.

O'Brien as an author remains embedded in the flesh of her female protagonists in order to avoid depicting, and perhaps experiencing, the terrors of separation, emergence and action on the surface of a world stripped of the mythological projections rampant in *Mother Ireland*.

In **"Rose,"** the speaker refers to her mother as a "gigantic sponge, a habitation in which she longed to sink and disappear forever and ever." As O'Brien's fiction advances it becomes apparent how strong the impulse is to "sink," how increasingly reluctant she is to be "lured out." This spectacle of fusion may frighten and repel the reader, and it does hinder artistic qualities of detachment and control, but it also makes reading what might be considered the worst of O'Brien a powerful encounter with the messy and unresolved in human experience. More lifelike than any art of lapidary perfection, its impact on the reader is visceral and personal. This sort of art fails to mitigate pain and confusion just as the mind often fails to dispel the anxieties of actual living. Many of O'Brien's narrators become haunting figures for the reader precisely because no implied author has pinpointed and filed away their misconceptions. Their neuroses aren't magically corrected by an ulterior voice of psychological normality. For example, in **"A Scandalous Woman"** an unreliable narrator, disappointed in marriage and deeply repressed, follows with pathological doggedness the career of a sexually precocious childhood friend, who eventually suffers and recovers from a mental breakdown. The parasitic motives of the frustrated narrator are not exposed through irony, but, if they were, it might lessen the uncomfortable effect the prose has on us. This self-deluded narration possesses a resonance not unlike that created by Fitzgerald's Nick Carraway, whose homo-erotic obsession with Jay Gatsby is also left throbbing under the surface of the text as an unconscious sexual drive.

O'Brien's most revealing disclosure in the Roth interview concerns a female compulsion to merge with the mother: "If you want to know what I regard as the principal crux of female despair, it is this: in the Greek myth of Oedipus and in Freud's exploration of it, the son's desire for his mother is admitted; the infant daughter also desires its mother but it is unthinkable either in myth, in fantasy or in fact, that the desire be consummated." O'Brien's most authentic writing centers around this secret wish, either demonstrating the catastrophic consequences of trying to realize the fusion, as in **"A House of My Dreams,"** or in presenting the growth that separation from a fantasized fusion promotes, the subject of **"Sister Imelda."** It is no coincidence that this story of a schoolgirl's moving beyond a reciprocated crush on a repressed and febrile nun is one of O'Brien's most finely crafted works, artistic control working hand-in-hand with autonomy. So much is the primal unity a fugitive ideal, the more it's sought the more it disperses, and the ego that chases the phantom is fragmented in the process. The speaker of **"House of my Dreams,"** who ends in mental breakdown, begins to caress another woman and says, "It was a strange sensation, as if touching gauze or some substance that was about to vanish into thin air." So too, those works in which the author fails to differentiate herself from her material, **"Night"** being the outstanding instance, tend to fragment for the reader and "vanish into thin air."

When the center of a work doesn't hold, we are presented with a troublesome problem of response. The rapidly disintegrating story seems to beg us for help to erect boundaries, and bestow integration. Or perhaps to be complicitous in the breakdown and suffer it too. Even the hint of such an invitation can leave some readers disgusted and cold, dismissing the work as an artistic failure. A detached but secure reader may regard even the manipulation as part of an appalling but convincing enactment of a real psychological condition. The prose unquestionably makes this powerful gesture of appeal to us, demanding reaction, either to affirm or reject the author. O'Brien's search for the innocence of recovered unity ends with this bid to merge with the reader which appears to replay some very old drama. We become the idealized other, pursued by a seductive rhetoric that intends to ensnare but may fly past us on the scent of more willing prey. (pp. 486-88)

> *Peggy O'Brien, "The Silly and the Serious: An Assessment of Edna O'Brien," in* The Massachusetts Review, *Vol. XXVIII, No. 3, Autumn, 1987, pp. 474-88.*

Jack Fuller   (essay date 1990)

[*Fuller is an American journalist, critic, and editor. In the following review of* Lantern Slides, *he admires the universality of O'Brien's Irish stories.*]

If Molly Bloom had James Joyce's gift for story and didn't ramble on so, she might have written fiction like Edna O'Brien's.

O'Brien's stories are earthy, wry, direct. They owe a debt to the Irish master, and they pay it. The title piece of this most recent collection [*Lantern Slides*]—set at a dinner party—is so honest about its antecedents in *Dubliners* that its main male character takes the name of Mr. Conroy, straight from "The Dead."

But O'Brien does not see Irish women, as Joyce saw Gerty McDowell on the beach, from a yearning distance. Her characters sometimes speak directly to the reader, sometimes not, but either way their voices are intimate and

presented without sentimentality or the wishfulness of lust.

O'Brien's women most commonly are people who have lost the love of their life, or the illusion of it. The Blazes Boylans of the world are no better today than when Joyce wrote. And the women have the same weary romanticism, believing that somehow, someday an Irishman might live up to his lies.

Many of the stories in this volume are a sort of Irish gothic. O'Brien is very hard on the national peculiarities and she has a taste for raw-edged tales about cruel towns and the indifferent city. One could read the first piece in the collection, **" 'Oft in a Stilly Night,' "** as a kind of commentary on Dylan Thomas' *Under Milk Wood.* Unlike Thomas' Welsh, the Irish characters in this "small somnolent village" are not forgiven through the miracle of sweet lyricism. O'Brien makes the drunks mean, the God-wracked ladies insane, the dalliance assaultive or at least crude. And in the end she asks, "Now I ask you what you would do? . . . You would probably drive on, is that it? Perhaps sequestered your own village is much the same. Perhaps everywhere is."

This is no author's vain boast of universality. O'Brien's stories have a reach way beyond the eccentricities of the land in which they are set. Hers are tales of people leaving love, of returning years later to find what is left. At their rawest, they are as cruel as a carving knife: the incestuous sister in **"Brother"** coolly planning to do away with his wan, newfound mate. And then O'Brien will surprise you with a moment so sweet and round that it seems it might redeem all humankind.

"Epitaph," for example, is a soliloquy of a woman whose love was spurned and then rekindled. In the end, she is the one who turns aside. But not in anger or despair.

> If was understood that we might meet in that other country. Might. . . . Meanwhile, I had that picture of you in my mind, my secret Odysseus returned from his wandering, reunited with his wife, his retinue, his dog. We said goodbye, three or four times; we clung. To think that it happened as cleanly as that.

The effects O'Brien achieves are so elegant that it is possible to overlook her subtlety.

Sometimes it is to be found in the perfect choice of word. A man and woman wander on the beach where they each once had tarried in love. The man has hopes, the woman memories. She describes the sand as being as white as saltpeter.

Sometimes it is the perfect detail: a woman visiting her emotionally distant father in a nursing home sits in the overheated bedroom as he shuffles off into the bathroom and fails to close the door. She finds herself "listening, while trying not to listen."

Sometimes the effects come from the shape of the piece as a whole. In **"Storm"** a mother on holiday has sharp words with her son and his girlfriend, they go off for a sail, a storm blows up and when they do not come home, she becomes frightened that she has lost them. The natural conditions mirror the tempest of her own relationship with them and her feelings of remorse. It is just that simple. And yet the grace is in the ending. The couple comes home, having eluded danger, and everyone acts as if nothing happened. " 'Tomorrow,' they say, as if there were no storm, no rift, as if the sea outside were a cradle lulling the world to a sweet, perpetual, guileless sleep."

Guilelessness is not the same as innocence, which is one of O'Brien's favorite themes. Nor is innocence like virginity, which can be lost but once. It is rather something that is eroded steadily by time.

In the story **"Another Time"** a famous woman pays a visit alone to a town of her youth and meets there a woman who, as a girl, walked away with her flame. The man, she learns, had spoken of her often in later years. "You were a feather in his cap, especially after you appeared on television," she is told. Another story, **"Dramas,"** as a whole is both an innocent farce and a tale of the end of innocence.

Ultimately, what makes these pieces so wonderful is that, like the masterpieces of the Irish literary tradition, they come straight from the soil of genuine experience. Convention-bound as Irish society is, its literature gets behind this to the sources of human behavior that convention attempts to reform or hide. Nor are literary conventions sacred either. You don't find very much easy affection or easy despair in O'Brien's pieces. Their elegance is in the way they render the complexity of human interchange and emotion.

It is peculiar that it was James Joyce who, more than anyone else, launched writers of fiction into a relentless and ultimately dead-ended pursuit of formal invention. Perhaps his own inventions were lighted with genius simply because, as an Irishman, he was still rooted in the rich, loamy earth of human concern (all too human, as he said), from which the value and deepest pleasures of literature grow.

O'Brien's work springs from the same fields. She is not particularly interested in chasing the chimera of structural novelty. Rather she has a more modest but more insatiable interest in finding ways to say things that are true. And time and again, in small ways and large, she succeeds. (pp. 1, 3)

> *Jack Fuller, "Wryly Irish," in* Chicago Tribune—Books, *May 27, 1990, pp. 1, 3.*

David Leavitt (essay date 1990)

[*Leavitt is an American short story writer whose work explores modern family relationships. In the following excerpt, he describes* Lantern Slides *as a superb collection of stories that delineates O'Brien's characteristic themes of human relationships and sorrows.*]

[O'Brien's stories] divide almost without exception into two types: those that describe the lives of worldly, urban women with a penchant for vacationing in exotic climes and (usually) an obsessive attachment to a charismatic, powerful and married man; and those in which Ms.

O'Brien—to borrow the title of an earlier collection—finds herself "returning" to the Ireland of her childhood. In these latter stories, we see once again the country girl, living in a blighted village with her house-proud mother and drunken father; but we also see, somewhere in the distance, the city woman, sitting at her writing table, puzzling out the mystery of how she got from there to here, and in the process delineating, with ever-increasing exactitude, the tragic world into which she was born.

Lantern Slides, her superb new collection, continues the quest for origin and explanation that has preoccupied Ms. O'Brien these past decades. Though she covers little new ground here, she also digs deeper into the old ground than ever before, unearthing a rich archeology. Tragedy is the central theme of the stories, but not the blind tragedy of car wrecks and earthquakes. Rather, what concerns Ms. O'Brien is those tragedies that come about as a result of ordinary passion, stupidity or stubbornness. The epigraph to the book—"Each human life must work through all the joys and sorrows, gains and losses, which make up the history of the world"—is from Thomas Mann, but it could just as well be from Shakespeare or Joyce, two omnipresent ghosts here, and it is echoed throughout the stories. "Ours was a small tragedy in comparison with the big ones," one narrator observes to her married lover, "the world gone off the rails, righteous chants of madmen, rapine, pillage; ordinary mortals, feeling as insignificant as gnats." But, as Ms. O'Brien shows us, ordinary mortals can love and suffer keenly.

In a story called **"Dramas,"** an ebullient, probably homosexual shopkeeper, arriving in a steely Irish village with the intention of starting a theatrical company, is quickly dissuaded from his original intention of producing Shakespeare or Chekhov: "The locals were suspicious, they did not want plays about dead birds and illegitimate children, or unhappy couples tearing at each other, because they had these scenarios aplenty." As the tension between the villagers' puritanism and the shopkeeper's flamboyance moves toward its inevitably awful climax, yet another episode of sordidness and humiliation is recorded in the O'Brien annals. High drama, we see, is not merely the province of the playwrights.

In **"Epitaph,"** a woman addresses the unreliable married lover with whom she has been obsessed for years, and who has been for years driving her to the brink of self-destruction. "You see, everyone is holding on," she tells him. "Just. If their skins were peeled off, or their chest bones opened, they would literally burst apart." Such ruthlessly surgical peeling and cracking might also describe Ms. O'Brien's method as a writer; the follies that can result from passion are subjected, in story after story, to an analysis so unsparing it verges on a kind of mutilation. Like the mother vacationing with her son and his girlfriend in **"Storm,"** Ms. O'Brien is constantly looking "into the abyss . . . frightened of the primitive forces that lurk there"; unlike the narrator, however, she never succumbs to the impulse to draw back.

In this literary universe, passions govern and casually destroy lives; cruelty and pain are as familiar as furniture. In " **'Oft in the Stilly Night,' "** a married woman whose .

shoes have been stolen by a "tinker woman" loses "her heart for retribution" upon seeing the unfortunate thief in a courtroom and asks the judge "in tearful tones to overlook [the crime] and to exercise clemency." But the judge will have none of it, will not even heed the woman's request that the tinker be allowed to keep the shoes, and the woman leaves the courtroom carrying them "limply, as if she would drop them the moment she got outside."

People often go mad in these stories. In one, an old sacristan is driven into a life of delusion for love of a priest, while in another a brother's repeated molestation of his sister compels her to plot the murder of his arriving bride. Elsewhere, tragedy results merely from a stubborn refusal to admit the truth, as in **"A Demon,"** in which a family making a visit first to a son in a monastery and then to a daughter who is ill in a convent endures with increasing anxiety and terror a journey fraught with mishaps—a late start, many wrong turns. Only in the end are the family members obliged to confront the true source of their anguish—not the journey but the daughter's mysterious "illness," which remains unnamed until its truly catastrophic implications can no longer be ignored.

The title story is the collection's masterpiece. A long, lilting paean to Joyce's own masterpiece, "The Dead," it travels the emotional terrain of a huge surprise party in contemporary Dublin, a celebration held to honor the birthday of a woman named Betty, whose husband has recently left her. The narrative voice—alternately wistful and funny—moves effortlessly among the points of view of the different guests, returning periodically, as if to center itself, to a young woman named Miss Lawless. (Most of Edna O'Brien's heroines could be named Miss Lawless.)

The stories that link the party guests usually begin with love and end with some kind of disaster or humiliation: a discovered tryst, a miscarriage, an abandonment. The owner of a flower shop that is about to go bankrupt searches frantically for a rich man to save her; a mentally ill girl whose "particular quirk was to keep walking, always walking, as if looking for something," wanders through on her way to somewhere else; a woman who has avenged herself on her philandering husband, and thereby earned the contempt of most of their friends, prays "with all her heart and soul for a seizure to finish her off, but she just grew thinner and thinner, and tighter and tighter, like a bottle brush."

Then "miniature trees with tiny lights as thin as buds" drop from the ceiling, "so that the room took on the wonder of a forest." A cake appears; a dog barks, suggesting the last-minute arrival of Betty's estranged husband, and the members of the crowd turn toward the door, "each rendered innocent by this moment of supreme suspense." As the story concludes, Miss Lawless, like the others, is caught up in the spell, the fantasy of the knight in shining armor arriving to save them all. "It was as if life were just beginning—tender, spectacular, all-embracing life—and she, like everyone, were jumping up to catch it. Catch it."

That repetition is vintage O'Brien—a stuttered last grasp at a fleeting sensation, and at the same moment an imploring plea to the reader, bringing to mind E. M. Forster's exhortation to "only connect." In the hands of a lesser writer, such a finale might seem melodramatic; but here, and elsewhere, Ms. O'Brien writes with a degree of assurance and commitment that can render even the most melodramatic gesture utterly credible.

With a few exceptions—**"Epitaph,"** most notably—I tend to find Ms. O'Brien's stories about cosmopolitan, contemporary women less satisfying than her Irish stories. Something is missing in them—a kind of gumption, a humorous vigor. Perhaps this is because the narrators of the city stories tend to speak into looking glasses and to live in the stasis of passionate attachments to married men that they cannot or will not break. The narrators of the Irish stories, by contrast, are engaged in investigations of the past—a past rich with fable and incident.

In a story called **"Another Time,"** a successful television announcer named Nelly decides to spend a holiday at an Irish hotel near her hometown, a hotel that, in her youth, she thought the height of glamour. There her past returns to her, "the rooms and landings of childhood, basins and slop buckets that oozed sadness." Nelly's homecoming prompts a rush of catharsis, "as if doors or windows were swinging open all around her and . . . she was letting go of some awful affliction."

For Edna O'Brien as well as for Nelly, the past—particularly the Irish past—provides a way into knowledge. Her stories unearth the primeval feelings buried just below the surface of nostalgia, using memories to illuminate both what is ridiculous and what is heroic about passion. Like Nelly, by going backward, Ms. O'Brien goes forward, "a river that winds its way back into its first beloved enclave before finally putting out to sea."

David Leavitt, "Small Tragedies and Ordinary Passions," in The New York Times Book Review, *June 24, 1990, p. 9.*

FURTHER READING

Biography

Kennedy, Ludovic. "Three Loves of Childhood—Irish Thoughts by Edna O'Brien." *The Listener* (3 June 1976): 701-02.
> Interview with O'Brien in which she discusses her childhood in Ireland, her religious upbringing, and her literary success in England.

Criticism

Champlin, Charles. "The Great American Short Story Rides Again." *Los Angeles Times Book Review* (30 June 1985): 1, 7.
> Review of *A Fanatic Heart,* praising O'Brien's "lyrical, painful, personal and occasionally slyly amusing recollections of a life begun in rural Ireland and continued in

London," her graceful language, and meticulous attention to detail.

Core, George. "Irish Affairs." *The Sewanee Review* LXXXIV, No. 1 (Winter 1976): ii-x.
    Compares the works of O'Brien to those of Sean O'Faolain, concluding that O'Brien is more successful than O'Faolain in expressing "the romantic soul caught in the web of modernity."

Doughty, Louise. "Restless Dreaming Souls." *The Times Literary Supplement,* No. 4549 (8-14 June 1990): 616.
    Commends O'Brien's convincing portrayal of personalities, idiosyncracies, and relationships in *Lantern Slides.*

Eckley, Grace. *Edna O'Brien.* Lewisburg, Pa.: Bucknell University Press, 1974, 88 p.
    Critical biography of O'Brien, focusing on her Irish heritage and her identity as a feminist writer.

Hope, Mary. Review of *Mrs. Reinhardt, and Other Stories,* by Edna O'Brien. *Spectator* 240, No. 7820 (20 May 1978): 23.
    Argues that *Mrs. Reinhardt* is a work of great depth and range, characterized by "rich and sure" writing and mature humor.

Wilbur, Ellen. "Love Tales Not Lightly Told." *The Christian Science Monitor* 82, No. 173 (2 August 1990): 12.
    Assesses the stories in *Lantern Slides,* stating that they "all deal in one way or another with love's ecstasy, its disappointment, and its destructive power."

Additional coverage of O'Brien's life and career is contained in the following sources published by Gale Research: *Contemporary Authors,* Vols. 1-4, rev. ed.; *Contemporary Authors New Revision Series,* Vol. 6; *Contemporary Literary Criticism,* Vols. 3, 5, 8, 13, 36, 65; *Dictionary of Literary Biography,* Vol. 14; and *Major 20th-Century Writers.*

Muriel Spark

1918-

(Full name Muriel Sarah Spark; has also written under the pseudonym Evelyn Cavallo) Scottish novelist, short story writer, poet, dramatist, essayist, biographer, editor, script-writer, and author of books for children.

INTRODUCTION

Recognized as an important figure in contemporary British literature, Spark is best known for her novels *The Prime of Miss Jean Brodie* and *The Mandelbaum Gate.* In much of her work Spark examines such topics as free will, psychological motivations, and moral issues, especially those pertaining to Catholicism. The supernatural and its intervention in everyday events is a dominant motif in Spark's short stories, and Tom Hubbard has observed: "Using various means, including the supernatural, the symbolic, and the subtle, Muriel Spark transfigures the commonplace and jolts us into seeing it in a new light."

Early in her writing career, Spark published poetry, short stories, and several biographies, including studies of such English authors as Mary Shelley, Emily Brontë, and John Masefield. In 1951 she won the *Observer* newspaper's short story prize for "The Seraph and the Zambesi," in which an angel disrupts a Christmas pageant and chides the participants for commercializing a religious holiday. Spark became a Roman Catholic in 1954, the year in which she began writing her first novel, and her conversion profoundly affected her work. While Spark's works are not predominantly centered on religious themes, they often reflect her belief that Catholicism has provided her with a "norm . . . something to measure from" when creating her fiction.

Spark's first collection of short fiction, *The Go-Away Bird, and Other Stories,* garnered praise for its economical prose style and convincing characterization. Several of the stories in this volume, including "The Seraph and the Zambesi" and "The Go-Away Bird," feature African settings based on Spark's observations while living in Rhodesia from 1937 to 1944. "The Go-Away Bird" has been praised in particular for its compelling portrayal of the tragic fate of a young woman whose feelings of loneliness and rootlessness impel her to return to the British colony where she grew up, in spite of several warnings that a family servant intends to harm her. Supernatural or inexplicable events often play a prominent role in Spark's stories. For example, in "The Portobello Road" the ghost of a Catholic woman returns to haunt the man who murdered her for threatening to reveal his efforts to enter a bigamous marriage. Incorporating supernatural elements with satire in another story, "The Black Madonna," Spark portrays a liberal white English couple who pray to a Madonna carved of black wood to help them conceive a child. When

the child is unaccountably born black, the couple rejects the baby despite their history of believing in racial tolerance. Critics have noted the influence of Henry James's novella *The Turn of the Screw* (1898) on Spark's story "The Twins," which focuses on two children who conspire to create mistrust among their parents and others by telling carefully constructed lies.

Spark's second collection, *Voices at Play,* includes four radio plays and six short stories, which, although thematically and technically related to her first collection, are generally considered less accomplished. Critics have, however, praised "The Ormolu Clock" for its depiction of the disturbing tensions between two innkeepers whose rival establishments face each other across a narrow path near the Austro-Yugoslavian border. Spark's next three volumes of short fiction consist primarily of reprints from her first two volumes but also include several stories previously published only in periodicals and such noted new pieces as "The Dragon." Throughout the 1960s and 1970s Spark concentrated on writing novels, but the publication in 1985 of *The Stories of Muriel Spark* renewed interest in her short fiction. Spark's short stories have been increasingly recognized as an important component in the development of her career as a novelist, as well as significant artistic achievements in their own right. In a review of *The Go-Away Bird, and Other Stories,* Aileen Pippett observed: "[Spark] communicates her special vision of the universe because she is a master of her craft, combining simple language with subtle construction, and because she has a perception of the reality of evil. Damnation and salvation are facts to her, and so is hocus-pocus. This mixture of mischief and mystery makes her work unique."

PRINCIPAL WORKS

SHORT FICTION

The Go-Away Bird, and Other Stories 1958
Voices at Play (short stories and radio scripts) 1961
Collected Stories I 1967
Bang-Bang You're Dead, and Other Stories 1983
The Stories of Muriel Spark 1985

OTHER MAJOR WORKS

Child of Light: A Reassessment of Mary Wollstonecraft Shelley (biography) 1951; also published as *Mary Shelley: A Biography* [revised edition], 1987
The Fanfarlo, and Other Verse (poetry) 1952
Emily Brontë: Her Life and Work [with Derek Stanford] (biography) 1953
John Masefield (biography) 1953
The Comforters (novel) 1957
Memento Mori (novel) 1958
Robinson (novel) 1958
The Bachelors (novel) 1960
The Ballad of Peckham Rye (novel) 1960
The Prime of Miss Jean Brodie (novel) 1961
Doctors of Philosophy (drama) 1962
The Girls of Slender Means (novel) 1963
The Mandelbaum Gate (novel) 1965
Collected Poems I (poetry) 1967; also published as *Going Up to Sotheby's, and Other Poems,* 1982
The Public Image (novel) 1968
The Driver's Seat (novel) 1970
Not to Disturb (novel) 1971
The Hothouse by the East River (novel) 1973
The Abbess of Crewe (novel) 1974
The Takeover (novel) 1976
Territorial Rights (novel) 1979
Loitering with Intent (novel) 1981
The Only Problem (novel) 1984
A Far Cry from Kensington (novel) 1988
Symposium (novel) 1990

Aileen Pippett (essay date 1960)

[*Pippett is an English critic who wrote* The Moth and the Stars *(1955), a biography of Virginia Woolf. In the following review, she praises the craftsmanship of the short fiction collected in* The Go-Away Bird, and Other Stories.]

Note well the name of Muriel Spark, readers were advised in 1957. Three years and three novels later, a collection of short stories indicates that this young British writer still sparkles. All the eleven stories [collected in *The Go-Away Bird, and Other Stories*] strike her distinctively frivolous-serious note. They are at once spine-chilling and comical, teasing the imagination, sticking like burrs to the memory. They tell of what indubitably happened, one is momentarily convinced, but in a very odd world.

Now, it is a prime function of the storyteller to open our eyes to a world that is indeed a very odd place. This Muriel Spark does to an uncanny degree. She communicates her special vision of the universe because she is a master of her craft, combining simple language with subtle construction, and because she has a perception of the reality of evil. Damnation and salvation are facts to her, and so is hocus-pocus. This mixture of mischief and mystery makes her work unique.

The title story ["**The Go-Away Bird**"] contains in its sixty pages a ballad of death and the maiden and material for half-a-dozen volumes of family chronicle about life in a British African colony and in post-war England. The small "go-away" cry of the insignificant gray-crested lourie is heard through all the contemporary hubbub.

Other stories are equally powerful and evocative. "**The Black Madonna**" is wryly concerned with the color problem in an English suburb. In "**The Twins**," Henry James' beautiful children reappear in our time to give a new turn of the screw, posing the question, who corrupted whom? "**The Pawnbroker's Wife**" describes a South African mother's fantastic attempts to make a foolish daughter socially acceptable; while "**Miss Pinkerton's Apocalypse**" is exuberant with certainty that a flying saucer is genuine Spode, and "**You Should Have Seen the Mess**" records the authentic voice of an English typist, eternally secure in smug stupidity.

"**The Portobello Road,**" the story of a haunting as told by a ghost, has a tremendous and characteristic punch line. The straying spirit, feckless in life and in death, recalls a "jolly snap" of her childhood friends at play "reflecting fearlessly in the face of the camera the glory of the world, as if it would never pass."

Other quiet comments have a similar shattering effect, like that of a shark's fin in the blue water of a bathing beach. For instance, a thoroughly odious woman is deservedly exposed at a cocktail party, and a participant in the riotous affair remarks, "I have forgotten her name but I shall remember it at the Bar of Judgment."

And I shall remember Muriel Spark gratefully for the glorious fantasy of the Seraph who gate-crashed a Nativity Masque, turned the majestic Victoria Falls to steam and who was last seen riding the Zambesi River, "among the rocks that look like crocodiles and the crocodiles that look like rocks."

Aileen Pippett, "Salvation and Hocus Pocus Are All Very Real," in The New York Times Book Review, *October 30, 1960, p. 4.*

Ann Birstein   (essay date 1960)

[*Birstein is an American educator, novelist, biographer, and critic. In the following review of* The Go-Away Bird, and Other Stories, *she praises the depth and emotional intensity of the longer pieces in the collection, especially "The Go-Away Bird" and "The Black Madonna."*]

Muriel Spark is the kind of writer so many people have discovered for themselves that she is finally reaching the wide audience she deserves. Not only is she good, at her best there is no one like her, and she writes in a voice that is distinctly her own. Mrs. Spark's special quality, because she *is* inimitable, is very hard to describe. It is a strange mixture of the most penetrating seriousness and also the illusion that, like some comedian famous for his timing, she is throwing away her best lines: "The Black Madonna had been given to the church by a recent convert. It was carved out of bog oak. . . . 'Looks a bit like contemporary art.' . . . 'It's old-*fashioned*. Else how'd it get sanctioned to be put up?' " To this very dark Virgin, Lou Parker decides to pray for a child. It is a natural decision, since Mrs. Parker is "not a snob, only sensible," and of such advanced opinions that she considers Jane Austen "too Victorian," and counts among her friends two very dark, shiny gentlemen from Jamaica. Naturally, however, when her prayers are rewarded by a pitch-black baby, it is all too much for her. She gives it away. And does the local priest think she has done a good thing? her husband asks, "No, not a *good* thing. In fact, he said it would have been a good thing if we could have kept the baby. But failing that, we did the *right* thing. Apparently, there's a difference."

It has been suggested that one of the reasons Mrs. Spark's work was slow to catch on in the beginning is that, like all very funny writers, she was not always taken seriously. This is true; but now that she has caught on, I think that perhaps a worse injustice is being done her, and that is the tendency to regard her as essentially a stylist and to refer to her work as "flawless" or "seamless." A dubious compliment, and the kind often paid to lady writers, who are not, as a group, inclined to chest thumping and other forms of literary violence. But the suggestion is that more attention is paid to making those little seams invisible than to anything else. Actually, Mrs. Spark is always deeply involved with her subject, and her range is extraordinary and sometimes terrifying. Those who have read her novel *Memento Mori* . . . know that death is a frequent and not unfriendly visitor in her work. In this collection [*The Go-Away Bird, and Other Stories*], the narrator of one story, **"The Portobello Road,"** is a girl murdered five years before; another concerns Selwyn MacGregor, "the nicest boy who ever committed the sin of whiskey," who contemplates corruption from his home by the side of a graveyard; and **"The Go-Away Bird"** itself, a lovely and subtle novella, is about a young girl doomed, no matter how much the call of a bird lures her away from Africa, to submit to a tragically ironic death there.

Mrs. Spark's habit is to hit lightly and then back away, and as a rule her aim is uncanny. Where she is most likely to miss is, I think, in some of her shorter work. Like all writers who attempt to turn our heads in a direction we had not thought of looking before, she needs time to accustom us to this unfamiliar perspective. Otherwise, the effect is not so much fleeting as too constricted, and there are several stories in this collection where one wishes she had lingered longer and tried for more. But where she does allow herself this latitude—as in **"The Go-Away Bird"** and **"The Black Madonna"**—the effect is unexpectedly powerful.

Ann Birstein, "An Uncanny Aim," in *The Reporter*, Vol. 23, No. 8, November 10, 1960, p. 55.

Time   (essay date 1960)

[*In the review below, the critic favorably appraises* The Go-Away Bird, and Other Stories.]

Sooner or later, readers of Muriel Spark's fiction come to understand that they have been hornswoggled in the very nicest way. The tactics of this talented Scot are essentially those of the confidence man. The Spark reader is entertained by an apparently straightforward, witty story—until the moment arrives when the rug is twitched from beneath his feet, or when a corps of spooks, bogies and supernatural agents start moving the furniture about, playing the devil with the shapes of common objects.

In [**"The Black Madonna"**], the first of these eleven short stories [collected in *The Go-Away Bird, and Other Stories*], a man and his wife, living a life of crushing respectability in an awful welfare-state township, pray to the Virgin to be relieved of their childlessness. Their prayers are answered. But the Madonna in their church, a figure carved from Irish bog oak, is black as ebony; so, too, is their first-born child. This merciless story makes plain that neither inheritance nor adultery with a Jamaican can explain the couple's embarrassingly Negroid blessing. For all its apparent defiance of realism, this kind of Spark fiction—typical of most tales in this collection—has honest intentions: to make vivid the author's conviction that the face of the world is a mask, and that the real hoax is on those who believe only what the eye can see. [**"The Go-Away Bird"**], really a short novel, is somewhat different from the others; it shows what Muriel Spark can accomplish when she forswears the stage properties of the semi-supernatural suspense story and moves her characters about with no strings attached. She tells the life and death of Daphne du Toit, an enchanting and entirely credible South African girl whose betrayed dreams illuminate a basic Spark theme—the cruelty of reality and the greater cruelty of the illusions that falsify it. (British author Spark herself spent 6½ years in Southern Rhodesia during World War II, working at "odd jobs, waiting to get home and trying to write.")

Daphne's childhood is haunted by the go-away bird, a grey-crested lourie, or parrot, whose eponymous cry seems to her a command to leave the provincial, semi-savage, secondhand and second-rate life of a British African colony for the authentic glories of historic England. Alas, her dreams are of a "land that was not, that is passed away"—the Rupert Brookeish Lubberland where the church clock stands at ten to 3, and there is honey still for tea, where life is a vision of white flannels on a vicarage lawn, and the Guard is always being changed but never for the worse.

In contrast to these dreams, life on the African home farm is twisted in a pattern of almost Faulknerian grotesquerie; Daphne's uncle is in bondage to his farm manager through an unavenged adultery a generation back; Auntie lies year long in a whisky fog with a loaded revolver at her bedside; her one friend is a boozy Cambridge expatriate who must, for his own reasons, falsify what "home" is like. Society at the local dorp is of inconceivable tedium, and only the natives in their kraals suggest that life lived on its own terms may be a good thing. When Daphne finally escapes to her never-never land. Author Spark moves to her fictional kill like a Mau Mau houseboy.

Daphne's English relations are a damply rotting family who call each other with gruesome whimsy names drawn from Gilbert & Sullivan and Kenneth Grahame. "Uncle Pooh-Bah," "Rat," etc. Then, belatedly, she is to be presented at court by a friend of a relative, a grizzly social harpy who earns her fat fee by staging lunches at the Ritz to meet other harpies and conscripted young men who turn out to be either too young or ineligible by reason of honest imbecility. Later chums are either married, queer or worse. Daphne goes back to the boredom of colonial clubland, and to a fate that is too painful to record. But the reader may be permitted to suspect that Author Spark enjoys it up to the last twist of the garrote.

With her novels *Memento Mori* and *The Ballad of Peckham Rye,* Muriel Spark, 42, won the kind of grateful acclaim that goes to an entertainer whom highbrows are not ashamed to be caught reading. This collection is another sign that the short story—which a few years back seemed exhausted in the banalities of realism plus mood—is still a natural form for those with a lively mind, a deft style and a crisp point to make. With other British writers such as Angus Wilson (whom she closely resembles) and V. S. Pritchett, Author Spark has in fact shown that the short story need not be just a thin slice of life cut by those who cannot carve a whole roast novel. (pp. 108, 110)

> *"Confidence Trickster," in* Time, *New York, Vol. LXXVI, No. 20, November 14, 1960, pp. 108, 110.*

Sybille Bedford (essay date 1960)

[*In the following review of* The Go-Away Bird, and Other Stories, *Bedford praises the collection while faulting what she views as the occasionally uneven quality of the shorter pieces.*]

Very good writing is often dull to read. Not so, the fates be praised, Muriel Spark's. She happens to be, by some rare concatenation of grace and talent, an artist, a serious—and a most accomplished—writer, a moralist engaged with the human predicament, wildly entertaining, and a joy to read. She also has a specialty, a trade-mark.

"I must explain," says a character in one of the stories [collected in **The Go-Away Bird, and Other Stories**], "that

I departed this life nearly five years ago." The character speaks casually if firmly. Readers of those wonderfully brilliant and original novels, *The Comforters,* and *Memento Mori,* have already experienced the always fresh shock of Muriel Spark's cool use of what to outsiders appears to be the supernatural. It is entirely deadpan—"No comment." (And, one must hasten to say, without a trace of whimsy.) The telephone speaks, the typewriter taps without the benefit of human voice or hand; like the Catholic Church, of which she is a member, Miss Spark never explains and never apologizes. She simply and quite literally has added, whenever convenient, the fourth dimension to otherwise sober and realistically tethered fiction.

Such employment of the *au delà* as a prop to plot was of course not at all unknown to the Victorians, but it is unusual in contemporary literature. Muriel Spark's way with it is her own; her result is a quickening of curiosity and suspense, the creation of highjinks, zest, and fun, without—felicitous achievement—impairing either the intrinsic sadness of her unusual themes or the psychological plausibility of her stories.

Perhaps the most dazzlingly told of these is **"The Portobello Road,"** the second longest story in the present volume. It opens with this lovely line, "One day in my young youth at high summer . . . " and for sheer virtuosity of presentment I cannot remember ever having read its equal. What managing of the operative fact! The unsuspecting reader can hardly fail to sit up with delighted shock and admiration at a certain point, which I shall be careful not to give away by one more word. Another favorite is **"The Black Madonna,"** a story about a childless couple installed in one of those new English " 'New Towns laid out in arcs and isosceles triangles" applying somewhat half-heartedly for a miracle; here we have an exhilarating blend of social exposition (wickedly observed and faultlessly delivered), poetic irony, and the trademark.

"The Go-Away Bird," the title story, novella length, is A Life, the swift sad ruthless tale of the happy youth and fate of a girl, an English girl raised in an African colony on literary dreams of England, and soon tripped up by several sets of inevitabilities. This Candide who is also a rather irritating schoolgirl stoic—"Oh I see," is her unvaried response to disillusion and disaster—grows up amongst white planters and native chiefs, sleepwalking in the eye of the storm of an old feud, is delayed by the war, sails at last for England, is betrayed at every turn, goes back to the colony, and is met by a long-laid fate.

The eight shorter stories of this volume are unequal, and what collection of short stories is not? But some are fantastic and some are bold and some are very funny, and nearly every one of them drives home its own nail. Perhaps the most enduring is **"The Twins,"** a blood-chilling puzzler, a kind of domestic *Turn of the Screw,* built with incredible concision on seemingly innocuous lines. I have, I hope, conveyed something of the author's remarkable literary skill, but have I said anything about the quality of the dialogue? Have I mentioned the wit, the conjuring of character, the insight? Have I begun to say how well she writes?

The fact is that Miss Spark has got about everything. (pp. 28-9)

Sybille Bedford, "Fantasy without Whimsy," in Saturday Review, *Vol. XLIII, No. 47, November 19, 1960, pp. 28-9.*

Samuel Hynes (essay date 1962)

[*An American critic and educator, Hynes has written and edited numerous studies of English literature and literary figures. In the following review of* Voices at Play, *Hynes, while offering limited praise for Spark's short fiction, unfavorably compares her work in this genre with her novels.*]

Of Mrs. Spark's many literary virtues, one which should not be overlooked is her extraordinary productivity. **Voices at Play** is her eighth book in less than six years, a record that puts her in the same league with Trollope and Arnold Bennett (to mention two mass-producers with whom she has no other affinity). Book-a-year writers are rare these days, and since Mrs. Spark's writing is at its best brilliant, and never less than entertaining, we must be grateful that she is also prolific.

This second collection of her shorter pieces demonstrates what the first, **The Go-Away Bird,** also suggested—that she can write adroit and subtle short stories, but that her *serious* form is the novel. Her short stories are valuable because she is an interesting and intelligent writer, but they don't belong to the same class of achievement as *The Comforters* and *Memento Mori.* They have some of the special qualities of her novels—the same delicately recorded rhythms of speech, the same awareness of the radical oddity of human behavior, the same sense of the unpredictability of ordinary existence—but all composing a lower level of significance.

For example, a number of these pieces are involved, in one way or another, with the supernatural, as most of the novels also are. But the supernatural here is the ghost-story variety—demon lovers and dead men's voices—and not the metaphysical sort that makes the novels so startlingly original. I should add at once that these supernatural pieces are well done; it is only in comparison with the longer fiction that they seem unimpressive.

Of the ten pieces in **Voices at Play,** three are set in Africa, where Mrs. Spark lived for some time. These seem more the products of memory than of imagination, and it may be worth noting that Mrs. Spark has never drawn upon this rather exotic personal background for her novels, though there are other African stories in **The Go-Away Bird.** In general, her stories have the qualities of memory—a few sharp details, the more-than-ordinary clarity that time gives to what it leaves us.

But sometimes the materials of memory carry their own significance, and a fine story results. **"The Ormolu Clock,"** for example, is a first-person recollection of an incident in an Austrian resort hotel; the narrator, a guest at the hotel, observes the triumph of her industrious, acquisitive landlady over the failing inn-keeper next door. The relationship is a complex one, and it is realized in the story entirely in terms of gestures and objects, the things a guest who knew neither of the principals might, if she were as perceptive as Mrs. Spark, observe. The story is economical and delicate, and entirely successful. But in other stories, the recollected details seem inadequate or contrived, and the results are less successful.

Voices at Play also includes four radio plays commissioned for the BBC's Third Programme. Mrs. Spark calls these "ear pieces," and they demonstrate further what her novels had already shown, that she has a marvelous ear for the shape and flow of speech. They must have been extremely effective when performed, but to the eye they seem a little bare, a little too much restricted by the limitations of the medium.

Perhaps the best way to describe these stories and plays is to say that they seem the by-products of a serious and original talent which has found its fullest expression in the larger form of the novel. The book is full of good writing, but Mrs. Spark's previous work has set a high standard, and by that standard **Voices at Play** is minor Spark. (pp. 285-86)

Samuel Hynes, "A Minor Spark," in The Commonweal, *Vol. LXXVI, No. 11, June 8, 1962, pp. 285-86.*

Harold W. Schneider (essay date 1962)

[*In the excerpt below, Schneider assesses* The Go-Away Bird, and Other Stories *and* Voices at Play, *noting that Spark's stories "entertain" and "enchant" but are rarely deeply moving.*]

On the surface [Muriel Spark] possesses all the writing virtues that should make her a master of the short story: she is able in the most crisp and economical prose quickly to develop believable characters and a situation in which the reader is immersed; she is skillful in developing personality through conversation and in finding exactly the right singularity of speech to make a character stand out as a type and as an individual at the same time (in one novel the attribution of the phrase "Well now" to an American couple, who use it many times but with different meanings to preface their remarks, made me conscious that I had been hearing the phrase used thus all my life without even noticing it); she is also able to handle point of view in any way that suits her, writing as omniscient author or in the character of a person in the story, either in the first person or as a consciousness described rather than describing; finally, she can construct her plots as tightly as her prose and bring them to their conclusions with no wasted effort. Because of these abilities there are no real failures among her stories, but one also feels there are not as many complete successes as there should be. The best of the stories are those that are almost novelettes, particularly **"The Go-Away Bird"** and **"The Portobello Road"** from her first volume and **"Bang-bang You're Dead"** from the most recent work, for it is in these that the characters attain something of a life and personality worth caring about, as well as the individuality that is usually present. Perhaps what is at fault is Mrs. Spark's striking cleverness, her utter competence, and occasionally even her willingness to flirt with the supernatural and the incredible. Her stories entertain and some times enchant by the presence of a fantastic, strange, or unknown world or scene (Mrs. Spark spent some years in Southern Rhodesia before World War II and many of her stories make use of what she saw and learned there), but while they please they are not always moving enough to be memorable.

Of the two volumes, *The Go-Away Bird, and Other Stories* (1958) clearly has the most memorable pieces. "The Twins," a story about the rather diabolical influence of a very young boy and girl, develops chillingly to its climax as the young woman narrator becomes aware that between the ages of five and twelve these precocious and evil children have gained complete control over their parents and their parents' relations with other people. Diabolically the twins, by constructing awkward situations through carefully planned lies, have made the parents so uncertain of each other and of outsiders that they accept whatever the twins say and act on it rather than on what the adults say. Not that the parents act meanly or badly to each other or to outsiders; they are simply very good people who cannot conceive of the evil in their children, and thus they make allowances for what seem the errors, pettiness, even nasty acts of other adults. This is a story of the triumph of evil over good—and the irony is that the evil comes from two beautiful and apparently guileless children. And there is a further irony: not only does the evil which triumphs over good come from the children; its triumph is largely good's own fault. Mrs. Spark surely means to show that such innocence as that of Jennie and Simon Reeves is not real goodness at all. Because they fail to recognize the evil in their children, they cannot cope with it and therefore do harm and injustice to themselves and their acquaintances. In order to combat evil, Mrs. Spark implies one must know it.

"The Twins" is fairly typical of Mrs. Spark's fiction, for it shows her concern with moral problems, sometimes even with unworldly "influences," her skill at quick characterizations, and her tight prose style. But the best and most compelling of the stories in this volume are the African tales. "The Pawnbroker's Wife," the least ambitious of these tales, is a realistic account of the triumph of a view of life over the real world. Again it is told by a woman narrator, who is forced to observe rather closely her landlady, abandoned wife of a pawnbroker, and the landlady's two unusual daughters. In their house on the sea front of South Africa this strange threesome force their lodgers to give them their attention through the discomfort they can inflict if the lodgers do not; the complication of the plot arises out of the stories the mother and daughters invent and force their lodgers to accept in silence to avoid expulsion from the house. "The Pawnbroker's Wife" is an amusing character study that succeeds at the same time in being a portrait edged in pathos. The second African tale, **"The Seraph and the Zambesi,"** indulges Mrs. Spark's penchant for the fantastic. It won first prize in the *Observer* competition in 1951 and can be counted this writer's first considerable success. In it the ubiquitous young woman narrator tells of Samuel Cramer, supposed poet and journalist of the nineteenth century, who is enjoying a reincarnation in the twentieth century as operator of a petrol pump on the Zambesi River near Victoria Falls. Cramer has written a nativity masque and is to play a seraph in it, but when on Christmas Eve the company assembles at Cramer's garage for the performance, the members find on the stage a strange insect-like being which radiates heat and claims to be a seraph. This creature is like a native's view of what a seraph might be:

> The eyes took up nearly the whole of the head, extending far over the cheekbones. From the back of the head came two muscular wings which from time to time folded themselves over the eyes, making a draught of scorching air. There was hardly any neck. Another pair of wings, tough and supple, spread from below the shoulders, and a third pair extended from the calves of the legs, appearing to sustain the body. The feet looked too fragile to bear up such a concentrated degree of being.

Cramer attempts unsuccessfully to persuade the seraph to leave, but he insists on his right as a seraph to stay to perform his own masque. Outside, young troopers, hearing that a leopard is supposedly in the garage, start a fire when they spray petrol inside to blind the beast. The story ends with the pursuit of the six-winged seraph up to the road to the river and the falls, which turns partly to steam from the heat of the seraph. This is an imaginative, wild and funny tale, quite different from either of the other African stories. In it Mrs. Spark plays with reality, creating her story out of her imagination and what must be scattered remnants of her African experience.

"The Go-Away Bird," the best of the lot, in its sixty pages tells the life story of Daphne du Toit, daughter of a Dutch father and an English mother in a British colony in Africa. Living with her mother's relatives after the death of her parents, Daphne grows up knowing that her guardian, Chakata Patterson, loves the natives but hates the Dutch; but she is twelve before she learns that he has continued to employ a Dutch man, Old Tuys, as manager of his farm because years before he wronged Tuys by making love to his promiscuous wife. Chakata's peculiar sense of honor makes him keep Old Tuys on even though Tuys has sworn revenge, has attempted to rape Mrs. Patterson, and is a constant threat to the women of the family. The inevitable action is now clear, but it does not come soon. Daphne longs to escape to England—fed on tales of that country by Donald Cloete, the often drunk Englishman who serves as clerk of the dorp; and urged on by the cry of the go-away bird, or grey-crested lourie, with its "go'way, go'way." But she does not get away before Old Tuys has made one attack upon her life while she is home from training college the Christmas between her sixteenth and seventeenth years. Even after this attack she must wait through years in Capetown when the war comes, during which time she meets and loses a fiancé in the war. And when in 1946 she finally comes to say goodbye to the Pattersons before she embarks for England, she undergoes yet another attack from Old Tuys. This time not a passing native but a man with a gun and on a bicycle (clearly Donald Cloete) saves her; Tuys is only wounded by Donald's shot. When Daphne says goodbye to Donald and thanks him, he says, "Don't return."

But life in England proves to offer no escape and no fulfill-ment. Her mother's family disappoint her, her social am-bitions turn to ashes before the commercial process by which they are to be achieved, a job as a teacher is taken from her because of the charges of the wife of the middle-aged barrister whose mistress she has become. At last, however, she meets someone she can love, Ralph Mercer, an admired popular novelist; and they become lovers for two years. When Ralph demands to know all about her, saying, "Love is an expedition of discovery into unex-plored territory," Daphne tells him of her past, of Chakata and their life in Africa, of the go-away bird. But Ralph's passion, less intense and lasting than Daphne's, cools rap-idly, and eventually he leaves their shared flat. When Daphne follows him to his mother's, he says, "Go away. . . . Go away and leave me in peace." Daphne re-turns to Africa. It is 1950.

The conclusion of the story comes swiftly. Only Chakata and Old Tuys are left on the farm and they are ill, Tuys senile from a stroke; the neighbors are mostly busy or are new and unknown. On the third day home, Daphne goes for a walk, sits down on a stone to rest, hears the familiar cry "Go'way, go'way," and herself cries, "God help me. Life is unbearable." Some time later Old Tuys returns to the house dragging what he says is a buck. Daphne's fu-neral is the next day, following the inquest.

There is another turn to the story. Ralph, who is too self-ish to be more than slightly moved by Daphne's death, makes a pilgrimage a year later to Africa to extend his sense of tragedy by learning more about Daphne. In an amusing irony he finds a new success among the surpris-ingly large number of persons here who are fans of his fic-tion. But when he visits Daphne's grave, from behind the grave he hears the cry, "Go'way, go'way," and again each day for the next six weeks in whatever place he is. Aban-doning his plan to stay in Africa, Ralph flees to England by plane, to the puzzlement of his new friends. The cry that could not save her has protected Daphne at last.

I have summarized this story in such detail because it seems to me the finest work of these two volumes of short stories—a haunting and deeply moving account, express-ing the tragic loneliness of a human soul not sure of what it wants from life, not finding its kindred spirit or its prop-er end. In it Mrs. Spark deftly depicts the unusual rela-tionship between Chakata and Old Tuys, the latter's ob-session, Daphne's sense of longing and her rootlessness, and the difference in the ways of life of the Africans and the English. This story shows best the author's eye for the particular detail, her close concern for the events she de-scribes, and her ability to place the reader in a situation and a scene essentially strange to him. Her technique of using a single phrase as a recurring motif is a device she does not use again with such success until her most recent novel. In **"The Go-Away Bird"** Mrs. Spark also abandons her first-person narrator with good result, for as omni-scient author she brings us closer to Daphne than would the point of view of an uninvolved onlooker. Her style is so spare it is almost flat, yet it serves her very well.

The other stories in this volume take place in England or Scotland and generally lack the compelling quality of these four, though some are more obviously funny and one or two quite touching. **"The Portobello Road"** concerns the lives of four young people who eventually pair off in their middle years. The story is witty, clever, entertaining; but it has what is here almost a fault: a too clever plot. At the end the story also has a surprising turn that smacks a bit of the methods of O. Henry. **"You Should Have Seen the Mess"** offers a delightful portrait of a lower middle-class girl brought up in the belief that "cleanliness is God-liness." Particularly amusing is the way Mrs. Spark makes this first-person narrator reflect the most conspicuous faults in the writing of the self-righteously half-educated. The story is notable in being Mrs. Spark's one attempt to satirize her first-person narrator entirely through the nar-rator's own language. **"Miss Pinkerton's Apocalypse"** is good Spark for another reason: it deals with the supernat-ural (flying saucers—real ones, Spode, in fact), but in a highly frolicsome way. Of the more serious stories **"The Black Madonna"** concerns the birth of a black child to a white Catholic couple. This event is complicated and made humorous by the couple's previous fairly close asso-ciation with two Negro students in self-conscious attempts at racial tolerance. The couple's tolerance suddenly breaks down and they put their baby out for adoption, even against the arguments of their priest and the evidence that the baby is their own. There is a humorous irony about all of the actions of the couple, even in their having prayed for a child to the Black Madonna, a modernistic statue of bog oak that was a Catholic convert's gift to their local church. The serious question raised is what is "right" and what is "good"—for the parents and the child. Surely Mrs. Spark means that, put to the test, one's tolerance and even one's faith may depend upon how much and in what way one is tested; that the courage to stand firm against the opinion of others is a rare thing. **"Come Along, Marjo-rie"** is a story of such exceptional courage, again in a reli-gious context. A young Catholic woman comes to an abbey in Worcestershire in a kind of personal retreat, and she so preserves her self-imposed vow of silence, prayer, and meditation that she annoys all of the lay visitors, called "pilgrims," and even the monks. When she finally does speak, it is to the young woman narrator: "The Lord is risen," Marjorie says. Later when Marjorie begins fast-ing, the authorities think she is going too far and they and the doctor take her away to an asylum. The important comment of the narrator occurs early in the story:

> I got the instant impression that she alone among the lay people, both pilgrims and Clois-ters, understood the purpose of the place. I did get that impression.

Voices at Play (1962), sub-titled "stories and ear-pieces," contains four radio plays and six short stories. There is in this volume a heavier run to fantasy, not usually very suc-cessful. "The Danger Zone," a radio piece which would do very well for "Twilight Zone," concerns the alliance the children of a Welsh village have with the strange for-eign children on the other side of the mountain. Its de-nouement is properly shocking and all quite pat. Similar to this piece are "The Interview" and "The Party Through the Wall"—they contain an overdose of imagination, their principal virtue is Mrs. Spark's superb ear for speech.

"The Dry River Bed" is an African ghost story, combining something of the spellbinding quality of **"The Go-Away Bird"** with the grotesque fantasy of **"The Seraph and the Zambesi."** The second African story, **"The Curtain Blown by the Breeze,"** might almost be the story of the promiscuous Mrs. Tuys of **"The Go-Away Bird."** More successful and more moving is **"Bang-bang You're Dead."** Sybil, the heroine who is from Africa, is showing reels of Kodachrome film (which have lain in her trunk for eighteen years and never before been seen) to her hosts in England. As she describes the people in the pictures, which include herself, she relives her life. The story exhibits Muriel Spark's ability to sum up the ironies of a life quickly and contains some reminiscent passages so deeply felt they must reflect their author's own experience. **"The Dark Glasses"** is a story rivaling **"The Twins"** in its chilling account of the relations of adults to children, though the pattern of evil is reversed. The other stories, more conventional in approach, form, and subject matter, might have been written by a Somerset Maugham somewhat more witty and economical than the one we know. There is a greater edge of satire than in Maugham, a bit more of a commitment to the characters, and a superb sense of style. (pp. 29-36)

> *Harold W. Schneider, "A Writer in Her Prime: The Fiction of Muriel Spark," in* Critique: Studies in Modern Fiction, *Vol. V, No. 2, Fall, 1962, pp. 28-45.*

Derek Stanford (essay date 1963)

[*Stanford is an English poet and critic who cowrote and edited several works with Spark. In the following excerpt from his* Muriel Spark: A Biographical and Critical Study, *Stanford discusses Spark's short fiction.*]

Muriel Spark's transition as a poet from the conventional to the original was less abrupt than one might believe. In South Africa she had been writing in what might be called a colonial-traditional Romantic manner, and so she continued when she came to this country until, about 1948, the yeast of change began to work within her.

Her short stories knew no such evolution. Fully grown and armed, like the new-born Sparti, they sprang forth in scandalous completeness from her brain. The mastery and freshness of her narrative gift was manifested right from the start. **"The Seraph and the Zambesi,"** which won the *Observer* short story competition, was all but her first essay in fiction. 'Essay' and 'attempt' are hardly words wherewith to describe this literary *putsch*. The triumph of the tale was almost an offence to the canonists of storytelling. It in nowise resembled the work of the tyro playing "sedulous ape" to some accepted master. Its style, its thought, its theme, were intransigent. And yet unlike so much experimental writing, there was nothing tentative about it. Its aim was perfect. Its very certainty upset some people.

As she began, so she continued. Her published stories number less than thirty; but each gets off to a fresh start. She imitates no other writer, nor does she repeat her own efforts. With each assault, she has made it news, created

a fresh apparatus of effect. Even such slighter pieces as **"Harper and Wilton," "Ladies and Gentlemen," "The Leaf-sweeper"** and **"The Girl I left behind me"** have an unadulterated look about them. A little of 'the old mixture,' 'the popular recipe' is never worked in. And the writing, as always, is spotless as new paint.

Bernard Shaw once declared that the secret of success in literature was to slap the public's face. Now there is nothing so unmannerly as face-slapping about Muriel Spark's fiction. The chastisement it administers is very much more subtle; more difficult to locate and repudiate.

First we feel it, maybe, as an astringency: a curious avoidance of the genial, of anything that might promote an *entente cordiale* between author and reader. Next, we realise that she does not share the same tastes and values as we do. That she is right and we are wrong can never, for one moment, be doubted by her. Her mastery depends upon her unqualified assumption of superiority. About this, in manner, there is nothing brash, nothing tiresomely assertive. She is an ironist of uncommon parts—irony, of course, being a language in which an élite communicates with its inferiors while still preserving *les convenances*. It is only when the heroine in one of these tales begins to proclaim her own thoughts a little, instead of merely serving to narrate events, that we become explicitly aware of this original smile of disdain. For the most part, this pride works smoothly and hiddenly. Only the uncertain need to insist, and Muriel Spark wears her arrogance as lightly as a grace. Thirdly, perhaps, we become aware that her world-picture is ours inverted. To make us see things as she sees them, it is necessary to stand the reader on his head.

Nor is this a matter of religious difference with the majority. A Roman Catholic, she has succeeded in offending the susceptibilities of certain of the faithful. Her story **"Come along, Marjorie,"** dealing with a religious House and Pilgrim Centre, was deeply resented by not a few representative pilgrims who thought they recognised likenesses.

Mr. T. S. Eliot once wrote anonymously that "The division between those who accept, and those who deny, Christian revelation I take to be the most profound difference between human beings . . . " The segregations affected by religion and ideology are great, but not so vast, I am convinced, as those established between temperament and temperament:

> There were ladies from Cork and thereabouts, ladies from Tyrone and Londonderry, all having come for a rest or a Retreat, and most bearing those neurotic stigmata of North or South accordingly. There were times when bitter bits of meaning would whistle across the space between North and South when they were gathered together outside of their common worship. Though all were Catholics, 'Temperament tells,' I told myself frequently. I did so often tell myself remarks like that to still my own nerves. [**"Come Along, Marjorie"**]

All her fiction can be taken as a polemic against togetherness; and in so far as all religions engender a sense of the collective, a sense of the group or fold, her work is apt to run counter to an ethos built up of fallacies and half-truths, and to set up certain resistances within it. It is never on articles of common doctrine that Muriel Spark runs foul of "the unco' guid." Rather it is the collective cosiness, which truth held in common may beget in its possessors, that causes this author's imaginative spine to arch like an irritated Persian cat's.

The narrator, the 'I' of **"Come Along, Marjorie,"** exists in a context of fiction, but is clearly a mouthpiece for the author. Muriel Spark, like the narrator, had spent some time convalescing from a nervous illness at a religious house similar to Watling Abbey.

At Watling Abbey, the narrator meets another convalescent. "Jennifer's neurosis took the form of 'same as.' We are all the same, she would assert, infuriating me because I knew God had made everyone unique—" none more so, indeed, than the narrator.

Arrived at Watling, the narrator looks round the platform and two other women (convalescent Pilgrims) joined her:

> . . . I made note that there was little in common between them and me except Catholicism, and then only in the mystical sense, for their religious apprehensions were different from mine. 'Different from' is the form my neurosis takes. I do like the differentiation of things, but it is apt to lead to nerve-racking pursuits. On the other hand, life led on the different-from level is always an adventure.

Jennifer's psychological egalitarianism is resented by the narrator, not only because of its false assumptions, but especially because it discounts her own superior identity.

Sometimes the uniqueness, the difference of the heroine causes her to question herself—to see this superiority in a negative light. Sybil (and the name, implying 'oracle', is significant) in **"Bang-bang You're Dead"** is seriously disquieted about her condition. Already, as a little girl, she has proved her superiority ("Sybil was precocious, her brain was like a blade") over Désirée, her twin in appearance ("She had discovered that dull children were apt to be spiteful"). Désirée grew up to be *femme moyenne sensuelle,* while Sybil, without moral effort, transcends sex.

The disturbing proofs of Sybil's superiority begin seriously when she realises, eighteen months after her marriage, that her husband is becoming a bore. "Other women," she remarks to herself, "do not wish to be married to a Mind. Yet I do . . . I am a freak and should not have married."

Providentially, Donald the husband is mauled by a lioness and dies. Sybil's friends urge her to marry again, and she tries to take an interest in such matters:

> On a few occasions Sybil attended these parties, working herself, as in a frenzy of self-discipline, into a state of carnal excitement about the men. She managed to do this only by an effortful sealing-off of all her critical faculties except those which assessed a good male voice and appearance. The hangovers were frightful.

The will (which others use to restrain their sensual feelings), Sybil has to employ to engender them. And the will fails to sustain the interest:

No, really, she thought; neither men nor women. It is a not caring for sexual relations. It is not merely a lack of pleasure in sex, it is dislike of the excitement. And it is not merely dislike, it is worse, it is boredom.

She felt a lonely emotion near to guilt.

At the end of the story, Sybil asks herself the question, "Am I a woman . . . or an intellectual monster? She was so accustomed to this question within herself that it needed no answer." This dissatisfaction which Sybil feels with herself makes no difference to her attitude of superiority towards others. She is not led to question her feelings for other people in the light of what she has learned about herself.

Sybil is presented as "quite famous," a source of interest to her friends ("Charming friends need not possess minds" is Sybil's assessment of them). She wonders why her husband did not explore her personality; but her only exploration of that of others is her search for a phrase with which to dismiss them. Just as she is lacking in feelings of sex, so she is lacking in feelings of friendship. Sybil's superiority is a mark of her self-isolation, her failure to relate to the world of others.

Like most of Muriel Spark's heroines, Sybil is an image of self-love. Because the two chief characters, Barry and Désirée, are satirically intended, and because they justify the satire spent upon them, it is easy for the reader to construe Sybil's contempt as an appropriate moral censure. It is when we see this attitude of disdain visited upon the minor figures of the story (the "charming friends" who "need not have minds") that we understand it is not an evaluative agent of moral judgment but the work of a superiority complex.

Sometimes, the operations of this superiority are hidden under the appearance of religious dictation. The heroine Needle in **"The Portobello Road"** acts apparently from religious motives. Her old associate George is going to marry her friend Kathleen, but Needle knew that George has been married in Africa to a black woman, now separated from him. George tells Needle that Kathleen is to marry him, and begs her to say nothing of his previous marriage. Needle says his action would be bigamy; she is duty bound to tell Kathleen. Whereupon George murders her. Afterwards, Needle supplements her Christian act of charity by coming back as a ghost to haunt him.

On the surface, it may appear that Needle's obligation to her religion made it incumbent on her to threaten a friend through his confession. From the context of the story, however, we see that Needle's feelings for George have always been hostile and disdainful. The religio-moral justification for her betrayal comes in most opportunely. Needle's 'treachery' is therefore a means of putting down George and asserting her own superiority.

And when we examine her other relationships, we find that Needle is another Sybil. Both end without husbands, and lovers belong to a discarded past. Friends admire her and cherish her company, which sentiments she repays by various gestures of rejection. And that which Needle abominates in George is his need of others, of friends, of 'togetherness.' Needle has little need of others, and resents those who voice the need themselves, since they make a call upon her which she is not prepared to answer.

Needle recalls how, at the Catholic Service of Confirmation, "The Bishop touches the candidate on the cheek, a symbolic reminder of the suffering a Christian is supposed to undertake." But any sufferings in the line of enduring one's neighbour, which might result from shouldering the burden of Christian charity, is unacceptable to Needle. Her preference is for martyrdom on ethical-doctrinal lines.

Needle and Sybil illustrate the way in which Muriel Spark's tastes and values differ from the reader's. The general assumption in fiction is that it is the heroine or hero who evokes our sympathetic feelings. It is Sybil and Needle, then, who should elicit our feelings of pity, approval and concern. But this is not what happens, according to many readers I have questioned. Needle and Sybil excite resistance, just as others excite resistance in them. Encased in the self-love of their own rightness or superiority, they do not attract us to identify ourselves with them or their self-willed fates. George is undoubtedly a weak fellow; a bigamist, too, in terms of the letters. Yet many will consider him a sight more human than the immaculate murdered Needle. Like Sybil, Needle symbolises the fine drilling-point of truth, and truth, of course, has to be paid for. When, therefore, George proceeds to stuff Needle's mouth with hay until she ceases to draw her righteous breath, certain readers—while willing to allow her martyrdom—feel no emotional resistance to George.

In Muriel Spark's more interesting shorter fiction, there appears a war between Philistines and Pharisees of the spirit. The Georges of this world, *hommes moyens sensuels,* represent the Philistines: the Needles and Sybils, the Pharisees. Middling and muddling men and women find themselves rebuked and called to judgment by these prim and fearful blue-stocking oracles. And there is something offensive to our common humanity in this judgment. Sybil and Needle, it would seem, have felt the call of sanctification. They have answered the call with determination—but without charity, humility or love. Saints they are not. Martyrs they are. Martyrs to the truth—and to their own self-love.

Needle is a religious prig with a diamond-edge of wit to her nature. Sybil is an artistic prig who sees others in terms of clichés. It is Muriel Spark's distinction to have created a prig among the celestial orders also. The angelic being in **"The Seraph and the Zambesi"** is a purist as to words and their usage. The literal preciseness of this holy monster's mind wrecks a nativity show and leads to the 'theatre' being burned down.

Of course, we agree with the Seraph that the Nativity masque put on by Cramer and the Fanfarlo is full of blasphemous implications, but of these the promoters are ignorant; and whether what the theologians call "invincible ignorance" should be punished has long been a fine consideration. The nativity masque represents the commercialisation of the spirit of Christmas—of all which the modern world understands by that term. In addition, the masque is not being performed to the greater glory of God, but to the greater profit and aggrandisement of Cramer and the Fanfarlo. Doubtless, Cramer needs to be corrected, but the shining righteous glow of the seraphic instructor does not give the happiest impression. The original angels of the Christmas story came to tell the shepherds not to be afraid, to speak of "Peace on earth and goodwill toward men." This seraph pays its visit to argue with Cramer pedantically:

> "—this is my show," continued Cramer.
>
> "Since when?" the Seraph said.
>
> "Right from the start," Cramer breathed at him.
>
> "Well, it's been mine from the Beginning," said the Seraph, "and the Beginning began first."

We get the point, but feel the Christian Faith could have been demonstrated more winningly.

"The Seraph and the Zambesi," "The Portobello Road," and **"Bang-bang You're dead"** are brilliant constructions; but the *rapport* which they establish with the reader is of an aesthetic and intellectual order. The sudden *frisson* of identification between character and reader does not take place. The fates of the heroines Needle and Sybil are too remote, too unrepresentative to engender much concern. And as far as **"The Seraph and the Zambesi"** goes, my feelings tend to be with Cramer against the wise-cracking 'abnormality' [Cramer's word for the Seraph] with wings. The miraculous can present itself as the friend or enemy of man. In Muriel Spark's writing it appears as the latter. [The critic adds in a footnote: The Black Madonna's 'miracle' (in the story of that name) is no unambiguous blessing.]

The one great exception to unattractive heroine creation occurs in the *novella* **"The Go-Away Bird,"** which I, personally, find her most sympathetic work. This long short-story I would rank with such masterpieces in the genre as Katherine Anne Porter's *Pale Horse, Pale Rider* and Lionel Trilling's *Of one time and place,* its length being adequate to the tragic content which is beautifully unfolded.

Both **"The Portobello Road"** and **"Bang-bang You're dead"** possess a tragic content which is never allowed to become explicit. The 'pity and the terror' remain latent, and the constant working of irony and satire prevent them from becoming manifest. (The characters in a tragic story must have a certain magnitude of spirit: in these two tales they lack this stature, since the operations of satire upon them prevent them from attaining tragic status.)

In **"The Go-away Bird,"** others besides the heroine Daphne are granted a liberal human status. Chakata (Daphne's Uncle), Old Tuys (her murderer) and Ralph Mercer (her lover) are all individuals in their own rights, not Aunt Sallies for the author's raking satire. Not that the comedy of manners is absent. The central drama and the major characters are tragically conceived; the minor plots and characters are satirically presented. A mordant economy of comment exists side by side with a music of fatality—a resonant quality which haunts the story like the repeated cry of the Go-away bird.

Daphne, like Sybil and Needle, is a subtle detector of the truth. Unlike them, it is not superiority of mind which makes her sensitive to its presence, but a radical innocence of nature which develops, by contrast, a nose for corruption. This innocence is far removed from ignorance or ingenuousness; and it is in no way complicated, or distorted, by notions of ethical or religious truth. Not that one can readily term Daphne a pagan, since that word carries today implications of the exotic and primitive.

Daphne is of her own time and place. From the oven of Africa, she dreams her dream of a rustic quasi-Edwardian England which experience teaches her to correct. Daphne differs from all Muriel Spark's heroines in that she desires to be taught, while the others have their tastes and criteria already established. Uncontaminated by abstract assumptions, she represents the pure soul confronting existence. That this confrontation implies a progressive disillusionment is the essence of this tragedy which is given formal finish by her death. We feel the tale is a paradigm of life.

Many of Muriel Spark's stories constitute a keen comedy of manners. The satire and observation in these pieces has no fixed social bias, but is dealt out freely to "U" and "non-U". **"The Black Madonna"** and **"You should have seen the mess"** are witty analyses of working-class behaviour-patterns in our affluent society. **"Daisy Overend"** is rife with middle-aged ex-debutante mannerisms. **"Come along, Marjorie,"** makes its amused comments on the lunatic fringe of Catholicism. **"The Pawnbroker's Wife"** is an exploration of *illusions de grandeur* in a woman with money but no education.

Other tales such as **"Miss Pinkerton's Apocalypse"** and **"A Sad Tale's Best for Winter"** defy too neat a categorisation. The flying-saucer which Miss Pinkerton sees is literally a saucer: "Spode" declares Miss Pinkerton. Selwyn Macgregor, in **"A Sad Tale's Best for Winter,"** lives by a churchyard and literally engages in "the contemplation of corruption."

"There is no health for me outside of honesty" Sybil ruefully persuaded herself in **"Bang-bang You're dead,"** and the simple sentence could be taken as expressing the author's general intention. Honesty, here, implies criticism; a criticism usually destructive and aggressive. The best of these stories come to us with the imprimatur of the Church—the one-woman Church Militant of Muriel Spark. (pp. 107-20)

> *Derek Stanford, in his* Muriel Spark: A Biographical and Critical Study, *Centaur Press Ltd., 1963, 184 p.*

Auberon Waugh (essay date 1967)

[*In the following excerpt, Waugh praises "The Black Madonna" and "The Curtain Blown by the Breeze" but generally finds Spark's short fiction inferior to her other literary achievements.*]

Collected Stories includes all the old favourites from **Voices at Play** and **The Go-Away Bird** with a few additions, 'The Black Madonna,' which tells of a liberal, Catholic couple who unaccountably give birth to a black baby, still remains, for the reviewer, the most enjoyable short story he has read in the English language. Another—**'The Curtain Blown by the Breeze'**—about an African small-town white community, has the most ingeniously described plot. But it is in another story, much less good than either of these, that I fancy Mrs Spark reveals the way in which she will preserve her sanity and her artistic integrity in the seductive role of a New York literary lioness.

In fact, **'The Seraph and the Zambesi'** appeared some time before her American life began. Those who read it then were puzzled, and 'puzzling' still seems the kindest adjective which is appropriate. It concerns Samuel Cramer, an unknown Romantic writer of the early nineteenth century whom Mrs Spark has chosen to reanimate and place in a Central African settlement in 1946. He runs a boarding house near the Victoria Falls; plans a Nativity play which is visited by a seraph from Heaven over whom they pour petrol which starts a fire. After a few extraordinarily pedestrian remarks, the seraph flies off and that is the end of the story. What are we to make of it?

The answer I would like to suggest is 'nothing.' Mrs Spark is not one to be frightened of the fantastic, but this is no more than an exercise in whimsy. I may be being uncommonly insensitive, but the story appeared to me to represent no more than a writer who had begun to taste the wine of critical acclaim and who had decided to push her luck. 'Don't ask a woman to read her reviews *and* write,' seemed to be the moral.

Until, that is, one has examined some of her later pieces. The only unpublished story included here—**'The Playhouse Called Remarkable'**—seems, at first glance, like **'The Seraph and the Zambesi,'** to be rubbish. A second reading tends to confirm this. In so far as it signifies anything, it is a pedantic, long-winded joke about the sources of artistic inspiration perhaps suggesting, in a somewhat whimsical fashion, that Art is the only remaining avenue of approach to God in this secular age. But is it not impossible, by any standards of logical or artistic consistency, to suspect that the author of *Memento Mori* could be guilty of such a banal, didactic intention? Who is she mocking? Obviously her reviewers. Equally certainly, the literary intelligentsia of London and New York. But I rather fancy that her mockery is aimed—far more than at the prevailing literary climate—at herself: at the whole idea that her superior imagination, powers of perception, ability to communicate—any of the qualities which might be supposed to comprise her creative vocation—are of the slightest importance. It is an awareness which must come to any Christian artist who is not, by nature, cast in the role of preacher. Non-Christian artists can make a religion of their talents, just as non-Christian critics worship at the shrine of Art, but for the Christian it is easier to see the falseness of this attitude than it is to decide the extent to which possession of these highly secular talents involves a responsibility to their source.

> *Auberon Waugh, "The Lost Leader," in* The Spectator, *Vol. 219, No. 7278, December 22, 1967, p. 783.*

Shirley Hazzard   (essay date 1968)

[*Hazzard is an Australian novelist, short story writer, and essayist who has spent most of her adult life in the United States and in Italy. In the following excerpt, she praises Spark's short stories and notes their importance in her development as a writer.*]

There are aspects of the obvious that can only be revealed to us by genius. It might, for instance, be said of Franz Kafka that he has enabled even those who have never read a line of his works to say of certain situations, "This is Kafkaesque," and to know what was implied. Something of such a singular view, that speaks a truth recognizable even to those who do not explore its origins, may be said to emanate from the works of Muriel Spark.

At this moment when, in all the arts, novelty is frequently confused with quality, Mrs. Spark's writings demonstrate how secondary—in fact, how incidental—are innovations of style and form to the work of the truly gifted: such innovation is a natural by-product of their originality rather than its main object. When the word "humorous" has little currency in literature or in life, her wit is employed to produce effects and insights only matched in contemporary fiction, in this reviewer's opinion, by the glittering jests of Vladimir Nabokov. At a time when our "tolerance" tends to take the form of general agreement that we are all capable of the worst crimes had we but the conditions for committing them, Mrs. Spark interests herself instead in our capacities for choice and in the use we make of them; and in those forces of good and evil that she picks out unerringly, often gleefully, beneath their worldly camouflage.

In all Muriel Spark's work there is a sense of high spirits and of, to use one of her own similes, "a mind like a blade." She does not posture instructively, nor does she shade her work to appease reviewers and gladden the hearts of publishing companies: she writes to entertain, in the highest sense of that word—to allow us the exercise of our intellect and imagination, to extend our self-curiosity and enrich our view.

Such are the pleasures to be derived from the first volume of a projected series of Mrs. Spark's collected stories [*Collected Stories I*] and from her new, short novel [*The Public Image*]. Short-story collections are often criticized as being "uneven"—presumably by those who prize uniformity in art—and it is not likely that these stories, some of them written years apart, should be of identical weight and tone. Mrs. Spark is a writer who has continually sought to develop and enlarge her art and, where necessary, to convulse it. It is precisely this "unevenness," this diversity and range of the stories, that makes the volume extraordinary, for the author is prepared to observe us under any circumstances and to recount her impressions in the form she finds appropriate.

The stories take place in Africa, in Hampstead, on the moon. Some of them hinge on a single crucial incident, others recount a multiplicity of events inexorably brought to their common fulfillment. Several contain a difficult element of the supernatural; others, like the delightful **"Alice Long's Dachshunds"** and **"Daisy Overend,"** go to the very roots of our nature. These stories—which, with their trains of thought that have been pursued in her novels, can now be viewed within the body of the writer's work—seem at times varied enough to have been written by different authors: yet each is totally, movingly recognizable as hers.

Palinurus in "The Unquiet Grave," speaks of "the art which is distilled and crystallized out of a lucid, curious and passionate imagination." It is this passionate curiosity that extends the art of Mrs. Spark beyond that detachment which can so readily become its own victim. The uniqueness and secrecy of each soul is fascinating to her: "I found that Jennifer's neurosis took the form of 'same as.' We are all the same, she would assert, infuriating me because I knew that God had made everyone unique." She will not let us vitiate our perceptions with sentiment, or allow us the doubtful refuge of clinical abstractions. If we are to encounter the blessed in disguise, we must also recognize those in love with their own good will or with the virtuous sense of their own guilt, those who would have us conform to their own concept of sensibility.

In one of the strongest stories in this collection, **"Bang-bang You're Dead,"** a woman finds herself complimenting a poet on verses she privately considers third-rate. "She did not know then," the author tells us, "that the price of allowing false opinions was the gradual loss of one's capacity for forming true ones." In the same story we are told, "There is no health, she thought, for me, outside of honesty." Mrs. Spark's literary strivings after this form of health can make the efforts of other authors seem as banal as a get-well card. No modern writer has given greater attention to our revelatory turns of phrase, or more richly conjured up the inflections of meaning in our language.

By the same token, her artistry in these stories is scrupulously disciplined. She does not indulge herself in enumerating sensations or cataloguing objects merely because she is aware of them: everything must bear on what she has to tell us. Nor does she seek, as narrator, to establish her own virtue as contrasted with the fallibility of those she writes about. There is no attempt, for example, in the fine first story in the collection, **"The Portobello Road,"** to palliate the stern decision that leads to the narrator's death: if we assume the writer to be human, we must allow her characteristics that will not always please us. In much of the book there is a complex sense of ultimate order which it may not be entirely fanciful to link to an Edinburgh upbringing.

One reads these brilliant stories with conscious pleasure in the author's fresh, independent gift and in the vitality of her intelligence. And with a sharing of her own delight. (pp. 1, 62)

Shirley Hazzard, " 'A Mind Like a Blade'," in The New York Times Book Review, *September 29, 1968, pp. 1, 62.*

Tom Hubbard   (essay date 1984)

[*In the following essay, Hubbard provides an overview of Spark's short fiction.*]

We profess to admire Muriel Spark; we vigorously defend

her from the charge of elegant trifling; we tend to falter, though, when we try to account for her steady output of short stories. Mrs. Spark is not of course unique in having such work played down or even ignored; we have not yet learned to accord the short story equal status with the novel. We still assume that only big is beautiful, or at least important, and are apparently content to regard these pieces as mere *jeux d'esprit,* tossed off in a twinkling for the *New Yorker* or *Winter's Tales.*

Even so, there is something odd about this neglect. If I may resort to parodied cliché—a manner relished by the authoress herself—Muriel Spark and the short story were meant for one another. She has produced many novels but only one of them, *The Mandelbaum Gate,* can be described as 'full-length'. That book is not one of her favourites and she has stated that she will never again write a long one. Like Sandy Stranger, Mrs. Spark prefers to act on the principle of economy; she is reluctant to fill 'a little glass with a pint of beer'. She's a distiller rather than a brewer; the little glass contains a fine malt. She has sound Scottish antecedents: [Robert Louis] Stevenson, one of her early loves, both preached and practised concision; going further back, there are the border ballads which Mrs. Spark admires for the 'sequence of events stated in such a way that they have the power to suggest what is left unsaid'. As a poet, long before she turned to fiction, she was well trained in compression; the next step, logically enough, was the short story, a half-way house between the poem and the novel. It is not surprising to find that many of her stories, for example **'The Ormolu Clock',** rely less on a resolvable plot than on the evocation of an atmosphere; they are poems in prose. On the other hand, she can handle a clear plot mechanism with considerable narrative skill; during her period of transition from poetry to fiction she wrote a study of the then Poet Laureate, John Masefield, and concentrated on his flair for telling a good story.

The short story is appropriate to her unremitting irony. There are two reasons for this. First, irony is most effective when it uses economical means; it must cut quickly and cleanly. Its temper is utterly opposed to the rhetorical and the overblown; indeed these tend to be its targets. Second, irony and the short story derive power from the setting of a situation and its consequent reversal. Muriel Spark thrives on such contradiction.

> I approve of the ceremonious accumulation of weather forecasts and barometer-readings that pronounce for a fine day, before letting rip on the statement: 'Nevertheless, it's raining.' . . . To have a great primitive crag [Edinburgh Castle Rock] rising up in the middle of populated streets of commerce, stately squares and winding closes, is like the statement of an unmitigated fact preceded by 'nevertheless'.

The 'nevertheless' principle had intrigued Scottish writers long before its particular expression by Muriel Spark. Burns mused on the best-laid schemes which 'gang aft agley'. In his analysis of irony [in *The Man Forbid, and Other Essays,* 1910], John Davidson wrote: 'By it our enterprises are whirled away from our most resolved intentions.' Perhaps the most familiar example in Mrs. Spark's

longer fiction is the frustration of Jean Brodie's schemes by her most trusted disciple. More readily than the shortest novel, however, the short story can be perceived as a totality. It can achieve a more concentrated power; expectations and illusions can be steadily but not too elaborately built up, and the effect of collapse, when it comes, is accordingly maximized. Raymond and Lou Parker in **'The Black Madonna'** pride themselves on a liberal, enlightened outlook which supposedly marks them off from their neighbours; *nevertheless,* when events take an unforeseen turn, they display their latent prejudices more dramatically than most. In **'The Fathers' Daughters',** Henry Castlemaine is a literary has-been; like his books, his devoted middle-aged daughter, Dora, is stuck on the shelf. The ambitious young critic Ben Donadieu is initially more interested in working on Kenneth Hope, a novelist who is as in fashion as Castlemaine is out of it. Hope's daughter, the 20-year-old Carmelita, is in her own way working on Ben. *Nevertheless,* at the end of the tale Ben undertakes to lead a Castlemaine revival and conveniently takes Dora on board as well.

In her short stories Muriel Spark can most trenchantly exploit her talent for surreal juxtaposition, which, far from being clever-clever gimmickry, is an essential part of her ironic method, her preoccupation with the 'nevertheless'. In **'The Curtain Blown by the Breeze',** the boerish Sonia Van der Merwe, encouraged to get-sophisticated-quick, surpasses the expectations of her female admirers who have only wanted a bit of bitchy fun at her expense. Her household in the middle of the African wilds is incongruously transformed into an island of pseudo-European vogue: 'It was less than a year before she got round to adding the Beardsley reproductions.' The juxtaposition is not in fact as bizarre as it seems; only a thin curtain separates the primitive from 'civilisation'; it can be blown at any time. Daphne du Toit in **'The Go-Away Bird'** duly departs for England and is initially taken by its twee charm; before long she learns that, no less than the veldt, it has its predators, and she herself is being stalked.

Mrs. Spark once remarked [in her study *John Masefield,* 1953] 'how sharp and lucid fantasy can be when it is deliberately intagliated on the surface of realism.' This applies to many of her short stories. She is perhaps at her most surreal when, by resorting without warning to the supernatural and the extra-terrestrial, she upsets the complacencies of the everyday. Samuel Cramer, the over-ripe romantic protagonist of a Baudelaire short story, is resurrected, in **'The Seraph and the Zambesi',** as a white settler going to seed in Rhodesia. Grotesque as this seems, it is all made plain in a matter-of-fact manner and, with convincing naturalism, Mrs. Spark builds up an atmosphere of tawdry and pretentious banality. Cramer is still pathetically and absurdly devoted to self-aggrandizement; having written a Nativity Masque, he prepares to mount it on a makeshift stage. Assuming that he has a right to exploit the celestial in the cause of the egotistical, he takes the part of the First Seraph; the performance has hardly begun when he is suddenly confronted by the real thing. Cramer protests that this is his show.

'Since when?' the Seraph said.

'Right from the start,' Cramer breathed at him.

'Well, it's been mine from the Beginning,' said the Seraph, 'and the Beginning began first.'

The Moon people, in **'The Playhouse Called Remarkable'**, are more benevolently inclined to the earthlings, who in turn give them rougher treatment than Cramer is able to inflict on the Seraph. Thematically related to *The Ballad of Peckham Rye*, the story tells of events just after Noah's Flood, when the Six Brothers of the Moon attempt to bring vision to the people of Hampstead. After initial successes they are eventually routed by the forces of populist philistinism—the 'tum tum ya movement'—as led by Johnnie Heath, assistant editor of the local rag and later Mayor. However, the Moon people's influence persists in the long run, as they have introduced literature, art and music to the world. A more recent story, **'The Executor'** concerns a Scotswoman on the make. Susan Kyle is a brisk Edinburgh bourgeoise who has always frowned on the irregular life-style of her uncle, a writer. She takes up her responsibilities for his literary remains—'archive as they called it'—with an enthusiasm that is something other than disinterestedly literary. During his lifetime she has already inventoried and sorted his papers, pleased with herself for having imposed order on his chaos.

> You didn't catch me filing away a letter from Angus Wilson or Saul Bellow in the same place as an ordinary "W" or "B", a Miss Mary Whitelaw or a Mrs. Jonathan Brown. I knew the value of these letters, they went into a famous-persons file, bulging, and of value.

The uncle dies and the archive is sold to a Foundation, but Susan keeps back the manuscript of ten chapters of an unfinished novel; she resolves to complete and publish it. Whenever she takes it up, however, and turns to the page headed 'Chapter Eleven', she finds it freshly inscribed in her uncle's hand. By this means the late writer tells her that he knows what she's up to. Terrified, she asks God to make her as 'strong and sensible' in a crisis as her heroine Margaret Thatcher. But the uncle persists in his supernatural needling; the Foundation rings up and queries Susan about the novel, to which many of the letters have referred. (In her efficient, philistine way, she had merely *filed* the letters; unconcerned with their content, she had not bothered to read them.) Susan's game is up and before she parts with the novel she notices her uncle's last inscription, a particularly cutting farewell.

'There are trap-doors and spring-guns in these two volumes, there are gins and pitfalls; and the precipitate reader may stumble unawares upon some nightmare not easily to be forgotten.' Stevenson's comment on Poe is equally applicable to Mrs. Spark. But the supernatural is not essential for her to create an atmosphere of menace. Her characters (and her readers) may be unnerved by some eccentric or misfit who turns out to be rather more sinister than quaint. Examples are Selwyn Macgregor, in ' **"A Sad Tale's Best for Winter"** ', and Hamilton in **'Alice Long's Dachshunds'**. **'The Ormolu Clock'** may well be Mrs. Spark's most disturbing short story, and not just because of Herr Stroh, a despised outcast. It describes the confident ascendancy of a hotelier, Frau Lublonitsch, and the accompanying decline of her business rival, the feckless Stroh. The narrator (who is not necessarily Mrs. Spark's mouthpiece) offers a sympathetic evocation of Frau Lublonitsch and her achievements. True, she works her girls fourteen hours a day, but they do the work 'cheerfully', and she mucks in more than anyone else. However, a note of unease is sounded at an early stage.

> Just as she turned to attack the day's work, I saw that she glanced at the sorry Hotel Stroh across the path. I saw her mouth turn down at the corners with the amusement of one who has a certain foreknowledge; I saw a landowner's recognition in her little black eyes.

It's all too smug and assured for our comfort. The tension rises, but doesn't snap, when Stroh's menacing quality becomes clear. The Lublonitsch and Stroh establishments face each other; the path which separates them leads to the Austro—Yugoslav border. Mrs. Spark, however, is not concerned with any iron curtain in the usual sense; in this story the frontier tension is between the domains of the two hoteliers. From his window Stroh stares into the narrator's room; he uses field-glasses—as much the equipment of the border guard as of the peeping Tom. The narrator trusts that Frau Lublonitsch or one of her sons will go across 'to deliver a protest'; the violation is territorial as much as personal and calls for a response at the highest diplomatic level.

There is no need for anything so explicit. In Frau Lublonitsch's opulent room there is a magnificently wrought clock, formerly in the possession of Stroh's grandfather 'when things were different' and which Stroh was forced to sell to her. She perches this clock on a ledge of her roof, and Stroh is accordingly warned. Time is running out for him, and this is an effective if cold and merciless way of reminding him. Offended as she has been by Stroh, the narrator does not join in the townspeople's gossiping at his expense; she wonders if he can live another winter. As for Frau Lublonitsch, the consensus view of her seems too cosy; the adoring community does not realize that she may be a more subtle menace than Stroh.

> She would take the Hotel Stroh. She would march on the bridge, and beyond it. The café would be hers, the swimming pool, the cinema. All the market place would be hers before she died in the scarlet bed under the gold-fringed canopy, facing her ormolu clock, her deed-boxes, and her ineffectual bottle of medicine.

Stroh loses his remaining guests and the story concludes thus:

> Everyone likes to be on the winning side. I saw the two new arrivals from the Hotel Stroh sitting secure under the Lublonitsch chestnut tree, taking breakfast, next morning. Herr Stroh, more sober than before, stood watching the scene from his doorway. I thought, why doesn't he spit on us, he's got nothing to lose? I saw again, in my mind's eye the ormolu clock set high in the sunset splendour. But I had not yet got over my fury with him for spying into my room, and was moved, all in one stroke, with high contempt and deep pity, feverish triumph and chilly fear.

This unresolved, ambiguous air prompts us to wonder where the real threat comes from—from an *individual,* Lublonitsch or Stroh—or from the *situation,* an international incident in microcosm.

Incidentally, **'The Ormolu Clock'** is evidence that the 'nevertheless' principle need not rely on an unexpected, sudden reversal. The unsettling effect is developed steadily throughout the piece; the appearance of the ormolu clock on the roof, and Stroh's reaction to it, may be considered a climax, but we have been prepared for it. Towards the end of **'The Pawnbroker's Wife'** Mrs. Jan Cloote spins her fantasy about a compass having been presented by a film star to her daughter. The narrator then reveals (to the reader, but not to Mrs. Cloote) that the compass had actually belonged to herself, and that she had been given it when she was 14. The attentive reader will recall that, earlier in the tale, the narrator had casually mentioned a compass which she had pawned and had never seen again. Such a reader enjoys the neatness with which the tale is constructed, but he will not be startled or shocked. This does not prevent the application of the 'nevertheless' principle to Mrs. Cloote, although she herself remains complacently ignorant of it.

Using various means, including the supernatural, the symbolic, and the subtle, Muriel Spark transfigures the commonplace and jolts us into seeing it in a new light. In this respect the 'nevertheless' can be related to Brecht's *Verfremdungseffekte,* usually translated as the 'estrangement' or (less satisfactorily) 'alienation' effect:

> If empathy makes something ordinary of a special event, alienation makes something special of an ordinary one. The most hackneyed everyday incidents are stripped of their monotony when represented as quite special. [Bertolt Brecht in *The Messingkauf Dialogues,* 1965]

Let us take a reader who unquestioningly accepts a stereotype of 'rebellious' working class and 'conservative' middle class. Much of what happens in actual experience will not register with this reader, either because it does not correspond to his preconceptions or is so familiar that he simply doesn't notice it. In the story **'You Should Have Seen the Mess'** the narrator, a young working-class girl, obsessed with respectability and cleanliness, is shocked by the free-and-easy behaviour of the middle-class people with whom she comes into contact. From her naïve point of view, such behaviour is worthy of notice. Perhaps our hypothetical reader would pass it by in real life; presented in this fictional form, and through eyes to which the familiar is unfamiliar, the phenomenon is brought to his attention. Our reader is admittedly an extreme case, himself a crude stereotype, but I think we can take the point that in this story Mrs. Spark is challenging certain expectations, and her 'nevertheless' principle is once again eloquently sustained.

Not the least of the reasons for this is that, like Brecht, Mrs. Spark eschews empathy; we do not 'identify' with the narrator of **'You Should Have Seen the Mess',** nor with anyone else in the story. If the girl sheds light on other people's lifestyles, they in turn shed light on her own lifestyle, and it too is rescued from being taken for granted.

Here is her response to Willy Morley, a well-off artist and bohemian, and his response to her.

> I could not deny that I liked Willy, in a way. There was something about him, I will say that. Mavis said, 'I hope he hasn't been making a pass at you, Lorna.' I said he had not done so, which was almost true, because he did not attempt to go to the full extent. It was always unhygienic when I went to Willy's place, and I told him so once, but he said, 'Lorna, you are a joy.'

We are made aware of implications missed by the girl, although ironically we receive the information only by means of her own reportage. Unable to accept a single point of view at its face value, we are freed from the limitations of the partial; we can respond to the situation in its totality and thus be capable of cool, objective criticism.

In consequence we can acquire an 'overview'. For both the Christian Spark and the Marxist Brecht, the 'overview' would seem to be the necessary alternative to a narrow, egoistic perspective. It can of course be argued that Christianity and Marxism are themselves subject to fallibility. Neither writer is a church- or party-hack, and one might prefer to relate Mrs. Spark's 'nevertheless' and Brecht's 'estrangement' to the practice of any artist of integrity and vision; he or she upsets existing relationships in order to create new ones, and reality can therefore be apprehended in ways previously unknown.

[Spark] is perhaps at her most surreal when, by resorting without warning to the supernatural and the extra-terrestrial, she upsets the complacencies of the everyday.

—Tom Hubbard

Even so, the faiths of Mrs. Spark and Brecht enable them to extract a phenomenon from its immediate context and to measure it against eternity or history. Both writers refuse to be satisfied by any notion that time can only be experienced while it is passing, that it is merely linear, one-dimensional.

It was her reading of Proust which revealed to Mrs. Spark just how the 'commonplace' could be 'estranged' from its normal setting and thus 'transfigured' into something 'special'. The Christian sacraments are based on 'the idea that the visible world is an active economy of outward signs embodying each an inward grace'. There is nothing new about that, writes Mrs. Spark [in her 1953 essay in the *Church of England Newspaper*], but the implications have been overlooked. With a mistaken dualism Christians have been too ready to see matter and spirit in conflict, assuming that spirit 'triumphs by virtue of disembodiment'. It is necessary to correct this by accepting 'that deep irony in which we are presented with the most unlikely people, places and things as repositories of invisible grace'; in other words, such people, places and things may appear trivial or irrelevant, 'nevertheless' they can lead us to spirituality. The taste of madeleine cake and tea may seem commonplace and therefore unworthy of mention, but for Proust's Marcel it always evokes his past 'in a special and meaningful way'; during his childhood, on Sunday mornings, his aunt would give him such refreshments, and the sensation has proved unexpectedly powerful, even 'sacramental'.

A mere tea-soaked crumb, then, can disrupt chronology and reveal eternity. Mrs. Spark quotes Proust's explanation:

> Let a sound, a scent already heard and breathed in the past be heard and breathed anew, simultaneously in the present and the past, real without being actual, ideal without being abstract, then instantly the permanent and characteristic essence hidden in things is freed and our true being which has for so long seemed dead but was not so in other ways awakens and revives, thanks to this celestial nourishment. An instant liberated from the order of time has recreated in us man liberated from the same order, so that he should be conscious of it.

In her own art Mrs. Spark makes use of the 'active economy of outward signs', transfiguring them in her own actively economical way. Each of her short stories is itself a liberated instant—an encapsulation of what is significant and authentic, rescued from the prevailing obscurity and mystification.

A wild bird whose call is 'go'way, go'way', a curtain blown by a breeze or a storm—such an 'outward sign' or symbol affords not only a neat title, but gives a short story a taut unity more subtle than can be achieved by the most ingeniously structured plot. As with Proust, however, these motifs are invaluable for reasons of content as much as those of form. The go-away bird is Daphne's link with the eternal; its cry unites her present and her past and transcends them. Try as she will to find some niche in this world, her exile is a calling, and it is the bird which calls. She leaves South Africa, but cannot leave the bird behind; in England he is grotesquely echoed and parodied by the budgerigar which is the unwelcome 'gift' to Daphne from her devious landlady. If the go-away bird gives Daphne an awareness that 'The fundamental things apply / As time goes by', the full significance of its cry is lost on such shallow, self-centred people as Ralph Mercer, popular novelist and Daphne's lover, who finds her a useful source of material then drops her. When she tells him about the bird, he is not interested; visiting South Africa after her death, he hears it first behind her grave, then more frequently in other places. It gives him the creeps and he scuttles back to England. Daphne—who is one of Mrs. Spark's few 'sympathetic' characters—has tended to *listen* to the bird; everyone else has explained her interest in terms of ornithology rather than eternity. We are told at the beginning of the story that 'It was possible to hear the bird, but very few did, for it was part of the background to everything.' Daphne is one of the very few, and can extract the essential from the clamour of the actual and the temporal.

An eternal—or, alternatively, historical—dimension is of particular advantage to the short story; it is enriched by the dialectical tension between such boundlessness and its own formal brevity. Mrs. Spark uses history to this effect in the autobiographical piece **'The First Year of My Life'**. Political and military events of the last year of World War I are juxtaposed with the simultaneous growth of an individual baby. The consequences are ironical as well as multidimensional; the infant's antics deflate the pomposities and pretensions of the public figures of the time. The curious result is that although the historical details provide such a broad sweep, they are also, paradoxically, belittled. The child may be tiny in comparison with 1918; may not 1918 appear even tinier in a larger scheme of things?

In the Proustian tradition, Mrs. Spark makes much of timeshifts and flashbacks. Again, this helps to achieve amplitude of content despite economy of form; a whole lifetime can be conveyed within thirty-odd pages, as in **'Bang-bang You're Dead'**. In this story the flashbacks are related whenever Sybil shows her friends another film of her life in Southern Africa. This juxtaposition of past and present results in the ironic contrast of grotesquely differing points of view; Sybil's friends interpret what they see in a naïvely optimistic manner, charmed by the apparent glamour and exoticism of it all. For Sybil, however, the camera has captured only the superficial appearance of a reality which she actually experienced and which was extremely ugly.

Another timeshift device is the initial presentation of a sequence of events, say a conversation, and its repetition later on in a different context. This enables the same material to be viewed from different perspectives; the second appearance might be more illuminating than the first—even ironically so. The device is familiar to readers of *The Prime of Miss Jean Brodie*. In a short story any repetition might, on first thoughts, seem to jeopardize the ideal of economy, but this apparent contradiction did not mar the border ballads, as Mrs. Spark has pointed out [in *John Masefield*]. This position is vindicated in her own **'A Member of the Family'**. The story opens with a chunk of dialogue between Richard and Trudy, in which he invites her to meet his mother. We are plunged straight into the situation; no words are wasted on introducing the pair. Then we are whisked back in time; the tale unfolds, we learn more about the characters, and a portion of that conversation is eventually repeated in its proper chronological sequence. This time, because of what we now know, and because the conversation is fresh in our memory, the repeated passage has acquired a tension absent at the beginning of the tale. What *will* happen when she meets his mother?

Tense—and also terse. The effect has been achieved subtly and suggestively. It would have been impossible if the events had been spelled out according to the clock, which shows time passing at only a single pace in a single direction.

Muriel Spark is not an escapist. Her work cannot be dismissed on the grounds of irresponsible frivolity or pseudo-mysticism. She believes in a dimension beyond the human, yet that impels her not to deny human life but to criticize it. The 'nevertheless' principle is not to be confused with negativity, which is the easier option preferred by lesser writers.

'An instant liberated from the order of time has recreated in us man liberated from the same order, so that he should be conscious of it.' An apparent fragment, such as a short story, contains the possibility of wholeness. Liberated itself, it attempts to liberate us; like all art, it asserts our freedom to confront seeming chaos with a totally integrated consciousness and our consequent ability to detect and create order. As I have tried to show, because of its form the short story has a particular responsibility to extract the essential from the nonessential.

I have just used the words 'freedom' and 'responsibility'; Muriel Spark is very much concerned with their interdependence. Self-fulfilment is not to be confused with self-indulgence. Proust explored the decadence of the late nineteenth century; Mrs. Spark has explored the rather less charming decadence of the middle and late years of the present century. In **'The Portobello Road'** the murdered Needle makes her posthumous way

> among the solemn crowds with their aimless purposes, their eternal life not far away, who push past the counters and stalls, who handle, buy, steal, touch, desire and ogle the merchandise. I hear the tinkling tills, I hear the jangle of loose change and tongues and children wanting to hold and have.

Mrs. Spark posits the individualism of being and becoming against the egoism of holding and having. The latter prefers contentment to challenge; it is not genuinely individualistic because it is happy to take the line of least resistance and conform to the false values, the bad faith of a mindless collective. Like the narrator of **'Come Along, Marjorie'**, Mrs. Spark prefers 'different from' to 'same as'. 'Different from' is a particularly important instance of the 'nevertheless' principle. Sybil in **'Bang-bang You're Dead'** finds that 'different from' is not a comfortable position. She reads the *Journals* of Kierkegaard, the founder of existentialism. In her own life she faces the existential challenge of being a genuine individual and not compromising with the conventional lie: 'the price of allowing false opinions was the gradual loss of one's capacity for forming true ones.'

Kierkegaard conceived that his task was 'to create difficulties everywhere'. Muriel Spark does likewise. Her 'nevertheless' principle is a constant threat to complacency. She does not disturb for disturbance's sake; her faith implies a commitment to positive moral values. Even the most coolly critical of her fictional protagonists is herself subject to criticism, even self-criticism; Sybil, for example, cannot be taken as embodying an ideal standard of human behaviour, and she knows it.

That point merits explanation. **'Bang-bang You're Dead'** has a discernibly Scottish flavour in its treatment of 'doubles'. Sybil and Désirée are extreme opposites in personality and outlook, but they resemble one another physically; are they the split parts of a possible unity? Sybil may be a person of 'integrity', insofar as that word is related to 'honesty', but not in the sense of 'wholeness'. Certainly

Désirée lacks depth and disinterestedness, but there is a want of sexuality, and even humanity, about Sybil. She herself recognizes this, and is troubled by self-questioning: 'Am I a woman . . . or an intellectual monster?'

The freedom to achieve integrity—in both senses of honesty and wholeness—is a challenge to any writer. If such freedom can be successfully exercised in art, there is encouragement for its exercise in real life. The reader of a Spark short story may wish to judge for himself if it aspires to [Hugh] MacDiarmid's 'multeity in unity', the ability to be 'at once infinitely great and infinitely small'; he may consider how far, indeed, such a liberated instant can recreate liberated man himself. (pp. 167-80)

> *Tom Hubbard, "The Liberated Instant: Muriel Spark and the Short Story," in* Muriel Spark: An Odd Capacity for Vision, *edited by Alan Bold, Vision and Barnes & Noble, 1984, pp. 167-82.*

Michiko Kakutani   (essay date 1985)

[*In the following review of* The Stories of Muriel Spark, *Kakutani discusses what she considers Spark's "dark view of human nature."*]

"I treated the story," says the narrator of one of Muriel Spark's recent novels, "with a light and heartless hand, as is my way when I have to give a perfectly serious account of things." It is a perfect description, of course, of Mrs. Spark's own adamantine style, and nowhere is that style more in evidence than in [*The Stories of Muriel Spark*]. Indeed, these tales serve as a kind of magnifying glass, heightening the distinctive qualities of Mrs. Spark's work: her cool, precise prose; her tricky, tricked-up plots, and her wicked, peremptory sense of humor. The weaknesses of her fiction, too, are thrown into relief here—we notice, more acutely, the author's willful tendency to withhold information, her reliance on arbitrary, neatly symbolic endings, and her reluctance to involve us emotionally in the lives of her people.

A convert to Catholicism, Mrs. Spark has always displayed a sharp moral sense and a fierce Olympian detachment in her fiction; the reader often has the sense that she is standing far away, looking down on her characters' mortal follies from a great distance as she mischievously twitches the strings of their destinies and moves them about with the same aplomb with which they attempt to manipulate one another through blackmail, deception and betrayal. In such novels as *The Comforters, Memento Mori* and *The Prime of Miss Jean Brodie,* this narrative strategy has yielded some deliciously funny metaphysical humor as well as some very clever satire; and there are moments in these stories when those same qualities snap, instantly, into focus. Mrs. Spark's portraits of the English and Dutch in Africa capture, with Waugh-like acerbity, the pretensions and hypocrisies of the colonial third world; and her depiction of the psychological games that develop within closed communities of people—a colony of expatriates, a trio of former schoolmates, a group of tenants in a rooming house—possesses a similar venomous vigor.

Still, one often suspects that Mrs. Spark doesn't care a lot for her characters—or, rather, that she doesn't like them terribly much—and this chilliness is accentuated in her shorter fiction. With the exception of **"The Go-Away Bird"**—a longish story that beautifully delineates the inexorable patterns of fate in an African girl's young life—these stories have a spindly, bony quality; they fold up on themselves like collapsible chairs, without giving us any sense of their people's inner lives, their past histories or their hopes and motivations. Irony is all in these stories—both the payoff and the raison d'être. **"The Fathers' Daughters,"** for instance, is an altogether predictable tale about a literary fortune hunter who dumps the daughter of one famous man for the daughter of another. **"The First Year of My Life"** is a slight, silly piece predicated on the conceit that babies are born omniscient—infants, Mrs. Spark writes, "know everything that is going on everywhere in the world; they can tune in to any conversation they choose, switch on to any scene"—and lose this knowledge as they grow older. And **"The Black Madonna"** is little more than a fancy illustration of that old maxim, you'd better be careful about what you pray for, because you might get what you want.

In **"The Black Madonna,"** a statue of the Madonna carved out of dark wood appears to grant the wishes of devout parishioners; a similar sense of the otherworldly intrudes in many of these stories. Even when the context is not overtly religious, the implication remains that the supernatural exists, that commonplace lives are subject to mysteries that passeth man's understanding. A little flying saucer glides into a living room in **"Miss Pinkerton's Apocalypse,"** and the heroine dispassionately notes that the saucer is Spode, and that it is being piloted by a tiny man the size of her finger. A real angel with three pairs of wings and huge, luminous eyes pays a visit to a Christmas pageant in **"The Seraph and the Zambesi,"** disrupting the local festivities. And evil incongruously embodied in the persons of two small children makes an unexpected appearance in **"The Twins."** Ghosts, also, figure prominently in several of the tales: in **"The Executor,"** the restless spirit of a writer haunts his dishonest niece; in **"The Leaf-Sweeper,"** a madman—who wants to deny the spirit of Christmas—meets up with an apparition of his alter-ego; and in **"The Portobello Road,"** a murdered woman keeps tabs on the people responsible for her death.

As in Mrs. Spark's novels, nasty, violent doings proliferate freely in these stories: people either live separately, "frolicking happily but not together," or they collide precipitously with one another, getting tied up in complicated stratagems that come to bloody conclusions. A woman nicknamed Needle is choked to death in a haystack after she vows to reveal an old friend's secret. A farmer returns from jail to find his wife with another man, and kills them both. Another man—in what may be a case of mistaken identity—shoots his would-be lover and then himself. Such endings may well ratify Mrs. Spark's distinctly dark view of human nature—an apparent belief in original sin, combined with a conviction that people are better off living independent lives, free of messy entanglements—but the reader too often feels that the author, unlike God, has already stacked the cards against her creations.

Michiko Kakutani, in a review of "The Stories of Muriel Spark," in The New York Times, *September 18, 1985, p. C23.*

Sharon Thompson   (essay date 1985)

[*In the following essay, Thompson analyzes Spark's short fiction and discusses her reputation.*]

When the rattle-tail end of a writer's career meets its slender forked tongue, it's an uncommon publishing event, particularly if the writer is female. [***The Stories of Muriel Spark***] from Dutton, preceded by Perigee reprints of more than half her novels, signifies Spark's pre-mortem positioning in the canon of those who will outlast the second millennium. A writer's chance at canonization depends on the interested parties. I count Catholics, feminists, misogynists, postmodernists, Fowlerites, and those with a simple taste for a wicked tongue among Spark's supporting factions. This odd coalition wouldn't last an hour at a faculty meeting, but it makes her a serious candidate for the immortality of the anthologized and syllabused. She's not on the top of many lists, but she's not on anyone's hit list either.

I'm cynical about the politics though not about the work. Among the chroniclers of women after the Second World War, and before (or outside of) second-wave feminism, she is one of the most successful at making *fictions* from the raw material of working women's lives. There are better realists than Spark, of course (she's not a realist at all), working female ground, and writers who are more moving, or who are mining deeper veins that may yield more subversive work. But at cutting fictions and polishing them to a high gloss, Spark reigns supreme. Her success is often attributed to a combination of modern material with the forms of parable and allegory, but while her work gains concentration and power from its relation to parable—particularly if it travels parable's liminal passage between detail and moral—it loses seriousness when it departs entirely from realism and shifts into the cartoon-devil country of allegory. Her genius is rather for the metaphysical short novel, and it is in the canniness with which she contrives to work a metaphor, a conceit, into a narrative that she takes my breath away. Spark is the John Donne of English fiction, a few centuries behind her time, but nonetheless interesting for it. If only she had Donne's inclination toward love, I'd be wholly of her party. (Sex appears in her work in isolation, like a peculiarly disgusting behavior engaged in by villains and those tainted by the residue of original sin.)

Because she has appeared as the one woman in so many male-dominated literary contexts, it's easy to forget that Spark came by her primary material the hard way. Her knowledge of the exigencies, pleasures, and vanities of a cosmopolitan working woman is firsthand. A veteran of the ill-paid life of the undereducated hack woman writer, Spark is reported to have been literally starving when some friends staked her on the promise that she go into therapy. Always one for the unexpected turn of character, she converted to Catholicism and satiric narrative instead of to "normalcy" as a consequence of her analytic hours with a Jungian priest. She began to write, as she once put it, "the way cows eat grass." Like all Spark analogies, it's on point in more ways than one. The Spark plot is a genre unto itself, and this explains, to a degree, her prolific output. And like genre novels her work is addictive. You get to enjoy going around the circuit, from the humorous set-up, through the slapstick muddle, to the tragedy brought on by lousy human nature. It's a bit like following up on a double Valium with a low voltage electric shock and an ax murder in the family.

Spark was 39 when her first novel, *The Comforters,* came out in 1957. Since then she has published a novel virtually every other year—17 in all. In one incredible year, three Spark novels came to market. Do we have to conclude that Catholicism cures writing blocks? As an ex-Catholic, I can't stand the thought—in my experience, Catholicism never cured anything. Conversion has, however. Leaving one culture for another grants permission to utterly scorn those left behind, to practice what Spark has called "the art of ridicule" to its outermost limits. In theory, any alternate culture would serve the same purpose, but for the satirist, Catholicism offers two highly congenial doctrines. The notion of original sin renders tolerable the otherwise discomfiting observation that there's something ridiculous and terrible about everyone. Redemption opens the enabling possibility of that exit from pessimism (not to mention Calvinism), the open window of grace. In tandem, these two doctrines permit Catholic satirists to criticize all of humanity without getting suicidally depressed.

Spark has made the most of this permission. She'll say anything about anyone. She'll turn a plot anywhichway, locate evil in any party. In *The Driver's Seat,* for example, a lonely spinster on the hunt for her "type" turns out to be plotting her own sex murder; her murderer becomes in effect her victim. It takes an iron stomach to write a plot like that. I've read angrier rhetoric in fiction by women, but outside of a few Dinesens, no angrier plot. It's stunning—actually scandalizing. In comparison, Rhys's novels, which I love, snivel and Lessing's slop. Spark has her weaknesses—a tendency toward the stereotype and the pat ending—but there isn't a sentimental bone in the body of her prose.

This collection spans almost 35 years and includes African as well as English and Scotch stories. (No New York stories unfortunately.) Most have appeared in previous collections, but there are some new ones—of which one or two are very fine. **"The Dragon"** and **"The Fortune Teller"** are her best parables yet about writing. (Her reputation as a critic's writer rests, largely, on an interpretation of her work as being about the act of creation—a scam on her part, I think, but in this case there's some real substance in the writing metaphor.)

Spark's African stories hold the fascination that current political events lend to fiction from an earlier time; reading them is a little like checking up on a fortune teller or a weathercaster: Can she make historical sense of such human injustice? Answer: yes and no. Spark is so convinced of the general human tendency toward evil that she runs low on explanations, though high on calamitous predictions. Her Africa is not [Nadine] Gordimer's; her take

on the continent is that of an outsider, a transient visitor. While Gordimer sees Africa as a homeland—and offers her vision of its lush beauty both as a partial explanation for the crazed will to possession and dominance acted upon so blatantly there as an argument for justice—Spark sees it as the polar opposite of home. "The place was not without its strange marvels," says one narrator, a British nurse, in a pure Sparkian sentence—that is, a sentence built very like a Spark novella, on the double flip negative, the syntax English allows to its cynics, its doubters, its withholding critical spirits. "I never got used to its travel-film colors except in the dry season when the dust made everything real." Real being foggy, washed-out England. But the whites remind each other that there are reasons to stay, invoking the most mundane motivations of low-echelon imperialism: "Heaps of servants. Cheap drinks. Birds, beasts, flowers."

In other stories, she is very good, as she always is in her novels, on young women of slender means. **"A Member of the Family"**—an early story printed originally in *Mademoiselle*—twists the girl-who-wants-to-get married plot. Trudy goes on vacation with Gwen, an acquaintance. Like well-matched satirists, the two are acutely aware of each other's flaws; rainy weather and a shortage of men sets them further on edge. A man turns up—Richard, an old friend of Gwen's—and Trudy and he begin a flirtation. When Trudy lies about her age, to him " . . . this remarkable statement was almost an invitation to a love affair." Back in London, Trudy keeps up her friendship with Gwen solely to keep tabs on Richard, and she sets her hopes for marrying Richard on a campaign to meet his mother. At last he invites her home, a success that turns out to signify the end of their relationship. Somewhat over-plotted and neat? Maybe, though in revealing not a murderer or a marriage, as the genre normally requires, but the erotic complications of familial bonds, the story pinches the expectations of its readers in the folds and turns of plot with bruising precision, a rare coup in women's fiction.

Spark also takes deadly aim at those couples who invite another woman on their vacations or to their homes for the weekend. Anyone who has ever been cast as a third wheel is revenged forever by **"Bang-Bang You're Dead"** and **"The Fortune Teller."** While triplets merit her most poisoned pen, she's a salutary dose for anyone who is unattached and feeling strange about it. In Spark, it's A-OK to be on your own. She regards coupling as an invitation to neurosis and parasitism at best, and to blackmail and general dastardliness at worst. Lovers or husbands and wives are not the only suspect couples. Even mother-and-son and employee-employer duos are on the sick side in her work. Hiring help is a weakness that enduring help will soon cure, and mothers would do well to oust their sons early on. That she gets away with this phobia against human connection without seeming downright mentally ill is a tribute to her mastery.

A few other stories in the collection are extraordinary. **"Alice Long's Dachshunds"** works on one's memories about the childhood terror of making a fatal error with a terrifying evocative power and then turns instead into a tale about an act of incomprehensible cruelty. It's another masterpiece of the story as spitball. The collection as a whole, however, makes it apparent that the short story is not Spark's form. A miniaturist, she has the economy of style the short story generally demands, but not the close perspective. She is preeminently a writer of surface, the most courteous of voyeurs. Her villains may open forbidden drawers with purloined or copied keys, sneak into bedrooms where they rifle through secret manuscripts. But Spark herself never takes an illicit look in a drawer, and she keeps away from the psychological as if it were contaminated. Her antipathy toward the couple makes the intimate group of almost no interest to her. She is a miniaturist of another ilk. Her ideal canvas is the microcosm, the association with a public face, the minivan of fools— the women's hotel, girl's school, an institution for the aging—and her ideal length is 224 pages, give or take. At 10 pages, she's frequently thin, and a puerile Catholicism shows through the bare spots. Too many ghosts roam these short plots. Divine retribution comes altogether too *ex-machina.* Other endings slide into base so easily they could have been written by a schoolgirl in 1910.

Again and again, I wished she had gained more, earlier, from two writers she has cited with admiration—Proust and Böll—or put her Catholicism to the severe tests of contemporary thought. But despite her trespasses against modernity, these stories teach something many far more philosophically sophisticated, good-politics narrative writers don't know: the uses of the double-helix plot and the biting tongue in bringing consciousness out of the general swoon. "Remember you must die" was the theme of one of her best-known novels, *Memento Mori,* and an acute recognition that we are not divine is the fuel of her wit, the underlying theme of all her work. For Spark it is a religious tenet. For the rest of us, it's a wake-up call of collective and individual mortality and human fallibility, the shot of adrenaline which comes from realizing that if not now, maybe never. When it is predictable and when it is not, Spark's work teaches this lesson: better cut to the quick with a sharp and unexpected blade than pound to the grave on the same dull point.

> Sharon Thompson, "The Canonization of Muriel Spark," in VLS, No. 39, October, 1985, p. 9.

Mona Knapp   (essay date 1986)

[*In the following review of* The Stories of Muriel Spark, *Knapp enthusiastically lauds Spark's short fiction.*]

Short stories have played a minor yet steady role in the long career of Muriel Spark, who began writing in the early 1950s, emerged to prominence with *The Prime of Miss Jean Brodie* in 1961, and still maintains her status as one of Britain's most admired novelists. [*The Stories of Muriel Spark*] spans chronologically the more than three decades of her career. Concurrently, it offers a representative sampling of the narrative devices and motifs typical of her work.

Many stories are set in Africa, where Spark lived for eight years. She does not present a large sociopolitical panora-

ma—in contrast, for example, to Gordimer or Lessing— but rather confines herself to the closed segment of private life experienced directly by the main figures. "The Go-Away Bird" captures best the alienation and emotional paralysis of the white colonialists and ends, as do many other stories, with one of them being brutally murdered. Spark's peculiarly individualized treatment of racial questions merges with her interest in Catholicism (she converted in 1954 and is often described as a Catholic writer) to produce the collection's best piece, "The Black Madonna." The title refers to an altarpiece in a rural English church carved of black wood which, it is rumored, can answer the prayers of childless couples. Spark's protagonists, a cultivated middle-aged white couple, pray to the ebony statue. They do indeed have a child—one so unusual it lays bare their true character and upturns their entire lives.

Semimagical and metaphysical events such as this are an element common to nearly all the stories. "The Portobello Road" is narrated by a ghost, who relates the story of her own murder and appears on occasion to haunt the murderer. In "The Executor" a bereaved niece is tormented by messages written to her daily in the hand of her deceased uncle, who is observing her from the world of the dead. "The First Year of My Life" describes just that, in a singularly inspired contrasting of personal and historical events from the viewpoint of a baby: "Apart from being born bedridden and toothless, unable to raise myself on the pillow . . . my bladder and my bowels totally out of control, I was further depressed by the curious behaviour of the two-legged mammals around me."

As demonstrated by the above quote, Spark has the gift of totally penetrating the viewpoint of her character. There is no omniscient narrator to help distinguish between delusion and faith, between the real and the supernatural. Her plots are brilliantly conceived and superbly executed in a flawless style. Of the twenty-seven stories printed here, the first twenty-one are identical to those contained in Spark's *Collected Stories 1* (1967). Only the last six are more recent (two date from 1985). Since all four previous collections of her stories are out of print, however, the volume fills a gap and should be warmly welcomed by her long-standing admirers as well as attract new readers to her work.

> Mona Knapp, in a review of "The Stories of Muriel Spark," in World Literature Today, Vol. 60, No. 3, Summer, 1986, p. 471.

Anita Brookner   (essay date 1987)

[*Brookner is an English art historian, novelist, and critic. In the following review of* The Stories of Muriel Spark, *Brookner compares and contrasts Spark's short stories with her novels.*]

Things mostly turn out for the worst in Muriel Spark's short stories, as they do in her novels, but with one important difference. In her novels, those masterly constructions full of dread, there is an awareness of the spiritual, even the theological import of most human errors. The journeys undertaken are directed to, or end up in, the heart of darkness, and however deranged or impervious her characters appear to be, some doom shadows them, in Venice, in the Maremma, in New York, in a peaceful village in France, as they wrestle with obscure destinies dressed up as simple or innocent preoccupations. At some point obsession takes over, and with obsession loss of control, of perspective, of peace of mind. All these accounts, which a lesser writer might have inflated to nightmare proportions, are couched in clean, even genteel prose, with detail abrupt and vivid enough to place the reader inside the action. For example, in *The Driver's Seat,* an elderly tourist in Italy is roughly taken in hand by an unwanted and inconvenient companion whose behaviour veers towards the embarrassing. The elderly tourist responds in a dazed and resolutely agreeable manner, but at some point brings out of her handbag 'a trembling pink tissue'. No other words are needed to convey the old lady's unease.

The inevitability of the novels, in which all is going to end badly, but with many agreeable stops along the way, has to do with predestination, which is, after all, a theological concept. In her last novel, *The Only Problem,* the Book of Job (which might indeed, for believers, encapsulate the only problem) was used to put the reader to some unusual thinking, without ever ceasing to be at once a mystery, an entertainment and a suspense story. Bright young things grown harshly middle-aged, effete expatriates, art historians of a recognisable kind, exiled movie stars, stateless persons who become more unsettled the farther they move from home, drift calmly into the worst possible thing that can happen to them. Estrangement takes them over. Lunatics abound, although their condition is not always apparent.

Lunatics, many of them escapees from the local asylum, also abound in the short stories. Ghosts are frequent. The surprising character of the short stories is their pre-rational content. A servant is efficient only when she communicates with a long dead paragon of a housekeeper. A fortune-teller is clairvoyantly dismantled by the aristocratic Frenchwoman in whose chateau she is staying. A flying saucer is identified by an antique dealer as Spode. A deadly pair of twins corrupt their perfectly ordinary parents. The notion (the word is Sparkish) of a soldier, manifestly dead, keeps cropping up in a train conveying an exhausted civil servant to her job in the Home Counties. A dead novelist taunts the niece who thinks she might finish his last book as an amusement by leaving constant messages for her on the blank page. A woman praying to a black Madonna carved out of bog oak gives birth to a black baby. None of this amounts to superstition, but underlying it all is a serious belief in the power of the irrational. All of this articulated in an unmistakably Scottish voice, except when the voice is unmistakably South African. 'Yere I was sitting yere on the bed feeding the baby and I look up at the window and so help me God it was a blerry nig standing outside with his face at the window'. Or alternatively, 'She wore her brown, for she was careful of the navy'.

She is heartlessly funny, for she never sets out to amuse. In the story called **'One of the Family',** Trudy carefully revises her age downwards in order to ensnare Richard. When he takes her home to meet his mother she thinks her hour has come, and is only mildly puzzled when he leaves for an evening without her. Invited down again, she meets a number of women of varying ages, all of whom mother has had to take on when Richard is once more up to his tricks. Poor Trudy, stuck at an unconvincing 22, has become one of the family. What married couples there are behave shamefully by advertising the married state to the benighted spinster who happens to be travelling in their wake. In the story called **'You should have seen the mess',** prudish Lorna likes a dainty life with all the extras and cannot abide uncleanliness. She is thus forced to leave her job in the solicitor's office when confronted with cracked teacups and rickety desks. 'I nearly passed a comment', says the menacing girl.

Mrs Spark conveys the agreeable illusion that if one is a writer strange things happen to one, just as fascinating characters tend to spring up in one's path. Many of these stories are written in the first person, in a deadpan voice that slips easily into one or other of her two favourite accents. They are sufficiently offhand to convince one that they are autobiographical, without ever dropping out of the realm of fiction. They are not recent: many hark back to the period of the 1940s, which is as much Muriel Spark's period as it is Elizabeth Bowen's. Readers of the *New Yorker,* in which most of these stories have appeared, cannot fail to take note of her tone, even in the homogenised all-purpose pages most favoured by that magazine. If anything, she shows up to lesser advantage in a book-length volume, simply by virtue of the fact that her style is so easily recognised and assimilated. It is easy to read these stories one after the other without noticing how surreal they truly are. And the surreal element is not entirely confined to the ghosts. One imagines Muriel Spark going about her business with pursed lips, receiving spirit messages from quite ordinary events, or perhaps imparting them where others see unconnected happenings or characters not always easy to classify. Things proceed by inadvertence or by indirection. There are no explanations.

Mrs Spark is an important writer, whose melancholy mischief is wholly serious. The mischief entertains: the melancholy must be reckoned with. In the stories the mischief—black mischief—is uppermost. In the novels the opposite is true. Sometimes, as in *The Driver's Seat,* possibly her finest novel, or *The Hothouse by the East River,* the melancholy takes on an edge of almost unbearable menace. Yet the style is compact, impassive, orderly, and economical: nothing is stretched beyond its natural limit. Indeed the narrative seems designed to unsettle the reader, so neatly is it contained within the relatively few pages to which these essentially, macabre stories are confined. She never goes over the edge, although she leaves the impression that everybody else is about to. Readers of the short stories reprinted in this volume will catch her drift, but it is to the novels that they must repair for a fuller exposition of her gifts. She will tease and tantalise them even there, but she will leave them thinking. For over and above amusement this writer conveys a wealth of matter, and it is matter that stretches both the nerves and the imagination. (pp. 29-30)

Anita Brookner, "Black Melancholy Mischief," in The Spectator, Vol. 258, No. 8284, April 18, 1987, pp. 29-30.

Valerie Shaw (essay date 1987)

[*In the following review of* The Stories of Muriel Spark, *Shaw praises Spark's narrative technique.*]

Nowadays, Muriel Spark is best known for her novels, and in particular for her creation of Miss Jean Brodie, a figure who has entered popular mythology in very much the same way as Mr Pickwick or Dr Jekyll. But it was as a poet that Spark began turning herself into a writer during the 1940s, and it was in the essentially poetic form of the short story that she first made readers sit up when she won the *Observer*'s 1951 Christmas story competition with her daringly experimental piece **'The Seraph and the Zambesi'**. Since then she has continued to publish short fiction in various magazines and annuals, notably the *New Yorker* and *Winter's Tales,* but **The Stories of Muriel Spark** is the first volume for 20 years to claim to have gathered together all of the stories—or tales as they might better be called, so powerful is the impression of a teller shaping and controlling each plot and character.

Unlike more traditional storytellers, however, Spark does not use voice to let us feel as if we were part of a cosy fireside group. Even though many of these stories have nursery-tale openings—'One day', or 'There was a man'—these rapidly turn quirky if not grotesque: 'One evening, a damp one in February, something flew in at the window', is how one story begins; another, 'One day a madman came into my little grandmother's shop at Watford'. The reader is disoriented, no matter where a particular story is set: colonial Africa in early items like **'Bang-Bang You're Dead'** and **'The Curtain Blown by the Breeze'**; postwar Hampstead in **'The Playhouse Called Remarkable'**, a satire against the philistine 'tum tum *ya'* approach to the arts; Spark's native Scotland in **'The Executor'**, where realism mingles with fantasy to capture with wonderful exactitude the blend of piety and greed in Scottish puritanism; contemporary Italy in **'The Dragon'**, the newest of the 27 stories in this collection, and also one of the most accomplished.

'The Dragon' is told in the first person, a method which suits Spark's brand of irony and is used in several other stories, such as **'The Portobello Road'** (in which a sprightly Catholic ghost takes its delight 'among the solemn crowds with their aimless purposes, their eternal life not far away') and the more acerbic **'Come Along, Marjorie'**, which derides chumminess of the religious variety. It also resembles another recent story, **'The Fortune-Teller'**, in being simultaneously a yarn and a parable about the writer's relationship to her art. The narrator of **'The Dragon'** makes dresses professionally as Spark makes novels and stories, priding herself on being 'first and foremost a needlewoman' and leaving it to other people to apply the grander titles of '*couturier,* dressmaker, designer'. Her insistence that 'it was my fascination with the needle and thread that earned me my reputation' is analagous to the exhilarating love of language which is always evident in

> **[One] of the many reasons why Spark's work lasts so well, and will continue to endure, is that she, like her compatriot [Robert Louis] Stevenson before her, knows how to unite art and entertainment. She can rejoice in her own specialness . . . while knowing that she will be read with pleasure by people outside the 'exclusive and small clientele' for which so much fashionable postmodernist fiction narrowly caters.**
>
> **—Valerie Shaw**

Spark's precisely cadenced phrases and her ear for idiom. Spark's literary reputation is for elegance and stylishness, but what **'The Dragon'** proposes is that worthwhile art begins in craftsmanship and never forgets it. What is more, 'design' is ultimately God's business, not man's.

Behind all of these stories, whether sharply comic as in so many instances, or more melancholy like the novella-length **'Go-Away Bird'** (which has been mysteriously omitted from the Contents page) lies an almost medieval sense of the world turned upside down. This applies to realistic stories as well as those which include supernatural elements, among which **'Another Pair of Hands'** is especially memorable for its gloriously noisy ghost who keeps a bachelor household running smoothly. Religious conviction is what gives these stories their characteristically detached manner, a cool quality which in Spark coexists with high-spirited joy, often tilting into hilarity, and which **'The Executor'** invites us to liken to a Brueghel painting, its colourful foreground crammed with self-engrossed worldly figures while in the distance the artist remains a vague 'speck on the horizon, always receding and always there'.

Perhaps this is why the reader will find no 'Author's Introduction', or indeed an Introduction of any sort, in this volume. The items are not arranged in chronological order of first appearance or according to any other discernible pattern. As a result, the air of enigma and ambiguity which is cultivated by individual stories encompasses the whole book, true to 'the power to suggest what is left unsaid' that Spark has found to be so marvellous about the ancient Scottish ballads. The stories are simply set before us, put there to be enjoyed—and not only by connoisseurs of literary *haute couture.* In fact, one of the many reasons why Spark's work lasts so well, and will continue to endure, is that she, like her compatriot [Robert Louis] Stevenson before her, knows how to unite art and entertainment. She can rejoice in her own specialness ('It wasn't everybody I would sew for', pronounces the dressmaker in **'The Dragon'**) while knowing that she will be read with pleasure by people outside the 'exclusive and small clientele' for which so much fashionable postmodernist fiction narrowly caters. (pp. 31-2)

Valerie Shaw, "Spark on the Horizon," in The Listener, *Vol. 117, No. 3009, April 30, 1987, pp. 31-2.*

Shena Mackay   (essay date 1987)

[*In the following review of* The Stories of Muriel Spark, *Mackay favorably appraises Spark's short fiction.*]

Like the late Hermione Gingold, who once remarked "I don't try to be funny, dear. It's just that I have a certain slant on life", Muriel Spark has a peculiar vision and a drily idiosyncratic ability to make people laugh. This collection [***The Stories of Muriel Spark***], appearing some thirty years after her early stories dazzled both critics and the reading public, makes up a small retrospective exhibition of her work; small because the twenty-seven stories printed here represent only a part of an impressively large *oeuvre*: since *The Comforters* in 1957, she has published sixteen novels, a play, a children's book, poetry and volumes of criticism and biography. *The Mandelbaum Gate* marked a departure from the insouciance of her earlier novels into, increasingly, obliqueness and abstraction, but the stories show no such development; the latest of them is as accomplished and accessible as the first: the collection opens with a story told by a ghost and closes with a woman breathing fire like a dragon. It is as though Muriel Spark sprang, fully armed, with her needle and her venom, from Edinburgh, whose presbyterian cadences, despite the Roman Catholicism of many of her characters, inform much of her prose. Like Hogg's Justified Sinner, a sometime resident of that city, she has always been concerned with manifestations of good and evil, malice and venom.

Thus, Needle, the ghostly narrator of **"The Portobello Road,"** reflects that

> there were times when, privately practising my writings about life, I knew the bitter side of my fortune. When I failed again and again to reproduce life in some satisfactory and perfect form, I was the more imprisoned, for all my carefree living, within my craving for this satisfaction. Sometimes in my impotence and need I secreted a venom which infected all my life for days on end and which spurted out indiscriminately.

It is Needle whose murder inspires the newspaper headline "Needle is found: in haystack!" That headline, once conceived, must have proved irresistible, and however the creative process worked, the idea has a lunatic charm. That Needle returns from the dead to torment her murderer is nothing out of the ordinary in Spark's world, where the supernatural is always padding along beside the mundane awaiting its opportunity to dismay and disconcert: a bossy Seraph sabotages a nativity play, a little man in a flying saucer—Spode or Royal Worcester—skims the ceiling of an antique dealer, a black Madonna bestows a black baby on a white couple, a ghost sweeps up the leaves in the gardens of the asylum and a mysterious soldier sells doom-laden "abstract funerals" for a few shillings.

Death, by whatever bizarre means, is never far from Spark's consciousness:

> "My address book", he was saying, "is becoming like a necropolis, so many people dying every month, this friend, that friend. You have to draw a line through their names. It's very sad."

> "I always use pencil," said a lady, a little younger, "then when people pass on I can rub them out."

Shades of *Memento Mori*. Spark has no compunction in rubbing out her characters, and they are seldom mourned; the five puppies in **"Alice Long's Dachshunds"**, found hanging in a row like the children in *Jude The Obscure* (although they met their fate at the hand of a drunken servant and not by a fraternal paw), are suspended there in the priest's hole in a chilling testimony to a child's expediency. Their owner's heart is broken, they were all she had, but the child, exonerated from the blame that she feared was hers, dances a triumphant sword-dance over the fire-irons: "Then her father starts to sing as well, loudly, tara rum-tum-tum, tara rum-tum-tum, clapping his hands while she dances the jig, and there isn't a thing anyone can do about it."

If that little girl's mother is shocked into remonstrance at this heartless jig, no such platitudes drop from the lips of the colonials, in the early stories set in a beautifully evoked post-war Africa of Ford V8s and flamboyant flowers, in relation to the deaths of "natives", "munts" or "blerry nigs". After Sonji Van der Merwe's husband, in **"The Curtain Blown by the Breeze"**, has blasted with a shotgun the twelve-year-old "piccanin" caught peeping through the window as she suckles her child, she writes to him in prison: "you have landed in jale with your bad temper you shoud of aimed at the legs." The appalling Afrikaners condemn themselves out of their own mouths, the natives, woolly-cropped and enigmatic, go about their work, and Spark makes no moral judgments; her people drift in and out of each other's lives like ghosts or *doppelgängers*, wreak havoc and pass on, or away, with few regrets. When the author *is* provoked to outrage, she uses as a device an omniscient baby, whose first wry smile is triggered by the complacent words of Asquith in the House of Commons at the end of the First World War. This comparatively recent story stands apart from the rest of the collection; for the most part the irony is less overt, and as she says of one of her characters, "To a delicate ear her tone might have resembled the stab of a pin stuck into a waxen image."

Shena Mackay, "Needlework Exhibition," in The Times Literary Supplement, *No. 4393, June 12, 1987, p. 627.*

FURTHER READING

Bibliography

Tominaga, Thomas T., and Schneidermeyer, Wilma. *Iris Murdoch and Muriel Spark: A Bibliography.* The Scarecrow

Author Bibliographies, no. 27. Metuchen, N.J.: Scarecrow
Press, 1976, 237 p.
    Lists primary and secondary sources through 1975.

Biography

Stanford, Derek. *Muriel Spark: A Biographical and Critical
Study.* Fontwell, England: Centaur Press, 1963, 184 p.
    Critical biography that includes personal reminiscence
    by Stanford and chapters on Spark's work as a poet,
    short story writer, novelist, radio scriptwriter, and critic.

Criticism

Greene, George. "Compulsion to Love." *The Kenyon Review*
XXXI, No. 2 (1969): 267-72.
    Review of *Collected Stories I.*

Additional coverage of Spark's life and career is contained in the following sources
published by Gale Research: *Concise Dictionary of British Literary Biography,* Vol. 7;
Contemporary Authors, Vols. 5-8, rev. ed.; *Contemporary Authors New Revision Series,*
Vol. 12; *Contemporary Literary Criticism,* Vols. 2, 3, 5, 8, 13, 18, 40; *Dictionary of Literary
Biography,* Vol. 15; and *Major 20th-Century Writers.*

Peter Taylor

1917-

(Full name Peter Hillsman Taylor) American short story writer, novelist, and dramatist.

INTRODUCTION

Taylor is considered one of the most accomplished short story writers in contemporary American literature. His stories are concerned exclusively with the lives of upper middle-class Southerners from the 1930s to the 1950s, a time when the industrialization and urbanization of the "New South" began to erode the genteel agrarian world of white society. While Taylor focuses these stories on a specific region, he is praised for achieving universal relevance in his works.

Taylor was born in Trenton, a small town in northwest Tennessee, to an upper middle-class family which for generations had been active in state politics. When Taylor was seven years old his family moved to Nashville and subsequently to St. Louis and then Memphis. This experience of displacement from a small town to urban centers, and the attendant confrontation between an older and a more modern milieu, is cited by commentators as the source of much of Taylor's fiction. A more immediate influence on the nature and development of Taylor as a fiction writer was his university education. Taylor is closely identified with the Southern Renaissance or Agrarian movement that his mentors at Vanderbilt University and Kenyon College, Allen Tate and John Crowe Ransom, helped to develop in the 1920s and 1930s. The Agrarians were a group of writers dedicated to preserving the way of life and traditional values of the South. They were concerned with social and political issues as well as literature: in particular, they attacked northern industrialism and sought to preserve the southern agricultural economy. Tate and Ransom later became prominent figures among the New Critics, who practiced close readings of poetry and insisted that criticism should be based on a study of the structure and texture of a given poem, not its content. From these critics, as well as his friendship with the poets Randall Jarrell and Robert Lowell, Taylor acquired an appreciation for poetry that profoundly influenced the composition of his stories.

In *A Long Fourth, and Other Stories* Taylor established the themes and milieu that he has continued to explore throughout his career. The title story, which is regarded as one of Taylor's best, delineates the changing values of a society and dramatizes the suffering of those unable to reconcile themselves to social change. The narrative centers on a prosperous Nashville woman and her attempts to prepare a memorable weekend for her son, who will visit her from New York before joining the army. Several circumstances undermine her plans and reveal the man-

ners and traditions that once provided order in her world to be powerless rituals of a way of life that no longer exists. Taylor's mastery of the short story form was secured with the publications of *The Widows of Thornton, Happy Families Are All Alike,* and *Miss Leonora When Last Seen, and Fifteen Other Stories.* The stories in these collections display Taylor's characteristically conversational prose style and chronicle the traumas of social change among the southern white gentry of the pre–Civil Rights era. Typical of Taylor's style is the gradual unfolding of a narrative in an indirect, ruminative fashion, using little action or dialogue. Through an accumulation of finely observed details that evoke the manners and morals of a particular period, Taylor builds tension and discloses his character's personalities.

It was not until the mid 1980s that Taylor earned the widespread recognition many critics thought his distinguished fiction has long deserved. *The Old Forest, and Other Stories,* a retrospective collection of Taylor's stories from the late 1930s to the 1980s, sparked new interest in the author's work and won the PEN/Faulkner award for fiction. Critics consistently praise Taylor's meticulous recreation of a world that, through his richly detailed descriptions of social manners and customs, becomes uniquely his own. Several commentators have observed that although Taylor's works are set in a particular time and place, their concern with perennial questions of morality and human nature transcend the restrictions of period fiction. As J. D. McClatchy has commented: "The South is his setting, but Taylor could as well be writing about any society in transition."

PRINCIPAL WORKS

SHORT FICTION

A Long Fourth, and Other Stories   1948
A Woman of Means   1950
The Widows of Thornton   1954
Happy Families Are All Alike   1959
Miss Leonora When Last Seen, and Fifteen Other Stories 1963
The Collected Stories of Peter Taylor   1969
In the Miro District, and Other Stories   1977
The Road, and Other Modern Stories   1979
The Old Forest, and Other Stories   1985

OTHER MAJOR WORKS

Tennessee Day in St. Louis   (drama)   1956
A Stand in the Mountains   (drama)   [first publication] 1971
Presences: Seven Dramatic Pieces   (drama)   [first publication] 1973
A Summons to Memphis   (novel)   1986

Robert Penn Warren   (essay date 1948)

[*Warren was considered one of the most distinguished men of letters in America. Consistently in the intellectual vanguard of American scholarship, he was associated with the Fugitive group of southern poets during the 1920s, whose stated intent was to create a literature utilizing the best qualities of modern and traditional art. After 1928, several of the Fugitives joined with other writers to form the Agrarians, a group dedicated to preserving the southern way of life and traditional southern values. Warren eventually left Agrarianism and went on to become a prominent founder of New Criticism, one of the most influential critical movements of the mid-twentieth century. The New Critics believed that a work of literature had to be examined as an object in itself through close analysis of symbol, image, and metaphor. Warren's work is strongly regional in character, often drawing its inspiration from the land, the people, and the history of the South. In the following excerpt from his introduction to* A Long Fourth, and Other Stories, *Warren characterizes the subject matter and principal themes of Taylor's work.*]

Peter Taylor's stories are officially about the contemporary, urban, middle-class world of the upper South, and he is the only writer who has taken this as his province. This world which he delineates so precisely provides a spe-

cial set of tensions and complications. For instance, the old-fashioned structure of family life still persists, disintegrating slowly under the pressures of modernity. Six of the stories in this volume—all except **"Rain in the Heart"**—are stories involving families, and all six are pictures of the disintegration of families. Lost simplicities and loyalties, the role of woman, the place of the Negro—these are topics which properly appear in the drama of this urban world. It is a world vastly uncertain of itself and the ground of its values, caught in a tangle of modern commercialism and traditions and conventions gone to seed, confused among pieties and pretensions. **"The Scoutmaster," "The Fancy Woman," "A Spinster's Tale,"** and especially **"A Long Fourth"** are rich fables of this situation.

So much for the material of these stories. But what of the level at which the storyteller takes the material and the cast of mind with which he views it? We have here not two questions, but one, for the cast of mind determines the level of interest. If Peter Taylor is concerned with the attrition of old loyalties, the breakdown of old patterns, and the collapse of old values, he regards the process without too much distress to his personal piety. The world he is treating, with its mixture of confusion and pretension, would appeal readily to a satiric eye. The older world from which it sprang more nearly knew, for better or worse, what it wanted, and was willing to pay the price; it was not confused in the same way, and if it had pretensions they were pretensions based on its own efforts and not on the true or false memory of the achievements of others. Because it was a human world it was subject to satire, but satire could scarcely strike it in its vitals. It could be damned more easily than it could be satirized. The new world invites satire, and there is often a satiric component in Peter Taylor's treatment of it. In the whole effect, however, he stops somewhere short of satire. Rather, he presents an irony blended of comedy and sympathetic understanding. Uncle Jake of **"The Scoutmaster"** and Harriet of **"A Long Fourth"** are comic creations, but comedy does not exhaust them. We find an awareness of character beyond what explicitly appears. Peter Taylor has a disenchanted mind, but a mind that nevertheless understands and values enchantment. The family affections and loyalties are real, and the memories compelling. It is sad that they cannot exist without being entangled with shoddiness, stupidity, and even cruelty.

The skeptical, ironic cast of mind prompts a peculiar respect for the material it treats. Such a mind hesitates to impose itself on the material and to organize a story like a theorem. It can be satisfied only with a deeper strategy than is common, a strategy that will lure the reader on to his confusion. The reader who can accept the challenge of such a writer may pass through confusion to revelation. He will have reached the revelation, however, with a fuller sense of the complexities of things and of the shadowy, unsaid, unreconciled meanings that must haunt every story worth writing or reading. For such a writer, or reader, fiction is experience, not a footnote. And Peter Taylor's stories are not footnotes.

This skeptical, ironic mind finds its appropriate level in the smaller collisions and crises of life. Only one story,

"The Fancy Woman," deals with violence, and even here the violent situation is refracted through the woman. In the end, it is the movement and temper of her being, and the ambivalence that this gives the story, that engage our interest. And in "Sky Line" and "Rain in the Heart," which lack the positive ironies of the other stories, we find the characteristic qualities of poised reserve. Perhaps the level at which Peter Taylor takes his drama accounts for the fact that his most successful and fully rendered characters are women—the fancy woman, the spinster, and Harriet of "A Long Fourth." The small observation, the casual word, the prized sentiment give the stuff that he works with and makes significant. The things that the menfolks live by are here too, but these things are, by and large, brought down to the scale of the household.

The style of these stories is one appropriate to the level of interest. With the exception of "Allegiance" it is a natural style, one based on conversation and the family tale, with the echo of the spoken word, with the texture of some narrator's mind. The narrator may be identified, as in "The Spinster's Tale," or he may have no formal existence, as in "The Fancy Woman" or "Rain in the Heart." But even in the last two stories we are fully aware of how Josie or the soldier would have told the story. This is what often makes the style of these stories seem neutral. The style is secreted from the inwardness of the material and is an extension of the material. It has no substance of its own and offers nothing to come between us and the story. This is not to say that such a style is the end of virtue, that there is no place for the style that dominates and, as it were, interprets the material. It is to say, simply, that such an "under-style" can have a virtue of its own and that the virtue here is organic and right.

The stories of *A Long Fourth* are by a very young man. To recur to this fact is not to apologize for the performance here. Instead, it is to congratulate ourselves that we can look forward to many more stories from Peter Taylor. In the fullness of time he will write many more stories, stories probably deeper, fuller, richer, and wiser than these. But it is not probable that those unwritten stories will be any truer than these. I have said that Peter Taylor has a disenchanted mind. In terms of his very disenchantment, however, he has succumbed to the last and most fatal enchantment: the enchantment of veracity. And that is what, in the end, makes the artist free. (pp. viii-x)

> *Robert Penn Warren, in an introduction to* A Long Fourth, and Other Stories *by Peter Taylor, Harcourt Brace Jovanovich, 1948, pp. vii-x.*

Hubert Creekmore   (essay date 1948)

[*In the following review of* A Long Fourth, and Other Stories, *Creekmore praises Taylor's portrayal of southern middle-class values in conflict with a changing society.*]

For a long time a considerable segment of readers has complained that Southern authors write only of the extremes of violence and degeneration in Southern life and never portray nice, moral people such as they, the readers, are. Peter Taylor's first book *A Long Fourth,* should come to them as a cheering and welcome confirmation of their existence.

Fortunately, the nice people in his seven long stories are just as interesting (if not as exciting) as those skeletons—the perverts, rapists, lynchers—who have escaped from the magnolia-scented closet of Southern suppression. Though their reality depends in large part on fundamental stigmata of the degeneration so often deplored, the neat balance of strength and weakness in the characters and the conventions of their social life give a humanness and fascination to the stories.

Peter Taylor's first story appeared in the little magazine *River* (Oxford, Miss.), but those in this collection were printed in what might be called the "literary axis" in America—*The Partisan, Sewanee, Kenyon* and *Southern* Reviews. No doubt Mr. Taylor's future work will reach a wide audience—to its delight and profit—for at 30 he has produced a book at once entertaining, perceptive and well written. He has a traditional, but rewarding, style, resembling conversation or the "atmosphere of family tale-telling," as Robert Penn Warren notes in his excellent introduction. The setting is "the urban, middle-class world of the upper South."

All but two of these stories concern the mores of family life in Nashville, Tenn., but they also, except when making a tangent with the ethos of their special social and political landscape, concern all United States family mores. The tensions, affection, longings, the "shoddiness, stupidity and even cruelty" are equally true for any family confronted with the attack of modern industrial forces on inherited standards. The disintegration which results from this clash flavors all seven of the stories, but in the five family stories a rueful, personal triumph of character remains to the older people. The effect of this triumph on their children produces the ironic effect with which most of the stories end.

In "The Scoutmaster" a daughter commits the social indiscretion of being discovered by her parents while virtually unchaperoned and kissing the man she loves. Nostalgia for "the golden days when a race of noble gentlemen and gracious ladies inhabited the land of the South" hangs blindly over the grown folk—so blindly that Uncle Jake, at a Scout meeting, can emerge adolescent enough to urge on the Scouts a return to the days before "the morals and the manners of the country had been corrupted."

The irony is double-edged (as in "A Long Fourth") because, although the realistic stand of the characters is false, their impulses and abortive altruisms are worthy and true; and in spite of this truth, they cannot satisfy both their human nature and their inherited standards except momentarily, and they end in a stalemate of romance about ideals and the past.

In addition to the ironic values and the family portrait, "A Long Fourth" reveals the despair of woman at separation from the man she has reared and the delicate, frustrating and perhaps eternal suspension in the relationship of white mistress and Negro servant, each of whom is losing her boy. "A Spinster's Tale" and "Sky Line" both mirror the deterioration of urban family life, the first through a girl's developing neurosis, the second through a boy's vision of shifting economic patterns. **"Allegiance,"** through an interview between a young soldier in London with his long-expatriated aunt, suggests an old Tennessee family crisis of jealousy, hatred and estrangement. In effect, it is the most subjective of the family stories.

The most objective of Mr. Taylor's stories (which might be called a family story by echo), and certainly the most amusing, is **"The Fancy Woman."** From Josie's viewpoint, we get glimpses of the rich man who is keeping her on his country place, of the dead wife and the two young sons. We also see, when a group of his friends arrive unexpectedly, the society which shaped this callous, selfish, arrogant man. "Josie observed their grooming. . . . Their figures were neatly corseted, and Josie felt that the little saggings under their chins and under the eyes . . . made them more charming; were, indeed, almost a part of their smartness."

The most personal story, **"Rain in the Heart,"** telling of a sergeant's evening with his bride, might be considered the beginning of the young generation's family life. But primarily it is the sergeant's struggle toward completeness of marriage and against the wartime "sense that no moment in his life had any relation to another. It was as though he were living a thousand lives."

Occasionally one has a feeling that the stories are rather attenuated, perhaps because their action is not violent but quiet—almost quotidian. This is especially true of the early parts of **"The Scoutmaster," "A Long Fourth"** and **"Rain in the Heart."** It is a tribute to Mr. Taylor's talent that by his rendering of atmosphere, nuances of character and barely perceptible conflicts he is able to keep such episodes from rebuffing the reader.

> Hubert Creekmore, *"Skeletons in the Magnolia-Tree,"* in The New York Times Book Review, *March 21, 1948, p. 6.*

Kenneth Clay Cathey (essay date 1953)

[*In the following essay, Cathey assesses the strengths and weaknesses of Taylor's early fiction.*]

Peter Taylor is at once among the most promising of our newer writers, and the most limited. His productions to date reveal a sensitive perception, a keen observation, and a remarkable ability to control his materials; yet the range of subjects upon which he has chosen to draw is surely one of the narrowest in present day literature. However, this range is an important and hitherto neglected one. As Robert Penn Warren has said, "Peter Taylor's stories are officially about the contemporary, urban, middle-class world of the upper South, and he is the only writer who has taken this as his province." Mr. Warren's list of qualifying adjectives might be made still more explicit by saying that Taylor writes about people in Nashville, Memphis, Chattanooga, St. Louis, and the hypothetical little town of Thornton, Tennessee. Moreover, these people always belong to old, traditional families, the land-owners-moved-to-the-city. There is a further circumscription within this

scope in that he has written only one story in which a real effort is made to characterize an adult male. Taylor seems to have intentionally restrained himself to showing the impact of his world upon women and children, especially women.

Nevertheless, the narrow limits of his range are completely overshadowed by the success of his efforts within them. The very restriction perhaps contributes to the fact that his tone of lively interest coupled with personal detachment never once falters. Taylor knows his fictional world intimately, but he himself is not part of it; he can depict its victories (such as they are) and its tragedies minutely, but he never becomes personally entangled in them. Almost, his tone reaches the Classical serenity. It is all the more remarkable that he achieved his artistic excellence at a very early age, his first story appearing when he was only twenty. Since then he has contributed to *The Southern Review*, and *Partisan Review*, *The Kenyon Review*, *The Sewanee Review* and *The New Yorker*. His total published output to the present consists of seventeen short stories, a novel and a play. Seven of his earlier stories were collected in *A Long Fourth and Other Stories* (1948).

In making an attempt to evaluate Taylor's accomplishments, the best point of departure seems to be an investigation of the structural variations evident in his later pieces as compared to his earlier ones. When he first began writing, his chief interest was, by his own admission, not so much in subject matter as in the search for what he called the "pure story." By this term he seems to have meant that he was seeking for a narrative situation which could be presented in a straightforward manner, without flashbacks or digressions, and with little or no exposition. The "pure story" would be one possessing a high degree of artistic immediacy; it would, in Henry James's words, present a direct impression of life. It can be speculated that the effort to obtain this immediacy first led Taylor into choosing as subject matter the world he knew best, the "middle-class South," and into concentrating on the elements of that world which would have the strongest direct appeal to the rank and file of readers, family affairs. By selecting such subject matter, and it is to be remarked that not a single piece of Taylor's work fails to consider the chief character or characters in relation to their family life, he assured himself that he would be dealing with a basic situation which required little exposition. Accordingly, his earlier stories, such as **"Skyline"** (1939) and **"Like the Sad Heart of Ruth"** (1941), show a tightness of structure and an avoidance of digressions which actually seem to threaten the artistic value of the work by hampering the clear expression of the meaning. In **"The Fancy Woman,"** (1940), for instance, the action begins (in the very first paragraph) on an evening, extends through all of the next day and ends on the second morning. In this space the characters indulge in no memories of what has preceded and make only occasional references to anything outside the immediate scene. Unfortunately this structure, constantly stressing the forward motion, leaves the author little or no time to make really clear just what the conflict in the story consists of, so that it seems closer to a sketch than a short story. In this connection it is helpful to remember Mark Schorer's distinction that "a short story makes some kind of complete dramatic statement whereas a sketch is content to give us an impression of a dramatic moment." Schorer thinks that the proper method of differentiating between the two is to have the action of a short story lead to some sort of moral revelation which becomes clear not only to the reader but also to at least one of the characters. In **"The Fancy Woman"** the central character, a prostitute, obviously does come to some such revelation; at the end she sits patiently on the bed and waits for her lover to break the door in and avenge himself for certain insults she has offered to his son. However, the reader is not at all certain just what is the revelation that causes her patient resignation, for the author has not clearly outlined the dramatic conflict during the earlier part of the story, although it is probable that the basic struggle is the woman's efforts to "break into" the society represented by her fairly wealthy lover. This failure to throw the conflict into high relief seems to be one of the chief faults of the fiction writers who in recent years have sought to follow James's admonition to present life directly. Perhaps the conflicts in ordinary life are seldom intense enough, except on the melodramatic level, to be artistically interesting. Yet the structure of Taylor's early stories is so tight, the progression so chronologically straightforward, that the struggles of his characters lack the vitality and intensification which alone can lead them to a true moral revelation within the circumscribed limits of the story. Taylor, in his search for the "pure" form, seems to have forgotten that no one stretch of time is more interesting than another except as it condenses, concentrates or intensifies the meaning of previous stretches. This intensification can only be introduced into the narrow bounds of the short story by properly handled exposition (i.e., information included for the purpose of making explicit all the complicating elements in the conflict). It is interesting to note how Taylor changed the structure of his stories as he grew older so as to allow himself more opportunity for connecting the immediate action of the story with the enveloping action.

"A Long Fourth" (1946) finds him trying for the first time to depict a truly dramatic conflict rather than a merely dramatized scene in which some traces of struggle are evident. The story runs to about twice the length (12,000 words) of his previous efforts and reveals a structure which is far different from the tight narratives of his earlier pieces. It opens with something of a leisurely pace in that the stream of consciousness of the central character is often used to supply exposition by means of flashbacks. In addition, **"A Long Fourth"** is the first of Taylor's stories to incorporate exposition stemming directly from the omniscient narrator. This variation of structure is important because it allows Taylor more opportunity to create the exact atmosphere of contemporary middle-class family relations in all their subtlety: doubly important when we realize that the family atmosphere is the real antagonistic force in all Taylor's works. **"A Long Fourth"** marks the first occasion on which he allowed himself enough structural freedom to include incidents that serve to illuminate the more recondite aspects of the setting. The events of this story seem at first reading to be a somewhat confused mass of happenings—some minor, some striking—which occur during a long, Fourth-of-July weekend while a mid-

dle-aged woman entertains various people and parties before her son goes off to the war. When new characters are introduced, Taylor shows no reluctance to stop his narrative long enough to sketch in the exact relation each bears to the central family group, especially to the mother. The story is impressive even at an initial reading for its vivid characterization and accurate rendering of the scene. Taylor's unusual power of observation transforms, as it were, the familiar, ordinary setting and turns it into something a bit magical, something easily remembered despite the dangers of banality from the subject. It is possibly one of his finest attributes that he can thus create an artistic world which is consistent within itself and yet bears so many points of resemblance to the real world that all of us know. The story is also outstanding in that it introduces an element which is of considerable importance in most of his work—the question of race relations and the status of Negroes in the modern South. The delicacy with which Taylor handles this theme is seen in the fact that it never once obtrudes itself so strongly into the central action that the piece becomes one of the "problem" stories of which we have had too many in recent fiction. As pointed out, Taylor's artistic world is consistent within itself: the presence of the Negro servants and their influence on some of the family activities is recognized, but the center of attention properly remains with the woman whose spiritual development is the real subject.

The chief fault of **"A Long Fourth"** is much the same as the difficulty which dogged him from the very beginning; he does not make clear just what is the influence of the conflict upon the central character. She clearly undergoes some moral revelation, for the author plainly states that she felt the final incident was "a larger and more general inquiry into her character than . . . ever . . . before." Unfortunately, the reader is not sure as to the specific nature of this inquiry, although we can speculate that it concerns her revaluation of the loyalties by which she has lived and which gave her existence meaning. The reader feels that the author knew clearly what he wanted to say but left part of it unsaid on the assumption that a "good" story should leave something to the reader's own power of interpretation. True, a good story is suggestively "incomplete," but the reader feels cheated when there is a distinct impression that the things left unsaid are consciously withheld by the author rather than stemming from a subject which is too universal to be totally comprehended by any single mind. Nevertheless, **"A Long Fourth"** marked an important stage of Taylor's development; in it he finally found his true subject, on which he could speak with authority, to be a depiction of the dissolving of traditional conceptions about family relationships: conceptions which included much that was useful, more that was hampering to modern life; much that was repulsive, more that was attractive to the sentiments of every one of us. In short, the story marks the clarification of Taylor's own view of life.

It is probable that at this time Taylor himself felt his chief weakness to be a vagueness in clearly outlining dramatic conflicts, for his next story, **"Allegiance"** (1947), is clearly constructed in such a way as to place the conflict at the center of attention. It does not plunge pell-mell into the action; rather it proceeds leisurely for a time, allowing the author space to present adequate exposition. The story opens with the entrance of a Nashville boy, in England with the American army, into the London parlor of an aunt who long ago shocked the entire family by completely severing all ties of kinship and going off to live a life of her own in a foreign country. Much use is made of the stream of consciousness technique in this opening section so as to allow the narrator (the boy) to indulge in flashbacks which set the scene by condensing the entire life history of the woman, who is the chief center of interest. He remembers her "romantic" quality and the aura of glamor which her independence lent her in the eyes of those who knew her as children. However, the dramatic structure of the story is shown by the fact that on the very first page the narrator reveals that this woman had in the past done some "grievous wrong" to his mother and that the family had been nursed on hatred of her (the aunt). This revelation immediately rouses a keen interest in the reader, an interest which is not disappointed, for the conflict is sharply illumined when the aunt soon afterwards makes the statement that the boy was always the member of his family most like herself, and he begins worrying over whether or not he is about to "betray someone or something." Having thus put into motion what seems to be the central action of the story, Taylor then wisely alternates between dialogue and reflections by the narrator in order to further characterize the aunt and introduce details about the boy's past, both of which help bring the story to an effective climax. The aunt alludes to the narrow provincialism of her Nashville family life, against which she had rebelled, and the reader expects the resolution of the conflict to make some more or less universal comment on family relationships that are too restrictive. Unfortunately, the story begins to fail at this point.

By attempting to concentrate the meaning of a woman's lifetime into a single dramatic moment, Taylor comes upon a methodological procedure which seems peculiarly fitted to the illumination of his chosen subject matter, the obligations and advantages of family bonds in a world of dissolving loyalties. However, he does not yet seem to be able fully to control this method, for he seriously neglects an adequate elaboration of the conflict itself after he has set the scene. Apparently what happened was that he became involved in the latter part of the story in an effort to show that "each moment and indeed everything in the life and body of the world must have in itself a latent magic which might be exploited." Although this is a very interesting idea (and one which recurs at other places in Taylor's work), the author fails to find objective correlatives for it in the action of the story, the last half of which is taken up with very subtle and introspective conjectures on the narrator's part as to whether or not the old lady's youthful rebellion was caused by a realization that the actual, the present moment, is more important than altruism or personal honor. The reader can only regret that this striking theme is expressed mostly by direct statement instead of being embodied artistically so as to show *why* the old lady came to such a conclusion. The dramatic possibilities latent in the situation could probably have been extended to an objective solution of the problem.

This lack of objectification is one of the chief faults of Taylor's earlier work and one which it is hard to see how he avoids even now since he practically never deals with violent action of any sort, preferring to draw his events from the quieter, everyday side of family affairs. Conversations, reunions, visits, minor domestic crises—these are the external substance of Taylor's stories. Therefore, **"Allegiance"** ends with several questions unanswered in the reader's mind; yet the skill with which the complication was built up and the vivid selection of details to suggest the atmosphere of an expatriate Southern lady's parlor in London (without allowing this atmosphere to dominate the drama, however) show that Taylor is beginning to achieve sufficient mastery of his structural techniques to allow him to center the reader's interest on what the story says about life rather than what it says about the author's private ideas (his point of departure), which is the mark of an artist as differentiated from a technician.

In the work that followed **"Allegiance"** Taylor showed evidences of intentional experiments with structure by venturing into the realm of another genre; in 1949 he published his only play, *The Death of a Kinsman*. The fact that he turned his attention to this form shortly after the appearance of **"Allegiance"** seems to indicate that he wanted to try something which he could perform with total freedom from all elements extraneous to the drama. The play is obviously experimental. It is incapable of holding an audience's attention throughout an actual stage performance since the entire first half accomplishes nothing but exposition, but it does succeed in making the essential conflict and its results very clear by the end. Like his stories, it deals with the effect of a close-knit family atmosphere on the central character—this time a maiden aunt who justifies her position of economic gratuitant by assiduously relieving the wife and mother of the burden of caring for the five children. The author makes it clear that both women realize they are playing "rôles" which descend from the traditional Southern composition of large families, the aunt's role having been actually obviated by modern economic changes which have made it possible for her to maintain a separate living if she so desired. For the first time, Taylor finds an adequate objectification of the antagonistic forces by introducing a housekeeper whose age, sex and lack of immediate family make her a counterbalance to the maiden aunt. The fact that this housekeeper can and does earn her own living is a constant reproach to Aunt Lida. Moreover, there is external conflict between the two since the housekeeper detests the other for her "hypocrisy" in accepting support which is really unnecessary. The conflict breaks into the open in a series of incidents connected with the funeral of a distant relative of the family who would have nothing to do with them while he was alive, but whom they feel obligated to bury because he was "kin" to them. This series of incidents fully elaborates the conflict and raises implications which are left to the reader to answer. In this case, however, the unanswered questions do not seem to be a mere temperamental reservation on the author's part.

The basic success of Taylor's dramatic experiment in *The Death of a Kinsman* would seem to indicate that he had finally perfected the essential elements of his structural technique, even though he still showed some clumsiness in handling exposition. It is a feature of first importance, though, that he realized both here and in **"Allegiance"** that whatever exposition is necessary to the full delineation of the dramatic conflict should not be sacrificed to an effort to "present a direct impression of life." Taylor was apparently ready at this time to enter upon a period of real artistic accomplishment in the highest sense of the word, combining a steady view of life with technical excellence. Instead he embarked upon another structural experiment which led to his greatest failure.

In 1950 he published his only long piece to date, *A Woman of Means,* which he always refers to as a novelette rather than a novel. It is hard to ascertain exactly why this work is so much less impressive than his better short stories. Perhaps it is because he reverted to a subject and method which he had used in some of his earliest efforts. Instead of dealing with a family in all its relations and connections with the social background, he concentrated on showing the development of a thirteen year old boy under the tutelage of a step-mother. To do this he adopted the first person singular point of view, which he handles less well than the omniscient viewpoint for which he shows a decided preference in the total body of his work. The structure of *A Woman of Means* shows serious faults. In reality it seems to be two short stories poorly woven together, for the reader's attention is sharply split between interest in the fortunes of the youthful narrator, who in the process of the story first comes to an awareness of his existence as an individual personality, and interest in the character of the stepmother, who suffers a nervous breakdown, possibly because of the boy's newly-declared independence. Unfortunately, the two storylines are not synthesized well enough for the reader to perceive any direct connection. There is an additional fault in that much of the earlier part of the work is taken up with exposition of the boy's life before his father's remarriage, exposition which really adds nothing to the understanding of his eventual psychological change. Or at least, it is exposition which could have been accomplished in a much shorter space, as Taylor himself proved by publishing a part of the novelette as a separate story in 1949. This story, **"Dudley for the Dartmouth Cup,"** presents as clear an insight into the boy's character and character-change as does the longer treatment in the novelette. (Taylor also published a central episode in the stepmother's life as a separate story, **"Casa Anna,"** 1948).

Perhaps the main trouble lay in the fact that Taylor was so accustomed to writing short stories that he really did not perceive the differences of structure demanded by the longer form, this difference being essentially (as Mark Schorer says) the depiction of a moral *evolution* instead of the moral *revelation* which is central to the short story. Taylor distinctly arranges the incidents in such a manner as to lead up to the two separate revelations that come to the two chief characters, but he does not embody the changes in enough objective incidents to show how the revelations affected the lives of the characters after they occurred. He comes closer to showing an evolution for the boy than for the step-mother; yet the woman's story occupies the position of greatest interest, the end of the book. As stated, these faults may be the result of Taylor's not

perceiving the true nature of novel (or novelette) structure; but it is more probable that they result from the effort to depict the psychology of an adolescent boy, which by its nature cannot help but seem rather too thin a subject to support a sustained effort now that the initial surge of interest in Freudian conceptions has died down.

From 1949 till 1951 Taylor was engaged in writing a series of nine stories for *The New Yorker,* among which are his finest efforts to date, especially **"Porte-Cochere," "Uncles," "What Do You Hear from 'Em," "Two Ladies in Retirement,"** and **"Bad Dreams."** For the most part, they deal with various aspects of the feminine view of Southern life and with the status of present day Negroes. This latter theme becomes increasingly important until it occupies the entire scene in Taylor's most recently published story, **"Bad Dreams,"** which is quite refreshing in that it views Negroes first of all as human and only secondarily as members of a minority race. Yet Taylor does not patronize them; in fact, he speaks privately of his interest in them as "anthropological" rather than "social." He refuses to be lured from his tone of calm detachment by either social problems or sentimentalism. It is not surprising that all the stories written after the appearance of his novelette show clear signs of the author's being more interested in content than form, since he had apparently realized that the short story was his forte and treated the technical aspects confidently. **"Bad Dreams"** and **"Two Ladies in Retirement,"** his most dramatically effective pieces, reveal central facets of Taylor's mature thought. Both are much like **"A Long Fourth"** in that a rather leisurely, expository opening emphasizes the fact that the atmosphere will be very important in the working out of the theme. However, in **"Bad Dreams"** a better job is done of dispersing the necessary exposition throughout the body of the action than in **"Two Ladies in Retirement."** Taylor shows unmistakable signs of having profited by the dramatic experiment of his play, for in both stories he outlines the conflict distinctly, embodies it in a sufficient number of incidents, and devotes enough space to the denouement to make clear to the reader the essential nature of the moral revelation that takes place. In these stories, with technical problems in the background, it becomes most strongly apparent what Taylor had been striving since the beginning of his career to say about the traditional family life of the South. The resolution of the action in each story shows that the women and Negroes (because of their subordinate rank) have been hampered in finding their true position in modern life by the hanging-on of old traditions directing their behavior into certain predetermined channels, and that these traditions do a basic injustice to the individual personality now that the external conditions on which they were founded have disappeared. The men of the South had escaped this hampering effect long ago by plunging into the business world, which was sharply differentiated from home life (this aspect of Taylor's thought is best seen in **"Uncles"**). As the author says of the central character in **"Two Ladies in Retirement"**—and he reveals his interest in subject matter in the later stories by an increasing tendency toward making direct statements of his thought—

> She had not asked to be born the unbeautiful, untalented heiress of a country family's fortune,

or to grow up to find that the country town that gave that fortune its only meaning was decaying and disappearing, even in a physical sense. The men of her generation, and of later generations, had gone to Nashville, Memphis, Louisville, and even to St. Louis, and had used their heads, their connections, their genteel manners to make their way to the top in the new order of things.

If they are to find any real happiness, both women and Negroes must give up their allegiance to the tradition without surrendering their loyalty to the basic family relationships embodied in it, this solution being arrived at by the women in **"Two Ladies in Retirement"** and by the Negroes in **"Bad Dreams."**

The most outstanding feature of Taylor's writing to date is that he has shown an almost uninterrupted improvement in both technique and content. Significantly, his very last story to appear is certainly his best from the standpoint of form, and probably from the standpoint of the ideas it expresses as well. His later efforts, impressive as artistic achievements in themselves, are even more impressive as portents of his future productions, coming as they do at a time when the authors of fiction (as Malcolm Cowley has pointed out) have realized the limitations of the older types of writing and are crying out for some new direction. Perhaps Peter Taylor can offer part of that direction by continuing to make valid statements about the external world we live in. (pp. 9-18)

Kenneth Clay Cathey, "Peter Taylor: An Evaluation," in The Western Review, *Vol. 18, No. 1, Autumn, 1953, pp. 9-19.*

Morgan Blum   (essay date 1962)

[*In the following excerpt, Blum discusses what he considers to be the "limitations" of Taylor's short stories.*]

The usual way a writer extends himself . . . results from a growth, a maturing in his powers or range of feeling, in his ability to treat the problems of advancing age, for example. Mr. Taylor has, from the beginning of his career, been able to imagine with such great verisimilitude people very different from himself in every way (in age, sex, race, fortune, and regional origin, for example) that few of the usual pathways to growth were available to him. As a writer, he matured young.

Mr. Taylor, then, does not limit himself in the persons he treats; they are not all variants of an autobiographical impulse. For the autobiographical limitation is one that the fiction writer imposes on himself only at great and telling risk. Coleridge must surely be right when he insists that writers of essentially limited power can sometimes treat successfully an autobiographical experience, but that one of the sure signs of genius is the writer's ability to render experience very different from his own.

If a rule can survive the harsh test the apparent exception exposes it to, it has, we are told, been proved a good rule. Two apparent exceptions to the rule I am about to talk about are *"Je Suis Perdu"* and **"1939,"** both from the 1959 volume, ***Happy Families Are All Alike.*** The rule in

question is not whether Mr. Taylor ever goes beyond the autobiographical; this can be demonstrated simply enough by citing one of the most beautiful of modern stories, **"Bad Dreams,"** where we have extended scenes of Negro life that no white person could have ever witnessed. And yet they tell more about the Negro than any of the hundred perfectly factual Negro scenes I have observed or heard reported. The rule in question is whether he is *ever* autobiographical.

"Je Suis Perdu" certainly *seems* autobiographical. The protagonist is finishing a year in France writing on a grant, just as Mr. Taylor did on a Fulbright. The fact that his character is a historian seems only the thinnest and most transparent of disguises for the author. But its ending is properly universal and reminds us of one of the reasons why Aristotle said that in dealing with the possible instead of the actual, tragedy is more philosophic than history. For what the ending deals with is the temptation to self-indulgence in all of us. It has, for example, a great deal to say about beatnik and Bohemian, though these lurk only on the story's fringe and never appear as actual characters, a great deal to say, that is, about work left undone or slovenly done, about human responsibilities unfulfilled, and about one antidote to these failings.

The ending comes about in this way. The protagonist has just completed a happy and successful year of work in Paris. But taking a last morning's walk, he finds himself assailed by the kind of black depression of spirit that some years earlier had been very common with him. Then he meets his daughter and baby son out walking with the French maid. And after a few moments of talk and laughter, some with the little girl sitting on his knee, he walks on to find the black mood gone. It has disappeared, linked perhaps in his mind with two other incidents that had earlier ended happily, one an affair of spilt milk and a shaved moustache within the time-span of the story, the other a remembered moment when his daughter, momentarily lost from him in a theatre crowd, cries out, *"Je suis perdu."* And he thinks, as the story ends:

> He found that he wanted the mood of despondency to return, and he knew it wouldn't for a long while. It was something [his daughter] had taken from him, something she had taken from him before and would take from him again and again—she and the little fellow in the carriage there, and their mother, too, even before they were born. They would never allow him to have it for days and days at a time, as he once did. He felt he had been cheated. But this was not a mood, it was only a thought. He felt a great loss—except he didn't really feel it, he only thought of it. And he felt, he *knew* that he had after all gotten to Paris too late . . . after he had already established steady habits of work . . . after he had acknowledged claims that others had on him . . . after there were ideas and truths and work and people that he loved better even than himself.

As I indicated earlier, this passage tells us a great deal about qualities that belong to someone very different from the protagonist—a great deal, that is, about pride and sloth and the kind of self-admiration that leaves a man free to think well of a great many of his own actions and attitudes while hating the being that is their source. But the scene is universalized beyond mere autobiography in a second way. The scenes of family life that show how the daughter "and the little fellow in the carriage there, and their mother, too" take away his moments of gloom or severity or fear have been wonderfully rendered; some of the dialogue is of its own sort almost unmatched in English. Above all, these scenes convince us—not only of their own reality, but of their power to destroy a black mood in the father, in almost anyone. And when an ending is so prepared for that it seems right and inevitable, what in the occasion that suggested it was perhaps mere autobiography, becomes, in the shape and effect of the finished story, appealing to all men of adequate sensibility.

"1939" is even more obviously autobiographical than *"Je Suis Perdu."* Mr. Taylor midway through the story speaks of it himself as a memoir. Its chief protagonist would, at first glance, seem to be Mr. Taylor, pure and simple, since he is a fiction writer who transferred to Kenyon to study under someone who is very much like Mr. John Crowe Ransom and since he is a senior at Kenyon in the fall of 1939 when Mr. Taylor was himself a senior there. But wherever Mr. Taylor's history conflicts with that of the protagonist, that discrepancy is ignored. I should like to cite one minor example of this and then one major one.

In order that one of the changes which the ending embodies should work, it is essential that all the students at Douglass House, where the protagonist lives, think of themselves as deeply independent of each other and of the rest of the campus with its fraternities and "fine old songs about early days at Kenyon." But Mr. Taylor had, distractingly enough for the purposes of the story, once belonged to a major national fraternity. And so he quite properly omits this awkward fact; it could, of course, have been explained away easily, but this would have been a pointless digression in a story already rich in apparent digressions that have in fact real points to make.

But the major change is even more interesting. Mr. Robert Penn Warren, in his wise introduction to *A Long Fourth,* tells us that Mr. Taylor had already, by the fall of 1939, published two fine stories and had written, in 1938 and 1939, two other stories that were subsequently published in *The Southern Review* and reprinted in *A Long Fourth.* In other words, Mr. Taylor was already a much more mature writer than the story's protagonist, an insecure and unpublished imitator of Henry James. And the difference is essential if the refrain *"Not Yet, not yet, not yet"*—which runs through the protagonist's mind at the story's end—is to be an effective conclusion, one, that is, which is consistent with the history of the character portrayed.

In another sense, however, Mr. Taylor has limited himself to the autobiographical. Mr. Taylor's world is always a world he has observed, peopled with folk he has observed. He never writes of times he has never known, as the historical novelist does. He never writes of an area he has never seen, as Saul Bellow consciously does in *Henderson the Rain King,* or of an activity he has never observed, as Stephen Crane consciously does in *The Red Badge of Courage.*

When the history of an earlier time enters a Taylor story, it always enters in a way that *he* could have experienced it—that is, as reading or legend or old folks' talk. Readers of *Tennessee Day in St. Louis* hear legends of Southern gentlemen-gamblers very much as Mr. Taylor may have heard them from the mouths of elders. (One guesses that such an elder in that play, Senator Cameron Caswell, may have been suggested at least in part by Mr. Taylor's grandfather, Bob Taylor, the hero of "The War of the Roses" in Tennessee politics.) And the description of the Dark Walk at Thornton, Tennessee, Mr. Taylor seems to have reconstructed from old legend and first-hand observations of his own. (Thornton, one guesses, shares more than a phoneme or two with Mr. Taylor's place of birth, Trenton, Tennessee.) But whatever the actual facts behind these hypotheses are—I suppose them inconsequential—the actual self-limitation that Mr. Taylor operates under here seems clear enough. He must work from first-hand observation. This means that, though the facts of one man's life may be suppressed or changed at will or created entirely or in part out of the imagination, Mr. Taylor must have known someone who shared his cultural heritage. For though an individual life may be altered as the needs of the story dictate and to the degree truth permits, the way of life which produced that character is a sacred thing, not to be violated. The symptoms reported are the symptoms observed, or they serve as the fundamental data on the basis of which the unobserved moment (e.g., a Negro family's talk when no white person is around) is constructed. An eye that looks and an imagination that builds—these are essential to Mr. Taylor's way of work, as they are, of course, to every other writer with the slightest pretensions to seriousness. The fundamental difference in the present instance is their absolute inseparability. The observed fact may always be recalcitrant and refuse to serve the needs of the story imagined. When this happens, that particular fact must go. But without closely observed details—the turn of phrase in a country-woman's mouth, the slightly offset quality of one man's chin as he sees it mirrored in his daughter's—without these things that at some point grew out of actual experience, Mr. Taylor does not write—at least not in any published book.

I believe that certain other matters excluded from Mr. Taylor's fiction up to now can be explained partially, but only partially, on this same basis, that they lie more or less outside of his experience. One such exclusion is that of violence; Mr. Robert Penn Warren had observed its exclusion in Mr. Taylor's early stories, and it seems even more completely excluded in the stories written since then. Or rather, to put the matter more precisely, such violence as there is takes place off stage. We may see its results in character or even in the debris strewn about a wrecked office, but we never see it as action.

Now, this seems at first glance a serious limitation in Mr. Taylor's work, whether self-imposed or not. After all, physical violence is by no means the private possession of Mr. Mickey Spillane; it can reveal what is most uniquely human, as well as what is merely bestial, in us all. In *War and Peace,* for example, the violent death of Petya Rostov expresses as well as any one action can all that Petya was at the moment and all that he aspired to. The diverse ways in which Dolohov and Denisov receive that death are vibrant with their own histories and the history of the human condition. But in Mr. Taylor, the absence of violence on stage is part and parcel of his general lack of interest in physical skills and physical experiences for their own sake. In general, both of Hemingway's "Big Two-Hearted River" stories with their quiet fishing and camping scenes, their relishing of sensation, have as little in common with Mr. Taylor's art as Tolstoy's or Hemingway's own battle scenes or the burning of the tobacco barns and the death of Benton Todd in Warren's *Night Rider*. (I hope it is clear that I am here speaking only of works and passages which I admire strongly.)

Again the apparent exception proves our rule. A fight of sorts does occur once on stage in Taylor's fiction. It takes place between the narrator (who resembles Taylor) and his friend Jim Prewitt (who resembles Robert Lowell) in the story "1939." An affair of shoulder blocks and shoves in the smoking compartment of a train, it is, viewed in isolation as mere physical action, dullness itself. But seen in context, as the product of all their frustrations over that long Thanksgiving weekend and of the immediate need of each to have the other obliterated from his sight, the scene is a wonderfully satisfying consequence of what has gone before, and at the same time makes possible a purgation of hostility that is necessary to the story's end. The point to be made here is twofold. On the one hand, Mr. Taylor has given us less than we get in some fights in fiction which, like his, have grave human import but which in addition seem splendid if thought of as action alone. On the other hand, what we get from him we get without distraction: we know what to look for, since a fight that is inconsequential in itself has consequence—if at all—only in terms of what has gone before or what is to come after.

Just as he avoids extremes in action, Mr. Taylor avoids extremes in characterization. He allows himself no male angels, no Alyosha Karamazov, and only a few female angels, who operate always in the restricted sphere of their own families—Laetitia Ramsey, Helen Ruth Lovell, the wife in "Cookie," the Flo Dear of "Two Ladies in Retirement" and *Tennessee Day in St. Louis*. But the absence of villains in his work is even more instructive. If we look for any embodiment of evil as powerful and intense as Mr. Hatch in Katherine Anne Porter's "Noon Wine," we simply look in vain. Our failure to find a true villain becomes especially revealing when we remember that Jesse Munroe in "A Friend and Protector" is guilty of a much longer list of crimes than Mr. Hatch. But Mr. Hatch's talk about chewing tobacco becomes, in retrospect, far more vicious than Jesse's activities as con man or procurer. For Mr. Hatch is both the doer of evil and the source of evil in others; and at the same time he himself is sourceless, without a history, and therefore unforgivable. Jesse Munroe, on the other hand, has a history. An accidental involvement in a murder among his fellow Negroes brings him apparently one but actually two white protectors, the narrator's Uncle Andrew and Aunt Margaret. And these two, occasionally aided and abetted by a Negro or two, bring about Jesse's ruin. For Uncle Andrew as Forgiving Saviour and Aunt Margaret as Doom-Pronouncing Judge provide all the food that Jesse's sense of guilt needs; he can undertake

his most vicious escapade with the sure feeling that each of his gods will give him at its end what he deserves. And they in turn need him, so that his ruin can satisfy the void left by "the pale *un*ruin of their own lives." This spreading of guilt—I shall come back to this in a later connection—characterizes Mr. Taylor's attempts to see people in their histories, with understanding and a measure of forgiveness. In fact, on those rare occasions when he makes his evildoer stand almost alone with no specific fellow being sharing his guilt but only society (the doctor-husband in "Cookie") or geography (the narrator in "A Walled Garden"), his figures are least satisfying. They cannot stand without histories, as Mr. Hatch can.

Mr. Taylor generally aims at a prose that resembles his villains in its lack of intensity. But it is a subtle instrument capable of rendering states of mind and feeling with great precision, of suggesting a character's point of view and even the "tone of voice" of his thought without ever being confined by this tone or the character's horizons. The following passage from "Two Ladies in Retirement" provides an interesting example of such a style. Because it is interesting as something more than style, we should see its place in the story. Miss Betty Pettigru, who had been an aggressive and dominant figure in Nashville society for many years, has come to live with her cousins the Tollivers to enjoy watching her three young "nephews" grow up and—in her own way—to help the process along. She soon finds herself involved in a feud for the boys' affections with Vennie, the old Negro cook.

Vance, the oldest of the three boys, is tremendously sensitive to what older people are and to the things they and their world value most. He senses both the war between Auntie Bet and Vennie and the sort of tactics that his "aunt" must have stooped to in the old social wars back in Tennessee, the tactics that he expects she can stoop to again in this new war. (He, also, has been wounded by Vennie.) And so he suggests, without quite phrasing the whole matter as a suggestion, since he himself is frightened by what he is saying, a thoroughly undetectable method of eavesdropping that Auntie Bet can use against Vennie. And she, in turn, is deeply humbled and mortified by what he must think of her if he supposes she can stoop to conniving with children and eavesdropping on a servant. On her bed upstairs she lies down and thinks of her old life in Nashville and what it must have done to her.

> It had just been life, plain and simple, where you did what good things you could and what bad things you must. As she looked back, it seemed that it had been hard for her to decide to leave Nashville only because it had meant facing the fact of the worthlessness of the goal she had set herself many years before—the goal set *for* her, really, by circumstances and by her personal limitations. What else could she have done with her life? She had not asked to be born in the days when Victoria was queen of England, when Southern womanhood was waited upon not by personal maids but by personal slaves. She had not asked to be born the unbeautiful, untalented heiress of a country family's fortune, or to grow up to find that the country town that gave that fortune its only meaning was decaying and dis-

appearing, even in a physical sense. The men of her generation, and of later generations, had gone to Nashville, Memphis, Louisville, and even to St. Louis, and had used their heads, their connections, and their genteel manners to make their way to the top in the new order of things. And wasn't that all *she* had done, and in the only way permissible for a Miss Pettigru from Thornton? Once the goal was defined, was it necessary that she should be any less ruthless than her male counterparts? In her generation, the ends justified the means. For men, at least, they did. Now, at last, Miss Betty saw how much like a man's life her own had been. She saw it in the eyes of the wounded, frightened child. She saw how it was that every day of her adult life had made her less a woman instead of more a woman. Or less somebody's old granny instead of more somebody's old granny. Wrong though it seemed, the things a man did to win happiness in the world—or in the only world Miss Betty knew—were of no consequence to the children he came home to at night, but every act, word, and thought of a woman was judged by and reflected in the children, in the husband, in all who loved her.

We can see in this passage how Mr. Taylor is in no way confined by Auntie Bet's point of view; he is able to be more articulate than she could possibly be at this terrible moment of sadness and self-knowledge. Still, we sense her thinking beneath his, so that we enjoy the best of both worlds. One phrase used twice in the passage, for example, is absolutely hers: "somebody's old granny." It is deeply and irrevocably hers because its very color has been fixed in her memory by that most perfect of fixatives, conscious hurt. The sentence that contained the hurting phrase was uttered by Mr. James Tolliver, a kindly and reasonably tactful man who never would have consciously given pain to Auntie Bet.

> "Vennie's like somebody's old granny, and since the world began, grannies have been hiding cookie jars for younguns."

What is interesting here is why the phrase hurt so much more than its gentle speaker ever guessed. The first reason is obvious but important; it italicizes Aunt Bet's singleness and childlessness. But another reason, somewhat less obvious, is far more important. Mr. Tolliver has uttered the phrase in answer to Aunt Bet's protest against Vennie's leaving three-layer chocolate cakes around for the boys to eat when Vance's complexion is already beginning to break out. Vennie's baking and her telling of old stories about Thornton, where she and the Tolliver family and Aunt Bet all had their origins, are her great weapons in her war with Miss Betty for the children's affections. Most significant, they are essentially a woman's weapons, skills that somebody's old granny might be expected to use when trying to win the interest and affections of the young. Miss Betty's weapons, on the contrary, are no different from those a man might wield, money and those things, such as treats, excursions, and a car, that money can buy. So simply recalling this phrase, and the weapons of war it suggests, serves as powerful evidence in Miss Betty's dis-

covery of the essential defeminization her way of life has brought her to.

Here, as elsewhere, Mr. Taylor's tremendous ability to give meaningful order to the parts of his stories plays a major part in the fiction's success. We are given everything we need to help us see why a character makes the key discovery that he does, but it is given with just enough indirection that we don't make our own discovery ahead of his. We might put the matter another way: Mr. Taylor's endings seem inevitable, but hardly predictable. As in a good detective story, the clues are all there; but they are given when our attention is aimed elsewhere. How Mr. Taylor differs from the typical detective story writer is pretty obvious: his clues root deep in character and human need and often in an entire way of life.

"The Little Cousins" is a classic of this sort of writing. The story is told of a time when its narrator, now grown up, was still a boy of nine, give or take one birthday. At its end he breaks down and weeps when his sister joins forces with Mary Elizabeth Caswell and when their colored nurse, Bessie Calhoun, disappears to take the train for Selma, Alabama, to attend her mother's funeral and her sister's wedding (*sic*). Until that moment, we have not fully realized how much this boy fears another loss like that of his dead mother, or to how great a degree Bessie has replaced his mother. We know his dependence on his sister much more clearly, but this too is a force we are likely to underestimate slightly. Yet every bit of evidence for every one of these discoveries appears much earlier in the story. To seize upon a single instance, Corinna's joining forces with Mary Elizabeth Caswell constitutes a terrible betrayal for her small brother. After all, Mary Elizabeth has functioned as the special example-and-rebuke, the older-child-who-did-it-better, that Bessie reserves for *Corinna*. The little brother suffers under Mary Elizabeth's example consciously only for Corinna's sake and unconsciously chiefly because sharing a common enemy will bring him closer to his sister. Thus, when on the night that Mary Elizabeth is crowned queen of the Veiled Prophet's Ball and Corinna willingly befriends her and speaks of experiences she has shared with her brother as if they were hers alone, he is understandably heartsick to see her betray him for an enemy who is his only because she *was* hers. But although Corinna's desertion of him for one portion of the adult world somehow catches the reader by surprise, it is carefully prepared for. We see it in her too grown-up vocabulary, in her fondness for "old best-sellers on the shelves of what had been [her] mother's sitting room," in her mothering of all the small neighbor children, whom she calls "the little cousins." And the laws that govern her age group, the glamour that surrounds Mary Elizabeth that night, all play their obvious parts in Corinna's turning away from a brother three years her junior.

Corinna's desertion is terrible to him for another reason: "she could always find the right words for my feelings as well as her own." Just as Corinna is the one who makes him articulate about his own frustrations, so Bessie Calhoun is the most clearly evident author of those frustrations. Cruel, arbitrary, forgiving, indulgent, she is of the essence *mother* for the boy. (For the reader, she is much more: perhaps the finest static character Mr. Taylor has created, and surely the funniest.)

"The Little Cousins" is a triumph in structure. Like **"Bad Dreams"** and **"Two Ladies in Retirement,"** everything in the story stands in a new perspective as a result of its ending. What was mere brick and four-by-four and mortar has now taken on fresh identity in the completed building. It is this that gives Mr. Taylor's best stories their perspicuity. The whole story stands clear in memory because each moment and incident was part of a total design and, the design remembered, the parts fall into place. (Mr. Taylor's stories are also perspicuous in the non-honorific, non-pejorative sense: a lazy reader would make fewer mistakes when he described those in Faulkner or in most Welty stories.)

This perspicuity answers, in part, the question why Mr. Taylor chose to limit himself in so many ways. By neglecting some things, he has been able to do others supremely well. If he does not give us magnificent action scenes, he is one of the few writers to approach Tolstoy's talents in two other significant respects: (1) the ability to see in every act a man or woman performs some expression of that being's total history; (2) the ability to create real families and extremely moving scenes of family life. More than this, Mr. Taylor has achieved a third thing that we have no right to expect of a work as wide-ranging and inclusive as *War and Peace:* he has produced short stories that are perspicuous and unified gems. (pp. 564-77)

> *Morgan Blum, "Peter Taylor: Self-Limitation in Fiction," in* The Sewanee Review, *Vol. LXX, No. 4, Autumn, 1962, pp. 559-78.*

Ashley Brown (essay date 1962)

[*Brown is an American educator, essayist, translator, and critic. In the following essay, he analyzes several of Taylor's early works.*]

Mr. Taylor has been publishing stories for twenty-five years now—his first two appeared in the little magazine *River* in 1937—and one is surprised that he is still sometimes referred to, despite his comparative youth, as a "young writer." In fact he was unusually gifted and assured even as an apprentice, and when *A Long Fourth and Other Stories* was published in 1948 he was already a leading member of his literary generation. Following Miss Welty's *A Curtain of Green* (1941) and J. F. Powers' *The Prince of Darkness and Other Stories* (1947), *A Long Fourth* was one of the best collections of short fiction which appeared during the forties. Meanwhile Mr. Taylor has quietly produced a small but impressive body of work which demands a critical presentation; he can no longer simply be put down as one of the young Southerners.

A Long Fourth was introduced by Robert Penn Warren, who described its subject as " . . . the contemporary, urban, middle-class world of the upper South. . . . It is a world vastly uncertain of itself and the ground of its values, caught in a tangle of modern commercialism and traditions and conventions gone to seed, confused among pie-

---

Taylor on symbolism in stories:

I think writing stories is rather like dreaming, and that if you have a certain temperament or sensibility, you'll have an affinity for certain symbols that will make the story have its impact. I resent a lot of the symbolic values in Joyce and other writers. For instance "The Dead" I think is a wonderful story, a naturalistic story, and I don't deny the interpretations that are put on it, the Christian interpretation on that and on "Araby," but I just sort of shrug and say, "Yes, that's there," and I'm sure it helped Joyce write the story maybe, but I think he wrote a good story almost in spite of those instead of because of them. I think that interpretation of "Araby" about the medieval search for the Grail—I can see it in there, but it's not what makes it a wonderful story. Or in "The Dead," I don't deny the interpretation of the crucifix, but I think it's fiction, I think it's the last scene when her lover dies out in the rain. I don't deny the symbols—I might, except that if you go through the story and look at the names of the characters, you'll see that it's very suspicious, that they are the right characters—Malins for . . . Eden, Freddy Malins is the character—from *mal,* you see. Joyce may have done all that, but I don't like that either, names—I try not to get a name that is too significant or symbolic.

> *Peter Taylor, in an interview with J. H. E. Paine,* Journal of the Short Story in English, *1987.*

---

ties and pretensions." Now Mr. Warren is correct but perhaps misleading about this. Is Mr. Taylor really picturing the urban middle-class South? Is he concerned primarily with the cultural milieu? Certainly many of the forms and manners of this society are "done" in the most precise detail even as they are dissolving; the future social historian will find a good source here. But Mr. Taylor is not directly interested (as writer) in the public institutions of church and state which have absorbed so much of the South's energy. He does not take us, for example, to the political rally or the adult Bible class. A Southerner is frequently reminded of these things. (In my state university a faculty group was recently informed by several of its members that Wednesday night is for prayer meetings and is therefore unsuitable for official university business.) Indeed one is struck by the lack of "public" life in Mr. Taylor's stories. Almost nobody goes to church or votes. Religion and politics are intended mainly for other people, like old Senator Caswell in the play *Tennessee Day in St. Louis,* who is considered quite absurd by the younger members of his family. (People *are* increasingly suspicious of politics: A friend of mine, who bears the name of one of the historic political families of the lower South, shocked his parents by successfully running for a minor office in New Haven, Connecticut.)

Yet Mr. Taylor is entirely true to a leading feature of Southern society. Mr. Warren pointed out that six of the seven stories in *A Long Fourth* involve the disintegration of family life. Here we arrive at the definition of Mr. Taylor's subject: it is precisely the family, its slow decline and its occasional survival, that he is concerned with. When he departs from this subject or works on its periphery, his fictional convention usually becomes reminiscence, as in **"1939,"** which is a charming memoir of Kenyon College in its little golden age of a generation ago, but to what purpose? Mr. Lytle (in *The Sewanee Review,* 1958) has described the family in *Tennessee Day in St. Louis* as the archetypal institution of Southern society; and he might have followed Aristotle in describing it as the basic equilibrium of *any* society. It is Mr. Taylor's special achievement, then, to have presented his characters almost entirely within this one institutional setting. Even **"Rain in the Heart"** (which Mr. Warren stated is outside the general subject) is about the bride and groom—implicitly the family—precariously surviving the war and its attendant social disruption. Mr. Lytle of course means the family in the largest sense: a configuration of humanity in which the several generations with their "connections" are a microcosm of the community. (Mr. Lytle would say that the family *is* the community.) Now it may be that the family in this sense is reaching the point of its disappearance. A young playwright and politician, Gore Vidal, who is close to the First Family itself, emphatically stated so last year, and certainly many issues in our national life are based on this (largely unarticulated) premise. In that case I should think that Mr. Taylor's stories would document for us an important phase of our recent history, and not only the history of the South.

We are concerned, however, with Mr. Taylor as an artist. The first thing to say about his early stories is that they exhibit a wide range of style and attack. There is no one style that the reader can point to and identify as Mr. Taylor's. Back of his work one can sense here and there his reading of Chekhov, the Joyce of *Dubliners,* occasionally James, and perhaps Miss Porter. These modern masters have long been read in many quarters, and Mr. Taylor must have absorbed his "sources" even before he started writing. But *A Long Fourth and Other Stories* does have some of the thematic unity of *Dubliners:* childhood, youth, marriage, and maturity: these are the headings which Joyce once gave to his fifteen stories. Similarly the stories in *A Long Fourth* chart the life of the family from childhood to old age. Again—to extend the comparison—Joyce's "The Dead," the culmination of his book, gathers up many of the situations in the earlier stories and dramatizes them at another level. And that is precisely what Mr. Taylor's title story does at the end of *his* book. These seven stories, as the author has grouped them, move through a series of rhetorical shifts which accurately control the various narrative contexts, and this is where the comparison with Joyce is most valid.

As an example of the skill with which Mr. Taylor manages his resources at an early stage of his career, we may take **"Sky Line,"** which dates from 1939. This is a story of loss, and it registers the deterioration of a family by way of a boy who lives in the vivid present and who would seem incapable of viewing his plight in any perspective outside his own. Mr. Taylor, that is, has deliberately scaled down the action to the sensory impressions which are so strongly felt by this adolescent, and, to intensify the case, he has rendered the story in the present tense. He has not even

permitted himself the kind of free-association with which Faulkner brings together past and present as a continuum in the first three parts of *The Sound and the Fury.* What is the justification of this method? The boy lives in an anonymous suburb (outside Memphis perhaps?) where history does not make itself felt and where time is measured by the space that is gradually filled:

> The new Catholic church is hardly finished in August when the new school building is started in the next block. The church is of yellow brick with a great round window above the main doorway. And for the new school the workmen are digging in the ground all through August. The lot they work in has always been covered with waist-high yellow grass, and every day the boy looks at the grass which the workmen have trampled down until it lies flat like the hair on a boy's head. He has never played in that lot with its high grass as he once used to do in the church lot, and has felt that it looked like "the central plains of Africa." But the workmen dig deep, and now the heaps of red dirt look like the "forbidding Caucasian mountains."

In this setting, during the Depression thirties, the boy Jim (whose family name is never stated) gropingly perceives the destruction of feeling and behavior. The very intensity of his perception, moment by moment, which at first seems to preclude any significance, in the end allows him to come to terms with his defeat. I suppose if Joyce or Faulkner were using this familiar situation, the boy would be "initiated" into his manhood through some ritualistic survival, but Mr. Taylor has excluded any appeal to history, and there is no one here who can properly direct the boy's instincts.

At the end of the story there is an ugly scene in which Jim, disillusioned with his father (who has finally married the mistress installed in his dead wife's place), is thwarted in an attempted sexual encounter with his new step-sister. (Jim, that is, wants to repeat his father's action.) The harsh images which invest the scene (the yellow "bilious" light, the "puffy" gray clouds, the girl's red cosmetics) prepare for her sarcastic laughter in "the room which once was his own." But this failure does not break him. For the first time his sensations converge into some kind of meaning, and the scene resolves as the storm erupts around them:

> He doesn't know how long the laughter lasts. The rain falls outside the open window, and now and again a raindrop splashes through the screen onto his face. At last it is almost night when the rain stops, and if there is any unnatural hue in the light, it is green. His heart has stopped pounding now, and all the heat has gone from his face. He has heard the hanging baskets beat against the house and felt the silence after their removal. He has heard the baseball smacking in the wet gloves of the men and seen the furniture auctioned on the lawn. The end of his grandmother, the death of his mother, the despair of his father, and the resignation of his new stepmother are all in his mind. The remarkable thing in the changed view from the window which had once been his lies in the tall apartment houses

which punctuate the horizon and in the boxlike, flat-roofed ones in his own neighborhood. Through this window the girl too, he knows, must have beheld changes. He takes his hand from the sill and massages his taut face on which the raindrops have dried.

When he faces her again, he says that they must prepare some sort of welcome, that they must get busy.

What I have tried to establish is that Mr. Taylor's method in this case has paid off handsomely. These characters *are* trapped in the present moment. The family must have come from somewhere and have some communal memories and inherited forms, but these things have dwindled away in this anonymous place. J. F. Powers in "Blue Island," a recent and more sardonic story of suburbia, has used a larger social reference than Mr. Taylor, but the effect of chaos is no more powerful.

Following **"Sky Line"** in *A Long Fourth* is **"A Spinster's Tale,"** which was written even earlier. Here the dissolution of the family is more gradual and more subtle in its revelation. The narrator, Elizabeth, a motherless child, is misplaced in a masculine household. Her gentle father and her amiably drunken brother and her uncles cannot replace the balance lost by the death of her mother. The equilibrium of this family, where old-fashioned courtly manners still prevail (it is Nashville in the first decade of the century), is deceptive, simply because the masculine courtesy has no true challenge from the other sex, and Elizabeth, being young, is discouraged by this masculine indirection:

> It was, I thought, their indifferent shifting from topic to topic that most discouraged me. Then I decided that it was the tremendous gaps that there seemed to be between the subjects that was bewildering to me. Still again I thought that it was the equal interest which they displayed for each subject that was dismaying. All things in the world were equally at home in their arguments. They exhibited equal indifference to the horrors that each topic might suggest; and I wondered whether or not their imperturbability was a thing that they had achieved.

The "ladylike" style of this story is beautifully sustained by Mr. Taylor. In a way it is a period style, where echoes of the old finishing-school and its Latinate education provide a kind of linguistic convention: "But I had learned not to concern myself with so general and so unreal a problem until I had cleared up more particular and real ones." The young lady in this story, that is, would appear to have a sensibility which is less perceptive than that of the boy in **"Sky Line."** But her prim response to events is nevertheless devastating in its results.

Through the center of the story moves Mr. Speed, a fallen gentleman of the community whose drunken pathos has long been tolerated with good humor by the men in Elizabeth's family, but who is a fearful affront to her. She is outside a closed circle in which the men, who live by a code of indirection, refuse to acknowledge the breakdown of civilized behavior which Mr. Speed represents. And of course there is no matriarch to provide the example of au-

thority on the feminine side. Thus Mr. Speed becomes to Elizabeth the symbol of brutality and indifference which she finds in *all* men. The innocent social rituals of her father and uncles, from which she is excluded, are to her the source of depravity: "As their voices grew louder and merrier, my courage slackened. It was then I first put into words the thought that in my brother and father I saw something of Mr. Speed. And I knew it was more than a taste for whisky they had in common." At the climax of the story Mr. Speed, during a heavy rain, beats on the door and is admitted by the servant. Elizabeth, reacting to his helpless rage with an "innocent" violence of her own, calls the police and has him humiliated—something her father would never do. The final paragraph brings to a focus everything which has gone wrong; the even tone of the speaker (a willed rage to order, as it were) conveys the horror that lurks below:

> I never discussed the events of that day with my father, and I never saw Mr. Speed again. But, despite the surge of pity I felt for the old man on our porch that afternoon, my hatred and fear of what he had stood for in my eyes has never left me. And since the day that I watched myself say "away" in the mirror, not a week has passed but that he has been brought to my mind by one thing or another. It was only the other night that I dreamed I was a little girl on Church Street again and that there was a drunk horse in our yard.

In **"The Fancy Woman"** (1940) the violence is real and the social dissolution is far more advanced. Here we are almost in John O'Hara's world, where the family exists merely as a convenient arrangement for "the best people"; it is not an institution in the old sense at all. But the attachments between the members of the family, being the expression of self-love, are passionate and indeed excessive, since there is no longer the configuration of humanity to balance the affections. The action in this case turns on the vanity of a rich Memphis business man who, having separated from his wife, brings a prostitute to his house and forces her to be the respectable hostess to his guests and his adolescent sons; but things do not work out so easily. (The wife, who has now taken a lover of her own, sends the boys to their father.) The situation of **"Sky Line"** is compounded; the brutality of feeling is almost total. The author approaches the subject by having the prostitute, Josie Carlson, near the post of observation, and he thus complicates the focus of the story in an unexpected manner. This girl is from the countryside and she retains in her own way a crude natural perception and even a sense of propriety which are lacking in the "refined" guests in her lover's house. But eventually she is the victim of her feelings; she cannot force herself to leave her equivocal rôle; and she will be broken:

> She locked her door and threw the big key across the room. She knocked the bottle of toilet water and the amber brush off the dressing table as she made room for the victrola. When she had started "Louisville Lady" playing she sat on the stool and began to wonder. "The kid's head was like a ball of gold, but I'm not gonna think about him ever once I get back to Memphis," she told her-

self. "No, by damn, but I wonder just what George'll do to me." She broke the blue seal of the whisky with her fingernail, and it didn't seem like more than twenty minutes or half an hour before George was beating and kicking on the door, and she was sitting on the stool and listening and just waiting for him to break the door, and wondering what he'd do to her.

Mr. Taylor has quite successfully conveyed the "feel" of this suburban milieu and this calculating family as they appear to Josie Carlson; but he has not sentimentalized her, that is, given in to her point of view; the language is finally the author's. Her judgment of the family is a partial one at best; and, as Mr. Warren says, "In the end, it is the movement and temper of her being, and the ambivalence that this gives the story, that engage our interest."

These early stories all end in incidental violence, but it is not the violence of tragedy. There is no hero anywhere in sight, and suffering is private and ironic as the social situation dwindles behind the individuals who emerge in the foreground. In the case of **"Sky Line"** especially I have stated that history no longer operates effectively; the characters do not have the dignity of a myth, of an historic rôle, however imperfect, behind them. (My political friend in New Haven once said, "It's rather nice to have a social myth in the background, even if no one lives up to it.") Sometimes they try to summon up a feeling for the heroic. For instance the young soldier in **"Rain in the Heart"** reads Civil War history while he is in service in Tennessee (fairly obviously, Chattanooga) during World War II. The foreign battlefield he may fight on seems "distant and almost abstract," and he tries to find a meaning in this Southern landscape:

> The sergeant's eyes had now grown so accustomed to the darkness inside and outside that he could look down between the trees on the slope of the ridge. He imagined there the line after line of Union soldiers that had once been thrown into the battle to take this ridge at all cost. The Confederate general's headquarters were not more than two blocks away. If he and she had been living in those days he would have seen ever so clearly the Cause for that fighting. And *this* battlefield would not be abstract. He would have stood here holding back the enemy from the very land which was his own, from the house in which she awaited him.

But like the protagonist in Mr. Tate's Ode, he must dismiss the heroic age as illusory. Some of these characters, however, live a kind of double existence; their memories of "the old times" (a very recurrent phrase) keep them from being altogether committed to the world around them. Mr. Taylor's later and more characteristic work, in fact, is essentially social comedy in which the incongruities of past and present offer an inexhaustible source of materials.

Such a work is **"A Long Fourth,"** the culmination of Mr. Taylor's first book. In this story Harriet Wilson, the good Nashville matriarch, is faced with a series of crises within her family which even her sympathetic husband "Sweetheart" cannot solve. Naturally affectionate, she does not

understand why her children should wish to be otherwise. Her daughters, who are very tall, do not attract many beaux, and Harriet reflects that "In her own day there had been more tall men, and tall women were then considered graceful." The daughters not only refuse to be conventional Southern belles; they are frequently coarse in their behavior. Son, the family's only heir, is likewise unconventional: a brilliant student at the university, he has gone to New York, where he is said to have "radical" ideas which get into the "disturbing" articles he is writing with such success. Now he is returning home for the long Fourth of July week end with his "friend" Miss Prewitt, who edits a birth-control magazine. The Wilsons, given this younger generation, would seem to have a dubious future. But Harriet is very proud of her son, and on the eve of his induction into the Army during World War II, she anticipates his home-coming with delight and apprehension. Mr. Taylor has a double-plot here. Harriet's beloved servant, Auntie Mattie, the Negro matriarch, has *her* troubles with her nephew BT, who is to Harriet a "sullen, stinking, thieving, fornicating" scoundrel; and like Son he is about to be inducted into the Service. When Auntie Mattie draws a comparison between Son's departure and BT's, Harriet is affronted and she withdraws in irrational anger:

> . . . she felt it her bounden duty to in some way make that black woman feel the grossness of her wrong and ultimately to drive her off the premises. And it was in this vein, this very declamatory language, this elevated tone with which Harriet expressed herself in the solitude of her room. She was unconsciously trying to use the language and the rhetoric of her mother and of the only books with which she had ever had much acquaintance. Between the moments when she even pictured Mattie's being tied and flogged or thought of Mama's uncle who shot all of his niggers before he would free them and of the Negro governor of North Carolina and the Negro senate rolling whisky barrels up the capitol steps, of the rape and uprisings in Memphis and the riots in Chicago, between these thoughts she would actually consider the virtue of her own wrath. And recalling her Greek classes at Miss Hood's school she thought without a flicker of humor of Achilles' indignation.

Her rage subsides, however, and, as the week end proceeds, it is increasingly difficult for her to make her moral discriminations according to received convention. Her ungainly daughters, for instance, present themselves in a more attractive way in her moment of crisis. Miss Prewitt, the "terrible woman of the future" (as Henry James would say), finally assumes the traditional rôle of romantic passion which Harriet would covet for her daughters. Son, the perfect gentleman, becomes the cold, indifferent observer of other people's weaknesses. And Mattie, out of her own confusions and sentiments, forces Harriet to a strange humility which brings no rewards:

> Mattie raised her eyes to her mistress, and there was neither forgiveness nor resentment in them. In her protruding lower lip and in her wide nostrils there was a defiance, but it was a defiance of the general nature of this world where she must pass her days, not of Harriet in particular.

In her eyes there was grief and there was something beyond grief. After a moment she did speak, and she told Harriet that she was going to sit here all night and that they had all better go on to bed in the house. Later when Harriet tried to recall the exact tone and words Mattie had used—as her acute ear would normally have allowed her to do—she could not reconstruct the speech at all. It seemed as though Mattie had used a special language common to both of them but one they had never before discovered and could now never recover. Afterward they faced each other in incommunicative silence for an indefinite time. Finally Harriet moved to the door again, but she looked back once more and she saw that besides the grief and hostility in Mattie's eyes there was an unspeakable loneliness for which she could offer no consolation.

This last scene in **"A Long Fourth"** is comparable to that last scene in "The Dead" where Gabriel Conroy is confronted with *his* vanities and illusions. The family social occasion, in each case, has ironically provided the setting for the revelation, but Mr. Taylor's situation contains a further irony: his Harriet Wilson in a sense *is* the family, whereas Joyce's Gabriel Conroy is mostly peripheral to the social situation—his ideas about other people's actions are ineffective and private.

"A Long Fourth" thus carries forward the situations of the earlier stories, and there is a new assurance about the author's practice which can be seen in his treatment of Harriet Wilson. As matriarch, she embodies many of the representative features of the Southern family, and her part in society is decisive. It is Mr. Taylor's contention that after the Civil War the men of the South, as they pursued money as an end in itself, largely abandoned their privileges as arbiters of civilization and left them to their wives and daughters. One of his later books, *The Widows of Thornton,* explores the results of this historic shift. But already in **"A Long Fourth"** one sees how the two matriarchs—white and black—control the ethos of the family, and the final scene is absolutely central to the subject. Harriet and Mattie, in fact, are the only persons who actually *suffer* the revelation of the family's failure.

In *A Woman of Means* (1950), a short novel, Mr. Taylor has extended the subject by way of the St. Louis matriarch, Anna Lauterbach, who is not Southern at all but who perhaps envies the Southern code which makes possible the importance of a woman like herself. She is deceived. She is very rich as the result of the money left to her by her father and her first husband, but she chooses to marry Gerald Dudley, the young business man from Tennessee, partly because she fancies that he represents something old-fashioned and substantial that she has lacked in her own money society, partly because she wants a son; and Gerald Dudley's son by *his* first marriage thus becomes an asset. But Anna cannot play the rôle of matriarch effectively—not under these conditions. She wants to be loved for herself; when she was a girl her father stressed her importance as a private person by naming his house Casa Anna; and this virtual cult of individual fulfillment does havoc to the social relationship. As for Gerald Dudley, his rejection of his Tennessee background is a matter

of "hard-headed" principle. If his attempt to live by "business ethics" in the St. Louis of the twenties is not altogether successful, that is not because he refuses to play the game. Since he is the husband of a rich woman, his position in her house and with her daughters is always equivocal, and this is symbolized by the billiard room, the only room in the house where he "seemed to have taken possession." His young son figures his career in this single image:

> My father was a picture of youthful virtue justly rewarded. The half-forgotten times when I had seen him in boarding house parlors, in small hotel rooms, on day coaches, returned to me for a minute now and made me aware of the complete elegance of this room. Then the thought that this wasn't anything but a poolroom, no matter how elaborately fitted out with red draperies and green plush couches, strengthened my first impression. And suddenly Father was saying, "You like it here, don't you, son?"
>
> "Yes, sir," I said. "Yes, sir."

It is the boy, Quintus Cincinnatus Lovell Dudley, who occupies the fictional center. He respects his father and loves his stepmother, and up to a point he has a charmed life. He is, as it were, a pawn in a game played by Gerald Dudley and his new wife. His "Southern-ness," which at first seems to exclude him from his class-mates at the Country Day School, presently becomes his advantage. (Like other Southerners in exile, he finds that the sentimental Northern image of the South can be turned to good account.) But the game eventually breaks down. Gerald Dudley fails in business through the treachery of his associates, and deprived of his "manhood" he acts irrationally towards his wife. She, always at the mercy of the men in her family (her indulgent father, then her erratic first husband), gives way under the strain and goes mad. These disasters are observed and indeed participated in by the boy. More than his father, he feels the pull of "the old times" in Tennessee from which he was wrenched, but which he too knows cannot sustain his father in his present predicament. At the end of the novel Mr. Taylor has the boy obsessively reading the newspaper stories about Charles Lindbergh, the hero of a "high-flying" decade, who says, as he is lifted from *The Spirit of St. Louis,* "Well, I made it." The successful modern Daedalus thus contrasts with the fallen Gerald Dudley, about whom one of the step-daughters delivers this comment:

> "Poor Father," she said, half in exasperation, half in sympathy. "Poor *man.*" Then she turned, facing him again, and I could hear her heels scrape on the tile floor of the conservatory. Neither of them spoke for a time. At last she said, "Of course, nobody's really to blame. It's only the circumstances, and this dreadful life here in St. Louis."

This family, brought together for a time under very precarious circumstances, will not even survive as a convenient arrangement; each of its members elects to make his own way in an uncertain social order.

One might call *A Woman of Means* the farthest extension of Mr. Taylor's subject; the dissolution of the family could hardly proceed beyond this point. But the subject is far from exhausted here, and Mr. Taylor has demonstrated in his later work that he can use it effectively at various levels at different moments in the historic decline. I should mention as examples of his versatility **"Bad Dreams"** in *The Widows of Thornton* (perhaps his most powerful story), **"Heads of Houses"** and **"Guests"** in *Happy Families Are All Alike,* and *Tennessee Day in St. Louis.* Sometimes one senses . . . that he has drawn the subject thin and dulled his perceptions, as though he wished to confer dignity on a family which has in fact already lost its equilibrium. Sometimes he falls into a nostalgia which is unwarranted; the phrase "the old times" occurs too often to be convincing, because Mr. Taylor is essentially ironic about history, and many of his characters have accepted the world as it is. Indeed there is scarcely any Southern writer who depends less on the great myth of the South as it has been raised by Faulkner and his generation, and perhaps in forfeiting this advantage Mr. Taylor has lost something. But I should think that he has gained something, too, because he has a special insight into the way our society presents itself at this moment, and his subject should continue to produce a rich yield. (pp. 588-602)

> Ashley Brown, *"The Early Fiction of Peter Taylor,"* in The Sewanee Review, *Vol. LXX, No. 4, Autumn, 1962, pp. 588-602.*

Jan Pinkerton   (essay date 1970)

[*Pinkerton is an American educator and critic. In the following essay, he argues that Taylor's regional writings possess universal themes and that Taylor is an advocate of social change.*]

Under the title "Southern-Fried," a writer in a national weekly recently reviewed *The Collected Stories of Peter Taylor* and proclaimed that we have had

> enough of eccentric or incestuous families tending their faded houses and lives, enough social events which the teen-aged children of "good" families attend in now-decadent mansions, enough about the humiliating behavior of not-so-nice relatives and "fancy ladies" who drink too much.

The reviewer concludes, in fact, that "Taylor's return to the same insipid, if not insidious, situations, events, remembrances and nostalgia finally implicates and indicts the author as much as his work." And Taylor's final error: "He does take these people seriously." The author is indicted, in other words, by his continuing to deal with—and to take seriously—the characters he draws from a presumably out-of-fashion regional setting.

It must be said, of course, that much of this pique is directed not at the region itself but at the social hierarchy associated with that region. The reviewer is attacking the depiction of what is supposedly a quaint form of snobbery. Yet, we might ask, how different are the class distinctions in Taylor's milieu from those in any other part of the country? Do they differ, in basic ways, from all the other forms of social stratification currently alive and flourishing in America? Certainly one of the stories scornfully referred to, **"The Fancy Woman,"** explores subtleties of social am-

bition that would be considered trenchant and incisive if the setting were not Memphis, Tennessee—or if the stereotypes evoked by that setting did not immediately click into readers' minds. In fact, the story documents, mainly by negative example, the criteria for determining a person's place within a social hierarchy—a matter which is as subtle and yet as all-prevailing today as it has ever been, and which finds distinct incarnations in such varied locales as the university campus, Harlem, or exurban Connecticut.

Yet perhaps this story has not been as well understood as it might be. Perhaps many of Taylor's stories, in fact, have been read in terms of stereotypes—and of consequent value judgments, both favorable and unfavorable—that a closer examination would demonstrate to be inaccurate. The current collection, although containing only about half the author's published stories, nevertheless provides an opportunity for discovering some of the special qualities that take him far beyond the generalizations usually offered to explain lesser-known Southern writers. Taylor draws upon a specific milieu, to be sure, but he frequently entertains ideas that contradict the dogmas popularly believed to be the point of all Southern literature. In terms of regional stereotypes, then, his stories should be seen, not as chronicles of more of the same "situations, events, remembrances and nostalgia," but as treatments of these matters that are controversial and even heretical. We have already suggested that certain "Southern" themes—of which Taylor makes considerable use—are not exclusively regional at all; we must now explain the specific heresies that Taylor propounds when he deals with these themes.

Another "regional" matter, then—beyond that of social stratification—is the presumed Southern attitude toward the past. The reviewer we have quoted implies that Taylor also, like all Southerners, is in love with the past; like the elderly Aunt Munsie, "the author too seems to believe that those really were the good ole days." That Taylor is nostalgic for the past is, to be sure, a standard critical statement made by even the most favorable readers; he has long been pronounced a writer of jeremiads lamenting the breakdown of traditional modes of life. But what the reviewer and most critics have failed to see is the distinction that must be made between Aunt Munsie and many of the other characters, on the one hand, and Taylor, the author, on the other. The character who mourns the past is usually shown by the author, through a variety of narrative techniques, to be limited in perception, to be ignoring obvious truths of the past, to be fantasizing an ideal age that never existed. We might add, of course, that such unrealistic thinking is not peculiar to one region. Yet it has, like the concept of a social hierarchy, been associated with the South—and has thereupon been judged harshly, along with the region itself. Taylor, however, is the analyzer of this phenomenon, not its true believer; he views the nostalgic stances of his characters with often-critical detachment, although ultimately he bestows the sympathy he always gives his imperfect human beings.

"Southern" themes of class-consciousness and of nostalgia, then, can be quickly spotted in Taylor's work but must not necessarily be identified with the author's own views.

Many of his stories, in fact, are far more deeply involved in other matters—in personal power plays, in the battle of the sexes, in the human compulsion to play roles, in frigidity, in the loneliness of women. These are issues that transcend region and make it difficult to pin-point any particular ideological formula on the part of the author, beyond the broad and generous outlook that he so clearly holds. There is, moreover, one further cliché from which he should be rescued: he is not the mourner of the decline of the family, that institution traditionally considered the stabilizer of a society. He often records the discontinuities of contemporary family life, but he does not imply that families of the past were superior or preferable; there were always conflicts and neuroses, he makes clear, and even a seemingly stable family façade has always been blighted by the basic and constant flaws in human nature.

Most of Taylor's stories, then, have a Southern setting; most include characters who express a nostalgia for older times; most take place within a disordered family situation. Yet, as we have indicated, the chief substance of the stories is not these more obvious characteristics. The earliest piece in the collection, **"A Spinster's Tale"** (1940), is the study of a girl's psychological warping, set within a family context, to be sure, but most logically because the topic depends on such a setting. The family is disordered, but in this instance it is by the death of the mother; the causes of disruption are medical, not sociological, and the tale is in no way inextricable from the region or paradigmatic of social breakdown. The story itself is of a girl's fears of masculinity and of her development into a formidable woman capable of dealing authoritatively and harshly with the masculine world. It is a tale of frigidity and of the inevitability of spinsterhood, a subject, incidentally, that has been more frequently associated with New England than with the South. Region, in other words, is secondary here, and any clichés, if they exist, are Freudian rather than Southern.

This early story is in many ways complementary to the latest story of the collection, **"Dean of Men"** (1969), the narrative of a man who is determined to succeed in a world of masculinity, to live among men—and not to follow the example of his father and grandfather, who had suffered defeats in business and politics and had retreated to a woman's world of family and household. "A man must somehow go on living among men," he tells his son, whose own ability to play a masculine role the narrator seems to doubt. As he tells tales from the life of both his father and grandfather, he makes clear that the family was at no time an ideal institution, despite the myth to the contrary; it might have served as a refuge, but it always had negative qualities: "People in my grandfather's day disliked admitting they did wretched things to each other at home or that there *were* family scenes in their families." We can conclude, then, that if there is a physical breakdown of the family in modern times, it is only an outward enactment of the disharmonies that have always existed. There is nothing in this story to convince the reader, in other words, that older times were better times. If Taylor is a "conservative" writer, as he has been called, it is not because he looks to the past but because his view of human nature is pessimistic, because he sees a constancy in

human nature, the chief characteristic of which is its imperfectability.

So the narrator of **"Dean of Men"** worries about his role as a man, and the narrator of **"A Spinster's Tale"** worries about how she, as a woman, will deal with men. We can identify, then, a basic theme in Taylor: a concern with role-playing and with personal identity. It is easy to say that this concern ties in, after all, with the breakdown of a stable society and of its chief institution, the family; in more stable times, one could say, role and identity were well governed and understood. But Taylor himself never gives support to such conclusions. Role-playing, a constant and universal human action, is the individual's carrying out of a particular mode of behavior offered by his society; excessive, or even pathological, role-playing can take place within a "stable" society as well as within one that is chaotic. The identity confusions that Taylor portrays, moreover, occur within contexts both of social rigidity and of social laxness. Regional or ideological formulae simply do not apply when a writer is drawing upon a broadly knowledgeable view of human nature.

Yet the claims of region still persist in Taylor's work; it is as inaccurate to deny them completely as it is to insist on their being the ultimate key to the interpretation of his stories. A valid connection with a Southern tradition, for instance, can be found in the manners of the region—the emphasis on forms of etiquette and protocol that persist more wholeheartedly in the South than in other parts of the country. Here is a connection with "role" that can account for Taylor's persistent use of the theme. When an individual participates in formal social codes, he is limiting his range of possible behavior and expression; perhaps a long-time participant develops a special sense of prescriptive role-playing—or perhaps he is merely more conscious of the procedures of living with others. For whatever reason, Taylor is constantly depicting the social formalities that seem to evolve easily into well-defined roles, and (as in **"Guests," "Heads of Houses,"** or **"Cookie"**) these formalities do not necessarily contribute to human happiness. They provide a measure of communication on one level, but they deny it on a deeper level. In a society with divisions between class, race, and sex, a social code can achieve a formal rapport between these divisions, but yet—as Taylor demonstrates with frequency and poignancy—it can exclude a more intimate rapport among those for whom such communion would relieve the loneliness and misunderstanding that bring misery to so many of Taylor's characters.

The ultimate statement on role-playing is to be found in **"Miss Leonora When Last Seen,"** the story of an eccentric small-town spinster given to taking automobile trips in which she assumes various identities: the "great lady" in the lace choker, the farmer's wife in dungarees, or, finally, the Memphis lady in stylish clothes looking for antiques or country hams. It is easy to say, of course, that Miss Leonora has lost her own identity because there is no longer a place for her in modern life or in a family that has dispersed. Yet her "real" self has always been problematic; no one has ever known her well, and the narrator admits that it is "hard for any two people to agree on what she is really like." Even in the past she had often been seen in terms of her external garments; she had at one time been identified by the uniform of a teacher at the Female Institute, and later by "what amounts to a uniform for our high-school teachers—the drab kind of street dresses that can be got through the mail-order catalogues." Nor does she herself see others except in terms of a generalized role; the narrator, formerly a student of hers, finds her seeming awareness of him to be flattering,

> until presently you realized it was merely of you as an individual in her scheme of things for Thomasville. She was still looking at me as though I were one of the village children that she would like so much to make something of.

When people are seen solely in terms of their roles—when human interaction is reduced to merely a kind of protocol—the result is loneliness and isolation. Miss Leonora, herself an abstraction and seeing others as abstractions, has always denied, and been denied, the benefits of human intimacy. The transition, then, from her earliest role as a member of the town's leading family to her latest role, that of a modern tourist, is not necessarily a change for the worse. The narrator of this story laments the change ("She will look too much like a thousand others") but he is shown to be an unremarkable man still committed to the small town; and it is the small town in which Miss Leonora has always been a "character"—but, as such, a public figure and not someone to whom others could relate on an individual or intimate basis. Perhaps her new facelessness, then, is essentially no different from the old; perhaps her new fluidity is even preferable to the stagnation of her previous life. We will return to what seems to be Taylor's heretical espousal of transience, of motion, even of uprootedness.

But there are other stories about the stifling dominance of role over individual personality. There is the example of Miss Patty Bean, for instance, in the story **"Their Losses."** She is one of three women, each with her own sense of loss, who meet on a train outside of Memphis. The loss that Miss Patty articulates is for a past order, although obviously there are other deficiencies in her life as well. Taylor, moreover, clearly not sharing her nostalgia for the past, makes her the most grotesque of the three women. She is bringing home from Washington a dying aunt, whom she sees as a symbol of past superiority; her people, she makes clear, were "not of *this* world but of *a* world that we have seen disappear. In mourning my family, I mourn that world's disappearance." Yet she feels no obligation to express love for these people as individuals; they are mourned solely for their roles in a larger abstraction: "How I regarded the members of my family as individuals is neither here nor there." It is obvious, in fact, that love was singularly lacking in Miss Patty's relations with others. Moreover, there are final revelations in the story: first, that the aunt has turned Roman Catholic; second, that she is a mental patient who does not remember the members of the family at all. Everything that Miss Patty has made her a symbol of is, ironically, not only dying, but also, like the aunt, alien and demented. Miss Patty's reverence for her family's role leads us to question the soundness of that

role—and the soundness and credibility of the world of the past as well.

Indeed the most grotesque of all the Taylor characters in this collection are also those most attached to an idealized past: the old Dorset brother and sister of **"Venus, Cupid, Folly and Time."** They, too, play roles ("We are all young, we all love one another") and, like Miss Leonora, they cast the young people of the town into collective roles. At their parties for the socially acceptable young people, they make no individual distinctions among them: they "made no effort to distinguish which of their guests was which. . . . The way they had gazed *at* the little face instead of into it had revealed their lack of interest in the individual child." It is, of course, the Dorsets' lack of individual distinctions that makes it possible for the children to add the extra guest, a procedure which itself involves role-playing among the young people and which brings the Dorsets' party-giving to its bizarre end. Thus the old people are defeated by being totally lost in abstraction, an abstract sense of their own lives, an abstract sense of the lives around them.

We cannot say, therefore, that Miss Leonora, Miss Patty, or the Dorsets are the way they are because the modern world has betrayed their mode of life. Taylor lays no blame on the times, on modernization, on industrialism, on a new commercial economy. In a number of stories he explains what did go wrong: it was the failure of these people either to initiate change or to respond to change. The Dorsets talk about proper breeding and they scorn the idea of money, but yet at the end of the story we learn how their own family had been established in Chatham:

> They were an obscure mercantile family who came to invest in a new Western city. Within two generations the business—no, the industry!—which they established made them rich beyond any dreams they could have had in the beginning. For half a century they were looked upon, if any family ever was, as our first family.

So it was money after all that made the Dorsets what they were. But most of the family moved on to other successful ventures, leaving behind only the old brother and sister who now claimed disgust at money and commercialism. If it is easy to speak of the breakdown of the stable Southern family and the loss of old virtues, Taylor clearly countermands such facile conclusions in this story. Instead of lamenting decaying families, he introduces the question, *Why* is this family decaying? And the answer is that this old brother and sister are the ones who have *not* picked up stakes and moved on elsewhere. It is for this reason that they are now sterile and decadent. The other members of the family, says the narrator, "knew that what they had in Chatham they could buy more of in other places. For them Chatham was an investment that had paid off." And so they moved on to Santa Barbara and Long Beach, Newport, or Long Island. It was commercialism that made this family in the first place; its decline, as embodied by the old bachelor and spinster, is *from* commercialism to gentility, not the other way around. In fact, admits the narrator, the spirit of the early Dorsets was really close to that of the rest of the people in Chatham: "The obvious difference was that we had to stay on here and pretend that our life had a meaning which it did not." That is precisely what the brother and sister had done. They were those without the vigor for further ventures, and so they settled down into make-believe, pretending that their way of life was the old way, the meaningful way. This, too, was role-playing. And the conclusion is unmistakable: all the "meaning" of the old order is pretense, an elaborate defensiveness on the part of those who are non-enterprising and defeatist.

The beginnings of this pretense, indeed, can be seen in the fact that some of these families, while spending their time elsewhere making money, nevertheless tried to block "progress" in their own home towns. Miss Leonora's family was guilty of this maneuver, and so was Mrs. Billingsby's family in **"Mrs. Billingsby's Wine."** The latter family tried to prevent street lights and sidewalks in the small town of Blackwell; yet "they went off long ago to Memphis and St. Louis and even Detroit and made or married stacks of money." One old-timer used to say, "Ever time they seen a dollar they taken after it and they never stopped a-running till they cotched it." Yet Mrs. Billingsby, one of those who left Blackwell, is gracious, personally kind. Money, obviously, does not harm one, the preaching of the Dorsets notwithstanding. Nor, apparently, does urban life. Mrs. Billingsby has left the small town, has lived in Memphis for forty years; and she has none of the eccentricity of the less-affluent Miss Leonora, who stayed behind. Their families pursued similar paths, seeking money and seeking urbanization, although both families tried to keep the new from the town of their origin; but Mrs. Billingsby, while less of a "character" than Miss Leonora, is surely more gracious than the spinster who indulges in ludicrous role-playing and sees the townspeople only as abstract role-players as well. Mrs. Billingsby, in fact—and this is one of the points of the story— remembers in individual terms the young woman from Blackwell who calls on her. And she is, of course, far removed from the bizarre Dorsets, who also stayed in the small town, speaking vehemently against money and commerce.

What is the moral of these stories? It seems to be: keep moving, be open to new experiences. The alternative is to stagnate. Yet is this a "Southern" theme or a Yankee theme? It sounds like the essence of the putative American experience, the official American code of conduct. The Southerners Taylor writes about, in other words, are those who stagnated because they did not move on, who fell into worship of an unreal past because they did not keep themselves refreshed by new ideas. This is Taylor's message, his heresy. He is a Southern writer who distrusts the past, a conservative writer who believes in change; those who see him as a stereotyped regionalist are themselves blinded by their clichéd responses to setting and style. (pp. 432-40)

> *Jan Pinkerton, "The Non-Regionalism of Peter Taylor," in* The Georgia Review, *Vol. XXIV, No. 4, Winter, 1970, pp. 432-40.*

Alfred Kazin (essay date 1971)

[*A highly respected American literary critic, Kazin is best known for his essay collections* The Inmost Leaf *(1955) and* Contemporaries *(1962), and particularly for* On Native Grounds *(1942), a study of American prose writing since the era of William Dean Howells. In the following excerpt, he characterizes the social background of Taylor's stories.*]

Taylor's fiction takes up directly the subtle moral disarrangements and dislocations within a seemingly immobile middle class. Taylor is all fiction writer and does not seem to want to be anything more. The "little inch of ivory" on which everything is worked out gives his stories an effect of necessity and realization. The shifts are entirely within the stories, do not take us through those harshly contrasting changes of time, scene, history which in many bigwriting Southern novelists embody violence to the person even when the novelist seems to be doing all the moving around.

Taylor loves to recite the brand names of candy companies and insurance companies. His subject *is* the executive middle class—its assurances subtly breaking down, the rearrangements being made under the surface. The top middle class seems to be authority in Nashville, but a key situation is the minimizing and subtle reversal of its authority. Authority actually has no power here; the surface of Taylor's stories, entirely domestic, often suburban, conceals the intense Brownian movement of emotions under the surface. Yet these dislocations or rearrangements of authority are more than usually quiet; the manner of a Taylor story is entirely part of the manners it describes, and seems to follow from them; Taylor has just left the party to think it over, but will rejoin it presently. We are in a world where an intense sense of duplication exists from person to person in the same family, from family to family in the same town, from the manner of the story to the matter, from the transparency and pure utility of Taylor's prose to these suburban Southern lives entirely absorbed in the details of living. The closeness of Taylor's workmanship perfectly reflects the habitual unconscious closeness of the group being emphasized here. The crisis usually turns on the sudden awareness of what all this routine has done. Illumination is all. There is almost never any decision forced by violence. There are usually no decisions. There is only the subtle displacement in silent minds still separate from each other.

But the disturbance to the woman in the family, the central domestic figure, registers the seemingly mild but irreversible shock to a "superior" way of life kept intact by family, money and routine. The "disturbance" to a woman is fundamental. The woman is left with the routine; the men have moved on. The men insist that families and traditions be kept up, but they are not there. In **"The Dark Walk,"** the most concentrated expression of this theme, the widow Sylvia Harrison realizes that "the husbands and fathers in those houses were not the tyrants of another day; . . . it seemed to Sylvia that the husbands had not been there at all. . . . Their lives had been changed in a way that the women's lives were not changed. The men of Nate's time had crossed over a border, had pushed into a new country, or had fled into a new country. And their brides lived as widows clinging to things the men would never come back to and from which they could not free themselves. . . ." Miss Betty in **"Two**

Ladies in Retirement," a story of women as genteel fossils and vestiges, fondly talks about people who had been "prominent in an important way." And Miss Bluemeyer, the old-maid housekeeper to the Wade family in the play *The Death of a Kinsman,* finally speaks out—"I understand a good deal of how this family business works. It makes a woman safe and sure being related this way and that way to everybody around her. And it keeps you from having to bother about anybody else, since they are not 'kinfolks.' " The women are getting mad in both senses of the word. The Negro women servants break out before their men do; in **"Bad Dreams"** the head of the family reflects that the butler's wife, "a good, hard-working, smart sort of a woman . . . at a moment's notice could get a look so bughouse-wild in her face that you felt you had to talk fast if you were going to keep her calm. Bert's mother had been that sort of woman too. In fact, he felt that most of the women he had ever had much to do with had been that sort. . . ."

There is far less violence in Peter Taylor than there is in Carson McCullers and Flannery O'Connor; but this seemingly intact world in which drama follows only from slight, soundless changes of consciousness has as its center a woman's sensibility precisely because of the contrast between the position she upholds and the slow, inner sapping of her life. The absence of "scenes," friction, strong movement of any kind, is the mark of a good breeding that seems to have worn the material smooth. The craftsmanship, like good manners, makes its points quietly; we are kept in a world in which nothing very much seems to happen only because Taylor is more chivalrous in writing about Southern ladies than they are in writing about themselves. (pp. 46-9)

Alfred Kazin, "The Secret of the South: Faulkner to Percy," in his Bright Book of Life: American Novelists & Storytellers from Hemingway to Mailer, *Atlantic-Little, Brown, 1973, pp. 21-68.*

Herschel Gower   (essay date 1977)

[*Gower is an American educator, nonfiction writer, and critic who has written primarily about the South. In the following essay, he focuses on the Nashville environs which feature prominently in Taylor's stories.*]

It is a matter of biological fact that Peter Taylor is descended from Taylors on both sides. His mother Katherine Taylor was a daughter of Governor Robert Taylor of Carter County, East Tennessee. His father Matthew Hillsman Taylor was a native of West Tennessee at the other end of the state. Peter was born in Trenton in 1917 and because of his father's business moved often from one section to another. Each area is rich in materials for fiction, but it is in Middle Tennessee that Peter Taylor has found a setting for many of his stories. It is Nashville, the capital of the state, that is often his *locus operandi,* the hub of his characters' actions. Nashville is often the place psychologically central to his first-person narrators. It functions as their point of reference, the place of established, stable values, the concentration of cultural mores.

One of Taylor's narrators contrasts the uplands of East Tennessee with Nashville:

The world [of Nashville] isn't the hard-bitten, Monkey Trial world of East Tennessee that everybody knows about but a gentler world in Middle Tennessee . . . which was known fifty years ago as the Nashville Basin and which in still earlier times, to the first settlers—our ancestors—was known somewhat romantically perhaps, and ironically, and incorrectly even, as the Miro District . . . so called in honor of Don Estevan Miro, last of the Spanish governors of Spanish Louisiana . . .

The city of Memphis—new, raw, bustling, a Mississippi River port and cotton town—is two hundred miles away. When Taylor was growing up he heard his mother characterizing the differences between East, Middle, and West Tennessee. In a recent interview, he said: "She was a great storyteller, with a delightful sense of humor. Her observations on the mores of Memphis, for instance, with its fast-paced commercialism and emphasis on 'progress', in contrast with Nashville's more conservative pace, always delighted me."

The importance of place in Southern fiction has already been explored by any number of critics. It can be noted here that in Taylor's formative years very real distinctions could still be made among the major cities of the three grand divisions of Tennessee. Some of these distinctions are now rapidly disappearing and one city tends to look like another from the Interstate Loop or the Belt Road. But each was once a recognizable entity with its own social "outlook," speech patterns, and political stance.

Who, then, are Taylor's people—characters—individuals—the blood and flesh of the stories? It has frequently been noted that he writes only about upper middle-class Southerners who are not involved in acts of bloodshed, lust, or violence. Taylor's characters, therefore, put the author in a class apart from most contemporary Southern authors. His characters live in the city, function as a family unit in spite of a great many urban tensions, and display good manners at home and in the social circles to which they belong. To generalize further: Taylor's characters make a conscious effort to keep the family intact, and one way of doing so is ritual—family dinners, entertainment in the home, a succession of visits from relatives. None of these rituals could be carried out in a cramped apartment or condominium with no servants, and certainly not with the falling away of good manners. As gentle folk, they have their problems with a changing world and with each other, but they are never discourteous in addressing another human being or confronting the world.

What they possess and hold on to and practice is a set of formal country manners reminiscent of Jane Austen and eighteenth century England. It is as though the country house in Miss Austen's rural society had packed up and moved (servants and all) to the West End section of Nashville and settled in Elliston Place or Acklen Park or the surburbs and gone right on with established rituals. As a class these people may appear an isolated group in the modern Southern city and seem foreigners to its main currents. The truth is that they have not lost their close connections with the country. They have not cut themselves off from their background. That means that they retain an interest in an outlying county and keep in touch with cousins, friends, and older family servants in a small town somewhere beyond the periphery of the Nashville Basin. In other words Taylor's urban dwellers still cling, however futilely, to agrarian and feudal concepts of land and place. The Episcopal Church is so much taken for granted that it is seldom mentioned.

Taylor's people have not moved from older cities like Charleston or Richmond to Nashville. The farm or plantation is the backdrop for their lives, past and present. I will cite, for example, an actual account written about Peter Taylor's real (not fictional) maternal great-grandfather and his farm in **"Happy Valley,"** Carter County, Tennessee. The year is 1858 and the author is Randal McGavock, a city-bred mayor of Nashville, who was often more faithful to his diary than to his wife. On May 15, 1858, McGavock, travelling in East Tennessee on legal business, got off the train at Johnson's Station . . .

> . . . where I found a horse for me to go over to Col. N. G. Taylor's in Carter Co. Col. Taylor lives on Buffalo creek—near Buffalo Mt.—and his farm is the picture of beauty. His wife is a very clever lady, and he is the prince of hospitality.

Col. and Mrs. Taylor were such good company and lavished so much hospitality on the Mayor that he stayed with them for three days. He went on to report the magnificent scenery thereabout and the presence of the two Taylor sons. These were of course young Robert (Bob) Taylor, Peter's grandfather, who served as a Democratic governor from 1897 to 1899, and Alfred (Alf) Taylor, who lost the race to his brother Bob in 1896, but who was finally elected a Republican governor in 1920. So even if one brother had to lose in Tennessee's "War of the Roses," both Bob and Alf eventually got to the Capitol City. They both left another of their father's farms on the Wautauga, described by McGavock as "very rich and beautiful," to settle for awhile in Nashville. But like Peter's characters, they never lost sight of the agrarian world of **"Happy Valley."**

Now we can move to a recurring theme in Taylor's fiction. In the interview with Louise Davis, Taylor said:

> The conflict that dominates many of my stories grows out of the shift of the Southern population from country life to city life. The real change in the world is represented there. When the South rises in industry, there are new elements in family life and mores.

All Southerners are aware of what he means by "new elements," but what strikes us about Taylor on first reading is the almost casual understatement he gives to a theme as momentous as this one. The changes from a rural to an urban South are slow and quietly modulated in the stories, but they are indeed there to be acknowledged, dealt with, and somehow accommodated.

Does Taylor, in his own quiet corner, pull a lot of punch-es? Does he make the transitions too gentle and far too easy? Does he lack "high seriousness"? Maybe so, maybe not. The fathers go off to work in insurance offices or law firms. They are spared the sweat of such industries as building stoves in North Nashville, or manufacturing shoes in East Nashville, or printing religious books for the masses, or operating piece-goods stores on the Public Square. In fact, an elderly cousin from the country, Cousin Johnny Kincaid, finds it strange that the head of the house in which he is staying, Edmund Harper of the story **"Guests,"** comes home at four in the afternoon with absolutely nothing to report about his day in the office. Did Harper and his ilk ever sweat at all?

Whether or not Taylor's characters live in what most of us commonly call "the real world" is perhaps beside the point. They simply try to avoid getting mixed up with the wrong set in Nashville or elsewhere. Their "problems" involve their own kind—problems enough of course. Even though several of the stories take place in the twenties and the years of the Great Depression, the characters simply ignore current matters like breadlines and soup kitchens, the soot that sifts down into Elliston Place from the foundries in North Nashville, the slums of South Nashville, the smell of the burning dump in Jim Town, and the poor children who swim for 15¢ in Cascade Plunge.

To be critical of Taylor's milieu would suggest criticism of Chekhov's or Turgenev's—two Russians with whom he has much in common. It is better to say that Taylor's people, with their sense of family history and their pride in belonging to a place, are now preoccupied with the preservation of their own families—not just with keeping intact somebody's family from off the street. They are also subconsciously, I believe, concerned with the preservation of their own class and its peculiar integrity. They are aware of the importance of having social intercourse with the "right people," going to good schools and getting proper educations and marrying people of their own class. Important too is their struggle to transplant the country to the city without severe losses to either the individual or the communal perspective. Part of the enveloping tension comes from their desire to capture the best of the two worlds—or thinking they can incorporate the two successfully. Consider the Edmund Harpers again:

> Three country nieces had been presented to Nashville society from the Harper house. Countless nephews had stayed there while working their way through the university—or as far through it as it seemed practicable for them to try to go . . . two of the three nieces had eloped with worthless louts from back home before their seasons in Nashville were half over. Most of the countless nephews had taken to a wild life . . . Worse still, the convalescents always outstayed their welcome, and Edmund had to support Henrietta in taking a firm hand when it was time for each poor old creature to return to his or her nearest kin in the country.

As Taylor tabulates them, the losses that families sustain in moving from one place to another or living from one age to another are painfully evident. Not only is the integrity of the family at stake, the "sacred" individuality of its incorrigible and "unreconstructed" members may be sacrificed. In ["**In the Miro District**"] we see the grandfather, Major Basil Manley, as a holdout against the urbanization of body and spirit. Whereas the Major's children had come to Nashville and now "saw everything in terms of Acklen Park," the grandfather insisted upon living apart from them and in a county that was only on the periphery of Middle Tennessee. This Major Manley, a veteran of the Civil War, insisted upon a life of his own "free of the rules and mores" of life in Nashville. The narrator (and grandson) explains:

> . . . he went on living in the drafty, unheated farmhouse that he and his father before him had been born in . . . That is to say, his farm and the county it was in were considered somewhat beyond the pale, not being in the handsome bluegrass, limestone country where livestock farms—and particularly horse farms—made the landscape a joy to look upon and where people had always held themselves well above other mortal Tennesseans. He preferred to go on living over there even after my father had bought our fine house in Acklen Park and set aside the room there for his exclusive occupancy.

This story is concerned with the family's attempts to "tame" the grandfather, divest him of his old-fashioned ways and bring him into town. A second theme in this story is the terrifying differences—always understated by Taylor—that exist between grandfather and grandson. Without them there would be no story, and, except superficially, the differences are never reconciled.

One of the many contradictions between the two generations is the way they look at women. The grandson explains:

> In our part of the world we were brought up on tales of the mysterious ways of Thomas Jefferson, whose mother and wife are scarcely mentioned in his writings, and Andrew Jackson and Sam Houston, whose reticence on the subject of women is beyond the comprehension of most men nowadays. Did they have too much respect for women? Were they perhaps, for all their courage in other domains, afraid of women or afraid of their own compelling feelings toward women? I didn't think all of this, of course, as I faced Grandfather Manley there in the hall, but I believe I felt it. It seemed to me that his generation and my own were a thousand years apart.

It is a mark of Peter Taylor's genius that an issue as embattled as the War Between the Sexes and one so often overplayed today can be expressed in queries as polite as these. It is part of his charm as a writer to deal with the great issues without agitation or violence. An emotion is sufficient unto the day and time thereof, especially when there is a ripple of humor somewhere beneath.

This brings me to the point of saying that Taylor is indeed very, very funny. As Robert Penn Warren pointed out thirty years ago in his introduction to *A Long Fourth and Other Stories:*

> If Peter Taylor is concerned with the attrition of

old loyalties, the breakdown of old patterns, and the collapse of old values, he regards the process without too much distress to his personal piety. The world he is treating, with its mixture of confusion and pretension, would appeal readily to a satiric eye.

Then Warren goes on to say that in spite of the humor invariably associated with satire, Taylor is not a satirist. "In the whole effect . . . he stops somewhere short of satire. Rather, he presents an irony blended of comedy and sympathetic understanding."

Part of the humor that arrests us . . . is the texture of the language and the rambling, anecdotal quality of the paragraphs. A story is seldom told as a straightforward experience, but with asides and digressions.

One contribution to the texture is the diction, which is faintly old-fashioned if not (at times) outright archaic. Taylor's people use phrases reminiscent of those suggested by Nancy Mitford twenty years ago when she and Alan Ross set the lexicographers buzzing over usages that they cavalierly designated "U" and "Non-U." As arbiters of distinctions between upper (or "U") and lower class (or "non-U") usage, the Honorable Nancy and Professor Ross cited "looking glass" and "writing paper" as Upper;

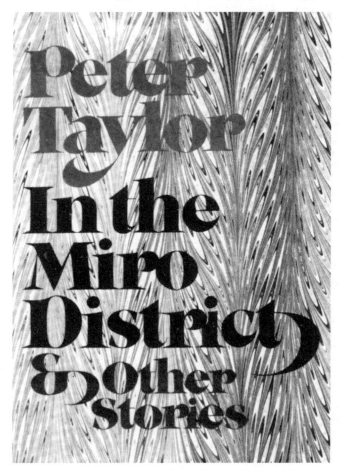

Dust jacket for Taylor's sixth short story collection, In the Miro District, and Other Stories.

they designated "mirror" and "stationery" as Non-Upper. It should be "spectacles," not "glasses," they said, and compiled their long lists of the levels of British diction in the twentieth century.

Taylor's people are also inclined to follow certain speech patterns. They will say "boarding school" instead of "prep school." Men have their "toddies" before dinner—not "cocktails." "It amounted to *truck* farming, though we did not even say the word," one narrator confides. The couples may have tete-a-tetes in a sun parlor but never in a Florida room. After dinner they play cards in the "sitting room," not the "living room." Their houses at Monteagle and Beersheba Springs are always cottages—never cabins—no matter how rustic or what the scale. They attend "coming-out parties" instead of "debut balls." They regularly say "fetch" for "bring." They "quarrel" but do not "fight." They report that "swearing" took place on certain occasions but they never repeat the exact words. Husbands and wives may refer to each other as Mr. or Mrs., especially with servants, and on formal occasions they may address each other directly by title. "Cousin" is the other title most frequently used in the stories, but Colonel, Major, Captain, and Governor follow in close order. Matters of money are never discussed in actual dollars and cents. The "very rich" are either "affluent" or "people of means." (Only the vulgar will tell you how much they spend on anything from a child's rattle to a mansion in Belle Meade.) No wife or husband will criticize the other to a third party or speak disparagingly of an offspring—no matter what the child may have done to warrant condemnation.

What is the fate of people like these gentlefolk living in Nashville who have appeared frequently between the covers of *The New Yorker*? Have they any future in a modern Southern city, either as individuals or a class? Are they merely "holdouts" meant to amuse us but not meant to move us very profoundly? Are they too fragile and anachronistic to haunt us for very long? Will they simply go the way of all country folk in the city and in another generation not remember who they are and where they are from and the difference between right and wrong without thinking?

I am not sure that the answers can be found in the collected stories of Peter Taylor. I *am* certain that there is no easy, simple answer to any of these troublesome questions about the future of Taylor's characters. All I can deduce from the Nashville stories is that people come into the city and after a while submit to its patterns. One narrator says:

> [Both my parents] believed that they acted always from the right instincts—right instincts which they shared with all the sensible and well-bred people they knew in Nashville. [Our small-town cousins] couldn't see what a city Nashville had become and didn't know what a difference that made in the way you looked at things. They thought too much of themselves and their pasts to observe that some places and some people in Tennessee had changed and had kept up with the times.

Part of keeping up with the times is marking a line down

the middle of the street to control traffic. Yet once upon a time:

> . . . everyone had equal rights on the streets of Thornton. A vehicle was a vehicle, and a person was a person, each with the right to move slowly as he pleased and to stop where and as often as he pleased. In the Thornton mind, there was no imaginary line down the middle of the street, and, indeed, no one there at that time had heard of drawing a real line on *any* street.

Old Aunt Munsie, the central character in this story, **"What You Hear From 'Em?,"** finally loses confidence in the future when her "white children" leave Thornton for big cities and have no intention of returning; when they, and her own child Crecie, conspire against her and her old ways; and finally when they all pretend they want her to join them in the city. She says flatly:

> "I ain't nothin' to 'em in Memphis, and they ain't nothin' to me in Nashville . . . A collie dog's a collie dog anywhar. But Aunt Munsie, she's just their Aunt Munsie here in Thornton."

The old woman, like certain wines, is not meant to travel and she knows it. What she also knows is that "concrete" relationships are necessary for the cementing of strong human ties.

In her capitulation to the times, Aunt Munsie softens into a stereotype:

> On the Square she would laugh and holler with the white folks the way they liked her to and the way Crecie and all the other oldtimers did, and she even took to trying a bandanna around her head—took to talking old-nigger foolishness, too . . .

Aunt Munsie declines sadly—without dignity or integrity. Her story approaches tragedy and becomes, finally, a kind of elegy for the softening and decline of the human spirit, a eulogy on the passing of an individual whose values ought to be sacred to the community of humankind.

In January, 1976, Taylor published a fine story in *The New Yorker* called **"The Captain's Son."** It is about, among other things, the marriage of two cousins, a girl from Nashville and a wealthy young man from Memphis. The girl's brother is the narrator:

> At our house [in Elliston Place] we tended to laugh at anything that was far in the past or far in the future. We were more or less taught to. And our mother and father would say they were glad neither of us children . . . took himself too seriously or set too great a store by who his forebears had been. We knew who we were without talking about it or thinking about it even. Simply to be what we were in Nashville, circa 1935, seemed good enough.

The narrator's summary of the family's "Nashville outlook" proves to be loaded with irony. His sister, having married "family," follows her husband into alcoholism under the very noses of the rest of the household. In their upstairs quarters the young couple drink silently day after day and the family flaw seems inbred; they live their lives trapped by a common weakness.

The bride's brother reports their "suburban decline" at the end of the story and drives home their plight as a general malaise of the city:

> . . . I know [other] couples just like them right here in Nashville. Something happened to them that nobody . . . could ever understand. And so they can't separate. They are too dependent on each other and on the good bourbon whiskey they drink together . . . If their livers stand up to it, they may actually survive to a very old age . . . [they] just might have the bad luck to live forever—the two of them, together in that expensive house they bought, perched among the houses just like it, out there on some godforsaken street in the flat and sunbaked and endlessly sprawling purlieus of Memphis.

The parents' "right instincts" about living in Nashville went wrong, of course, and proved all but disastrous for the cousins who became man and wife.

The second turn of irony in **"The Captain's Son"** is the plight of the narrator himself. He moves out of the family home and quietly declares his independence. We hear him report how he took an apartment in a suburban development off Hillsboro Road. In a casual aside he mentions another fact: "I have never married." So with the deaths of the mother and father within a few months of each other, with the sister childless, the Tolliver family is depleted. The lonely survivors have succumbed to the ways of the city and almost become "atoms anonymous." Occasionally the brother and sister exchange letters and look back to happier times. Some of her letters to him make no sense at all, but neither of them has lost the ability to look back. The past, however blurred, is not obliterated.

Many of the stable characters look back too—with an agreeable lack of self-pity and sentimentality—and some of them try going back to the country or the mountains for short spells. We have to remember, however, that most of the stories are set in the twenties, thirties, and forties—not the sixties and seventies. Taylor's characters do not look ahead to a later, more complex time or consciously try to come to grips with what may be in store for them and their descendants in the Super-City. His people are simply not given to town-and-social planning, predicting the future, or intellectualizing on man's fate as a city-dweller. They may be concerned with Time Past and Time Present, but they are not ruffled by the omens of Time Future. They accept loneliness and separation and the loss of **"Happy Valley."** But they complain very little. Even while looking back, they do not howl over their losses; they present a fairly genial, good-natured face to a changing world and to each other. As a class they have not as yet been totally fragmented or assimilated into the ways of the city.

Unlike some of the people John Updike, Philip Roth, and Walker Percy write about, Taylor's Nashvillians are human beings who elicit compassion from us but do not strike us with terror. There is always the chance, however, that given another twenty years they will be just as terrible

as the others. Perhaps Taylor is saying, finally, that by another generation these people will have outlived their Nashville period and come to the end of their uneasy period of Grace. As is the usual way of artists, Taylor has recorded a fragile company just in the nick of time. (pp. 37-47)

> *Herschel Gower, "The Nashville Stories," in* Shenandoah, *Vol. XXVIII, No. 2, Winter, 1977, pp. 37-47.*

Jane Barnes Casey   (essay date 1978)

[*Casey is an American novelist, short story writer, and critic. In the following essay, she analyzes* In the Miro District, and Other Stories *in order to assess Taylor's modification of recurrent themes in his works.*]

As an author, Peter Taylor is more often praised than understood. The respect his work inspires frequently seems taken in by appearances, by the fact that in a formal sense, his material *seems* fixed. His stories usually take place in Tennessee—in Memphis or Nashville or Chatham; the characters are drawn from the upper middle class or from the Negro servant class; people are seen in terms of the family, rarely as isolated individuals or divorced ones or even single ones; the stories occur before 1960, and some take place around the turn of the century, while others are governed by the events and history of the 19th century, particularly, of course, the Civil War.

Yet the limitations Mr. Taylor sets on his work barely contain the shifting, probing attitude he constantly turns on his material. He is a great craftsman, but of a foxy sort, intent on working as much complexity as possible into the world behind his simple surfaces. In his best stories, his masterpieces, every detail is present in all its vital controversy; every part hums with its own inner fullness, as well as in its relation to every other part. He is a master of contradiction, though we have only to mention this quality when Mr. Taylor's single-mindedness must be accounted for. His work has always been concerned with the conflict between affectionate, civil society and chaos, regardless of whether the disorder is sexual, drunken, or natural. From **"A Spinster's Tale"** when this chaos appears in the form of Mr. Speed, who's compared to a "loose horse," through **"There"** when the theme is recast as all that's mortally, tragically unattainable, through **"In the Miro District"** with its extraordinary descriptions of the 1811 earthquake, Mr. Taylor has never been far from his preoccupation with the social world and the forces which threaten it.

The purpose of this essay is to discuss the way Mr. Taylor's handling of his recurrent themes has changed and evolved toward his newest collection of stories, ***In The Miro District.*** The book invites us to look back. Tonally, particularly in the experimental prose poems, the book evokes the author's earliest stories when he wrote out of oneness with the domestic context he so lovingly described. Reading **"The Hand of Emmagene"** with its casual, unforced pace, its love of furniture and china and cooking, it is impossible not to think of **"A Long Fourth,"** one of Mr. Taylor's most lusciously written first stories, full of sympathetic descriptions of the characters, family routines, and relationships. Both **"The Hand of Emmagene"** and **"A Long Fourth"** have marriage at their moral center, but the difference between the marriages is enormous. In **"A Long Fourth,"** Harriet and Sweetheart's happy union is what creates the fullness of tone. Their freshness and purity and unexamined goodness is the measure by which we know the problems in the story. As Harriet's hysteria testifies, it is, in many ways, an inadequate measure. But much as Harriet wants to deny the connection between Son and BT, the black cook's nephew, they are equivalents. BT is bestial and incompetent when compared to his aunt, just as Son is unfruitful in comparison to his parents. The South in which Harriet and Sweetheart bloomed has somehow been reduced to rampant carnality, on the one hand, and sterile respectability or sterile radicalism, on the other. We end by feeling both the sadness and confusion that Harriet and Sweetheart feel about the tragic problem of race and the inability of the younger generation to proceed. But just because the emotions we feel are in the old-fashioned style of Harriet and Sweetheart, we also feel Mr. Taylor's oneness with them: his sense of the modern world as acid, biting into the soft medium he loves.

By contrast, in **"The Hand of Emmagene,"** the narrator's marriage is stable and happy, but the narrator and his wife differ from Sweetheart and Harriet in having real knowledge of the world. Whereas Harriet has a romantic hope for Son and her daughters, one which skirts the issue of sex, in the prose poem, the narrator and his wife are good people, but they are not innocent. Though the poet is moved by horror, as well as sympathy for Emmagene, these are the wholesome emotions of someone who trusts reason, who sees extremism from the perspective of normal affection and sexuality. Between **"A Long Fourth"** and **"The Hand of Emmagene,"** marriage has grown tough enough to bear the stresses of the modern world, though the question of whether society can pass happy marriage from one generation to the next seems to have withered away. Emmagene is certainly a failure in this regard, but she is a freak too. In fact, she is all that is freakish and uncompromising in human experience, as opposed to what is unsuitable, say, or unacceptable.

Originally, Mr. Taylor seemed to give himself to Southern society, even though it was doomed, but his loyalty has undergone a transformation. While he continues to regard marriage as central, the conditions for its survival are more mythic than regional. What is interesting is that what appears to have made the reaffirmation of marriage possible is an avowal of sex as part of love; more importantly, this avowal is synonymous with an affirmation of masculinity.

In The Miro District is basically about men. In two of the stories, the central characters are young men involved in rites of passage. Until this collection, Mr. Taylor has written more from the female point of view, using it as a screen through which he has observed disorder. Almost without exception, disorder has been associated with men trampling the social restraints enforced or represented by women. In his earliest stories, in **"A Spinster's Tale"** and **"The Fancy Woman,"** through Betsy's frailty and Josie's

vulnerability, we see the destructiveness, the cruelty, the violence of the male. And in later stories, such as **"At the Drugstore,"** Matt Donelson subdues what is brutal and anti-social in himself out of a sense of duty to women.

"At the Drugstore" is nonetheless a melancholy story, written in a dry, analytical, even agonized style. In it strong moral impulses run neck and neck with disillusion, and the unresolved tension between the two gives the story its dominant quality—a haunting, straw fragrance like that of pressed flowers. It's a story which shows what Mr. Taylor has gone through to arrive at the consonance of *In The Miro District,* and like **"A Long Fourth,"** it also takes place around a homecoming. Unlike Son, Matt Donelson has successfully gone on to have a family of his own, one which he thinks he is proud of. To his surprise, on his first day home, he finds himself on the way to the drugstore in a kind of numbed, neurotic fog. Once there, his apparent purpose—the purchase of shaving lotion—turns out to be an excuse for a deeper confrontation. On one level, his attention is caught by the relation of the pharmacist and his son; on another level, Matt is preoccupied with recollections of school days and the curiosity he felt about Mr. Conway and his female assistants. Matt identifies with the son's difficulties with his father, but he is also jealous of him for being so at home in what is expected of him.

Matt's disaffection with his family emerges in his awareness, while the causes of his alienation arise in his memory. He relives his terror and fascination as he recalls how a school mate once wrote "Mr. Conway sleeps with his mother" in full view on the mirror behind the counter. It's not too much to say that Matt seems to raise up and resolve his Oedipal dilemma in the course of his visit to the drugstore. When he goes home, he brings with him an awareness of all the forbidden sexuality which underlies family life and conflicts with domesticity. At the same time, he assumes authority in and for himself, having come to terms with his father. Matt now views his life and his choices with his own eyes, without the aid or illusion of tradition, and though he conceives of his choice as bleak, lying as it does between a brutal, selfish self and a resigned one, he commits himself to continuity, society, and civil discipline.

BT's carnality and Son's radical ideas meet with a positive outcome in Matt's dilemma. He becomes more suited to his life by realizing his nature, though this is one of Mr. Taylor's most mercurial stories, and the closer we come to explaining it, the more mysterious it remains at the core. The question is: has the hero in fact realized his nature? Isn't there a way in which he treats his carnal self to the same morality he finds so eroded in family life? He construes his inner outlaw as guilty of wanting to sleep with his mother, of wanting to despoil the relationship which is the basis for honor and purity and love in all other relationships. Yet to conceive of sexuality in terms of this kind of Freudian original guilt is to punish himself by a code he has come to doubt. The story goes to great lengths to suggest that marriage, for Matt's class anyway, is a form being emptied of real emotional content. The contemporary world is seen as defined by change, by the exact undoing of the family though it represents "all the good sense and reasonableness that made life worth-while—or even tolerable."

What makes this story bleak is not that Matt has to choose between the lesser of two evils. That bleakness is present, but there is a deeper bleakness stemming from a sense that bourgeois morality is insufficient—it cannot embrace the whole complexity; nonetheless, it is all there is to see us through the chaos between birth and death. There is a flaw in this reasoning—perhaps snarl is a better word because Mr. Taylor has gone on to untangle it in his new book. The snarl, as I see it, is in the contradiction between the potential Matt discovers in himself and his impulse to label it critically. The story suggests that Matt is torn between two equally powerful parts of himself, one anti-social, the other not, and yet in fact, these impulses are not treated equally, or not experienced equally. Matt looks beyond taboo, but he suppresses what he sees. The story is structured in terms of a Freudian analysis of Matt's experience, committing him from the start to a responsible, social resolution. The content of the story is not quite what it purports to be: Matt's self-discovery is prejudged. It's been found guilty of being savage before the narrative begins.

In **"A Long Fourth,"** Mr. Taylor wrote out of identification with the large-hearted goodness of Harriet and Sweetheart; they were emblems of a coherent social world in which the younger generation had gone astray. In **"At the Drugstore,"** the author writes from the point of view of the younger generation, struggling to find a morality which will enable them to do as much good for others as Harriet and Sweetheart were able to do. *In The Miro District* shows Mr. Taylor as having arrived at the goal he set for Matt Donelson. The interior conflicts have once more been realigned and subtly expanded beyond the scope of narrow Freudian arguments, though at the same time, *In The Miro District* seems specifically organized to recapitulate Mr. Taylor's career, while demonstrating step by step his move from narrowest possible vision to the broadest, most humane one.

The first story in the collection, **"The Captain's Son,"** appears to be a deliberate caricature of all the elements normally associated with "Southern" fiction: complex family ties, historical skeletons in the closet, dark sexual problems. Not only does it seem to be a deliberate caricature of a genre, but it also seems to be a wholly negative one. In an author who once treated the same society so sympathetically, it is hard not to feel that **"The Captain's Son"** is literally a regional critique. The villain—though Tolliver proclaims it and Lila's family deny it—is in everybody's breast. The villain is snobbery in one form or another, though the guilt is equally divided between Tolliver, who wants to retreat by marrying, and his father-in-law, who allows him, even compels Tolliver to marry into the household.

Each man believes he represents good breeding; both act out of noblesse oblige, though they emphasize different aspects of it. Tolliver's Deep South Planter background celebrates class differences and glories in its own privileges. His father-in-law, as a good liberal democrat, wants to mask inequalities in class and wealth. This doesn't stop him from honoring them in his heart—so much so that he

takes control of his daughter's marriage lest Tolliver "turn out to be a high liver and a big spender and so, during times when nearly everybody was hard up, be a source of embarrassment to us all."

Both Tolliver and his father-in-law want to preserve a way of life, but they are willing to do it at the expense of life itself: Tolliver, after all, is impotent. Not coincidentally, Tolliver will not or cannot find employment. His impotence and joblessness are reflections of each other, and the connection of the two is the most powerful expression so far in Mr. Taylor's work of male despair in the modern world. Yet this depair is entirely associated with the rigid enforcement of Southernness—the deference of men to the social necessities of marriage. In **"The Captain's Son,"** however, marriage is no perpetuation but a sacrifice of the couple who marry.

Looking back from this collection, it's as if Southern chivalry toward women had been strained until it snapped, until what is Jamesian in Mr. Taylor's sensibility had been revolutionized by a Laurentian awareness. For as long as women hold the moral reins in his stories, men suffer from emasculation. As opposed to the castrating women in much American fiction, the women in Mr. Taylor's earlier stories do not undermine their men personally. There are, in fact, many real heroines, among them Miss Lenore and the amazing Aunt Munsie in **"What You Hear From."** The problem is an historical or cultural one for men. Women's lives are more meaningful because they remain morally potent in the domestic sphere; meanwhile the possibility of moral potency in the political sphere has been lost for men in a world where they have no real effectiveness. It is a world described in **"Dean of Men,"** in which the political power of the hero's grandfather has shrunk to the paltry gray arena of college administration.

Women are not blamed for the demoralization of men, but there is a coincidence between strong women and unhappy men, at least until *In The Miro District.* To some extent, this condition prevailed as long as Mr. Taylor preserved the notion that the woman's domain was the house and family, while man's was the exterior one of commerce and politics. More precisely, this condition prevailed as long as Mr. Taylor accepted women as the carriers of the social conscience. The honor of Southern womanhood and her purity were once part of a successful ethical arrangement in which men let women have charge of the spiritual accounts. **"A Long Fourth"** is a portrait of that world in its final phase. But the trade off, the swapping of covert for overt power, ceases to be that; increasingly, as men's crucial energy is no longer invested in the affairs of the world, the restraint exercised by and for women is entirely negative.

In **"At the Drugstore,"** the man's problem is what to do about this energy. It is a source of potency and vitality, but in its disengagement from meaningful work, it is also lawlessly sexual. As a Southerner, Mr. Taylor seems to have been concerned with the question of how a man can go on being a man in the modern world without undermining the moral basis of society—without, in other words, rebelling against the woman's role as it has been traditionally defined. Though the sexes are assigned roles in this dilemma, the problem is deeper than sex. It is the great modern problem of how to incorporate the most vital, but also the most anarchic urges into civilized life. Is it possible for the individual to be completely alive without adding to the existing chaos and suffering?

Tolliver's failure as a man seems to be laid at the doorstep of a Southern conspiracy to perpetuate the most trivial, most murderous aspects of itself. The next story, **"Daphne's Lover,"** returns to the theme of **"At the Drugstore,"** but treats it without bias. **"Daphne's Lover"** is about sexuality and contrasts Frank Lacy's life of affairs and marriages with the narrator's devoted monogamy. Having admitted the power of male desire or passion, the next question is whether any sort of reasonably decent social order can survive it. Once the restraint of custom has given way, is there anything to stem the flood of erotic selfishness?

In **"A Long Fourth,"** the choice was between unleashed sensuality and arid abstraction; **"At the Drugstore"** brought the beast and the intellect together, but with a sense that both were aspects of the fallen nature of man—guilty and picayune—all there was in the absence of immutable truths and, simultaneously, not enough. **"Daphne's Lover"** transcends these painful limitations, having at its core the image of Daphne eternally pursued by Apollo. Though *Ode on a Grecian Urn* is neither quoted nor alluded to, the story is haunted by its cultural ghost, by our inevitable association between figures frozen in the chase and Keats's lines:

> More happy love! more happy, happy love!
> For ever warm and still to be enjoy'd;
> For ever panting and for ever young;
> All breathing human passion far above . . .

Mr. Taylor's story lifts carnality into the realm of the imagination, into the timeless ideal which can only remain perfect in art. But as Daphne only escaped Apollo by becoming a tree, so Mr. Taylor suggests there is no escape from desire as long as we are human and for just as long, our experience of it will be incomplete. We are born with built-in restrictions on what we are capable of doing. Willy-nilly, we are types.

This given is what replaces the restraints of Southern gallantry and good manners. It governs us more strictly than any psychoanalytic theory. Whether, like Frank Lacy, we give our urges their full expression or, like the narrator of **"Daphne's Lover,"** we marry once and happily, we are only going to know one half of all there is to know of love. The whole is in our imaginations. We may find it rendered whole in art or we may try to complete our limited experience through friendship, as the narrator does with Frank; but we are born subject to the laws of our own natures which will rule us whether we want them to or not. For this reason "a healthy imagination is like a healthy appetite. If you do not feed it the lives of your friends, I maintain, then you are apt to feed it your own life, to live in your own imagination rather than upon it."

But there is another dimension to **"Daphne's Lover,"** one it is necessary to mention as it helps pave the way to the final story, **"In the Miro District."** Frank Lacy, the rake figure in **"Daphne's Lover,"** is also the most sympathetic.

While the narrator is outraged by the little girl who dresses up and blows kisses out the window, Frank seems to understand and tolerate her wildness. When she writes her flirtatious graffiti on his back fence, Frank simply paints it over, unruffled by her teasing but moved to protect her from people who might misunderstand her (such as the narrator who calls her a "whore"). Frank is also friends with Janet Turner, another high-spirited girl of whom Mr. Taylor observes (in a line that contains a world of variation on decorum and goodness), "Alone with a boy she was a model of propriety, but in public she was difficult."

As a character, Janet harks back to Josie of **"The Fancy Woman,"** a high-spirited, sexually unconventional girl who sleeps with a married man. Her problem is that she accepts the conventional male estimate of a girl who does what she's doing. She sees herself as a slut, though the author sees her as a social victim who is unfairly made to think too little of herself. Though her lover's son appreciates her romantic qualities (and is himself too young to understand why she does not), the society as a whole does not tolerate unmarried or extramarital sex.

In **"Daphne's Lover,"** Janet is a freer agent than Josie, unafraid to be herself, though she also dies young: she remains an outsider. Unlike Josie, she is not a romantic figure. She is utterly independent, but in a way which makes her sexually unattractive (or threatening) to the men in the story. For the author, the question seems to be whether or not a romantic attitude toward women could survive without the system. Though Mr. Taylor had pictured the morality invested in women as more and more of a dead weight, still that stone shores up illusion. If family life and civilization might fall apart without the woman as its conscience, so would sweetness and imagination and fun.

But when the girl spends the weekend with the young narrator in **"In the Miro District,"** the event is both romantic and natural. It involves not the slightest social embarrassment for either the girl or the boy; being in love is enough to justify sleeping together (their embarrassment is only over being caught). Mr. Taylor writes as simply and directly of their weekend as if there had never been anything in his work to suggest that such an occurrence was ever forbidden. It's as if the book's progress were towards a full airing of things as they really were, beginning with a cry from the heart on behalf of the male, moving through a recognition of masculine passion and then, necessarily to the admission that women are passionate too. If Southern chivalry has snapped, it's because in some way it was false or reduced to empty appearances. The easy atmosphere of the narrator's love-making suggests that sleeping with respectable girls was something people did when they were in love, though society felt it was important not to admit what really went on. Yet Mr. Taylor himself seems to have waited to tell the truth and has only been released by finding a moral framework large enough to hold the broken pieces of the old order.

"In the Miro District" provides this in its profound and economic use of the narrator's relation to his grandfather's frequently repeated stories. These stories are the crux of Mr. Taylor's story. They are unvarnished tales of "the eternal chaos we live in," and the grandfather insists on telling them instead of the Civil War stories he is expected to tell. His account of seeing his law partner shot and his own surrealistic escape into the swamps, his recounting of the hallucinations which made him imagine he was living through the New Madrid Earthquake (described to him by his own father), these stories are his witness to the mysterious violence in which human history pathetically, frailly unfolds. The grandfather's association with the earthquake links him with a time before his own, and through that time to the early American South when French and Spanish settlers were swept away "like so many Adams and Eves before the wrath of their Maker." In this final image, his experience is associated with the human condition since the beginning of time. What he knows about it is terrifying, but he won't suppress that truth. He refuses to submit to the stylized, domesticated version of chaos entertained by Southern society in its endless retelling of the Civil War. He lays no claim to his privileges as a Civil War veteran; he will not allow himself to be promoted in their artificial military ranks, and he will not let his real experience be altered so that it can adorn his daughter's living room.

When the narrator drunkenly begs his grandfather to tell about Reelfoot Lake, he then goes on to mock the old man's stories by telling them himself. But as he does, the boy—without realizing it—actually imagining the opposite—is acting out the moral of his grandfather's tales. He is himself behaving crazily; but in this, as an outlaw, he also demonstrates his resemblance to the old man. The boy sees the beginning of his independence in the moment when he flings back what he's listened to all the times the strange pair has been forced together. And yet it is precisely his defiance that shows him to be his grandfather's equivalent. It is what sets them both apart from the generation between them—a generation living by a modified version of the code the grandfather still strictly observes.

By his code, an absolute distinction is made between public and private life. The grandfather, for instance, never drinks in public as his daughter and son-in-law do. To him, there is never any excuse for liquor, though he might indulge in it out of weakness. If he does, it does not make liquor any better. Between his generation and the boy's, drinking has become socially acceptable in a way the grandfather finds appalling. And his grandson matches the old man's absolute morality—by taking his parents' liberalism to its natural conclusion—by doing whatever he feels like doing in public, to whatever extreme. The boy is willing to admit openly and completely what they will only half admit.

The grandfather and grandson clash on three occasions: when the old man arrives and finds him drunk, when he arrives and discovers the boy and a bunch of friends in bed with girls who aren't so nice, when he arrives and interrupts the narrator and his best (nice) girl while they are making love in the grandfather's bed. On the first two occasions, the grandfather is firm but sympathetic. When he finds the boy drunk, he tries to calm him down and sober him up. When he finds the girls in his daughter's house, he sends them packing, but he treats them in an understanding fashion and even helps his grandson clean up.

When he finds the respectable girl naked in his wardrobe, he leaves and is not seen again until he's put on the social costume his family has wanted him to adopt all along.

The fact that he chooses to draw the line at the respectable girl creates an interesting ambiguity. Does the boy go too far when he denigrates Southern womanhood (as opposed to Southern tarthood)? Or does it finally become clear to the old man that the boy will continue to break the fraying rules until he finds moral zero? Will he try murder next to see if that's rock bottom? It is not entirely clear whether the grandfather is disturbed by what the boy has done or of what he might do. Until then the grandfather has refused to stand for conventional wisdom, but now he moves into his daughter's house and allows himself to be trotted out at dinner parties as a Civil War relic.

Given the drift of the whole collection, the grandfather's resignation is probably meant as his acknowledgement that traditional moral authority, based on the Southern woman's honor, is dead in his grandson's generation. For him, the woman's importance has been so deep he will not even speak of his wife by her first name. The absolute privacy of their relationship, its mysterious and sacred quality has been the balance to God's mysterious and terrifying relation to man. In the old Christian world, at home and in nature, the male was ruled by powers higher than himself. The grandfather's faith lay in a sense that the outer chaos was governed by a retributive God, and that the society which successfully brought his kidnappers to trial was one whose laws bore some real relation to what was just.

But just as woman's honor is dead, so is God in the grandson's generation. From the grandfather's point of view, there is no stopping anyone from doing anything. When he sees his own code dismissed by his grandson, the old man assumes the entire world of spirit has collapsed. There are no beliefs, but there is nothing to inspire them either. At that point, the grandfather lays his authority at the service of the liberal society he regards as hypocritical. It is his way of demonstrating to his grandson that conventions, though they are only rules (not principles, not absolutes) are still better than nothing.

And yet this is not entirely a story of defeat. When Aunt Munsie in **"What You Hear From 'Em"** puts on a bandana and "took to talking old-nigger foolishness," when Miss Leonora puts on all but the rhinestone glasses of the silly old lady tourist, one feels they have really been broken in the tug-of-war between the old moral order and uprooted contemporary society. **"In the Miro District"** revolves around the same conflict, but the outcome is different: if one world has clearly passed away, another has come in its place. It has always been part of Mr. Taylor's complexity that he saw how the new order brought new possibilities too. In **"Mrs. Billingsby's Wine,"** his heroine profits from the inexorable democracy that undermines social order and high principles by making no one person or ideal better than any other. In part, the appeal of **"Mrs. Billingsby's Wine"** is that it blithely contradicts two of the author's most powerful stories—**"What You Hear From 'Em"** and **"Miss Leonora When Last Seen."** But it is also appealing because of what seems to be a mischievous reversal of what has come to be the obligatory progress of the modern short story. Instead of getting sadder and sadder as things move along, the heroine of **"Mrs. Billingsby's Wine"** gets happier and happier and ends by realizing that she'd had what she wants all along.

Still, this very element of mischief makes the happy ending seem possible because anything is possible and not because the new world is run according to a coherent design. The method Mr. Taylor uses in **"Mrs. Billingsby's Wine"** is the same one he employs elsewhere to point up a more demoralized truth. In **"Mrs. Billingsby's Wine,"** he carefully shows how the young woman and the older one are humanly equal—alike in their vitality and goodness and in their being at ease in the experience of their different generations. The story—like so many of Mr. Taylor's stories—is a tissue in which the parts of the subject become so enmeshed that we finally feel there is no difference between things that seemed opposite at the start. It is not that opposites become indistinguishable but rather that they become equivalents. Son and BT are an example, Tolliver and his father-in-law are another.

In **"A Long Fourth,"** the likeness of BT and Son suggests that it doesn't matter which alternative one picks: they are equally bad. In **"The Captain's Son,"** the opposing parties are equally to blame. The sources of tension in these stories are slowly transformed in a way which often emphasizes the futility of their having been distinguished in the first place. Mr. Taylor repeatedly raises moral dilemmas only to show they can't be solved because there are no black and white moral categories. Yet when we come to **"In the Miro District,"** the equivalence of grandfather and grandson is ultimately what makes the story one of renewal.

The boy imagines that the greatest difference between him and his grandfather lies in their attitude toward love. "He might know everything else in the world, including every other noble feeling which I would never be able to experience. He might be morally correct about everything else in the world, but he was not morally correct about love between a man and woman." Just as the boy wrongly imagines he is freeing himself by spewing back his grandfather's stories, he errs when he congratulates himself on knowing more about women than the old man. In fact, for both of them, love is central, though the grandfather refuses to speak of it while the boy insists on being frank. The grandfather's romantic silence about sex and his grandson's open acceptance of it are mirror opposites, but this means the boy's view is just as good as the old man's and more: **"In the Miro District"** shows the boy to be as deeply and inescapably part of a universal order as his grandfather.

For the boy, this order is one that has developed through the collection—it is the one that governs Frank Lacy and the narrator of **"The Hand of Emmagene."** It is an order in which the disruptive side of human nature is subject to the laws of human reason. The author's willingness to trust fallible human reason seems to arise from a sinewy faith in the survival of an order larger than man and one which resembles the Christian universe, though the Christian vocabulary has been washed away.

Mr. Taylor insinuates this impression by having the boy as his narrator. He slowly circles through his grandfather's stories, telling them again and again, each time with different emphasis, in a spare, almost heartlessly serene language that the reader unconsciously identifies with the old man's voice. This, of course, contributes to the interchangeableness of the two characters, but even more remarkable is the way the device confuses our sense of the universes in which the two men dwell. The boy's imagery stresses the Christianity of his grandfather's world but in the broadest possible terms. It is not the Christianity of Christ's Resurrection or compassion. It is actually only Christian in the sense that a God oversees the universe—that there is a Maker of an Adam and Eve. If we articulate all that's implied in the boy's tone, the Maker is a thoroughly disinterested One who tended to be identified with Christian terms in the grandfather's day, but who always was and always will be a Force beyond our control. The hard edge of the boy's voice seems to imply there has never been a hope of salvation, though there has always been a God. Beneath his boastful recounting of his youthful escapades, the boy speaks with an ancient sense of the helplessness of man, seeing it stretch backward to the beginning, feeling it there, undermining the present.

"Men, women and children, during the first bad shock, hung on to trees like squirrels. In one case a tree infested with people was seen to fall across a newly made ravine, and the poor wretches hung there for hours until there was a remission in the earth's undulation. Whole families were seen to disappear into round holes twenty feet wide, and the roaring of the upheaval was so loud their screams could not be heard." The horror of the scene is timeless. The soundless agony of the Earthquake's victims is made to seem like the lost agony of all the victims in history, all those who've perished inexplicably and horribly from the first Flood through the holocausts of our own time. They die in the darkness that runs alongside the bright, lit, fragile world of unwitting survivors.

Human social life has always seemed precarious to Mr. Taylor, but at first its greatest threat was human violence. Gradually, his allegiance to a specific social order has yielded to his growing insight into the total insecurity in which custom must survive. In his most recent story, **"In the Miro District,"** custom itself is questioned as a stable vessel, or rather our need for it to be fixed is questioned. **"In the Miro District"** is about the revolution in custom between the grandfather's day and his grandson's. Both live according to entirely different conventions, but the difference is one of detail. For both men, custom has not changed in its essential reference to love. The woman who once had all value vested in her honor still represents all that's important. Once her importance was expressed by not acknowledging her passionateness, now the opposite is true.

But there has been no loss of hope or of fulfillment. The ease attending the young lovers in **"In the Miro District"** derives from the eternal nature of love. Where Mr. Taylor once seemed to fear chaos, he now seems to trust the order inherent in experience: an order that does not depend on social restraint for its existence. Through his career, he has altered and refined his questions, viewing the problem of order and disorder from different, even opposing, perspectives, testing the sanity of reason and the vitality of the irrational, mixing them until his questions have given way—not so much to answers as to moral sureness. (pp. 213-30)

Jane Barnes Casey, "A View of Peter Taylor's Stories," in The Virginia Quarterly Review, Vol. 54, No. 2, Spring, 1978, pp. 213-30.

Peter Taylor with Barbara Thompson (interview date 1987)

[In the following excerpt, Taylor discusses recurring themes in his short stories and how his southern upbringing has influenced his writing.]

[Thompson]: Why did you become a writer, a storyteller?

[Taylor]: I think a great part of it was the storytelling in the family. I was lucky to come along out of this family of storytellers. My grandfather was famous for his tales. There used to be cartoons about him in the Washington papers—standing in the Senate cloakroom telling stories to the other senators. He was of the generation just following the Civil War; he was a little boy then. His father was of the war generation. He, that great grandfather, was a lawyer, a clergyman, a landowner. He went to Princeton and was a Unionist. In fact, he was Commissioner of Indian Affairs under the first President Johnson. He was enlightened and freed his slaves. But his wife was for the Confederacy, more or less. Her brother was a Confederate senator from Tennessee. That's why the younger children of the next generation were afterwards to become Democrats and the older children Republicans. We grew up, in my generation, with political battles, sometimes bloody, at home between those great-uncles and aunts. But I think it did give me a sense of history, a sense of the past. I began to make up stories about these things, the old houses, Robert E. Lee, southern things that I was obsessed by even then, at eight or nine. And I did have considerable imagination, of course, and so when I began to make up stories about my forebears, I began, you know, to exercise my power over them. *That's* one of the satisfactions of writing fiction! One of the reasons that all of this was so interesting to me was that we lived outside the South, away from what we thought of as the South, and yet there was constant talk at our table about Tennessee, constant plans for going back there at Christmas, at Easter, at every holiday. This was when we lived in St. Louis. We considered that far up north! My mother and father thought Nashville was the center of the world. When we lived away from there it was either because my father was in business in St. Louis or my grandfather in politics in Washington. There are no more loyal Southerners than those who grew up *just* outside the South or in the border states. We lived in a little South of our own in St. Louis. We had a houseful of servants from my father's farm in the cotton country of West Tennessee, and the adults—black and white—would talk about the South, about the way things used to be there. We had very intelligent people working for us. Lucille, who really ran the house, had been to college for two or three

years, and had taught school. That was the tragic thing in those days: even when the negroes went off to college, there was really nothing they could do with their education—especially during the Depression years—and they would come back home and go into service. Lucille would talk to me about my writing and my efforts to paint. I had more conversations with her than with my mother on those subjects—and of course far more than with my father. Lucille had more influence on me when I was a child than any other adult, unless it were her cousin Basil Manly Taylor, who was our butler. It has always been difficult for me to see how people who grew up in the South, brought up by people like Lucille Taylor and B. M. Taylor, could be guilty of race prejudice. The people that loved me most and that I loved most when I was growing up, I think, were these people. (pp. 47-8)

Many of the early stories are in a woman's voice or from a woman's point of view.

When I first began writing stories I wrote about blacks a great deal, and I wrote about women. I didn't begin with any conscious philosophy, but I had a store of stories that I knew, that I had been told, and I felt I had to write them. I discovered in writing them that certain people were always getting the short end. I found the blacks being exploited by the white women, and the white women being exploited by the white men. In my stories that always came through to me and from the stories themselves I began to understand what I really thought.

As Lawrence said, not to trust the teller, but trust the tale.

I quote Frank O'Connor to my students, that when you are writing a story, at some point the story must take over. You are not going to be able to control it. I think this is true. O'Connor said he thought Joyce controls his stories too tightly—"Who ever heard of a Joyce story taking over?" he asked—and that there is a deadness about them. You have got to keep the story opened up, let the story take over at some point.

Do you always know the ending when you begin?

I know one ending. But before I've worked on a story very long I know another. That's part of the fun of it. You begin with one thing, but the story itself may change your mind by the end. I always have some idea, but I think it's important to keep your story free when you are writing it, rather than working mechanically towards a fixed ending. I often reverse my understanding in the course of writing a story. Perhaps my real feelings come out as I write.

In ways you hadn't imagined?

That happens to me more often than not. I didn't know what was going to happen in **"The Old Forest."** I didn't plan all the business of the hunt for Lee Ann or understand its significance. The significance began to emerge as I was writing it, along with my true feelings about the characters. The story came from something I remembered. I did have such an accident in the family car, and there were some incidents and characters like those I describe . . . There was a girl like Lee Ann and there was another set of young people that I sometimes ran with; the accident occurred a few blocks from where she lived, and she was involved in it. But it was only after I began writing the story that I realized the significance of that girl. Obviously it was too carefully plotted, at last, to have happened that way. Then another story of mine called **"Guests,"** an earlier one about a family who have cousins visiting them from the country. I hadn't planned for anyone to die when I was writing the beginning of the story, but then it suddenly seemed the only way the story *could* end.

What do you begin with, in those cases where it isn't a remembered event or an old family tale?

I often begin with a character or a situation I've observed or even with a joke I've heard. Often a very serious story has begun with a joke. If a joke or anecdote sticks in my mind for years I know there must be something in it that means something to me that I am not conscious of. This is what I mean when I say I feel one learns about oneself from writing fiction. If a story has stuck with me for years, even a dirty story, a dirty joke, I'll think the story must contain some profound meaning for me and about me . . . I'll give you an example. There's a story called **"Heads of Houses."** Ten years before I wrote it I knew a couple who went to stay in the summer with the wife's parents up in the mountains of Tennessee. The two couples got on each other's nerves terribly. Their summer together was a disaster, more or less, and so the young husband pretended he had received a telegram or letter—I think this got into the story—calling him back to the university where he taught. When they set out for home and were starting to drive down the mountainside, they looked back and saw the father and mother and bachelor brother join hands and dance in a circle on the lawn—they were so glad the young couple had gone! And, you understand, the young couple had been feeling guilty about leaving. When I began the story, the very point of it was to be that dancing on the lawn. That's what had originally appealed to me. But when I finished it, it was all wrong. When I saw how wrong it was I tore up the story without ever looking at it again. Then I wrote it again from scratch—in quite a different form. When I wrote it the first time it was the story of the two couples; in the background was the brother, the one who danced with the parents in a circle. That was really his only role. But by the time I got the story worked out the second time, I saw how he was really the most sympathetic character in it. Everyone else is enjoying (or suffering) a rich family life, but the old bachelor brother is not having any life at all. And by the time I finished the second version there wasn't even any dancing on the lawn. The parents and the brother are too preoccupied with the significance of the moment. The brother simply stands there juggling apples. So the important image I began with never got into the story at all. Then there is a story called **"The Hand of Emmagene,"** about a girl who cuts off her hand. Well, I'd heard that story fifteen years before, at least. It was told to me by the same woman, Lucy Hooke, who told me the story of **"Heads of Houses."** She was a marvelous storyteller—you know how some people have a great talent for telling a story but can't write one. Just as many writers can't actually *tell* a story. Well, Lucy Hooke told me about the severed hand. It was her brother who found it, I think. It was a young woman's hand. Why had she done it? What had happened? In real life she was

a girl from East Tennessee, which is generally considered the puritanical part of the state, up-country. Nobody knew why she cut off her hand. That's the mystery we were left with. I only knew that I must imagine why some young woman would do such a thing, what it signified. But I didn't know how to use it, or what it meant to me. Or how I would fit something like that into the quiet world of the stories I usually write. And then at last I realized that what I had to do to dramatize it was to put it against the background of the most conventional people I could think of, just perfectly plain and unimaginative people. And in dramatizing it I found its significance, at least twenty-five years after the event. I have another story called **"Her Need."** I have rewritten it since *In the Miro District* appeared. I was walking early one morning in Charlottesville and saw a young woman, thirty-five or so, with her teenage son beside her in her car speeding along through the residential streets, driving him somewhere. I began to speculate upon what they were doing, where they were going. I went home and wrote the story that day. Sometimes you have a story that's been in your mind a long time. I have one story that I haven't written yet that I want to write. I recently thought about it reading Trollope's *Barchester Towers*. I want to bring out the story of the people who leave a town, leave the world they have always lived in and go off and become something else. What reminded me of it was the Stanhopes in Trollope, who had been off in Italy and then came back to Barchester. They are very continental, all their manners are different, and they are rather resented and thought odd by everybody. It's a big part of the novel. Well, I have seen that happen. People would go off and become very rich someplace else and when they would come back to Nashville or Memphis or St. Louis, they weren't quite accepted. I don't know quite what it means: the people who resented them all wanted to be rich themselves. But if somebody went off and got to be president of U.S. Steel or owned it or something, the people back home rather rejected them. I'll get some little theme like that and go over it and over it and wonder why it interests me and what there is in it, ask myself where does that lead and what does it signify? Is this just a frivolous interest or a profound one? What is marvelous is when your frivolous interests (your interests in the world, just representing it and imitating life) coincide with some serious theme that you are concerned with; when the two coincide, that's what's marvelous and fun. Then sometimes a story stays in your mind for a long time and refuses to yield the significance it has for you. It's like trying to discover what your dreams mean.

When did you know that you were going to be a writer?

When I finished school I received a scholarship to Columbia University. But it didn't cover all my expenses; my father was dead set against my accepting it. It created a great crisis in the family. My mother was all for my going—for doing whatever I chose to do. She went out to the stores and outfitted me, even packed the wardrobe trunk. But my father held out against it. He was determined that I should go to Vanderbilt, where he had gone to college. I was equally determined that I shouldn't go to Vanderbilt. So, instead, I went out to Southwestern there in Memphis and took some courses and at the same time got work at the newspaper. That was the greatest piece of good luck for me, because there in Tennessee during the Depression some of the best writers in the country (or in the English-speaking world) were teaching: Allen Tate, John Crowe Ransom, Robert Penn Warren. I knew all those people when I was very young. Also Katherine Anne Porter and Andrew Lytle. Allen Tate particularly made a great impression on me. I had him as my freshman English instructor at Southwestern and he was electrifying. He talked about the *art* of fiction, taking it seriously as a form. It was his genius as a teacher that he made young people feel the importance of literature, the importance of art. That came just at the right moment for me. I had already realized that I had a welter of stories I wished to tell. I had written stories, I had written poems, but I had no real principles of writing. When I became interested in the formal qualities, art and life itself meant something. Later in life, Allen Tate and I quarrelled. I think he did me a great injury. But I was able to forgive him because that injury counted for almost nothing compared to what he taught me when I was young. The next summer I took a writing course with Tate, in fiction, and that was the real beginning. Allen liked my stories immensely. He wrote letters to Robert Penn Warren about them—at that time Warren and Cleanth Brooks were editing *The Southern Review*—and sent him two of my stories, without my knowledge. That was very like Tate. He was ever generous with young people, to the end of his life. I know he sent those stories because in Warren's preface to my first book he mentions that he had rejected them and expresses regret for having done so. Actually it was very wise of him and I am grateful to him for it now. But then I am grateful to him for so many things. One can't have a better friend than Robert Penn Warren, or a more delightful companion. I saw that first story just the other day, in an old copy of a magazine called *River*. When Warren didn't take those stories, I sent it to a man who'd written to me from Oxford, Mississippi. His magazine ran just a few issues, but my first story and Eudora Welty's were in that issue.

What came next?

Allen Tate persuaded me I should go that next year to Vanderbilt. At Vanderbilt, I met John Crowe Ransom. He was a great poet. One never doubted that. But you never got to know him well—that is, not when you were a student. Later on we became good friends, played bridge together every week for years, but not in the early days. He was very different from Tate, who dramatized everything, even his friendships with students. Ransom's way was the opposite. He was all understatement. You would go to his office for a conference on a story, bring the story for him to read, and he would say almost nothing. What he *would* say was very much to the point and counted a great deal with me, but you had to prod him, pull it out and listen carefully. He had pertinent things to say, but he hated what he sometimes called "evangelical teaching." Ransom was a disciplinarian in his way and narrow: he had little interest in fiction and tried his best to persuade me to write poetry. I remember I wrote a story in which I included a little poem. The poem was necessary to the story, I believe. I kept that paper for years because he wrote on it "*B* for

the story, *A* for the little poem." That was his way of pressing me to write poetry. And I have to say that Ransom prevailed, because the first thing I ever published was a poem, the year I graduated from Kenyon. He was the best kind of teacher or the best for me at that time—a satisfying, reassuring person to talk to about one's work just because he *was* so impersonal. When you gave him a poem to read the first thing he did was to look at the poem and tap on the desk to make sure the meter was correct. Then he carefully checked the rhyme scheme. He would not discuss other elements of the poem until he had done that. It seems now that what he taught me about writing was compression. And compression is what I have set great store by as a short-story writer. He was so questioning of every detail in the manuscript before him that you felt compelled to make everything functional and to be ready to defend it. That habit carried over into story writing. I believe that's one reason I write stories instead of novels. As Faulkner is said to have said, everyone wants to write poetry in the beginning but if you can't write poetry you write short stories, and if you can't write short stories you write novels. Well, that's too easy, but still there is some truth in it. And, of course, when I was at Kenyon I was writing poems in self-defense. The general interest there at that time was all in poetry, not at all in fiction. I've referred to Ransom's interest, of course, but it must be remembered I was rooming with Robert Lowell. And Randall Jarrell was there, too. Jarrell knew a great deal about fiction, but his chief concern was with poetry.

Was Jarrell an important influence?

He had tremendous influence on me for several years, most of all on my reading. I think I began reading Chekhov under his influence back at Vanderbilt, but I'm not sure. He was the first serious literary person I knew who read Chekhov stories and could talk about them. Other people would tell you they read or admired Chekhov but they didn't really know his stories. Very few people have read them even now. I think it's because his stories have the compression of poetry. Most readers don't know how he is to be read. He gives the illusion that he is just telling a simple tale. Readers often feel it's not much of a tale, that "nothing happens." But actually every line is *packed*. I don't know how much I have been influenced by him. I don't ever consciously think, "Ah, this is a Chekhov effect!" But anything you admire so much is bound to affect you. Without knowing it, you are going to steal from it, or be influenced by its subtle structure and statement. That's one reason for a young writer to read a master. But one goes through phases. Most people do. Everybody should. After Chekhov it was James for me. Since Jarrell didn't like his fiction, James became one of our great subjects for debate. He would make condescending remarks about James, say really silly things and bend double with laughter. Finally it got so we avoided the subject. I went through a period when I read nothing but James. Lowell and I tried to read *The Golden Bowl* aloud! It is very hard to do. I suppose I absorbed something from Chekhov— people have pointed out evidence of it in my work, Jarrell especially did—but James I *consciously* learned from. I imitated him. And then I had to unlearn some of it. I think it is good to imitate for a time, but then you have to discard what you can't use. In the long run, a good writer doesn't have to worry about stealing or borrowing. What he can make his own he will keep without giving it a thought. What he can't he will discard.

Which were the Jamesian stories?

I'm almost afraid to say, for fear that his influence doesn't show in the least. **"A Spinster's Tale"** would certainly be one, although other people may not see it. I was experimenting in those days in different ways. One of my ghost plays seems a direct steal from "The Jolly Corner," but I didn't realize it until I had almost finished writing it. It is the one where a man comes back to St. Louis to see his old girlfriend and comes upon himself as he might have been had he married that girl. It is perilously near "The Jolly Corner." Then I had a Lawrence period. I still consider Lawrence's short stories the greatest stories of this century. I keep going back to them. The feeling for nature in them is quite wonderful. It is rather the opposite of James. That is one of the things Jarrell would say about James, that in all of James you could never imagine finding a description of a landscape. I have dug out a few. But there are not many. (pp. 50-9)

Do you ever do research for a story?

No, I feel very strongly against that. I read Southern history because I *like* reading it. Then suddenly I'll find it appearing in something I write. But as soon as I have a body of ideas and put them in a story *consciously,* that just kills it for me. When I have done it at times, it *has* killed it. I have a number of stories I've never put in a collection and never would put in a collection, partly because it seemed to me they never came to life on their own. I had forced some idea, something Freudian or political or some idea about history. (pp. 60-1)

I know you haven't written memoirs, but do you write critical essays or reviews?

The last review I wrote was a review of Allen Tate's *The Fathers,* which came out, I think, in 1939. I resolved early that if I was going to teach I was never going to write criticism, and I won't. It's too hard. Why, writing criticism takes as much time as writing fiction and is a much less serious business! Teaching takes as much of my life as I want to give to generalization. And I like teaching so much better than I like writing criticism. It involves you with other people. I do all my teaching in conference, one to one. Teaching is always done best *vis-à-vis.* I worked in New York for a time at Henry Holt, just as a first reader, and I realized I disliked reading all those manuscripts from people I would never see or know anything about. It is so much more fun to see really bright young people trying to write and learning to read intelligently, and seeing them develop, being involved with them. So much of your life as a writer is isolating. When I think of that, I can hardly wait for my next teaching stint at some college or university. And then, too, I have a horror of defining, of limiting. Everything seems to me to be such a cliché as soon as I say it. The other problem is that as soon as I make a point, I am sure I can disprove it; I'm sure that the opposite is also true.

You once said something in that context about Flaubert.

Yes, well, of course, who can write fiction in this century without feeling some pressure from Flaubert. And some of the writers I've been influenced by, to them Flaubert was God. His was the Word. He was the Master. But you know, often I think of Flaubert's rules and regulations and wish to see if I can successfully defy them. To see how much the narrator can generalize and how much he can come in and exercise his omniscience, how far I can impose the narrator on the narrative. Because, you know, I believe if one thing can be proved by some esthetic theory, then there is inevitably another theory that can prove the opposite. The delightful thing about writing stories is that you can have it both ways. You can mull it over and cover up and deceive the reader until finally he accepts your way of doing it. The best thing of all is that you don't have to be consistent, particularly from one story to another. When I was still an undergraduate I wrote a story called **"The Spinster's Tale."** The next story after that was called **"The Fancy Woman,"** in which I absolutely reversed the characters and the subject. What I wished to present in that first story was a discovery of evil, how the shock of it affected a woman's whole life. And in the other story the character was so far corrupted that she couldn't believe in her discovery of innocence. She was beyond any possibility of accepting it. Maybe that is not the right way to write, but I often bounce from one idea to another. So often ideas for stories are born out of other stories. You write one and you see some little minor theme in there that you wish to develop further.

When I was reading your stories chronologically, I was conscious that many of them seemed concerned with revising some view of the past, or with present events in which the past is a vital element.

I think that's one way of thinking about one's fiction. Saying, well, what if I looked at it from this other point of view? Taking stories one has heard and trying to make sense of them, trying to learn what in the closest analysis and profoundest speculation they might mean. In the beginning I wrote many stories about women. Southern women, old ladies, a lot of them. Each story came out of some incident, out of some strong feeling. I am always trying to discover in a story what it is that I am *really* trying to say about the subject and why it interests me, what it means and what I can do with it. In **"Miss Leonora When Last Seen,"** for instance, I was trying to imagine what it was like to have *been* one of those women. To reflect *that* side, that world. I had seen such women, and I wanted to discover what they meant, what their lives meant. The women that I had seen were the most cultivated people I knew, so much more cultivated than the men in that society. And they had ideas—not explicit ideas but inceptions of ideas as to what the world should be like, what their roles were to be. I had grown up with just so many old ladies: my father, being a lawyer, looked after the estates and affairs of many of them; wherever we were living they'd come to visit us, with their wardrobe trunks. They were delightful, extremely intelligent people. They stood for the intellectual and cultural life of the society.

Jane Barnes suggests in her essay about you that after

"Miss Leonora" you began to explore the masculine side of life, and of your own nature.

I think she hits the nail on the head. In the beginning my sympathy had been all with women, but after that I thought, well, what if I look at it from the men's point of view of that world. My wife says I'm much softer, easier on my father now when I tell stories . . . that his role changes in them from the way I used to tell them. When I was first married, my father and I had battles. On their visits, my father would insist on staying in bed and having his breakfast brought to him. I would rage and say, "He can't *do* that!" and Eleanor would say, "Oh yes." She would take his meals up, or my mother would. She remembers my raging—but I had other feelings about him, also.

I remember an early story, "Porte-Cochère," in which the father seems very like the man in "The Gift of the Prodigal" but less sympathetically viewed.

The man in the later stories is much more sympathetic than the character in the earlier. I like that story dramatically—that's what I was trying to do then, learn to write a dramatic story—but I feel I never got inside that man in "Porte-Cochère." I had someone tell me just this week that it's mechanically fine, dramatically witty, the language is satisfactory, but something is missing, something about getting inside the character. I don't think the reader is engaged in that story emotionally. I think the new stories have that. I like to think I have made some progress. One makes advances. You *do!* You come to see what your story is like. That's part of the fun: to see how you can get the other elements that are not your natural interests or concerns primarily. In that earlier story I was trying to force it really dramatically. He was not a character of the sort I was interested in at that time. I could probably write that story better now because I have more interest in that sort of person, maybe because since then I have seen my father and others grow old. And grown old myself. I can be more sympathetic.

After "Miss Leonora" the next story was—

"Venus, Cupid, Folly and Time." Ford Madox Ford says at some point you have to begin to make up stories. Up until then in some stories—the most anthologized like **"What You Hear from 'Em?"**—there's not a word that's made up. But **"Venus, Cupid, Folly and Time"** begins a change in my writing. It is less ironic, less funny, with fewer genteel characters, more eccentrics. (pp. 61-8)

I remember your saying that "Venus, Cupid, . . . " was your first plotted story—"made" rather than evolved. You started with an effect to be achieved rather than a tale to be told?

I really had in mind almost an allegory. One of the things it's about is incest—not just the brother and sister, but all the young people. It's a form of incest to want to marry only in your class, your own background exactly. That was the world I had grown up in. I had seen my brothers and sisters in it. Some of those young people—it was very sad—*couldn't* marry anyone but that way, and never married because there was nobody in that set the right age.

They had other chances to marry, but nobody that would fit; it had to be "in the family," so to speak. It *is* a sort of incest to marry within a class, especially when it's within a class in a certain town. People didn't like it as well if their families married somebody from Cincinnati or New Orleans; it had to be somebody from Memphis or Nashville. That was what my idea was. I had a much clearer synopsis for that story in my mind than I usually do. That really was a turning point.

You often start with just an image, or a single sentence, don't you? In "The Fancy Woman" it was that first sentence—"He wanted no more of her drunken palaver"?

Yes. I feel justified in doing that because if you have any profound thoughts or views they will emerge from within the story inevitably. I still believe that. I tell young writers not to worry about writing a profound story because, as James said, a profound mind will produce a profound story and a superficial mind will produce a superficial story. Remember Tolstoy's saying that Chekhov was so given to truth that he could not possibly have presented anything but the truth. And he said—Tolstoy said—that it's very much the way it was when he was learning to ride a bicycle. He was learning in a huge gymnasium, and there was one lady, standing in the middle, walking around there, and he kept saying to himself "whatever I do I must not run into that woman." And he circled around her—he could hardly ride the bicycle—and ran her down. That's the way Chekhov is with the truth, whatever he *tries* to do . . .

And telling the truth is, finally, what writing is about? That wonderful quote from Montaigne about speaking the truth, not as much as you know but as much as you dare—and daring more as you grow older.

I think trying to write is a religious exercise. You are trying to understand life, and you can only get the illusion of doing it fully by writing. That is, it's the only way I can come to understand things fully. When I create, when I put my own mark on something and form it, I begin to know the whole truth about it, how it was put together. Then you can begin to change things around. You know all this after you have written a lot. You really know. And it has become the most important thing in your life. It has nothing to do with craft, or even art, in a way. It is making sense of life. It is coming to understand yourself. That's what I love about Katherine Anne Porter. She managed to interpret the events of her life in her stories, just by writing them down. She knew what she was really like—and that represents the highest intelligence in the world, to know what you really are. She did. You think of a storyteller as not very intellectual at all—or I do—but someone who writes stories and lets his intelligence come out *that* way. But she was intellectual in the ordinary sense, too. Her essays are just amazing. Though she knew her art—there was no question about that—she was my idea of the unprofessional. I feel strongly against professionalism, against someone's feeling he has to write a book every year to keep his name before the public. I see people processing themselves, torturing themselves, for that, rather than writing out of a compulsion some story from their own experience, their own feelings. That's the way you should write, unless you are just practicing. I tell young writers to steal a plot or an idea or whatever, just to get going. See how a character comes out, how you fit it into your life. . . . You see great writers doing it too. Certainly some of James's stories came right out of Trollope. And some came from Hawthorne. It's just so clear to me that James took the work of Hawthorne and Trollope and of all kinds of writers and made of them a much greater work. I really don't think you should make money writing. Oh, I'm not going to turn down money, but people worrying about how they are going to make a living writing ought to worry about making a living some other way on the periphery, doing something congenial to them like teaching or editing. We hear a lot of complaints from writers now, especially from PEN, about the situation of the writer—well, it's *always* been awful! I think you should write for yourself, for the joy of it, the pleasure of it, and for the satisfaction that you have in learning about your life. (pp. 69-71)

In the last years you've been writing stories in a new form. Prose poems? What do you call them?

Lowell always spoke of them as "story poems" in his homey way. That's better. I have learned not to speak of them as poems, myself. I call them broken-line prose. I began writing them when I was trying to make things shorter. I am always trying for compression. It fascinates me that my stories get longer and longer when I'm always trying to make them shorter. I began by wanting to get interest in every line, every sentence. I felt if a line is broken, if where the line ends means something, you get another emphasis. When a sentence just ends at that line, you get one kind of rhythm, one emphasis, but if it ends in the middle of the line, you get something else, the run-on lines, enjambment. All these are techniques of poetry. Oh, the sentences mean what they mean, but the fact that they're put together in a line gives another emphasis, the way it does in poetry. You have the two kinds of syntax, the line endings and the run-on line, and the regular syntax of the language. You can be saying a lot more in a short space. This was my feeling when I began writing them, not really *knowing* what I was doing. For years I had been very sanctimonious, saying, "I like poetry to be poetry and fiction to be fiction." In my case that's a sure sign that someday I'm going to change my mind and do just the opposite. So I began by writing just a few lines that way, in the story called **"Three Heroines."** The story itself was easy to write because it's almost literally what happened: an account of my going home, and my mother and the woman that had always looked after her. The story just fell into place, and I was able to work on the lines, working out the form. I submitted that story, **"The Gift of the Prodigal,"** to *The New Yorker* in that form. I knew all along they wouldn't like it that way. I didn't like it either; I did it sort of for fun. They wrote back at once, saying they'd like to print it, but they'd like me to put it in the other form. I said I would, but that I'd like the right, if I put it in a book, to put it back in the original form. I haven't done so, however. Every story in **In the Miro District** was written in that form originally. That is, I began them all that way, but if I got halfway through and found that it got too long or I couldn't sustain the concept or that the line ends were

not significant, no longer functional, then I'd give it up. It had become artificial. But most of the time I think it puts more emphasis on the texture if you think in terms of lines, if you think of the intrinsic importance of each sentence. That is my ideal in writing, that each sentence should have an intrinsic interest, and then that it should have an interest in terms of the whole story. That is the satisfaction that you get in poetry, and this is the way I think of writing a story. Even the novel-like thing I'm writing now is being written in that form. (pp. 72-3)

You once spoke of the short story as a dramatic form, more akin to playwriting than to the writing of novels.

The short-story writer is concerned with compression, with saying as much as he can in a short space, just as the poet is. So he has to choose the right dramatic moment for the presentation. If he can do that in writing a story, he can have as big a canvas as he would with a novel. That's the genius of the short-story writer—finding precisely the right moment in the vital interplay between the characters. The same is true for playwrights. In a play everything has to be done in a particular scene, at a particular time, and you have to choose that. That's the business of the dramatist. (p. 74)

You spoke earlier of trying to shorten and compress, but I have the impression that your most recent stories are often very long.

I'm not trying now to write short stories. A really short story has to be concerned with a limited kind of experience, and be limited in time, I think. But if your tendency is to write longer and longer stories, then you should go ahead, I think. For one thing, I've gotten terribly interested in plot, a thing I scorned when I was a young man. When people would mention plot to me, or structure even, I was repelled. I thought there was something crass about plot. I had no interest in it. But I've learned through the years that there's something very useful in it, that there is a kind of emphasis you can achieve with plot used properly. It *punctuates!* It can say, "Well, we've gone this far" and then "this far." (p. 76)

How would you like to be remembered?

I would like to have as many of my stories as possible survive and be read and liked. At my age it's hard not to want to feel that your last book is your best book. And I'd like to feel that what I'm doing now is still better. When I look back on my earlier things I understand why a lot of them were ignored. They're not bad, they're not slick or cheap in any way, but I lacked knowledge of how to say what I wanted to say, and lacked knowledge of what I wanted to say. I always had the inclination to tell a story, but in my early stories I never pressed hard enough to know what it meant, as I think I do now. I wasted many years of effort writing things that were not the kinds of stories I should have been writing. I'm not ashamed of any of them, but I wish I'd written other stories that I would like to write now. (p. 80)

Peter Taylor and Barbara Thompson, in an interview in The Paris Review, *Vol. 29, No. 104, Fall, 1987, pp. 45-82.*

J. A. Bryant, Jr.   (essay date 1987)

[*Bryant is an American educator and critic. In the following essay, he discusses Taylor's examination of the idealization of southern culture and heritage through the upper middle-class characters he portrays.*]

In the past, reviews of Peter Taylor's books have often begun with the observation that his work has been neglected by the general reader. The popular reception last year of his second novel, *A Summons to Memphis,* has probably put an end to that; yet *A Summons to Memphis* is not essentially different from most of the memorable shorter works that have preceded it. Like **"In the Miro District"** and **"The Old Forest,"** two of the more recent stories that critics justifiably call masterpieces, it is ostensibly a protracted reminiscence presented with covert artfulness by a mature narrator who has witnessed and been a party to the disintegration of a modern Southern family. In all three the narrator manipulates the time sequence of his story in much the same fashion, focussing like any good storyteller on a single event but all the while seeming to allow what appears to be a compulsive digressiveness free rein. In this way the unfolding story comes to us enriched both by a network of attendant circumstance authentically and vividly presented and by commentary that creates a visible authority for the story. Moreover, the credibility of that commentary is enhanced for readers who can bring to it a familiarity with the various localities that appear in the stories and with the principal details of Taylor's career. Thus when the narrator in these stories speaks of Acklen Park, Elliston Place, Belle Meade, West End, and Division Street in Nashville and unfailingly places and describes such locations accurately, readers who know Nashville and something of Taylor's life there slip readily into the illusion that what they are getting is an authentic reminiscence. Similarly readers from Memphis may be gratified by the mere mention of such names as Overton Park, Adams Street, and Bristol Highway. The fact is that Taylor from the beginning has applied his talent to the world he has known and has unhesitatingly retained intact not only place names but much of the other data he has

observed, including, one suspects, a good many personal family relationships.

To say that he has done this as a result of some deliberate strategy, however, would be misleading. What may have begun as strategy in Taylor's earliest work has persisted as integrity in the work of his maturity. For almost thirty years now, with an indifference to critical opinion that can be equated with courage, he has been putting together honest, often photographically accurate, images of the Tennessee he knows to show the effects of cultural inheritance on its people. In several of his best stories he has dealt with a spurious regional identity that persists in the minds of many southerners, particularly affluent urban southerners, who imagine they are preserving an authentic and uniquely southern way of life when actually they are perpetuating customs and values based upon a myth that has been generated largely by sentimental novelists. These modern southerners find it possible to believe in an Old South populated for the most part by benevolent slaveholders, landed gentry, who imported their culture from England and France, and who sent their sons to Yale and Harvard, and brought up their daughters to be models of manners and decorum. In the myth as in life the Civil War impoverished these early southerners and several generations of their descendants, but the War itself survives in their minds as a glorious age of chivalry, one not likely to come again in this decadent modern world. For such as these, who consider *Gone With the Wind* a tribute to their own past, the Civil War has become more golden than bloody.

Several of Taylor's mentors at Vanderbilt had recognized the widespread acceptance of this romantic view when they called themselves Fugitives and firmly repudiated the caricatures that were then as now flourishing among defenders of antebellum society. Nevertheless, most readers saw the Fugitives as simply new "southern writers" and undiscriminatingly lumped them together with the popular romanticists, unaware that several had already undertaken a more perceptive critique of southern life in poetry and fiction—that John Ransom, for example, with customary irony had treated of the southern myth in such pieces as "Captain Carpenter" and "Antique Harvesters" or that Allen Tate had dealt obliquely with the same matter in his widely misunderstood "Ode to the Confederate Dead" and made it one of the concerns of his novel *The Fathers.* Taylor, whether by accident or design, followed soon after in this largely unhonored course initiated by his Vanderbilt predecessors. Since then he has looked squarely at the south he knows best, appreciated the complex mixture of vigor, pride, and guilt in its distinctive variant of American culture, and recreated it in fictional work that in the end may prove to be a more durable critique than any offered by formal historians.

Taylor's south—or more precisely, Taylor's Tennessee—is not a spiritual wasteland. He sees much of its southern inheritance as healthy, admirable, and even elegant, but he regards as damaging that self-serving historical apologetic which pretenders to prominence and power use, sometimes without quite realizing what they are doing, to justify their claims. As Taylor portrays them, social aspirants in Nashville and Memphis apply their romantic apologetic in much the same way. In both cities those not born to a "big house," to use a phrase presumably applied by slaves to plantation manor houses, often find it necessary first to dignify or even suppress their memory of a more modest origin, then to create an appropriate big house of their own in some fashionable section or suburb, and thereafter to support vigorously such distinctions in class and custom as will call attention to their position and guarantee its continuation. In other ways the versions of the myth may vary from one city to the other, and they may not be entirely compatible; for at least until recently large cities in the South, sometimes counties even, have cherished distinctive versions of the regional myth with correspondingly distinctive modes of conduct that tend to preserve their individuality.

This, or something like it, is the process that has resulted in the idealization of a past life, more or less unconscious, by the families that Taylor presents in *A Summons to Memphis* and in the two long stories which serve as title stories in his most recent collections. All these have connections in a small town or rural area by which they can claim to have derived from the plantation south and feel superior to the vast body of artisans, shop keepers, workers, and servants who make up the bulk of the population; and all feel threatened when circumstances challenge the protective wall of romantic myth that gives color, dignity, and meaning to their lives. In *A Summons to Memphis* the elder Carver is a man from the respectable West Tennessee small town of Thornton (the Trenton of Taylor's youth), who early in life made his way to Nashville, married into an established family, fared well in business, and in time acquired an imposing "estate" on the fashionable Franklin Pike south of town. He has continued to think of West Tennessee as his old home and considers the property he still owns there as the agrarian base of his Nashville family. Nevertheless, when financial reverses require him to make a move, he bypasses Thornton and settles in Memphis. The effect on his family is traumatic. Deprived of its customary roots, the family appears to disintegrate; the once fun-loving wife declines into invalidism, the older son rushes into World War II and an early death, and two daughters, failing to find suitable husbands, remain "eternal young ladies" even as they advance into middle age. The younger son, Phillip, who serves as narrator, abandons Memphis, becomes an editor and a collector of rare books and settles in a Manhattan apartment with a Jewish mistress fourteen years his junior.

As the story progresses, attempts by the sisters, first, to prevent their father's second marriage and then to discourage what turns out to be his abortive attempt to revisit an old business associate and erstwhile enemy in Nashville, make it necessary for Phillip to return home. His visits there also prompt him to re-examine family relationships and adopt a more charitable view of his father's vagaries. Nevertheless he returns to New York and his ageing mistress to live out a life of serenity in their apartment filled with dusty books. *A Summons to Memphis,* it turns out, is not so much the story of a family that disintegrated as it is of one that found itself immured in a local fantasy and could not disintegrate. Had the Carver family been able to remain in Nashville, it might have disintegrated naturally into other Nashville families and so never faced the pain of alienation and atrophy that its inability to adapt to Memphis made inevitable. As it was, it remained an expatriated Nashville family, from which the elder Carver tried vainly to escape after his wife died and from which the sons did escape, one to war and death and the other to a solipsistic existence in faceless upper Manhattan.

Taylor depicted a similar resistence to change in one of his earliest stories, first published in *New Republic* in 1941 as "Like the Sad Heart of Ruth." Later he included it as "The Walled Garden" in both *Happy Families Are All Alike* (1959) and *The Old Forest* (1985). His use of this story as late as 1985 suggests its utility as a symbol of the situation which he had been exploring throughout his career in more realistic settings. "The Walled Garden" is a dramatic monologue, faintly reminiscent of Robert Browning, that a Memphis matron delivers to a young man who has presumed to call on her daughter. She receives the young man on the terrace of her home, which overlooks a garden she has created to serve as an oasis in the dusty terrain of West Tennessee, and begins by establishing that her guest knows nothing of flowers and gardening. Then she tells him bluntly, ". . . my daughter has finally made her life with me in this little garden plot, and year by year she has come to realize how little else there is hereabouts to compare with it." Her monologue continues with several variations on this theme and culminates in a chilling account of how years ago she broke the girl's spirit and turned her from a wild-eyed innocent into a cultural stereotype.

Nothing quite so melodramatic happens in "The Old Forest" but the later story may be read as an exploration of the situation which the early one presents. By contrast, it ends more or less happily in an enlightenment that eventually prompts another Memphis couple to escape from their garden. The event which makes that escape possible takes place in 1937 and is narrated by Nat Ramsey, now a man in his sixties and approaching retirement as a college teacher. Shortly before his marriage Nat was involved in an accident in Overton Park. A girl who happened to be with him at the time was a working girl with no pretensions to important family connections. Both were unhurt, but the girl inexplicably left the scene of the accident and disappeared in the direction of a part of the park known as the Old Forest because of its stand of ancient trees. The young man's fiancee, Caroline Braxley, aware that in class-conscious Memphis no marriage can take place until Nat's girl from the lower strata can be found and shown to be without claim upon him, joins vigorously in the search and by successfully second-guessing the vanished girl's motives discovers her whereabouts. The young woman, it turns out, has been fearful that publicity might reveal her connection with a grossly unattractive grandmother, who operates a disreputable Memphis night spot. That detail, of course, is a matter of no consequence to proper Memphis. As soon as the girl has been accounted for, she is forgotten, and plans for the marriage continue. Some years later Nat and Caroline, now comfortably established in Memphis life, recognize that they can no longer live in the walled garden that the city must forever be for them and escape to an academic life elsewhere. Nevertheless, the narrator's preoccupation with a trivial escapade thirty years after the event suggests that their escape, though real enough geographically, may have been not unlike Phillip Carver's escape to a life of rare book collecting.

Taylor has written stories of genuine escape, notably **"The Dark Walk,"** which he used as the concluding piece in *The Widows of Thornton,* his second collection, published in 1954; but most are not so happy, and some are accounts of how people help to build the walls that imprison them. The best example of this—probably the best story that he has written—is **"In the Miro District,"** the concluding piece in the collection of 1977 that bears its name. Taylor had anticipated the theme and action of **"In the Miro District"** in another story in *The Widows of Thorton:* **"What You Hear From 'Em."** In that one we have the unforgettable portrait of Aunt Munsie, an old Negro woman who raises pigs and pulls her slop wagon through the streets of Thornton in Olympian disregard of her fellow citizens' sensibilities and her own safety in the small-town traffic. The conclusion is analogous to the conclusion of **"In the Miro District."** Munsie grows old, her white patrons never return to Thornton from their reconstituted lives in Nashville and Memphis, and the town passes an ordinance forbidding the keeping of swine within its corporate limits. Deprived of her usual means of survival she surrenders her dignity and accepts the kind of role that the citizens of Thornton expect black people to assume: she takes to wearing a bandanna on her head and talking about the Bell Witch, and claims to remember how Forrest rode into town and saved all the cotton at the depot. Behind this stereotypical facade, Munsie's walled garden, she lives on for twenty years as a colorful old darkey whom the townspeople can understand and tolerate.

The victim of self-immurement in **"In the Miro District"** is an elderly Tennessean who after the death of his wife declines to give up his home but agrees reluctantly to "keep things" in a downstairs bedroom at the Nashville establishment of his daughter and son-in-law. He visits there infrequently, however, and on two occasions manages to arrive when the teen-aged grandson, having been left alone, is entertaining—once a party composed of four couples and another time, in his grandfather's downstairs room, his best girl. In the first episode the grandfather, on discovering couples naked and drunk in the upstairs bedrooms, "cleans house" with a sternness not altogether devoid of humor; but when he discovers the boy misbehaving with a "decent" girl in the room furnished with his favorite but unfashionable golden-oak pieces, rocker, wardrobe, and large folding-bed, he decides that surrender on his part may be preferable to letting his grandson's continuing profligacy go unchallenged. So he moves to Nashville permanently, on Nashville's terms.

This is where the old man begins to build the garden that becomes his prison. Before giving up he had preferred to go about in country work clothes. Usually instead of a tie he wore a gold collar button at his neck, and he refused to hide his weak chin with a proper beard. His daughter had hoped that he would furnish his room with some of the rosewood and walnut pieces that she knew he possessed, but she said nothing when he brought instead the plain things he and his wife had bought in the early years of their marriage. He refused to talk about the Civil War, saying that he had acquired his officer's rank only at a Confederate reunion. On occasion he would talk about his experiences with the notorious nightriders, who in years after the War had infested the area around Reelfoot Lake, and tell of the accounts he had heard or read of the great earthquake in 1811 which had created that lake and devastated the region. In short, he retained his identity as a member of the generation that had endured the War and survived the anarchy which followed, and with something like a frontiersman's honesty manifested a silent contempt for the younger generation's romanticizing and pseudo-sophistication in manners and morals.

Now, as an antique on exhibit, he grows the expected beard and dresses in a black serge suit, white shirt with starched collar, and a black shoe-string tie. Once he taught his grandson to refer to the area around Nashville as the Miro District (the name of the last Spanish governor who laid claim to it), saying that "only an antique Spanish name could do justice to the grandeur which Nashvillians [claim] for themselves." Now he himself has consented to act as a symbol of the only claim to grandeur that Nashvillians can understand; and the grandson, advanced to college age but none the wiser, brings friends home from Sewanee and takes pleasures in listening with them to the old man's reflections about strategy in the War Between the States and his tales of Shiloh, Vicksburg, Stone River, Franklin, and Chickamauga. Sometimes, though, the boy wonders whether he himself is any closer to the rehabilitated grandfather than those admiring visitors who sit at his feet.

Thus, though poles apart in social station and means, Aunt Munsie and the grandfather of **"In the Miro District"** both submit to the fantasies of the generations that come after them. Their stories hold up for inspection an aspect of the contemporary South that is seldom recognized by those who live in fashionable urban settings, but it represents a kind of self-deception that has counterparts in other regions of the United States and indeed in changing cultures everywhere. As its chronicler in Tennessee Taylor has achieved a universality in his work that is rapidly being acknowledged and applauded. Current admirers sometimes compare his achievment either to that of Eudora Welty among modern writers or to Chekhov among the older masters. Comparison with the latter is more appropriate because, having like Chekhov committed himself to telling the truth, Taylor consistently rejects both the obligation to entertain and the temptation to judge. He is not a raconteur, though he sometimes uses the persona of one, and he is not a satirist; but like Chekhov he has the ability to comprehend the anxiety, sometimes only latent, that can stultify any society which has failed, for whatever reason, to confront the true nature of the past that has produced it. Some would call the consequences of such a failure tragic; Chekhov insisted on calling them comic. The label one uses is not important so long as the author in question has the talent to present his perceptions fully in intelligible wholes. Taylor, it is now clear, has that talent in abundance. (pp. 65-72)

J. A. Bryant, Jr., "Peter Taylor and the Walled Gardens," in Journal of the Short Story in English, No. 9, Autumn, 1987, pp. 65-72.

Roland Sodowsky and Gargi Roysircar Sodowsky (essay date 1988)

[*In the following essay, the authors present two differing psychological interpretations of "A Spinster's Tale."*]

Several critics have noted the depth and richness of the characters in Peter Taylor's work, a complexity which makes his stories particularly apt for psychological interpretation. An especially good example is **"A Spinster's Tale,"** in which the protagonist, Betsy, may be seen from a Freudian point of view as being trapped by the forces of parent-child relationships and sexual fears or from an Adlerian point of view as choosing and controlling the unsocial direction of her life.

Set in an upper-class home in Nashville around 1900, **"Spinster's Tale"** is narrated by an unmarried woman named Elizabeth who recalls events beginning with her mother's death and ending about a year later, shortly after her fourteenth birthday. Her mother has died a few days after bearing a stillborn child. Elizabeth, called Betsy by her eighteen-year-old brother, lives with her father, brother, and several servants. During a moment of grief one afternoon about six months after her mother's death, the girl observes an old man passing the house, red-faced, drunk, stumbling and cursing. Seeing this man, Mr. Speed, causes her to become "dry-eyed in my fright" and to remember vividly the burial of the stillborn infant and a few minutes spent with her mother just before her death. Betsy recognizes Mr. Speed as a "permanent and formidable figure in my life which I would be called upon to deal with," and thereafter she observes him from the parlor window each time he passes, even though the sight of him makes her teeth chatter. Much of the rest of the story consists of variations of this basic pattern in which the terrified girl watches the old man, anticipating the day when he will come to her door.

In one variation, Betsy stands at the door of her bedroom late at night while her drunken brother, whom she intuits as a less menacing version of Mr. Speed, climbs the stairs. With apparent incestuous intent, she entices him into her bedroom. Thinking about the encounter later, she wishes she had made him aware of "some unmentionable trouble" they have in common. In another variation, she learns the unwelcome lesson that her brother and Mr. Speed are more alike than she had thought. In another, just after the girl's father and uncles jokingly accuse her of flirting with a boy, Mr. Speed appears outside and she becomes hysterical.

In the final variation, Mr. Speed, caught in a rainstorm, actually enters the house, frightening both Betsy and Lucy, a maid. After letting him in, the maid flees up the stairs, but Betsy calls the police. The old man tries to leave but falls from the porch and is knocked unconscious. The police find him thus a few minutes later and take him away.

"Spinster's Tale" is replete with objects and actions for which, in his discussion of dream symbols in *The Interpretation of Dreams,* Sigmund Freud assigns various sexual meanings. A study of Betsy's reactions to these symbols suggests that despite the lonely girl's desperate attempts to deal with the phenomena these symbols represent, she cannot adjust to them. Instead, she projects her unacceptable, frightening sexual impulses to external dangers. Thus she fears maleness and male sexuality and thereby copes projectively and unconsciously with her fears, although in a deviant manner.

Except for a flashback to the burial of the stillborn infant, the girl is never seen outside the house, which she repeatedly describes as "shadowy," the dream-like setting thus making an interpretation in Freudian terms especially appropriate. Although her father, brother, and the servants also occupy the house, she persistently calls it "my house," "my door," to which Mr. Speed will eventually come, reminding one of Freud's symbolization of persons as male organs, of the house as body, doors as apertures, and rooms as female; churches too are equated with the vagina, and Betsy's house is on Church Street. Mr. Speed carries a top coat, a later version of the cloak, one of Freud's phallic symbols, and a heavy walking cane, also phallic, with which he beats the trees or pokes at the "soft sod along the sidewalk." When the March wind blows off his hat, another male genital symbol, it rolls across the lawn toward the house. And when he finally does come to the door, he raps on it with his cane. Once inside, however, he throws the cane on the floor in an apparent gesture of defeat.

Betsy unconsciously defends herself, displacing her guilty, fearful attraction for Mr. Speed upon her brother, a safer target. She remembers her brother in terms of phallic images. He shows her "a box of cigarettes which a girl had given him"; he chases after and returns Mr. Speed's hat, thus identifying himself more closely in Betsy's eyes with the old man; in her white nightgown, symbolizing chastity, she watches her brother from her bedroom doorway as he comes up the stairs, stumbling like Mr. Speed, "putting his white forefinger to his red face"; after he has climbed the stairs, an act symbolizing coitus, and entered her room, she remembers "something like a longing for my brother to strike me," but since he does not and therefore does not symbolically enter her, she presumably has failed to cope with her fears.

She also remembers the box, a female symbol, containing the stillborn infant when it is buried, and she associates it in a rapid sequence of images with Mr. Speed, who apparently epitomizes maleness, with her last moments with her mother, and with her mother's death, which her "memory did not dwell upon." When Mr. Speed finally enters the house, one assumes Betsy cannot help but react as she does. The maid Lucy, who could be but is not Betsy's surrogate mother, pleads with Betsy to climb the stairs, that is, to perform, in Freudian terms, a symbolic coital act. Instead, she reacts unconsciously, circling defensively behind Mr. Speed to telephone the police, thereby repressing her desire for the male "invasion." A few minutes later Mr. Speed's "limp body" is taken away.

Betsy sees herself as having acted with a mixture of cruelty and courage, and instead of being fearful of or attracted to Mr. Speed, she both despises and pities the old man lying unconscious in the mud. In the last paragraph the narrator says, " . . . my hatred of what he had stood for in my eyes has never left me . . . not a week has passed but that he has been brought to my mind by one thing or another." The child Betsy may appear to have been victorious, but in Freudian terms the adult Elizabeth is the regressing victim of the girl's failure to overcome her terror.

An Adlerian point of view leads to a different conclusion. According to Alfred Adler, the biological and environmental "givens"—for example, Betsy's plain looks, adolescent stirrings, and isolation in a discouraging male world—are re-created by a person with her "private logic" to attain "success": "Experiences, traumata, and sexual developmental mechanisms cannot yield an explanation, but the perspective in which they are regarded . . . which subordinates all life to the final goal, can do so." In *Superiority and Social Interest* Adler sees the neurotic as striving toward a goal of superiority in order to overcome past and current feelings of inferiority. Rather than reacting automatically to events which determine her to be a spinster, Betsy is actively carving out her niche in the world, a niche that in her eyes is inferior to none. Betsy's fear of heterosexual intimacy, for example, may express the direction she is taking to attain her goal of superiority over men.

From this point of view, the incidents from her puberty that the narrator recalls are important not in themselves but because she remembers them and because of the way the girl Betsy chooses to respond to them. In *Individual Psychology* Adler says, "There are no chance memories. Out of the incalculable number of impressions which meet an individual, he chooses to remember only those which he feels, however darkly, to have a bearing on his situation." The narrator's selective *re*-collection of pubescent experiences mirrors her present biases and view of life, and, as the story's title suggests (**"A Spinster's Tale"**), her reconstruction of events does not necessarily correspond to the historical truth. The purposeful delving into the past has the power of repetitive rehearsals or of a self-fulfilling prophecy, expressing the narrator's intention of continuing with the symbolic, spinster-like life of her youth. These memories, Adler says, a person " . . . repeats to himself . . . to keep him concentrated on his goal, and to prepare him by means of past experiences, so that he will meet the future with an already tested style of action."

When Betsy is frightened by Mr. Speed, her ultimate symbol of maleness, for example, she construes the image of her dead mother, whom she remembers as wan, smiling, gentle, and religious—the opposite of the stumbling drunk. By symbiotically escaping into this idealized memory, Betsy sidesteps a social problem—confrontation with the old man and thereby with males in general—thus avoiding possible defeat or humiliation in a relationship. In choosing "not to dwell upon" the memory of her mother's death, Betsy thus denies it, as well as the challenges

of adolescence, i.e. the stepping toward new freedom and adult responsibilities. Betsy calls her memories of her mother "sudden and inexplicable," but they are neither: they manifest her preference for nonexistence, passivity, and social withdrawal. After seeing Mr. Speed the first time, Betsy stands "cold and silent," a metaphorical and literal expression of her chosen life style.

Betsy recalls that her mother severely condemned drinking before her death, an attitude not shared by her brother or by her father, who has toddies with her uncles every Saturday afternoon. Her father calls "Old Speed" a "rascal" with "merry tolerance," but simultaneously warns her brother of the consequences of drinking by using Mr. Speed as a bad example. Betsy cannot identify with her father's contradictory attitude and the well-defined masculine pattern he establishes in the house. She wonders whether he ever thinks of her mother, since he never mentions her. She seems to accuse him of indifference, saying " . . . in a year I had forgotten how he treated her when she had been alive." Unable to establish satisfactory alliances with her brother or father, she replaces the human tendency for *gemeinschaftsgefühl* with an attitude of distrust and poor regard for her surviving family members and, ultimately, the world at large.

The development of this attitude appears clearly in the sibling rivalry between Betsy and her brother. Sober, he teases her mercilessly. Drunk, he tries to make her a conspirator by offering the passive, watchful girl candy, but she sees him as "giggling," "bouncing," and "silly" and refuses to compromise the attitude about drinking that she has adopted from her mother. [In his *Psychodynamics, Psychotherapy, and Counseling*] Rudolf Dreikurs, the popularizer of Adler in the United States, says such sibling differences indicate competition and the development of different personalities. Betsy, feeling intellectually ignored by her father and class-valedictorian brother, sees her brother as the "boss" and herself as inadequate. To compete with her brother's ruling style, she chooses the feminine avoiding style, a typical example of familial confrontation between two Adlerian types. She requests, for example, her father and brother "not to talk about war, which seemed to [her father] a natural enough request for a young lady to make." While father and son argue on a vast diversity of male-oriented topics, Betsy quietly observes her brother or slips away because she finds the contentious dialogue unbearable.

Dreikurs points out that where one sibling succeeds, a competing sibling gives up; and where the sibling fails (the brother's intemperance, for example), the competitor moves in, thus finding a place and significance in the family. Betsy's behavior fits this pattern. Adler says a woman feels equal to a man she perceives as superior if she can experience herself in her "masculine protest" to be "equally superior" to him. This striving for compensatory superiority reflects an exaggerated perception of male power and recognition such as Betsy sees in her small world on Church Street. Not being brave enough to confront them, Betsy resorts to what Adler calls "depreciation tendency" (the neurotic's tendency to enhance self-esteem by disparaging others) in order to maneuver her brother and Mr.

Speed, to sneak into power struggles with them, and to inflict sly revenge in their weak moments. Betsy's nearly incestuous encounter with her brother, for example, in which she appears uncharacteristically confident and well-rehearsed, may be an attempt to compromise him and thus gain a "victory" and revenge. Her desire for him to strike her could be seen as her search for confirmation of suspected male violence and cruelty.

Betsy has long been preparing for the "eventuality" to settle completely with Mr. Speed. The narrator recalls, "And the sort of preparation that I had been able to make [was] the clearance of all restraints and inhibitions regarding Mr. Speed in my own mind and in my relationship with my world. . . ." The "restraints" and "inhibitions" that Betsy rids herself of are the foundations of Adler's *gemeinschaftsgefühl*. Instead of giving the drunk Mr. Speed shelter in her house from the rain, Betsy, in a tone of pretended innocence, calls the police. She is keenly aware that she deals with Mr. Speed, "however wrongly," all by herself, that is, unsocially. Her father's curt remark, "I regret that the bluecoats were called," underscores the disparity in father and daughter's life attitudes.

The passive-aggressive Betsy begins to find her place and power in her family by her success in hurting others through her one-upmanship games. She discovers a way to supervise her father's household staff by snooping around, springing out upon the unsuspecting servants, and intimidating them by threatening to call her father or the police. The narrator recalls, "In this way, from day to day, I began to take my place as mistress in our motherless household."

Betsy's life-style is that of a cautious, contriving busybody. Even in her nightly dreams she allows no mysteries or loose ends and "pieces together" these dreams into a "form of logic." The fearful Betsy grows into the controlling Betsy who says, "I would complete an unfinished dream and wouldn't know in the morning what part I dreamed and what part pieced together." In one such dream a "big" Betsy, in control of everything, watches "little" Betsy "trembling and weeping." Betsy then makes a "very considerable discovery" about herself—that instead of being fearful she can be feared. Betsy is not the victim of causality, but rather the pilot of her dreams and of the direction of her life as well. In her own terms, she has achieved "equal superiority" over Mr. Speed, her brother, and therefore all men. Just as the pubescent Betsy pieces together her dreams into patterns which suit her, the adult narrator continues to piece together her life in ways that, according to her private logic, reveal her to be superior and successful.

That **"A Spinster's Tale"** can sustain two such disparate interpretations of its protagonist demonstrates, we feel, the profundity of Taylor's characterization. We see in the story the dynamics of familial relationships, and little else, either shaping a girl and the woman to be or being used by the girl to shape the woman she chooses to be. The ambiguity in Taylor's fine story is satisfying, like truth. (pp. 49-54)

Roland Sodowsky and Gargi Roysircar So-

dowsky, "Determined Failure, Self-Styled Success: Two Views of Betsy in Peter Taylor's 'Spinster's Tale'," in Studies in Short Fiction, *Vol. 25, No. 1, Winter, 1988, pp. 49-54.*

Walter Shear   (essay date 1989)

[*In the following essay, Shear analyzes the effect that crossing social boundaries has on characters throughout Taylor's short stories.*]

Though acknowledged as one of the masters of the short story in English, Peter Taylor has, in an era of voluminous critical activity, received comparatively little attention. One reason may be that his pictures of Southern society are so satisfying simply as descriptive characterizations; we are convinced by his deceptively smooth style that he has accurately recorded a particular class of Southern sensibility as it existed in the middle of the twentieth century. Taylor himself has mentioned that his friend Randall Jarrell urged him to keep writing his kind of story because the Southern society of their era was disappearing. In spite of all this, what remains particularly intriguing in the typical Taylor story is the way the sure, deft strokes of social description—the assurance of a seemingly shared cultural reality—steadily uncover a dialectic which centers on resistance. And while varieties of reluctance in the narrative convince us that to exist socially is to experience fate, the stories continue to insist that social life, whatever its distresses, is the only life possible.

As Jan Pinkerton has noted, Taylor's society has throughout definite lines drawn between class, race, and sex; there are also, less insistently perhaps, generational lines, lines between the values of the past and those of the present, and, in some stories, lines between public and private behavior and between city life and country life. While such boundaries apprise a reader of the orders in Taylor's conception of the traditional, they also serve, by setting up categories within which and among which individuals must exist, to suggest, in modes simultaneously symbolic and externally real, the social organization of the characters' psychic life. The fact that these categories imply social definitions of identity introduces the esthetic potentiality for an investigation of the problematics of social being, with emphasis on the relationship of social being to notions of human nature.

Since the narratives accent sensibility and awareness, the drama of the fiction is not the abrupt one of a completely altered relationship to society, but that of the settling or unsettling of one's social allegiances and social powers. At the heart of the drama is a subtle violation. To cross social boundary lines, to become involved socially, physically, and imaginatively with those outside one's socially defined self is to encounter the other, to consciously or unconsciously enter that sphere the culture has declared different from, if not alien to, the self. Thus the inclination of Taylor's narratives toward grotesque images, ironic bits of humor, and strange extensions of logic, all of which suggest that a price is continually being paid, one which has been paid in the past as well, for the current coherent state of affairs. In its more radical overtones, the narration asks us to imagine life as a drama of gestures and to ask ourselves how many assumptions are necessary for communal existence—and why. Thus everything ordinary in Taylor's society seems capable of an extraordinary relationship; the uncanny consistently haunts the quotidian.

In Taylor's fiction history is an explanation that becomes a mystery. Time has not merely passed, it has altered the grounds of existence for the characters. At the end of **"Guests"** Edmund Harper wonders over an absent culture that has come to seem *literally* vital:

> ". . . something in the life out there didn't satisfy you [Cousin Johnny] the way it should. The country wasn't itself any more. And something was wrong for me here. By 'country' we mean the old world . . . the old ways, the old life, where people had real grandfathers and real children, and where love was something that could endure the light of day. . . . Our trouble was . . . we were lost without our old realities. . . . We couldn't discover what it is people keep alive for without them. . . . Other people seem to know some reason why it is better to be alive than dead this April morning. I will have to find it out."

As in this passage, spatial dimensions are often used to make definite temporal distinctions. Describing the original conception of **The Widows of Thornton,** Taylor stated, "I wanted to give the reader the impression that every character carried in his head a map of that simple country town [Thornton, Tennessee] while going about his life in the complex city." Picking up the title of this Taylor volume, Albert J. Griffith describes this tendency to cling to "things the rest of the world values no more" as a metaphoric, spiritual widowhood. In a practical sense one can say that these individuals simply need to adjust to social changes, yet their personal dramas suggest ways that a specific time and place may become a home for the psyche, creating such a feeling of natural existence for the self that, once absent, no amount of adjusting can recapture. Thus some cultures which may no longer exist or which, in the tricks memory and the mind can play, may never have actually existed, contain a vividness of valuing that no other milieu can equal. Aunt Munsie, the Tolliver's former servant in **"What You Hear From 'Em?"**, believes that the values of reality must have a literal ground to exist, articulating the importance of land-owning but believing "it was not really to own land that Thad and Will ought to come back to Thornton. It was more that if they were going to be rich, they ought to come home, where their granddaddy had owned land and where their money counted for something. How could they ever be rich anywhere else?"

In at least one story it is the future that marks the impossible boundary of otherness. In **"Miss Leonora When Last Seen,"** the assigning of values to the past, viewed from the perspective of an outsider, seems a strangling, heartless nostalgia: here Miss Leonora's family is accused of doing "all it could to impede the growth and progress of our town. . . . Their one idea was always to keep the town unspoiled, unspoiled by railroads or factories or even county politics. Perhaps they should not be blamed for wanting to keep the town unspoiled. Yet I am not quite

sure about that." Eventually the narrator comes to see that in Miss Leonora's case the barrier has been not the town's past but the town's future, as she conceived that future and as she tried to live it with her strangely impersonal personal relationship to her students. Nonetheless, it is still a temporal barrier. The narrator notes her "awareness of you, the individual before her, a very flattering awareness until presently you realized it was merely of you as an individual in her scheme of things for Thomasville. She was still looking at me as though I were one of the village children that she would like so much to make something of." Even as he begins to imaginatively participate in her perspective, the narrator starts to back away from what he feels is an alien vision, demonstrating the discomfort he feels throughout the story in his role as go-between, someone who is denied a value perspective of his own. In this case, as a result of simply the idea of change, his home town environment becomes alienated from him. More typically, Taylor's domestic environments serve to convey that impulse in the mind to seek feelings connected with its natural home. And as tendency, the impulse may limit or inhibit the character's experience of otherness, or, with the persistent sense of loss of home, make it pervasive.

As early as 1970, Jan Pinkerton argued that a basic theme to Taylor's fiction was a concern "with role-playing and with personal identity." The very titles of Taylor's stories—**"Dean of Men," "A Spinster's Tale," "The Fancy Woman," "A Wife of Nashville," "Heads of Houses"**—call attention to the importance of social role-playing in his characters' lives. Esthetically, social roles also provide the structural dimensions for the stories, supplying the narrative an essential point of departure and a place of return. Yet even though they furnish the "normality" against which otherwise is measured, in many of Taylor's stories there is a tension created by the "playing" of the social role. As articulated in **"The Death of a Kinsman,"** the tension may be rooted in arguments about modes of social being. In the story-play Mrs. Wade puts role-playing in a traditional context, not, however, without a tone of irony: ". . . Aunt Lida and I have played our roles so perfectly, as we've always seen them played in Tennessee: She, the maiden aunt, responsible and capable; I, the beautiful young wife, the bearer of children, the reigning Queen." She is countered by Mrs. Bluemeyer, who, as cultural outsider, declares: "I was a queer sort who couldn't make herself do it. . . . All along I have seen you are a really brainy woman and yet to see you here saying the things you say and playacting all the time." Bluemeyer goes on to complain to Aunt Lida, ". . . I have seen right along that you are really the same as I in lots of your feelings, Miss Wade, that you are really lost and alone in the world, but you would not have it so, you just wouldn't." Each speaker senses the desperation of everyday existence, but in the context of the story Bluemeyer's cry for her kind of authenticity does not recognize Lida's appreciation of the values and nuances in communal intimacies.

At times Taylor's narratives lead to a despair in social role-playing, the self's melancholy about its social acquiescence, a metaphysical suspicion that this performing of function may be a form of nonbeing and that unused individuality may become another version of otherness. At the end of **"A Wife of Nashville"** Helen Ruth perceives that "everything that happened in life only demonstrated in some way the lonesomeness that people felt. . . . she would even talk about the 'so much else' that had been missing from her life and that she had not been able to name, and about the foolish mysteriés she had so nobly accepted upon her reconciliation with John R [her husband]. To her, these things were all one now, they were her loneliness, the loneliness from which everybody knowingly or unknowingly suffered."

In several stories there is a rejection by society of the roles the characters have chosen. Miss Leonora, who tries to perform a culturally uplifting role for her community, is forced to acknowledge her defeat: "I was unrealistic. I tried to be to you children [she is speaking to an adult male] what I thought you needed to have somebody be. That's a mistake always. One has to try to be with people what they want one to be." But her other roles in the story simply serve to bring out comically the basic incompatibility she has with her world. The two college students in **"1939"** suffer the same comic fate. They regard the "real world" with ambiguity (as beneath them but necessary as the source of raw experience) and thus set themselves up to have their creative writer pose not so much mocked as swallowed up. Their girl friends jilt them simply by being involved, experiencing the world by making commitments to it in a way that the boys cannot. The final words of the story—*"Not yet, not yet, not yet"*—sum up the response of the world to their aspiration for being; their roles are less right or wrong than merely premature.

In some stories the characters are objective, self-conscious, almost fatalistic about their being for others. Henry Parker in **"Heads of Houses"** has "learned to think of himself sometimes as others thought of him, and to play the role he was assigned," but he cultivates an inner consciousness as "a man capable of thinking inside this role assigned him, and not, for the time being, as a man whose other life was so much more real and so much more complicated. . . ." The narrator of **"The Old Forest"** looks at others playing roles, manifesting male social roles deliberately, in the context of historical perspective: "They were a generation of American men who were perhaps the last to grow up in a world where women were absolutely subjected and under the absolute protection of men. . . . And so these men of position and power had to act as surrogate fathers during a transitional period. It was a sort of communal fatherhood they were acting out."

This tendency to exist for others is probably the basic reason for the lack of vivid individuals in Taylor's fiction. Individualism in the form of a character standing apart from others, someone not merely different from his/her fellow being, but in some obsessive fashion indifferent to them—this quality scarcely exists in Taylor's stories. Indeed, so few characters, especially in the early fiction, stand out as idiosyncratic, rebellious, strident, or actively vital, that the society seems to be invisibly oppressing all overt libido impulses and to be exuding a taut but pervasive disapproval of all sharp expressions of personality. What one remembers about the Taylor narrative is usually not the character, but the relationships the character is involved in.

Often the narrative carries the notion of social roles so far that one perceives character as the medium through which society manifests itself.

The male professor in **"Je Suis Perdu"** is perhaps the Taylor character who feels most acutely that his role-playing has become a metaphysical issue. His satisfactions in his life in Paris and his work accomplished slide into moody discontents. He is, for example, stricken by "the bad thought . . . that he was no longer *going to be* this or that. He *was*. It was a matter of *being*. And to *be* meant, or seemed to mean at such a moment, to *be over with*." At the end of the story the feeling of a waning vitality leads to be a strangely bland reaction to the problematics of social obligation:

> He felt a great loss—except he didn't really feel it, he only thought of it. And he felt, he *knew* that he had after all gotten to Paris too late . . . after he had already established steady habits of work . . . after he had acknowledged claims that others had on him . . . after there were ideas and truths and work and people that he loved better even than himself.

Although the last phrase seems to salvage his situation with hint of the small nobility of his domestic and social self-sacrifice, earlier in the passage a concern to be correct about thinking and feeling uncovers a regret which grudgingly acknowledges the attraction of self-indulgence. The style itself subtly articulates the problem of social being as the tendency to cover existential frustrations in suppressive rationalizing. Still, one's sense of a "problem" rather than a "solution" in this particular conclusion depends on the degree of irony that one perceives in the style. The case of the professor's altruism certainly suggests Jane Barnes Casey's idea that Taylor's stories raise "the question of how a man can go on being a man in the modern world without undermining the moral basis of society. . . ." But in a broader sense it also demonstrates the kind of deep, pervasive anxiety over social role—the sense that social obligation may inherently inhibit or diminish being—that surfaces periodically in the fiction.

Given the characters' unease, it is understandable that Taylor's plots would feature a wide variety of encounters with the other. The fact that the stable middle class virtues of social existence—social responsibility and imaginative sympathy—are double-edged for Taylor forces the fiction to move toward the private arena of sensibility rather than toward the actual possibilities and difficulties of public life. Instead of being an extension and enrichment of social responsibility, imaginative sympathy tends to be a compensation, the mental experience of the other stirring an emotional vitality that a social existence has seemingly renounced. In some cases, however, the imaginative experience can act reciprocally to strengthen identity, and thereby become a positive element. Thus there are broad implications in statements like that of the narrator of **"Daphne's Lover"** who feels "as if once I knew what my life was to be I needed to participate more wholeheartedly in the lives of others."

The source of the emotional vitality in imaginative sympathy seems to lie exactly in the awareness of difference. Taylor has stated in regard to being, "It's a problem that has always fascinated me: you can't help wondering at times, if you'd been made just a little bit differently, and if life had treated you differently, you might have ended up this person or that person." In his fiction the characters do occasionally seem to come to a greater sense of themselves after an encounter with what is different or alien in others. It is a position articulated by Will Perkins at the end of **"Promise of Rain"**: "I had just discovered what it means to see the world through another man's eyes. . . . it is only then that the world, as you have seen it through your own eyes, will begin to tell you things about yourself." As the narrator in **"Daphne's Lover"** suggests, such activity with acquaintances may be instinctive for many: "if one has any imagination whatsoever, one has always to participate to some degree in the experience of one's friends." But, as this story illustrates, the distinctiveness of beings and the sense of a distance from even those apparently close can result in a feedback to the problematics of one's own existence.

At the heart of the drama of personal relationships in most of Taylor's stories is a rhythm evolving out of sensitivity to the difference and sameness in the other. In the midst of the overt social battle between the Harpers and their guests (**"Guests"**), Edmund Harper discovers the basis of his own imaginative version of the drama: "Here is such a person as I might have been, and I am such a one as he might have been." It is in fact the tension between sameness and difference that has effectively strangled social interaction. Edmund wonders to find "a part of himself always reaching out and wanting to communicate with them and another part forever holding back, as though afraid of what *would* be communicated."

While the narrative surface of the story concerns the social peculiarities of the country cousins, the Kincaids, in their visit to the Harpers, the city/country contrast here is sufficiently extreme to force manners, gestures, language itself into a dramatization of the need/denial bind of otherness. Henrietta Harper's insistent social hospitality toward her country cousins, while a somewhat discomforting experience for her and even more so for Edmund, her husband, becomes a plea for the old social intimacies of a more rural community, a life the couple abandoned many years ago. It is a gesture both accepted and resisted in the provincially-defensive responses of Annie Kincaid, whose dogged protection of the intimacy and the way of life she and her husband share is carried to the point where she refuses to inform her hosts that her husband is a dying man. As the tension grows, Edmund comes to the conclusion that Cousin Annie is doing more than just defensively redrawing lines of privacy on enemy turf: "She had had the offensive from the beginning and she was winning battle after battle. Every discomfort that Cousin Johnny suffered in silence, every dish he did without, every custom he had to conform to that was 'bad for him' was a victory over Henrietta, and gave the old lady deeper satisfaction just because Henrietta might not be aware of it." As a result of her action, each "gift" of hospitality is transformed into the demand of the other and the social visit becomes a deadly psychological struggle.

It is Cousin Johnny's discomfort and bizarrely sudden death which provide the pathetically stark background for this social comedy. As suggested by the Harper's struggle over the best way to address him—their more personal "Johnny" is immediately encountered by Annie's more formal "Mr. Kincaid"—Cousin Johnny becomes literally the victim of what he has come to represent, reduced at last to that social cipher which the realization of otherness exposes. Like several other deaths in Taylor's fiction, his becomes the occasion as well for mourning dead communal ties.

In other Taylor stories the sense of overt differences and covert sameness induces the psychological mechanism of projection, which brings out the complex interactions inherent in the relationships themselves. The narrator's reaction to Mr. Speed in **"A Spinster's Tale"** and Franny's love/fear fascination with Miles in **"Reservations: A Love Story"** both demonstrate characters seeing their own anxieties and fascinations in another, beginning to act out these psychological fixations, and, as a result, discovering, almost half-consciously, something about themselves. Before encountering Miles, Franny had dreamed of "the dark handsome man she was always going to meet on a train coming back from boarding school at Christmas or during the summer at Lake Michigan." The fact that Miles is from outside her world makes him to some degree the embodiment of that psychic stranger who represents her desire, and this is not a small part of her willingness to marry him. Yet at the same time she is disturbed enough by his literal strangeness to have the family hire a detective to investigate his past. His resultant social stability establishes sufficient sameness for the marriage to take place, but it also makes him less her desire and more literally himself.

Because of the snow, they are forced to spend their wedding night at the hotel where Miles has been living, a strange territory that she attempts to make psychologically familiar by mistaking strangers for people she knows. When she is accidentally locked in the bathroom, the literal barrier provokes a probing exchange between bride and bridegroom in which each sees the other less idealistically and senses himself/herself as less innocent than the notion of selfless love would imply. It is also a scene that makes them both feel a little more hemmed in by their own desires. The innocence their wedding night surrenders is the idea of themselves as detached, but loyal individuals, without calculating desires. In Taylor's games of boundaries, marriage, a basic form of social commitment to what was totally other, becomes at this stage a shelter for a new form of innocence: "Silently they were toasting their own bliss and happiness, confident that it would never again be shadowed by the irrelevances of the different circumstances of their upbringings or by the possibly impure and selfish motives that had helped to bring them together."

In **"A Spinster's Tale"** the character of the title feels even in the shelter of her family an increasing revulsion for what she perceives as the uninhibited, and perhaps tasteless, masculine world. Eventually, the town drunk, Mr. Speed, comes to be the embodiment of all this grotesque sexual otherness. Despite her terror of this bete noire, when finally she is forced to confront him she coolly summons the police to drag the pathetic drunk away. In the end she concludes, "I was frightened by the thought of cruelty which I found I was capable of, a cruelty which seemed inextricably mixed with what I called courage." In the confrontation the raw but vague danger that Speed represented is somehow transferred to a negative otherness within her, and to some degree she becomes what she fears. Her sense of the negative inside is like that of Matt Donelson in the story **"At the Drugstore."** After his experience with Mr. Conway, the pharmacist, and the rather nasty childhood memories this invokes, Matt feels that in penetrating "beyond all the good sense and reasonableness that made life worthwhile," "he was now confronted by a thing that had a face and a will of its own," a glimpse of a kind of threat to civilized values existing within him. Jane Barnes Casey argues that Matt subdues what is "brutal and anti-social in himself" but goes home with an awareness of "all the forbidden sexuality which underlies family life and conflicts with domesticity."

Sometimes the keener feeling for the push and pull of social categories which is the result of otherness in action leads to a despair over being what one is. When this attitude produces an extreme overcompensation in the form of imaginative participation, it can result in the kind of abandonment—or even betrayal—of self suggested by the last sentence of **"The Gift of the Prodigal"** where the seemingly disapproving father reveals his true relationship to his son: "I am listening gratefully to all he will tell me about himself, about any life that is not my own." The darkest side of this form of the parasitical is starkly sketched out in the destructive relationship between the Nelsons and their Negro servant Jesse (**"A Friend and Protector"**):

> . . . Jesse's outside activities had been not only *his,* but *ours* too . . . Uncle Andrew, with his double or triple standard . . . had most certainly forced Jesse's destruction upon him, and Aunt Margaret had made the complete destruction possible and desirous to him with her censorious words and looks. But they did it because they had to, because they were so dissatisfied with the pale *un*ruin of their own lives. They did it because something would not let them ruin their own lives as they wanted and felt a need to do—as I have often felt a need to do, myself.

And even in the less disastrous narratives characters can emerge periodically from the struggle with otherness to view their social activities with detached resignation. In such a moment Miss Betty in **"Two Ladies in Retirement"** speculates on how her life has gradually crossed a gender line:

> Once the goal was defined, was it necessary that she should be any less ruthless than her male counterparts? In her generation, the ends justified the means. For men, at least, they did. Now, at last, Miss Betty saw how much like a man's life her own had been. She saw it in the eyes of the wounded, frightened child. She saw how it was that every day of her adult life had made her less a woman instead of more a woman. . . . Wrong though it seemed, the things a man did

to win happiness in the world—or in the only world Miss Betty knew—were of no consequence to the children he came home to at night, but every act, word, and thought of a woman was judged by and reflected in the children, in the husband, in all who loved her.

In her case the sense of an unfair world works against her regret for a traditional role and, since she feels hers is the only social role change left her, she remains as competitive as she feels she has to be. The self-conscious reaction by the narrator in **"Dean of Men"** is to suppress his feelings as well, to break with what he sees as family history and remain in a competitive world he no longer believes in. Like his father and grandfather before him, he feels betrayed by his fellow males, colleagues in his academic community, but where as his father and grandfather responded by remaining in the circle of their family, he resolves to submit to his masculine fate and, despite personal reluctance and loss of faith, return to the world of men.

Since Taylor is on one level a social historian, it is not surprising that some of his most successful stories play the modern crossing of gender lines, the movements into different roles and strange value areas, against the more recalcitrant lines of class and social distinction. Working about the triangle of an upper middle class engaged couple, Caroline Braxley and Nat Ramsey, and a young independent working woman, Lee Ann Deehart, **"The Old Forest"** employs sexual and economic differences to explore the characters' senses of their free will and fate. When Nat's sexually-innocent squiring of Lee Ann shortly before his marriage leads to an auto accident, Lee Ann suddenly, abruptly, flees the scene into the woods. As far as Nat is concerned she seems to have disappeared, and he must find her. Representing the otherness of nature and the opposite of social constraints, the forest is ambivalent. Historically, it is associated with the pioneer woman's "last refuge from the brute she lived alone with in the wilderness," but it also invokes the danger of isolation and loneliness. Lee Ann's impulsive escape into the forest as an initial hiding place accents her desire for risky freedoms and indeed parallels her venturing as a woman of the late 1930s into the predominantly masculine world of business.

Caroline also views Lee Ann's dash into the woods as a kind of social freedom, perhaps a masculine kind of power that Lee Ann has gained "literally to disappear from the glaring light of day while the whole world, so to speak, looked on." It achieves a kind of anonymity that Caroline has been denied. Yet as the plot follows Nat's tracking Lee Ann down, society's pursuit of her, and thus the acknowledgement of its obligation to her, is paralleled by her own acknowledgement of social tie as she returns at last to her grandmother, with whom she has previously seemed unconnected. Both Nat and Lee Ann seem to move back to their social roles with a sense that they have reached the limits of their freedom. In his involvement with the two women Nat has half-consciously used a form of masculine freedom which his society has made available; however, Lee Ann's disappearance has forced him to recognize the depth of socially-imposed obligation in their overtly casual relationship. Further, his relatively passive role throughout makes him aware of an emotionally-inhibited relationship to all the otherness he will encounter in later life: " . . . I knew, then, at thirty-seven, that I was only going to try to comprehend intellectually the world about me and beyond me and that I had failed somehow at some time to reach out and grasp direct experience of a larger life which no amount of intellectualizing could compensate for."

Strangely it is Caroline, the one who had in the situation seemed most vulnerable socially, who acts most effectively and gains the clearest sense of the only kind of power she believes she can ever have, "the power of a woman in a man's world." As she perceives her situation, "it was a question of how very much I had to lose and how little power I had to save myself. Because *I* had set *myself* free the way other girls have. . . . Power, or strength, is what everybody must have if he—if she—is to survive in any kind of world. I have to protect and use whatever strength I have." Given the circumstances of Taylor's fiction, this kind of willingness and ability to work within a world's limits is a remarkably positive attribute.

The one Taylor story, **"Venus, Cupid, Folly and Time,"** which looks at various attempts, playful and serious, to ignore, subvert, and distort boundaries exudes an atmosphere of decadence from beginning to end. Here the narrative is centered about a seeming initiation party for young people, an occasion whose secret motto is "This is what it is to be young forever"; it is an absolutely contradictory social gathering. When the party-givers, the rather ancient Dorsets, proclaim to the assembled adolescents, "We are all young, we all love one another," and " . . . love can make us all young forever," they defy time by denying otherness. Further, their traditional party has by now become a kind of scheme for claiming a social elitism they do not possess. The more that the snobbish Dorsets insist on casting out those with social differences—"that boy upstairs didn't belong amongst us"—the more they call attention to their introverted sociability and create suspicion of their own relationship.

It is the very falsity of the atmosphere that provokes the sharpness in the alternative versions of artful pretensions. In exposing the Dorsets, Ned's disguise interacts with the other art work in the house not simply to evoke modes of social evasion, but to further demonstrate the mean-spiritedness of trickery, and the way the pent-up imagination can burst out to betray and mock life's possibilities. At the heart of the cruel revelation is the incest idea, raised to consciousness as an oblique attack on the Dorsets, but there for all to comprehend. As the ultimate gender line, it challenges the notion of civilized boundaries by playing the family-outsider distinction against the importance of sexual difference. Sexuality thus imagined is tied vividly to the idea of social violation. The tremors from this excursion into the forbidden turn the party into chaos, and ultimately destroy the party as a social tradition, but the narrative stresses the terrible potency of the thought in the lives of younger brother and sister, Ned and Emily Meriwether: "the Dorset's party . . . marked the end of their childhood intimacy and the beginning of a shyness, a reserve, even an animosity between them that was destined

to be a sorrow forever to the two sensible parents. . . . " Thus, in a strangely ironic configuration, the conclusion of the story implies a literal and somewhat petulant demonstration of Levi-Strauss's concept that the incest taboo leads to the creation of society.

In this story, and indeed in most of his others, the effect of Taylor's fiction is that of abstract art. Despite the vivid detail and convincing texture of a social reality, the author's analysis of society is as dependent on sociological and psychological assumption as on observation. Taylor in fact creates Southern society of the 1940s and 1950s in large part according to his own myth. As he views its operation in a traditional society, the encounter with otherness typically sends characters back to traditional and/or more familiar social roles. Since Taylor assumes that society will inevitably change with the passage of time, the characters' awareness of social role often involves fitting it into a temporal perspective. The characters' responses may vary from surrender, regression or resignation to a more or less realistic assessment of one's social position. It may also to a greater or lesser degree invoke the notion that there is inherently as much of perversity in social adjustment as in the refusal to acknowledge change. The challenging dimension of this social dynamic for the characters involved is characterized most vividly in **"The Old Forest"** with the metaphor of social reality as fatalistic journey:

> And it occurred to me now that when Caroline said go as fast as you can she really meant to take us all the way back into our past and begin the journey all over again, not merely from a point of four days ago or from the days of our childhood but from a point in our identity that would require a much deeper delving and a more radical turn.

Few, of course, can twist the perspective on their own identity in such a "radical" manner, but typically character exploration in Taylor's stories charts out the labyrinth of social being in amazing depth. The miracle of his calm narration is its deft coherence in weaving among the tensions created by what a person is, what a person can be, and what a person cannot be. The encounter with the other leads inevitably back, not to the discovery of the self, but to the discovery of the self 's seemingly-permanent relationship to society. (pp. 50-62)

Walter Shear, "Peter Taylor's Fiction: The Encounter with the Other," in The Southern Literary Journal, *Vol. XXI, No. 2, Spring, 1989, pp. 50-63.*

David M. Robinson (essay date 1990)

[In the following essay, Robinson examines the significance of the past in "The Old Forest."]

Peter Taylor's achievement in fiction rests on his mastery of a retrospective narration with a dual purpose: detailed social observation that marks the best fiction of manners, and an accompanying depth of psychological revelation that transcends social forms. The paradigm of Taylor's best fiction is the recollection of an event deep in the past of the narrator or the community, which is reported with

---

Goodwin recalling Taylor as his writing teacher:

I was one of twenty or so students in his fiction writing class, and we studied him, as students always study their teachers. One of the women in the class was fascinated by his beautiful, well-made clothes, his tweeds and neck-scarves and English shoes; she was fascinated because he was so obviously not a dandy or a snob, and one day it came to her he looked like an elegant mountaineer. She was right. Peter has broad hands and large, expressive features; he has a comfortable walk as if he is always moving down a slight incline. His face is lined but calm and open, and his eyes are a light blue; my classmate found it easy to imagine him on a ridge, wearing buckskins and resting on his musket, gazing into Appalachian distances. That seemed romantic to me, but I do believe, as Bellow does, that landscape shapes faces, and hill people acquire the look of their hills, ocean people of their oceans. Peter does look like Tennessee.

Stephen Goodwin, in his "Like Nothing Else In Tennessee," Shenandoah, 1977.

---

a consciousness of its personal significance or with an attempt to assess that significance. The past holds Taylor's characters powerfully, molding their identity while inhibiting their free development. The struggle for identity and the struggle with the past are, as Taylor portrays them, very much the same. The power of Taylor's narration comes in part from the almost hypnotic engagement of his narrator with the past, and the intensity of the attempt to understand it. It is not the past, however, but the act of remembering, of retelling, and of reinterpreting the past in the retelling that reminds us that the work of self-creation is still in progress. The events of the past continue to have resonance in the present because they are still being assimilated. Taylor distances his narrators from their earlier selves and exploits that distance to achieve his psychological portraits. But as the narrator moves toward self-analysis, the distance of the past becomes illusory, for the past comes to dictate even the terms by which he attempts to recreate it and to recreate himself.

In **"The Old Forest,"** arguably the best of Taylor's stories, Nat Ramsey describes his own struggle for maturity in the midst of the demise of the upper-class Memphis of 1937. Nat's recollection begins with an explanation of why, when he "was already formally engaged," he "sometimes went out on the town with girls of a different sort." Nat has much to say about that "sort" of girl in the course of the story, remembering that these women were "facetiously and somewhat arrogantly referred to as the Memphis demimonde." The casual social brutality of the phrase designated "a girl who was not in the Memphis debutante set." Such labeling marked out those women who might lack the right social status for marriage but also suggested an air of the exotic in the otherwise absolutely predictable lives of Nat and his friends.

These women are interesting and stimulating companions, "bright girls certainly and some of them even highly intelligent," who "read books, . . . looked at pictures,

and . . . were apt to attend any concert or play that came to Memphis," not "the innocent, untutored types that we generally took to dances at the Memphis Country Club and whom we eventually looked forward to marrying." As we see Nat come into closer contact with these women, his sense of their strength and complexity grows. He discovers that in addition to a "physical beauty and a bookishness," qualities that we might associate with the traditionally feminine, they also had "a certain toughness of mind and a boldness of spirit." They are modern women, who, though still restricted by the persisting division of sexual roles, were in the process of transforming those roles.

Curiously, Nat comes to identify the symbol of this transformation as the Old Forest, "a densely wooded area which is actually the last surviving bit of primeval forest that once grew right up to the bluffs above the Mississippi River." A week before his marriage, Nat has driven near the forest with Lee Ann Deehart, one of the "demimondaines," when his car collides with a skidding truck on a frozen road. Nat is mildly injured in the accident, but before anyone can arrive to give assistance, Lee Ann walks away from the car and into the Old Forest, disappearing for four days. Lee Ann's disappearance raises the threat of scandal and endangers Nat's engagement to one of the Memphis Country Club girls, Caroline Braxley. In his attempt to find Lee Ann, he confronts her world and begins to learn the limitations of his own.

Lee Ann is associated with the Old Forest because it represents what is beyond the control of Nat's ordered life. "Here are giant oak and yellow poplar trees older than the memory of the earliest white settler." Surrounded by the man-made city, the forest has not submitted to that power. In escaping into the forest, Lee Ann unwittingly proves how tenuous Nat's control of his life is. It is a lesson that experience continues to repeat for him. Almost casually dropped in the middle of his reminiscence is this stunning list of personal tragedies: the loss of two brothers in the Korean War, the death of his parents in a fire at his home, and the accidental deaths of two of his teenage children. It would seem that the incident with Lee Ann would pale to insignificance when weighed against those pains, but, in fact, these instances of loss and grief augment its importance. Here Nat began to learn his mortal limitations. As Nat remembers it, "life *was* different" in the Memphis of 1937. It is not life that has changed, of course, but his perception of the boundary of the possible. "Our tranquil, upper-middle-class world of 1937 did not have the rest of the world crowding in on it so much." But the remark tells us more about Nat's maturing consciousness of tragedy than about the degree to which persons of his class were insulated from experience. Lee Ann's walk into the forest proves how fragile Nat's world really was.

Nat's sense of vulnerability begins to grow after he realizes the gravity of his situation, and the forest looms in his mind, embodying the threatening forces that delimit his social world. "More than the density of the underbrush, more than its proximity to the Zoo, where certain unsavory characters often hung out, it was the great size and antiquity of the forest trees somehow and the old rumors that white settlers had once been ambushed there by

Chickasaw Indians that made me feel that if anything had happened to the girl, it had happened there." Nat is ironically right that "something" had happened to Lee Ann, though it was not the violence that he had feared. Her disappearance is an assertion of independence from the grips of Nat's world, which will attempt to exert a benevolent but nonetheless firm claim on her in the aftermath of the wreck.

Her disappearance, though we eventually find it to be considerably more complex, carries the resonance of women's resistance to paternalistic authority of which Nat finds himself a rather reluctant emissary. He recognizes the symbolic threat of the forest to the world made by his male ancestors, and he realizes with some discomfort that his own fear is similar to that of generations of men in Memphis, who "have feared and wanted to destroy [the forest] for a long time and whose destruction they are still working at even in this latter day." That destructive impulse is the push to modernization, the drive behind the steady development and conquest of the land. "It has only recently been saved by a narrow margin from a great highway that men wished to put through there—saved by groups of women determined to save this last bit of the old forest from the axes of modern men."

As a persisting wilderness, the forest thus represents a counterforce to masculine control, and, in a larger sense, to all forms of social control. Nat's meditation on the symbolic connotations of the forest is punctuated by stories of "mad pioneer women, driven mad by their loneliness and isolation, who ran off into the forest" to be later "captured by Indians." The Old Forest reminds Nat that "civilization" is male civilization, and he begins to discover how deeply implicated in that civilization he is. As the Memphis city fathers reach out in a show of concern for Lee Ann's welfare, they also enact their own insecurity in the viability of their social structure, and their guilt over its basis in oppression.

But Nat is worried about more than Lee Ann's fate. He wonders "if all this might actually lead to my beautiful, willowy Caroline Braxley's breaking off our engagement." But the story's heightened tension about this point is at least superficially without basis. Nat had described Caroline early in the story as his wife of many years. Our knowledge that the incident did not end Nat's engagement emphasizes the particular burden of Taylor's retrospective narration. By minimizing the tension over the consequences of Nat's accident, he has focused it instead on Nat's tone as he recalls those events. The question is not whether he will marry, but what the marriage will mean to him.

As Nat flounders in the exigencies of Lee Ann's disappearance, Caroline begins to demonstrate a capacity to meet the gravity of the situation. Her stature grows as the story progresses. When she eventually takes over the search, Nat docilely cooperates with her. So it seems that his life continues for most of the next forty years. Caroline's "good judgment in all matters relating to our marriage," Nat says, "has never failed her—or us." But despite Nat's persuasive depiction of his concern that his engagement might be ruined, he undermines our faith in his absolute

contentment in his relation with Caroline when he describes the customs of engagement and marriage in upper-class Memphis. Engagement "was in no sense so unalterably binding as it had been in our parents' day," he explains, adding that "it was not considered absolutely dishonorable for either party to break off the plans merely because he or she had had a change of heart." Even more ominously, Nat admits that "the thought pleased me—that is, the ease with which an engagement might be ended." Afraid on the one hand that he will not be able to marry Caroline, he is also afraid that he *will* marry her. While visiting with Caroline and her parents, he admits "indulging in a perverse fantasy, a fantasy in which Caroline had broken off our engagement and I was standing up pretty well, was even seeking consolation in the arms, so to speak, of a safely returned Lee Ann Deehart." Nat's fantasy suggests his attraction to Lee Ann, but it tells us more about his vague sense of confinement in the world that he inhabits. If Caroline represents a secure place in that world, Lee Ann represents escape. His dreams of Lee Ann are indeed fantasy—she had earlier treated the possibility of their marriage with humorous contempt—but like all fantasies, they are revealing. They suggest Nat's stirring of resistance to the predictable course of his life. He never directs that resentment toward Caroline, for whom he has profound respect. He resists instead the sure movement of the machinery that will take him through a "good" marriage and into a predictable life in his father's business. One of the story's ironies is that the crisis transforms what might have seemed a marriage of convenience into a meaningful and durable relationship.

The accident sets in motion a process of maturing. This accounts for his returning in memory to it after so many years. When Nat finally tells Caroline that Lee Ann had been in the car with him, he is surprised to find that she already knows this. Her reaction convinces him to go ahead and tell an "uncensored version of the accident." Caroline's capacity to take command of the situation impresses Nat, who is characteristically in a state of indecisiveness. " 'You do know, don't you,' she went on after a moment, 'that you are going to have to *find* Lee Ann? And you probably are going to need help." Caroline understands that Lee Ann's disappearance might force an end to her engagement. In recognizing her relative powerlessness in the situation, a fact that is only beginning to dawn on Nat, Caroline finds the source of a surprising strength. Nat's eventual comprehension of her complex and courageous reaction to the events is an essential aspect of the maturity that he achieves.

Caroline might have been expected to play an unsavory part in the story, a manipulative individual attempting to assert the requisites of privilege. But in Taylor's deft touch, she begins to capture our sympathy and seize the moral momentum of the story, supplying the drifting Nat with both a will and a purpose in finding Lee Ann. Her motives are not disinterested, but her courage in the face of the possible disaster contrasts favorably with Nat's fantasy-punctuated passivity. While Nat has begun to awaken to the ways that Memphis Country Club life insulates him from experience, Caroline is more keenly aware of those limits and of their concomitant restrictions to her

capacity of choice. As Nat eventually comes to understand, Caroline's social position carries a burden with it,
a knowledge of "what was going to be expected of [her]
in making a marriage and bringing up a family there in
Memphis." Lee Ann represented a threat to those expectations, competing for the husbands that were the requirements for survival as it had been defined to Caroline.
While it is the narrowness of the definition of success and
not girls of a lower social standing that are the real threat
to Caroline and her peers, Taylor builds a measure of sympathy for her. He depicts Caroline and Nat as people
trapped in a value system as it crumbles. However we
scorn those values, it is hard to blame them for the world
into which they were born. Taylor has written a devastating indictment of the narrowness of the upper class but has
treated the people of that class with fair-minded sympathy. While Caroline's quest seems superficially like the attempt to protect her privilege, it is much closer to an effort
to overcome the vulnerability that Nat's accident has revealed to her—the restricted scope of her possibilities for
self-definition. The story thus develops around the hunt
for Lee Ann, but its actual fuel is this struggle for self-
definition that the hunt initiates, not only in Nat, but also
in Caroline.

Since the source of their insulation from experience is their
social class, Nat and Caroline experience their search for
self-definition in versions of humiliation, as the perspectives and protections of their upbringing are stripped away
in their dealings with Lee Ann's friends. Lee Ann's circle
has a good-natured scorn for Nat and his friends, and in
order to communicate with them at all Nat and Caroline
must repeatedly meet that scorn. It leaves their inherited
view of the world, already shaky, impossible to sustain. As
they surrender that view, their move toward self-
understanding advances. Nat searches for Lee Ann in the
company of Memphis police, making the rounds of her
friends and inquiring of her whereabouts. Nat is thus immersed in the world of these women, and he finds himself
fascinated by the comparative freedom of their lives.

> At any rate, they were all freed from old re-
> straints put on them by family and community,
> liberated in each case, so it seems to me, by sheer
> strength of character, liberated in many re-
> spects, but above all else—and I cannot say how
> it came about—liberated sexually. . . . They
> were not promiscuous—not most of them—but
> they slept with the men they were in love with
> and they did not conceal the fact.

The issue of Nat's possible sexual involvement with Lee
Ann is always present to the police, who ask him at one
point if she is pregnant. Even after he has told them she
is not, he finds himself later asking one of her friends,
Nancy Minnifee, the same question, thereby opening himself to the deepest humiliation of the search. "Nancy's
mouth dropped open. Then she laughed aloud. Presently
she said, 'Well, one thing's certain, Nat. It wouldn't be any
concern of yours if she were.'" Nat's blunder reveals the
kind of overbearing assumption that provides Lee Ann
and her friends with fuel for their resentment and at least
part of the motive for Lee Ann's defiant flight.

Nat's second day of searching is in the company of his fa-

ther, the mayor, and the newspaper editor—
representatives of the Memphis establishment who were
the last generation "to grow up in a world where women
were absolutely subjected and under the absolute protection of men." Nat sees in retrospect, and perhaps begins
to see during the time of the events, that they were protecting a patriarchy that they sensed was being threatened
from within. "They thought of these girls as the daughters
of men who had abdicated their authority and responsibility as fathers," and of themselves as "surrogate fathers,"
acting to hold the fabric of the society that they knew together. "It was a sort of communal fatherhood they were
acting out." While Nat has been formed by his father's
world, and clings to it with part of himself, he is also stifled and finds in himself some resistance to it. But the very
structure of authority that has molded him is beginning
to change, making his ambivalence even more complex.
As Nat recalls, "I actually heard my father saying, 'That's
what the whole world is going to be like someday.' He
meant like the life such girls as Lee Ann were making for
themselves." Lee Ann represents, to Nat, a future which
is both attractive and frightening.

Nat's relations with Lee Ann and her friends have been
one expression of his tentative reluctance to follow the expected course of life. Another small mode of resistance has
been his persistence in studying Latin poetry, a subject in
which his interest is less than passionate and his skill minimal. His continuing in the study baffles his family, and he
himself professes not to understand his motivations fully.
But it is precisely because it is extraneous, even an encumbrance, to the expected that he persists in it. When Caroline finds him at home after the accident, a copy of his
Latin text nearby, her greeting is revealing. "I hope you
see now what folly your pursuit of Latin poetry is." This
petty defiance of the expected in his study of Latin was an
attempt at self-possession, and, although he drops it, this
mild nonconformity grows in more meaningful ways during the crisis.

This helps to explain Nat's fascination with Lee Ann,
which grows in proportion to her defiance of the Memphis
order. His dating of the "demimondaines" has been a flirting with the forbidden, a safe way to test the limits of the
social restrictions. But as Nat begins to search for Lee
Ann, the gravity of conflict in those relations becomes
clear. Lee Ann's friends call to warn him to leave her
alone. These only add to his curiosity to find her. Yet he
is simultaneously pushed toward a closer intimacy with
Caroline. After the day of searching with his father, Nat
and Caroline "tell each other how much we loved each
other and how we would let nothing on earth interfere
with our getting married." While the pledge reassures Nat
somewhat, he is still plagued by the phone calls that he has
kept secret and eventually tells Caroline of them. "And
before I left that night she got me to tell her all I knew
about 'that whole tribe of city girls.'" That Nat trusts
Caroline deeply enough to be frank, and that she accepts
his "confessions" with a non-judgmental determination to
make good use of them, is an indication of the growing
strength of their relationship. For Nat gives her not only
"an account of my innocent friendship with Lee Ann Dee-

hart" but also "an account of my earlier relations, which were not innocent, with a girl named Fern Morris."

While Nat's relationship with Caroline grows deeper, so does his confusion about his feelings for Lee Ann. In their frank discussion, he had held one thing back from Caroline, a growing sense that in his search for her he was "discovering what my true feelings toward Lee Ann had been during the past two years." He had begun to feel, he admitted, "that [Lee Ann] was the girl I ought and wanted to be marrying." The story's central question is whether this is escapist wish-projection. Is he attracted to Lee Ann because she is what he cannot have, or is he belatedly learning the truth of his own feelings? Even as he entertained them, he "realized the absolute folly of such thoughts and the utter impossibility of any such conclusion to present events." While this at first seems like a confession of Nat's weak inability to resist the pressure of conformity, other evidence suggests that the impossibility of the fantasy, and thus its essential safety, is part of its appeal. It is not that he lacks the courage to act on his attraction for Lee Ann but that his attraction to her depends on his conviction that he will never be able to enact it.

One remark about his relationship with Lee Ann is particularly significant:

> I had never dared insist upon the occasional advances I had naturally made to her, because she had always seemed too delicate, too vulnerable, for me to think of suggesting a casual sexual relationship with her. She had seemed too clever and too intelligent for me to deceive her about my intentions or my worth as a person. And I imagined I relished the kind of restraint there was between us because it was so altogether personal and not one placed upon us by any element or segment of society, or by any outside circumstances whatever.

But of course the contours of their entire relationship had been determined by the class barriers that existed between them. Nat was destined to marry a woman from his social set, and he and Lee Ann understood this from the outset of their friendship. There would never have been such a friendship except for the distance that social structures had decreed between them. The impossibility of marriage had had the effect of freeing them from some aspects of sexual tension. But to consider that freedom as an indication that no "element or segment of society" had placed restraints on them is the kind of obtuseness that marks Nat as still seriously immature.

Caroline's emergence as a central figure in the story is the result of her capacity to replace Lee Ann as an embodiment of reality for Nat. In her presence, "my thoughts and fantasies of the day before seemed literally like something out of a dream that I might have had." Nat grows toward a more mature self-knowledge through his rejection of immature fantasy.

Nat's explanation of his relations with the "city girls," and his sexual affair with Fern Morris, provide Caroline with the information to negotiate successfully the hostile territory of Lee Ann's network of friends. To act on the information, Caroline also must go through a certain humilia-

tion, parading her vulnerability before these hostile women and openly struggling to regain what she once might have regarded hers by right—her coming marriage. Caroline's humiliation undermines the perspective from which she has hitherto seen the world and thus makes a fuller self-development possible. She must finally appeal to Nat's former lover, Fern Morris, who offers her a clue to Lee Ann's location. It is Lee Ann's possession of a snapshot of a woman whom Nat has known as the proprietor of a nightclub, Mrs. Power. She was a woman with "a huge goiter on her neck" who "was never known to smile." This sinister figure is Lee Ann's grandmother, to whom she has returned a few days after the accident. But Lee Ann has tried to keep her connection with Mrs. Power a secret because of the social embarrassment that it might cause her. Her motive for hiding is not to avoid the scandal of having been caught with Nat, nor is it to make herself an obstacle to Nat's marriage. Caroline deduces the complex motivations behind Lee Ann's disappearance when Nat tells her what he knows of Lee Ann's past at a number of boarding schools away from Memphis. " 'They kept her away from home,' Caroline speculated. 'And so when she had finished school she wasn't prepared for the kind of 'family' she had. That's why she moved out on them and lived in a boarding house." Lee Ann's motives in disappearing thus turn out to be very different from those that Nat had surmised. Her flight is less a defiance of the social order than an indication of her fear to be exposed to it. It is primarily to avoid social embarrassment that she tried to protect her past from discovery and publication.

Caroline's discovery of Lee Ann's whereabouts is the catalyst for the self-confrontations that form the climax of the story. When they find Lee Ann at the apartment above her grandmother's nightclub, Caroline tells Nat to stay in the car while she goes up to talk to Lee Ann. Although we may suspect that her gesture is in part motivated by a jealous insecurity, its operative motive is Caroline's recognition that Nat may inhibit her communication with Lee Ann. But Lee Ann's near presence prompts Nat to a painful moment of self-analysis. As he waits in the car, he imagines his separation from Lee Ann as a sign of his closure to experience. Should he accept that closure? To leave the car and enter her apartment, against Caroline's instructions, would be the culminating act in Nat's growing defiance of the course of his life.

> I suddenly realized—at that early age—that there was experience to be had in life that I might never know anything about except through hearsay and through books. I felt that this was my last moment to reach out and understand something of the world that was other than my own narrow circumstances and my own narrow nature.

This interpretation of his course of development is an advance over his earlier misdirected feelings of love for Lee Ann. "The notion I had had yesterday that I was in love with her and wanted to marry her didn't really adequately express the emotions that her disappearance had stirred in me." As Nat has come to understand something of Lee Ann's suffering, he has come to see her as a symbol of experience, an alternative to the sheltered life he has led. His decision to stay in the car, ending his pursuit of Lee Ann, thus becomes an important moment of self-definition. "It may be that the moment of my great failure was when I continued to sit there in the car and did not force my way into the house where the old woman with the goiter lived and where it now seemed Lee Ann had been hiding for four days." While we may grant that Nat's feeling of crisis is genuine and that it locates an essential element of his personality, it is not hard to see that his impulse to burst into Lee Ann's house—an action that represented for him an active grasping of experience—would have been a ludicrous and tragic mistake. Whether from good judgment, loyalty to Caroline, or simple cowardice, Nat remains in the car. His inaction is an act of wisdom—or at least an avoidance of folly. What could he have said to Lee Ann that would have constructively addressed her situation? What could he have said that she would not have rightly rebuffed? His feeling that it is within his power to reestablish some connection with her, if that is what his impulse to enter her house means, is a sad overestimation of his capacity to exert control over experience. Nat's failure was not that he did not burst into Lee Ann's room, grasping for the experience of life that she represented to him. It was in labeling as a failure an act that was, under the circumstances, the only decent one that he could have taken. While Nat does indeed grow in recognizing the narrowness of his own experience, he has not yet achieved a full and tragic acceptance of the limits from within which he must pursue experience. Nat's failure to act is appropriate. His real failure, and one which he seems to labor to understand as he recalls the incident, is not to recognize the appropriateness of the decision.

There is some evidence, although it is by no means conclusive, that Nat may have grown toward an acceptance of the limits of experience, and thus learned in a small way to meet it more constructively. He refers to it as his "extraordinary decision" to leave his career in business at age thirty-seven and "go back to the university and prepare myself to become a teacher." The decision is a break in the pattern of life that had been established for him by his parents and that had been preserved in the final success of his four-day search to locate Lee Ann. Nat qualifies the impact of the decision with frank self-assessment: "But I knew then, at thirty-seven, that I was only going to try to comprehend intellectually the world about me and beyond me and that I had failed somehow at some time to reach out and grasp direct experience of a larger life which no amount of intellectualizing could compensate for." While many of Taylor's readers may be loath to accept the pursuit of a teaching career as a signpost of personal growth, it is exactly that for Nat, despite his mild denigration of it. Nat is less a victim of his inability to act than of his tendency to romanticize some vague notion about the grasping of experience. There is something of a Proustian flourish in Nat's romantic sense of his failure to grasp experience and his retreat into the intellectual life to analyze that failure. Insofar as this bespeaks immaturity, the story charts an arrested self-development. But without exaggerating the significance of his change—it is a vocational change which occurs after his father dies, leaving him financially secure—Nat does eventually alter the course of

his life in a delayed but seemingly genuine effort to understand. His accident with Lee Ann at least shook the foundations of his comfortable ignorance and accelerated a process in which his recognition of his narrow personal and social experience became a stimulus to self-improvement.

One strand of the story, however, works against this building indictment of the past—Nat's nostalgia for the lost world of Memphis. The story resists a linear reduction to any thematic certainty. Nat himself is no complete convert to modernity, but he continues to yearn with part of himself for the world that his accident shattered. "Our tranquil, upper-middle-class world of 1937 did not have the rest of the world crowding in on it so much," he recalls. Nat's desire for the past, despite the lessons of his experience, is itself problematic for any definitive thematic reading of the story, but it is augmented by the fact that Taylor creates a similar nostalgic reaction in his readers. **"The Old Forest"** evokes an attraction for the Memphis of the 1930s in its oblique glimpses of the lives of the upper class, despite the fact that the logic of the narrative condemns that world and shows it empty. Consider Nat's account of his dinner with the Braxleys the day after the accident. During the evening, Nat is taken by one of the Braxley's black servants to receive a telephone call from his father. "As he preceded me the length of the living room and then gently guided me across the hall to the telephone in the library, I believe he would have put his hand under my elbow to help me—as if a real invalid—if I had allowed him to." Obviously the suggestion of infantile dependency accurately reflects the weaker parts of Nat's character. But the social trappings of the Braxley house, particularly the brief image of the plantation South that Nat's dependence on the faithful servant evokes, cuts both ways in the story. It is precisely the kind of life that has damagingly restricted Nat and Caroline's vision of the world, against which they must struggle to attain a mature identity. But it is also a potentially seductive hook into the world of rare privilege. Nat is quite explicit about his attraction to this now extinct world when he recounts being driven home by the Braxley's servant, Robert. Nat falls asleep on the brief drive home and has to be awakened when they arrive.

> I remember how warmly I thanked him for bringing me home, even shaking his hand, which was a rather unusual thing to do in those days. I felt greatly refreshed and restored and personally grateful to Robert for it. There was not, in those days in Memphis, any time or occasion when one felt more secure and relaxed than when one had given oneself over completely to the care and protection of the black servants who surrounded us and who created and sustained for the most part the luxury which distinguished the lives we lived then from the lives we live now.

That modern lives are indeed different is, at least in part, a lamentable fact for Nat, even though he goes on to admit the injustice of the arrangements that made his former luxury possible. "They [the servants] did so for us, whatever their motives and however degrading our demands and our acceptance of their attentions may have been to them." There remains some part of Nat which has not been weaned from the comfortable and ultimately unjust innocence of his upper-class childhood. That has, of course, made the achievement of such maturity as he has all the more difficult. And it has made him a much more compelling subject for fiction. It behooves us to recognize that Nat's nostalgia is an oblique affirmation of the very world that his experience has proven to be both crippling and unsustainable. Insofar as his evocation of that nostalgia is an appealing part of the texture of the story, Nat's dilemma is the reader's as well, who must reject the lost world of Memphis even as he or she responds to its allure.

Although we know much less about it, Lee Ann's change after the accident is also significant. After her talk with Caroline, a profile emerges of a woman pushed by the circumstances of her past toward self-knowledge. As she hid in the Old Forest after the accident, Lee Ann realized that "she had no choice but to go back to the real world." The forest had been for her a momentary shelter from the crisis of self-knowledge that the accident threatened. Her return to the "real world" meant the acceptance of her grandmother and, as that implies, an acceptance of herself. Her friendship with Nat, who lived in a social and economic world that was unattainable for her, is one of the things that she had to abandon in her return. Nat's search for her had thus been an insistent attempt to reconfirm a destructive connection that she wished to abandon. As he sits in the car to wait for Caroline, Nat still does not understand that he is a potential obstruction to Lee Ann's process of healing.

While Caroline has been the catalyst for these crises, Nat has been largely unaware of the stress that she feels. He begins to realize her pain only as they drive away from Lee Ann's house, having resolved her disappearance and insured that there will be no damaging publicity. In this moment of success, Caroline reveals for the first time the vulnerability which drove her. Caroline asks Nat to drive "as far and as fast" out of town as he could, a revealing gesture of escape from Memphis. As she tells him what she has learned of Lee Ann's past, she "burst into weeping that began with a kind of wailing and grinding of teeth that one ordinarily associates more with a very old person in great physical pain, a wailing that became mixed almost immediately with a sort of hollow laughter in which there was no mirth." Caroline's wail is prompted in part by her sympathy for Lee Ann, but it is also self-directed, a recognition of the fundamental emptiness of the social forms that she has preserved in finding Lee Ann. Caroline confessed "her own feelings of jealousy and resentment of the girl—of *that* girl and of all those other girls, too," whom she had confronted as friends of Lee Ann. Her resentment transcends romantic jealousy, and is rooted in her sense of imprisonment within the social forms that she has striven to preserve. Caroline is disturbed "not with what [Lee Ann] might be to you but with her freedom to jump out of your car, her freedom *from* you, her freedom to run off into the woods. . . ." What follows this declaration of resentment is an important exchange that anchors the story firmly in the context of social commentary, even as it details the psychological development of its central characters.

"*You* would like to be able to do that?" I interrupted. It seemed so unlike her role as I understood it.

"*Any*body would, wouldn't they?" she said, not looking at me but at the endless stretch of concrete that lay straight ahead. "*Men* have always been able to do it," she said.

Nat has presented Lee Ann and her friends as modern women who have taken control of their lives in ways that were impossible to previous generations. The conflict over Lee Ann's disappearance is not merely one between Nat and Lee Ann but between Lee Ann's generation of women and the male power structure. In her assertion of survival, Caroline has been forced ironically to reaffirm that power structure, and her conversation with Lee Ann has brought that home to her. Like Nat, she sees Lee Ann perhaps for more than she is, a figure of freedom whose existence outside the Memphis upper class is a reminder of her own confinement within it. She describes Lee Ann and her friends as women "who have made their break with the past." "How I do admire and envy them! And how little you understand them, Nat." Caroline understands her difference from women like Lee Ann, and the achievement of that knowledge, however painful, confirms her strength and intelligence.

Caroline has recognized the way her choice has been restricted by her sex and social position, and she resorts to the language of power to explain her motivation. "Don't you see, it was a question of how very much I had to lose and how little power I had to save myself. Because *I* had not set *my*self free the way those other girls have. One makes that choice at a much earlier age than this, I'm afraid." Like Lee Ann, Caroline has recognized that an acceptance of even a restrictive past is necessary and can be a progressive and affirming step. Throughout his fiction, Taylor suggests that the past cannot be ignored, and that the attempt to do so is ultimately destructive.

Caroline has come to recognize that "Power, or strength, is what everybody must have some of if he—if she—is to survive in any kind of world." In preserving her own power through preserving her engagement, she is also helping Lee Ann to gain a new power in her restoration to her family on more open terms. Caroline has come to see that power may arise from the very circumstances that have made for weakness. "I know now what the only kind of power I can ever have must be," she tells Nat. "You mean the power of a woman in a man's world," Nat replies. Restricted as this power is, Caroline's capacity to exercise it with a knowledge of its limits is her source of strength. And her explanation of it forces Nat to a deeper understanding that his strength must also come from an exercise of power in a world in which his own situation is limited. Thus he concludes with a recognition of the "support and understanding" that she gave him "when I made the great break in my life in my late thirties." These are not dramatic victories of self-assertion or the overcoming of adverse events. They are closer to forms of accommodation with experience, assertions of self within tragically limited spheres of action. Taylor's fiction revolves on his analysis of the tragedy of human limits, both psychological and social. But Nat tells a story in which the response to experience, not the negation of experience, bears the emphasis. Even in his telling, he continues to respond. (pp. 63-77)

> David M. Robinson, "Engaging the Past: Peter Taylor's 'The Old Forest'," in The Southern Literary Journal, *Vol. XXII, No. 2, Spring, 1990, pp. 63-77.*

FURTHER READING

Bibliography

Griffin, Carl H. "Peter Taylor." In *Andrew Little, Walker Percy, Peter Taylor: A Reference Guide,* edited by Victor Kramer, Patricia Bailey, Carol G. Dana, and Carl H. Griffin, pp. 187-243. Boston: G. K. Hall & Co., 1983.
> Comprehensive bibliography which lists secondary writings chronologically by year.

Wright, Stuart T. *Peter Taylor: A Descriptive Bibliography, 1934-1987.* Charlottesville: The University of Virginia, 1988, 228 p.
> Bibliography of editions and appearances of Taylor's works.

Criticism

Baumbach, Jonathan. "Peter Taylor." In *Moderns and Contemporaries: Nine Masters of the Short Story,* edited by Jonathan Baumbach and Arthur Edelstein, pp. 343-44. New York: Random House, 1968.
> Critical introduction to "Venus, Cupid, Folly, and Time" and "Two Pilgrims."

Eisinger, Chester E. "The Conservative Imagination." In his *Fiction of the Forties,* pp. 146-230. Chicago: The University of Chicago Press, 1963.
> Examines Taylor's *A Long Fourth, and Other Stories* and *A Woman of Means.*

Griffith, Albert J. *Peter Taylor.* Rev. ed. Boston: Twayne Publishers, 1990, 192 p.
> Biographical and critical study.

Holman, David Marion. "Peter Taylor." In *The History of Southern Literature,* edited by Louis D. Rubin, Jr., pp. 494-96. Baton Rouge: Louisiana State University Press, 1985.
> Description of Taylor's writings, dividing them into two categories: "The first group . . . might be termed modern tales of manners; the second consists of psychological tales in the tradition of the southern grotesque."

Matthews, Jack. "Peter Taylor's Most Recent Fiction." *The Kenyon Review* 8, No. 1 (Winter 1986): 118-19.
> Favorable review of *The Old Forest, and Other Stories.*

Miller, Karl. "Memphis Blues." *London Review of Books* 7, No. 15 (5 September 1985): 15.
> Review of *The Old Forest, and Other Stories* in which Miller praises Taylor's skill in portraying southern upper middle-class society.

Peden, William. "Metropolis, Village, and Suburbia: The Short Fiction of Manners." In his *The American Short Story: Continuity and Change, 1940-1975,* pp. 30-68. Boston: Houghton Mifflin Company, 1975.
> Discusses the major recurrent themes of Taylor's short story collections *A Long Fourth, and Other Stories, The Widows of Thornton, Happy Families Are All Alike,* and *Miss Leonora When Last Seen.*

Pinkerton, Jan. "The Vagaries of Taste and Peter Taylor's 'A Spinster's Tale'." *Kansas Quarterly* 9, No. 2 (Spring 1977): 81-5.
> Examines "A Spinster's Tale" in order to demonstrate how critical evaluations of literary works are determined by their subject matter and their author's reputation.

Robinson, Clayton. "Peter Taylor." In *Literature of Tennessee,* edited by Ray Willbanks, pp. 149-61. n.p.: Mercer University Press, 1984.
> Overview of Taylor as a short story writer, novelist, and dramatist. Robinson praises Taylor's early fiction but expresses disappointment at his later dramas and short stories.

Robison, James Curry, ed. *Peter Taylor: A Study of the Short Fiction.* Boston: Twayne Publishers, 1988, 183 p.
> Includes a lengthy critical study by Robison and previously published essays and reminiscences by writers such as Robert Penn Warren and Allen Tate.

Towers, Robert. "A Master of the Miniature Novel." *The New York Times Book Review* (17 February 1985): 1, 26.
> Review of *The Old Forest, and Other Stories,* praising Taylor for "an exactitude of observation and loving attention to the minutiae of class behavior that characterizes so much of our best writing in the realist mode."

Voss, Arthur. "Peter Taylor." In his *The American Short Story: A Critical Survey,* pp. 352-53. Norman: University of Oklahoma Press, 1973.
> Outlines Taylor's works and themes.

Walker, Jeffrey. "1945-1956: Post-World War II Manners and Mores." In *The American Short Story, 1945-1980: A Critical History,* edited by Gordon Weaver, pp. 16-18. Boston: Twayne Publishers, 1983.
> Focuses on Taylor's first two collections of stories, *A Long Fourth, and Other Stories* and *The Widows of Thornton.*

Walkiewicz, E. P. "1957-1969: Toward Diversity of Form." In *The American Short Story, 1945-1980: A Critical History,* edited by Gordon Weaver, pp. 44-6. Boston: Twayne Publishers, 1983.
> Examines "Taylor's fondness for the supernatural, the slightly surreal, and the grotesque."

Williamson, Alan. "Identity and the Wider Eros: A Reading of Peter Taylor's Stories." *Shenandoah* 30, No. 1 (Fall 1978): 71-84.
> Examines the concepts of identity and eroticism as exemplified in Taylor's stories.

Young, Thomas Daniel. *Tennessee Writers.* Knoxville: University of Tennessee Press, 1981, 92-9.

>Outlines the major subjects and themes of Taylor's writings and presents "A Long Fourth" as an illustration of the characteristic issues found in Taylor's short stories.

Additional coverage of Taylor's life and career is contained in the following sources published by Gale Research: *Contemporary Authors* Vol. 13-16; *Contemporary Authors New Revision Series,* Vol. 9; *Contemporary Literary Criticism,* Vols. 1, 4, 18, 37, 44, 50, 71; *Dictionary of Literary Biography Yearbook: 1981;* and *Major 20th-Century Writers.*

Appendix:

Select Bibliography of General Sources on Short Fiction

BOOKS OF CRITICISM

Allen, Walter. *The Short Story in English.* New York: Oxford University Press, 1981, 413 p.

Aycock, Wendell M., ed. *The Teller and the Tale: Aspects of the Short Story* (Proceedings of the Comparative Literature Symposium, Texas Tech University, Volume XIII). Lubbock: Texas Tech Press, 1982, 156 p.

Averill, Deborah. *The Irish Short Story from George Moore to Frank O'Connor.* Washington, D.C.: University Press of America, 1982, 329 p.

Bates, H. E. *The Modern Short Story: A Critical Survey.* Boston: Writer, 1941, 231 p.

Bayley, John. *The Short Story: Henry James to Elizabeth Bowen.* Great Britain: The Harvester Press Limited, 1988, 197 p.

Bennett, E. K. *A History of the German Novelle: From Goethe to Thomas Mann.* Cambridge: At the University Press, 1934, 296 p.

Bone, Robert. *Down Home: A History of Afro-American Short Fiction from Its Beginning to the End of the Harlem Renaissance.* Rev. ed. New York: Columbia University Press, 1988, 350 p.

Bruck, Peter. *The Black American Short Story in the Twentieth Century: A Collection of Critical Essays.* Amsterdam: B. R. Grüner Publishing Co., 1977, 209 p.

Burnett, Whit, and Burnett, Hallie. *The Modern Short Story in the Making.* New York: Hawthorn Books, 1964, 405 p.

Canby, Henry Seidel. *The Short Story in English.* New York: Henry Holt and Co., 1909, 386 p.

Current-García, Eugene. *The American Short Story before 1850: A Critical History.* Twayne's Critical History of the Short Story, edited by William Peden. Boston: Twayne Publishers, 1985, 168 p.

Flora, Joseph M., ed. *The English Short Story, 1880-1945: A Critical History.* Twayne's Critical History of the Short Story, edited by William Peden. Boston: Twayne Publishers, 1985, 215 p.

Foster, David William. *Studies in the Contemporary Spanish-American Short Story.* Columbia, Mo.: University of Missouri Press, 1979, 126 p.

George, Albert J. *Short Fiction in France, 1800-1850.* Syracuse, N.Y.: Syracuse University Press, 1964, 245 p.

Gerlach, John. *Toward an End: Closure and Structure in the American Short Story.* University, Ala.: The University of Alabama Press, 1985, 193 p.

Hankin, Cherry, ed. *Critical Essays on the New Zealand Short Story.* Auckland: Heinemann Publishers, 1982, 186 p.

Hanson, Clare, ed. *Re-Reading the Short Story.* London: MacMillan Press, 1989, 137 p.

Harris, Wendell V. *British Short Fiction in the Nineteenth Century.* Detroit: Wayne State University Press, 1979, 209 p.

Huntington, John. *Rationalizing Genius: Ideological Strategies in the Classic American Science Fiction Short Story.* New Brunswick: Rutgers University Press, 1989, 216 p.

Kilroy, James F., ed. *The Irish Short Story: A Critical History.* Twayne's Critical History of the Short Story, edited by William Peden. Boston: Twayne Publishers, 1984, 251 p.

Lee, A. Robert. *The Nineteenth-Century American Short Story.* Totowa, N. J.: Vision / Barnes & Noble, 1986, 196 p.

Leibowitz, Judith. *Narrative Purpose in the Novella.* The Hague: Mouton, 1974, 137 p.

Lohafer, Susan. *Coming to Terms with the Short Story.* Baton Rouge: Louisiana State University Press, 1983, 171 p.

Lohafer, Susan, and Clarey, Jo Ellyn. *Short Story Theory at a Crossroads.* Baton Rouge: Louisiana State University Press, 1989, 352 p.

Mann, Susan Garland. *The Short Story Cycle: A Genre Companion and Reference Guide.* New York: Greenwood Press, 1989, 228 p.

Matthews, Brander. *The Philosophy of the Short Story.* New York: Longmans, Green and Co., 1901, 83 p.

May, Charles E., ed. *Short Story Theories.* Athens, Oh.: Ohio University Press, 1976, 251 p.

McClave, Heather, ed. *Women Writers of the Short Story: A Collection of Critical Essays.* Englewood Cliffs, N. J.: Prentice-Hall, 1980, 171 p.

Moser, Charles, ed. *The Russian Short Story: A Critical History.* Twayne's Critical History of the Short Story, edited by William Peden. Boston: Twayne Publishers, 1986, 232 p.

New, W. H. *Dreams of Speech and Violence: The Art of the Short Story in Canada and New Zealand.* Toronto: The University of Toronto Press, 1987, 302 p.

Newman, Frances. *The Short Story's Mutations: From Petronius to Paul Morand.* New York: B. W. Huebsch, 1925, 332 p.

O'Connor, Frank. *The Lonely Voice: A Study of the Short Story.* Cleveland: World Publishing Co., 1963, 220 p.

O'Faolain, Sean. *The Short Story.* New York: Devin-Adair Co., 1951, 370 p.

Orel, Harold. *The Victorian Short Story: Development and Triumph of a Literary Genre.* Cambridge: Cambridge University Press, 1986, 213 p.

O'Toole, L. Michael. *Structure, Style and Interpretation in the Russian Short Story.* New Haven: Yale University Press, 1982, 272 p.

Pattee, Fred Lewis. *The Development of the American Short Story: An Historical Survey.* New York: Harper and Brothers Publishers, 1923, 388 p.

Peden, Margaret Sayers, ed. *The Latin American Short Story: A Critical History.* Twayne's Critical History of the Short Story, edited by William Peden. Boston: Twayne Publishers, 1983, 160 p.

Peden, William. *The American Short Story: Continuity and Change, 1940-1975.* Rev. ed. Boston: Houghton Mifflin Co., 1975, 215 p.

Reid, Ian. *The Short Story.* The Critical Idiom, edited by John D. Jump. London: Methuen and Co., 1977, 76 p.

Rhode, Robert D. *Setting in the American Short Story of Local Color, 1865-1900.* The Hague: Mouton, 1975, 189 p.

Rohrberger, Mary. *Hawthorne and the Modern Short Story: A Study in Genre.* The Hague: Mouton and Co., 1966, 148 p.

Shaw, Valerie, *The Short Story: A Critical Introduction.* London: Longman, 1983, 294 p.

Stephens, Michael. *The Dramaturgy of Style: Voice in Short Fiction.* Carbondale, Ill.: Southern Illinois University Press, 1986, 281 p.

Stevick, Philip, ed. *The American Short Story, 1900-1945: A Critical History.* Twayne's Critical History of the Short Story, edited by William Peden, Boston: Twayne Publishers, 1984, 209 p.

Summers, Hollis, ed. *Discussion of the Short Story.* Boston: D. C. Heath and Co., 1963, 118 p.

Vannatta, Dennis, ed. *The English Short Story, 1945-1980: A Critical History.* Twayne's Critical History of the Short Story, edited by William Peden. Boston: Twayne Publishers, 1985, 206 p.

Voss, Arthur. *The American Short Story: A Critical Survey.* Norman, Okla.: University of Oklahoma Press, 1973, 399 p.

Ward, Alfred C. *Aspects of the Modern Short Story: English and American.* London: University of London Press, 1924, 307 p.

Weaver, Gordon, ed. *The American Short Story, 1945-1980: A Critical History.* Twayne's Critical History of the Short Story, edited by William Peden. Boston: Twayne Publishers, 1983, 150 p.

West, Ray B., Jr. *The Short Story in America, 1900-1950.* Chicago: Henry Regnery Co., 1952, 147 p.

Williams, Blanche Colton. *Our Short Story Writers.* New York: Moffat, Yard and Co., 1920, 357 p.

Wright, Austin McGiffert. *The American Short Story in the Twenties.* Chicago: University of Chicago Press, 1961, 425 p.

CRITICAL ANTHOLOGIES

Atkinson, W. Patterson, ed. *The Short-Story.* Boston: Allyn and Bacon, 1923, 317 p.

Baldwin, Charles Sears, ed. *American Short Stories.* New York: Longmans, Green and Co., 1904, 333 p.

Charters, Ann, ed. *The Story and Its Writer: An Introduction to Short Fiction.* New York: St. Martin's Press, 1983, 1239 p.

Current-García, Eugene, and Patrick, Walton R., eds. *American Short Stories: 1820 to the Present.* Key Editions, edited by John C. Gerber. Chicago: Scott, Foresman and Co., 1952, 633 p.

Fagin, N. Bryllion, ed. *America through the Short Story.* Boston: Little, Brown, and Co., 1936, 508 p.

Frakes, James R., and Traschen, Isadore, eds. *Short Fiction: A Critical Collection.* Prentice-Hall English Literature Series, edited by Maynard Mack. Englewood Cliffs, N.J.: Prentice-Hall, 1959, 459 p.

Gifford, Douglas, ed. *Scottish Short Stories, 1800-1900.* The Scottish Library, edited by Alexander Scott. London: Calder and Boyars, 1971, 350 p.

Gordon, Caroline, and Tate, Allen, eds. *The House of Fiction: An Anthology of the Short Story with Commentary.* Rev. ed. New York: Charles Scribner's Sons, 1960, 469 p.

Greet, T. Y., et. al. *The Worlds of Fiction: Stories in Context.* Boston: Houghton Mifflin Co., 1964, 429 p.

Gullason, Thomas A., and Caspar, Leonard, eds. *The World of Short Fiction: An International Collection.* New York: Harper and Row, 1962, 548 p.

Havighurst, Walter, ed. *Masters of the Modern Short Story.* New York: Harcourt, Brace and Co., 1945, 538 p.

Litz, A. Walton, ed. *Major American Short Stories.* New York: Oxford University Press, 1975, 823 p.

Matthews, Brander, ed. *The Short-Story: Specimens Illustrating Its Development.* New York: American Book Co., 1907, 399 p.

Menton, Seymour, ed. *The Spanish American Short Story: A Critical Anthology.* Berkeley and Los Angeles: University of California Press, 1980, 496 p.

Mzamane, Mbulelo Vizikhungo, ed. *Hungry Flames, and Other Black South African Short Stories.* Longman African Classics. Essex: Longman, 1986, 162 p.

Schorer, Mark, ed. *The Short Story: A Critical Anthology.* Rev. ed. Prentice-Hall English Literature Series, edited by Maynard Mack. Englewood Cliffs, N. J.: Prentice-Hall, 1967, 459 p.

Simpson, Claude M., ed. *The Local Colorists: American Short Stories, 1857-1900.* New York: Harper and Brothers Publishers, 1960, 340 p.

Stanton, Robert, ed. *The Short Story and the Reader.* New York: Henry Holt and Co., 1960, 557 p.

West, Ray B., Jr., ed. *American Short Stories.* New York: Thomas Y. Crowell Co., 1959, 267 p.

Short Story Criticism Indexes

Literary Criticism Series
Cumulative Author Index

SSC Cumulative Nationality Index
SSC Cumulative Title Index

This Index Includes References to Entries in These Gale Series

Concise Dictionary of American Literary Biography contains illustrated entries on major American authors selected and updated from the *Dictionary of Literary Biography*.

Contemporary Literary Criticism presents excerpts of criticism on the works of novelists, poets, dramatists, short story writers, scriptwriters, and other creative writers who are now living or who have died since 1960.

Twentieth-Century Literary Criticism contains critical excerpts by the most significant commentators on poets, novelists, short story writers, dramatists, and philosophers who died between 1900 and 1960.

Nineteenth-Century Literature Criticism offers significant passages from criticism on authors who died between 1800 and 1899.

Literature Criticism from 1400 to 1800 compiles significant passages from the most noteworthy criticism on authors of the fifteenth through eighteenth centuries.

Classical and Medieval Literature Criticism offers excerpts of criticism on the works of world authors from classical antiquity through the fourteenth century.

Short Story Criticism compiles excerpts of criticism on short fiction by writers of all eras and nationalities.

Poetry Criticism presents excerpts of criticism on the works of poets from all eras, movements, and nationalities.

Drama Criticism contains excerpts of criticism on dramatists of all nationalities and periods of literary history.

Children's Literature Review includes excerpts from reviews, criticism, and commentary on works of authors and illustrators who create books for children.

Contemporary Authors Series encompasses five related series. *Contemporary Authors* provides biographical and bibliographical information on more than 97,000 writers of fiction and nonfiction. *Contemporary Authors New Revision Series* provides completely updated information on authors covered in *CA*. *Contemporary Authors Permanent Series* consists of listings for deceased and inactive authors. *Contemporary Authors Autobiography Series* presents specially commissioned autobiographies by leading contemporary writers. *Contemporary Authors Bibliographical Series* contains primary and secondary bibliographies as well as analytical bibliographical essays by authorities on major modern authors.

Dictionary of Literary Biography encompasses four related series. *Dictionary of Literary Biography* furnishes illustrated overviews of authors' lives and works. *Dictionary of Literary Biography Documentary Series* illuminates the careers of major figures through a selection of literary documents, including letters, interviews, and photographs. *Dictionary of Literary Biography Yearbook* summarizes the past year's literary activity and includes updated entries on individual authors. *Concise Dictionary of American Literary Biography* comprises six volumes of revised and updated sketches on major American authors that were originally presented in *Dictionary of Literary Biography*.

Major 20th-Century Writers contains in four volumes both newly written and completely updated *CA* sketches on over one thousand of the most influential authors of our time.

Something about the Author Series encompasses three related series. *Something about the Author* contains well-illustrated biographical sketches on juvenile and young adult authors and illustrators from all eras. *Something about the Author Autobiography Series* presents specially commissioned autobiographies by prominent authors and illustrators of books for children and young adults. *Authors & Artists for Young Adults* provides high school and junior high school students with profiles of their favorite creative artists.

Yesterday's Authors of Books for Children contains heavily illustrated entries on children's writers who died before 1961. Complete in two volumes.

Literary Criticism Series
Cumulative Author Index

This index lists all author entries in the Gale Literary Criticism Series and includes cross-references to other Gale sources. References in the index are identified as follows:

AAYA: *Authors & Artists for Young Adults,* Volumes 1-7
BLC: *Black Literature Criticism,* Volumes 1-3
CA: *Contemporary Authors* (original series), Volumes 1-136
CAAS: *Contemporary Authors Autobiography Series,* Volumes 1-15
CABS: *Contemporary Authors Bibliographical Series,* Volumes 1-3
CANR: *Contemporary Authors New Revision Series,* Volumes 1-35
CAP: *Contemporary Authors Permanent Series,* Volumes 1-2
CA-R: *Contemporary Authors* (first revision), Volumes 1-44
CDALB: *Concise Dictionary of American Literary Biography,* Volumes 1-6
CLC: *Contemporary Literary Criticism,* Volumes 1-71
CLR: *Children's Literature Review,* Volumes 1-25
CMLC: *Classical and Medieval Literature Criticism,* Volumes 1-9
DC: *Drama Criticism,* Volumes 1-2
DLB: *Dictionary of Literary Biography,* Volumes 1-114
DLB-DS: *Dictionary of Literary Biography Documentary Series,* Volumes 1-9
DLB-Y: *Dictionary of Literary Biography Yearbook,* Volumes 1980-1990
LC: *Literature Criticism from 1400 to 1800,* Volumes 1-19
NCLC: *Nineteenth-Century Literature Criticism,* Volumes 1-35
PC: *Poetry Criticism,* Volumes 1-4
SAAS: *Something about the Author Autobiography Series,* Volumes 1-14
SATA: *Something about the Author,* Volumes 1-68
SSC: *Short Story Criticism,* Volumes 1-10
TCLC: *Twentieth-Century Literary Criticism,* Volumes 1-45
WLC: *World Literature Criticism, 1500 to the Present,* Volumes 1-6
YABC: *Yesterday's Authors of Books for Children,* Volumes 1-2

Ayrton, Michael 1921-1975 . . . . CLC 7
   See also CANR 9, 21; CA 5-8R;
   obituary CA 61-64

Azorin 1874-1967 . . . . CLC 11
   See also Martinez Ruiz, Jose

Azuela, Mariano 1873-1952 . . . . TCLC 3
   See also CA 104

"Bab" 1836-1911
   See Gilbert, (Sir) W(illiam) S(chwenck)

Babel, Isaak (Emmanuilovich)
   1894-1941 . . . . TCLC 2, 13
   See also CA 104

Babits, Mihaly 1883-1941 . . . . TCLC 14
   See also CA 114

Babur 1483-1530 . . . . LC 18

Bacchelli, Riccardo 1891-1985 . . . . . CLC 19
   See also CA 29-32R; obituary CA 117

Bach, Richard (David) 1936- . . . . CLC 14
   See also CANR 18; CA 9-12R; SATA 13

Bachman, Richard 1947-
   See King, Stephen (Edwin)

Bachmann, Ingeborg 1926-1973 . . . . . CLC 69
   See also CA 93-96; obituary CA 45-48

Bacon, Sir Francis 1561-1626 . . . . LC 18

Bacovia, George 1881-1957 . . . . TCLC 24

Bagehot, Walter 1826-1877 . . . . . . NCLC 10
   See also DLB 55

Bagnold, Enid 1889-1981 . . . . CLC 25
   See also CANR 5; CA 5-8R;
   obituary CA 103; SATA 1, 25; DLB 13

Bagryana, Elisaveta 1893- . . . . CLC 10

Bailey, Paul 1937- . . . . CLC 45
   See also CANR 16; CA 21-24R; DLB 14

Baillie, Joanna 1762-1851 . . . . NCLC 2

Bainbridge, Beryl
   1933- . . . . CLC 4, 5, 8, 10, 14, 18, 22, 62
   See also CANR 24; CA 21-24R; DLB 14

Baker, Elliott 1922- . . . . CLC 8, 61
   See also CANR 2; CA 45-48

Baker, Nicholson 1957- . . . . CLC 61

Baker, Russell (Wayne) 1925- . . . . . . CLC 31
   See also CANR 11; CA 57-60

Bakshi, Ralph 1938- . . . . CLC 26
   See also CA 112

Bakunin, Mikhail (Alexandrovich)
   1814-1876 . . . . NCLC 25

Baldwin, James (Arthur)
   1924-1987 . . . . . CLC 1, 2, 3, 4, 5, 8, 13,
      15, 17, 42, 50, 67; DC 1; SSC 10
   See also BLC 1; WLC 1; CANR 3,24;
   CA 1-4R; obituary CA 124; CABS 1;
   SATA 9, 54; DLB 2, 7, 33; DLB-Y 87;
   CDALB 1941-1968; AAYA 4

Ballard, J(ames) G(raham)
   1930- . . . . CLC 3, 6, 14, 36; SSC 1
   See also CANR 15; CA 5-8R; DLB 14

Balmont, Konstantin Dmitriyevich
   1867-1943 . . . . TCLC 11
   See also CA 109

Balzac, Honore de
   1799-1850 . . . . NCLC 5, 35; SSC 5
   See also WLC 1

Bambara, Toni Cade 1939- . . . . CLC 19
   See also BLC 1; CANR 24; CA 29-32R;
   DLB 38; AAYA 5

Bandanes, Jerome 1937- . . . . CLC 59

Banim, John 1798-1842 . . . . NCLC 13

Banim, Michael 1796-1874 . . . . . NCLC 13

Banks, Iain 1954- . . . . CLC 34
   See also CA 123

Banks, Lynne Reid 1929- . . . . CLC 23
   See also Reid Banks, Lynne

Banks, Russell 1940- . . . . CLC 37
   See also CANR 19; CA 65-68

Banville, John 1945- . . . . CLC 46
   See also CA 117, 128; DLB 14

Banville, Theodore (Faullain) de
   1832-1891 . . . . NCLC 9

Baraka, Imamu Amiri
   1934- . . . CLC 1, 2, 3, 5, 10, 14, 33; PC 4
   See also Jones, (Everett) LeRoi
   See also BLC 1; CANR 27; CA 21-24R;
   CABS 3; DLB 5, 7, 16, 38; DLB-DS 8;
   CDALB 1941-1968

Barbellion, W. N. P. 1889-1919 . . . TCLC 24

Barbera, Jack 1945- . . . . CLC 44
   See also CA 110

Barbey d'Aurevilly, Jules Amedee
   1808-1889 . . . . NCLC 1

Barbusse, Henri 1873-1935 . . . . TCLC 5
   See also CA 105; DLB 65

Barea, Arturo 1897-1957 . . . . TCLC 14
   See also CA 111

Barfoot, Joan 1946- . . . . CLC 18
   See also CA 105

Baring, Maurice 1874-1945 . . . . TCLC 8
   See also CA 105; DLB 34

Barker, Clive 1952- . . . . CLC 52
   See also CA 121

Barker, George (Granville)
   1913- . . . . CLC 8, 48
   See also CANR 7; CA 9-12R; DLB 20

Barker, Howard 1946- . . . . CLC 37
   See also CA 102; DLB 13

Barker, Pat 1943- . . . . CLC 32
   See also CA 117, 122

Barlow, Joel 1754-1812 . . . . NCLC 23
   See also DLB 37

Barnard, Mary (Ethel) 1909- . . . . . . CLC 48
   See also CAP 2; CA 21-22

Barnes, Djuna (Chappell)
   1892-1982 . . . CLC 3, 4, 8, 11, 29; SSC 3
   See also CANR 16; CA 9-12R;
   obituary CA 107; DLB 4, 9, 45

Barnes, Julian 1946- . . . . CLC 42
   See also CANR 19; CA 102

Barnes, Peter 1931- . . . . CLC 5, 56
   See also CA 65-68; DLB 13

Baroja (y Nessi), Pio 1872-1956 . . . . TCLC 8
   See also CA 104

Barondess, Sue K(aufman) 1926-1977
   See Kaufman, Sue
   See also CANR 1; CA 1-4R;
   obituary CA 69-72

Barrett, (Roger) Syd 1946-
   See Pink Floyd

Barrett, William (Christopher)
   1913- . . . . CLC 27
   See also CANR 11; CA 13-16R

Barrie, (Sir) J(ames) M(atthew)
   1860-1937 . . . . TCLC 2
   See also CLR 16; YABC 1; CA 104;
   DLB 10

Barrol, Grady 1953-
   See Bograd, Larry

Barry, Philip (James Quinn)
   1896-1949 . . . . TCLC 11
   See also CA 109; DLB 7

Barth, John (Simmons)
   1930- . . . . . . CLC 1, 2, 3, 5, 7, 9, 10, 14,
      27, 51; SSC 10
   See also CANR 5, 23; CA 1-4R; CABS 1;
   DLB 2

Barthelme, Donald
   1931-1989 . . . . . CLC 1, 2, 3, 5, 6, 8, 13,
      23, 46, 59; SSC 2
   See also CANR 20; CA 21-24R, 129;
   SATA 7; DLB 2; DLB-Y 80

Barthelme, Frederick 1943- . . . . CLC 36
   See also CA 114, 122; DLB-Y 85

Barthes, Roland 1915-1980 . . . . CLC 24
   See also obituary CA 97-100

Barzun, Jacques (Martin) 1907- . . . CLC 51
   See also CANR 22; CA 61-64

Bashevis, Isaac 1904-1991
   See Singer, Isaac Bashevis

Bashkirtseff, Marie 1859-1884 . . . NCLC 27

Basho, Matsuo 1644-1694 . . . . PC 3

Bass, Kingsley B. 1935-

Bassani, Giorgio 1916- . . . . CLC 9
   See also CA 65-68

Bataille, Georges 1897-1962 . . . . CLC 29
   See also CA 101; obituary CA 89-92

Bates, H(erbert) E(rnest)
   1905-1974 . . . . CLC 46; SSC 10
   See also CANR 34; CA 93-96;
   obituary CA 45-48

Baudelaire, Charles
   1821-1867 . . . . NCLC 6, 29; PC 1
   See also WLC 1

Baudrillard, Jean 1929- . . . . CLC 60

Baum, L(yman) Frank 1856-1919 . . . TCLC 7
   See also CLR 15; CA 108; SATA 18;
   DLB 22

Baumbach, Jonathan 1933- . . . . . . CLC 6, 23
   See also CAAS 5; CANR 12; CA 13-16R;
   DLB-Y 80

Bausch, Richard (Carl) 1945- . . . . . . CLC 51
   See also CA 101

Baxter, Charles 1947- . . . . CLC 45
   See also CA 57-60

Baxter, James K(eir) 1926-1972 . . . . CLC 14
   See also CA 77-80

Bayer, Sylvia 1909-1981
   See Glassco, John

Beagle, Peter S(oyer) 1939- . . . . CLC 7
   See also CANR 4; CA 9-12R; DLB-Y 80

Cunningham, Julia (Woolfolk)
1916- .... **CLC 12**
See also CANR 4, 19; CA 9-12R; SAAS 2;
SATA 1, 26

Cunningham, Michael 1952- .... **CLC 34**

Currie, Ellen 19??- .... **CLC 44**

Dabrowska, Maria (Szumska)
1889-1965 .... **CLC 15**
See also CA 106

Dabydeen, David 1956?- .... **CLC 34**
See also CA 106

Dacey, Philip 1939- .... **CLC 51**
See also CANR 14; CA 37-40R

Dagerman, Stig (Halvard)
1923-1954 .... **TCLC 17**
See also CA 117

Dahl, Roald 1916- .... **CLC 1, 6, 18**
See also CLR 1, 7; CANR 6; CA 1-4R;
SATA 1, 26

Dahlberg, Edward 1900-1977... **CLC 1, 7, 14**
See also CA 9-12R; obituary CA 69-72;
DLB 48

Daly, Elizabeth 1878-1967........ **CLC 52**
See also CAP 2; CA 23-24;
obituary CA 25-28R

Daly, Maureen 1921- .... **CLC 17**
See also McGivern, Maureen Daly
See also SAAS 1; SATA 2

Daniken, Erich von 1935-
See Von Daniken, Erich

Dannay, Frederic 1905-1982
See Queen, Ellery
See also CANR 1; CA 1-4R;
obituary CA 107

D'Annunzio, Gabriele
1863-1938 .... **TCLC 6, 40**
See also CA 104

Dante (Alighieri)
See Alighieri, Dante

Danvers, Dennis 1947- .... **CLC 70**

Danziger, Paula 1944- .... **CLC 21**
See also CLR 20; CA 112, 115; SATA 30,
36

Dario, Ruben 1867-1916 .... **TCLC 4**
See also Sarmiento, Felix Ruben Garcia
See also CA 104

Darley, George 1795-1846 .... **NCLC 2**

Daryush, Elizabeth 1887-1977.... **CLC 6, 19**
See also CANR 3; CA 49-52; DLB 20

Daudet, (Louis Marie) Alphonse
1840-1897 .... **NCLC 1**

Daumal, Rene 1908-1944 .... **TCLC 14**
See also CA 114

Davenport, Guy (Mattison, Jr.)
1927- .... **CLC 6, 14, 38**
See also CANR 23; CA 33-36R

Davidson, Donald (Grady)
1893-1968 .... **CLC 2, 13, 19**
See also CANR 4; CA 5-8R;
obituary CA 25-28R; DLB 45

Davidson, John 1857-1909 .... **TCLC 24**
See also CA 118; DLB 19

Davidson, Sara 1943- .... **CLC 9**
See also CA 81-84

Davie, Donald (Alfred)
1922- .... **CLC 5, 8, 10, 31**
See also CAAS 3; CANR 1; CA 1-4R;
DLB 27

Davies, Ray(mond Douglas) 1944- .. **CLC 21**
See also CA 116

Davies, Rhys 1903-1978.......... **CLC 23**
See also CANR 4; CA 9-12R;
obituary CA 81-84

Davies, (William) Robertson
1913- .... **CLC 2, 7, 13, 25, 42**
See also WLC 2; CANR 17; CA 33-36R;
DLB 68

Davies, W(illiam) H(enry)
1871-1940 .... **TCLC 5**
See also CA 104; DLB 19

Davis, Frank Marshall 1905-1987
See also BLC 1; CA 123, 125; DLB 51

Davis, H(arold) L(enoir)
1896-1960 .... **CLC 49**
See also obituary CA 89-92; DLB 9

Davis, Rebecca (Blaine) Harding
1831-1910 .... **TCLC 6**
See also CA 104; DLB 74

Davis, Richard Harding
1864-1916 .... **TCLC 24**
See also CA 114; DLB 12, 23, 78, 79

Davison, Frank Dalby 1893-1970 ... **CLC 15**
See also obituary CA 116

Davison, Peter 1928- .... **CLC 28**
See also CAAS 4; CANR 3; CA 9-12R;
DLB 5

Davys, Mary 1674-1732............. **LC 1**
See also DLB 39

Dawson, Fielding 1930- .... **CLC 6**
See also CA 85-88

Day, Clarence (Shepard, Jr.)
1874-1935 .... **TCLC 25**
See also CA 108; DLB 11

Day, Thomas 1748-1789............ **LC 1**
See also YABC 1; DLB 39

Day Lewis, C(ecil)
1904-1 .... **CLC 1, 6, 10**
See also CAP 1; CA 15-16;
obituary CA 33-36R; DLB 15, 20

Dazai Osamu 1909-1948 .... **TCLC 11**
See also Tsushima Shuji

De Crayencour, Marguerite 1903-1987
See Yourcenar, Marguerite

Deer, Sandra 1940- .... **CLC 45**

De Ferrari, Gabriella 19??- .... **CLC 65**

Defoe, Daniel 1660?-1731 .... **LC 1**
See also WLC 2; SATA 22; DLB 39

De Hartog, Jan 1914- .... **CLC 19**
See also CANR 1; CA 1-4R

Deighton, Len 1929- ...... **CLC 4, 7, 22, 46**
See also Deighton, Leonard Cyril
See also DLB 87

Deighton, Leonard Cyril 1929-
See Deighton, Len
See also CANR 19; CA 9-12R

De la Mare, Walter (John)
1873-1956 .... **TCLC 4**
See also CLR 23; WLC 2; CA 110;
SATA 16; DLB 19

Delaney, Shelagh 1939- .... **CLC 29**
See also CA 17-20R; DLB 13

Delany, Mary (Granville Pendarves)
1700-1788 .... **LC 12**

Delany, Samuel R(ay, Jr.)
1942- .... **CLC 8, 14, 38**
See also BLC 1; CANR 27; CA 81-84;
DLB 8, 33

de la Ramee, Marie Louise 1839-1908
See Ouida
See also SATA 20

De la Roche, Mazo 1885-1961 ..... **CLC 14**
See also CA 85-88; DLB 68

Delbanco, Nicholas (Franklin)
1942- .... **CLC 6, 13**
See also CAAS 2; CA 17-20R; DLB 6

del Castillo, Michel 1933- .... **CLC 38**
See also CA 109

Deledda, Grazia 1871-1936 .... **TCLC 23**
See also CA 123

Delibes (Setien), Miguel 1920- ... **CLC 8, 18**
See also CANR 1; CA 45-48

DeLillo, Don
1936- .... **CLC 8, 10, 13, 27, 39, 54**
See also CANR 21; CA 81-84; DLB 6

De Lisser, H(erbert) G(eorge)
1878-1944 .... **TCLC 12**
See also CA 109

Deloria, Vine (Victor), Jr. 1933- .... **CLC 21**
See also CANR 5, 20; CA 53-56; SATA 21

Del Vecchio, John M(ichael)
1947- .... **CLC 29**
See also CA 110

de Man, Paul 1919-1983 .... **CLC 55**
See also obituary CA 111; DLB 67

De Marinis, Rick 1934- .... **CLC 54**
See also CANR 9, 25; CA 57-60

Demby, William 1922- .... **CLC 53**
See also BLC 1; CA 81-84; DLB 33

Denby, Edwin (Orr) 1903-1983 .... **CLC 48**
See also obituary CA 110

Dennis, John 1657-1734............ **LC 11**

Dennis, Nigel (Forbes) 1912- .... **CLC 8**
See also CA 25-28R; obituary CA 129;
DLB 13, 15

De Palma, Brian 1940- .... **CLC 20**
See also CA 109

De Quincey, Thomas 1785-1859 ... **NCLC 4**

Deren, Eleanora 1908-1961
See Deren, Maya
See also obituary CA 111

Deren, Maya 1908-1961........... **CLC 16**
See also Deren, Eleanora

Derleth, August (William)
1909-1971 .... **CLC 31**
See also CANR 4; CA 1-4R;
obituary CA 29-32R; SATA 5; DLB 9

Derrida, Jacques 1930- .... **CLC 24**
See also CA 124, 127

Desai, Anita 1937- . . . . **CLC 19, 37**
See also CA 81-84

De Saint-Luc, Jean 1909-1981
See Glassco, John

De Sica, Vittorio 1902-1974 . . . . . . **CLC 20**
See also obituary CA 117

Desnos, Robert 1900-1945 . . . . **TCLC 22**
See also CA 121

Destouches, Louis-Ferdinand-Auguste
1894-1961
See Celine, Louis-Ferdinand
See also CA 85-88

Deutsch, Babette 1895-1982 . . . . **CLC 18**
See also CANR 4; CA 1-4R;
obituary CA 108; SATA 1;
obituary SATA 33; DLB 45

Devenant, William 1606-1649 . . . . **LC 13**

Devkota, Laxmiprasad
1909-1959 . . . . **TCLC 23**
See also CA 123

DeVoto, Bernard (Augustine)
1897-1955 . . . . **TCLC 29**
See also CA 113; DLB 9

De Vries, Peter
1910- . . . . **CLC 1, 2, 3, 7, 10, 28, 46**
See also CA 17-20R; DLB 6; DLB-Y 82

Dexter, Pete 1943- . . . . **CLC 34, 55**
See also CA 127

Diamano, Silmang 1906-
See Senghor, Leopold Sedar

Diamond, Neil (Leslie) 1941- . . . . **CLC 30**
See also CA 108

Dick, Philip K(indred)
1928-1982 . . . . **CLC 10, 30**
See also CANR 2, 16; CA 49-52;
obituary CA 106; DLB 8

Dickens, Charles
1812-1870 . . . . **NCLC 3, 8, 18, 26**
See also WLC 2; SATA 15; DLB 21, 55, 70

Dickey, James (Lafayette)
1923- . . . . **CLC 1, 2, 4, 7, 10, 15, 47**
See also CANR 10; CA 9-12R; CABS 2;
DLB 5; DLB-Y 82; DLB-DS 7

Dickey, William 1928- . . . . **CLC 3, 28**
See also CANR 24; CA 9-12R; DLB 5

Dickinson, Charles 1952- . . . . **CLC 49**

Dickinson, Emily (Elizabeth)
1830-1886 . . . . **NCLC 21; PC 1**
See also WLC 2; SATA 29; DLB 1;
CDALB 1865-1917

Dickinson, Peter (Malcolm de Brissac)
1927- . . . . **CLC 12, 35**
See also CA 41-44R; SATA 5; DLB 87

Didion, Joan 1934- . . . . . **CLC 1, 3, 8, 14, 32**
See also CANR 14; CA 5-8R; DLB 2;
DLB-Y 81, 86; CDALB 1968-1987

Dillard, Annie 1945- . . . . **CLC 9, 60**
See also CANR 3; CA 49-52; SATA 10;
DLB-Y 80

Dillard, R(ichard) H(enry) W(ilde)
1937- . . . . **CLC 5**
See also CAAS 7; CANR 10; CA 21-24R;
DLB 5

Dillon, Eilis 1920- . . . . **CLC 17**
See also CLR 26; CAAS 3; CANR 4;
CA 9-12R; SATA 2

Dinesen, Isak
1885-1962 . . . . **CLC 10, 29; SSC 7**
See also Blixen, Karen (Christentze
Dinesen)
See also CANR 22

Ding Ling 1904-1986 . . . . **CLC 68**

Disch, Thomas M(ichael) 1940- . . . **CLC 7, 36**
See also CAAS 4; CANR 17; CA 21-24R;
SATA 54; DLB 8

Disraeli, Benjamin 1804-1881 . . . . . **NCLC 2**
See also DLB 21, 55

Dixon, Paige 1911-
See Corcoran, Barbara

Dixon, Stephen 1936- . . . . **CLC 52**
See also CANR 17; CA 89-92

Doblin, Alfred 1878-1957 . . . . **TCLC 13**
See also Doeblin, Alfred

Dobrolyubov, Nikolai Alexandrovich
1836-1861 . . . . **NCLC 5**

Dobyns, Stephen 1941- . . . . **CLC 37**
See also CANR 2, 18; CA 45-48

Doctorow, E(dgar) L(aurence)
1931- . . . . . **CLC 6, 11, 15, 18, 37, 44, 65**
See also CANR 2, 33; CA 45-48; DLB 2,
28; DLB-Y 80; CDALB 1968-1987

Dodgson, Charles Lutwidge 1832-1898
See Carroll, Lewis
See also YABC 2

Dodson, Owen 1914-1983
See also BLC 1; CANR 24; CA 65-68;
obituary CA 110; DLB 76

Doeblin, Alfred 1878-1957 . . . . **TCLC 13**
See also CA 110; DLB 66

Doerr, Harriet 1910- . . . . **CLC 34**
See also CA 117, 122

Domini, Rey 1934-
See Lorde, Audre

Donaldson, Stephen R. 1947- . . . . . . **CLC 46**
See also CANR 13; CA 89-92

Donleavy, J(ames) P(atrick)
1926- . . . . **CLC 1, 4, 6, 10, 45**
See also CANR 24; CA 9-12R; DLB 6

Donnadieu, Marguerite 1914-
See Duras, Marguerite

Donne, John 1572?-1631 . . . . . . **LC 10; PC 1**
See also WLC 2

Donnell, David 1939?- . . . . **CLC 34**

Donoso, Jose 1924- . . . . **CLC 4, 8, 11, 32**
See also CA 81-84

Donovan, John 1928- . . . . **CLC 35**
See also CLR 3; CA 97-100; SATA 29

Doolittle, Hilda 1886-1961
See H(ilda) D(oolittle)
See also CA 97-100; DLB 4, 45

Dorfman, Ariel 1942- . . . . **CLC 48**
See also CA 124

Dorn, Ed(ward Merton) 1929- . . . **CLC 10, 18**
See also CA 93-96; DLB 5

Dos Passos, John (Roderigo)
1896-1970 . . . **CLC 1, 4, 8, 11, 15, 25, 34**
See also WLC 2; CANR 3; CA 1-4R;
obituary CA 29-32R; DLB 4, 9;
DLB-DS 1

Dostoevsky, Fyodor
1821-1881 . . . . **NCLC 2, 7, 21, 33; SSC 2**
See also WLC 2

Doughty, Charles (Montagu)
1843-1926 . . . . **TCLC 27**
See also CA 115; DLB 19, 57

Douglas, George 1869-1902 . . . . **TCLC 28**

Douglas, Keith 1920-1944 . . . . **TCLC 40**
See also DLB 27

Douglass, Frederick 1817?-1895 . . . **NCLC 7**
See also BLC 1; WLC 2; SATA 29; DLB 1,
43, 50, 79; CDALB 1640-1865

Dourado, (Waldomiro Freitas) Autran
1926- . . . . **CLC 23, 60**
See also CA 25-28R

Dove, Rita 1952- . . . . **CLC 50**
See also CA 109

Dowson, Ernest (Christopher)
1867-1900 . . . . **TCLC 4**
See also CA 105; DLB 19

Doyle, (Sir) Arthur Conan
1859-1930 . . . . **TCLC 7, 26**
See also WLC 2; CA 104, 122; SATA 24;
DLB 18, 70

Dr. A 1933-
See Silverstein, Alvin and Virginia B(arbara
Opshelor) Silverstein

Drabble, Margaret
1939- . . . . **CLC 2, 3, 5, 8, 10, 22, 53**
See also CANR 18; CA 13-16R; SATA 48;
DLB 14

Drayton, Michael 1563-1631 . . . . **LC 8**

Dreiser, Theodore (Herman Albert)
1871-1945 . . . . **TCLC 10, 18, 35**
See also WLC 2; CA 106; SATA 48;
DLB 9, 12; DLB-DS 1;
CDALB 1865-1917

Drexler, Rosalyn 1926- . . . . **CLC 2, 6**
See also CA 81-84

Dreyer, Carl Theodor 1889-1968 . . . . **CLC 16**
See also obituary CA 116

Drieu La Rochelle, Pierre
1893-1945 . . . . **TCLC 21**
See also CA 117; DLB 72

Droste-Hulshoff, Annette Freiin von
1797-1848 . . . . **NCLC 3**

Drummond, William Henry
1854-1907 . . . . **TCLC 25**
See also DLB 92

Drummond de Andrade, Carlos 1902-1987
See Andrade, Carlos Drummond de

Drury, Allen (Stuart) 1918- . . . . **CLC 37**
See also CANR 18; CA 57-60

Dryden, John 1631-1700 . . . . **LC 3**
See also WLC 2

Duberman, Martin 1930- . . . . **CLC 8**
See also CANR 2; CA 1-4R

Dubie, Norman (Evans, Jr.) 1945- . . **CLC 36**
See also CANR 12; CA 69-72

Fowles, John (Robert)
1926- .... **CLC 1, 2, 3, 4, 6, 9, 10, 15, 33**
See also CANR 25; CA 5-8R; SATA 22;
DLB 14

Fox, Paula 1923-............... **CLC 2, 8**
See also CLR 1; CANR 20; CA 73-76;
SATA 17; DLB 52

Fox, William Price (Jr.) 1926- ..... **CLC 22**
See also CANR 11; CA 17-20R; DLB 2;
DLB-Y 81

Foxe, John 1516?-1587............. **LC 14**

Frame (Clutha), Janet (Paterson)
1924- .... **CLC 2, 3, 6, 22, 66**
See also Clutha, Janet Paterson Frame

France, Anatole 1844-1924 .... **TCLC 9**
See also Thibault, Jacques Anatole Francois

Francis, Claude 19??-............ **CLC 50**

Francis, Dick 1920- .... **CLC 2, 22, 42**
See also CANR 9; CA 5-8R; DLB 87

Francis, Robert (Churchill)
1901-1987 .... **CLC 15**
See also CANR 1; CA 1-4R;
obituary CA 123

Frank, Anne 1929-1945 .... **TCLC 17**
See also WLC 2; CA 113; SATA 42

Frank, Elizabeth 1945-............ **CLC 39**
See also CA 121, 126

Franklin, (Stella Maria Sarah) Miles
1879-1954 .... **TCLC 7**
See also CA 104

Fraser, Antonia (Pakenham)
1932- .... **CLC 32**
See also CA 85-88; SATA 32

Fraser, George MacDonald 1925-.... **CLC 7**
See also CANR 2; CA 45-48

Fraser, Sylvia 1935-.............. **CLC 64**
See also CANR 1, 16; CA 45-48

Frayn, Michael 1933-...... **CLC 3, 7, 31, 47**
See also CA 5-8R; DLB 13, 14

Fraze, Candida 19??- .... **CLC 50**
See also CA 125

Frazer, Sir James George
1854-1941 .... **TCLC 32**
See also CA 118

Frazier, Ian 1951-................ **CLC 46**
See also CA 130

Frederic, Harold 1856-1898...... **NCLC 10**
See also DLB 12, 23

Frederick the Great 1712-1786 ...... **LC 14**

Fredman, Russell (Bruce) 1929-
See also CLR 20

Fredro, Aleksander 1793-1876..... **NCLC 8**

Freeling, Nicolas 1927- .... **CLC 38**
See also CANR 1, 17; CA 49-52; DLB 87

Freeman, Douglas Southall
1886-1953 .... **TCLC 11**
See also CA 109; DLB 17

Freeman, Judith 1946-............ **CLC 55**

Freeman, Mary (Eleanor) Wilkins
1852-1930 .... **TCLC 9; SSC 1**
See also CA 106; DLB 12, 78

Freeman, R(ichard) Austin
1862-1943 .... **TCLC 21**
See also CA 113; DLB 70

French, Marilyn 1929-...... **CLC 10, 18, 60**
See also CANR 3; CA 69-72

Freneau, Philip Morin 1752-1832 .. **NCLC 1**
See also DLB 37, 43

Friedman, B(ernard) H(arper)
1926-...................... **CLC 7**
See also CANR 3; CA 1-4R

Friedman, Bruce Jay 1930-.... **CLC 3, 5, 56**
See also CANR 25; CA 9-12R; DLB 2, 28

Friel, Brian 1929-........... **CLC 5, 42, 59**
See also CA 21-24R; DLB 13

Friis-Baastad, Babbis (Ellinor)
1921-1970 .... **CLC 12**
See also CA 17-20R; SATA 7

Frisch, Max (Rudolf)
1911- ...... **CLC 3, 9, 14, 18, 32, 44**
See also CA 85-88; DLB 69

Fromentin, Eugene (Samuel Auguste)
1820-1876 .... **NCLC 10**

Frost, Robert (Lee)
1874-1963 ... **CLC 1, 3, 4, 9, 10, 13, 15,
26, 34, 44; PC 1**
See also WLC 2; CA 89-92; SATA 14;
DLB 54; DLB-DS 7; CDALB 1917-1929

Fry, Christopher 1907-....... **CLC 2, 10, 14**
See also CANR 9; CA 17-20R; DLB 13

Frye, (Herman) Northrop
1912-1991 .... **CLC 24, 70**
See also CANR 8; CA 5-8R;
obituary CA 133; DLB 67, 68

Fuchs, Daniel 1909- .... **CLC 8, 22**
See also CAAS 5; CA 81-84; DLB 9, 26, 28

Fuchs, Daniel 1934-.............. **CLC 34**
See also CANR 14; CA 37-40R

Fuentes, Carlos
1928-...... **CLC 3, 8, 10, 13, 22, 41, 60**
See also WLC 2; CANR 10; CA 69-72

Fugard, Athol 1932-... **CLC 5, 9, 14, 25, 40**
See also CA 85-88

Fugard, Sheila 1932- .... **CLC 48**
See also CA 125

Fuller, Charles (H., Jr.)
1939-.................. **CLC 25; DC 1**
See also BLC 2; CA 108, 112; DLB 38

Fuller, John (Leopold) 1937-...... **CLC 62**
See also CANR 9; CA 21-22R; DLB 40

Fuller, (Sarah) Margaret
1810-1850 .... **NCLC 5**
See also Ossoli, Sarah Margaret (Fuller
marchesa d')
See also DLB 1, 59, 73; CDALB 1640-1865

Fuller, Roy (Broadbent) 1912-.... **CLC 4, 28**
See also CA 5-8R; DLB 15, 20

Fulton, Alice 1952-............... **CLC 52**
See also CA 116

Furabo 1644-1694
See Basho, Matsuo

Furphy, Joseph 1843-1912........ **TCLC 25**

Futabatei Shimei 1864-1909....... **TCLC 44**

Futrelle, Jacques 1875-1912 ...... **TCLC 19**
See also CA 113

Gaboriau, Emile 1835-1873 ...... **NCLC 14**

Gadda, Carlo Emilio 1893-1973 .... **CLC 11**
See also CA 89-92

Gaddis, William
1922- .... **CLC 1, 3, 6, 8, 10, 19, 43**
See also CAAS 4; CANR 21; CA 17-20R;
DLB 2

Gaines, Ernest J. 1933- ...... **CLC 3, 11, 18**
See also BLC 2; CANR 6, 24; CA 9-12R;
DLB 2, 33; DLB-Y 80;
CDALB 1968-1988

Gaitskill, Mary 1954-............. **CLC 69**
See also CA 128

Gale, Zona 1874-1938 .... **TCLC 7**
See also CA 105; DLB 9, 78

Gallagher, Tess 1943-.......... **CLC 18, 63**
See also CA 106

Gallant, Mavis
1922- .... **CLC 7, 18, 38; SSC 5**
See also CA 69-72; DLB 53

Gallant, Roy A(rthur) 1924- .... **CLC 17**
See also CANR 4; CA 5-8R; SATA 4

Gallico, Paul (William) 1897-1976 ... **CLC 2**
See also CA 5-8R; obituary CA 69-72;
SATA 13; DLB 9

Galsworthy, John 1867-1933.... **TCLC 1, 45**
See also WLC 2; brief entry CA 104;
DLB 10, 34, 98

Galt, John 1779-1839............ **NCLC 1**

Galvin, James 1951-.............. **CLC 38**
See also CANR 26; CA 108

Gamboa, Frederico 1864-1939..... **TCLC 36**

Gann, Ernest K(ellogg) 1910- ...... **CLC 23**
See also CANR 1; CA 1-4R

Garcia Lorca, Federico
1898-1936 ..... **TCLC 1, 7; DC 2; PC 3**
See also WLC 2; CA 131;
brief entry CA 104; DLB 108

Garcia Marquez, Gabriel (Jose)
1928- ... **CLC 2, 3, 8, 10, 15, 27, 47, 55,
68; SSC 8**
See also WLC 3; CANR 10, 28;
CA 33-36R; AAYA 3

Gardam, Jane 1928-.............. **CLC 43**
See also CLR 12; CANR 2, 18; CA 49-52;
SATA 28, 39; DLB 14

Gardner, Herb 1934- .... **CLC 44**

Gardner, John (Champlin, Jr.)
1933-1982 .... **CLC 2, 3, 5, 7, 8, 10, 18,
28, 34; SSC 7**
See also CA 65-68; obituary CA 107;
obituary SATA 31, 40; DLB 2; DLB-Y 82

Gardner, John (Edmund) 1926-..... **CLC 30**
See also CANR 15; CA 103

Gardons, S. S. 1926-
See Snodgrass, W(illiam) D(e Witt)

Garfield, Leon 1921-.............. **CLC 12**
See also CA 17-20R; SATA 1, 32

Garland, (Hannibal) Hamlin
1860-1940 .... **TCLC 3**
See also CA 104; DLB 12, 71, 78

Garneau, Hector (de) Saint Denys
1912-1943 .... **TCLC 13**
See also CA 111; DLB 88

Hoffmann, E(rnst) T(heodor) A(madeus)
    1776-1822 . . . . NCLC 2
    See also SATA 27; DLB 90

Hoffmann, Gert   1932- . . . . CLC 54

Hofmannsthal, Hugo (Laurenz August
    Hofmann Edler) von
    1874-1929 . . . . TCLC 11
    See also CA 106; DLB 81

Hogg, James   1770-1835 . . . . NCLC 4

Holbach, Paul Henri Thiry, Baron d'
    1723-1789 . . . . LC 14

Holberg, Ludvig   1684-1754 . . . . LC 6

Holden, Ursula   1921- . . . . CLC 18
    See also CAAS 8; CANR 22; CA 101

Holderlin, (Johann Christian) Friedrich
    1770-1843 . . . . NCLC 16; PC 4

Holdstock, Robert (P.)   1948- . . . . CLC 39

Holland, Isabelle   1920- . . . . CLC 21
    See also CANR 10, 25; CA 21-24R;
    SATA 8

Holland, Marcus   1900-1985
    See Caldwell, (Janet Miriam) Taylor
    (Holland)

Hollander, John   1929- . . . . . . CLC 2, 5, 8, 14
    See also CANR 1; CA 1-4R; SATA 13;
    DLB 5

Holleran, Andrew   1943?- . . . . CLC 38

Hollinghurst, Alan   1954- . . . . CLC 55
    See also CA 114

Hollis, Jim   1916-
    See Summers, Hollis (Spurgeon, Jr.)

Holmes, John Clellon   1926-1988 . . . . CLC 56
    See also CANR 4; CA 9-10R;
    obituary CA 125; DLB 16

Holmes, Oliver Wendell
    1809-1894 . . . . NCLC 14
    See also SATA 34; DLB 1;
    CDALB 1640-1865

Holt, Victoria   1906-
    See Hibbert, Eleanor (Burford)

Holub, Miroslav   1923- . . . . CLC 4
    See also CANR 10; CA 21-24R

Homer   c. 8th century B.C.- . . . . CMLC 1

Honig, Edwin   1919- . . . . CLC 33
    See also CAAS 8; CANR 4; CA 5-8R;
    DLB 5

Hood, Hugh (John Blagdon)
    1928- . . . . CLC 15, 28
    See also CANR 1; CA 49-52; DLB 53

Hood, Thomas   1799-1845 . . . . NCLC 16

Hooker, (Peter) Jeremy   1941- . . . . . . CLC 43
    See also CANR 22; CA 77-80; DLB 40

Hope, A(lec) D(erwent)   1907- . . . . CLC 3, 51
    See also CA 21-24R

Hope, Christopher (David Tully)
    1944- . . . . CLC 52
    See also CA 106

Hopkins, Gerard Manley
    1844-1889 . . . . NCLC 17
    See also DLB 35, 57

Hopkins, John (Richard)   1931- . . . . . . CLC 4
    See also CA 85-88

Hopkins, Pauline Elizabeth
    1859-1930 . . . . TCLC 28
    See also BLC 2; DLB 50

Horgan, Paul   1903- . . . . CLC 9, 53
    See also CANR 9; CA 13-16R; SATA 13;
    DLB-Y 85

Horovitz, Israel   1939- . . . . CLC 56
    See also CA 33-36R; DLB 7

Horvath, Odon von   1901-1938 . . . . TCLC 45
    See also brief entry CA 118; DLB 85

Horwitz, Julius   1920-1986 . . . . CLC 14
    See also CANR 12; CA 9-12R;
    obituary CA 119

Hospital, Janette Turner   1942- . . . . . CLC 42
    See also CA 108

Hostos (y Bonilla), Eugenio Maria de
    1893-1903 . . . . TCLC 24
    See also CA 123

Hougan, Carolyn   19??- . . . . CLC 34

Household, Geoffrey (Edward West)
    1900-1988 . . . . CLC 11
    See also CA 77-80; obituary CA 126;
    SATA 14, 59; DLB 87

Housman, A(lfred) E(dward)
    1859-1936 . . . . TCLC 1, 10; PC 2
    See also CA 104, 125; DLB 19

Housman, Laurence   1865-1959 . . . . . TCLC 7
    See also CA 106; SATA 25; DLB 10

Howard, Elizabeth Jane   1923- . . . CLC 7, 29
    See also CANR 8; CA 5-8R

Howard, Maureen   1930- . . . . . CLC 5, 14, 46
    See also CA 53-56; DLB-Y 83

Howard, Richard   1929- . . . . . . CLC 7, 10, 47
    See also CANR 25; CA 85-88; DLB 5

Howard, Robert E(rvin)
    1906-1936 . . . . TCLC 8
    See also CA 105

Howe, Fanny   1940- . . . . CLC 47
    See also CA 117; SATA 52

Howe, Julia Ward   1819-1910 . . . . . TCLC 21
    See also CA 117; DLB 1

Howe, Tina   1937- . . . . CLC 48
    See also CA 109

Howell, James   1594?-1666 . . . . LC 13

Howells, William Dean
    1837-1920 . . . . TCLC 7, 17, 41
    See also brief entry CA 104; DLB 12, 64,
    74, 79; CDALB 1865-1917

Howes, Barbara   1914- . . . . CLC 15
    See also CAAS 3; CA 9-12R; SATA 5

Hrabal, Bohumil   1914- . . . . CLC 13, 67
    See also CAAS 12; CA 106

Hubbard, L(afayette) Ron(ald)
    1911-1986 . . . . CLC 43
    See also CANR 22; CA 77-80;
    obituary CA 118

Huch, Ricarda (Octavia)
    1864-1947 . . . . TCLC 13
    See also CA 111; DLB 66

Huddle, David   1942- . . . . CLC 49
    See also CA 57-60

Hudson, W(illiam) H(enry)
    1841-1922 . . . . TCLC 29
    See also CA 115; SATA 35

Hueffer, Ford Madox   1873-1939
    See Ford, Ford Madox

Hughart, Barry   1934- . . . . CLC 39

Hughes, David (John)   1930- . . . . CLC 48
    See also CA 116, 129; DLB 14

Hughes, Edward James   1930-
    See Hughes, Ted

Hughes, (James) Langston
    1902-1967 . . . . CLC 1, 5, 10, 15, 35, 44;
    PC 1; SSC 6
    See also BLC 2; CLR 17; CANR 1;
    CA 1-4R; obituary CA 25-28R; SATA 4,
    33; DLB 4, 7, 48, 51, 86;
    CDALB 1929-1941

Hughes, Richard (Arthur Warren)
    1900-1976 . . . . CLC 1, 11
    See also CANR 4; CA 5-8R;
    obituary CA 65-68; SATA 8;
    obituary SATA 25; DLB 15

Hughes, Ted   1930- . . . . . CLC 2, 4, 9, 14, 37
    See also CLR 3; CANR 1; CA 1-4R;
    SATA 27, 49; DLB 40

Hugo, Richard F(ranklin)
    1923-1982 . . . . CLC 6, 18, 32
    See also CANR 3; CA 49-52;
    obituary CA 108; DLB 5

Hugo, Victor Marie
    1802-1885 . . . . NCLC 3, 10, 21
    See also SATA 47

Huidobro, Vicente   1893-1948 . . . . . TCLC 31

Hulme, Keri   1947- . . . . CLC 39
    See also CA 125

Hulme, T(homas) E(rnest)
    1883-1917 . . . . TCLC 21
    See also CA 117; DLB 19

Hume, David   1711-1776 . . . . LC 7

Humphrey, William   1924- . . . . CLC 45
    See also CA 77-80; DLB 6

Humphreys, Emyr (Owen)   1919- . . . . CLC 47
    See also CANR 3, 24; CA 5-8R; DLB 15

Humphreys, Josephine   1945- . . . . CLC 34, 57
    See also CA 121, 127

Hunt, E(verette) Howard (Jr.)
    1918- . . . . CLC 3
    See also CANR 2; CA 45-48

Hunt, (James Henry) Leigh
    1784-1859 . . . . NCLC 1

Hunt, Marsha   1946- . . . . CLC 70

Hunter, Evan   1926- . . . . CLC 11, 31
    See also CANR 5; CA 5-8R; SATA 25;
    DLB-Y 82

Hunter, Kristin (Eggleston)   1931- . . . CLC 35
    See also CLR 3; CANR 13; CA 13-16R;
    SATA 12; DLB 33

Hunter, Mollie (Maureen McIlwraith)
    1922- . . . . CLC 21
    See also McIlwraith, Maureen Mollie
    Hunter

Hunter, Robert   ?-1734 . . . . LC 7

Hurston, Zora Neale
    1901?-1960 . . . . CLC 7, 30, 61; SSC 4
    See also BLC 2; CA 85-88; DLB 51, 86

Author Index

Montagu, Lady Mary (Pierrepont) Wortley
     1689-1762 . . . . **LC 9**

Montague, John (Patrick)
     1929- . . . . **CLC 13, 46**
     See also CANR 9; CA 9-12R; DLB 40

Montaigne, Michel (Eyquem) de
     1533-1592 . . . . **LC 8**

Montale, Eugenio 1896-1981 . . . **CLC 7, 9, 18**
     See also CANR 30; CA 17-20R;
     obituary CA 104

Montesquieu, Charles-Louis de Secondat
     1689-1755 . . . . **LC 7**

Montgomery, Marion (H., Jr.)
     1925- . . . . **CLC 7**
     See also CANR 3; CA 1-4R; DLB 6

Montgomery, Robert Bruce 1921-1978
     See Crispin, Edmund
     See also CA 104

Montherlant, Henri (Milon) de
     1896-1972 . . . . **CLC 8, 19**
     See also CA 85-88; obituary CA 37-40R;
     DLB 72

Monty Python . . . . **CLC 21**

Moodie, Susanna (Strickland)
     1803-1885 . . . . **NCLC 14**

Mooney, Ted 1951- . . . . **CLC 25**

Moorcock, Michael (John)
     1939- . . . . **CLC 5, 27, 58**
     See also CAAS 5; CANR 2, 17; CA 45-48;
     DLB 14

Moore, Brian
     1921- . . . . **CLC 1, 3, 5, 7, 8, 19, 32**
     See also CANR 1, 25; CA 1-4R

Moore, George (Augustus)
     1852-1933 . . . . **TCLC 7**
     See also CA 104; DLB 10, 18, 57

Moore, Lorrie 1957- . . . . **CLC 39, 45, 68**
     See also Moore, Marie Lorena

Moore, Marianne (Craig)
     1887-1972 . . . **CLC 1, 2, 4, 8, 10, 13, 19,**
                                      47; PC 4
     See also CANR 3; CA 1-4R;
     obituary CA 33-36R; SATA 20; DLB 45;
     DLB-DS 7; CDALB 1929-1941

Moore, Marie Lorena 1957-
     See Moore, Lorrie
     See also CA 116

Moore, Thomas 1779-1852 . . . . **NCLC 6**

Morand, Paul 1888-1976 . . . . **CLC 41**
     See also obituary CA 69-72; DLB 65

Morante, Elsa 1918-1985 . . . . **CLC 8, 47**
     See also CA 85-88; obituary CA 117

Moravia, Alberto
     1907- . . . . **CLC 2, 7, 11, 18, 27, 46**
     See also Pincherle, Alberto

More, Hannah 1745-1833 . . . . **NCLC 27**

More, Henry 1614-1687 . . . . **LC 9**

More, Sir Thomas 1478-1535 . . . . **LC 10**

Moreas, Jean 1856-1910 . . . . **TCLC 18**

Morgan, Berry 1919- . . . . **CLC 6**
     See also CA 49-52; DLB 6

Morgan, Edwin (George) 1920- . . . . . **CLC 31**
     See also CANR 3; CA 7-8R; DLB 27

Morgan, (George) Frederick
     1922- . . . . **CLC 23**
     See also CANR 21; CA 17-20R

Morgan, Janet 1945- . . . . **CLC 39**
     See also CA 65-68

Morgan, Lady 1776?-1859 . . . . . . **NCLC 29**

Morgan, Robin 1941- . . . . **CLC 2**
     See also CA 69-72

Morgan, Seth 1949-1990 . . . . **CLC 65**
     See also CA 132

Morgenstern, Christian (Otto Josef Wolfgang)
     1871-1914 . . . . **TCLC 8**
     See also CA 105

Moricz, Zsigmond 1879-1942 . . . . . **TCLC 33**

Morike, Eduard (Friedrich)
     1804-1875 . . . . **NCLC 10**

Mori Ogai 1862-1922 . . . . **TCLC 14**
     See also Mori Rintaro

Mori Rintaro 1862-1922
     See Mori Ogai
     See also CA 110

Moritz, Karl Philipp 1756-1793 . . . . . . **LC 2**

Morris, Julian 1916-
     See West, Morris L.

Morris, Steveland Judkins 1950-
     See Wonder, Stevie
     See also CA 111

Morris, William 1834-1896 . . . . **NCLC 4**
     See also DLB 18, 35, 57

Morris, Wright (Marion)
     1910- . . . . **CLC 1, 3, 7, 18, 37**
     See also CANR 21; CA 9-12R; DLB 2;
     DLB-Y 81

Morrison, James Douglas 1943-1971
     See Morrison, Jim
     See also CA 73-76

Morrison, Jim 1943-1971 . . . . **CLC 17**
     See also Morrison, James Douglas

Morrison, Toni 1931- . . . . . **CLC 4, 10, 22, 55**
     See also BLC 3; CANR 27; CA 29-32R;
     SATA 57; DLB 6, 33; DLB-Y 81;
     CDALB 1968-1987; AAYA 1

Morrison, Van 1945- . . . . **CLC 21**
     See also CA 116

Mortimer, John (Clifford)
     1923- . . . . **CLC 28, 43**
     See also CANR 21; CA 13-16R; DLB 13

Mortimer, Penelope (Ruth) 1918- . . . . **CLC 5**
     See also CA 57-60

Mosher, Howard Frank 19??- . . . . . . **CLC 62**

Mosley, Nicholas 1923- . . . . **CLC 43, 70**
     See also CA 69-72; DLB 14

Moss, Howard
     1922-1987 . . . . **CLC 7, 14, 45, 50**
     See also CANR 1; CA 1-4R;
     obituary CA 123; DLB 5

Motion, Andrew (Peter) 1952- . . . . . . **CLC 47**
     See also DLB 40

Motley, Willard (Francis)
     1912-1965 . . . . **CLC 18**
     See also CA 117; obituary CA 106; DLB 76

Mott, Michael (Charles Alston)
     1930- . . . . **CLC 15, 34**
     See also CAAS 7; CANR 7, 29; CA 5-8R

Mowat, Farley (McGill) 1921- . . . . . **CLC 26**
     See also CLR 20; CANR 4, 24; CA 1-4R;
     SATA 3, 55; DLB 68; AAYA 1

Mphahlele, Es'kia 1919-
     See Mphahlele, Ezekiel

Mphahlele, Ezekiel 1919- . . . . **CLC 25**
     See also BLC 3; CANR 26; CA 81-84

Mqhayi, S(amuel) E(dward) K(rune Loliwe)
     1875-1945 . . . . **TCLC 25**
     See also BLC 3

Mrozek, Slawomir 1930- . . . . **CLC 3, 13**
     See also CAAS 10; CANR 29; CA 13-16R

Mtwa, Percy 19??- . . . . **CLC 47**

Mueller, Lisel 1924- . . . . **CLC 13, 51**
     See also CA 93-96

Muir, Edwin 1887-1959 . . . . **TCLC 2**
     See also CA 104; DLB 20

Muir, John 1838-1914 . . . . **TCLC 28**

Mujica Lainez, Manuel
     1910-1984 . . . . **CLC 31**
     See also CA 81-84; obituary CA 112

Mukherjee, Bharati 1940- . . . . **CLC 53**
     See also CA 107; DLB 60

Muldoon, Paul 1951- . . . . **CLC 32**
     See also CA 113, 129; DLB 40

Mulisch, Harry (Kurt Victor)
     1927- . . . . **CLC 42**
     See also CANR 6, 26; CA 9-12R

Mull, Martin 1943- . . . . **CLC 17**
     See also CA 105

Munford, Robert 1737?-1783 . . . . **LC 5**
     See also DLB 31

Munro, Alice (Laidlaw)
     1931- . . . . **CLC 6, 10, 19, 50; SSC 3**
     See also CA 33-36R; SATA 29; DLB 53

Munro, H(ector) H(ugh) 1870-1916
     See Saki
     See also CA 104; DLB 34

Murasaki, Lady c. 11th century- . . . **CMLC 1**

Murdoch, (Jean) Iris
     1919- . . . . . . **CLC 1, 2, 3, 4, 6, 8, 11, 15,**
                                      22, 31, 51
     See also CANR 8; CA 13-16R; DLB 14

Murphy, Richard 1927- . . . . **CLC 41**
     See also CA 29-32R; DLB 40

Murphy, Sylvia 19??- . . . . **CLC 34**

Murphy, Thomas (Bernard) 1935- . . . **CLC 51**
     See also CA 101

Murray, Les(lie) A(llan) 1938- . . . . . **CLC 40**
     See also CANR 11, 27; CA 21-24R

Murry, John Middleton
     1889-1957 . . . . **TCLC 16**
     See also CA 118

Musgrave, Susan 1951- . . . . **CLC 13, 54**
     See also CA 69-72

Musil, Robert (Edler von)
     1880-1942 . . . . **TCLC 12**
     See also CA 109; DLB 81

Musset, (Louis Charles) Alfred de
     1810-1857 . . . . **NCLC 7**

Myers, Walter Dean 1937- .... CLC 35
See also BLC 3; CLR 4, 16; CANR 20;
CA 33-36R; SAAS 2; SATA 27, 41;
DLB 33; AAYA 4

Myers, Walter M. 1937-
See Myers, Walter Dean

Nabokov, Vladimir (Vladimirovich)
1899-1977 .... CLC 1, 2, 3, 6, 8, 11, 15,
23, 44, 46, 64
See also CANR 20; CA 5-8R;
obituary CA 69-72; DLB 2; DLB-Y 80;
DLB-DS 3; CDALB 1941-1968

Nagy, Laszlo 1925-1978............ CLC 7
See also CA 129; obituary CA 112

Naipaul, Shiva(dhar Srinivasa)
1945-1985 .... CLC 32, 39
See also CA 110, 112; obituary CA 116;
DLB-Y 85

Naipaul, V(idiadhar) S(urajprasad)
1932- .... CLC 4, 7, 9, 13, 18, 37
See also CANR 1; CA 1-4R; DLB-Y 85

Nakos, Ioulia 1899?-
See Nakos, Lilika

Nakos, Lilika 1899?- .... CLC 29

Nakou, Lilika 1899?-
See Nakos, Lilika

Narayan, R(asipuram) K(rishnaswami)
1906- .... CLC 7, 28, 47
See also CA 81-84

Nash, (Frediric) Ogden 1902-1971 .. CLC 23
See also CAP 1; CA 13-14;
obituary CA 29-32R; SATA 2, 46;
DLB 11

Nathan, George Jean 1882-1958 ... TCLC 18
See also CA 114

Natsume, Kinnosuke 1867-1916
See Natsume, Soseki
See also CA 104

Natsume, Soseki 1867-1916..... TCLC 2, 10
See also Natsume, Kinnosuke

Natti, (Mary) Lee 1919-
See Kingman, (Mary) Lee
See also CANR 2; CA 7-8R

Naylor, Gloria 1950- .... CLC 28, 52
See also BLC 3; CANR 27; CA 107;
AAYA 6

Neff, Debra 1972-............... CLC 59

Neihardt, John G(neisenau)
1881-1973 .... CLC 32
See also CAP 1; CA 13-14; DLB 9, 54

Nekrasov, Nikolai Alekseevich
1821-1878 .... NCLC 11

Nelligan, Emile 1879-1941........ TCLC 14
See also CA 114; DLB 92

Nelson, Willie 1933-.............. CLC 17
See also CA 107

Nemerov, Howard 1920- ... CLC 2, 6, 9, 36
See also CANR 1, 27; CA 1-4R; CABS 2;
DLB 5, 6; DLB-Y 83

Neruda, Pablo
1904-1973 .... CLC 1, 2, 5, 7, 9, 28, 62;
PC 4
See also CAP 2; CA 19-20;
obituary CA 45-48

Nerval, Gerard de 1808-1855...... NCLC 1

Nervo, (Jose) Amado (Ruiz de)
1870-1919 .... TCLC 11
See also CA 109

Neufeld, John (Arthur) 1938- ...... CLC 17
See also CANR 11; CA 25-28R; SAAS 3;
SATA 6

Neville, Emily Cheney 1919-....... CLC 12
See also CANR 3; CA 5-8R; SAAS 2;
SATA 1

Newbound, Bernard Slade 1930-
See Slade, Bernard
See also CA 81-84

Newby, P(ercy) H(oward)
1918- .... CLC 2, 13
See also CA 5-8R; DLB 15

Newlove, Donald 1928- .... CLC 6
See also CANR 25; CA 29-32R

Newlove, John (Herbert) 1938-..... CLC 14
See also CANR 9, 25; CA 21-24R

Newman, Charles 1938-.......... CLC 2, 8
See also CA 21-24R

Newman, Edwin (Harold) 1919- .... CLC 14
See also CANR 5; CA 69-72

Newton, Suzanne 1936- .... CLC 35
See also CANR 14; CA 41-44R; SATA 5

Nexo, Martin Andersen
1869-1954 .... TCLC 43

Nezval, Vitezslav 1900-1958 ...... TCLC 44
See also CA 123

Ngema, Mbongeni 1955- .... CLC 57

Ngugi, James Thiong'o 1938-
See Ngugi wa Thiong'o

Ngugi wa Thiong'o 1938-... CLC 3, 7, 13, 36
See also Ngugi, James (Thiong'o); Wa
Thiong'o, Ngugi
See also BLC 3

Nichol, B(arrie) P(hillip) 1944-..... CLC 18
See also CA 53-56; DLB 53

Nichols, John (Treadwell) 1940-.... CLC 38
See also CAAS 2; CANR 6; CA 9-12R;
DLB-Y 82

Nichols, Peter (Richard)
1927-.................. CLC 5, 36, 65
See also CANR 33; CA 104; DLB 13

Nicolas, F.R.E. 1927-
See Freeling, Nicolas

Niedecker, Lorine 1903-1970.... CLC 10, 42
See also CAP 2; CA 25-28; DLB 48

Nietzsche, Friedrich (Wilhelm)
1844-1900 .... TCLC 10, 18
See also CA 107, 121

Nievo, Ippolito 1831-1861 .... NCLC 22

Nightingale, Anne Redmon 1943-
See Redmon (Nightingale), Anne
See also CA 103

Nin, Anais
1903-1977 ..... CLC 1, 4, 8, 11, 14, 60;
SSC 10
See also CANR 22; CA 13-16R;
obituary CA 69-72; DLB 2, 4

Nissenson, Hugh 1933-.......... CLC 4, 9
See also CANR 27; CA 17-20R; DLB 28

Niven, Larry 1938-............... CLC 8
See also Niven, Laurence Van Cott
See also DLB 8

Niven, Laurence Van Cott 1938-
See Niven, Larry
See also CANR 14; CA 21-24R

Nixon, Agnes Eckhardt 1927-...... CLC 21
See also CA 110

Nizan, Paul 1905-1940........... TCLC 40
See also DLB 72

Nkosi, Lewis 1936-............... CLC 45
See also BLC 3; CANR 27; CA 65-68

Nodier, (Jean) Charles (Emmanuel)
1780-1844 .... NCLC 19

Nolan, Christopher 1965-.......... CLC 58
See also CA 111

Nordhoff, Charles 1887-1947...... TCLC 23
See also CA 108; SATA 23; DLB 9

Norman, Marsha 1947- .... CLC 28
See also CA 105; CABS 3; DLB-Y 84

Norris, (Benjamin) Frank(lin)
1870-1902 .... TCLC 24
See also CA 110; DLB 12, 71;
CDALB 1865-1917

Norris, Leslie 1921-............... CLC 14
See also CANR 14; CAP 1; CA 11-12;
DLB 27

North, Andrew 1912-
See Norton, Andre

North, Christopher 1785-1854
See Wilson, John

Norton, Alice Mary 1912-
See Norton, Andre
See also CANR 2; CA 1-4R; SATA 1, 43

Norton, Andre 1912- .... CLC 12
See also Norton, Mary Alice
See also DLB 8, 52

Norway, Nevil Shute 1899-1960
See Shute (Norway), Nevil
See also CA 102; obituary CA 93-96

Norwid, Cyprian Kamil
1821-1883 .... NCLC 17

Nossack, Hans Erich 1901-1978..... CLC 6
See also CA 93-96; obituary CA 85-88;
DLB 69

Nova, Craig 1945-............... CLC 7, 31
See also CANR 2; CA 45-48

Novak, Joseph 1933-
See Kosinski, Jerzy (Nikodem)

Novalis 1772-1801 .... NCLC 13

Nowlan, Alden (Albert) 1933-...... CLC 15
See also CANR 5; CA 9-12R; DLB 53

Noyes, Alfred 1880-1958 .... TCLC 7
See also CA 104; DLB 20

Nunn, Kem 19??-................. CLC 34

Nye, Robert 1939- .... CLC 13, 42
See also CANR 29; CA 33-36R; SATA 6;
DLB 14

Nyro, Laura 1947- .... CLC 17

Oates, Joyce Carol
1938- ..... CLC 1, 2, 3, 6, 9, 11, 15, 19,
33, 52; SSC 6
See also CANR 25; CA 5-8R; DLB 2, 5;
DLB-Y 81; CDALB 1968-1987

Author Index

Piccolo, Lucio 1901-1969......... **CLC 13**
See also CA 97-100

Pickthall, Marjorie (Lowry Christie)
1883-1922 .... **TCLC 21**
See also CA 107; DLB 92

Pico della Mirandola, Giovanni
1463-1494 .... **LC 15**

Piercy, Marge
1936- .... **CLC 3, 6, 14, 18, 27, 62**
See also CAAS 1; CANR 13; CA 21-24R

Pilnyak, Boris 1894-1937?....... **TCLC 23**

Pincherle, Alberto 1907- .... **CLC 11, 18**
See also Moravia, Alberto
See also CA 25-28R

Pineda, Cecile 1942-.............. **CLC 39**
See also CA 118

Pinero, Miguel (Gomez)
1946-1988 .... **CLC 4, 55**
See also CANR 29; CA 61-64;
obituary CA 125

Pinero, Sir Arthur Wing
1855-1934 .... **TCLC 32**
See also CA 110; DLB 10

Pinget, Robert 1919- .... **CLC 7, 13, 37**
See also CA 85-88; DLB 83

Pink Floyd...................... **CLC 35**

Pinkney, Edward 1802-1828 ..... **NCLC 31**

Pinkwater, D(aniel) M(anus)
1941-...................... **CLC 35**
See also Pinkwater, Manus
See also CLR 4; CANR 12; CA 29-32R;
SAAS 3; SATA 46; AAYA 1

Pinkwater, Manus 1941-
See Pinkwater, D(aniel) M(anus)
See also SATA 8

Pinsky, Robert 1940- .... **CLC 9, 19, 38**
See also CAAS 4; CA 29-32R; DLB-Y 82

Pinter, Harold
1930- ..... **CLC 1, 3, 6, 9, 11, 15, 27, 58**
See also CA 5-8R; DLB 13

Pirandello, Luigi 1867-1936..... **TCLC 4, 29**
See also CA 104

Pirsig, Robert M(aynard) 1928- ... **CLC 4, 6**
See also CA 53-56; SATA 39

Pisarev, Dmitry Ivanovich
1840-1868 .... **NCLC 25**

Pix, Mary (Griffith) 1666-1709 ...... **LC 8**
See also DLB 80

Plaidy, Jean 1906-
See Hibbert, Eleanor (Burford)

Plant, Robert 1948- .... **CLC 12**

Plante, David (Robert)
1940- .... **CLC 7, 23, 38**
See also CANR 12; CA 37-40R; DLB-Y 83

Plath, Sylvia
1932-1963 .... **CLC 1, 2, 3, 5, 9, 11, 14, 17, 50, 51, 62; PC 1**
See also CAP 2; CA 19-20; DLB 5, 6;
CDALB 1941-1968

Plato 428? B.C.-348? B.C........ **CMLC 8**

Platonov, Andrei (Platonovich)
1899-1951 .... **TCLC 14**
See also Klimentov, Andrei Platonovich
See also CA 108

Platt, Kin 1911- .... **CLC 26**
See also CANR 11; CA 17-20R; SATA 21

Plimpton, George (Ames) 1927-..... **CLC 36**
See also CA 21-24R; SATA 10

Plomer, William (Charles Franklin)
1903-1973 .... **CLC 4, 8**
See also CAP 2; CA 21-22; SATA 24;
DLB 20

Plumly, Stanley (Ross) 1939- ...... **CLC 33**
See also CA 108, 110; DLB 5

Poe, Edgar Allan
1809-1849 ... **NCLC 1, 16; PC 1; SSC 1**
See also SATA 23; DLB 3, 59, 73, 74;
CDALB 1640-1865

Pohl, Frederik 1919- .... **CLC 18**
See also CAAS 1; CANR 11; CA 61-64;
SATA 24; DLB 8

Poirier, Louis 1910-
See Gracq, Julien
See also CA 122, 126

Poitier, Sidney 1924?- .... **CLC 26**
See also CA 117

Polanski, Roman 1933- .... **CLC 16**
See also CA 77-80

Poliakoff, Stephen 1952- .... **CLC 38**
See also CA 106; DLB 13

Police, The...................... **CLC 26**

Pollitt, Katha 1949- .... **CLC 28**
See also CA 120, 122

Pollock, Sharon 19??-.............. **CLC 50**
See also DLB 60

Pomerance, Bernard 1940-........ **CLC 13**
See also CA 101

Ponge, Francis (Jean Gaston Alfred)
1899-...................... **CLC 6, 18**
See also CA 85-88; obituary CA 126

Pontoppidan, Henrik 1857-1943 ... **TCLC 29**
See also obituary CA 126

Poole, Josephine 1933-............. **CLC 17**
See also CANR 10; CA 21-24R; SAAS 2;
SATA 5

Popa, Vasko 1922- .... **CLC 19**
See also CA 112

Pope, Alexander 1688-1744......... **LC 3**

Porter, Connie 1960- .... **CLC 70**

Porter, Gene Stratton 1863-1924 .. **TCLC 21**
See also CA 112

Porter, Katherine Anne
1890-1980 ..... **CLC 1, 3, 7, 10, 13, 15, 27; SSC 4**
See also CANR 1; CA 1-4R;
obituary CA 101; obituary SATA 23, 39;
DLB 4, 9; DLB-Y 80

Porter, Peter (Neville Frederick)
1929-................... **CLC 5, 13, 33**
See also CA 85-88; DLB 40

Porter, William Sydney 1862-1910
See Henry, O.
See also YABC 2; CA 104; DLB 12, 78, 79;
CDALB 1865-1917

Post, Melville D. 1871-1930 ..... **TCLC 39**
See also brief entry CA 110

Potok, Chaim 1929-....... **CLC 2, 7, 14, 26**
See also CANR 19; CA 17-20R; SATA 33;
DLB 28

Potter, Dennis (Christopher George)
1935-...................... **CLC 58**
See also CA 107

Pound, Ezra (Loomis)
1885-1972 ..... **CLC 1, 2, 3, 4, 5, 7, 10, 13, 18, 34, 48, 50; PC 4**
See also CA 5-8R; obituary CA 37-40R;
DLB 4, 45, 63; CDALB 1917-1929

Povod, Reinaldo 1959-............ **CLC 44**

Powell, Adam Clayton, Jr. 1908-1972
See also BLC 3; CA 102;
obituary CA 33-36R

Powell, Anthony (Dymoke)
1905-................. **CLC 1, 3, 7, 9, 10, 31**
See also CANR 1; CA 1-4R; DLB 15

Powell, Dawn 1897-1965 .... **CLC 66**
See also CA 5-8R

Powell, Padgett 1952-............. **CLC 34**
See also CA 126

Powers, J(ames) F(arl)
1917-........ **CLC 1, 4, 8, 57; SSC 4**
See also CANR 2; CA 1-4R

Powers, John J(ames) 1945-
See Powers, John R.

Powers, John R. 1945-............ **CLC 66**
See also Powers, John J(ames)
See also CA 69-72

Pownall, David 1938-............. **CLC 10**
See also CA 89-92; DLB 14

Powys, John Cowper
1872-1963 .... **CLC 7, 9, 15, 46**
See also CA 85-88; DLB 15

Powys, T(heodore) F(rancis)
1875-1953 .... **TCLC 9**
See also CA 106; DLB 36

Prager, Emily 1952-.............. **CLC 56**

Pratt, E(dwin) J(ohn) 1883-1964 .... **CLC 19**
See also obituary CA 93-96; DLB 92

Premchand 1880-1936 .... **TCLC 21**

Preussler, Otfried 1923-.......... **CLC 17**
See also CA 77-80; SATA 24

Prevert, Jacques (Henri Marie)
1900-1977 .... **CLC 15**
See also CANR 29; CA 77-80;
obituary CA 69-72; obituary SATA 30

Prevost, Abbe (Antoine Francois)
1697-1763 .... **LC 1**

Price, (Edward) Reynolds
1933-......... **CLC 3, 6, 13, 43, 50, 63**
See also CANR 1; CA 1-4R; DLB 2

Price, Richard 1949- .... **CLC 6, 12**
See also CANR 3; CA 49-52; DLB-Y 81

Prichard, Katharine Susannah
1883-1969 .... **CLC 46**
See also CAP 1; CA 11-12

Priestley, J(ohn) B(oynton)
1894-1984 .... **CLC 2, 5, 9, 34**
See also CA 9-12R; obituary CA 113;
DLB 10, 34, 77; DLB-Y 84

Prince (Rogers Nelson) 1958?- ..... **CLC 35**

Rogers, Sam 1943-
See Shepard, Sam

Rogers, Thomas (Hunton) 1931- .... CLC 57
See also CA 89-92

Rogers, Will(iam Penn Adair)
1879-1935 .... TCLC 8
See also CA 105; DLB 11

Rogin, Gilbert 1929- .... CLC 18
See also CANR 15; CA 65-68

Rohan, Koda 1867-1947 .... TCLC 22
See also CA 121

Rohmer, Eric 1920- .... CLC 16
See also Scherer, Jean-Marie Maurice

Rohmer, Sax 1883-1959 .... TCLC 28
See also Ward, Arthur Henry Sarsfield
See also CA 108; DLB 70

Roiphe, Anne (Richardson)
1935- .... CLC 3, 9
See also CA 89-92; DLB-Y 80

Rolfe, Frederick (William Serafino Austin
Lewis Mary) 1860-1913..... TCLC 12
See also CA 107; DLB 34

Rolland, Romain 1866-1944 ...... TCLC 23
See also CA 118; DLB 65

Rolvaag, O(le) E(dvart)
1876-1931 .... TCLC 17
See also CA 117; DLB 9

Romains, Jules 1885-1972 .... CLC 7
See also CA 85-88

Romero, Jose Ruben 1890-1952 ... TCLC 14
See also CA 114

Ronsard, Pierre de 1524-1585 .... LC 6

Rooke, Leon 1934- .... CLC 25, 34
See also CANR 23; CA 25-28R

Roper, William 1498-1578 .... LC 10

Rosa, Joao Guimaraes 1908-1967 ... CLC 23
See also obituary CA 89-92

Rosen, Richard (Dean) 1949- ...... CLC 39
See also CA 77-80

Rosenberg, Isaac 1890-1918 ...... TCLC 12
See also CA 107; DLB 20

Rosenblatt, Joe 1933- .... CLC 15
See also Rosenblatt, Joseph

Rosenblatt, Joseph 1933-
See Rosenblatt, Joe
See also CA 89-92

Rosenfeld, Samuel 1896-1963
See Tzara, Tristan
See also obituary CA 89-92

Rosenthal, M(acha) L(ouis) 1917- ... CLC 28
See also CAAS 6; CANR 4; CA 1-4R;
SATA 59; DLB 5

Ross, (James) Sinclair 1908- .... CLC 13
See also CA 73-76; DLB 88

Rossetti, Christina Georgina
1830-1894 .... NCLC 2
See also SATA 20; DLB 35

Rossetti, Dante Gabriel
1828-1882 .... NCLC 4
See also DLB 35

Rossetti, Gabriel Charles Dante 1828-1882
See Rossetti, Dante Gabriel

Rossner, Judith (Perelman)
1935- .... CLC 6, 9, 29
See also CANR 18; CA 17-20R; DLB 6

Rostand, Edmond (Eugene Alexis)
1868-1918 .... TCLC 6, 37
See also CA 104, 126

Roth, Henry 1906- .... CLC 2, 6, 11
See also CAP 1; CA 11-12; DLB 28

Roth, Joseph 1894-1939 .... TCLC 33
See also DLB 85

Roth, Philip (Milton)
1933- ...... CLC 1, 2, 3, 4, 6, 9, 15, 22,
31, 47, 66
See also CANR 1, 22; CA 1-4R; DLB 2, 28;
DLB-Y 82; CDALB 1968-1988

Rothenberg, James 1931- .... CLC 57

Rothenberg, Jerome 1931- .... CLC 6, 57
See also CANR 1; CA 45-48; DLB 5

Roumain, Jacques 1907-1944 ..... TCLC 19
See also BLC 3; CA 117, 125

Rourke, Constance (Mayfield)
1885-1941 .... TCLC 12
See also YABC 1; CA 107

Rousseau, Jean-Baptiste 1671-1741 ... LC 9

Rousseau, Jean-Jacques 1712-1778... LC 14

Roussel, Raymond 1877-1933 ..... TCLC 20
See also CA 117

Rovit, Earl (Herbert) 1927- .... CLC 7
See also CANR 12; CA 5-8R

Rowe, Nicholas 1674-1718 .... LC 8

Rowson, Susanna Haswell
1762-1824 .... NCLC 5
See also DLB 37

Roy, Gabrielle 1909-1983 ...... CLC 10, 14
See also CANR 5; CA 53-56;
obituary CA 110; DLB 68

Rozewicz, Tadeusz 1921- .... CLC 9, 23
See also CA 108

Ruark, Gibbons 1941- .... CLC 3
See also CANR 14; CA 33-36R

Rubens, Bernice 192?- .... CLC 19, 31
See also CA 25-28R; DLB 14

Rubenstein, Gladys 1934-
See Swan, Gladys

Rudkin, (James) David 1936- ...... CLC 14
See also CA 89-92; DLB 13

Rudnik, Raphael 1933- .... CLC 7
See also CA 29-32R

Ruiz, Jose Martinez 1874-1967
See Azorin

Rukeyser, Muriel
1913-1980 .... CLC 6, 10, 15, 27
See also CANR 26; CA 5-8R;
obituary CA 93-96; obituary SATA 22;
DLB 48

Rule, Jane (Vance) 1931- .... CLC 27
See also CANR 12; CA 25-28R; DLB 60

Rulfo, Juan 1918-1986 .... CLC 8
See also CANR 26; CA 85-88;
obituary CA 118

Runyon, (Alfred) Damon
1880-1946 .... TCLC 10
See also CA 107; DLB 11

Rush, Norman 1933- .... CLC 44
See also CA 121, 126

Rushdie, (Ahmed) Salman
1947- .... CLC 23, 31, 55, 59
See also CA 108, 111

Rushforth, Peter (Scott) 1945- ..... CLC 19
See also CA 101

Ruskin, John 1819-1900 .... TCLC 20
See also CA 114; SATA 24; DLB 55

Russ, Joanna 1937- .... CLC 15
See also CANR 11; CA 25-28R; DLB 8

Russell, George William 1867-1935
See A. E.
See also CA 104

Russell, (Henry) Ken(neth Alfred)
1927- .... CLC 16
See also CA 105

Russell, Mary Annette Beauchamp 1866-1941
See Elizabeth

Russell, Willy 1947- .... CLC 60

Rutherford, Mark 1831-1913 ...... TCLC 25
See also CA 121; DLB 18

Ruyslinck, Ward 1929- .... CLC 14

Ryan, Cornelius (John) 1920-1974 ... CLC 7
See also CA 69-72; obituary CA 53-56

Ryan, Michael 1946- .... CLC 65
See also CA 49-52; DLB-Y 82

Rybakov, Anatoli 1911?- .... CLC 23, 53
See also CA 126

Ryder, Jonathan 1927-
See Ludlum, Robert

Ryga, George 1932- .... CLC 14
See also CA 101; obituary CA 124; DLB 60

Sévigné, Marquise de Marie de
Rabutin-Chantal 1626-1696..... LC 11

Saba, Umberto 1883-1957 .... TCLC 33

Sabato, Ernesto 1911- .... CLC 10, 23
See also CA 97-100

Sacher-Masoch, Leopold von
1836?-1895 .... NCLC 31

Sachs, Marilyn (Stickle) 1927- ..... CLC 35
See also CLR 2; CANR 13; CA 17-20R;
SAAS 2; SATA 3, 52

Sachs, Nelly 1891-1970 .... CLC 14
See also CAP 2; CA 17-18;
obituary CA 25-28R

Sackler, Howard (Oliver)
1929-1982 .... CLC 14
See also CA 61-64; obituary CA 108; DLB 7

Sacks, Oliver 1933- .... CLC 67
See also CANR 28; CA 53-56

Sade, Donatien Alphonse Francois, Comte de
1740-1814 .... NCLC 3

Sadoff, Ira 1945- .... CLC 9
See also CANR 5, 21; CA 53-56

Safire, William 1929- .... CLC 10
See also CA 17-20R

Sagan, Carl (Edward) 1934- .... CLC 30
See also CANR 11; CA 25-28R; SATA 58

Sagan, Francoise
1935- .... CLC 3, 6, 9, 17, 36
See also Quoirez, Francoise
See also CANR 6; DLB 83

SSC Cumulative Nationality Index

Title Index

Title Index

Title Index

Title Index